THE
WEALTH OF NATIONS

THE
WEALTH OF
NATIONS

ADAM SMITH

Introduction by Alan B. Krueger

Edited, with notes and Marginal Summary,
by Edwin Cannan

BANTAM CLASSIC

THE WEALTH OF NATIONS
A Bantam Book

PUBLISHING HISTORY
The Wealth of Nations was originally published in 1776.
This edition is based on the fifth edition as edited and
annotated by Edwin Cannan in 1904.
Bantam Classic Edition/March 2003

Published by
Bantam Dell
A Division of Random House, Inc.
New York, New York

ISBN 0-553-58597-5

Manufactured in the United States of America
Published simultaneously in Canada

OPM   10   9   8   7   6   5

CONTENTS

BOOK IV

Of Systems of political Economy

CHAPTER III

[From "Introduction and Plan of the Work" to "Public Debts," the Contents are printed in the present edition as they appeared in eds. 3–5. Eds. 1 and 2 neither enumerate the chapter "Conclusion of the Mercantile System," nor divide Bk. V., ch. i., Pt. iii., Art. 1st into sections, since the chapter and one of the two sections appeared first in ed. 3. Eds. 1 and 2 also read "Inequalities in Wages and Profits arising from the Nature of the different Employments of both" at Bk. I., ch. x., Pt. 1.]

INTRODUCTION

Alan B. Krueger, Princeton University

NO BOOK has had more influence on economists' thinking and economic policy—and by extension on the world population's material well-being—than *An Inquiry Into the Nature and Causes of the Wealth of Nations* by Adam Smith. Skeptics of this claim might point out that many of the ideas in *The Wealth of Nations* can be traced to earlier thinkers and that Smith borrowed liberally from his French contemporaries. It has also become popular to find ancient Chinese philosophers who, unbeknownst to Smith, advanced related ideas two thousand years previously. Yet *The Wealth of Nations* has rightly earned its reputation as the founding work of modern economics. The genius of *The Wealth of Nations* lies in Adam Smith's abilities as a great synthesizer, great observer, and great storyteller. And most important of all, Smith was a great economic theorist. He saw economic behavior as primarily guided by the fundamental force of self-interest, and he conceived of the economy as a system in which regular patterns emerged from people interacting in markets on their own accord, without interference from outside authorities. Order, not chaos, would result if individuals were left to their own devices in Adam Smith's conception of the economy.

The notion that the social sciences, and economics in particular, can be studied like physics and chemistry, by breaking down human behavior into a small number of fundamental forces and modeling how individuals and organizations interact in such an environment, has survived and thrived to this day. What makes it work so brilliantly in Smith's hands is that Smith was a nuanced thinker. He was not nearly as doctrinaire a defender of unfettered free enterprise as many of his late-twentieth-century followers have made him out to be. He could—and often did—persuasively argue opposite sides of the same issue. He recognized that human judgment was not infallible. For example, he argued, "The contempt of risk and the presumptuous hope of success, are in no period of life more active than at the age at which young people chuse their professions" (p. 151). He also worried incessantly that giant corporations would come to dominate particular industries and, led by self-interest, use their influence with government to unfairly thwart their competitors and suppress the wages of their workers.

Nevertheless, Adam Smith could strip away complexity and focus on the fundamental forces at work, and he argued that such forces would conspire to produce the greatest common good under conditions of perfect liberty and perfect competition, without the actors involved intending this fortuitous result or even being aware of the role they played in bringing it about. Smith viewed competition as economically efficient: "Every individual is continually exerting himself to find out the most advantageous employment for whatever capital he can command. It is his own advantage, indeed, and not that of the society which he has in view. But the study of his own advantage naturally, or rather necessarily, leads him to prefer that employment which is most advantageous to the society" (pp. 569–570).

Central to Smith's thinking was the notion of equilibrium: the economy would reach a balance in which buyers and sellers, workers and firms, would have no incentive to change their economic behavior (i.e., quantities supplied or demanded) in light of the set of prices and wages that would be grounded out in the market by the pursuit of individuals' self-interest. "The proposition that resources seek their most profitable uses, so that in equilibrium the rates of return to a resource in various uses will be equal," the Nobel laureate George Stigler once wrote, "is still the most important substantive proposition in all of economics" (Stigler, 1976, p. 1201).

That Adam Smith would become the father of modern economics must have seemed rather improbable when he was born in 1723 in Kirkcaldy, a small town on the east coast of Scotland. (The exact date of Smith's birth is unknown. He was baptized on June 5, 1723.) His father, a well-to-do Scotsman also named Adam Smith, died before Smith was born. He was raised by his mother, a caring woman from a prominent family to whom he remained devoted throughout his life, with the help of his deceased father's friends (as specified in his father's will). Smith was a sickly infant and child, and he suffered from colic, an affliction normally confined to infants, throughout his entire life. His health prevented him from partaking in sports; instead, as a schoolboy he gravitated toward reading the classics and history. His contemporary and first biographer, Dugald Stewart, recounted that Smith was kidnapped by marauding vagrants when he was about three years old, and briefly held captive until rescued by his uncle, whom Stewart called "the happy instrument of preserving to the world a genius, which was destined, not only to extend the boundaries of science, but to enlighten and reform the commercial policy of Europe" (Stewart, 1793, pp. 2–3).

The adolescent genius attended university in Glasgow when he was fourteen years old, the normal age of matriculation early in the eighteenth century. At the time, Glasgow was a hotbed of the Scottish Enlightenment. In addition to housing a fine university, Glasgow was also a center for trade in livestock ("a continual fair or market" in Smith's words), which some biographers believe provided grist for his future economic theorizing. Smith was a dedicated and serious, if somewhat shy and awkward, student. He was fond of many of his teachers. In particular, his professor of moral philosophy, Francis Hutcheson, had a profound, "never to be forgotten" impact on Smith, and quite possibly served as a role model for his career.

In the summer of 1740 Smith completed his studies at Glasgow and attended Balliol College at Oxford University in England. There he stayed for the next six years. Smith's experience at the elite Oxford campus was not as rewarding as his time spent at Glasgow, however. The Oxford tradition, which continues to this day, is to allow students more free time for self-instruction than is allowed in American colleges; certainly the dedication to teaching was less than what Smith was accustomed to at Glasgow. According to Ross (1995; p. 75), while at Oxford Adam Smith "reckoned that it is each man's interest to live as much at ease as possible, and if someone's rewards are the same whether he performs or does not perform an onerous duty, he will either neglect it or perform it as slackly as his superiors permit. . . . Thus, it came about, Smith argued, that the Oxford professors had given up even the pretence of teaching for many years." It may well be that Smith's Oxford experience ignited his belief in the virtues of competition.

Smith returned home to Kirkcaldy after leaving Oxford. It took him nearly five years to find a teaching position. In 1751, Smith was unanimously elected to the Chair of Logic at his former school, Glasgow University. He assumed the Chair of Moral Philosophy after another professor retired a year later. Revered as a popular and dedicated teacher of logic, rhetoric, and moral philosophy, Smith remained a professor at Glasgow University until 1764. Famously absentminded and overheard to talk to himself while he was alone, Professor Smith avidly played a card game known as whist (similar to bridge) in his leisure hours. He later described these years as "by far the happiest and most honourable period of my life" (Stewart, 1793, p. 112). He also assumed administrative positions, including Dean of Faculty in 1761.

While at Glasgow he published his first book, in 1759, *The Theory of Moral Sentiments,* a tract that explains human morality through the sentiment of sympathy. The book was well received—with high praise from Edmund Burke and David Hume, Smith's long-time friend—and established Smith's reputation as a man of letters. After gaining notoriety from *Moral Sentiments,* Smith was invited by Charles Townshend to become a travelling tutor to his stepson, the third duke of Buccleuch.

Perhaps growing weary of academic politics and restless in

Glasgow, and tempted by a generous stipend and promise of a pension, Smith left Glasgow in 1764 to become a tutor to the eighteen-year-old Buccleuch. Smith and Buccleuch embarked on a grand tour of France and Switzerland, taking up primary residence in Toulouse, France. They must have made quite a pair: the absentminded Smith with his broken French and his teenage charge, visiting the intellectual salons of Paris and Geneva. Serving as a private tutor left Smith with an unexpected amount of free time, every professor's dream. He used his time to befriend many of the great French intellectuals of the day, including d'Alembert, Turgot, Voltaire, and—most consequential of all—François Quesnay, author of *Tableau Économique*, an economic model of the flow of the macroeconomy.[1] Unfortunately, his time in France was cut short by the death of Hew Campbell Scott, the duke's brother, who had joined them for study.

Smith returned with the duke to London in the fall of 1766, and devoted the next ten years to researching and writing *The Wealth of Nations*, supporting himself on the annuity provided by the Duke of Buccleuch. Most of the time he spent in Kirkcaldy, with his mother, who lived to the age of ninety. Smith wrote a friend in 1780, "Upon my return to Britain I retired to a small Town in Scotland the place of my nativity, where I continued to live for six years in great tranquility, and almost in complete retirement. During this time I amused myself principally with writing my Enquiry concerning the Wealth of Nations."[2] What an amusement! The volume published in London on March 8, 1776, consumed nearly 1,100 pages, and drew extensively on modern and ancient history, philosophy, firsthand observation, published reports—all of which were marshaled to generate and support keen insights into economic theory.

The student who is about to read *The Wealth of Nations* for

---

[1] Smith had intended to dedicate *The Wealth of Nations* to Quesnay, but Quesnay died shortly before the book went to press.

[2] Letter to Andreas Holt quoted in Ross (1995; p. 227).

the first time is lucky. The book is eminently readable. Smith's clear, evocative writing style resembles that of one of his favorite authors, Jonathan Swift, author of *Gulliver's Travels*. His attention to detail and breadth of knowledge are remarkable. Economics is not the dismal science in Smith's hands.

The first chapter of *The Wealth of Nations* provides a vivid description of the division of labor, through a careful case study of a pin factory. Smith attributes the improvement in labor productivity, the key ingredient in economic growth, to an ever more specialized division of labor. "The greatest improvement in the productive powers of labour, and the greater part of the skill, dexterity, and judgment with which it is anywhere directed, or applied," he observed, "seem to have been the effects of the division of labour" (p. 9). In modern terms, his discussion of the division of labor can best be thought of as a description of a production function. Assigning individuals more specialized tasks increases output per unit of input. Leaving the classroom and visiting the factory floor paid immeasurable dividends for Smith's analysis, a lesson that is often lost on modern economists.[3]

Probably the most famous (and selectively cited) passage in *The Wealth of Nations* concerns Smith's reference to the *invisible hand*. This reference occurs only once in the book, toward the end of the following long paragraph (p. 572):

> But the annual revenue of every society is always precisely equal to the exchangeable value of the whole annual produce of its industry, or rather is precisely the same thing with that exchangeable value. As every individual, therefore, endeavours as much as he can both to employ his capital in the support of domestic industry, and so to direct that industry that its produce may be of the greatest value; every individual necessarily labours to rend the annual revenue

[3]It is worth noting, however, that the National Bureau of Economic Research has recently organized visits to factory floors in many industries to expose academic economists to the workings of the modern factory floor. These visits are appropriately called "pin factory" visits, in homage to Smith.

of the society as great as he can. He generally, indeed, neither intends to promote the public interest, nor knows how much he is promoting it. By preferring the support of domestic to that of foreign industry, he intends only his own security; and by directing that industry in such a manner as its produce may be of the greatest value, he intends only his own gain, and he is in this, as in many other cases, led by an invisible hand to promote an end which was no part of his intention. Nor is it always the worse for the society that it was no part of it. By pursuing his own interest he frequently promotes that of the society more effectually than when he really intends to promote it. I have never known much good done by those who affected to trade for the public good. It is an affectation, indeed, not very common among merchants, and very few words need be employed in dissuading them from it.

Smith's specific point is that restrictions on imports, supported by merchants and manufacturers in some industries, work to the advantage of those industries but not to the general good of society.

Many liberal and conservative economists have interpreted Smith's reference to the invisible hand broadly, as indicating his commitment to the idea that individual exchange in the marketplace inexorably leads to the greatest good for society. Emma Rothschild challenges this commonplace twentieth-century interpretation, suggesting that "Smith did not especially esteem the invisible hand" (Rothschild, 2001, p. 116). She even goes so far as to suggest that Smith used the famous metaphor as an ironic joke, in the tradition of Jonathan Swift. She does not dispute that Smith was a great defender of individual freedom. She also acknowledges that the ideas that individuals' actions have unintended consequences and that these unintended consequences sometimes promote the public good permeate *The Wealth of Nations*. The thrust of her argument is that, interpreted in the context of the late eighteenth century and Smith's other writings, he would be skeptical of the twentieth-century elevation of the invisible hand to the central concept of his thinking. This conclusion is partly speculative and has enraged critics, but there can be little doubt that Smith's faith in the power of an invisible hand has been exaggerated by modern commentators. He persistently worried that merchants and manufacturers, pursuing their own self-interest, would orchestrate government regulation and patronage to their advantage, knocking the benevolent invisible hand off course. This worry applies with equal force to contemporary politics as well. Moreover, Rothschild emphasizes that Smith used the metaphor only once in *The Wealth of Nations*, applied it rather narrowly, and presented it with more than his usual number of caveats and qualifications.

To be sure, Smith worried about the encroachment of government on economic activity. And his concerns were directed at least as much toward parish councils, church wardens, big corporations, guilds, and established religious institutions as to the national government; after all, these institutions were part and parcel of eighteenth-century government. He was nonetheless frequently tolerant of government intervention when the aim was to reduce poverty. For example, concerning labor regulation, Smith passionately argued, "When the regulation, therefore, is in support of the workmen, it is always just and equitable; but it is sometimes otherwise when in favour of the masters" (p. 195). He also saw a tacit conspiracy on the part of employers "always and everywhere" to keep wages as low as possible.

Smith was a Rawlsian before the philosopher John Rawls, proclaiming: "No society can surely be flourishing and happy, of which the far greater part of the members are poor and miserable. It is but equity, besides, that they who feed, clothe and lodge the whole body of the people, should have such a share of the produce of their own labour as to be themselves tolerably well fed, clothed and lodged." (pp. 110–111)

He clearly had a big heart and much compassion for the disadvantaged. This generated inevitable conflict in his own thinking. One must decide how much efficiency should be sacrificed to improve the lot of those who feed, clothe, and lodge the rest of society, if that is a goal of economic policy. The answer is not easy for one individual, nor universally accepted across individuals. Smith wrestled with this dilemma. As a consequence, some of Smith's arguments were at times ambiguous or in conflict, despite his precise prose. In fact, at the turn of the nineteenth century Adam Smith's arguments were invoked by Samuel Whitbread in favor of a minimum wage and by William Pitt against it.

A similar conflict arises concerning progressive taxation, meaning a tendency for tax rates to rise with an individual's income. Smith favored low taxes and argued that subjects "ought to contribute toward the support of the government, as nearly as possible, in proportion to their respective abilities" (p. 1043). This sounds like a flat tax. Yet he also argued, "It is not very unreasonable that the rich should contribute to the public expence, not only in proportion to their revenue, but something more than in that proportion" (p. 1065). Indeed, Smith supported a tax on luxury carriages, anathema to the idea of a flat tax.

Smith also supported universal government-financed education—not for reasons of efficiency or redistribution, but because he believed the division of labor destined people to perform monotonous, mind-numbing tasks that eroded their intelligence. His economic policy had social and moral objectives, not just the maximization of national income. Smith was very much a product of the Enlightenment.

In *The Wealth of Nations* Smith describes people as usually rational decision makers, although sometimes seduced by "romantic hopes" to disregard the dangers inherent in their decisions. In a very real sense, the origin of "behavioral economics," an emerging field in economics that questions whether individuals act rationally to maximize their individual utility, can be traced back to Adam Smith.

He thought the market was ubiquitous and uniquely human, writing: "The propensity to truck, barter and exchange one thing for another . . . is common to all men, and to be found in no other race of animals" (p. 22). He would undoubtedly be shocked to discover that twentieth-century economists have found that animals such as rats and pigeons respond to economic incentives in laboratory settings, and generally seem capable of displaying consistent economic behavior. Nevertheless, the documented pressure for market activity to develop in virtually all human environments, from Communism to prisoner-of-war camps, does seem a remarkable human tendency. Constraints can be imposed on a market, but the rise of a market seems virtually unavoidable.

Smith's keenest observations on the operation of markets pertained to the labor market. In chapter X he established the idea of *equalizing differences*: "The whole of the advantages and disadvantages of the different employments of labour and stock must, in the same neighborhood, be either perfectly equal or continually tending to equality" (p. 138). This has become the fundamental equilibrium concept of modern labor economics, animating the theory of compensating differential for work amenities and the theory of human capital. He proposed five reasons why wages differ in different employments: (1) "The wages of labour vary with the ease or hardship, the cleanliness or dirtiness, the honourableness or dishonourableness of the employment." (2) "The wages of labour vary with the easiness and cheapness, or the difficulty and expence of learning the business." (3) "The wages of labour in different occupations vary with the constancy or inconstancy of employment." (4) "The wages of labour vary according to the small or great trust which must be reposed in the workmen." (5) "The wages of labour in different employments vary according to the probability or improbability of success in them" (pp. 140–147).

The first, third, and fifth reasons can be thought of as compensating differentials: in a market with perfect mobility and full information (at least on the margin), undesirable attributes of particular employments will be counterbalanced by higher wages to recruit a sufficient number of workers into those professions. The second reason is a straightforward statement of equilibrium in human capital theory. The fourth explanation, while consistent with compensating differentials, is probably more appropriately considered a forerunner of efficiency wage theory, where workers are paid a wage premium to ensure their trust. As Smith highlighted, trust is not an issue when it comes to self-employed workers; imperfect monitoring and shirking are not a problem when a worker is his or her own boss.

While one must resist judging eighteenth-century philosophers from the standpoint of twenty-first-century morality and experience, given Smith's keen insights into the labor market and his vigorous defense of individual liberty, his meek stand on slavery must be considered a disappointment. Smith observed that "The experience of all ages and nations, I believe, demonstrates that the work done by slaves, though it appears to cost only their maintenance, is in the end the dearest of any. A person who can acquire no property, can have no other interest but to eat as much, and to labour as little as possible. Whatever work he does beyond what is sufficient to purchase his own maintenance, can be squeezed out of him by violence only, and not by any interest of his own" (p. 493). This analysis implies that slavery would be less profitable than wage labor, a situation that cannot persist for long in equilibrium. Yet slavery showed no tendency to abate by peaceful means in the southern American colonies. Moreover, Smith argued that the decision of the Quakers in Pennsylvania to free their slaves implied that they must have been few in number, for, "Had they made any considerable part of their [the Quakers'] property, such a resolution could never have been agreed to" (p. 494). And Smith's argument that the cost of slave labor was unexpectedly dear is inconsistent with his conclusion that sugar plantations, which heavily used slave labor, were more profitable than corn cultivation, which was not produced with much slave labor in the English colonies. In any event, Smith did not enunciate a principled stand against slavery, an odious deviation from perfect liberty.

Adam Smith foresaw the potential for the American colonies to become a great economic power in *The Wealth of Nations*. It is doubtful that he foresaw the influence that his work would have on the development of America, however. While Smith corresponded with Benjamin Franklin, and may well have met him in Scotland or England, his influence on the founding fathers was far-reaching. Samuel Adams, Thomas Jefferson, James Madison, and Alexander Hamilton all studied *The Wealth of Nations*. Madison, in particular, was persuaded by Smith's work to argue for full religious liberty in *The Federalist Papers*. A couple of years ago, my research assistant, Melissa Clark, discovered that George Washington also owned a copy of *The Wealth of Nations*, by noticing his signature on the table of contents to the fourth edition of the book, published in January 1789 and currently housed in Princeton University's Firestone Library.[4]

Smith was fifty-three years old when *The Wealth of Nations* was first published.[5] He had moved to London to oversee the final stages of publication of the book and to be with his dear friend David Hume at the end of Hume's life. Smith remained in London for two years after the publication of the book. In 1778 he moved back to Scotland, having been appointed commissioner of customs for Edinburgh, serving on the board his father had served on. Still a bachelor, he lived quietly with his mother and a maiden cousin in a pleasant stone house, and he looked after the nine-year-old son of another cousin. Adam Smith died in Edinburgh on July 17, 1790. Ironically, Smith was disappointed that he had not accomplished more in his lifetime. In all likelihood, he died firmly believing that *The Theory of Moral Sentiments* was his most important and influential work (Ross, 1995, p. 177).

If scholarship is to be judged by its impact on future generations, then there is no question that *The Wealth of Nations*

[4]Smith made no alteration save adding an acknowledgment in the fourth edition. The fifth edition, published later in 1789, was the last Smith revised himself.

[5]Perhaps by coincidence, the most influential subsequent works in economics were published by men of approximately the same age. John Maynard Keynes was fifty-three in the year *The General Theory of Employment, Interest and Money* was published; Karl Marx was forty-nine when *Das Kapital* was published; and Milton Friedman was forty-five when *A Theory of the Consumption Function* was published and fifty-one when *A Monetary History of the United States* was published (written with Anna J. Schwartz, who was forty-eight). So much for the idea that economists are past their peak productivity before middle age.

remains an unparalleled success. Indeed, most of postwar economics can be thought of as an effort to determine theoretically and empirically when, and under what conditions, Adam Smith's invisible hand turns out to be all thumbs. The modern theory of information economics highlights that the first welfare theorem, which holds that in a competitive equilibrium no one can be made better off without making someone else worse off, does not apply if information is imperfect or asymmetric. Likewise, unattended externalities (i.e., spillovers from a private transaction that affect more than those parties directly involved in the transaction) mean that government intervention can improve a laissez-faire equilibrium. Transaction costs and irrational decision making could also reduce the economy from peak efficiency. And the exercise of noncompetitive market power, such as collusion among employers in the product or labor market, can reduce the efficiency of a market economy, as Smith warned.

The challenge for modern economists has been to quantify the importance of deviations from the benchmark model of perfect liberty that Smith provided, and to determine whether alternative government would in some sense produce better results than the status quo. This is very much an agenda that Adam Smith laid out. It is testimony to the slow progress of economic science and the prescient genius of Adam Smith that his conception of equilibrium remains at the forefront of economics, some 225 years later. I suspect Smith would also be proud that *The Wealth of Nations* continues to have a profound influence on scholars in fields outside of economics, especially in philosophy, history, and sociology.

RECOMMENDED READINGS

Heilbroner, Robert L. (Ed.) *The Essential Adam Smith*. London: W.W. Norton and Company, 1987. Contains important essays as well as key excerpts from Smith's longer works, including *The Wealth of Nations*. Selected personal correspondences are also included.

Heilbroner, Robert L. *The Worldly Philosophers*. New York: Simon & Schuster, 1999. A classic text on the history of economic thought and the men who shaped it. In addition to a substantial section on Adam Smith, this book discusses the lives and ideas of Karl Marx, John Maynard Keynes, David Ricardo, and others.

Hollander, Samuel. *The Economics of Adam Smith*. Toronto: University of Toronto Press, 1973. Develops and analyzes the economic models that underlie and are implied by Smith's writings.

Malloy, Robin Paul and Jerry Evensky. (Eds.) *Adam Smith and the Philosophy of Law and Economics*. Dordrecht: Kluwer Academic Publishers, 1994. A collection of essays from such academic disciplines as law, legal history, economics, and philosophy that explores Adam Smith's contribution to the philosophy of law and economics.

Rae, John. *Life of Adam Smith*. New York: Augustus M. Kelley, 1965. Originally published in 1895, this was the first large-scale biography of Adam Smith. The 1965 reprint contains a helpful *Comprehensive Guide to John Rae's Life of Adam Smith* by Jacob Viner that outlines Smith's life and points out errors and omissions in Rae's original work.

Ross, Ian S. *The Life and Times of Adam Smith*. Oxford: Clarendon Press, 1995. A well-researched biography of Smith's life from birth to death. Ross focuses on the events of Smith's life and the people he was in contact with, and discusses how these events and people may have shaped Adam Smith's philosophical views.

Rothschild, Emma. *Economic Sentiments: Adam Smith, Condorcet and the Enlightenment*. Cambridge, MA: Harvard University Press, 2001. A reinterpretation of the ideas of Adam Smith and the Marquis du Condorcet that emphasizes the interconnections between their views of economics and politics in the context of the eighteenth-century Enlightenment.

Stewart, Dugald. *An Account of the Life and Writings of the Author,* 1793. Stewart, a philosopher in his own right, contributed this memoir of Smith to later editions of *Essays on Philosophical Subjects* and *The Wealth of Nations.*

Stigler, George. "The Successes and Failures of Professor Smith." *Journal of Political Economy*, 84(6), 1976, pp. 1199–1213. A short, well-written account of the economic theories of Smith. Stigler focuses on the relative importance of each of these theories in shaping economic thought and the degree to which each theory has been accepted or rejected by subsequent generations of economists.

Weinstein, Jack Russell. *On Adam Smith.* Wadsworth: Belmont, CA, 2001. A short primer on Adam Smith's philosophy and thinking for students of Smith or those interested in basic economics.

Wightman, W. L. D. (Ed.) *Essays on Philosophical Subjects.* Indianapolis: Liberty Classics, 1982. As Adam Smith neared death, he had many of his writings that he did not consider worthy of publication destroyed. After his death, some of his remaining essays were collected into this book in 1795.

THE
WEALTH OF NATIONS

INTRODUCTION AND PLAN OF THE WORK

THE ANNUAL[1] labour of every nation is the fund which orig-

The produce of annual labour supplies annual consumption,

inally supplies it with all the necessaries and conveniences of life[2] which it annually consumes, and which consist always either in the immediate produce of that labour, or in what is purchased with that produce from other nations.

better or worse according to the proportion of produce to people,

According therefore, as this produce, or what is purchased with it, bears a greater or smaller proportion to the number of those who are to consume it, the nation will be better or worse supplied with all the necessaries and conveniencies for which it has occasion.[3]

which proportion is regulated by the skill, etc., of the labour and the proportion of useful labourers,

But this proportion must in every nation be regulated by two different circumstances; first, by the skill, dexterity, and judgment with which its labour is generally applied;[4] and, secondly, by the proportion between the number of those who are employed in useful labour, and that of those who are not so em-

---

[1] [This word, with "annually" just below, at once marks the transition from the older British economists' ordinary practice of regarding the wealth of a nation as an accumulated fund. Following the physiocrats, Smith sees that the important thing is how much can be produced in a given time.]

[2] [Cp. with this phrase Locke, *Some Considerations of the Consequences of the Lowering of Interest and Raising the Value of Money*, ed. of 1696, p. 66, "the intrinsic natural worth of anything consists in its fitness to supply the necessities or serve the conveniencies of human life."]

[3] [The implication that the nation's welfare is to be reckoned by the average welfare of its members, not by the aggregate, is to be noticed.]

[4] [Ed. 1 reads "with which labour is generally applied in it."]

ployed.[5] Whatever be the soil, climate, or extent of territory of any particular nation, the abundance or scantiness of its annual supply must, in that particular situation, depend upon those two circumstances.

The abundance or scantiness of this supply too seems to depend more upon the former of those two circumstances than

and more by the skill, etc., than by the proportion of useful labourers, as is shown by the greater produce of civilised societies.

upon the latter. Among the savage nations of hunters and fishers, every individual who is able to work, is more or less employed in useful labour, and endeavours to provide, as well as he can, the necessaries and conveniencies of life, for himself, or[6] such of his family or tribe as are either too old, or too young, or too infirm to go a hunting and fishing. Such nations, however, are so miserably poor, that from mere want, they are frequently reduced, or, at least, think themselves reduced, to the necessity sometimes of directly destroying, and sometimes of abandoning their infants, their old people, and those afflicted with lingering diseases, to perish with hunger, or to be devoured by wild beasts. Among civilized and thriving nations, on the contrary, though a great number of people do not labour at all, many of whom consume the produce of ten times, frequently of a hundred times more labour than the greater part of those who work; yet the produce of the whole labour of the society is so great, that all are often abundantly supplied, and a workman, even of the lowest and poorest order, if he is frugal and industrious, may enjoy a greater share of the necessaries and conveniencies of life than it is possible for any savage to acquire.

The causes[7] of this improvement, in the productive powers of labour, and the order, according to which its produce is nat-

---

[5] [This second circumstance may be stretched so as to include the duration and intensity of the labour of those who are usefully employed, but another important circumstance, the quantity and quality of the accumulated instruments of production, is altogether omitted.]

[6] [Ed. 1 reads "and."]

[7] [Only one cause, the division of labour, is actually treated.]

The causes of improvement and natural distribution are the subject of Book I.

Capital stock, which regulates the proportion of useful labourers, is treated of in Book II.

urally distributed among the different ranks and conditions of men in the society, make the subject of the First Book of this Inquiry.

Whatever be the actual state of the skill, dexterity, and judgment with which labour is applied in any nation, the abundance or scantiness of its annual supply must depend, during the continuance of that state, upon the proportion between the number of those who are annually employed in useful labour, and that of those who are not so employed. The number of useful and productive[8] labourers, it will hereafter appear, is every where in proportion to the quantity of capital stock which is employed in setting them to work, and to the particular way in which it is so employed. The Second Book, therefore, treats of the nature of capital stock, of the manner in which it is gradually accumulated, and of the different quantities of labour which it puts into motion, according to the different ways in which it is employed.

Nations tolerably well advanced as to skill, dexterity, and judgment, in the application of labour, have followed very different plans in the general conduct or direction of it; and those plans have not all been equally favourable to the greatness of its produce. The policy of some nations has given extraordinary encouragement to the industry of the country; that of others to the industry of towns. Scarce any nation has dealt equally and impartially with every sort of industry. Since the downfall of the Roman empire, the policy of Europe has been more favourable to arts, manufactures, and commerce, the industry of towns; than to agriculture, the industry of the country. The circumstances

The circumstances which led Europe to encourage the industry of the towns and discourage agriculture are dealt with in Book III.

---

[8] [This word slips in here as an apparently unimportant synonym of "useful," but subsequently ousts "useful" altogether, and is explained in such a way that unproductive labour may be useful; see esp. below p. 423.]

which seem to have introduced and established this policy are explained in the Third Book.

Though those different plans were, perhaps, first introduced by the private interests and prejudices of particular orders of men, without any regard to, or foresight of, their consequences upon the general welfare of the society; yet they have given occasion to very different theories of political œconomy; of which some magnify the importance of that industry which is carried on in towns, others of that which is carried on in the country. Those theories have had a considerable influence, not only upon the opinions of men of learning, but upon the public conduct of princes and sovereign states. I have endeavoured, in the Fourth Book, to explain, as fully and distinctly as I can, those different theories, and the principal effects which they have produced in different ages and nations.

The theories to which different policies have given rise are explained in Book IV.

To explain[9] in what has consisted the revenue of the great body of the people, or what has been the nature[10] of those funds, which, in different ages and nations, have supplied their annual consumption, is the object of[11] these Four first Books. The Fifth and last Book treats of the revenue of the sovereign, or commonwealth. In this book I have endeavoured to show; first, what are the necessary expences of the sovereign, or commonwealth; which of those expences ought to be defrayed by the general contribution of the whole society; and which of them, by that of some particular part only, or of some particular members of it:[12] secondly, what are the different methods in which the whole society may be made to contribute towards defraying the expences incumbent on the whole society, and

The expenditure, revenue and debts of the sovereign are treated of in Book V.

---

[9] [Ed. 1 does not contain "to explain."]

[10] [Ed. 1 reads "what is the nature."]

[11] [Ed. 1 reads "is treated of in."]

[12] [Ed. 1 reads "of the society."]

what are the principal advantages and inconveniencies of each of those methods: and, thirdly and lastly, what are the reasons and causes which have induced almost all modern governments to mortgage some part of this revenue, or to contract debts, and what have been the effects of those debts upon the real wealth, the annual produce of the land and labour of the society.[13]

---

[13] [Read in conjunction with the first two paragraphs, this sentence makes it clear that the wealth of a nation is to be reckoned by its *per capita* income. But this view is often temporarily departed from in the course of the work.]

BOOK I

OF THE CAUSES OF IMPROVEMENT IN THE
PRODUCTIVE POWERS OF LABOUR, AND OF THE
ORDER ACCORDING TO WHICH ITS PRODUCE IS
NATURALLY DISTRIBUTED AMONG THE
DIFFERENT RANKS OF THE PEOPLE.

CHAPTER I

OF THE DIVISION OF LABOUR[1]

Division of labour is the great cause of its increased powers, as may be better understood from a particular example,

THE GREATEST improvement[2] in the productive powers of labour, and the greater part of the skill, dexterity, and judgment with which it is any where directed, or applied, seem to have been the effects of the division of labour.

The effects of the division of labour, in

---

[1] [This phrase, if used at all before this time, was not a familiar one. Its presence here is probably due to a passage in Mandeville, *Fable of the Bees*, pt. ii. (1729), dial. vi., p. 335: "CLEO ... when once men come to be governed by written laws, all the rest comes on apace ... No number of men, when once they enjoy quiet, and no man needs to fear his neighbour, will be long without learning to divide and subdivide their labour. HOR. I don't understand you. CLEO. Man, as I have hinted before, naturally loves to imitate what he sees others do, which is the reason that savage people all do the same thing: this hinders them from meliorating their condition, though they are always wishing for it: but if one will wholly apply himself to the making of bows and arrows, whilst another provides food, a third builds huts, a fourth makes garments, and a fifth utensils, they not only become useful to one another, but the callings and employments themselves will, in the same number of years, receive much greater improvements, than if all had been promiscuously followed by every one of the five. HOR. I believe you are perfectly right there; and the truth of what you say is in nothing so conspicuous as it is in watchmaking, which is come to a higher degree of perfection than it would have been arrived at yet, if the whole had always remained the employment of one person; and I am persuaded that even the plenty we have of clocks and watches, as well as the exactness and beauty they may be made of, are chiefly owing to the division that has been made of that art into many branches." Joseph Harris, *Essay upon Money and Coins*, 1757, pt. i., § 12, treats of the "usefulness of distinct trades," or "the advantages accruing to mankind from their betaking themselves severally to different occupations," but does not use the phrase "division of labour."]

[2] [Ed. 1 reads "improvements."]

the general business of society, will be more easily understood, by considering in what manner it operates in some particular manufactures. It is commonly supposed to be carried furthest in some very trifling ones; not perhaps that it really is carried further in them than in others of more importance: but in those trifling manufactures which are destined to supply the small wants of but a small number of people, the whole number of workmen must necessarily be small; and those employed in every different branch of the work can often be collected into the same workhouse, and placed at once under the view of the spectator. In those great manufactures, on the contrary, which are destined to supply the great wants of the great body of the people, every different branch of the work employs so great a number of workmen, that it is impossible to collect them all into the same workhouse. We can seldom see more, at one time, than those employed in one single branch. Though in such manufactures,[3] therefore, the work may really be divided into a much greater number of parts, than in those of a more trifling nature, the division is not near so obvious, and has accordingly been much less observed.

To take an example, therefore,[4] from a very trifling manufacture; but one in which the division of labour has been very often taken notice of, the trade of the pin-maker; a workman not educated to this business (which the division of labour has rendered a distinct trade),[5] nor acquainted with the use of the machinery employed in it (to the invention of which the same division of labour has probably given occasion), could scarce, perhaps, with his utmost industry, make one pin in a day, and certainly could not make twenty. But in the way in which this

such as pin-making.

---

[3] [Ed. 1 reads "Though in them."]

[4] [Another and perhaps more important reason for taking an example like that which follows is the possibility of exhibiting the advantages of division of labour in statistical form.]

[5] [This parenthesis would alone be sufficient to show that those are wrong who believe Smith did not include the separation of employments in "division of labour."]

business is now carried on, not only the whole work is a peculiar trade, but it is divided into a number of branches, of which the greater part are likewise peculiar trades. One man draws out the wire, another straights it, a third cuts it, a fourth points it, a fifth grinds it at the top for receiving the head; to make the head requires two or three distinct operations; to put it on, is a peculiar business, to whiten the pins is another; it is even a trade by itself to put them into the paper; and the important business of making a pin is, in this manner, divided into about eighteen distinct operations, which, in some manufactories, are all performed by distinct hands, though in others the same man will sometimes perform two or three of them.[6] I have seen a small manufactory of this kind where ten men only were employed, and where some of them consequently performed two or three distinct operations. But though they were very poor, and therefore but indifferently accommodated with the necessary machinery, they could, when they exerted themselves, make among them about twelve pounds of pins in a day. There are in a pound upwards of four thousand pins of a middling size. Those ten persons, therefore, could make among them upwards of forty-eight thousand pins in a day. Each person, therefore, making a tenth part of forty-eight thousand pins, might be considered as making four thousand eight hundred pins in a day. But if they had all wrought separately and independently, and without any of them having been educated to this peculiar business, they certainly could not each of them have made twenty, perhaps not one pin in a day; that is, certainly, not the two hundred and fortieth, perhaps not the four thousand eight hundredth part of what they are at present capable of performing, in consequence

---

[6] [In Adam Smith's *Lectures*, p. 164, the business is, as here, divided into eighteen operations. This number is doubtless taken from the *Encyclopédie*, tom. v. (published in 1755), *s.v.* Épingle. The article is ascribed to M. Delaire, "qui décrivait la fabrication de l'épingle dans les ateliers même des ouvriers," p. 807. In some factories the division was carried further. E. Chambers, *Cyclopædia*, vol. ii., 2nd ed., 1738, and 4th ed., 1741, *s.v.* Pin, makes the number of separate operations twenty-five.]

of a proper division and combination of their different operations.

In every other art and manufacture, the effects of the division of labour are similar to what they are in this very trifling one; though, in many of them, the labour can neither be so much subdivided, nor reduced to so great a simplicity of operation. The division of labour, however, so far as it can be introduced, occasions, in every art, a proportionable increase of the productive powers of labour. The separation of different trades and employments from one another, seems to have taken place, in consequence of this advantage. This separation too is generally carried furthest in those countries which enjoy the highest degree of industry and improvement; what is the work of one man in a rude state of society, being generally that of several in an improved one. In every improved society, the farmer is generally nothing but a farmer; the manufacturer, nothing but a manufacturer. The labour too which is necessary to produce any one complete manufacture, is almost always divided among a great number of hands. How many different trades are employed in each branch of the linen and woollen manufactures, from the growers of the flax and the wool, to the bleachers and smoothers of the linen, or to the dyers and dressers of the cloth! The nature of agriculture, indeed, does not admit of so many subdivisions of labour, nor of so complete a separation of one business from another, as manufactures. It is impossible to separate so entirely, the business of the grazier from that of the corn-farmer, as the trade of the carpenter is commonly separated from that of the smith. The spinner is almost always a distinct person from the weaver; but the ploughman, the harrower, the sower of the seed, and the reaper of the corn, are often the same. The occasions for those different sorts of labour returning with the different seasons of the year, it is impossible that one man should be constantly employed in any one of them. This impossibility of making so complete and entire a separation of all the different branches of labour employed in agriculture, is perhaps the reason why the improvement of the

The effect is similar in all trades and also in the division of employments.

productive powers of labour in this art, does not always keep
pace with their improvement in manufactures. The most opulent nations, indeed, generally excel all their neighbours in
agriculture as well as in manufactures; but they are commonly
more distinguished by their superiority in the latter than in the
former. Their lands are in general better cultivated, and having
more labour and expence bestowed upon them, produce more
in proportion to the extent and natural fertility of the ground.
But this[7] superiority of produce is seldom much more than in
proportion to the superiority of labour and expence. In agriculture, the labour of the rich country is not always much more
productive than that of the poor; or, at least, it is never so much
more productive, as it commonly is in manufactures. The corn
of the rich country, therefore, will not always, in the same degree of goodness, come cheaper to market than that of the
poor. The corn of Poland, in the same degree of goodness, is as
cheap as that of France, notwithstanding the superior opulence
and improvement of the latter country. The corn of France is, in
the corn provinces, fully as good, and in most years nearly
about the same price with the corn of England, though, in opulence and improvement, France is perhaps inferior to England.
The corn-lands of England, however, are better cultivated than
those of France, and the corn-lands[8] of France are said to be
much better cultivated than those of Poland. But though the
poor country, notwithstanding the inferiority of its cultivation,
can, in some measure, rival the rich in the cheapness and goodness of its corn, it can pretend to no such competition in its
manufactures; at least if those manufactures suit the soil, climate, and situation of the country. The silks of France are better and cheaper than those of England, because the silk
manufacture, at least under the high duties upon the importation of raw silk, does not so well suit the climate of England as
that of France.[9] But the hard-ware and the coarse woollens of
England are beyond all comparison superior to those of

[7] [Ed. 1 reads "the."]

[8] [Ed. 1 reads "the lands" here and in the line above.]

[9] [Ed. 1 reads "because the silk manufacture does not suit the climate of England."]

France, and much cheaper too in the same degree of goodness.[10] In Poland there are said to be scarce any manufactures
of any kind, a few of those coarser household manufactures excepted, without which no country can well subsist.

This great increase of the quantity of work, which, in consequence of the division of labour, the same number of people
are capable of performing,[11] is owing to three different circum-

*The advantage is
due to three
circumstances,*

stances; first, to the increase of dexterity in
every particular workman; secondly, to the
saving of the time which is commonly lost in
passing from one species of work to another;
and lastly, to the invention of a great number of machines
which facilitate and abridge labour, and enable one man to do
the work of many.[12]

First, the improvement of the dexterity of the workman necessarily increases the quantity of the work he can perform; and
the division of labour, by reducing every man's business to

*(1) improved
dexterity,*

some one simple operation, and by making
this operation the sole employment of his
life, necessarily increases very much the
dexterity of the workman. A common smith, who, though accustomed to handle the hammer, has never been used to make

[10] [In *Lectures*, p. 164, the comparison is between English and French "toys," *i.e.*,
small metal articles.]

[11] [Ed. 1 places "in consequence of the division of labour" here instead of in the
line above.]

[12] ["Pour la célérité du travail et la perfection de l'ouvrage, elles dépendent en-
tièrement de la multitude des ouvriers rassemblés. Lorsqu'une manufacture est
nombreuse, chaque operation occupe un homme différent. Tel ouvrier ne fait et ne
fera de sa vie qu'une seule et unique chose; tel autre une autre chose; d'où il arrive
que chacune s'exécute bien et promptement, et que l'ouvrage le mieux fait est encore celui qu'on a à meilleur marché. D'ailleurs le goût et la façon se perfection-
nent nécessairement entre un grand nombre d'ouvriers, parce qu'il est difficile
qu'il ne s'en rencontre quelques-uns capables de réfléchir, de combiner, et de trou-
ver enfin le seul moyen qui puisse les mettre audessus de leurs semblables; le
moyen ou d'épargner la matière, ou d'allonger le temps, ou de surfaire l'industrie,
soit par une machine nouvelle, soit par une manœuvre plus commode."—
Encyclopédie, tom i. (1751), p. 717, *s.v.* Art. All three advantages mentioned in the
text above are included here.]

nails, if upon some particular occasion he is obliged to attempt it, will scarce, I am assured, be able to make above two or three hundred nails in a day, and those too very bad ones.[13] A smith who has been accustomed to make nails, but whose sole or principal business has not been that of a nailer, can seldom with his utmost diligence make more than eight hundred or a thousand nails in a day. I have seen several boys under twenty years of age who had never exercised any other trade but that of making nails, and who, when they exerted themselves, could make, each of them, upwards of two thousand three hundred nails in a day.[14] The making of a nail, however, is by no means one of the simplest operations. The same person blows the bellows, stirs or mends the fire as there is occasion, heats the iron, and forges every part of the nail: In forging the head too he is obliged to change his tools. The different operations into which the making of a pin, or of a metal button,[15] is subdivided, are all of them much more simple, and the dexterity of the person, of whose life it has been the sole business to perform them, is usually much greater. The rapidity with which some of the operations of those manufactures are performed, exceeds what the human hand could, by those who had never seen them, be supposed capable of acquiring.

Secondly, the advantage which is gained by saving the time commonly lost in passing from one sort of work to another, is much greater than we should at first view be apt to imagine it.

(2) saving of time, It is impossible to pass very quickly from one kind of work to another, that is carried on in a different place, and with quite different tools. A country weaver,[16] who cultivates a small farm, must lose a good deal of time in passing from his loom to the field, and from the field to

---

[13] [In *Lectures*, p. 166, "a country smith not accustomed to make nails will work very hard for three or four hundred a day and those too very bad."]

[14] [In *Lectures*, p. 166, "a boy used to it will easily make two thousand and those incomparably better."]

[15] [In *Lectures*, p. 255, it is implied that the labour of making a button was divided among eighty persons.]

[16] [The same example occurs in *Lectures*, p. 166.]

his loom. When the two trades can be carried on in the same workhouse, the loss of time is no doubt much less. It is even in this case, however, very considerable. A man commonly saunters a little in turning his hand from one sort of employment to another. When he first begins the new work he is seldom very keen and hearty; his mind, as they say, does not go to it, and for some time he rather trifles than applies to good purpose. The habit of sauntering and of indolent careless application, which is naturally, or rather necessarily acquired by every country workman who is obliged to change his work and his tools every half hour, and to apply his hand in twenty different ways almost every day of his life; renders him almost always slothful and lazy, and incapable of any vigorous application even on the most pressing occasions. Independent, therefore, of his deficiency in point of dexterity, this cause alone must always reduce considerably the quantity of work which he is capable of performing.

Thirdly, and lastly, every body must be sensible how much labour is facilitated and abridged by the application of proper machinery. It is unnecessary to give any example.[17] I shall only

and (3) application of machinery, invented by workmen,

observe, therefore,[18] that the invention of all those machines by which labour is so much facilitated and abridged, seems to have been originally owing to the division of labour. Men are much more likely to discover easier and readier methods of attaining any object, when the whole attention of their minds is directed towards that single object, than when it is dissipated among a great variety of things. But in consequence of the division of labour, the whole of every man's attention comes naturally to be directed towards some one very simple object. It is naturally to be expected, therefore, that some one or other of those who are employed in each particular branch of labour should soon find out easier and readier

[17] [Examples are given in *Lectures*, p. 167: "Two men and three horses will do more in a day with the plough than twenty men without it. The miller and his servant will do more with the water mill than a dozen with the hand mill, though it too be a machine."]

[18] [Ed. 1 reads "I shall, therefore, only observe."]

methods of performing their own particular work, wherever the nature of it admits of such improvement. A great part of the machines made use of[19] in those manufactures in which labour is most subdivided, were originally the inventions of common workmen, who, being each of them employed in some very simple operation, naturally turned their thoughts towards finding out easier and readier methods of performing it. Whoever has been much accustomed to visit such manufactures, must frequently have been shewn very pretty machines, which were the inventions of such[20] workmen, in order to facilitate and quicken their own particular part of the work. In the first fire-engines,[21] a boy was constantly employed to open and shut alternately the communication between the boiler and the cylinder, according as the piston either ascended or descended. One of those boys, who loved to play with his companions, observed that, by tying a string from the handle of the valve which opened this communication to another part of the machine, the valve would open and shut without his assistance, and leave him at liberty to divert himself with his play-fellows. One of the greatest improvements that has been made upon this machine, since it was first invented, was in this manner the discovery of a boy who wanted to save his own labour.[22]

All the improvements in machinery, however, have by no

[19] [Ed. 1 reads "machines employed."]

[20] [Ed. 1 reads "of common."]

[21] [*I.e.*, steam-engines.]

[22] [This pretty story is largely, at any rate, mythical. It appears to have grown out of a misreading (not necessarily by Smith) of the following passage: "They used before to work with a buoy in the cylinder enclosed in a pipe, which buoy rose when the steam was strong, and opened the injection, and made a stroke; thereby they were capable of only giving six, eight or ten strokes in a minute, till a boy, Humphry Potter, who attended the engine, added (what he called scoggan) a catch that the beam Q always opened; and then it would go fifteen or sixteen strokes in a minute. But this being perplexed with catches and strings, Mr. Henry Beighton, in an engine he had built at Newcastle-on-Tyne in 1718, took them all away, the beam itself simply supplying all much better."—J. T. Desaguliers, *Course of Experimental Philosophy*, vol. ii., 1744, p. 533. From pp. 469, 471, it appears that hand labour was originally used before the "buoy" was devised.]

means been the inventions of those who had occasion to use the machines. Many improvements have been made by the in-

or by machine-makers and philosophers.

genuity of the makers of the machines, when to make them became the business of a peculiar trade; and some by that of those who are called philosophers or men of speculation, whose trade it is not to do any thing, but to observe every thing; and who, upon that account, are often capable of combining together the powers of the most distant and dissimilar objects.[23] In the progress of society, philosophy or speculation becomes, like every other employment, the principal or sole trade and occupation of a particular class of citizens. Like every other employment too, it is subdivided into a great number of different branches, each of which affords occupation to a peculiar tribe or class of philosophers; and this subdivision of employment in philosophy, as well as in every other business, improves dexterity, and saves time. Each individual becomes more expert in his own peculiar branch, more work is done upon the whole, and the quantity of science is considerably increased by it.[24]

It is the great multiplication of the productions of all the

---

[23] [In *Lectures*, p. 167, the invention of the plough is conjecturally attributed to a farmer and that of the hand-mill to a slave, while the invention of the water-wheel and the steam-engine is credited to philosophers. Mandeville is very much less favourable to the claims of the philosophers: "They are very seldom the same sort of people, those that invent arts and improvements in them and those that inquire into the reason of things: this latter is most commonly practised by such as are idle and indolent, that are fond of retirement, hate business and take delight in speculation; whereas none succeed oftener in the first than active, stirring and laborious men, such as will put their hand to the plough, try experiments and give all their attention to what they are about."—*Fable of the Bees*, pt. ii. (1729), dial. iii., p. 151. He goes on to give as examples the improvements in soap-boiling, grain-dyeing, etc.]

[24] [The advantage of producing particular commodities wholly or chiefly in the countries most naturally fitted for their production is recognised below, p. 573, but the fact that division of labour is necessary for its attainment is not noticed. The fact that division of labour allows different workers to be put exclusively to the kind of work for which they are best fitted by qualities not acquired by education and practice, such as age, sex, size and strength, is in part ignored and in part de-

different arts, in consequence of the division of labour, which occasions, in a well-governed society, that universal opulence

Hence the universal opulence of a well-governed society,

which extends itself to the lowest ranks of the people. Every workman has a great quantity of his own work to dispose of beyond what he himself has occasion for; and every other workman being exactly in the same situation, he is enabled to exchange a great quantity of his own goods for a great quantity, or, what comes to the same thing, for the price of a great quantity of theirs. He supplies them abundantly with what they have occasion for, and they accommodate him as amply with what he has occasion for, and a general plenty diffuses itself through all the different ranks of the society.

Observe the accommodation of the most common artificer or day-labourer in a civilized and thriving country, and you will perceive that the number of people of whose industry a

even the day-labourer's coat being the produce of a vast number of workmen.

part, though but a small part, has been employed in procuring him this accommodation, exceeds all computation. The woollen coat, for example, which covers the day-labourer, as coarse and rough as it may appear, is the produce of the joint labour of a great multitude of workmen. The shepherd, the sorter of the wool, the wool-comber or carder, the dyer, the scribbler, the spinner, the weaver, the fuller, the dresser, with many others, must all join their different arts in order to complete even this homely production. How many merchants and carriers, besides, must have been employed in transporting the materials from some of those workmen to others who often live in a very distant part of the country! how much commerce and navigation in particular, how many ship-builders, sailors, sailmakers, rope-makers, must have been employed in order to bring together the different drugs made use of by the dyer, which often come from the remotest corners of the world!

nied below, pp. 24–25, 26. The disadvantage of division of labour or specialisation is dealt with below, pp. 987–989.]

What a variety of labour too is necessary in order to produce the tools of the meanest of those workmen! To say nothing of such complicated machines as the ship of the sailor, the mill of the fuller, or even the loom of the weaver, let us consider only what a variety of labour is requisite in order to form that very simple machine, the shears with which the shepherd clips the wool. The miner, the builder of the furnace for smelting the ore, the feller of the timber, the burner of the charcoal to be made use of in the smelting-house, the brick-maker, the brick-layer, the workmen who attend the furnace, the mill-wright, the forger, the smith, must all of them join their different arts in order to produce them. Were we to examine, in the same manner, all the different parts of his dress and household furniture, the coarse linen shirt which he wears next his skin, the shoes which cover his feet, the bed which he lies on, and all the different parts which compose it, the kitchen-grate at which he prepares his victuals, the coals which he makes use of for that purpose, dug from the bowels of the earth, and brought to him perhaps by a long sea and a long land carriage, all the other utensils of his kitchen, all the furniture of his table, the knives and forks, the earthen or pewter plates upon which he serves up and divides his victuals, the different hands employed in preparing his bread and his beer, the glass window which lets in the heat and the light, and keeps out the wind and the rain, with all the knowledge and art requisite for preparing that beautiful and happy invention, without which these northern parts of the world could scarce have afforded a very comfortable habitation, together with the tools of all the different workmen employed in producing those different conveniencies; if we examine, I say, all these things, and consider what a variety of labour is employed about each of them, we shall be sensible that without the assistance and co-operation of many thousands, the very meanest person in a civilized country could not be provided, even according to, what we very falsely imagine, the easy and simple manner in which he is commonly accommodated. Compared, indeed, with the more extravagant luxury of the great, his accommodation must no doubt appear extremely simple and easy; and yet it may be true, perhaps, that the accommodation of an European prince does not always so much exceed that of an industrious and frugal peasant, as the accommodation of the latter exceeds that of many an African king, the absolute master of the lives and liberties of ten thousand naked savages.[25]

[25] [This paragraph was probably taken bodily from the MS. of the author's lectures. It appears to be founded on Mun, *England's Treasure by Forraign Trade*, chap. iii., at end; Locke, *Civil Government*, §43; Mandeville, *Fable of the Bees*, pt. i., Remark P, 2nd ed., 1723, p. 182, and perhaps Harris, *Essay upon Money and Coins*, pt. i., §12. See *Lectures*, pp. 161–162 and notes.]

CHAPTER II

OF THE PRINCIPLE WHICH GIVES OCCASION
TO THE DIVISION OF LABOUR

THIS DIVISION of labour, from which so many advantages are derived, is not originally the effect of any human wisdom, which foresees and intends that general opulence to which it gives occasion.[1] It is the necessary, though very slow and gradual, consequence of a certain propensity in human nature which has in view no such extensive utility; the propensity to truck, barter, and exchange one thing for another.

The division of labour arises from a propensity in human nature to exchange.

Whether this propensity be one of those original principles in human nature, of which no further account can be given; or whether, as seems more probable, it be the necessary consequence of the faculties of reason and speech, it belongs not to our present subject to enquire. It is common to all men, and to be found in no other race of animals, which seem to know neither this nor any other species of contracts. Two greyhounds, in running down the same hare, have sometimes the appearance of acting in some sort of concert. Each turns her towards his companion, or endeavours to intercept her when his companion turns her towards himself. This, however, is not the effect of any contract, but of the accidental con-

This propensity is found in man alone.

---

[1] [*I.e.*, it is not the effect of any conscious regulation by the state or society, like the "law of Sesostris," that every man should follow the employment of his father, referred to in the corresponding passage in *Lectures*, p. 168. The denial that it is the effect of individual wisdom recognising the advantage of exercising special natural talents comes lower down, p. 24–25.]

currence of their passions in the same object at that particular time. Nobody ever saw a dog make a fair and deliberate exchange of one bone for another with another dog.[2] Nobody ever saw one animal by its gestures and natural cries signify to another, this is mine, that yours; I am willing to give this for that. When an animal wants to obtain something either of a man or of another animal, it has no other means of persuasion but to gain the favour of those whose service it requires. A puppy fawns upon its dam, and a spaniel endeavours by a thousand attractions to engage the attention of its master who is at dinner, when it wants to be fed by him. Man sometimes uses the same arts with his brethren, and when he has no other means of engaging them to act according to his inclinations, endeavours by every servile and fawning attention to obtain their good will. He has not time, however, to do this upon every occasion. In civilized society he stands at all times in need of the co-operation and assistance of great multitudes, while his whole life is scarce sufficient to gain the friendship of a few persons. In almost every other race of animals each individual, when it is grown up to maturity, is entirely[3] independent, and in its natural state has occasion for the assistance of no other living creature. But man has almost constant occasion for the help of his brethren, and it is in vain for him to expect it from their benevolence only. He will be more likely to prevail if he can interest their self-love in his favour, and shew them that it is for their own advantage to do for him what he requires of them. Whoever offers to another a bargain of any kind, proposes to do this. Give me that which I want, and you shall have this which you want, is the meaning of every such offer; and it is in this manner that we obtain from one another the far greater part of those good offices which we stand in need of. It is not from the benevolence of the butcher, the brewer, or the baker, that we expect our dinner, but from their regard to their

[2] [It is by no means clear what object there could be in exchanging one bone for another.]

[3] [Misprinted "intirely" in eds. 1–5. "Entirely" occurs a little lower down in all eds.]

own interest. We address ourselves, not to their humanity but
to their self-love, and never talk to them of our own necessities
but of their advantages. Nobody but a beggar chuses to depend
chiefly upon the benevolence of his fellow-citizens. Even a
beggar does not depend upon it entirely. The charity of well-
disposed people, indeed, supplies him with the whole fund of
his subsistence. But though this principle ultimately provides
him with all the necessaries of life which he has occasion for, it
neither does nor can provide him with them as he has occasion
for them. The greater part of his occasional wants are supplied
in the same manner as those of other people, by treaty, by
barter, and by purchase. With the money which one man gives
him he purchases food. The old cloaths which another bestows
upon him he exchanges for other old cloaths which suit him
better, or for lodging, or for food, or for money, with which he
can buy either food, cloaths, or lodging, as he has occasion.[4]

As it is by treaty, by barter, and by purchase, that we obtain
from one another the greater part of those mutual good offices
which we stand in need of, so it is this same
trucking disposition which originally gives
occasion to the division of labour. In a tribe
of hunters or shepherds a particular person
makes bows and arrows, for example, with
more readiness and dexterity than any other. He frequently exchanges them for cattle or for venison with his companions;
and he finds at last that he can in this manner get more cattle
and venison, than if he himself went to the field to catch them.
From a regard to his own interest, therefore, the making of
bows and arrows grows to be his chief business, and he becomes a sort of armourer. Another excels in making the frames
and covers of their little huts or moveable houses. He is accustomed to be of use in this way to his neighbours, who reward
him in the same manner with cattle and with venison, till at last
he finds it his interest to dedicate himself entirely to this employment, and to become a sort of house-carpenter. In the
same manner a third becomes a smith or a brazier; a fourth a

*It is encouraged
by self-interest
and leads to divi-
sion of labour,*

[4] [The paragraph is repeated from *Lectures*, p. 169. It is founded on Mandeville,
Fable of the Bees, pt. ii. (1729), dial. vi., pp. 421, 422.]

tanner or dresser of hides or skins, the principal part of the clothing of savages. And thus the certainty of being able to exchange all that surplus part of the produce of his own labour, which is over and above his own consumption, for such parts of the produce of other men's labour as he may have occasion for, encourages every man to apply himself to a particular occupation, and to cultivate and bring to perfection whatever talent or genius he may possess for that particular species of business.[5]

The difference of natural talents in different men is, in reality, much less than we are aware of; and the very different genius which appears to distinguish men of *thus giving rise to* different professions, when grown up to ma- *differences of* turity, is not upon many occasions so much *talent more* the cause, as the effect of the division of *important than* labour.[6] The difference between the most *the natural* dissimilar characters, between a philosopher *differences,* and a common street porter, for example, seems to arise not so much from nature, as from habit, custom, and education. When they came into the world, and for the first six or eight years of their existence, they were, perhaps,[7] very much alike, and neither their parents nor playfellows could perceive any remarkable difference. About that age, or soon after, they come to be employed in very different occupations. The difference of talents comes then to be taken notice of, and widens by degrees, till at last the vanity of the philosopher is willing to acknowledge scarce any resemblance. But without the disposition to truck, barter, and exchange, every man must have procured to himself every necessary and conveniency of life which he wanted. All must have had the same duties to perform, and the same work to do, and there could have been no

[5] [*Lectures*, pp. 169–170.]

[6] [This is apparently directed against Harris, *Money and Coins*, pt. i., §11, and is in accordance with the view of Hume, who asks readers to "consider how nearly equal all men are in their bodily force, and even in their mental powers and faculties, ere cultivated by education."—"Of the Original Contract," in *Essays, Moral and Political*, 1748, p. 291.]

[7] ["Perhaps" is omitted in eds. 2 and 3, and restored in the errata to ed. 4.]

such difference of employment as could alone give occasion to any great difference of talents.[8]

As it is this disposition which forms that difference of talents, so remarkable among men of different professions, so it
and rendering those differences useful.
is this same disposition which renders that difference useful. Many tribes of animals acknowledged to be all of the same species, derive from nature a much more remarkable distinction of genius, than what, antecedent to custom and education, appears to take place among men. By nature a philosopher is not in genius and disposition half so different from a street porter, as a mastiff is from a greyhound, or a greyhound from a spaniel, or this last from a shepherd's dog. Those different tribes of animals, however, though all of the same species, are of scarce any use to one another. The strength of the mastiff is not in the least supported either by the swiftness of the greyhound, or by the sagacity of the spaniel, or by the docility of the shepherd's dog. The effects of those different geniuses and talents, for want of the power or disposition to barter and exchange, cannot be brought into a common stock, and do not in the least contribute to the better accommodation and conveniency of the species. Each animal is still obliged to support and defend itself, separately and independently, and derives no sort of advantage from that variety of talents with which nature has distinguished its fellows. Among men, on the contrary, the most dissimilar geniuses are of use to one another; the different produces of their respective talents, by the general disposition to truck, barter, and exchange, being brought, as it were, into a common stock, where every man may purchase whatever part of the produce of other men's talents he has occasion for.

[8] [*Lectures*, pp. 170–171.]

CHAPTER III

THAT THE DIVISION OF LABOUR IS LIMITED BY THE EXTENT OF THE MARKET

AS IT is the power of exchanging that gives occasion to the division of labour, so the extent of this division must always be

Division of labour is limited by the extent of the power of exchanging.

limited by the extent of that power, or, in other words, by the extent of the market. When the market is very small, no person can have any encouragement to dedicate himself entirely to one employment, for want of the power to exchange all that surplus part of the produce of his own labour, which is over and above his own consumption, for such parts of the produce of other men's labour as he has occasion for.

There are some sorts of industry, even of the lowest kind, which can be carried on no where but in a great town. A porter,

Various trades cannot be carried on except in towns.

for example, can find employment and subsistence in no other place. A village is by much too narrow a sphere for him; even an ordinary market town is scarce large enough to afford him constant occupation. In the lone houses and very small villages which are scattered about in so desert a country as the Highlands of Scotland, every farmer must be butcher, baker and brewer for his own family. In such situations we can scarce expect to find even a smith, a carpenter, or a mason, within less than twenty miles of another of the same trade. The scattered families that live at eight or ten miles distance from the nearest of them, must learn to perform themselves a great number of little pieces of work, for which, in more populous countries, they would call in the assistance of those workmen. Country workmen are almost every where obliged to apply themselves to all the different branches of industry that have so much affinity to one another as to be employed about the same sort of materials. A country carpenter deals in every sort of work that is made of wood: a country smith in every sort of work that is made of iron. The former is not only a carpenter, but a joiner, a cabinet maker, and even a carver in wood, as well as a wheelwright, a ploughwright, a cart and waggon maker. The employments of the latter are still more various. It is impossible there should be such a trade as even that of a nailer in the remote and inland parts of the Highlands of Scotland. Such a workman at the rate of a thousand nails a day, and three hundred working days in the year, will make three hundred thousand nails in the year. But in such a situation it would be impossible to dispose of one thousand, that is, of one day's work in the year.

As by means of water-carriage a more extensive market is opened to every sort of industry than what land-carriage alone

Water-carriage widens the market,

can afford it, so it is upon the sea-coast, and along the banks of navigable rivers, that industry of every kind naturally begins to subdivide and improve itself, and it is frequently not till a long time after that those improvements extend themselves to the inland parts of the country. A broad-wheeled waggon, attended by two men, and drawn by eight horses, in about six weeks time carries and brings back between London and Edinburgh near four ton weight of goods. In about the same time a ship navigated by six or eight men, and sailing between the ports of London and Leith, frequently carries and brings back two hundred ton weight of goods. Six or eight men, therefore, by the help of water-carriage, can carry and bring back in the same time the same quantity of goods between London and Edinburgh, as fifty broad-wheeled waggons, attended by a hundred men, and drawn by four hundred horses.[1] Upon two

[1] [The superiority of carriage by sea is here considerably less than in *Lectures*, p. 172, but is still probably exaggerated. W. Playfair, ed. of *Wealth of Nations*, 1805, vol. i., p. 29, says a waggon of the kind described could carry eight tons, but, of course, some allowance must be made for thirty years of road improvement.]

hundred tons of goods, therefore, carried by the cheapest land-carriage from London to Edinburgh, there must be charged the maintenance of a hundred men for three weeks, and both the maintenance, and, what is nearly equal to the maintenance, the wear and tear of four hundred horses as well as of fifty great waggons. Whereas, upon the same quantity of goods carried by water, there is to be charged only the maintenance of six or eight men, and the wear and tear of a ship of two hundred tons burthen, together with the value of the superior risk, or the difference of the insurance between land and water-carriage. Were there no other communication between those two places, therefore, but by land-carriage, as no goods could be transported from the one to the other, except such whose price was very considerable in proportion to their weight, they could carry on but a small part of that commerce which at present subsists[2] between them, and consequently could give but a small part of that encouragement which they at present mutually afford to each other's industry. There could be little or no commerce of any kind between the distant parts of the world. What goods could bear the expence of land-carriage between London and Calcutta?[3] Or if there were[4] any so precious as to be able to support this expence, with what safety could they be transported through the territories of so many barbarous nations? Those two cities, however, at present carry on a very considerable commerce with each other,[5] and by mutually affording a market, give a good deal of encouragement to each other's industry.

Since such, therefore, are the advantages of water-carriage, it is natural that the first improvements of art and industry should be made where this conveniency opens the whole world for a market to the produce of every sort of labour, and that

[2] [Ed. 1 reads "which is at present carried on."]

[3] [Playfair, *op. cit.*, p. 30, says that equalising the out and home voyages goods were carried from London to Calcutta by sea at the same price (12s per cwt.) as from London to Leeds by land.]

[4] [Ed. 1 reads "was."]

[5] [Ed. 1 reads "carry on together a very considerable commerce."]

and so the first improvements are on the seacoast or navigable rivers,

they should always be much later in extending themselves into the inland parts of the country. The inland parts of the country can for a long time have no other market for the greater part of their goods, but the country which lies round about them, and separates them from the seacoast, and the great navigable rivers. The extent of their market, therefore, must for a long time be in proportion to the riches and populousness of that country, and consequently their improvement must always be posterior to the improvement of that country. In our North American colonies the plantations have constantly followed either the sea-coast or the banks of navigable rivers, and have scarce any where extended themselves to any considerable distance from both.

The nations that, according to the best authenticated history, appear to have been first civilized, were those that dwelt

for example among the ancient nations on the Mediterranean coast.

round the coast of the Mediterranean sea. That sea, by far the greatest inlet that is known in the world, having no tides, nor consequently any waves except such as are caused by the wind only,[6] was, by the smoothness of its surface, as well as by the multitude of its islands, and the proximity of its neighbouring shores, extremely favourable to the infant navigation of the world; when, from their ignorance of the compass, men were afraid to quit the view of the coast, and from the imperfection of the art of ship-building, to abandon themselves to the boisterous waves of the ocean. To pass beyond the pillars of Hercules, that is, to sail out of the Streights of Gibraltar, was, in the antient world, long considered as a most wonderful and dangerous exploit of navigation. It was late before even the Phenicians and Carthaginians, the most skilful navigators and ship-builders of those old times, attempted it, and they were for a long time the only nations that did attempt it.

Of all the countries on the coast of the Mediterranean sea, Egypt seems to have been the first in which either agriculture

---

[6] [This shows a curious belief in the wave-producing capacity of the tides.]

Improvements first took place in Egypt, or manufactures were cultivated and improved to any considerable degree. Upper Egypt extends itself nowhere above a few miles from the Nile, and in Lower Egypt that great river breaks itself into many different canals,[7] which, with the assistance of a little art, seem to have afforded a communication by water-carriage, not only between all the great towns, but between all the considerable villages, and even to many farm-houses in the country; nearly in the same manner as the Rhine and the Maese do in Holland at present. The extent and easiness of this inland navigation was probably one of the principal causes of the early improvement of Egypt.

The improvements in agriculture and manufactures seem likewise to have been of very great antiquity in the provinces *Bengal and China;* of Bengal in the East Indies, and in some of the eastern provinces of China; though the great extent of this antiquity is not authenticated by any histories of whose authority we, in this part of the world, are well assured. In Bengal the Ganges and several other great rivers form a great number of navigable canals[8] in the same manner as the Nile does in Egypt. In the Eastern provinces of China too, several great rivers form, by their different branches, a multitude of canals, and by communicating with one another afford an inland navigation much more extensive than that either of the Nile or the Ganges, or perhaps than both of them put together. It is remarkable that neither the antient Egyptians, nor the Indians, nor the Chinese, encouraged foreign commerce, but seem all to have derived their great opulence from this inland navigation.

All the inland parts of Africa, and all that part of Asia which lies any considerable way north of the Euxine and Caspian seas, the antient Scythia, the modern Tartary and Siberia, seem in all ages of the world to have been in the same barbarous and uncivilized state in which we find them at present. The sea of

[7] [It is only in recent times that this word has become applicable especially to artificial channels; see Murray, *Oxford English Dictionary, s.v.*]

[8] [Ed. 1 reads "break themselves into many canals."]

while Africa, Tartary and Siberia, and also Bavaria, Austria and Hungary are backward.

Tartary is the frozen ocean which admits of no navigation, and though some of the greatest rivers in the world run through that country,[9] they are at too great a distance from one another to carry commerce and communication through the greater part of it. There are in Africa none of those great inlets, such as the Baltic and Adriatic seas in Europe, the Mediterranean and Euxine seas in both Europe and Asia, and the gulphs of Arabia, Persia, India, Bengal, and Siam, in Asia, to carry maritime commerce into the interior parts of that great continent: and the great rivers of Africa are at too great a distance from one another to give occasion to any considerable inland navigation. The commerce besides which any nation can carry on by means of a river which does not break itself into any great number of branches or canals, and which runs into another territory before it reaches the sea, can never be very considerable; because it is always in the power of the nations who possess that other territory to obstruct the communication between the upper country and the sea. The navigation of the Danube is of very little use to the different states of Bavaria, Austria and Hungary, in comparison of what it would be if any[10] of them possessed the whole of its course till it falls into the Black Sea.[11]

[9] [The real difficulty is that the mouths of the rivers are in the Arctic Sea, so that they are separated. One of the objects of the Siberian railway is to connect them.]

[10] [Ed. 1 reads "any one" here.]

[11] [The passage corresponding to this chapter is comprised in one paragraph in *Lectures*, p. 172.]

CHAPTER IV

OF THE ORIGIN AND USE OF MONEY

WHEN THE division of labour has been once thoroughly established, it is but a very small part of a man's wants which the

Division of labour being established, every man lives by exchanging.

produce of his own labour can supply. He supplies the far greater part of them by exchanging that surplus part of the produce of his own labour, which is over and above his own consumption, for such parts of the produce of other men's labour as he has occasion for. Every man thus lives by exchanging, or becomes in some measure a merchant, and the society itself grows to be what is properly a commercial society.

But when the division of labour first began to take place, this power of exchanging must frequently have been very

Difficulties of barter lead to the selection of one commodity as money,

much clogged and embarrassed in its operations. One man, we shall suppose, has more of a certain commodity than he himself has occasion for, while another has less. The former consequently would be glad to dispose of, and the latter to purchase, a part of this superfluity. But if this latter should chance to have nothing that the former stands in need of, no exchange can be made between them. The butcher has more meat in his shop than he himself can consume, and the brewer and the baker would each of them be willing to purchase a part of it. But they have nothing to offer in exchange, except the different productions of their respective trades, and the butcher is already provided with all the bread and beer which he has immediate occasion for. No exchange can, in this case, be made between them. He

cannot be their merchant, nor they his customers; and they
are all of them thus mutually less serviceable to one another.
In order to avoid the inconveniency of such situations, every
prudent man in every period of society, after the first establishment of the division of labour, must naturally have endeavoured to manage his affairs in such a manner, as to have at all
times by him, besides the peculiar produce of his own industry,
a certain quantity of some one commodity or other, such as he
imagined few people would be likely to refuse in exchange for
the produce of their industry.[1]

Many different commodities, it is probable, were successively both thought of and employed for this purpose. In the
rude ages of society, cattle are said to have
for example, been the common instrument of commerce;
cattle, salt, shells, and, though they must have been a most in-
cod, tobacco, convenient one, yet in old times we find
sugar, leather things were frequently valued according to
and nails. the number of cattle which had been given in
exchange for them. The armour of Diomede, says Homer, cost
only nine oxen; but that of Glaucus cost an hundred oxen.[2] Salt
is said to be the common instrument of commerce and exchanges in Abyssinia;[3] a species of shells in some parts of the
coast of India; dried cod at Newfoundland; tobacco in
Virginia;[4] sugar in some of our West India colonies; hides or
dressed leather in some other countries; and there is at this day
a village in Scotland where it is not uncommon, I am told, for a

---

[1] [The paragraph has a close resemblance to Harris, *Money and Coins*, pt. i., §§19,
20.]

[2] [*Iliad*, vi., 236: quoted with the same object in Pliny, *Hist. Nat.*, lib. xxxiii., cap.
i.; Pufendorf, *De jure naturæ et gentium*, lib. v., cap. v., § 1; Martin-Leake,
Historical Account of English Money, 2nd ed., 1745, p. 4 and elsewhere.]

[3] [Montesquieu, *Esprit des lois*, liv. xxii., chap. i., note.]

[4] [W. Douglass, *A Summary Historical and Political of the First Planting,
Progressive Improvements and Present State of the British Settlements in North
America*, 1760, vol. ii., p. 364. Certain law officers' fees in Washington were still
computed in tobacco in 1888.—J.J. Lalor, *Cyclopædia of Political Science*, 1888,
s.v. Money, p. 879.]

workman to carry nails instead of money to the baker's shop or the ale-house.[5]

In all countries, however, men seem at last to have been determined by irresistible reasons to give the preference, for this employment, to metals above every other commodity.[6] Metals can not only be kept with as little loss as any other commodity, scarce any thing being less perishable than they are, but they can likewise, without any loss, be divided into any number of parts, as by fusion those parts can easily be reunited again; a quality which no other equally durable commodities possess, and which more than any other quality renders them fit to be the instruments of commerce and circulation. The man who wanted to buy salt, for example, and had nothing but cattle to give in exchange for it, must have been obliged to buy salt to the value of a whole ox, or a whole sheep, at a time. He could seldom buy less than this, because what he was to give for it could seldom be divided without loss; and if he had a mind to buy more, he must, for the same reasons, have been obliged to buy double or triple the quantity, the value, to wit, of two or three oxen, or of two or three sheep. If, on the contrary, instead of sheep or oxen, he had metals to give in exchange for it, he could easily proportion the quantity of the metal to the precise quantity of the commodity which he had immediate occasion for.

Metals were eventually preferred because durable and divisible.

Different metals have been made use of by different nations

---

[5] [Playfair, ed. of *Wealth of Nations*, 1805, vol. i., p. 36, says the explanation of this is that factors furnish the nailers with materials, and during the time they are working give them a credit for bread, cheese and chandlery goods, which they pay for in nails when the iron is worked up. The fact that nails are metal is forgotten at the beginning of the next paragraph in the text above.]

[6] [For earlier theories as to these reasons see Grotius, *De jure belli et pacis*, lib. ii., cap. xii., § 17; Pufendorf, *De jure naturæ et gentium*, lib. v., cap. i., § 13; Locke, *Some Considerations*, 2nd ed., 1696, p. 31; Law, *Money and Trade*, 1705, ch. i.; Hutcheson, *System of Moral Philosophy*, 1755, vol. ii., pp. 55, 56; Montesquieu, *Esprit des lois*, liv. xxii., ch. ii.; Cantillon, *Essai sur la Nature du Commerce en général*, 1755, pp. 153, 355–357; Harris, *Money and Coins*, pt. i., §§ 22–27, and cp. *Lectures*, pp. 182–185.]

Iron, copper, gold and silver, for this purpose. Iron was the common instrument of commerce among the antient Spartans; copper among the antient Romans; and gold and silver among all rich and commercial nations.

Those metals seem originally to have been made use of for this purpose in rude bars, without any stamp or coinage. Thus *were at first used in unstamped bars,* we are told by Pliny,[7] upon the authority of Timæus, an antient historian, that, till the time of Servius Tullius, the Romans had no coined money, but made use of unstamped bars of copper, to purchase whatever they had occasion for. These rude bars, therefore, performed at this time the function of money.

The use of metals in this rude state was attended with two very considerable inconveniencies; first with the trouble of *and afterwards stamped to show quantity and fineness;* weighing;[8] and, secondly, with that[9] of assaying them. In the precious metals, where a small difference in the quantity makes a great difference in the value, even the business of weighing, with proper exactness, requires at least very accurate weights and scales. The weighing of gold in particular is an operation of some nicety. In the coarser metals, indeed, where a small error would be of little consequence, less accuracy would, no doubt, be necessary. Yet we should find it excessively troublesome, if every time a poor man had occasion either to buy or sell a farthing's worth of goods, he was obliged to weigh the farthing. The operation of assaying is still more difficult, still more tedious, and, unless a part of the metal is fairly melted in the crucible, with proper dissolvents, any conclusion that can be drawn from it, is ex-

---

[7] Plin. Nist. Nat. lib. 33. cap. 3. ["Servius rex primus signavit aes. Antea rudi usos Romæ Timæus tradit." Ed. 1 reads "authority of one Remeus, an antient author," Remeus being the reading in the edition of Pliny in Smith's library, cp. Bonar's *Catalogue of the Library of Adam Smith*, 1894, p. 87. Ed. 1 does not contain the note.]

[8] [Ed. 1 reads "weighing them."]

[9] [Ed. 1 reads "with the trouble."]

tremely uncertain. Before the institution of coined money, however, unless they went through this tedious and difficult operation, people must always have been liable to the grossest frauds and impositions, and instead of a pound weight of pure silver, or pure copper, might receive in exchange for their goods, an adulterated composition of the coarsest and cheapest materials, which had, however, in their outward appearance, been made to resemble those metals. To prevent such abuses, to facilitate exchanges, and thereby to encourage all sorts of industry and commerce, it had been found necessary, in all countries that have made any considerable advances towards improvement, to affix a public stamp upon certain quantities of such particular metals, as were in those countries commonly made use of to purchase goods. Hence the origin of coined money, and of those public offices called mints;[10] institutions exactly of the same nature with those of the aulnagers and stampmasters of woollen and linen cloth.[11] All of them are equally meant to ascertain, by means of a public stamp, the quantity and uniform goodness of those different commodities when brought to market.

The first public stamps of this kind that were affixed to the current metals, seem in many cases to have been intended to

stamps to show fineness being introduced first, ascertain, what it was both most difficult and most important to ascertain, the goodness or fineness of the metal, and to have resembled the sterling mark which is at present affixed to plate and bars of silver, or the Spanish mark which is sometimes affixed to ingots of gold, and which being struck only

---

[10] [Aristotle, *Politics*, 1257a, 38–41; quoted by Pufendorf, *De jure naturæ et gentium*, lib. v., cap. i., § 12.]

[11] [The aulnager measured woollen cloth in England under 25 Ed. III., st. 4, c. 1. See John Smith, *Chronicon Rusticum-Commerciale or Memoirs of Wool*, 1747, vol. i., p. 37. The stampmasters of linen cloth in the linen districts of Scotland were appointed under 10 Ann., c. 21, to prevent "divers abuses and deceits" which "have of late years been used in the manufactures of linen cloth . . . with respect to the lengths, breadths and unequal sorting of yarn, which leads to the great debasing and undervaluing of the said linen cloth both at home and in foreign parts."
—*Statutes of the Realm*, vol. ix., p. 682.]

upon one side of the piece, and not covering the whole surface, ascertains the fineness, but not the weight of the metal. Abraham weighs to Ephron the four hundred shekels of silver which he had agreed to pay for the field of Machpelah.[12] They are said however to be the current money of the merchant, and yet are received by weight and not by tale, in the same manner as ingots of gold and bars of silver are at present. The revenues of the antient Saxon kings of England are said to have been paid, not in money but in kind, that is, in victuals and provisions of all sorts. William the Conqueror introduced the custom of paying them in money.[13] This money, however, was, for a long time, received at the exchequer, by weight and not by tale.[14]

The inconveniency and difficulty of weighing those metals with exactness gave occasion to the institution of coins, of

and coinage to show weight later.

which the stamp, covering entirely both sides of the piece and sometimes the edges too, was supposed to ascertain not only the fineness, but the weight of the metal. Such coins, therefore, were received by tale as at present, without the trouble of weighing.

The denominations of those coins seem originally to have expressed the weight or quantity of metal contained in them. In

The names of coins originally expressed their weight.

the time of Servius Tullius, who first coined money at Rome,[15] the Roman As or Pondo contained a Roman pound of good copper. It was divided in the same manner as our

Troyes pound, into twelve ounces, each of which contained a real ounce of good copper. The English pound sterling in the time of Edward I., contained a pound,

---

[12] [Genesis xxiii. 16.]

[13] ["King William the First, for the better pay of his warriors, caused the *firmes* which till his time had for the most part been answered in victuals, to be converted in *pecuniam numeratam.*"—Lowndes, *Report containing an Essay for the Amendment of the Silver Coins*, 1695, p. 4. Hume, whom Adam Smith often follows, makes no such absurd statement, *History*, ed. of 1773, vol. i., pp. 225, 226.]

[14] [Lowndes, *Essay*, p. 4.]

[15] [Above, p. 36.]

Tower weight, of silver of a known fineness. The Tower pound seems to have been something more than the Roman pound, and something less than the Troyes pound. This last was not introduced into the mint of England till the 18th of Henry VIII. The French livre contained in the time of Charlemagne a pound, Troyes weight, of silver of a known fineness. The fair of Troyes in Champaign was at that time frequented by all the nations of Europe, and the weights and measures of so famous a market were generally known and esteemed. The Scots money pound contained, from the time of Alexander the First to that of Robert Bruce, a pound of silver of the same weight and fineness with the English pound sterling. English, French, and Scots pennies too, contained all of them originally a real pennyweight of silver, the twentieth part of an ounce, and the two-hundred-and-fortieth part of a pound. The shilling too seems originally to have been the denomination of a weight. *When wheat is at twelve shillings the quarter*, says an antient statute of Henry III. *then wastel bread of a farthing shall weigh eleven shillings and four pence.*[16] The proportion, however, between the shilling and either the penny on the one hand, or the pound on the other, seems not to have been so constant and uniform as that between the penny and the pound. During the first race of the kings of France, the French sou or shilling appears upon different occasions to have contained five, twelve, twenty, and forty pennies.[17] Among the antient Saxons a shilling appears at one time to have contained only five pennies,[18] and it is not im-

[16] [The Assize of Bread and Ale, 51 Hen. III., contains an elaborate scale beginning, "When a quarter of wheat is sold for xii d. then wastel bread of a farthing shall weigh vi l. and xvi s." and goes on to the figures quoted in the text above. The statute is quoted at second-hand from Martin Folkes' *Table of English Silver Coins* with the same object by Harris, *Essay upon Money and Coins*, pt. i., § 29, but Harris does not go far enough in the scale to bring in the penny as a weight. As to this scale see below, pp. 243–244, 248, 249.]

[17] [Ed. I reads "twenty, forty and forty-eight pennies." Garnier, *Recherches sur la nature et les causes de la richesse des nations, par Adam Smith*, 1802, tom. v., p. 55, in a note on this passage says that the sou was always twelve deniers.]

[18] [Hume, *History of England*, ed. of 1773, i., p. 226. Fleetwood, *Chronicon Preciosum*, 1707, p. 30. These authorities say there were 48 shillings in the pound, so that 240 pence would still make £1.]

probable that it may have been as variable among them as among their neighbours, the antient Franks. From the time of Charlemagne among the French,[19] and from that of William the Conqueror among the English,[20] the proportion between the pound, the shilling, and the penny, seems to have been uniformly the same as at present, though the value of each has been very different. For in every country of the world, I believe, the avarice and injustice of princes and sovereign states, abusing the confidence of their subjects, have by degrees diminished the real quantity of metal, which had been originally contained in their coins. The Roman As, in the latter ages of the Republic, was reduced to the twenty-fourth part of its original value, and, instead of weighing a pound, came to weigh only half an ounce.[21] The English pound and penny contain at present about a third only; the Scots pound and penny about a thirty-sixth; and the French pound and penny about a sixty-sixth part of their original value.[22] By means of those operations the princes and sovereign states which performed them were enabled, in appearance, to pay their debts and to fulfil their engagements with a smaller quantity of silver than would otherwise have been requisite. It was indeed in appearance only; for their creditors were really defrauded of a part of what was due to them. All other debtors in the state were allowed the same privilege, and might pay with the same nominal sum of the new and debased coin whatever they had borrowed in the old. Such operations, therefore, have always proved favourable to the debtor, and ruinous to the creditor, and have sometimes produced a greater and more universal revolution in the fortunes of private persons, than could have been occasioned by a very great public calamity.[23]

[19] [Harris, *Money and Coins*, pt. i., § 29.]

[20] ["It is thought that soon after the Conquest a pound sterling was divided into twenty shillings."—Hume, *History of England*, ed. of 1773, vol. i., p. 227.]

[21] [Pliny, *Hist. Nat.*, lib. xxxiii., cap. iii.; see below, pp. 1186–1187.]

[22] [Harris, *Money and Coins*, pt. i., § 30, note, makes the French livre about one seventieth part of its original value.]

[23] [The subject of debased and depreciated coinage occurs again below, pp. 50,

It is in this manner that money has become in all civilized nations the universal instrument of commerce, by the intervention of which goods of all kinds are bought and sold, or exchanged for one another.[24]

What are the rules which men naturally observe in exchanging them either for money or for one another, I shall now proceed to examine. These rules determine what may be called the relative or exchangeable value of goods.

The next inquiry is what rules determine exchangeable value.

The word VALUE, it is to be observed, has two different meanings, and sometimes expresses the utility of some particular object, and sometimes the power of purchasing other goods which the possession of that object conveys. The one may be called "value in use;" the other, "value in exchange." The things which have the greatest value in use have frequently little or no value in exchange; and on the contrary, those which have the greatest value in exchange have frequently little or no value in use. Nothing is more useful than water: but it will purchase scarce any thing; scarce any thing can be had in exchange for it. A diamond, on the contrary, has scarce any value in use; but a very great quantity of other goods may frequently be had in exchange for it.[25]

Value may mean either value in use or value in exchange.

264, 694–703, 1184–1189. One of the reasons why gold and silver became the most usual forms of money is dealt with below, pp. 234–235.]

[24] [In *Lectures*, pp. 182–190, where much of this chapter is to be found, money is considered "first as the measure of value and then as the medium of permutation or exchange." Money is said to have had its origin in the fact that men naturally fell upon one commodity with which to compare the value of all other commodities. When this commodity was once selected it became the medium of exchange. In this chapter money comes into use from the first as a medium of exchange, and its use as a measure of value is not mentioned. The next chapter explains that it is vulgarly used as a measure of value because it is used as an instrument of commerce or medium of exchange.]

[25] [*Lectures*, p. 157. Law, *Money and Trade*, 1705, ch. i. (followed by Harris, *Money and Coins*, pt. i., § 3), contrasts the value of water with that of diamonds. The cheapness of water is referred to by Plato, *Euthydem*. 304 B., quoted by Pufendorf, *De jure naturæ et gentium*, lib. v., cap. i., § 6; cp. Barbeyrac's note on § 4.]

Three questions,

In order to investigate the principles which regulate the exchangeable value of commodities, I shall endeavour to shew,

(1) wherein consists the real price of commodities, (2) what are the different parts of this price, (3) why the market price sometimes diverges from this price,

First, what is the real measure of this exchangeable value; or, wherein consists the real price of all commodities.

Secondly, what are the different parts of which this real price is composed or made up.

And, lastly, what are the different circumstances which sometimes raise some or all of these different parts of price above, and sometimes sink them below their natural or ordinary rate; or, what are the causes which sometimes hinder

will be answered in the next three chapters.

the market price, that is, the actual price of commodities, from coinciding exactly with what may be called their natural price. I shall endeavour to explain, as fully and distinctly as I can, those three subjects in the three following chapters, for which I must very earnestly entreat both the patience and attention of the reader: his patience in order to examine a detail which may perhaps in some places appear unnecessarily tedious; and his attention in order to understand what may, perhaps, after the fullest explication which I am capable of giving of it, appear still in some degree obscure. I am always willing to run some hazard of being tedious in order to be sure that I am perspicuous; and after taking the utmost pains that I can to be perspicuous, some obscurity may still appear to remain upon a subject[26] in its own nature extremely abstracted.

[26] [Ed. 1 reads "subject which is."]

CHAPTER V

OF THE REAL AND NOMINAL PRICE OF COMMODITIES, OR OF THEIR PRICE IN LABOUR, AND THEIR PRICE IN MONEY

EVERY MAN is rich or poor according to the degree in which he can afford to enjoy the necessaries, conveniencies, and amusements of human life.[1] But after the division of labour has once thoroughly taken place, it is but a very small part of these with which a man's own labour can supply him. The far greater part of them he must derive from the labour of other people, and he must be rich or poor according to the quantity of that labour which he can command, or which he can afford to purchase. The value of any commodity, therefore, to the person who possesses it, and who means not to use or consume it himself, but to exchange it for other commodities, is equal to the quantity of labour which it enables him to purchase or command. Labour, therefore, is the real measure of the exchangeable value of all commodities.

Labour is the real measure of exchangeable value,

The real price of every thing, what every thing really costs to the man who wants to acquire it, is the toil and trouble of acquiring it. What every thing is really worth to the man who has acquired it, and who wants to dispose of it or exchange it for something else, is the toil and trouble which it can save to himself, and which it can impose upon other people. What is

and the first price paid for all things.

---

[1] ["La richesse en elle-même n'est autre chose que la nourriture, les commodités et les agréments de la vie."—Cantillon, *Essai*, pp. 1, 2.]

bought with money or with goods is purchased by labour,[2] as much as what we acquire by the toil of our own body. That money or those goods indeed save us this toil. They contain the value of a certain quantity of labour which we exchange for what is supposed at the time to contain the value of an equal quantity. Labour was the first price, the original purchase-money that was paid for all things. It was not by gold or by silver, but by labour, that all the wealth of the world was originally purchased; and its value, to those who possess it, and who want to exchange it for some new productions, is precisely equal to the quantity of labour which it can enable them to purchase or command.

Wealth, as Mr. Hobbes says, is power.[3] But the person who either acquires, or succeeds to a great fortune, does not neces-

Wealth is power of purchasing labour.

sarily acquire or succeed to any political power, either civil or military. His fortune may, perhaps, afford him the means of acquiring both, but the mere possession of that fortune does not necessarily convey to him either. The power which that possession immediately and directly conveys to him is the power of purchasing; a certain command over all the labour, or over all the produce of labour which is then in the market. His fortune is greater or less, precisely in proportion to the extent of this power; or to the quantity either of other men's labour, or, what is the same thing, of the produce of other men's labour, which it enables him to purchase or command. The exchangeable value of every thing must always be precisely equal to the extent of this power which it conveys to its owner.[4]

But though labour be the real measure of the exchangeable value of all commodities, it is not that by which their value is

---

[2] ["Everything in the world is purchased by labour."—Hume, "Of Commerce," in *Political Discourses*, 1752, p. 12.]

[3] ["Also riches joined with liberality is Power, because it procureth friends and servants: without liberality not so, because in this case they defend not but expose men to envy as a prey."—*Leviathan*, I., x.]

[4] [This paragraph appears first in Additions and Corrections and ed. 3.]

But value is not commonly estimated by labour, because labour is difficult to measure,

commonly estimated. It is often difficult to ascertain the proportion between two different quantities of labour. The time spent in two different sorts of work will not always alone determine this proportion. The different degrees of hardship endured, and of ingenuity exercised, must likewise be taken into account. There may be more labour in an hour's hard work than in two hours easy business; or in an hour's application to a trade which it cost ten years labour to learn, than in a month's industry at an ordinary and obvious employment. But it is not easy to find any accurate measure either of hardship or ingenuity. In exchanging indeed the different productions of different sorts of labour for one another, some allowance is commonly made for both. It is adjusted, however, not by any accurate measure, but by the higgling and bargaining of the market, according to that sort of rough equality which, though not exact, is sufficient for carrying on the business of common life.[5]

Every commodity besides, is more frequently exchanged for, and thereby compared with, other commodities than with

and commodities are more frequently exchanged for other commodities,

labour. It is more natural therefore, to estimate its exchangeable value by the quantity of some other commodity than by that of the labour which it can purchase. The greater part of people too understand better what is meant by a quantity of a particular commodity, than by a quantity of labour. The one is a plain palpable object; the other an abstract notion, which, though it can be made sufficiently intelligible, is not altogether so natural and obvious.

But when barter ceases, and money has become the common instrument of commerce, every particular commodity is more frequently exchanged for money than for any other commodity. The butcher seldom carries his beef or his mutton to the baker, or the brewer, in order to exchange them for bread or

[5] [The absence of any reference to the lengthy discussion of this subject in chap. x. is curious.]

especially money, which is therefore more frequently used in estimating value.

for beer; but he carries them to the market, where he exchanges them for money, and afterwards exchanges that money for bread and for beer. The quantity of money which he gets for them regulates too the quantity of bread and beer which he can afterwards purchase. It is more natural and obvious to him, therefore, to estimate their value by the quantity of money, the commodity for which he immediately exchanges them, than by that of bread and beer, the commodities for which he can exchange them only by the intervention of another commodity; and rather to say that his butcher's meat is worth threepence or fourpence a pound, than that it is worth three or four pounds of bread, or three or four quarts of small beer. Hence it comes to pass, that the exchangeable value of every commodity is more frequently estimated by the quantity of money, than by the quantity either of labour or of any other commodity which can be had in exchange for it.

Gold and silver, however, like every other commodity, vary in their value, are sometimes cheaper and sometimes dearer, sometimes of easier and sometimes of more difficult purchase. The quantity of labour which any particular quantity of them can purchase or command, or the quantity of other goods which it will exchange for, depends always upon the fertility or barrenness of the mines which happen to be known about the time when such exchanges are trade. The discovery of the abundant mines of America reduced, in the sixteenth century, the value of gold and silver in Europe to about a third of what it had been before.[6] As it cost less labour to bring those metals from the mine to the market, so when they were brought thither[7] they could purchase or command less labour; and this revolution in their value, though perhaps the greatest, is by no

But gold and silver vary in value, sometimes costing more and sometimes less labour, whereas equal labour always means equal sacrifice to the labourer,

[6] [Below, pp. 260–261.]

[7] [Ed. 1 reads "there."]

means the only one of which history gives some account. But as a measure of quantity, such as the natural foot, fathom, or handful, which is continually varying in its own quantity, can never be an accurate measure of the quantity of other things; so a commodity which is itself continually varying in its own value, can never be an accurate measure of the value of other commodities. Equal quantities of labour, at all times and places, may be said to be[8] of equal value to the labourer. In his ordinary state of health, strength and spirits; in the ordinary degree of his skill and dexterity,[9] he must always lay down the same portion of his ease, his liberty, and his happiness. The price which he pays must always be the same, whatever may be the quantity of goods which he receives in return for it. Of these, indeed, it may sometimes purchase a greater and sometimes a smaller quantity; but it is their value which varies, not that of the labour which purchases them. At all times and places that is dear which it is difficult to come at, or which it costs much labour to acquire; and that cheap which is to be had easily, or with very little labour. Labour alone, therefore, never varying in its own value, is alone the ultimate and real standard by which the value of all commodities can at all times and places be estimated and compared. It is their real price; money is their nominal price only.

But though equal quantities of labour are always of equal value to the labourer, yet to the person who employs him they appear sometimes to be of greater and sometimes of smaller value. He purchases them sometimes with a greater and sometimes with a smaller quantity of goods, and to him the price of labour seems to vary like that of all other things. It appears to him dear in the one case, and cheap in the other. In reality, however, it is the goods which are cheap in the one case, and dear in the other.

although the employer regards labour as varying in value.

---

[8] [Ed. 1 reads "Equal quantities of labour must at all times and places be."]

[9] [The words from "In his ordinary state of health" to "dexterity" appear first in ed. 2.]

In this popular sense, therefore, labour, like commodities, may be said to have a real and a nominal price. Its real price

So regarded, labour has a real and a nominal price.

may be said to consist in the quantity of the necessaries and conveniencies of life which are given for it; its nominal price, in the quantity of money. The labourer is rich or poor, is well or ill rewarded in proportion to the real, not to the nominal price of his labour.

The distinction between the real and the nominal price of commodities and labour, is not a matter of mere speculation,

The distinction between real and nominal is some-times useful in practice,

but may sometimes be of considerable use in practice. The same real price is always of the same value; but on account of the variations in the value of gold and silver, the same nominal price is sometimes of very different values. When a landed estate, therefore, is

sold with a reservation of a perpetual rent, if it is intended that this rent should always be of the same value, it is of importance to the family in whose favour it is reserved, that it should not consist in a particular sum of money.[10] Its value would in this case be liable to variations of two different kinds; first, to those which arise from the different quantities of gold and silver which are contained at different times in coin of the same denomination; and, secondly, to those which arise from the different values of equal quantities of gold and silver at different times.

Princes and sovereign states have frequently fancied that they had a temporary interest to diminish the quantity of pure

since the amount of metal in coins tends to diminish,

metal contained in their coins; but they seldom have fancied that they had any to augment it. The quantity of metal contained in the coins, I believe of all nations, has, accordingly, been almost continually diminish-

[10] ["Be above all things careful how you make any composition or agreement for any long space of years to receive a certain price of money for the corn that is due to you, although for the present it may seem a tempting bargain."—Fleetwood, *Chronicon Preciosium*, p. 174.]

ing, and hardly ever augmenting.[11] Such variations therefore tend almost always to diminish the value of a money rent.

The discovery of the mines of America diminished the value of gold and silver in Europe. This diminution, it is com-

and the value of gold and silver to fall.

monly supposed, though I apprehend without any certain proof, is still going on gradually,[12] and is likely to continue to do so for a long time. Upon this supposition, therefore, such variations are more likely to diminish, than to augment the value of a money rent, even though it should be stipulated to be paid, not in such a quantity of coined money of such a denomination (in so many pounds sterling, for example), but in so many ounces either of pure silver, or of silver of a certain standard.

The rents which have been reserved in corn have preserved their value much better than those which have been reserved in

English rents reserved in money have fallen to a fourth since 1586,

money, even where the denomination of the coin has not been altered. By the 18th of Elizabeth[13] it was enacted, that a third of the rent of all college leases should be reserved in corn, to be paid, either in kind, or according to the current prices at the nearest public market. The money arising from this corn rent, though originally but a third of the whole, is in the present times, according to Doctor Blackstone, commonly near double of what arises from the

[11] [Above, pp. 39–40.]

[12] [Below, pp. 293–295.]

[13] [C. 6, which applies to Oxford, Cambridge, Winchester and Eton, and provides that no college shall make any lease for lives or years of tithes, arable land or pasture without securing that at least one-third of "tholde" (presumably the whole not the old) rent should be paid in corn. The Act was promoted by Sir Thomas Smith to the astonishment, it is said, of his fellow-members of Parliament, who could not see what difference it would make. "But the knight took the advantage of the present cheapness; knowing hereafter grain would grow dearer, mankind daily multiplying, and licence being lately given for transportation. So that at this day much emolument redoundeth to the colleges in each university, by the passing of this Act; and though their rents stand still, their revenues do increase."—Fuller, *Hist. of the University of Cambridge*, 1655, p. 144, quoted in Strype, *Life of the learned Sir Thomas Smith*, 1698, p. 192.]

other two-thirds.[14] The old money rents of colleges must, according to this account, have sunk almost to a fourth part of their ancient value; or are worth little more than a fourth part of the corn which they were formerly worth. But since the reign of Philip and Mary the denomination of the English coin has undergone little or no alteration, and the same number of pounds, shillings and pence have contained very nearly the same quantity of pure silver. This degradation, therefore, in the value of the money rents of colleges, has arisen altogether from the degradation in the value of silver.

When the degradation in the value of silver is combined with the diminution of the quantity of it contained in the coin

and similar Scotch and French rents almost to nothing.

of the same denomination, the loss is frequently still greater. In Scotland, where the denomination of the coin has undergone much greater alterations than it ever did in England, and in France, where it has undergone still greater than it ever did in Scotland,[15] some ancient rents, originally of considerable value, have in this manner been reduced almost to nothing.

Equal quantities of labour will at distant times be purchased more nearly with equal quantities of corn, the subsistence of

Corn rents are more stable than money rents,

the labourer, than with equal quantities of gold and silver, or perhaps of any other commodity. Equal quantities of corn, therefore, will, at distant times, be more nearly of the same real value, or enable the possessor to purchase or command more nearly the same quantity of the labour of other people. They will do this, I say, more nearly than equal quantities of almost any other commodity; for even equal quantities of corn will not do it exactly. The subsistence of the labourer, or the real price of labour, as I shall endeavour to show hereafter,[16] is very different upon different occasions; more liberal in a society advancing to opulence, than in one that is standing still;

[14] [*Commentaries*, 1765, vol. ii., p. 322.]

[15] [Above, p. 39.]

[16] [Below, pp. 96–104.]

and in one that is standing still, than in one that is going backwards. Every other commodity, however, will at any particular time purchase a greater or smaller quantity of labour in proportion to the quantity of subsistence which it can purchase at that time. A rent therefore reserved in corn is liable only to the variations in the quantity of labour which a certain quantity of corn can purchase. But a rent reserved in any other commodity is liable, not only to the variations in the quantity of labour which any particular quantity of corn can purchase, but to the variations in the quantity of corn which can be purchased by any particular quantity of that commodity.

Though the real value of a corn rent, it is to be observed however, varies much less from century to century than that of *but liable to much larger annual variations,* a money rent, it varies much more from year to year. The money price of labour, as I shall endeavour to show hereafter,[17] does not fluctuate from year to year with the money price of corn, but seems to be every where accommodated, not to the temporary or occasional, but to the average or ordinary price of that necessary of life. The average or ordinary price of corn again is regulated, as I shall likewise endeavour to show hereafter,[18] by the value of silver, by the richness or barrenness of the mines which supply the market with that metal, or by the quantity of labour which must be employed, and consequently of corn which must be consumed, in order to bring any particular quantity of silver[19] from the mine to the market. But the value of silver, though it sometimes varies greatly from century to century, seldom varies much from year to year, but frequently continues the same, or very nearly the same, for half a century or a century together. The ordinary or average money price of corn, therefore, may, during so long a period, continue the same or very nearly the same too, and along with it the money price of labour, provided, at least, the society continues, in other respects, in the same or nearly in the same condition.

[17] [Below, pp. 105, 118, 119, 120.]

[18] [Below, chap. xi., see esp. pp. 260–261.]

[19] [Ed. 1 reads "it."]

In the mean time the temporary and occasional price of corn may frequently be double, one year, of what it had been the year before, or fluctuate, for example, from five and twenty to fifty shillings the quarter.[20] But when corn is at the latter price, not only the nominal, but the real value of a corn rent will be double of what it is when at the former, or will command double the quantity either of labour or of the greater part of other commodities; the money price of labour, and along with it that of most other things, continuing the same during all these fluctuations.

Labour, therefore, it appears evidently, is the only universal, as well as the only accurate measure of value, or the only standard by which we can compare the values of different commodities at all times and at all places. We cannot estimate, it is allowed, the real value of different commodities from century to century by the quantities of silver which were given for them. We cannot estimate it from year to year by the quantities of corn. By the quantities of labour we can, with the greatest accuracy, estimate it both from century to century and from year to year. From century to century, corn is a better measure than silver, because from century to century, equal quantities of corn will command the same quantity of labour more nearly than equal quantities of silver. From year to year, on the contrary, silver is a better measure than corn, because equal quantities of it will more nearly command the same quantity of labour.[21]

so that labour is the only universal standard.

But though in establishing perpetual rents, or even in letting very long leases, it may be of use to distinguish between real

[20] [Ed. 1 places the "for example" here.]

[21] ["In England and this part of the world, wheat being the constant and most general food, not altering with the fashion, not growing by chance: but as the farmers sow more or less of it, which they endeavour to proportion, as near as can be guessed to the consumption, abstracting the overplus of the precedent year in their provision for the next; and *vice versa*, it must needs fall out that it keeps the nearest proportion to its consumption (which is more studied and designed in this than other commodities) of anything, if you take it for seven or twenty years together: though perhaps the scarcity of one year, caused by the accidents of the season,

and nominal price; it is of none in buying and selling, the more

But in ordinary transactions money is sufficient,

common and ordinary transactions of human life.

At the same time and place the real and the nominal price of all commodities are exactly in proportion to one another. The more or less money you get for any commodity, in the London mar-

being perfectly accurate at the same time and place,

ket, for example, the more or less labour it will at that time and place enable you to purchase or command. At the same time and place, therefore, money is the exact measure

of the real exchangeable value of all commodities. It is so, however, at the same time and place only.

Though at distant places, there is no regular proportion between the real and the money price of commodities, yet the merchant who carries goods from the one to the other has

and the only thing to be considered in transactions between distant places.

nothing to consider but their money price, or the difference between the quantity of silver for which he buys them, and that for which he is likely to sell them. Half an ounce of silver at Canton in China may command a greater quantity both of labour and of the

necessaries and conveniencies of life, than an ounce at London. A commodity, therefore, which sells for half an ounce of silver at Canton may there be really dearer, of more real importance to the man who possesses it there, than a commodity which sells for an ounce at London is to[22] the man who pos-

---

may very much vary it from the immediately precedent or following. Wheat, therefore, in this part of the world (and that grain which is the constant general food of any other country) is the fittest measure to judge of the altered value of things in any long tract of time: and therefore wheat here, rice in Turkey, etc., is the fittest thing to reserve a rent in, which is designed to be constantly the same for all future ages. But money is the best measure of the altered value of things in a few years: because its vent is the same and its quantity alters slowly. But wheat, or any other grain, cannot serve instead of money: because of its bulkiness and too quick change of its quantity."—Locke, *Some Considerations of the Consequences of the Lowering of Interest and Raising the Value of Money*, ed. of 1696, pp. 74, 75.]

[22] [Ed. 1 reads "than one which sells for an ounce at London to."]

sesses it at London. If a London merchant, however, can buy at Canton for half an ounce of silver, a commodity which he can afterwards sell at London for an ounce, he gains a hundred per cent. by the bargain, just as much as if an ounce of silver was at London exactly of the same value as at Canton. It is of no importance to him that half an ounce of silver at Canton would have given him the command of more labour and of a greater quantity of the necessaries and conveniencies of life than an ounce can do at London. An ounce at London will always give him the command of double the quantity of all these, which half an ounce could have done there, and this is precisely what he wants.

As it is the nominal or money price of goods, therefore, which finally determines the prudence or imprudence of all purchases and sales, and thereby regulates almost the whole business of common life in which price is concerned, we cannot wonder that it should have been so much more attended to than the real price.

So it is no wonder that money price has been more attended to.

In such a work as this, however, it may sometimes be of use to compare the different real values of a particular commodity at different times and places, or the different degrees of power over the labour of other people which it may, upon different occasions, have given to those who possessed it. We must in this case compare, not so much the different quantities of silver for which it was commonly sold, as the different quantities of labour which those different quantities of silver could have purchased. But the current prices of labour at distant times and places can scarce ever be known with any degree of exactness. Those of corn, though they have in few places been regularly recorded, are in general better known and have been more frequently taken notice of by historians and other writers. We must generally, therefore, content ourselves with them, not as being always exactly in the same proportion as the current prices of labour, but as being the nearest approximation which can commonly be had to that proportion. I shall

In this work corn prices will sometimes be used.

hereafter have occasion to make several comparisons of this kind.[23]

In the progress of industry, commercial nations have found it convenient to coin several different metals into money; gold

Several metals have been coined, but only one is used as the standard, and that usually the one first used in commerce,

for larger payments, silver for purchases of moderate value, and copper, or some other coarse metal, for those of still smaller consideration. They have always, however, considered one of those metals as more peculiarly the measure of value than any of the other two; and this preference seems generally to have been given to the metal which they happened first to make use of as the instrument of commerce. Having once begun to use it as their standard, which they must have done when they had no other money, they have generally continued to do so even when the necessity was not the same.

The Romans are said to have had nothing but copper money till within five years before the first Punic war,[24] when they first

as the Romans used copper,

began to coin silver. Copper, therefore, appears to have continued always the measure of value in that republic. At Rome all accounts appear to have been kept, and the value of all estates to have been computed, either in *Asses* or in *Sestertii*. The *As* was always the denomination of a copper coin. The word *Sestertius* signifies two *Asses* and a half. Though the *Sestertius*, therefore, was originally[25] a silver coin, its value was estimated in copper. At Rome, one who owed a great deal of money, was said to have a great deal of other people's copper.[26]

The northern nations who established themselves upon the ruins of the Roman empire, seem to have had silver money from the first beginning of their settlements, and not to have

---

[23] [Below, chap. xi. *passim*.]

[24] Pliny, lib. xxxiii. c. 3. [This note is not in ed. 1.]

[25] [Eds. 1 and 2 read "always."]

[26] [Habere aes alienum.]

known either gold or copper coins for several ages thereafter. There were silver coins in England in the time of the Saxons; *and modern European nations silver.* but there was little gold coined till the time of Edward III. nor any copper till that of James I. of Great Britain. In England, therefore, and for the same reason, I believe, in all other modern nations of Europe, all accounts are kept, and the value of all goods and of all estates is generally computed in silver: and when we mean to express the amount of a person's fortune, we seldom mention the number of guineas, but the number of pounds sterling[27] which we suppose would be given for it.

Originally, in all countries, I believe, a legal tender of payment could[28] be made only in the coin of that metal,[29] which *The standard metal originally was the only legal tender,* was peculiarly considered as the standard or measure of value. In England, gold was not considered as a legal tender for a long time after it was coined into money. The proportion between the values of gold and silver money was not fixed by any public law or proclamation; but was left to be settled by the market. If a debtor offered payment in gold, the creditor might either reject such payment altogether, or accept of it at such a valuation of the gold as he and his debtor could agree upon. Copper is not at present a legal tender, except in the change of the smaller silver coins. In this state of things the distinction between the metal which was the standard, and that which was not the standard, was something more than a nominal distinction.

In process of time, and as people became gradually more familiar with the use of the different metals in coin, and consequently better acquainted with the proportion between their respective values, it has in most countries, I believe, been found convenient to ascertain this proportion, and to declare by a

---

[27] [Ed. 1 does not contain "sterling."]

[28] [Ed. 1 places the "originally" here.]

[29] [Ed. 1 places the "only" here.]

later the proportion between the values of the two metals is declared by law, and both are legal tender, the distinction between them ceasing to be of importance,

public law[30] that a guinea, for example, of such a weight and fineness, should exchange for one-and-twenty shillings, or be a legal tender for a debt of that amount.[31] In this state of things, and during the continuance of any one regulated proportion of this kind, the distinction between the metal which is the standard, and that which is not the standard, becomes little more than a nominal distinction.[32]

In consequence of any change, however, in this regulated proportion, this distinction becomes, or at least seems to be-

except when a change is made in the regulated proportion.

come, something more than nominal again. If the regulated value of a guinea, for example, was either reduced to twenty, or raised to two-and-twenty shillings, all accounts being kept and almost all obligations for debt being expressed in silver money, the greater part of payments could in either case be made with the same quantity of silver money as before; but would require very different quantities of gold money; a greater in the one case, and a smaller in the other. Silver would appear to be more invariable in its value than gold. Silver would appear to measure the value of gold, and gold would not appear to measure the value of silver. The value of gold would seem to depend upon the quantity of silver

[30] [The Act, 19 Hen. VII., c. 5, ordered that certain gold coins should pass for the sums for which they were coined, and 5 and 6 Ed. VI. prescribed penalties for giving or taking more than was warranted by proclamation. The value of the guinea was supposed to be fixed by the proclamation of 1717, for which see *Economic Journal*, March, 1898. Lead tokens were coined by individuals in the reign of Elizabeth. James I. coined copper farthing tokens, but abstained from proclaiming them as money of that value. In 1672 copper halfpennies were issued, and both halfpennies and farthings were ordered to pass as money of those values in all payments under sixpence.—Harris, *Money and Coins*, pt. i., § 39; Liverpool, *Treatise on the Coins of the Realm*, 1805, pp. 130, 131.]

[31] [Ed. 1 reads "sum."]

[32] [*I.e.*, if 21 pounds may be paid with 420 silver shillings or with gold guineas it does not matter whether a "pound" properly signifies 20 silver shillings or $\frac{20}{21}$ of a gold guinea.]

which it would exchange for; and the value of silver would not seem to depend upon the quantity of gold which it would exchange for. This difference, however, would be altogether owing to the custom of keeping accounts, and of expressing the amount of all great and small sums rather in silver than in gold money. One of Mr. Drummond's notes for five-and-twenty or fifty guineas would, after an alteration of this kind, be still payable with five-and-twenty or fifty guineas in the same manner as before. It would, after such an alteration, be payable with the same quantity of gold as before, but with very different quantities of silver. In the payment of such a note, gold would appear to be more invariable in its value than silver. Gold would appear to measure the value of silver, and silver would not appear to measure the value of gold. If the custom of keeping accounts, and of expressing promissory notes and other obligations for money in this manner, should ever become general, gold, and not silver, would be considered as the metal which was peculiarly the standard or measure of value.

In reality, during the continuance of any one regulated proportion, between the respective values of the different metals in coin, the value of the most precious metal regulates the value of the whole coin.[33] Twelve copper pence contain half a pound, avoirdupois, of copper, of not the best quality, which, before it is coined, is seldom worth seven-pence in silver. But as by the regulation twelve such pence are ordered to exchange for a shilling, they are in the market considered as worth a shilling, and a shilling can at any time be had for them. Even before the late reformation of the gold coin of Great Britain,[34] the gold, that part of it at least which circulated in

During the continuance of a regulated proportion, the value of the most precious metal regulates the value of the whole coinage, as in Great Britain,

[33] [This happens to have been usually, though not always, true, but it is so simply because it has usually happened that the most precious metal in use as money has been made or become the standard. Gold was already the standard in England, though the fact was not generally recognised; see Harris, *Money and Coins*, pt. ii., §§ 36, 37, and below, pp. 699–703.]

[34] [In 1774.]

London and its neighbourhood, was in general less degraded below its standard weight than the greater part of the silver. One-and-twenty worn and defaced shillings, however, were considered as equivalent to a guinea, which perhaps, indeed, was worn and defaced too, but seldom so much so. The late regulations[35] have brought the gold coin as near perhaps to its standard weight as it is possible to bring the current coin of any nation; and the order, to receive no gold at the public offices but by weight, is likely to preserve it so, as long as that order is enforced. The silver coin still continues in the same worn and degraded state as before the reformation of the gold coin. In the market, however, one-and-twenty shillings of this degraded silver coin are still considered as worth a guinea of this excellent gold coin.

The reformation of the gold coin has evidently raised the value of the silver coin which can be exchanged for it.

In the English mint a pound weight of gold is coined into forty-four guineas and a half, which, at one-and-twenty shillings the guinea, is equal to forty-six pounds fourteen shillings and six-pence. An ounce of such gold coin, therefore, is worth 3 *l*. 17 *s*. 10½ *d*. in silver. In England no duty or seignorage is paid upon the coinage, and he who carries a pound weight or an ounce weight of standard gold bullion to the mint, gets back a pound weight or an ounce weight of gold in coin, without any deduction. Three pounds seventeen shillings and ten-pence half-penny an ounce, therefore, is said to be the mint price of gold in England, or the quantity of gold coin which the mint gives in return for standard gold bullion.

where the reformation of the gold coin has raised the value of the silver coin.

Before the reformation of the gold coin, the price of standard gold bullion in the market had for many years been upwards of 3 *l*. 18 *s*. sometimes 3 *l*. 19 *s*. and very frequently 4 *l*. an ounce; that sum, it is probable, in the worn and degraded gold coin, seldom containing more than an ounce of standard

<hr>

[35] [These regulations, issued in 1774, provided that guineas should not pass when they had lost a certain portion of their weight, varying with their age.—Liverpool, *Coins of the Realm*, p. 216, note.]

gold. Since the reformation of the gold coin, the market price of standard gold bullion seldom exceeds 3 *l.* 17 *s.* 7 *d.* an ounce. Before the reformation of the gold coin, the market price was always more or less above the mint price. Since that reformation, the market price has been constantly below the mint price. But that market price is the same whether it is paid in gold or in silver coin. The late reformation of the gold coin, therefore, has raised not only the value of the gold coin, but likewise that of the silver coin in proportion to gold bullion, and probably too in proportion to all other commodities; though the price of the greater part of other commodities being influenced by so many other causes, the rise in the value either of gold or silver coin in proportion to them, may not be so distinct and sensible.

In the English mint a pound weight of standard silver bullion is coined into sixty-two shillings, containing, in the same manner, a pound weight of standard silver. Five shillings and two-pence an ounce, therefore, is said to be the mint price of silver in England, or the quantity of silver coin which the mint gives in return for standard silver bullion. Before the reformation of the gold coin, the market price of standard silver bullion was, upon different occasions, five shillings and four-pence, five shillings and five-pence, five shillings and six-pence, five shillings and seven-pence, and very often five shillings and eight-pence an ounce. Five shillings and seven-pence, however, seems to have been the most common price. Since the reformation of the gold coin, the market price of standard silver bullion has fallen occasionally to five shillings and three-pence, five shillings and four-pence, and five shillings and five-pence an ounce; which last price it has scarce ever exceeded. Though the market price of silver bullion has fallen considerably since the reformation of the gold coin, it has not fallen so low as the mint price.

In the proportion between the different metals in the English coin, as copper is rated very much above its real value, so silver is rated somewhat below it. In the market of Europe, in the French coin and in the Dutch coin, an

Silver is rated below its value in England.

ounce of fine gold exchanges for about fourteen ounces of fine silver. In the English coin, it exchanges for about fifteen ounces, that is, for more silver than it is worth according to the common estimation of Europe.[36] But as the price of copper in bars is not, even in England, raised by the high price of copper in English coin, so the price of silver in bullion is not sunk by the low rate of silver in English coin. Silver in bullion still preserves its proper proportion to gold; for the same reason that copper in bars preserves its proper proportion to silver.[37]

Upon the reformation of the silver coin in the reign of William III. the price of silver bullion still continued to be somewhat above the mint price. Mr. Locke imputed this high price to the permission of exporting silver bullion, and to the prohibition of exporting silver coin.[38] This permission of exporting, he said, rendered the demand for silver bullion greater than the demand for silver coin. But the number of people who want silver coin for the common uses of buying and selling at home, is surely much greater than that of those who want silver bullion either for the use of exportation or for any other use. There subsists at present a like permission of exporting gold bullion, and a like prohibition of exporting gold coin; and yet the price of gold bullion has fallen below the mint price. But in the English coin silver was then, in the same manner as now, under-rated in proportion to gold; and the gold coin (which at that time too was

Locke's explanation of the high price of silver bullion is wrong.

---

[36] [Magens, *Universal Merchant*, ed. Horsley, 1753, pp. 53–55, gives the proportions thus: French coin, 1 to $14\frac{5803}{12279}$, on line Dutch, 1 to 14 $\frac{82550}{154425}$, English, 1 to $15\frac{14295}{68200}$.]

[37] [Full weight silver coins would not remain in circulation, as the bullion in them was worth more reckoned in guineas and in the ordinary old and worn silver coins than the nominal amount stamped on them.]

[38] [Locke, *Further Considerations Concerning Raising the Value of Money*, 2nd ed., 1695, pp. 58–60. The exportation of foreign coin (misprinted "kind" in Pickering) or bullion of gold or silver was permitted by 15 Car. II., c. 7, on the ground that it was "found by experience that" money and bullion were "carried in greatest abundance (as to a common market) to such places as give free liberty for exporting the same" and in order "the better to keep in and increase the current coins" of the kingdom.]

not supposed to require any reformation) regulated then, as well as now, the real value of the whole coin. As the reformation of the silver coin did not then reduce the price of silver bullion to the mint price, it is not very probable that a like reformation will do so now.

Were the silver coin brought back as near to its standard weight as the gold, a guinea, it is probable, would, according to the present proportion, exchange for more silver in coin than it would purchase in bullion. The silver coin containing its full standard weight, there would in this case be a profit in melting it down, in order, first, to sell the bullion for gold coin, and afterwards to exchange this gold coin for silver coin to be melted down in the same manner. Some alteration in the present proportion seems to be the only method of preventing this inconveniency.

If the silver coin were reformed, it would be melted.

The inconveniency perhaps would be less if silver was rated in the coin as much above its proper proportion to gold as it is at present rated below it; provided it was at the same time enacted that silver should not be a legal tender for more than the change of a guinea; in the same manner as copper is not a legal tender for more than the change of a shilling. No creditor could in this case be cheated in consequence of the high valuation of silver in coin; as no creditor can at present be cheated in consequence of the high valuation of copper. The bankers only would suffer by this regulation. When a run comes upon them they sometimes endeavour to gain time by paying in sixpences, and they would be precluded by this regulation from this discreditable method of evading immediate payment. They would be obliged in consequence to keep at all times in their coffers a greater quantity of cash than at present; and though this might no doubt be a considerable inconveniency to them, it would at the same time be a considerable security to their creditors.[39]

Silver ought to be rated higher and should not be legal tender for more than a guinea.

[39] [Harris, writing nearly twenty years earlier, had said, "it would be a ridiculous

Three pounds seventeen shillings and ten-pence halfpenny (the mint price of gold) certainly does not contain, even in our present excellent gold coin, more than an ounce of standard gold, and it may be thought, therefore, should not purchase more standard bullion. But gold in coin is more convenient than gold in bullion, and though, in England, the coinage is free, yet the gold which is carried in bullion to the mint, can seldom be returned in coin to the owner till after a delay of several weeks. In the present hurry of the mint it could not be returned till after a delay of several months. This delay is equivalent to a small duty, and renders gold in coin somewhat more valuable than an equal quantity of gold in bullion.[40] If in the English coin silver was rated according to its proper proportion to gold, the price of silver bullion would probably fall below the mint price even without any reformation of the silver coin; the value even of the present worn and defaced silver coin being regulated by the value of the excellent gold coin for which it can be changed.

If it were properly rated, silver bullion would fall below the mint price without any recoinage.

A small seignorage or duty upon the coinage of both gold and silver would probably increase still more the superiority of those metals in coin above an equal quantity of either of them in bullion. The coinage would in this case increase the value of the metal coined in proportion to the extent of this small duty; for the same reason that the fashion increases the value of plate in proportion to the price of that fashion. The superiority of coin above bullion would prevent the melting down of the coin, and would discourage its exportation. If upon any public exigency

A seignorage would prevent melting and discourage exportation.

and vain attempt to make a standard integer of gold, whose parts should be silver; or to make a motley standard, part gold and part silver."—*Money and Coins*, pt. i., § 36.]

[40] [*I.e.*, an ounce of standard gold would not actually fetch £3 17s. 10½d. if sold for cash down.]

it should become necessary to export the coin, the greater part of it would soon return again of its own accord. Abroad it could sell only for its weight in bullion. At home it would buy more than that weight. There would be a profit, therefore, in bringing it home again. In France a seignorage of about eight per cent. is imposed upon the coinage,[41] and the French coin, when exported, is said to return home again of its own accord.[42]

The occasional fluctuations in the market price of gold and silver bullion arise from the same causes as the like fluctuations in that of all other commodities. The frequent loss of those metals from various accidents by sea and by land, the continual waste of them in gilding and plating, in lace and embroidery, in the wear and tear of coin, and in that of plate;[43] require, in all countries which possess no mines of their own, a continual importation, in order to repair this loss and this waste. The merchant importers, like all other merchants, we may believe, endeavour, as well as they can, to suit their occasional importations to what, they judge, is likely to be the immediate demand. With all their attention, however, they sometimes over-do the business, and sometimes under-do it. When they import more bullion than is wanted, rather than incur the risk and trouble of exporting it again, they are sometimes willing to sell a part of it for something less than the ordinary or average price. When, on the other hand, they import less than is wanted, they get something more than this price. But when, under all those occasional fluctuations, the market price either of gold or silver bullion continues for several years together steadily and constantly, either more or less

Fluctuations in the market price of gold and silver are due to ordinary commercial causes, but steady divergence from mint price is due to the state of the coin.

[41] [This erroneous statement is repeated below, pp. 600, 601, and on p. 697, where the calculations on which it is based are given. See the note on that passage.]

[42] [The question of seignorage is further discussed at some length in the chapter on Commercial Treaties, pp. 695–703.]

[43] [Ed. 1 reads "in the tear and wear of coin, and in the tear and wear of plate."]

above, or more or less below the mint price: we may be assured that this steady and constant, either superiority or inferiority of price, is the effect of something in the state of the coin, which, at that time, renders a certain quantity of coin either of more value or of less value than the precise quantity of bullion which it ought to contain. The constancy and steadiness of the effect, supposes a proportionable constancy and steadiness in the cause.

The money of any particular country is, at any particular time and place, more or less an accurate measure of value according as the current coin is more or less

The price of goods is adjusted to the actual contents of the coinage.

exactly agreeable to its standard, or contains more or less exactly the precise quantity of pure gold or pure silver which it ought to contain. If in England, for example, forty-four guineas and a half contained exactly a pound weight of standard gold, or eleven ounces of fine gold and one ounce of alloy, the gold coin of England would be as accurate a measure of the actual value of goods at any particular time and place as the nature of the thing would admit. But if, by rubbing and wearing, forty-four guineas and a half generally contain less than a pound weight of standard gold; the diminution, however, being greater in some pieces than in others; the measure of value comes to be liable to the same sort of uncertainty to which all other weights and measures are commonly exposed. As it rarely happens that these are exactly agreeable to their standard, the merchant adjusts the price of his goods, as well as he can, not to what those weights and measures ought to be, but to what, upon an average, he finds by experience they actually are. In consequence of a like disorder in the coin, the price of goods comes, in the same manner, to be adjusted, not to the quantity of pure gold or silver which the coin ought to contain, but to that which, upon an average, it is found by experience it actually does contain.

By the money-price of goods, it is to be observed, I understand always the quantity of pure gold or silver for which they are sold, without any regard to the denomination of the coin. Six shillings and eight-pence, for example, in the time of Edward I., I consider as the same money-price with a pound sterling in the present times; because it contained, as nearly as we can judge, the same quantity of pure silver.

CHAPTER VI

OF THE COMPONENT PARTS OF
THE PRICE OF COMMODITIES

IN THAT early and rude state of society which precedes both the accumulation of stock and the appropriation of land, the

Quantity of labour is originally the only rule of value,

proportion between the quantities of labour necessary for acquiring different objects seems to be the only circumstance which can afford any rule for exchanging them for one another. If among a nation of hunters, for example, it usually costs twice the labour to kill a beaver which it does to kill a deer, one beaver should naturally exchange for or be worth two deer. It is natural that what is usually the produce of two days or two hours labour, should be worth double of what is usually the produce of one day's or one hour's labour.

If the one species of labour should be more severe than the

allowance being made for superior hardship,

other, some allowance will naturally be made for this superior hardship; and the produce of one hour's labour in the one way may frequently exchange for that of two hours labour in the other.

Or if the one species of labour requires an uncommon degree of dexterity and ingenuity, the esteem which men have for such

and for uncommon dexterity and inge- nuity.

talents, will naturally give a value to their produce, superior to what would be due to the time employed about it. Such talents can seldom be acquired but in consequence of long application, and the superior value of their produce may frequently be no more than a reasonable compensation for the time and labour which must be spent in acquiring them. In the advanced state of society, allowances of this kind, for superior hardship and superior skill, are commonly made in the wages of labour; and something of the same kind must probably have taken place in its earliest and rudest period.

In this state of things, the whole produce of labour belongs to the labourer; and[1] the quantity of labour commonly employed in acquiring or producing any commodity, is the only circumstance which can regulate the quantity of labour which it ought commonly to purchase, command, or exchange for.

The whole produce then belongs to the labourer,

As soon as stock has accumulated in the hands of particular persons, some of them will naturally employ it in setting to work industrious people, whom they will supply with materials and subsistence, in order to make a profit by the sale of their work, or by what their labour adds to the value of the materials. In exchanging the complete manufacture either for money, for labour, or for other goods, over and above what may be sufficient to pay the price of the materials, and the wages of the workmen, something must be given for the profits of the undertaker of the work who hazards his stock in this adventure. The value which the workmen add to the materials, therefore, resolves itself in this case into two parts, of which the one pays their wages, the other the profits of their employer upon the whole stock of materials and wages which he advanced. He could have no interest to employ them, unless he expected from the sale of their work something more than what was sufficient to replace his stock to him; and he could have no interest to employ a great stock rather than a small one, unless his profits were to bear some proportion to the extent of his stock.

but when stock is used, something must be given for the profits of the undertaker, and the value of work resolves itself into wages and profits.

The profits of stock, it may perhaps be thought, are only a different name for the wages of a particular sort of labour, the labour of inspection and direction. They are, however, alto-

---

[1] [Ed. 1 does not contain "the whole produce of labour belongs to the labourer; and." The words, however, occur in all eds. at p. 91 below.]

Profits are not merely wages of inspection and direction.

gether different, are regulated by quite sufficient principles, and bear no proportion to the quantity, the hardship, or the ingenuity of this supposed labour of inspection and direction. They are regulated altogether by the value of the stock employed, and are greater or smaller in proportion to the extent of this stock. Let us suppose, for example, that in some particular place, where the common annual profits of manufacturing stock are ten per cent. there are two different manufactures, in each of which twenty workmen are employed at the rate of fifteen pounds a year each, or at the expence of three hundred a year in each manufactory. Let us suppose too, that the coarse materials annually wrought up in the one cost only seven hundred pounds, while the finer materials in the other cost seven thousand. The capital annually employed[2] in the one will in this case amount only to one thousand pounds; whereas that employed in the other will amount to seven thousand three hundred pounds. At the rate of ten per cent. therefore, the undertaker of the one will expect an yearly profit of about one hundred pounds only; while that of the other will expect about seven hundred and thirty pounds. But though their profits are so very different, their labour of inspection and direction may be either altogether or very nearly the same. In many great works, almost the whole labour of this kind is[3] committed to some principal clerk. His wages properly express the value of this labour of inspection and direction. Though in settling them some regard is had commonly, not only to his labour and skill, but to the trust which is reposed in him, yet they never bear any regular proportion to the capital of which he oversees the management; and the owner of this capital, though he is thus discharged of almost all labour, still expects that his profits should bear a regular proportion to his capital.[4] In the price of commodities, therefore, the profits of stock constitute a compo-

---

[2] ["The capital annually employed" is the working expenses for twelve months, not the capital in the usual modern sense.]

[3] [Ed. 1 inserts "frequently."]

[4] [Eds. 1 and 2 read "proportion to it."]

nent part[5] altogether different from the wages of labour, and regulated by quite different principles.

In this state of things, the whole produce of labour does not always belong to the labourer. He must in most cases share it

The labourer shares with the employer, and labour alone no longer regulates value.

with the owner of the stock which employs him. Neither is the quantity of labour commonly employed in acquiring or producing any commodity, the only circumstance[6] which can regulate the quantity which it ought commonly to purchase, command, or exchange for. An additional quantity, it is evident, must be due for the profits of the stock which advanced the wages and furnished the materials of that labour.

As soon as the land of any country has all become private property, the landlords, like all other men, love to reap where

When land has all become private property, rent constitutes a third component part of the price of most commodities.

they never sowed,[7] and demand a rent even for its natural produce. The wood of the forest, the grass of the field, and all the natural fruits of the earth, which, when land was in common, cost the labourer only the trouble of gathering them, come, even to him,[8] to have an additional price fixed upon them. He must give up to the landlord a portion of what his labour either

collects or produces. This portion, or, what comes to the same thing, the price of this portion, constitutes the rent of land, and in the price of the greater part of commodities makes a third component part.[9]

---

[5] [Ed. 1 reads "profits of stock are a source of value."]

[6] [Ed. 1 reads from the beginning of the paragraph: "In this state of things, therefore, the quantity of labour commonly employed in acquiring or producing any commodity is by no means the only circumstance."]

[7] [Buchanan, ed. *Wealth of Nations*, 1814, vol. i., p. 80, says: "They do so. But the question is why this apparently unreasonable demand is so generally complied with. Other men love also to reap where they never sowed, but the landlords alone, it would appear, succeed in so desirable an object."]

[8] [Ed. 1 does not contain "the labourer" and "even to him."]

[9] [Ed. 1 in place of these two sentences reads: "Men must then pay for the licence

The real value of all the different component parts of price, it must be observed, is measured[10] by the quantity of labour which they can, each of them, purchase or command. Labour measures the value not only of that part of price which resolves itself into labour, but of that which resolves itself into rent, and of that which resolves itself into profit.

The real value of all three parts is measured by labour.

In every society the price of every commodity finally resolves itself into some one or other, or all of those three parts; and in every improved society, all the three enter more or less, as component parts, into the price of the far greater part of commodities.

In an improved society all three parts are generally present,

In the price of corn, for example, one part pays the rent of the landlord, another pays the wages or maintenance of the labourers and labouring cattle[11] employed in producing it, and the third pays the profit of the farmer. These three parts seem either immediately or ultimately to make up the whole price of corn. A

for example, in corn,

to gather them; and in exchanging them either for money, for labour, or for other goods, over and above what is due, both for the labour of gathering them, and for the profits of the stock which employs that labour, some allowance must be made for the price of the licence, which constitutes the first rent of land. In the price therefore of the greater part of commodities the rent of land comes in this manner to constitute a third source of value. In this state of things, neither the quantity of labour commonly employed in acquiring or producing any commodity, nor the profits of the stock which advanced the wages and furnished the materials of that labour, are the only circumstances which can regulate the quantity of labour which it ought commonly to purchase, command or exchange for. A third circumstance must likewise be taken into consideration; the rent of the land; and the commodity must commonly purchase, command or exchange for, an additional quantity of labour, in order to enable the person who brings it to market to pay this rent."]

[10] [Ed. 1 reads "The real value of all the different component parts of price is in this manner measured."]

[11] [Smith overlooks the fact that his inclusion of the maintenance of labouring cattle here as a sort of wages requires him to include it in the national income or "wealth of the nation," and therefore to reckon the cattle themselves as part of the nation.]

fourth part, it may perhaps be thought, is necessary for replacing the stock of the farmer, or for compensating the wear and tear[12] of his labouring cattle, and other instruments of husbandry. But it must be considered that the price of any instrument of husbandry, such as a labouring horse, is itself made up of the same three parts; the rent of the land upon which he is reared, the labour of tending and rearing him, and the profits of the farmer who advances both the rent of this land, and the wages of this labour. Though the price of the corn, therefore, may pay the price as well as the maintenance of the horse, the whole price still resolves itself either immediately or ultimately into the same three parts of rent, labour,[13] and profit.

In the price of flour or meal, we must add to the price of the corn, the profits of the miller, and the wages of his servants; in *in flour or meal,* the price of bread, the profits of the baker, and the wages of his servants; and in the price of both, the labour of transporting the corn from the house of the farmer to that of the miller, and from that of the miller to that of the baker, together with the profits of those who advance the wages of that labour.

The price of flax resolves itself into the same three parts as that of corn. In the price of linen we must add to this price the *and in flax.* wages of the flax-dresser, of the spinner, of the weaver, of the bleacher, &c. together with the profits of their respective employers.

As any particular commodity comes to be more manufactured, that part of the price which resolves itself into wages and *Rent is a smaller proportion in highly manufactured commodities.* profit, comes to be greater in proportion to that which resolves itself into rent. In the progress of the manufacture, not only the number of profits increase, but every subsequent profit is greater than the foregoing; because the capital from which it is derived

---

[12] [Ed. 1 reads "tear and wear."]

[13] [The use of "labour" instead of the more natural "wages" here is more probably the result of its use five lines higher up than of any feeling of difficulty about the maintenance of cattle. On pp. 78, 80 below "rent, labour and profit" and "rent, wages and profit" are both used; see below, pp. 424–425, and note.]

must always be greater. The capital which employs the weavers, for example, must be greater than that which employs the spinners; because it not only replaces that capital with its profits, but pays, besides, the wages of the weavers; and the profits must always bear some proportion to the capital.[14]

In the most improved societies, however, there are always a few commodities of which the price resolves itself into two parts

A few commodities have only two or even one of the three component parts.

only, the wages of labour, and the profits of stock; and a still smaller number, in which it consists altogether in the wages of labour. In the price of sea-fish, for example, one part pays the labour of the fishermen, and the other the profits of the capital employed in the fishery. Rent very seldom makes any part of it, though it does sometimes, as I shall shew hereafter.[15] It is otherwise, at least through the greater part of Europe, in river fisheries. A salmon fishery pays a rent, and rent, though it cannot well be called the rent of land, makes a part of the price of a salmon as well as wages and profit. In some parts of Scotland a few poor people make a trade of gathering, along the sea-shore, those little variegated stones commonly known by the name of Scotch Pebbles. The price which is paid to them by the stone-cutter is altogether the wages of their labour; neither rent nor profit make any part of it.

But the whole price of any commodity must still finally resolve itself into some one or other, or all of those three parts; as

But all must have at least one,

whatever part of it remains after paying the rent of the land, and the price of the whole labour employed in raising, manufacturing, and bringing it to market, must necessarily be profit to somebody.[16]

[14] [The fact that the later manufacturer has to replace what is here called the capital, *i.e.*, the periodical expenditure of the earlier manufacturer, does not necessarily require him to have a greater capital to deal with the same produce. It need not be greater if he requires less machinery and buildings and a smaller stock of materials.]

[15] [Below, p. 200.]

[16] [Only true if "commodity" be understood to include solely goods which constitute income.]

As the price or exchangeable value of every particular commodity, taken separately, resolves itself into some one or other,

and the price of the whole annual produce resolves itself into wages, profits and rent,

or all of those three parts; so that of all the commodities which compose the whole annual produce of the labour of every country, taken complexly, must resolve itself into the same three parts, and be parcelled out among different inhabitants of the country, either as the wages of their labour, the profits of their stock, or the rent of their land.[17] The whole of what is annually either collected or produced by the labour of every society, or what comes to the same thing, the whole price of it, is in this manner originally distributed among some of its different members. Wages, profit, and rent, are the three original sources of all revenue as well as of all exchangeable value. All other revenue[18] is ultimately derived from some one or other of these.

Whoever derives his revenue from a fund which is his own, must draw it either from his labour, from his stock, or from his

which are the only original kinds of revenue.

land. The revenue derived from labour is called wages. That derived from stock, by the person who manages or employs it, is called profit. That derived from it by the person who does not employ it himself, but lends it to another, is called the interest or the use of money. It is the compensation which the borrower pays to the lender, for the profit which he has an opportunity of making by the use of the money. Part of that profit naturally belongs to the borrower, who runs the risk and takes the trouble of employing it; and part to the lender, who affords him the opportunity of making this profit. The interest of money is always a derivative revenue, which, if it is not paid from the profit which is made by the use of the money, must be paid from some other source of revenue, unless per-

---

[17] [The "whole annual produce" must be taken to mean the income and not the whole mass of goods produced, including those which perish or are used up in the creation of others.]

[18] [Some parts of this "other revenue," viz., interest and taxes, are mentioned in the next paragraph. It is perhaps also intended to include the rent of houses; see below, pp. 356, 357.]

haps the borrower is a spendthrift, who contracts a second debt in order to pay the interest of the first. The revenue which proceeds altogether from land, is called rent, and belongs to the landlord. The revenue of the farmer is derived partly from his labour, and partly from his stock. To him, land is only the instrument which enables him to earn the wages of this labour, and to make the profits of this stock. All taxes, and all the revenue which is founded upon them, all salaries, pensions, and annuities of every kind, are ultimately derived from some one or other of those three original sources of revenue, and are paid either immediately or mediately from the wages of labour, the profits of stock, or the rent of land.

When those three different sorts of revenue belong to different persons, they are readily distinguished; but when they *They are sometimes confounded,* belong to the same they are sometimes confounded with one another, at least in common language.

A gentleman who farms a part of his own estate, after paying the expence of cultivation, should gain both the rent of the *for example, a gentleman farmer's rent is called profit,* landlord and the profit of the farmer. He is apt to denominate, however, his whole gain, profit, and thus confounds rent with profit, at least in common language. The greater part of our North American and West Indian planters are in this situation. They farm, the greater part of them, their own estates, and accordingly we seldom hear of the rent of a plantation, but frequently of its profit.

Common farmers seldom employ any overseer to direct the general operations of the farm. They generally too work a good *a common farmer's wages are called profit,* deal with their own hands, as ploughmen, harrowers, &c. What remains of the crop after paying the rent, therefore, should not only replace to them their stock employed in cultivation, together with its ordinary profits, but pay them the wages which are due to them, both as labourers and overseers. Whatever remains, however, after paying the rent and keeping up the stock, is called profit. But wages evidently make a part of it. The farmer, by saving these wages, must necessarily gain them. Wages, therefore, are in this case confounded with profit.

An independent manufacturer, who has stock enough both to purchase materials, and to maintain himself till he can carry his work to market, should gain both the wages of a journeyman who works under a master, and the profit which that mas-

and so are an independent manufacturer's wages,

ter makes by the sale of the journeyman's work.[19] His whole gains, however, are commonly called profit, and wages are, in this case too, confounded with profit.[20]

A gardener who cultivates his own garden with his own hands, unites in his own person the three different characters, of landlord, farmer, and labourer. His produce, therefore, should pay him the rent of the first, the profit of the second, and

while the rent and profit of a gardener cultivating his own land are considered earnings of labour.

the wages of the third. The whole, however, is commonly considered as the earnings of his labour. Both rent and profit are, in this case, confounded with wages.

As in a civilized country there are but few commodities of which the exchangeable value arises from labour only, rent and profit

contributing largely to that of the far greater part of them, so the annual produce of its labour will always be sufficient to

A great part of the annual produce goes to the idle; the proportion regulates the increase or diminution of the produce.

purchase or command a much greater quantity of labour than what was employed in raising, preparing, and bringing that produce to market. If the society were[21] annually to employ all the labour which it can annually purchase, as the quantity of labour would increase greatly every year, so the produce of every succeeding year would be of vastly

greater value than that of the foregoing. But there is no country in which the whole annual produce is employed in maintaining

[19] [Ed. 1 reads "sale of his work."]

[20] [Below, pp. 154–156.]

[21] [Eds. 1–3 read "was."]

the industrious. The idle every where consume a great part of it; and according to the different proportions in which it is annually divided between those two different orders of people, its ordinary or average value must either annually increase, or diminish, or continue the same from one year to another.

CHAPTER VII

OF THE NATURAL AND MARKET PRICE OF COMMODITIES[1]

THERE IS in every society or neighbourhood an ordinary or average rate both of wages and profit in every different employment of labour and stock. This rate is naturally regulated, as I shall show hereafter,[2] partly by the general circumstances of the society, their riches or poverty, their advancing, stationary, or declining condition; and partly by the particular nature of each employment.

Ordinary or average rates of wages, profit,

There is likewise in every society or neighbourhood an ordinary or average rate of rent, which is regulated too, as I shall show hereafter,[3] partly by the general circumstances of the society or neighbourhood in which the land is situated, and partly by the natural or improved fertility of the land.

and rent

These ordinary or average rates may be called the natural rates of wages, profit, and rent, at the time and place in which they commonly prevail.

may be called natural rates,

When the price of any commodity is neither more nor less than what is sufficient to pay the rent of the land, the wages of the labour, and the profits of the stock employed

to pay which a commodity is sold at its natural price,

---

[1] [The chapter follows *Lectures*, pp. 173–182, very closely.]

[2] [Below, chaps. viii. and ix.]

[3] [Below, chap. xi.]

in raising, preparing, and bringing it to market, according to their natural rates, the commodity is then sold for what may be called its natural price.

The commodity is then sold precisely for what it is worth, or for what it really costs the person who brings it to market;

or for what it really costs, which includes profit, for though in common language what is called the prime cost of any commodity does not comprehend the profit of the person who is to sell it again, yet if he sells it at a price which does not allow him the ordinary rate of profit in his neighbourhood, he is evidently a loser by the trade; since by employing his stock in some other way he might have made that profit. His profit, besides, is his revenue, the proper fund of his subsistence. As, while he is preparing and bringing the goods to market, he advances to his workmen their wages, or their subsistence; so he advances to himself, in the same manner, his own subsistence, which is generally suitable to the profit which he may reasonably expect from the sale of his goods. Unless they yield him this profit, therefore, they do not repay him what they may very properly be said to have really cost him.

Though the price, therefore, which leaves him this profit, is not always the lowest at which a dealer may sometimes sell his

since no one will go on selling without profit. goods, it is the lowest at which he is likely to sell them for any considerable time; at least where there is perfect liberty,[4] or where he may change his trade as often as he pleases.

The actual price at which any commodity is commonly sold

Market price is called its market price. It may either be above, or below, or exactly the same with its natural price.

is regulated by the quantity brought to market and the effectual demand. The market price of every particular commodity is regulated by the proportion between the quantity which is actually brought to market, and the demand of those who are willing to pay the natural price of

4 [The same phrase occurs below, pp. 88, 138, 139.]

the commodity, or the whole value of the rent, labour, and profit,[5] which must be paid in order to bring it thither. Such people may be called the effectual demanders, and their demand the effectual demand; since it may be sufficient to effectuate the bringing of the commodity to market. It is different from the absolute demand. A very poor man may be said in some sense to have a demand for a coach and six; he might like to have it; but his demand is not an effectual demand, as the commodity can never be brought to market in order to satisfy it.

When the quantity of any commodity which is brought to market falls short of the effectual demand, all those who are

When the quantity brought falls short of the effectual demand, the market price rises above the natural;

willing to pay the whole value of the rent, wages, and profit, which must be paid in order to bring it thither, cannot be supplied with the quantity which they want. Rather than want it altogether, some of them will be willing to give more. A competition will immediately begin among them, and the market price will rise more or less above the natural price, according as either the greatness of the deficiency, or the wealth and wanton luxury of the competitors, happen to animate more or less the eagerness of the competition. Among competitors of equal wealth and luxury the same deficiency[6] will generally occasion a more or less eager competition, according as the acquisition of the commodity happens to be of more or less importance to them.[7] Hence the exorbitant price of the necessaries of life during the blockade of a town or in a famine.

When the quantity brought to market exceeds the effectual demand, it cannot be all sold to those who are willing to pay the whole value of the rent, wages and profit, which must be

---

[5] [Above, p. 72 and note 13.]

[6] [Ed. 1, beginning three lines higher up, reads "according as the greatness of the deficiency increases more or less the eagerness of this competition. The same deficiency."]

[7] [Ed. 1 reads "the competitors."]

when it exceeds the effectual demand the market price falls below the natural;

paid in order to bring it thither. Some part must be sold to those who are willing to pay less, and the low price which they give for it must reduce the price of the whole. The market price will sink more or less below the natural price, according as the greatness of the excess increases more or less the competition of the sellers, or according as it happens to be more or less important to them to get immediately rid of the commodity. The same excess in the importation of perishable, will occasion a much greater competition than in that of durable commodities; in the importation of oranges, for example, than in that of old iron.

When the quantity brought to market is just sufficient to supply the effectual demand and no more, the market price nat-

when it is just equal to the effectual demand the market and natural price coincide.

urally comes to be either exactly, or as nearly as can be judged of, the same with the natural price. The whole quantity upon hand can be disposed of for this price, and cannot be disposed of for more. The competition of the different dealers obliges them all to accept of this price, but does not oblige them to accept of less.

The quantity of every commodity brought to market naturally suits itself to the effectual demand. It is the interest of all

It naturally suits itself to the effectual demand.

those who employ their land, labour, or stock, in bringing any commodity to market, that the quantity never should exceed the effectual demand; and it is the interest of all other people that it never should fall short of that demand.[8]

If at any time it exceeds the effectual demand, some of the

When it exceeds that demand, some of the component parts of its price are below their natural rate;

component parts of its price must be paid below their natural rate. If it is rent, the interest of the landlords will immediately prompt them to withdraw a part of their land; and if it is wages or profit, the interest of the labourers in the one case, and of their employers in the other, will prompt them to

[8] [Ed. 1 reads "fall short of it."]

withdraw a part of their labour or stock from this employment. The quantity brought to market will soon be no more than sufficient to supply the effectual demand. All the different parts of its price will rise to their natural rate, and the whole price to its natural price.

If, on the contrary, the quantity brought to market should at any time fall short of the effectual demand, some of the component parts of its price must rise above their natural rate. If it is rent, the interest of all other landlords will naturally prompt them to prepare more land for the raising of this commodity; if it is wages or profit, the interest of all other labourers and dealers will soon prompt them to employ more labour and stock in preparing and bringing it to market. The quantity brought thither will soon be sufficient to supply the effectual demand. All the different parts of its price will soon sink to their natural rate, and the whole price to its natural price.

when it falls short, some of the component parts are above their natural rate.

The natural price, therefore, is, as it were, the central price, to which the prices of all commodities are continually gravitating. Different accidents may sometimes keep them suspended a good deal above it, and sometimes force them down even somewhat below it. But whatever may be the obstacles which hinder them from settling in this center of repose and continuance, they are constantly tending towards it.

Natural price is the central price to which actual prices gravitate.

The whole quantity of industry annually employed in order to bring any commodity to market, naturally suits itself in this manner to the effectual demand. It naturally aims at bringing always that precise quantity thither which may be sufficient to supply, and no more than supply, that demand.

Industry suits itself to the effectual demand,

But in some employments the same quantity of industry will in different years produce very different quantities of commodities;[9] while in others it will produce always the same,

[9] [See below, pp. 160, 161.]

but the quantity produced by a given amount of industry sometimes fluctuates. or very nearly the same. The same number of labourers in husbandry will, in different years, produce very different quantities of corn, wine, oil, hops, &c. But the same number of spinners and weavers will every year produce the same or very nearly the same quantity of linen and woollen cloth. It is only the average produce of the one species of industry which can be suited in any respect to the effectual demand; and as its actual produce is frequently much greater and frequently much less than its average produce, the quantity of the commodities brought to market will sometimes exceed a good deal, and sometimes fall short a good deal, of the effectual demand. Even though that demand therefore should continue always the same, their market price will be liable to great fluctuations, will sometimes fall a good deal below, and sometimes rise a good deal above, their natural price. In the other species of industry, the produce of equal quantities of labour being always the same, or very nearly the same, it can be more exactly suited to the effectual demand. While that demand continues the same, therefore, the market price of the commodities is likely to do so too, and to be either altogether, or as nearly as can be judged of, the same with the natural price. That the price of linen and woollen cloth is liable neither to such frequent nor to such great variations as the price of corn, every man's experience will inform him. The price of the one species of commodities varies only with the variations in the demand: That of the other varies not only with the variations in the demand, but with the much greater and more frequent variations in the quantity of what is brought to market in order to supply that demand.

The occasional and temporary fluctuations in the market price of any commodity fall chiefly upon those parts of its *The fluctuations fall on wages and profit more than on rent,* price which resolve themselves into wages and profit. That part which resolves itself into rent is less affected by them. A rent certain in money is not in the least affected by them either in its rate or in its value. A rent which consists either in a certain proportion or in a certain quantity of the rude produce, is no doubt affected in its yearly value by all the occasional and temporary fluctuations in the market price of that rude produce; but it is seldom affected by them in its yearly rate. In settling the terms of the lease, the landlord and farmer endeavour, according to their best judgment, to adjust that rate, not to the temporary and occasional, but to the average and ordinary price of the produce.

Such fluctuations affect both the value and the rate either of wages or of profit, according as the market happens to be either

affecting them in different proportions according to the supply of commodities and labour.

over-stocked or under-stocked with commodities or with labour; with work done, or with work to be done. A public mourning raises the price of black cloth[10] (with which the market is almost always under-stocked upon such occasions), and augments the profits of the merchants who possess any considerable quantity of it. It has no effect upon the wages of the weavers. The market is under-stocked with commodities, not with labour; with work done, not with work to be done. It raises the wages of journeymen taylors. The market is here under-stocked with labour. There is an effectual demand for more[11] labour, for more work to be done than can be had. It sinks the price of coloured silks and cloths, and thereby reduces the profits of the merchants who have any considerable quantity of them upon hand. It sinks too the wages of the workmen employed in preparing such commodities, for which all demand is stopped for six months, perhaps for a twelvemonth. The market is here over-stocked both with commodities and with labour.

But though the market price of every particular commodity

But market price may be kept above natural for a long time,

is in this manner continually gravitating, if one may say so, towards the natural price, yet sometimes particular accidents, sometimes natural causes, and sometimes particular regulations of police, may, in many

[10] [Repeated below, p. 160.]

[11] [Ed. 1 does not contain "more."]

commodities, keep up the market price, for a long time together, a good deal above the natural price.

When by an increase in the effectual demand, the market
price of some particular commodity happens to rise a good

*in consequence of
want of general
knowledge of high
profits,*

deal above the natural price, those who employ their stocks in supplying that market are
generally careful to conceal this change. If it
was. commonly known, their great profit
would tempt so many new rivals to employ
their stocks in the same way, that, the effectual demand being
fully supplied, the market price would soon be reduced to the
natural price, and perhaps for some time even below it. If the
market is at a great distance from the residence of those who
supply it, they may sometimes be able to keep the secret for
several years together, and may so long enjoy their extraordinary profits without any new rivals. Secrets of this kind, however, it must be acknowledged, can seldom be long kept; and
the extraordinary profit can last very little longer than they are
kept.

Secrets in manufactures are capable of being longer kept
than secrets in trade. A dyer who has found the means of pro-

*or in consequence
of secrets in
manufactures,*

ducing a particular colour with materials
which cost only half the price of those commonly made use of, may, with good management, enjoy the advantage of his discovery
as long as he lives, and even leave it as a legacy to his posterity.
His extraordinary gains arise from the high price which is paid
for his private labour. They properly consist in the high wages
of that labour. But as they are repeated upon every part of his
stock, and as their whole amount bears, upon that account, a
regular proportion to it, they are commonly considered as extraordinary profits of stock.[12]

Such enhancements of the market price are evidently the ef-

[12] [They are called profits simply because all the gains of the master-manufacturer
are called profits. They can scarcely be said to have been "considered" at all; if
they had been, they would doubtless have been pronounced to be, in the words of
the next paragraph, "the effects of a particular accident," namely, the possession of
peculiar knowledge on the part of the dyer.]

which may operate for long periods,

or in consequence of scarcity of peculiar soils,

fects of particular accidents, of which, however, the operation may sometimes last for many years together.

Some natural productions require such a singularity of soil and situation, that all the land in a great country, which is fit for producing them, may not be sufficient to supply the effectual demand. The whole quantity brought to market, therefore, may be disposed of to those who are willing to give more than what is sufficient to pay the rent of the land which produced them, together with the wages of the labour, and the profits of the stock which were employed in preparing and bringing them to market, according to their natural rates. Such commodities may continue for whole centuries together to be sold at this high price;[13] and that part of it which resolves itself into the rent of land is in this case the part which is generally paid above its natural rate. The rent of the land which affords such singular and esteemed productions, like the rent of some vineyards in France of a peculiarly happy soil and situation, bears no regular proportion to the rent of other equally fertile and equally well-cultivated land in its neighbourhood. The wages of the labour and the profits of the stock employed in bringing such commodities to market, on the contrary, are seldom out of their natural proportion to those of the other employments of labour and stock in their neighbourhood.

which may continue for ever.

Such enhancements of the market price are evidently the effect of natural causes which may hinder the effectual demand from ever being fully supplied, and which may continue, therefore, to operate for ever.

A monopoly has the same effect as a trade secret,

A monopoly granted either to an individual or to a trading company has the same effect as a secret in trade or manufactures. The monopolists, by keeping the market constantly understocked, by never fully supplying the effec-

[13] [Ed. 1 places "for whole centuries together" here instead of where printed.]

tual demand, sell their commodities much above the natural price, and raise their emoluments, whether they consist in wages or profit, greatly above their natural rate.

The price of monopoly is upon every occasion the highest which can be got. The natural price, or the price of free competition, on the contrary, is the lowest which can be taken, not upon every occasion indeed, but for any considerable time together. The one is upon every occasion the highest which can be squeezed out of the buyers, or which, it is supposed, they will consent to give: The other is the lowest which the sellers can commonly afford to take, and at the same time continue their business.

the price of monopoly being the highest which can be got.

The exclusive privileges of corporations, statutes of apprenticeship,[14] and all those laws which restrain, in particular employments, the competition to a smaller number than might otherwise go into them, have the same tendency, though in a less degree. They are a sort of enlarged monopolies, and may frequently, for ages together, and in whole classes of employments, keep up the market price of particular commodities above the natural price, and maintain both the wages of the labour and the profits of the stock employed about them somewhat above their natural rate.

Corporation privileges, etc., are enlarged monopolies.

Such enhancements of the market price may last as long as the regulations of police which give occasion to them.

The market price of any particular commodity, though it may continue long above, can seldom continue long below, its natural price. Whatever part of it was paid below the natural rate, the persons whose interest it affected would im-

Market price is seldom long below natural price,

[14] [See below, pp. 163–179. Playfair, in a note on this passage, ed. *Wealth of Nations*, 1805, vol. i., p. 97, says: "This observation about corporations and apprenticeships scarcely applies at all to the present day. In London, for example, the freemen only can carry on certain businesses within the city: there is not one of those businesses that may not be carried on elsewhere, and the produce sold in the city. If Mr. Smith's principle applied, goods would be dearer in Cheapside than in Bond Street, which is not the case."]

mediately feel the loss, and would immediately withdraw either so much land, or so much labour, or so much stock, from being employed about it, that the quantity brought to market would soon be no more than sufficient to supply the effectual demand. Its market price, therefore, would soon rise to the natural price. This at least would be the case where there was perfect liberty.[15]

The same statutes of apprenticeship and other corporation laws indeed, which, when a manufacture is in prosperity, enable the workman to raise his wages a good deal above their natural rate, sometimes oblige him, when it decays, to let them down a good deal below it. As in the one case they exclude many people from his employment, so in the other they exclude him from many employments. The effect of such regulations, however, is not near so durable in sinking the workman's wages below, as in raising them above, their natural rate. Their operation in the one way may endure for many centuries, but in the other it can last no longer than the lives of some of the workmen who were bred to the business in the time of its prosperity. When they are gone, the number of those who are afterwards educated to the trade will naturally suit itself to the effectual demand. The police must be as violent as that of Indostan or ancient Egypt[16] (where every man was bound by a principle of religion to follow the occupation of his father, and was supposed to commit the most horrid sacrilege if he changed it for another), which can in any particular employment, and for several generations together, sink either the wages of labour or the profits of stock below their natural rate.

though apprenticeship and corporation laws sometimes reduce wages much below the natural rate for a certain period.

This is all that I think necessary to be observed at present concerning the deviations, whether occasional or permanent, of the market price of commodities from the natural price.

---

[15] [Above, p. 79, and below, pp. 138, 139.]

[16] [In *Lectures*, p. 168, the Egyptian practice is attributed to "a law of Sesostris."]

Natural price varies with the natural rate of wages, profit and rent.

The natural price itself varies with the natural rate of each of its component parts, of wages, profit, and rent; and in every society this rate varies according to their circumstances, according to their riches or poverty, their advancing, stationary, or declining condition. I shall, in the four following chapters, endeavour to explain, as fully and distinctly as I can, the causes of those different variations.

Wages will be dealt with in chapter vii.,

First, I shall endeavour to explain what are the circumstances which naturally determine the rate of wages, and in what manner those circumstances are affected by the riches or poverty, by the advancing, stationary, or declining state of the society.

profit in chapter ix.,

Secondly, I shall endeavour to show what are the circumstances which naturally determine the rate of profit, and in what manner too those circumstances are affected by the like variations in the state of the society.

differences of wages and profit in chapter x.,

Though pecuniary wages and profit are very different in the different employments of labour and stock; yet a certain proportion seems commonly to take place between both the pecuniary wages in all the different employments of labour, and the pecuniary profits in all the different employments of stock. This proportion, it will appear hereafter, depends partly upon the nature of the different employments, and partly upon the different laws and policy of the society in which they are carried on. But though in many respects dependent upon the laws and policy, this proportion seems to be little affected by the riches or poverty of that society; by its advancing, stationary, or declining condition; but to remain the same or very nearly the same in all those different states. I shall, in the third place, endeavour to explain all the different circumstances which regulate this proportion.

and rent in chapter xi.

In the fourth and last place, I shall endeavour to show what are the circumstances which regulate the rent of land, and which either raise or lower the real price of all the different substances which it produces.

CHAPTER VIII

OF THE WAGES OF LABOUR

THE PRODUCE of labour constitutes the natural recompence or wages of labour.

Produce is the natural wages of labour.

In that original state of things, which precedes both the appropriation of land and the accumulation of stock, the whole produce of labour belongs to the labourer.[1] He has neither landlord nor master to share with him.

Originally the whole belonged to the labourer.

Had this state continued, the wages of labour would have augmented with all those improvements in its productive powers, to which the division of labour gives occasion. All things would gradually have become cheaper.[2] They would have been produced by a smaller quantity of labour; and as the commodities produced by equal quantities of labour would naturally in this state of things be exchanged for one another, they would have been purchased likewise with the produce of a smaller quantity.

If this had continued, all things would have become cheaper,

though in appearance many things might have become dearer.

But though all things would have become cheaper in reality, in appearance many things might have become dearer than before, or have been exchanged for a greater

[1] [The same nine words occur above, p. 68, in ed. 2 and later eds.]

[2] [The word "cheaper" is defined by the next sentence as "produced by a smaller quantity of labour."]

quantity of other goods.[3] Let us suppose, for example, that in the greater part of employments the productive powers of labour had been improved to tenfold, or that a day's labour could produce ten times the quantity of work which it had done originally; but that in a particular employment they had been improved only to double, or that a day's labour could produce only twice the quantity of work which it had done before. In exchanging the produce of a day's labour in the greater part of employments, for that of a day's labour in this particular one, ten times the original quantity of work in them would purchase only twice the original quantity in it. Any particular quantity in it, therefore, a pound weight, for example, would appear to be five times dearer than before.[4] In reality,[5] however, it would be twice as cheap. Though it required five times the quantity of other goods to purchase it, it would require only half the quantity of labour either to purchase or to produce it. The acquisition, therefore, would be twice as easy[6] as before.

But this original state of things, in which the labourer enjoyed the whole produce of his own labour, could not last

This state was ended by the appropriation of land and accumulation of stock, beyond the first introduction of the appropriation of land and the accumulation of stock. It was at an end, therefore, long before the most considerable improvements were made in the productive powers of labour, and it would be to no purpose to trace further what might have been its effects upon the recompence or wages of labour.

As soon as land becomes private property, the landlord demands a share of almost all the produce which[7] the labourer

---

[3] [It would be less confusing if the sentence ran: "But though all things would have become cheaper in the sense just attributed to the word, yet in the sense in which the words cheaper and dearer are ordinarily used many things might have become dearer than before."]

[4] [*I.e.*, "would in the ordinary sense of the word be five times dearer than before."]

[5] [*I.e.*, "in the sense attributed to the word above."]

[6] [If the amount of labour necessary for the acquisition of a thing measures its value, "twice as cheap" means simply, twice as easy to acquire.]

[7] [Ed. 1 reads "of whatever produce."]

can either raise, or collect from it. His rent makes the first de-

rent being the first deduction, duction from the produce of the labour which is employed upon land.

It seldom happens that the person who tills the ground has wherewithal to maintain himself till he reaps the harvest. His maintenance is generally advanced to

and profit the second, both in agriculture, him from the stock of a master, the farmer who employs him, and who would have no interest to employ him, unless he was to share in the produce of his labour, or unless

his stock was to be replaced to him with a profit. This profit makes a second deduction from the produce of the labour which is employed upon land.

The produce of almost all other labour is liable to the like deduction of profit. In all arts and manufactures the greater

and other arts and manufactures. part of the workmen stand in need of a master to advance them the materials of their work, and their wages and maintenance till it

be compleated.[8] He shares in the produce of their labour, or in the value which it adds to the materials upon which it is bestowed; and in this share consists his profit.[9]

It sometimes happens, indeed, that a single independent workman has stock sufficient both to purchase the materials of

The independent workman gets profits as well as wages, his work, and to maintain himself till it be compleated. He is both master and workman, and enjoys the whole produce of his own labour, or the whole value which it adds

to the materials upon which it is bestowed. It includes what are usually two distinct revenues, belonging to two distinct persons, the profits of stock, and the wages of labour.

Such cases, however, are not very frequent, and in every

but this case is infrequent. part of Europe, twenty workmen serve under a master for one that is independent; and the wages of labour are every where understood

[8] [The provision of tools to work with and buildings to work in is forgotten.]

[9] [Cp. with this account that given at the beginning of chap. vi., pp. 67–68 above.]

to be, what they usually are, when the labourer is one person, and the owner of the stock which employs him another.

What are the common wages of labour, depends every where upon the contract usually made between those two parties, whose interests are by no means the same. The workmen desire to get as much, the masters to give as little as possible. The former are disposed to combine in order to raise, the latter in order to lower the wages of labour.

Wages depend on contract between masters and workmen.

It is not, however, difficult to foresee which of the two parties must, upon all ordinary occasions, have the advantage in the dispute, and force the other into a compliance with their terms. The masters, being fewer in number, can combine much more easily; and the law, besides, authorises, or at least does not prohibit their combinations,[10] while it prohibits those of the workmen.[11] We have no acts of parliament against combining to lower the price of work; but many against combining to raise it. In all such disputes the masters can hold out much longer. A landlord, a farmer, a master manufacturer, or merchant, though they did not employ a single workman, could generally live a year or two upon the stocks which they have already acquired. Many workmen could not subsist a week, few could subsist a month, and scarce any a year without employment. In the long-run the workman may be as necessary to his master as his master is to him, but the necessity is not so immediate.

The masters have the advantage,

We rarely hear, it has been said, of the combinations of masters, though frequently of those of workmen. But whoever imagines, upon this account, that masters rarely combine, is as ignorant of the world as of the subject. Masters are always and

[10] [Ed. 1 reads, "The masters being fewer in number can not only combine more easily, but the law authorises their combinations, or at least does not prohibit them."]

[11] [*E.g.*, 7 Geo. I., stat. 1, c. 13, as to London tailors; 12 Geo. I., c. 34, as to wool-combers and weavers; 12 Geo. I., c. 35, as to brick and tile makers within fifteen miles of London; 22 Geo. II., c. 27, § 12, as to persons employed in the woollen manufacture and many others.]

every where in a sort of tacit, but constant and uniform combi-

though less is heard of masters' combinations than of workmen's. nation, not to raise the wages of labour above their actual rate. To violate this combination is every where a most unpopular action, and a sort of reproach to a master among his neighbours and equals. We seldom, indeed, hear of this combination, because it is the usual, and one may say, the natural state of things which nobody ever hears of. Masters too sometimes enter into particular combinations to sink the wages of labour even below this rate. These are always conducted with the utmost silence and secrecy, till the moment of execution, and when the workmen yield, as they sometimes do, without resistance, though severely felt by them, they are never heard of by other people. Such combinations, however, are frequently resisted by a contrary defensive combination of the workmen; who sometimes too, without any provocation of this kind, combine of their own accord to raise the price of their labour. Their usual pretences[12] are, sometimes the high price of provisions; sometimes the great profit which their masters make by their work. But whether their combinations be offensive or defensive, they are always abundantly heard of. In order to bring the point to a speedy decision, they have always recourse to the loudest clamour, and sometimes to the most shocking violence and outrage. They are desperate, and act with the folly and extravagance of desperate men, who must either[13] starve, or frighten their masters into an immediate compliance with their demands. The masters upon these occasions are just as clamorous upon the other side, and never cease to call aloud for the assistance of the civil magistrate, and the rigorous execution of those laws which have been enacted with so much severity against the combinations of servants, labourers, and journeymen. The workmen, accordingly, very seldom derive any advantage from the violence of those tumultuous combinations, which, partly from the interposition

[12] [The word is used as elsewhere in Adam Smith without the implication of falsity now attached to it: a pretence is simply something put forward.]

[13] [Ed. 1 does not contain "either."]

of the civil magistrate, partly from the superior steadiness of the masters, partly from the necessity which the greater part of the workmen are under of submitting for the sake of present subsistence, generally end in nothing, but the punishment or ruin of the ring-leaders.

But though in disputes with their workmen, masters must generally have the advantage, there is however a certain rate below which it seems impossible to reduce, for any considerable time, the ordinary wages even of the lowest species of labour.

But masters cannot reduce wages below a certain rate, namely, subsistence for a man and something over for a family.

A man must always live by his work, and his wages must at least be sufficient to maintain him. They must even upon most occasions be somewhat more; otherwise it would be impossible for him to bring up a family, and the race of such workmen could not last beyond the first generation. Mr. Cantillon seems, upon this account, to suppose that the lowest species of common labourers must every where earn at least double their own maintenance, in order that one with another they may be enabled to bring up two children; the labour of the wife, on account of her necessary attendance on the children, being supposed no more than sufficient to provide for herself.[14] But one-half the children born, it is computed, die before the age of manhood.[15] The poorest labourers, therefore, according to this account, must, one with another, attempt to rear at least four children, in order that two may have an equal chance of living to that age. But the necessary maintenance of four children, it is supposed, may be nearly equal to that of one man. The labour of an able-bodied slave, the same author adds, is computed to be worth double his maintenance; and that of the meanest labourer, he thinks, cannot be worth less than that of

---

[14] [*Essai sur la nature du commerce en général*, 1755, pp. 42–47. The "seems" is not meaningless, as Cantillon is unusually obscure in the passage referred to. It is not clear whether he intends to include the woman's earnings or not.]

[15] [*I.e.*, before completing their seventeenth year, as stated by Dr. Halley, quoted by Cantillon, *Essai*, pp. 42, 43.]

an able-bodied slave. Thus far at least seems certain, that, in order to bring up a family, the labour of the husband and wife together must, even in the lowest species of common labour, be able to earn something more than what is precisely necessary for their own maintenance; but in what proportion, whether in that above mentioned, or in any other, I shall not take upon me to determine.[16]

There are certain circumstances, however, which sometimes give the labourers an advantage, and enable them to raise their wages considerably above this rate; evidently the lowest which is consistent with common humanity.

Wages may be considerably above this rate,

When in any country the demand for those who live by wages; labourers, journeymen, servants of every kind, is continually increasing; when every year furnishes employment for a greater number than had been employed the year before, the workmen have no occasion to combine in order to raise their wages. The scarcity of hands occasions a competition among masters, who bid against one another, in order to get workmen,[17] and thus voluntarily break through the natural combination of masters not to raise wages.

when there is an increasing demand for labourers,

The demand for those who live by wages, it is evident, cannot increase but in proportion to the increase of the funds which are destined for the payment of wages. These funds are of two kinds; first, the revenue which is over and above what is necessary for the maintenance;[18] and secondly, the stock which is

which is caused by an increase of the funds destined for the payment of wages. The funds

---

[16] [Cantillon himself, p. 44, says: "C'est une matière qui n'admet pas un calcul exact, et dans laquelle la précision n'est pas même fort nécessaire, il suffit qu'on ne s'y éloigne pas beaucoup de la réalité."]

[17] [Ed. 1 reads "them."]

[18] [There is no attempt to define "maintenance," and consequently the division of a man's revenue into what is necessary for his maintenance and what is over and above is left perfectly vague.]

consist of — over and above what is necessary for the employment of their masters.

When the landlord, annuitant, or monied man, has a greater revenue than what he judges sufficient to maintain his own *surplus revenue,* family, he employs either the whole or a part of the surplus in maintaining one or more menial servants.[19] Increase this surplus, and he will naturally increase the number of those servants.

When an independent workman, such as a weaver or shoemaker, has got more stock than what is sufficient to purchase *and surplus stock.* the materials of his own work, and to maintain himself till he can dispose of it, he naturally employs one or more journeymen with the surplus, in order to make a profit by their work. Increase this surplus, and he will naturally increase the number of his journeymen.

The demand for those who live by wages, therefore, necessarily increases with the increase of the revenue and stock of *The demand for* every country, and cannot possibly increase *labourers there-* without it. The increase of revenue and stock *fore increases with* is the increase of national wealth.[20] The de- *the increase of* mand for those who live by wages, therefore, *national wealth.* naturally increases with the increase of national wealth, and cannot possibly increase

High wages are without it.
occasioned by the It is not the actual greatness of national
increase, not by wealth, but its continual increase, which oc-
the actual great- casions a rise in the wages[21] of labour. It is
ness of national not, accordingly, in the richest countries, but
wealth. in the most thriving, or in those which are

---

[19] [It seems to be implied here that keeping a menial servant, even to perform the most necessary offices (*e.g.*, to nurse the infant child of a widower), is not "maintaining" a family.]

[20] [Above, in the Introduction and Plan of the Work, the wealth of a nation was treated as synonymous with its annual produce, and there has been hitherto no suggestion that its stock must be considered.]

[21] [Apparently this is a slip for "occasions high wages." At any rate the next sentences require this assertion and not that actually made.]

growing rich the fastest, that the wages of labour are highest. England is certainly, in the present times, a much richer[22] country than any part of North America. The wages of labour, however, are much higher in North America than in any part of England. In the province of New York, common labourers earn[23] three shillings and sixpence currency, equal to two shillings sterling, a day; ship carpenters, ten shillings and sixpence currency, with a pint of rum worth sixpence sterling, equal in all to six shillings and sixpence sterling; house carpenters and bricklayers, eight shillings currency, equal to four shillings and sixpence sterling; journeymen taylors, five shillings currency, equal to about two shillings and ten-pence sterling. These prices are all above the London price; and wages are said to be as high in the other colonies as in New York. The price of provisions is every where in North America much lower than in England. A dearth has never been known there. In the worst seasons, they have always had a sufficiency for themselves, though less for exportation. If the money price of labour, therefore, be higher than it is any where in the mother country, its real price, the real command of the necessaries and conveniencies of life which it conveys to the labourer, must be higher in a still greater proportion.

But though North America is not yet so rich as England, it is much more thriving, and advancing with much greater rapidity to the further acquisition of riches. The most decisive mark of the prosperity of any country is the increase of the number of its inhabitants. In Great Britain, and most other European countries, they are not supposed to double in less than five hundred years. In the British colonies in North America, it has been found, that they double in twenty

North America is more thriving than England.

----

[22] [The method of calculating wealth by the amount of annual produce per head adopted above, in the Introduction and Plan of the Work, is departed from here and below, p. 101, and frequently in later passages, in favour of the calculation by amount of capital wealth.]

[23] This was written in 1773, before the commencement of the late disturbances. [Ed. 1 does not contain this note; eds. 2 and 3 read "present disturbances."]

or five-and-twenty years.[24] Nor in the present times is this increase principally owing to the continual importation of new inhabitants, but to the great multiplication of the species. Those who live to old age, it is said, frequently see there from fifty to a hundred, and sometimes many more, descendants from their own body. Labour is there so well rewarded that a numerous family of children, instead of being a burthen is a source of opulence and prosperity to the parents. The labour of each child, before it can leave their house, is computed to be worth a hundred pounds clear gain to them. A young widow with four or five young children, who, among the middling or inferior ranks of people in Europe, would have so little chance for a second husband, is there frequently courted as a sort of fortune. The value of children is the greatest of all encouragements to marriage. We cannot, therefore, wonder that the people in North America should generally marry very young. Notwithstanding the great increase occasioned by such early marriages, there is a continual complaint of the scarcity of hands in North America. The demand for labourers, the funds destined for maintaining them, increase, it seems, still faster than they can find labourers to employ.

Though the wealth of a country should be very great, yet if it has been long stationary, we must not expect to find the wages of labour very high in it. The funds destined for the payment of wages, the revenue and stock of its inhabitants, may be of the greatest extent; but if they have continued for several

---

[24] [Petty, *Political Arithmetic*, 1699, p. 18, made the period for England 360 years. Gregory King, quoted by Davenant, *Works*, ed. Whitworth, 1771, vol. ii., p. 176, makes it 435 years in the past and probably 600 in the future. In 1703 the population of Virginia was 60,000, in 1755 it was 300,000, and in 1765 it was 500,000, "by which they appear to have doubled their numbers every twenty years as nigh as may be."—*The Present State of Great Britain and North America with regard to Agriculture, Population, Trade and Manufactures*, 1767, p. 22, note. "The original number of persons who in 1643 had settled in New England was 21,200. Ever since, it is reckoned that more have left them than have gone to them. In the year 1760 they were increased to half a million. They have therefore all along doubled their own number in twenty-five years."—Richard Price, *Observations on Reversionary Payments*, etc., 1771, pp. 204, 205. The statement as to America is repeated below, p. 530.]

Wages are not high in a stationary country however rich.

centuries of the same, or very nearly of the same extent, the number of labourers employed every year could easily supply, and even more than supply, the number wanted the following year. There could seldom be any scarcity of hands, nor could the masters be obliged to bid against one another in order to get them. The hands, on the contrary, would, in this case, naturally multiply beyond their employment. There would be a constant scarcity of employment, and the labourers would be obliged to bid against one another in order to get it. If in such a country the wages of labour had ever been more than sufficient to maintain the labourer, and to enable him to bring up a family, the competition of the labourers and the interest of the masters would soon reduce them to this lowest rate which is consistent with common humanity. China has been long one of the richest, that is, one of the most fertile, best cultivated, most industrious, and most populous countries in the world.[25] It seems, however, to have been long stationary. Marco Polo, who visited it more than five hundred years ago,[26] describes its cultivation, industry, and populousness, almost in the same terms in which they are described by travellers in the present times. It had perhaps, even long before his time, acquired that full complement of riches which the nature of its laws and institutions permits it to acquire. The accounts of all travellers, inconsistent in many other respects, agree in the low wages of labour, and in the difficulty which a labourer finds in bringing up a family in China. If by digging the ground a whole day he can get what will purchase a small quantity of rice in the evening, he is contented. The condition of artificers is, if possible, still worse. Instead of waiting indolently in their work-houses, for the calls of their customers, as in Europe, they are continually running about the streets with the tools of their respective trades, offering

---

[25] [Here we have a third method of calculating the riches or wealth of a country, namely by the amount of produce per acre.

[26] [The date of his arrival was 1275.]

their service, and as it were begging employment.[27] The poverty of the lower ranks of people in China far surpasses that of the most beggarly nations in Europe. In the neighbourhood of Canton many hundred, it is commonly said, many thousand families have no habitation on the land, but live constantly in little fishing boats upon the rivers and canals. The subsistence which they find there is so scanty that they are eager to fish up the nastiest garbage thrown overboard from any European ship. Any carrion, the carcase of a dead dog or cat, for example, though half putrid and stinking, is as welcome to them as the most wholesome food to the people of other countries. Marriage is encouraged in China, not by the profitableness of children, but by the liberty of destroying them. In all great towns several are every night exposed in the street, or drowned like puppies in the water. The performance of this horrid office is even said to be the avowed business by which some people earn their subsistence.[28]

[27] ["Les artisans courent les villes du matin au soir pour chercher pratique," Quesnay, *Éphémérides du citoyen*, Mars, 1767; *Œuvres*, ed. Oncken, 1888, p. 581.]

[28] ["Cependant quelque sobre et quelque industrieux que soit le peuple de la Chine, le grand nombre de ses habitants y cause beaucoup de misère. On en voit de si pauvres, que ne pouvant fournir a leurs enfants les aliments nécessaires, ils les exposent dans les rues, surtout lorsque les mères tombent malades, ou qu'elles manquent de lait pour les nourrir. Ces petits innocents sont condamnés en quelque manière à la mort presque au même instant qu'ils ont commencé de vivre: cela frappe dans les grandes villes, comme Peking, Canton; car dans les autres villes à peine s'en aperçoit-on.

"C'est ce qui a porté les missionnaires a entretenir dans ces endroits très peuplés, un nombre de catéchistes, qui en partagent entre eux tous les quartiers, et les parcourent tous les matins, pour procurer la grâce du baptême à une multitude d'enfants moribonds.

"Dans la même vue on a quelquefois gagné des sages-femmes infidèles afin qu'elles permissent à des filles chrétiennes de ses suivre dans les différentes maisons où elles sont appelées: car il arrive quelquefois que les Chinois se trouvant hors d'état de nourrir une nombreuse famille, engagent ces sages femmes à étouffer dans un bassin plein d'eau les petites filles aussitôt qu'elles sont nées; ces chrétiennes ont soin de les baptiser, et par ce moyen ces tristes victimes de l'indigence de leurs parents trouvent la vie éternelle dans ces mêmes eaux, qui leur ravissent une vie courte et périssable."—Du Halde, *Description géographique*,

China, however, though it may perhaps stand still, does not seem to go backwards. Its towns are no-where deserted by

China is not going backwards and labourers there keep up their numbers.

their inhabitants. The lands which had once been cultivated are no-where neglected. The same or very nearly the same annual labour must therefore continue to be performed, and the funds destined for maintaining it must not, consequently, be sensibly diminished. The lowest class of labourers, therefore, notwithstanding their scanty subsistence, must some way or another make shift to continue their race so far as to keep up their usual numbers.

But it would be otherwise in a country where the funds destined for the maintenance of labour were sensibly decaying.

In a declining country this would not be the case.

Every year the demand for servants and labourers would, in all the different classes of employments, be less than it had been the year before. Many who had been bred in the superior classes, not being able to find employment in their own business, would be glad to seek it in the lowest. The lowest class being not only overstocked with its own workmen, but with the overflowings of all the other classes, the competition for employment would be so great in it, as to reduce the wages of labour to the most miserable and scanty subsistence of the labourer. Many would not be able to find employment even upon these hard terms, but would either starve, or be driven to seek a subsistence either by begging, or by the perpetration perhaps of the greatest enormities. Want, famine, and mortality would immediately prevail in that class, and from thence extend themselves to all the superior classes, till the number of inhabitants in the country was reduced to what could easily be maintained by the revenue and stock which remained in it, and which had escaped either the tyranny or calamity which had destroyed the rest. This perhaps is nearly the present state of

historique, chronologique, politique et physique de l'empire de la Chine et de la Tartarie chinoise, 1735, tom. ii., pp. 73, 74. The statement in the text above that drowning babies is a special business is possibly founded on a mistranslation of "sages-femmes."]

Bengal, and of some other of the English settlements in the East Indies. In a fertile country which had before been much depopulated, where subsistence, consequently, should not be very difficult, and where, notwithstanding, three or four hundred thousand people die of hunger in one year, we may be assured that the funds destined for the maintenance of the labouring poor are fast decaying. The difference between the genius of the British constitution which protects and governs North America, and that of the mercantile company which oppresses and domineers in the East Indies, cannot perhaps be better illustrated than by the different state of those countries.

The liberal reward of labour, therefore, as it is the necessary effect, so it is the natural symptom of increasing national wealth. The scanty maintenance of the labouring poor, on the other hand, is the natural symptom that things are at a stand, and their starving condition that they are going fast backwards.

In Great Britain the wages of labour seem, in the present times, to be evidently more than what is precisely necessary to enable the labourer to bring up a family. In order to satisfy ourselves upon this point it will not be necessary to enter into any tedious or doubtful calculation of what may be the lowest sum upon which it is possible to do this. There are many plain symptoms that the wages of labour are no-where in this country regulated by this lowest rate which is consistent with common humanity.

In Great Britain wages are above the lowest rate,

First, in almost every part of Great Britain there is a distinction, even in the lowest species of labour, between summer and winter wages. Summer wages are always highest. But on account of the extraordinary expence of fewel, the maintenance of a family is most expensive in winter. Wages, therefore, being highest when this expence is lowest, it seems evident that they are not regulated by what is necessary for this expence; but by the quantity and supposed value of the work. A labourer, it may be said indeed, ought to save part of his summer wages in order to defray his winter expence; and that through the whole year they do not exceed

since (1) there is a difference between winter and summer wages,

what is necessary to maintain his family through the whole year. A slave, however, or one absolutely dependent on us for immediate subsistence, would not be treated in this manner. His daily subsistence would be proportioned to his daily necessities.

Secondly, the wages of labour do not in Great Britain fluctuate with the price of provisions. These vary everywhere from year to year, frequently from month to month. But in many places the money price of labour remains uniformly the same sometimes for half a century together. If in these places, therefore, the labouring poor can maintain their families in dear years, they must be at their ease in times of moderate plenty, and in affluence in those of extraordinary cheapness. The high price of provisions during these ten years past has not in many parts of the kingdom been accompanied with any sensible rise in the money price of labour. It has, indeed, in some; owing probably more to the increase of the demand for labour than to that of the price of provisions.

(2) wages do not fluctuate with the price of provisions,

Thirdly, as the price of provisions varies more from year to year than the wages of labour, so, on the other hand, the wages of labour vary more from place to place than the price of provisions. The prices of bread and butcher's meat are generally the same or very nearly the same through the greater part of the united kingdom. These and most other things which are sold by retail, the way in which the labouring poor buy all things, are generally fully as cheap or cheaper in great towns than in the remoter parts of the country, for reasons which I shall have occasion to explain hereafter.[29] But the wages of labour in a great town and its neighbourhood are frequently a fourth or a fifth part, twenty or five-and-twenty per cent. higher than at a few miles distance. Eighteen pence a day may be reckoned the common price of labour in London and its neighbourhood. At a few miles dis-

(3) wages vary more from place to place than the price of provisions,

[29] [Below, p. 156.]

tance it falls to fourteen and fifteen pence. Ten pence may be reckoned its price in Edinburgh and its neighbourhood. At a few miles distance it falls to eight pence, the usual price of common labour through the greater part of the low country of Scotland, where it varies a good deal less than in England.[30] Such a difference of prices, which it seems is not always sufficient to transport a man from one parish to another, would necessarily occasion so great a transportation of the most bulky commodities, not only from one parish to another, but from one end of the kingdom, almost from one end of the world to the other, as would soon reduce them more nearly to a level. After all that has been said of the levity and inconstancy of human nature, it appears evidently from experience that a man is of all sorts of luggage the most difficult to be transported. If the labouring poor, therefore, can maintain their families in those parts of the kingdom where the price of labour is lowest, they must be in affluence where it is highest.

Fourthly, the variations in the price of labour not only do not correspond either in place or time with those in the price of provisions, but they are frequently quite opposite.

and (4) frequently wages and the price of provisions vary in opposite directions, as grain is cheaper and wages are higher in England than in Scotland;

Grain, the food of the common people, is dearer in Scotland than in England, whence Scotland receives almost every year very large supplies. But English corn must be sold dearer in Scotland, the country to which it is brought, than in England, the country from which it comes; and in proportion to its quality it cannot be sold dearer in Scotland than the Scotch corn that comes to the same market in competition with it. The quality of grain depends chiefly upon the quantity of flour or meal which it yields at the mill, and in this respect English grain is so much superior to the Scotch, that, though often dearer in appearance, or in proportion to the measure of its bulk, it is generally cheaper in reality, or in proportion to its

---

[30] [The difference between England and Scotland in this respect is attributed to the English law of settlement below, p. 193.]

quality, or even to the measure of its weight. The price of labour, on the contrary, is dearer in England than in Scotland. If the labouring poor, therefore, can maintain their families in the one part of the united kingdom, they must be in affluence in the other. Oatmeal indeed supplies the common people in Scotland with the greatest and the best part of their food, which is in general much inferior to that of their neighbours of the same rank in England.[31] This difference, however, in the mode of their subsistence is not the cause, but the effect, of the difference in their wages; though, by a strange misapprehension, I have frequently heard it represented as the cause. It is not because one man keeps a coach while his neighbour walks a-foot, that the one is rich and the other poor; but because the one is rich he keeps a coach, and because the other is poor he walks a-foot.

During the course of the last century, taking one year with another, grain was dearer in both parts of the united kingdom than during that of the present. This is a matter of fact which cannot now admit of any reasonable doubt; and the proof of it is, if possible, still more decisive with regard to Scotland than with regard to England. It is in Scotland supported by the evidence of the public fiars, annual valuations made upon oath, according to the actual state of the markets, of all the different sorts of grain in every different county of Scotland. If such direct proof could require any collateral evidence to confirm it, I would observe that this has likewise been the case in France, and probably in most other parts of Europe. With regard to France there is the clearest proof.[32] But though it is certain that in both parts of the united kingdom grain was somewhat dearer in the last century than in the present, it is equally certain that labour was much cheaper. If the labouring poor, therefore, could bring up their families then, they must be much more at their ease now. In the last century, the most usual day-wages of common

and in the last century grain was dearer and wages were lower than in this;

---

[31] [The inferiority of oatmeal is again insisted on below, p. 220.]

[32] [Authorities are quoted below, p. 325.]

labour through the greater part of Scotland were sixpence in summer and five-pence in winter. Three shillings a week, the same price very nearly, still continues to be paid in some parts of the Highlands and Western Islands. Through the greater part of the low country the most usual wages of common labour are now eight-pence a day; ten-pence, sometimes a shilling about Edinburgh, in the counties which border upon England, probably on account of that neighbourhood, and in a few other places where there has lately been a considerable rise in the demand for labour, about Glasgow, Carron, Ayr-shire, &c. In England the improvements of agriculture, manufactures and commerce began much earlier than in Scotland. The demand for labour, and consequently its price, must necessarily have increased with those improvements. In the last century, accordingly, as well as in the present, the wages of labour were higher in England than in Scotland. They have risen too considerably since that time, though, on account of the greater variety of wages paid there in different places, it is more difficult to ascertain how much. In 1614, the pay of a foot soldier was the same as in the present times, eight pence a day.[33] When it was first established it would naturally be regulated by the usual wages of common labourers, the rank of people from which foot soldiers are commonly drawn. Lord Chief Justice Hales,[34] who wrote in the time of Charles II. computes the necessary expence of a labourer's family, consisting of six persons, the father and mother, two children able to do something, and two not able, at ten shillings a week, or twenty-six pounds a year. If they cannot earn this by their labour, they must make it up, he supposes, either by begging or stealing. He appears to have enquired very carefully into this subject.[35] In 1688, Mr.

[33] [Hume, *History*, ed. of 1773, vol. vi., p. 178, quoting Rymer's *Foedera* tom. xvi., p. 717. This was for service in Germany.]

[34] [Sir Matthew Hale.]

[35] See his scheme for the maintenance of the Poor, in Burn's History of the Poor-laws. [This note appears first in ed. 2. Hale's *Discourse Touching Provision for the Poor* was printed in 1683. It contains no internal evidence of the careful inquiry attributed to it above.]

Gregory King, whose skill in political arithmetic is so much extolled by Doctor Davenant,[36] computed the ordinary income of labourers and out-servants to be fifteen pounds a year to a family, which he supposed to consist, one with another, of three and a half persons.[37] His calculation, therefore, though different in appearance, corresponds very nearly at bottom with that of judge Hales. Both suppose the weekly expence of such families to be about twenty pence a head. Both the pecuniary income and expence of such families have increased considerably since that time through the greater part of the kingdom; in some places more, and in some less; though perhaps scarce any where so much as some exaggerated accounts of the present wages of labour have lately represented them to the public. The price of labour, it must be observed, cannot be ascertained very accurately any where, different prices being often paid at the same place and for the same sort of labour, not only according to the different abilities of the workmen, but according to the easiness or hardness of the masters. Where wages are not regulated by law, all that we can pretend to determine is what are the most usual; and experience seems to show that law can never regulate them properly, though it has often pretended to do so.

The real recompence of labour, the real quantity of the necessaries and conveniencies of life which it can procure to the labourer, has, during the course of the present century, increased perhaps in a still greater proportion than its money price. Not only grain has become somewhat cheaper, but many other things, from which the industrious poor derive an agreeable and wholesome variety of food, have become a great deal cheaper. Potatoes, for example, do not at present, through the greater part of the kingdom, cost half the price which they used to do thirty or forty years ago.

while other necessaries and conveniencies have also become cheaper.

[36] [Davenant, *Essay upon the probable Methods of Making a People Gainers in the Balance of Trade*, 1699, pp. 15, 16; in *Works*, ed. Whitworth, vol. ii, p. 175.]

[37] [Scheme D in Davenant, *Balance of Trade*, in *Works* Scheme B, vol. ii., p. 184. See below, p. 267, note.]

The same thing may be said of turnips, carrots, cabbages; things which were formerly never raised but by the spade, but which are now commonly raised by the plough. All sort of garden stuff too has become cheaper. The greater part of the apples and even of the onions consumed in Great Britain were in the last century imported from Flanders. The great improvements in the coarser manufactures of both linen and woollen cloth furnish the labourers with cheaper and better cloathing; and those in the manufactures of the coarser metals, with cheaper and better instruments of trade, as well as with many agreeable and convenient pieces of household furniture. Soap, salt, candles, leather, and fermented liquors, have, indeed, become a good deal dearer; chiefly from the taxes which have been laid upon them. The quantity of these, however, which the labouring poor are under any necessity of consuming, is so very small, that the increase in their price does not compensate the diminution in that of so many other things. The common complaint that luxury extends itself even to the lowest ranks of the people, and that the labouring poor will not now be contented with the same food, cloathing and lodging which satisfied them in former times, may convince us that it is not the money price of labour only, but its real recompence, which has augmented.

Is this improvement in the circumstances of the lower ranks of the people to be regarded as an advantage or as an inconveniency to the society?[38] The answer seems at first sight abundantly plain. Servants, labourers and workmen of different kinds, make up the far greater part of every great political society. But what improves the circumstances of the greater part can never be regarded as an inconveniency to the whole. No society can surely be flourishing

High earnings of labour are an advantage to the society.

---

[38] [Berkeley, *Querist*, 5th ed., 1752, qu. 2, asks "whether a people can be called poor where the common sort are well fed, clothed and lodged." Hume, "On Commerce," says: "The greatness of a state and the happiness of its subjects, however independent they may be supposed in some respects, are commonly allowed to be inseparable with regard to commerce."—*Political Discourses*, 1752, p. 4.]

and happy, of which the far greater part of the members are poor and miserable. It is but equity, besides, that they who feed, cloath and lodge the whole body of the people, should have such a share of the produce of their own labour as to be themselves tolerably well fed, cloathed and lodged.

Poverty, though it no doubt discourages, does not always prevent marriage. It seems even to be favourable to generation.

Poverty does not prevent births, A half-starved Highland woman frequently bears more than twenty children, while a pampered fine lady is often incapable of bearing any, and is generally exhausted by two or three. Barrenness, so frequent among women of fashion, is very rare among those of inferior station. Luxury in the fair sex, while it inflames perhaps the passion for enjoyment, seems always to weaken, and frequently to destroy altogether, the powers of generation.

But poverty, though it does not prevent the generation, is extremely unfavourable to the rearing of children. The tender

but is unfavourable to the rearing of children, plant is produced, but in so cold a soil, and so severe a climate, soon withers and dies. It is not uncommon, I have been frequently told, in the Highlands of Scotland for a mother who has borne twenty children not to have two alive. Several officers of great experience have assured me, that so far from recruiting their regiment, they have never been able to supply it with drums and fifes from all the soldiers' children that were born in it. A greater number of fine children, however, is seldom seen any where than about a barrack of soldiers. Very few of them, it seems, arrive at the age of thirteen or fourteen. In some places one half the children born die before they are four years of age; in many places before they are seven; and in almost all places before they are nine or ten. This great mortality, however, will every where be found chiefly among the children of the common people, who cannot afford to tend them with the same care as those of better station. Though their marriages are generally more fruitful than those of people of fashion, a smaller proportion of their children arrive at maturity. In foundling hospitals, and among the children brought up by parish charities, the mortality is still greater than among those of the common people.

Every species of animals naturally multiplies in proportion to the means of their subsistence, and no species can ever mul-

and so restrains multiplication,

tiply beyond it. But in civilized society it is only among the inferior ranks of people that the scantiness of subsistence can set limits to the further multiplication of the human species; and it can do so in no other way than by destroying a great part of the children which their fruitful marriages produce.

The liberal reward of labour, by enabling them to provide better for their children, and consequently to bring up a greater

while the liberal reward of labour encourages it

number, naturally tends to widen and extend those limits. It deserves to be remarked too, that it necessarily does this as nearly as possible in the proportion which the demand for labour requires.[39] If this demand is continually increasing, the reward of labour must necessarily encourage in such a manner the marriage and multiplication of labourers, as may enable them to supply that continually increasing demand by a continually increasing population. If the reward[40] should at any time be less than what was requisite for this purpose, the deficiency of hands would soon raise it; and if it should at any time be more, their excessive multiplication would soon lower it to this necessary rate. The market would be so much under-stocked with labour in the one case, and so much over-stocked in the other, as would soon force back its price to that proper rate which the circumstances of the society required. It is in this manner that the demand for men, like that for any other commodity, necessarily regulates the production of men; quickens it when it goes on too slowly, and stops it when it advances too fast. It is this demand which regulates and determines the state of propagation in all the different countries of the world, in North America, in Europe, and in China; which renders it rap-

[39] [Cantillon, *Essai*, pt. i., ch. ix., title, "Le nombre de laboureurs, artisans et autres qui travaillent dans un état se proportionne naturellement au besoin qu'on en a."]

[40] [Ed. 1 reads "If it."]

idly progressive in the first, slow and gradual in the second, and altogether stationary in the last.[41]

The wear and tear[42] of a slave, it has been said, is at the expence of his master; but that of a free servant is at his own expence. The wear and tear of the latter, however, is, in reality, as much at the expence of his master as that of the former. The wages paid to journeymen and servants of every kind must be such as may enable them, one with another, to continue the race of journeymen and servants, according as the increasing, diminishing, or stationary demand of the society may happen to require. But though the wear and tear of a free servant be equally at the expence of his master, it generally costs him much less than that of a slave. The fund destined for replacing or repairing, if I may say so, the wear and tear of the slave, is commonly managed by a negligent master or careless overseer. That destined for performing the same office with regard to the free man, is managed by the free man himself. The disorders which generally prevail in the œconomy of the rich, naturally introduce themselves into the management of the former: The strict frugality and parsimonious attention of the poor as naturally establish themselves in that of the latter. Under such different management, the same purpose must require very different degrees of expence to execute it. It appears, accordingly, from the experience of all ages and nations, I believe, that the work done by freemen comes cheaper in the end than that performed by slaves. It is found to do so even at Boston, New York, and Philadelphia, where the wages of common labour are so very high.

as the wear and tear of the free man must be paid for just like that of the slave, though not so extravagantly.

The liberal reward of labour, therefore, as it is the effect of

[41] [Berkeley, *Querist*, qu. 62, asks "whether a country inhabited by people well fed, clothed and lodged would not become every day more populous? And whether a numerous stock of people in such circumstances would not constitute a flourishing nation?"]

[42] [Ed. 1 reads "tear and wear" here and in the three other cases where the phrase is used in this paragraph.]

High wages increase population. increasing wealth, so it is the cause of increasing population. To complain of it, is to lament over the necessary effect and cause of the greatest public prosperity.

It deserves to be remarked, perhaps, that it is in the progressive state, while the society is advancing to the further acquisition, rather than when it has acquired its full complement of

The progressive state is the best for the labouring poor. riches, that the condition of the labouring poor, of the great body of the people, seems to be the happiest and the most comfortable. It is hard in the stationary, and miserable in the declining state. The progressive state is in reality the cheerful and the hearty state to all the different orders of the society. The stationary is dull; the declining melancholy.

The liberal reward of labour, as it encourages the propagation, so it increases the industry of the common people. The wages of labour are the encouragement of industry, which, like

High wages encourage industry. every other human quality, improves in proportion to the encouragement it receives. A plentiful subsistence increases the bodily strength of the labourer, and the comfortable hope of bettering his condition, and of ending his days perhaps in ease and plenty, animates him to exert that strength to the utmost. Where wages are high, accordingly, we shall always find the workmen more active, diligent, and expeditious, than where they are low; in England, for example, than in Scotland; in the neighbourhood of great towns, than in remote country places. Some workmen, indeed, when they can earn in four days what will maintain them through the week, will be idle the other three. This, however, is by no means the case with the greater part.[43] Workmen, on the contrary, when they are liberally paid by the piece, are very apt to over-work themselves, and to ruin their health and constitution in a few years. A carpenter in London, and in some other places, is not supposed to last in his utmost vigour above eight years. Something of the same kind happens in many other trades, in which the workmen are paid

---

[43] [This is a more favourable view than that taken in *Lectures*, p. 257.]

by the piece; as they generally are in manufactures, and even in country labour, wherever wages are higher than ordinary. Almost every class of artificers is subject to some peculiar infirmity occasioned by excessive application to their peculiar species of work. Ramuzzini, an eminent Italian physician, has written a particular book concerning such diseases.[44] We do not reckon our soldiers the most industrious set of people among us. Yet when soldiers have been employed in some particular sorts of work, and liberally paid by the piece, their officers have frequently been obliged to stipulate with the undertaker, that they should not be allowed to earn above a certain sum every day, according to the rate at which they were paid. Till this stipulation was made, mutual emulation and the desire of greater gain, frequently prompted them to over-work themselves, and to hurt their health by excessive labour. Excessive application during four days of the week, is frequently the real cause of the idleness of the other three, so much and so loudly complained of. Great labour, either of mind or body, continued for several days together, is in most men naturally followed by a great desire of relaxation, which, if not restrained by force or by some strong necessity, is almost irresistible. It is the call of nature, which requires to be relieved by some indulgence, sometimes of ease only, but sometimes too of dissipation and diversion. If it is not complied with, the consequences are often dangerous, and sometimes fatal, and such as almost always, sooner or later, bring on the peculiar infirmity of the trade. If masters would always listen to the dictates of reason and humanity, they have frequently occasion rather to moderate, than to animate the application of many of their workmen. It will be found, I believe, in every sort of trade, that the man who works so moderately, as to be able to work constantly, not only preserves his health the longest, but, in the course of the year, executes the greatest quantity of work.

In cheap years, it is pretended, workmen are generally more idle, and in dear ones more industrious than ordinary. A plenti-

[44] [*De morbis artificum diatriba*, 1700, translated into English (*A Treatise on the Diseases of Tradesmen*) by R. James, 1746.]

ful subsistence therefore, it has been concluded, relaxes, and a scanty one quickens their industry. That a little more plenty than ordinary may render some workmen idle, cannot well be doubted; but that it should have this effect upon the greater part, or that men in general should work better when they are ill fed than when they are well fed, when they are disheartened than when they are in good spirits, when they are frequently sick than when they are generally in good health, seems not very probable. Years of dearth, it is to be observed, are generally among the common people years of sickness and mortality, which cannot fail to diminish the produce of their industry.

The opinion that cheap years encourage idleness is erroneous.

In years of plenty, servants frequently leave their masters, and trust their subsistence to what they can make by their own industry. But the same cheapness of provisions, by increasing the fund which is destined for the maintenance of servants, encourages masters, farmers especially, to employ a greater number. Farmers upon such occasions expect more profit from their corn by maintaining a few more labouring servants, than by selling it at a low price in the market. The demand for servants increases, while the number of those who offer to supply that demand diminishes. The price of labour, therefore, frequently rises in cheap years.

Wages are high in cheap years,

In years of scarcity, the difficulty and uncertainty of subsistence make all such people eager to return to service. But the high price of provisions, by diminishing the funds destined for the maintenance of servants, disposes masters rather to diminish than to increase the number of those they have. In dear years too, poor independent workmen frequently consume the little stocks with which they had used to supply themselves with the materials of their work, and are obliged to become journeymen for subsistence. More people want employment than can easily get it; many are willing to take it upon lower terms than ordinary, and the wages of both servants and journeymen frequently sink in dear years.

and low in dear years,

Masters of all sorts, therefore, frequently make better bargains with their servants in dear than in cheap years, and find

so that masters commend dear years.

them more humble and dependent in the former than in the latter. They naturally, therefore, commend the former as more favourable to industry. Landlords and farmers, besides, two of the largest classes of masters, have another reason for being pleased with dear years. The rents of the one and the profits of the other depend very much upon the price of provisions. Nothing can be more absurd, however, than to imagine that men in general should work less when they work for themselves, than when they work for other people. A poor independent workman will generally be more industrious than even a journeyman who works by the piece. The one enjoys the whole produce of his own industry; the other shares it with his master. The one, in his separate independent state, is less liable to the temptations of bad company, which in large manufactories so frequently ruin the morals of the other. The superiority of the independent workman over those servants who are hired by the month or by the year, and whose wages and maintenance are the same whether they do much or do little, is likely to be still greater. Cheap years tend to increase the proportion of independent workmen to journeymen and servants of all kinds, and dear years to diminish it.

A French author of great knowledge and ingenuity, Mr. Messance, receiver of the tailles[45] in the election of St. Etienne, endeavours to show that the poor do more work in cheap than in dear years, by comparing the quantity and value of the goods made upon those different occasions in three different manufactures; one of coarse woollens carried on at Elbeuf; one of linen, and another of silk, both which extend through the whole generality of Rouen.[46] It appears from his account,

[45] [Misprinted "taillies" in eds. 3–5.]

[46] [*Recherches sur la population des généralités d'Auvergne, de Lyon, de Rouen, et de quelques provinces et villes du royaume, avec des réflexions sur la valeur du bled tant en France qu'en Angleterre, depuis 1674 jusqu'en 1764*, par M. Messance, receveur des tailles de l'élection de Saint-Etienne, 1766, pp. 287–292, 305–308.]

Messance shows that in some French manufactures more is produced in cheap years.

which is copied from the registers of the public offices, that the quantity and value of the goods made in all those three manufactures has generally been greater in cheap than in dear years; and that it has always been greatest in the cheapest, and least in the dearest years. All the three seem to be stationary manufactures, or which, though their produce may vary somewhat from year to year, are upon the whole neither going backwards nor forwards.

The manufacture of linen in Scotland, and that of coarse woollens in the west riding of Yorkshire, are growing manufac-

No connexion is visible between dearness or cheapness of the years and the variations in Scotch linen and Yorkshire woollen manufactures.

tures, of which the produce is generally, though with some variations, increasing both in quantity and value. Upon examining, however, the accounts which have been published of their annual produce, I have not been able to observe that its variations have had any sensible connection with the dearness or cheapness of the seasons. In 1740, a year of great scarcity, both manufactures, in-

deed, appear to have declined very considerably. But in 1756, another year of great scarcity, the Scotch manufacture made more than ordinary advances. The Yorkshire manufacture, indeed, declined, and its produce did not rise to what it had been in 1755 till 1766, after the repeal of the American stamp act. In that and the following year it greatly exceeded what it had ever been before, and it has continued to advance[47] ever since.

The produce depends on other circumstances, and more of it escapes being reckoned in cheap years.

The produce of all great manufactures for distant sale must necessarily depend, not so much upon the dearness or cheapness of the seasons in the countries where they are carried on, as upon the circumstances which affect the demand in the countries where they are consumed; upon peace or war, upon the prosperity or declension of other rival manu-

---

[47] [Ed. 1 reads "continued to do so."]

factures, and upon the good or bad humour of their principal customers. A great part of the extraordinary work, besides, which is probably done in cheap years, never enters the public registers of manufactures. The men servants who leave their masters become independent labourers. The women return to their parents, and commonly spin in order to make cloaths for themselves and their families. Even the independent workmen do not always work for public sale, but are employed by some of their neighbours in manufactures for family use. The produce of their labour, therefore, frequently makes no figure in those public registers of which the records are sometimes published with so much parade, and from which our merchants and manufacturers would often vainly pretend to announce the prosperity or declension of the greatest empires.

Though the variations in the price of labour, not only do not always correspond with those in the price of provisions, but are frequently quite opposite, we must not, upon this account, imagine that the price of provisions has no influence upon that of labour. The money price of labour is necessarily regulated by two circumstances; the demand for labour, and the price of the necessaries and conveniencies of life. The demand for labour, according as it happens to be increasing, stationary, or declining, or to require an increasing, stationary, or declining population, determines the quantity of the necessaries and conveniencies of life which must be given to the labourer; and the money price of labour is determined by what is requisite for purchasing this quantity. Though the money price of labour, therefore, is sometimes high where the price of provisions is low, it would be still higher, the demand continuing the same, if the price of provisions was high.

There is, however, a connexion between the price of labour and that of provisions.

It is because the demand for labour increases in years of sudden and extraordinary plenty, and diminishes in those of sudden and extraordinary scarcity, that the money price of labour sometimes rises in the one, and sinks in the other.

In a year of sudden and extraordinary plenty, there are funds in the hands of many of the employers of industry, sufficient to maintain and employ a greater number of industrious people than had been employed the year before; and this extraordinary number cannot always be had. Those masters, therefore, who want more workmen, bid against one another, in order to get them, which sometimes raises both the real and the money price of their labour.

The contrary of this happens in a year of sudden and extraordinary scarcity. The funds destined for employing industry are less than they had been the year *In years of plenty there is a greater demand for labour,* before. A considerable number of people are thrown out of employment, who bid against one another, in order to get it, which sometimes lowers both the real and the money price of labour. In 1740, a year of extraordinary scarcity, many people were willing to work for bare subsistence. In the succeeding years of plenty, it was more difficult to get labourers and servants.

The scarcity of a dear year, by diminishing the demand for labour, tends to lower its price, as the high price of provisions *and in years of scarcity a less demand,* tends to raise it. The plenty of a cheap year, on the contrary, by increasing the demand, tends to raise the price of labour, as the cheapness of provisions tends to lower it. In the ordinary variations of the price of provisions, those two opposite causes seem to counterbalance one another; which is probably in part the reason why the wages of labour are everywhere so much more steady and permanent than the price of provisions.

The increase in the wages of labour necessarily increases the price of many commodities, by increasing that part of it *and the effect of variations in the price of provisions is thus counterbalanced.* which resolves itself into wages, and so far tends to diminish their consumption both at home and abroad. The same cause, however, which raises the wages of labour, the increase of stock, tends to increase its productive powers, and to make a smaller quantity of labour produce a greater quantity of work. The owner of the stock which employs a great number of labourers, necessarily endeavours, for his own advantage, to make such a proper divi-

Increase of wages increases prices, but the cause of increased wages tends to diminish prices.

sion and distribution of employment, that they may be enabled to produce the greatest quantity of work possible. For the same reason, he endeavours to supply them with the best machinery which either he or they can think of. What takes place among the labourers in a particular workhouse, takes place, for the same reason, among those of a great society. The greater their number, the more they naturally divide themselves into different classes and subdivisions of employment. More heads are occupied in inventing the most proper machinery for executing the work of each, and it is, therefore, more likely to be invented. There are many commodities, therefore, which, in consequence of these improvements, come to be produced by so much less labour than before, that the increase of its price is more than compensated by the diminution of its quantity.[48]

---

[48] [Ed. 1 reads "that the increase of its price does not compensate the diminution of its quantity." The meaning is that the increase in the amount paid for a given quantity of labour is more than counterbalanced by the diminution in the quantity required. The statement is repeated below, pp. 328, 329.]

CHAPTER IX

OF THE PROFITS OF STOCK

Profits depend on increase and decrease of wealth, THE RISE and fall in the profits of stock depend upon the same causes with the rise and fall in the wages of labour, the increasing or declining state of the wealth of the society; but those causes affect the one and the other very differently.

The increase of stock, which raises wages, tends to lower profit. When the stocks of many rich merchants are turned into *falling with the increase of wealth.* the same trade, their mutual competition naturally tends to lower its profit; and when there is a like increase of stock in all the different trades carried on in the same society, the same competition must produce the same effect in them all.[1]

It is not easy, it has already been observed, to ascertain what are the average wages of labour even in a particular place, and *The rate is difficult to ascertain,* at a particular time. We can, even in this case, seldom determine more than what are the most usual wages. But even this can seldom be done with regard to the profits of stock. Profit is so very fluctuating, that the person who carries on a particular trade cannot always tell you himself what is the average of his annual profit. It is affected, not only by every variation of price in the commodities which he deals in, but by the good or bad fortune both of his rivals and of his customers, and by a thousand other accidents to which goods when carried either by sea or by land,

[1] [This statement is somewhat amplified below, p. 451, where the increasing intensity of the competition between the owners of capital is attributed to the gradually increasing difficulty of finding "a profitable method of employing any new capital."]

or even when stored in a warehouse, are liable. It varies, therefore, not only from year to year, but from day to day, and almost
from hour to hour. To ascertain what is the average profit of all
the different trades carried on in a great kingdom, must be
much more difficult; and to judge of what it may have been formerly, or in remote periods of time, with any degree of precision, must be altogether impossible.

But though it may be impossible to determine with any degree of precision, what are or were the average profits of stock,

*but may be in-
ferred from the
rate of interest,*
either in the present, or in ancient times,
some notion may be formed of them from
the interest of money.[2] It may be laid down
as a maxim, that wherever a great deal can
be made by the use of money, a great deal will commonly be
given for the use of it; and that wherever little can be made by
it, less will commonly be given for it.[3] According, therefore, as
the usual market rate of interest varies in any country, we may
be assured that the ordinary profits of stock must vary with it,
must sink as it sinks, and rise as it rises. The progress of interest, therefore, may lead us to form some notion of the progress
of profit.

By the 37th of Henry VIII.[4] all interest above ten per cent.
was declared unlawful. More, it seems, had sometimes been
taken before that. In the reign of Edward VI. religious zeal prohibited all interest.[5] This prohibition, however, like all others of

---

[2] [Defined above, pp. 74, 75.]

[3] [But that interest will not always bear the same proportion to profit is recognised
below, pp. 134, 135–136.]

[4] [C. 9, "an act against usury." On the ground that previous Acts and laws had been
obscure it repeals them all, and prohibits the repurchase of goods sold within three
months before, and the obtaining by any device more than 10 per cent. per annum
for forbearing payment of money. Its real effect was to legalise interest up to 10
per cent.]

[5] [5 & 6 Ed. VI., c. 20, forbade all interest, and repealed 37 Hen. VIII., c. 9, alleging in its preamble that that Act was not intended to allow usury, as "divers persons blinded with inordinate love of themselves" imagined, but was intended
against all usury, "and yet nevertheless the same was by the said act permitted for
the avoiding of a more ill and inconvenience that before that time was used."]

which has fallen in England, the same kind, is said to have produced no effect, and probably rather increased than diminished the evil of usury. The statute of Henry VIII. was revived by the 13th of Elizabeth, cap. 8.[6] and ten per cent. continued to be the legal rate of interest till the 21st of James I.[7] when it was restricted to eight per cent. It was reduced to six per cent. soon after the restoration,[8] and by the 12th of Queen Anne,[9] to five per cent. All these different statutory regulations seem to have been made with great propriety. They seem to have followed and not to have gone before the market rate of interest, or the rate at which people of good credit usually borrowed. Since the time of Queen Anne, five

[6] [On the ground that 5 & 6 Ed. VI., c. 20, "hath not done so much good as was hoped it should but rather the said vice of usury and especially by way of sale of wares and shifts of interest hath much more exceedingly abounded to the utter undoing of many gentlemen, merchants, occupiers and others."]

[7] [C. 17, which alleges that the fall of prices which had taken place made the maintenance of "so high a rate" as 10 per cent. prejudicial to agriculture and commerce, and therefore reduces the maximum to 8 per cent. for the future. It concludes with the very empty proviso that "no words in this law contained shall be construed or expounded to allow the practice of usury in point of religion or conscience."]

[8] [It had already been so reduced by a Commonwealth Act of Parliament, passed in August, 1651, which adopts the reasons given by 21 Jac. I., c. 17. But of course this, like other Acts of the Commonwealth, had to be ignored by the Restoration Parliament, which, by 12 Car. II., c. 13, re-made the reduction on the grounds that the abatement of interest from 10 per cent. "in former times hath been found by notable experience beneficial to the advancement of trade and improvement of lands by good husbandry, with many other considerable advantages to this nation, especially the reducing of it to a nearer proportion with foreign states with whom we traffic," and because "in fresh memory the like fall from eight to six in the hundred by a late constant practice hath found the like success to the general contentment of this nation as is visible by several improvements," while "it is the endeavour of some at present to reduce it back again in practice to the allowance of the statute still in force to eight in the hundred to the great discouragement of ingenuity and industry in the husbandry trade and commerce of this nation."]

[9] [By 12 Ann. st. 2, c. 16, which speaks of the benefit to trade and agriculture resulting from the earlier reductions, of the burdens which the war had laid on landowners, and of the decay of foreign trade owing to the high interest and profit of money at home, which things made it "absolutely necessary to reduce the high rate of interest" to a nearer proportion with the interest allowed in foreign states.]

per cent. seems to have been rather above than below the market rate. Before the late war,[10] the government borrowed at three per cent.;[11] and people of good credit in the capital, and in many other parts of the kingdom, at three and a half, four, and four and a half per cent.

Since the time of Henry VIII. the wealth and revenue of the country have been continually advancing, and, in the course of their progress, their pace seems rather to have been gradually accelerated than retarded. They seem, not only to have been going on, but to have been going on faster and faster.[12] The wages of labour have been continually increasing during the same period, and in the greater part of the different branches of trade and manufactures the profits of stock have been diminishing.

while wealth has been increasing.

It generally requires a greater stock to carry on any sort of trade in a great town than in a country village. The great stocks employed in every branch of trade, and the number of rich competitors, generally reduce the rate of profit in the former below what it is in the latter. But the wages of labour are generally higher in a great town than in a country village. In a thriving town the people who have great stocks to employ, frequently cannot get the number of workmen they want, and therefore bid against one another in order to get as many as they can, which raises the wages of labour, and lowers the profits of stock. In the remote parts of the country there is fre-

Profits are lower in towns, where there is much stock, than in the country, where there is little.

[10] [That of 1756–1763.]

[11] [Holders of 4 per cent. annuities who declined to accept in exchange new stock bearing interest for some years at 3½ and afterwards at 3 per cent. were paid off by means of money raised by a 3 per cent. loan in 1750. See Sinclair, *History of the Public Revenue*, 1785, pt. ii., p. 113. From that time till the beginning of 1755 the 3 per cents. were usually above par. Then they gradually sank to 63 in January, 1762; rose to 96 in March, 1763; fell again to 80 in October, 1764; after that they were seldom above 90 before the publication of the *Wealth of Nations* (Sinclair, *op. cit.*, pt. iii., 1790, Appendix iii.). The policy of a legal regulation of interest is discussed below, pp. 455–456.]

[12] [Below, pp. 439–441.]

quently not stock sufficient to employ all the people, who therefore bid against one another in order to get employment, which lowers the wages of labour, and raises the profits of stock.

In Scotland, though the legal rate of interest is the same as in England, the market rate is rather higher. People of the best

Interest is higher in Scotland, a poor country, than in England.

credit there seldom borrow under five per cent. Even private bankers in Edinburgh give four per cent. upon their promissory notes, of which payment either in whole or in part may be demanded at pleasure. Private bankers in London give no interest for the money which is deposited with them. There are few trades which cannot be carried on with a smaller stock in Scotland than in England. The common rate of profit, therefore, must be somewhat greater. The wages of labour, it has already been observed, are lower in Scotland than in England.[13] The country too is not only much poorer, but the steps by which it advances to a better condition, for it is evidently advancing, seem to be much slower and more tardy.[14]

The legal rate of interest in France has not, during the course of the present century, been always regulated by the

So too in France, a country probably less rich than England,

market rate.[15] In 1720 interest was reduced from the twentieth to the fiftieth penny, or from five to two per cent. In 1724 it was raised to the thirtieth penny, or to $3\frac{1}{3}$ per cent. In 1725 it was again raised to the twentieth penny, or to five per cent. In 1766, during the administration of Mr. Laverdy, it was reduced to the twenty-fifth penny, or to four per cent. The Abbe Terray raised it afterwards to the old rate of five per cent. The supposed purpose of many of

[13] [Above, p. 107.]

[14] [Below, p. 258.]

[15] See Denisart, Article Taux des Intérêts, tom. iii. p. 18. [J. B. Denisart, *Collection de décisions nouvelles et de notions relatives à la jurisprudence actuelle*, 7th ed., 1771, *s.v.* Intérêt, subdivision Taux des Intérêts. This does not go so far as the reduction of 1766. The note appears first in ed. 2.]

those violent reductions of interest was to prepare the way for reducing that of the public debts; a purpose which has sometimes been executed. France is perhaps in the present times not so rich a country as England; and though the legal rate of interest has in France frequently been lower than in England, the market rate has generally been higher; for there, as in other countries, they have several very safe and easy methods of evading the law.[16] The profits of trade, I have been assured by British merchants who had traded in both countries, are higher in France than in England; and it is no doubt upon this account that many British subjects chuse rather to employ their capitals in a country where trade is in disgrace, than in one where it is highly respected. The wages of labour are lower in France than in England. When you go from Scotland to England, the difference which you may remark between the dress and countenance of the common people in the one country and in the other, sufficiently indicates the difference in their condition. The contrast is still greater when you return from France. France, though no doubt a richer country than Scotland, seems not to be going forward so fast. It is a common and even a popular opinion in the country, that it is going backwards; an opinion which, I apprehend, is ill-founded even with regard to France, but which nobody can possibly entertain with regard to Scotland, who sees the country now, and who saw it twenty or thirty years ago.

The province of Holland, on the other hand, in proportion to the extent of its territory and the number of its people, is a richer country than England. The government there borrows at two per cent., and private people of good credit at three. The wages of labour are said to be higher in Holland than in England, and the Dutch, it is well known, trade upon lower profits than any people in Europe. The trade of Holland, it has been pretended by some people, is decaying, and it may perhaps be true that some particular branches of it are so. But these symptoms seem to indi-

but lower in Holland, which is richer than England.

---

[16] [Below, p. 456.]

cate sufficiently that there is no general decay. When profit diminishes, merchants are very apt to complain that trade decays; though the diminution of profits is the natural effect of its prosperity, or of a greater stock being employed in it than before. During the late war the Dutch gained the whole carrying trade of France, of which they still retain a very large share. The great property which they possess both in the French and English funds, about forty millions, it is said, in the latter (in which I suspect, however, there is a considerable exaggeration);[17] the great sums which they lend to private people in countries where the rate of interest is higher than in their own, are circumstances which no doubt demonstrate the redundancy of their stock, or that it has increased beyond what they can employ with tolerable profit in the proper business of their own country: but they do not demonstrate that that business has decreased. As the capital of a private man, though acquired by a particular trade, may increase beyond what he can employ in it, and yet that trade continue to increase too; so may likewise the capital of a great nation.

In our North American and West Indian colonies, not only the wages of labour, but the interest of money, and consequently the profits of stock, are higher than in England. In the different colonies both the legal and the market rate of interest

[17] [Postlethwayt, *Dictionary of Commerce*, 2nd ed., 1757, vol. i., p. 877, *s.v.* Funds, says that the amount of British funds held by foreigners has been estimated by some at one-fifth and by others at one-fourth of the whole debt. But Magens, *Universal Merchant* (ed. Horsley), 1753, p. 13, thought it "more than probable that foreigners are not concerned in anything like one-fourth." He had been informed "that most of the money which the Dutch have here is in Bank, East India and South Sea stocks, and that their interest in them might amount to one-third of the whole." Fairman, *Account of the Public Funds*, 7th ed., 1824, p. 229, quotes "an account drawn up in the year 1762, showing how much of the several funds transferable at the Bank of England then stood in the names of foreigners," which is also in Sinclair, *History of the Public Revenue*, pt. iii., 1790, p. 366. From this it appears that foreigners held £4,627,858 of Bank stock and £10,328,537 in the other funds, which did not include South Sea and East India stock. Fairman had reason to believe that the South Sea holding amounted to £2,500,000 and the East Indian to more than £500,000, which would make in all about £18,000,000. In 1806, he says, the total claiming exemption from income tax (foreigners were exempt) was £18,500,000, but this did not include Bank stock.]

run from six to eight per cent. High wages of labour and high

In the peculiar case of new colonies high wages and high profits go together, but profits gradually diminish.

profits of stock, however, are things, perhaps, which scarce ever go together, except in the peculiar circumstances of new colonies. A new colony must always for some time be more under-stocked in proportion to the extent of its territory, and more under-peopled in proportion to the extent of its stock, than the greater part of our countries. They have more land than they have stock to cultivate. What they have, therefore, is applied to the cultivation only of what is most fertile and most favourably situated, the land[18] near the sea shore, and along the banks of navigable rivers. Such land too is frequently purchased at a price below the value even of its natural produce. Stock employed in the purchase and improvement of such lands must yield a very large profit, and consequently afford to pay a very large interest. Its rapid accumulation in so profitable an employment enables the planter to increase the number of his hands faster than he can find them in a new settlement. Those whom he can find, therefore, are very liberally rewarded. As the colony increases, the profits of stock gradually diminish. When the most fertile and best situated lands have been all occupied, less profit can be made by the cultivation of what is inferior both in soil and situation, and less interest can be afforded for the stock which is so employed. In the greater part of our colonies, accordingly, both the legal and the market rate of interest have been considerably reduced during the course of the present century. As riches, improvement, and population have increased, interest has declined. The wages of labour do not sink with the profits of stock. The demand for labour increases with the increase of stock whatever be its profits; and after these are diminished, stock may not only continue to increase, but to increase much faster than before. It is with industrious nations who are advancing in the acquisition of riches, as with industrious individuals. A great stock, though with small profits, generally

18 [Eds. 1–3 read "lands."]

increases faster than a small stock with great profits. Money, says the proverb, makes money. When you have got a little, it is often easy to get more. The great difficulty is to get that little. The connection between the increase of stock and that of industry, or of the demand for useful labour, has partly been explained already,[19] but will be explained more fully hereafter[20] in treating of the accumulation of stock.

The acquisition of new territory, or of new branches of trade, may sometimes raise the profits of stock, and with them

New territories and trades may raise profits even in a country advancing in riches.

the interest of money, even in a country which is fast advancing in the acquisition of riches. The stock of the country not being sufficient for the whole accession of business, which such acquisitions present to the different people among whom it is divided, is applied to those particular branches only which afford the greatest profit. Part of what had before been employed in other trades, is necessarily withdrawn from them, and turned into some of the new and more profitable ones. In all those old trades, therefore, the competition comes to be less than before. The market comes to be less fully supplied with many different sorts of goods. Their price necessarily rises more or less, and yields a greater profit to those who deal in them, who can, therefore, afford to borrow at a higher interest. For some time after the conclusion of the late war, not only private people of the best credit, but some of the greatest companies in London, commonly borrowed at five per cent. who before that had not been used to pay more than four, and four and a half per cent. The great accession both of territory and trade, by our acquisitions in North America and the West Indies, will sufficiently account for this, without supposing any diminution in the capital stock of the society. So great an accession of new business to be carried on by the old stock, must necessarily have diminished the quantity employed in a great number of particular branches, in which the competition

[19] [Above, pp. 91–97.]

[20] [Below, pp. 422–446.]

being less, the profits must have been greater. I shall hereafter[21] have occasion to mention the reasons which dispose me to believe that the capital stock of Great Britain was not diminished even by the enormous expence of the late war.

The diminution of the capital stock of the society, or of the funds destined for the maintenance of industry, however, as it

Diminution of capital stock raises profits.

lowers the wages of labour, so it raises the profits of stock, and consequently the interest of money. By the wages of labour being lowered, the owners of what stock remains in the society can bring their goods at less expence to market than before, and less stock being employed in supplying the market than before, they can sell them dearer.[22] Their goods cost them less, and they get more for them. Their profits, therefore, being augmented at both ends, can well afford a large interest. The great fortunes so suddenly and so easily acquired in Bengal and the other British settlements in the East Indies, may satisfy us that, as the wages of labour are very low, so the profits of stock are very high in those ruined countries. The interest of money is proportionably so. In Bengal, money is frequently lent to the farmers at forty, fifty, and sixty per cent. and the succeeding crop is mortgaged for the payment. As the profits which can afford such an interest must eat up almost the whole rent of the landlord, so such enormous usury must in its turn eat up the greater part of those profits. Before the fall of the Roman republic, a usury of the same kind seems to have been common in the provinces, under the ruinous administration of their proconsuls. The virtuous Brutus lent money in Cyprus at eight-and-forty[23] per cent. as we learn from the letters of Cicero.[24]

[21] [Below, pp. 440–442, 1183–1184.]

[22] [Eds. 1 and 2 read "cheaper."]

[23] [Ed. 1 reads "five and forty," 8 having probably been misread as 5.]

[24] [*Ad Atticum*, VI., i., 5, 6. Cicero had arranged that a six-year-old debt should be repaid with interest at the rate of 12 per cent. per annum, the principal being increased by that amount for each of the six years. This would have very nearly doubled the principal, but Brutus, through his agent, kept asking for 48 per cent.,

In a country which had acquired that full complement of riches which the nature of its soil and climate, and its situation

In a country as rich as it possibly could be, profits as well as wages would be very low,

with respect to other countries, allowed it to acquire; which could, therefore, advance no further, and which was not going backwards, both the wages of labour and the profits of stock would probably be very low. In a country fully peopled in proportion to what either its territory could maintain or its stock employ, the competition for employment would necessarily be so great as to reduce the wages of labour to what was barely sufficient to keep up the number of labourers, and, the country being already fully peopled, that number could never be augmented. In a country fully stocked in proportion to all the business it had to transact, as great a quantity of stock would be employed in every particular branch as the nature and extent of the trade would admit. The competition, therefore, would every-where be as great, and consequently the ordinary profit as low as possible.

But perhaps no country has ever yet arrived at this degree of opulence. China seems to have been long stationary, and had

but there has never yet been any such country.

probably long ago acquired that full complement of riches which is consistent with the nature of its laws and institutions. But this complement may be much inferior to what, with other laws and institutions, the nature of its soil, climate, and situation might admit of. A country which neglects or despises foreign commerce, and which admits the vessels of foreign nations into one or two of its ports only, cannot transact the same quantity of business which it might do with different laws and institutions. In a country too, where, though the rich or the owners of large capitals enjoy a good deal of security, the poor or the owners of small capitals enjoy scarce any, but are liable, under the pretence of justice, to be pillaged and plundered at any time by the inferior mandarines, the quantity

which would have multiplied it by more than fifteen. However, Cicero asserted that the 12 per cent. would have satisfied the cruellest usurers.]

of stock employed in all the different branches of business transacted within it, can never be equal to what the nature and extent of that business might admit. In every different branch, the oppression of the poor must establish the monopoly of the rich, who, by engrossing the whole trade to themselves, will be able to make very large profits. Twelve per cent. accordingly is said to be the common interest of money in China, and the ordinary profits of stock must be sufficient to afford this large interest.

A defect in the law may sometimes raise the rate of interest considerably above what the condition of the country, as to

Interest is raised by defective enforcement of contracts,

wealth or poverty, would require. When the law does not enforce the performance of contracts, it puts all borrowers nearly upon the same footing with bankrupts or people of doubtful credit in better regulated countries. The uncertainty of recovering his money makes the lender exact the same usurious interest which is usually required from bankrupts. Among the barbarous nations who over-ran the western provinces of the Roman empire, the performance of contracts was left for many ages to the faith of the contracting parties.[25] The courts of justice of their kings seldom intermeddled in it. The high rate of interest which took place in those ancient times may perhaps be partly accounted for from this cause.

When the law prohibits interest altogether, it does not prevent it. Many people must borrow, and nobody will lend with-

and by prohibition.

out such a consideration for the use of their money as is suitable, not only to what can be made by the use of it, but to the difficulty and danger of evading the law. The high rate of interest among all Mahometan nations is accounted for by Mr. Montesquieu, not from their poverty, but partly from this,[26] and partly from the difficulty of recovering the money.[27]

[25] [*Lectures*, pp. 130–134.]

[26] [*I.e.*, the danger of evading the law.]

[27] [*Esprit des lois*, liv. xxii., ch. 19, "L'usure augmente dans les pays mahométans

The lowest ordinary rate of profit must always be something more than what is sufficient to compensate the occasional losses to which every employment of stock is exposed. It is this surplus only which is neat or clear profit. What is called gross profit comprehends frequently, not only this surplus, but what is retained for compensating such extraordinary losses. The interest which the borrower can afford to pay is in proportion to the clear profit only.

The lowest rate of profit must be more than enough to compensate losses,

The lowest ordinary rate of interest must, in the same manner, be something more than sufficient to compensate the occasional losses to which lending, even with tolerable prudence, is exposed. Were it not more, charity or friendship could be the only motives for lending.

and so must the lowest rate of interest.

In a country which had acquired its full complement of riches, where in every particular branch of business there was the greatest quantity of stock that could be employed in it, as the ordinary rate of clear profit would be very small, so the usual market rate of interest which could be afforded out of it, would be so low as to render it impossible for any but the very wealthiest people to live upon the interest of their money. All people of small or middling fortunes would be obliged to superintend themselves the employment of their own stocks. It would be necessary that almost every man should be a man of business, or engage in some sort of trade. The province of Holland seems to be approaching near to this state. It is there unfashionable not to be a man of business.[28] Necessity makes it usual for almost every

In a country as rich as it possibly could be interest would be so low that only the wealthiest people could live on it.

à proportion de la sévérité de la défense: le prêteur s'indemnise du péril de la contravention. Dans ces pays d'Orient, la plupart des hommes n'ont rien d'assuré; il n'y a presque point de rapport entre la possession actuelle d'une somme et l'espérance de la ravoir après l'avoir prêtée: l'usure y augmente donc a proportion du péril de l'insolvabilité."]

[28] [Joshua Gee, *Trade and Navigation of Great Britain Considered*, 1729, p. 128,

man to be so, and custom every where regulates fashion. As it is ridiculous not to dress, so is it, in some measure, not to be employed, like other people. As a man of a civil profession seems awkward in a camp or a garrison, and is even in some danger of being despised there, so does an idle man among men of business.

The highest ordinary rate of profit may be such as, in the price of the greater part of commodities, eats up the whole of

The highest rate of profit would eat up all rent and leave only wages.

what should go to the rent of the land, and leaves only what is sufficient to pay the labour of preparing and bringing them to market, according to the lowest rate at which labour can any-where be paid, the bare subsistence of the labourer. The workman must always have been fed in some way or other while he was about the work; but the landlord may not always have been paid. The profits of the trade which the servants of the East India Company carry on in Bengal may not perhaps be very far from this rate.[29]

The proportion which the usual market rate of interest ought to bear to the ordinary rate of clear profit, necessarily

The proportion of interest to profit rises and falls with the rate of profit.

varies as profit rises or falls. Double interest is in Great Britain reckoned, what the merchants call, a good, moderate, reasonable profit; terms which I apprehend mean no more than a common and usual profit. In a country where the ordinary rate of clear profit is eight or ten per cent., it may be reasonable that one half of it should go to interest, wherever business is carried on with borrowed money. The stock is at the risk of the borrower, who, as it were, insures it to the lender; and four or five per cent. may, in the greater part of trades, be both a sufficient profit upon the risk of this insurance, and a sufficient recompence for the trouble of employing the stock. But the proportion between interest and clear profit might not be the same in

notices the fact of the Dutch being all engaged in trade and ascribes it to the deficiency of valuable land.]

[29] [See below, pp. 810–814.]

countries where the ordinary rate of profit was either a good deal lower, or a good deal higher. If it were a good deal lower, one half of it perhaps could not be afforded for interest; and more might be afforded if it were a good deal higher.

In countries which are fast advancing to riches, the low rate of profit may, in the price of many commodities, compensate the high wages of labour, and enable those countries to sell as cheap as their less thriving neighbours, among whom the wages of labour may be lower.

In reality high profits tend much more to raise the price of work than high wages. If in the linen manufacture, for example, the wages of the different working people, the flax-dressers, the spinners, the weavers, &c.

Countries with low profits can sell as cheap as those with low wages; and in reality high profits tend to raise prices more than high wages.

should, all of them, be advanced two pence a day; it would be necessary to heighten the price of a piece of linen only by a number of two pences equal to the number of people that had been employed about it, multiplied by the number of days during which they had been so employed. That part of the price of the commodity which resolved itself into wages would, through all the different stages of the manufacture, rise only in arithmetical proportion to this rise of wages. But if the profits of all the different employers of those working people should be raised five per cent. that part of the price of the commodity which resolved itself into profit, would, through all the different stages of the manufacture, rise in geometrical proportion to this rise of profit. The employer of the flax-dressers would in selling his flax require an additional five per cent. upon the whole value of the materials and wages which he advanced to his workmen. The employer of the spinners would require an additional five per cent. both upon the advanced price of the flax and upon the wages of the spinners. And the employer of the weavers would require a like five per cent. both upon the advanced price of the linen yarn and upon the wages of the weavers. In raising the price of commodities the rise of wages operates in the same manner as simple interest does in the accumulation of debt. The rise of profit operates like compound interest.[30] Our merchants and master-manufacturers complain much of the bad effects of high wages in raising the price, and thereby lessening the sale of their goods both at home and abroad. They say nothing concerning the bad effects of high profits. They are silent with regard to the pernicious effects of their own gains. They complain only of those of other people.[31]

---

[30] [According to the view of the subject here set forth, if the three employers each spend £100 in wages and materials, and profits are at first 5 per cent. and then rise to 10 per cent., the finished commodity must rise from £331 0s. 3d. to £364 2s., while if, on the other hand, the wages rise from £100 to £105, the commodity will only rise to £347 11s. 3d. It is assumed either that profits mean profits on turn-over and not on capital per annum, or else that the employers each have their capital turned over once a year. But even when one or other of these assumptions is granted, it is clear that the "simple interest" may easily be greater than the "compound." In the examples just given we doubled profits, but only added one-twentieth to wages. If we double wages and leave profits at 5 per cent., the commodity should rise from £331 0s. 3d. to £662 0s. 6d.]

[31] [This paragraph is not in ed. 1; the epigram at the end, however, did not make its appearance here for the first time in ed. 2, since it occurs in a slightly less polished form below, p. 762.]

CHAPTER X

OF WAGES AND PROFIT IN THE DIFFERENT EMPLOYMENTS OF LABOUR AND STOCK[1]

THE WHOLE of the advantages and disadvantages of the different employments of labour and stock must, in the same

Advantages and disadvantages tend to equality where there is perfect liberty.

neighbourhood, be either perfectly equal or continually tending to equality. If in the same neighbourhood, there was any employment evidently either[2] more or less advantageous than the rest, so many people would crowd into it in the one case, and so many would desert it in the other, that its advantages would soon return to the level of other employments. This at least would be the case in a society where things were left to follow their natural course, where there was perfect liberty,[3] and where every man was perfectly free both to chuse what occupation he thought proper, and to change it as often as he thought proper. Every man's interest would prompt him to seek the advantageous, and to shun the disadvantageous employment.

Pecuniary wages and profit, indeed, are every-where in

[1] [The general design of this chapter, as well as many of its details, was doubtless suggested by Cantillon, *Essai*, pt. 1, chaps. vii. and viii. The first of these chapters is headed: "Le travail d'un laboureur vaut moins que celui d'un artisan," and the second: "Les artisans gagnent les uns plus les autres moins selon les cas et les circonstances différentes." The second ends thus: "Par ces inductions et cent autres qu'on pourrait tirer de l'expérience ordinaire, on peut voir facilement que la différence de prix qu'on paie pour le travail journalier est fondée sur des raisons naturelles et sensibles."]

[2] [Ed. 1 reads "either evidently."]

[3] [Above, pp. 79, 88.]

Europe extremely different according to the different employments of labour and stock. But this
difference arises partly from certain circumstances in the employments themselves,
which, either really, or at least in the imaginations of men, make up for a small pecuniary gain in some, and counter-balance a
great one in others; and partly from the policy of Europe, which no-where leaves things
at perfect liberty.

Actual differences of pecuniary wages and profits are due partly to counterbalancing circumstances and partly to want of perfect liberty.

The particular consideration of those circumstances and of
that policy will divide this chapter into two parts.

PART I

INEQUALITIES ARISING FROM THE NATURE OF THE EMPLOYMENTS THEMSELVES[4]

The five following are the principal circumstances which,
so far as I have been able to observe, make up for a small
pecuniary gain in some employments, and
counter-balance a great one in others: first,
the agreeableness or disagreeableness of the
employments themselves; secondly, the eas-
iness and cheapness, or the difficulty and expence of learning
them; thirdly, the constancy or inconstancy of employment in
them; fourthly, the small or great trust which must be reposed
in those who exercise them; and fifthly, the probability or improbability of success in them.

There are five counterbalancing circumstances:

---

[4] [The foregoing introductory paragraphs would lead a logical reader to expect part 1 of the chapter to be entitled: "Inequalities of pecuniary wages and profit which merely counterbalance inequalities of other advantages and disadvantages." The rather obscure title actually chosen is due to the fact that nearly a quarter of the part is occupied by a discussion of three further conditions which must be present in addition to "perfect freedom" in order to bring about the equality of total advantages and disadvantages. The chapter would have been clearer if this discussion had been placed at the beginning, but it was probably an afterthought.]

First, The wages of labour vary with the ease or hardship, the cleanliness or dirtiness, the honourableness or dishonourableness of the employment. Thus in most places, take the year round, a journeyman taylor earns less than a journeyman weaver. His work is much easier. A journeyman weaver earns less than a journeyman smith. His work is not always easier, but it is much cleanlier. A journeyman blacksmith, though an artificer, seldom earns so much in twelve hours as a collier, who is only a labourer, does in eight. His work is not quite so dirty, is less dangerous, and is carried on in day-light, and above ground. Honour makes a great part of the reward of all honourable professions. In point of pecuniary gain, all things considered, they are generally under-recompensed, as I shall endeavour to show by and by.[5] Disgrace has the contrary effect. The trade of a butcher is a brutal and an odious business; but it is in most places more profitable than the greater part of common trades. The most detestable of all employments, that of public executioner, is, in proportion to the quantity of work done, better paid than any common trade whatever.

(1) Wages vary with the agreeableness of the employment.

Hunting and fishing, the most important employments of mankind in the rude state of society, become in its advanced state their most agreeable amusements, and they pursue for pleasure what they once followed from necessity. In the advanced state of society, therefore, they are all very poor people who follow as a trade, what other people pursue as a pastime. Fishermen have been so since the time of[6] Theocritus. A poacher is every-where a very poor man in Great Britain. In countries where the rigour of the law suffers no poachers, the licensed hunter is not in a much better condition. The natural taste for those employments makes more people follow them than can live comfortably by them,

Some very agreeable employments are exceedingly ill paid.

[5] [Below, pp. 146–149.]

[6] See Idyllium xxi. [This merely describes the life of two poor fishermen. The note appears first in ed. 2.]

and the produce of their labour, in proportion to its quantity, comes always too cheap to market to afford anything but the most scanty subsistence to the labourers.

Disagreeableness and disgrace affect the profits of stock in the same manner as the wages of labour. The keeper of an inn

The same thing is true of profits.

or tavern, who is never master of his own house, and who is exposed to the brutality of every drunkard, exercises neither a very agreeable nor a very creditable business. But there is scarce any common trade in which a small stock yields so great a profit.

(2) Wages vary with the cost of learning the business.

Secondly, The wages of labour vary with the easiness and cheapness, or the difficulty and expence of learning the business.

When any expensive machine is erected, the extraordinary work to be performed by it before it is worn out, it must be expected, will replace the capital laid out upon it, with at least the[7] ordinary profits. A man educated at the expence of much labour and time to any of those employments which require extraordinary dexterity and skill, may be compared to one of those expensive machines. The work which he learns to perform, it must be expected, over and above the usual wages of common labour, will replace to him the whole expence of his education, with at least the ordinary profits of an equally valuable capital. It must do this too in a reasonable time, regard being had to the very uncertain duration of human life, in the same manner as to the more certain duration of the machine.

The difference between the wages of skilled labour and those of common labour, is founded upon this principle.

The policy of Europe considers the labour of all mechanics, artificers, and manufacturers, as skilled labour; and that of all country labourers as common labour. It seems to suppose that

The cost of apprenticeship accounts for the

of the former to be of a more nice and delicate nature than that of the latter. It is so perhaps in some cases; but in the greater part it

---

[7] [Ed. 1 reads "its."]

wages of manufac- is quite otherwise, as I shall endeavour to
turers being shew by and by.[8] The laws and customs of
higher than those Europe, therefore, in order to qualify any
of country person for exercising the one species of
labourers. labour, impose the necessity of an apprenticeship, though with different degrees of rigour in different
places. They leave the other free and open to every body.
During the continuance of the apprenticeship, the whole
labour of the apprentice belongs to his master. In the mean
time he must, in many cases, be maintained by his parents or
relations, and in almost all cases must be cloathed by them.
Some money too is commonly given to the master for teaching
him his trade. They who cannot give money, give time, or become bound for more than the usual number of years; a consideration which, though it is not always advantageous to the
master, on account of the usual idleness of apprentices, is always disadvantageous to the apprentice. In country labour, on
the contrary, the labourer, while he is employed about the easier, learns the more difficult parts of his business, and his own
labour maintains him through all the different stages of his employment. It is reasonable, therefore, that in Europe the wages
of mechanics, artificers, and manufacturers, should be somewhat higher than those of common labourers.[9] They are so accordingly, and their superior gains make them in most places
be considered as a superior rank of people. This superiority,
however, is generally very small; the daily or weekly earnings
of journeymen in the more common sorts of manufactures,
such as those of plain linen and woollen cloth, computed at an
average, are, in most places, very little more than the day
wages of common labourers. Their employment, indeed, is
more steady and uniform, and the superiority of their earnings,
taking the whole year together, may be somewhat greater.
It seems evidently, however, to be no greater than what is

---

[8] [Below, pp. 173, 174.]

[9] [This argument seems to be modelled closely on Cantillon, *Essai*, pp. 23, 24, but
probably also owes something to Mandeville, *Fable of the Bees*, pt. ii., dialogue
vi., vol. ii., p. 423. Cp. *Lectures*, pp. 173–175.]

sufficient to compensate the superior expence of their education.

Education in the ingenious arts and in the liberal professions, is still more tedious and expensive. The pecuniary recompence, therefore, of painters and sculptors, of lawyers and physicians, ought[10] to be much more liberal: and it is so accordingly.

Education for liberal professions is more costly and the pecuniary recompense consequently higher. Profits are not much affected by this circumstance.

The profits of stock seem to be very little affected by the easiness or difficulty of learning the trade in which it is employed. All the different ways in which stock is commonly employed in great towns seem, in reality, to be almost equally easy and equally difficult to learn. One branch either of foreign or domestic trade, cannot well be a much more intricate business than another.

(3) Wages vary with constancy of employment.

Thirdly, The wages of labour in different occupations vary with the constancy or inconstancy of employment.[11]

Employment is much more constant in some trades than in others. In the greater part of manufactures, a journeyman may be pretty sure of employment almost every day in the year that he is able to work. A mason or bricklayer,

[10] [The "ought" is equivalent to "it is reasonable they should be" in the previous paragraph, and to "must" in "must not only maintain him while he is idle" on p. 119. Cp. "doivent" in Cantillon, *Essai*, p. 24: "Ceux donc qui emploient des artisans ou gens de métier, doivent nécessairement payer leur travail plus haut que celui d'un laboureur ou manœuvre." The meaning need not be that it is ethically right that a person on whose education much has been spent should receive a large reward, but only that it is economically desirable, since otherwise there would be a deficiency of such persons.]

[11] [The treatment of this head would have been clearer if it had begun with a distinction between "day-wages" (mentioned lower down on the page) and annual earnings. The first paragraph of the argument claims that annual earnings as well as day-wages will be higher in the inconstant employment so as to counterbalance the disadvantage or repulsive force of having "anxious and desponding moments." In the subsequent paragraphs, however, this claim is lost sight of, and the discussion proceeds as if the thesis was that annual earnings are equal though day-wages may be unequal.]

on the contrary, can work neither in hard frost nor in foul weather, and his employment at all other times depends upon the occasional calls of his customers. He is liable, in consequence, to be frequently without any. What he earns, therefore, while he is employed, must not only maintain him while he is idle, but make him some compensation for those anxious and desponding moments which the thought of so precarious a situation must sometimes occasion. Where the computed earnings of the greater part of manufacturers, accordingly, are nearly upon a level with the day wages of common labourers, those of masons and bricklayers are generally from one half more to double those wages. Where common labourers earn four and five shillings a week, masons and bricklayers frequently earn seven and eight; where the former earn six, the latter often earn nine and ten, and where the former earn nine and ten, as in London, the latter commonly earn fifteen and eighteen. No species of skilled labour, however, seems more easy to learn than that of masons and bricklayers. Chairmen in London, during the summer season, are said sometimes to be employed as bricklayers. The high wages of those workmen, therefore, are not so much the recompence of their skill, as the compensation for the inconstancy of their employment.

A house carpenter seems to exercise rather a nicer and more ingenious trade than a mason. In most places, however, for it is not universally so, his day-wages are somewhat lower. His employment, though it depends much, does not depend so entirely upon the occasional calls of his customers; and it is not liable to be interrupted by the weather.

When the trades which generally afford constant employment, happen in a particular place not to do so, the wages of the workmen always rise a good deal above their ordinary proportion to those of common labour. In London almost all journeymen artificers are liable to be called upon and dismissed by their masters from day to day, and from week to week, in the same manner as day-labourers in other places. The lowest order of artificers, journeymen taylors, accordingly, earn their half a crown a day,[12]

[12] [Below, pp. 195, 196.]

though eighteen pence may be reckoned the wages of common labour. In small towns and country villages, the wages of journeymen taylors frequently scarce equal those of common labour; but in London they are often many weeks without employment, particularly during the summer.

When the inconstancy of employment is combined with the hardship, disagreeableness, and dirtiness of the work, it sometimes raises the wages of the most common labour above those of the most skilful artificers. A collier working by the piece is supposed, at Newcastle, to earn commonly about double, and in many parts of Scotland about three times the wages of common labour. His high wages arise altogether from the hardship, disagreeableness, and dirtiness of his work. His employment may, upon most occasions, be as constant as he pleases. The coal-heavers in London exercise a trade which in hardship, dirtiness, and disagreeableness, almost equals that of colliers; and from the unavoidable irregularity in the arrivals of coalships, the employment of the greater part of them is necessarily very inconstant. If colliers, therefore, commonly earn double and triple the wages of common labour, it ought not to seem unreasonable that coal-heavers should sometimes earn four and five times those wages. In the enquiry made into their condition a few years ago, it was found that at the rate at which they were then paid, they could earn from six to ten shillings a day. Six shillings are about four times the wages of common labour in London, and in every particular trade, the lowest common earnings may always be considered as those of the far greater number. How extravagant soever those earnings may appear, if they were more than sufficient to compensate all the disagreeable circumstances of the business, there would soon be so great a number of competitors as, in a trade which has no exclusive privilege, would quickly reduce them to a lower rate.

Constancy does not affect profits. The constancy or inconstancy of employment cannot affect[13] the ordinary profits of stock in any particular trade. Whether the

---

[13] [Misprinted "effect" in ed. 5.]

stock is or is not constantly employed depends, not upon the trade, but the trader.[14]

(4) Wages vary with the trust to be reposed.

Fourthly, The wages of labour vary according to the small or great trust which must be reposed in the workmen.[15]

The wages of goldsmiths and jewellers are everywhere superior to those of many other workmen, not only of equal, but of much superior ingenuity; on account of the precious materials with which they are intrusted.

We trust our health to the physician; our fortune and sometimes our life and reputation to the lawyer and attorney. Such confidence could not safely be reposed in people of a very mean or low condition. Their reward must be such, therefore, as may give them that rank in the society which so important a trust requires. The long time and the great expence which must be laid out in their education, when combined with this circumstance, necessarily enhance still further the price of their labour.

Profits are unaffected by trust.

When a person employs only his own stock in trade, there is no trust; and the credit which he may get from other people, depends, not upon the nature of his trade, but upon their opinion

---

[14] [That "stock" consists of actual objects seems to be overlooked here. The constancy with which such objects can be employed is various: the constancy with which the hearse of a village is employed depends on the number of deaths, which may be said to be "the trade," and is certainly not "the trader." There is no difference of profits corresponding to differences of day-wages due to unequal constancy of employment, for the simple reason that "profits" are calculated by their amount per annum, but the rural undertaker, liable to long interruption of business in healthy seasons, may just as well as the bricklayer be supposed to receive "some compensation for those anxious and desponding moments which the thought of so precarious a situation must sometimes occasion."]

[15] [The argument foreshadowed in the introductory paragraphs of the chapter requires an allegation that it is a disadvantage to a person to have trust reposed in him, but no such allegation is made. Cantillon, *Essai*, p. 27, says: "lorsqu'il faut de la capacité et de la confiance, on paie encore le travail plus cher, comme aux jouailliers, teneurs de compte, caissiers, et autres." Hume, *History*, ed. of 1773, vol. viii., p. 323, says: "It is a familiar rule in all business that every man should be paid in proportion to the trust reposed in him and the power which he enjoys."]

of his fortune, probity, and prudence. The different rates of profit, therefore, in the different branches of trade, cannot arise from the different degrees of trust reposed in the traders.[16]

(5) Wages vary with the probability of success.

Fifthly, The wages of labour in different employments vary according to the probability or improbability of success in them.[17]

The probability that any particular person shall ever be qualified for the employment to which he is educated, is very different in different occupations. In the greater part of mechanic trades, success is almost certain; but very uncertain in the liberal professions. Put your son apprentice to a shoemaker, there is little doubt of his learning to make a pair of shoes: But send him to study the law, it is at least twenty to one if ever he makes such proficiency as will enable him to live by the business. In a perfectly fair lottery, those who draw the prizes ought to gain all that is lost by those who draw the blanks. In a profession where twenty fail for one that succeeds, that one ought to gain all that should have been gained by the unsuccessful twenty. The counsellor at law who, perhaps, at near forty years of age, begins to make something by his profession, ought to receive the retribution, not only of his own so tedious and expensive education, but of that of more than twenty others who are never likely to make any thing by it. How extravagant soever the fees of counsellors at law may sometimes appear, their real retribution is never equal to this.[18] Compute in any particular place, what is likely to be annually gained, and what is likely to be annually spent, by all the different workmen in any common trade, such as that of shoe-

[16] [But some trades, e.g., that of a banker, may be necessarily confined to persons of more than average trustworthiness, and this may raise the rate of profit above the ordinary level if such persons are not sufficiently plentiful.]

[17] [The argument under this head, which is often misunderstood, is that pecuniary wages are (on the average, setting great gains against small ones) less in trades where there are high prizes and many blanks. The remote possibility of obtaining one of the high prizes is one of the circumstances which "in the imaginations of men make up for a small pecuniary gain" (p. 139). Cantillon, Essai, p. 24, is not so subtle, merely making remuneration proportionate to risk.]

[18] [Lectures, p. 175.]

makers or weavers, and you will find that the former sum will generally exceed the latter. But make the same computation with regard to all the counsellors and students of law, in all the different inns of court, and you will find that their annual gains bear but a very small proportion to their annual expence, even though you rate the former as high, and the latter as low, as can well be done. The lottery of the law, therefore, is very far from being a perfectly fair lottery; and that, as well as many other liberal and honourable professions, is,[19] in point of pecuniary gain, evidently under-recompenced.

Those professions keep their level, however, with other oc-cupations, and, notwithstanding these discouragements, all the most generous and liberal spirits are eager to crowd into them. Two different causes con-tribute to recommend them. First, the desire of the reputation which attends upon supe-rior excellence in any of them; and, sec-ondly, the natural confidence which every man has more or less, not only in his own abilities, but in his own good fortune.

Law and similar professions are nevertheless crowded.

To excel in any profession, in which but few arrive at medi-ocrity, is the most decisive mark of what is called genius or su-perior talents. The public admiration which attends upon such distinguished abilities, makes always a part of their reward; a greater or smaller in proportion as it is higher or lower in degree. It makes a consid-erable part of that reward[20] in the profession of physic; a still greater perhaps in that of law; in poetry and philosophy it makes almost the whole.

Public admiration makes a part of the reward of su-perior abilities,

There are some very agreeable and beautiful talents of which the possession commands a certain sort of admiration; but of which the exercise for the sake of gain is considered, whether from reason or prejudice, as a sort of public prostitu-tion. The pecuniary recompence, therefore, of those who exer-cise them in this manner, must be sufficient, not only to pay for

[19] [Eds. 1–4 read "are."]

[20] [Ed. 1 reads "of it."]

except in the peculiar case of players, opera singers, &c.

the time, labour, and expence of acquiring the talents, but for the discredit which attends the employment of them as the means of subsistence. The exorbitant rewards of players, opera-singers, opera-dancers, &c. are founded upon those two principles; the rarity and beauty of the talents, and the discredit of employing them in this manner. It seems absurd at first sight that we should despise their persons, and yet reward their talents with the most profuse liberality. While we do the one, however, we must of necessity do the other. Should the public opinion or prejudice ever alter with regard to such occupations, their pecuniary recompence would quickly diminish. More people would apply to them, and the competition would quickly reduce the price of their labour. Such talents, though far from being common, are by no means so rare as is imagined. Many people possess them in great perfection, who disdain to make this use of them; and many more are capable of acquiring them, if any thing could be made honourably by them.

The over-weening conceit which the greater part of men have of their own abilities, is an ancient evil remarked by the

The greater part of men have an over-weening conceit of their abilities:

philosophers and moralists of all ages. Their absurd presumption in their own good fortune, has been less taken notice of. It is, however, if possible, still more universal. There is no man living who, when in tolerable health and spirits, has not some share of it. The chance of gain is by every man more or less over-valued, and the chance of loss is by most men under-valued, and by scarce any man, who is in tolerable health and spirits, valued more than it is worth.

That the chance of gain is naturally over-valued, we may learn from the universal success of lotteries. The world neither ever saw, nor ever will see, a perfectly fair lottery; or one in

lotteries show that the chance of gain is overvalued,

which the whole gain compensated the whole loss; because the undertaker could make nothing by it. In the state lotteries the tickets are really not worth the price which is paid by the original subscribers, and yet commonly sell in the market for twenty, thirty, and sometimes forty per cent. advance. The vain hope of gaining some of the great prizes is the sole cause of this demand. The soberest people scarce look upon it as a folly to pay a small sum for the chance of gaining ten or twenty thousand pounds; though they know that even that small sum is perhaps twenty or thirty per cent. more than the chance is worth. In a lottery in which no prize exceeded twenty pounds, though in other respects it approached much nearer to a perfectly fair one than the common state lotteries, there would not be the same demand for tickets. In order to have a better chance for some of the great prizes, some people purchase several tickets, and others, small shares in a still greater number. There is not, however, a more certain proposition in mathematics, than that the more tickets you adventure upon, the more likely you are to be a loser. Adventure upon all the tickets in the lottery, and you lose for certain; and the greater the number of your tickets the nearer you approach to this certainty.

That the chance of loss is frequently undervalued, and scarce ever valued more than it is worth, we may learn from the very moderate profit of insurers. In order to *and the moderate profit of insurers shows that the chance of loss is undervalued.* make insurance, either from fire or sea-risk, a trade at all, the common premium must be sufficient to compensate the common losses, to pay the expence of management, and to afford such a profit as might have been drawn from an equal capital employed in any common trade. The person who pays no more than this, evidently pays no more than the real value of the risk, or the lowest price at which he can reasonably expect to insure it. But though many people have made a little money by insurance, very few have made a great fortune; and from this consideration alone, it seems evident enough, that the ordinary balance of profit and loss is not more advantageous in this, than in other common trades by which so many people make fortunes. Moderate, however, as the premium of insurance commonly is, many people despise the risk too much to care to pay it. Taking the whole kingdom at an average, nineteen houses in twenty, or rather, perhaps, ninety-nine in a hundred, are not insured from fire. Sea risk is more alarming to the greater part of people, and the proportion of ships insured to those not insured is much greater. Many sail, however, at all seasons, and even in time of war, without any insurance. This may sometimes perhaps be done without any imprudence. When a great company, or even a great merchant, has twenty or thirty ships at sea, they may, as it were, insure one another. The premium saved upon them all, may more than compensate such losses as they are likely to meet with in the common course of chances. The neglect of insurance upon shipping, however, in the same manner as upon houses, is, in most cases, the effect of no such nice calculation, but of mere thoughtless rashness and presumptuous contempt of the risk.

The contempt of risk and the presumptuous hope of success, are in no period of life more active than at the age at which young people chuse their professions. *Young people are particularly prone to overvalue the chance of gain and undervalue the risk of loss.* How little the fear of misfortune is then capable of balancing the hope of good luck, appears still more evidently in the readiness of the common people to enlist as soldiers, or to go to sea, than in the eagerness of those of better fashion to enter into what are called the liberal professions.

What a common soldier may lose is obvious enough. Without regarding the danger, however, young volunteers never enlist so readily as at the beginning of *For this reason soldiers are poorly paid,* a new war; and though they have scarce any chance of preferment, they figure to themselves, in their youthful fancies, a thousand occasions of acquiring honour and distinction which never occur. These romantic hopes make the whole price of their blood. Their pay is less than that of common labourers, and in actual service their fatigues are much greater.

The lottery of the sea is not altogether so disadvantageous as that of the army. The son of a creditable labourer or artificer may frequently go to sea with his father's consent; but if he en-

and sailors not much better. lists as a soldier, it is always without it. Other people see some chance of his making something by the one trade: nobody but himself sees any of his making any thing by the other. The great admiral is less the object of public admiration than the great general, and the highest success in the sea service promises a less brilliant fortune and reputation than equal success in the land. The same difference runs through all the inferior degrees of preferment in both. By the rules of precedency a captain in the navy ranks with a colonel in the army: but he does not rank with him in the common estimation. As the great prizes in the lottery are less, the smaller ones must be more numerous. Common sailors, therefore, more frequently get some fortune and preferment than common soldiers; and the hope of those prizes is what principally recommends the trade. Though their skill and dexterity are much superior to that of almost any artificers, and though their whole life is one continual scene of hardship and danger, yet for all this dexterity and skill, for all those hardships and dangers, while they remain in the condition of common sailors, they receive scarce any other recompence but the pleasure of exercising the one and of surmounting the other. Their wages are not greater than those of common labourers at the port which regulates the rate of seamen's wages. As they are continually going from port to port, the monthly pay of those who sail from all the different ports of Great Britain, is more nearly upon a level than that of any other workmen in those different places; and the rate of the port to and from which the greatest number sail, that is the port of London, regulates that of all the rest. At London the wages of the greater part of the different classes of workmen are about double those of the same classes at Edinburgh. But the sailors who sail from the port of London seldom earn above three or four shillings a month more than those who sail from the port of Leith, and the difference is frequently not so great. In time of peace, and in the merchant service, the London price is from a guinea to about seven-and-twenty shillings the calendar month. A common labourer in London, at the rate of nine or ten shillings a week, may earn in the calendar month from forty to five-and-forty shillings. The sailor, indeed, over and above his pay, is supplied with provisions. Their value, however, may not perhaps always exceed the difference between his pay and that of the common labourer; and though it sometimes should, the excess will not be clear gain to the sailor, because he cannot share it with his wife and family, whom he must maintain out of his wages at home.

The dangers and hair-breadth escapes of a life of adventures, instead of disheartening young people, seem frequently

Dangers which can be surmounted attract, though mere unwholesomeness repels.

to recommend a trade to them. A tender mother, among the inferior ranks of people, is often afraid to send her son to school at a sea-port town, lest the sight of the ships and the conversation and adventures of the sailors should entice him to go to sea. The distant prospect of hazards, from which we can hope to extricate ourselves by courage and address, is not disagreeable to us, and does not raise the wages of labour in any employment. It is otherwise with those in which courage and address can be of no avail. In trades which are known to be very unwholesome, the wages of labour are always remarkably high. Unwholesomeness is a species of disagreeableness, and its effects upon the wages of labour are to be ranked under that general head.

In all the different employments of stock, the ordinary rate of profit varies more or less with the certainty or uncertainty of

Profits vary with certainty of return.

the returns. These are in general less uncertain in the inland than in the foreign trade, and in some branches of foreign trade than in others; in the trade to North America, for example, than in that to Jamaica. The ordinary rate of profit always rises more or less with the risk. It does not, however, seem to rise in proportion to it, or so as to compensate it completely. Bankruptcies are most frequent in the most hazardous trades. The most hazardous of all trades, that of a smuggler, though when the adventure succeeds it is likewise the most profitable, is the infallible road to bankruptcy. The presumptuous hope of success seems to act here as upon all other occasions, and to entice so many adventurers into those hazardous trades, that their competition reduces the[21] profit below what is sufficient to compensate the risk. To compensate it completely, the common returns ought, over and above the ordinary profits of stock, not only to make up for all occasional losses, but to afford a surplus profit to the adventurers of the same nature with the profit of insurers. But if the common returns were sufficient for all this, bankruptcies would not be more frequent in these than in other trades.[22]

Of the five circumstances, therefore, which vary the wages of labour, two only affect the profits of stock; the agreeable-

Profits are less unequal than wages, and their inequality is often only due to the inclusion of wages,

ness or disagreeableness of the business, and the risk or security with which it is attended. In point of agreeableness or disagreeableness, there is little or no difference in the far greater part of the different employments of stock; but a great deal in those of labour; and the ordinary profit of stock, though it rises with the risk, does not always seem to rise in proportion to it. It should follow from all this, that, in the same society or neighbourhood, the average and ordinary rates of profit in the different employments of stock should be more nearly upon a level than the pecuniary wages of the different sorts of labour. They are so accordingly. The difference between the earnings of a common labourer and those of a well employed lawyer or physician, is evidently much greater than that between the ordinary profits in any two different branches of trade. The apparent difference, besides, in the profits of different trades, is generally a deception arising from our not always distinguishing what ought to be considered as wages, from what ought to be considered as profit.[23]

Apothecaries profit is become a bye-word, denoting some-

---

[21] [Eds. 4 and 5 read "their," doubtless a misprint.]

[22] [The fact is overlooked that the numerous bankruptcies may be counterbalanced by the instances of great gain. Below, on pp. 173–174, the converse mistake is made of comparing great successes and leaving out of account great failures.]

[23] [Above, pp. 75, 76.]

thing uncommonly extravagant. This great apparent profit,

as in the case of the profit of an apothecary,

however, is frequently no more than the reasonable wages of labour. The skill of an apothecary is a much nicer and more delicate matter than that of any artificer whatever; and the trust which is reposed in him is of much greater importance. He is the physician of the poor in all cases, and of the rich when the distress or danger is not very great. His reward, therefore, ought to be suitable to his skill and his trust, and it arises generally from the price at which he sells his drugs. But the whole drugs which the best employed apothecary, in a large market town, will sell in a year, may not perhaps cost him above thirty or forty pounds. Though he should sell them, therefore, for three or four hundred, or at a thousand per cent. profit, this may frequently be no more than the reasonable wages of his labour charged, in the only way in which he can charge them, upon the price of his drugs. The greater part of the apparent profit is real wages disguised in the garb of profit.

In a small sea-port town,²⁴ a little grocer will make forty or fifty per cent. upon a stock of a single hundred pounds, while a

or country grocer.

considerable wholesale merchant in the same place will scarce make eight or ten per cent. upon a stock of ten thousand. The trade of the grocer may be necessary for the conveniency of the inhabitants, and the narrowness of the market may not admit the employment of a larger capital in the business. The man, however, must not only live by his trade, but live by it suitably to the qualifications which it requires. Besides possessing a little capital, he must be able to read, write, and account, and must be a tolerable judge too of, perhaps, fifty or sixty different sorts of goods, their prices, qualities, and the markets where they are to be had cheapest. He must have all the knowledge, in short, that is necessary for a great merchant, which nothing hinders him from becoming but the want of a sufficient capital. Thirty or forty pounds a year cannot be considered as too great a recompence

²⁴ [Doubtless Kirkcaldy was in Smith's mind.]

for the labour of a person so accomplished. Deduct this from the seemingly great profits of his capital, and little more will remain, perhaps, than the ordinary profits of stock. The greater part of the apparent profit is, in this case too, real wages.

The difference between the apparent profit of the retail and that of the wholesale trade, is much less in the capital than in small towns and country villages. Where ten thousand pounds

The greater difference between retail and whole-sale profits in town than country is due to the same cause.

can be employed in the grocery trade, the wages of the grocer's labour make but a very trifling addition to the real profits of so great a stock. The apparent profits of the wealthy retailer, therefore, are there more nearly upon a level with those of the wholesale merchant. It is upon this account that goods sold by retail are generally as cheap and fre-

quently much cheaper in the capital than in small towns and country villages.[25] Grocery goods, for example, are generally much cheaper; bread and butcher's meat frequently as cheap. It costs no more to bring grocery goods to the great town than to the country village; but it costs a great deal more to bring corn and cattle, as the greater part of them must be brought from a much greater distance. The prime cost of grocery goods, there-fore, being the same in both places, they are cheapest where the least profit is charged upon them. The prime cost of bread and butcher's meat is greater in the great town than in the country village; and though the profit is less, therefore they are not always cheaper there, but often equally cheap. In such arti-cles as bread and butcher's meat, the same cause, which dimin-ishes apparent profit, increases prime cost. The extent of the market, by giving employment to greater stocks, diminishes apparent profit; but by requiring supplies from a greater dis-tance, it increases prime cost. This diminution of the one and increase of the other seem, in most cases, nearly to counter-balance one another; which is probably the reason that, though the prices of corn and cattle are commonly very different in different parts of the kingdom, those of bread and butcher's

[25] [Above, p. 105.]

meat are generally very nearly the same through the greater part of it.

Though the profits of stock both in the wholesale and retail trade are generally less in the capital than in small towns and country villages, yet great fortunes are frequently acquired from small beginnings in the former, and scarce ever in the latter. In small towns and country villages, on account of the narrowness of the market, trade cannot always be extended as stock extends.

The lesser rate of profit in towns yields larger fortunes, but these mostly arise from speculation.

In such places, therefore, though the rate of a particular person's profits may be very high, the sum or amount of them can never be very great, nor consequently that of his annual accumulation. In great towns, on the contrary, trade can be extended as stock increases, and the credit of a frugal and thriving man increases much faster than his stock. His trade is extended in proportion to the amount of both, and the sum or amount of his profits is in proportion to the extent of his trade, and his annual accumulation in proportion to the amount of his profits. It seldom happens, however, that great fortunes are made even in great towns by any one regular, established, and well-known branch of business, but in consequence of a long life of industry, frugality, and attention. Sudden fortunes, indeed, are sometimes made in such places by what is called the trade of speculation. The speculative merchant exercises no one regular, established, or well known branch of business. He is a corn merchant this year, and a wine merchant the next, and a sugar, tobacco, or tea merchant the year after. He enters into every trade when he foresees that it is likely to be more than commonly profitable, and he quits it when he foresees that its profits are likely to return to the level of other trades. His profits and losses, therefore, can bear no regular proportion to those of any one established and well-known branch of business. A bold adventurer may sometimes acquire a considerable fortune by two or three successful speculations; but is just as likely to lose one by two or three unsuccessful ones. This trade can be carried on no where but in great towns. It is only in places of the most extensive commerce and correspondence that the intelligence requisite for it can be had.

The five circumstances above mentioned, though they occasion considerable inequalities in the wages of labour and profits of stock, occasion none in the whole of the advantages and disadvantages, real or imaginary, of the different employments of either. The nature of those circumstances is such, that they make up for a small pecuniary gain in some, and counter-balance a great one in others.

The five circumstances thus counterbalance difference of pecuniary gains,

In order, however, that this equality may take place in the whole of their advantages or disadvantages, three things are requisite even where there is the most perfect freedom. First, the employments must be well known and long established in the neighbourhood; secondly, they must be in their ordinary, or what may be called their natural state; and, thirdly, they must be the sole or principal employments of those who occupy them.

but three things are necessary as well as perfect freedom:

First, this equality can take place only in those employments which are well known, and have been long established in the neighbourhood.

(1) the employments must be well known and long established,

Where all other circumstances are equal, wages are generally higher in new than in old trades. When a projector attempts to establish a new manufacture, he must at first entice his workmen from other employments by higher wages than they can either earn in their own trades, or than the nature of his work would otherwise require, and a considerable time must pass away before he can venture to reduce them to the common level. Manufactures for which the demand arises altogether from fashion and fancy, are continually changing, and seldom last long enough to be considered as old established manufactures. Those, on the contrary, for which the demand arises chiefly from use or necessity, are less liable to change, and the same form or fabric may continue in demand for whole

since new trades yield higher wages,

centuries together. The wages of labour, therefore, are likely to be higher in manufactures of the former, than in those of the latter kind. Birmingham deals chiefly in manufactures of the former kind; Sheffield in those of the latter; and the wages of labour in those two different places, are said to be suitable to this difference in the nature of their manufactures.

The establishment of any new manufacture, of any new branch of commerce, or of any new practice in agriculture, is always a speculation, from which the projector promises him-

and higher profits: self extraordinary profits. These profits sometimes are very great, and sometimes, more frequently, perhaps, they are quite otherwise; but in general they bear no regular proportion to those of other old trades in the neighbourhood. If the project succeeds, they are commonly at first very high. When the trade or practice becomes thoroughly established and well known, the competition reduces them to the level of other trades.

Secondly, This equality in the whole of the advantages and

(2) the employ-ments must be in their natural state, disadvantages of the different employments of labour and stock, can take place only in the ordinary, or what may be called the natural state of those employments.

The demand for almost every different species of labour is sometimes greater and sometimes less than usual. In the one case the advantages of the employment rise above, in the other

since the demand for labour in each employment varies from time to time they fall below the common level. The demand for country labour is greater at hay-time and harvest, than during the greater part of the year; and wages rise with the demand. In time of war, when forty or fifty thousand sailors are forced from the merchant service into that of the king, the demand for sailors to merchant ships necessarily rises with their scarcity, and their wages upon such occasions commonly rise from a guinea and seven-and-twenty shillings, to forty shillings and three pounds a month. In a decaying manufacture, on the contrary, many workmen, rather than quit their old trade, are contented with smaller wages than would otherwise be suitable to the nature of their employment.

The profits of stock vary with the price of the commodities in which it is employed. As the price of any commodity rises

and profits fluctuate with the price of the commodity produced:

above the ordinary or average rate, the profits of at least some part of the stock that is employed in bringing it to market, rise above their proper level, and as it falls they sink below it. All commodities are more or less liable to variations of price, but some are much more so than others. In all commodities which are produced by human industry, the quantity of industry annually employed is necessarily regulated by the annual demand, in such a manner that the average annual produce may, as nearly as possible, be equal to the average annual consumption. In some employments, it has already been observed,[26] the same quantity of industry will always produce the same, or very nearly the same quantity of commodities. In the linen or woollen manufactures, for example, the same number of hands will annually work up very nearly the same quantity of linen and woollen cloth. The variations in the market price of such commodities, therefore, can arise only from some accidental variation in the demand. A public mourning raises the price of black cloth.[27] But as the demand for most sorts of plain linen and woollen cloth is pretty uniform, so is likewise the price. But there are other employments in which the same quantity of industry will not always produce the same quantity of commodities. The same quantity of industry, for example, will, in different years, produce very different quantities of corn, wine, hops, sugar, tobacco, &c. The price of such commodities, therefore, varies not only with the variations of demand, but with the much greater and more frequent variations of quantity, and is consequently extremely fluctuating. But the profit of some of the dealers must necessarily fluctuate with the price of the commodities. The operations of the speculative merchant are principally employed about such commodities. He endeavours to buy them up when he foresees that

---

[26] [Above, pp. 82–83.]

[27] [The illustration has already been used above, p. 84.]

their price is likely to rise, and to sell them when it is likely to fall.

and (3) the employments must be the principal employment of those who occupy them, since people maintained by one employment will work cheap at another, like the Scotch cotters,

Thirdly, This equality in the whole of the advantages and disadvantages of the different employments of labour and stock, can take place only in such as are the sole or principal employments of those who occupy them.

When a person derives his subsistence from one employment, which does not occupy the greater part of his time; in the intervals of his leisure he is often willing to work at another for less wages than would otherwise suit the nature of the employment.

There still subsists in many parts of Scotland a set of people called Cotters or Cottagers, though they were more frequent some years ago than they are now. They are a sort of out-servants of the landlords and farmers. The usual reward which they receive from their masters is a house, a small garden for pot herbs, as much grass as will feed a cow, and, perhaps, an acre or two of bad arable land. When their master has occasion for their labour, he gives them, besides, two pecks of oatmeal a week, worth about sixteen pence sterling. During a great part of the year he has little or no occasion for their labour, and the cultivation of their own little possession is not sufficient to occupy the time which is left at their own disposal. When such occupiers were more numerous than they are at present, they are said to have been willing to give their spare time for a very small recompence to any body, and to have wrought for less wages than other labourers. In ancient times they seem to have been common all over Europe. In countries ill cultivated and worse inhabited, the greater part of the landlords and farmers could not otherwise provide themselves with the extraordinary number of hands, which country labour requires at certain seasons. The daily or weekly recompence which such labourers occasionally received from their masters, was evidently not the whole price of their labour. Their small tenement made a considerable part of it. This daily or weekly recompence, however, seems to have been considered as the whole of it, by many writers who have collected the prices of labour and provisions in ancient times, and who have taken pleasure in representing both as wonderfully low.

The produce of such labour comes frequently cheaper to market than would otherwise be suitable to its nature. Stockings in many parts of Scotland are knit much cheaper than they can any-where be wrought upon the loom. They are the work of servants and labourers, who derive the principal part of their subsistence from some other employment. More than a thousand pair of Shetland stockings are annually imported into Leith, of which the price is from five pence to seven pence a pair. At Learwick, the small capital of the Shetland islands, ten pence a day, I have been assured, is a common price of common labour. In the same islands they knit worsted stockings to the value of a guinea a pair and upwards.

Shetland knitters,

The spinning of linen yarn is carried on in Scotland nearly in the same way as the knitting of stockings, by servants who are chiefly hired for other purposes. They earn but a very scanty subsistence, who endeavour to get their whole livelihood by either of those trades. In most parts of Scotland she is a good spinner who can earn twenty pence a week.

Scotch linen spinners,

In opulent countries the market is generally so extensive that any one trade is sufficient to employ the whole labour and stock of those who occupy it. Instances of people's living by one employment, and at the same time deriving some little advantage from another, occur chiefly in poor countries. The following instance, however, of something of the same kind is to be found in the capital of a very rich one. There is no city in Europe, I believe, in which house-rent is dearer than in London, and yet I know no capital in which a furnished apartment can be hired so cheap. Lodging is not only much cheaper in London than in Paris; it is much cheaper than in Edinburgh of the same degree of goodness; and what may seem extraordinary, the dearness of house-rent is the cause of the cheapness

and London lodging house keepers.

of lodging. The dearness of house-rent in London arises, not only from those causes which render it dear in all great capitals, the dearness of labour, the dearness of all the materials of building, which must generally be brought from a great distance, and above all the dearness of ground-rent, every landlord acting the part of a monopolist, and frequently exacting a higher rent for a single acre of bad land in a town, than can be had for a hundred of the best in the country; but it arises in part from the peculiar manners and customs of the people which oblige every master of a family to hire a whole house from top to bottom. A dwelling-house in England means every thing that is contained under the same roof. In France, Scotland, and many other parts of Europe, it frequently means no more than a single story. A tradesman in London is obliged to hire a whole house in that part of the town where his customers live. His shop is upon the ground-floor, and he and his family sleep in the garret; and he endeavours to pay a part of his house-rent by letting the two middle stories to lodgers. He expects to maintain his family by his trade, and not by his lodgers. Whereas, at Paris and Edinburgh, the people who let lodgings have commonly no other means of subsistence; and the price of the lodging must pay, not only the rent of the house, but the whole expence of the family.

PART II

INEQUALITIES OCCASIONED BY THE POLICY OF EUROPE

Such are the inequalities in the whole of the advantages and disadvantages of the different employments of labour and stock, which the defect of any of the three requisites above-mentioned must occasion, even where there is the most perfect liberty. But the policy of Europe, by not leaving things at perfect liberty, occasions other inequalities of much greater importance.

The policy of Europe occasions more important inequalities

It does this chiefly in the three following ways. First, by restraining the competition in some employments to a smaller number than would otherwise be disposed to enter into them; *in three ways:* secondly, by increasing it in others beyond what it naturally would be; and, thirdly, by obstructing the free circulation of labour and stock, both from employment to employment and from place to place.

First, The policy of Europe occasions a very important inequality in the whole of the advantages and disadvantages of the different employments of labour and stock, by restraining the competition in some employments to a smaller number than might otherwise be disposed to enter into them.

(1) It restricts competition in some employments,

The exclusive privileges of corporations are the principal means it makes use of for this purpose.

The exclusive privilege of an incorporated trade necessarily restrains the competition, in the town where it is established, to those who are free of the trade. To have served an apprenticeship in the town, under a master properly qualified, is commonly the necessary requisite for obtaining this freedom. The bye-laws of the corporation regulate sometimes the number of apprentices which any master is allowed to have, and almost always the number of years which each apprentice is obliged to serve. The intention of both regulations is to restrain the competition to a much smaller number than might otherwise be disposed to enter into the trade. The limitation of the number of apprentices restrains it directly. A long term of apprenticeship restrains it more indirectly, but as effectually, by increasing the expence of education.

principally by giving exclusive privileges to corporations, which require long apprenticeship and limit the number of apprentices.

In Sheffield no master cutler can have more than one apprentice at a time, by a bye-law of the corporation. In Norfolk and Norwich no master weaver can have more than two apprentices, under pain of forfeiting five pounds a month to the king.[28] No master hatter can have more than two apprentices

---

[28] [Under 13 and 14 Car. II., c. 5, § 18.]

any-where in England, or in the English plantations, under pain of forfeiting five pounds a month, half to the king, and half to him who shall sue in any court of record.[29] Both these regulations, though they have been confirmed by a public law of the kingdom, are evidently dictated by the same corporation spirit which enacted the bye-law of Sheffield.[30] The silk weavers in London had scarce been incorporated a year when they enacted a bye-law, restraining any master from having more than two apprentices at a time. It required a particular act of parliament to rescind this bye-law.[31]

Seven years seem anciently to have been, all over Europe, the usual term established for the duration of apprenticeships in the greater part of incorporated trades. All such incorporations were

Seven years is the usual period of apprenticeship.

anciently called universities; which indeed is the proper Latin name for any incorporation whatever. The university of smiths, the university of taylors, &c. are expressions which we commonly meet with in the old charters of ancient towns.[32] When those particular incorporations which are now peculiarly called universities were first established, the term of years which

[29] [8 Eliz., c. 11, § 8; 1 Jac. I., c. 17, § 3; 5 Geo. II., c. 22.]

[30] [But 8 Eliz., c. 11, was enacted "at the lamentable suit and complaint" not of the hatters but of the cap-makers, who alleged that they were being impoverished by the excessive use of hats, which were made of foreign wool, and the extension to the colonies of the restriction on apprentices by 5 Geo. II., c. 22, was doubtless suggested by the English hatters' jealousy of the American hatters, so that this regulation was not dictated by quite the same spirit as the Sheffield by-law.]

[31] [The preamble of 13 and 14 Car. II., c. 15, says that the company of silk throwers in London were incorporated in 1629, and the preamble of 20 Car. II., c. 6, says that the trade had lately been obstructed because the company had endeavoured to put into execution a certain by-law made by them nearly forty years since, restricting the freemen to 160 spindles and the assistants to 240. The act 20 Car. II., c. 6, accordingly declares this by-law void. It also enacts that "no by-law already made or hereafter to be made by the said company shall limit the number of apprentices to less than three."]

[32] ["In Italy a mestiere or company of artisans and tradesmen was sometimes styled an *ars* or *universitas*.... The company of mercers of Rome are styled *universitas merciariorum*, and the company of bakers there *universitas pistorum*."— Madox, *Firma Burgi*, 1726, p. 32.]

it was necessary to study, in order to obtain the degree of master of arts, appears evidently to have been copied from the term of apprenticeship in common trades, of which the incorporations were much more ancient. As to have wrought seven years under a master properly qualified, was necessary, in order to entitle any person to become a master, and to have himself apprentices in a common trade; so to have studied seven years under a master properly qualified, was necessary to entitle him to become a master, teacher, or doctor (words anciently synonymous) in the liberal arts, and to have scholars or apprentices (words likewise originally synonymous) to study under him.

By the 5th of Elizabeth, commonly called the Statute of Apprenticeship,[33] it was enacted, that no person should for the future exercise any trade craft, or mystery at that time exercised in England, unless he had previously served to it an apprenticeship of seven years at least; and what before had been the bye-law of many particular corporations, became in England the general and public law of all trades carried on in market towns. For though the words of the statute are very general, and seem plainly to include the whole kingdom, by interpretation its operation has been limited to market towns, it having been held that in country villages a person may exercise several different trades, though he has not served a seven years apprenticeship to each, they being necessary for the conveniency of the inhabitants, and the number of people frequently not being sufficient to supply each with a particular set of hands.[34]

The Statute of Apprenticeship, which required it everywhere in England, has been confined to market towns,

and to trades existing when it was passed.

By a strict interpretation of the words too the operation of this statute has been limited to those trades which were established in England before the 5th of Elizabeth, and has

---

[33] [C. 4, § 31.]

[34] ["It hath been held that this statute doth not restrain a man from using several trades, so as he had been an apprentice to all; wherefore it indemnifies all petty chapmen in little towns and villages because their masters kept the same mixed trades before."—Matthew Bacon, *New Abridgement of the Law*, 3rd ed., 1768, vol. iii., p. 553, *s.v.* Master and servant.]

never been extended to such as have been introduced since that time.[35] This limitation has given occasion to several distinctions which, considered as rules of police, appear as foolish as can well be imagined. It has been adjudged, for example, that a coach-maker can neither himself make nor employ journeymen to make his coach-wheels; but must buy them of a master wheel-wright; this latter trade having been exercised in England before the 5th of Elizabeth.[35a] But a wheel-wright, though he has never served an apprenticeship to a coach-maker, may either himself make or employ journeymen to make coaches; the trade of a coach-maker not being within the statute, because not exercised in England at the time when it was made.[36] The manufacturers of Manchester, Birmingham, and Wolverhampton, are many of them, upon this account, not within the statute; not having been exercised in England before the 5th of Elizabeth.

In France, the duration of apprenticeships is different in different towns and in different trades. In Paris, five years is the

The term varies in France, term required in a great number; but before any person can be qualified to exercise the trade as a master, he must, in many of them, serve five years more as a journeyman. During this latter term he is called the companion[37] of his master, and the term itself is called his companionship.[38]

In Scotland there is no general law which regulates universally the duration of apprenticeships. The

and Scotland, where the regulations are less oppressive. term is different in different corporations. Where it is long, a part of it may generally be redeemed by paying a small fine. In most towns too a very small fine is sufficient to purchase the freedom of any corporation. The weavers of linen

---

[35] [*Ibid.*, vol. iii., p. 552.]

[35a] [*Ibid.*, vol. i., p. 553.]

[36] [Bacon (*ibid.*, iii., 553), however, says distinctly: "A coachmaker within this statute," on the authority of Ventris' *Reports*, p. 346.]

[37] [Compagnon.]

[38] [Compagnonnage.]

and hempen cloth, the principal manufactures of the country, as well as all other artificers subservient to them, wheel-makers, reel-makers, &c. may exercise their trades in any town corporate without paying any fine. In all towns corporate all persons are free to sell butcher's meat upon any lawful day of the week. Three years is in Scotland a common term of apprenticeship, even in some very nice trades; and in general I know of no country in Europe in which corporation laws are so little oppressive.

The property which every man has in his own labour, as it is the original foundation of all other property,[39] so it is the most sacred and inviolable. The patrimony of a poor man lies in the strength and dexterity of his hands; and to hinder him from employing this strength and dexterity in what manner he thinks proper without injury to his neighbour, is a plain violation of this most sacred property. It is a manifest encroachment upon the just liberty both of the workman, and of those who might be disposed to employ him. As it hinders the one from working at what he thinks proper, so it hinders the others from employing whom they think proper. To judge whether he is fit to be employed, may surely be trusted to the discretion of the employers whose interest it so much concerns. The affected anxiety of the law-giver lest they should employ an improper person, is evidently as impertinent as it is oppressive.

All such regulations are as impertinent as oppressive.

The institution of long apprenticeships can give no security that insufficient workmanship shall not frequently be exposed to public sale. When this is done it is generally the effect of fraud, and not of inability; and the longest apprenticeship can give no security against fraud. Quite different regulations are necessary to prevent this abuse. The sterling mark upon plate, and the stamps upon linen[40] and

Long apprenticeships are no security against bad work,

---

[39] [Contrast with this the account of the origin of property in the *Lectures*, pp. 107–127.]

[40] [Of Scotch manufacture, 10 Ann., c. 21; 13 Geo. I., c. 26.]

woollen cloth,[41] give the purchaser much greater security than any statute of apprenticeship. He generally looks at these, but never thinks it worth while to enquire whether the workmen had served a seven years apprenticeship.

The institution of long apprenticeships has no tendency to form young people to industry. A journeyman who works by

and do not form young people to industry.

the piece is likely to be industrious, because he derives a benefit from every exertion of his industry. An apprentice is likely to be idle, and almost always is so, because he has no immediate interest to be otherwise. In the inferior employments, the sweets of labour consist altogether in the recompence of labour. They who are soonest in a condition to enjoy the sweets of it, are likely soonest to conceive a relish for it, and to acquire the early habit of industry. A young man naturally conceives an aversion to labour, when for a long time he receives no benefit from it. The boys who are put out apprentices from public charities are generally bound for more than the usual number of years, and they generally turn out very idle and worthless.

Apprenticeships were altogether unknown to the ancients. The reciprocal duties of master and apprentice make a consid-

Apprenticeships were unknown to the ancients.

erable article in every modern code.[42] The Roman law is perfectly silent with regard to them. I know no Greek or Latin work (I might venture, I believe, to assert that there is none) which expresses the idea we now annex to the word Apprentice, a servant bound to work at a particular trade for the benefit of a master, during a term of years, upon condition that the master shall teach him that trade.

Long apprenticeships are altogether unnecessary. The arts, which are much superior to common trades, such as those of making clocks and watches, contain no such mystery as to require a long course of instruction. The first invention of such

[41] [39 Eliz., c. 20; 43 Eliz., c. 10, § 7.]

[42] [The article on apprentices occupies twenty-four pages in Richard Burn's *Justice of the Peace*, 1764.]

*Long apprentice-
ships are
altogether
unnecessary.*

beautiful machines, indeed, and even that of some of the instruments employed in making them, must, no doubt, have been the work of deep thought and long time, and may justly be considered as among the happiest efforts of human ingenuity. But when both have been fairly invented and are well understood, to explain to any young man, in the completest manner, how to apply the instruments and how to construct the machines, cannot well require more than the lessons of a few weeks: perhaps those of a few days might be sufficient. In the common mechanic trades, those of a few days might certainly be sufficient. The dexterity of hand, indeed, even in common trades, cannot be acquired without much practice and experience. But a young man would practise with much more diligence and attention, if from the beginning he wrought as a journeyman, being paid in proportion to the little work which he could execute, and paying in his turn for the materials which he might sometimes spoil through awkwardness and inexperience. His education would generally in this way be more effectual, and always less tedious and expensive. The master, indeed, would be a loser. He would lose all the wages of the apprentice, which he now saves, for seven years together. In the end, perhaps, the apprentice himself would be a loser. In a trade so easily learnt he would have more competitors, and his wages, when he came to be a complete workman, would be much less than at present. The same increase of competition would reduce the profits of the masters as well as the wages of the workmen. The trades, the crafts, the mysteries,[43] would all be losers. But the public would be a gainer, the work of all artificers coming in this way much cheaper to market.

It is to prevent this reduction of price, and consequently of wages and profit, by restraining that free competition which

---

[43] [The last two terms seem to be used rather contemptuously. Probably Smith had fresh in his recollection the passage in which Madox ridicules as a "piece of puerility" the use of the English word "misterie," derived from "the Gallick word mestera, mistera and misteria," as if it "signified something μυστηριῶδες, mysterious."—*Firma Burgi*, 1726, pp. 33–35.]

Corporations were established to keep up prices and consequently wages and profit; would most certainly occasion it, that all corporations, and the greater part of corporation laws, have been established. In order to erect a corporation, no other authority in ancient times was requisite in many parts of Europe, but that of the town corporate in which it was established. In England, indeed, a charter from the king was likewise necessary. But this prerogative of the crown seems to have been reserved rather for extorting money from the subject, than for the defence of the common liberty against such oppressive monopolies. Upon paying a fine to the king, the charter seems generally to have been readily granted; and when any particular class of artificers or traders thought proper to act as a corporation without a charter, such adulterine guilds, as they were called, were not always disfranchised upon that account, but obliged to fine annually to the king for permission to exercise their usurped privileges.[44] The immediate inspection of all corporations, and of the bye-laws which they might think proper to enact for their own government, belonged to the town corporate in which they were established; and whatever discipline was exercised over them, proceeded commonly, not from the king, but from that greater incorporation of which those subordinate ones were only parts or members.[45]

The government of towns corporate was altogether in the hands of traders and artificers; and it was the manifest interest *by means of which the towns gained at the expense of the country,* of every particular class of them, to prevent the market from being over-stocked, as they commonly express it, with their own particular species of industry; which is in reality to keep it always under-stocked. Each class was eager to establish regulations proper for this purpose, and, provided it was allowed to do so, was willing to consent that every other class should do the same. In conse-

---

[44] See Madox, *Firma Burgi*, p. 26, &c. This note appears first in ed. 2.

[45] "Peradventure from these secular gilds or in imitation of them sprang the method or practice of gildating and embodying whole towns."—Madox, *Firma Burgi*, p. 27.

quence of such regulations, indeed, each class was obliged to buy the goods they had occasion for from every other within the town, somewhat dearer than they otherwise might have done. But in recompence, they were enabled to sell their own just as much dearer; so that so far it was as broad as long, as they say; and in the dealings of the different classes within the town with one another, none of them were losers by these regulations. But in their dealings with the country they were all great gainers; and in these latter dealings consists the whole trade which supports and enriches every town.

Every town draws its whole subsistence, and all the materials of its industry, from the country. It pays for these chiefly in two ways: first, by sending back to the country a part of those materials wrought up and manufactured; in which case their price is augmented by the wages of the workmen, and the profits of their masters or immediate employers: secondly, by sending to it a part both of the rude and manufactured produce, either of other countries, or of distant parts of the same country, imported into the town; in which case too the original price of those goods is augmented by the wages of the carriers or sailors, and by the profits of the merchants who employ them. In what is gained upon the first of those two branches of commerce, consists the advantage which the town makes by its manufactures; in what is gained upon the second, the advantage of its inland and foreign trade. The wages of the workmen, and the profits of their different employers, make up the whole of what is gained upon both. Whatever regulations, therefore, tend to increase those wages and profits beyond what they otherwise would be, tend to enable the town to purchase, with a smaller quantity of its labour, the produce of a greater quantity of the labour of the country. They give the traders and artificers in the town an advantage over the landlords, farmers, and labourers in the country, and break down that natural equality which would otherwise take place in the commerce which is carried on between them. The whole annual produce of the labour of the so-

being enabled to get the produce of a larger quantity of country labour in exchange for the produce of a smaller quantity of their own,

ciety is annually divided between those two different sets of people. By means of those regulations a greater share of it is given to the inhabitants of the town than would otherwise fall to them; and a less to those of the country.

The price which the town really pays for the provisions and

as the exports of a town are the real price of its imports.

materials annually imported into it, is the quantity of manufactures and other goods annually exported from it. The dearer the latter are sold, the cheaper the former are bought. The industry of the town becomes more, and that of the country less advantageous.

That the industry which is carried on in towns is, everywhere in Europe, more advantageous than that which is carried

That town industry is better paid is shown by the large fortunes made in it.

on in the country, without entering into any very nice computations, we may satisfy ourselves by one very simple and obvious observation. In every country of Europe we find, at least, a hundred people who have acquired great fortunes from small beginnings by trade and manufactures, the industry which properly belongs to towns, for one who has done so by that which properly belongs to the country, the raising of rude produce by the improvement and cultivation of land. Industry, therefore, must be better rewarded, the wages of labour and the profits of stock must evidently be greater in the one situation than in the other.[46] But stock and labour naturally seek the most advantageous employment. They naturally, therefore, resort as much as they can to the town, and desert the country.

The inhabitants of a town, being collected into one place,

Combination is easy to the inhabitants of a town,

can easily combine together. The most insignificant trades carried on in towns have accordingly, in some place or other, been incorporated; and even where they have never been incorporated, yet the corporation spirit, the jealousy of

[46] [The argument is unsound in the absence of any proof that the more numerous successes are not counterbalanced by equally numerous failures; cp. above p. 154, note.]

strangers, the aversion to take apprentices, or to communicate the secret of their trade, generally prevail in them, and often teach them, by voluntary associations and agreements, to prevent that free competition which they cannot prohibit by byelaws. The trades which employ but a small number of hands, run most easily into such combinations. Half a dozen woolcombers, perhaps, are necessary to keep a thousand spinners and weavers at work. By combining not to take apprentices they can not only engross the employment, but reduce the whole manufacture into a sort of slavery to themselves, and raise the price of their labour above what is due to the nature of their work.

The inhabitants of the country, dispersed in distant places, cannot easily combine together.[47] They have not only never been incorporated, but the corporation spirit never has prevailed among them. No apprenticeship has ever been thought necessary to qualify for husbandry, the great trade of the country. After what are called the fine arts, and the liberal professions, however, there is perhaps no trade which requires so great a variety of knowledge and experience. The innumerable volumes which have been written upon it in all languages, may satisfy us, that among the wisest and most learned nations, it has never been regarded as a matter very easily understood. And from all those volumes we shall in vain attempt to collect that knowledge of its various and complicated operations, which is commonly possessed even by the common farmer; how contemptuously soever the very contemptible authors of some of them may sometimes affect to speak of him. There is scarce any common mechanic trade, on the contrary, of which all the operations may not be as completely and distinctly explained in a pamphlet of a very few pages, as it is possible for words illustrated by figures to explain them. In the history of the arts, now publishing by the French academy of

and difficult to those of the country, who are dispersed and not governed by the corporation spirit. No apprenticeship is prescribed for farming, though a difficult art,

[47] [Below, p. 832.]

sciences,[48] several of them are actually explained in this manner. The direction of operations, besides, which must be varied with every change of the weather, as well as with many other accidents, requires much more judgment and discretion, than that of those which are always the same or very nearly the same.

Not only the art of the farmer, the general direction of the operations of husbandry, but many inferior branches of country labour, require much more skill and experience than the greater part of mechanic trades. The man who works upon brass and iron, works with instruments and upon materials of which the temper is always the same, or very nearly the same. But the man who ploughs the ground with a team of horses or oxen, works with instruments of which the health, strength, and temper, are very different upon different occasions. The condition of the materials which he works upon too is as variable as that of the instruments which he works with, and both require to be managed with much judgment and discretion. The common ploughman, though generally regarded as the pattern of stupidity and ignorance, is seldom defective in this judgment and discretion. He is less accustomed, indeed, to social intercourse than the mechanic who lives in a town. His voice and language are more uncouth and more difficult to be understood by those who are not used to them. His understanding, however, being accustomed to consider a greater variety of objects, is generally much superior to that of the other, whose whole attention from morning till night is commonly occupied in performing one or two very simple operations. How much the lower ranks of people in the country are really superior to those of the town, is well known to every man whom either business or curiosity has led to converse much with both.[49] In China and Indostan accordingly both the rank and the wages of

or for the inferior branches of country labour, which require more skill than most mechanic trades.

[48] [*Descriptions des Arts et Métiers faites ou approuvées par Messieurs de l'Académie Royale des Sciences*, 1761–88.]

[49] [*Lectures*, p. 255.]

country labourers are said to be superior to those of the greater part of artificers and manufacturers. They would probably be so everywhere, if corporation laws and the corporation spirit did not prevent it.

The superiority which the industry of the towns has everywhere in Europe over that of the country, is not altogether ow-

The superiority of town industry is enhanced by other regulations, such as high duties on foreign manufactures.

ing to corporations and corporation laws. It is supported by many other regulations. The high duties upon foreign manufactures and upon all goods imported by alien merchants, all tend to the same purpose. Corporation laws enable the inhabitants of towns to raise their prices, without fearing to be under-sold by the free competition of their own coun-

trymen. Those other regulations secure them equally against that of foreigners. The enhancement of price occasioned by both is everywhere finally paid by the landlords, farmers, and labourers of the country, who have seldom opposed the establishment of such monopolies. They have commonly neither inclination nor fitness to enter into combinations; and the clamour and sophistry of merchants and manufacturers easily persuade them that the private interest of a part, and of a subordinate part of the society, is the general interest of the whole.

In Great Britain the superiority of the industry of the towns over that of the country, seems to have been greater formerly

The superiority has declined in Great Britain.

than in the present times. The wages of country labour approach nearer to those of manufacturing labour, and the profits of stock employed in agriculture to those of trading

and manufacturing stock, than they are said to have done in the last century, or in the beginning of the present. This change may be regarded as the necessary, though very late consequence of the extraordinary encouragement given to the industry of the towns. The stock accumulated in them comes in time to be so great, that it can no longer be employed with the ancient profit in that species of industry which is peculiar to them. That industry has its limits like every other; and the increase of stock, by increasing the competition, necessarily reduces the profit. The lowering of profit in the town forces out stock to the country, where, by creating a new demand for country labour, it necessarily raises its wages. It then spreads itself, if I may say so, over the face of the land, and by being employed in agriculture is in part restored to the country, at the expence of which, in a great measure, it had originally been accumulated in the town. That every-where in Europe the greatest improvements of the country have been owing to such overflowings of the stock originally accumulated in the towns, I shall endeavour to show hereafter;[50] and at the same time to demonstrate, that though some countries have by this course attained to a considerable degree of opulence, it is in itself necessarily slow, uncertain, liable to be disturbed and interrupted by innumerable accidents, and in every respect contrary to the order of nature and of reason. The interests, prejudices, laws and customs which have given occasion to it, I shall endeavour to explain as fully and distinctly as I can in the third and fourth books of this inquiry.

People of the same trade seldom meet together, even for merriment and diversion, but the conversation ends in a conspiracy against the public, or in some contrivance to raise prices. It is impossible indeed to prevent such meetings, by any law which either could be executed, or would be consistent with liberty and justice. But though the law cannot hinder people of the same trade from sometimes assembling together, it ought to do nothing to facilitate such assemblies; much less to render them necessary.

Meetings of people in the same trade ought not to be facilitated,

A regulation which obliges all those of the same trade in a particular town to enter their names and places of abode in a public register, facilitates such assemblies. It connects individuals who might never otherwise be known to one another, and gives every man of the trade a direction where to find every other man of it.

as by registration of traders,

A regulation which enables those of the same trade to tax

---

[50] [Below, pp. 519–535.]

by the establishment of funds for the sick, widows and orphans,

themselves in order to provide for their poor, their sick, their widows and orphans, by giving them a common interest to manage, renders such assemblies necessary.

An incorporation not only renders them necessary, but makes the act of the majority binding upon the whole. In a free trade an effectual combination cannot be es-

or by incorporation.

tablished but by the unanimous consent of every single trader,[51] and it cannot last longer than every single trader continues of the same mind. The majority of a corporation can enact a bye-law with proper penalties, which will limit the competition more effectually and more durably than any voluntary combination whatever.

The pretence that corporations are necessary for the better government of the trade, is without any foundation. The real

Corporations are unnecessary, and corrupt the workmen.

and effectual discipline which is exercised over a workman, is not that of his corporation, but that of his customers. It is the fear of losing their employment which restrains his frauds and corrects his negligence. An

exclusive corporation necessarily weakens the force of this discipline. A particular set of workmen must then be employed, let them behave well or ill. It is upon this account, that in many large incorporated towns no tolerable workmen are to be found, even in some of the most necessary trades. If you would have your work tolerably executed, it must be done in the suburbs, where the workmen, having no exclusive privilege, have nothing but their character to depend upon, and you must then smuggle it into the town as well as you can.

It is in this manner that the policy of Europe, by restraining the competition in some employments to a smaller number than would otherwise be disposed to enter into them, occasions a very important inequality in the whole of the advantages and disadvantages of the different employments of labour and stock.

[51] [Ed. 1 reads "single member of it" here and in the next line.]

(2) The policy of Europe increases competition in some trades.

Secondly, The policy of Europe, by increasing the competition in some employments beyond what it naturally would be, occasions another inequality of an opposite kind in the whole of the advantages and disadvantages of the different employments of labour and stock.

It has been considered as of so much importance that a proper number of young people should be educated for certain

It cheapens the education of the clergy and thereby reduces their earnings;

professions, that, sometimes the public, and sometimes the piety of private founders have established many pensions, scholarships, exhibitions, bursaries, &c. for this purpose, which draw many more people into

those trades than could otherwise pretend to follow them. In all christian countries, I believe, the education of the greater part of churchmen is paid for in this manner. Very few of them are educated altogether at their own expence. The long, tedious, and expensive education, therefore, of those who are, will not always procure them a suitable reward, the church being crowded with people who, in order to get employment, are willing to accept of a much smaller recompence than what such an education would otherwise have entitled them to; and in this manner the competition of the poor takes away the reward of the rich. It would be indecent, no doubt, to compare either a curate or a chaplain with a journeyman in any common trade. The pay of a curate or chaplain, however, may very properly be considered as of the same nature with the wages of a journeyman. They are, all three, paid for their work according to the contract which they may happen to make with their respective superiors. Till after the middle of the fourteenth century, five merks, containing about as much silver as ten pounds of our present money, was in England the usual pay of a curate[52] or stipendiary parish priest, as we find it regulated by the decrees of several different national councils.[53] At the same period four pence a day, contain-

[52] [Eds. 4 and 5 erroneously insert "a" here.]

[53] [According to Richard Burn's *Ecclesiastical Law*, 1763, *s.v.* Curates, six marks

ing the same quantity of silver as a shilling of our present money, was declared to be the pay of a master mason, and three pence a day, equal to nine pence of our present money, that of a journeyman mason.[54] The wages of both these labourers, therefore, supposing them to have been constantly employed, were much superior to those of the curate. The wages of the master mason, supposing him to have been without employment one third of the year, would have fully equalled them. By the 12th of Queen Anne, c. 12, it is declared, "That whereas for want of sufficient maintenance and encouragement to curates, the cures have in several places been meanly supplied, the bishop is, therefore, empowered to appoint by writing under his hand and seal a sufficient certain stipend or allowance, not exceeding fifty and not less than twenty pounds a year."[55] Forty pounds a year is reckoned at present very good pay for a curate, and notwithstanding this act of parliament, there are many curacies under twenty pounds a year. There are journeymen shoemakers in London who earn forty pounds a year, and there is scarce an industrious workman of any kind in that metropolis who does not earn more than twenty. This last sum indeed does not exceed what is frequently earned by common labourers in many country parishes. Whenever the law has attempted to regulate the wages of workmen, it has always been rather to lower them than to raise them. But the law has upon many occasions attempted to raise the wages of curates, and for the dignity of the church, to oblige the rectors of parishes to give them more than the wretched maintenance which they themselves might be willing to accept of. And in both cases the law seems to have been equally ineffectual, and has never either been able to raise the wages of curates, or to sink those of labourers to the degree that was intended; because it has never been able to hinder either the one from being willing to accept

was the pay ordered by a constitution of Archbishop Islip till 1378, when it was raised to eight.]

[54] See the Statute of labourers, 25 Ed. III. [Below, pp. 241, 242. The note is not in ed. 1.]

[55] [The quotation is not intended to be *verbatim*, in spite of the inverted commas.]

of less than the legal allowance, on account of the indigence of their situation and the multitude of their competitors; or the other from receiving more, on account of the contrary competition of those who expected to derive either profit or pleasure from employing them.

The great benefices and other ecclesiastical dignities support the honour of the church, notwithstanding the mean circumstances of some of its inferior members. The respect paid to the profession too makes some compensation even to them for the meanness of their pecuniary recompence. In England, and in all Roman Catholic countries, the lottery of the church is in reality much more advantageous than is necessary. The example of the church of Scotland, of Geneva, and of several other protestant churches, may satisfy us, that in so creditable a profession, in which education is so easily procured, the hopes of much more moderate benefices will draw a sufficient number of learned, decent, and respectable men into holy orders.

so that it is only the great benefices, etc., which support the honour of the English and Roman Catholic Churches.

In professions in which there are no benefices, such as law and physic, if an equal proportion of people were educated at the public expence, the competition would soon be so great, as to sink very much their pecuniary reward. It might then not be worth any man's while to educate his son to either of those professions at his own expence. They would be entirely abandoned to such as had been educated by those public charities, whose numbers and necessities would oblige them in general to content themselves with a very miserable recompence, to the entire degradation of the now respectable professions of law and physic.

The same cause, if present, would lower the reward of lawyers and physicians,

That unprosperous race of men commonly called men of letters, is pretty much in the situation which lawyers and physicians probably would be in upon the foregoing supposition. In every part of Europe the greater part of them have been educated for the church, but have been hindered by different reasons from

as it has done that of men of letters,

entering into holy orders. They have generally, therefore, been educated at the public expence, and their numbers are everywhere so great as commonly to reduce the price of their labour to a very paultry recompence.

Before the invention of the art of printing, the only employment by which a man of letters could make any thing by his talents, was that of a public or private[56] teacher, or by communicating to other people the curious and useful knowledge which he had acquired himself: And this is still surely a more honourable, a more useful, and in general even a more profitable employment than that other of writing for a bookseller, to which the art of printing has given occasion. The time and study, the genius, knowledge, and application requisite to qualify an eminent teacher of the sciences, are at least equal to what is necessary for the greatest practitioners in law and physic. But the usual reward of the eminent teacher bears no proportion to that of the lawyer or physician; because the trade of the one is crowded with indigent people who have been brought up to it at the public expence; whereas those of the other two are incumbered with very few who have not been educated at their own. The usual recompence, however, of public and private teachers, small as it may appear, would undoubtedly be less than it is, if the competition of those yet more indigent men of letters who write for bread was not taken out of the market. Before the invention of the art of printing, a scholar and a beggar seem to have been terms very nearly synonymous. The different governors of the universities before that time appear to have often granted licences to their scholars to beg.[57]

In ancient times, before any charities of this kind had been established for the education of indigent people to the learned professions, the rewards of eminent teachers appear to have been much more considerable. Isocrates, in

and that of teachers,

who were much better paid in ancient times.

---

[56] [Ed. 1 does not contain "or private."]

[57] [Hume, *History*, ed. of 1773, vol. iii., p. 403, quotes 11 Hen. VII., c. 22, which forbids students to beg without permission from the chancellor.]

what is called his discourse against the sophists, reproaches the teachers of his own times with inconsistency. "They make the most magnificent promises to their scholars, says he, and undertake to teach them to be wise, to be happy, and to be just, and in return for so important a service they stipulate the paultry reward of four or five minæ. They who teach wisdom, continues he, ought certainly to be wise themselves; but if any man were[58] to sell such a bargain for such a price, he would be convicted of the most evident folly."[59] He certainly does not mean here to exaggerate the reward, and we may be assured that it was not less than he represents it. Four minæ were equal to thirteen pounds six shillings and eight pence: five minæ to sixteen pounds thirteen shillings and four pence. Something not less than the largest of those two sums, therefore, must at that time have been usually paid to the most eminent teachers at Athens. Isocrates himself demanded ten minæ,[60] or thirty-three pounds six shillings and eight pence, from each scholar. When he taught at Athens, he is said to have had an hundred scholars. I understand this to be the number whom he taught at one time, or who attended what we would call one course of lectures, a number which will not appear extraordinary from so great a city to so famous a teacher, who taught too what was at that time the most fashionable of all sciences, rhetoric. He must have made, therefore, by each course of lectures, a thousand minæ, or *3,333l. 6s. 8d.* A thousand minæ, accordingly, is said by Plutarch in another place, to have been his Didactron, or usual price of teaching.[61] Many other eminent teachers in

[58] [Eds. 1–3 read "was."]

[59] [§§ 3, 4. A very free but not incorrect translation. Arbuthnot, *Tables of Ancient Coins, Weights and Measures*, 2nd ed., 1754, p. 198, refers to but does not quote the passage as his authority for stating the reward of a sophist at four or five minæ. He treats the mina as equal to £3 4s. 7d., which at the rate of 62s. to the pound troy is considerably too low.]

[60] [Plutarch, *Demosthenes*, c. v., § 3; *Isocrates*, § 30.]

[61] [Arbuthnot, *Tables of Ancient Coins*, p. 198, says, "Isocrates had from his disciples a didactron or reward of 1, 000 minæ, £3,229 3s. 4d.," and quotes "Plut. in Isocrate," which says nothing about a "didactron," but only that Isocrates charged ten minæ and had 100 pupils.—§§ 9, 12, 30.]

those times appear to have acquired great fortunes. Gorgias made a present to the temple of Delphi of his own statue in solid gold.[62] We must not, I presume, suppose that it was as large as the life. His way of living, as well as that of Hippias and Protagoras, two other eminent teachers of those times, is represented by Plato as splendid even to ostentation.[63] Plato himself is said to have lived with a good deal of magnificence. Aristotle, after having been tutor to Alexander, and most munificently rewarded, as it is universally agreed, both by him and his father Philip,[64] thought it worth while, notwithstanding, to return to Athens, in order to resume the teaching of his school. Teachers of the sciences were probably in those times less common than they came to be in an age or two afterwards, when the competition had probably somewhat reduced both the price of their labour and the admiration for their persons. The most eminent of them, however, appear always to have enjoyed a degree of consideration much superior to any of the like profession in the present times. The Athenians sent Carneades the academic, and Diogenes the stoic, upon a solemn embassy to Rome; and though their city had then declined from its former grandeur, it was still an independent and considerable republic. Carneades too was a Babylonian by birth,[65] and as there never was a people more jealous of admitting foreigners to public offices than the Athenians, their consideration for him must have been very great.

Perhaps this cheapness of teaching is no disadvantage to the public.

This inequality is upon the whole, perhaps, rather advantageous than hurtful to the public. It may somewhat degrade the profession of a public teacher; but the cheapness of

[62] [This story is from Pliny, *H. N.*, xxxiii., cap. iv., who remarks, "Tantus erat docendae oratoriae quaestus," but the commentators point out that earlier authorities ascribe the erection of the statue not to Gorgias, but to the whole of Greece.]

[63] [It is difficult to discover on what passage this statement is based.]

[64] [Plutarch, *Alexander*.]

[65] [This is a slip. Carneades was a native of Cyrene, and it was his colleague Diogenes who was a Babylonian by birth.]

literary education is surely an advantage which greatly over-balances this trifling inconveniency. The public too might derive still greater benefit from it, if the constitution of those schools and colleges, in which education is carried on, was more reasonable than it is at present through the greater part of Europe.[66]

Thirdly, The policy of Europe, by obstructing the free circulation of labour and stock both from employment to employment, and from place to place, occasions in some cases a very inconvenient inequality in the whole of the advantages and disadvantages of their different employments.

(3) The policy of Europe obstructs the free circulation of labour.

The statute of apprenticeship[67] obstructs the free circulation of labour from one employment to another, even in the same place. The exclusive privileges of corporations obstruct it from one place to another, even in the same employment.

Apprenticeship and corporation privileges obstruct circulation from employment to employment and from place to place.

It frequently happens that while high wages are given to the workmen in one manufacture, those in another are obliged to content themselves with bare subsistence. The one is in an advancing state, and has, therefore, a continual demand for new hands: The other is in a declining state, and the super-abundance of hands is continually increasing. Those two manufactures may sometimes be in the same town, and sometimes in the same neighbourhood, without being able to lend the least assistance to one another. The statute of apprenticeship may oppose it in the one case, and both that and an exclusive corporation in the other. In many different manufactures, however, the operations are so much alike, that the workmen could easily change trades with one another, if those absurd laws did not hinder them. The arts

So that the changes of employment necessary to equalise wages are prevented.

[66] [Below, pp. 962–979.]

[67] [Above, p. 165.]

of weaving plain linen and plain silk, for example, are almost entirely the same. That of weaving plain woollen is somewhat different; but the difference is so insignificant, that either a linen or a silk weaver might become a tolerable workman in a very few days. If any of those three capital manufactures, therefore, were decaying, the workmen might find a resource in one of the other two which was in a more prosperous condition; and their wages would neither rise too high in the thriving, nor sink too low in the decaying manufacture. The linen manufacture indeed is, in England, by a particular statute,[68] open to every body; but as it is not much cultivated through the greater part of the country, it can afford no general resource to the workmen of other decaying manufactures, who, wherever the statute of apprenticeship takes place, have no other choice but either to come upon the parish, or to work as common labourers, for which, by their habits, they are much worse qualified than for any sort of manufacture that bears any resemblance to their own. They generally, therefore, chuse to come upon the parish.

Whatever obstructs the free circulation of labour from one employment to another, obstructs that of stock likewise; the quantity of stock which can be employed in any branch of business depending very much upon that of the[69] labour which can be employed in it. Corporation laws, however, give less obstruction to the free circulation of stock from one place to another than to that of labour. It is every-where much easier for a wealthy merchant to obtain the privilege of trading in a town corporate, than for a poor artificer to obtain that of working in it.

What obstructs the circulation of labour also obstructs that of stock.

The obstruction which corporation laws give to the free circulation of labour is common, I believe, to every part of Europe. That which is given to it by the poor laws is, so far as I know,[70] peculiar to England. It consists in the difficulty which a

[68] [15 Car. II., c. 15.]

[69] [Ed. 1 does not contain "the."]

[70] [Ed. 1 places the "is" here.]

In England the circulation of labour is further obstructed by the poor law. poor man finds in obtaining a settlement, or even in being allowed to exercise his industry in any parish but that to which he belongs. It is the labour of artificers and manufacturers only of which the free circulation is obstructed by corporation laws. The difficulty of obtaining settlements obstructs even that of common labour. It may be worth while to give some account of the rise, progress, and present state of this disorder, the greatest perhaps of any in the police of England.

When by the destruction of monasteries the poor had been deprived of the charity of those religious houses, after some *Each parish was to support its own poor under 43 Eliz., c. 2;* other ineffectual attempts for their relief, it was enacted by the 43d of Elizabeth, c. 2. that every parish should be bound to provide for its own poor; and that overseers of the poor should be annually appointed, who, with the churchwardens, should raise, by a parish rate, competent sums for this purpose.

By this statute the necessity of providing for their own poor was indispensably imposed upon every parish. Who were to be considered as the poor of each parish, became, therefore, a *these were determined by 13 and 14 Car. II. to be such as had resided forty days, within which time, however, a new inhabitant might be removed.* question of some importance. This question, after some variation, was at last determined by the 13th and 14th of Charles II.[71] when it was enacted, that forty days undisturbed residence should gain any person a settlement in any parish; but that within that time it should be lawful for two justices of the peace, upon complaint made by the churchwardens or overseers of the poor, to remove any new inhabitant to the parish where he was last legally settled;[72] unless he either rented a tenement of ten pounds a year, or could give such security for the discharge of the parish

[71] [C. 12.]

[72] [This account of the provisions of the Acts regarding settlement, though not incorrect, inverts the order of the ideas which prompted them. The preamble com-

where he was then living, as those justices should judge sufficient.

Some frauds, it is said, were committed in consequence of this statute; parish officers sometimes bribing their own poor

Notice in writing was required from the new inhabitant by 1 James II.

to go clandestinely to another parish and by keeping themselves concealed for forty days to gain a settlement there, to the discharge of that to which they properly belonged. It was enacted, therefore, by the 1st of James II.[73] that the forty days undisturbed residence of any person necessary to gain a settlement, should be accounted only from the time of his delivering notice in writing, of the place of his abode and the number of his family, to one of the churchwardens or overseers of the parish where he came to dwell.

But parish officers, it seems, were not always more honest with regard to their own, than they had been with regard to

Such notice was to be published in church under 3 W. III.

other parishes, and sometimes connived at such intrusions, receiving the notice, and taking no proper steps in consequence of it. As every person in a parish, therefore, was supposed to have an interest to prevent as much as possible their being burdened by such intruders, it was further enacted by the 3d of William III.[74] that the forty days residence should be accounted only from the publication of such notice in writing on Sunday in the church, immediately after divine service.

plains that owing to defects in the law "poor people are not restrained from going from one parish to another and therefore do endeavour to settle themselves in those parishes where there is the best stock," and so forth, and the Act therefore gives the justices power, "within forty days after any such person or persons coming so to settle as aforesaid," to remove them "to such parish where he or they were last legally settled either as a native, householder, sojourner, apprentice or servant for the space of forty days at the least." The use of the term "settlement" seems to have originated with this Act.]

[73] [C. 17, "An act for reviving and continuance of several acts." The reason given is that "such poor persons at their first coming to a parish do commonly conceal themselves." Nothing is said either here or in Burn's *Poor Law* or *Justice of the Peace* about parish officers bribing their poor to go to another parish.]

[74] [3 W. and M., c. 11, § 3.]

"After all," says Doctor Burn, "this kind of settlement, by continuing forty days after publication of notice in writing, is very seldom obtained; and the design of the acts is not so much for gaining of settlements, as for the avoiding of them by persons coming into a parish clandestinely: for the giving of notice is only putting a force upon the parish to remove. But if a person's situation is such, that it is doubtful whether he is actually removeable or not, he shall by giving of notice compel the parish either to allow him a settlement uncontested, by suffering him to continue forty days; or, by removing him, to try the right."[75]

This statute, therefore, rendered it almost impracticable for a poor man to gain a new settlement in the old way, by forty

There were four other ways of gaining a settlement,

days inhabitancy. But that it might not appear to preclude altogether the common people of one parish from ever establishing themselves with security in another, it appointed four other ways by which a settlement might be gained without any notice delivered or published. The first was, by being taxed to parish rates and paying them; the second, by being elected into an annual parish office, and serving in it a year; the third, by serving an apprenticeship in the parish; the fourth, by being hired into service there for a year, and continuing in the same service during the whole of it.[76]

Nobody can gain a settlement by either of the two first ways, but by the public deed of the whole parish, who are

two of which were impossible to all poor men,

too well aware of the consequences to adopt any newcomer who has nothing but his labour to support him, either by taxing him to parish rates, or by electing him into a parish office.

No married man can well gain any settlement in either of the two last ways. An apprentice is scarce ever married; and it is expressly enacted, that no married servant shall gain any set-

[75] [Richard Burn, *Justice of the Peace*, 1764, vol. ii., p. 253.]

[76] [§§ 6, 8.]

and the other two to all married men, tlement by being hired for a year.[77] The principal effect of introducing settlement by service, has been to put out in a great measure the old fashion of hiring for a year, which before had been so customary in England, that even at this day, if no particular term is agreed upon, the law intends that every servant is hired for a year. But masters are not always willing to give their servants a settlement by hiring them in this manner; and servants are not always willing to be so hired, because, as every last settlement discharges all the foregoing, they might thereby lose their original settlement in the places of their nativity, the habitation of their parents and relations.

No independent workman, it is evident, whether labourer or artificer, is likely to gain any new settlement either by appren-

and to all independent workmen. ticeship or by service. When such a person, therefore, carried his industry to a new parish, he was liable to be removed, how healthy and industrious soever, at the caprice of any churchwarden or overseer, unless he either rented a tenement of ten pounds a year, a thing impossible for one who has nothing but his labour to live by; or could give such security for the discharge of the parish as two justices of the peace should judge sufficient. What security they shall require, indeed, is left altogether to their discretion; but they cannot well require less than thirty pounds, it having been enacted, that the purchase even of a freehold estate of less than thirty pounds value, shall not gain any person a settlement, as not being sufficient for the discharge of the parish.[78] But this is a security which scarce any man who lives by labour can give; and much greater security is frequently demanded.

In order to restore in some measure that free circulation of labour which those different statutes had almost entirely taken away,[79] the invention of certificates was fallen upon.

[77] [§ 7 confines settlement by service to unmarried persons without children.]

[78] [By 9 Geo. I., c. 7.]

[79] [The Act, 13 & 14 Car. II., c. 12, giving the justices power to remove the immi-

By the 8th and 9th of William III.[80] it was enacted, that if any person should bring a certificate from the parish where he was last legally settled, subscribed by the churchwardens and overseers of the poor, and allowed by two justices of the peace, that every other parish should be obliged to receive him; that he should not be removeable merely upon account of his being likely to become chargeable, but only upon his becoming actually chargeable, and that then the parish which granted the certificate should be obliged to pay the expence both of his maintenance and of his removal. And in order to give the most perfect security to the parish where such certificated man should come to reside, it was further enacted by the same statute,[81] that he should gain no settlement there by any means whatever, except either by renting a tenement of ten pounds a year, or by serving upon his own account in an annual parish office for one whole year; and consequently neither by notice, nor by service, nor by apprenticeship, nor by paying parish rates. By the 12th of Queen Anne too, stat. I. c. 18. it was further enacted, that neither the

Certificates were invented to enable persons to reside in a parish without being immediately removable and without gaining a settlement.

grant within forty days was certainly obstructive to the free circulation of labour, but the other statutes referred to in the text, by making the attainment of a settlement more difficult, would appear to have made it less necessary for a parish to put in force the power of removal, and therefore to have assisted rather than obstructed the free circulation of labour. The poor law commissioners of 1834, long after the power of removal had been abolished in 1795, found the law of settlement a great obstruction to the free circulation of labour, because men were afraid of gaining a new settlement, not because a new settlement was denied them.]

[80] [C. 30, "An act for supplying some defects in the laws for the relief of the poor of this kingdom." The preamble recites, "Forasmuch as many poor persons chargeable to the parish, township or place where they live, merely for want of work, would in any other place when sufficient employment is to be had maintain themselves and families without being burdensome to any parish, township or place." But certificates were invented long before this. The Act 13 & 14 Car. II., c. 12, provides for their issue to persons going into another parish for harvest or any other kind of work, and the preamble of 8 & 9 W. III., c. 30, shows that they were commonly given. Only temporary employment, however, was contemplated, and, on the expiration of the job, the certificated person became removable.]

[81] [Rather by the explanatory Act, 9 & 10 W. III., c. 11.]

servants nor apprentices of such certificated man should gain
any settlement in the parish where he resided under such certificate.[82]

How far this invention has restored that free circulation of
labour which the preceding statutes had almost entirely taken
away, we may learn from the following very judicious observa-

*Certificates were
required by the
new parish but re-
fused by the old.*

tion of Doctor Burn. "It is obvious," says he,
"that there are divers good reasons for requiring certificates with persons coming to
settle in any place; namely, that persons residing under them can gain no settlement,
neither by apprenticeship, nor by service, nor by giving notice,
nor by paying parish rates; that they can settle neither apprentices nor servants; that if they become chargeable, it is certainly known whither to remove them, and the parish shall be
paid for the removal, and for their maintenance in the mean
time; and that if they fall sick, and cannot be removed, the
parish which gave the certificate must maintain them: none of
all which can be without a certificate. Which reasons will hold
proportionally for parishes not granting certificates in ordinary cases; for it is far more than an equal chance, but that they
will have the certificated persons again, and in a worse condition."[83] The moral of this observation seems to be, that certificates ought always to be required by the parish where any poor
man comes to reside, and that they ought very seldom to be
granted by that which he proposes to leave. "There is somewhat of hardship in this matter of certificates," says the same
very intelligent Author, in his History of the Poor Laws, "by
putting it in the power of a parish officer, to imprison a man as
it were for life; however inconvenient it may be for him to continue at that place where he has had the misfortune to acquire
what is called a settlement, or whatever advantage he may propose to himself by living elsewhere."[84]

[82] [All these statutes are conveniently collected in Richard Burn's *History of the
Poor Laws*, 1764, pp. 94–100.]

[83] [Burn, *Justice of the Peace*, 1764, vol. ii., p. 274.]

[84] [Burn, *History of the Poor Laws*, 1764, pp. 235, 236, where it is observed that

Though a certificate carries along with it no testimonial of good behaviour, and certifies nothing but that the person belongs to the parish to which he really does belong, it is altogether discretionary in the parish officers either to grant or to refuse it. A mandamus was once moved for, says Doctor Burn, to compel the churchwardens and overseers to sign a certificate; but the court of King's Bench rejected the motion as a very strange attempt.[85]

The courts declined to force overseers to give a certificate.

The very unequal price of labour which we frequently find in England in places at no great distance from one another, is probably owing to the obstruction which the law of settlements gives to a poor man who would carry his industry from one parish to another without a certificate. A single man, indeed, who is healthy and industrious, may sometimes reside by sufferance without one; but a man with a wife and family who should attempt to do so, would in most parishes be sure of being removed, and if the single man should afterwards marry, he would generally be removed likewise.[86] The scarcity of hands in one parish, therefore, cannot always be relieved by their superabundance in another, as it is constantly in Scotland, and, I believe, in all other countries where there is no difficulty of settlement. In such countries, though wages may sometimes rise a little in the neighbourhood of a great town, or wherever else there is an extraordinary demand for labour, and sink gradually as the distance from such places increases, till they fall back to the common rate of the country; yet we never meet with those sudden and unaccountable differences in the wages of neighbour-

This law is the cause of the very unequal price of labour in England,

"it was the easy method of obtaining a settlement by a residency of forty days that brought parishes into a state of war against the poor and against one another," and that if settlement were reduced to the place of birth or of inhabitancy for one or more years, certificates would be got rid of.]

[85] [Burn, *Justice*, vol. ii., p. 209. The date given is 1730.]

[86] [Since the fact of the father having no settlement would not free the parish from the danger of having at some future time to support the children.]

ing places which we sometimes find in England, where it is often more difficult for a poor man to pass the artificial boundary of a parish, than an arm of the sea or a ridge of high mountains, natural boundaries which sometimes separate very distinctly different rates of wages in other countries.

To remove a man who has committed no misdemeanour from the parish where he chuses to reside, is an evident violation of natural liberty and justice. The common people of England, however, so jealous of their liberty, but like the common people of most other countries never rightly understanding wherein it consists, have now for more than a century together suffered themselves to be exposed to this oppression without a remedy. Though men of reflection too have sometimes complained of the law of settlements as a public grievance; yet it has never been the object of any general popular clamour, such as that against general warrants, an abusive practice undoubtedly, but such a one as was not likely to occasion any general oppression. There is scarce a poor man in England of forty years of age, I will venture to say, who has not in some part of his life felt himself most cruelly oppressed[87] by this ill-contrived law of settlements.

and an evident violation of natural liberty, though tamely submitted to.

I shall conclude this long chapter with observing, that though anciently it was usual to rate wages, first by general laws extending over the whole kingdom, and afterwards by particular orders of the justices of peace in every particular county, both these practices have now gone entirely into disuse. "By the experience of above four hundred years," says Doctor Burn, "it seems time to lay aside all endeavours to bring under strict regulations, what in

Wages were anciently rated by law or by justices of peace.

---

[87] [Some evidence in support of this assertion would have been acceptable. Sir Frederic M. Eden, *State of the Poor*, 1797, vol. i., pp. 296–298, may be consulted on the other side. William Hay's *Remarks on the Laws Relating to the Poor*, 1735, which Eden regards as giving a very exaggerated view of the obstruction caused by the law of settlement, was in the Edinburgh Advocates' Library in 1776, and Adam Smith may have seen it.]

its own nature seems incapable of minute limitation: for if all persons in the same kind of work were to receive equal wages, there would be no emulation, and no room left for industry or ingenuity."[88]

Particular acts of parliament, however, still attempt sometimes to regulate wages in particular trades and in particular

London taylors' wages are still rated by law.

places. Thus the 8th of George III.[89] prohibits under heavy penalties all master taylors in London, and five miles round it, from giving, and their workmen from accepting, more than two shillings and sevenpence halfpenny a day, except in the case of a general mourning. Whenever the legislature attempts to regulate the differences between masters and their workmen, its counsellors are always the masters. When the regulation, therefore, is in favour of the workmen, it is always just and equitable; but it is sometimes otherwise when in favour of the masters. Thus the law which obliges the masters in several different trades to pay their workmen in money and not in goods, is quite just and equitable.[90] It imposes no real hardship upon the masters. It only obliges them to pay that value in money, which they pretended to pay, but did not al-

---

[88] [*History of the Poor Laws*, p. 130, loosely quoted. After "limitation" the passage runs, "as thereby it leaves no room for industry or ingenuity; for if all persons in the same kind of work were to receive equal wages there would be no emulation."]

[89] [7 Geo. I., stat. 1, c. 13, was passed, according to its preamble, because journeymen taylors had lately departed from their service without just cause, and had entered into "combinations to advance their wages to unreasonable prices, and lessen their usual hours of work, which is of evil example, and manifestly tends to the prejudice of trade, to the encouragement of idleness, and to the great increase of the poor." It prescribed hours, 6 A.M. to 8 P.M., and wages, 2s. a day in the second quarter and 1s. 8d. for the rest of the year. Quarter sessions might alter these rates. This Act was amended by 8 Geo. III., c. 17, under which the hours were to be 6 A.M. to 7 P.M., and wages a maximum of 2s. 7½d. a day. Masters inside the area were forbidden to pay more to workers outside the area than was allowed by the Act within it.]

[90] [1 Ann., stat. 2, c. 18, applied to workmen in the woollen, linen, fustian, cotton and iron manufacture; 13 Geo. II., c. 8, to manufacturers of gloves, boots, shoes and other leather wares. The second of these Acts only prohibits ruck payments when made without the request and consent of the workmen.]

ways really pay, in goods. This law is in favour of the work-men; but the 8th of George III. is in favour of the masters. When masters combine together in order to reduce the wages of their workmen, they commonly enter into a private bond or agreement, not to give more than a certain wage under a cer-tain penalty. Were the workmen to enter into a contrary combi-nation of the same kind, not to accept of a certain wage under a certain penalty, the law would punish them very severely; and if it dealt impartially, it would treat the masters in the same manner. But the 8th of George III. enforces by law that very regulation which masters sometimes attempt to establish by such combinations. The complaint of the workmen, that it puts the ablest and most industrious upon the same footing with an ordinary workman, seems perfectly well founded.

In ancient times too it was usual to attempt to regulate the profits of merchants and other dealers, by rating the price both

Attempts were also made to regu-late profits by fixing prices, and the assize of bread still remains.

of provisions and other goods. The assize of bread is, so far as I know, the only remnant of this ancient usage. Where there is an ex-clusive corporation, it may perhaps be proper to regulate the price of the first neces-sary of life. But where there is none, the competition will regulate it much better than any assize. The method of fixing the assize of bread established by the 31st of George II.[91] could not be put in practice in Scotland, on account of a defect in the law; its execution depending upon the office of clerk of the market, which does not exist there. This defect was not remedied till the 3d of George III.[92] The want of an as-size occasioned no sensible inconveniency, and the establish-ment of one in the few places where it has yet taken place, has produced no sensible advantage. In the greater part of the towns of Scotland, however, there is an incorporation of bakers who claim exclusive privileges, though they are not very strictly guarded.

The proportion between the different rates both of wages

[91] [C. 29.]

[92] [C. 6. The preamble relates the defect.]

and profit in the different employments of labour and stock, seems not to be much affected, as has already been observed,[93] by the riches or poverty, the advancing, stationary, or declining state of the society. Such revolutions in the public welfare, though they affect the general rates both of wages and profit, must in the end affect them equally in all different employments. The proportion between them, therefore, must remain the same, and cannot well be altered, at least for any considerable time, by any such revolutions.

The inequalities of wages and profits are not much affected by the advancing or declining state of the society.

---

[93] [Above, p. 89.]

CHAPTER XI

OF THE RENT OF LAND

RENT, CONSIDERED as the price paid for the use of land, is naturally the highest which the tenant can afford to pay in the actual circumstances of the land. In adjusting the terms of the lease, the landlord endeavours to leave him no greater share of the produce than what is sufficient to keep up the stock from which he furnishes the seed, pays the labour, and purchases and maintains the cattle and other instruments of husbandry, together with the ordinary profits of farming stock in the neighbourhood. This is evidently the smallest share with which the tenant can content himself without being a loser, and the landlord seldom means to leave him any more. Whatever part of the produce, or, what is the same thing, whatever part of its price, is over and above this share, he naturally endeavours to reserve to himself as the rent of his land, which is evidently the highest the tenant can afford to pay in the actual circumstances of the land. Sometimes, indeed, the liberality, more frequently the ignorance, of the landlord, makes him accept of somewhat less than this portion; and sometimes too, though more rarely, the ignorance of the tenant makes him undertake to pay somewhat more, or to content himself with somewhat less, than the ordinary profits of farming stock in the neighbourhood. This portion, however, may still be considered as the natural rent of land, or the rent for which it is naturally meant that land should for the most part be let.

Rent is the produce which is over what is necessary to pay the farmer ordinary profit.

The rent of land, it may be thought, is frequently no more than a reasonable profit or interest for the stock laid out by the landlord upon its improvement. This, no doubt, may be partly

It is not merely interest on stock laid out in improvements,

the case upon some occasions; for it can scarce ever be more than partly the case. The landlord demands a rent even for unimproved land, and the supposed interest or profit upon the expence of improvement is generally an addition to this original rent: Those improvements, besides, are not always made by the stock of the landlord, but sometimes by that of the tenant. When the lease comes to be renewed, however, the landlord commonly demands the same augmentation of rent, as if they had been all made by his own.

He sometimes demands rent for what is altogether incapable of human improvement. Kelp is a species of sea-weed,

and is sometimes obtained for land incapable of improvement, such as rocks where kelp grows;

which, when burnt, yields an alkaline salt, useful for making glass, soap, and for several other purposes. It grows in several parts of Great Britain, particularly in Scotland, upon such rocks only as lie within the high water mark, which are twice every day covered with the sea, and of which the produce, therefore, was never augmented by human industry. The landlord, however, whose estate is bounded by a kelp shore of this kind, demands a rent for it as much as for his corn fields.

The sea in the neighbourhood of the islands of Shetland is more than commonly abundant in fish, which make a great part

and for the opportunity to fish.

of the subsistence of their inhabitants. But in order to profit by the produce of the water, they must have a habitation upon the neighbouring land. The rent of the landlord is in proportion, not to what the farmer can make by the land, but to what he can make both by the land and by[1] the water. It is partly paid in sea-fish; and one of the very few instances in which rent makes a part of the price of that commodity, is to be found in that country.

The rent of land, therefore, considered as the price paid for the use of the land, is naturally a monopoly price. It is not at all

---

[1] ["By" appears first in ed. 3.]

proportioned to what the landlord may have laid out upon the
improvement of the land, or to what he can
afford to take; but to what the farmer can afford to give.

It is therefore a monopoly price.

Such parts only of the produce of land can commonly be
brought to market of which the ordinary price is sufficient to
replace the stock which must be employed in
bringing them thither, together with its ordinary profits. If the ordinary price is more
than this, the surplus part of it will naturally
go to the rent of the land. If it is not more,
though the commodity may be brought to
market, it can afford no rent to the landlord.
Whether the price is, or is not more, depends upon the demand.

Whether particular parts of produce fetch a price sufficient to yield a rent depends on the demand.

There are some parts of the produce of land for which the
demand must always be such as to afford a greater price than
what is sufficient to bring them to market;
and there are others for which it either may
or may not be such as to afford this greater
price. The former must always afford a rent
to that landlord. The latter sometimes may,
and sometimes may not, according to different circumstances.

Some parts are always in sufficient demand; others sometimes are and sometimes are not.

Rent, it is to be observed, therefore, enters into the composition of the price of commodities in a different way from
wages and profit. High or low wages and
profit, are the causes of high or low price;
high or low rent is the effect of it. It is because high or low wages and profit must be
paid, in order to bring a particular commod-
ity to market, that its price is high or low. But it is because its
price is high or low; a great deal more, or very little more, or
no more, than what is sufficient to pay those wages and profit,
that it affords a high rent, or a low rent, or no rent at all.

Wages and profit are causes of price; rent is an effect.

The particular consideration, first, of those parts of the produce of land which always afford some rent; secondly, of those
which sometimes may and sometimes may not afford rent; and,
thirdly, of the variations which, in the different periods of im-

The chapter is divided into three parts.

provement, naturally take place, in the relative value of those two different sorts of rude produce, when compared both with one another and with manufactured commodities, will divide this chapter into three parts.

PART I

OF THE PRODUCE OF LAND WHICH ALWAYS AFFORDS RENT

As men, like all other animals, naturally multiply in proportion to the means of their subsistence, food is always, more or less, in demand. It can always purchase or command a greater or smaller quantity of labour, and somebody can always be found

Food can always purchase as much labour as it can maintain.

who is willing to do something in order to obtain it. The quantity of labour, indeed, which it can purchase, is not always equal to what it could maintain, if managed in the most economical manner, on account of the

high wages which are sometimes given to labour. But it can always purchase such a quantity of labour as it can maintain, according to the rate at which that sort of labour is commonly maintained in the neighbourhood.

But land, in almost any situation, produces a greater quan-

Almost all land produces more than enough food to maintain the labour and pay the profits, and therefore yields rent.

tity of food than what is sufficient to maintain all the labour necessary for bringing it to market, in the most liberal way in which that labour is ever maintained. The surplus too is always more than sufficient to replace the stock which employed that labour, together with its profits. Something, therefore, always remains for a rent to the landlord.

The most desart moors in Norway and Scotland produce some sort of pasture for cattle, of which the milk and the increase are always more than sufficient, not only to maintain all the labour necessary for tending them, and to pay the ordinary profit to the farmer or owner of the herd or flock; but to afford some small rent to the landlord. The rent increases in proportion to the goodness of the pasture. The same extent of ground not only maintains a greater number of cattle, but as they are brought within a smaller compass, less labour becomes requisite to tend them, and to collect their produce. The landlord gains both ways; by the increase of the produce, and by the diminution of the labour which must be maintained out of it.

The rent of land not only varies with its fertility, whatever be its produce, but with its situation, whatever be its fertility.[2]

The rent varies with situation as well as with fertility. Land in the neighbourhood of a town gives a greater rent than land equally fertile in a distant part of the country. Though it may cost no more labour to cultivate the one than the other, it must always cost more to bring the produce of the distant land to market. A greater quantity of labour, therefore, must be maintained out of it; and the surplus, from which are drawn both the profit of the farmer and the rent of the landlord, must be diminished. But in remote parts of the country the rate of profits, as has already been shown,[3] is generally higher than in the neighbourhood of a large town. A smaller proportion of this diminished surplus, therefore, must belong to the landlord.

Good roads, canals, and navigable rivers, by diminishing the expence of carriage, put the remote parts of the country *Good roads, etc., diminish differences of rent.* more nearly upon a level with those in the neighbourhood of the town. They are upon that account the greatest of all improvements. They encourage the cultivation of the remote, which must always be the most extensive circle of the country. They are advantageous to the town, by breaking down the monopoly of the country in its neighbourhood. They are advantageous even to that part of the country. Though they introduce some rival commodities into the old market, they open many new markets to its produce. Monopoly, besides, is a

[2] [Eds. 1 and 2 read "The rent of land varies with its fertility, whatever be its produce, and with its situation, whatever be its fertility."]

[3] [Above, p. 125–126.]

great enemy to good management, which can never be universally established but in consequence of that free and universal competition which forces everybody to have recourse to it for the sake of self-defence. It is not more than fifty years ago, that some of the counties in the neighbourhood of London petitioned the parliament against the extension of the turnpike roads into the remoter counties. Those remoter counties, they pretended, from the cheapness of labour, would be able to sell their grass and corn cheaper in the London market than themselves, and would thereby reduce their rents, and ruin their cultivation. Their rents, however, have risen, and their cultivation has been improved since that time.

A corn field of moderate fertility produces a much greater quantity of food for man, than the best pasture of equal extent.

Corn land yields a larger supply of food after maintaining labour than pasture. Though its cultivation requires much more labour, yet the surplus which remains after replacing the seed and maintaining all that labour, is likewise much greater. If a pound of butcher's-meat, therefore, was never supposed to be worth more than a pound of bread, this greater surplus would every-where be of greater value, and constitute a greater fund both for the profit of the farmer and the rent of the landlord. It seems to have done so universally in the rude beginnings of agriculture.

But the relative values of those two different species of food, bread, and butcher's-meat, are very different in the different periods of agriculture. In its rude beginnings, the unimproved wilds, which then occupy the far greater part of the country, are all abandoned to cattle. There is more butcher's-meat than bread, and bread, therefore, is the food for which there is the greatest competition, and which consequently brings the greatest price. At Buenos Ayres, we are told by Ulloa, four reals, one-and-twenty pence halfpenny sterling, was, forty or fifty years ago, the ordinary price of an ox, chosen from a herd of two or three hundred.[4] He says nothing of the price of

In early times meat is cheaper than bread,

---

[4] [Vol. i., p. 532, in the French translation of Juan and Ulloa's work, *Voyage his-*

bread, probably because he found nothing remarkable about it.
An ox there, he says, costs little more than the labour of catching him. But corn can no-where be raised without a great deal
of labour, and in a country which lies upon the river Plate, at
that time the direct road from Europe to the silver mines of
Potosi, the money price of labour could not be very cheap. It is
otherwise when cultivation is extended over the greater part of
the country. There is then more bread than butcher's-meat. The
competition changes its direction, and the price of butcher's-
meat becomes greater than the price of bread.

By the extension besides of cultivation the unimproved
wilds become insufficient to supply the demand for butcher's-
meat. A great part of the cultivated lands must be employed in

*but later on it
becomes dearer,*

rearing and fattening cattle, of which the
price, therefore, must be sufficient to pay,
not only the labour necessary for tending
them, but the rent which the landlord and the profit which the
farmer could have drawn from such land employed in tillage.
The cattle bred upon the most uncultivated moors, when
brought to the same market, are, in proportion to their weight
or goodness, sold at the same price as those which are reared
upon the most improved land. The proprietors of those moors
profit by it, and raise the rent of their land in proportion to the
price of their cattle. It is not more than a century ago that in
many parts of the highlands of Scotland, butcher's-meat was as
cheap or cheaper than even bread made of oat-meal. The union
opened the market of England to the highland cattle. Their ordinary price is at present about three times greater than at the
beginning of the century, and the rents of many highland estates have been tripled and quadrupled in the same time.[5] In
almost every part of Great Britain a pound of the best
butcher's-meat is, in the present times, generally worth more
than two pounds of the best white bread; and in plentiful years
it is sometimes worth three or four pounds.

torique de l'Amérique méridionale par don George Juan et don Antoine de Ulloa,
1752. The statement is repeated in almost the same words, substituting "three or
four hundred" for "two or three hundred," below, p. 253–254.]

[5] [See below, pp. 222, 299.]

It is thus that in the progress of improvement the rent and profit of unimproved pasture come to be regulated in some *and pasture yields* measure by the rent and profit of what is im-*as good a rent as* proved, and these again by the rent and profit *corn land,* of corn. Corn is an annual crop. Butcher's-meat, a crop which requires four or five years to grow. As an acre of land, therefore, will produce a much smaller quantity of the one species of food than of the other, the inferiority of the quantity must be compensated by the superiority of the price. If it was more than compensated, more corn land would be turned into pasture; and if it was not compensated, part of what was in pasture would be brought back into corn.

This equality, however, between the rent and profit of grass and those of corn; of the land of which the immediate produce *and sometimes a* is food for cattle, and of that of which the *greater one,* immediate produce is food for men; must be understood to take place only through the greater part of the improved lands of a great country. In some particular local situations it is quite otherwise, and the rent and profit of grass are much superior to what can be made by corn.

Thus in the neighbourhood of a great town, the demand for milk and for forage to horses, frequently contribute, together *as in the neigh-* with the high price of butcher's-meat, to *bourhood of a* raise the value of grass above what may be *great town,* called its natural proportion to that of corn. This local advantage, it is evident, cannot be communicated to the lands at a distance.

Particular circumstances have sometimes rendered some countries so populous, that the whole territory, like the lands in *or all over a* the neighbourhood of a great town, has not *populous country* been sufficient to produce both the grass and *which imports* the corn necessary for the subsistence of *corn, such as* their inhabitants. Their lands, therefore, have *Holland and* been principally employed in the production *ancient Italy,* of grass, the more bulky commodity, and which cannot be so easily brought from a great distance; the corn, the food of the great body of the people, has been chiefly imported from foreign countries. Holland is at present in this situation, and a considerable part of ancient Italy seems to have been so during the prosperity of the Romans. To feed well, old Cato said, as we are told by Cicero, was the first and most profitable thing in the management of a private estate; to feed tolerably well, the second; and to feed ill, the third. To plough, he ranked only in the fourth place of profit and advantage.[6] Tillage, indeed, in that part of ancient Italy which lay in the neighbourhood of Rome, must have been very much discouraged by the distributions of corn which were frequently made to the people, either gratuitously, or at a very low price. This corn was brought from the conquered provinces, of which several, instead of taxes, were obliged to furnish a tenth part of their produce at a stated price, about sixpence a peck, to the republic.[7] The low price at which this corn was distributed to the people, must necessarily have sunk the price of what could be brought to the Roman market from Latium, or the ancient territory of Rome, and must have discouraged its cultivation in that country.

In an open country too, of which the principal produce is corn, a well-enclosed piece of grass will frequently rent higher than any corn field in its neighbourhood. It is convenient for the maintenance of the cattle employed in the cultivation of the corn, and its high rent is, in this case, not so properly paid from the value of its own produce, as from that of the corn lands which are cultivated by means of it. It is likely to fall, if ever the neighbouring lands are completely enclosed. The present high rent of enclosed land in Scotland seems owing to the scarcity of enclosure, and will probably last no longer than that scarcity. The advantage of enclosure is greater for pasture than for corn. It saves the labour of guarding the cattle, which feed better too when they are not liable to be disturbed by their keeper or his dog.

and occasionally in a country where enclosure is unusual.

But where there is no local advantage of this kind, the rent

[6] [Cicero, *De officiis*, lib. ii. *ad fin.* Quoted in *Lectures*, p. 229.]

[7] [See below, pp. 296, 297.]

Ordinarily the rent of corn land regulates that of pasture.

and profit of corn, or whatever else is the common vegetable food of the people, must naturally regulate, upon the land which is fit for producing it, the rent and profit of pasture.

The use of the artificial grasses, of turnips, carrots, cabbages, and the other expedients which have been fallen upon to

Improved methods of feeding cattle lower meat in proportion to bread.

make an equal quantity of land feed a greater number of cattle than when in natural grass, should somewhat reduce, it might be expected, the superiority which, in an improved country, the price of butcher's-meat naturally has over that of bread. It seems

accordingly to have done so; and there is some reason for believing that, at least in the London market, the price of butcher's-meat in proportion to the price of bread, is a good deal lower in the present times than it was in the beginning of the last century.

In the appendix to the Life of Prince Henry, Doctor Birch has given us an account of the prices of butcher's-meat as

The price of meat was higher at the beginning of the seventeenth century

commonly paid by that prince. It is there said that the four quarters of an ox weighing six hundred pounds usually cost him nine pounds ten shillings, or thereabouts; that is, thirty-one shillings and eight pence per hundred pounds weight.[8] Prince Henry died

on the 6th of November 1612, in the nineteenth year of his age.[9]

In March 1764, there was a parliamentary inquiry into the causes of the high price of provisions at that time. It was

than in 1763–4;

then, among other proof to the same purpose, given in evidence by a Virginia merchant, that in March 1763, he had victualled his ships for twenty-four or twenty-five shillings the hundred weight of beef, which he considered as the ordinary price; whereas, in

[8] [*The Life of Henry Prince of Wales*, by Thomas Birch, D.D., 1760, p. 346.]

[9] [*Ibid.*, p. 271.]

that dear year, he had paid twenty-seven shillings for the same weight and sort.[10] This high price in 1764 is, however, four shillings and eight pence cheaper than the ordinary price paid by prince Henry; and it is the best beef only, it must be observed, which is fit to be salted for those distant voyages.

The price paid by prince Henry amounts to $3\frac{1}{5}d$. per pound weight of the whole carcase, coarse and choice pieces taken together; and at that rate the choice pieces could not have been sold by retail for less than $4\frac{1}{2}d$. or $5d$. the pound.

In the parliamentary inquiry in 1764, the witness stated the price of the choice pieces of the best beef to be to the consumer $4d$. and $4\frac{1}{4}d$. the pound; and the coarse pieces in general to be from seven farthings to $2\frac{1}{2}d$. and $2\frac{3}{4}d$.; and this they said was in general one half-penny dearer than the same sort of pieces had usually been sold in the month of March.[11] But even this high price is still a good deal cheaper than what we can well suppose the ordinary retail price to have been in the time of prince Henry.

whereas wheat was cheaper. During the twelve first years of the last century, the average price of the best wheat at the Windsor market was $1l$. $18s$. $9\frac{1}{2}d$. the quarter of nine Winchester bushels.

But in the twelve years preceding 1764, including that year, the average price of the same measure of the best wheat at the same market was $2l$. $1s$. $9\frac{1}{2}d$.[12]

In the twelve first years of the last century, therefore, wheat

---

[10] [*A Report from the Committee who, upon the 8th day of February, 1764, were appointed to inquire into the Causes of the High Price of Provisions with the proceedings of the House thereupon.* Published by order of the House of Commons, 1764, paragraph 4, where, however, there is no definite statement to the effect that the Virginia merchant, Mr. Capel Hanbury, considered 24s. or 25s. as the ordinary price.]

[11] [*Report from the Committee*, paragraph 3 almost *verbatim*. The Committee resolved "that the high price of provisions of late has been occasioned partly by circumstances peculiar to the season and the year, and partly by the defect of the laws in force for convicting and punishing all persons concerned in forestalling cattle in their passage to market."]

[12] [These prices are deduced from the tables at the end of the chapter.]

appears to have been a good deal cheaper, and butcher's-meat a good deal dearer, than in the twelve years preceding 1764, including that year.

In all great countries the greater part of the cultivated lands are employed in producing either food for men or food for cat-

The rent and profit of corn land and pasture regulate those of all other land.

tle. The rent and profit of these regulate the rent and profit of all other cultivated land. If any particular produce afforded less, the land would soon be turned into corn or pasture; and if any afforded more, some part of the lands in corn or pasture would soon be turned to that produce.

Those productions, indeed, which require either a greater

The apparently greater rent or profit of some other kinds is only interest on greater expense,

original expence of improvement, or a greater annual expence of cultivation, in order to fit the land for them, appear commonly to afford, the one a greater rent, the other a greater profit than corn or pasture. This superiority, however, will seldom be found to amount to more than a reasonable interest or compensation for this superior expence.

In a hop garden, a fruit garden, a kitchen garden, both the rent of the landlord, and the profit of the farmer, are generally

as in hop, and fruit gardens;

greater than in a corn or grass field. But to bring the ground into this condition requires more expence. Hence a greater rent becomes due to the landlord. It requires too a more attentive and skilful management. Hence a greater profit becomes due to the farmer. The crop too, at least in the hop and fruit garden, is more precarious. Its price, therefore, besides compensating all occasional losses, must afford something like the profit of insurance.[13] The circumstances of gardeners, generally mean, and always moderate, may satisfy us that their great ingenuity is not commonly over-recompenced. Their delightful art is practised by so many rich people for amusement, that little ad-

---

[13] [Only if the extra risk deters people from entering the business, and according to pp. 153, 154 above it would not.]

vantage is to be made by those who practise it for profit; because the persons who should naturally be their best customers, supply themselves with all their most precious productions.

The advantage which the landlord derives from such improvements seems at no time to have been greater than what ────────── was sufficient to compensate the original expence of making them. In the ancient hus*kitchen gardens;* pence of making them. In the ancient husbandry, after the vineyard, a well-watered kitchen garden seems to have been the part of the farm which was supposed to yield the most valuable produce. But Democritus, who wrote upon husbandry about two thousand years ago, and who was regarded by the ancients as one of the fathers of the art, thought they did not act wisely who enclosed a kitchen garden. The profit, he said, would not compensate the expence of a stone wall; and bricks (he meant, I suppose, bricks baked in the sun) mouldered with the rain, and the winter storm, and required continual repairs. Columella, who reports this judgment of Democritus, does not controvert it, but proposes a very frugal method of enclosing with a hedge of brambles[14] and briars, which, he says, he had found by experience to be both a lasting and an impenetrable fence;[15] but which, it seems, was not commonly known in the time of Democritus. Palladius adopts the opinion of Columella, which had before been recommended by Varro.[16] In the judgment of those ancient improvers, the produce of a kitchen garden had, it seems, been little more than sufficient to pay the extraordinary culture and the expence of watering; for in countries so near the sun, it was thought proper, in those times as in the present, to have the command of a stream of water, which could be conducted to every bed in

───────────────

[14] [Ed. 1 reads "thorns."]

[15] [Columella, *De re rustica*, xi., 3, but the recommendation of the fence is "Et haec quidem claudendi horti ratio maxime est antiquis probata."]

[16] [Gesnerus' edition of Columella in *Scriptores rei rustiae* in Adam Smith's library (see Bonar's *Catalogue, s.v.* Gesnerus), commenting on the passage referred to above, quotes the opinions of Varro, *De re rustica*, i., 14, and Palladius, *De re rustica*, i., 34.]

the garden. Through the greater part of Europe, a kitchen garden is not at present supposed to deserve a better enclosure than that recommended by Columella. In Great Britain, and some other northern countries, the finer fruits cannot be brought to perfection but by the assistance of a wall. Their price, therefore, in such countries, must be sufficient to pay the expence of building and maintaining what they cannot be had without. The fruit-wall frequently surrounds the kitchen garden, which thus enjoys the benefit of an enclosure which its own produce could seldom pay for.

That the vineyard, when properly planted and brought to perfection, was the most valuable part of the farm, seems to *and vineyards.* have been an undoubted maxim in the ancient agriculture, as it is in the modern through all the wine countries. But whether it was advantageous to plant a new vineyard, was a matter of dispute among the ancient Italian husbandmen, as we learn from Columella. He decides, like a true lover of all curious cultivation, in favour of the vineyard, and endeavours to show, by a comparison of the profit and expence, that it was a most advantageous improvement.[17] Such comparisons, however, between the profit and expence of new projects, are commonly very fallacious; and in nothing more so than in agriculture. Had the gain actually made by such plantations been commonly as great as he imagined it might have been, there could have been no dispute about it. The same point is frequently at this day a matter of controversy in the wine countries. Their writers on agriculture, indeed, the lovers and promoters of high cultivation, seem generally disposed to decide with Columella in favour of the vineyard. In France the anxiety of the proprietors of the old vineyards to prevent the planting of any new ones, seems to favour their opinion, and to indicate a consciousness in those who must have the experience, that this species of cultivation is at present in that country more profitable than any other. It seems at the same time, however, to indicate another opinion, that this superior profit can last no longer than the laws which

[17] [*De re rustica*, iii., 3.]

at present restrain the free cultivation of the vine. In 1731, they obtained an order of council, prohibiting both the planting of new vineyards, and the renewal of those old ones, of which the cultivation had been interrupted for two years, without a particular permission from the king, to be granted only in consequence of an information from the intendant of the province, certifying that he had examined the land, and that it was incapable of any other culture. The pretence of this order was the scarcity of corn and pasture, and the super-abundance of wine. But had this super-abundance been real, it would, without any order of council, have effectually prevented the plantation of new vineyards, by reducing the profits of this species of cultivation below their natural proportion to those of corn and pasture. With regard to the supposed scarcity of corn occasioned by the multiplication of vineyards, corn is nowhere in France more carefully cultivated than in the wine provinces, where the land is fit for producing it; as in Burgundy, Guienne, and the Upper Languedoc. The numerous hands employed in the one species of cultivation necessarily encourage the other, by affording a ready market for its produce. To diminish the number of those who are capable of paying for it, is surely a most unpromising expedient for encouraging the cultivation of corn. It is like the policy which would promote agriculture by discouraging manufactures.

The rent and profit of those productions, therefore, which require either a greater original expence of improvement in order to fit the land for them, or a greater annual expence of cultivation, though often much superior to those of corn and pasture, yet when they do no more than compensate such extraordinary expence, are in reality regulated by the rent and profit of those common crops.

It sometimes happens, indeed, that the quantity of land *Land fitted for a particular produce may have a monopoly,* which can be fitted for some particular produce, is too small to supply the effectual demand. The whole produce can be disposed of to those who are willing to give somewhat more than what is sufficient to pay the whole rent, wages and profit necessary for raising and bringing it to

market, according to their natural rates, or according to the
rates at which they are paid in the greater part of other cultivated land. The surplus part of the price which remains after
defraying the whole expence of improvement and cultivation
may commonly, in this case, and in this case only, bear no regular proportion to the like surplus in corn or pasture, but may
exceed it in almost any degree; and the greater part of this excess naturally goes to the rent of the landlord.

The usual and natural proportion, for example, between the
rent and profit of wine and those of corn and pasture, must be
such as that understood to take place only with regard to
which produces those vineyards which produce nothing but
wine of a particu- good common wine, such as can be raised
lar flavour, almost any-where, upon any light, gravelly,
or sandy soil, and which has nothing to recommend it but its strength and wholesomeness. It is with such
vineyards only that common land of the country can be
brought into competition; for with those of a peculiar quality it
is evident that it cannot.

The vine is more affected by the difference of soils than any
other fruit tree. From some it derives a flavour which no culture or management can equal, it is supposed, upon any other.
This flavour, real or imaginary, is sometimes peculiar to the
produce of a few vineyards; sometimes it extends through the
greater part of a small district, and sometimes through a considerable part of a large province. The whole quantity of such
wines that is brought to market falls short of the effectual demand, or the demand of those who would be willing to pay the
whole rent, profit and wages necessary for preparing and
bringing them thither, according to the ordinary rate, or according to the rate at which they are paid in common vineyards. The whole quantity, therefore, can be disposed of to
those who are willing to pay more, which necessarily raises
the[18] price above that of common wine. The difference is
greater or less, according as the fashionableness and scarcity
of the wine render the competition of the buyers more or less

[18] [Ed. 1 reads "their."]

eager. Whatever it be, the greater part of it goes to the rent of the landlord. For though such vineyards are in general more carefully cultivated than most others, the high price of the wine seems to be, not so much the effect, as the cause of this careful cultivation. In so valuable a produce the loss occasioned by negligence is so great as to force even the most careless to attention. A small part of this high price, therefore, is sufficient to pay the wages of the extraordinary labour bestowed upon their cultivation, and the profits of the extraordinary stock which puts that labour into motion.

The sugar colonies possessed by the European nations in the West Indies, may be compared to those precious vineyards.

or the West Indian sugar colonies, Their whole produce falls short of the effectual demand of Europe, and can be disposed of to those who are willing to give more than what is sufficient to pay the whole rent, profit and wages necessary for preparing and bringing it to market, according to the rate at which they are commonly paid by any other produce. In Cochin-china the finest white sugar commonly sells for three piastres the quintal, about thirteen shillings and sixpence of our money, as we are told by Mr. Poivre,[19] a very careful observer of the agriculture of that country. What is there called the quintal weighs from a hundred and fifty to two hundred Paris pounds, or a hundred and seventy-five Paris pounds at a medium,[20] which reduces the price of the hundred weight English to about eight shillings sterling, not a fourth part of what is commonly paid for the brown or muskavada sugars imported from our colonies, and not a sixth part of what is paid for the finest white sugar. The greater part of the cultivated lands in Cochin-china are employed in producing corn and

[19] Voyages d'un Philosophe [*ou observations sur les mœurs et les arts des peuples de l'Afrique, de l'Asie, et de l'Amérique*, 1768, pp. 92, 93. The note appears first in ed. 2].

[20] [The French original says the Cochin-China quintal "équivaut à 150 L. 200 de nos livres, poids de marc," which cannot possibly bear the meaning ascribed to it in the text. Probably the 150 L. are pounds equal to 1⅕ of the pounds poids de marc. This would make the cwt. English worth only about seven shillings.]

rice, the food of the great body of the people. The respective prices of corn, rice, and sugar, are there probably in the natural proportion, or in that which naturally takes place in the different crops of the greater part of cultivated land, and which recompences the landlord and farmer, as nearly as can be computed, according to what is usually the original expence of improvement and the annual expence of cultivation. But in our sugar colonies the price of sugar bears no such proportion to that of the produce of a rice or corn field either in Europe or in America. It is commonly said, that a sugar planter expects that the rum and the molasses should defray the whole expence of his cultivation, and that his sugar should be all clear profit. If this be true, for I pretend not to affirm it, it is as if a corn farmer expected to defray the expence of his cultivation with the chaff and the straw, and that the grain should be all clear profit. We see frequently societies of merchants in London and other trading towns, purchase waste lands in our sugar colonies, which they expect to improve and cultivate with profit by means of factors and agents; notwithstanding the great distance and the uncertain returns, from the defective administration of justice in those countries. Nobody will attempt to improve and cultivate in the same manner the most fertile lands of Scotland, Ireland, or the corn provinces of North America, though from the more exact administration of justice in these countries, more regular returns might be expected.

In Virginia and Maryland the cultivation of tobacco is preferred, as more profitable, to that of corn. Tobacco might *and in a less degree the tobacco plantations of Virginia and Maryland.* be cultivated with advantage through the greater part of Europe; but in almost every part of Europe it has become a principal subject of taxation, and to collect a tax from every different farm in the country where this plant might happen to be cultivated, would be more difficult, it has been supposed, than to levy one upon its importation at the customhouse. The cultivation of tobacco has upon this account been most absurdly prohibited through the greater part of Europe,[21] which necessarily gives a sort of monopoly to the countries where it is allowed; and as Virginia and Maryland produce the greatest quantity of it, they share largely, though with some competitors, in the advantage of this monopoly. The cultivation of tobacco, however, seems not to be so advantageous as that of sugar. I have never even heard of any tobacco plantation that was improved and cultivated by the capital of merchants who resided in Great Britain, and our tobacco colonies send us home no such wealthy planters as we see frequently arrive from our sugar islands. Though from the preference given in those colonies to the cultivation of tobacco above that of corn, it would appear that the effectual demand of Europe for tobacco is not completely supplied, it probably is more nearly so than that for sugar: And though the present price of tobacco is probably more than sufficient to pay the whole rent, wages and profit necessary for preparing and bringing it to market, according to the rate at which they are commonly paid in corn land; it must not be so much more as the present price of sugar. Our tobacco planters, accordingly, have shewn the same fear of the super-abundance of tobacco, which the proprietors of the old vineyards in France have of the super-abundance of wine. By act of assem-

---

[21] [Tobacco growing in England, Ireland, and the Channel Islands was prohibited by 12 Car. II., c. 34, the preamble of which alleges that the lords and commons have considered "of how great concern and importance it is that the colonies and plantations of this kingdom in America be defended, maintained and kept up, and that all due and possible encouragement be given unto them, and that not only in regard great and considerable dominions and countries have been thereby gained and added to the imperial crown of this realm, but for that the strength and welfare of this kingdom do very much depend upon them in regard of the employment of a very considerable part of its shipping and seamen, and of the vent of very great quantities of its native commodities and manufactures as also of its supply with several considerable commodities which it was wont formerly to have only from foreigners and at far dearer rates, and forasmuch as tobacco is one of the main products of several of those plantations and upon which their welfare and subsistence and the navigation of this kingdom and vent of its commodities thither do much depend; And in regard it is found by experience that the tobaccos planted in these parts are not so good and wholesome for the takers thereof, and that by the planting thereof Your Majesty is deprived of a considerable part of your revenue." The prohibition was extended to Scotland by 22 Geo. III., c. 73.]

bly they have restrained its cultivation to six thousand plants,
supposed to yield a thousand weight of tobacco, for every negro between sixteen and sixty years of age.[22] Such a negro,
over and above this quantity of tobacco, can manage, they
reckon, four acres of Indian corn.[23] To prevent the market from
being overstocked too, they have sometimes, in plentiful years,
we are told by Dr. Douglas,[24] (I suspect he has been ill informed) burnt a certain quantity of tobacco for every negro, in
the same manner as the Dutch are said to do of spices.[25] If such
violent methods are necessary to keep up the present price of
tobacco, the superior advantage of its culture over that of corn,
if it still has any, will not probably be of long continuance.

It is in this manner that the rent of the cultivated land, of
which the produce is human food, regulates
the rent of the greater part of other cultivated
land. No particular produce can long afford
less; because the land would immediately be
turned to another use: And if any particular
produce commonly affords more, it is be-
cause the quantity of land which can be fitted for it is too small
to supply the effectual demand.

*So the rent of
cultivated land
producing food
regulates that of
most of the rest,*

In Europe corn is the principal produce of
land which serves immediately for human
food. Except in particular situations, therefore, the rent of corn land regulates in
Europe that of all other cultivated land.
Britain need envy neither the vineyards of

*and in Europe the
rent of corn land
regulates that of
other cultivated
land producing
food.*

[22] [William Douglass, M.D., *A Summary, Historical and Political, of the First
Planting, Progressive Improvements and Present State of the British Settlements
in North America*, 1760, vol. ii., pp. 359, 360 and 373.]

[23] [*Ibid.*, p. 374, but the phrase is "an industrious man" not "such a negro."]

[24] [Douglas's Summary, vol. ii., pp. 372, 373. This note appears first in ed 2. In the
text of ed. 1. the name is spelt "Douglass."]

[25] [This saying about the Dutch and spices is repeated below, pp. 662, 807.
Douglass, vol. ii., p. 372, in a note to the statement that Virginia and Maryland occasionally produce more than they can sell to advantage, which immediately precedes his account of the occasional burning of tobacco, says: "This is sometimes
the case with the Dutch East India spices and the West India sugars."]

France nor the olive plantations of Italy. Except in particular situations, the value of these is regulated by that of corn, in which the fertility of Britain is not much inferior to that of either of those two countries.

If in any country the common and favourite vegetable food of the people should be drawn from a plant of which the most common land, with the same or nearly the same culture, produced a much greater quantity than the most fertile does of corn, the rent of the landlord, or the surplus quantity of food which would remain to him, after paying the labour and replacing the stock of the farmer together with its ordinary profits, would necessarily be much greater. Whatever was the rate at which labour was commonly maintained in that country, this greater surplus could always maintain a greater quantity of it, and consequently enable the landlord to purchase or command a greater quantity of it. The real value of his rent, his real power and authority, his command of the necessaries and conveniencies of life with which the labour of other people could supply him, would necessarily be much greater.

If the common food was such as to produce a greater surplus, rent would be higher:

A rice field produces a much greater quantity of food than the most fertile corn field. Two crops in the year from thirty to sixty bushels each, are said to be the ordinary produce of an acre. Though its cultivation, therefore, requires more labour, a much greater surplus remains after maintaining all that labour. In those rice countries, therefore, where rice is the common and favourite vegetable food of the people, and where the cultivators are chiefly maintained with it, a greater share of this greater surplus should belong to the landlord than in corn countries. In Carolina, where the planters, as in other British colonies, are generally both farmers and landlords, and where rent consequently is confounded with profit, the cultivation of rice is found to be more profitable than that of corn, though their fields produce only one crop in the year, and though, from the prevalence of the customs of Europe, rice is not there the common and favourite vegetable food of the people.

for example, rice,

A good rice field is a bog at all seasons, and at one season a bog covered with water. It is unfit either for corn, or pasture, or vineyard, or, indeed, for any other vegetable produce that is very useful to men: And the lands which are fit for those purposes, are not fit for rice. Even in the rice countries, therefore, the rent of rice lands cannot regulate the rent of the other cultivated land which can never be turned to that produce.

The food produced by a field of potatoes is not inferior in quantity to that produced by a field of rice, and much superior

or potatoes. to what is produced by a field of wheat. Twelve thousand weight of potatoes from an acre of land is not a greater produce than two thousand weight of wheat. The food or solid nourishment, indeed, which can be drawn from each of those two plants, is not altogether in proportion to their weight, on account of the watery nature of potatoes. Allowing, however, half the weight of this root to go to water, a very large allowance, such an acre of potatoes will still produce six thousand weight of solid nourishment, three times the quantity produced by the acre of wheat. An acre of potatoes is cultivated with less expence than an acre of wheat; the fallow, which generally precedes the sowing of wheat, more than compensating the hoeing and other extraordinary culture which is always given to potatoes. Should this root ever become in any part of Europe, like rice in some rice countries, the common and favourite vegetable food of the people, so as to occupy the same proportion of the lands in tillage which wheat and other sorts of grain for human food do at present, the same quantity of cultivated land would maintain a much greater number of people, and the labourers being generally fed with potatoes, a greater surplus would remain after replacing all the stock and maintaining all the labour employed in cultivation. A greater share of this surplus too would belong to the landlord. Population would increase, and rents would rise much beyond what they are at present.

The land which is fit for potatoes, is fit for almost every other useful vegetable. If they occupied the same proportion of cultivated land which corn does at present, they would regulate, in the same manner, the rent of the greater part of other cultivated land.

In some parts of Lancashire it is pretended, I have been told, that bread of oatmeal is a heartier food for labouring people than wheaten bread, and I have frequently heard the same doctrine held in Scotland. I am, however, somewhat doubtful of the truth of it. The common people in Scotland, who are fed with oatmeal, are in general neither so strong nor so handsome as the same rank of people in England, who are fed with wheaten bread. They neither work so well, nor look so well; and as there is not the same difference between the people of fashion in the two countries, experience would seem to show, that the food of the common people in Scotland is not so suitable to the human constitution as that of their neighbours of the same rank in England.[26] But it seems to be otherwise with potatoes. The chairmen, porters, and coal-heavers in London, and those unfortunate women who live by prostitution, the strongest men and the most beautiful women perhaps in the British dominions, are said to be, the greater part of them, from the lowest rank of people in Ireland, who are generally fed with this root. No food can afford a more decisive proof of its nourishing quality, or of its being peculiarly suitable to the health of the human constitution.

Wheat is probably a better food than oats,

but not than potatoes.

It is difficult to preserve potatoes through the year, and impossible to store them like corn, for two or three years together. The fear of not being able to sell them before they rot, discourages their cultivation, and is, perhaps, the chief obstacle to their ever becoming in any great country, like bread, the principal vegetable food of all the different ranks of the people.

Potatoes however, are perishable.

---

[26] [The inferiority of oatmeal has already been asserted above, pp. 106, 107.]

PART II

Of the Produce of Land which sometimes does, and sometimes does not, afford Rent

Human food seems to be the only produce of land which always and necessarily affords some rent to the landlord. Other sorts of produce sometimes may and sometimes may not, according to different circumstances.

After food, cloathing and lodging are the two great wants of mankind.

The materials of cloathing and lodging, at first super-abundant, come in time to afford a rent.

Land in its original rude state can afford the materials of cloathing and lodging to a much greater number of people than it can feed. In its improved state it can sometimes feed a greater number of people than it can supply with those materials; at least in the way in which they require them, and are willing to pay for them. In the one state, therefore, there is always a super-abundance of those materials, which are frequently, upon that account, of little or no value. In the other there is often a scarcity, which necessarily augments their value. In the one state a great part of them is thrown away as useless, and the price of what is used is considered as equal only to the labour and expence of fitting it for use, and can, therefore, afford no rent to the landlord. In the other they are all made use of, and there is frequently a demand for more than can be had. Somebody is always[27] willing to give more for every part of them than what is sufficient to pay the expence of bringing them to market. Their price, therefore, can always afford some rent to the landlord.

The skins of the larger animals were the original materials of cloathing. Among nations of hunters and shepherds, therefore, whose food consists chiefly in the flesh of those animals, every

For example, hides and wool,

[27] [This "always" is qualified almost to the extent of contradiction on pp. 224–225, below.]

man, by providing himself with food, provides himself with the materials of more cloathing than he can wear. If there was no foreign commerce, the greater part of them would be thrown away as things of no value. This was probably the case among the hunting nations of North America, before their country was discovered by the Europeans, with whom they now exchange their surplus peltry, for blankets, fire-arms, and brandy, which gives it some value. In the present commercial state of the known world, the most barbarous nations, I believe, among whom land property is established, have some foreign commerce of this kind, and find among their wealthier neighbours such a demand for all the materials of cloathing, which their land produces, and which can neither be wrought up nor consumed at home, as raises their price above what it costs to send them to those wealthier neighbours.[28] It affords, therefore, some rent to the landlord. When the greater part of the highland cattle were consumed on their own hills, the exportation of their hides made the most considerable article of the commerce of that country, and what they were exchanged for afforded some addition to the rent of the highland estates.[29] The wool of England, which in old times could neither be consumed nor wrought up at home, found a market in the then wealthier and more industrious country of Flanders, and its price afforded something to the rent of the land which produced it. In countries not better cultivated than England was then, or than the highlands of Scotland are now, and which had no foreign commerce, the materials of cloathing would evidently be so super-abundant, that a great part of them would be thrown away as useless, and no part could afford any rent to the landlord.

The materials of lodging cannot always be transported to so great a distance as those of cloathing, and do not so readily become an object of foreign commerce. When *stone and timber.* they are super-abundant in the country which produces them, it frequently happens, even in the present com-

---

[28] [Ed. I reads "thither."]

[29] [Above, p. 204, and below, p. 298–299.]

mercial state of the world, that they are of no value to the land-lord. A good stone quarry in the neighbourhood of London would afford a considerable rent. In many parts of Scotland and Wales it affords none. Barren timber for building is of great value in a populous and well-cultivated country, and the land which produces it affords a considerable rent. But in many parts of North America the landlord would be much obliged to any body who would carry away the greater part of his large trees. In some parts of the highlands of Scotland the bark is the only part of the wood which, for want of roads and water-carriage, can be sent to market. The timber is left to rot upon the ground. When the materials of lodging are so super-abundant, the part made use of is worth only the labour and expence of fitting it for that use. It affords no rent to the landlord, who generally grants the use of it to whoever takes the trouble of asking it. The de-mand of wealthier nations, however, sometimes enables him to get a rent for it. The paving of the streets of London has enabled the owners of some barren rocks on the coast of Scotland to draw a rent from what never afforded any before. The woods of Norway and of the coasts of the Baltic, find a market in many parts of Great Britain which they could not find at home, and thereby afford some rent to their proprietors.

Countries are populous, not in proportion to the number of people whom their produce can cloath and lodge, but in pro-portion to that of those whom it can feed. When food is pro-

Population depends on food;

vided, it is easy to find the necessary cloathing and lodging. But though these are at hand, it may often be difficult to find food. In some parts even of the British dominions what is called A House, may be built by one day's labour of one man. The sim-plest species of cloathing, the skins of animals, require some-what more labour to dress and prepare them for use. They do not, however, ~~~~ a great deal. Among savage and bar-barous nati~~~~ dth or little more th~~~~ part of ~~~~ hole year, will b~~~~ vide ~~~~ ing and lodg~~~~ greater ~~~~ the other nin~~~~ frequently ~~~~ provid~~~~

But when by the improvement and cultivation of land the labour of one family can provide food for two, the labour of half the society becomes sufficient to provide food for the whole. The other half, therefore, or at least the greater part of them, can be employed in providing other things, or in satisfying the other wants and fancies of mankind. Cloathing and lodging, household furniture, and what is called Equipage, are the principal objects of the greater part of those wants and fancies. The rich man consumes no more food than his poor neighbour. In quality it may be very different, and to select and prepare it may require more labour and art; but in quantity it is very nearly the same. But compare the spacious palace and great wardrobe of the one, with the hovel and the few rags of the other, and you will be sensible that the difference between their cloathing, lodging, and household furniture, is almost as great in quantity as it is in quality. The desire of food is limited in every man by the narrow capacity of the human stomach; but the desire of the conveniencies and ornaments of building, dress, equipage, and household furniture, seems to have no limit or certain boundary. Those, therefore, who have the command of more food than they themselves can consume, are always willing to exchange the surplus, or, what is the same thing, the price of it, for gratifications of this other kind. What is over and above satisfying the limited desire, is given for the amusement of those desires which cannot be satisfied, but seem to be altogether endless. The poor, in order to obtain food, exert themselves to gratify those fancies of the rich, and to obtain it more certainly, they vie with one another in the cheapness and perfection of their work. The number of workmen increases with the increasing quantity of food, or with the growing improvement and culti-

_____ ds; and as the nature of their business admits _____ ivisions of labour, the quantity of materials _____ k up, increases in a much greater propor- _____ bers. Hence arises a demand for every sort _____ man invention can employ, either usefully

so the demand for the materials of cloathing and lodging is increased by greater ease of obtaining food,

or ornamentally, in building, dress, equipage, or household furniture; for the fossils and minerals contained in the bowels of the earth, the precious metals, and the precious stones.

Food is in this manner, not only the original source of rent, but every other part of the produce of land which afterwards affords rent, derives that part of its value from the improvement of the powers of labour in producing food by means of the improvement and cultivation of land.[30]

which thus makes them afford rent.

Those other parts of the produce of land, however, which afterwards afford rent, do not afford it always. Even in improved and cultivated countries, the demand for them is not always such as to afford a greater price than what is sufficient to pay the labour, and replace, together with its ordinary profits, the stock which must be employed in bringing them to market. Whether it is or is not such, depends upon different circumstances.

They do not, however, even then always afford rent:

Whether a coal-mine, for example, can afford any rent, depends partly upon its fertility, and partly upon its situation.

for example, some coal-mines are too barren to afford rent,

A mine of any kind may be said to be either fertile or barren, according as the quantity of mineral which can be brought from it by a certain quantity of labour, is greater or less than what can be brought by an equal quantity from the greater part of other mines of the same kind.

Some coal-mines advantageously situated, cannot be wrought on account of their barrenness. The produce does not pay the expence. They can afford neither profit nor rent.

There are some of which the produce is barely sufficient to pay the labour,[31] and replace, together with its ordinary profits, the stock employed in working them. They afford some profit

---

[30] [This and the two preceding paragraphs appear to be based on the dissertation on the natural wants of mankind in *Lectures*, pp. 157–161; cp. *Moral Sentiments*, 1759, p. 349.]

[31] [Misprinted "labourer" in ed. 5.]

to the undertaker of the work, but no rent to the landlord. They can be wrought advantageously by nobody but the landlord, who being himself undertaker of the work, gets the ordinary profit of the capital which he employs in it. Many coal-mines in Scotland are wrought in this manner, and can be wrought in no other. The landlord will allow nobody else to work them without paying some rent, and nobody can afford to pay any.

Other coal-mines in the same country sufficiently fertile, cannot be wrought on account of their situation. A quantity of *or too disadvanta-* mineral sufficient to defray the expence of *geously situated.* working, could be brought from the mine by the ordinary, or even less than the ordinary quantity of labour: But in an inland country, thinly inhabited, and without either good roads or water-carriage, this quantity could not be sold.

Coals are a less agreeable fewel than wood: they are said *The price of coal* too to be less wholesome. The expence of *is kept down by* coals, therefore, at the place where they are *that of wood,* consumed, must generally be somewhat less than that of wood.

The price of wood again varies with the state of agriculture, nearly in the same manner, and exactly for the same reason, as *which varies with* the price of cattle. In its rude beginnings the *the state of* greater part of every country is covered with *agriculture.* wood, which is then a mere incumbrance of no value to the landlord, who would gladly give it to any body for the cutting. As agriculture advances, the woods are partly cleared by the progress of tillage, and partly go to decay in consequence of the increased number of cattle. These, though they do not increase in the same proportion as corn, which is altogether the acquisition of human industry, yet multiply under the care and protection of men; who store up in the season of plenty what may maintain them in that of scarcity, who through the whole year furnish them with a greater quantity of food than uncultivated nature provides for them, and who by destroying and extirpating their enemies, secure them in the free enjoyment of all that she provides Numerous herds of cattle, when allowed to wander through the woods, though they do not destroy the old trees, hinder any young ones from coming up, so that in the course of a century or two the whole forest goes to ruin. The scarcity of wood then raises its price. It affords a good rent, and the landlord sometimes finds that he can scarce employ his best lands more advantageously than in growing barren timber, of which the greatness of the profit often compensates the lateness of the returns. This seems in the present times to be nearly the state of things in several parts of Great Britain, where the profit of planting is found to be equal to that of either corn or pasture. The advantage which the landlord derives from planting, can nowhere exceed, at least for any considerable time, the rent which these could afford him; and in an inland country which is highly cultivated, it will frequently not fall much short of this rent. Upon the sea-coast of a well-improved country, indeed, if coals can conveniently be had for fewel,[32] it may sometimes be cheaper to bring barren timber for building from less cultivated foreign countries, than to raise it at home. In the new town of Edinburgh, built within these few years,[33] there is not, perhaps, a single stick of Scotch timber.

Whatever may be the price of wood, if that of coals is such that the expence of a coal-fire is nearly equal to that of a wood

But in the coal countries coal is everywhere much below this price.

one, we may be assured, that at that place, and in these circumstances, the price of coals is as high as it can be. It seems to be so in some of the inland parts of England, particularly in Oxfordshire, where it is usual, even in the fires of the common people, to mix coals and wood together, and where the difference in the expence of those two sorts of fewel cannot, therefore, be very great.

Coals, in the coal countries, are every-where much below this highest price. If they were not, they could not bear the ex-

---

[32] [Ed. 1 reads "if it can conveniently get coals for fewel."]

[33] [The North Bridge was only made passable in 1772: in 1778 the buildings along Princes Street had run to a considerable length, and St. Andrew's Square and the streets connected with it were almost complete. A plan of that date shows the whole block between Queen Street and Princes Street (Arnot, *History of Edinburgh*, 1779, pp. 233, 315, 318, 319).]

pence of a distant carriage, either by land or by water. A small quantity only could be sold, and the coal masters and coal proprietors find it more for their interest to sell a great quantity at a price somewhat above the lowest, than a small quantity at the highest. The most fertile coal-mine too, regulates the price of coals at all the other mines in its neighbourhood.[34] Both the proprietor and the undertaker of the work find, the one that he can get a greater rent, the other that he can get a greater profit, by somewhat underselling all their neighbours. Their neighbours are soon obliged to sell at the same price, though they cannot so well afford it, and though it always diminishes, and sometimes takes away altogether both their rent and their profit. Some works are abandoned altogether; others can afford no rent, and can be wrought only by the proprietor.

The lowest price at which coals can be sold for any considerable time, is, like that of all other commodities, the price

The lowest possible price is that which only replaces stock with profits.

which is barely sufficient to replace, together with its ordinary profits, the stock which must be employed in bringing them to market. At a coal-mine for which the landlord can get no rent, but which he must either work himself or let it alone altogether, the price of coals must generally be nearly about this price.

Rent, even where coals afford one, has generally a smaller share in their price than in that of most other parts of the rude

Rent forms a smaller proportion of the price of coal than of that of most other rude produce.

produce of land. The rent of an estate above ground, commonly amounts to what is supposed to be a third of the gross produce; and it is generally a rent certain and independent of the occasional variations in the crop. In coal-mines a fifth of the gross produce is a very great rent; a tenth the common rent, and

[34] [Buchanan (ed. of *Wealth of Nations*, vol. i., p. 279), commenting on this passage, remarks judiciously: "It is not by the produce of one coal mine, however fertile, but by the joint produce of all the coal mines that can be worked, that the price of coals is fixed. A certain quantity of coals only can be consumed at a certain price. If the mines that can be worked produce more than this quantity the price will fall; if they produce less it will rise."]

it is seldom a rent certain, but depends upon the occasional variations in the produce. These are so great, that in a country where thirty years purchase is considered as a moderate price for the property for a landed estate, ten years purchase is regarded as a good price for that of a coal-mine.

The value of a coal-mine to the proprietor frequently depends[35] as much upon its situation as upon its fertility. That of a

The situation of a metallic mine is less important than that of a coal mine,

metallic mine depends more upon its fertility, and less upon its situation. The coarse, and still more the precious metals, when separated from the ore, are so valuable that they can generally bear the expence of a very long land, and of the most distant sea carriage. Their market is not confined to the countries in the neighbourhood of the mine but extends to the whole world. The copper of Japan makes an article of commerce in Europe;[36] the iron of Spain in that of Chili and Peru. The silver of Peru finds its way, not only to Europe, but from Europe to China.

The price of coals in Westmorland or Shropshire can have little effect on their price at Newcastle; and their price in the

metals from all parts of the world being brought into competition.

Lionnois can have none at all. The productions of such distant coal-mines can never be brought into competition with one another. But the productions of the most distant metallic mines frequently may, and in fact commonly are. The price, therefore, of the coarse, and still more that of the precious metals, at the most fertile mines in the world, must necessarily more or less affect their price at every other in it. The price of copper in Japan must have some influence upon its price at the copper mines in Europe. The price of silver in Peru, or the quantity either of labour or of other goods which it will purchase there, must have some influence on its price, not only at the silver mines of Europe, but at those of China. After the discovery of the mines of Peru, the silver

---

[35] [Ed. 1 reads "depends frequently."]

[36] [Ed. 1 reads "article in the commerce of Europe."]

mines of Europe were, the greater part of them, abandoned. The value of silver was so much reduced that their produce could no longer pay the expence of working them, or replace, with a profit, the food, cloaths, lodging and other necessaries which were consumed in that operation. This was the case too with the mines of Cuba and St. Domingo, and even with the ancient mines of Peru, after the discovery of those of Potosi.

The price of every metal at every mine, therefore, being regulated in some measure by its price at the most fertile mine in the world that is actually wrought, it can at *Rent has therefore a small share in the price of metals.* the greater part of mines do very little more than pay the expence of working, and can seldom afford a very high rent to the landlord. Rent, accordingly, seems at the greater part of mines to have but a small share in the price of the coarse, and a still smaller in that of the precious metals. Labour and profit make up the greater part of both.

A sixth part of the gross produced may be reckoned the average rent of the tin mines of Cornwall, the most fertile that are known in the world, as we are told by the *Tin and lead mines pay a sixth in Cornwall and Scotland.* Rev. Mr. Borlace, vice-warden of the stannaries. Some, he says, afford more, and some do not afford so much.[37] A sixth part of the gross produce is the rent too of several very fertile lead mines in Scotland.

In the silver mines of Peru, we are told by Frezier and Ulloa, the proprietor frequently exacts no other acknowledgment from the undertaker of the mine, but that he *The silver mines of Peru formerly paid a fifth,* will grind the ore at his mill, paying him the ordinary multure or price of grinding.[38] Till 1736, indeed, the tax of the king of Spain amounted to one-fifth of the standard silver, which till then

---

[37][*Natural History of Cornwall*, by William Borlase, 1758, p. 175, but nothing is there said as to the landlord sometimes receiving more than one-sixth.]

[38] ["Those who are willing to labour themselves easily obtain of the miner a vein to work on; what they get out of it is their own, paying him the King's duty and the hire of the mill, which is so considerable that some are satisfied with the profit it yields without employing any to work for them in the mines."—Frezier, *Voyage to*

might be considered as the real rent of the greater part of the silver mines of Peru, the richest which have been known in the world. If there had been no tax, this fifth would naturally have belonged to the landlord, and many mines might have been wrought which could not then be wrought, because they could not afford this tax.[39] The tax of the duke of Cornwall upon tin is supposed to amount to more than five per cent. or one-twentieth part of the value;[40] and whatever may be his proportion, it would naturally too belong to the proprietor of the mine, if tin was duty free. But if you add one-twentieth to one-sixth, you will find that the whole average rent of the tin mines of Cornwall, was[41] to the whole average rent of the silver mines of Peru, as thirteen to twelve. But the silver mines of Peru are not now able to pay even this low rent, and the tax upon silver

and now only a tenth, was, in 1736, reduced from one-fifth to one-tenth.[42] Even this tax upon silver too gives more temptation to smuggling than the tax of one-twentieth upon tin; and smuggling must be much easier in the precious than in the bulky commodity. The tax of the king of Spain accordingly is said to be very ill paid, and that of the duke of Cornwall very well. Rent, therefore, it is probable, makes a greater part of the price of tin at the most fertile tin

---

the South Sea and along the Coasts of Chile and Peru in the Years 1712, 1713 and 1714, with a Postscript by Dr. Edmund Halley, 1717, p. 109. For Ulloa see below, p. 233, note.]

[39] [In place of these two sentences ed. 1 reads, "The tax of the King of Spain, indeed, amounts to one-fifth of the standard silver, which may be considered as the real rent of the greater part of the silver mines of Peru, the richest which are known in the world. If there was no tax, this fifth would naturally belong to the landlord, and many mines might be wrought which cannot be wrought at present, because they cannot afford this tax."]

[40] [The sum of more than £10,000 paid on £190,954 worth of produce is mentioned by Borlase. The duty was 4s. per cwt.—*Natural History of Cornwall,* p. 183.]

[41] [Ed. I reads "is."]

[42] [The reduction is mentioned again below, pp. 274, 291. Ed. I does not contain this sentence, and begins the next with "The high tax upon silver, too, gives much greater temptation to smuggling than the low tax upon tin."]

mines, than it does of silver at the most fertile silver mines in the world. After replacing the stock employed in working those different mines, together with its ordinary profits, the residue which remains to the proprietor, is greater it seems in the coarse, than in the precious metal.

Neither are the profits of the undertakers of silver mines commonly very great in Peru. The same most respectable and *while profits are small.* well informed authors acquaint us, that when any person undertakes to work a new mine in Peru, he is universally looked upon as a man destined to bankruptcy and ruin, and is upon that account shunned and avoided by every body.[43] Mining, it seems, is considered there in the same light as here, as a lottery, in which the prizes do not compensate the blanks, though the greatness of some tempts many adventurers to throw away their fortunes in such unprosperous projects.

As the sovereign, however, derives a considerable part of his revenue from the produce of silver mines, the law in Peru gives *Mining is encouraged in Peru by the interest of the sovereign.* every possible encouragement to the discovery and working of new ones. Whoever discovers a new mine, is entitled to measure off two hundred and forty-six feet in length, according to what he supposes to be the direction of the vein, and half as much in breadth.[44] He becomes proprietor of this portion of the mine, and can work it without paying any acknowledgment to the landlord. The interest of the duke of Cornwall has given occasion to a regulation nearly of the same kind in that ancient dutchy. In waste and uninclosed

[43] ["Quand un homme témoigne avoir dessein de fouiller dans quelque mine, les autres le regardent comme un extravagant qui court à sa perte, et qui risque une ruine certaine pour des espérances éloignées et très-douteuses. Ils tâchent de le détourner de son dessein, et s'ils n'y peuvent réussir, ils le fuyent en l'évitant, comme s'ils craignaient qu'il ne leur communiquât son mal."—*Voyage historique de l'Amérique méridionale par don George Juan et par don Antoine de Ulloa,* 1752, tom. i., p. 379. The statement relates to the province of Quito, and the condition of things is contrasted with that prevailing in Peru proper. For Frezier see next page, note 47.]

[44] [Frezier, *Voyage,* p. 109.]

lands any person who discovers a tin mine, may mark out its limits to a certain extent, which is called bounding a mine. The bounder becomes the real proprietor of the mine, and may either work it himself, or give it in lease to another, without the consent of the owner of the land, to whom, however, a very small acknowledgment must be paid upon working it.[45] In both regulations the sacred rights of private property are sacrificed to the supposed interests of public revenue.

The same encouragement is given in Peru to the discovery and working of new gold mines; and in gold the king's tax amounts only to a twentieth part of the standard metal. It was once a fifth, and afterwards a tenth, as in silver; but it was found that the work could not bear even the lowest of these two taxes.[46] If it is rare, however, say the same authors, Frezier and Ulloa, to find a person who has made his fortune by a silver, it is still much rarer to find one who has done so by a gold mine.[47] This twentieth part seems to be the whole rent which is paid by the greater part of the gold mines in Chili and Peru. Gold too is much more liable to be smuggled than even silver; not only on account of the superior value of the metal in proportion to its bulk, but on account of the peculiar way in which nature produces it. Silver is very seldom found virgin, but, like most other metals, is generally

The gold mines of Peru now pay only a twentieth in rent.

---

[45] [Borlase, *Natural History of Cornwall*, pp. 167, 175. If the land was "bounded" (bounding could only take place on "wastrel or common") the lord of the soil received only a fifteenth.]

[46] [Ed. 1 reads "It was once a fifth, as in silver, but it was found the work could not bear it."]

[47] ["It is more rare to see a gold miner rich than a silver miner or of any other metal."—Frezier, *Voyage*, p. 108. There seems nothing in either Frezier or Ulloa to indicate that they took the gloomy view of the prospects of the gold and silver miner which is ascribed to them in the text. From this and the curious way in which they are coupled together, here and above (pp. 230–231, 232), and also the fact that no mention is made of the title of either of their books, it seems probable that Smith is quoting from memory or from notes which had become mixed. It is possible that he confused Frezier with Ulloa's collaborator, Don George Juan, but Ulloa is quoted without Frezier above, p. 203, and below, p. 254.]

mineralized with some other body, from which it is impossible to separate it in such quantities as will pay for the expence, but by a very laborious and tedious operation, which cannot well be carried on but in workhouses erected for the purpose, and therefore exposed to the inspection of the king's officers. Gold, on the contrary, is almost always found virgin. It is sometimes found in pieces of some bulk; and even when mixed in small and almost insensible particles with sand, earth, and other extraneous bodies, it can be separated from them by a very short and simple operation, which can be carried on in any private house by any body who is possessed of a small quantity of mercury. If the king's tax, therefore, is but ill paid upon silver, it is likely to be much worse paid upon gold; and rent must make a much smaller part of the price of gold, than even of that of silver.

The lowest price at which the precious metals can be sold, or the smallest quantity of other goods for which they can be

The lowest price of the precious metals must replace stock with ordinary profits,

exchanged during any considerable time, is regulated by the same principles which fix the lowest ordinary price of all other goods. The stock which must commonly be employed, the food, cloaths, and lodging which must commonly be consumed in bringing them from the mine to the market, determine it. It must at least be sufficient to replace that stock, with the ordinary profits.

Their highest price, however, seems not to be necessarily determined by any thing but the actual scarcity or plenty of

but their highest price is determined by their scarcity.

those metals themselves. It is not determined by that of any other commodity, in the same manner as the price of coals is by that of wood, beyond which no scarcity can ever raise it. Increase the scarcity of gold to a certain degree, and the smallest bit of it may become more precious than a diamond, and exchange for a greater quantity of other goods.

The demand for those metals arises partly from their utility, and partly from their beauty. If you except iron, they are more useful than, perhaps, any other metal. As they are less liable to

The demand for them arises from their utility and beauty:

rust and impurity, they can more easily be kept clean; and the utensils either of the table or the kitchen are often upon that account more agreeable when made of them. A silver boiler is more cleanly that a lead, copper, or tin one; and the same quality would render a gold boiler still better than a silver one. Their principal merit, however, arises from their beauty, which renders them peculiarly fit for the ornaments of dress and furniture. No paint or dye can give

and the merit of beauty is enhanced by their scarcity.

so splendid a colour as gilding. The merit of their beauty is greatly enhanced by their scarcity. With the greater part of rich people, the chief enjoyment of riches consists in the parade of riches, which in their eye is never so complete as when they appear to possess those decisive marks of opulence which nobody can possess but themselves. In their eyes the merit of an object which is in any degree either useful or beautiful, is greatly enhanced by its scarcity, or by the great labour which it requires to collect any considerable quantity of it, a labour which nobody can afford to pay but themselves. Such objects they are willing to purchase at a higher price than things much more beautiful and useful, but more common. These qualities of utility, beauty, and scarcity, are the original foundation of the high price of those metals, or of the great quantity of other goods for which they can every-where be exchanged. This value was antecedent to and independent of their being employed as coin, and was the quality which fitted them for that employment. That employment, however, by occasioning a new demand, and by diminishing the quantity which could be employed in any other way, may have afterwards contributed to keep up or increase their value.

The demand for precious stones arises altogether from their beauty enhanced by their scarcity.

The demand for the precious stones arises altogether from their beauty. They are of no use, but as ornaments; and the merit of their beauty is greatly enhanced by their scarcity, or by the difficulty and expence of getting them from the mine. Wages and profit accordingly make up, upon most occasions, almost the whole of their high price. Rent comes in but for a very small share; frequently for no share; and the most fertile mines only afford any considerable rent. When Tavernier, a jeweller, visited the diamond mines of Golconda and Visiapour, he was informed that the sovereign of the country, for whose benefit they were wrought, had ordered all of them to be shut up, except those which yielded the largest and finest stones.[48] The others, it seems, were to the proprietor not worth the working.

As the price both of the precious metals and of the precious stones is regulated all over the world by their price at the most fertile mine in it, the rent which a mine of either can afford to its proprietor is in proportion, not to its absolute, but to what may be called its relative fertility, or to its superiority over other mines of the same kind. If new mines were discovered as much superior to those of Potosi as they were superior to those of Europe, the value of silver might be so much degraded as to render even the mines of Potosi not worth the working. Before the discovery of the Spanish West Indies, the most fertile mines in Europe may have afforded as great a rent to their proprietor as the richest mines in Peru do at present. Though the quantity of silver was much less, it might have exchanged for an equal quantity of other goods, and the proprietor's share might have enabled him to purchase or command an equal quantity either of labour or of commodities. The value both of the produce and of the rent, the real revenue which they afforded both to the public and to the proprietor, might have been the same.

The rent of mines of precious metals and precious stones is in proportion to their relative and not to their absolute fertility.

[48] [*The Six Voyages of John Baptista Tavernier, a noble man of France now living, through Turkey into Persia and the East Indies*, translated by J. P., 1678, does not appear to contain any such statement. Possibly it is merely founded on Tavernier's remark that "there was a mine discovered between Coulour and Raolconda, which the King caused to be shut up again by reason of some cheats that were used there; for they found therein that sort of stones which had this green outside, fair and transparent, and which appeared more fair than the others, but when they came to the mill they crumbled to pieces" (pt. ii., p. 138). In eds. 4 and 5 "yielded" is misprinted "yield."]

The most abundant mines either of the precious metals or of the precious stones could add little to the wealth of the world. A produce of which the value is principally derived from its scarcity, is necessarily degraded by its abundance. A service of plate, and the other frivolous ornaments of dress and furniture, could be purchased for a smaller quantity of labour, or for a smaller quantity of commodities; and in this would consist the sole advantage which the world could derive from that abundance.

Abundant supplies would add little to the wealth of the world.

It is otherwise in estates above ground. The value both of their produce and of their rent is in proportion to their absolute, and not to their relative fertility. The land which produces a certain quantity of food, cloaths, and lodging, can always feed, cloath, and lodge a certain number of people; and whatever may be the proportion of the landlord, it will always give him a proportionable command of the labour of those people, and of the commodities with which that labour can supply him. The value of the most barren lands is not diminished by the neighbourhood of the most fertile. On the contrary, it is generally increased by it. The great number of people maintained by the fertile lands affords a market to many parts of the produce of the barren, which they could never have found among those whom their own produce could maintain.

But in estates above ground both produce and rent are regulated by absolute fertility.

Whatever increases the fertility of land in producing food, increases not only the value of the lands upon which the improvement is bestowed, but contributes likewise to increase that of many other lands, by creating a new demand for their produce. That abundance of food, of which, in consequence of the improvement of land, many people have the disposal beyond what they themselves can consume, is the great cause of the demand both for the precious metals and the precious stones, as well as for every other conveniency and ornament of dress, lodging, household furniture, and equipage. Food not only constitutes the principal part of the riches of the

Abundance of food raises the value of other produce.

world, but it is the abundance of food which gives the principal part of their value to many other sorts of riches. The poor inhabitants of Cuba and St. Domingo, when they were first discovered by the Spaniards, used to wear little bits of gold as ornaments in their hair and other parts of their dress. They seemed to value them as we would do any little pebbles of somewhat more than ordinary beauty, and to consider them as just worth the picking up, but not worth the refusing to any body who asked them. They gave them to their new guests at the first request, without seeming to think that they had made them any very valuable present. They were astonished to observe the rage of the Spaniards to obtain them; and had no notion that there could anywhere be a country in which many people had the disposal of so great a superfluity of food, so scanty always among themselves, that for a very small quantity of those glittering baubles they would willingly give as much as might maintain a whole family for many years. Could they have been made to understand this, the passion of the Spaniards would not have surprised them.

PART III

OF THE VARIATIONS IN THE PROPORTION BETWEEN THE RESPECTIVE VALUES OF THAT SORT OF PRODUCE WHICH ALWAYS AFFORDS RENT, AND OF THAT WHICH SOMETIMES DOES AND SOMETIMES DOES NOT AFFORD RENT

The increasing abundance of food, in consequence of increasing improvement and cultivation, must necessarily increase the demand for every part of the produce of land which is not food, and which can be applied either to use or to ornament. In the whole progress of improvement, it might therefore be expected, there should be only one variation in the comparative values of those two different sorts of produce. The value of that sort which sometimes does and sometimes does not afford rent, should con-

The general course of progress is for produce other than food to become dearer,

stantly rise in proportion to that which always affords some
rent. As art and industry advance, the materials of cloathing
and lodging, the useful fossils and minerals of the earth, the
precious metals and the precious stones should gradually come
to be more and more in demand, should gradually exchange for
a greater and a greater quantity of food, or in other words,
should gradually become dearer and dearer. This accordingly
has been the case with most of these things upon most occasions, and would have been the case with all of them upon all
occasions, if particular accidents had not upon some occasions
increased the supply of some of them, in a still greater proportion than the demand.

The value of a free-stone quarry, for example, will necessarily increase with the increasing improvement and population of the country round about it; especially
but there are
interruptions,
if it should be the only one in the neighbourhood. But the value of a silver mine, even
though there should not be another within a thousand miles of
it, will not necessarily increase with the improvement of the
country in which it is situated. The market for the produce of a
free-stone quarry can seldom extend more than a few miles
round about it, and the demand must generally be in proportion
as in the case
of silver,
to the improvement and population of that
small district. But the market for the produce
of a silver mine may extend over the whole
known world. Unless the world in general, therefore, be advancing in improvement and population, the demand for silver
might not be at all increased by the improvement even of a
large country in the neighbourhood of the mine. Even though
when new fertile
mines are
discovered.
the world in general were improving, yet, if,
in the course of its improvement, new mines
should be discovered, much more fertile
than any which had been known before,
though the demand for silver would necessarily increase, yet
the supply might increase in so much a greater proportion, that
the real price of that metal might gradually fall; that is, any
given quantity, a pound weight of it, for example, might gradually purchase or command a smaller and a smaller quantity of

labour, or exchange for a smaller and a smaller quantity of corn, the principal part of the subsistence of the labourer.

The great market for silver is the commercial and civilized part of the world.

If by the general progress of improvement the demand of this market should increase, while at the same time the supply did not increase in the same proportion, the value of silver would gradually rise in proportion to that of corn. Any given quantity of silver would exchange for a greater and a greater quantity of corn; or, in other words, the average money price of corn would gradually become cheaper and cheaper.

Silver would grow dearer in the general progress of improvement,

If, on the contrary, the supply by some accident should increase for many years together in a greater proportion than the demand, that metal would gradually become cheaper and cheaper; or, in other words, the average money price of corn would, in spite of all improvements, gradually become dearer and dearer.

but might grow cheaper if some accident increased the supply for many years together:

But if, on the other hand, the supply of the metal should increase nearly in the same proportion as the demand, it would continue to purchase or exchange for nearly the same quantity of corn, and the average money price of corn would, in spite of all improvements, continue very nearly the same.

or remain stationary if demand and supply increased equally.

These three seem to exhaust all the possible combinations of events which can happen in the progress of improvement; and during the course of the four centuries preceding the present, if we may judge by what has happened both in France and Great Britain, each of those three different combinations seem[49] to have taken place in the European market, and nearly in the same order too in which I have here set them down.

These three things have happened during the last 400 years.

[49] [Ed. 1 reads "seems."]

DIGRESSION CONCERNING THE VARIATIONS IN THE VALUE OF SILVER DURING THE COURSE OF THE FOUR LAST CENTURIES

First Period

In 1350, and for some time before, the average price of the quarter of wheat in England seems not to have been estimated

From 1350 to 1570 silver gradually fell.

lower than four ounces of silver, Tower-weight, equal to about twenty shillings of our present money. From this price it seems to have fallen gradually to two ounces of silver, equal to about ten shillings of our present money, the price at which we find it estimated in the beginning of the sixteenth century, and at which it seems to have continued to be estimated till about 1570.[50]

In 1350, being the 25th of Edward III, was enacted what is called, The statute of labourers.[51] In the preamble it complains

In 1350 wheat was 4 oz. of silver per quarter,

much of the insolence of servants, who endeavoured to raise their wages upon their masters.[52] It therefore ordains, that all servants and labourers should for the future be contented with the same wages and liveries (liveries in those

---

[50] [The evidence for this statement, which does not agree with the figures in the table at the end of the chapter, is given in the next eleven paragraphs.]

[51] [Already quoted above, p. 180.]

[52] [It speaks of the Act of 1349, which ordered a continuance of wages at the level of 20 Edward III., and five or six years before (1347 or 1348 to 1353), as having been passed "against the malice of servants which were idle and not willing to serve after the pestilence without taking excessive wages," and gives as the reason for new provisions "forasmuch as it is given the King to understand in this present Parliament by the petition of the commonalty that the said servants having no regard to the said ordinance, but to their ease and singular covetise, do withdraw themselves to serve great men and other, unless they have livery and wages to the double or treble of that they were wont to take the said twentieth year and before, to the great damage of the great men and impoverishing of all the said commonalty, whereof the said commonalty prayeth remedy."]

times signified, not only cloaths, but provisions) which they had been accustomed to receive in the 20th year of the king, and the four preceding years;[53] that upon this account their livery wheat should no-where be estimated higher than ten-pence a bushel, and that it should always be in the option of the master to deliver them either the wheat or the money. Tenpence a bushel, therefore, had, in the 25th of Edward III, been reckoned a very moderate price of wheat, since it required a particular statute to oblige servants to accept of it in exchange for their usual livery of provisions; and it had been reckoned a reasonable price ten years before that, or in the 16th year of the king, the term to which the statute refers. But in the 16th year of Edward III, ten-pence contained about half an ounce of silver, Tower-weight, and was nearly equal to half a crown of our present money.[54] Four ounces of silver, Tower-weight, therefore, equal to six shillings and eight-pence of the money of those times, and to near twenty shillings of that of the present, must have been reckoned a moderate price for the quarter of eight bushels.

This statute is surely a better evidence of what was reckoned in those times a moderate price of grain, than the prices *and was not less than that at the beginning of the century,* of some particular years which have generally been recorded by historians and other writers on account of their extraordinary dearness or cheapness, and from which, therefore, it is difficult to form any judgment concerning what may have been the ordinary price.[55] There are, besides, other reasons for believing, that in the beginning of the fourteenth century, and for some time before, the common price of wheat was not less than four ounces of silver the quarter, and that of other grain in proportion.

In 1309, Ralph de Born, prior of St. Augustine's, Canter-

---

[53] [*I.e.*, four years before the twentieth year.]

[54] [This and the other reductions of ancient money to the eighteenth century standard are probably founded on the table in Martin Folkes, *Table of English Silver Coins*, 1745, p. 142.]

[55] [*E.g.*, Fleetwood's prices in the table at the end of the chapter.]

bury, gave a feast upon his installation-day, of which William
Thorn has preserved, not only the bill of fare, but the prices of
many particulars. In that feast were consumed, 1st, Fifty-three
quarters of wheat, which cost nineteen pounds, or seven
shillings and two-pence a quarter, equal to about one-and-
twenty shillings and six-pence of our present money; 2dly,
Fifty-eight quarters of malt, which cost seventeen pounds ten
shillings, or six shillings a quarter, equal to about eighteen
shillings of our present money: 3dly, Twenty quarters of oats,
which cost four pounds, or four shillings a quarter, equal to
about twelve shillings of our present money.[56] The prices of
malt and oats seem here to be higher than their ordinary proportion to the price of wheat.

These prices are not recorded on account of their extraordinary dearness or cheapness, but are mentioned accidentally as
the prices actually paid for large quantities of grain consumed
at a feast which was famous for its magnificence.

In 1262, being the 51st of Henry III, was revived an ancient
statute called, *The Assize of Bread and Ale*,[57] which, the king

and for some time   says in the preamble, had been made in the
before.   times of his progenitors sometime kings of
                     England. It is probably, therefore, as old at
least as the time of his grandfather Henry II, and may have
been as old as the conquest. It regulates the price of bread according as the prices of wheat may happen to be, from one
shilling to twenty shillings the quarter of the money of those
times. But statutes of this kind are generally presumed to provide with equal care for all deviations from the middle price,
for those below it as well as those above it. Ten shillings, therefore, containing six ounces of silver, Tower-weight, and equal
to about thirty shillings of our present money, must, upon this

---

[56] [Fleetwood, *Chronicon Preciosum*, 1707, pp. 83–85.]

[57] [The date 1262 is wrong, as 51 Hen. III. ran from October 28, 1266, to October
27, 1267. But the editions of the statutes which ascribe the statute to 51 Hen. III.
appear to have no good authority for doing so; see *Statutes of the Realm*, vol. i., p.
199, notes. The statute has already been quoted above, p. 39, and is quoted again
below, p. 249.]

supposition, have been reckoned the middle price of the quarter of wheat when this statute was first enacted, and must have continued to be so in the 51st of Henry III. We cannot therefore be very wrong[58] in supposing that the middle price was not less than one-third of the highest price at which this statute regulates the price of bread, or than six shillings and eight-pence of the money of those times, containing four ounces of silver, Tower-weight.

From these different facts, therefore, we seem to have some reason to conclude, that about the middle of the fourteenth century, and for a considerable time before, the average or ordinary price of the quarter of wheat was not supposed to be less than four ounces of silver, Tower-weight.

From about the middle of the fourteenth to the beginning of the sixteenth century, what was reckoned the reasonable and

From that it sank gradually to 2 oz. at the beginning of the sixteenth century and remained at that till 1570.

moderate, that is the ordinary or average price of wheat, seems to have sunk gradually to about one-half of this price; so as at last to have fallen to about two ounces of silver, Tower-weight, equal to about ten shillings of our present money. It continued to be estimated at this price till about 1570.

In the household book of Henry, the fifth earl of Northumberland, drawn up in 1512, there are two different estimations of wheat. In one of them it is computed at six shillings and eight-pence the quarter, in the other at five shillings and eight-pence only.[59] In 1512, six shillings and eight-pence contained only two ounces of silver, Tower-weight, and were equal to about ten shillings of our present money.

From the 25th of Edward III, to the beginning of the reign of Elizabeth, during the space of more than two hundred years,

---

[58] [Ed. 1 reads "very far wrong."]

[59] [*The Regulations and Establishment of the Household of Henry Algernon Percy, the fifth Earl of Northumberland, at his castles of Wresill and Lekinfield in Yorkshire, begun anno domini MDXII.*, 1770, pp. 2, 4, but there are not really two estimations. It seems clear that "vs. viijd." on p. 4 is merely a misprint or mistake for "vis. viijd.," since 118 qrs. 2 bushels are reckoned at £39 8s. 4d.]

six shillings and eight-pence, it appears from several different statutes, had continued to be considered as what is called the moderate and reasonable, that is the ordinary or average price of wheat. The quantity of silver, however, contained in that nominal sum was, during the course of this period, continually diminishing, in consequence of some alterations which were made in the coin. But the increase of the value of silver had, it seems, so far compensated the diminution of the quantity of it contained in the same nominal sum, that the legislature did not think it worth while to attend to this circumstance.

Thus in 1436 it was enacted, that wheat might be exported without a licence when the price was so low as six shillings and eight-pence.[60] And in 1463 it was enacted, that no wheat should be imported if the price was not above six shillings and eight-pence the quarter.[61] The legislature had imagined, that when the price was so low, there could be no inconveniency in exportation, but that when it rose higher, it became prudent to allow of importation. Six shillings and eight-pence, therefore, containing about the same quantity of silver as thirteen shillings and four-pence of our present money (one third part less than the same nominal sum contained in the time of Edward III), had in those times been considered as what is called the moderate and reasonable price of wheat.

In 1554, by the 1st and 2d of Philip and Mary;[62] and in 1558, by the 1st of Elizabeth,[63] the exportation of wheat was in the same manner prohibited, whenever the price of the quarter should exceed six shillings and eight-pence, which did not then contain two penny worth more silver than the same nominal sum does at present. But it had soon been found that to re-

[60] [15 Hen. VI., c. 2.]

[61] [3 Ed. IV., c. 2.]

[62] [1 and 2 P. and M., c. 5, § 7. Licences for exportation, however, are recognised by the Act.]

[63] [1 Eliz., c. 11, § 11, which, however, merely partially exempts Norfolk and Suffolk from regulations intended to prevent exportation from places where no custom-house existed.]

strain the exportation of wheat till the price was so very low, was in reality, to prohibit it altogether. In 1562, therefore, by the 5th of Elizabeth,[64] the exportation of wheat was allowed from certain ports whenever the price of the quarter should not exceed ten shillings, containing nearly the same quantity of silver as the nominal sum does at present. This price had at this time, therefore, been considered as what is called the moderate and reasonable price of wheat. It agrees nearly with the estimation of the Northumberland book in 1512.

That in France the average price of grain was, in the same manner, much lower in the end of the fifteenth and beginning

The same fall has been observed in France.

of the sixteenth century, than in the two centuries preceding, has been observed both by Mr. Duprè de St. Maur,[65] and by the elegant author of the Essay on the police of grain.[66] Its price, during the same period, had probably sunk in the same manner through the greater part of Europe.

This rise in the value of silver, in proportion to that of corn, may either have been owing altogether to the increase of the

It may have been due to the increase of demand for silver or to a diminution of supply.

demand for that metal, in consequence of increasing improvement and cultivation, the supply in the mean time continuing the same as before: Or, the demand continuing the same as before, it may have been owing altogether to the gradual diminution of the supply; the greater part of the mines which were then known in the world, being much exhausted, and consequently the expence of working them much increased: Or it may have been owing partly to the one and partly to the other

---

[64] [5 Eliz., c. 5, § 17.]

[65] ["Neither his *Recherches sur la valeur des Monnoies et sur les prix des grains avant et après le concile de Francfort*, 1762, nor his *Essai sur les Monnoies, ou réflexions sur le rapport entre l'argent et les denrées*, 1746, contain any clear justification for this reference.]

[66] [From 1446 to 1515 "le blé fut plus bas que dans les siècles précédents."—*Essai sur la police générale des grains sur leur prix et sur les effets de l'agriculture*, 1755 (by C. J. Herbert), pp. 259, 260.]

of those two circumstances. In the end of the fifteenth and beginning of the sixteenth centuries, the greater part of Europe
was approaching towards a more settled form of government
than it had enjoyed for several ages before. The increase of security would naturally increase industry and improvement; and
the demand for the precious metals, as well as for every other
luxury and ornament, would naturally increase with the increase of riches. A greater annual produce would require a
greater quantity of coin to circulate it; and a greater number of
rich people would require a greater quantity of plate and other
ornaments of silver. It is natural to suppose too, that the greater
part of the mines which then supplied the European market
with silver, might be a good deal exhausted, and have become
more expensive in the working. They had been wrought many
of them from the time of the Romans.

It has been the opinion, however, of the greater part of those
who have written upon the prices of commodities in ancient
times, that, from the Conquest, perhaps from the invasion of
Julius Cæsar, till the discovery of the mines
of America, the value of silver was continually diminishing. This opinion they seem to
have been led into, partly by the observations which they had occasion to make upon
the prices both of corn and of some other
parts of the rude produce of land; and partly by the popular notion, that as the quantity of silver naturally increases in every
country with the increase of wealth, so its value diminishes as
its quantity increases.

*Most writers,
however, have
supposed that the
value of silver
continually fell.*

In their observations upon the prices of corn, three different
circumstances seem frequently to have misled them.

First, In ancient times almost all rents were paid in kind; in
a certain quantity of corn, cattle, poultry, &c. It sometimes
happened, however, that the landlord would stipulate,[67] that he
should be at liberty to demand of the tenant, either the annual
payment in kind, or a certain sum of money instead of it. The
price at which the payment in kind was in this manner ex-

[67] [Ed. 1 reads "with the tenant" here and omits "of the tenant" at end of line.]

They have been misled in their observations on the price of corn, (1) by confusing conversion prices with market prices;

changed for a certain sum of money, is in Scotland called the conversion price. As the option is always in the landlord to take either the substance or the price, it is necessary for the safety of the tenant, that the conversion price should rather be below than above the average market price. In many places, accordingly, it is not much above one-half of this price. Through the greater part of Scotland this custom still continues with regard to poultry, and in some places with regard to cattle. It might probably have continued to take place too with regard to corn, had not the institution of the public fiars put an end to it. These are annual valuations, according to the judgment of an assize, of the average price of all the different sorts of grain, and of all the different qualities of each, according to the actual market price in every different county. This institution rendered it sufficiently safe for the tenant, and much more convenient for the landlord, to convert, as they call it, the corn rent, rather at what should happen to be the price of the fiars of each year,[68] than at any certain fixed price. But the writers who have collected the prices of corn in ancient times, seem frequently to have mistaken what is called in Scotland the conversion price for the actual market price. Fleetwood acknowledges, upon one occasion, that he had made this mistake. As he wrote his book, however, for a particular purpose, he does not think proper to make this acknowledgment till after transcribing this conversion price fifteen times.[69] The price is eight shillings the quarter of wheat. This sum in 1423, the year at which he begins with it, contained the same quantity of silver as sixteen shillings of our present money. But in 1562, the year at which he ends with it, it contained no more than the same nominal sum does at present.

[68] [Ed. 1 reads "rent at the price of the fiars of each year rather."]

[69] [*Chronicon Preciosum*, 1707, pp. 121, 122. Fleetwood does not "acknowledge any mistake," but says that though the price was not the market price it might have been "well agreed upon." His "particular purpose" was to prove that in order to qualify for a fellowship a man might conscientiously swear his income to be much less than it was.]

Secondly, They have been misled by the slovenly manner in which some ancient statutes of assize had been sometimes transcribed by lazy copiers; and sometimes perhaps actually composed by the legislature.

(2) by the slovenly transcription of ancient statutes of assize;

The ancient statutes of assize seem to have begun always with determining what ought to be the price of bread and ale when the price of wheat and barley were at the lowest, and to have proceeded gradually to determine what it ought to be, according as the prices of those two sorts of grain should gradually rise above this lowest price. But the transcribers of those statutes seem frequently to have thought it sufficient, to copy the regulation as far as the three or four first and lowest prices; saving in this manner their own labour, and judging, I suppose, that this was enough to show what proportion ought to be observed in all higher prices.

Thus in the assize of bread and ale, of the 51st of Henry III, the price of bread was regulated according to the different prices of wheat, from one shilling to twenty shillings the quarter, of the money of those times. But in the manuscripts from which all the different editions of the statutes, preceding that of Mr. Ruffhead, were printed, the copiers had never transcribed this regulation beyond the price of twelve shillings.[70] Several writers, therefore, being misled by this faulty transcription, very naturally concluded that the middle price, or six shillings the quarter, equal to about eighteen shillings of our present money, was the ordinary or average price of wheat at that time.

In the statute of Tumbrel and Pillory,[71] enacted nearly about the same time, the price of ale is regulated according to every sixpence rise in the price of barley, from two shillings to four shillings the quarter. That four shillings, however, was not considered as the highest price to which barley might frequently

[70] [The statement is too sweeping. See *Statutes of the Realm*, vol. i., pp. xxiv and 199, notes. Ruffhead's edition began to be published in 1762.]

[71] [Judicium Pillorie, temp. incert., ascribed to 51 Hen. III., stat. 6.]

or by misunder-
standings of those
statutes;

rise in those times, and that these prices were only given as an example of the proportion which ought to be observed in all other prices, whether higher or lower, we may infer from the last words of the statute; "et sic deinceps crescetur vel diminuetur per sex denarios." The expression is very slovenly, but the meaning is plain enough; "That the price of ale is in this manner to be increased or diminished according to every sixpence rise or fall in the price of barley." In the composition of this statute the legislature itself seems to have been as negligent as the copiers were in the transcription of the other.

In an ancient manuscript of the Regiam Majestatem, an old Scotch law book, there is a statute of assize, in which the price of bread is regulated according to all the different prices of wheat, from ten-pence to three shillings the Scotch boll, equal to about half an English quarter. Three shillings Scotch, at the time when this assize is supposed to have been enacted, were equal to about nine shilling sterling of our present money. Mr. Ruddiman[72] seems[73] to conclude from this that three shillings was the highest price to which wheat ever rose in those times, and that ten-pence, a shilling, or at most two shillings, were the ordinary prices. Upon consulting the manuscript, however, it appears evidently, that all these prices are only set down as examples of the proportion which ought to be observed between the respective prices of wheat and bread. The last words of the statute are "reliqua judicabis secundum præscripta habendo respectum ad pretium bladi." "You shall judge of the remaining cases according to what is above written having a respect to the price of corn."[74]

---

[72] [Eds. 1 and 2 read "Rudiman."]

[73] [See his preface to Anderson's Diplomata Scotiae. *Selectus diplomatum et numismatum Scotiae thesaurus*, 1739, p. 82, and in the translation, *An Introduction to Mr. James Anderson's* Diplomata Scotiae, by Thomas Ruddiman, M.A., Edinburgh, 1773, pp. 170, 174, 228. The note appears first in ed. 2.]

[74] [The manuscript appears to be the Alexander Foulis MS., now 25. 4. 10. in the

Thirdly, They seem to have been misled too by the very low price at which wheat was sometimes sold in very ancient

and (3) by attributing too much importance to excessively low prices.

times; and to have imagined, that as its lowest price was then much lower than in later times, its ordinary price must likewise have been much lower. They might have found, however, that in those ancient times, its highest price was fully as much above, as its lowest price was below any thing that had ever been known in later times. Thus in 1270, Fleetwood gives us two prices of the quarter of wheat.[75] The one is four pounds sixteen shillings of the money of those times, equal to fourteen pounds eight shillings of that of the present; the other is six pounds eight shillings, equal to nineteen pounds four shillings of our present money. No price can be found in the end of the fifteenth, or beginning of the sixteenth century, which approaches to the extravagance of these. The price of corn, though at all times liable to variation,[76] varies most in those turbulent and disorderly societies, in which the interruption of all commerce and communication hinders the plenty of one part of the country from relieving the scarcity of another. In the disorderly state of England under the Plantagenets, who governed it from about the middle of the twelfth, till towards the end of the fifteenth century, one district might be in plenty, while another at no great distance, by having its crop destroyed either by some accident of the seasons, or by the incursion of some neighbouring baron, might be suffering all the horrors of a famine; and yet if the lands of some hostile lord were interposed between them, the one might not be able to give the least assis-

Edinburgh Advocates' Library, No. viii. of the MSS., described in *Acts of the Parliaments of Scotland*, vol. i. The exact words are "Memorandum quod reliqua judicabis secundum praedicta habendo respectum ad praescripta bladi precium duplicando."]

[75] [*Chronicon Preciosum*, p. 78. Fleetwood quotes the author of *Antiq. Britan* in *Vita Joh. Pecham* as saying that "provisions were so scarce that parents did eat their own children."]

[76] [Eds. 1 to 3 read "variations."]

tance to the other. Under the vigorous administration of the Tudors, who governed England during the latter part of the fifteenth, and through the whole of the sixteenth century, no baron was powerful enough to dare to disturb the public security.

The reader will find at the end of this chapter all the prices of wheat which have been collected by Fleetwood from 1202

The figures at the end of the chapter confirm this account.

to 1597, both inclusive, reduced to the money of the present times, and digested according to the order of time, into seven divisions of twelve years each. At the end of each division too, he will find the average price of the twelve years of which it consists. In that long period of time, Fleetwood has been able to collect the prices of no more than eighty years, so that four years are wanting to make out the last twelve years. I have added, therefore, from the accounts of Eton College, the prices of 1598, 1599, 1600, and 1601.[77] It is the only addition which I have made. The reader will see, that from the beginning of the thirteenth, till after the middle of the sixteenth century, the average price of each twelve years grows gradually lower and lower; and that towards the end of the sixteenth century it begins to rise again. The prices, indeed, which Fleetwood has been able to collect, seem to have been those chiefly which were remarkable for extraordinary dearness or cheapness; and I do not pretend that any very certain conclusion can be drawn from them. So far, however, as they prove any thing at all, they confirm the account which I have been endeavouring to give. Fleetwood himself, however, seems, with most other writers, to have believed,[78] that during all this period the value of silver, in consequence of its increasing abundance, was continually diminishing. The prices of corn which he himself has collected, certainly do not agree with this opinion. They agree perfectly

[77] [See the table, pp. 340–348 below.]

[78] [This appears to be merely an inference from the fact that he does not take notice of fluctuations.]

with that of Mr. Duprè de St. Maur,[79] and with that which I have been endeavouring to explain. Bishop Fleetwood and Mr. Duprè de St. Maur are the two authors who seem to have collected, with the greatest diligence and fidelity, the prices of things in ancient times. It is somewhat curious that, though their opinions are so very different, their facts, so far as they relate to the price of corn at least, should coincide so very exactly.

It is not, however, so much from the low price of corn, as from that of some other parts of the rude produce of land, that the most judicious writers have inferred the great value of silver in those very ancient times. Corn, it has been said, being a sort of manufacture, was, in those rude ages, much dearer in proportion than the greater part of other commodities; it is meant, I suppose, than the greater part of unmanufactured commodities; such as cattle, poultry, game of all kinds, &c. That in those times of poverty and barbarism these were proportionably much cheaper than corn, is undoubtedly true. But this cheapness was not the effect of the high value of silver, but of the low value of those commodities. It was not because silver would in such times purchase or represent a greater quantity of labour, but because[80] such commodities would purchase or represent a much smaller quantity than in times of more opulence and improvement. Silver must certainly be cheaper in Spanish America than in Europe; in the country where it is produced, than in the country to which it is brought, at the expence of a long carriage both by land and by sea, of a freight and an insurance. One-and-twenty pence halfpenny sterling, however, we are told by Ulloa, was, not many years ago, at Buenos Ayres, the price of an ox chosen from a herd of three or four hun-

Sometimes the value of silver has been measured by the price of cattle, poultry, etc. But the low price of these things shows their cheapness, not the dearness of silver,

---

[79][Above, pp. 244, 245.]

[80] [Ed. 1 reads "that" instead of "because," here and also two lines above.]

dred.[81] Sixteen shillings sterling, we are told by Mr. Byron, was the price of a good horse in the capital of Chili.[82] In a country naturally fertile, but of which the far greater part is altogether uncultivated, cattle, poultry, game of all kinds, &c. as they can be acquired with a very small quantity of labour, so they will purchase or command but a very small quantity. The low money price for which they may be sold, is no proof that the real value of silver is there very high, but that the real value of those commodities is very low.

Labour, it must always be remembered, and not any particular commodity or set of commodities, is the real measure of the value both of silver and of all other commodities.

for labour is the real measure.

But in countries almost waste, or but thinly inhabited, cattle, poultry, game of all kinds, &c. as they are the spontaneous productions of nature, so she frequently produces them in much greater quantities than the consumption of the inhabitants requires. In such a state of things the supply commonly exceeds the demand. In different states of society, in different stages of improvement, therefore, such commodities will represent, or be equivalent to, very different quantities of labour.

Cattle, poultry, etc., are produced by very different quantities of labour at different times,

In every state of society, in every stage of improvement, corn is the production of human industry. But the average produce of every sort of industry is always suited, more or less exactly, to the average consumption; the average supply to the average demand. In every different stage of improvement, besides, the raising of equal quantities of corn in the same soil and climate, will, at an average, require nearly

whereas corn scarcely varies at all,

[81] [*Voyage historique de l'Amérique méridionale*, vol. i., p. 552, where, however, the number of cattle is two or three hundred, as correctly quoted above, pp. 203.]

[82] [*Narrative of the Hon. John Byron, containing an account of the Great Distresses suffered by himself and his companions on the Coast of Patagonia from 1740 to 1746, 1768*, pp. 212, 220.]

equal quantities of labour; or what comes to the same thing, the price of nearly equal quantities; the continual increase of the productive powers of labour in an improving[83] state of cultivation being more or less counterbalanced by the continually increasing price of cattle, the principal instruments of agriculture. Upon all these accounts, therefore, we may rest assured, that equal quantities of corn will, in every state of society, in every stage of improvement, more nearly represent, or be equivalent to, equal quantities of labour, than equal quantities of any other part of the rude produce of land. Corn, accordingly, it has already been observed,[84] is, in all the different stages of wealth and improvement, a more accurate measure of value than any other commodity or set of commodities. In all those different stages, therefore, we can judge better of the real value of silver, by comparing it with corn, than by comparing it with any other commodity, or set of commodities.

Corn, besides, or whatever else is the common and favourite vegetable food of the people, constitutes, in every civilized country, the principal part of the subsistence of the labourer. In consequence of the extension of agriculture, the land of every country produces a much greater quantity of vegetable than of animal food, and the labourer every-where lives chiefly upon the wholesome food that is cheapest and most abundant. Butcher's-meat, except in the most thriving countries, or where labour is most highly rewarded, makes but an insignificant part of his subsistence; poultry makes a still smaller part of it, and game no part of it. In France, and even in Scotland, where labour is somewhat better rewarded than in France, the labouring poor seldom eat butcher's-meat, except upon holidays, and other extraordinary occasions. The money price of labour, therefore, depends much more upon the average money price of corn, the subsistence of the labourer, than upon that of butcher's-meat, or of any other part of the rude produce of land. The real value of gold and silver,

and also regulates the money price of labour.

---

[83] [Misprinted "improved" in ed. 5.]

[84] [Above, p. 54.]

therefore, the real quantity of labour which they can purchase or command, depends much more upon the quantity of corn which they can purchase or command, than upon that of butcher's-meat, or any other part of the rude produce of land.

Such slight observations, however, upon the prices either of corn or of other commodities, would not probably have misled so many intelligent authors, had they not been influenced, at the same time, by the popular notion,[85] that as the quantity of silver naturally increases in every country with the increase of wealth, so its value diminishes as its quantity increases. This notion, however, seems to be altogether groundless.

The authors were also misled by the notion that silver falls in value as its quantity increases.

The quantity of the precious metals may increase in any country from two different causes: either, first, from the increased abundance of the mines which supply it; or, secondly, from the increased wealth of the people, from the increased produce of their annual labour. The first of these causes is no doubt necessarily connected with the diminution of the value of the precious metals; but the second is not.

When more abundant mines are discovered, a greater quantity of the precious metals is brought to market, and the quantity of the necessaries and conveniences of life for which they must be exchanged being the same as before, equal quantities of the metals must be exchanged for smaller quantities of commodities. So far, therefore, as the increase of the quantity of the precious metals in any country arises from the increased abundance of the mines, it is necessarily connected with some diminution of their value.

Increase of quantity arising from greater abundance of the mines is connected with diminution of value,

When, on the contrary, the wealth of any country increases, when the annual produce of its labour becomes gradually greater and greater, a greater quantity of coin becomes necessary in order to circulate a greater quantity of commodities:

---

[85] [Ed. 1 reads "had they not been agreeable to the popular notion."]

but increase of quantity resulting from the increased wealth of a country is not.

and the people, as they can afford it, as they have more commodities to give for it, will naturally purchase a greater and a greater quantity of plate. The quantity of their coin will increase from necessity; the quantity of their plate from vanity and ostentation, or from the same reason that the quantity of fine statues, pictures, and of every other luxury and curiosity, is likely to increase among them. But as statuaries and painters are not likely to be worse rewarded in times of wealth and prosperity, than in times of poverty and depression, so gold and silver are not likely to be worse paid for.

The price of gold and silver, when the accidental discovery of more abundant mines does not keep it down, as it naturally

Gold and silver are dearer in a rich country,

rises with the wealth of every country, so, whatever be the state of the mines, it is at all times naturally higher in a rich than in a poor country. Gold and silver, like all other commodities, naturally seek the market where the best price is given for them, and the best price is commonly given for every thing in the country which can best afford it. Labour, it must be remembered, is the ultimate price which is paid for every thing, and in countries where labour is equally well rewarded, the money price of labour will be in proportion to that of the subsistence of the labourer. But gold and silver will naturally exchange for a greater quantity of subsistence in a rich than in a poor country, in a country which abounds with subsistence, than in one which is but indifferently supplied with it. If the two countries are at a great distance, the difference may be very great; because though the metals naturally fly from the

as may be shown by comparing China with Europe and Scotland with England as to the price of subsistence.

worse to the better market, yet it may be difficult to transport them in such quantities as to bring their price nearly to a level in both. If the countries are near, the difference will be smaller, and may sometimes be scarce perceptible; because in this case the transportation will be easy. China is a much richer country than any part of Europe, and the difference between the price of subsistence in China and in Europe is very great. Rice in China is much cheaper than wheat is any-where in Europe. England is a much richer country than Scotland; but the difference between the money-price of corn in those two countries is much smaller, and is but just perceptible. In proportion to the quantity or measure, Scotch corn generally appears to be a good deal cheaper than English; but in proportion to its quality, it is certainly somewhat dearer. Scotland receives almost every year very large supplies from England, and every commodity must commonly be somewhat dearer in the country to which it is brought than in that from which it comes. English corn, therefore, must be dearer in Scotland than in England, and yet in proportion to its quality, or to the quantity and goodness of the flour or meal which can be made from it, it cannot commonly be sold higher there than the Scotch corn which comes to market in competition with it.

The difference between the money price of labour in China and in Europe, is still greater than that between the money price of subsistence; because the real recompence of labour is higher in Europe than in China, the greater part of Europe being in an improving state, while China seems to be standing still. The money price of labour is lower in Scotland than in England, because the real recompence of labour is much lower; Scotland, though advancing to greater wealth, is advancing much more slowly than England.[86] The frequency of emigration from Scotland, and the rarity of it from England, sufficiently prove that the demand for labour is very different in the two countries.[87] The proportion between the real recompence of labour in different countries, it must be remembered, is naturally regulated, not by their actual wealth or poverty, but by their advancing, stationary, or declining condition.

Gold and silver are cheapest among the poorest nations.

Gold and silver, as they are naturally of the greatest value among the richest, so they

---

[86] [Above, p. 126.]

[87] [This sentence is not in ed. 1.]

The fact that corn is dearer in towns is due to its dearness there, not to the cheapness of silver,

are naturally of the least value among the poorest nations. Among savages, the poorest of all nations, they are of scarce any value.

In great towns corn is always dearer than in remote parts of the country. This, however, is the effect, not of the real cheapness of silver, but of the real dearness of corn. It does not cost less labour to bring silver to the great town than to the remote parts of the country; but it costs a great deal more to bring corn.

In some very rich and commercial countries, such as Holland and the territory of Genoa, corn is dear for the same

and this is true also in Holland, Genoa, etc.

reason that it is dear in great towns. They do not produce enough to maintain their inhabitants. They are rich in the industry and skill of their artificers and manufacturers; in every sort of machinery which can facilitate and abridge labour; in shipping, and in all the other instruments and means of carriage and commerce: but they are poor in corn, which, as it must be brought to them from distant countries, must, by an addition to its price, pay for the carriage from those countries. It does not cost less labour to bring silver to Amsterdam than to Dantzick; but it costs a great deal more to bring corn. The real cost of silver must be nearly the same in both places; but that of corn must be very different. Diminish the real opulence either of Holland or of the territory of Genoa, while the number of their inhabitants remains the same: diminish their power of supplying themselves from distant countries; and the price of corn, instead of sinking with that diminution in the quantity of their silver, which must necessarily accompany this declension either as its cause or as its effect, will rise to the price of a famine. When we are in want of necessaries we must part with all superfluities, of which the value, as it rises in times of opulence and prosperity, so it sinks in times of poverty and distress. It is otherwise with necessaries. Their real price, the quantity of labour which they can purchase or command, rises in times of poverty and distress, and sinks in times of opulence and prosperity, which are always times of great abundance; for they could not otherwise be times of opulence and prosperity. Corn is a necessary, silver is only a superfluity.

Whatever, therefore, may have been the increase in the quantity of the precious metals, which, during the period be-

So no increase of silver due to the increase of wealth could have reduced its value.

tween the middle of the fourteenth and that of the sixteenth century, arose from the increase of wealth and improvement, it could have no tendency to diminish their value either in Great Britain, or in any other part of Europe. If those who have collected the prices of things in ancient times, therefore, had, during this period, no reason to infer the diminution of the value of silver, from any observations which they had made upon the prices either of corn or of other commodities, they had still less reason to infer it from any supposed increase of wealth and improvement.

Second Period

No doubt exists as to the second period,

But how various soever may have been the opinions of the learned concerning the progress of the value of silver during this first period, they are unanimous concerning it during the second.

From about 1570 to about 1640, during a period of about seventy years, the variation in the proportion between the

silver sank, and a quarter of corn came to be worth 6 oz. or 8 oz. of silver.

value of silver and that of corn, held a quite opposite course. Silver sunk in its real value, or would exchange for a smaller quantity of labour than before; and corn rose in its nominal price, and instead of being commonly sold for about two ounces of silver the quarter, or about ten shillings of our present money, came to be sold for six and eight ounces of silver the quarter, or about thirty and forty shillings of our present money.

The discovery of abundant mines of America, seems to have been the sole cause of this diminution in the value of silver in proportion to that of corn. It is accounted for accord-

This was owing to the discovery of the abundant American mines. ingly in the same manner by every body; and there never has been any dispute either about the fact, or about the cause of it. The greater part of Europe was, during this period, advancing in industry and improvement, and the demand for silver must consequently have been increasing. But the increase of the supply had, it seems, so far exceeded that of the demand, that the value of that metal sunk considerably. The discovery of the mines of America, it is to be observed, does not seem to have had any very sensible effect upon the prices of things in England till after 1570; though even the mines of Potosi had been discovered more than twenty years before.[88]

From 1595 to 1620, both inclusive, the average price of the quarter of nine bushels of the best wheat at Windsor market, *Wheat rose at Windsor market.* appears from the accounts of Eton College,[89] to have been 2*l.* 1*s.* 6*d.* $\frac{9}{13}$. From which sum, neglecting the fraction, and deducting a ninth, or 4*s.* 7*d.* $\frac{1}{3}$, the price of the quarter of eight bushels comes out to have been 1*l.* 16*s.* 10*d.* $\frac{2}{3}$. And from this sum, neglecting likewise the fraction, and deducting a ninth, or 4*s.* 1*d.* $\frac{1}{6}$, for the difference between the price of the best wheat and that of the middle wheat,[90] the price of the middle wheat comes out to have been about 1*l.* 12*s.* 8*d.* $\frac{2}{6}$, or about six ounces and one-third of an ounce of silver.

From 1621 to 1636, both inclusive, the average price of the same measure of the best wheat at the same market, appears, from the same accounts, to have been 2*l.* 10*s.*; from which making the like deductions as in the foregoing case, the average price of the quarter of eight bushels of middle wheat

---

[88] [In 1545. Ed. 1 reads "thirty" instead of "twenty." In ed. 2 the correction is in the errata. See below p.274, notes 128 and 129.]

[89] [See the table at the end of the chapter, p. 345.]

[90] [The deduction of this ninth is recommended by Charles Smith, *Three Tracts on the Corn Trade and Corn Laws*, 2nd ed., 1766, p. 104, because, "it hath been found that the value of all the wheat fit for bread, if mixed together, would be eight-ninths of the value of the best wheat."]

comes out to have been 1*l*. 19*s*. 6*d*. or about seven ounces and two-thirds of an ounce of silver.

Third Period

Between 1630 and 1640, or about 1636, the effect of the discovery of the mines of America in reducing the value of silver,

The effect of the discovery of the American mines was complete about 1636.

appears to have been completed, and the value of that metal seems never to have sunk lower in proportion to that of corn than it was about that time. It seems to have risen somewhat in the course of the present century, and it had probably begun to do so even some time before the end of the last.

From 1637 to 1700, both inclusive, being the sixty-four last years of the last century, the average price of the quarter of

From 1637 to 1700 there was a very slight rise of wheat at Windsor,

nine bushels of the best wheat at Windsor market, appears, from the same accounts, to have been 2*l*. 11*s*. 0*d*. ⅓; which is only 1*s*. 0*d*. ⅓ dearer than it had been during the sixteen years before. But in the course of these sixty-four years there happened two events which must have produced a much greater scarcity of corn than what the course of the seasons would otherwise have occasioned, and which, therefore, without supposing any further reduction in the value of silver, will much more than account for this very small enhancement of price.

The first of these events was the civil war, which, by discouraging tillage and interrupting commerce, must have raised

due to the civil war,

the price of corn much above what the course of the seasons would otherwise have occasioned. It must have had this effect more or less at all the different markets in the kingdom, but particularly at those in the neighbourhood of London, which require to be supplied from the greatest distance. In 1648, accordingly, the price of the best wheat at Windsor market, appears, from the same accounts, to have been 4*l*. 5*s*. and in 1649 to have been 4*l*. the quarter of nine bushels. The excess of those two years above 2*l*. 10*s*. (the average price of the sixteen years preceding 1637) is 3*l*. 5*s*.; which divided among the sixty-four last years of the last century, will alone very nearly account for that small enhancement of price which seems to have taken place in them. These, however, though the highest, are by no means the only high prices which seem to have been occasioned by the civil wars.

The second event was the bounty upon the exportation of corn, granted in 1688.[91] The bounty, it has been thought by

the bounty on the exportation of corn,

many people, by encouraging tillage, may, in a long course of years, have occasioned a greater abundance, and consequently a greater cheapness of corn in the home-market, than what would otherwise have taken place there. How far the bounty could produce this effect at any time, I shall examine hereafter;[92] I shall only observe at present, that[93] between 1688 and 1700, it had not time to produce any such effect.[94] During this short period its only effect must have been, by encouraging the exportation of the surplus produce of every year, and thereby hindering the abundance of one year from compensating the scarcity of another, to raise the price in the home-market. The scarcity which prevailed in England from 1693 to 1699, both inclusive, though no doubt principally owing to the badness of the seasons, and, therefore, extending through a considerable part of Europe, must have been some-

[91] [By 1 W. & M., c. 12, "An act for the encouraging the exportation of corn," the preamble of which alleges that "it hath been found by experience, that the exportation of corn and grain into foreign parts, when the price thereof is at a low rate in this kingdom, hath been a great advantage not only to the owners of land but to the trade of this kingdom in general." It provides that when malt or barley does not exceed 24s. per Winchester quarter, rye 32s. and wheat 48s. in any port, every person exporting such corn on an English ship with a crew at least two-thirds English shall receive from the Customs 2s. 6d. for every quarter of barley or malt, 3s. 6d. for every quarter of rye and 5s. for every quarter of wheat.]

[92] [Below, pp. 637–665.]

[93] [In place of "How far the bounty could produce this effect at any time, I shall examine hereafter; I shall only observe at present, that," ed. 1 reads simply "But."]

[94] [For "not" ed. 1 reads "no," and for "any such" it reads "this."]

what enhanced by the bounty. In 1699, accordingly, the further exportation of corn was prohibited for nine months.[95]

There was a third event which occurred in the course of the same period, and which, though it could not occasion any

and the clipping and wearing of the coin,

scarcity of corn, nor, perhaps, any augmentation in the real quantity of silver which was usually paid for it, must necessarily have occasioned some augmentation in the nominal sum. This event was the great debasement[96] of the silver coin, by clipping and wearing. This evil had begun in the reign of Charles II. and had gone on continually increasing till 1695; at which time, as we may learn from Mr. Lowndes, the current silver coin was, at an average, near five-and-twenty per cent. below its standard value.[97] But the nominal sum which constitutes the market-price of every commodity is necessarily regulated, not so much by the quantity of silver, which, according to the standard, ought to be contained in it, as by that which, it is found by experience, actually is contained in it. This nominal sum, therefore, is necessarily higher when the coin is much

[95] [The Act 10 Will. III., c. 3, prohibits exportation for one year from 10th February, 1699. The mistake "nine months" is probably due to a misreading of C. Smith, *Tracts on the Corn Trade*, p. 9, wheat "growing, and continuing dearer till 1698, the exportation was forbid for one year, and then for nine months the bounty was suspended" (cp. pp. 44, 119). As a matter of fact, the bounty was suspended by 11 & 12 Will. III., c. 1, from 9th February, 1699, to 29th September, 1700, or not much more than seven months and a half. The Act 11 & 12 Will. III., c. 1, alleges that the Act granting the bounty "was grounded upon the highest wisdom and prudence and has succeeded to the greatest benefit and advantage to the nation by the greatest encouragement of tillage," and only suspends it because "it appears that the present stock and quantity of corn in this kingdom may not be sufficient for the use and service of the people at home should there be too great an exportation into parts beyond the seas, which many persons may be prompted to do for their own private advantage and the lucre of the said bounty."—*Statutes of the Realm*, vol. vii., p. 544.]

[96] [For "debasement" ed. 1 reads "degradation."]

[97] [Lowndes says on p. 107 of his *Report Containing an Essay for the Amendment of the Silver Coins*, 1695, "the moneys commonly current are diminished near one-half, to wit, in a proportion something greater than that of ten to twenty-two." But in the text above, the popular estimate, as indicated by the price of silver bullion, is accepted, as in the next paragraph.]

debased[98] by clipping and wearing, than when near to its standard value.

In the course of the present century, the silver coin has not at any time been more below its standard weight than it is at present. But though very much defaced, its value has been kept up by that of the gold coin for which it is exchanged.[99] For though before the late re-coinage, the gold coin was a good deal defaced too, it was less so than the silver. In 1695, on the contrary, the value of the silver coin was not kept up by the gold coin; a guinea then commonly exchanging for thirty shillings of the worn and clipt silver.[100] Before the late re-coinage of the gold, the price of silver bullion was seldom higher than five shillings and seven-pence an ounce, which is but five-pence above the mint price. But in 1695, the common price of silver bullion was six shillings and five-pence an ounce,[101] which is fifteen-pence above the mint price. Even before the late re-coinage of the gold,[102] therefore, the coin, gold and silver together, when compared with silver bullion, was not supposed to be more than eight per cent. below its standard value. In 1695, on the contrary, it had been supposed to be near five-and-twenty per cent. below that value. But in the beginning of the present century, that is, immediately after the great re-coinage in King William's time, the greater part of the current silver coin must have been still nearer to its standard weight than it is at present. In the course of the present century too there has been no great public calamity, such as the civil war, which could either discourage tillage, or interrupt the interior com-

which was then much greater than in the present century.

Moreover the bounty has been long enough in existence to produce any possible effect in lowering the price of corn.

---

[98] [Ed. 1 reads "degraded."]

[99] [See above, p. 59.]

[100] [Lowndes, *Essay*, p. 88.]

[101] [Lowndes's *Essay on the Silver Coin*, p. 68. This note appears first in ed. 2.]

[102] [Above, p. 59.]

merce of the country. And though the bounty which has taken place through the greater part of this century, must always raise the price of corn somewhat higher than it otherwise would be in the actual state of tillage;[103] yet as, in the course of this century, the bounty has had full time to produce all the good effects commonly imputed to it, to encourage tillage, and thereby to increase the quantity of corn in the home market, it may, upon the principles of a system which I shall explain and examine hereafter,[104] be supposed to have done something to lower the price of that commodity the one way, as well as to raise it the other. It is by many people supposed to have done more.[105] In the sixty-four first[106] years of the present century accordingly, the average price of the quarter of nine bushels of the best wheat at Windsor market, appears, by the accounts of Eton College, to have been 2*l.* 0*s.* 6*d.* $^{19}\!/_{32}$,[107] which is about ten shillings and sixpence, or more than five-and-twenty per cent. cheaper[108] than it had been during the sixty-four last years of the last century; and about nine shillings and sixpence cheaper than it had been during the sixteen years preceding 1636, when the discovery of the abundant mines of America may be supposed to have produced its full effect; and about one shilling cheaper than it had been in the twenty-six years preceding 1620, before that discovery can well be supposed to have produced its full effect. According to this account, the average price of middle wheat, during these sixty-four first years of the

---

[103] [The meaning is "given a certain area and intensity of cultivation, the bounty will raise the price of corn."]

[104] [Ed. 1 does not contain "upon the principles of a system which I shall explain hereafter." The reference is presumably to pp. 637–651.]

[105] [Ed. 1 reads here "a notion which I shall examine hereafter."]

[106] [Doubtless by a misprint ed. 5 omits "first." The term is used again at the end of the paragraph and also on pp. 269, 270.]

[107] [See the table at the end of the chapter: $^{19}\!/_{32}$ is a mistake for $^{9}\!/_{32}$.]

[108] [The 25 per cent. is erroneously reckoned on the £2 0s. 6$^{19}\!/_{32}$d. instead of on the £2 11s. 0½d. The fall of price is really less than 21 per cent.]

present century, comes out to have been about thirty-two shillings the quarter of eight bushels.

The value of silver, therefore, seems to have risen some-

Silver has risen somewhat since the beginning of the century, and the rise began before;

what in proportion to that of corn during the course of the present century, and it had probably begun to do so even some time before the end of the last.

In 1687, the price of the quarter of nine bushels of the best wheat at Windsor market was 1*l*. 5*s*. 2*d*., the lowest price at which it had ever been from 1595.

In 1688, Mr. Gregory King, a man famous for his knowledge in matters of this kind, estimated the average price of

as is shown by Mr. King's calculations.

wheat in years of moderate plenty to be to the grower 3*s*. 6*d*. the bushel, or eight-and-twenty shillings the quarter.[109] The grower's price I understand to be the same with what is sometimes called the contract price, or the price at which a farmer contracts for a certain number of years to deliver a certain quantity of corn to a dealer. As a contract of this kind saves the farmer the expence and trouble of marketing, the contract price is generally lower than what is supposed to be the average market price. Mr. King had judged eight-and-twenty shillings the quarter to be at that time the ordinary contract price in years of moderate plenty. Before the scarcity occasioned by the late extraordinary course of bad seasons, it was, I have been assured,[110] the ordinary contract price in all common years.

[109] [The date is taken from the heading of Scheme D in Davenant, *Essay upon the Probable Means of Making a People Gainers in the Balance of Trade*, 1699, p. 22, *Works*, ed. Whitworth, 1771, vol. ii., p. 184. Cp. *Natural and Political Observations and Conclusions upon the State and Condition of England*, by Gregory King, Esq., Lancaster, H., in George Chalmers' *Estimate of the Comparative Strength of Great Britain*, 1802, p. 429; in Davenant, *Balance of Trade*, pp. 71, 72, *Works*, vol. ii., p. 217. Davenant says "this value is what the same is worth upon the spot where the corn grew; but this value is increased by the carriage to the place where it is at last spent, at least ¼ part more."]

[110] [Ed. 1 does not contain this parenthesis.]

In 1688 was granted the parliamentary bounty upon the exportation of corn.[111] The country gentlemen, who then composed a still greater proportion of the legislature than they do at present, had felt that the money price of corn was falling. The bounty was an expedient to raise it artificially to the high price at which it had frequently been sold in the times of Charles I. and II. It was to take place, therefore, till wheat was so high as forty-eight shillings the quarter; that is twenty shillings, or ⅚ths dearer than Mr. King had in that very year estimated the grower's price to be in times of moderate plenty. If his calculations deserve any part of the reputation which they have obtained very universally, eight-and-forty shillings the quarter was a price which, without some such expedient as the bounty, could not at that time be expected, except in years of extraordinary scarcity. But the government of King William was not then fully settled. It was in no condition to refuse any thing to the country gentlemen, from whom it was at that very time soliciting the first establishment of the annual land-tax.

The value of silver, therefore, in proportion to that of corn, had probably risen somewhat before the end of the last century; and it seems to have continued to do so during the course of the greater part of the present; though the necessary operation of the bounty must have hindered that rise from being so sensible as it otherwise would have been in the actual state of tillage.

Apart from its effect in extending tillage, the bounty raises the price of corn, both in times of plenty and of scarcity.

In plentiful years the bounty, by occasioning an extraordinary exportation, necessarily raises the price of corn above what it otherwise would be in those years. To encourage tillage, by keeping up the price of corn even in the most plentiful years, was the avowed end of the institution.

In years of great scarcity, indeed, the bounty has generally been suspended. It must, however, have had some effect even[112] upon the prices of many of those years.

---

[111] [Above, p. 263, note.]

[112] [Ed. 5, doubtless by a misprint, omits "even."]

By the extraordinary exportation which it occasions in years of plenty, it must frequently hinder the plenty of one year from compensating the scarcity of another.

Both in years of plenty and in years of scarcity, therefore, the bounty raises the price of corn above what it naturally would be in the actual state of tillage. If, during the sixty-four first years of the present century, therefore, the average price has been lower than during the sixty-four last years of the last century, it must, in the same state of tillage, have been much more so, had it not been for this operation of the bounty.

But without the bounty, it may be said, the state of tillage would not have been the same. What may have been the effects

It is said to have extended tillage (and so to have reduced the price), but the rise of silver has not been peculiar to England.

of this institution upon the agriculture of the country, I shall endeavour to explain hereafter,[113] when I come to treat particularly of bounties. I shall only observe at present, that this rise in the value of silver, in proportion to that of corn, has not been peculiar to England. It has been observed to have taken place in France during the same period, and nearly in the same proportion too, by three very faithful, diligent, and laborious collectors of the prices of corn, Mr. Duprè de St. Maur, Mr. Messance, and the author of the Essay on the police of grain.[114] But in France, till 1764, the exportation of grain was by law prohibited; and it is somewhat difficult to suppose, that nearly the same diminution of price which took place in one country, notwithstanding this prohibition, should in another be owing to the extraordinary encouragement given to exportation.

It would be more proper, perhaps, to consider this variation in the average money price of corn as the effect rather of some

---

[113] [Below, pp. 637–651.]

[114] [The references to Duprè de St. Maur and the *Essay* (see above, p. 246, note), as well as the whole argument of the paragraph, are from Messance, *Recherches sur la population des généralités d'Auvergne*, etc., p. 281. Messance's quotations are from Duprè's *Essai sur les Monnoies*, 1746, p. 68, and Herbert's *Essai sur la police générale des grains*, 1755, pp. ix, 77, 189; cp. below, p. 325.]

The alteration should be regarded as a rise of silver rather than a fall of corn.

gradual rise in the real value of silver in the European market, than of any fall in the real average value of corn. Corn, it has already been observed,[115] is at distant periods of time a more accurate measure of value than either silver, or perhaps any other commodity.

When, after the discovery of the abundant mines of America, corn rose to three and four times its former money price, this change was universally ascribed, not to any rise in the real value of corn, but to a fall in the real value of silver. If during the sixty-four first years of the present century, therefore, the average money price of corn has fallen somewhat below what it had been during the greater part of the last century, we should in the same manner impute this change, not to any fall in the real value of corn, but to some rise in the real value of silver in the European market.

The high price of corn during these ten or twelve years past, indeed, has occasioned a suspicion[116] that the real value of silver still continues to fall in the European market. This high price of corn, however, seems evidently to have been the effect

The recent high price of corn is merely the effect of unfavourable seasons.

of the extraordinary unfavourableness of the seasons, and ought therefore to be regarded, not as a permanent, but as a transitory and occasional event. The seasons for these ten or twelve years past have been unfavourable through the greater part of Europe; and the disorders of Poland have very much increased the scarcity in all those countries, which, in dear years, used to be supplied from that market. So long a course of bad seasons, though not a very common event, is by no means a singular one; and whoever has enquired much into the history of the prices of corn in former times, will be at no loss to recollect several other examples of the same kind. Ten years of extraordinary scarcity, besides, are not more wonderful than ten years of extraordinary plenty. The low price of corn from 1741 to 1750, both inclu-

[115] [Above, pp. 50, 51.]

[116] [Examined below, pp. 294, 295.]

sive, may very well be set in opposition to its high price during these last eight or ten years. From 1741 to 1750, the average price of the quarter of nine bushels of the best wheat at Windsor market, it appears from the accounts of Eton College, was only 1*l.* 13*s.* 9*d.* ⅘, *which is nearly* 6*s.* 3*d.* below the average price of the sixty-four first years of the present century.[117] The average price of the quarter of eight bushels of middle wheat, comes out, according to this account, to have been, during these ten years, only 1*l.* 6*s.* 8*d.*[118]

Between 1741 and 1750, however, the bounty must have hindered the price of corn from falling so low in the home market as it naturally would have done. During these ten years

The bounty kept up the price between 1741 and 1750.

the quantity of all sorts of grain exported, it appears from the custom-house books, amounted to no less than eight millions twenty-nine thousand one hundred and fifty-six quarters one bushel. The bounty paid for this amounted to 1,514,962*l.* 17*s.* 4*d.* ½.[119] In 1749 accordingly, Mr. Pelham, at that time prime minister, observed to the House of Commons, that for the three years[120] preceding, a very extraordinary sum had been paid as bounty for the exportation of

---

[117] [See the table at the end of the chapter.]

[118] [This figure is obtained, as recommended by Charles Smith (*Tracts on the Corn Trade*, 1766, p. 104), by deducting one-ninth for the greater size of the Windsor measure and one-ninth from the remainder for the difference between best and middling wheat.]

[119] ["Tract 3d," referred to a few lines farther on, only gives the quantities of each kind of grain exported in each year (pp. 110, 111), so that if the figures in the text are taken from it they must have been obtained by somewhat laborious arithmetical operations. The particulars are as follows:—

	Exported.		Bounty payable.		
	Qr.	Bush.			
Wheat	3,784,524	1	£946,131	0	7½
Rye	765,056	6	133,884	18	7½
Barley, malt and oats	3,479,575	2	434,946	18	1½
	8,029,156	1	£1,514,962	17	4½]

[120] ["Years" is apparently a mistake for "months." "There is such a superabundance of corn that incredible quantities have been lately exported. I should be

The sudden change at 1750 was due to accidental variation of the seasons.

corn. He had good reason to make this observation, and in the following year he might have had still better. In that single year the bounty paid amounted to no less than 324,176*l*. 10*s*. 6*d*.[121] It is unnecessary to observe how much this forced exportation must have raised the price of corn above what it otherwise would have been in the home market.

At the end of the accounts annexed to this chapter the reader will find the particular account of those ten years separated from the rest. He will find there too the particular account of the preceding ten years, of which the average is likewise below, though not so much below, the general average of the sixty-four first years of the century. The year 1740, however, was a year of extraordinary scarcity. These twenty years preceding 1750, may very well be set in opposition to the twenty preceding 1770. As the former were a good deal below the general average of the century, notwithstanding the intervention of one or two dear years: so the latter have been a good deal above it, notwithstanding the intervention of one or two cheap ones, of 1759, for example. If the former have not been as much below the general average, as the latter have been above it, we ought probably to impute it to the bounty. The change has evidently been too sudden to be ascribed to any change in the value of silver, which is always slow and gradual. The suddenness of the effect can be accounted for only by a cause which can operate suddenly, the accidental variation of the seasons.

The money price of labour in Great Britain has, indeed, risen during the course of the present century. This, however,

afraid to mention what quantities have been exported if it did not appear upon our custom-house books; but from them it appears that lately there was in three months' time above £220,000 paid for bounties upon corn exported."— *Parliamentary History* (Hansard), vol. xiv., p. 589.]

[121] See Tracts on the Corn Trade; Tract 3d. [This note appears first in ed. 2. The exports for 1750 are given in C. Smith, *op. cit.*, p. 111, as 947,602 qr. 1 bush. of wheat, 99,049 qr. 3 bush. of rye, and 559,538 qr. 5 bush. of barley, malt and oats. The bounty on these quantities would be £324,176 10s.]

The rise in the price of labour has been due to increase of demand for labour, not to a diminution in the value of silver.

seems to be the effect, not so much of any diminution in the value of silver in the European market, as of an increase in the demand for labour in Great Britain, arising from the great, and almost universal prosperity of the country. In France, a country not altogether so prosperous, the money price of labour has, since the middle of the last century, been observed to sink gradually with the average money price of corn. Both in the last century and in the present, the day-wages of common labour are there said to have been pretty uniformly about the twentieth part of the average price of the septier of wheat, a measure which contains a little more than four Winchester bushels. In Great Britain the real recompence of labour, it has already been shown,[122] the real quantities[123] of the necessaries and conveniencies of life which are given to the labourer, has increased considerably during the course of the present century. The rise in its money price seems to have been the effect, not of any diminution of the value of silver in the general market of Europe, but of a rise in the real price of labour in the particular market of Great Britain, owing to the peculiarly happy circumstances of the country.

For some time after the first discovery of America, silver would continue to sell at its former, or not much below its for-

The decrease in the rent and profit of mines of gold and silver

mer price. The profits of mining would for some time be very great, and much above their natural rate. Those who imported that metal into Europe, however, would soon find that the whole annual importation could not be disposed of at this high price. Silver would gradually exchange for a smaller and a smaller quantity of goods. Its price would sink gradually lower and lower till it fell to its natural price; or to what was just sufficient to pay, according to their natural rates, the wages of the labour, the profits of the stock,

[122] [Above, pp. 107–110.]

[123] [Ed. 1, perhaps correctly, reads "quantity."]

and the rent of the land, which must be paid in order to bring it from the mine to the market. In the greater part of the silver mines of Peru, the tax of the king of Spain, amounting to a tenth[124] of the gross produce, eats up, it has already been observed,[125] the whole rent of the land. This tax was originally a half; it soon afterwards fell to a third, then to a fifth, and at last to a tenth, at which rate it still continues.[126] In the greater part of the silver mines of Peru, this, it seems, is all that remains, after replacing the stock of the undertaker of the work, together with its ordinary profits; and it seems to be universally acknowledged that these profits, which were once very high, are now as low as they can well be, consistently with carrying on the works.

The tax of the king of Spain was reduced to a fifth part of the registered silver in 1504,[127] one-and-forty years before 1545,[128] the date of the discovery of the mines of Potosi. In the course of ninety years,[129] or before 1636, these mines, the most fertile in all America, had time sufficient to produce their full effect, or to reduce the value of silver in the European market as low as it could well fall, while it continued to pay this tax to the king of Spain. Ninety years[130] is time sufficient to reduce any commodity, of which there is no monopoly, to its natural price, or to the lowest price at which, while it pays a particular tax, it can continue to be sold for any considerable time together.

The price of silver in the European market might perhaps have fallen still lower, and it might have become necessary ei-

---

[124] [Ed. 1 reads "fifth."]

[125] [Above, pp. 231, 233.]

[126] [Ed. 1 reads "fell to a third and then to a fifth, at which rate it still continues."]

[127] Solorzano, vol. ii. [Solorzano-Pereira, *De Indiarum Jure*, Madrid, 1777, lib. v., cap. 1., §§ 22, 23; vol. ii., p. 883, col. 2. Ed. 1 does not contain the note.]

[128] [Ed. 1 reads "one and thirty years before 1535." The date 1545 is given in Solorzano, *op. cit.*, vol. ii., p. 882, col. 2.]

[129] [Ed. 1 reads "In the course of a century."]

[130] [Ed. 1 reads "A hundred years."]

has been stayed by the gradual enlargement of the market, ther to reduce the tax upon it, not only to one tenth, as in 1736, but to one twentieth,[131] in the same manner as that upon gold, or to give up working the greater part of the American mines which are now wrought. The gradual increase of the demand for silver, or the gradual enlargement of the market for the produce of the silver mines of America, is probably the cause which has prevented this from happening, and which has not only kept up the value of silver in the European market, but has perhaps even raised it somewhat higher than it was about the middle of the last century.

Since the first discovery of America, the market for the produce of its silver mines has been growing gradually more and more extensive.

First, The market of Europe has become gradually more and more extensive. Since the discovery of America, the greater *(1) in Europe,* part of Europe has been much improved. England, Holland, France and Germany; even Sweden, Denmark, and Russia, have all advanced considerably both in agriculture and in manufactures. Italy seems not to have gone backwards. The fall of Italy preceded the conquest of Peru. Since that time it seems rather to have recovered a little. Spain and Portugal, indeed, are supposed to have gone backwards. Portugal, however, is but a very small part of Europe, and the declension of Spain is not, perhaps, so great as is commonly imagined. In the beginning of the sixteenth century, Spain was a very poor country, even in comparison with France, which has been so much improved since that time. It was the well-known remark of the Emperor Charles V. who had travelled so frequently through both countries, that every thing abounded in France, but that every thing was wanting in Spain. The increasing produce of the agriculture and manufactures of Europe must necessarily have required a gradual increase in the quantity of silver coin to circulate it; and the increasing number

---

[131] [Ed. 1 reads "lower" instead of "reduce," and does not contain "not only to one-tenth, as in 1736, but to one-twentieth." See above, p. 231, note.]

of wealthy individuals must have required the like increase in the quantity of their plate and other ornaments of silver.

Secondly, America is itself a new market for the produce of its own silver mines; and as its advances in agriculture, industry,

(2) in America itself,

and population, are much more rapid than those of the most thriving countries in Europe, its demand must increase much more rapidly. The English colonies are altogether a new market, which partly for coin and partly for plate, requires a continually augmenting supply of silver through a great continent where there never was any demand before. The greater part too of the Spanish and Portuguese colonies are altogether new markets. New Granada, the Yucatan, Paraguay, and the Brazils were, before discovered by the Europeans, inhabited by savage nations, who had neither arts nor agriculture. A considerable degree of both has now been introduced into all of them. Even Mexico and Peru, though they cannot be considered as altogether new markets, are certainly much more extensive ones than they ever were before. After all the wonderful tales which have been published concerning the splendid state of those countries in ancient times, whoever reads, with any degree of sober judgment, the history of their first discovery and conquest, will evidently discern that, in arts, agriculture, and commerce, their inhabitants were much more ignorant than the Tartars of the Ukraine are at present. Even the Peruvians, the more civilized nation of the two, though they made use of gold and silver as ornaments, had no coined money of any kind. Their whole commerce was carried on by barter, and there was accordingly scarce any division of labour among them. Those who cultivated the ground were obliged to build their own houses, to make their own household furniture, their own clothes, shoes, and instruments of agriculture. The few artificers among them are said to have been all maintained by the sovereign, the nobles, and the priests, and were probably their servants or slaves. All the ancient arts of Mexico and Peru have never furnished one single manufacture to Europe.[132] The

---

[132] [Below, p. 719. Raynal, *Histoire philosophique*, Amsterdam ed. 1773, tom. iii., pp. 113, 116, takes the same view of the Peruvians.]

Spanish armies, though they scarce ever exceeded five hundred men, and frequently did not amount to half that number, found almost every-where great difficulty in procuring subsistence. The famines which they are said to have occasioned almost wherever they went, in countries too which at the same time are represented as very populous and well-cultivated, sufficiently demonstrate that the story of this populousness and high cultivation is in a great measure fabulous. The Spanish colonies are under a government in many respects less favourable to agriculture, improvement and population, than that of the English colonies.[133] They seem, however, to be advancing in all these much more rapidly than any country in Europe. In a fertile soil and happy climate, the great abundance and cheapness of land, a circumstance common to all new colonies, is, it seems, so great an advantage as to compensate many defects in civil government. Frezier, who visited Peru in 1713, represents Lima as containing between twenty-five and twenty-eight thousand inhabitants.[134] Ulloa, who resided in the same country between 1740 and 1746, represents it as containing more than fifty thousand.[135] The difference in their accounts of the populousness of several other principal towns in Chili and Peru is nearly the same;[136] and as there seems to be no reason to doubt of the good information of either, it marks an increase which is scarce inferior to that of the English colonies. America, therefore, is a new market for the produce of its own silver mines, of which the demand must increase much more rapidly than that of the most thriving country in Europe.

Thirdly, The East Indies is another market for the produce of the silver mines of America, and a market which, from the

[133] [Below, pp. 719–746, *passim*.]

[134] [*Voyage to the South Sea*, p. 218, but the number mentioned is twenty-five to thirty thousand.]

[135] [*Voyage historique*, tom. i., pp. 443, 445: "sixteen to eighteen thousand persons of Spanish extraction, a comparatively small number of Indians and half-breeds, the greater part of the population being negroes and mulattoes."]

[136] [*E.g.*, Santiago and Callao, Frezier, *Voyage*, pp. 102, 202; Juan and Ulloa, *Voyage historique*, vol. i., p. 468; vol. ii., p. 49.]

_____
and (3) in the East Indies,
_____

time of the first discovery of those mines, has been continually taking off a greater and a greater quantity of silver. Since that time, the direct trade between America and the East Indies, which is carried on by means of the Acapulco ships,[137] has been continually augmenting, and the indirect intercourse by the way of Europe has been augmenting in a still greater proportion. During the sixteenth century, the Portuguese were the only European nation who carried on any regular trade to the East Indies. In the last years of that century the Dutch began to encroach upon this monopoly, and in a few years expelled them from their principal settlements in India. During the greater part of the last century those two nations divided the most considerable part of the East India trade between them; the trade of the Dutch continually augmenting in a still greater proportion than that of the Portuguese declined. The English and French carried on some trade with India in the last century, but it has been greatly augmented in the course of the present. The East India trade of the Swedes and Danes began in the course of the present century. Even the Muscovites now trade regularly with China by a sort of caravans which go over land through Siberia and Tartary to Pekin. The East India trade of all these nations, if we except that of the French, which the last war had well nigh annihilated, has been almost continually augmenting. The increasing consumption of East India goods in Europe is, it seems, so great, as to afford a gradual increase of employment to them all. Tea, for example, was a drug very little used in Europe before the middle of the last century. At present the value of the tea annually imported by the English East India Company, for the use of their own countrymen, amounts to more than a million and a half a year; and even this is not enough; a great deal more being constantly smuggled into the country from the ports of Holland, from Gottenburg in Sweden, and from the coast of France too, as long as the

_____

[137] [Originally one ship, and, after 1720, two ships, were allowed to sail between Acapulco in Mexico and the Philippines. For the regulations applied to the trade see Uztariz, *Theory and Practice of Commerce and Maritime Affairs*, trans. by John Kippax, 1751, vol. i., pp. 206–208.]

French East India Company was in prosperity. The consumption of the porcelain of China, of the spiceries of the Moluccas, of the piece goods of Bengal, and of innumerable other articles, has increased very nearly in a like proportion. The tonnage accordingly of all the European shipping employed in the East India trade, at any one time during the last century, was not, perhaps, much greater than that of the English East India Company before the late reduction of their shipping.[138]

But in the East Indies, particularly in China and Indostan, the value of the precious metals, when the Europeans first began to trade to those countries, was much

where the value of gold and silver was, and still is, higher than in Europe.

higher than in Europe; and it still continues to be so. In rice countries, which generally yield two, sometimes three crops in the year, each of them more plentiful than any common crop of corn, the abundance of food must be much greater than in any corn country of equal extent. Such countries are accordingly much more populous. In them too the rich, having a greater super-abundance of food to dispose of beyond what they themselves can consume, have the means of purchasing a much greater quantity of the labour of other people. The retinue of a grandee in China or Indostan accordingly is, by all accounts, much more numerous and splendid than that of the richest subjects in Europe. The same super-abundance of food, of which they have the disposal, enables them to give a greater quantity of it for all those singular and rare productions which nature furnishes but in very small quantities; such as the precious metals and the precious stones, the great objects of the competition of the rich. Though the mines, therefore, which supplied the Indian market had been as abundant as those which supplied the European, such com-

---

[138] ["In order to prevent the great consumption of timber fit for the construction of large ships of war, the East India Company were prohibited from building, or allowing to be built for their service, any new ships, till the shipping in their employment should be reduced under 45,000 tons, or employing any ships built after 18th March, 1772. But they are at liberty to build any vessel whatever in India or the colonies, or to charter any vessel built in India or the colonies, 12 Geo. III., c. 54."—Macpherson, *Annals of Commerce*, 1805, A.D. 1772, vol. iii., pp. 521, 522.]

modities would naturally exchange for a greater quantity of food in India than in Europe. But the mines which supplied the Indian market with the precious metals seem to have been a god deal less abundant, and those which supplied it with the precious stones a good deal more so, than the mines which supplied the European. The precious metals, therefore, would naturally exchange in India for somewhat a greater quantity of the precious stones, and for a much greater quantity of food[139] than in Europe. The money price of diamonds, the greatest of all superfluities, would be somewhat lower, and that of food, the first of all necessaries, a great deal lower in the one country than in the other. But the real price of labour, the real quantity of the necessaries of life which is given to the labourer, it has already been observed,[140] is lower both in China and Indostan, the two great markets of India, than it is through the greater part of Europe. The wages of the labourer will there purchase a smaller quantity of food; and as the money price of food is much lower in India than in Europe, the money price of labour is there lower upon a double account; upon account both of the small quantity of food which it will purchase, and of the low price of that food. But in countries of equal art and industry, the money price of the greater part of manufactures will be in proportion to the money price of labour; and in manufacturing art and industry, China and Indostan, though inferior, seem not to be much inferior to any part of Europe. The money price of the greater part of manufactures, therefore, will naturally be much lower in those great empires than it is any-where in Europe. Through the greater part of Europe too the expence of land-carriage increases very much both the real and nominal price of most manufactures. It costs more labour, and therefore more money, to bring first the materials, and afterwards the complete manufacture to market. In China and Indostan the extent and variety of inland navigations save the greater part of this labour, and consequently of this money, and thereby re-duce still lower both the real and the nominal price of the

[139] [Ed. 1 places "in India" here instead of two lines above.]

[140] [Above, pp. 103, 104.]

greater part of their manufactures. Upon all these accounts, the precious metals are a commodity which it always has been, and still continues to be, extremely advantageous to carry from Europe to India. There is scarce any commodity which brings a better price there; or which, in proportion to the quantity of labour and commodities which it costs in Europe, will purchase or command a greater quantity of labour and commodities in India. It is more advantageous too to carry silver thither than gold; because in China, and the greater part of the other markets of India, the proportion between fine silver and fine gold is but as ten, or at most as twelve,[141] to one; whereas in Europe it is as fourteen or fifteen to one. In China, and the greater part of the other markets of India, ten, or at most twelve, ounces of silver will purchase an ounce of gold; in Europe it requires from fourteen to fifteen ounces. In the cargoes, therefore, of the greater part of European ships which sail to India, silver has generally been one of the most valuable articles.[142] It is the most valuable article in the Acapulco ships which sail to Manilla. The silver of the new continent seems in this manner to be one of the principal commodities[143] by which the commerce between the two extremities of the old one is carried on, and it is by means of it, in a great measure,[144] that those distant parts of the world are connected with one another.

In order to supply so very widely extended a market, the

The supply of silver must provide for waste quantity of silver annually brought from the mines must not only be sufficient to support that continual increase both of coin and of

---

[141] [Ed. 1 does not contain "or at most as twelve" here and two lines lower down.]

[142] [Newton, in his *Representation to the Lords of the Treasury*, 1717 (reprinted in the *Universal Merchant*, quoted on p. 283), says that in China and Japan the ratio is 9 or 10 to 1 and in India 12 to 1, and this carries away the silver from all Europe. Magens, in a note to this passage (*Universal Merchant*, p. 90), says that down to 1732 such quantities of silver went to China to fetch back gold that the price of gold in China rose and it became no longer profitable to send silver there.]

[143] [Ed. 1 reads "be the principal commodity."]

[144] [Ed. 1 reads "chiefly."]

as well as increase of plate and coin. plate which is required in all thriving countries; but to repair that continual waste and consumption of silver which takes place in all countries where that metal is used.

The continual consumption of the precious metals in coin by wearing, and in plate both by wearing and cleaning, is very

Waste is considerable. sensible; and in commodities of which the use is so very widely extended, would alone require a very great annual supply. The consumption of those metals in some particular manufactures, though it may not perhaps be greater upon the whole than this gradual consumption, is, however, much more sensible, as it is much more rapid. In the manufactures of Birmingham alone, the quantity of gold and silver annually employed in gilding and plating, and thereby disqualified from ever afterwards appearing in the shape of those metals, is said to amount to more than fifty thousand pounds sterling. We may from thence form some notion how great must be the annual consumption in all the different parts of the world, either in manufactures of the same kind with those of Birmingham, or in laces, embroideries, gold and silver stuffs, the gilding of books, furniture, &c. A considerable quantity too must be annually lost in transporting those metals from one place to another both by sea and by land. In the greater part of the governments of Asia, besides, the almost universal custom of concealing treasures in the bowels of the earth, of which the knowledge frequently dies with the person who makes the concealment, must occasion the loss of a still greater quantity.

Six millions of gold and silver are imported at Cadiz and Lisbon, The quantity of gold and silver imported at both Cadiz and Lisbon (including not only what comes under register, but what may be supposed to be smuggled) amounts, according to the best accounts,[145] to about six millions sterling a year.

---

[145] [The same words are used below, p. 558.]

According to Mr. Meggens[146] the annual importation of the precious metals into Spain, at an average of six years;

as shown by Magens,

viz. from 1748 to 1753, both inclusive; and into Portugal, at an average of seven years; viz. from 1747 to 1753, both inclusive;[147] amounted in silver to 1,101,107 pounds weight; and in gold to 49,940 pounds weight. The silver, at sixty-two shillings the pound Troy, amounts to 3,413,431*l.* 10*s.*[148] sterling. The gold, at forty-four guineas and a half the pound Troy, amounts to 2,333,446*l.* 14*s.* sterling. Both together amount to 5,746,878*l.* 4*s.* sterling. The account of what was imported under register, he assures us is exact. He gives us the detail of the particular places from which the gold and silver were brought, and of the particular quantity of each metal, which, according to the register, each of them afforded. He makes an allowance too for the quantity of each metal which he supposes may have been smuggled. The great experience of this judicious merchant renders his opinion of considerable weight.

Raynal,

According to the eloquent and, sometimes, well-informed Author of the Philosophical

[146] Postscript to the *Universal Merchant*, p. 15 and 16. This Postscript was not printed till 1756, three years after the publication of the book, which has never had a second edition. The postscript is, therefore, to be found in few copies: It corrects several errors in the book. [This note appears first in ed. 2. The title of the work referred to is *Farther Explanations of some particular subjects relating to Trade, Coin, and Exchanges, contained in the Universal Merchant*, by N. M., 1756. On p. 1 N. M. claims the authorship of the book "published by Mr. Horsley under the too pompous title of *The Universal Merchant*." In the dedication of *The Universal Merchant*, 1753, William Horsley, the editor, says the author "though an alien by birth is an Englishman by interest." Sir James Steuart, who calls him "Mr. Megens," says he lived long in England and wrote the *Universal Merchant* in German, from which it had been translated (*Inquiry into the Principles of Political Economy*, 1767, vol. ii., pp. 158, 292). The *Gentleman's Magazine* for August, 1764, p. 398, contains in the obituary, under date August 18, 1764, "Nicolas Magens Esq. a merchant worth £100,000."]

[147] [The two periods are really five years, April, 1748, to April, 1753, and six years, January, 1747, to January, 1753, but the averages are correct, being taken from Magens.]

[148] [The 10s. here should be 14s., and one line lower down the 14s. should be 10s.]

and Political History of the Establishment of the Europeans in
the two Indies, the annual importation of registered gold and
silver into Spain, at an average of eleven years; viz. from 1754
to 1764, both inclusive; amounted to 13,984,185¾[149] piastres of
ten reals. On account of what may have been smuggled, however, the whole annual importation, he supposes, may have
amounted to seventeen millions of piastres; which, at 4s. 6d.
the piastre, is equal to 3,825,000l. sterling. He gives the detail
too of the particular places from which the gold and silver were
brought, and of the particular quantities of each metal which,
according to the register, each of them afforded.[150] He informs
us too, that if we were to judge of the quantity of gold annually
imported from the Brazils into Lisbon by the amount of the tax
paid to the king of Portugal, which it seems is one-fifth of the
standard metal, we might value it at eighteen millions of cruza-
does, or forty-five millions of French livres, equal to about two
millions sterling. On account of what may have been smuggled,
however, we may safely, he says, add to this sum an eighth
more, or 250,000l. sterling, so that the whole will amount to
2,250,000l. sterling.[151] According to this account, therefore, the
whole annual importation of the precious metals into both
Spain and Portugal, amounts to about 6,075,000l. sterling.

Several other very well authenticated, though manuscript,[152]
accounts, I have been assured, agree, in making this whole an-
and other authors.   nual importation amount at an average to
about six millions sterling; sometimes a lit-
tle more, sometimes a little less.

The annual importation of the precious metals into Cadiz
and Lisbon, indeed, is not equal to the whole annual produce of
the mines of America. Some part is sent annually by the
Acapulco ships to Manilla; some part is employed in the contraband trade which the Spanish colonies carry on with those

---

[149] [Misprinted 13,984, 185⅚ in ed. 2 and later editions.]

[150] [Raynal, *Histoire philosophique et politique des établissemens et du commerce des Européens dans les deux Indes*, Amsterdam ed., 1773, tom. iii., p. 310.]

[151] [Raynal, *Histoire philosophique*, Amsterdam ed., 1773, tom. iii., p. 385.]

[152] [Ed. 1 does not contain "though manuscript."]

This is not the whole of the annual supply, but by far the greater part.

of other European nations; and some part, no doubt, remains in the country. The mines of America, besides, are by no means the only gold and silver mines in the world. They are, however, by far the most abundant. The produce of all the other mines which are known, is insignificant, it is acknowledged, in comparison with theirs; and the far greater part of their produce, it is likewise acknowledged, is annually imported into Cadiz and Lisbon. But the consumption of Birmingham alone, at the rate of fifty thousand pounds a year,[153] is equal to the hundred-and-twentieth part of this annual importation at the rate of six millions a year. The whole annual consumption of gold and silver, therefore, in all the different countries of the world where those metals are used, may perhaps be nearly equal to the whole annual produce. The remainder may be no more than sufficient to supply the increasing demand of all thriving countries. It may even have fallen so far short of this demand as somewhat to raise the price of those metals in the European market.

The quantity of brass and iron annually brought from the mine to the market is out of all proportion greater than that of

Brass and iron increase, but we do not expect them to fall in value. Why then gold and silver?

gold and silver. We do not, however, upon this account, imagine that those coarse metals are likely to multiply beyond the demand, or to become gradually cheaper and cheaper. Why should we imagine that the precious metals are likely to do so? The coarse metals, indeed, though harder, are put to much harder uses, and, as they are of less value, less care is employed in their preservation. The precious metals, however, are not necessarily immortal any more than they, but are liable too to be lost, wasted, and consumed in a great variety of ways.

The price of all metals, though liable to slow and gradual variations, varies less from year to year than that of almost any other part of rude produce of land; and the price of the pre-

---

153 [Above, p. 282.]

In consequence of their durability the metals, especially gold and silver, vary little in value from year to year.

cious metals is even less liable to sudden variations than that of the coarse ones. The durableness of metals is the foundation of this extraordinary steadiness of price. The corn which was brought to market last year, will be all or almost all consumed long before the end of this year. But some part of the iron which was brought from the mine two or three hundred years ago, may be still in use, and perhaps some part of the gold which was brought from it two or three thousand years ago. The different masses of corn which in different years must supply the consumption of the world, will always be nearly in proportion to the respective produce of those different years. But the proportion between the different masses of iron which may be in use in two different years, will be very little affected by any accidental difference in the produce of the iron mines of those two years; and the proportion between the masses of gold will be still less affected by any such difference in the produce of the gold mines. Though the produce of the greater part of metallic mines, therefore, varies, perhaps, still more from year to year than that of the greater part of corn-fields, those variations have not the same effect upon the price of the one species of commodities, as upon that of the other.

VARIATIONS IN THE PROPORTION BETWEEN THE RESPECTIVE VALUES OF GOLD AND SILVER

Before the discovery of the mines of America, the value of fine gold to fine silver was regulated in the different mints of Europe, between the proportions of one to ten and one to twelve; that is, an ounce of fine gold was supposed to be worth from ten to twelve ounces of fine silver. About the middle of the last century it came to be regulated, between the proportions of one to fourteen and one to fifteen; that is, an ounce of fine gold came to be supposed worth between fourteen and fifteen ounces of fine sil-

After the discovery of the American mines silver fell in proportion to gold.

ver. Gold rose in its nominal value, or in the quantity of silver which was given for it. Both metals sunk in their real value, or in the quantity of labour which they could purchase; but silver sunk more than gold. Though both the gold and silver mines of America exceeded in fertility all those which had ever been known before, the fertility of the silver mines had, it seems, been proportionably still greater than that of the gold ones.

The great quantities of silver carried annually from Europe to India, have, in some of the English settlements, gradually

It is higher in the East. reduced the value of that metal in proportion to gold. In the mint of Calcutta, an ounce of fine gold is supposed to be worth fifteen ounces of fine silver, in the same manner as in Europe. It is in the mint perhaps rated too high for the value which it bears in the market of Bengal. In China, the proportion of gold to silver still continues as one to ten, or one to twelve.[154] In Japan, it is said to be as one to eight.[155]

The proportion between the quantities of gold and silver annually imported into Europe, according to Mr. Meggen's ac-

Magens seems to think the proportion of value should be the same as the proportion of quantity, count, is as one to twenty-two nearly,[156] that is, for one ounce of gold there are imported a little more than twenty-two ounces of silver. The great quantity of silver sent annually to the East Indies, reduces, he supposes, the quantities of those metals which remain in Europe to the proportion of one to fourteen or fifteen, the proportion of their values. The proportion between their values, he seems to think,[157] must necessarily be the same as that between their quantities, and would therefore be as one to twenty-two, were it not for this greater exportation of silver.

[154] [Ed. 1 does not contain "or one to twelve."]

[155] [Cantillon gives one to ten for China and one to eight for Japan, *Essai*, p. 365.]

[156] [Above, p. 283. The exact figure given by Magens, *Farther Explanations*, p. 16, is 1 to 22⅒.]

[157] [*Ibid.*, p. 17.]

But the ordinary proportion between the respective values of two commodities is not necessarily the same as that between the quantities of them which are commonly in the market. The price *but this is absurd.* of an ox, reckoned at ten guineas, is about threescore times the price of a lamb, reckoned at 3s. 6d. It would be absurd, however, to infer from thence, that there are commonly in the market threescore lambs for one ox: and it would be just as absurd to infer, because an ounce of gold will commonly purchase from fourteen to fifteen ounces of silver, that there are commonly in the market only fourteen or fifteen ounces of silver for one ounce of gold.

The quantity of silver commonly in the market, it is probable, is much greater in proportion to that of gold, than the *The whole of a cheap commodity is commonly worth more than the whole of a dear one, and this is the case with silver and gold.* value of a certain quantity of gold is to that of an equal quantity of silver. The whole quantity of a cheap commodity brought to market, is commonly not only greater, but of greater value, than the whole quantity of a dear one. The whole quantity of bread annually brought to market, is not only greater, but of greater value than the whole quantity of butcher's-meat; the whole quantity of butcher's-meat, than the whole quantity of poultry; and the whole quantity of poultry, than the whole quantity of wild fowl. There are so many more purchases for the cheap than for the dear commodity, that, not only a greater quantity of it, but a greater value, can commonly be disposed of. The whole quantity, therefore, of the cheap commodity must commonly be greater in proportion to the whole quantity of the dear one, than the value of a certain quantity of the dear one, is to the value of an equal quantity of the cheap one. When we compare the precious metals with one another, silver is a cheap, and gold a dear commodity. We ought naturally to expect, therefore, that there should always be in the market, not only a greater quantity, but a greater value of silver than of gold. Let any man, who has a little of both, compare his own silver with his gold plate, and he will probably find, that, not only the quantity, but the value of the former greatly exceeds that of the latter. Many people, besides, have a good deal of silver who have no gold plate, which, even with those who have it, is generally confined to watchcases, snuff-boxes, and such like trinkets, of which the whole amount is seldom of great value. In the British coin, indeed, the value of the gold preponderates greatly, but it is not so in that of all countries. In the coin of some countries the value of the two metals is nearly equal. In the Scotch coin, before the union with England, the gold preponderated very little, though it did somewhat,[158] as it appears by the accounts of the mint. In the coin of many countries the silver preponderates. In France, the largest sums are commonly paid in that metal, and it is there difficult to get more gold than what is necessary to carry about in your pocket. The superior value, however, of the silver plate above that of the gold, which takes place in all countries, will much more than compensate the preponderancy of the gold coin above the silver, which takes place only in some countries.

Though, in one sense of the word, silver always has been, and probably always will be, much cheaper than gold; yet in

Gold is nearer its lowest possible price than silver.

another sense, gold may, perhaps, in the present state of the Spanish[159] market, be said to be somewhat cheaper than silver. A commodity may be said to be dear or cheap, not only according to the absolute greatness or smallness of its usual price, but according as that price is more or less above the lowest for which it is possible to bring it to market for any considerable time together. This lowest price is that which barely replaces, with a moderate profit, the stock which must be employed in bringing the commodity thither. It is the price

---

[158] See Ruddiman's Preface to Anderson's Diplomata, &c. Scotiæ [*Selectus diplomatum et numismatum thesaurus* (quoted above, p. 250), pp. 84, 85; and in the translation, pp. 175, 176. But the statement that gold preponderated is founded merely on the fact that the value of the gold coined in the periods 16th December, 1602, to 19th July, 1606, and 20th September, 1611, to 14th April, 1613, was greater than that of the silver coined in the same time, which proves nothing about the proportions in the whole stock of coin. The statement is repeated below, p. 379. The note appears first in ed. 2.]

[159] [Ed. 1 reads "European."]

which affords nothing to the landlord, of which rent makes not any component part, but which resolves itself altogether into wages and profit. But, in the present state of the Spanish[160] market, gold is certainly somewhat nearer to this lowest price than silver. The tax of the King of Spain upon gold is only one-twentieth part of the standard metal, or five per cent.; whereas his tax upon silver amounts to one-tenth part of it, or to ten per cent.[161] In these taxes too, it has already been observed,[162] consists the whole rent of the greater part of the gold and silver mines of Spanish America; and that upon gold is still worse paid than that upon silver. The profits of the undertakers of gold mines too, as they more rarely make a fortune, must, in general, be still more moderate than those of the undertakers of silver mines.[163] The price of Spanish gold, therefore, as it affords both less rent and less profit, must, in the Spanish[164] market, be somewhat nearer to the lowest price for which it is possible to bring it thither, than the price of Spanish silver. When all expences are computed, the whole quantity of the one metal, it would seem, cannot, in the Spanish market, be disposed of so advantageously as the whole quantity of the other.[165] The tax, indeed, of the King of Portugal[166] upon the gold of the Brazils, is the same with the ancient tax[167] of the King of Spain upon the silver of Mexico and Peru; or one-fifth part of the standard metal.[168] It may, therefore, be uncertain whether to the general market of Europe the whole mass of American

[160] [Ed. 1 reads "European."]

[161] [Ed. 1 reads "one fifth part of it, or to twenty per cent."]

[162] [Above, pp. 229, 274.]

[163] [Above, p. 233.]

[164] [Ed. 1 reads "European."]

[165] [Ed. 1 places the "it would seem" after "computed," omits "in the Spanish market," and puts the whole sentence at the end of the paragraph.]

[166] [Ed. 1 places the "indeed" here.]

[167] [Ed. 1 reads "that."]

[168] [Above, p. 284.]

gold comes at a price[169] nearer to the lowest for which it is possible to bring it thither, than the whole mass of American silver.

Diamonds are nearer still.

The price of diamonds and other precious stones may, perhaps, be still nearer to the lowest price at which it is possible to bring them to market, than even the price of gold.[170]

Though it is not very profitable, that any part of a tax which is not only imposed upon one of the most proper subjects of taxation, a mere luxury and superfluity, but which affords so very important a revenue, as the tax upon silver, will ever be given up as long as it is possible to pay it; yet the same impossibility of paying it, which in 1736 made it necessary to reduce it from one-fifth to one-tenth,[171] may in time make it necessary to reduce it still further; in the same manner as it made it necessary to reduce the tax upon gold to one-twentieth.[172] That the silver mines of

It may be necessary to reduce still further the tax on silver in Spanish America.

---

[169] [Ed. 1 reads "It must still be true, however, that the whole mass of American gold comes to the European market at a price."]

[170] [Ed. 1 contains another paragraph, "Were the king of Spain to give up his tax upon silver, the price of that metal might not, upon that account, sink immediately in the European market. As long as the quantity brought thither continued the same as before, it would still continue to sell at the same price. The first and immediate effect of this change, would be to increase the profits of mining, the undertaker of the mine now gaining all that he had been used to pay to the king. These great profits would soon tempt a greater number of people to undertake the working of new mines. Many mines would be wrought which cannot be wrought at present, because they cannot afford to pay this tax, and the quantity of silver brought to market would, in a few years be so much augmented, probably, as to sink its price about one-fifth below its present standard. This diminution in the value of silver would again reduce the profits of mining nearly to their present rate."]

[171] [Above, pp. 231, 274.]

[172] [Ed. 1 reads from the beginning of the paragraph, "It is not indeed very probable, that any part of a tax which affords so important a revenue, and which is imposed, too, upon one of the most proper subjects of taxation, will ever be given up as long as it is possible to pay it. The impossibility of paying it, however, may in time make it necessary to diminish it, in the same manner as it made it necessary to diminish the tax upon gold."]

Spanish America, like all other mines, become gradually more expensive in the working, on account of the greater depths at which it is necessary to carry on the works, and of the greater expence of drawing out the water and of supplying them with fresh air at those depths, is acknowledged by every body who has enquired into the state of those mines.

These causes, which are equivalent to a growing scarcity of silver (for a commodity may be said to grow scarcer when it becomes more difficult and expensive to collect a certain quantity of it), must, in time, produce one or other of the three following events. The increase of the expence must either, first, be compensated altogether by a proportionable increase in the price of the metal; or, secondly, it must be compensated altogether by a proportionable diminution of the tax upon silver; or, thirdly, it must be compensated partly by the one, and partly by the other of those two expedients. This third event is very possible. As gold rose in its price in proportion to silver, notwithstanding a great diminution of the tax upon gold; so silver might rise in its price in proportion to labour and commodities, notwithstanding an equal diminution of the tax upon silver.

The greater cost of raising silver must lead to an increase of its price, or a reduction of the tax upon it, or both.

Such successive reductions of the tax, however, though they may not prevent altogether, must certainly retard, more or less, the rise of the value of silver in the European market. In consequence of such reductions, many mines may be wrought which could not be wrought before, because they could not afford to pay the old tax; and the quantity of silver annually brought to market must always be somewhat greater, and, therefore, the value of any given quantity somewhat less, than it otherwise would have been. In consequence of the reduction in 1736, the value of silver in the European market, though it may not at this day be lower than before that reduction, is, probably, at least ten per cent. lower than it would

The reduction of the tax in the past makes silver at least 10 per cent. lower than it would otherwise have been.

have been, had the Court of Spain continued to exact the old tax.[173]

That, notwithstanding this reduction, the value of silver has, during the course of the present century, begun to rise somewhat in the European market, the facts and arguments which have been alleged above, dispose me to believe, or more properly to suspect and conjecture; for the best opinion which I can form upon this subject scarce, perhaps, deserves the name of belief. The rise, indeed, supposing there has been any, has hitherto[174] been so very small, that after all that has been said, it may, perhaps, appear to many people uncertain, not only whether this event has actually taken place; but whether the contrary may not have taken place, or whether the value of silver may not still continue to fall in the European market.

Silver has probably risen somewhat in the present century.

It must be observed, however, that whatever may be the supposed annual importation of gold and silver, there must be a certain period, at which the annual consumption of those metals will be equal to that annual importation. Their consumption must increase as their mass increases, or rather in a much greater proportion. As their mass increases, their value diminishes. They are more used, and less cared for, and their consumption consequently increases in a greater proportion than their mass. After a certain period, therefore, the annual consumption of those metals must, in this manner, become equal to their annual importation, provided that importation is not continually increasing; which, in the present times, is not supposed to be the case.

The annual consumption must at length equal the annual importation,

If, when the annual consumption has become equal to the

[173] [This paragraph appears first in ed. 2.]

[174] [Ed. 1 reads from the beginning of the paragraph, "That the first of these three events has already begun to take place, or that silver has, during the course of the present century, begun to rise somewhat in its value in the European market, the facts and arguments which have been alledged above dispose me to believe. The rise, indeed, has hitherto."]

and will then accommodate itself to changes in the importation.

annual importation, the annual importation should gradually diminish, the annual consumption may, for some time, exceed the annual importation. The mass of those metals may gradually and insensibly diminish, and their value gradually and insensibly rise, till the annual importation becoming again stationary, the annual consumption will gradually and insensibly accommodate itself to what that annual importation can maintain.[175]

GROUNDS OF THE SUSPICION THAT THE VALUE OF SILVER STILL CONTINUES TO DECREASE

Gold and silver are supposed to be still falling because they are increasing in quantity and some sorts of rude produce are rising.

The increase of the wealth of Europe, and the popular notion that, as the quantity of the precious metals naturally increases with the increase of wealth, so their value diminishes as their quantity increases, may, perhaps,[176] dispose many people to believe that their value still continues to fall in the European market; and the still gradually increasing price of many parts of the rude produce of land may[177] confirm them still further in this opinion.

That that increase in[178] the quantity of the precious metals,

It has already been shown that the increase of the metals need not diminish their value:

which arises in any country[179] from the increase of wealth, has no tendency to diminish their value, I have endeavoured to show already.[180] Gold and silver naturally resort to a rich country, for the same reason that all sorts of luxuries and curiosities resort to it;

[175] [The last two paragraphs appear first in Additions and Corrections and ed. 3.]

[176] [Ed. 1 reads "may besides."]

[177] [Ed. 1 reads "perhaps" here.]

[178] [Ed. 1 reads "That the increase of."]

[179] [Ed. 1 places the "which arises" here.]

[180] [Above, p. 256 ff.]

not because they are cheaper there than in poorer countries, but because they are dearer, or because a better price is given for them. It is the superiority of price which attracts them, and as soon as that superiority ceases, they necessarily cease to go thither.

If you except corn and such other vegetables as are raised altogether by human industry, that all other sorts of rude pro-

and the rise of cattle, etc., is due to a rise in their real price, not to a fall of silver.

duce, cattle, poultry, game of all kinds, the useful fossils and minerals of the earth, &c. naturally grow dearer as the society advances in wealth and improvement, I have endeavoured to show already.[181] Though such commodities, therefore, come to exchange for a greater quantity of silver than before, it will not from thence follow that silver has become really cheaper, or will purchase less labour than before, but that such commodities have become really dearer, or will purchase more labour than before. It is not their nominal price only, but their real price which rises in the progress of improvement. The rise of their nominal price is the effect, not of any degradation of the value of silver, but of the rise in their real price.

DIFFERENT EFFECTS OF THE PROGRESS OF IMPROVEMENT UPON THREE DIFFERENT SORTS OF RUDE PRODUCE

These different sorts of rude produce may be divided into three classes. The first comprehends those which it is scarce in the

The real price of three sorts of rude produce rises in the progress of improvement:

power of human industry to multiply at all. The second, those which it can multiply in proportion to the demand. The third, those in which the efficacy of industry is either limited or uncertain. In the progress of wealth and improvement, the real price of the first may rise to any degree of extravagance, and seems not to be limited by any certain boundary. That of the second, though it may rise greatly, has, however, a certain boundary beyond

---

[181] [Above, pp. 238–240.]

which it cannot well pass for any considerable time together. That of the third, though its natural tendency is to rise in the progress of improvement, yet in the same degree of improvement it may sometimes happen even to fall, sometimes to continue the same, and sometimes to rise more or less, according as different accidents render the efforts of human industry, in multiplying this sort of rude produce, more or less successful.

First Sort

The first sort of rude produce of which the price rises in the progress of improvement, is that which it is scarce in the power

(1) The sort which cannot be multiplied by human industry, such as game.

of human industry to multiply at all. It consists in those things which nature produces only in certain quantities, and which being of a very perishable nature, it is impossible to accumulate together the produce of many different seasons. Such are the greater part of rare and singular birds and fishes, many different sorts of game, almost all wild-fowl, all birds of passage in particular, as well as many other things. When wealth and the luxury which accompanies it increase, the demand for these is likely to increase with them, and no effort of human industry may be able to increase the supply much beyond what it was before this increase of the demand. The quantity of such commodities, therefore, remaining the same, or nearly the same, while the competition to purchase them is continually increasing, their price may rise to any degree of extravagance, and seems not to be limited by any certain boundary. If woodcocks should become so fashionable as to sell for twenty guineas a-piece, no effort of human industry could increase the number of those brought to market, much beyond what it is at present. The high price paid by the Romans, in the time of their greatest grandeur, for rare birds and fishes, may in this manner easily be accounted for. These prices were not the effects of the low value of silver in those times, but of the high value of such rarities and curiosities as human industry could not multiply at pleasure. The real value of silver was higher at Rome, for some time before and after the fall of the republic, than it is through the greater part of Europe at present. Three sestertii, equal to about sixpence sterling, was the price which the republic paid for the modius or peck of the tithe wheat of Sicily. This price, however, was probably below the average market price, the obligation to deliver their wheat at this rate being considered as a tax upon the Sicilian farmers. When the Romans, therefore, had occasion to order more corn than the tithe of wheat amounted to, they were bound by capitulation to pay for the surplus at the rate of four sestertii, or eight-pence sterling, the peck;[182] and this had probably been reckoned the moderate and reasonable, that is, the ordinary or average contract price of those times; it is equal to about one-and-twenty shillings the quarter. Eight-and-twenty shillings the quarter was, before the late years of scarcity, the ordinary contract price of English wheat, which in quality is inferior to the Sicilian, and generally sells for a lower price in the European market. The value of silver, therefore, in those ancient times, must have been to its value in the present, as three to four inversely; that is, three ounces of silver would then have purchased the same quantity of labour and commodities which four ounces will do at present. When we read in Pliny, therefore, that Seius[183] bought a white nightingale, as a present for the empress Agrippina, at the price of six thousand sestertii, equal to about fifty pounds of our present money; and that Asinius Celer[184] purchased a surmullet at the price of eight thousand sestertii, equal to about sixty-six pounds thirteen shillings and four-pence of our present money; the extravagance of those prices, how much soever it may surprise us, is apt, notwithstanding, to appear to us about one-third less than it really was. Their real price, the quantity of labour and subsistence which was given away for

---

[182] [As mentioned above, p. 206. Cicero, *In Verr.*, Act. II., lib. iii., c. 70, is the authority.]

[183] Lib. x. c. 29. ["Scio sestertiis sex candidam alioquin, quod est prope inusitatum, venisse, quae Agrippinae Claudii principis conjugi dono daretur." "Seius" seems to be the result of misreading "Scio."]

[184] Lib. ix. c. 17. [This and the previous note appear first in ed. 2.]

them, was about one-third more than their nominal price is apt to express to us in the present times. Seius gave for the nightingale the command of a quantity of labour and subsistence equal to what 66*l.* 13*s.* 4*d.* would purchase in the present times; and Asinius Celer gave for the surmullet the command of a quantity equal to what 88*l.* 17*s.* 9*d.* ⅓, would purchase. What occasioned the extravagance of those high prices was, not so much the abundance of silver, as the abundance of labour and subsistence, of which those Romans had the disposal, beyond what was necessary for their own use. The quantity of silver, of which they had the disposal, was a good deal less than what the command of the same quantity of labour and subsistence would have procured to them in the present times.

Second Sort

The second sort of rude produce of which the price rises in the progress of improvement, is that which human industry can multiply in proportion to the demand. It consists in those useful plants and animals, which, in uncultivated countries, nature produces with such profuse abundance, that they are of little or no value, and which, as cultivation advances, are therefore forced to give place to some more profitable produce. During a long period in the progress of improvement, the quantity of these is continually diminishing, while at the same time the demand for them is continually increasing. Their real value, therefore, the real quantity of labour which they will purchase or command, gradually rises, till at last it gets so high as to render them as profitable a produce as any thing else which human industry can raise upon the most fertile and best cultivated land. When it has got so high it cannot well go higher. If it did, more land and more industry would soon be employed to increase their quantity.

(2) The sort which can be multiplied at will, e.g. cattle, poultry.

When the price of cattle, for example, rises so high that it is as profitable to cultivate land in order to raise food for them, as in order to raise food for man, it cannot well go higher. If it did, more corn land would soon be turned into pasture. The exten-

When it becomes profitable to cultivate land to yield food for cattle, the price of cattle cannot go higher.

sion of tillage, by diminishing the quantity of wild pasture, diminishes the quantity of butcher's-meat which the country naturally produces without labour or cultivation, and by increasing the number of those who have either corn, or, what comes to the same thing, the price of corn, to give in exchange for it, increases the demand. The price of butcher's-meat, therefore, and consequently of cattle, must gradually rise till it gets so high, that it becomes as profitable to employ the most fertile and best cultivated lands in raising food for them as in raising corn. But it must always be late in the progress of improvement before tillage can be so far extended as to raise the price of cattle to this height; and till it has got to this height, if the country is advancing at all, their price must be continually rising. There are, perhaps, some parts of Europe in which the price of cattle has not yet got to this height. It had not got to this height in any part of Scotland before the union.[185] Had the Scotch cattle been always confined to the market of Scotland, in a country in which the quantity of land, which can be applied to no other purpose but the feeding of cattle, is so great in proportion to what can be applied to other purposes, it is scarce possible, perhaps, that their price could ever have risen so high as to render it profitable to cultivate land for the sake of feeding them. In England, the price of cattle, it has already been observed,[186] seems, in the neighbourhood of London, to have got to this height about the beginning of the last century; but it was much later probably before it got to it through the greater part of the remoter counties; in some of which, perhaps, it may scarce yet have got to it. Of all the different substances, however, which compose this second sort of rude produce, cattle is, perhaps, that of which the price, in the progress of improvement, first rises to this height.

Till the price of cattle, indeed, has got to this height, it seems scarce possible that the greater part, even of those lands

---

[185] [Above, pp. 204, 222.]

[186] [Above, p. 207, and cp. below, p. 305.]

which are capable of the highest cultivation, can be completely cultivated. In all farms too distant from any town to carry manure from it, that is, in the far greater part of those of every extensive country, the quantity of well-cultivated land must be in proportion to the quantity of manure which the farm itself produces; and this again must be in proportion to the stock of cattle which are maintained upon it. The land is manured either by pasturing the cattle upon it, or by feeding them in the stable, and from thence carrying out their dung to it. But unless the price of the cattle be sufficient to pay both the rent and profit of cultivated land, the farmer cannot afford to pasture them upon it; and he can still less afford to feed them in the stable. It is with the produce of improved and cultivated land only, that cattle can be fed in the stable; because to collect the scanty and scattered produce of waste and unimproved lands would require too much labour and be too expensive. If the price of the cattle, therefore, is not sufficient to pay for the produce of improved and cultivated land, when they are allowed to pasture it, that price will be still less sufficient to pay for that produce when it must be collected with a good deal of additional labour, and brought into the stable to them. In these circumstances, therefore, no more cattle can, with profit, be fed in the stable than what are necessary for tillage. But these can never afford manure enough for keeping constantly in good condition, all the lands which they are capable of cultivating. What they afford being insufficient for the whole farm, will naturally be reserved for the lands to which it can be most advantageously or conveniently applied; the most fertile, or those, perhaps, in the neighbourhood of the farm-yard. These, therefore, will be kept constantly in good condition and fit for tillage. The rest will, the greater part of them, be allowed to lie waste, producing scarce any thing but some miserable pasture, just sufficient to keep alive a few straggling, half-starved cattle; the farm, though much understocked in proportion to what would be necessary for its complete cultivation, being very frequently overstocked in proportion to its actual produce. A portion of this waste land, however, after

It must go to this height in order to secure complete cultivation.

having been pastured in this wretched manner for six or seven years together, may be ploughed up, when it will yield, perhaps, a poor crop or two of bad oats, or of some other coarse grain, and then, being entirely exhausted, it must be rested and pastured again as before, and another portion ploughed up to be in the same manner exhausted and rested again in its turn. Such accordingly was the general system of management all over the low country of Scotland before the union. The lands which were kept constantly well manured and in good condition, seldom exceeded a third or a fourth part of the whole farm, and sometimes did not amount to a fifth or a sixth part of it. The rest were never manured, but a certain portion of them was in its turn, notwithstanding, regularly cultivated and exhausted. Under this system of management, it is evident, even that part of the lands of Scotland which is capable of good cultivation, could produce but little in comparison of what it may be capable of producing. But how disadvantageous soever this system may appear, yet before the union the low price of cattle seems to have rendered it almost unavoidable. If, notwithstanding a great rise in their price, it still continues to prevail through a considerable part of the country, it is owing, in many places, no doubt, to ignorance and attachment to old customs, but in most places to the unavoidable obstructions which the natural course of things opposes to the immediate or speedy establishment of a better system: first, to the poverty of the tenants, to their not having yet had time to acquire a stock of cattle sufficient to cultivate their lands more completely, the same rise of price which would render it advantageous for them to maintain a greater stock, rendering it more difficult for them to acquire it; and, secondly, to their not having yet had time to put their lands in condition to maintain this greater stock properly, supposing they were capable of acquiring it. The increase of stock and the improvement of land are two events which must go hand in hand, and of which the one can no-where much outrun the other. Without some increase of stock, there can be scarce any improvement of land, but there can be no considerable increase of stock but in consequence of a considerable improvement of land; because otherwise the land could not maintain it. These natural obstructions to the establishment of a better system, cannot be removed but by a long course of frugality and industry; and half a century or a century more, perhaps, must pass away before the old system, which is wearing out gradually, can be completely abolished through all the different parts of the country. Of all the commercial[187] advantages, however, which Scotland has derived from the union with England, this rise in the price of cattle is, perhaps, the greatest. It has not only raised the value of all highland estates, but it has, perhaps, been the principal cause of the improvement of the low country.

In all new colonies the great quantity of waste land, which can for many years be applied to no other purpose but the feeding of cattle, soon renders them extremely abundant, and in every thing great cheapness is the necessary consequence of great abundance. Though all the cattle of the European colonies in America were originally carried from Europe, they soon multiplied so much there, and became of so little value, that even horses were allowed to run wild in the woods without any owner thinking it worth while to claim them. It must be a long time after the first establishment of such colonies, before it can become profitable to feed cattle upon the produce of cultivated land. The same causes, therefore, the want of manure, and the disproportion between the stock employed in cultivation, and the land which it is destined to cultivate, are likely to introduce there a system of husbandry not unlike that which still continues to take place in so many parts of Scotland. Mr. Kalm, the Swedish traveller, when he gives an account of the husbandry of some of the English colonies in North America, as he found it in 1749, observes, accordingly, that he can with difficulty discover there the character of the English nation, so well skilled in all the different branches of agriculture. They make scarce any manure for their corn fields, he says; but when one piece of ground has been exhausted by continual cropping, they clear and cultivate

Consequently new colonies are poorly cultivated.

---

[187] [Eds. 1–3 read "of all commercial."]

another piece of fresh land; and when that is exhausted, proceed to a third. Their cattle are allowed to wander through the woods and other uncultivated grounds, where they are half-starved; having long ago extirpated almost all the annual grasses by cropping them too early in the spring, before they had time to form their flowers, or to shed their seeds.[188] The annual grasses were, it seems, the best natural grasses in that part of North America; and when the Europeans first settled there, they used to grow very thick, and to rise three or four feet high. A piece of ground which, when he wrote, could not maintain one cow, would in former times, he was assured, have maintained four, each of which would have given four times the quantity of milk which that one was capable of giving. The poorness of the pasture had, in his opinion, occasioned the degradation of their cattle, which degenerated sensibly from one generation to another. They were probably not unlike that stunted breed which was common all over Scotland thirty or forty years ago, and which is now so much mended through the greater part of the low country, not so much by a change of the breed, though that expedient has been employed in some places, as by a more plentiful method of feeding them.

Though it is late, therefore, in the progress of improvement before cattle can bring such a price as to render it profitable to

Cattle are the first of this second sort of rude produce to bring in the price necessary to secure cultivation,

cultivate land for the sake of feeding them; yet of all the different parts which compose this second sort of rude produce, they are perhaps the first which bring this price; because till they bring it, it seems impossible that improvement can be brought near even to that degree of perfection to which it has arrived in many parts of Europe.

[188] Kalm's Travels, vol. i. p. 343, 344. [*Travels into North America, containing its natural history and a circumstantial account of its Plantations and Agriculture in general, with the civil, ecclesiastical and commercial state of the country, the manners of the inhabitants and several curious and important remarks on various subjects*, by Peter Kalm, Professor of Œconomy in the University of Aobo, in Swedish Finland, and member of the S. Royal Academy of Sciences. Translated by John Reinhold Forster, F.A.S., 3 vols. 1770. The note appears first in ed. 2.]

As cattle are among the first, so perhaps venison is among the last parts of this sort of rude produce which bring this

and venison is the last;

price. The price of venison in Great Britain, how extravagant soever it may appear, is not near sufficient to compensate the expence of a deer park, as is well known to all those who have had any experience in the feeding of deer. If it was otherwise, the feeding of deer would soon become an article of common farming; in the same manner as the feeding of those small birds called Turdi was among the ancient Romans. Varro and Columella assure us that it was a most profitable article.[189] The fattening of ortolans, birds of passage which arrive lean in the country, is said to be so in some parts of France. If venison continues in fashion, and the wealth and luxury of Great Britain increase as they have done for some time past, its price may very probably rise still higher than it is at present.

Between that period in the progress of improvement which brings to its height the price of so necessary an article as cattle,

other things are intermediate,

and that which brings to it the price of such a superfluity as venison, there is a very long interval, in the course of which many other sorts of rude produce gradually arrive at their highest price, some sooner and some later, according to different circumstances.

Thus in every farm the offals of the barn and stables will maintain a certain number of poultry. These, as they are fed

such as poultry,

with what would otherwise be lost, are a mere save-all; and as they cost the farmer scarce any thing, so he can afford to sell them for very little. Almost all that he gets is pure gain, and their price can scarce be so low as to discourage him from feeding this number. But in countries ill cultivated, and, therefore, but thinly inhabited, the poultry, which are thus raised without expence, are often fully sufficient to supply the whole demand. In this state of things, therefore, they are often as cheap as butcher's-meat, or

[189] [Varro, *De re rustica*, iii., 2, and Columella, *De re rustica*, viii., 10, *ad fin.*, where Varro is quoted.]

any other sort of animal food. But the whole quantity of poultry, which the farm in this manner produces without expence, must always be much smaller than the whole quantity of butcher's-meat which is reared upon it; and in times of wealth and luxury what is rare, with only nearly equal merit, is always preferred to what is common. As wealth and luxury increase, therefore, in consequence of improvement and cultivation, the price of poultry gradually rises above that of butcher's-meat, till at last it gets so high that it becomes profitable to cultivate land for the sake of feeding them. When it has got to this height, it cannot well go higher. If it did, more land would soon be turned to this purpose. In several provinces of France, the feeding of poultry is considered as a very important article in rural œconomy, and sufficiently profitable to encourage the farmer to raise a considerable quantity of Indian corn and buck-wheat for this purpose. A middling farmer will there sometimes have four hundred fowls in his yard. The feeding of poultry seems scarce yet to be generally considered as a matter of so much importance in England. They are certainly, however, dearer in England than in France, as England receives considerable supplies from France. In the progress of improvement, the period at which every particular sort of animal food is dearest, must naturally be that which immediately precedes the general practice of cultivating land for the sake of raising it. For some time before this practice becomes general, the scarcity must necessarily raise the price. After it has become general, new methods of feeding are commonly fallen upon, which enable the farmer to raise upon the same quantity of ground a much greater quantity of that particular sort of animal food. The plenty not only obliges him to sell cheaper, but in consequence of these improvements he can afford to sell cheaper; for if he could not afford it, the plenty would not be of long continuance. It has been probably in this manner that the introduction of clover, turnips, carrots, cabbages, &c. has contributed to sink the common price of butcher's-meat in the London market somewhat below what it was about the beginning of the last century.

The hog, that finds his food among ordure, and greedily de-

vours many things rejected by every other useful animal, is, ––––––––––– like poultry, originally kept as a save-all. As
hogs, ––––––––––– long as the number of such animals, which
can thus be reared at little or no expence, is fully sufficient to
supply the demand, this sort of butcher's-meat comes to market
at a much lower price than any other. But when the demand
rises beyond what this quantity can supply, when it becomes
necessary to raise food on purpose for feeding and fattening
hogs, in the same manner as for feeding and fattening other
cattle, the price necessarily rises, and becomes proportionably
either higher or lower than that of other butcher's-meat, according as the nature of the country, and the state of its agriculture, happen to render the feeding of hogs more or less
expensive than that of other cattle. In France, according to Mr.
Buffon, the price of pork is nearly equal to that of beef.[190] In
most parts of Great Britain it is at present somewhat higher.

The great rise in the price both of hogs and poultry has in
Great Britain been frequently imputed to the diminution of the
number of cottagers and other small occupiers of land; an
event which has in every part of Europe been the immediate
forerunner of improvement and better cultivation, but which at
the same time may have contributed to raise the price of those
articles, both somewhat sooner and somewhat faster than it
would otherwise have risen. As the poorest family can often
maintain a cat or a dog, without any expence, so the poorest
occupiers of land can commonly maintain a few poultry, or a
sow and a few pigs, at very little. The little offals of their own
table, their whey, skimmed milk and butter-milk, supply those
animals with a part of their food, and they find the rest in the
neighbouring fields without doing any sensible damage to any
body. By diminishing the number of those small occupiers,
therefore, the quantity of this sort of provisions which is thus
produced at little or no expence, must certainly have been a
good deal diminished, and their price must consequently have
been raised both sooner and faster than it would otherwise
have risen. Sooner or later, however, in the progress of im-

[190] [*Histoire Naturelle*, vol. v. (1755), p. 122.]

provement, it must at any rate have risen to the utmost height to which it is capable of rising; or to the price which pays the labour and expence of cultivating the land which furnishes them with food as well as these are paid upon the greater part of other cultivated land.

The business of the dairy, like the feeding of hogs and poultry, is originally carried on as a save-all. The cattle necessarily

milk, butter and cheese.

kept upon the farm, produce more milk than either the rearing of their own young, or the consumption of the farmer's family requires; and they produce most at one particular season. But of all the productions of land, milk is perhaps the most perishable. In the warm season, when it is most abundant, it will scarce keep four-and-twenty hours. The farmer, by making it into fresh butter, stores a small part of it for a week: by making it into salt butter, for a year: and by making it into cheese, he stores a much greater part of it for several years. Part of all these is reserved for the use of his own family. The rest goes to market, in order to find the best price which is to be had, and which can scarce be so low as to discourage him from sending thither whatever is over and above the use of his own family. If it is very low, indeed, he will be likely to manage his dairy in a very slovenly and dirty manner, and will scarce perhaps think it worth while to have a particular room or building on purpose for it, but will suffer the business to be carried on amidst the smoke, filth, and nastiness of his own kitchen; as was the case of almost all the farmers dairies in Scotland thirty or forty years ago, and as is the case of many of them still. The same causes which gradually raise the price of butcher's-meat, the increase of the demand, and, in consequence of the improvement of the country, the diminution of the quantity which can be fed at little or no expence, raise, in the same manner, that of the produce of the dairy, of which the price naturally connects with that of butcher's-meat, or with the expence of feeding cattle. The increase of price pays for more labour, care, and cleanliness. The dairy becomes more worthy of the farmer's attention, and the quality of its produce gradually improves. The price at last gets so high that it becomes worth while to employ some of the most fertile and best cultivated lands in feeding cattle merely for the purpose of the dairy; and when it has got to this height, it cannot well go higher. If it did, more land would soon be turned to this purpose. It seems to have got to this height through the greater part of England, where much good land is commonly employed in this manner. If you except the neighbourhood of a few considerable towns, it seems not yet to have got to this height anywhere in Scotland, where common farmers seldom employ much good land in raising food for cattle merely for the purpose of the dairy. The price of the produce, though it has risen very considerably within these few years, is probably still too low to admit of it. The inferiority of the quality, indeed, compared with that of the produce of English dairies, is fully equal to that of the price. But this inferiority of quality is, perhaps, rather the effect of this lowness of price than the cause of it. Though the quality was much better, the greater part of what is brought to market could not, I apprehend, in the present circumstances of the country, be disposed of at a much better price; and the present price, it is probable, would not pay the expence of the land and labour necessary for producing a much better quality. Through the greater part of England, notwithstanding the superiority of price, the dairy is not reckoned a more profitable employment of land than the raising of corn, or the fattening of cattle, the two great objects of agriculture. Through the greater part of Scotland, therefore, it cannot yet be even so profitable.

The lands of no country, it is evident, can ever be completely cultivated and improved, till once the price of every produce, which human industry is obliged to raise upon them, has got so high as to pay for the expence of complete improvement and cultivation. In order to do this, the price of each particular produce must be sufficient, first, to pay the rent of good corn land, as it is that which regulates the rent of the greater part of other cultivated land; and secondly, to pay the labour and expence of the farmer as well as they are commonly paid upon good corn-land; or, in other words, to replace with the or-

The rise of price, being necessary for good cultivation, should be regarded with satisfaction.

dinary profits the stock which he employs about it. This rise in the price of each particular produce, must evidently be previous to the improvement and cultivation of the land which is destined for raising it. Gain is the end of all improvement, and nothing could deserve that name of which loss was to be the necessary consequence. But loss must be the necessary consequence of improving land for the sake of a produce of which the price could never bring back the expence. If the complete improvement and cultivation of the country be, as it most certainly is, the greatest of all public advantages, this rise in the price of all those different sorts of rude produce, instead of being considered as a public calamity, ought to be regarded as the necessary forerunner and attendant of the greatest of all public advantages.

This rise too in the nominal or money-price of all those different sorts of rude produce has been the effect, not of any

It is due not to a fall of silver but to a rise in the real price of the produce.

degradation in the value of silver, but of a rise in their real price. They have become worth, not only a greater quantity of silver, but a greater quantity of labour and subsistence than before. As it costs a greater quantity of labour and subsistence to bring them to market, so when they are brought thither, they represent or are equivalent to a greater quantity.

Third Sort

The third and last sort of rude produce, of which the price naturally rises in the progress of improvement, is that in which the

(3) The sort of regard to which the efficacy of industry is limited or uncertain,

efficacy of human industry, in augmenting the quantity, is either limited or uncertain. Though the real price of this sort of rude produce, therefore, naturally tends to rise in the progress of improvement, yet, according as different accidents happen to render the

efforts of human industry more or less successful in augmenting the quantity, it may happen sometimes even to fall, sometimes to continue the same in very different periods of improvement, and sometimes to rise more or less in the same period.

There are some sorts of rude produce which nature has rendered a kind of appendages to other sorts; so that the quantity of the one which any country can afford, is necessarily limited by that of the other. The quantity of wool or of raw hides, for example, which any country can afford, is necessarily limited by the number of great and small cattle that are kept in it. The state of its improvement, and the nature of its agriculture, again necessarily determine this number.

e.g. wool and hides, which are appendages to other sorts of produce.

The same causes, which, in the progress of improvement, gradually raise the price of butcher's-meat, should have the same effect, it may be thought, upon the prices of wool and raw hides, and raise them too nearly in the same proportion. It probably would be so, if in the rude beginnings of improvement the market for the latter commodities was confined within as narrow bounds as that for the former. But the extent of their respective markets is commonly extremely different.

Wool and hides in early times have a larger market open to them than butcher's-meat.

The market for butcher's-meat is almost every-where confined to the country which produces it. Ireland, and some part of British America indeed, carry on a considerable trade in salt provisions; but they are, I believe, the only countries in the commercial world which do so, or which export to other countries any considerable part of their butcher's-meat.

The market for wool and raw hides, on the contrary, is in the rude beginnings of improvement very seldom confined to the country which produces them. They can easily be transported to distant countries, wool without any preparation, and raw hides with very little: and as they are the materials of many manufactures, the industry of other countries may occasion a demand for them, though that of the country which produces them might not occasion any.

In countries ill cultivated, and therefore but thinly inhabited, the price of the wool and the hide bears always a much greater proportion to that of the whole beast, than in countries where,

In thinly inhabited countries the wool and hide are more valuable in proportion to the carcase. improvement and population being further advanced, there is more demand for butcher's-meat. Mr. Hume observes, that in the Saxon times, the fleece was estimated at two-fifths of the value of the whole sheep, and that this was much above the proportion of its present estimation.[191] In some provinces of Spain, I have been assured, the sheep is frequently killed merely for the sake of the fleece and the tallow. The carcase is often left to rot upon the ground, or to be devoured by beasts and birds of prey. If this sometimes happens even in Spain, it happens almost constantly in Chili, at Buenos Ayres,[192] and in many other parts of Spanish America, where the horned cattle are almost constantly killed merely for the sake of the hide and the fallow. This too used to happen almost constantly in Hispaniola, while it was infested by the Buccaneers, and before the settlement, improvement, and populousness of the French plantations (which now extend round the coast of almost the whole western half of the island) had given some value to the cattle of the Spaniards, who still continue to possess, not only the eatern part of the coast, but the whole inland and mountainous part of the country.

Though in the progress of improvement and population, the price of the whole beast necessarily rises, yet the price of the

In the progress of improvement the wool and hide should rise, though not so much as the carcase. carcase is likely to be much more affected by this rise than that of the wool and the hide. The market for the carcase, being in the rude state of society confined always to the country which produces it, must necessarily be extended in proportion to the improvement and population of that country. But the market for the wool and the hides even of a barbarous country often extending to the whole commercial world, it can very seldom be enlarged in the same proportion.

[191] [*History*, ed. of 1773, vol. i., p. 226.]

[192] [Juan and Ulloa, *Voyage historique*, 2de ptie, liv. i., chap. v., vol. i., p. 552.]

The state of the whole commercial world can seldom be much affected by the improvement of any particular country; and the market for such commodities may remain the same, or very nearly the same, after such improvements, as before. It should, however, in the natural course of things rather upon the whole be somewhat extended in consequence of them. If the manufactures, especially, of which those commodities are the materials, should ever come to flourish in the country, the market, though it might not be much enlarged, would at least be brought much nearer to the place of growth than before; and the price of those materials might at least be increased by what had usually been the expence of transporting them to distant countries. Though it might not rise therefore in the same proportion as that of butcher's-meat, it ought naturally to rise somewhat, and it ought certainly not to fall.

In England, however, notwithstanding the flourishing state of its woollen manufacture, the price of English wool has

But in England wool has fallen since 1339. fallen very considerably since the time of Edward III. There are many authentic records which demonstrate that during the reign of that prince (towards the middle of

the fourteenth century, or about 1339) what was reckoned the moderate and reasonable price of the tod or twenty-eight pounds of English wool was not less than ten shillings of the money of those times,[193] containing, at the rate of twenty-pence the ounce, six ounces of silver Tower-weight, equal to about thirty shillings of our present money. In the present times, one-and-twenty shillings the tod may be reckoned a good price for very good English wool. The money-price of wool, therefore, in the time of Edward III, was to its money-price in the present times as ten to seven. The superiority of its real price was still greater. At the rate of six shillings and eight-pence the quarter, ten shillings was in those ancient times the price of twelve

---

[193] See Smith's Memoirs of Wool, vol. i. c. 5, 6, and 7; also, vol. ii. c. 176. [Ed. 1 does not give the volumes and chapters. The work was *Chronicon Rusticum-Commerciale, or Memoirs of Wool, etc.*, by John Smith, and published 1747; see below, p. 827.]

bushels of wheat. At the rate of twenty-eight shillings the quarter, one-and-twenty shillings is in the present times the price of six bushels only. The proportion between the real prices of ancient and modern times, therefore, is as twelve to six, or as two to one. In those ancient times a tod of wool would have purchased twice the quantity of subsistence which it will purchase at present; and consequently twice the quantity of labour, if the real recompence of labour had been the same in both periods.

This degradation both in the real and nominal value of wool, could never have happened in consequence of the natural course of things. It has accordingly been the effect of violence and artifice: First, of the absolute prohibition of exporting wool from England;[194] Secondly, of the permission of importing it from Spain[195] duty free; Thirdly, of the prohibition of exporting it from Ireland to any other country but England. In consequence of these regulations, the market for English wool, instead of being somewhat extended in consequence of the improvement of England, has been confined to the home market, where the wool of several other countries[196] is allowed to come into competition with it, and where that of Ireland is forced into competition with it. As the woollen manufactures too of Ireland are fully as much discouraged as is consistent with justice and fair dealing, the Irish can work up but a small part of their own wool at home, and are, therefore, obliged to send a greater proportion of it to Great Britain, the only market they are allowed.

This has been caused by artificial regulations.

I have not been able to find any such authentic records concerning the price of raw hides in ancient times. Wool was commonly paid as a subsidy to the king, and its valuation in that subsidy ascertains, at least in some degree, what was its ordinary price.

The real price of hides at present is somewhat lower than in the fifteenth century,

---

[194] [See below, p. 822, and Smith's *Memoirs of Wool*, vol. i., pp. 159, 170, 182.]

[195] [Eds. 1 and 2 read "importing it from all other countries."]

[196] [Eds. 1 and 2 read "wool of all other countries."]

But this seems not to have been the case with raw hides. Fleetwood, however, from an account in 1425, between the prior of Burcester Oxford and one of his canons, gives us their price, at least as it was stated, upon that particular occasion; viz. five ox hides at twelve shillings; five cow hides at seven shillings and three pence: thirty-six sheep skins of two years old at nine shillings; sixteen calves skins at two shillings.[197] In 1425, twelve shillings contained about the same quantity of silver as four-and-twenty shillings of our present money. An ox hide, therefore, was in this account valued at the same quantity of silver as 4s ⅘ths of our present money. Its nominal price was a good deal lower than at present. But at the rate of six shillings and eight-pence the quarter, twelve shillings would in those times have purchased fourteen bushels and four-fifths of a bushel of wheat, which, at three and six-pence the bushel, would in the present times cost 51s. 4d. An ox hide, therefore, would in those times have purchased as much corn as ten shillings and three-pence would purchase at present. Its real value was equal to ten shillings and three-pence of our present money. In those ancient times, when the cattle were half starved during the greater part of the winter, we cannot suppose that they were of a very large size. An ox hide which weighs four stone of sixteen pounds averdupois, is not in the present times reckoned a bad one; and in those ancient times would probably have been reckoned a very good one. But at half a crown the stone, which at this moment (February 1773) I understand to be the common price, such a hide would at present cost only ten shillings. Though its nominal price, therefore, is higher in the present than it was in those ancient times, its real price, the real quantity of subsistence which it will purchase or command, is rather somewhat lower. The price of cow hides, as stated in the above account, is nearly in the common proportion to that of ox hides. That of sheep skins is a good deal above it. They had probably been sold with the wool. That of calves skins, on the contrary, is greatly below it. In countries

---

[197] [*Chronicon preciosum*, ed. of 1707, p. 100, quoting from Kennet's *Par. Ant.* Burcester is the modern Bicester.]

where the price of cattle is very low, the calves, which are not intended to be reared in order to keep up the stock, are generally killed very young; as was the case in Scotland twenty or thirty years ago. It saves the milk, which their price would not pay for. Their skins, therefore, are commonly good for little.

The price of raw hides is a good deal lower at present than it was a few years ago; owing probably to the taking off the duty upon seal skins, and to the allowing, for a limited time, the importation of raw hides from Ireland and from the plantations duty free, which was done in 1769.[198] Take the whole of the present century at an average, their real price has probably been somewhat higher than it was in those ancient times. The nature of the commodity renders it not quite so proper for being transported to distant markets as wool. It suffers more by keeping. A salted hide is reckoned inferior to a fresh one, and sells for a lower price. This circumstance must necessarily have some tendency to sink the price of raw hides produced in a country which does not manufacture them, but is obliged to export them; and comparatively to raise that of those produced in a country which does manufacture them. It must have some tendency to sink their price in a barbarous, and to raise it in an improved and manufacturing country. It must have had some tendency therefore to sink it in ancient, and to raise it in modern times. Our tanners besides have not been quite so successful as our clothiers, in convincing the wisdom of the nation, that the safety of the commonwealth depends upon the prosperity of their particular manufacture. They have accordingly been much less favoured. The exportation of raw hides has, indeed, been prohibited, and declared a nuisance:[199] but their importation from foreign

but their average price during the present century is probably higher.

They are not so easily transported as wool,

---

[198] [9 Geo. III., c. 39, for five years; continued by 14 Geo. III., c. 86, and 21 Geo. III., c. 29.]

[199] [By 5 Eliz., c. 22; 8 Eliz., c. 14; 18 Eliz., c. 9; 13 and 14 Car. II., c. 7, which last uses the words "common and public nuisance." See Blackstone, *Commentaries*, vol. iv., pp. 167–169.]

and tanners have not been so much favoured by legislation as clothiers.

countries has been subjected to a duty;[200] and though this duty has been taken off from those of Ireland and the plantations (for the limited time of five years only), yet Ireland has not been confined to the market of Great Britain for the sale of its surplus hides, or of those which are not manufactured at home. The hides of common cattle have but within these few years been put among the enumerated commodities which the plantations can send nowhere but to the mother country; neither has the commerce of Ireland been in this case oppressed hitherto, in order to support the manufactures of Great Britain.

Whatever regulations tend to sink the price either of wool or of raw hides below what it naturally would be, must, in an im-

Regulations which sink the price of wool or hides in an improved country raise the price of meat,

proved and cultivated country, have some tendency to raise the price of butcher's-meat. The price both of the great and small cattle, which are fed on improved and cultivated land, must be sufficient to pay the rent which the landlord, and the profit which the farmer has reason to expect from improved and cul-

tivated land. If it is not, they will soon cease to feed them. Whatever part of this price, therefore, is not paid by the wool and the hide, must be paid by the carcase. The less there is paid for the one, the more must be paid for the other. In what manner this price is to be divided upon the different parts of the beast, is indifferent to the landlords and farmers, provided it is all paid to them. In an improved and cultivated country, therefore, their interest as landlords and farmers cannot be much affected by such regulations, though their interest as consumers

but not in an unimproved country.

may, by the rise in the price of provisions.[201] It would be quite otherwise, however, in an unimproved and uncultivated country, where the greater part of the lands could be applied

---

[200] [9 Ann., c. 11.]

[201] [This passage, from the beginning of the paragraph, is quoted at length below, p. 828.]

to no other purpose but the feeding of cattle, and where the wool and the hide made the principal part of the value of those cattle. Their interest as landlords and farmers would in this case be very deeply affected by such regulations, and their interest as consumers very little. The fall in the price of the wool and the hide, would not in this case raise the price of the carcase; because the greater part of the lands of the country being applicable to no other purpose but the feeding of cattle, the same number would still continue to be fed. The same quantity of butcher's-meat would still come to market. The demand for it would be no greater than before. Its price, therefore, would be the same as before. The whole price of cattle would fall, and along with it both the rent and the profit of all those lands of which cattle was the principal produce, that is, of the greater part of the lands of the country. The perpetual prohibition of the exportation of wool, which is commonly, but very falsely, ascribed to Edward III,[202] would, in the then circumstances of the country, have been the most destructive regulation which could well have been thought of. It would not only have reduced the actual value of the greater part of the lands of the kingdom, but by reducing the price of the most important species of small cattle, it would have retarded very much its subsequent improvement.

The wool of Scotland fell very considerably in its price in consequence of the union with England, by which it was excluded from the great market of Europe, and confined to the narrow one of Great Britain. The value of the greater part of the lands in the southern counties of Scotland, which are chiefly a sheep country, would have been very deeply affected by this event, had not the rise in the price of butcher's-meat fully compensated the fall in the price of wool.

The Union sank the price of Scotch wool, while it raised the price of Scotch meat.

As the efficacy of human industry, in increasing the quan-

---

[202] [John Smith, *Memoirs of Wool*, vol. i., p. 25, explains that the words "It shall be felony to carry away any wool out of the realm until it be otherwise ordained" do not imply a perpetual prohibition.]

tity either of wool or of raw hides, is limited, so far as it depends upon the produce of the country where it is exerted; so it

The efficacy of industry in increasing wool and hides is both limited and uncertain.

is uncertain so far as it depends upon the produce of other countries. It so far depends, not so much upon the quantity which they produce, as upon that which they do not manufacture; and upon the restraints which they may or may not think proper to impose upon the exportation of this sort of rude produce. These circumstances, as they are altogether independent of domestic industry, so they necessarily render the efficacy of its efforts more or less uncertain. In multiplying this sort of rude produce, therefore, the efficacy of human industry is not only limited, but uncertain.

In multiplying another very important sort of rude produce, the quantity of fish that is brought to market, it is likewise both

The same thing is true of fish, which naturally rise in the progress of improvement.

limited and uncertain. It is limited by the local situation of the country, by the proximity or distance of its different provinces from the sea, by the number of its lakes and rivers, and by what may be called the fertility or barrenness of those seas, lakes and rivers, as to this sort of rude produce. As population increases, as the annual produce of the land and labour of the country grows greater and greater, there come to be more buyers of fish, and those buyers too have a greater quantity and variety of other goods, or, what is the same thing, the price of a greater quantity and variety of other goods, to buy with. But it will generally be impossible to supply the great and extended market without employing a quantity of labour greater than in proportion to what had been requisite for supplying the narrow and confined one. A market which, from requiring only one thousand, comes to require annually ten thousand ton of fish, can seldom be supplied without employing more than ten times the quantity of labour which had before been sufficient to supply it. The fish must generally be sought for at a greater distance, larger vessels must be employed, and more expensive machinery of every kind made use of. The real price of this commodity, therefore, naturally rises in the progress of improvement. It has accordingly done so, I believe, more or less in every country.

Though the success of a particular day's fishing may be a very uncertain matter, yet, the local situation of the country being supposed, the general efficacy of industry in bringing a certain quantity of fish to market, taking the course of a year, or of several years together, it may perhaps be thought, is certain enough; and it, no doubt, is so. As it depends more, however, upon the local situation of the country than upon the state of its wealth and industry; as upon this account it may in different countries be the same in very different periods of improvement, and very different in the same period; its connection with the state of improvement is uncertain, and it is of this sort of uncertainty that I am here speaking.

The connexion of success in fishing with the state of improvement is uncertain.

In increasing minerals the efficacy of industry is not limited but uncertain.

In increasing the quantity of the different minerals and metals which are drawn from the bowels of the earth, that of the more precious ones particularly, the efficacy of human industry seems not to be limited, but to be altogether uncertain.

The quantity of the precious metals in a country depends on its power of purchasing and the fertility of the mines.

The quantity of the precious metals which is to be found in any country is not limited by any thing in its local situation, such as the fertility or barrenness of its own mines. Those metals frequently abound in countries which possess no mines. Their quantity in every particular country seems to depend upon two different circumstances; first, upon its power of purchasing, upon the state of its industry, upon the annual produce of its land and labour, in consequence of which it can afford to employ a greater or a smaller quantity of labour and subsistence in bringing or purchasing such superfluities as gold and silver, either from its own mines or from those of other countries; and, secondly, upon the fertility or barrenness of the mines which may happen at any particular time to supply the commercial world with those metals. The quantity of those metals in the countries most remote from the mines, must be more or less affected by this fertility or barrenness, on account of the easy and cheap transportation of those metals, of their small bulk and great value. Their quantity in China and Indostan must have been more or less affected by the abundance of the mines of America.

So far as their quantity in any particular country depends upon the former of those two circumstances (the power of purchasing), their real price, like that of all

So far as it depends on the former circumstance the real price is likely to rise with improvement;

other luxuries and superfluities, is likely to rise with the wealth and improvement of the country, and to fall with its poverty and depression. Countries which have a great quantity of labour and subsistence to spare, can afford to purchase any particular quantity of those metals at the expence of a greater quantity of labour and subsistence, than countries which have less to spare.

so far as it depends on the latter circumstance the real price will vary with the fertility of the mines,

So far as their quantity in any particular country depends upon the latter of those two circumstances (the fertility or barrenness of the mines which happen to supply the commercial world) their real price, the real quantity of labour and subsistence which they will purchase or exchange for, will, no doubt, sink more or less in proportion to the fertility, and rise in proportion to the barrenness, of those mines.

The fertility or barrenness of the mines, however, which may happen at any particular time to supply the commercial

which has no connexion with the state of industry.

world, is a circumstance which, it is evident, may have no sort of connection with the state of industry in a particular country. It seems even to have no very necessary connection with that of the world in general. As arts and commerce, indeed, gradually spread themselves over a greater and a greater part of the earth, the search for new mines, being extended over a wider surface, may have somewhat a better chance for being successful, than when confined within narrower bounds. The discovery of new mines, however, as the old ones come to be gradually exhausted, is a matter of the greatest uncertainty, and such as no human skill or industry can ensure. All indications, it is acknowledged, are doubtful, and the actual discovery and successful working of a new mine can alone ascertain the reality of its value, or even of its existence. In this search there seem to be no certain limits either to the possible success, or to the possible disappointment of human industry. In the course of a century or two, it is possible that new mines may be discovered more fertile than any that have ever yet been known; and it is just equally possible that the most fertile mine then known may be more barren than any that was wrought before the discovery of the mines of America. Whether the one or the other of those two events may happen to take place, is of very little importance to the real wealth and prosperity of the world, to the real value of the annual produce of the land and labour of mankind. Its nominal value, the quantity of gold and silver by which this annual produce could be expressed or represented, would, no doubt, be very different; but its real value, the real quantity of labour which it could purchase or command, would be precisely the same. A shilling might in the one case represent no more labour than a penny does at present; and a penny in the other might represent as much as a shilling does now. But in the one case he who had a shilling in his pocket, would be no richer than he who has a penny at present; and in the other he who had a penny would be just as rich as he who has a shilling now. The cheapness and abundance of gold and silver plate, would be the sole advantage which the world could derive from the one event, and the dearness and scarcity of those trifling superfluities the only inconveniency it could suffer from the other.

CONCLUSION OF THE DIGRESSION CONCERNING
THE VARIATIONS IN THE VALUE OF SILVER

The greater part of the writers who have collected the money prices of things in ancient times, seem to have considered the low money price of corn, and of goods in general, or, in other words, the high value of gold and silver, as a proof, not only of the scarcity of those metals, but of the poverty and barbarism of the country at the time when it took place. This notion is connected

The high value of the precious metals is no proof of poverty and barbarism,

with the system of political œconomy which represents national wealth as consisting in the abundance, and national poverty in the scarcity, of gold and silver; a system which I shall endeavour to explain and examine at great length in the fourth book of this enquiry. I shall only observe at present, that the high value of the precious metals can be no proof of the poverty or barbarism of any particular country at the time when it took place. It is a proof only of the barrenness of the mines which happened at that time to supply the commercial world. A poor country, as it cannot afford to buy more, so it can as little afford to pay dearer for gold and silver than a rich one; and the value of those metals, therefore, is not likely to be higher in the former than in the latter. In China, a country much richer than any part of Europe,[203] the value of the precious metals is much higher than in any part of Europe. As the wealth of Europe, indeed, has increased greatly since the discovery of the mines of America, so the value of gold and silver has gradually diminished. This diminution of their value, however, has not been owing to the increase of the real wealth of Europe, of the annual produce of its land and labour, but to the accidental discovery of more abundant mines than any that were known before. The increase of the quantity of gold and silver in Europe, and the increase of its manufactures and agriculture, are two events which, though they have happened

[203] [The same words occur above, p. 258.]

nearly about the same time, yet have arisen from very different causes, and have scarce any natural connection with one another. The one has arisen from a mere accident, in which neither prudence nor policy either had or could have any share: The other from the fall of the feudal system, and from the establishment of a government which afforded to industry the only encouragement which it requires, some tolerable security that it shall enjoy the fruits of its own labour. Poland, where the feudal system still continues to take place, is at this day as beggarly a country as it was before the discovery of America. The money price of corn, however, has risen; the real value of the precious metals has fallen in Poland, in the same manner as in other parts of Europe. Their quantity, therefore, must have increased there as in other places, and nearly in the same proportion to the annual produce of its land and labour. This increase of the quantity of those metals, however, has not, it seems, increased that annual produce, has neither improved the manufactures and agriculture of the country, nor mended the circumstances of its inhabitants. Spain and Portugal, the countries which possess the mines, are after Poland, perhaps, the two most beggarly countries in Europe. The value of the precious metals, however, must be lower in Spain and Portugal than in any other part of Europe; as they come from those countries to all other parts of Europe, loaded, not only with a freight and an insurance, but with the expence of smuggling, their exportation being either prohibited, or subjected to a duty. In proportion to the annual produce of the land and labour, therefore, their quantity must be greater in those countries than in any other part of Europe: Those countries, however, are poorer than the greater part of Europe. Though the feudal system has been abolished in Spain and Portugal, it has not been succeeded by a much better.

As the low value of gold and silver, therefore, is no proof of the wealth and flourishing state of the country where it takes place; so neither is their high value, or the low money price either of goods in general, or of corn in particular, any proof of its poverty and barbarism.

But though the low money price either of goods in general, or of corn in particular, be no proof of the poverty or barbarism of the times, the low money price of some particular sorts of goods, such as cattle, poultry, game of all kinds, &c[204] in proportion to that of corn, is a most decisive one. It clearly demonstrates, first, their great abundance in proportion to that of corn, and consequently the great extent of the land which they occupied in proportion to what was occupied by corn; and, secondly, the low value of this land in proportion to that of corn land, and consequently the uncultivated and unimproved state of the far greater part of the lands of the country. It clearly demonstrates that the stock and population of the country did not bear the same proportion to the extent of its territory, which they commonly do in civilized countries, and that society was at that time, and in that country, but in its infancy. From the high or low money price either of goods in general, or of corn in particular, we can infer only that the mines which at that time happened to supply the commercial world with gold and silver, were fertile or barren, not that the country was rich or poor. But from the high or low money price of some sorts of goods in proportion to that of others, we can infer, with a degree of probability that approaches almost to certainty, that it was rich or poor, that the greater part of its lands were improved or unimproved, and that it was either in a more or less barbarous state, or in a more or less civilized one.

but the low price of cattle, poultry, game, &c., is a proof of poverty or barbarism.

Any rise in the money price of goods which proceeded altogether from the degradation of the value of silver, would affect all sorts of goods equally, and raise their price universally a third, or a fourth, or a fifth part higher, according as silver happened to lose a third, or a fourth, or a fifth part of its former value.[205] But the rise in the price of pro-

A rise of price due entirely to degradation of silver would affect all goods equally, but corn has risen much less than other provisions,

---

[204] [Ed. 1 does not contain "&c."]

[205] [The arithmetic is slightly at fault. It should be, "happened to lose a fourth, a fifth, or a sixth part of its former value."]

visions, which has been the subject of so much reasoning and conversation, does not affect all sorts of provisions equally. Taking the course of the present century at an average, the price of corn, it is acknowledged, even by those who account for this rise by the degradation of the value of silver, has risen much less than that of some other sorts of provisions. The rise in the price of those other sorts of provisions, therefore, cannot be owing altogether to the degradation of the value of silver. Some other causes must be taken into the account, and those which have been above assigned, will, perhaps, without having recourse to the supposed degradation of the value of silver, sufficiently explain this rise in those particular sorts of provisions of which the price has actually risen in proportion to that of corn.

As to the price of corn itself, it has, during the sixty-four first years of the present century, and before the late extraordinary course of bad seasons, been somewhat lower than it was during the sixty-four last years of the preceding century. This fact is attested, not only by the accounts of Windsor market,[206] but by the public fiars[207] of all the different counties of Scotland, and by the accounts of several different markets in France, which have been collected with great diligence and fidelity by Mr. Messance,[208] and by Mr. Duprè de St. Maur.[209] The evidence is more complete than could well have been expected in a matter which is naturally so very difficult to be ascertained.

and has indeed been somewhat lower in 1701–64 than in 1637–1700

As to the high price of corn during these last ten or twelve years, it can be sufficiently accounted for from the badness of the seasons, without supposing any degradation in the value of silver.

while its recent high price has been due only to bad seasons.

[206] [Below, pp. 346–348.]

[207] [Above, p. 107.]

[208] [*Recherches sur la Population*, pp. 293–304.]

[209] [*Essai sur les monnoies ou réflexions sur le rapport entre l'argent et les denrées*, 1746, esp. p. 181 of the "Variations dans les prix."]

The opinion, therefore, that silver is continually sinking in its value, seems not to be founded upon any good observations, either upon the prices of corn, or upon those of other provisions.

The same quantity of silver, it may, perhaps, be said, will in

The distinction between a rise of prices and a fall in the value of silver is not useless:

the present times, even according to the account which has been here given, purchase a much smaller quantity of several sorts of provisions than it would have done during some part of the last century; and to ascertain whether this change be owing to a rise in the value of those goods, or to a fall in the value of silver, is only to establish a vain and useless distinction, which can be of no sort of service to the man who has only a certain quantity of silver to go to market with, or a certain fixed revenue in money. I certainly do not pretend that the knowledge of this distinction will enable him to buy cheaper. It may not, however, upon that account be altogether useless.

it affords an easy proof of the prosperity of the country,

It may be of some use to the public by affording an easy proof of the prosperous condition of the country. If the rise in the price of some sorts of provisions be owing altogether to a fall in the value of silver, it is owing to a circumstance from which nothing can be inferred but the fertility of the American mines. The real wealth of the country, the annual produce of its land and labour, may, notwithstanding this circumstance, be either gradually declining, as in Portugal and Poland; or gradually advancing, as in most other parts of Europe. But if this rise in the price of some sorts of provisions be owing to a rise in the real value of the land which produces them, to its increased fertility; or, in consequence of more extended improvement and good cultivation, to its having been rendered fit for producing corn; it is owing to a circumstance which indicates in the clearest manner the prosperous and advancing state of the country. The land constitutes by far the greatest, the most important, and the most durable part of the wealth of every extensive country. It may surely be of some use, or, at least, it may give some satisfaction to the Public, to have so decisive a proof of the increasing value of by far the greatest, the most important, and the most durable part of its wealth.

It may too be of some use to the Public in regulating the pecuniary reward of some of its inferior servants. If this rise in the price of some sorts of provisions be owing to a fall in the value of silver, their pecuniary reward, provided it was not too large before, ought certainly to be augmented in proportion to the extent of this fall. If it is not augmented, their real recompence will evidently be so much diminished. But if this rise of price is owing to the increased value in consequence of the improved fertility of the land which produces such provisions, it becomes a much nicer matter to judge either in what proportion any pecuniary reward ought to be augmented, or whether it ought to be augmented at all. The extension of improvement and cultivation, as it necessarily raises more or less, in proportion to the price of corn, that of every sort of animal food, so it as necessarily lowers that of, I believe, every sort of vegetable food. It raises the price of animal food; because a great part of the land which produces it, being rendered fit for producing corn, must afford to the landlord and farmer the rent and profit of corn land. It lowers the price of vegetable food; because, by increasing the fertility of the land, it increases its abundance. The improvements of agriculture too introduce many sorts of vegetable food, which, requiring less land and not more labour than corn, come much cheaper to market. Such are potatoes and maize, or what is called Indian corn, the two most important improvements which the agriculture of Europe, perhaps, which Europe itself, has received from the great extension of its commerce and navigation. Many sorts of vegetable food, besides, which in the rude state of agriculture are confined to the kitchen-garden, and raised only by the spade, come in its improved state to be introduced into common fields, and to be raised by the plough: such as turnips, carrots, cabbages, &c. If in the progress of improvement, therefore, the real price of one species of food necessarily rises, that of another as necessarily

and may be of use in regulating the wages of the inferior servants of the state.

falls, and it becomes a matter of more nicety to judge how far the rise in the one may be compensated by the fall in the other. When the real price of butcher's-meat has once got to its height (which, with regard to every sort, except, perhaps, that of hogs flesh, it seems to have done through a great part of England more than a century ago), any rise which can afterwards happen in that of any other sort of animal food, cannot much affect the circumstances of the inferior ranks of people. The circumstances of the poor through a great part of England cannot surely be so much distressed by any rise in the price of poultry, fish, wild-fowl, or venison, as they must be relieved by the fall in that of potatoes.

In the present season of scarcity the high price of corn no

The poor are more distressed by the artificial rise of some manufactures than by the natural rise of rude produce other than corn.

doubt distresses the poor. But in times of moderate plenty, when corn is at its ordinary or average price, the natural rise in the price of any other sort of rude produce cannot much affect them. They suffer more, perhaps, by the artificial rise which has been occasioned by taxes in the price of some manufactured commodities; as of salt, soap, leather, candles, malt, beer, and ale, &c.

EFFECTS OF THE PROGRESS OF IMPROVEMENT UPON THE REAL PRICE OF MANUFACTURES

It is the natural effect of improvement, however, to diminish gradually the real price of almost all manufactures. That of the

But the natural effect of improvement is to diminish the price of manufactures.

manufacturing workmanship diminishes, perhaps, in all of them without exception. In consequence of better machinery, of greater dexterity, and of a more proper division and distribution of work, all of which are the natural effects of improvement, a much smaller quantity of labour becomes requisite for executing any particular piece of work; and though, in consequence of the flourishing circumstances of the society, the real price of labour should rise very considerably, yet the great diminution of the quantity will generally much more than compensate the greatest rise which can happen in the price.[210]

There are, indeed, a few manufactures, in which the necessary rise in the real price of the rude materials will more than

In a few manufactures the rise in the price of raw material counter-balances improvement in execution,

compensate all the advantages which improvement can introduce into the execution of the work. In carpenters and joiners work, and in the coarser sort of cabinet work, the necessary rise in the real price of barren timber, in consequence of the improvement of land, will more than compensate all the advantages which can be derived from the best machinery, the greatest dexterity, and the most proper division and distribution of work.

But in all cases in which the real price of the rude materials either does not rise at all, or does not rise very much, that of the

but in other cases price falls considerably.

manufactured commodity sinks very considerably. This diminution of price has, in the course of the present and preceding century,

Since 1600 this has been most remarkable in manufactures made of the coarser metals.

been most remarkable in those manufactures of which the materials are the coarser metals. A better movement of a watch, that about the middle of the last century could have been bought for twenty pounds, may now perhaps be had for twenty shillings. In the work of cutlers and locksmiths, in all

the toys[211] which are made of the coarser metals, and in all those goods which are commonly known by the name of Birmingham and Sheffield ware, there has been, during the same period, a very great reduction of price, though not altogether so great as in watch-work. It has, however, been sufficient to astonish the workmen of every other part of Europe, who in many cases acknowledge that they can produce no work of equal goodness for double, or even for triple the price. There are perhaps no manufactures in which the division of

---

[210] [Above, pp. 120, 121.]

[211] [*Lectures*, pp. 159, 164.]

labour can be carried further, or in which the machinery employed admits of a greater variety of improvements, than those of which the materials are the coarser metals.

In the clothing manufacture there has, during the same period, been no such sensible reduction of price. The price of su-

Clothing has not fallen much in the same period,

perfine cloth, I have been assured, on the contrary, has, within these five-and-twenty or thirty years, risen somewhat in proportion to its quality; owing, it was said, to a considerable rise in the price of the material, which consists altogether of Spanish wool. That of the Yorkshire cloth, which is made altogether of English wool, is said indeed, during the course of the present century, to have fallen a good deal in proportion to its quality. Quality, however, is so very disputable a matter, that I look upon all information of this kind as somewhat uncertain. In the clothing manufacture, the division of labour is nearly the same now as it was a century ago, and the machinery employed is not very different. There may, however, have been some small improvements in both, which may have occasioned some reduction of price.

But[212] the reduction will appear much more sensible and un-

but very considerably since the fifteenth century.

deniable, if we compare the price of this manufacture in the present times with what it was in a much remoter period, towards the end of the fifteenth century, when the labour was probably much less subdivided, and the machinery employed much more imperfect, than it is at present.

In 1487, being the 4th of Henry VII.[213] it was enacted, that "whosoever shall sell by retail a broad yard of the finest scar-

Fine cloth has fallen to less than one-third of its price in 1487,

let grained, or of other grained cloth of the finest making, above sixteen shillings, shall forfeit forty shillings for every yard so sold." Sixteen shillings, therefore, containing about the same quantity of silver as four-and-twenty shillings of our present money, was, at that time,

[212] [Ed. 1 does not contain "but."]

[213] [C. 8.]

reckoned not an unreasonable price for a yard of the finest cloth; and as this is a sumptuary law, such cloth, it is probable, had usually been sold somewhat dearer. A guinea may be reckoned the highest price in the present times. Even though the quality of the cloths, therefore, should be supposed equal, and that of the present times is most probably much superior, yet, even upon this supposition, the money price of the finest cloth appears to have been considerably reduced since the end of the fifteenth century. But its real price has been much more reduced. Six shillings and eight-pence was then, and long afterwards, reckoned the average price of a quarter of wheat. Sixteen shillings, therefore, was the price of two quarters and more than three bushels of wheat. Valuing a quarter of wheat in the present times at eight-and-twenty shillings, the real price of a yard of fine cloth must, in those times, have been equal to at least three pounds six shillings and sixpence of our present money. The man who bought it must have parted with the command of a quantity of labour and subsistence equal to what that sum would purchase in the present times.

The reduction in the real price of the coarse manufacture, though considerable, has not been so great as in that of the fine.

In 1463, being the 3d of Edward IV.[214] it was enacted, that "no servant in husbandry, nor common labourer, nor servant to any artificer inhabiting out of a city or burgh, shall use or wear in their clothing any cloth above two shillings the broad yard." In the 3d of Edward IV. two shillings contained very nearly the same quantity of silver as four of our present money. But the Yorkshire cloth which is now sold at four shillings the yard, is probably much superior to any that was then made for the wearing of the very poorest order of common servants. Even the money price of their clothing, therefore, may, in proportion to the quality, be somewhat cheaper in the present than it was in those ancient times. The real price is certainly a good deal cheaper. Ten-pence was

and coarse cloth has fallen to less than one half of its price in 1463.

[214] [C. 5. The quotations from this Act and from 4 Hen. VII., c. 8, are not quite *verbatim*.]

then reckoned what is called the moderate and reasonable price of a bushel of wheat. Two shillings, therefore, was the price of two bushels and near two pecks of wheat, which in the present times, at three shillings and sixpence the bushel, would be worth eight shillings and nine-pence. For a yard of this cloth the poor servant must have parted with the power of purchasing a quantity of subsistence equal to what eight shillings and nine-pence would purchase in the present times. This is a sumptuary law too, restraining the luxury and extravagance of the poor. Their clothing, therefore, had commonly been much more expensive.

The same order of people are, by the same law, prohibited from wearing hose, of which the price should exceed fourteen-

Hose have fallen very considerably since 1463,

pence the pair, equal to about eight-and-twenty pence of our present money. But fourteen-pence was in those times the price of a bushel and near two pecks of wheat; which, in the present times, at three and sixpence the bushel, would cost five shillings and three-pence. We should in the present times consider this as a very high price for a pair of stockings to a servant of the poorest and lowest order. He must, however, in those times have paid what was really equivalent to this price for them.

In the time of Edward IV. the art of knitting stockings was probably not known in any part of Europe. Their hose were

when they were made of common cloth.

made of common cloth, which may have been one of the causes of their dearness. The first person that wore stockings in England is said to have been Queen Elizabeth. She received them as a present from the Spanish ambassador.[215]

---

[215] ["Dr. Howell in his *History of the World*, vol. ii., p. 222, relates 'that Queen Elizabeth, in this third year of her reign, was presented with a pair of black knit silk stockings by her silk woman, Mrs. Mountague, and thenceforth she never wore cloth ones any more.' This eminent author adds 'that King Henry VIII., that magnificent and expensive Prince, wore ordinarily cloth hose, except there came from Spain, by great chance, a pair of silk stockings; for Spain very early abounded in silk. His son, King Edward VI., was presented with a pair of long Spanish silk stockings by his merchant, Sir Thomas Gresham, and the present was

Both in the coarse and in the fine woollen manufacture, the machinery employed was much more imperfect in those an-

The machinery for making cloth has been much improved,

cient, than it is in the present times. It has since received three very capital improvements, besides, probably, many smaller ones of which it may be difficult to ascertain either the number or the importance. The three capital improvements are: first, the exchange of the rock and spindle for the spinning-wheel, which, with the same quantity of labour, will perform more than double the quantity of work. Secondly, the use of several very ingenious machines which facilitate and abridge in a still greater proportion the winding of the worsted and woollen yarn, or the proper arrangement of the warp and woof before they are put into the loom; an operation which, previous to the inventions of those machines, must have been extremely tedious and troublesome. Thirdly, The employment of the fulling mill for thickening the cloth, instead of treading it in water. Neither wind nor water mills of any kind were known in England so early as the beginning of the sixteenth century, nor, so far as I know, in any other part of Europe north of the Alps. They had been introduced into Italy some time before.

The consideration of these circumstances may, perhaps, in some measure explain to us why the real price both of the

which explains the fall of price.

coarse and of the fine manufacture, was so much higher in those ancient, than it is in the present times. It cost a greater quantity of labour to bring the goods to market. When they were brought thither, therefore, they must have purchased or exchanged for the price of a greater quantity.

The coarse manufacture probably was, in those ancient

then much taken notice of.' Thus it is plain that the invention of knit silk stockings originally came from Spain. Others relate that one William Rider, an apprentice on London Bridge, seeing at the house of an Italian merchant a pair of knit worsted stockings from Mantua, made with great skill a pair exactly like them, which he presented in the year 1564 to William Earl of Pembroke, and were the first of that kind worn in England."—Adam Anderson, *Historical and Chronological Deduction of the Origin of Commerce*, 1764, A.D. 1561.]

times, carried on in England, in the same manner as it always

The coarse manufacture was a houshold one,

has been in countries where arts and manufactures are in their infancy. It was probably a houshold manufacture, in which every different part of the work was occasionally performed by all the different members of almost every private family; but so as to be their work only when they had nothing else to do, and not to be the principal business from which any of them derived the greater part of their subsistence. The work which is performed in this manner, it has already been observed,[216] comes always much cheaper to market than that

but the fine was carried on in Flanders by people who subsisted on it, and was subject to customs duty,

which is the principal or sole fund of the workman's subsistence. The fine manufacture, on the other hand, was not in those times carried on in England, but in the rich and commercial country of Flanders; and it was probably conducted then, in the same manner as now, by people who derived the whole, or the principal part of their subsistence from it. It was besides a foreign manufacture, and must have paid some duty, the ancient custom of tonnage and poundage at least, to the king. This duty, indeed, would not probably be very great. It was not then the policy of Europe to restrain, by high duties, the importation of foreign manufactures, but rather to encourage it, in order that merchants might be enabled to supply, at as easy a rate as possible, the great men with the conveniencies and luxuries which they wanted, and which the industry of their own country could not afford them.

which explains why the coarse was in those times lower in proportion to the fine.

The consideration of these circumstances may perhaps in some measure explain to us why, in those ancient times, the real price of the coarse manufacture was, in proportion to that of the fine, so much lower than in the present times.

---

[216] [Above, pp. 161, 162.]

CONCLUSION OF THE CHAPTER

I shall conclude this very long chapter with observing[217] that every improvement in the circumstances of the society tends either directly or indirectly to raise the real rent of land, to increase the real wealth of the landlord, his power of purchasing the labour, or the produce of the labour of other people.

Every improvement in the circumstances of society raises rent.

The extension of improvement and cultivation tends to raise it directly. The landlord's share of the produce necessarily increases with the increase of the produce.

That rise in the real price of those parts of the rude produce of land, which is first the effect of extended improvement and cultivation, and afterwards the cause of their being still further extended, the rise in the price of cattle, for example, tends too to raise the rent of land directly, and in a still greater proportion. The real value of the landlord's share, his real command of the labour of other people, not only rises with the real value of the produce, but the proportion of his share to the whole produce rises with it. That produce, after the rise in its real price, requires no more labour to collect it than before. A smaller proportion of it will, therefore, be sufficient to replace, with the ordinary profit, the stock which employs that labour. A greater proportion of it must, consequently, belong to the landlord.[218]

Extension of improvement and cultivation raises it directly,

and so does the rise in the price of cattle, &c.

All those improvements in the productive powers of labour, which tend directly to reduce the real price of manufactures, tend indirectly to raise the real rent of land. The landlord exchanges that part of his rude produce, which is over and above his own con-

Improvements which reduce the price of manufactures raise it indirectly,

---

[217] [Towards the end of chapter x. the same words occur, omitting "very."]

[218] [The opposite of this is stated on p. 428 below.]

sumption, or what comes to the same thing, the price of that part of it, for manufactured produce. Whatever reduces the real price of the latter, raises that of the former. An equal quantity of the former becomes thereby equivalent to a greater quantity of the latter; and the landlord is enabled to purchase a greater quantity of the conveniencies, ornaments, or luxuries, which he has occasion for.

Every increase in the real wealth of the society, every increase in the quantity of useful labour employed within it, tends indirectly to raise the real rent of land.

and so does every increase in the quantity of useful labour employed.

A certain proportion of this labour naturally goes to the land. A greater number of men and cattle are employed in its cultivation, the produce increases with the increase of the stock which is thus employed in raising it, and the rent increases with the produce.

The contrary circumstances, the neglect of cultivation and improvement, the fall in the real price of any part of the rude produce of land, the rise in the real price of manufactures from the decay of manufacturing art and industry, the declension of the real wealth of the society, all tend, on the

The contrary circumstances lower rent.

other hand, to lower the real rent of land, to reduce the real wealth of the landlord, to diminish his power of purchasing either the labour, or the produce of the labour of other people.

The whole annual produce of the land and labour of every country, or what comes to the same thing, the whole price of that annual produce, naturally divides itself, it has already been observed,[219] into three parts; the rent of land, the wages of labour, and the profits of stock; and constitutes a revenue to three different orders of people;

There are three parts of produce and three original orders of society.

to those who live by rent, to those who live by wages, and to those who live by profit. These are the three great, original and constituent orders of every civilized society, from whose revenue that of every other order is ultimately derived.

---

[219] [Above, p. 71.]

The interest of the first of those three great orders, it appears from what has been just now said, is strictly and insepa-

The interest of the proprietors of land is insepara- bly connected with the general inter- est of the society. rably connected with the general interest of the society. Whatever either promotes or obstructs the one, necessarily promotes or obstructs the other. When the public deliberates concerning any regulation of commerce or police, the proprietors of land never can mislead it, with a view to promote the interest of their own particular order; at least, if they have any tolerable knowledge of that interest. They are, indeed, too often defective in this tolerable knowledge. They are the only one of the three orders whose revenue costs them neither labour nor care, but comes to them, as it were, of its own accord, and independent of any plan or project of their own. That indolence, which is the natural effect of the ease and security of their situation, renders them too often, not only ignorant, but incapable of that application of mind which is necessary in order to foresee and understand the consequences of any public regulation.

The interest of the second order, that of those who live by wages, is as strictly connected with the interest of the society as that of the first. The wages of the labourer, it has already

So also is that of those who live by wages, been shewn,[220] are never so high as when the demand for labour is continually rising, or when the quantity employed is every year increasing considerably. When this real wealth of the society becomes stationary, his wages are soon reduced to what is barely enough to enable him to bring up a family, or to continue the race of labourers. When the society declines, they fall even below this. The order of proprietors may, perhaps, gain more by the prosperity of the society, than that of labourers: but there is no order that suffers so cruelly from its decline. But though the interest of the labourer is strictly connected with that of the society, he is incapable either of comprehending that interest, or of understanding its connexion with his own. His condition leaves him no time to receive the

220 [Above, pp. 98–100.]

necessary information, and his education and habits are commonly such as to render him unfit to judge even though he was fully informed. In the public deliberations, therefore, his voice is little heard and less regarded, except upon some particular occasions, when his clamour is animated, set on, and supported by his employers, not for his, but their own particular purposes.

His employers constitute the third order, that of those who live by profit. It is the stock that is employed for the sake of

but the interest of those who live by profit has not the same connexion with the general interest of the society.

profit, which puts into motion the greater part of the useful labour of every society. The plans and projects of the employers of stock regulate and direct all the most important operations of labour, and profit is the end proposed by all those plans and projects. But the rate of profit does not, like rent and wages, rise with the prosperity, and fall with the declension, of the society. On the contrary, it is naturally low in rich, and high in poor countries, and it is always highest in the countries which are going fastest to ruin. The interest of this third order, therefore, has not the same connexion with the general interest of the society as that of the other two. Merchants and master manufacturers are, in this order, the two classes of people who commonly employ the largest capitals, and who by their wealth draw to themselves the greatest share of the public consideration. As during their whole lives they are engaged in plans and projects, they have frequently more acuteness of understanding than the greater part of country gentlemen. As their thoughts, however, are commonly exercised rather about the interest of their own particular branch of business, than about that of the society, their judgment, even when given with the greatest candour (which it has not been upon every occasion), is much more to be depended upon with regard to the former of those two objects, than with regard to the latter. Their superiority over the country gentleman is, not so much in their knowledge of the public interest, as in their having a better knowledge of their own interest than he has of his. It is by this superior knowledge of their own interest that they have frequently imposed upon his generosity, and persuaded him to give up both his own interest and that of the public, from a very simple but honest conviction, that their interest, and not his, was the interest of the public. The interest of the dealers, however, in any particular branch of trade or manufactures, is always in some respects different from, and even opposite to, that of the public. To widen the market and to narrow the competition, is always the interest of the dealers. To widen the market may frequently be agreeable enough to the interest of the public; but to narrow the competition must always be against it, and can serve only to enable the dealers, by raising their profits above what they naturally would be, to levy, for their own benefit, an absurd tax upon the rest of their fellow-citizens. The proposal of any new law or regulation of commerce which comes from this order, ought always to be listened to with great precaution, and ought never to be adopted till after having been long and carefully examined, not only with the most scrupulous, but with the most suspicious attention. It comes from an order of men, whose interest is never exactly the same with that of the public, who have generally an interest to deceive and even to oppress the public, and who accordingly have, upon many occasions, both deceived and oppressed it.

Years XII.	Price of the Quarter of Wheat each Year.[221]			Average of the different Prices of the same Year.			The average Price of each Year in Money of the present Times.[222]		
	£.	s.	d.	£.	s.	d.	£.	s.	d.
1202	—	12	—	—	—	—	1	16	—
	—	12	—						
1205	—	13	4	—	13	5	2	—	3
	—	15	—						
1223	—	12	—	—	—	—	1	16	—
1237	—	3	4	—	—	—	—	10	—
1243	—	2	—	—	—	—	—	6	—
1244	—	2	—	—	—	—	—	6	—
1246	—	16	—	—	—	—	2	8	—
1247	—	13	4	—	—	—	2	—	—
1257	1	4	—	—	—	—	3	12	—
	1	—	—						
1258	—	15	—	—	17	—	2	11	—
	—	16	—						
1270	4	16	—				16	16	—
	6	8	—	5	12	—			
1286	—	2	8				1	8	—
	—	16	—	—	9	4			
Total,							35	9	3
Average Price,							2	19	1¼

[221] [As is explained above, p. 252, the prices from 1202 to 1597 are collected from Fleetwood (*Chronicon Preciosum*, 1707, pp. 77–124), and from 1598 to 1601 they are from the Eton College account without any reduction for the size of the Windsor quarter or the quality of the wheat, and consequently identical with those given in the table on p. 345 below, as to which see note.]

[222] [In the reduction of the ancient money to the eighteenth century standard the table in Martin Folkes (*Table of English Silver Coins*, 1745, p. 142) appears to have been followed. Approximate figures are aimed at (*e.g.*, the factor 3 does duty both for 2.906 and 2.871), and the error is not always uniform, *e.g.*, between 1464 and 1497 some of the sums appear to have been multiplied by the approximate 1½ and others by the exact 1.55.]

Years XII.	Price of the Quarter of Wheat each Year.			Average of the different Prices of the same Year.			The average Price of each Year in Money of the present Times.		
	£.	s.	d.	£.	s.	d.	£.	s.	d.
1287	—	3	4	—	—	—	1	10	—
	—	—	8						
	—	1	—						
	—	1	4						
	—	1	6						
1288	—	1	8	—	3	—¼²²³	—	9	—¾
	—	2	—						
	—	3	4						
	—	9	4						
	—	12	—						
	—	6	—						
1289	—	2	—	—	10	1¾	1	10	4¾²²⁴
	—	10	8						
	1	—	—						
1290	—	16	—²²⁵	—	—	—	2	8	—
1294	—	16	—	—	—	—	2	8	—
1302	—	4	—	—	—	—	—	12	—
1309	—	7	2	—	—	—	1	1	6
1315	1	—	—	—	—	—	3	—	—
	1	—	—						
	1	10	—						
1316	1	12	—	1	10	6	4	11	6
	2	—	—						
	2	4	—						
	—	14	—						
1317	2	13	—²²⁶	1	19	6	5	18	6
	4	—	—						
	—	6	8						
1336	—	2	—	—	—	—	—	6	—
1338	—	3	4	—	—	—	—	10	—
Total,							23	4	11¼
Average Price,							1	18	8

²²³ [This should be 2s. 7¼d. The mistake is evidently due to the 3s. 4d. belonging to the year 1287 having been erroneously added in.]

²²⁴ [*Sic* in all editions. More convenient to the unpractised eye in adding up than "¼."]

²²⁵ ["And sometime xxs. as H. Knighton."—Fleetwood, *Chronicon Preciosum*, p. 82.]

²²⁶ [Miscopied: it is £2 13s. 4d. in Fleetwood, *op. cit.*, p. 92.]

Years XII.	Price of the Quarter of Wheat each Year.			Average of the different Prices of the same Year.			The average Price of each Year in Money of the present Times.		
	£.	s.	d.	£.	s.	d.	£.	s.	d.
1339	—	9	—	—	—	—	1	7	—
1349	—	2	—	—	—	—	—	5	2
1359	1	6	8	—	—	—	3	2	2
1361	—	2	—	—	—	—	—	4	8
1363	—	15	—	—	—	—	1	15	—
	1	—	—						
1369	1	4	—	1	2	—	2	9	4[227]
1379	—	4	—	—	—	—	—	9	4
1387	—	2	—	—	—	—	—	4	8
	—	13	4						
1390	—	14	—	—	14	5	1	13	7
	—	16	—						
1401	—	16	—	—	—	—	1	17	4
	—	4	4¼						
1407	—	3	4	—	3	10	—	8	11
1416	—	16	—	—	—	—	1	12	—
						Total,	23	4	11¼
						Average Price,	1	5	9½

	£.	s.	d.	£.	s.	d.	£.	s.	d.
1423	—	8	—	—	—	—	—	16	—
1425	—	4	—	—	—	—	—	8	—
1434	1	6	8	—	—	—	2	13	4
1435	—	5	4	—	—	—	—	10	8
	1	—	—						
1439	1	6	8	1	3	4	2	6	8
1440	1	4	—	—	—	—	2	8	—
	—	4	4						
1444	—	4	—	—	4	2	—	8	4
1445	—	4	6	—	—	—	—	9	—
1447	—	8	—	—	—	—	—	16	—
1448	—	6	8	—	—	—	—	13	4
1449	—	5	—	—	—	—	—	10	—
1451	—	8	—	—	—	—	—	16	—
						Total,	12	15	4
						Average Price,	1	1	3½

227 [Obviously a mistake for £2 11s. 4d.]

Years XII.	Price of the Quarter of Wheat each Year.			Average of the different Prices of the same Year.			The average Price of each Year in Money of the present Times.		
	£.	s.	d.	£.	s.	d.	£.	s.	d.
1453	—	5	4	—	—	—	—	10	8
1455	—	1	2	—	—	—	—	2	4
1457	—	7	8	—	—	—	—	15	4
1459	—	5	—	—	—	—	—	10	—
1460	—	8	—	—	—	—	—	16	—
	—	2	—						
1463	—	1	8	—	1	10	—	3	8
1464	—	6	8	—	—	—	—	10	—
1486	1	4	—	—	—	—	1	17	—
1491	—	14	8	—	—	—	1	2	—
1494	—	4	—	—	—	—	—	6	—
1495	—	3	4	—	—	—	—	5	—
1497	1	—	—	—	—	—	1	11	—
					Total,		8	9	—
					Average Price,		—	14	1

	£.	s.	d.	£.	s.	d.	£.	s.	d.
1499	—	4	—	—	—	—	—	6	—
1504	—	5	8	—	—	—	—	8	6
1521	1	—	—	—	—	—	1	10	—
1551	—	8	—	—	—	—	—	2	—
1553	—	8	—	—	—	—	—	8	—
1554	—	8	—	—	—	—	—	8	—
1555	—	8	—	—	—	—	—	8	—
1556	—	8	—	—	—	—	—	8	—
	—	4	—						
1557	—	5	—						
	—	8	—	—	17	8½[228]	—	17	8½
	2	13	4						
1558	—	8	—	—	—	—	—	8	—
1559	—	8	—	—	—	—	—	8	—
1560	—	8	—	—	—	—	—	8	—
					Total,		6	0	2½
					Average Price,		—	10	0½[229]

[228] [This should be 17s. 7d. here and in the next column. Eds. 1 and 2 read "12s. 7d.," a mistake of £1 having been made in the addition.]

[229] [This should obviously be 10s. ½d. Eds. 1 and 2 read "£6 5s. 1d." for the total and "10s. 5d." for the average, in consequence of the mistake mentioned in the preceding note.]

Years XII.	Price of the Quarter of Wheat each Year.			Average of the different Prices of the same Year.			The average Price of each Year in Money of the present Times.		
	£.	s.	d.	£.	s.	d.	£.	s.	d.
1561	—	8	—	—	—	—	—	8	—
1562	—	8	—	—	—	—	—	8	—
	2	16	—						
1574	1	4	—	2	—	—	2	—	—
1587	3	4	—	—	—	—	3	4	—
1594	2	16	—	—	—	—	2	16	—
1595	2	13	—230	—	—	—	2	13	—
1596	4	—	—	—	—	—	4	—	—
1597	5	4	—						
	4	—	—	4	12	—	4	12	—
1598	2	16	8	—	—	—	2	16	8
1599	1	19	2	—	—	—	1	19	2
1600	1	17	8	—	—	—	1	17	8
1601	1	14	10231	—	—	—	1	14	10
Total,							28	9	4
Average Price,							2	7	5½232

---

230 [Miscopied: it is £2 13s. 4d. in Fleetwood, *Chronicon Preciosum*, p. 123.]

231 [See p. 340, note 221.]

232 [Eds. 1 and 2 read £2 4s. 9½d., the 89s. left over after dividing the pounds having been inadvertently divided by 20 instead of by 12.]

Prices of the Quarter of nine Bushels of the best or highest period Wheat at Windsor Market, on Lady-Day and Michaelmas, from 1595 to 1764, both inclusive; the Price of each Year being the Medium between the highest Prices of those Two Market-days.[233]

Years		£	s.	d.	Years		£	s.	d.
1595,	—	2	0	0	1621,	—	1	10	4
1596,	—	2	8	0	1622,	—	2	18	8
1597,	—	3	9	6	1623,	—	2	12	0
1598,	—	2	16	8	1624,	—	2	8	0
1599,	—	1	19	2	1625,	—	2	12	0
1600,	—	1	17	8	1626,	—	2	9	4
1601,	—	1	14	10	1627,	—	1	16	0
1602,	—	1	9	4	1628,	—	1	8	0
1603,	—	1	15	4	1629,	—	2	2	0
1604,	—	1	10	8	1630,	—	2	15	8
1605,	—	1	15	10	1631,	—	3	8	0
1606,	—	1	13	0	1632,	—	2	13	4
1607,	—	1	16	8	1633,	—	2	18	0
1608,	—	2	16	8	1634,	—	2	16	0
1609,	—	2	10	0	1635,	—	2	16	0
1610,	—	1	15	10	1636,	—	2	16	8
1611,	—	1	18	8		16)40	0	0	
1612,	—	2	2	4		2	10	0	
1613,	—	2	8	8					
1614,	—	2	1	8½					
1615,	—	1	18	8					
1616,	—	2	0	4					
1617,	—	2	8	8					
1618,	—	2	6	8					
1619,	—	1	15	4					
1620,	—	1	10	4					
	26)54	0	6½						
	2	1	6⅚₃						

[233] [The list of prices, but not the division into periods, is apparently copied from Charles Smith (*Tracts on the Corn Trade*, 1766, pp. 97–102, cp. pp. 43, 104), who, however, states that it had been previously published, p. 96.]

Wheat per quarter.				Wheat per quarter.			
Years		£	s.	d.	Years	£	s.	d.
1637,	—	2	13	0	Brought over,	79	14	10
1638,	—	2	17	4	1671, —	2	2	0
1639,	—	2	4	10	1672, —	2	1	0
1640,	—	2	4	8	1673, —	2	6	8
1641,	—	2	8	0	1674, —	3	8	8
1642,	Wanting in the account. The year 1646 supplied by Bishop Fleetwood	0	0	0	1675, —	3	4	8
1643,		0	0	0	1676, —	1	18	0
1644,		0	0	0	1677, —	2	2	0
1645,		0	0	0	1678, —	2	19	0
1646,	—	2	8	0	1679, —	3	0	0
1647,	—	3	13	8	1680, —	2	5	0
1648,	—	4	5	0	1681, —	2	6	8
1649,	—	4	0	0	1682, —	2	4	0
1650,	—	3	16	8	1683, —	2	0	0
1651,	—	3	13	4	1684, —	2	4	0
1652,	—	2	9	6	1685, —	2	6	8
1653,	—	1	15	6	1686, —	1	14	0
1654,	—	1	6	0	1687, —	1	5	2
1655,	—	1	13	4	1688, —	2	6	0
1656,	—	2	3	0	1689, —	1	10	0
1657,	—	2	6	8	1690, —	1	14	8
1658,	—	3	5	0	1691, —	1	14	0
1659,	—	3	6	0	1692, —	2	6	8
1660,	—	2	16	6	1693, —	3	7	8
1661,	—	3	10	0	1694, —	3	4	0
1662,	—	3	14	0	1695, —	2	13	0
1663,	—	2	17	0	1696, —	3	11	0
1664,	—	2	0	6	1697, —	3	0	0
1665,	—	2	9	4	1698, —	3	8	4
1666,	—	1	16	0	1699, —	3	4	0
1667,	—	1	16	0	1700, —	2	0	0
1668,	—	2	0	0				
1669,	—	2	4	4	60)153		1	8
1670,	—	2	1	8		2	11	0½
Carry over,		79	14	10				

| Wheat per quarter. | | | | Wheat per quarter. | | | |
Years		£	s.	d.	Years	£	s.	d.
1701,	—	1	17	8	Brought over,	69	8	8
1702,	—	1	9	6	1734, —	1	18	10
1703,	—	1	16	0	1735, —	2	3	0
1704,	—	2	6	6	1736, —	2	0	4
1705,	—	1	10	0	1737, —	1	18	0
1706,	—	1	6	0	1738, —	1	15	6
1707,	—	1	8	6	1739, —	1	18	6
1708,	—	2	1	6	1740, —	2	10	8
1709,	—	3	18	6	1741, —	2	6	8
1710,	—	3	18	0	1742, —	1	14	0
1711,	—	2	14	0	1743, —	1	4	10
1712,	—	2	6	4	1744, —	1	4	10
1713,	—	2	11	0	1745, —	1	7	6
1714,	—	2	10	4	1746, —	1	19	0
1715,	—	2	3	0	1747, —	1	14	0
1716,	—	2	8	0	1748, —	1	17	0
1717,	—	2	5	8	1749, —	1	17	0
1718,	—	1	18	10	1750, —	1	12	6
1719,	—	1	15	0	1751, —	1	18	6
1720,	—	1	17	0	1752, —	2	1	10
1721,	—	1	17	6	1753, —	2	4	8
1722,	—	1	16	0	1754, —	1	14	8
1723,	—	1	14	8	1755, —	1	13	10
1724,	—	1	17	0	1756, —	2	5	3
1725,	—	2	8	6	1757, —	3	0	0
1726,	—	2	6	0	1758, —	2	10	0
1727,	—	2	2	0	1759, —	1	19	10
1728,	—	2	14	6	1760, —	1	16	6
1729,	—	2	6	10	1761, —	1	10	3
1730,	—	1	16	6	1762, —	1	19	0
1731,	—	1	12	10	1763, —	2	0	9
1732,	—	1	6	8	1764, —	2	6	9
1733,	—	1	8	4				
					64)129		13	6
Carry over,		69	8	8		2	0	6 $\frac{19}{32}$.[234]

[234] [This should be $\frac{9}{23}$.]

Wheat per quarter.					Wheat per quarter.			
Years		£	s.	d.	Years		£	s.	d.
1731,	—	1	12	10	1741,	—	2	6	8
1732,	—	1	6	8	1742,	—	1	14	0
1733,	—	1	8	4	1743,	—	1	4	10
1734,	—	1	18	10	1744,	—	1	4	10
1735,	—	2	3	0	1745,	—	1	7	6
1736,	—	2	0	4	1746,	—	1	19	0
1737,	—	1	18	0	1747,	—	1	14	10
1738,	—	1	15	6	1748,	—	1	17	0
1739,	—	1	18	6	1749,	—	1	17	0
1740,	—	2	10	8	1750,	—	1	12	6
	10)18		12	8		10)16		18	2
	1		17	3⅕		1		13	9⅖

BOOK II

OF THE NATURE, ACCUMULATION, AND EMPLOYMENT OF STOCK

Introduction

IN THAT rude state of society in which there is no division of labour, in which exchanges are seldom made, and in which

In the rude state of society stock is unnecessary.

every man provides every thing for himself, it is not necessary that any stock should be accumulated or stored up beforehand, in order to carry on the business of the society. Every man endeavours to supply by his own industry his own occasional wants as they occur. When he is hungry, he goes to the forest to hunt; when his coat is worn out, he clothes himself with the skin of the first large animal he kills: and when his hut begins to go to ruin, he repairs it, as well as he can, with the trees and the turf that are nearest it.

But when the division of labour has once been thoroughly introduced, the produce of a man's own labour can supply but a

Division of labour makes it necessary.

very small part of his occasional wants. The far greater part of them are supplied by the produce of other mens labour, which he purchases with the produce, or what is the same thing, with the price of the produce of his own. But this purchase cannot be made till such time as the produce of his own labour has not only been completed, but sold. A stock of goods of different kinds, therefore, must be stored up somewhere sufficient to maintain him, and to supply him with the materials and tools of his work, till such time, at least, as both these events can be brought about. A weaver cannot apply himself entirely to his peculiar business, unless there is beforehand stored up somewhere, either in his own possession or in that of some other person, a stock sufficient to maintain him, and to supply him with the materials and tools of his work, till he has not only completed but sold his web. This accumulation must, evidently, be previous to his applying his industry for so long a time to such a peculiar business.[1]

As the accumulation of stock must, in the nature of things, be previous to the division of labour, so labour can be more

Accumulation of stock and division of labour advance together.

and more subdivided[2] in proportion only as stock is previously more and more accumulated. The quantity of materials which the same number of people can work up, increases in a great proportion as labour comes to be more and more subdivided; and as the operations of each workman are gradually reduced to a greater degree of simplicity, a variety of new machines come to be invented for facilitating and abridging those operations. As the division of labour advances, therefore, in order to give constant employment to an equal number of workmen, an equal stock of provisions, and a greater stock of materials and tools than what would have been necessary in a ruder state of things, must be accumulated beforehand. But the number of workmen in every branch of business generally increases with the division of labour in that branch, or rather it is the increase of their number which enables them to class and subdivide themselves in this manner.

As the accumulation of stock is previously necessary for

Accumulation causes the same quantity of industry to produce more.

carrying on this great improvement in the productive powers of labour, so that accumulation naturally leads to this improvement. The person who employs his stock in maintaining labour, necessarily wishes to employ it in such a manner as to produce as

---

[1] [*Lectures*, p. 181.]

[2] [Eds. 1 and 2 place the "only" here.]

great a quantity of work as possible. He endeavours, therefore, both to make among his workmen the most proper distribution of employment, and to furnish them with the best machines which he can either invent or afford to purchase. His abilities in both these respects are generally in proportion to the extent of his stock, or to the number of people whom it can employ. The quantity of industry, therefore, not only increases in every country with the increase of the stock which employs it, but, in consequence of that increase, the same quantity of industry produces a much greater quantity of work.

Such are in general the effects of the increase of stock upon industry and its productive powers.

In the following book I have endeavoured to explain the nature of stock, the effects of its accumulation into capitals of different kinds, and the effects of the differ-

This Book treats of the nature of stock, the effects of its accumulation, and its different employments. ent employments of those capitals. This book is divided into five chapters. In the first chapter, I have endeavoured to show what are the different parts or branches into which the stock, either of an individual, or of a great society, naturally divides itself. In the second, I have endeavoured to explain the nature and operation of money considered as a particular branch of the general stock of the society. The stock which is accumulated into a capital, may either be employed by the person to whom it belongs, or it may be lent to some other person. In the third and fourth chapters, I have endeavoured to examine the manner in which it operates in both these situations. The fifth and last chapter treats of the different effects which the different employments of capital immediately produce upon the quantity both of national industry, and of the annual produce of land and labour.

CHAPTER I

OF THE DIVISION OF STOCK

WHEN THE stock which a man possesses is no more than sufficient to maintain him for a few days or a few weeks, he seldom thinks of deriving any revenue from it. He consumes it as sparingly as he can, and endeavours by his labour to acquire something which may supply its place before it be consumed altogether. His revenue is, in this case, derived from his labour only. This is the state of the greater part of the labouring poor in all countries.

A man does not think of obtaining revenue from a small stock,

But when he possesses stock sufficient to maintain him for months or years, he naturally endeavours to derive a revenue from the greater part of it; reserving only so much for his immediate consumption as may maintain him till this revenue begins to come in. His whole stock, therefore, is distinguished into two parts. That part which, he expects, is to afford him this revenue, is called his capital. The other is that which supplies his immediate consumption; and which consists either, first, in that portion of his whole stock which was originally reserved for this purpose; or, secondly, in his revenue, from whatever source derived, as it gradually comes in; or, thirdly, in such things as had been purchased by either of these in former years, and which are not yet entirely consumed; such as a stock of clothes, household furniture, and the like. In one, or other, or all of these three articles, consists the stock which men commonly reserve for their own immediate consumption.

but when he has more than enough for immediate consumption, he endeavours to derive a revenue from the rest, using it either as

There are two different ways in which a capital may be employed so as to yield a revenue or profit to its employer.

First, it may be employed in raising, manufacturing, or purchasing goods, and selling them again with a profit. The capital employed in this manner yields no revenue or profit to its employer, while it either remains in his possession, or continues in the same shape. The goods of the merchant yield him no revenue or profit till he sells them for money, and the money yields him as little till it is again exchanged for goods. His capital is continually going from him in one shape, and returning to him in another, and it is only by means of such circulation, or successive exchanges, that it can yield him any profit. Such capitals, therefore, may very properly be called circulating capitals.

(1) circulating capital,

Secondly, it may be employed in the improvement of land, in the purchase of useful machines and instruments of trade, or in such-like things as yield a revenue or profit without changing masters, or circulating any further. Such capitals, therefore, may very properly be called fixed capitals.

or (2) fixed capital.

Different occupations require very different proportions between the fixed and circulating capitals employed in them.

Different proportions of fixed and circulating capital are required in different trades.

The capital of a merchant, for example, is altogether a circulating capital. He has occasion for no machines or instruments of trade, unless his shop, or warehouse, be considered as such.

Some part of the capital of every master artificer or manufacturer must be fixed in the instruments of his trade. This part, however, is very small in some, and very great in others. A master taylor requires no other instruments of trade but a parcel of needles. Those of the master shoemaker are a little, though but a very little, more expensive. Those of the weaver rise a good deal above those of the shoemaker. The far greater part of the capital of all such master artificers, however, is circulated, either in the wages of their workmen, or in the price of their materials, and repaid with a profit by the price of the work.

In other works a much greater fixed capital is required. In a great iron-work, for example, the furnace for melting the ore, the forge, the slitt-mill, are instruments of trade which cannot be erected without a very great expence. In coal-works, and mines of every kind, the machinery necessary both for drawing out the water and for other purposes, is frequently still more expensive.

That part of the capital of the farmer which is employed in the instruments of agriculture is a fixed; that which is employed in the wages and maintenance of his labouring servants, is a circulating capital. He makes a profit of the one by keeping it in his own possession, and of the other by parting with it. The price or value of his labouring cattle is a fixed capital in the same manner as that of the instruments of husbandry: Their maintenance is a circulating capital in the same manner as that of the labouring servants. The farmer makes his profit by keeping the labouring cattle, and by parting with their maintenance. Both the price and the maintenance of the cattle which are bought in and fattened, not for labour, but for sale, are a circulating capital. The farmer makes his profit by parting with them. A flock of sheep or a herd of cattle that, in a breeding country, is bought in, neither for labour, nor for sale, but in order to make a profit by their wool, by their milk, and by their increase, is a fixed capital: The profit is made by keeping them. Their maintenance is a circulating capital. The profit is made by parting with it; and it comes back with both its own profit, and the profit upon the whole price of the cattle, in the price of the wool, the milk, and the increase. The whole value of the seed too is properly a fixed capital. Though it goes backwards and forwards between the ground and the granary, it never changes masters, and therefore does not properly circulate.

The stock of a society is divided in the same way into

The farmer makes his profit, not by its sale, but by its increase.

The general stock of any country or society is the same with that of all its inhabitants or members, and therefore naturally divides itself into the same three portions, each of which has a distinct function or office.

The First, is that portion which is reserved for immediate consumption, and of which the characteristic is that it affords no revenue or profit. It consists in the stock of food, clothes, household furniture, &c., which have been purchased by their proper consumers, but which are not yet entirely consumed. The whole stock of mere dwelling houses too subsisting at any one time in the country, make a part of this first portion. The stock that is laid out in a house, if it is to be the dwelling-house of the proprietor, ceases from that moment to serve in the function of a capital, or to afford any revenue to its owner. A dwelling-house, as such, contributes nothing to the revenue of its inhabitant; and though it is, no doubt, extremely useful to him, it is as his clothes and household furniture are useful to him, which, however, make a part of his expence, and not of his revenue. If it is to be let to a tenant for rent, as the house itself can produce nothing,[1] the tenant must always pay the rent out of some other revenue which he derives either from labour, or stock, or land. Though a house, therefore, may yield a revenue to its proprietor, and thereby serve in the function of a capital to him, it cannot yield any to the public, nor serve in the function of a capital to it, and the revenue of the whole body of the people can never be in the smallest degree increased by it. Clothes, and household furniture, in the same manner, sometimes yield a revenue, and thereby serve in the function of a capital to particular persons. In countries where masquerades are common, it is a trade to let out masquerade dresses for a night. Upholsterers frequently let furniture by the month or by the year. Undertakers let the furniture of funerals by the day and by the week. Many people let

(1) the portion reserved for immediate consumption,

---

[1] ["Ce n'est pas cette maison qui produit elle-même ces mille francs.... Le loyer d'une maison n'est point pour la société une augmentation de revenu, une création de richesses nouvelles, il n'est au contraire qu'un mouvement, qu'un changement de main."—Mercier de la Rivière, *L'Ordre naturel et essentiel des Sociétés politiques*, 12mo ed., 1767, vol. ii., p. 123, or in Daire's *Physiocrates*, p. 487.]

furnished houses, and get a rent, not only for the use of the house, but for that of the furniture. The revenue, however, which is derived from such things, must always be ultimately drawn from some other source of revenue. Of all parts of the stock, either of an individual, or of a society, reserved for immediate consumption, what is laid out in houses is most slowly consumed. A stock of clothes may last several years: a stock of furniture half a century or a century: but a stock of houses, well built and properly taken care of, may last many centuries. Though the period of their total consumption, however, is more distant, they are still as really a stock reserved for immediate consumption as either clothes or household furniture.

The Second of the three portions into which the general

(2) the fixed capital, which consists of

stock of the society divides itself, is the fixed capital; of which the characteristic is, that it affords a revenue or profit without circulating or changing masters. It consists chiefly of the four following articles:

(a) useful machines,

First, of all useful machines and instruments of trade which facilitate and abridge labour:

(b) profitable buildings,

Secondly, of all those profitable buildings which are the means of procuring a revenue, not only to their proprietor who lets them for a rent, but to the person who possesses them and pays that rent for them; such as shops, warehouses, workhouses, farmhouses, with all their necessary buildings; stables, granaries, &c. These are very different from mere dwelling houses. They are a sort of instruments of trade, and may be considered in the same light:

Thirdly, of the improvements of land, of what has been profitably laid out in clearing, draining, enclosing, manuring,

(c) improvements of land,

and reducing it into the condition most proper for tillage and culture. An improved farm may very justly be regarded in the same light as those useful machines which facilitate and abridge labour, and by means of which, an equal circulating capital can afford a much greater revenue to its employer. An improved farm is equally advantageous and more durable than any of those machines, frequently requiring no other repairs than the most profitable application of the farmer's capital employed in cultivating it:

Fourthly, of the acquired and useful abilities of all the inhabitants or members of the society. The acquisition of such

and (d) acquired and useful abilities,

talents, by the maintenance of the acquirer during his education, study, or apprenticeship, always costs a real expence, which is a capital fixed and realized, as it were, in his person. Those talents, as they make a part of his fortune, so do they likewise of that of the society to which he belongs. The improved dexterity of a workman may be considered in the same light as a machine or instrument of trade which facilitates and abridges labour, and which, though it costs a certain expence, repays that expence with a profit.[2]

The Third and last of the three portions into which the general stock of the society naturally divides itself, is the circulat-

and (3) the circulating capital, which consists of

ing capital; of which the characteristic is, that it affords a revenue only by circulating or changing masters. It is composed likewise of four parts:

First, of the money by means of which all the other three are

(a) the money,

circulated and distributed to their proper consumers:[3]

(b) the stock of provisions in the possession of the sellers,

Secondly, of the stock of provisions which are in the possession of the butcher, the grazier, the farmer, the corn-merchant, the brewer, &c. and from the sale of which they expect to derive a profit:

(c) the materials of clothes, furniture, and buildings,

Thirdly, of the materials, whether altogether rude, or more or less manufactured, of clothes, furniture and building, which are not yet made up into any of those three shapes, but which remain in the hands of the

[2] [But in bk. i., ch. x., the remuneration of improved dexterity is treated as wages.]

[3] [Ed. 1 reads "users and consumers" here and seventeen lines lower.]

growers, the manufacturers, the mercers, and drapers, the timber-merchants, the carpenters and joiners, the brick-makers, &c.

Fourthly, and lastly, of the work which is made up and completed, but which is still in the hands of the merchant or manu-

and (d) completed work in the hands of the merchant or manufacturer.

facturer, and not yet disposed of or distributed to the proper consumers; such as the finished work which we frequently find ready-made in the shops of the smith, the cabinet-maker, the goldsmith, the jeweller, the china-merchant, &c. The circulating capital consists in this manner, of the provisions, materials, and finished work of all kinds that are in the hands of their respective dealers, and of the money that is necessary for circulating and distributing them to those who are finally to use, or to consume them.

Of these four parts three, provisions, materials, and finished

The last three parts of the circu-lating capital are regularly with-drawn from it.

work, are, either annually, or in a longer or shorter period, regularly withdrawn from it, and placed either in the fixed capital or in the stock reserved for immediate consumption.

Every fixed capital is both originally de-

Every fixed capital is derived from and supported by a circulating capital,

rived from, and requires to be continually supported by a circulating capital. All useful machines and instruments of trade are origi-nally derived from a circulating capital, which furnishes the materials of which they are made, and the maintenance of the work-men who make them. They require too a capital of the same kind to keep them in constant repair.

No fixed capital can yield any revenue but by means of a circulating capital. The most useful machines and instruments

and cannot yield any revenue without it.

of trade will produce nothing without the circulating capital which affords the materi-als they are employed upon, and the mainte-nance of the workmen who employ them. Land, however improved, will yield no revenue without a cir-culating capital, which maintains the labourers who cultivate and collect its produce.

The end of both fixed and circulating capital is to maintain and augment the other part of the stock.

To maintain and augment the stock which may be reserved for immediate consumption, is the sole end and purpose both of the fixed and circulating capitals. It is this stock which feeds, clothes, and lodges the people. Their riches or poverty depends upon the abundant or sparing supplies which those two capitals can afford to the stock reserved for immediate consumption.

The circulating capital is kept up by the produce of land, mines, and fisheries,

So great a part of the circulating capital being continually withdrawn from it, in order to be placed in the other two branches of the general stock of the society; it must in its turn require continual supplies, without which it would soon cease to exist. These supplies are principally drawn from three sources, the produce of land, of mines, and of fisheries. These afford continual supplies of provisions and materials, of which part is afterwards wrought up into finished work, and by which are replaced the provisions, materials and finished work continually withdrawn from the circulating capital. From mines too is drawn what is necessary for maintaining and augmenting that part of it which consists in money. For though, in the ordinary course of business, this part is not, like the other three, necessarily withdrawn from it, in order to be placed in the other two branches of the general stock of the society, it must, however, like all other things, be wasted and worn out at last, and sometimes too be either lost or sent abroad, and must, therefore, require continual, though, no doubt, much smaller supplies.

which require both fixed and circulating capitals to cultivate them,

Land, mines, and fisheries, require all both a fixed and a circulating capital to cultivate them: and their produce replaces with a profit, not only those capitals, but all the others in the society. Thus the farmer annually replaces to the manufacturer the provisions which he had consumed and the materials which he had wrought up the year before; and the manufacturer replaces to the farmer the finished work which he had wasted and worn out in the same time. This is the real exchange that is annually made between those two orders of people, though it seldom happens that the rude produce of the one and the manufactured produce of the other, are directly bartered for one another; because it seldom happens that the farmer sells his corn and his cattle, his flax and his wool, to the very same person of whom he chuses to purchase the clothes, furniture, and instruments of trade which he wants. He sells, therefore, his rude produce for money, with which he can purchase, wherever it is to be had, the manufactured produce he has occasion for. Land even replaces, in part at least, the capitals with which fisheries and mines are cultivated. It is the produce of land which draws the fish from the waters; and it is the produce of the surface of the earth which extracts the minerals from its bowels.

The produce of land, mines, and fisheries, when their natural fertility is equal, is in proportion to the extent and proper application of the capitals employed about them. When the capitals are equal and equally well applied, it is in proportion to their natural fertility.

and, when their fertility is equal, yield produce proportionate to the capital employed.

In all countries where there is tolerable security, every man of common understanding will endeavour to employ whatever stock he can command, in procuring either present enjoyment or future profit. If it is employed in procuring present enjoyment, it is a stock reserved for immediate consumption. If it is employed in procuring future profit, it must procure this profit either by staying with him, or by going from him. In the one case it is a fixed, in the other it is a circulating capital. A man must be perfectly crazy who, where there is tolerable security, does not employ all the stock which he commands, whether it be his own or borrowed of other people, in some one or other of those three ways.

Where there is tolerable security all stock is employed in one or other of the three ways.

In those unfortunate countries, indeed, where men are continually afraid of the violence of their superiors, they frequently bury and conceal a great part of their stock, in order to have it always at hand to carry with them to some place of

But in countries where violence prevails much stock is buried and concealed.

safety, in case of their being threatened with any of those disasters to which they consider themselves as at all times exposed. This is said to be a common practice in Turkey, in Indostan, and, I believe, in most other governments of Asia. It seems to have been a common practice among our ancestors during the violence of the feudal government. Treasure-trove was in those times considered as no contemptible part of the revenue of the greatest sovereigns in Europe. It consisted in such treasure as was found concealed in the earth, and to which no particular person could prove any right. This was regarded in those times as so important an object, that it was always considered as belonging to the sovereign, and neither to the finder nor to the proprietor of the land, unless the right to it had been conveyed to the latter by an express clause in his charter. It was put upon the same footing with gold and silver mines, which, without a special clause in the charter, were never supposed to be comprehended in the general grant of the lands, though mines of lead, copper, tin, and coal were, as things of smaller consequence.

CHAPTER II

OF MONEY CONSIDERED AS A PARTICULAR BRANCH OF THE GENERAL STOCK OF THE SOCIETY, OR OF THE EXPENCE OF MAINTAINING THE NATIONAL CAPITAL

IT HAS been shewn in the first Book, that the price of the greater part of commodities resolves itself into three parts, of which one pays the wages of the labour, another the profits of the stock, and a third the rent of the land which had been employed in producing and bringing them to market: that there are, indeed, some commodities of which the price is made up of two of those parts only, the wages of labour, and the profits of stock: and a very few in which it consists altogether in one, the wages of labour: but that the price of every commodity necessarily resolves itself into some one, or other, or all of these three parts; every part of it which goes neither to rent nor to wages, being necessarily profit to somebody.

Prices are divided into three parts, wages, profits, and rent,

Since this is the case, it has been observed, with regard to every particular commodity, taken separately; it must be so with regard to all the commodities which compose the whole annual produce of the land and labour of every country, taken complexly. The whole price or exchangeable value of that annual produce, must resolve itself into the same three parts, and be parcelled out among the different inhabitants of the country, either as the wages of their labour, the profits of their stock, or the rent of their land.

and the whole annual produce is divided into the same three parts;

But though the whole value of the annual produce of the

but we may distinguish between gross and net revenue.

land and labour of every country is thus divided among and constitutes a revenue to its different inhabitants; yet as in the rent of a private estate we distinguish between the gross rent and the neat rent, so may we likewise in the revenue of all the inhabitants of a great country.

The gross rent of a private estate comprehends whatever is paid by the farmer; the neat rent, what remains free to the land-

Gross rent is the whole sum paid by the farmer; net rent what is left free to the landlord.

lord, after deducting the expence of management, of repairs, and all other necessary charges; or what, without hurting his estate, he can afford to place in his stock reserved for immediate consumption, or to spend upon his table, equipage, the ornaments of his house and furniture, his private enjoyments and amusements. His real wealth is in proportion, not to his gross, but to his neat rent.

The gross revenue of all the inhabitants of a great country, comprehends the whole annual produce of their land and

Gross revenue is the whole annual produce: net revenue what is left free after deducting the maintenance of fixed and circulating capital.

labour; the neat revenue, what remains free to them after deducting the expence of maintaining; first, their fixed; and, secondly, their circulating capital; or what, without encroaching upon their capital, they can place in their stock reserved for immediate consumption, or spend upon their subsistence, conveniences, and amusements. Their real wealth too is in proportion, not to their gross, but to their neat revenue.

The whole expence of maintaining the fixed capital, must evidently be excluded from the neat revenue of the society.

The whole expence of maintaining the fixed capital must be excluded,

Neither the materials necessary for supporting their useful machines and instruments of trade, their profitable buildings, &c. nor the produce of the labour necessary for fashioning those materials into the proper form, can ever make any part of it. The price of that labour may indeed make a part of it; as the workmen so employed may place the whole value of their wages in their stock reserved for immediate consumption. But in other sorts of labour, both the price and the produce go to this stock, the price to that of the workmen, the produce to that of other people, whose subsistence, conveniencies, and amusements, are augmented by the labour of those workmen.

The intention of the fixed capital is to increase the productive powers of labour, or to enable the same number of labourers to perform a much greater quantity of work. In a farm where all the necessary buildings, fences, drains, communications, &c. are in the most perfect good order, the same number of labourers and labouring cattle will raise a much greater produce, than in one of equal extent and equally good ground, but not furnished with equal conveniencies. In manufactures the same number of hands, assisted with the best machinery, will work up a much greater quantity of goods than with more imperfect instruments of trade. The expence which is properly laid out upon a fixed capital of any kind, is always repaid with great profit, and increases the annual produce by a much greater value than that of the support which such improvements require. This support, however, still requires a certain portion of that produce. A certain quantity of materials, and the labour of a certain number of workmen, both of which might have been immediately employed to augment the food, clothing and lodging, the subsistence and conveniencies of the society, are thus diverted to another employment, highly advantageous indeed, but still different from this one. It is upon this account that all such improvements in mechanics, as enable the same number of workmen to perform an equal quantity of work with cheaper and simpler machinery than had been usual before, are always regarded as advantageous to every society. A certain quantity of materials, and the labour of a certain number of workmen, which had before been employed in supporting a more complex and expensive machinery, can afterwards be applied to

since the only object of the fixed capital is to increase the productive powers of labour,

and any cheapening or simplification is regarded as a good.

augment the quantity of work which that or any other machinery is useful only for performing. The undertaker of some great manufactory who employs a thousand a-year in the maintenance of his machinery, if he can reduce this expence to five hundred, will naturally[1] employ the other five hundred in purchasing an additional quantity of materials to be wrought up by an additional number of workmen. The quantity of that work, therefore, which his machinery was useful only for performing, will naturally be augmented, and with it all the advantage and conveniency which the society can derive from that work.

The expence of maintaining the fixed capital in a great country, may very properly be compared to that of repairs in a

The cost of maintaining the fixed capital is like the cost of repairs on an estate,

private estate. The expence of repairs may frequently be necessary for supporting the produce of the estate, and consequently both the gross and the neat rent of the landlord. When by a more proper direction, however, it can be diminished without occasioning any diminution of produce, the gross rent remains at least the same as before, and the neat rent is necessarily augmented.

But though the whole expence of maintaining the fixed capital is thus necessarily excluded from the neat revenue of the

but the expence of maintaining the last three parts of the circulating capital is not to be deducted,

society, it is not the same case with that of maintaining the circulating capital. Of the four parts of which this latter capital is composed, money, provisions, materials, and finished work, the three last, it has already been observed, are regularly withdrawn from it, and placed either in the fixed capital of the

society, or in their stock reserved for immediate consumption. Whatever portion of those consumable goods is not employed in maintaining the former, goes all to the latter, and makes a part of the neat revenue of the society. The maintenance of those three parts of the circulating capital, therefore, with-

---

[1] [There seems no reason whatever for supposing that this is necessarily the "natural" action.]

draws no portion of the annual produce from the neat revenue of the society, besides what is necessary for maintaining the fixed capital.

The circulating capital of a society is in this respect different from that of an individual. That of an individual is totally

the circulating capital of the society being different in this respect from that of an individual.

excluded from making any part of his neat revenue, which must consist altogether in his profits. But though the circulating capital of every individual makes a part of that of the society to which he belongs, it is not upon that account totally excluded from making a part likewise of their neat revenue. Though the whole goods in a merchant's shop must by no means be placed in his own stock reserved for immediate consumption, they may in that of other people, who, from a revenue derived from other funds, may regularly replace their value to him, together with its profits, without occasioning any diminution either of his capital or of theirs.[2]

The maintenance of the money alone must be deducted.

Money, therefore, is the only part of the circulating capital of a society, of which the maintenance can occasion any diminution in their neat revenue.

The fixed capital, and that part of the circulating capital which consists in money, so far as they affect the revenue of the society, bear a very great resemblance to one another.

First, as those machines and instruments of trade, &c. require a certain expence, first to erect them, and afterwards to

The money resembles the fixed capital, since

support them, both which expences, though they make a part of the gross, are deductions from the neat revenue of the society; so the stock of money which circulates in any country must require a certain expence, first to collect it, and afterwards to support it, both which expences, though they

[2] [In this paragraph the capital or stock of goods is confused with the goods themselves. The goods of which the stock consists may become revenue, but the stock itself cannot. The maintenance of a stock, even of perishable and consumable goods, does form a charge on the labour of the society.]

make a part of the gross, are, in the same manner, deductions from the neat revenue of the society. A certain quantity of very

(1) the maintenance of the stock of money is part of the gross but not of the net revenue,

valuable materials, gold and silver, and of very curious labour, instead of augmenting the stock reserved for immediate consumption, the subsistence, conveniencies, and amusements of individuals, is employed in supporting that great but expensive instrument of commerce, by means of which every individual in the society has his subsistence, conveniencies, and amusements, regularly distributed to him in their proper proportion.

Secondly, as the machines and instruments of trade, &c. which compose the fixed capital either of an individual or of a

and (2) the money itself forms no part of the net revenue.

society, make no part either of the gross or of the neat revenue of either; so money, by means of which the whole revenue of the society is regularly distributed among all its different members, makes itself no part of

that revenue. The great wheel of circulation is altogether different from the goods which are circulated by means of it. The revenue of the society consists altogether in those goods, and not in the wheel which circulates them. In computing either the gross or the neat revenue of any society, we must always, from their whole annual circulation of money and goods, deduct the whole value of the money, of which not a single farthing can ever make any part of either.[3]

It is the ambiguity of language only which can make this proposition appear either doubtful or paradoxical. When prop-

It only appears to do so from the ambiguity of language,

erly explained and understood, it is almost self-evident.

When we talk of any particular sum of money, we sometimes mean nothing but the metal pieces of which it is composed; and

sometimes we include in our meaning some obscure reference to the goods which can be had in exchange for it, or to the

were not for the use of the old-fashioned term "circulation" instead of the
produce," the explanation which follows would be unnecessary. No one
spected of a desire to add all the money to the annual produce.]

power of purchasing which the possession of it conveys. Thus when we say, that the circulating money of England has been *sums of money being often used to indicate the goods purchasable as well as the coins themselves.* computed at eighteen millions, we mean only to express the amount of the metal pieces, which some writers have computed, or rather have supposed to circulate in that country. But when we say that a man is worth fifty or a hundred pounds a-year, we mean commonly to express not only the amount of the metal pieces which are annually paid to him, but the value of the goods which he can annually purchase or consume. We mean commonly to ascertain what is or ought to be his way of living, or the quantity and quality of the necessaries and conveniences of life in which he can with propriety indulge himself.

When, by any particular sum of money, we mean not only to express the amount of the metal pieces of which it is composed, *We must not add both together.* but to include in its signification some obscure reference to the goods which can be had in exchange for them, the wealth or revenue which it in this case denotes, is equal only to one of the two values which are thus intimated somewhat ambiguously by the same word, and to the latter more properly than to the former, to the money's worth more properly than to the money.

Thus if a guinea be the weekly pension of a particular person, he can in the course of the week purchase with it a certain *If a man has a guinea a week he enjoys a guinea's worth of subsistence, &c.* quantity of subsistence, conveniencies, and amusements. In proportion as this quantity is great or small, so are his real riches, his real weekly revenue. His weekly revenue is certainly not equal both to the guinea, and to what can be purchased with it, but only to one or other of those two equal values; and to the latter more properly than to the former, to the guinea's worth rather than to the guinea.

If the pension of such a person was paid to him, not in gold, but in a weekly bill for a guinea, his revenue surely would n~

so properly consist in the piece of paper, as in what he could

and his real
revenue is that
subsistence, &c.

get for it. A guinea may be considered as a bill for a certain quantity of necessaries and conveniences upon all the tradesmen in the neighbourhood. The revenue of the person to whom it is paid, does not so properly consist in the piece of gold, as in what he can get for it, or in what he can exchange it for. If it could be exchanged for nothing, it would, like a bill upon a bankrupt, be of no more value than the most useless piece of paper.

Though the weekly or yearly revenue of all the different inhabitants of any country, in the same manner, may be, and in

The same is true
of all the inhabi-
tants of a country.

reality frequently is paid to them in money, their real riches, however, the real weekly or yearly revenue of all of them taken together, must always be great or small in proportion to the quantity of consumable goods which they can all of them purchase with this money. The whole revenue of all of them taken together is evidently not equal to both the money and the consumable goods; but only to one or other of those two values, and to the latter more properly than to the former.

Though we frequently, therefore, express a person's revenue by the metal pieces which are annually paid to him, it is because the amount of those pieces regulates the extent of his power of purchasing, or the value of the goods which he can annually afford to consume. We still consider his revenue as consisting in this power of purchasing or consuming, and not in the pieces which convey it.

But if this is sufficiently evident even with regard to an individual, it is still more so with regard to a

The coins
annually paid to
an individual of-
ten equal his
revenue, but the
stock of coin in a
ciety is never
l to its whole
e.

society. The amount of the metal pieces which are annually paid to an individual, is often precisely equal to his revenue, and is upon that account the shortest and best expression of its value. But the amount of the metal pieces which circulate in a society, can never be equal to the revenue of all its members. As the same guinea which pays the weekly pension of one man to-day, may pay that of another to-morrow, and that of a third the day thereafter, the amount of the metal pieces which annually circulate in any country, must always be of much less value than the whole money pensions annually paid with them. But the power of purchasing, or[4] the goods which can successively be bought with the whole of those money pensions as they are successively paid, must always be precisely of the same value with those pensions; as must likewise be the revenue of the different persons to whom they are paid. That revenue, therefore, cannot consist in those metal pieces, of which the amount is so much inferior to its value, but in the power of purchasing, in the goods which can successively be bought with them as they circulate from hand to hand.

Money, therefore, the great wheel of circulation, the great instrument of commerce, like all other instruments of trade,

Money is therefore no part of the revenue of the society.

though it makes a part and a very valuable part of the capital, makes no part of the revenue of the society to which it belongs; and though the metal pieces of which it is composed, in the course of their annual circulation, distribute to every man the revenue which properly belongs to him, they make themselves no part of that revenue.

Thirdly, and lastly, the machines and instruments of trade, &c. which compose the fixed capital, bear this further resem-

(3) Every saving in the cost of maintaining the stock of money is an improvement.

blance to that part of the circulating capital which consists in money; that as every saving in the expence of erecting and supporting those machines, which does not diminish the productive powers of labour, is an improvement of the neat revenue of the society; so every saving in the expence of collecting and supporting that part of the circulating capital which consists in money, is an improvement of exactly the same kind.

It is sufficiently obvious, and it has partly too been explained already, in what manner every saving in the expence of

---

[4] [Ed. 1 does not contain "or."]

supporting the fixed capital is an improvement of the neat revenue of the society. The whole capital of the undertaker of every work is necessarily divided between his fixed and his circulating capital. While his whole capital remains the same, the smaller the one part, the greater must necessarily be the other. It is the circulating capital which furnishes the materials and wages of labour, and puts industry into motion. Every saving, therefore, in the expence of maintaining the fixed capital, which does not diminish the productive powers of labour, must increase the fund which puts industry into motion, and consequently the annual produce of land and labour, the real revenue of every society.

The substitution of paper in the room of gold and silver money, replaces a very expensive instrument of commerce

The substitution of paper for gold money is an improvement.

with one much less costly, and sometimes equally convenient. Circulation comes to be carried on by a new wheel, which it costs less both to erect and to maintain than the old one. But in what manner this operation is performed, and in what manner it tends to increase either the gross or the neat revenue of the society, is not altogether so obvious, and may therefore require some further explication.

Bank notes are the best sort of paper money.

There are several different sorts of paper money; but the circulating notes of banks and bankers are the species which is best known, and which seems best adapted for this purpose.

When the people of any particular country have such confidence in the fortune, probity, and prudence of a particular banker, as to believe that he is always ready to pay upon demand such of his promissory notes as are likely to be at any time presented to him; those notes come to have the same currency as gold and silver money, from the confidence that such money can at any time be had for them.

A particular banker lends among his customers his own \missory notes, to the extent, we shall suppose, of a hundred \nd pounds. As those notes serve all the purposes of \is debtors pay him the same interest as if he had lent them so much money. This interest is the source of his gain.

When a banker lends out £100,000 in notes and keeps in hand only £20,000 in gold and silver, £80,000 in gold and silver is spared from the circulation:

Though some of those notes are continually coming back upon him for payment, part of them continue to circulate for months and years together. Though he has generally in circulation, therefore, notes to the extent of a hundred thousand pounds, twenty thousand pounds in gold and silver may, frequently, be a sufficient provision for answering occasional demands. By this operation, therefore, twenty thousand pounds in gold and silver perform all the functions which a hundred thousand could otherwise have performed. The same exchanges may be made, the same quantity of consumable goods may be circulated and distributed to their proper consumers, by means of his promissory notes, to the value of a hundred thousand pounds, as by an equal value of gold and silver money. Eighty thousand pounds of gold and silver, therefore, can, in this manner, be spared from the circulation of the country; and if different operations of the same kind should, at the same time, be carried on by many different banks and bankers, the whole circulation may thus be conducted with a fifth part only of the gold and silver which would otherwise have been requisite.

Let us suppose, for example, that the whole circulating money of some particular country amounted, at a particular

and if many bankers do the same, four-fifths of the gold and silver previously circulating may be sent abroad,

time, to one million sterling, that sum being then sufficient for circulating the whole annual produce of their land and labour. Let us suppose too, that some time thereafter, different banks and bankers issued promissory notes, payable to the bearer, to the extent of one million, reserving in their different coffers two hundred thousand pounds for answering occasional demands. There would remain, therefore, in circulation, eight hundred thousand pounds in gold and silver, and a million of bank notes, or eighteen hundred thousand pounds of paper and money together. But the annual produce of the land and labour of the country had before required only one million to circulate and distribute it to its proper consumers, and that annual produce cannot be immediately augmented by those operations of banking. One million, therefore, will be sufficient to circulate it after them. The goods to be bought and sold being precisely the same as before, the same quantity of money will be sufficient for buying and selling them. The channel of circulation, if I may be allowed such an expression, will remain precisely the same as before. One million we have supposed sufficient to fill that channel. Whatever, therefore, is poured into it beyond this sum, cannot run in it, but must overflow. One million eight hundred thousand pounds are poured into it. Eight hundred thousand pounds, therefore, must overflow, that sum being over and above what can be employed in the circulation of the country. But though this sum cannot be employed at home, it is too valuable to be allowed to lie idle. It will, therefore, be sent abroad, in order to seek that profitable employment which it cannot find at home. But the paper cannot go abroad; because at a distance from the banks which issue it, and from the country in which payment of it can be exacted by law, it will not be received in common payments. Gold and silver, therefore, to the amount of eight hundred thousand pounds will be sent abroad, and the channel of home circulation will remain filled with a million of paper, instead of the million of those metals which filled it before.

But though so great a quantity of gold and silver is thus sent *and exchanged for goods,* abroad, we must not imagine that it is sent abroad for nothing, or that its proprietors make a present of it to foreign nations. They will exchange it for foreign goods of some kind or another, in order to supply the consumption either of some other foreign country, or of their own.

either to supply the consumption of another country, in which case the profit will be an addition to the net revenue of the country, If they employ it in purchasing goods in one foreign country in order to supply the consumption of another, or in what is called the carrying trade, whatever profit they make will be an addition to the neat revenue of their own country. It is like a new fund, created for carrying on a new trade; domestic business being now transacted by paper, and the gold and silver being converted into a fund for this new trade.

or to supply home consumption (1) of luxuries, (2) of materials, tools and provisions wherewith industrious people are maintained and employed.

If they employ it in purchasing foreign goods for home consumption, they may either, first, purchase such goods as are likely to be consumed by idle people who produce nothing, such as foreign wines, foreign silks, &c.; or, secondly, they may purchase an additional stock of materials, tools, and provisions, in order to maintain and employ an additional number of industrious people, who re-produce, with a profit, the value of their annual consumption.

If to supply luxuries, prodigality and consumption are increased;

So far as it is employed in the first way, it promotes prodigality, increases expence and consumption without increasing production, or establishing any permanent fund for supporting that expence, and is in every respect hurtful to the society.

So far as it is employed in the second way, it promotes industry; and though it increases the consumption of the society,

if to supply materials, &c., a permanent fund for supporting consumption is provided.

it provides a permanent fund for supporting that consumption, the people who consume re-producing, with a profit, the whole value of their annual consumption. The gross revenue of the society, the annual produce of their land and labour, is increased by the whole value which the labour of those workmen adds to the materials upon which they are employed; and their neat revenue by what remains of this value, after deducting what is necessary for supporting the tools and instruments of their trade.

The greater part of the gold and silver sent abroad purchases materials, &c.

That the greater part of the gold and silver which, being forced abroad by those operations of banking, is employed in purchasing foreign goods for home consumption, is and must be employed in purchasing those of this second kind, seems not only probable but almost unavoidable. Though some particular men may sometimes increase their expence very considerably though their revenue does not increase at all, we may be assured that no class or order of men ever does so; because, though the principles of common prudence do not always govern the conduct of every individual, they always influence that of the majority of every class or order. But the revenue of idle people, considered as a class or order, cannot, in the smallest degree, be increased by those operations of banking. Their expence in general, therefore, cannot be much increased by them, though that of a few individuals among them may, and in reality sometimes is. The demand of idle people, therefore, for foreign goods, being the same, or very nearly the same, as before, a very small part of the money, which being forced abroad by those operations of banking, is employed in purchasing foreign goods for home consumption, is likely to be employed in purchasing those for their use. The greater part of it will naturally be destined for the employment of industry, and not for the maintenance of idleness.

When we compute the quantity of industry which the circulating capital of any society can employ, we must always have regard to those parts of it only, which consist in provisions, materials, and finished work: the other, which consists in money, and which serves only to circulate those three, must always be deducted. In order to put industry into motion, three things are requisite; materials to work upon, tools to work with, and the wages or recompence for the sake of which the work is done. Money is neither a material to work upon, nor a tool to work with; and though the wages of the workman are commonly paid to him in money, his real revenue, like that of all other men, consists, not in the money, but in the money's worth; not in the metal pieces, but in what can be got for them.

The quantity of industry which the circulating capital can employ is determined by the provisions, materials, and finished work, and not at all by the quantity of money.

The quantity of industry which any capital can employ, must, evidently, be equal to the number of workmen whom it can supply with materials, tools, and a maintenance suitable to the nature of the work. Money may be requisite for purchasing the materials and tools of the work, as well as the maintenance of the workmen. But the quantity of industry which the whole capital can employ, is certainly not equal both to the money which purchases, and to the materials, tools, and maintenance, which are purchased with it; but only to one or other of those two values, and to the latter more properly than to the former.

When paper is substituted in the room of gold and silver money, the quantity of the materials, tools, and maintenance, which the whole circulating capital can supply, may be increased by the whole value of gold and silver which used to be employed in purchasing them. The whole value of the great wheel of circulation and distribution, is added to the goods which are circulated and distributed by means of it. The operation, in some measure, resembles that of the undertaker of some great work, who, in consequence of some improvement in mechanics, takes down his old machinery, and adds the difference between its price and that of the new to his circulating capital, to the fund from which he furnishes materials and wages to his workmen.[5]

The substitution of paper for gold and silver increases the materials, tools, and maintenance at the expence of the gold and silver money.

What is the proportion which the circulating money of any country bears to the whole value of the annual produce circulated by means of it, it is, perhaps, impossible to determine. It has been computed by different authors at a fifth, at a tenth, at a twentieth, and at a thirtieth part of that value.[6] But how small soever the proportion which the circulating money may bear to the whole value of the annual produce, as but a part, and frequently but a small part, of that

The quantity of money bears a small proportion to the whole produce, but a large one to that part destined to maintain industry.

[5] [Above, pp. 364, 365.]

[6] [Petty's estimate in *Verbum Sapienti* is £40,000,000 for the income and £6,000,000 for the coin. Gregory King's estimate is £43,500,000 for the income and no less than £11,500,000 for the coin, in Geo. Chalmers, *Estimate*, 1802, pp. 423, 427.]

produce, is ever destined for the maintenance of industry, it must always bear a very considerable proportion to that part. When, therefore, by the substitution of paper, the gold and silver necessary for circulation is reduced to, perhaps, a fifth part of the former quantity, if the value of only the greater part of the other four-fifths be added to the funds which are destined for the maintenance of industry, it must make a very considerable addition to the quantity of that industry, and, consequently, to the value of the annual produce of land and labour.

An operation of this kind has, within these five-and-twenty or thirty years, been performed in Scotland, by the erection of

An operation of this kind has been carried out in Scotland with excellent effects.

new banking companies in almost every considerable town, and even in some country villages.[7] The effects of it have been precisely those above described. The business of the country is almost entirely carried on by means of the paper of those different banking companies, with which purchases and payments of all kinds are commonly made Silver very seldom appears except in the change of a twenty shillings bank note, and gold still seldomer. But though the conduct of all those different companies has not been unexceptionable, and has accordingly required an act of parliament to regulate it; the country,[8] notwithstanding, has evidently derived great benefit from their trade. I have heard it asserted, that the trade of the city of Glasgow, doubled in about fifteen years after the first erection of the banks there; and that the trade of Scotland has more than quadrupled since the first erection of the two public banks at Edinburgh, of which the one, called The Bank of Scotland, was established by act of parliament in 1695; the other, called The Royal Bank, by royal charter in 1727.[9] Whether the trade, either of Scotland in general, or of the city of Glasgow in particular, has really increased in so great a proportion, during so short a period, I do not pretend to know. If either of them has increased in this pro-

[7] [Below, pp. 392–393.]

[8] [Misprinted "contrary" in ed. 5.]

[9] [Adam Anderson, *Commerce*, A.D. 1695.]

portion, it seems to be an effect too great to be accounted for by the sole operation of this cause. That the trade and industry of Scotland, however, have increased very considerably during this period, and that the banks have contributed a good deal to this increase, cannot be doubted.

The value of the silver money which circulated in Scotland before the union, in 1707, and which, immediately after it, was brought into the bank of Scotland in order to be re-coined, amounted to 411,117*l*. 10*s*. 9*d*. sterling. No account has been got of the gold coin; but it appears from the ancient accounts of the mint of Scotland, that the value of the gold annually coined somewhat exceeded that of the silver.[10] There were a good many people too upon this occasion, who, from a diffidence of repayment, did not bring their silver into the bank of Scotland: and there was, besides, some English coin, which was not called in.[11] The whole value of the gold and silver, therefore, which circulated in Scotland before the union, cannot be estimated at less than a million sterling. It seems to have constituted almost the whole circulation of that country; for though the circulation of the bank of Scotland, which had then no rival, was considerable, it seems to have made but a very small part of the whole. In the present times the whole circulation of Scotland cannot be estimated at less than two millions, of which that part which consists in gold and silver, most probably, does not amount to half a million. But though the circulating gold and silver of Scotland have suffered so great a diminution during this period, its real riches and prosperity do not appear to have suffered any. Its agricul-

There was at the Union at least a million sterling of gold and silver money, and now there is not half a million.

---

[10] See Ruddiman's Preface to Anderson's Diplomata, &c. Scotiæ. [pp. 84, 85. See above, p. 289, note.]

[11] ["The folly of a few misers or the fear that people might have of losing their money, or various other dangers and accidents, prevented very many of the old Scots coins from being brought in," *op. cit.*, p. 175. Ruddiman in a note, *op. cit.*, p. 231, says: "The English coin was also ordained to be called in," but does not include it in his estimate of not less than £900,000, p. 176.]

ture, manufactures, and trade, on the contrary, the annual produce of its land and labour, have evidently been augmented.

It is chiefly by discounting bills of exchange, that is, by advancing money upon them before they are due, that the greater

Notes are ordinarily issued by discounting bills, part of banks and bankers issue their promissory notes. They deduct always, upon whatever sum they advance, the legal interest till the bill shall become due. The payment of the bill, when it becomes due, replaces to the bank the value of what had been advanced, together with a clear profit of the interest. The banker who advances to the merchant whose bill he discounts, not gold and silver, but his own promissory notes, has the advantage of being able to discount to a greater amount by the whole value of his promissory notes, which he finds by experience, are commonly in circulation. He is thereby enabled to make his clear gain of interest on so much a larger sum.

The commerce of Scotland, which at present is not very great, was still more inconsiderable when the two first banking

but the Scotch banks invented the system of cash accounts, companies were established; and those companies would have had but little trade, had they confined their business to the discounting of bills of exchange. They invented, therefore, another method of issuing their promissory notes; by granting, what they called, cash accounts, that is by giving credit to the extent of a certain sum (two or three thousand pounds, for example), to any individual who could procure two persons of undoubted credit and good landed estate to become surety for him, that whatever money should be advanced to him, within the sum for which the credit had been given, should be repaid upon demand, together with the legal interest. Credits of this kind are, I believe, commonly granted by banks and bankers in all different parts of the world. But the easy terms upon which the Scotch banking companies accept of re-payment are, so far as I know, peculiar to them, and have, perhaps, been the principal cause, both of the great trade of those companies, and of the benefit which the country has received from it.

Whoever has a credit of this kind with one of those companies, and borrows a thousand pounds upon it, for example, may
which enable them repay this sum piece-meal, by twenty and
to issue notes thirty pounds at a time, the company dis-
readily, counting a proportionable part of the interest
of the great sum from the day on which each
of those small sums is paid in, till the whole be in this manner
repaid. All merchants, therefore, and almost all men of business, find it convenient to keep such cash accounts with them,
and are thereby interested to promote the trade of those companies, by readily receiving their notes in all payments, and by
encouraging all those with whom they have any influence to do
the same. The banks, when their customers apply to them for
money, generally advance it to them in their own promissory
notes. These the merchants pay away to the manufacturers for
goods, the manufacturers to the farmers for materials and provisions, the farmers to their landlords for rent, the landlords repay them to the merchants for the conveniencies and luxuries
with which they supply them, and the merchants again return
them to the banks in order to balance their cash accounts, or to
replace what they may have borrowed of them; and thus almost
the whole money business of the country is transacted by
means of them. Hence the great trade of those companies.

By means of those cash accounts every merchant can, without imprudence, carry on a greater trade than he otherwise
could do. If there are two merchants, one in
and make it London, and the other in Edinburgh, who
possible for every employ equal stocks in the same branch of
merchant to carry trade, the Edinburgh merchant can, without
on a greater trade imprudence, carry on a greater trade, and
than he otherwise give employment to a greater number of
could. people than the London merchant. The
London merchant must always keep by him a considerable
sum of money, either in his own coffers, or in those of his
banker, who gives him no interest for it, in order to answer the
demands continually coming upon him for payment of the
goods which he purchases upon credit. Let the ordinary
amount of this sum be supposed five hundred pounds. The

value of the goods in his warehouse must always be less by five hundred pounds than it would have been, had he not been obliged to keep such a sum unemployed. Let us suppose that he generally disposes of his whole stock upon hand, or of goods to the value of his whole stock upon hand, once in the year. By being obliged to keep so great a sum unemployed, he must sell in a year five hundred pounds worth less goods than he might otherwise have done. His annual profits must be less by all that he could have made by the sale of five hundred pounds worth more goods; and the number of people employed in preparing his goods for the market, must be less by all those that five hundred pounds more stock could have employed. The merchant in Edinburgh, on the other hand, keeps no money unemployed for answering such occasional demands. When they actually come upon him, he satisfies them from his cash account with the bank, and gradually replaces the sum borrowed with the money or paper which comes in from the occasional sales of his goods. With the same stock, therefore, he can, without imprudence, have at all times in his warehouse a larger quantity of goods than the London merchant; and can thereby both make a greater profit himself, and give constant employment to a greater number of industrious people who prepare those goods for the market. Hence the great benefit which the country has derived from this trade.

The facility of discounting bills of exchange, it may be thought indeed, gives the English merchants a conveniency equivalent to the cash accounts of the Scotch merchants. But the Scotch merchants, it must be remembered, can discount their bills of exchange as easily as the English merchants; and have, besides, the additional conveniency of their cash accounts.

The Scotch banks can of course discount bills when required.

The whole paper money of every kind which can easily circulate in any country never can exceed the value of the gold and silver, of which it supplies the place, or which (the commerce being supposed the same) would circulate there, if there was no paper money. If twenty shilling notes, for example, are the lowest paper money current in Scotland, the whole of that currency which can easily circulate there cannot exceed the sum of gold and silver which would be necessary for transacting the annual exchanges of twenty shillings value and upwards usually transacted within that country. Should the circulating paper at any time exceed that sum, as the excess could neither be sent abroad nor be employed in the circulation of the country, it must immediately return upon the banks to be exchanged for gold and silver. Many people would immediately perceive that they had more of this paper than was necessary for transacting their business at home, and as they could not send it abroad, they would immediately demand payment of it from the banks. When this superfluous paper was converted into gold and silver, they could easily find a use for it by sending it abroad; but they could find none while it remained in the shape of paper. There would immediately, therefore, be a run upon the banks to the whole extent of this superfluous paper, and, if they shewed any difficulty or backwardness in payment, to a much greater extent; the alarm, which this would occasion, necessarily increasing the run.

The whole of the paper money can never exceed the gold and silver which would have been required in its absence.

Over and above the expences which are common to every branch of trade; such as the expence of house-rent, the wages of servants, clerks, accountants, &c.; the expences peculiar to a bank consist chiefly in two articles: First, in the expence of keeping at all times in its coffers, for answering the occasional demands of the holders of its notes, a large sum of money, of which it loses the interest: And, secondly, in the expence of replenishing those coffers as fast as they are emptied by answering such occasional demands.

The peculiar expenses of a bank are (1) the keeping and (2) the replenishing of a stock of money with which to repay notes.

A banking company, which issues more paper than can be employed in the circulation of the country, and of which the excess is continually returning upon them for payment, ought to increase the quantity of gold and silver, which they keep at all times in

A bank which issues too much paper will much increase both the first

their coffers, not only in proportion to this excessive increase of their circulation, but in a much greater proportion; their notes returning upon them much faster than in proportion to the excess of their quantity. Such a company, therefore, ought to increase the first article of their expence, not only in proportion to this forced increase of their business, but in a much greater proportion.

The coffers of such a company too, though they ought to be filled much fuller, yet must empty themselves much faster than

and the second expense,

if their business was confined within more reasonable bounds, and must require, not only a more violent, but a more constant and uninterrupted exertion of expence in order to replenish them. The coin too, which is thus continually drawn in such large quantities from their coffers, cannot be employed in the circulation of the country. It comes in place of a paper which is over and above what can be employed in that circulation, and is therefore over and above what can be employed in it too. But as that coin will not be allowed to lie idle, it must, in one shape or another, be sent abroad, in order to find that profitable employment which it cannot find at home; and this continual exportation of gold and silver, by enhancing the difficulty, must necessarily enhance still further the expence of the bank, in finding new gold and silver in order to replenish those coffers, which empty themselves so very rapidly. Such a company therefore, must, in proportion to this forced increase of their business, increase the second article of their expence still more than the first.

Let us suppose that all the paper of a particular bank, which the circulation of the country can easily absorb and employ,

as may be shown by an example.

amounts exactly to forty thousand pounds; and that for answering occasional demands, this bank is obliged to keep at all times in its coffers ten thousand pounds in gold and silver. Should this bank attempt to circulate forty-four thousand pounds, the four thousand pounds which are over and above what the circulation can easily absorb and employ, will return upon it almost as fast as they are issued. For answering occasional demands, therefore, this bank ought to keep at all times in its coffers, not ten thousand pounds only, but fourteen thousand pounds. It will thus gain nothing by the interest of the four thousand pounds excessive circulation; and it will lose the whole expence of continually collecting four thousand pounds in gold and silver, which will be continually going out of its coffers as fast as they are brought into them.

Had every particular banking company always understood

Banks have sometimes not. understood this,

and attended to its own particular interest, the circulation never could have been overstocked with paper money. But every particular banking company has not always understood or attended to its own particular interest, and the circulation has frequently been overstocked with paper money.

By issuing too great a quantity of paper, of which the excess was continually returning, in order to be exchanged for gold

e.g., the Bank of England,

and silver, the bank of England was for many years together obliged to coin gold to the extent of between eight hundred thousand pounds and a million a year; or at an average, about eight hundred and fifty thousand pounds.[12] For this great coinage the bank (in consequence of the worn and degraded state into which the gold coin had fallen a few years ago) was frequently obliged to purchase gold bullion at the high price of four pounds an ounce, which it soon after issued in coin at 3*l.* 17*s.* 10½*d.* an ounce, losing in this manner between two and a half and three per cent. upon the coinage of so very large a sum. Though the bank therefore paid no seignorage, though the government was properly at the expence of the coinage, this liberality of government did not prevent altogether the expence of the bank.

The Scotch banks, in consequence of an excess of the same

[12] [From 1766 to 1772 inclusive the coinage averaged about £810,000 per annum. The amount for "ten years together" is stated below, pp. 695, 702, to have been upwards of £800,000 a year, though the average for the ten years 1763–1772 was only £760,000. But the inclusion of the large coinage of 1773, *viz.,* £1,317,645, would raise these averages considerably. See the figures at the end of each year in Macpherson, *Annals of Commerce.*]

kind, were all obliged to employ constantly agents at London
to collect money for them, at an expence which was seldom

*and the Scotch
banks.*

below one and a half or two per cent. This
money was sent down by the waggon, and
insured by the carriers at an additional ex-
pence of three quarters per cent. or fifteen shillings on the hundred pounds. Those agents were not always able to replenish
the coffers of their employers so fast as they were emptied. In
this case the resource of the banks was, to draw upon their correspondents in London bills of exchange to the extent of the
sum which they wanted. When those correspondents afterwards drew upon them for the payment of this sum, together
with the interest and a commission, some of those banks, from
the distress into which their excessive circulation had thrown
them, had sometimes no other means of satisfying this draught
but by drawing a second set of bills either upon the same, or
upon some other correspondents in London; and the same
sum, or rather bills for the same sum, would in this manner
make sometimes more than two or three journies: the debtor
bank, paying always the interest and commission upon the
whole accumulated sum. Even those Scotch banks which
never distinguished themselves by their extreme imprudence,
were sometimes obliged to employ this ruinous resource.

The gold coin which was paid out either by the bank of
England, or by the Scotch banks, in exchange for that part of
their paper which was over and above what could be employed
in the circulation of the country, being likewise over and above
what could be employed in that circulation, was sometimes
sent abroad in the shape of coin, sometimes melted down and
sent abroad in the shape of bullion, and sometimes melted
down and sold to the bank of England at the high price of four
pounds an ounce. It was the newest, the heaviest, and the best
pieces only which were carefully picked out of the whole coin,
and either sent abroad or melted down. At home, and while
they remained[13] in the shape of coin, those heavy pieces were
of no more value than the light: But they were of more value

[13] [Misprinted "remain" in ed. 5.]

abroad, or when melted down into bullion, at home. The bank of England, notwithstanding their great annual coinage, found to their astonishment, that there was every year the same scarcity of coin as there had been the year before; and that notwithstanding the great quantity of good and new coin which was every year issued from the bank, the state of the coin, instead of growing better and better, became every year worse and worse. Every year they found themselves under the necessity of coining nearly the same quantity of gold as they had coined the year before, and from the continual rise in the price of gold bullion, in consequence of the continual wearing and clipping of the coin, the expence of this great annual coinage became every year greater and greater. The bank of England, it is to be observed, by supplying its own coffers with coin, is indirectly obliged to supply the whole kingdom, into which coin is continually flowing from those coffers in a great variety of ways. Whatever coin therefore was wanted to support this excessive circulation both of Scotch and English paper money, whatever vacuities this excessive circulation occasioned in the necessary coin of the kingdom, the bank of England was obliged to supply them. The Scotch banks, no doubt, paid all of them very dearly for their own imprudence and inattention. But the bank of England paid very dearly, not only for its own imprudence, but for the much greater imprudence of almost all the Scotch banks.

The excessive circulation was caused by overtrading.

The over-trading of some bold projectors in both parts of the united kingdom, was the original cause of this excessive circulation of paper money.

A bank ought not to advance more than the amount which merchants would otherwise have to keep by them in cash.

What a bank can with propriety advance to a merchant or undertaker of any kind, is not either the whole capital with which he trades, or even any considerable part of that capital; but that part of it only, which he would otherwise be obliged to keep by him unemployed, and in ready money for answering occasional demands. If the paper money which the bank advances never exceeds this value, it can never exceed the value of the gold and silver, which would necessarily circulate in the country if there was no paper money; it can never exceed the quantity which the circulation of the country can easily absorb and employ.

When a bank discounts to a merchant a real bill of exchange drawn by a real creditor upon a real debtor, and which, as soon as it becomes due, is really paid by that debtor; it only advances to him a part of the value which he would otherwise be obliged to keep by him unemployed and in ready money for answering occasional demands. The payment of the bill, when it becomes due, replaces to the bank the value of what it had advanced, together with the interest. The coffers of the bank, so far as its dealings are confined to such customers, resemble a water pond, from which, though a stream is continually running out, yet another is continually running in, fully equal to that which runs out; so that, without any further care or attention, the pond keeps always equally, or very near equally full. Little or no expence can ever be necessary for replenishing the coffers of such a bank.

This limit is observed when only real bills of exchange are discounted.

A merchant, without over-trading, may frequently have occasion for a sum of ready money, even when he has no bills to discount. When a bank, besides discounting his bills, advances him likewise upon such occasions, such sums upon his cash account, and accepts of a piece meal repayment as the money comes in from the occasional sale of his goods, upon the easy terms of the banking companies of Scotland; it dispenses him entirely from the necessity of keeping any part of his stock by him unemployed and in ready money for answering occasional demands. When such demands actually come upon him, he can answer them sufficiently from his cash account. The bank, however, in dealing with such customers, ought to observe with great attention, whether in the course of some short period (of four, five, six, or eight months, for example) the sum of the repayments which it commonly receives from them, is, or is not, fully equal to that

Cash accounts should be carefully watched to secure the same end,

of the advances which it commonly makes to them. If, within
the course of such short periods, the sum of the repayments
from certain customers is, upon most occasions, fully equal to
that of the advances, it may safely continue to deal with such
customers. Though the stream which is in this case continually
running out from its coffers may be very large, that which is
continually running into them must be at least equally large; so
that without any further care or attention those coffers are
likely to be always equally or very near equally full; and scarce
ever to require any extraordinary expence to replenish them. If,
on the contrary, the sum of the repayments from certain other
customers falls commonly very much short of the advances
which it makes to them, it cannot with any safety continue to
deal with such customers, at least if they continue to deal with
it in this manner. The stream which is in this case continually
running out from its coffers is necessarily much larger than
that which is continually running in; so that, unless they are replenished by some great and continual effort of expence, those
coffers must soon be exhausted altogether.

The banking companies of Scotland, accordingly, were for a
long time very careful to require frequent
as they were for a long time by the Scotch banks, which required frequent and regular operations,
and regular repayments from all their cus-
tomers, and did not care to deal with any
person, whatever might be his fortune or
credit, who did not make, what they called,
frequent and regular operations with them.
By this attention, besides saving almost en-
tirely the extraordinary expence of replenishing their coffers,
they gained two other very considerable advantages.

First, by this attention they were enabled to make some tolerable judgment concerning the thriving or declining circumstance of their debtors, without being
and thus (1) were able to judge of the circumstances of their debtors,
obliged to look out for any other evidence
besides what their own books afforded them;
men being for the most part either regular or
irregular in their repayments according as
their circumstances are either thriving or declining. A private
man who lends out his money to perhaps half a dozen or a

dozen of debtors, may, either by himself or his agents, observe
and enquire both constantly and carefully into the conduct and
situation of each of them. But a banking company, which lends
money to perhaps five hundred different people, and of which
the attention is continually occupied by objects of a very different kind, can have no regular information concerning the
conduct and circumstances of the greater part of its debtors beyond what its own books afford it.[14] In requiring frequent and
regular repayments from all their customers, the banking companies of Scotland had probably this advantage in view.

Secondly, by this attention they secured themselves from
the possibility of issuing more paper money than what the cir-

*and (2) were
secured against
issuing too much
paper.*

culation of the country could easily absorb
and employ. When they observed, that
within moderate periods of time the repayments of a particular customer were upon
most occasions fully equal to the advances
which they had made to him, they might be assured that the paper money which they had advanced to him, had not at any
time exceeded the quantity of gold and silver which he would
otherwise have been obliged to keep by him for answering occasional demands; and that, consequently, the paper money,
which they had circulated by this means, had not at any time
exceeded the quantity of gold and silver which would have circulated in the country, had there been no paper money. The frequency, regularity and amounts of his repayments would
sufficiently demonstrate that the amount of their advances had
at no time exceeded that part of his capital which he would otherwise have been obliged to keep by him unemployed and in
ready money for answering occasional demands; that is, for
the purpose of keeping the rest of his capital in constant employment. It is this part of his capital only which, within moderate periods of time, is continually returning to every dealer in
the shape of money, whether paper or coin, and continually going from him in the same shape. If the advances of the bank

---

[14] [But as Playfair (ed. of *Wealth of Nations*, vol. i., p, 472) points out, the more
customers a bank has the more it is likely to know the transactions of each of
them.]

had commonly exceeded this part of his capital, the ordinary amount of his repayments could not, within moderate periods of time, have equalled the ordinary amount of its advances. The stream which, by means of his dealings, was continually running into the coffers of the bank, could not have been equal to the stream which, by means of the same dealings, was continually running out. The advances of the bank paper, by exceeding the quantity of gold and silver which, had there been no such advances, he would have been obliged to keep by him for answering occasional demands, might soon come to exceed the whole quantity of gold and silver which (the commerce being supposed the same) would have circulated in the country had there been no paper money; and consequently to exceed the quantity which the circulation of the country could easily absorb and employ; and the excess of this paper money would immediately have returned upon the bank in order to be exchanged for gold and silver. This second advantage, though equally real, was not perhaps so well understood by all the different banking companies of Scotland as the first.

When, partly by the conveniency of discounting bills, and partly by that of cash accounts, the creditable traders of any country can be dispensed from the necessity of keeping any part of their stock by them unemployed and in ready money for answering occasional demands, they can reasonably expect no farther assistance from banks and bankers, who, when they have gone thus far, cannot, consistently with their own interest and safety, go farther. A bank cannot, consistently with its own interest, advance to a trader the whole or even the greater part of the circulating capital with which he trades; because, though that capital is continually returning to him in the shape of money, and going from him in the same shape, yet the whole of the returns is too distant from the whole of the outgoings, and the sum of his repayments could not equal the sum of its advances within such moderate periods of time as suit the conveniency of a bank. Still less could a bank afford to advance him any considerable part of his fixed capital; of the capital which the undertaker of

Bankers' loans ought to be only for moderate periods of time.

an iron forge, for example, employs in erecting his forge and smelting-house, his work-houses and warehouses, the dwelling-houses of his workmen, &c.; of the capital which the undertaker of a mine employs in sinking his shafts, in erecting engines for drawing out the water, in making roads and waggon-ways, &c.; of the capital which the person who undertakes to improve land employs in clearing, draining, enclosing, manuring and ploughing waste and uncultivated fields, in building farm-houses, with all their necessary appendages of stables, granaries, &c. The returns of the fixed capital are in almost all cases much slower than those of the circulating capital; and such expences, even when laid out with the greatest prudence and judgment, very seldom return to the undertaker till after a period of many years, a period by far too distant to suit the conveniency of a bank. Traders and other undertakers may, no doubt, with great propriety, carry on a very considerable part of their projects with borrowed money. In justice to their creditors, however, their own capital ought, in this case, to be sufficient to ensure, if I may say so, the capital of those creditors; or to render it extremely improbable that those creditors should incur any loss, even though the success of the project should fall very much short of the expectation of the projectors. Even with this precaution too, the money which is borrowed, and which it is meant should not be repaid till after a period of several years, ought not to be borrowed of a bank, but ought to be borrowed upon bond or mortgage, of such private people as propose to live upon the interest of their money, without taking the trouble themselves to employ the capital; and who are upon that account willing to lend that capital to such people of good credit as are likely to keep it for several years. A bank, indeed, which lends its money without the expence of stampt paper, or of attornies fees for drawing bonds and mortgages, and which accepts of repayment upon the easy terms of the banking companies of Scotland; would, no doubt, be a very convenient creditor to such traders and undertakers. But such traders and undertakers would, surely, be most inconvenient debtors to such a bank.

It is now more than five-and-twenty years since the paper

money issued by the different banking companies of Scotland was fully equal, or rather was somewhat more than fully equal, to what the circulation of the country could easily absorb and employ.[15] Those companies, therefore, had so long ago given all the assistance to the traders and other undertakers of Scotland which it is possible for banks and bankers, consistently with their own interest, to give. They had even done somewhat more. They had over-traded a little, and had brought upon themselves that loss, or at least that diminution of profit, which in this particular business never fails to attend the smallest degree of over-trading. Those traders and other undertakers, having got so much assistance from banks and bankers, wished to get still more. The banks, they seem to have thought, could extend their credits to whatever sum might be wanted, without incurring any other expence besides that of a few reams of paper. They complained of the contracted views and dastardly spirit of the directors of those banks, which did not, they said, extend their credits in proportion to the extension of the trade of the country; meaning, no doubt, by the extension of that trade the extension of their own projects beyond what they could carry on, either with their own capital, or with what they had credit to borrow of private people in the usual way of bond or mortgage. The banks, they seem to have thought, were in honour bound to supply the deficiency, and to provide them with all the capital which they wanted to trade with. The banks, however, were of a different opinion, and upon their refusing to extend their credits, some of those traders had recourse to an expedient which, for a time, served their purpose, though at a much greater expence, yet as effectually as the utmost extension of bank credits could have done. This expedient was no other than the well-known shift of drawing and re-drawing; the shift to which unfortunate traders have sometimes recourse when they are upon the brink of bankruptcy. The practice of raising

More than twenty-five years ago the proper amount of paper money had been reached in Scotland,

but the traders were not content,

---

[15] [Above, p. 378.]

money in this manner had been long known in England, and
during the course of the late war, when the *and some of them resorted to drawing and redrawing,* high profits of trade afforded a great temptation to over-trading, is said to have been carried on to a very great extent. From England it was brought into Scotland, where, in proportion to the very limited commerce, and to the very moderate capital of the country, it was soon carried on to a much greater extent than it ever had been in England.

The practice of drawing and re-drawing is so well known to all men of business, that it may perhaps be thought unnecessary to give any account of it. But as this *which shall be explained.* book may come into the hands of many people who are not men of business, and as the effects of this practice upon the banking trade are not perhaps generally understood even by men of business themselves, I shall endeavour to explain it as distinctly as I can.

The customs of merchants, which were established when the barbarous laws of Europe did not enforce the performance of their contracts, and which during the *Bills of exchange have extraordinary legal privileges.* course of the two last centuries have been adopted into the laws of all European nations, have given such extraordinary privileges to bills of exchange, that money is more readily advanced upon them, than upon any other species of obligation; especially when they are made payable within so short a period as two or three months after their date. If, when the bill becomes due, the acceptor does not pay it as soon as it is presented, he becomes from that moment a bankrupt. The bill is protested, and returns upon the drawer, who, if he does not immediately pay it, becomes likewise a bankrupt. If, before it came to the person who presents it to the acceptor for payment, it had passed through the hands of several other persons, who had successively advanced to one another the contents of it either in money or goods, and who to express that each of them had in his turn received those contents had all of them in their order endorsed, that is, written their names upon the back of the bill; each endorser becomes in his turn liable to the owner of the bill for those contents, and, if he fails to pay, he becomes too from that moment a bankrupt. Though the drawer, acceptor, and endorsers of the bill should, all of them, be persons of doubtful credit; yet still the shortness of the date gives some security to the owner of the bill. Though all of them may be very likely to become bankrupts; it is a chance if they all become so in so short a time. The house is crazy, says a weary traveller to himself, and will not stand very long; but it is a chance if it falls to-night, and I will venture, therefore, to sleep in it to-night.

The trader A in Edinburgh, we shall suppose, draws a bill upon B in London, payable two months after date. In reality B in London owes nothing to A in Edinburgh; but he agrees to accept of A's bill, upon condition that before the term of payment he shall redraw upon A in Edinburgh for the same sum, together with the interest and a commission, another bill payable likewise two months after date. B accordingly, before the expiration of the first two months, re-draws this bill upon A in Edinburgh; who again, before the expiration of the second two months, draws a second bill upon B in London, payable likewise two months after date; and before the expiration of the third two months, B in London re-draws upon A in Edinburgh another bill, payable also two months after date. This practice has sometimes gone on, not only for several months, but for several years together, the bill always returning upon A in Edinburgh, with the accumulated interest and commission of all the former bills. The interest was five per cent. in the year, and the commission was never less than one half per cent. on each draught. This commission being repeated more than six times in the year, whatever money A might raise by this expedient must necessarily have cost him something more than eight per cent. in the year, and sometimes a great deal more; when either the price of the commission happened to rise, or when he was obliged to pay compound interest upon the interest and commission of former bills. This practice was called raising money by circulation.

So two persons, one in London and one in Edinburgh, would draw bills on each other.

In a country where the ordinary profits of stock in the greater part of mercantile projects are supposed to run between

Much money was raised in this expensive way.

six and ten per cent., it must have been a very fortunate speculation of which the returns could not only repay the enormous expence at which the money was thus borrowed for carrying it on; but afford, besides, a good surplus profit to the projector. Many vast and extensive projects, however, were undertaken, and for several years carried on without any other fund to support them besides what was raised at this enormous expence. The projectors, no doubt, had in their golden dreams the most distinct vision of this great profit. Upon their awaking, however, either at the end of their projects, or when they were no longer able to carry them on, they very seldom, I believe, had the good fortune to find it.[16]

The bills which A in Edinburgh drew upon B in London, he regularly discounted two months before they were due with

[16] The method described in the text was by no means either the most common or the most expensive one in which those adventurers sometimes raised money by circulation. It frequently happened that A in Edinburgh would enable B in London to pay the first bill of exchange by drawing, a few days before it became due, a second bill at three months date upon the same B in London. This bill, being payable to his own order, A sold in Edinburgh at par; and with its contents purchased bills upon London payable at sight to the order of B, to whom he sent them by the post. Towards the end of the late war, the exchange between Edinburgh and London was frequently three per cent. against Edinburgh, and those bills at sight must frequently have cost A that premium. This transaction therefore being repeated at least four times in the year, and being loaded with a commission of at least one half per cent. upon each repetition, must at that period have cost A at least fourteen per cent. in the year. At other times A would enable B to discharge the first bill of exchange by drawing, a few days before it became due, a second bill at two months date; not upon B, but upon some third person, C, for example, in London. This other bill was made payable to the order of B, who, upon its being accepted by C, discounted it with some banker in London; and A enabled C to discharge it by drawing, a few days before it became due, a third bill, likewise at two months date, sometimes upon his first correspondent B, and sometimes upon some fourth or fifth person, D or E, for example. This third bill was made payable to the order of C; who, as soon as it was accepted, discounted it in the same manner with some banker in London. Such operations being repeated at least six times in the year, and being loaded with a commission of at least one-half per cent. upon each repetition, together with the legal interest of five per cent., this method of raising

some bank or banker in Edinburgh; and the bills which B in
London redrew upon A in Edinburgh, he as regularly dis-
                        counted either with the bank of England,
The bill on   or with some other bankers in London.
London would   Whatever was advanced upon such circulat-
be discounted in   ing bills, was, in Edinburgh, advanced in the
Edinburgh, and   paper of the Scotch banks, and in London,
the bill on   when they were discounted at the bank of
Edinburgh   England, in the paper of that bank. Though
discounted in   the bills upon which this paper had been ad-
London,   vanced, were all of them repaid in their turn
as soon as they became due; yet the value which had been
really advanced upon the first bill, was never really returned to
the banks which advanced it; because, before each bill became
due, another bill was always drawn to somewhat a greater
amount than the bill which was soon to be paid; and the discounting of this other bill was essentially necessary towards
the payment of that which was soon to be due. This payment,
therefore, was altogether fictitious. The stream, which, by
means of those circulating bills of exchange, had once been
made to run out from the coffers of the banks, was never replaced by any stream which really run into them.

The paper which was issued upon those circulating bills of
exchange, amounted, upon many occasions, to the whole fund
                        destined for carrying on some vast and ex-
and each was   tensive project of agriculture, commerce, or
always replaced   manufactures; and not merely to that part of
by another.   it which, had there been no paper money, the
projector would have been obliged to keep by him, unem-

money, in the same manner as that described in the text, must have cost A something more than eight per cent. By saving, however, the exchange between
Edinburgh and London it was less expensive than that mentioned in the foregoing
part of this note; but then it required an established credit with more houses than
one in London, an advantage which many of these adventurers could not always
find it easy to procure. [This note appears first in ed. 2. Playfair observes that the
calculation of the loss of 14 per cent. by the first method is wrong, since "if A at
Edinburgh negotiated his bills on London at 3 per cent. loss, he would gain as
much in purchasing bills on London with the money."—Ed. of *Wealth of Nations*,
vol. i., p. 483, note.]

ployed and in ready money for answering occasional demands.

The amount thus advanced by the banks was in excess of the limit laid down above, but this was not perceived at first.

The greater part of this paper was, consequently, over and above the value of the gold and silver which would have circulated in the country, had there been no paper money. It was over and above, therefore, what the circulation of the country could easily absorb and employ, and upon that account immediately returned upon the banks in order to be exchanged for gold and silver, which they were to find as they could. It was a capital which those projectors had very artfully contrived to draw from those banks, not only without their knowledge or deliberate consent, but for some time, perhaps, without their having the most distant suspicion that they had really advanced it.

When two people, who are continually drawing and redrawing upon one another, discount their bills always with the

When the banks found it out they made difficulties about discounting,

same banker, he must immediately discover what they are about, and see clearly that they are trading, not with any capital of their own, but with the capital which he advances to them. But this discovery is not altogether so easy when they discount their bills sometimes with one banker, and sometimes with another, and when the same two persons do not constantly draw and re-draw upon one another, but occasionally run the round of a great circle of projectors, who find it for their interest to assist one another in this method of raising money, and to render it, upon that account, as difficult as possible to distinguish between a real and a fictitious bill of exchange; between a bill drawn by a real creditor upon a real debtor, and a bill for which there was properly no real creditor but the bank which discounted it; nor any real debtor but the projector who made use of the money. When a banker had even made this discovery, he might sometimes make it too late, and might find that he had already discounted the bills of those projectors to so great an extent, that, by refusing to discount any more, he would necessarily make them all bankrupts, and thus, by ruining them, might perhaps ruin himself. For his own interest and safety, therefore, he might find it necessary, in this very perilous situation, to go on for some time, endeavouring, however, to withdraw gradually, and upon that account making every day greater and greater difficulties about discounting, in order to force those projectors by degrees to have recourse, either to other bankers, or to other methods of raising money; so as that he himself might, as soon as possible, get out of the circle. The difficulties, accordingly, which the bank of England, which the principal bankers in London, and which even the more prudent Scotch banks began, after a certain time, and when all of them had already gone too far, to make about discounting, not only alarmed, but enraged in the highest degree those projectors. Their own distress, of *which alarmed and enraged the projectors;* which this prudent and necessary reserve of the banks was, no doubt, the immediate occasion, they called the distress of the country; and this distress of the country, they said, was altogether owing to the ignorance, pusillanimity, and bad conduct of the banks, which did not give a sufficiently liberal aid to the spiritual undertakings of those who exerted themselves in order to beautify, improve, and enrich the country. It was the duty of the banks, they seemed to think, to lend for as long a time, and to as great an extent as they might wish to borrow. The banks, however, by refusing in this manner to give more credit to those, to whom they had already given a great deal too much, took the only method by which it was now possible to save either their own credit, or the public credit of the country.

In the midst of this clamour and distress, a new bank[17] was established in Scotland for the express purpose of relieving the

[17] [The Ayr bank's head office was at Ayr, but it had branches at Edinburgh and Dumfries. A detailed history of it is to be found in *The Precipitation and Fall of Messrs. Douglas, Heron and Company, late Bankers in Air with the Causes of their Distress and Ruin investigated and considered by a Committee of Inquiry appointed by the Proprietors*, Edinburgh, 1778. From this it appears that Smith's account of the proceedings of the bank is extremely accurate, a fact which is doubtless due to his old pupil, the Duke of Buccleuch, having been one of the principal shareholders. Writing to Pulteney on 5th September, 1772, Smith says, "though I have had no concern myself in the public calamities, some of the friends in whom I interest myself the most have been deeply concerned in them; and my

distress of the country. The design was generous; but the exe-

then the Ayr bank was established and advanced money very freely,

cution was imprudent, and the nature and causes of the distress which it meant to relieve, were not, perhaps, well understood. This bank was more liberal than any other had ever been, both in granting cash accounts, and in discounting bills of exchange. With regard to the latter, it seems to have made scarce any distinction between real and circulating bills, but to have discounted all equally. It was the avowed principle of this bank to advance, upon any reasonable security, the whole capital which was to be employed in those[18] improvements of which the returns are the most slow and distant, such as the improvements of land. To promote such improvements was even said to be the chief of the public spirited purposes for which it was instituted. By its liberality in granting cash accounts, and in discounting bills of exchange, it, no doubt, issued great quantities of its bank notes. But those bank notes being, the greater part of them, over and above what the circulation of the country could easily absorb and employ, returned upon it, in order to be exchanged for gold and silver, as fast as they were issued. Its coffers were never well filled. The capital which had been subscribed to this bank at two different subscriptions, amounted to one hundred

but soon got into difficulties,

and sixty thousand pounds, of which eighty per cent. only was paid up. This sum ought to have been paid in at several different instalments. A great part of the proprietors, when they paid in their first instalment, opened a cash account with the bank; and the directors, thinking themselves obliged to treat their own

---

attention has been a good deal occupied about the most proper method of extricating them." The extrication was effected chiefly by the sale of redeemable annuities. See Rae, *Life of Adam Smith*, 1895, pp. 253–255; David Macpherson, *Annals of Commerce*, vol. iii., pp. 525, 553; *House of Commons' Journals*, vol. xxxiv., pp. 493–495, and the Act of Parliament, 14 Geo. III., c. 21. The East India Company opposed the bill on the ground that the bonds to be issued would compete with theirs, but their opposition was defeated by a vote of 176 to 36 in the House of Commons, *Journals*, vol. xxxix., p. 601.]

[18] [Ed. 1 does not contain "those."]

proprietors with the same liberality with which they treated all other men, allowed many of them to borrow upon this cash account what they paid in, upon all their subsequent instalments. Such payments, therefore, only put into one coffer, what had the moment before been taken out of another. But had the coffers of this bank been filled ever so well, its excessive circulation must have emptied them faster than they could have been replenished by any other expedient but the ruinous one of drawing upon London, and when the bill became due, paying it, together with interest and commission, by another draught upon the same place. Its coffers having been filled so very ill, it is said to have been driven to this resource within a very few months after it began to do business. The estates of the proprietors of this bank were worth several millions, and by their subscription to the original bond or contract of the bank, were really pledged for answering all its engagements.[19] By means of the great credit which so great a pledge necessarily gave it, it was, notwithstanding its too liberal conduct, enabled to carry on business for more than two years. When it was obliged to stop, it had in the circulation about two hundred thousand pounds in bank notes. In order to support the circulation of those notes, which were continually returning upon it as fast as they were issued, it had been constantly in the practice of drawing bills of exchange upon London, of which the number and value were continually increasing, and, when it stopt, amounted to upwards of six hundred thousand pounds. This bank, therefore, had, in little more than the course of two years, advanced to different people upwards of eight hundred thousand pounds at five per cent. Upon the two hundred thousand pounds which it circulated in bank notes, this five per cent. might, perhaps, be considered as clear gain, without any other deduction besides the expence of management. But upon upwards of six hundred thousand pounds, for which it was continually drawing bills of exchange upon London, it was paying, in the way of interest

and was obliged to stop in two years.

---

[19] [Macpherson, *op. cit.*, p. 525, says the partners were the Dukes of Buccleuch and Queensberry, the Earl of Dumfries, Mr. Douglas and many other gentlemen.]

and commission, upwards of eight per cent., and was consequently losing more than three per cent. upon more than three-fourths of all its dealings.

The operations of this bank seem to have produced effects quite opposite to those which were intended by the particular persons who planned and directed it. They

Its action and failure increased the distress of projectors and the country generally,

seem to have intended to support the spirited undertakings, for as such they considered them, which were at that time carrying on in different parts of the country; and at the same time, by drawing the whole banking business to themselves, to supplant all the other Scotch banks; particularly those established at Edinburgh, whose backwardness in discounting bills of exchange had given some offence. This bank, no doubt, gave some temporary relief to those projectors, and enabled them to carry on their projects for about two years longer than they could otherwise have done. But it thereby only enabled them to get so much deeper into debt, so that when ruin came, it fell so much the heavier both upon them and upon their creditors. The operations of this bank, therefore, instead of relieving, in reality aggravated in the long-run the distress which those projectors had brought both upon themselves and upon their country. It would have been much better for themselves, their creditors and their country, had the greater part of them been obliged to stop two years sooner than they actually did. The temporary re-

but relieved the other Scotch banks.

lief, however, which this bank afforded to those projectors, proved a real and permanent relief to the other Scotch banks. All the dealers in circulating bills of exchange, which those other banks had become so backward in discounting, had recourse to this new bank, where they were received with open arms. Those other banks, therefore, were enabled to get very easily out of that fatal circle, from which they could not otherwise have disengaged themselves without incurring a considerable loss, and perhaps too even some degree of discredit.

In the long-run, therefore, the operations of this bank increased the real distress of the country which it meant to relieve; and effectually relieved from a very great distress those rivals whom it meant to supplant.

At the first setting out of this bank, it was the opinion of some people, that how fast soever its coffers might be emptied,

Another plan would have been to raise money on the securities pledged by borrowers: it might easily replenish them by raising money upon the securities of those to whom it had advanced its paper. Experience, I believe, soon convinced them that this method of raising money was by much too slow to answer their purpose; and that coffers which originally were so ill filled, and which emptied themselves so very fast, could be replenished by no other expedient but the ruinous one of drawing bills upon London, and when they became due, paying them by other draughts upon the same place with accumulated interest and commission. But though they had been able by this method to raise money as fast as they wanted it; yet, instead of making a profit, they must have suffered a loss by every such operation; so that

this would have been a losing business, in the long-run they must have ruined themselves as a mercantile company, though, perhaps, not so soon as by the more expensive practice of drawing and re-drawing. They could still have made nothing by the interest of the paper, which, being over and above what the circulation of the country could absorb and employ, returned upon them, in order to be exchanged for gold and silver, as fast as they issued it; and for the payment of which they were themselves continually obliged to borrow money. On the contrary, the whole expence of this borrowing, of employing agents to look out for people who had money to lend, of negotiating with those people, and of drawing the proper bond or assignment, must have fallen upon them, and have been so much clear loss upon the balance of their accounts. The project of replenishing their coffers in this manner may be compared to that of a man who had a water-pond from which a stream was continually running out, and into which no stream was continually running, but who proposed to keep it always equally full by employing a number of people to go continually with buckets to a well at some miles distance in order to bring water to replenish it.

But though this operation had proved, not only practicable, but profitable to the bank as a mercantile company; yet the country could have derived no benefit from it; but, on the contrary, must have suffered a very considerable loss by it. This operation could not augment in the smallest degree the quantity of money to be lent. It could only have erected this bank into a sort of general loan office for the whole country. Those who wanted to borrow, must have applied to this bank, instead of applying to the private persons who had lent it their money. But a bank which lends money, perhaps, to five hundred different people, the greater part of whom its directors can know very little about, is not likely to be more judicious in the choice of its debtors, than a private person who lends out his money among a few people whom he knows, and in whose sober and frugal conduct he thinks he has good reason to confide. The debtors of such a bank, as that whose conduct I have been giving some account of, were likely, the greater part of them, to be chimerical projectors, the drawers and re-drawers of circulating bills of exchange, who would employ the money in extravagant undertakings, which, with all the assistance that could be given them, they would probably never be able to complete, and which, if they should be completed, would never repay the expence which they had really cost, would never afford a fund capable of maintaining a quantity of labour equal to that which had been employed about them. The sober and frugal debtors of private persons, on the contrary, would be more likely to employ the money borrowed in sober undertakings which were proportioned to their capitals, and which, though they might have less of the grand and the marvellous, would have more of the solid and the profitable, which would repay with a large profit whatever had been laid out upon them, and which would thus afford a fund capable of maintaining a much greater quantity of labour than that which had been employed about them. The success of this operation, therefore, without increasing in the smallest degree

and even if profitable would have been hurtful to the country.

the capital of the country, would only have transferred a great part of it from prudent and profitable, to imprudent and un-profitable undertakings.

That the industry of Scotland languished for want of money to employ it, was the opinion of the famous Mr. Law. By estab-lishing a bank of a particular kind, which he seems to have imagined might issue paper to the amount of the whole value of all the lands in the country, he proposed to remedy this want of money. The parliament of Scotland, when he first proposed his project, did not think proper to adopt it.[20] It was afterwards adopted, with some variations, by the duke of Orleans, at that time re-gent of France. The idea of the possibility of multiplying paper money to almost any extent, was the real foundation of what is called the Mississippi scheme, the most extravagant project both of banking and stock-jobbing that, perhaps, the world ever saw. The different operations of this scheme are explained so fully, so clearly, and with so much order and distinctness, by Mr. Du Verney, in his Examination of the Political Reflections upon Commerce and Finances of Mr. Du Tot,[21] that I shall not give any account of them.[22] The principles upon which it was founded are explained by Mr. Law himself, in a discourse con-cerning money and trade, which he published in Scotland when he first proposed his project.[23] The splendid, but vision-

Law's scheme has been suffi-ciently explained by Du Verney and Du Tot.

[20] [*Lectures*, p. 211. The bookseller's preface to the 2nd ed. of *Money and Trade* (below, note 23) says the work consists of "some heads of a scheme which Mr. Law proposed to the Parliament of Scotland in the year 1705."]

[21] [These two books are in Bonar, *Catalogue of Adam Smith's library*, pp. 35, 36. Du Tot's is *Réflexions politiques sur les Finances et le Commerce, ou l'on examine quelles ont été sur les revenus, les denrées, le change étranger et conséquemment sur notre commerce, les influences des augmentations et des diminutions des valeurs numéraires des monnoyes*, La Haye, 1754. Du Verney's is *Examen du livre intitulé "Réflexions politiques sur les Finances et le Commerce,"* La Haye, 1740.]

[22] [In *Lectures* there is an account, apparently derived from Du Verney, which ex-tends over eight pages, 211–218.]

[23] [*Money and Trade Considered, with a Proposal for Supplying the Nation with Money*, 1705.]

ary ideas which are set forth in that and some other works upon the same principles, still continue to make an impression upon many people, and have, perhaps, in part, contributed to that excess of banking, which has of late been complained of both in Scotland and in other places.

The bank of England is the greatest bank of circulation in Europe. It was incorporated, in pursuance of an act of parliament, by a charter under the great seal, dated *The bank of* the 27th of July, 1694. It at that time ad-*England was* vanced to government the sum of one mil-*established in* lion two hundred thousand pounds, for an *1694,* annuity of one hundred thousand pounds: or for 96,000*l.* a year interest, at the rate of eight per cent., and 4,000*l.* a year for the expence of management. The credit of the new government, established by the Revolution, we may believe, must have been very low, when it was obliged to borrow at so high an interest.

In 1697 the bank was allowed to enlarge its capital stock by an ingraftment of 1,001,171*l.* 10*s.* Its whole capital *enlarged its stock* stock, therefore, amounted at this time to *in 1697,* 2,201,171*l.* 10*s.* This engraftment is said to have been for the support of public credit. In 1696, tallies had been at forty, and fifty, and sixty per cent. discount, and bank notes at twenty per cent.[24] During the great recoinage of the silver, which was going on at this time, the bank had thought proper to discontinue the payment of its notes, which necessarily occasioned their discredit.

In pursuance of the 7th Anne, c. vii. the bank advanced and paid into the exchequer, the sum of 400,000*l.*; making in all the *in 1708,* sum of 1,600,000*l.* which it had advanced upon its original annuity of 96,000*l.* interest and 4,000*l.* for expence of management. In 1708, therefore, the credit of government was as good as that of private persons, since it could borrow at six per cent. interest, the common legal and market rate of those times. In pursuance of the

---

[24] [James Postlethwayt's History of the Public Revenue, page 301. *History of the Public Revenue from 1688 to 1753, with an Appendix to 1758,* by James Postlethwayt, F.R.S., 1759; see also below, p. 1160.]

same act, the bank cancelled exchequer bills to the amount of 1,775,027*l*. 17*s*. 10½*d*. at six per cent. interest, and was at the same time allowed to take in subscriptions for doubling its capital. In 1708, therefore, the capital of the bank amounted to 4,402,343*l*.; and it had advanced to government the sum of 3,375,027*l*. 17*s*. 10½*d*.

By a call of fifteen per cent. in 1709, there was paid in and

in 1709 and 1710, made stock 656,204*l*. 1*s*. 9*d*.; and by another of ten per cent. in 1710, 501,448*l*. 12*s*. 11*d*. In consequence of those two calls, therefore, the bank capital amounted to 5,559,995*l*. 14*s*. 8*d*.

In pursuance of the 3d George I. c. 8. the bank delivered up two millions of exchequer bills to be cancelled. It had at this

in 1717 and later. time, therefore, advanced to government 5,375,027*l*. 17*s*. 10*d*.[25] In pursuance of the 8th George I. c. 21. the bank purchased of the South Sea Company, stock to the amount of 4,000,000*l*.: and in 1722, in consequence of the subscriptions which it had taken in for enabling it to make this purchase, its capital stock was increased by 3,400,000*l*. At this time, therefore, the bank had advanced to the public 9,375,027*l*. 17*s*. 10½*d*.; and its capital stock amounted only to 8,959,995*l*. 14*s*. 8*d*. It was upon this occasion that the sum which the bank had advanced to the public, and for which it received interest, began first to exceed its capital stock, or the sum for which it paid a dividend to the proprietors of bank stock; or, in other words, that the bank began to have an undivided capital, over and above its divided one. It has continued to have an undivided capital of the same kind ever since. In 1746, the bank had, upon different occasions, advanced to the public 11,686,800*l*. and its divided capital had been raised by different calls and subscriptions to 10,780,000*l*.[26] The state of those two sums has continued to be

---

[25] [These three lines are not in ed. 1.]

[26] [From "it was incorporated," on p. 406, to this point is an abstract of the "Historical State of the Bank of England," in Postlethwayt's *History of the Public Revenue*, pp. 301–310. The totals are taken from the bottom of Postlethwayt's pages.]

the same ever since. In pursuance of the 4th of George III. c. 25. the bank agreed to pay to government for the renewal of its charter 110,000*l.* without interest or repayment. This sum, therefore, did not increase either of those two other sums.

The dividend of the bank has varied according to the variations in the rate of the interest which it has, at different times, received for the money it had advanced to the public, as well as according to other circumstances. This rate of interest has gradually been reduced from eight to three per cent. For some years past the bank dividend has been at five and a half per cent.

The rate of interest received by it from the public has been reduced from 8 to 3 per cent. and its dividend has lately been 5½ per cent.

The stability of the bank of England is equal to that of the British government. All that it has advanced to the public must be lost before its creditors can sustain any loss. No other banking company in England can be established by act of parliament, or can consist of more than six members. It acts, not only as an ordinary bank, but as a great engine of state. It receives and pays the greater part of the annuities which are due to the creditors of the public, it circulates exchequer bills, and it advances to government the annual amount of the land and malt taxes, which are frequently not paid up till some years thereafter. In those different operations, its duty to the public may sometimes have obliged it, without any fault of its directors, to overstock the circulation with paper money. It likewise discounts merchants bills, and has, upon several different occasions, supported the credit of the principal houses, not only of England, but of Hamburgh and Holland. Upon one occasion, in 1763, it is said to have advanced for this purpose, in one week, about 1,600,000*l.*; a great part of it in bullion. I do not, however, pretend to warrant either the greatness of the sum, or the shortness of the time. Upon other occasions, this great company has been reduced to the necessity of paying in sixpences.[27]

It acts as a great engine of state.

---

[27] [In 1745. Magens, *Universal Merchant*, p. 31, suggests that there may have been suspicions that the money was being drawn out for the support of the rebellion.]

It is not by augmenting the capital of the country, but by rendering a greater part of that capital active and productive

The operations of banking turn dead stock into productive capital,

than would otherwise be so, that the most judicious operations of banking can increase the industry of the country. That part of his capital which a dealer is obliged to keep by him unemployed, and in ready money for answering occasional demands, is so much dead stock, which, so long as it remains in this situation, produces nothing either to him or to his country. The judicious operations of banking enable him to convert this dead stock into active and productive stock; into materials to work upon, into tools to work with, and into provisions and subsistence to work for; into stock which produces something both to himself[28] and to his country. The gold and silver money which circulates in any country, and by means of which the produce of its land and labour is annually circulated and distributed to the proper consumers, is, in the same manner as the ready money of the dealer, all dead stock. It is a very valuable part of the capital of the country, which produces nothing to the country. The judicious operations of banking, by substituting paper in the room of a great part of this gold and silver, enables the country to convert a great part of this dead stock into active and productive stock; into stock which produces something to the country. The gold and silver money which circulates in any country may very properly be compared to a highway, which, while it circulates and carries to market all the grass and corn of the country, produces itself not a single pile of either. The judicious operations of banking, by providing, if I may be allowed so violent a metaphor, a sort

but make commerce and industry somewhat less secure.

of waggon-way through the air; enable the country to convert, as it were, a great part of its highways into good pastures and cornfields, and thereby to increase very considerably the annual produce of its land and labour. The commerce and industry of the country, however, it must be acknowledged, though they may be somewhat aug-

---

[28] [Eds. 1 and 2 read "him."]

mented, cannot be altogether so secure, when they are thus, as it were, suspended upon the Dædalian wings of paper money, as when they travel about upon the solid ground of gold and silver. Over and above the accidents to which they are exposed from the unskilfulness of the conductors of this paper money, they are liable to several others, from which no prudence or skill of those conductors can guard them.

An unsuccessful war, for example, in which the enemy got possession of the capital, and consequently of that treasure which supported the credit of the paper money, would occasion a much greater confusion in a country where the whole circulation was carried on by paper, than in one where the greater part of it was carried on by gold and silver. The usual instrument of commerce having lost its value, no exchanges could be made but either by barter or upon credit. All taxes having been usually paid in paper money, the prince would not have wherewithal either to pay his troops, or to furnish his magazines; and the state of the country would be much more irretrievable than if the greater part of its circulation had consisted in gold and silver. A prince, anxious to maintain his dominions at all times in the state in which he can most easily defend them, ought, upon this account, to guard, not only against that excessive multiplication of paper money which ruins the very banks which issue it; but even against that multiplication of it, which enables them to fill the greater part of the circulation of the country with it.

Precautions should be taken to prevent the greater part of the circulation being filled with paper.

The circulation of every country may be considered as divided into two different branches; the circulation of the dealers with one another, and the circulation between the dealers and the consumers. Though the same pieces of money, whether paper or metal, may be employed sometimes in the one circulation and sometimes in the other; yet as both are constantly going on at the same time, each requires a certain stock of money of one kind or another, to carry it on. The value of

Circulation may be divided into that between dealers and that between dealers and consumers.

the goods circulated between the different dealers, never can
exceed the value of those circulated between the dealers and
the consumers; whatever is bought by the dealers, being ultimately destined to be sold to the consumers. The circulation
between the dealers, as it is carried on by wholesale, requires
generally a pretty large sum for every particular transaction.
That between the dealers and the consumers, on the contrary,
as it is generally carried on by retail, frequently requires but
very small ones, a shilling, or even a halfpenny, being often
sufficient. But small sums circulate much faster than large
ones. A shilling changes masters more frequently than a
guinea, and a halfpenny more frequently than a shilling.
Though the annual purchases of all the consumers, therefore,
are at least equal in value to those of all the dealers, they can
generally be transacted with a much smaller quantity of
money; the same pieces, by a more rapid circulation, serving
as the instrument of many more purchases of the one kind than
of the other.

Paper money may be so regulated, as either to confine itself
very much to the circulation between the different dealers, or
to extend itself likewise to a great part of
that between the dealers and the consumers.
Where no bank notes are circulated under
ten pounds value, as in London,[29] paper
money confines itself very much to the circulation between the dealers. When a ten
pound bank note comes into the hands of a
consumer, he is generally obliged to change it at the first shop
where he has occasion to purchase five shillings worth of
goods; so that it often returns into the hands of a dealer, before
the consumer has spent the fortieth part of the money. Where
bank notes are issued for so small sums as twenty shillings, as
in Scotland, paper money extends itself to a considerable part
of the circulation between dealers and consumers. Before the
act of parliament, which put a stop to the circulation of ten and

*The circulation
of paper may be
confined to the
former by not
allowing notes for
small sums.*

---

[29] [The Bank of England issued none under £20 till 1759, when £15 and £10 notes
were introduced.—Anderson, *Commerce*, A.D. 1759.]

five shilling notes,[30] it filled a still greater part of that circulation. In the currencies of North America, paper was commonly issued for so small a sum as a shilling, and filled almost the whole of that circulation. In some paper currencies of Yorkshire, it was issued even for so small a sum as a sixpence.

Where the issuing of bank notes for such very small sums is allowed and commonly practised, many mean people are both enabled and encouraged to become bankers.

The issue of such notes enables mean people to become bankers.

A person whose promissory note for five pounds, or even for twenty shillings, would be rejected by every body, will get it to be received without scruple when it is issued for so small a sum as a sixpence. But the frequent bankruptcies to which such beggarly bankers must be liable, may occasion a very considerable inconveniency, and sometimes even a very great calamity, to many poor people who had received their notes in payment.

It were better, perhaps, that no bank notes were issued in any part of the kingdom for a smaller sum than five pounds.

None for less than £5 should be issued.

Paper money would then, probably, confine itself, in every part of the kingdom, to the circulation between the different dealers, as much as it does at present in London, where no bank notes are issued under ten pounds value; five pounds being, in most parts of the kingdom, a sum which, though it will purchase, perhaps, little more than half the quantity of goods, is as much considered, and is as seldom spent all at once, as ten pounds are amidst the profuse expence of London.

Where paper money, it is to be observed, is pretty much confined to the circulation between dealers and dealers, as at London, there is always plenty of gold and silver. Where it extends itself to a considerable part of the circulation between dealers and consumers, as in Scotland, and still more in North America, it banishes gold and

This would secure the circulation of plenty of gold and silver,

[30] [5 Geo. III., c. 49.]

silver almost entirely from the country; almost all the ordinary transactions of its interior commerce being thus carried on by paper. The suppression of ten and five shilling bank notes, somewhat relieved the scarcity of gold and silver in Scotland; and the suppression of twenty shilling notes, would probably relieve it still more. Those metals are said to have become more abundant in America, since the suppression of some of their paper currencies. They are said, likewise, to have been more abundant before the institution of those currencies.

Though paper money should be pretty much confined to the circulation between dealers and dealers, yet banks and bankers might still be able to give nearly the same assistance to the industry and commerce of the country, as they had done when paper money filled almost the whole circulation. The ready money which a dealer is obliged to keep by him, for answering occasional demands, is destined altogether for the circulation between himself and other dealers, of whom he buys goods. He has no occasion to keep any by him for the circulation between himself and the consumers, who are his customers, and who bring ready money to him, instead of taking any from him. Though no paper money, therefore, was allowed to be issued, but for such sums as would confine it pretty much to the circulation between dealers and dealers; yet, partly by discounting real bills of exchange, and partly by lending upon cash accounts, banks and bankers might still be able to relieve the greater part of those dealers from the necessity of keeping any considerable part of their stock by them, unemployed and in ready money, for answering occasional demands. They might still be able to give the utmost assistance which banks and bankers can, with propriety, give to traders of every kind.

and would not prevent banks from giving sufficient assistance to traders.

To restrain private people, it may be said, from receiving in payment the promissory notes of a banker, for any sum whether great or small, when they themselves are willing to receive them; or, to restrain a banker from issuing such notes, when all his neighbours are willing to accept

A law against small notes would be a violation of natural liberty

necessary for the security of the society. of them, is a manifest violation of that natural liberty which it is the proper business of law, not to infringe, but to support. Such regulations may, no doubt, be considered as in some respect a violation of natural liberty. But those exertions of the natural liberty of a few individuals, which might endanger the security of the whole society, are, and ought to be, restrained by the laws of all governments; of the most free, as well as of the most despotical. The obligation of building party walls, in order to prevent the communication of fire, is a violation of natural liberty, exactly of the same kind with the regulations of the banking trade which are here proposed.

A paper money consisting in bank notes, issued by people of undoubted credit, payable upon demand without any condition, and in fact always readily paid as soon *Paper money payable on demand is equal to gold and silver,* as presented, is, in every respect, equal in value to gold and silver money; since gold and silver money can at any time be had for it. Whatever is either bought or sold for such paper, must necessarily be bought or sold as cheap as it could have been for gold and silver.

The increase of paper money, it has been said, by augmenting the quantity, and consequently diminishing the value of *and does not raise prices;* the whole currency, necessarily augments the money price of commodities. But as the quantity of gold and silver, which is taken from the currency, is always equal to the quantity of paper which is added to it, paper money does not necessarily increase the quantity of the whole currency. From the beginning of the last century to the present time, provisions never were cheaper in Scotland than in 1759, though, from the circulation of ten and five shilling bank notes, there was then more paper money in the country than at present. The proportion between the price of provisions in Scotland and that in England, is the same now as before the great multiplication of banking companies in Scotland. Corn is, upon most occasions, fully as cheap in England as in France; though there is a great deal of paper money in England, and scarce any in France. In 1751 and in

1752, when Mr. Hume published his Political Discourses,[31] and soon after the great multiplication of paper money in Scotland, there was a very sensible rise in the price of provisions, owing, probably, to the badness of the seasons, and not to the multiplication of paper money.

It would be otherwise, indeed, with a paper money consisting in promissory notes, of which the immediate payment depended, in any respect, either upon the good will of those who issued them; or upon a condition which the holder of the notes might not always have it in his power to fulfil; or of which the payment was not exigible till after a certain number of years, and which in the mean time bore no interest. Such a paper money would, no doubt, fall more or less below the value of gold and silver, according as the difficulty or uncertainty of obtaining immediate payment was supposed to be greater or less; or according to the greater or less distance of time at which payment was exigible.

but paper not repayable on demand would fall below gold and silver,

Some years ago the different banking companies of Scotland were in the practice of inserting into their bank notes, what they called an Optional Clause, by which they promised payment to the bearer, either as soon as the note should be presented, or, in the option of the directors, six months after such presentment, together with the legal interest for the said six months. The directors of some of those banks sometimes took advantage of this optional clause, and sometimes threatened those who demanded gold and silver in exchange for a considerable number of their notes, that they would take advantage of it, unless such demanders would content themselves with a part of what they demanded. The promissory notes of those banking companies constituted at that time the far greater part

as happened in Scotland during the prevalence of the Optional Clause,

[31] [The reference is probably to the passages in the "Discourse of Money," and the "Discourse of the Balance of Trade," where Hume censures paper money as the cause of a rise of prices.—*Political Discourses*, 1752, pp. 43–45, 89–91; cp. *Lectures*, p. 197.]

of the currency of Scotland, which this uncertainty of payment necessarily degraded below the value of gold and silver money. During the continuance of this abuse (which prevailed chiefly in 1762, 1763, and 1764), while the exchange between London and Carlisle was at par, that between London and Dumfries would sometimes be four per cent. against Dumfries, though this town is not thirty miles distant from Carlisle. But at Carlisle, bills were paid in gold and silver; whereas at Dumfries they were paid in Scotch bank notes, and the uncertainty of getting those bank notes exchanged for gold and silver coin had thus degraded them four per cent. below the value of that coin. The same act of parliament which suppressed ten and five shilling bank notes, suppressed likewise this optional clause,[32] and thereby restored the exchange between England and Scotland to its natural rate, or to what the course of trade and remittances might happen to make it.

In the paper currencies of Yorkshire, the payment of so small a sum as a sixpence sometimes depended upon the con-

and must have happened in regard to the Yorkshire currencies when small sums were repayable in guineas. dition that the holder of the note should bring the change of a guinea to the person who issued it; a condition, which the holders of such notes might frequently find it very difficult to fulfil, and which must have degraded this currency below the value of gold and silver money. An act of parliament, ac-

cordingly, declared all such clauses unlawful, and suppressed, in the same manner as in Scotland, all promissory notes, payable to the bearer, under twenty shillings value.[33]

The paper currencies of North America consisted, not in bank notes payable to the bearer on demand, but in a government paper, of which the payment was not exigible till several years after it was issued: And though the colony governments paid no interest to the holders of this paper, they declared it to be, and in fact rendered it, a legal tender of payment for the full

---

[32] [5 Geo. III., c. 49; referred to above, p. 412.]

[33] [15 Geo. III., c. 51.]

The North American paper currencies consisted of government notes repayable at a distant date,

value for which it was issued. But allowing the colony security to be perfectly good, a hundred pounds payable fifteen years hence, for example, in a country where interest is at six per cent. is worth little more than forty pounds ready money. To oblige a creditor, therefore, to accept of this as full payment for a debt of a hundred pounds actually paid down in ready money, was an act of such violent injustice, as has scarce, perhaps, been attempted by the government of any other country which pretended to be free. It bears the evident marks of having originally been, what the honest and down-right Doctor Douglass assures us it was, a scheme of fraudulent debtors to cheat their creditors.[34] The government of Pennsylvania, indeed, pretended, upon their first emission of paper money, in 1722, to render their paper of equal value with gold and silver, by enacting penalties against all those who made any difference in the price of their goods when they sold them for a colony paper, and when they sold them for gold and silver; a regulation equally tyrannical, but much less effectual than that which it was meant to support. A positive law may render a shilling a legal tender for a guinea; because it may direct the courts of justice to discharge the debtor who has made that tender. But no positive law can oblige a person who sells goods, and who is at liberty to sell or not to sell, as he pleases, to accept of a shilling as equivalent to a guinea in the price of

and depreciated the currency to a great degree.

them. Notwithstanding any regulation of this kind, it appeared by the course of exchange with Great Britain, that a hundred pounds sterling was occasionally considered as equivalent, in some of the colonies, to a hundred and thirty

[34] ["A knavish device of fraudulent debtors of the loan money to pay off their loans at a very depreciated value." William Douglass, M.D., *Summary, Historical and Political, of the First Planting, Progressive Improvements, and Present State of the British Settlements in North America*, 1760, vol. ii., p. 107. The author uses strong language in many places about what he calls "this accursed affair of plantation paper currencies," vol. ii., p. 13, note (*s*); cp. vol. i., pp. 310, 359; vol. ii., pp. 254–255, 334–335.]

pounds, and in others to so great a sum as eleven hundred pounds currency; this difference in the value arising from the difference in the quantity of paper emitted in the different colonies, and in the distance and probability of the term of its final discharge and redemption.

They were therefore justly prohibited.

No law, therefore, could be more equitable than the act of parliament, so unjustly complained of in the colonies, which declared that no paper currency to be emitted there in time coming, should be a legal tender of payment.[35]

Pennsylvania was always more moderate in its emissions of paper money than any other of our colonies. Its paper currency

Pennsylvania was moderate in its issues, and its currency never went below the real par.

accordingly is said never to have sunk below the value of the gold and silver which was current in the colony before the first emission of its paper money. Before that emission, the colony had raised the denomination of its coin, and had, by act of assembly, ordered five shillings sterling to pass in the colony for six and three-pence, and afterwards for six and eight-pence. A pound colony currency, therefore, even when that currency was gold and silver, was more than thirty per cent. below the value of a pound sterling, and when that currency was turned into paper, it was seldom much more than thirty per cent. below that value. The pretence for raising the denomination of the coin, was to prevent the exportation of gold and silver, by making equal quantities of those metals pass for greater sums in the colony than they did in the mother country. It was found, however, that the price of all goods from the mother country rose exactly in proportion as they raised the denomination of their coin, so that their gold and silver were exported as fast as ever.

The colonial paper was somewhat supported by being received in payment of taxes.

The paper of each colony being received in the payment of the provincial taxes, for the full value for which it had been issued, it necessarily derived from this use some additional value, over and above what it would have had, from the real or supposed distance of the term of its final discharge and redemption. This additional value was greater or less, according as the quantity of paper issued was more or less above what could be employed in the payment of the taxes of the particular colony which issued it. It was in all the colonies very much above what could be employed in this manner.

A prince, who should enact that a certain proportion of his taxes should be paid in a paper money of a certain kind, might thereby give a certain value to this paper money; even though the term of its final discharge and redemption should depend altogether upon the will of the prince. If the bank which issued this paper was careful to keep the quantity of it always somewhat below what could easily be employed in this manner, the demand for it might be such as to make it even bear a premium, or sell for somewhat more in the market than the quantity of gold or silver currency for which it was issued. Some people account in this manner for what is called the Agio of the bank of Amsterdam, or for the superiority of bank money over current money; though this bank money, as they pretend, cannot be taken out of the bank at the will of the owner. The greater part of foreign bills of exchange must be paid in bank money, that is, by a transfer in the books of the bank; and the directors of the bank, they allege, are careful to keep the whole quantity of bank money always below what this use occasions a demand for. It is upon this account, they say, that bank money sells for a premium, or bears an agio of four or five per cent. above the same nominal sum of the gold and silver currency of the country. This account of the bank of Amsterdam, however, it will appear hereafter,[36] is in a great measure chimerical.[37]

A requirement that certain taxes should be paid in particular paper money might give that paper a certain value even if it was irredeemable.

---

[36] [Below, pp. 602–614. See also the "Advertisement" or preface to the 4th ed., above.]

[37] [Ed. 1 reads "This account of the Bank of Amsterdam, however, I have reason to believe, is altogether chimerical."]

A paper currency which falls below the value of gold and silver coin, does not thereby sink the value of those metals, or occasion equal quantities of them[38] to exchange for a smaller quantity of goods of any other kind. The proportion between the value of gold and silver and that of goods of any other kind, depends in all cases, not upon the nature or quantity of any particular paper money, which may be current in any particular country, but upon the richness or poverty of the mines, which happen at any particular time to supply the great market of the commercial world with those metals. It depends upon the proportion between the quantity of labour which is necessary in order to bring a certain quantity of gold and silver to market, and that which is necessary in order to bring thither a certain quantity of any other sort of goods.

A paper currency depreciated below the value of the coin does not sink the value of gold and silver.

If bankers are restrained from issuing any circulating bank notes or notes payable to the bearer, for less than a certain sum; and if they are subjected to the obligation of an immediate and unconditional payment of such bank notes as soon as presented, their trade may, with safety to the public, be rendered in all other respects perfectly free. The late multiplication of banking companies in both parts of the united kingdom, an event by which many people have been much alarmed, instead of diminishing, increases the security of the public. It obliges all of them to be more circumspect in their conduct, and, by not extending their currency beyond its due proportion to their cash, to guard themselves against those malicious runs, which the rivalship of so many competitors is always ready to bring upon them. It restrains the circulation of each particular company within a narrower circle, and reduces their circulating notes to a smaller number. By dividing the whole circulation into a

The only restrictions on banking which are necessary are the prohibition of small bank notes and the requirement that all notes shall be repaid on demand.

---

[38] [Ed. 1 reads "sink the value of gold and silver, or occasion equal quantities of those metals."]

greater number of parts, the failure of any one company, an accident which, in the course of things, must sometimes happen, becomes of less consequence to the public. This free competition too obliges all bankers to be more liberal in their dealings with their customers, lest their rivals should carry them away. In general, if any branch of trade, or any division of labour, be advantageous to the public, the freer and more general the competition, it will always be the more so.

CHAPTER III

OF THE ACCUMULATION OF CAPITAL, OR OF PRODUCTIVE AND UNPRODUCTIVE LABOUR

THERE IS one sort of labour which adds to the value of the subject upon which it is bestowed: there is another which has no such effect. The former, as it produces a value, may be called productive; the latter, unproductive[1] labour. Thus the labour of a manufacturer adds, generally, to the value of the materials which he works upon, that of his own maintenance, and of his master's profit. The labour of a menial servant, on the contrary, adds to the value of nothing. Though the manufacturer has his wages advanced to him by his master, he, in reality, costs him no expence, the value of those wages being generally restored, together with a profit, in the improved value of the subject upon which his labour is bestowed. But the maintenance of a menial servant never is restored. A man grows rich by employing a multitude of manufacturers: he grows poor, by maintaining a multitude of menial servants.[2] The labour of the latter, however, has its value, and deserves its reward as well as that of the former. But the labour

There are two sorts of labour, productive and unproductive.

[1] Some French authors of great learning and ingenuity have used those words in a different sense. In the last chapter of the fourth book I shall endeavour to show that their sense is an improper one.

[2] [In the argument which follows in the text the fact is overlooked that this is only true when the manufacturers are employed to produce commodities for sale and when the menial servants are employed merely for the comfort of the employer. A man may and often does grow poor by employing people to make "particular subjects or vendible commodities" for his own consumption, and an innkeeper may and often does grow rich by employing menial servants.]

of the manufacturer fixes and realizes itself in some particular subject or vendible commodity, which lasts for some time at least after that labour is past. It is, as it were, a certain quantity of labour stocked and stored up to the employed, if necessary, upon some other occasion. That subject, or what is the same thing, the price of that subject, can afterwards, if necessary, put into motion a quantity of labour equal to that which had originally produced it. The labour of the menial servant, on the contrary, does not fix or realize itself in any particular subject or vendible commodity. His services generally perish in the very instant of their performance, and seldom leave any trace or value behind them, for which an equal quantity of service could afterwards be procured.

The labour of some of the most respectable orders in the society is, like that of menial servants, unproductive of any value, and does not fix or realize itself in any

Many kinds of labour besides menial service are unproductive.

permanent subject, or vendible commodity, which endures after that labour is past, and for which an equal quantity of labour could afterwards be procured. The sovereign, for example, with all the officers both of justice and war who serve under him, the whole army and navy, are unproductive labourers. They are the servants of the public, and are maintained by a part of the annual produce of the industry of other people. Their service, how honourable, how useful,[3] or how necessary soever, produces nothing for which an equal quantity of service can afterwards be procured. The protection, security, and defence of the commonwealth, the effect of their labour this year, will not purchase its protection, security, and defence for the year to come. In the same class must be ranked, some both of the gravest and most important, and some of the most frivolous professions: churchmen, lawyers, physicians, men of letters of all kinds; players, buffoons, musicians, opera-singers, opera-dancers, &c. The labour of the meanest of these has a certain value, regulated by the very same principles

---

[3] [But in the "Introduction and Plan of the Work," "useful" is coupled with "productive," and used as equivalent to it.]

which regulate that of every other sort of labour; and that of the noblest and most useful, produces nothing which could afterwards purchase or procure an equal quantity of labour. Like the declamation of the actor, the harangue of the orator, or the tune of the musician, the work of all of them perishes in the very instant of its production.

Both productive and unproductive labourers, and those who do not labour at all, are all equally maintained by the annual

The proportion of the produce employed in maintaining productive hands determines the next year's produce.

produce of the land and labour of the country. This produce, how great so-ever, can never be infinite, but must have certain limits. According, therefore, as a smaller or greater proportion of it is in any one year employed in maintaining unproductive hands, the more in the one case and the less in the other will remain for the productive, and the next year's produce will be greater or smaller accordingly; the whole annual produce, if we except the spontaneous productions of the earth, being the effect of productive labour.

Though the whole annual produce of the land and labour of every country, is, no doubt, ultimately destined for supplying

Part of the produce replaces capital, part constitutes profit and rent.

the consumption of its inhabitants, and for procuring a revenue to them; yet when it first comes either from the ground, or from the hands of the productive labourers, it naturally divides itself into two parts. One of them, and frequently the largest, is, in the first place, destined for replacing a capital, or for renewing the provisions, materials, and finished work, which had been withdrawn from a capital; the other for constituting a revenue either to the owner of this capital, as the profit of his stock; or to some other person, as the rent of his land. Thus, of the produce of land, one part replaces the capital of the farmer; the other pays his profit and the rent of the landlord; and thus constitutes a revenue both to the owner of this capital, as the profits of his stock; and to some other person, as the rent of his land. Of the produce of a great manufactory, in the same manner, one part, and that always the largest, replaces the capital of the undertaker of the work; the other pays his profit, and thus constitutes a revenue to the owner of this capital.[4]

That part of the annual produce of the land and labour of any country which replaces a capital, never is immediately

That which replaces capital employs none but productive hands,

employed to maintain any but productive hands. It pays the wages of productive labour only. That which is immediately destined for constituting a revenue either as profit or as rent, may maintain indifferently either productive or unproductive hands.

Whatever part of his stock a man employs as a capital, he always expects is to be replaced to him with a profit. He employs it, therefore, in maintaining productive hands only; and after having served in the function of a capital to him, it constitutes a revenue to them. Whenever he employs any part of it in maintaining unproductive hands of any kind, that part is, from that moment, withdrawn from his capital, and placed in his stock reserved for immediate consumption.

Unproductive labourers, and those who do not labour at all, are all maintained by revenue; either, first, by that part of the

while unproductive hands and those who do not labour are supported by revenue.

annual produce which is originally destined for constituting a revenue to some particular persons, either as the rent of land or as the profits of stock; or, secondly, by that part which, though originally destined for replacing a capital and for maintaining productive labourers only, yet when it comes into their

hands, whatever part of it is over and above their necessary subsistence, may be employed in maintaining indifferently either productive or unproductive hands. Thus, not only the great landlord or the rich merchant, but even the common workman, if his wages are considerable, may maintain a menial servant; or he may sometimes go to a play or a puppet-show, and so contribute his share towards maintaining one set of unproductive labourers; or he may pay some taxes, and thus help to

---

[4] [It must be observed that in this paragraph produce is not used in the ordinary economic sense of income or net produce, but as including all products, *e.g.*, the oil used in weaving machinery as well as the cloth.]

maintain another set, more honourable and useful, indeed, but equally unproductive. No part of the annual produce, however, which had been originally destined to replace a capital, is ever directed towards maintaining unproductive hands, till after it has put into motion its full complement of productive labour, or all that it could put into motion in the way in which it was employed. The workman must have earned his wages by work done, before he can employ any part of them in this manner. That part too is generally but a small one. It is his spare revenue only, of which productive labourers have seldom a great deal. They generally have some, however; and in the payment of taxes the greatness of their number may compensate, in some measure, the smallness of their contribution. The rent of land and the profits of stock are every-where, therefore, the principal sources from which unproductive hands derive their subsistence. These are the two sorts of revenue of which the owners have generally most to spare. They might both maintain indifferently either productive or unproductive hands. They seem, however, to have some predilection for the latter. The expence of a great lord feeds generally more idle than industrious people. The rich merchant, though with his capital he maintains industrious people only, yet by his expence, that is, by the employment of his revenue, he feeds commonly the very same sort as the great lord.

The proportion, therefore, between the productive and unproductive hands, depends very much in every country upon the proportion between that part of the annual produce, which, as soon as it comes either from the ground or from the hands of the productive labourers, is destined for replacing a capital, and that which is destined for constituting a revenue, either as rent, or as profit. This proportion is very different in rich from what it is in poor countries.

So the proportion of productive hands depends on the proportion between profit with rent and the part of produce which replaces capital.

Thus, at present, in the opulent countries of Europe, a very large, frequently the largest portion of the produce of the land, is destined for replacing the capital of the rich and independent farmer; the other for paying his profits, and the rent of the landlord. But anciently, during the prevalency of the feudal government, a very small portion of the produce was sufficient to replace the capital employed in cultivation. It consisted commonly in a few wretched cattle, maintained altogether by the spontaneous produce of uncultivated land, and which might, therefore, be considered as a part of that spontaneous produce. It generally too belonged to the landlord, and was by him advanced to the occupiers of the land. All the rest of the produce properly belonged to him too, either as rent for his land, or as profit upon this paultry capital. The occupiers of land were generally bondmen, whose persons and effects were equally his property. Those who were not bondmen were tenants at will, and though the rent which they paid was often nominally little more than a quit-rent, it really amounted to the whole produce of the land. Their lord could at all times command their labour in peace, and their service in war. Though they lived at a distance from his house, they were equally dependent upon him as his retainers who lived in it. But the whole produce of the land undoubtedly belongs to him, who can dispose of the labour and service of all those whom it maintains. In the present state of Europe, the share of the landlord seldom exceeds a third, sometimes not a fourth part of the whole produce of the land. The rent of land, however, in all the improved parts of the country, has been tripled and quadrupled since those ancient times; and this third or fourth part of the annual produce is, it seems, three or four times greater than the whole had been before. In the progress of improvement, rent, though it increases in proportion to the extent, diminishes in proportion to the produce of the land.

Rent anciently formed a larger proportion of the produce of agriculture than now.

In the opulent countries of Europe, great capitals are at present employed in trade and manufactures. In the ancient state, the little trade that was stirring, and the few homely and coarse manufactures that were carried on, required but very small capitals. These,

Profits were anciently a larger share of the produce of manufactures, however, must have yielded very large profits. The rate of interest was no-where less than ten per cent. and their profits must have been sufficient to afford this great interest. At present the rate of interest, in the improved parts of Europe, is no-where higher than six per cent. and in some of the most improved it is so low as four, three, and two per cent. Though that part of the revenue of the inhabitants which is derived from the profits of stock is always much greater in rich than in poor countries, it is because the stock is much greater: in proportion to the stock the profits are generally much less.[5]

That part of the annual produce, therefore, which, as soon as it comes either from the ground, or from the hands of the productive labourers, is destined for replacing a capital, is not only much greater in rich than in poor countries, but bears a much greater proportion to that which is immediately destined for constituting a revenue either as rent or as profit. The funds destined for the maintenance of productive labour, are not only much greater in the former than in the latter, but bear a much greater proportion to those which, though they may be employed to maintain either productive or unproductive hands, have generally a predilection for the latter.

so the proportion of produce required for replacing capital is greater than it was.

The proportion between those different funds necessarily determines in every country the general character of the inhabitants as to industry or idleness. We are more industrious than our forefathers; because in the present times the funds destined for the maintenance of industry, are much greater in proportion to those which are likely to be employed in the maintenance of idleness, than they were two or three centuries ago. Our ancestors were idle for want of a sufficient encouragement to industry. It is

The proportion between the funds determines whether the inhabitants of the country shall be industrious or idle.

---

[5] [The question first propounded, whether profits form a larger proportion of the produce, is wholly lost sight of. With a stock larger in proportion to the produce, a lower rate of profit may give a larger proportion of the produce.]

better, says the proverb, to play for nothing, than to work for nothing. In mercantile and manufacturing towns, where the inferior ranks of people are chiefly maintained by the employment of capital, they are in general industrious, sober, and thriving; as in many English, and in most Dutch towns. In those towns which are principally supported by the constant or occasional residence of a court, and in which the inferior ranks of people are chiefly maintained by the spending of revenue, they are in general idle, dissolute, and poor; as at Rome, Versailles, Compiegne, and Fontainbleau. If you except Rouen and Bourdeaux, there is little trade or industry in any of the parliament towns of France;[6] and the inferior ranks of people, being chiefly maintained by the expence of the members of the courts of justice, and of those who come to plead before them, are in general idle and poor. The great trade of Rouen and Bourdeaux seems to be altogether the effect of their situation. Rouen is necessarily the entrepôt of almost all the goods which are brought either from foreign countries, or from the maritime provinces of France, for the consumption of the great city of Paris. Bourdeaux is in the same manner the entrepôt of the wines which grow upon the banks of the Garonne, and of the rivers which run into it, one of the richest wine countries in the world, and which seems to produce the wine fittest for exportation, or best suited to the taste of foreign nations. Such advantageous situations necessarily attract a great capital by the great employment which they afford it; and the employment of this capital is the cause of the industry of those two cities. In the other parliament towns of France, very little more capital seems to be employed than what is necessary for supplying their own consumption; that is, little more than the smallest capital which can be employed in them. The same thing may be said of Paris, Madrid, and Vienna. Of those three cities, Paris is by far the most industrious: but Paris itself is the principal market of all the manufactures established at Paris, and its own consumption is the principal object of all the trade

[6] [*Viz.*, Paris, Toulouse, Grenoble, Bordeaux, Dijon, Rouen, Aix, Rennes, Pau, Metz, Besançon and Douai.—*Encyclopédie*, tom. xii., 1765, *s.v.* Parlement.]

which it carries on. London, Lisbon, and Copenhagen, are, perhaps, the only three cities in Europe, which are both the constant residence of a court, and can at the same time be considered as trading cities, or as cities which trade not only for their own consumption, but for that of other cities and countries. The situation of all the three is extremely advantageous, and naturally fits them to be the entrepôts of a great part of the goods destined for the consumption of distant places. In a city where a great revenue is spent, to employ with advantage a capital for any other purpose than for supplying the consumption of that city, is probably more difficult than in one in which the inferior ranks of people have no other maintenance but what they derive from the employment of such a capital. The idleness of the greater part of the people who are maintained by the expence of revenue, corrupts, it is probable, the industry of those who ought to be maintained by the employment of capital, and renders it less advantageous to employ a capital there than in other places. There was little trade or industry in Edinburgh before the union. When the Scotch parliament was no longer to be assembled in it, when it ceased to be the necessary residence of the principal nobility and gentry of Scotland, it became a city of some trade and industry. It still continues, however, to be the residence of the principal courts of justice in Scotland, of the boards of customs and excise, &c. A considerable revenue, therefore, still continues to be spent in it. In trade and industry it is much inferior to Glasgow, of which the inhabitants are chiefly maintained by the employment of capital.[7] The inhabitants of a large village, it has sometimes been observed, after having made considerable progress in manufactures, have become idle and poor, in consequence of a great lord's having taken up his residence in their neighbourhood.

The proportion between capital and revenue, therefore, seems everywhere to regulate the proportion between industry and idleness. Wherever capital predominates, industry pre-

[7] [In Lectures, pp. 154–156, the idleness of Edinburgh and such like places compared with Glasgow is attributed simply to the want of independence in the inhabitants. The introduction of revenue and capital is the fruit of study of the physiocratic doctrines.]

Increase or diminution of the capital of a country consequently increases or diminishes its annual produce.

vails: wherever revenue, idleness. Every increase or diminution of capital, therefore, naturally tends to increase or diminish the real quantity of industry, the number of productive hands, and consequently the exchangeable value of the annual produce of the land and labour of the country, the real wealth and revenue of all its inhabitants.

Capitals are increased by parsimony, and diminished by prodigality and misconduct.

Whatever a person saves from his revenue he adds to his capital, and either employs it himself in maintaining an addi-

Capitals are increased by parsimony or saving.

tional number of productive hands, or enables some other person to do so, by lending it to him for an interest, that is, for a share of the profits. As the capital of an individual can be increased only by what he saves from his annual revenue or his annual gains, so the capital of a society, which is the same with that of all the individuals who compose it, can be increased only in the same manner.

Parsimony, and not industry, is the immediate cause of the increase of capital. Industry, indeed, provides the subject which parsimony accumulates. But whatever industry might acquire, if parsimony did not save and store up, the capital would never be the greater.

Parsimony, by increasing the fund which is destined for the maintenance of productive hands, tends to increase the number of those hands whose labour adds to the value of the subject upon which it is bestowed. It tends therefore to increase the exchangeable value of the annual produce of the land and labour of the country. It puts into motion an additional quantity of industry, which gives an additional value to the annual produce.

What is annually saved is as regularly consumed as what is annually spent, and nearly in the same time too;[8] but it is con-

___

[8] [This paradox is arrived at through a confusion between the remuneration of the labourers who produce the additions to the capital and the additions themselves. What is really saved is the additions to the capital, and these are not consumed.]

sumed by a different set of people. That portion of his revenue
which a rich man annually spends, is in most cases consumed
by idle guests, and menial servants, who
leave nothing behind them in return for their
consumption. That portion which he annually saves, as for the sake of the profit it is
immediately employed as a capital, is consumed in the same
manner, and nearly in the same time too, but by a different set
of people, by labourers, manufacturers, and artificers, who reproduce with a profit the value of their annual consumption.
His revenue, we shall suppose, is paid him in money. Had he
spent the whole, the food, clothing, and lodging, which the
whole could have purchased, would have been distributed
among the former set of people. By saving a part of it, as that
part is for the sake of the profit immediately employed as a
capital either by himself or by some other person, the food,
clothing, and lodging, which may be purchased with it, are
necessarily reserved for the latter. The consumption is the
same, but the consumers are different.

What is saved is consumed by productive hands.

By what a frugal man annually saves, he not only affords
maintenance to an additional number of productive hands, for
that or the ensuing year, but, like the founder
of a public workhouse, he establishes as it
were a perpetual fund for the maintenance of
an equal number in all times to come. The
perpetual allotment and destination of this
fund, indeed, is not always guarded by any
positive law, by any trust-right or deed of mortmain. It is always guarded, however, by a very powerful principle, the plain
and evident interest of every individual to whom any share of it
shall ever belong. No part of it can ever afterwards be employed to maintain any but productive hands, without an evident loss to the person who thus perverts it from its proper
destination.

The frugal man establishes a perpetual fund for the employment of productive hands.

The prodigal perverts it in this manner.
By not confining his expence within his income, he encroaches upon his capital. Like
him who perverts the revenues of some pi-

The prodigal perverts such funds to other uses.

ous foundation to profane purposes, he pays the wages of idle-ness with those funds which the frugality of his forefathers had, as it were, consecrated to the maintenance of industry. By diminishing the funds destined for the employment of produc-tive labour, he necessarily diminishes, so far as it[9] depends upon him, the quantity of that labour which adds a value to the subject upon which it is bestowed, and, consequently, the value of the annual produce of the land and labour of the whole country, the real wealth and revenue of its inhabitants. If the prodigality of some was not compensated by the frugality of others, the conduct of every prodigal, by feeding the idle with the bread of the industrious, tends not only to beggar himself, but to impoverish his country.

Though the expence of the prodigal should be altogether in home-made, and no part of it in foreign commodities, its effect upon the productive funds of the society would still be the same. Every year there would still be a certain quantity of food and clothing, which ought to have maintained productive, employed in maintaining unpro-ductive hands. Every year, therefore, there would still be some diminution in what would otherwise have been the value of the annual produce of the land and labour of the country.

Whether he spends on home or for-eign commodities makes no difference.

This expence, it may be said indeed, not being in foreign goods, and not occasioning any exportation of gold and silver, the same quantity of money would remain in the country as before. But if the quantity of food and clothing, which were thus con-sumed by unproductive, had been distrib-uted among productive hands, they would have reproduced, together with a profit, the full value of their consumption. The same quantity of money would in this case equally have remained in the country, and there would besides have been a reproduction of an equal value of

If he had not spent there would have been just as much money in the country and the goods produced by productive hands as well.

[9] [Ed. 1 does not contain "it."]

consumable goods. There would have been two values instead of one.

The same quantity of money, besides, cannot long remain in any country in which the value of the annual produce dimin-

Besides, when the annual produce diminishes, money will go abroad;

ishes. The sole use of money is to circulate consumable goods. By means of it, provisions, materials, and finished work, are bought and sold, and distributed to their proper consumers. The quantity of money, therefore, which can be annually employed in any country, must be determined by the value of the consumable goods annually circulated within it. These must consist either in the immediate produce of the land and labour of the country itself, or in something which had been purchased with some part of that produce. Their value, therefore, must diminish as the value of that produce diminishes, and along with it the quantity of money which can be employed in circulating them. But the money which by this annual diminution of produce is annually thrown out of domestic circulation, will not be allowed to lie idle. The interest of whoever possesses it, requires that it should be employed. But having no employment at home, it will, in spite of all laws and prohibitions, be sent abroad, and employed in purchasing consumable goods which may be of some use at home. Its annual exportation will in this manner continue for some time to add something to the annual consumption of the country beyond the value of its own annual produce. What in the days of its prosperity had been saved from that annual produce, and employed in purchasing gold and silver, will contribute for some little time to support its consumption in adversity. The exportation of gold and silver is, in this case, not the cause, but the effect of its declension, and may even, for some little time, alleviate the misery of that declension.

and on the other hand money will come in when the annual produce increases.

The quantity of money, on the contrary, must in every country naturally increase as the value of the annual produce increases. The value of the consumable goods annually circulated within the society being greater, will require a greater quantity of money to circulate them. A part of the increased produce, therefore, will naturally be employed in purchasing, wherever it is to be had, the additional quantity of gold and silver necessary for circulating the rest. The increase of those metals will in this case be the effect, not the cause, of the public prosperity. Gold and silver are purchased every-where in the same manner. The food, clothing, and lodging, the revenue and maintenance of all those whose labour or stock is employed in bringing them from the mine to the market, is the price paid for them in Peru as well as in England. The country which has this price to pay, will never be long without the quantity of those metals which it has occasion for; and no country will ever long retain a quantity which it has no occasion for.

Whatever, therefore, we may imagine the real wealth and revenue of a country to consist in, whether in the value of the annual produce of its land and labour, as plain reason seems to dictate; or in the quantity of the precious metals which circulate within it, as vulgar prejudices suppose; in either view of the matter, every prodigal appears to be a public enemy, and every frugal man a public benefactor.

So even if the real wealth of a country consisted of its money, the prodigal would be a public enemy.

The effects of misconduct are often the same as those of prodigality. Every injudicious and unsuccessful project in agriculture, mines, fisheries, trade, or manufactures, tends in the same manner to diminish the funds destined for the maintenance of productive labour. In every such project, though the capital is consumed by productive hands only, yet, as by the injudicious manner in which they are employed, they do not reproduce the full value of their consumption, there must always be some diminution in what would otherwise have been the productive funds of the society.

Injudicious employment of capital has the same effect as prodigality.

Frugality and prudence predominate.

It can seldom happen, indeed, that the circumstances of a great nation can be much affected either by the prodigality or misconduct of individuals; the profusion or imprudence of some, being always more than compensated by the frugality and good conduct of others.

With regard to profusion, the principle which prompts to expence, is the passion for present enjoyment; which, though

Prodigality is more intermittent than the desire to better our condition.

sometimes violent and very difficult to be restrained, is in general only momentary and occasional. But the principle which prompts to save, is the desire of bettering our condition, a desire which, though generally calm and dispassionate, comes with us from the womb, and never leaves us till we go into the grave. In the whole interval which separates those two moments, there is scarce perhaps a single instant[10] in which any man is so perfectly and completely satisfied with his situation, as to be without any wish of alteration or improvement of any kind. An augmentation of fortune is the means by which the greater part of men propose and wish to better their condition. It is the means the most vulgar and the most obvious; and the most likely way of augmenting their fortune, is to save and accumulate some part of what they acquire, either regularly and annually, or upon some extraordinary occasions. Though the principle of expence, therefore, prevails in almost all men upon some occasions, and in some men upon almost all occasions, yet in the greater part of men, taking the whole course of their life at an average, the principle of frugality seems not only to predominate, but to predominate very greatly.

With regard to misconduct, the number of prudent and successful undertakings is every-where much greater than that of

Imprudent undertakings are small in number compared to prudent ones.

injudicious and unsuccessful ones. After all our complaints of the frequency of bankruptcies, the unhappy men who fall into this misfortune make but a very small part of the whole number engaged in trade, and all other sorts of business; not much more perhaps than one in a thousand. Bankruptcy is perhaps the great-

---

[10] [Misprinted "instance" in ed. 5, and consequently in some modern editions.]

est and most humiliating calamity which can befal an innocent man. The greater part of men, therefore, are sufficiently careful to avoid it. Some, indeed, do not avoid it; as some do not avoid the gallows.

Great nations are never impoverished[11] by private, though they sometimes are by public prodigality and misconduct. The

Public prodigality and imprudence are more to be feared than private,

whole, or almost the whole public revenue, is in most countries employed in maintaining unproductive hands. Such are the people who compose a numerous and splendid court, a great ecclesiastical establishment, great fleets and armies, who in time of peace produce nothing, and in time of war acquire nothing which can compensate the expence of maintaining them, even while the war lasts. Such people, as they themselves produce nothing, are all maintained by the produce of other men's labour. When multiplied, therefore, to an unnecessary number, they may in a particular year consume so great a share of this produce, as not to leave a sufficiency for maintaining the productive labourers, who should reproduce it next year. The next year's produce, therefore, will be less than that of the foregoing, and if the same disorder should continue, that of the third year will be still less than that of the second. Those unproductive hands, who should be maintained by a part only of the spare revenue of the people, may consume so great a share of their whole revenue, and therefore oblige so great a number to encroach upon their capitals, upon the funds destined for the maintenance of productive labour, that all the frugality and good conduct of individuals may not be able to compensate the waste and degradation of produce occasioned by this violent and forced encroachment.

but are counteracted by private frugality and prudence.

This frugality and good conduct, however, is upon most occasions, it appears from experience, sufficient to compensate, not only the private prodigality and misconduct

---

[11] ["Impoverished" is here equivalent to "made poor," *i.e.*, ruined, not merely to "made poorer."]

of individuals, but the public extravagance of government. The uniform, constant, and uninterrupted effort of every man to better his condition, the principle from which public and national, as well as private opulence is originally derived, is frequently powerful enough to maintain the natural progress of things toward improvement, in spite both of the extravagance of government, and of the greatest errors of administration. Like the unknown principle of animal life, it frequently restores health and vigour to the constitution, in spite, not only of the disease, but of the absurd prescriptions of the doctor.

The annual produce of the land and labour of any nation can be increased in its value by no other means, but by increasing either the number of its productive labourers, or the productive powers of those labourers who had before been employed. The number of its productive labourers, it is evident, can never be much increased, but in consequence of an increase of capital, or of the funds destined for maintaining them. The productive powers of the same number of labourers cannot be increased, but in consequence either of some addition and improvement to those machines and instruments which facilitate and abridge labour; or of a more proper division and distribution of employment. In either case an additional capital is almost always required. It is by means of an additional capital only, that the undertaker of any work can either provide his workmen with better machinery, or make a more proper distribution of employment among them. When the work to be done consists of a number of parts, to keep every man constantly employed in one way, requires a much greater capital than where every man is occasionally employed in every different part of the work. When we compare, therefore, the state of a nation at two different periods, and find, that the annual produce of its land and labour is evidently greater at the latter than at the former, that its lands are better cultivated, its manufacturers more numerous and more flourishing, and its trade more extensive, we may be as-

To increase the produce of a nation an increase of capital is necessary.

If, therefore the produce has increased, we may be sure the capital has increased.

sured that its capital must have increased during the interval between those two periods, and that more must have been added to it by the good conduct of some, than had been taken from it either by the private misconduct of others, or by the public extravagance of government. But we shall find this to have been the case of almost all nations, in all tolerably quiet and peaceful times, even of those who have not enjoyed the most prudent and parsimonious governments. To form a right judgment of it, indeed, we must compare the state of the country at periods somewhat distant from one another. The progress is frequently so gradual, that, at near periods, the improvement is not only not sensible, but from the declension either of certain branches of industry, or of certain districts of the country, things which sometimes happen though the country in general be[12] in great prosperity, there frequently arises a suspicion, that the riches and industry of the whole are decaying.

This has been the case of almost all nations in peaceable times.

The annual produce of the land and labour of England, for example, is certainly much greater than it was, a little more than a century ago, at the restoration of Charles II. Though, at present, few people, I believe, doubt of this, yet during this period, five years have seldom passed away in which some book or pamphlet has not been published, written too with such abilities as to gain some authority with the public, and pretending to demonstrate that the wealth of the nation was fast declining, that the country was depopulated, agriculture neglected, manufactures decaying, and trade undone. Nor have these publications been all party pamphlets, the wretched offspring of falsehood and venality. Many of them have been written by very candid and very intelligent people; who wrote nothing but what they believed, and for no other reason but because they believed it.

England for example from 1660 to 1776,

The annual produce of the land and labour of England again, was certainly much greater at the restoration, than we

---

[12] [Ed. 1 reads "is."]

or from 1558 to 1660. can suppose it to have been about an hundred years before, at the accession of Elizabeth. At this period too, we have all reason to believe, the country was much more advanced in improvement, than it had been about a century before, towards the close of the dissensions between the houses of York and Lancaster. Even then it was, probably, in a better condition than it had been at the Norman conquest, and at the Norman conquest, than during the confusion of the Saxon Heptarchy. Even at this early period, it was certainly a more improved country than at the invasion of Julius Cæsar, when its inhabitants were nearly in the same state with the savages in North America.

In each of those periods, however, there was, not only much private and public profusion, many expensive and unnecessary *though there was much public and private profusion, and many other disorders and misfortunes occurred.* wars, great perversion of the annual produce from maintaining productive to maintain unproductive hands; but sometimes, in the confusion of civil discord, such absolute waste and destruction of stock, as might be supposed, not only to retard, as it certainly did, the natural accumulation of riches, but to have left the country, at the end of the period, poorer than at the beginning. Thus, in the happiest and most fortunate period of them all, that which has passed since the restoration, how many disorders and misfortunes have occurred, which, could they have been foreseen, not only the impoverishment, but the total ruin of the country would have been expected from them? The fire and the plague of London, the two Dutch wars, the disorders of the revolution, the war in Ireland, the four expensive French wars of 1688, 1702,[13] 1742, and 1756, together with the two rebellions of 1715 and 1745. In the course of the four French wars, the nation has contracted more than a hundred and forty-five millions of debt, over and above all the other extraordinary annual expence which they occasioned, so that the whole cannot be computed at less than two hundred millions. So great a share of the annual produce of the land and

---

[13] [Ed. 1 reads "1701."]

labour of the country, has, since the revolution, been employed upon different occasions, in maintaining an extraordinary number of unproductive hands. But had not those wars given this particular direction to so large a capital, the greater part of it would naturally have been employed in maintaining productive hands, whose labour would have replaced, with a profit, the whole value of their consumption. The value of the annual produce of the land and labour of the country, would have been considerably increased by it every year, and every year's increase would have augmented still more that of the following year.[14] More houses would have been built, more lands would have been improved, and those which had been improved before would have been better cultivated, more manufactures would have been established, and those which had been established before would have been more extended; and to what height the real wealth and revenue of the country might, by this time, have been raised, it is not perhaps very easy even to imagine.

But though the profusion of government must, undoubtedly, have retarded the natural progress of England towards wealth and improvement, it has not been *Private frugality and prudence have silently counteracted these circumstances.* able to stop it. The annual produce of its land and labour is, undoubtedly, much greater at present than it was either at the restoration or at the revolution. The capital, therefore, annually employed in cultivating this land, and in maintaining this labour, must likewise be much greater. In the midst of all the exactions of government, this capital has been silently and gradually accumulated by the private frugality and good conduct of individuals, by their universal, continual, and uninterrupted effort to better their own condition. It is this effort, protected by law and allowed by liberty to exert itself in the manner that is most advantageous, which has maintained the progress of England towards opulence and improvement in almost all former times, and which, it is to be hoped, will do so in all future times. England, however, as it

[14] [Ed. 1 reads "the next year."]

has never been blessed with a very parsimonious government, so parsimony has at no time been the characteristical virtue of its inhabitants. It is the highest impertinence and presumption, therefore, in kings and ministers, to pretend to watch over the economy of private people, and to restrain their expence, either by sumptuary laws, or by prohibiting the importation of foreign luxuries. They are themselves always, and without any exception, the greatest spendthrifts in the society. Let them look well after their own expence, and they may safely trust private people with theirs. If their own extravagance does not ruin the state, that of their subjects never will.

As frugality increases, and prodigality diminishes the public capital, so the conduct of those whose expence just equals their revenue, without either accumulating or encroaching, neither increases nor diminishes it. Some modes of expence, however, seem to contribute more to the growth of public opulence than others.

Apart from increase or diminution of capital different kinds of expense may be distinguished.

The revenue of an individual may be spent, either in things which are consumed immediately, and in which one day's expence can neither alleviate nor support that of another; or it may be spent in things more durable, which can therefore be accumulated, and in which every day's expence may, as he chuses, either alleviate or support and heighten the effect of that of the following day. A man of fortune, for example, may either spend his

An individual who spends on durable commodities will be richer than one who spends on perishable ones.

revenue in a profuse and sumptuous table, and in maintaining a great number of menial servants, and a multitude of dogs and horses; or contenting himself with a frugal table and few attendants, he may lay out the greater part of it in adorning his house or his country villa, in useful or ornamental buildings, in useful or ornamental furniture, in collecting books, statues, pictures; or in things more frivolous, jewels, baubles, ingenious trinkets of different kinds; or, what is most trifling of all, in amassing a great wardrobe of fine clothes, like the favourite and minister of a great prince who died a few years ago.[15] Were two men of equal fortune to spend their revenue, the one chiefly in the one way, the other in the other, the magnificence of the person whose expence had been chiefly in durable commodities, would be continually increasing, every day's expence contributing something to support and heighten the effect of that of the following day: that of the other, on the contrary, would be no greater at the end of the period than at the beginning. The former too would, at the end of the period, be the richer man of the two. He would have a stock of goods of some kind or other, which, though it might not be worth all that it cost, would always be worth something. No trace or vestige of the expence of the latter would remain, and the effects of ten or twenty years profusion would be as completely annihilated as if they had never existed.

As the one mode of expence is more favourable than the other to the opulence of an individual, so is it likewise to that

The same thing is true of a nation.

of a nation. The houses, the furniture, the clothing of the rich, in a little time, become useful to the inferior and middling ranks of people. They are able to purchase them when their superiors grow weary of them, and the general accommodation of the whole people is thus gradually improved, when this mode of expence becomes universal among men of fortune. In countries which have long been rich, you will frequently find the inferior ranks of people in possession both of houses and furniture perfectly good and entire, but of which neither the one could have been built, nor the other have been made for their use. What was formerly a seat of the family of Seymour,

[15] [As suggested by Germain Garnier's note on this passage (*Recherches sur la Nature et les Causes de la Richesse des Nations*, 1892, tom. ii., p. 346), this was doubtless the Count of Bruhl, Minister and Great Chamberlain to the King of Poland, who left at his death 365 suits of clothes, all very rich. Jonas Hanway (*Historical Account of the British Trade over the Caspian Sea, with a Journal of Travels from London through Russia into Persia, and back through Russia, Germany and Holland*, 1753, vol.ii., p. 230) says this count had 300 or 400 suits of rich clothes, and had "collected all the finest colours of all the finest cloths, velvets, and silks of all the manufactures, not to mention the different kinds of lace and embroideries of Europe," and also pictures and books, at Dresden. He died in 1764.]

is now an inn upon the Bath road.[16] The marriage-bed of James the First of Great Britain, which his Queen brought with her from Denmark, as a present fit for a sovereign to make to a sovereign, was, a few years ago, the ornament of an ale-house at Dunfermline.[17] In some ancient cities, which either have been long stationary, or have gone somewhat to decay, you will sometimes scarce find a single house which could have been built for its present inhabitants. If you go into those houses too, you will frequently find many excellent, though antiquated pieces of furniture, which are still very fit for use, and which could as little have been made for them. Noble palaces, magnificent villas, great collections of books, statues, pictures, and other curiosities, are frequently both an ornament and an honour, not only to the neighbourhood, but to the whole country to which they belong. Versailles is an ornament and an honour to France, Stowe and Wilton to England. Italy still continues to command some sort of veneration by the number of monuments of this kind which it possesses, though the wealth which produced them has decayed, and though[18] the genius which planned them seems to be extinguished, perhaps from not having the same employment.

The expence too, which is laid out in durable commodities, is favourable, not only to accumulation, but to frugality. If a
The former expence is easier to bring to an end, person should at any time exceed in it, he can easily reform without exposing himself to the censure of the public. To reduce very much the number of his servants, to reform his table from great profusion to great frugality, to lay down his equipage after he has once set it up, are changes which cannot escape the observation of his neighbours, and which are supposed to imply some acknowledgement of preceding bad

---

[16] [This was the Castle Inn at Marlborough, which ceased to be an inn and became Marlborough College in 1843, thus undergoing another vicissitude.]

[17] [The innkeeper, Mrs. Walker, a zealous Jacobite, refused an offer of fifty guineas for the bed, but presented it about 1764 to the Earl of Elgin (John Fernie, *History of the Town and Parish of Dunfermline*, 1815, p. 71), and its remains now form a mantel-piece in the dining-room at Broomhall, near Dunfermline.]

[18] [Ed. 1 does not contain "though."]

conduct. Few, therefore, of those who have once been so unfortunate as to launch out too far into this sort of expence, have afterwards the courage to reform, till ruin and bankruptcy oblige them. But if a person has, at any time, been at too great an expence in building, in furniture, in books or pictures, no imprudence can be inferred from his changing his conduct. These are things in which further expence is frequently rendered unnecessary by former expence; and when a person stops short, he appears to do so, not because he has exceeded his fortune, but because he has satisfied his fancy.

The expence, besides, that is laid out in durable commodities, gives maintenance, commonly, to a greater number of

and gives maintenance to more people.

people, than that which is employed in the most profuse hospitality. Of two or three hundred weight of provisions, which may sometimes be served up at a great festival, one-half, perhaps, is thrown to the dunghill, and there is always a great deal wasted and abused. But if the expence of this entertainment had been employed in setting to work masons, carpenters, upholsterers, mechanics, &c.[19] a quantity of provisions, of equal value, would have been distributed among a still greater number of people, who would have bought them in penny-worths and pound weights, and not have lost or thrown away a single ounce of them. In the one way, besides, this expence maintains productive, in the other unproductive hands. In the one way, therefore, it increases, in the other, it does not increase, the exchangeable value of the annual produce of the land and labour of the country.

I would not, however, by all this be understood to mean, that the one species of expence always betokens a more liberal or generous spirit than the other. When a man of fortune spends

It does not follow that it betokens a more generous spirit.

his revenue chiefly in hospitality, he shares the greater part of it with his friends and companions; but when he employs it in purchasing such durable commodities, he often spends the whole upon his own person, and

---

[19] [Ed. 1 does not contain "&c."]

gives nothing to any body without an equivalent. The latter species of expence, therefore, especially when directed towards frivolous objects, the little ornaments of dress and furniture, jewels, trinkets, gewgaws, frequently indicates, not only a trifling, but a base and selfish disposition. All that I mean is, that the one sort of expence, as it always occasions some accumulation of valuable commodities, as it is more favourable to private frugality, and, consequently, to the increase of the public capital, and as it maintains productive, rather than unproductive hands, conduces more than the other to the growth of public opulence.

CHAPTER IV

OF STOCK LENT AT INTEREST

THE STOCK which is lent at interest is always considered as a capital by the lender. He expects that in due time it is to be restored to him, and that in the mean time the borrower is to pay him a certain annual rent for the use of it. The borrower may use it either as a capital, or as a stock reserved for immediate consumption. If he uses it as a capital, he employs it in the maintenance of productive labourers, who reproduce the value with a profit. He can, in this case, both restore the capital and pay the interest without alienating or encroaching upon any other source of revenue. If he uses it as a stock reserved for immediate consumption, he acts the part of a prodigal, and dissipates in the maintenance of the idle, what was destined for the support of the industrious. He can, in this case, neither restore the capital nor pay the interest, without either alienating or encroaching upon some other source of revenue, such as the property or the rent of land.

Stock lent at interest is a capital to the lender, but may or may not be so to the borrower.

The stock which is lent at interest is, no doubt, occasionally employed in both these ways, but in the former much more frequently than in the latter. The man who borrows in order to spend will soon be ruined, and he who lends to him will generally have occasion to repent of his folly. To borrow or to lend for such a purpose, therefore, is in all cases, where gross usury is out of the question, contrary to the interest of both parties; and though it no doubt happens sometimes that people do both the one and the other; yet, from the regard that all men have

Generally it is so to the borrower,

for their own interest, we may be assured, that it cannot happen so very frequently as we are sometimes apt to imagine. Ask any rich man of common prudence, to which of the two sorts of people he has lent the greater part of his stock, to those who, he thinks, will employ it profitably, or to those who will spend it idly, and he will laugh at you for proposing the question. Even among borrowers, therefore, not the people in the world most famous for frugality, the number of the frugal and industrious surpasses considerably that of the prodigal and idle.

The only people to whom stock is commonly lent, without their being expected to make any very profitable use of it, are

except in case of mortgages effected by country gentlemen.

country gentlemen who borrow upon mortgage. Even they scarce ever borrow merely to spend. What they borrow, one may say, is commonly spent before they borrow it. They have generally consumed so great a quantity of goods, advanced to them upon credit by shopkeepers and tradesmen, that they find it necessary to borrow at interest in order to pay the debt. The capital borrowed replaces the capitals of those shopkeepers and tradesmen, which the country gentlemen could not have replaced from the rents of their estates. It is not properly borrowed in order to be spent, but in order to replace a capital which had been spent before.

Almost all loans at interest are made in money, either of paper, or of gold and silver. But what the borrower really wants,

Loans are made in money, but what the borrower wants and gets is goods.

and what the lender really supplies him with, is not the money, but the money's worth, or the goods which it can purchase. If he wants it as a stock for immediate consumption, it is those goods only which he can place in that stock. If he wants it as a capital for employing industry, it is from those goods only that the industrious can be furnished with the tools, materials, and maintenance, necessary for carrying on their work. By means of the loan, the lender, as it were, assigns to the borrower his right to a certain portion of the annual produce of the land and labour of the country, to be employed as the borrower pleases.[1]

The quantity of stock, therefore, or, as it is commonly expressed, of money which can be lent at interest in any country,

So the quantity of stock which can be lent is determined by the value of that part of the produce which replaces such capital as the owner does not himself employ.

is not regulated by the value of the money, whether paper or coin, which serves as the instrument of the different loans made in that country, but by the value of that part of the annual produce which, as soon as it comes either from the ground, or from the hands of the productive labourers, is destined not only for replacing a capital, but such a capital as the owner does not care to be at the trouble of employing himself. As such capitals are commonly lent out and paid back in money, they constitute what is called the monied interest. It is distinct, not only from the landed, but from the trading and manufacturing interests, as in these last the owners themselves employ their own capitals. Even in the monied interest, however, the money is, as it were, but the deed of assignment, which conveys from one hand to another those capitals which the owners do not care to employ themselves. Those capitals may be greater in almost any proportion, than the amount of the money which serves as the instrument of

This may be much greater than the actual money employed.

their conveyance; the same pieces of money successively serving for many different loans, as well as for many different purchases. A, for example, lends to W a thousand pounds, with which W immediately purchases of B a thousand pounds worth of goods. B having no occasion for the money himself, lends the identical pieces to X, with which X immediately purchases of C another thousand pounds worth of goods. C in the same manner, and for the same reason, lends them to Y, who again purchases goods with them of D. In this manner the same pieces, either of coin or of paper, may, in the course of a few days, serve as the instrument

[1] [*Lectures*, p. 220.]

of three different loans, and of three different purchases, each of which is, in value, equal to the whole amount of those pieces. What the three monied men A, B, and C, assign to the three borrowers, W, X, Y, is the power of making those purchases. In this power consist both the value and the use of the loans. The stock lent by the three monied men, is equal to the value of the goods which can be purchased with it, and is three times greater than that of the money with which the purchases are made. Those loans, however, may be all perfectly well secured, the goods purchased by the different debtors being so employed, as, in due time, to bring back, with a profit, an equal value either of coin or of paper. And as the same pieces of money can thus serve as the instrument of different loans to three, or for the same reason, to thirty times their value, so they may likewise successively serve as the instrument of repayment.

A capital lent at interest may, in this manner, be considered as an assignment from the lender to the borrower of a certain considerable portion of the annual produce; upon condition that the borrower in return shall, during the continuance of the loan, annually assign to the lender a smaller portion, called the interest; and at the end of it, a portion equally considerable with that which had originally been assigned to him, called the repayment. Though money, either coin or paper, serves generally as the deed of assignment both to the smaller, and to the more considerable portion, it is itself altogether different from what is assigned by it.

The money is altogether different from what is actually assigned either as principal or interest.

In proportion as that share of the annual produce which, as soon as it comes either from the ground, or from the hands of the productive labourers, is destined for replacing a capital, increases in any country, what is called the monied interest naturally increases with it. The increase of those particular capitals from which the owners wish to derive a revenue, without being at the trouble of employing them themselves, naturally accompanies

The stock to be lent at interest naturally grows as the whole quantity of stock increases.

the general increase of capitals; or, in other words, as stock increases, the quantity of stock to be lent at interest grows gradually greater and greater.

As the quantity of stock to be lent at interest increases, the interest, or the price which must be paid for the use of that stock, necessarily diminishes, not only from those general causes which make the market price of things commonly diminish as their quantity increases, but from other causes which are peculiar to this particular case. As capitals increase in any country, the profits which can be made by employing them necessarily diminish. It becomes gradually more and more difficult to find within the country a profitable method of employing any new capital. There arises in consequence a competition between different capitals, the owner of one endeavouring to get possession of that employment which is occupied by another. But upon most occasions he can hope to justle that other out of this employment, by no other means but by dealing upon more reasonable terms. He must not only sell what he deals in somewhat cheaper, but in order to get it to sell, he must sometimes too buy it dearer. The demand for productive labour, by the increase of the funds which are destined for maintaining it, grows every day greater and greater. Labourers easily find employment, but the owners of capitals find it difficult to get labourers to employ. Their competition raises the wages of labour, and sinks the profits of stock. But when the profits which can be made by the use of a capital are in this manner diminished, as it were, at both ends, the price which can be paid for the use of it, that is, the rate of interest, must necessarily be diminished with them.

Interest falls as the quantity of stock to be lent increases,

because profits diminish as it becomes more difficult to find a profitable method of employing new capital.

Mr. Locke, Mr. Law, and Mr. Montesquieu, as well as many other writers,[2] seem to have imagined that the increase of the

---

[2] [Locke, *Some Considerations*, ed. of 1696, pp. 6, 10, 11, 81; Law, *Money and Trade*, 2nd ed., 1720, p. 17; Montesquieu, *Esprit des Lois*, liv. xxii., ch. vi. Locke

quantity of gold and silver, in consequence of the discovery of

The notion that it was the discovery of the West Indies which lowered interest has been refuted by Hume.

the Spanish West Indies, was the real cause of the lowering of the rate of interest through the greater part of Europe. Those metals, they say, having become of less value themselves, the use of any particular portion of them necessarily became of less value too, and consequently the price which could be paid for it. This notion, which at first sight seems so plausible, has been so fully exposed by Mr. Hume,[3] that it is, perhaps, unnecessary to say anything more about it. The following very short and plain argument, however, may serve to explain more distinctly the fallacy which seems to have misled those gentlemen.

Before the discovery of the Spanish West Indies, ten per cent. seems to have been the common rate of interest through

If £100 are now required to purchase what £50 would have purchased then, £10 must now be required to purchase what £5 would have purchased then.

the greater part of Europe. It has since that time in different countries sunk to six, five, four, and three per cent. Let us suppose that in every particular country the value of silver has sunk precisely in the same proportion as the rate of interest; and that in those countries, for example, where interest has been reduced from ten to five per cent., the same quantity of silver can now purchase just half the quantity of goods which it could have purchased before. This supposition will not, I believe, be found any-where agreeable to the truth; but it is the most favourable to the opinion which we are going to examine; and even upon this supposition it is utterly impossible that the lowering of the value of silver could have the smallest tendency to lower the rate of interest. If a hundred pounds are in those

and Law suppose that the rate rises and falls with the quantity of money, and Montesquieu specifically attributes the historical fall to the discovery of the American mines. Cantillon disapproves of the common and received idea that an increase of effective money diminishes the rate of interest.—*Essai*, pp. 282–285; see *Lectures*, pp. 219, 220.]

[3] [In his essay, "Of Interest," in *Political Discourses*, 1752.]

countries now of no more value than fifty pounds were then, ten pounds must now be of no more value than five pounds were then. Whatever were the causes which lowered the value of the capital, the same must necessarily have lowered that of the interest, and exactly in the same proportion. The proportion between the value of the capital and that of the interest, must have remained the same, though the rate had never been altered. By altering the rate, on the contrary, the proportion between those two values is necessarily altered. If a hundred pounds now are worth no more than fifty were then, five pounds now can be worth no more than two pounds ten shillings were then. By reducing the rate of interest, therefore, from ten to five per cent., we give for the use of a capital, which is supposed to be equal to one-half of its former value, an interest which is equal to one-fourth only of the value of the former interest.

Any increase in the quantity of silver, while that of the commodities circulated by means of it remained the same, could

An increase in the quantity of silver could only diminish its value.

have no other effect than to diminish the value of that metal. The nominal value of all sorts of goods would be greater, but their real value would be precisely the same as before. They would be exchanged for a greater number of pieces of silver; but the quantity of labour which they could command, the number of people whom they could maintain and employ, would be precisely the same. The capital of the country would be the same, though a greater number of pieces might be requisite for conveying any equal portion of it from one hand to another. The deeds of assignment, like the conveyances of a verbose attorney, would be more cumber-

Nominal wages would be greater, but real wages the same; profits would be the same nominally and really.

some, but the thing assigned would be precisely the same as before, and could produce only the same effects. The funds for maintaining productive labour being the same, the demand for it would be the same. Its price or wages, therefore, though nominally greater, would really be the same. They would be paid in a greater number of pieces of silver; but they would purchase only the same quantity of goods. The profits of stock would be the same both nominally and really. The wages of labour are commonly computed by the quantity of silver which is paid to the labourer. When that is increased, therefore, his wages appear to be increased, though they may sometimes be no greater than before. But the profits of stock are not computed by the number of pieces of silver with which they are paid, but by the proportion which those pieces bear to the whole capital employed. Thus in a particular country five shillings a week are said to be the common wages of labour, and ten per cent. the common profits of stock. But the whole capital of the country being the same as before, the competition between the different capitals of individuals into which it was divided would likewise be the same. They would all trade with the same advantages and disadvantages. The common proportion between capital and profit, therefore, would be the same, and consequently the common interest of money; what can commonly be given for the use of money being necessarily regulated by what can commonly be made by the use of it.

Any increase in the quantity of commodities annually circulated within the country, while that of the money which circulated them remained the same, would, on

An increase in the goods annually circulated would cause a fall of profits and consequently of interest.

the contrary, produce many other important effects, besides that of raising the value of the money. The capital of the country, though it might nominally be the same, would really be augmented. It might continue to be expressed by the same quantity of money, but it would command a greater quantity of labour. The quantity of productive labour which it could maintain and employ would be increased, and consequently the demand for that labour. Its wages would naturally rise with the demand, and yet might appear to sink. They might be paid with a smaller quantity of money, but that smaller quantity might purchase a greater quantity of goods than a greater had done before. The profits of stock would be diminished both really and in appearance. The whole capital of the country being augmented, the competition between the different capitals of which it was composed, would naturally be augmented along with it. The owners of those particular capitals would be obliged to content themselves with a smaller proportion of the produce of that labour which their respective capitals employed. The interest of money, keeping pace always with the profits of stock, might, in this manner, be greatly diminished, though the value of money, or the quantity of goods which any particular sum could purchase, was greatly augmented.

In some countries the interest of money has been prohibited by law. But as something can every-where be made by the use of money, something ought every-where to be paid for the use of it. This regulation, instead of preventing, has been found from experience to increase the evil of usury; the debtor being obliged to pay, not only for the use of the money, but for the risk which his creditor runs by accepting a compensation for that use. He is obliged, if one may say so, to insure his creditor from the penalties of usury.

The prohibition of interest is wrong, and increases the evil of usury.

In countries where interest is permitted, the law, in order to prevent the extortion of usury, generally fixes the highest rate which can be taken without incurring a penalty. This rate ought always to be somewhat above the lowest market price, or the price which is commonly paid for the use of money by those who can give the most undoubted security. If this legal rate should be fixed below the lowest market rate, the effects of this fixation must be nearly the same as those of a total prohibition of interest. The creditor will not lend his money for less than the use of it is worth, and the debtor must pay him for the risk which he runs by accepting the full value of that use. If it is fixed precisely at the lowest market price, it ruins with honest people, who respect the laws of their country, the credit of all those who cannot give the very best security, and obliges them to have recourse to exorbitant usurers. In a country, such as Great Britain, where money is lent to government at three per cent. and to private people upon good security at four, and

Where a maximum rate is fixed, this should be somewhat above the market rate on good security,

four and a half, the present legal rate, five per cent., is perhaps, as proper as any.

The legal rate, it is to be observed, though it ought to be somewhat above, ought not to be much above the lowest mar-

but not much above, or the greater part of loans would be to prodigals and projectors.

ket rate. If the legal rate of interest in Great Britain, for example, was fixed so high as eight or ten per cent., the greater part of the money which was to be lent, would be lent to prodigals and projectors, who alone would be willing to give this high interest. Sober people, who will give for the use of money no more than a part of what they are likely to make by the use of it, would not venture into the competition. A great part of the capital of the country would thus be kept out of the hands which were most likely to make a profitable and advantageous use of it, and thrown into those which were most likely to waste and destroy it. Where the legal rate of interest, on the contrary, is fixed but a very little above the lowest market rate, sober people are universally preferred, as borrowers, to prodigals and projectors. The person who lends money gets nearly as much interest from the former as he dares to take from the latter, and his money is much safer in the hands of the one set of people, than in those of the other. A great part of the capital of the country is thus thrown into the hands in which it is most likely to be employed with advantage.

No law can reduce the common rate of interest below the lowest ordinary market rate at the time when that law is made.

No law can reduce interest below the market rate.

Notwithstanding the edict of 1766, by which the French king attempted to reduce the rate of interest from five to four per cent., money contined to be lent in France at five per cent., the law being evaded in several different ways.[4]

The ordinary market price of land, it is to be observed, depends every-where upon the ordinary market rate of interest.[5]

[4] [Above, p. 127.]

[5] [This seems obvious, but it was distinctly denied by Locke, *Some Considerations*, pp. 83, 84.]

The person who has a capital from which he wishes to derive a revenue, without taking the trouble to employ it himself, delib-

The number of years' purchase commonly paid for land depends on the rate of interest.

erates whether he should buy land with it, or lend it out at interest. The superior security of land, together with some other advantages which almost every-where attend upon this species of property, will generally dispose him to content himself with a smaller revenue from land, than what he might have by lending out his money at interest. These advantages are sufficient to compensate a certain difference of revenue; but they will compensate a certain difference only; and if the rent of land should fall short of the interest of money by a greater difference, nobody would buy land, which would soon reduce its ordinary price. On the contrary, if the advantages should much more than compensate the difference, every body would buy land, which again would soon raise its ordinary price. When interest was at ten per cent., land was commonly sold for ten and twelve years purchase. As interest sunk to six, five, and four per cent., the price of land rose to twenty, five and twenty, and thirty years purchase. The market rate of interest is higher in France than in England; and the common price of land is lower. In England it commonly sells at thirty; in France at twenty years purchase.

CHAPTER V

OF THE DIFFERENT EMPLOYMENT OF CAPITALS

THOUGH ALL capitals are destined for the maintenance of productive labour only, yet the quantity of that labour, which

The quantity of labour put in motion and the value added to the annual produce by capitals vary with their employment.

equal capitals are capable of putting into motion, varies extremely according to the diversity of their employment; as does likewise the value which that employment adds to the annual produce of the land and labour of the country.

A capital may be employed in four different ways: either, first, in procuring the rude produce annually required for the use and consumption of the society; or, secondly, in manufacturing and preparing that rude produce for immediate use and consumption; or, thirdly,

There are four different ways of employing capital,

in transporting either the rude or manufactured produce from the places where they abound to those where they are wanted; or, lastly, in dividing particular portions of either into such small parcels as suit the occasional demands of those who want them. In the first way are employed the capitals of all those who undertake the improvement or cultivation of lands, mines, or fisheries; in the second, those of all master manufacturers; in the third, those of all wholesale merchants; and in the fourth, those of all retailers. It is difficult to conceive that a capital should be employed in any way which may not be classed under some one or other of those four.

all of which are necessary:

Each of those four methods of employing a capital is essentially necessary either to the existence or extension of the other three, or to the general conveniency of the society.

Unless a capital was employed in furnishing rude produce *(1) procuring rude produce,* to a certain degree of abundance, neither manufactures nor trade of any kind could exist.

Unless a capital was employed in manufacturing that part of the rude produce which requires a good deal of preparation before it can be fit for use and consumption, it *(2) manufacturing,* either would never be produced, because there could be no demand for it; or if it was produced spontaneously, it would be of no value in exchange, and could add nothing to the wealth of the society.

Unless a capital was employed in transporting, either the rude or manufactured produce, from the places where it *(3) transportation,* abounds to those where it is wanted, no more of either could be produced than was necessary for the consumption of the neighbourhood. The capital of the merchant exchanges the surplus produce of one place for that of another, and thus encourages the industry and increases the enjoyments of both.

Unless a capital was employed in breaking and dividing certain portions either of the rude or manufactured produce, *and (4) distribution.* into such small parcels as suit the occasional demands of those who want them, every man would be obliged to purchase a greater quantity of the goods he wanted, than his immediate occasions required. If there was no such trade as a butcher, for example, every man would be obliged to purchase a whole ox or a whole sheep at a time. This would generally be inconvenient to the rich, and much more so to the poor. If a poor workman was obliged to purchase a month's or six months provisions at a time, a great part of the stock which he employs as a capital in the instruments of his trade, or in the furniture of his shop, and which yields him a revenue, he would be forced to place in that part of his stock which is reserved for immediate consumption, and which yields him no revenue. Nothing can be more convenient for such a person than to be able to purchase his subsistence from day to day, or even from hour to hour, as he wants it. He is thereby enabled to employ almost his whole stock as a capital. He is thus enabled to furnish work to a greater value, and the profit, which he makes by it in this way, much more than compensates the additional price which the profit of the retailer imposes upon the goods. The prejudices of some political writers against shopkeepers and tradesmen, are altogether without foundation. So far is it from being necessary, either to tax them, or to restrict their numbers, that they can never be multiplied so as to hurt the publick, though they may so as to hurt one another. The quantity of grocery goods, for example, which can be sold in a particular town, is limited by the demand of that town and its[1] neighbourhood. The capital, therefore, which can be employed in the grocery trade cannot exceed what is sufficient to purchase that quantity. If this capital is divided between two different grocers, their competition will tend to make both of them sell cheaper, than if it were in the hands of one only; and if it were divided among twenty, their competition would be just so much the greater, and the chance of their combining together, in order to raise the price, just so much the less. Their competition might perhaps ruin some of themselves; but to take care of this is the business of the parties concerned, and it may safely be trusted to their discretion. It can never hurt either the consumer, or the producer; on the contrary, it must tend to make the retailers both sell cheaper and buy dearer, than if the whole trade was monopolized by one or two persons. Some of them, perhaps, may sometimes decoy a weak customer to buy what he has no occasion for. This evil, however, is of too little importance to deserve the publick attention, nor would it necessarily be prevented by restricting their numbers. It is not the multitude of ale-houses, to give the most suspicious example, that occasions a general disposition to drunkenness among the common people; but that disposition arising from other causes necessarily gives employment to a multitude of ale-houses.

The persons whose capitals are employed in any of those

---

[1] [Ed. 1 does not contain "its."]

four ways are themselves productive labourers. Their labour, when properly directed, fixes and realizes itself in the subject

The employers of such capitals are productive labourers:

or vendible commodity upon which it is bestowed, and generally adds to its price the value at least of their own maintenance and consumption. The profits of the farmer, of the manufacturer, of the merchant, and retailer, are all drawn from the price of the goods which the two first produce, and the two last buy and sell. Equal capitals, however, employed in each of those four different ways, will immediately[2] put into motion very different quantities of productive labour, and augment too in very different proportions the value of the annual produce of the land and labour of the society to which they belong.

The capital of the retailer replaces, together with its profits, that of the merchant of whom he purchases goods, and thereby

the capital of the retailer employs only himself;

enables him to continue his business. The retailer himself is the only productive labourer whom it immediately employs. In his profits, consists the whole value which its employment adds to the annual produce of the land and labour of the society.

The capital of the wholesale merchant replaces, together with their profits, the capitals of the farmers and manufactur-

the capital of the merchant employs sailors and carriers;

ers of whom he purchases the rude and manufactured produce which he deals in, and thereby enables them to continue their respective trades. It is by this service chiefly that he contributes indirectly to support the productive labour of the society, and to increase the value of its annual produce. His capital employs too the sailors and carriers who transport his goods from one place to another, and it augments the price of those goods by the value, not only of his profits, but of their wages. This is all the productive labour which it immediately puts into motion, and all the value which it immediately adds to the annual produce. Its operation in

---

[2] [Ed. 1 does not contain "immediately" here or eight lines lower down.]

both these respects is a good deal superior to that of the capital of the retailer.

Part of the capital of the master manufacturer is employed as a fixed capital in the instruments of his trade, and replaces,

the capital of the manufacturer employs his workmen;

together with its profits, that of some other artificer of whom he purchases them. Part of his circulating capital is employed in purchasing materials, and replaces, with their profits, the capitals of the farmers and miners of whom he purchases them. But a great part of it is always, either annually, or in a much shorter period, distributed among the different workmen whom he employs. It augments the value of those materials by their wages, and by their masters profits upon the whole stock of wages, materials, and instruments of trade employed in the business. It puts immediately[3] into motion, therefore, a much greater quantity of productive labour, and adds a much greater value to the annual produce of the land and labour of the society, than an equal capital in the hands of any wholesale merchant.

No equal capital puts into motion a greater quantity of productive labour than that of the farmer. Not only his labouring

the capital of the farmer employs his servants and his cattle, and adds a much greater value to the annual produce than other capital.

servants, but his labouring cattle, are productive labourers. In agriculture too nature labours along with man; and though her labour costs no expence, its produce has its value, as well as that of the most expensive workmen. The most important operations of agriculture seem intended, not so much to increase, though they do that too, as to direct the fertility of nature towards the production of the plants most profitable to man. A field overgrown with briars and brambles may frequently produce as great a quantity of vegetables as the best cultivated vineyard or corn field. Planting and tillage frequently regulate more than they animate the active fertility of nature; and after all their labour, a great part of the work always remains to be done by her.

---

[3] [Ed. 1 does not contain "immediately."]

The labourers and labouring cattle, therefore, employed in agriculture, not only occasion, like the workmen in manufactures, the reproduction of a value equal to their own consumption, or to the capital which employs them, together with its owners profits; but of a much greater value. Over and above the capital of the farmer and all its profits, they regularly occasion the reproduction of the rent of the landlord. This rent may be considered as the produce of those powers of nature, the use of which the landlord lends to the farmer. It is greater or smaller according to the supposed extent of those powers, or in other words, according to the supposed natural or improved fertility of the land. It is the work of nature which remains after deducting or compensating every thing which can be regarded as the work of man. It is seldom less than a fourth, and frequently more than a third of the whole produce. No equal quantity of productive labour employed in manufactures can ever occasion so great a reproduction. In them nature does nothing; man does all; and the reproduction must always be in proportion to the strength of the agents that occasion it. The capital employed in agriculture, therefore, not only puts into motion a greater quantity of productive labour than any equal capital employed in manufactures, but in proportion too to the quantity of productive labour which it employs, it adds a much greater value to the annual produce of the land and labour of the country, to the real wealth and revenue of its inhabitants. Of all the ways in which a capital can be employed, it is by far the most advantageous to the society.

The capitals employed in the agriculture and in the retail trade of any society, must always reside within that society. Their employment is confined almost to a precise spot, to the farm, and to the shop of the retailer. They must generally too, though there are some exceptions to this, belong to resident members of the society.

Capitals employed in agriculture and retail trade must reside within the country;

The capital of a wholesale merchant, on the contrary, seems to have no fixed or necessary residence anywhere, but may

the capital of the merchant may reside anywhere;

wander about from place to place, according as it can either buy cheap or sell dear.

The capital of the manufacturer must no doubt reside where the manufacture is carried on; but where this shall be is not always necessarily determined. It may frequently be at a great distance both from the

the capital of the manufacturer must be where the manufacture is, but that is not necessarily determined.

place where the materials grow, and from that where the complete manufacture is consumed. Lyons is very distant both from the places which afford the materials of its manufactures, and from those which consume them. The people of fashion in Sicily are cloathed in silks made in other countries, from the materials which their own pro-

duces. Part of the wool of Spain is manufactured in Great Britain, and some part of that cloth is afterwards sent back to Spain.

Whether the merchant whose capital exports the surplus produce of any society be a native or a foreigner, is of very

Whether the merchant who exports belongs to the country or not makes little difference.

little importance. If he is a foreigner, the number of their productive labourers is necessarily less than if he had been a native by one man only; and the value of their annual produce, by the profits of that one man. The sailors or carriers whom he employs may still belong indifferently either to his coun-

try, or to their country, or to some third country, in the same manner as if he had been a native. The capital of a foreigner gives a value to their surplus produce equally with that of a native, by exchanging it for something for which there is a demand at home. It as effectually replaces the capital of the person who produces that surplus, and as effectually enables him to continue his business; the service by which the capital of a wholesale merchant chiefly contributes to support the productive labour, and to augment the value of the annual produce of the society to which he belongs.

It is of more consequence that the capital of the manufacturer should reside within the country. It necessarily puts into

motion a greater quantity of productive labour, and adds a
greater value to the annual produce of the
land and labour of the society. It may, however, be very useful to the country, though it
should not reside within it. The capitals of
the British manufacturers who work up the
flax and hemp annually imported from the
coasts of the Baltic, are surely very useful to
the countries which produce them. Those
materials are a part of the surplus produce of
those countries which, unless it was annually
exchanged for something which is in demand there, would be
of no value, and would soon cease to be produced. The merchants who export it, replace the capitals of the people who
produce it, and thereby encourage them to continue the production; and the British manufacturers replace the capitals of
those merchants.

The capital of the manufacturer will put into motion more native labour if it resides within the country, but may be useful even if outside it.

A particular country, in the same manner as a particular
person, may frequently not have capital sufficient both to improve and cultivate all its lands, to manufac-
ture and prepare their whole rude produce
for immediate use and consumption, and to
transport the surplus part either of the rude
or manufactured produce to those distant
markets where it can be exchanged for
something for which there is a demand at
home. The inhabitants of many different parts of Great Britain
have not capital sufficient to improve and cultivate all their
lands. The wool of the southern counties of Scotland is, a great
part of it, after a long land carriage through very bad roads,
manufactured in Yorkshire, for want of a capital to manufacture it at home. There are many little manufacturing towns in
Great Britain, of which the inhabitants have not capital sufficient to transport the produce of their own industry to those
distant markets where there is demand and consumption for it.
If there are any merchants among them, they are properly only
the agents of wealthier merchants who reside in some of the
greater commercial cities.

Particular coun- tries often have not enough capital for cultivation, manufactures, and transportation.

When the capital of any country is not sufficient for all those three purposes, in proportion as a greater share of it is

In such cases the larger the proportion employed in agriculture, the larger will be the annual produce.

employed in agriculture, the greater will be the quantity of productive labour which it puts into motion within the country; as will likewise be the value which its employment adds to the annual produce of the land and labour of the society. After agriculture, the capital employed in manufactures puts into motion the greatest quantity of productive labour, and adds the greatest value to the annual produce. That which is employed in the trade of exportation, has the least effect of any of the three.

The country, indeed, which has not capital sufficient for all those three purposes, has not arrived at that degree of opulence

The quickest way to make the capital sufficient for all these purposes is to begin with the most profitable.

for which it seems naturally destined. To attempt, however, prematurely and with an insufficient capital, to do all the three, is certainly not the shortest way for a society, no more than it would be for an individual, to acquire a sufficient one. The capital of all the individuals of a nation, has its limits in the same manner as that of a single individual, and is capable of executing only certain purposes. The capital of all the individuals of a nation is increased in the same manner as that of a single individual, by their continually accumulating and adding to it whatever they save out of their income. It is likely to increase the fastest, therefore, when it is employed in the way that affords the greatest revenue to all the inhabitants of the country, as they will thus be enabled to make the greatest savings. But the revenue of all the inhabitants of

That they have done so is the principal cause of the progress of the American colonies.

the country is necessarily in proportion to the value of the annual produce of their land and labour.

It has been the principal cause of the rapid progress of our American colonies towards wealth and greatness, that almost their whole capitals have hitherto been employed in agriculture.⁴ They have no manufactures, those houshold and coarser manufactures excepted which necessarily accompany the progress of agriculture, and which are the work of the women and children in every private family. The greater part both of the exportation and coasting trade of America, is carried on by the capitals of merchants who reside in Great Britain. Even the stores and warehouses from which goods are retailed in some provinces, particularly in Virginia and Maryland, belong many of them to merchants who reside in the mother country, and afford one of the few instances of the retail trade of a society being carried on by the capitals of those who are not resident members of it. Were the Americans, either by combination or by any other sort of violence, to stop the importation of European manufactures, and, by thus giving a monopoly to such of their own countrymen as could manufacture the like goods, divert any considerable part of their capital into this employment, they would retard instead of accelerating the further increase in the value of their annual produce, and would obstruct instead of promoting the progress of their country towards real wealth and greatness. This would be still more the case, were they to attempt, in the same manner, to monopolize to themselves their whole exportation trade.

The course of human prosperity, indeed, seems scarce ever to have been of so long continuance as to enable any

Great countries have scarcely ever acquired sufficient capital for all those purposes.

great country to acquire capital sufficient for all those three purposes; unless, perhaps, we give credit to the wonderful accounts of the wealth and cultivation of China, of those of antient Egypt, and of the antient state of Indostan. Even those three countries, the wealthiest, according to all accounts, that ever were in the world, are chiefly renowned for their superiority in agriculture and manufactures. They do not appear to have been eminent for foreign trade. The antient Egyptians had a superstitious antipathy to

⁴ [Below, pp. 529–530.]

the sea;[5] a superstition nearly of the same kind prevails among the Indians; and the Chinese have never excelled in foreign commerce. The greater part of the surplus produce of all those three countries seems to have been always exported by foreigners, who gave in exchange for it something else for which they found a demand there, frequently gold and silver.

It is thus that the same capital will in any country put into motion a greater or smaller quantity of productive labour, and add a greater or smaller value to the annual produce of its land and labour, according to the different proportions in which it is employed in agriculture, manufactures, and wholesale trade. The difference too is very great, according to the different sorts of wholesale trade in which any part of it is employed.

Different kinds of wholesale trade employ different quantities of productive labour and add different amounts to the annual produce.

All wholesale trade, all buying in order to sell again by wholesale, may be reduced to three different sorts. The home trade, the foreign trade of consumption, and the carrying trade. The home trade is employed in purchasing in one part of the same country, and selling in another, the produce of the industry of that country. It comprehends both the inland and the coasting trade. The foreign trade of consumption is employed in purchasing foreign goods for home consumption. The carrying trade is employed in transacting the commerce of foreign countries, or in carrying the surplus produce of one to another.

There are three different kinds of trade: home, foreign and carrying.

The capital which is employed in purchasing in one part of the country in order to sell in another the produce of the industry of that country, generally replaces by every such operation two distinct capitals that had both been employed in the agricul-

Capital employed in buying in one part of the country

---

[5] [Possibly the supposed authority for this statement is Montesquieu, *Esprit des Lois*, liv. xxi., ch. vi.: "L'Egypte éloignée par la religion et par les mœurs de toute communication avec les étrangers, ne faisait guere de commerce au-dehors.... Les Egyptiens furent si peu jaloux du commerce du dehors qu'ils laissèrent celui de la mer rouge à toutes les petites nations qui y eurent quelque port."]

to sell in another replaces two domestic capitals. ture or manufactures of that country, and thereby enables them to continue that employment. When it sends out from the residence of the merchant a certain value of commodities, it generally brings back in return at least an equal value of other commodities. When both are the produce of domestick industry, it necessarily replaces by every such operation two distinct capitals, which had both been employed in supporting productive labour, and thereby enables them to continue that support. The capital which sends Scotch manufactures to London, and brings back English corn and manufactures to Edinburgh, necessarily replaces, by every such operation, two British capitals which had both been employed in the agriculture or manufactures of Great Britain.

The capital employed in purchasing foreign goods for home-consumption, when this purchase is made with the produce of domestick industry, replaces too, by *Capital employed in importation replaces one domestic and one foreign capital.* every such operation, two distinct capitals; but one of them only is employed in supporting domestick industry. The capital which sends British goods to Portugal, and brings back Portuguese goods to Great Britain, replaces by every such operation only one British capital. The other is a Portuguese one. Though the returns, therefore, of the foreign trade of consumption should be as quick as those of the home-trade, the capital employed in it will give but one-half the encouragement to the industry or productive labour of the country.

But the returns of the foreign trade of consumption are very seldom so quick as those of the home-trade. The returns of the *Its returns are not so quick as those of home trade.* home-trade generally come in before the end of the year, and sometimes three or four times in the year. The returns of the foreign trade of consumption seldom come in before the end of the year, and sometimes not till after two or three years. A capital, therefore, employed in the home-trade will sometimes make twelve operations, or be sent out and returned twelve times, before a capital employed in the foreign trade of consumption has made one. If the capitals are equal, therefore, the one will give four and twenty times more encouragement and support to the industry of the country than the other.[6]

The foreign goods for home-consumption may sometimes be purchased, not with the produce of domestick industry, but with some other foreign goods. These last, however, must have been purchased either immediately with the produce of domestick industry, or with something else that had been purchased with it; for the case of war and conquest excepted, foreign goods can never be acquired but in exchange for something that had been produced at home, either immediately, or after two or more different exchanges. The effects, therefore, of a capital employed in such a round-about foreign trade of consumption, are, in every respect, the same as those of one employed in the most direct trade of the same kind, except that the final returns are likely to be still more distant, as they must depend upon the returns of two or three distinct foreign trades. If the flax and hemp of Riga are purchased with the tobacco of Virginia, which had been purchased with British manufactures, the merchant must wait for the returns of two distinct foreign trades before he can employ the same capital in re-purchasing a like quantity of British manufactures. If the tobacco of Virginia had been purchased, not with British manufactures, but with the sugar and rum of Jamaica which had been purchased with those manufactures, he must wait for the returns of three. If those two or three distinct foreign trades should happen to be carried on by two or three distinct merchants, of whom the second buys the goods imported by the first, and the third buys those imported by the second, in order to export them again, each merchant indeed will in this case receive the returns of his own capital more quickly; but the final returns of the whole capital employed in the trade will be just as slow as ever. Whether the whole capital employed in such a round-about trade belong to one merchant

Roundabout foreign trade has the same effect as direct.

[6] [If this doctrine as to the advantage of quick returns had been applied earlier in the chapter, it would have made havoc of the argument as to the superiority of agriculture.]

or to three, can make no difference with regard to the country, though it may with regard to the particular merchants. Three times a greater capital must in both cases be employed, in order to exchange a certain value of British manufactures for a certain quantity of flax and hemp, than would have been necessary, had the manufactures and the flax and hemp been directly exchanged for one another. The whole capital employed, therefore, in such a round-about foreign trade of consumption, will generally give less encouragement and support to the productive labour of the country, than an equal capital employed in a more direct trade of the same kind.

Whatever be the foreign commodity with which the foreign goods for home-consumption are purchased, it can occasion no essential difference either in the nature of the trade, or in the encouragement and support which it can give to the productive labour of the country from which it is carried on. If they are purchased with the gold of Brazil, for example, or with the silver of Peru, this gold and silver, like the tobacco of Virginia, must have been purchased with something that either was the produce of the industry of the country, or that had been purchased with something else that was so. So far, therefore, as the productive labour of the country is concerned, the foreign trade of consumption which is carried on by means of gold and silver, has all the advantages and all the inconveniences of any other equally round-about foreign trade of consumption, and will replace just as fast or just as slow the capital which is immediately employed in supporting that productive labour. It seems even to have one advantage over any other equally round-about foreign trade. The transportation of those metals from one place to another, on account of their small bulk and great value, is less expensive than that of almost any other foreign goods of equal value. Their freight is much less, and their insurance not greater; and no goods, besides, are less liable to suffer by the carriage.[7] An equal quantity of foreign goods,

Foreign trade carried on by means of gold and silver is in no way different from the rest.

---

[7] [The second part of this sentence is not in Ed. 1.]

therefore, may frequently be purchased with a smaller quantity of the produce of domestick industry, by the intervention of gold and silver, than by that of any other foreign goods. The demand of the country may frequently, in this manner, be supplied more completely and at a smaller expence than in any other. Whether, by the continual exportation of those metals, a trade of this kind is likely to impoverish the country from which it is carried on, in any other way, I shall have occasion to examine at great length hereafter.[8]

That part of the capital of any country which is employed in the carrying trade, is altogether withdrawn from porting the

Capital employed in the carrying trade replaces two foreign capitals.

productive labour of that particular country, to support that of some foreign countries. Though it may replace by every operation two distinct capitals, yet neither of them belongs[9] to that particular country. The capital of the Dutch merchant, which carries the corn of Poland to Portugal, and brings back the fruits and wines of Portugal to Poland, replaces by every such operation two capitals, neither of which had been employed in supporting the productive labour of Holland; but one of them in supporting that of Poland, and the other that of Portugal. The profits only return regularly to Holland, and constitute the whole addition which this trade necessarily makes to the annual produce of the land and labour of that country. When, indeed, the carrying trade of

It may employ ships and sailors belonging to the country, but this is not always the case,

any particular country is carried on with the ships and sailors of that country, that part of the capital employed in it which pays the freight, is distributed among, and puts into motion, a certain number of productive labourers of that country. Almost all nations that have had any considerable share of the carrying trade have, in fact, carried it on in this manner. The trade itself has probably derived its name from it, the people of such countries being the carriers to other countries. It does not,

---

[8] [Bk. iv.]

[9] [Ed. 1 reads "belong."]

however, seem essential to the nature of the trade that it should be so. A Dutch merchant may, for example, employ his capital in transacting the commerce of Poland and Portugal, by carrying part of the surplus produce of the one to the other, not in Dutch, but in British bottoms. It may be presumed, that he actually does so upon some particular occasions. It is upon this account, however, that the carrying trade has been supposed peculiarly advantageous to such a country as Great Britain, of which the defence and security depend upon the number of its sailors and shipping. But the same capital may employ as many sailors and shipping, either in the foreign trade of consumption, or even in the home-trade, when carried on by coasting vessels, as it could in the carrying trade. The number of sailors and shipping which any particular capital can employ, does not depend upon the nature of the trade, but partly upon the bulk of the goods in proportion to their value, and partly upon the distance of the ports between which they are to be carried; chiefly upon the former of those two circumstances. The coal-trade from Newcastle to London, for example, employs more shipping than all the carrying trade of England, though the ports are at no great distance. To force, therefore, by extraordinary encouragements, a larger share of the capital of any country into the carrying trade, than what would naturally go to it, will not always necessarily increase the shipping of that country.

and equal capital employed in importation or coasting trade may employ as many ships and men.

Capital in home trade therefore supports more productive labour than capital employed in foreign trade, which, however, supports more than capital in the carrying trade.

The capital, therefore, employed in the home-trade of any country will generally give encouragement and support to a greater quantity of productive labour in that country, and increase the value of its annual produce more than an equal capital employed in the foreign trade of consumption: and the capital employed in this latter trade has in both these respects a still greater advantage over an equal capital employed in the carrying trade. The riches, and so far as power depends upon riches, the power of every country, must always be in proportion to the value of its annual produce, the fund from which all taxes must ultimately be paid. But the great object of the political œconomy of every country, is to increase the riches and power of that country. It ought, therefore, to give no preference nor superior encouragement to the foreign trade of consumption above the home trade, nor to the carrying trade above either of the other two. It ought neither to force nor to allure into either of those two channels, a greater share of the capital of the country than what would naturally flow into them of its own accord.

Political economy ought consequently not to allure capital into the foreign or the carrying trade

Each of those different branches of trade, however, is not only advantageous, but necessary and unavoidable, when the course of things, without any constraint or violence, naturally introduces it.

though each is advantageous when naturally introduced.

When the produce of any particular branch of industry exceeds what the demand of the country requires, the surplus must be sent abroad, and exchanged for something for which there is a demand at home. Without such exportation, a part of the productive labour of the country must cease,[10] and the value of its annual produce diminish. The land and labour of Great Britain produce generally more corn, woollens, and hard ware, than the demand of the home-market requires. The surplus part of them, therefore, must be sent abroad, and exchanged for something for which there is a demand at home. It is only by means of such exportation, that this surplus can acquire a value sufficient to compensate the labour and expence of producing it. The neighbourhood of the sea coast, and the banks of all navigable rivers are advantageous situations for industry, only be-

The surplus of the produce of particular branches of industry must be sent abroad.

[10] [But why may not the labour be diverted to the production of "something for which there is a demand at home"? The "corn, woollens and hardware" immediately below perhaps suggest that it is supposed the country has certain physical characteristics which compel its inhabitants to produce particular commodities.]

cause they facilitate the exportation and exchange of such surplus produce for something else which is more in demand there.

When the foreign goods which are thus purchased with the surplus produce of domestic industry exceed the demand of the home-market, the surplus part of them must be sent abroad again, and exchanged for something more in demand at home. About ninety-six thousand hogsheads of tobacco are annually purchased in Virginia and Maryland, with a part of the surplus produce of British industry. But the demand of Great Britain does not require, perhaps, more than fourteen thousand.[11] If the remaining eighty-two thousand, therefore, could not be sent abroad and exchanged for something more in demand at home, the importation of them must cease immediately, and with it the productive labour of all those inhabitants of Great Britain, who are at present employed in preparing the goods with which these eighty-two thousand hogsheads are annually purchased. Those goods, which are part of the produce of the land and labour of Great Britain, having no market at home, and being deprived of that which they had abroad, must cease to he produced. The most round-about foreign trade of consumption, therefore, may, upon some occasions, be as necessary for supporting the productive labour of the country, and the value of its annual produce, as the most direct.

Foreign goods obtained in exchange must often be re-exported.

When the capital stock of any country is increased to such a degree, that it cannot be all employed in supplying the consumption, and supporting the productive labour of that particular country, the surplus part of it naturally disgorges itself into the carrying trade, and is employed in performing the same offices to other countries. The carrying trade is the natural effect and symptom of great na-

When the other employments are full, the surplus capital disgorges itself into the carrying trade, which is a symptom rather than a cause of great national wealth.

[11] [Below, p. 630. The figures 96,000 and 13,500 are given in the continuation of Anderson's *Commerce*, A.D. 1775, ed. of 1801, vol. iv., p. 187.]

tional wealth; but it does not seem to be the natural cause of it. Those statesmen who have been disposed to favour it with particular encouragements, seem to have mistaken the effect and symptom for the cause. Holland, in proportion to the extent of the land and the number of its inhabitants, by far the richest country in Europe, has, accordingly, the greatest share of the carrying trade of Europe. England, perhaps the second richest country of Europe, is likewise supposed to have a considerable share of it; though what commonly passes for the carrying trade of England, will frequently, perhaps, be found to be no more than a round-about foreign trade of consumption. Such are, in a great measure, the trades which carry the goods of the East and West Indies, and of America, to different European markets. Those goods are generally purchased either immediately with the produce of British industry, or with something else which had been purchased with that produce, and the final returns of those trades are generally used or consumed in Great Britain. The trade which is carried on in British bottoms between the different ports of the Mediterranean, and some trade of the same kind carried on by British merchants between the different ports of India, make, perhaps, the principal branches of what is properly the carrying trade of Great Britain.

The extent of the home-trade and of the capital which can be employed in it, is necessarily limited by the value of the surplus produce of all those distant places within the country which

The possible extent of the carrying trade is much the greatest.

have occasion to exchange their respective productions with one another. That of the foreign trade of consumption, by the value of the surplus produce of the whole country and of what can be purchased with it. That of the carrying trade, by the value of the surplus produce of all the different countries in the world. Its possible extent, therefore, is in a manner infinite in comparison of that of the other two, and is capable of absorbing the greatest capitals.

The consideration of his own private profit, is the sole motive which determines the owner of any capital to employ it either in agriculture, in manufactures, or in some particular branch of the wholesale or retail trade. The different quantities of productive labour which it may put into motion, and the different values which it may add to the annual produce of the land and labour of the society, according as it is employed in one or other of those different ways, never enter into his thoughts. In countries, therefore, where agriculture is the most profitable of all employments, and farming and improving the most direct roads to a splendid fortune, the capitals of individuals will naturally be employed in the manner most advantageous to the whole society. The profits of agriculture, however, seem to have no superiority over those of other employments in any part of Europe. Projectors, indeed, in every corner of it, have within these few years amused the public with most magnificent accounts of the profits to be made by the cultivation and improvement of land. Without entering into any particular discussion of their calculations, a very simple observation may satisfy us that the result of them must be false. We see every day the most splendid fortunes that have been acquired in the course of a single life by trade and manufactures, frequently from a very small capital, sometimes from no capital. A single instance of such a fortune acquired by agriculture in the same time, and from such a capital, has not, perhaps, occurred in Europe during the course of the present century. In all the great countries of Europe, however, much good land still remains uncultivated, and the greater part of what is cultivated, is far from being improved to the degree of which it is capable. Agriculture, therefore, is almost everywhere capable of absorbing a much greater capital than has ever yet been employed in it. What circumstances in the policy of Europe have given the trades which are carried on in towns so great an advantage over that which is carried on in the country, that private persons frequently find it more for their advantage to employ their capitals in the most distant carrying trades of Asia and America, than in the improvement and cultivation of the most fertile fields in their own neighbourhood, I shall endeavour to explain at full length in the two following books.

Agriculture does not yield sufficient profit to attract all the capital which it might absorb.

The reason will be explained in the next two books.

BOOK III

OF THE DIFFERENT PROGRESS OF OPULENCE
IN DIFFERENT NATIONS

CHAPTER I

OF THE NATURAL PROGRESS OF OPULENCE

THE GREAT commerce of every civilized society, is that carried on between the inhabitants of the town and those of the country. It consists in the exchange of rude for manufactured produce, either immediately, or by the intervention of money, or of some sort of paper which represents money. The country supplies the town with the means of subsistence, and the materials of manufacture. The town repays this supply by sending back a part of the manufactured produce to the inhabitants of the country. The town, in which there neither is nor can be any reproduction of substances,[1] may very properly be said to gain its whole wealth and subsistence from the country. We must not, however, upon this account, imagine that the gain of the town is the loss of the country. The gains of both are mutual and reciprocal, and the division of labour is in this, as in all other cases, advantageous to all the different persons employed in the various occupations into which it is subdivided. The inhabitants of the country purchase of the town a greater quantity of manufactured goods, with the produce of a much smaller quantity of their own labour, than they must have employed had they attempted to prepare them themselves. The town affords a market for the surplus produce of the country, or what is over and above the maintenance of the cultivators, and it is there that the inhabitants of the country exchange it for

The great commerce is that between town and country, which is obviously advantageous to both.

[1] [The error that agriculture produces substances and manufacture only alters them is doubtless at the bottom of much of the support gained by the theory of productive and unproductive labour.]

something else which is in demand among them. The greater
the number and revenue of the inhabitants of the town, the
more extensive is the market which it affords to those of
the country; and the more extensive that market, it is always
the more advantageous to a great number. The corn which
grows within a mile of the town, sells there for the same price
with that which comes from twenty miles distance. But the
price of the latter must generally, not only pay the expence of
raising and bringing it to market, but afford too the ordinary
profits of agriculture to the farmer. The proprietors and cultivators of the country, therefore, which lies in the neighbourhood
of the town, over and above the ordinary profits of agriculture,
gain, in the price of what they sell, the whole value of the carriage of the like produce that is brought from more distant
parts, and they save, besides, the whole value of this carriage
in the price of what they buy. Compare the cultivation of the
lands in the neighbourhood of any considerable town, with that
of those which lie at some distance from it, and you will easily
satisfy yourself how much the country is benefited by the commerce of the town. Among all the absurd speculations that
have been propagated concerning the balance of trade, it has
never been pretended that either the country loses by its commerce with the town, or the town by that with the country
which maintains it.

As subsistence is, in the nature of things, prior to conveniency and luxury, so the industry which procures the former,
_____ must necessarily be prior to that which min-
The cultivation of isters to the latter. The cultivation and im-
the country must provement of the country, therefore, which
be prior to the affords subsistence, must, necessarily, be
increase of the affords subsistence, must, necessarily, be
town, prior to the increase of the town, which fur-
_____ nishes only the means of conveniency and
luxury. It is the surplus produce of the country only, or what is
over and above the maintenance of the cultivators, that constitutes the subsistence of the town, which can therefore increase only with the increase of this surplus produce. The
town, indeed, may not always derive its whole subsistence
from the country in its neighbourhood, or even from the terri-

though the town may sometimes be distant from the country from which it derives its subsistence.

tory to which it belongs, but from very distant countries; and this, though it forms no exception from the general rule, has occasioned considerable variations in the progress of opulence in different ages and nations.

That order of things which necessity imposes in general, though not in every particular country, is, in every particular country, promoted by the natural inclinations of man.

This order of things is favoured by the natural preference of man for agriculture.

If human institutions had never thwarted those natural inclinations, the towns could no-where have increased beyond what the improvement and cultivation of the territory in which they were situated could support; till such time, at least, as the whole of that territory was completely cultivated and improved. Upon equal, or nearly equal profits, most men will chuse to employ their capitals rather in the improvement and cultivation of land, than either in manufactures or in foreign trade. The man who employs his capital in land, has it more under his view and command, and his fortune is much less liable to accidents, than that of the trader, who is obliged frequently to commit it, not only to the winds and the waves, but to the more uncertain elements of human folly and injustice, by giving great credits in distant countries to men, with whose character and situation he can seldom be thoroughly acquainted. The capital of the landlord, on the contrary, which is fixed in the improvement of his land, seems to be as well secured as the nature of human affairs can admit of. The beauty of the country besides, the pleasures of a country life, the tranquillity of mind which it promises, and wherever the injustice of human laws does not disturb it, the independency which it really affords, have charms that more or less attract every body; and as to cultivate the ground was the original destination of man, so in every stage of his existence he seems to retain a predilection for this primitive employment.

Without the assistance of some artificers, indeed, the cultivation of land cannot be carried on, but with great inconve-

niency and continual interruption. Smiths, carpenters, wheel-
wrights, and plough-wrights, masons, and bricklayers, tanners,
shoemakers, and taylors, are people, whose
service the farmer has frequent occasion for.
Such artificers too stand, occasionally, in
need of the assistance of one another; and as
their residence is not, like that of the farmer,
necessarily tied down to a precise spot, they
naturally settle in the neighbourhood of one
another, and thus form a small town or village. The butcher, the brewer, and the baker,
soon join them, together with many other artificers and retailers, necessary or useful for
supplying their occasional wants, and who contribute still further to augment the town. The inhabitants of the town and
those of the country are mutually the servants of one another.
The town is a continual fair or market, to which the inhabitants
of the country resort, in order to exchange their rude for manufactured produce.[2] It is this commerce which supplies the inhabitants of the town both with the materials of their work, and
the means of their subsistence. The quantity of the finished
work which they sell to the inhabitants of the country, necessarily regulates the quantity of the materials and provisions
which they buy. Neither their employment nor subsistence,
therefore, can augment, but in proportion to the augmentation
of the demand from the country for finished work; and this demand can augment only in proportion to the extension of improvement and cultivation. Had human institutions, therefore,
never disturbed the natural course of things, the progressive
wealth and increase of the towns would, in every political society, be consequential, and in proportion to the improvement
and cultivation of the territory or country.

In our North American colonies, where uncultivated land is
still to be had upon easy terms, no manufactures for distant
sale have ever yet been established in any of their towns. When

Cultivators require the assistance of artificers, who settle together and form a village, and their employment augments with the improvement of the country.

---

[2] [This passage, from the beginning of the paragraph, may well have been suggested by Cantillon, *Essai*, pp. 11–22.]

an artificer has acquired a little more stock than is necessary for carrying on his own business in supplying the neighbour-ing country, he does not, in North America, attempt to establish with it a manufacture for more distant sale, but employs it in the pur-chase and improvement of uncultivated land. From artificer he becomes planter, and nei-ther the large wages nor the easy subsistence which that country affords to artificers, can bribe him rather to work for other people than for himself. He feels that an artificer is the servant of his customers, from whom he derives his subsis-tence; but that a planter who cultivates his own land, and de-rives his necessary subsistence from the labour of his own family, is really a master, and independent of all the world.

In the American colonies an artifi-cer who has ac-quired sufficient stock becomes a planter instead of manufacturing for distant sale,

In countries, on the contrary, where there is either no uncul-tivated land, or none that can be had upon easy terms, every ar-tificer who has acquired more stock than he can employ in the occasional jobs of the neighbourhood, endeavours to prepare work for more distant sale. The smith erects some sort of iron, the weaver some sort of linen or woollen manufactory. Those different manufactures come, in process of time, to be gradually subdivided, and thereby im-proved and refined in a great variety of ways, which may easily be conceived, and which it is therefore unnecessary to explain any further.

as in countries where no unculti-vated land can be procured.

In seeking for employment to a capital, manufactures are, upon equal or nearly equal profits, naturally preferred to for-eign commerce, for the same reason that agriculture is naturally preferred to manu-factures. As the capital of the landlord or farmer is more secure than that of the manu-facturer, so the capital of the manufacturer, being at all times more within his view and command, is more secure than that of the foreign merchant. In every period, in-deed, of every society, the surplus part both of the rude and manufactured produce, or that for which there is no demand at

Manufactures are naturally pre-ferred to foreign commerce.

home, must be sent abroad in order to be exchanged for something for which there is some demand at home. But whether the capital, which carries this surplus produce abroad, be a foreign or a domestic one, is of very little importance. If the society has not acquired sufficient capital both to cultivate all its lands, and to manufacture in the completest manner the whole of its[3] rude produce, there is even a considerable advantage that that rude produce should[4] be exported by a foreign capital, in order that the whole stock of the society may be employed in more useful purposes. The wealth of ancient Egypt, that of China and Indostan, sufficiently demonstrate that a nation may attain a very high degree of opulence, though the greater part of its exportation trade be carried on by foreigners. The progress of our North American and West Indian colonies would have been much less rapid, had not capital but what belonged to themselves been employed in exporting their surplus produce.

According to the natural course of things, therefore, the greater part of the capital of every growing society is, first, directed to agriculture, afterwards to manufactures, and last of all to foreign commerce. This order of things is so very natural, that in every society that had any territory, it has always, I believe, been in some degree observed. Some of their lands must have been cultivated before any considerable towns could be established, and some sort of coarse industry of the manufacturing kind must have been carried on in those towns, before they could well think of employing themselves in foreign commerce.

So the natural course of things is first agriculture, then manufactures, and finally foreign commerce.

But though this natural order of things must have taken place in some degree in every such society, it has, in all the modern states of Europe, been, in many respects, entirely inverted. The foreign commerce of some of their cities has in-

But this order has been in many respects inverted.

---

[3] [Ed. 1 reads "their."]

[4] [Ed. 1 reads "considerable advantage that it should."]

troduced all their finer manufactures, or such as were fit for distant sale; and manufactures and foreign commerce together, have given birth to the principal improvements of agriculture. The manners and customs which the nature of their original government introduced, and which remained after that government was greatly altered, necessarily forced them into this unnatural and retrograde order.

CHAPTER II

OF THE DISCOURAGEMENT OF AGRICULTURE IN THE ANCIENT STATE OF EUROPE AFTER THE FALL OF THE ROMAN EMPIRE

WHEN THE German and Scythian nations over-ran the western provinces of the Roman empire, the confusions which followed so great a revolution lasted for several centuries. The rapine and violence which the barbarians exercised against the ancient inhabitants, interrupted the commerce between the towns and the country. The towns were deserted, and the country was left uncultivated, and the western provinces of Europe, which had enjoyed a considerable degree of opulence under the Roman empire, sunk into the lowest state of poverty and barbarism. During the continuance of those confusions, the chiefs and principal leaders of those nations, acquired or usurped to themselves the greater part of the lands of those countries. A great part of them was uncultivated; but no part of them, whether cultivated or uncultivated, was left without a proprietor. All of them were engrossed, and the greater part by a few great proprietors.

After the fall of the Roman Empire all the land of Western Europe was engrossed, chiefly by large proprietors.

This original engrossing of uncultivated lands, though a great, might have been but a transitory evil. They might soon have been divided again, and broke into small parcels either by succession or by alienation. The law of primogeniture hindered them from being divided by succession: the introduction of en-

Primogeniture and entails prevented the great estates being divided.

tails prevented their being broke into small parcels by alienation.[1]

When land, like moveables, is considered as the means only of subsistence and enjoyment, the natural law of succession divides it, like them, among all the children of the family; of all of whom the subsistence and enjoyment may be supposed equally dear to the father. This natural law of succession accordingly took place among the Romans, who made no more distinction between elder and younger, between male and female, in the inheritance of lands, than we do in the distribution of moveables. But when land was considered as the means, not of subsistence merely, but of power and protection, it was thought better that it should descend undivided to one. In those disorderly times, every great landlord was a sort of petty prince. His tenants were his subjects. He was their judge, and in some respects their legislator in peace, and their leader in war. He made war according to his own discretion, frequently against his neighbours, and sometimes against his sovereign. The security of a landed estate, therefore, the protection which its owner could afford to those who dwelt on it, depended upon its greatness. To divide it was to ruin it, and to expose every part of it to be oppressed and swallowed up by the incursions of its neighbours. The law of primogeniture, therefore, came to take place, not immediately, indeed, but in process of time, in the succession of landed estates, for the same reason that it has generally taken place in that of monarchies, though not always at their first institution. That the power, and consequently the security of the monarchy, may not be weakened by division, it must descend entire to one of the children. To which of them so important a preference shall be given, must be determined by some general rule, founded not upon the doubtful distinctions of personal merit, but upon some plain and evident difference which can admit of no dis-

Primogeniture was introduced because every great landlord was a petty prince.

[1] [Primogeniture and entails are censured as inimical to agriculture in *Lectures*, pp. 120, 124, 228.]

pute. Among the children of the same family, there can be no indisputable difference but that of sex, and that of age. The male sex is universally preferred to the female; and when all other things are equal, the elder every-where takes place of the younger. Hence the origin of the right of primogeniture, and of what is called lineal succession.[2]

Laws frequently continue in force long after the circumstances, which first gave occasion to them, and which could alone render them reasonable, are no more. In the present state of Europe, the proprietor of a single acre of land is as perfectly secure of his possession as the proprietor of a hundred thousand. The right of primogeniture, however, still continues to be respected, and as of all institutions it is the fittest to support the pride of family distinctions, it is still likely to endure for many centuries. In every other respect, nothing can be more contrary to the real interest of a numerous family, than a right which in order to enrich one, beggars all the rest of the children.

It is now unreasonable, but supports the pride of family distinctions.

Entails are the natural consequences of the law of primogeniture. They were introduced to preserve a certain lineal succession, of which the law of primogeniture first gave the idea, and to hinder any part of the original estate from being carried out of the proposed line either by gift, or devise, or alienation; either by the folly, or by the misfortune of any of its successive owners. They were altogether unknown to the Romans. Neither their substitutions nor fideicommisses bear any resemblance to entails, though some French lawyers have thought proper to dress the modern institution in the language and garb[3] of those antient ones.[4]

Entails have the same origin,

and are now absurd.

When great landed estates were a sort of principalities, entails might not be unreasonable. Like what are called the fundamental

[2] [*Lectures*, pp. 117–118.]

[3] [Ed. 1 reads "form."]

[4] [In *Lectures*, p. 123, the Roman origin of entails appears to be accepted.]

laws of some monarchies, they might frequently hinder the security of thousands from being endangered by the caprice or extravagance of one man. But in the present state of Europe, when small as well as great estates derive their security from the laws of their country, nothing can be more completely absurd. They are founded upon the most absurd of all suppositions, the supposition that every successive generation of men have not an equal right to the earth, and to all that it possesses; but that the property of the present generation should be restrained and regulated according to the fancy of those who died perhaps five hundred years ago.[5] Entails, however, are still respected through the greater part of Europe, in those countries particularly in which noble birth is a necessary qualification for the enjoyment either of civil or military honours. Entails are thought necessary for maintaining this exclusive privilege of the nobility to the great offices and honours of their country; and that order having usurped one unjust advantage over the rest of their fellow-citizens, lest their poverty should render it ridiculous, it is thought reasonable that they should have another. The common law of England, indeed, is said to abhor perpetuities, and they are accordingly more restricted there than in any other European monarchy; though even England is not altogether without them. In Scotland more than one-fifth, perhaps more than one-third part of the whole lands of the country, are at present supposed to be[6] under strict entail.

Great tracts of uncultivated land were, in this manner, not only engrossed by particular families, but the possibility

Great proprietors are seldom great improvers.

of their being divided again was as much as possible precluded for ever. It seldom happens, however, that a great proprietor is a great improver. In the disorderly times which gave birth to those barbarous institutions, the great proprietor was sufficiently employed in defending his own territo-

---

[5] [This passage follows *Lectures*, p. 124, rather closely, reproducing even the repetition of "absurd."]

[6] [Ed. 1 does not contain "supposed to be."]

ries, or in extending his jurisdiction and authority over those of
his neighbours. He had no leisure to attend to the cultivation
and improvement of land. When the establishment of law and
order afforded him this leisure, he often wanted the inclination,
and almost always the requisite abilities. If the expence of his
house and person either equalled or exceeded his revenue, as it
did very frequently, he had no stock to employ in this manner.
If he was an œconomist, he generally found it more profitable
to employ his annual savings in new purchases, than in the improvement of his old estate. To improve land with profit, like
all other commercial projects, requires an exact attention to
small savings and small gains, of which a man born to a great
fortune, even though naturally frugal, is very seldom capable.
The situation of such a person naturally disposes him to attend
rather to ornament which pleases his fancy, than to profit for
which he has so little occasion. The elegance of his dress, of
his equipage, of his house, and household furniture, are objects
which from his infancy he has been accustomed to have some
anxiety about. The turn of mind which this habit naturally
forms, follows him when he comes to think of the improvement of land. He embellishes perhaps four or five hundred
acres in the neighbourhood of his house, at ten times the expence which the land is worth after all his improvements; and
finds that if he was to improve his whole estate in the same
manner, and he has little taste for any other, he would be a
bankrupt before he had finished the tenth part of it. There still
remain in both parts of the united kingdom some great estates
which have continued without interruption in the hands of the
same family since the times of feudal anarchy. Compare the
present condition of those estates with the possessions of
the small proprietors in their neighbourhood, and you will require no other argument to convince you how unfavourable
such extensive property is to improvement.[7]

If little improvement was to be expected from such great
proprietors, still less was to be hoped for from those who occupied the land under them. In the ancient state of Europe, the

[7] [This remark follows *Lectures*, p. 228. Cp. below, pp. 519, 520, 530.]

occupiers of land were all tenants at will. They were all or almost all slaves; but their slavery was of a milder kind

The occupiers were not likely to improve, as they were slaves attached to the land and incapable of acquiring property. than that known among the ancient Greeks and Romans, or even in our West Indian colonies. They were supposed to belong more directly to the land than to their masters. They could, therefore, be sold with it, but not separately. They could marry, provided it was with the consent of their master; and he could not afterwards dissolve the

marriage by selling the man and wife to different persons. If he maimed or murdered any of them, he was liable to some penalty, though generally but to a small one. They were not, however, capable of acquiring property. Whatever they acquired was acquired to their master, and he could take it from them at pleasure. Whatever cultivation and improvement could be carried on by means of such slaves, was properly carried on by their master. It was at his expence. The seed, the cattle, and the instruments of husbandry were all his. It was for his benefit. Such slaves could acquire nothing but their daily maintenance. It was properly the proprietor himself, therefore, that, in this case, occupied his own lands, and cultivated them by his own bondmen. This species of slavery still subsists in Russia, Poland, Hungary, Bohemia, Moravia, and other parts of Germany. It is only in the western and south-western provinces of Europe, that it has gradually been abolished altogether.[8]

But if great improvements are seldom to be expected from great proprietors, they are least of all to be expected when they

Slave labour is the dearest of all. employ slaves for their workmen. The experience of all ages and nations, I believe, demonstrates that the work done by slaves,

though it appears to cost only their maintenance, is in the end the dearest of any. A person who can acquire no property, can have no other interest but to eat as much, and to labour as little as possible. Whatever work he does beyond what is sufficient

---

[8] ["A small part of the West of Europe is the only portion of the globe that is free from slavery," "and is nothing in comparison with the vast continents where it still prevails."—*Lectures*, p. 96.]

to purchase his own maintenance, can be squeezed out of him by violence only, and not by any interest of his own. In ancient Italy, how much the cultivation of corn degenerated, how unprofitable it became to the master when it fell under the management of slaves, is remarked by both Pliny and Columella.[9] In the time of Aristotle it had not been much better in ancient Greece. Speaking of the ideal republic described in the laws of Plato, to maintain five thousand idle men (the number of warriors supposed necessary for its defence) together with their women and servants, would require, he says, a territory of boundless extent and fertility, like the plains of Babylon.[10]

The pride of man makes him love to domineer, and nothing mortifies him so much as to be obliged to condescend to persuade his inferiors. Wherever the law allows

At present sugar and tobacco can afford slave cultivation, corn cannot.

it, and the nature of the work can afford it, therefore, he will generally prefer the service of slaves to that of freemen. The planting of sugar and tobacco can afford the expence of slave cultivation. The raising of corn, it seems, in the present times, cannot. In the English colonies, of which the principal produce is corn, the far greater part of the work is done by freemen. The late resolution of the Quakers in Pennsylvania to set at liberty all their negro slaves,[11] may satisfy us that their number cannot be very great. Had they made any considerable part of their property, such a resolution could never have been agreed to. In our sugar colonies, on the contrary, the whole work is done by slaves, and in our tobacco colonies a very great part of it. The profits of a sugar-plantation in any of our West Indian colonies are generally much greater than those of any other cultivation that is known either in Europe or America: And the profits of a tobacco plantation, though inferior to those of sugar, are superior to those

---

[9] [Pliny, *H. N.*, lib. xviii., cap. iv.; Columella, *De re rustica*, lib. i., præfatio.]

[10] [*Politics*, 1265a.]

[11] [Raynal, *Historie philosophique* (Amsterdam ed.), tom. vi., pp. 368–388.]

of corn, as has already been observed.[12] Both can afford the expence of slave cultivation, but sugar can afford it still better than tobacco. The number of negroes accordingly is much greater, in proportion to that of whites, in our sugar than in our tobacco colonies.

To the slave cultivators of ancient times, gradually succeeded a species of farmers known at present in France by the name of metayers. They are called in Latin, *Coloni Partiarii*. They have been so long in disuse in England that at present I know no English name for them. The proprietor furnished them with the seed, cattle, and instruments of husbandry, the whole stock, in short, necessary for cultivating the farm. The produce was divided equally between the proprietor and the farmer, after setting aside what was judged necessary for keeping up the stock, which was restored to the proprietor when the farmer either quitted, or was turned out of the farm.[13]

The slaves were succeeded by metayers,

Land occupied by such tenants is properly cultivated at the expence of the proprietor, as much as that occupied by slaves. There is, however, one very essential difference between them. Such tenants, being freemen, are capable of acquiring property, and having a certain proportion of the produce of the land, they have a plain interest that the whole produce should be as great as possible, in order that their own proportion may be so. A slave, on the contrary, who can acquire nothing but his maintenance, consults his own ease by making the land produce as little as possible over and above that maintenance. It is probable that it was partly upon account of this advantage, and partly upon account of the encroachments which the sovereign, always jealous of the great lords, gradually encouraged their villains to make upon their authority, and which seem at last to have been such as rendered this species of servitude altogether inconvenient, that tenure in villanage gradually wore out through the greater part of

who are very different in that they can acquire property.

[12] [Above, pp. 215, 216; *Lectures*, p. 225.]

[13] [*Ibid.*, pp. 100, 101.]

Europe. The time and manner, however, in which so important a revolution was brought about, is one of the most obscure points in modern history. The church of Rome claims great merit in it; and it is certain that so early as the twelfth century, Alexander III.[14] published a bull for the general emancipation of slaves. It seems, however, to have been rather a pious exhortation, than a law to which exact obedience was required from the faithful. Slavery continued to take place almost universally for several centuries afterwards, till it was gradually abolished by the joint operation of the two interests above mentioned, that of the proprietor on the one hand, and that of the sovereign on the other. A villain enfranchised, and at the same time allowed to continue in possession of the land, having no stock of his own, could cultivate it only by means of what the landlord advanced to him, and must, therefore, have been what the French call a metayer.

It could never, however, be the interest even of this last species of cultivators to lay out, in the further improvement of the land, any part of the little stock which they might save from their own share of the produce, because the lord, who laid out nothing, was to get one-half of whatever it produced. The tithe, which is but a tenth of the produce, is found to be a very great hindrance to improvement. A tax, therefore, which amounted to one-half, must have been an effectual bar to it. It might be the interest of a metayer to make the land produce as much as could be brought out of it by means of the stock furnished by the proprietor; but it could never be his interest to mix any part of his own with it. In France, where five parts out of six of the whole kingdom are said to be still occupied by this species of cultivators,[15] the proprietors complain that their metayers take every opportunity of employing the master's cattle rather in carriage than in culti-

But they could have no interest to employ stock in improvement.

---

[14] [Raynal, *Histoire philosophique* (Amsterdam ed.), tom. i., p. 12. In *Lectures*, pp. 101, 102, Innocent III. appears in error for Alexander III.]

[15] [Probably Quesnay's estimate; cp. his article on "Fermiers" in the *Encyclopédie*, reprinted in his *Œuvres*, ed. Oncken, 1888, pp. 160, 171.]

vation; because in the one case they get the whole profits to themselves, in the other they share them with their landlord. This species of tenants still subsists in some parts of Scotland. They are called steel-bow[16] tenants. Those ancient English tenants, who are said by Chief Baron Gilbert and Doctor Blackstone to have been rather bailiffs of the landlord than farmers properly so called, were probably of the same kind.[17]

To this species of tenancy succeeded, though by very slow degrees, farmers properly so called, who cultivated the land

Metayers were followed by farmers, who sometimes find it to their interest to improve when they have a lease, but leases were long insecure.

with their own stock, paying a rent certain to the landlord. When such farmers have a lease for a term of years, they may sometimes find it for their interest to lay out part of their capital in the further improvement of the farm; because they may sometimes expect to recover it, with a large profit, before the expiration of the lease. The possession even of such farmers, however, was long extremely precarious, and still is so in many parts of Europe. They could before the expiration of their term be legally outed of their lease, by a new purchaser; in England, even by the fictitious action of a common recovery. If they were turned out illegally by the violence of their master, the action by which they obtained redress was extremely imperfect. It did not always re-instate them in the possession of the land, but gave them damages which never amounted to the real loss. Even in England, the country perhaps of Europe where the yeomanry has always been most respected, it was not till about the 14th of Henry the VIIth that the action of ejectment was in-

---

[16] [Garnier is certainly wrong in suggesting in his note, "ce nom vient probablement de la manière dont ils étaient autrefois armés en guerre."—*Recherches*, etc., tom. ii., p. 428. "Bow" is the farming stock; "steel" is said to indicate the nature of the contract, and eisern vieh and bestia ferri are quoted as parallels by Cosmo Innes, *Lectures on Scotch Legal Antiquities*, 1872, pp. 245, 266.]

[17] [Gilbert, *Treatise of Tenures*, 3rd ed., 1757, pp. 34 and 54; Blackstone, *Commentaries*, vol. ii., pp. 141, 142. The whole paragraph follows *Lectures*, p. 226, rather closely.]

vented,[18] by which the tenant recovers, not damages only but possession, and in which his claim is not necessarily concluded by the uncertain decision of a single assize. This action has been found so effectual a remedy that, in the modern practice, when the landlord has occasion to sue for the possession of the land, he seldom makes use of the actions which properly belong to him as landlord, the writ of right or the writ of entry,[19] but sues in the name of his tenant, by the writ of ejectment. In England, therefore, the security of the tenant is equal to that of the proprietor. In England besides a lease for life of forty shillings a year value is a freehold, and entitles the lessee to vote for a member of parliament; and as a great part of the yeomanry have freeholds of this kind, the whole order becomes respectable to their landlords on account of the political consideration which this gives them.[20] There is, I believe, nowhere in Europe, except in England, any instance of the tenant building upon the land of which he had no lease, and trusting that the honour of his landlord would take no advantage of so important an improvement. Those laws and customs so favourable to the yeomanry, have perhaps contributed more to the present grandeur of England, than all their boasted regulations of commerce taken together.

> The forty-shilling freeholder vote in England contributes to the security of the farmer.

The law which secures the longest leases against successors of every kind is, so far as I know, peculiar to Great Britain. It was introduced into Scotland so early as 1449, by a law of James the IId.[21] Its beneficial influence, however, has been much obstructed by entails; the heirs of entail being generally restrained from letting leases for

> The law of Scotland is not quite so favourable.

---

[18] [M. Bacon, *New Abridgment of the Law*, 3rd ed., 1768, vol. ii., p. 160, *s.v.* Ejectment; cp. *Lectures*, p. 227.]

[19] [Blackstone, *Commentaries*, iii., 197.]

[20] [*Lectures*, pp. 227–228.]

[21] [Acts of 1449, c. 6, "ordained for the safety and favour of the poor people that labours the ground."]

any long term of years, frequently for more than one year. A late act of parliament[22] has, in this respect, somewhat slackened their fetters, though they are still by much too strait. In Scotland, besides, as no leasehold gives a vote for a member of parliament, the yeomanry are upon this account less respectable to their landlords than in England.

In other parts of Europe, after it was found convenient to secure tenants both against heirs and purchasers, the term of their security was still limited to a very short period; in France, for example, to nine years from the commencement of the lease. It has in that country, indeed, been lately extended to twenty-seven,[23] a period still too short to encourage the tenant to make the most important improvements. The proprietors of land were anciently the legislators of every part of Europe. The laws relating to land, therefore, were all calculated for what they supposed the interest of the proprietor. It was for his interest, they had imagined, that no lease granted by any of his predecessors should hinder him from enjoying, during a long term of years, the full value of his land. Avarice and injustice are always shortsighted, and they did not foresee how much this regulation must obstruct improvement, and thereby hurt in the long-run the real interest of the landlord.[24]

In the rest of Europe the farmer is less secure.

The farmers too, besides paying the rent, were anciently, it was supposed, bound to perform a great number of services to the landlord, which were seldom either specified in the lease, or regulated by any precise rule, but by the use and wont of the manor or barony. These services, therefore, being almost entirely arbitrary, subjected the tenant to many vexations. In Scotland the abolition of all services, not precisely stipulated in the lease,[25] has in the course of a few

Customary services were vexatious to the farmer,

---

[22] [10 Geo. III., c. 51.]

[23] [Below, p. 863.]

[24] [*Lectures*, pp. 226, 227.]

[25] [20 Geo. II., c. 50, § 21.]

years very much altered for the better the condition of the yeomanry of that country.

The public services to which the yeomanry were bound, were not less arbitrary than the private ones. *and so also were compulsory labour on the roads,* To make and maintain the high roads, a servitude which still subsists, I believe, every-where, though with different degrees of oppression in different countries, was not the only one.

When the king's troops, when his household or his officers *purveyance* of any kind passed through any part of the country, the yeomanry were bound to provide them with horses, carriages, and provisions, at a price regulated by the purveyor. Great Britain is, I believe, the only monarchy in Europe where the oppression of purveyance has been entirely abolished. It still subsists in France and Germany.

The public taxes to which they were subject were as irregular and oppressive as the services. The ancient lords, though *and tallages.* extremely unwilling to grant themselves any pecuniary aid to their sovereign, easily allowed him to tallage, as they called it, their tenants,[26] and had not knowledge enough to foresee how much this must in the end affect their own revenue. The taille, as it still subsists in France, may serve as an example of those ancient tallages. It is a tax upon the supposed profits of the farmer, which they estimate by the stock that he has upon the farm. It is his interest, therefore, to appear to have as little as possible, and consequently to employ as little as possible in its cultivation, and none in its improvement. Should any stock happen to accumulate in the hands of a French farmer, the taille is almost equal to a prohibition of its ever being employed upon the land. This tax besides is supposed to dishonour whoever is subject to it, and to degrade him below, not only the rank of a gentleman, but that of a burgher, and whoever rents the lands of another becomes subject to it. No gentleman, nor even any burgher

[26] [*Lectures*, p. 227.]

who[27] has stock, will submit to this degradation. This tax, therefore, not only hinders the stock which accumulates upon the land from being employed in its improvement, but drives away all other stock from it. The ancient tenths and fifteenths,[28] so usual in England in former times, seem, so far as they affected the land, to have been taxes of the same nature with the taille.

Under all these discouragements, little improvement could be expected from the occupiers of land. That order of people,

Even under the best laws the farmer is at a disadvantage in improving,

with all the liberty and security which law can give, must always improve under great disadvantages. The farmer compared with the proprietor, is as a merchant who trades with borrowed money compared with one who trades with his own. The stock of both may improve, but that of the one, with only equal good conduct, must always improve more slowly than that of the other, on account of the large share of the profits which is consumed by the interest of the loan. The lands cultivated by the farmer must, in the same manner, with only equal good conduct, be improved more slowly than those cultivated by the proprietor; on account of the large share of the produce which is consumed in the rent, and which, had the farmer been proprietor, he might have employed in the further improvement of the land.[29] The station of a farmer besides is, from the nature of things, inferior to that of a proprietor. Through the greater part of Europe the yeomanry are regarded as an inferior rank of people, even to the better sort of tradesmen and mechanics, and in all parts of Europe to the great merchants and master manufacturers. It can seldom happen, therefore, that a man of any considerable stock should quit the superior, in order to place himself in an inferior station. Even in the present state of

---

[27] [Ed. 1 reads "that."]

[28] [Originally tenths and fifteenths of movable goods; subsequently fixed sums levied from the parishes, and raised by them like other local rates; see Cannan, *History of Local Rates*, 1896, pp. 13–14, 18–20, 22 note, 23 note.]

[29] [*Lectures*, p. 226.]

Europe, therefore, little stock is likely to go from any other profession to the improvement of land in the way of farming.

but large farmers are the principal improvers after small proprietors. More does perhaps in Great Britain than in any other country, though even there the great stocks which are, in some places, employed in farming, have generally been acquired by farming, the trade, perhaps, in which of all others stock is commonly acquired most slowly. After small proprietors, however, rich and great farmers are, in every country, the principal improvers. There are more such perhaps in England than in any other European monarchy. In the republican governments of Holland and of Berne in Switzerland, the farmers are said to be not inferior to those of England.[30]

The ancient policy of Europe was, over and above all this, unfavourable to the improvement and cultivation of land,

The common prohibition of the export of corn and the restraints on internal trade in agricultural produce were further discouragements to agriculture. whether carried on by the proprietor or by the farmer; first, by the general prohibition of the exportation of corn without a special licence, which seems to have been a very universal regulation; and secondly, by the restraints which were laid upon the inland commerce, not only of corn but of almost every other part of the produce of the farm, by the absurd laws against engrossers, regraters, and forestallers, and by the privileges of fairs and markets.[31] It has already been observed in what manner the prohibition of the exportation of corn, together with some encouragement given to the importation of foreign corn, obstructed the cultivation of ancient Italy, naturally the most fertile country in Europe, and at that time the seat of the greatest empire in the world.[32]

[30] [*Essays on Husbandry* (by Walter Harte), 1764, pp. 69–80.]

[31] [Below, pp. 660–674.]

[32] [Above, pp. 205–206; *Lectures*, p. 229.]

To what degree such restraints upon the inland commerce of this commodity, joined to the general prohibition of exportation, must have discouraged the cultivation of countries less fertile, and less favourably circumstanced, it is not perhaps very easy to imagine.

CHAPTER III

OF THE RISE AND PROGRESS OF CITIES AND TOWNS
AFTER THE FALL OF THE ROMAN EMPIRE

THE INHABITANTS of cities and towns were, after the fall of the Roman empire, not more favoured than those of the country. They consisted, indeed, of a very different order of people from the first inhabitants of the ancient republics of Greece and Italy. These last were composed chiefly of the proprietors of lands, among whom the public territory was originally divided, and who found it convenient to build their houses in the neighbourhood of one another, and to surround them with a wall, for the sake of common defence. After the fall of the Roman empire, on the contrary, the proprietors of land seem generally to have lived in fortified castles on their own estates, and in the midst of their own tenants and dependants. The towns were chiefly inhabited by tradesmen and mechanics, who seem in those days to have been of servile, or very nearly of servile condition. The privileges which we find granted by ancient charters to the inhabitants of some of the principal towns in Europe, sufficiently shew what they were before those grants. The people to whom it is granted as a privilege, that they might give away their own daughters in marriage without the consent of their lord, that upon their death their own children, and not their lord, should succeed to their goods, and that they might dispose of their own effects by will, must, before those grants, have been either altogether, or very nearly in the same state of villanage with the occupiers of land in the country.

They seem, indeed, to have been a very poor, mean set of

The townsmen were not at first favoured more than the countrymen.

people, who used to travel about with their goods from place to place, and from fair to fair, like the hawkers and pedlars of the present times.[1]

They were very nearly of servile condition,

In all the different countries of Europe then, in the same manner as in several of the Tartar governments of Asia at present, taxes used to be levied upon the persons and goods of travellers, when they passed through certain manors, when they went over certain bridges, when they carried about their goods from place to place in a fair, when they erected in it a booth or stall to sell them in. These different taxes were known in England by the names of passage, pontage, lastage, and stallage. Sometimes the king, sometimes a great lord, who had, it seems, upon some occasions, authority to do this, would grant to particular traders, to such particularly as lived in their own demesnes, a general exemption from such taxes. Such traders, though in other respects of servile, or very nearly of servile condition, were upon this account called Free-traders. They in return usually paid to their protector a sort of annual poll-tax. In those days protection was seldom granted without a valuable consideration, and this tax might, perhaps, be considered as compensation for what their patrons might lose by their exemption from other taxes. At first, both those poll-taxes and those exemptions seem to have been altogether personal, and to have affected only particular individuals, during either their lives, or the pleasure of their protectors. In the very imperfect accounts which have been published from Domesday-book, of several of the towns of England, mention is frequently made sometimes of the tax which particular burghers paid, each of them, either to the king, or to some other great lord, for this sort of protection; and sometimes of the general amount only of all those taxes.[2]

[1] [*Lectures*, p. 233.]

[2] See Brady's historical treatise of Cities and Burroughs, p. 3, &c. [Robert Brady, *Historical Treatise of Cities and Burghs or Boroughs*, 2nd ed., 1711. See, for the statements as to the position of townsmen and traders contained in these two paragraphs, esp. pp. 16, 18, and Appendix, p. 8. Cp. Hume, *History*, ed. of 1773, vol. i., p. 205, where Domesday and Brady are both mentioned. The note appears first in ed. 2.]

But how servile soever may have been originally the condition of the inhabitants of the[3] towns, it appears evidently, that they arrived at liberty and independency much earlier than the occupiers of land in the country. That part of the king's revenue which arose from such poll-taxes in any particular town, used commonly to be let in farm, during a term of years for a rent certain, sometimes to the sheriff of the county, and sometimes to other persons. The burghers themselves frequently got credit enough to be admitted to farm the revenues of this sort which arose out of their own town, they becoming jointly and severally answerable for the whole rent.[4] To let a farm in this manner was quite agreeable to the usual œconomy of, I believe, the sovereigns of all the different countries of Europe; who used frequently to let whole manors to all the tenants of those manors, they becoming jointly and severally answerable for the whole rent.[5] but in return being allowed to collect it in their own way, and to pay it into the king's exchequer by the hands of their own bailiff, and being thus altogether freed from the insolence of the king's officers; a circumstance in those days regarded as of the greatest importance.

but arrived at liberty much earlier than the country people, acquiring the farm of their town,

At first, the farm of the town was probably let to the burghers, in the same manner as it had been to other farmers, for a term of years only. In process of time, however, it seems to have become the general practice to grant it to them in fee, that is for ever, reserving a rent certain never after-

first for a term of years and afterwards in perpetuity,

---

[3] [Ed. 1 does not contain "the."]

[4] See Madox Firma Burgi, [1726,] p. 18. also [Madox,] History [and Antiquities] of the Exchequer, chap. 10. sect. v. p. 223, first edition [1711. But the statement in the text above that the farm was in place of poll taxes is not supported by *Firma Burgi*, p. 251, where Madox says the "yearly ferme of towns arose out of certain locata or demised things that yielded issues or profit," *e.g.*, assised rents, pleas, perquisites, custom of goods, fairs, markets, stallage, aldermanries, tolls and wharfage. It was only if these fell short of the farm, that a direct contribution from the townsmen would be levied. The note appears first in ed. 2.]

[5] [An instance is given in *Firma Burgi*, p. 21.]

wards to be augmented. The payment having thus become perpetual, the exemptions, in return for which it was made, naturally became perpetual too. Those exemptions, therefore, ceased to be personal, and could not afterwards be considered as belonging to individuals as individuals, but as burghers of a particular burgh, which upon this account, was called a Free burgh, for the same reason that they had been called Free-burghers or Free-traders.

Along with this grant, the important privileges above mentioned, that they might give away their own daughters in mar-

as well as other privileges equivalent to freedom,

riage, that their children should succeed to them, and that they might dispose of their own effects by will, were generally bestowed upon the burghers of the town to whom it was given. Whether such privileges had before been usually granted along with the freedom of trade, to particular burghers, as individuals, I know not. I reckon it not improbable that they were, though I cannot produce any direct evidence of it. But however this may have been, the principal attributes of villanage and slavery being thus taken away from them, they now, at least, became really free in our present sense of the word Freedom.

Nor was this all. They were generally at the same time erected into a commonalty or corporation, with the privilege of having

and a government of their own.

magistrates and a town-council of their own, of making bye-laws for their own government, of building walls for their own defence, and of reducing all their inhabitants under a sort of military discipline, by obliging them to watch and ward; that is, as anciently understood, to guard and defend those walls against all attacks and surprises by night as well as by day. In England they were generally exempted from suit to the hundred and county courts; and all such pleas as should arise among them, the pleas of the crown excepted, were left to the decision of their own magistrates. In other countries much greater and more extensive jurisdictions were frequently granted to them.[6]

It might, probably, be necessary to grant to such towns as

---

[6] See Madox *Firma Burgi:* See also Pfeffel in the remarkable events under

were admitted to farm their own revenues, some sort of compulsive jurisdiction to oblige their own citizens to make payment. In those disorderly times it might have been extremely inconvenient to have left them to seek this sort of justice from any other tribunal. But it must seem extraordinary that the sovereigns of all the different countries of Europe, should have exchanged in this manner for a rent certain, never more to be augmented, that branch of their revenue, which was, perhaps, of all others the most likely to be improved by the natural course of things, without either expence or attention of their own:[7] and that they should, besides, have in this manner voluntarily erected a sort of independent republics in the heart of their own dominions.

It seems strange that sovereigns should have abandoned the prospect of increased revenue and have erected independent republics,

In order to understand this, it must be remembered, that in those days the sovereign of perhaps no country in Europe was able to protect, through the whole extent of his dominions, the weaker part of his subjects from the oppression of the great lords. Those whom the law could not protect, and who were not strong enough to defend themselves, were obliged either to have recourse to the protection of some great lord, and in order to obtain it to become either his slaves or vassals; or to enter into a league of mutual defence for the common protection of one another. The inhabitants of cities and burghs, considered as single individuals, had no power to defend themselves; but by entering into a league of mutual defence with their neighbours, they were capable of making no contemptible resistance. The lords despised the burghers, whom they considered not only as of a different order, but as a parcel of emancipated slaves, almost of a different

but the towns were the natural allies of the sovereign against the lords.

Frederic II. and his successors of the house of Suabia. [This note appears first in ed. 2. In Pfeffel's *Nouvel Abrégé chronologique de l'histoire et du droit public d'Allemagne*, 1776, "Evénements remarquables sous Frédéric II." is a chapter heading, and subsequent chapters are headed in the same way. For the references to the power of the towns, see the index, *s.v.* Villes at the end of tom. i.]

[7] [*Lectures*, p. 40.]

species from themselves. The wealth of the burghers never failed to provoke their envy and indignation, and they plundered them upon every occasion without mercy or remorse. The burghers naturally hated and feared the lords. The king hated and feared them too; but though perhaps he might despise, he had no reason either to hate or fear the burghers. Mutual interest, therefore, disposed them to support the king, and the king to support them against the lords. They were the enemies of his enemies, and it was his interest to render them as secure and independent of those enemies as he could. By granting them magistrates of their own, the privilege of making bye-laws for their own government, that of building walls for their own defence, and that of reducing all their inhabitants under a sort of military discipline, he gave them all the means of security and independency of the barons which it was in his power to bestow. Without the establishment of some regular government of this kind, without some authority to compel their inhabitants to act according to some certain plan or system, no voluntary league of mutual defence could either have afforded them any permanent security, or have enabled them to give the king any considerable support. By granting them the farm of their town in fee, he took away from those whom he wished to have for his friends, and, if one may say so, for his allies, all ground of jealousy and suspicion that he was ever afterwards to oppress them, either by raising the farm rent of their towns, or by granting it to some other farmer.

The princes who lived upon the worst terms with their barons, seem accordingly to have been the most liberal in grants of this kind to their burghs. King John of England, for example, appears to have been a most munificent benefactor to his towns.[8] Philip the First of France lost all authority over his barons. Towards the end of his reign, his son Lewis, known afterwards by the name of Lewis the Fat, consulted, according to Father Daniel, with the bishops of the royal

The sovereigns who quarrelled most with the barons were the most liberal to the towns.

---

[8] See Madox [*Firma Burgi*, pp. 35, 150. The note is not in ed. 1.]

demesnes, concerning the most proper means of restraining the violence of the great lords.[9] Their advice consisted of two different proposals. One was to erect a new order of jurisdiction by establishing magistrates and a town council in every considerable town of his demesnes. The other was to form a new militia, by making the inhabitants of those towns, under the command of their own magistrates, march out upon proper occasions to the assistance of the king. It is from this period, according to the French antiquarians,[10] that we are to date the institution of the magistrates and councils of cities in France. It was during the unprosperous reigns of the princes of the house of Suabia that the greater part of the free towns of Germany received the first grants of their privileges, and that the famous Hanseatic league first became formidable.[11]

The militia of the cities seems, in those times, not to have been inferior to that of the country, and as they could be more

The city militia was often able to overpower the neighbouring lords, as in Italy and Switzerland.

readily assembled upon any sudden occasion, they frequently had the advantage in their disputes with the neighbouring lords. In countries, such as Italy and Switzerland, in which on account either of their distance from the principal seat of government, of the natural strength of the country itself, or of some other reason, the sovereign came to lose the whole of his authority, the cities generally became independent republics,

---

[9] ["L'excommunication de Philippe I. et son inapplication aux affaires avaient presque ruiné toute son autorité en France....Les plus puissants vassaux de France étaient devenus plus que jamais indociles à l'égard du souverain....Louis le Gros, a qui Philippe son père avait abandonné la conduite de l'état sur les dernières années de sa vie, délibera avec les évêques du domaine royal, des moyens de remédier à ces maux, et imagina avec eux une nouvelle police pour la levée des troupes, et une nouvelle forme de justice dans les villes pour empêcher l'impunité des crimes."—G. Daniel, *Histoire de France*, 1755, vol. iii., pp. 512–513. A description of the new institutions follows, pp. 513–514.]

[10] [Possibly Du Cange (who is referred to in the margin of Daniel, p. 514, and by Hume, *History*, ed. 1773, vol. ii., p. 118), *Glossarium, s.v.* Commune, communia, etc., "Primus vero ejus modi *Communias* in Francia Ludov. VII. [? VI.] rex multiplicavit et auxit."]

[11] See Pfeffel. [Reference above, p. 507 note. The note is not in ed. 1.]

and conquered all the nobility in their neighbourhood; obliging them to pull down their castles in the country, and to live, like other peaceable inhabitants, in the city. This is the short history of the republic of Berne, as well as of several other cities in Switzerland. If you except Venice, for of that city the history is somewhat different, it is the history of all the considerable Italian republics, of which so great a number arose and perished, between the end of the twelfth and the beginning of the sixteenth century.

In countries such as France or England, where the authority of the sovereign, though frequently very low, never was destroyed altogether, the cities had no opportunity of becoming entirely independent. They became, however, so considerable, that the sovereign could impose no tax upon them, besides the stated farm-rent of the town, without their own consent. They were, therefore, called upon to send deputies to the general assembly of the states of the kingdom, where they might join with the clergy and the barons in granting, upon urgent occasions, some extraordinary aid to the king. Being generally too more favourable to his power, their deputies seem, sometimes, to have been employed by him as a counter-balance in those assemblies to the authority of the great lords.[12] Hence the origin of the representation of burghs in the states general of all the great monarchies in Europe.

In France and England the cities could not be taxed without their own consent.

Order and good government, and along with them the liberty and security of individuals, were, in this manner, established in cities, at a time when the occupiers of land in the country were exposed to every sort of violence. But men in this defenceless state naturally content themselves with their necessary subsistence; because to acquire more might only tempt the injustice of their oppressors. On the con-

In consequence of this greater security of the towns industry flourished and stock accumulated there earlier than in the country.

---

[12] [Ed. 1 places "in those assemblies" here instead of in the line above; see *Lectures*, p. 41.]

trary, when they are secure of enjoying the fruits of their industry, they naturally exert it to better their condition and to acquire not only the necessaries, but the conveniencies and elegancies of life. That industry, therefore, which aims at something more than necessary subsistence, was established in cities long before it was commonly practised by the occupiers of land in the country. If in the hands of a poor cultivator, oppressed with the servitude of villanage, some little stock should accumulate, he would naturally conceal it with great care from his master, to whom it would otherwise have belonged, and take the first opportunity of running away to a town. The law was at that time so indulgent to the inhabitants of towns, and so desirous of diminishing the authority of the lords over those of the country, that if he could conceal himself there from the pursuit of his lord for a year, he was free for ever.[13] Whatever stock, therefore, accumulated in the hands of the industrious part of the inhabitants of the country, naturally took refuge in cities, as the only sanctuaries in which it could be secure to the person that acquired it.

The inhabitants of a city, it is true, must always ultimately derive their subsistence, and the whole materials and means of

Cities on the seacoast or on navigable rivers are not dependent on the neighbouring country.

their industry, from the country. But those of a city, situated near either the seacoast or the banks of a navigable river, are not necessarily confined to derive them from the country in their neighbourhood. They have a much wider range, and may draw them from the most remote corners of the world, either in exchange for the manufactured produce of their own industry, or by performing the office of carriers between distant countries, and exchanging the produce of one for that of another. A city might in this manner grow up to great wealth and splendor, while not only the country in its neighbourhood, but all those to which it traded, were in poverty and wretchedness. Each of those countries, perhaps, taken singly, could afford it but a small part, either of its subsistence, or of its employment;

[13] [*Lectures*, p. 40.]

but all of them taken together could afford it both a great sub-sistence and a great employment. There were, however, within the narrow circle of the commerce of those times, some countries that were opulent and industrious. Such was the Greek empire as long as it subsisted, and that of the Saracens during the reigns of the Abassides. Such too was Egypt till it was conquered by the Turks, some part of the coast of Barbary, and all those provinces of Spain which were under the government of the Moors.

The cities of Italy seem to have been the first in Europe which were raised by commerce to any considerable degree of

The cities of Italy were the first to grow opulent, being centrally situated and benefited by the crusades.

opulence. Italy lay in the centre of what was at that time the improved and civilized part of the world. The crusades, too, though, by the great waste of stock and destruction of inhabitants which they occasioned, they must necessarily have retarded the progress of the greater part of Europe, were extremely favourable to that of some Italian cities. The great armies which marched from all parts to the conquest of the Holy Land, gave extraordinary encouragement to the shipping of Venice, Genoa, and Pisa, sometimes in transporting them thither, and always in supplying them with provisions. They were the commissaries, if one may say so, of those armies; and the most destructive frenzy that ever befell the European nations,[14] was a source of opulence to those republics.

The cities imported manufactures and luxuries from richer countries, which were paid for by rude produce.

The inhabitants of trading cities, by importing the improved manufactures and expensive luxuries of richer countries, afforded some food to the vanity of the great proprietors, who eagerly purchased them with great quantities of the rude produce of their own lands. The commerce of a great

---

[14] ["The most signal and most durable monument of human folly that has yet appeared in any age or nation," Hume, *History*, ed. of 1773, vol. i., p. 292; "this universal frenzy," *ibid.*, p. 298, of ed. 1770, vol. i., p. 327, but in his 1st ed. Hume wrote "universal madness."]

part of Europe in those times, accordingly, consisted chiefly in the exchange of their own rude, for the manufactured produce of more civilized nations. Thus the wool of England used to be exchanged for the wines of France, and the fine cloths of Flanders, in the same manner as the corn of[15] Poland is at this day exchanged for the wines and brandies of France, and for the silks and velvets of France and Italy.

A taste for the finer and more improved manufactures, was in this manner introduced by foreign commerce into countries where no such works were carried on. But when this taste became so general as to occasion a considerable demand, the merchants, in order to save the expence of carriage, naturally endeavoured to establish some manufactures of the same kind in their own country. Hence the origin of the first manufactures for distant sale that seem to have been established in the western provinces of Europe, after the fall of the Roman empire.

Demand for such manufactured articles having become considerable, their manufacture was established in the cities.

No large country, it must be observed, ever did or could subsist without some sort of manufactures being carried on in it; and when it is said of any such country that it has no manufactures, it must always be understood of the finer and more improved, or of such as are fit for distant sale. In every large country, both the clothing and houshold furniture of the far greater part of the people, are the produce of their own industry. This is even more universally the case in those poor countries which are commonly said to have no manufactures, than in those rich ones that are said to abound in them. In the latter, you will generally find, both in the clothes and houshold furniture of the lowest rank of people, a much greater proportion of foreign productions than in the former.

All countries have some manufactures.

Those manufactures which are fit for distant sale, seem to have been introduced into different countries in two different ways.

---

[15] [Misprinted "in" in ed. 5.]

Sometimes they have been introduced, in the manner above mentioned, by the violent operation, if one may say so, of the stocks of particular merchants and undertakers, who established them in imitation of some foreign manufactures of the same kind. Such manufactures, therefore, are the offspring of foreign commerce, and such seem to have been the ancient manufactures of silks, velvets, and brocades, which flourished in Lucca, during[16] the thirteenth century. They were banished from thence by the tyranny of one of Machiavel's heroes, Castruccio Castracani. In 1310, nine hundred families were driven out of Lucca, of whom thirty-one retired to Venice, and offered to introduce there the silk manufacture.[17] Their offer was accepted; many privileges were conferred upon them, and they began the manufacture with three hundred workmen. Such too seem to have been the manufactures of fine cloths that anciently flourished in Flanders, and which were introduced into England in the beginning of the reign of Elizabeth; and such are the present silk manufactures of Lyons and Spital-fields. Manufactures introduced in this manner are generally employed upon foreign materials, being[18] imitations of foreign manufactures. When the Venetian manufacture was first established, the materials were all brought from Sicily and the Levant. The more ancient manufacture of Lucca was likewise carried on with foreign materials. The cultivation of mulberry trees, and the breeding of silkworms, seem[19] not to have been common in the northern parts of Italy before the sixteenth century. Those arts were not introduced

Sometimes manufactures for distant sale are introduced in imitation of foreign manufactures.

[16] [Ed. 1 reads "that were introduced into Venice in the beginning of."]

[17] See Sandi Istoria Civile de Vinezia, Part 2. vol. i. page 247, and 256. [Vettor Sandi, *Principi di storia civile della Republica di Venezia*, Venice, 1755. The pages should be 257, 258. This note and the three sentences in the text which the reference covers, from "They were banished" to "three hundred workmen," appear first in ed. 2.]

[18] [Ed. 1 reads "being in."]

[19] [Ed. 1 reads "seems."]

into France till the reign of Charles IX.[20] The manufactures of Flanders were carried on chiefly with Spanish and English wool. Spanish wool was the material, not of the first woollen manufacture of England, but of the first that was fit for distant sale. More than one half the materials of the Lyons manufacture is at this day foreign silk; when it was first established, the whole or very nearly the whole was so. No part of the materials of the Spital-fields manufacture is ever likely to be the produce of England. The seat of such manufactures, as they are generally introduced by the scheme and project of a few individuals, is sometimes established in a maritime city, and sometimes in an inland town, according as their interest, judgment or caprice happen to determine.

At other times manufactures for distant sale grow up naturally, and as it were of their own accord, by the gradual refinement of those household and coarser manufactures which must at all times be carried on even in the poorest and rudest countries. Such manufactures are generally employed upon the materials which the country produces, and they seem frequently to have been first refined and improved in such inland countries as were, not indeed at a very great, but at a considerable distance from the sea coast, and sometimes even from all water carriage. An inland country naturally fertile and easily cultivated, produces a great surplus of provisions beyond what is necessary for maintaining the cultivators, and on account of the expence of land carriage, and inconveniency of river navigation, it may frequently be difficult to send this surplus abroad. Abundance, therefore, renders provisions cheap, and encourages a great number of workmen to settle in the neighbourhood, who find that their industry can there procure them

Sometimes they have grown up out of the coarser home manufactures.

[20] [Ed. 1 (beginning eight lines higher up), "When the Venetian manufacture flourished, there was not a mulberry tree, nor consequently a silkworm, in all Lombardy. They brought the materials from Sicily and from the Levant, the manufacture itself being in imitation of those carried on in the Greek empire. Mulberry trees were first planted in Lombardy in the beginning of the sixteenth century, by the encouragement of Ludovico Sforza, Duke of Milan."]

more of the necessaries and conveniencies of life than in other places. They work up the materials of manufacture which the land produces, and exchange their finished work, or what is the same thing the price of it, for more materials and provisions. They give a new value to the surplus part of the rude produce, by saving the expence of carrying it to the water side, or to some distant market; and they furnish the cultivators with something in exchange for it that is either useful or agreeable to them, upon easier terms than they could have obtained it before. The cultivators get a better price for their surplus produce, and can purchase cheaper other conveniencies which they have occasion for. They are thus both encouraged and enabled to increase this surplus produce by a further improvement and better cultivation of the land; and as the fertility of the land had given birth to the manufacture, so the progress of the manufacture reacts upon the land, and increases still further its fertility. The manufacturers first supply the neighbourhood, and afterwards, as their work improves and refines, more distant markets. For though neither the rude produce, nor even the coarse manufacture, could, without the greatest difficulty, support the expence of a considerable land carriage, the refined and improved manufacture easily may. In a small bulk it frequently contains the price of a great quantity of rude produce. A piece of fine cloth, for example, which weighs only eighty pounds, contains in it, the price, not only of eighty pounds weight of wool, but sometimes of several thousand weight of corn, the maintenance of the different working people, and of their immediate employers. The corn, which could with difficulty have been carried abroad in its own shape, is in this manner virtually exported in that of the complete manufacture, and may easily be sent to the remotest corners of the world. In this manner have grown up naturally, and as it were of their own accord, the manufactures of Leeds, Halifax, Sheffield, Birmingham, and Wolverhampton. Such manufactures are the offspring of agriculture. In the modern history of Europe, their extension and improvement have generally been posterior to those which were the offspring of foreign commerce. England was noted for the manufacture of fine cloths made of Spanish wool, more than a century before any of those which now flourish in the places above mentioned were fit for foreign sale. The extension and improvement of these last could not take place but in consequence of the extension and improvement of agriculture, the last and greatest effect of foreign commerce, and of the manufactures immediately introduced by it, and which I shall now proceed to explain.

CHAPTER IV

HOW THE COMMERCE OF THE TOWNS CONTRIBUTED TO THE IMPROVEMENT OF THE COUNTRY

The rise of towns benefited the country,

THE INCREASE and riches of commercial and manufacturing towns, contributed to the improvement and cultivation of the countries to which they belonged, in three different ways.

First, by affording a great and ready market for the rude produce of the country, they gave encouragement to its cultivation and further improvement. This benefit

because they afforded (1) a ready market for its produce,

was not even confined to the countries in which they were situated, but extended more or less to all those with which they had any dealings. To all of them they afforded a market for some part either of their rude or manufactured produce, and consequently gave some encouragement to the industry and improvement of all. Their own country, however, on account of its neighbourhood, necessarily derived the greatest benefit from this market. Its rude produce being charged with less carriage, the traders could pay the growers a better price for it, and yet afford it as cheap to the consumers as that of more distant countries.

(2) because merchants bought land in the country and improved it,

Secondly, the wealth acquired by the inhabitants of cities was frequently employed in purchasing such lands as were to be sold, of which a great part would frequently be uncultivated. Merchants are commonly ambitious of becoming country gentlemen, and when they do, they are generally the best of all improvers. A merchant is accustomed to employ his money chiefly in profitable projects; whereas a mere country gentleman is accustomed to employ it chiefly in expence. The one often sees his money go from him and return to him again with a profit: the other, when once he parts with it, very seldom expects to see any more of it. Those different habits naturally affect their temper and disposition in every sort of business. A merchant is commonly a bold; a country gentleman, a timid undertaker. The one is not afraid to lay out at once a large capital upon the improvement of his land, when he has a probable prospect of raising the value of it in proportion to the expence. The other, if he has any capital, which is not always the case, seldom ventures to employ it in this manner. If he improves at all, it is commonly not with a capital, but with what he can save out of his annual revenue. Whoever has had the fortune to live in a mercantile town situated in an unimproved country, must have frequently observed how much more spirited the operations of merchants were in this way, than those of mere country gentlemen.[1] The habits, besides, of order, economy and attention, to which mercantile business naturally forms a merchant, render him much fitter to execute, with profit and success, any project of improvement.

Thirdly, and lastly, commerce and manufactures gradually introduced order and good government, and with them, the lib-

and (3) because order and good government were introduced.

erty and security of individuals, among the inhabitants of the country, who had before lived almost in a continual state of war with their neighbours, and of servile dependency upon their superiors. This, though it has been the least observed, is by far the most important of all their effects. Mr. Hume[2] is the only writer who, so far as I know, has hitherto taken notice of it.

In a country which has neither foreign commerce, nor any

[1] [Above, pp. 491–492.]

[2] ["Of Commerce" and "Of Luxury" in *Political Discourses*, 1752, and *History*, ed. of 1773, vol. iii., p. 400.]

of the finer manufactures, a great proprietor, having nothing
for which he can exchange the greater part of the produce of

*Before foreign
commerce and fine
manufactures are
introduced great
proprietors are
surrounded
by bands of
retainers,*

his lands which is over and above the maintenance of the cultivators, consumes the
whole in rustic hospitality at home. If this
surplus produce is sufficient to maintain a
hundred or a thousand men, he can make use
of it in no other way than by maintaining a
hundred or a thousand men. He is at all
times, therefore, surrounded with a multi-
tude of retainers and dependants, who having no equivalent to
give in return for their maintenance, but being fed entirely by
his bounty, must obey him, for the same reason that soldiers
must obey the prince who pays them. Before the extension of
commerce and manufactures in Europe, the hospitality of the
rich and the great, from the sovereign down to the smallest
baron, exceeded every thing which in the present times we can
easily form a notion of. Westminster hall was the dining-room
of William Rufus, and might frequently, perhaps, not be too
large for his company. It was reckoned a piece of magnificence
in Thomas Becket, that he strowed the floor of his hall with
clean hay or rushes in the season, in order that the knights and
squires, who could not get seats, might not spoil their fine
clothes when they sat down on the floor to eat their dinner.[3] The
great earl of Warwick is said to have entertained every day at
his different manors, thirty thousand people; and though the
number here may have been exaggerated, it must, however,
have been very great to admit of such exaggeration.[4] A hospitality nearly of the same kind was exercised not many years
ago in many different parts of the highlands of Scotland. It
seems to be common in all nations to whom commerce
and manufactures are little known. I have seen, says Doctor

[3] [Evidently from Hume, *History*, ed. of 1773, vol. i., p. 384.]

[4] ["No less than 30,000 persons are said to have daily lived at his board in the different manors and castles which he possessed in England."—Hume, *History*, ed.
of 1773, vol. iii., p. 182. In *Lectures*, p. 42, it had been "40,000 people, besides
tenants."]

Pocock, an Arabian chief dine in the streets of a town where he had come to sell his cattle, and invite all passengers, even common beggars, to sit down with him and partake of his banquet.[5]

The occupiers of land were in every respect as dependent upon the great proprietor as his retainers. Even such of them as

and tenants at will were just as dependent as retainers.

were not in a state of villanage, were tenants at will, who paid a rent in no respect equivalent to the subsistence which the land afforded them. A crown, half a crown, a sheep, a lamb, was some years ago in the highlands of Scotland a common rent for lands which maintained a family. In some places it is so at this day; nor will money at present purchase a greater quantity of commodities there than in other places. In a country where the surplus produce of a large estate must be consumed upon the estate itself, it will frequently be more convenient for the proprietor, that part of it be consumed at a distance from his own house, provided they who consume it are as dependent upon him as either his retainers or his menial servants. He is thereby saved from the embarrassment of either too large a company or too large a family. A tenant at will, who possesses land sufficient to maintain his family for little more than a quit-rent, is as dependent upon the proprietor as any servant or retainer whatever, and must obey him with as little reserve. Such a proprietor, as he feeds his servants and retainers at his own house, so he feeds his tenants at their houses. The subsistence of both is derived from his bounty, and its continuance depends upon his good pleasure.

The power of the ancient barons was founded on this.

Upon the authority which the great proprietors necessarily had in such a state of things over their tenants and retainers, was founded the power of the ancient barons. They necessarily became the judges in

[5] ["An Arab prince will often dine in the street, before his door, and call to all that pass, even beggars, in the usual expression, Bismillah, that is, In the name of God; who come and sit down, and when they have done, give their Hamdellilah, that is, God be praised. For the Arabs are great levellers, put everybody on a footing with them; and it is by such generosity and hospitality that they maintain their interest."—Richard Pococke, *Description of the East*, 1743, vol. i., p. 183.]

peace, and the leaders in war, of all who dwelt upon their estates. They could maintain order and execute the law within their respective demesnes, because each of them could there turn the whole force of all the inhabitants against the injustice of any one. No other person had sufficient authority to do this. The king in particular had not. In those ancient times he was little more than the greatest proprietor in his dominions, to whom, for the sake of common defence against their common enemies, the other great proprietors paid certain respects. To have enforced payment of a small debt within the lands of a great proprietor, where all the inhabitants were armed and accustomed to stand by one another, would have cost the king, had he attempted it by his own authority, almost the same effort as to extinguish a civil war. He was, therefore, obliged to abandon the administration of justice through the greater part of the country, to those who were capable of administering it; and for the same reason to leave the command of the country militia to those whom that militia would obey.

It is a mistake to imagine that those territorial jurisdictions took their origin from the feudal law. Not only the highest jurisdictions both civil and criminal, but the power of levying troops, of coining money, and even that of making bye-laws for the government of their own people, were all rights possessed allodially by the great proprietors of land several centuries before even the name of the feudal law was known in Europe. The authority and jurisdiction of the Saxon lords in England, appear[6] to have been as great before the conquest, as that of any of the Norman lords after it. But the feudal law is not supposed to have become the common law of England till after the conquest.[7] That the most extensive authority and jurisdictions were possessed by the great lords in France allodially, long before the feudal law was introduced into that country, is a matter of fact that admits of no doubt. That authority and those jurisdictions all necessarily flowed

It was anterior to and independent of the feudal law.

---

[6] [Eds. 1 and 2 read "appears."]

[7] [Hume, *History*, ed. of 1773, i., 224.]

from the state of property and manners just now described. Without remounting to the remote antiquities of either the French or English monarchies, we may find in much later times many proofs that such effects must always flow from such causes. It is not thirty years ago since Mr. Cameron of Lochiel, a gentleman of Lochabar in Scotland, without any legal warrant whatever, not being what was then called a lord of regality, nor even a tenant in chief, but a vassal of the duke of Argyle, and without being so much as a justice of peace, used, notwithstanding, to exercise the highest criminal jurisdiction over his own people. He is said to have done so with great equity, though without any of the formalities of justice; and it is not improbable that the state of that part of the country at that time made it necessary for him to assume this authority in order to maintain the public peace. That gentleman, whose rent never exceeded five hundred pounds a year, carried, in 1745, eight hundred of his own people into the rebellion with him.[8]

The introduction of the feudal law, so far from extending, may be regarded as an attempt to moderate the authority of the

It was moderated by the feudal law, great allodial lords.[9] It established a regular subordination, accompanied with a long train of services and duties, from the king down to the smallest proprietor. During the minority of the proprietor, the rent, together with the management of his lands, fell into the hands of his immediate superior, and, consequently, those of all great proprietors into the hands of the king, who was charged with the maintenance and education of the pupil, and who, from his authority as guardian, was supposed to have a right of disposing of him in marriage, provided it was in a manner not unsuitable to his rank. But though this institution necessarily tended to strengthen the authority of the

[8] ["The Highlands of Scotland have long been entitled by law to every privilege of British subjects; but it was not till very lately that the common people could in fact enjoy those privileges."—Hume, *History*, vol. i., p. 214, ed. of 1773. Cp. *Lectures*, p. 116.]

[9] [*Lectures*, pp. 38, 39.]

king, and to weaken that of the great proprietors, it could not do either sufficiently for establishing order and good government among the inhabitants of the country; because it could not alter sufficiently that state of property and manners from which the disorders arose. The authority of government still continued to be, as before, too weak in the head and too strong in the inferior members, and the excessive strength of the inferior members was the cause of the weakness of the head. After the institution of feudal subordination, the king was as incapable of restraining the violence of the great lords as before. They still continued to make war according to their own discretion, almost continually upon one another, and very frequently upon the king; and the open country still continued to be a scene of violence, rapine, and disorder.

But what all the violence of the feudal institutions could never have effected, the silent and insensible operation of

and undermined by foreign commerce. foreign commerce and manufactures gradually brought about. These gradually furnished the great proprietors with something for which they could exchange the whole surplus produce of their lands, and which they could consume themselves without sharing it either with tenants or retainers. All for ourselves, and nothing for other people, seems, in every age of the world, to have been the vile maxim of the masters of mankind. As soon, therefore, as they could find a method of consuming the whole value of their rents themselves, they had no disposition to share them with any other persons. For a pair of diamond buckles perhaps, or for something as frivolous and useless, they exchanged the maintenance, or what is the same thing, the price of the maintenance of a thousand men for a year, and with it the whole weight and authority which it could give them. The buckles, however, were to be all their own, and no other human creature was to have any share of them; whereas in the more ancient method of expence they must have shared with at least a thousand people. With the judges that were to determine the preference, this difference was perfectly decisive; and thus, for the gratification of the most childish, the meanest and the most sordid of all vanities, they gradually bartered their whole power and authority.[10]

In a country where there is no foreign commerce, nor any of the finer manufactures, a man of ten thousand a year cannot

At present a rich man maintains in all as many persons as an ancient baron, but he contributes only a small portion of the maintenance of each person.

well employ his revenue in any other way than in maintaining, perhaps, a thousand families, who are all of them necessarily at his command. In the present state of Europe, a man of ten thousand a year can spend his whole revenue, and he generally does so, without directly maintaining twenty people, or being able to command more than ten footmen not worth the commanding.

Indirectly, perhaps, he maintains as great or even a greater number of people than he could have done by the ancient method of expence. For though the quantity of precious productions for which he exchanges his whole revenue be very small, the number of workmen employed in collecting and preparing it, must necessarily have been very great. Its great price generally arises from the wages of their labour, and the profits of all their immediate employers. By paying that price he indirectly pays all those wages and profits, and thus indirectly contributes to the maintenance of all the workmen and their employers. He generally contributes, however, but a very small proportion to that of each, to very few perhaps a tenth, to many not a hundredth, and to some not a thousandth, nor even a ten thousandth part of their whole annual maintenance. Though he contributes, therefore, to the maintenance of them all, they are all more or less independent of him, because generally they can all be maintained without him.

When the great proprietors of land spend their rents in maintaining their tenants and retainers, each of them maintains entirely all his own tenants and all his own retainers. But when they spend them in maintaining tradesmen and artificers, they may, all of them taken together, perhaps, maintain as great, or, on account of the waste which attends rustic hospitality, a

[10] [Hume, *History*, ed. of 1773, vol. iii., p. 400; vol. v., p. 488.]

greater number of people than before. Each of them, however, taken singly, contributes often but a very small share to the maintenance of any individual of this greater number. Each tradesman or artificer derives his subsistence from the employment, not of one, but of a hundred or a thousand different customers. Though in some measure obliged to them all, therefore, he is not absolutely dependent upon any one of them.

The personal expence of the great proprietors having in this manner gradually increased, it was impossible that the number of their retainers should not as gradually diminish, till they were at last dismissed altogether. The same cause gradually led them to dismiss the unnecessary part of their tenants. Farms were enlarged, and the occupiers of land, notwithstanding the complaints of depopulation, reduced to the number necessary for cultivating it, according to the imperfect state of cultivation and improvement in those times. By the removal of the unnecessary mouths, and by exacting from the farmer the full value of the farm, a greater surplus, or what is the same thing, the price of a greater surplus, was obtained for the proprietor, which the merchants and manufacturers soon furnished him with a method of spending upon his own person in the same manner as he had done the rest. The same cause continuing to operate, he was desirous to raise his rents above what his lands, in the actual state of their improvement, could afford. His tenants could agree to this upon one condition only, that they should be secured in their possession, for such a term of years as might give them time to recover with profit whatever they should lay out in the further improvement of the land. The expensive vanity of the landlord made him willing to accept of this condition; and hence the origin of long leases.

To meet their new expenses the great proprietors dismissed their retainers and their unnecessary tenants, and gave the remaining tenants long leases,

Even a tenant at will, who pays the full value of the land, is not altogether dependent upon the landlord. The pecuniary advantages which they receive from one another, are mutual and

thus making them independent.

equal, and such a tenant will expose neither his life nor his fortune in the service of the proprietor. But if he has a lease for a
long term of years, he is altogether independent; and his landlord must not expect from him even the most trifling service
beyond what is either expressly stipulated in the lease, or imposed upon him by the common and known law of the country.

The tenants having in this manner become independent,
and the retainers being dismissed, the great proprietors were

*The great propri-
etors thus became
insignificant.*

no longer capable of interrupting the regular
execution of justice, or of disturbing the
peace of the country. Having sold their birth-
right, not like Esau for a mess of pottage in
time of hunger and necessity, but in the wantonness of plenty,
for trinkets and baubles, fitter to be the play-things of children
than the serious pursuits of men, they became as insignificant
as any substantial burgher or tradesman in a city. A regular
government was established in the country as well as in the
city, nobody having sufficient power to disturb its operations in
the one, any more than in the other.

It does not, perhaps, relate to the present subject, but I cannot help remarking it, that very old families, such as have pos-

*Old families are
rare in commer-
cial countries.*

sessed some considerable estate from father
to son for many successive generations, are
very rare in commercial countries. In countries which have little commerce, on the con-
trary, such as Wales or the highlands of Scotland, they are very
common. The Arabian histories seem to be all full of genealo-
gies, and there is a history written by a Tartar Khan, which has
been translated into several European languages, and which
contains scarce any thing else;[11] a proof that ancient families
are very common among those nations. In countries where a
rich man can spend his revenue in no other way than by main-

---

[11] [*Histoire généalogique des Tatars traduite du manuscript Tartare D'Abulgasi-
Bayadur-chan et enrichie d'un grand nombre de remarques authentiques et très
curieuses sur le véritable estat present de l'Asie septentrionale avec les cartes
géographiques nécessaires*, par D., Leyden, 1726. The preface says some Swedish
officers imprisoned in Siberia had it translated into Russian and then retranslated
it themselves into various other languages.]

taining as many people as it can maintain, he is not apt to run out, and his benevolence it seems is seldom so violent as to attempt to maintain more than he can afford. But where he can spend the greatest revenue upon his own person, he frequently has no bounds to his expence, because he frequently has no bounds to his vanity, or to his affection for his own person. In commercial countries, therefore, riches, in spite of the most violent regulations of law to prevent their dissipation, very seldom remain long in the same family. Among simple nations, on the contrary, they frequently do without any regulations of law: for among nations of shepherds, such as the Tartars and Arabs, the consumable nature of their property necessarily renders all such regulations impossible.

A revolution of the greatest importance to the public happiness, was in this manner brought about by two different orders of people, who had not the least intention to serve the public. To gratify the most childish vanity was the sole motive of the great proprietors. The merchants and artificers, much less ridiculous, acted merely from a view to their own interest, and in pursuit of their own pedlar principle of turning a penny wherever a penny was to be got. Neither of them had either knowledge or foresight of that great revolution which the folly of the one, and the industry of the other, was gradually bringing about.

A revolution was thus insensibly brought about,

and commerce and manufactures became the cause of the improvement of the country. This order of things is both slow and uncertain compared with the natural order, as may be shown by the rapid progress of the North American colonies,

It is thus that through the greater part of Europe the commerce and manufactures of cities, instead of being the effect, have been the cause and occasion of the improvement and cultivation of the country.

This order, however, being contrary to the natural course of things, is necessarily both slow and uncertain. Compare the slow progress of those European countries of which the wealth depends very much upon their commerce and manufactures, with the rapid advances of our North American colonies, of which the wealth is founded altogether in agricul-

ture. Through the greater part of Europe, the number of inhabitants is not supposed to double in less than five hundred years.
In several of our North American colonies, it is found to double in twenty or five-and-twenty years.[12] In Europe the law of
primogeniture, and perpetuities of different kinds, prevent the
division of great estates, and thereby hinder the multiplication
of small proprietors. A small proprietor, however, who knows
every part of his little territory, who[13] views it all with[14] the affection which property, especially small property, naturally in-
spires, and who upon that account takes pleasure not only in
cultivating but in adorning it, is generally of all improvers the
most industrious, the most intelligent, and the most successful.[15] The same regulations, besides, keep so much land out of
the market, that there are always more capitals to buy than
there is land to sell, so that what is sold always sells at a monopoly price. The rent never pays the interest of the purchase-
money, and is besides burdened with repairs and other
occasional charges, to which the interest of money is not liable. To purchase land is every-where in Europe a most unprofitable employment of a small capital. For the sake of the
superior security, indeed, a man of moderate circumstances,
when he retires from business, will sometimes chuse to lay out
his little capital in land. A man of profession too, whose revenue is derived from another source, often loves to secure his
savings in the same way. But a young man, who, instead of applying to trade or to some profession, should employ a capital
of two or three thousand pounds in the purchase and cultivation of a small piece of land, might indeed expect to live very
happily, and very independently, but must bid adieu, forever, to
all hope of either great fortune or great illustration, which by a
different employment of his stock he might have had the same
chance of acquiring with other people. Such a person too,
though he cannot aspire at being proprietor, will often disdain

[12] [Above, p. 100, note.]

[13] [Ed. 5 omits "who" by a misprint.]

[14] [Eds. 2–5 read "with all," doubtless a corruption.]

[15] [Cp. above, pp. 491–492.]

to be a farmer. The small quantity of land, therefore, which is brought to market, and the high price of what is brought thither,[16] prevents a great number of capitals from being employed in its cultivation and improvement which would otherwise have taken that direction. In North America, on the contrary, fifty or sixty pounds is often found a sufficient stock to begin a plantation with. The purchase and improvement of uncultivated land, is there the most profitable employment of the smallest as well as of the greatest capitals, and the most direct road to all the fortune and illustration which can be acquired in that country. Such land, indeed, is in North America to be had almost for nothing, or at a price much below the value of the natural produce; a thing impossible in Europe, or, indeed, in any country where all lands have long been private property. If landed estates, however, were divided equally among all the children, upon the death of any proprietor who left a numerous family, the estate would generally be sold. So much land would come to market, that it could no longer sell at a monopoly price. The free rent of the land would go nearer to pay the interest of the purchase-money, and a small capital might be employed in purchasing land as profitably as in any other way.

England, on account of the natural fertility of the soil, of the great extent of the[17] sea-coast in proportion to that of the whole

and the slow progress of England in agriculture in spite of favours accorded to it

country, and of the many navigable rivers which run through it, and afford the conveniency of water carriage to some of the most inland parts of it, is perhaps as well fitted by nature as any large country in Europe, to be the seat of foreign commerce, and manufactures for distant sale, and of all the improvements which these can occasion. From the beginning of the reign of Elizabeth too, the English legislature has been peculiarly attentive to the interests of commerce and manufactures, and in reality there is no country in Europe, Holland itself not

[16] [Ed. 1 does not contain "thither."]

[17] [Ed. 1 does not contain "the."]

excepted, of which the law is, upon the whole, more favourable to this sort of industry. Commerce and manufactures have accordingly been continually advancing during all this period. The cultivation and improvement of the country has, no doubt, been gradually advancing too: But it seems to have followed slowly, and at a distance, the more rapid progress of commerce and manufactures. The greater part of the country must probably have been cultivated before the reign of Elizabeth; and a very great part of it still remains uncultivated, and the cultivation of the far greater part, much inferior to what it might be. The law of England, however, favours agriculture not only indirectly by the protection of commerce, but by several direct encouragements. Except in times of scarcity, the exportation of corn is not only free, but encouraged by a bounty. In times of moderate plenty, the importation of foreign corn is loaded with duties that amount to a prohibition. The importation of live cattle, except from Ireland, is prohibited at all times,[18] and it is but of late that it was permitted from thence.[19] Those who cultivate the land, therefore, have a monopoly against their countrymen for the two greatest and most important articles of land produce, bread and butcher's meat. These encouragements, though at bottom, perhaps, as I shall endeavour to show hereafter,[20] altogether illusory, sufficiently demonstrate at least the good intention of the legislature to favour agriculture. But what is of much more importance than all of them, the yeomanry of England are rendered as secure, as independent, and as respectable as law can make them. No country, therefore, in which the right of primogeniture takes place, which pays tithes, and where perpetuities, though contrary to the spirit of the law, are admitted in some cases, can give more encouragement to agriculture than England. Such, however, notwithstanding, is the state of its cultivation. What would it have been, had the law given no direct encouragement to agriculture besides what arises indirectly from the progress of commerce,

[18] [18 Car. II., c. 2.]

[19] [32 Geo. II., c. 11, § 1; 5 Geo. III., c. 10; 12 Geo. III., c. 2.]

[20] [Below, pp. 576–580, 660–687.]

and had left the yeomanry in the same condition as in most other countries of Europe? It is now more than two hundred years since the beginning of the reign of Elizabeth, a period as long as the course of human prosperity usually endures.

France seems to have had a considerable share of foreign commerce near a century before England was distinguished as a commercial country. The marine of France *and the still* was considerable, according to the notions *slower progress of* of the times, before the expedition of *France,* Charles the VIIIth to Naples.[21] The cultivation and improvement of France, however, is, upon the whole, inferior to that of England. The law of the country has never given the same direct encouragement to agriculture.

The foreign commerce of Spain and Portugal to the other parts of Europe, though chiefly carried on in foreign ships, is very considerable. That to their colonies is *Spain and* carried on in their own, and is much greater, *Portugal.* on account of the great riches and extent of those colonies. But it has never introduced any considerable manufactures for distant sale into either of those countries, and the greater part of both still remains uncultivated. The foreign commerce of Portugal is of older standing than that of any great country in Europe, except Italy.

Italy is the only great country of Europe which seems to have been cultivated and improved in every part, by means of foreign commerce and manufactures for distant sale. Before the invasion of Charles the VIIIth, Italy, according to

---

[21] [It seems likely that Charles VIII. is here (though not on the next page) confused with Charles of Anjou, brother of St. Louis. At any rate Hénault (who is quoted below, p. 791) says: "Notre marine aussitôt détruite que créée sous Philippe Auguste, s'était bien rétablie sous S. Louis si, comme le dit un historien, ce prince embarqua soixante-mille hommes à Aigues-mortes ... quant à la première expédition, Joinville dit qu'au départ de Chypre pour la conquête de Damiette, il y avait dix-huit cents vaisseaux tant grands que petits. S. Louis avait aussi mis en mer une flotte considérable pour défendre les côtes de Poitou contre la flotte de Henri III., et son frère Charles d'Anjou en avait une de quatre-vingts voiles, composée de galères et de vaisseaux, lors de son expédition de Naples."—*Nouvel Abrégé chronologique de l'Histoire de France*, 1768, tom. i., p. 201, A.D. 1299. This puts the French marine 200 years earlier.]

Guicciardin,[22] was cultivated not less in the most mountainous and barren parts of the country, than in the plainest and most fertile. The advantageous situation of the country, and the great number of independent states which at that time subsisted in it, probably contributed not a little to this general cultivation. It is not impossible too, notwithstanding this general expression of one of the most judicious and reserved of modern historians, that Italy was not at that time better cultivated than England is at present.

Italy alone was improved throughout by foreign commerce and exported manufactures.

The capital, however, that is acquired to any country by commerce and manufactures, is all a very precarious and uncertain possession, till some part of it has been secured and realised in the cultivation and improvement of its lands. A merchant, it has been said very properly, is not necessarily the citizen of any particular country. It is in a great measure indifferent to him from what place he carries on his trade; and a very trifling disgust will make him remove his capital, and together with it all the industry which it supports, from one country to another. No part of it can be said to belong to any particular country, till it has been spread as it were over the face of that country, either in buildings, or in the lasting improvement of lands. No vestige now remains of the great wealth, said to have been possessed by the greater part of the Hans towns, except in the obscure histories of the thirteenth and fourteenth centuries. It is even uncertain where some of them were situated, or to what towns in Europe the Latin names given to some of them belong. But though the misfortunes of Italy in the end of the fifteenth and beginning of the sixteenth centuries greatly diminished the commerce and

The national capital acquired by commerce and manufactures is an uncertain possession till realised in the improvement of land.

[22] ["Perchè ridotta tutta in somma pace e tranquillità, coltivata non meno ne' luoghi più montuosi, e più sterili, che nelle pianure, e regioni sue più fertili, nè sottoposta ad altro Imperio, che de' suoi medesimi, non solo era abbondantissima d' abitatori, e di richezze."—Guicciardini, *Della Istoria d'Italia*, Venice, 1738, vol. i., p. 2.]

manufactures of the cities of Lombardy and Tuscany, those countries still continue to be among the most populous and best cultivated in Europe. The civil wars of Flanders, and the Spanish government which succeeded them, chased away the great commerce of Antwerp, Ghent, and Bruges. But Flanders still continues to be one of the richest, best cultivated, and most populous provinces of Europe. The ordinary revolutions of war and government easily dry up the sources of that wealth which arises from commerce only. That which arises from the more solid improvements of agriculture, is much more durable, and cannot be destroyed but by those more violent convulsions occasioned by the depredations of hostile and barbarous nations continued for a century or two together; such as those that happened for some time before and after the fall of the Roman empire in the western provinces of Europe.

BOOK IV

OF SYSTEMS OF POLITICAL ŒCONOMY

Introduction

POLITICAL ŒCONOMY, considered as a branch of the science of a statesman or legislator, proposes two distinct objects:

The first object of political œconomy is to provide subsistence for the people.

first, to provide a plentiful revenue or subsistence for the people, or more properly to enable them to provide such a revenue or subsistence for themselves; and secondly, to supply the state or commonwealth with a revenue sufficient for the public services. It proposes to enrich both the people and the sovereign.

The different progress of opulence in different ages and nations, has given occasion to two different systems of political

Two different systems proposed for this end will be explained.

œconomy, with regard to enriching the people. The one may be called the system of commerce, the other that of agriculture. I shall endeavour to explain both as fully and distinctly as I can, and shall begin with the system of commerce. It is the modern system, and is best understood in our own country and in our own times.

CHAPTER I

OF THE PRINCIPLE OF THE COMMERCIAL OR MERCANTILE SYSTEM

THAT WEALTH consists in money, or in gold and silver, is a popular notion which naturally arises from the double function

Wealth and money in common language are considered synonymous.

of money, as the instrument of commerce, and as the measure of value. In consequence of its being the instrument of commerce, when we have money we can more readily obtain whatever else we have occasion for, than by means of any other commodity. The great affair, we always find, is to get money. When that is obtained, there is no difficulty in making any subsequent purchase. In consequence of its being the measure of value, we estimate that of all other commodities by the quantity of money which they will exchange for. We say of a rich man that he is worth a great deal, and of a poor man that he is worth very little money. A frugal man, or a man eager to be rich, is said to love money; and a careless, a generous, or a profuse man, is said to be indifferent about it. To grow rich is to get money; and wealth and money, in short, are, in common language, considered as in every respect synonymous.

A rich country, in the same manner as a rich man, is supposed to be a country abounding in money; and to heap up

Similarly the Tartars thought wealth consisted of cattle.

gold and silver in any country is supposed to be the readiest way to enrich it. For some time after the discovery of America, the first enquiry of the Spaniards, when they arrived upon any unknown coast, used to be, if there was any gold or silver to be found in the neighbourhood? By the information which they received, they judged whether it was worth while to make a settlement there, or if the country was worth the conquering. Plano Carpino, a monk sent ambassador from the king of France to one of the sons of the famous Gengis Khan, says that the Tartars used frequently to ask him, if there was plenty of sheep and oxen in the kingdom of France?[1] Their enquiry had the same object with that of the Spaniards. They wanted to know if the country was rich enough to be worth the conquering. Among the Tartars, as among all other nations of shepherds, who are generally ignorant of the use of money, cattle are the instruments of commerce and the measures of value. Wealth, therefore, according to them, consisted in cattle, as according to the Spaniards it consisted in gold and silver. Of the two, the Tartar notion, perhaps, was the nearest to the truth.

Mr. Locke remarks a distinction between money and other moveable goods. All other moveable goods, he says, are of so consumable a nature that the wealth which consists in them cannot be much depended on, and a nation which abounds in them one year may, without any exportation, but merely by their own waste and extravagance, be in great want of them the next. Money, on the contrary, is a steady friend, which, though it may travel about from hand to hand, yet if it can be kept from going out of the country, is not very liable to be wasted and consumed. Gold and silver, therefore, are, according to him, the most solid and substantial part of the moveable wealth of a nation, and to multiply those metals ought, he

Locke thought gold and silver the most substantial part of the wealth of a nation.

---

[1] [There seems to be a confusion between Plano-Carpini, a Franciscan sent as legate by Pope Innocent IV. in 1246, and Guillaume de Rubruquis, another Franciscan sent as ambassador by Louis IX. in 1253. As is pointed out by Rogers in a note on this passage, the reference appears to be to Rubruquis, *Voyage en Tartarie et à la Chine*, chap. xxxiii. The great Khan's secretaries, Rubruquis states, on one occasion displayed curiosity about France: "s'enquérant s'il y avait force bœufs, moutons, et chevaux, comme s'ils eussent déjà été tous prêts d'y venir et emmener tout." Plano-Carpini and Rubruquis are both in Bergeron's *Voyages faits principalement en Asie dans les xii., xiii., xiv. et xv. siècles*, La Haye, 1735.]

thinks, upon that account, to be the great object of its political œconomy.[2]

Others admit that if a nation could be separated from all the world, it would be of no consequence how much, or how little money circulated in it. The consumable *Others say that it is necessary to have much money in order to maintain fleets and armies abroad.* goods which were circulated by means of this money, would only be exchanged for a greater or a smaller number of pieces; but the real wealth or poverty of the country, they allow, would depend altogether upon the abundance or scarcity of those consumable goods. But it is otherwise, they think, with countries which have connections with foreign nations, and which are obliged to carry on foreign wars, and to maintain fleets and armies in distant countries. This, they say, cannot be done, but by sending abroad money to pay them with; and a nation cannot send much money abroad, unless it has a good deal at home. Every such nation, therefore, must endeavour in time of peace to accumulate gold and silver, that, when occasion requires, it may have wherewithal to carry on foreign wars.

In consequence of these popular notions, all the different nations of Europe have studied, though to little purpose, every *So all European nations have tried to accumulate gold and silver.* possible means of accumulating gold and silver in their respective countries. Spain and Portugal, the proprietors of the principal mines which supply Europe with those metals, have either prohibited their exporation under the severest penalties, or subjected it to a considerable duty.[3] The like prohibition seems anciently to have made a part of the policy of most other European nations. It is even to be found, where we should least of all expect[4] to find it, in some

---

[2] [There is very little foundation for any part of this paragraph. It perhaps originated in an inaccurate recollection of pp. 17, 18 and 77–79 of *Some Considerations* (1696 ed.), and §§ 46–50 of *Civil Government*. It was probably transferred bodily from the *Lectures* without verification. See *Lectures*, p. 198.]

[3] [See below, p. 644, note 18.]

[4] [Ed. 1 reads "expect least of all."]

old Scotch acts of parliament, which forbid under heavy penal-

At first by a prohibition of exploration,

ties the carrying gold or silver *forth of the kingdom.*[5] The like policy anciently took place both in France and England.

When those countries became commercial, the merchants found this prohibition, upon many occasions, extremely inconvenient. They could frequently buy

but merchants found this inconvenient,

more advantageously with gold and silver than with any other commodity, the foreign goods which they wanted, either to import into their own, or to carry to some other for-

eign country. They remonstrated, therefore, against this prohibition as hurtful to trade.

They represented, first, that the exportation of gold and silver in order to purchase foreign goods, did not always diminish

and therefore argued that exportation did not always diminish the stock in the country,

the quantity of those metals in the kingdom. That, on the contrary, it might frequently increase that quantity;[6] because, if the consumption of foreign goods was not thereby increased in the country, those goods might be re-exported to foreign countries, and,

being there sold for a large profit, might bring back much more treasure than was originally sent out to purchase them. Mr. Mun compares this operation of foreign trade to the seed-time and harvest of agriculture. "If we only behold," says he, "the actions of the husbandman in the seed time, when he casteth away much good corn into the ground, we shall account him rather a madman than a husbandman. But when we consider his labours in the harvest, which is the end of his endeavours, we shall find the worth and plentiful increase of his actions."[7]

---

[5] [The words "forth of the realm" occur in (January) 1487, c. 11. Other Acts are 1436, c. 13; 1451, c. 15; 1482, c. 8.]

[6] [Ed. 1 reads "increase it."]

[7] [*England's Treasure by Forraign Trade, or the Ballance of our Forraign Trade is the Rule of our Treasure*, 1664, chap. iv., *ad fin.*, which reads, however, "we will rather accompt him a mad man."]

They represented, secondly, that this prohibition could not hinder the exportation of gold and silver, which, on account

and that the metals could be retained only by attention to the balance of trade.

of the smallness of their bulk in proportion to their value, could easily be smuggled abroad.[8] That this exportation could only be prevented by a proper attention to, what they called, the balance of trade.[9] That when the country exported to a greater value than it imported, a balance became due to it from foreign nations, which was necessarily paid to it in gold and silver, and thereby increased the quantity of those metals in the kingdom. But that when it imported to a greater value than it exported, a contrary balance became due to foreign nations, which was necessarily paid to them in the same manner, and thereby diminished that quantity. That in this case to prohibit the exportation of those metals could not prevent it, but only by making it more dangerous, render it more expensive. That the exchange was thereby turned more against the country which owed the balance, than it otherwise might have been; the merchant who purchased a bill upon the foreign country being obliged to pay the banker who sold it, not only for the natural risk, trouble and expence of sending the money thither, but for the extraordinary risk arising from the prohibition. But that the more the exchange was against any country, the more the balance of trade became necessarily against it; the money of that country becoming necessarily of so much less value, in comparison with that of the country to which the balance was due. That if the exchange between England and Holland, for example, was five per cent. against England, it would require a hundred and five ounces of silver in England to purchase a bill for a hundred ounces of silver in Holland: that a hundred and five ounces of silver in England, therefore, would be worth only a hundred

[8] [Mun, *England's Treasure*, chap. vi.]

[9] ["Among other things relating to trade there hath been much discourse of the balance of trade; the right understanding whereof may be of singular use."—Josiah Child, *New Discourse of Trade*, 1694, p. 152, chap. ix., introducing an explanation. The term was used before Mun's work was written. See Palgrave's *Dictionary of Political Economy, s.v.* Balance of Trade, History of the theory.]

ounces of silver in Holland, and would purchase only a proportionable quantity of Dutch goods: but that a hundred ounces of silver in Holland, on the contrary, would be worth a hundred and five ounces in England, and would purchase a proportionable quantity of English goods: that the English goods which were sold to Holland would be sold so much cheaper; and the Dutch goods which were sold to England, so much dearer, by the difference of the exchange; that the one would draw so much less Dutch money to England, and the other so much more English money to Holland, as this difference amounted to: and that the balance of trade, therefore, would necessarily be so much more against England, and would require a greater balance of gold and silver to be exported to Holland.

Those arguments were partly solid and partly sophistical. They were solid so far as they asserted that the exportation of

Their arguments were partly sophistical,

gold and silver in trade might frequently be advantageous to the country. They were solid too, in asserting that no prohibition could prevent their exportation, when private people found any advantage in exporting them. But they were sophistical in supposing, that either to preserve or to augment the quantity of those metals required more the attention of government, than to preserve or to augment the quantity of any other useful commodities, which the freedom of trade, without any such attention, never fails to supply in the proper quantity. They were sophistical too, perhaps, in asserting that the high price of exchange necessarily increased, what they called, the unfavourable balance of trade, or occasioned the exportation of a greater quantity of gold and silver. That high price, indeed, was extremely disadvantageous to the merchants who had any money to pay in foreign countries. They paid so much dearer for the bills which their bankers granted them upon those countries. But though the risk arising from the prohibition might occasion some extraordinary expence to the bankers, it would not necessarily carry any more money out of the country. This expence would generally be all laid out in the country, in smuggling the money out of it, and could seldom occasion the exportation of a single six-pence beyond the precise sum drawn for. The high price of exchange too would naturally dispose the merchants to endeavour to make their exports nearly balance their imports, in order that they might have this high exchange to pay upon as small a sum as possible. The high price of exchange, besides, must necessarily have operated as a tax, in raising the price of foreign goods, and thereby diminishing their consumption.[10] It would tend, therefore, not to increase, but to diminish, what they called, the unfavourable balance of trade, and consequently the exportation of gold and silver.

Such as they were, however, those arguments convinced the people to whom they were addressed. They were addressed by merchants to parliaments, and to the councils of princes, to no-

but they convinced parliaments and councils.

bles, and to country gentlemen; by those who were supposed to understand trade, to those who were conscious to themselves that they knew nothing about the matter. That foreign trade enriched the country, experience demonstrated to the nobles and country gentlemen, as well as to the merchants; but how, or in what manner, none of them well knew. The merchants knew perfectly in what manner it enriched themselves. It was their business to know it. But to know in what manner it enriched the country, was no part of their business. This subject never came into their consideration, but when they had occasion to apply to their country for some change in the laws relating to foreign trade. It then became necessary to say something about the beneficial effects of foreign trade, and the manner in which those effects were obstructed by the laws as they then stood. To the judges who were to decide the business, it appeared a most satisfactory account of the matter, when they were told that foreign trade brought money into the country, but that the laws in question hindered it from bringing so much as it otherwise would do. Those arguments therefore produced the wished-for effect. The prohibition of exporting gold and silver was in France and England confined to the coin of those

---

[10] [This sentence appears first in ed. 2. Ed. 1 begins the next sentence, "The high price of exchange therefore would tend."]

respective countries. The exportation of foreign coin and of bullion was made free. In Holland, and in some other places, this liberty was extended even to the coin of the country. The attention of government was turned away from guarding against the exportation of gold and silver, to watch over the balance of trade, as the only cause which could occasion any augmentation or diminution of those metals.

The exportation of foreign coin and bullion was permitted by France and England, and the exportation of Dutch coin by Holland.

From one fruitless care it was turned away to another care much more intricate, much more embarrassing, and just equally fruitless. The title of Mun's book, England's Treasure in[11] Foreign Trade, became a fundamental maxim in the political œconomy, not of England only, but of all other commercial countries. The inland or home trade, the most important of all, the trade in which an equal capital affords the greatest revenue, and creates the greatest employment to the people of the country, was considered as subsidiary only to foreign trade. It neither brought money into the country, it was said, nor carried any out of it. The country therefore could never become either richer or poorer by means of it, except so far as its prosperity or decay might indirectly influence the state of foreign trade.

That treasure was obtained by foreign trade became a received maxim.

A country that has no mines of its own must undoubtedly draw its gold and silver from foreign countries, in the same manner as one that has no vineyards of its own must draw its wines. It does not seem necessary, however, that the attention of government should be more turned towards the one than towards the other object. A country that has wherewithal to buy wine, will always get the wine which it has occasion for; and a country that has wherewithal to buy gold and silver, will never be in want of those metals. They are to be bought for a certain price like all other commodities, and as they are the price of all other com-

Gold and silver will be imported without any attention of government.

---

[11] ["In" is a mistake for "by."]

modities, so all other commodities are the price of those metals. We trust with perfect security that the freedom of trade, without any attention of government, will always supply us with the wine which we have occasion for: and we may trust with equal security that it will always supply us with all the gold and silver which we can afford to purchase or to employ, either in circulating our commodities, or in other uses.

The quantity of every commodity which human industry can either purchase or produce, naturally regulates itself in

They can be imported more easily than other commodities when there is an effectual demand.

every country according to the effectual demand, or according to the demand of those who are willing to pay the whole rent, labour and profits which must be paid in order to prepare and bring it to market. But no commodities regulate themselves more easily or more exactly according to this effectual demand than gold and silver; because, on account of the small bulk and great value of those metals, no commodities can be more easily transported from one place to another, from the places where they are cheap, to those where they are dear, from the places where they exceed, to those where they fall short of this effectual demand. If there were in England, for example, an effectual demand for an additional quantity of gold, a packet-boat could bring from Lisbon, or from wherever else it was to be had, fifty tuns of gold, which could be coined into more than five millions of guineas. But if there were[12] an effectual demand for grain to the same value, to import it would require, at five guineas a tun, a million of tuns of shipping, or a thousand ships of a thousand tuns each. The navy of England would not be sufficient.

When their quantity exceeds the demand it is impossible to prevent their exportation,

When the quantity of gold and silver imported into any country exceeds the effectual demand, no vigilance of government can prevent their exportation. All the sanguinary laws of Spain and Portugal are not able to keep their gold and silver at home.

---

[12] [Here and four lines higher eds. 1–3 read "if there was."]

The continual importations from Peru and Brazil exceed the effectual demand of those countries, and sink the price of those

and it would be equally impossible to prevent their importation if the supply fell short of the effectual demand.

metals there below that in the neighbouring countries. If, on the contrary, in any particular country their quantity fell short of the effectual demand, so as to raise their price above that of[13] the neighbouring countries, the government would have no occasion to take any pains to import them. If it were[14] even to take pains to prevent their importation, it would not be able to effectuate it. Those metals, when the Spartans had got wherewithal to purchase them, broke through all the barriers which the laws of Lycurgus opposed to their entrance into Lacedemon. All the sanguinary laws of the customs are not able to prevent the importation of the teas of the Dutch and Gottenburgh East India companies; because somewhat cheaper than those of the British company. A pound of tea, however, is about a hundred times the bulk of one of the highest prices, sixteen shillings, that is commonly paid for it in silver, and more than two thousand times the bulk of the same price in gold, and consequently just so many times more difficult to smuggle.

It is partly owing to the easy transportation of gold and silver from the places where they abound to those where they are

It is this ease of transportation which makes the value of gold and silver so uniform.

wanted, that the price of those metals does not fluctuate continually like that of the greater part of other commodities, which are hindered by their bulk from shifting their situation, when the market happens to be either over or under-stocked with them. The price

of those metals, indeed, is not altogether exempted from variation, but the changes to which it is liable are generally slow, gradual, and uniform. In Europe, for example, it is supposed, without much foundation, perhaps, that, during the course of the present and preceding century, they have been constantly,

[13] [Ed. 1 reads "in."]

[14] [Eds. 1–3 read "if it was."]

but gradually, sinking in their value, on account of the continual importations from the Spanish West Indies.[15] But to make any sudden change in the price of gold and silver, so as to raise or lower at once, sensibly and remarkably, the money price of all other commodities, requires such a revolution in commerce as that occasioned by the discovery of America.

If, notwithstanding all this, gold and silver should at any time fall short in a country which has wherewithal to purchase them, there are more expedients for supplying their place, than that of almost any other commodity. If the materials of manufacture are wanted, industry must stop. If provisions are wanted, the people must starve. But if money is wanted, barter will supply its place, though with a good deal of inconveniency. Buying and selling upon credit, and the different dealers compensating their credits with one another, once a month or once a year, will supply it with less inconveniency. A well-regulated paper money will supply it, not only without any inconveniency, but, in some cases, with some advantages.[16] Upon every account, therefore, the attention of government never was so unnecessarily employed, as when directed to watch over the preservation or increase of the quantity of money in any country.

If they did fall short, their place could be supplied by paper.

No complaint, however, is more common than that of a scarcity of money. Money, like wine, must always be scarce with those who have neither wherewithal to buy it, nor credit to borrow it. Those who have either, will seldom be in want either of the money, or of the wine which they have occasion for. This complaint, however, of the scarcity of money, is not always confined to improvident spendthrifts. It is sometimes general through a whole mercantile town, and the country in its neighbourhood.

The common complaint of scarcity of money only means difficulty in borrowing.

---

[15] [The absence of any reference to the long Digression in bk. i., chap. xi., suggests that this passage was written before the Digression was incorporated in the work. Contrast the reference below, p. 638.]

[16] [Ed. 1 reads "not only without any inconveniency but with very great advantages."]

Over-trading is the common cause of it. Sober men, whose projects have been disproportioned to their capitals, are as likely to have neither wherewithal to buy money, nor credit to borrow it as prodigals whose expence has been disproportioned to their revenue. Before their projects can be brought to bear, their stock is gone, and their credit with it. They run about everywhere to borrow money, and every body tells them that they have none to lend. Even such general complaints of the scarcity of money do not always prove that the usual number of gold and silver pieces are not circulating in the country, but that many people want those pieces who have nothing to give for them. When the profits of trade happen to be greater than ordinary, over-trading becomes a general error both among great and small dealers. They do not always send more money abroad than usual, but they buy upon credit both at home and abroad, an unusual quantity of goods, which they send to some distant market, in hopes that the returns will come in before the demand for payment. The demand comes before the returns, and they have nothing at hand, with which they can either purchase money, or give solid security for borrowing. It is not any scarcity of gold and silver, but the difficulty which such people find in borrowing, and which their creditors find in getting payment, that occasions the general complaint of the scarcity of money.

It would be too ridiculous to go about seriously to prove, that wealth does not consist in money, or in gold and silver; but in what money purchases, and is valuable only for purchasing. Money, no doubt, makes always a part of the national capital; but it has already been shown[17] that it generally makes but a small part, and always the most unprofitable part of it.

Money makes but a small part of the national capital.

It is not because wealth consists more essentially in money than in goods, that the merchant finds it generally more easy to buy goods with money, than to buy money with goods; but be-

---

[17] [This probably refers to p. 377, though the object there is rather to insist on the largeness of the saving effected by dispensing with money, and pp. 363–372.]

cause money is the known and established instrument of com-

It is easier to buy than to sell simply because money is the instrument of commerce.

merce, for which every thing is readily given in exchange, but which is not always with equal readiness to be got in exchange for every thing. The greater part of goods besides are more perishable than money, and he may frequently sustain a much greater loss by keeping them. When his goods are upon hand too, he is more liable to such demands for money as he may not be able to answer, than when he has got their price in his coffers. Over and above all this, his profit arises more directly from selling than from buying, and he is upon all these accounts generally much more anxious to exchange his goods for money, than his money for goods. But though a particular merchant, with abundance of goods in his warehouse, may sometimes be ruined by not being able to sell them in time, a nation or country is not liable to the same accident. The whole capital of a merchant frequently consists in perishable goods destined for purchasing money. But it is but a very small part of the annual produce of the land and labour of a country which can ever be destined for purchasing gold and silver from their neighbours. The far greater part is circulated and consumed among themselves; and even of the surplus which is sent abroad, the greater part is generally destined for the purchase of other foreign goods. Though gold and silver, therefore, could not be had in exchange for the goods destined to purchase them, the nation would not be ruined. It might, indeed, suffer some loss and inconveniency, and be forced upon some of those expedients which are necessary for supplying the place of money. The annual produce of its land and labour, however, would be the same, or very nearly the same, as usual, because the same, or very nearly the same consumable capital would be employed in maintaining it. And though goods do not always draw money so readily as money draws goods, in the long-run they draw it more necessarily than even it draws them. Goods can serve many other purposes besides purchasing money, but money can serve no other purpose besides purchasing goods. Money, therefore, necessarily runs after goods, but goods do not always or necessarily run after money. The man who buys, does not always mean to sell again, but frequently to use or to consume; whereas he who sells, always means to buy again. The one may frequently have done the whole, but the other can never have done more than the one-half of his business. It is not for its own sake that men desire money, but for the sake of what they can purchase with it.

Consumable commodities, it is said, are soon destroyed; whereas gold and silver are of a more durable nature, and, were it not for this continual exportation, might be

The durability of a commodity is no reason for accumulating more of it than is wanted.

accumulated for ages together, to the incredible augmentation of the real wealth of the country. Nothing, therefore, it is pretended, can be more disadvantageous to any country, than the trade which consists in the exchange of such lasting for such perishable commodities. We do not, however, reckon that trade disadvantageous which consists in the exchange of the hard-ware of England for the wines of France; and yet hard-ware is a very durable commodity, and were it not[18] for this continual exportation, might too be accumulated for ages together, to the incredible augmentation of the pots and pans of the country. But it readily occurs that the number of such utensils is in every country necessarily limited by the use which there is for them; that it would be absurd to have more pots and pans than were necessary for cooking the victuals usually consumed there; and that if the quantity of victuals were to increase, the number of pots and pans would readily increase along with it, a part of the increased quantity of victuals being employed in purchasing them, or in maintaining an additional number of workmen whose business it was to make them. It should as readily occur that the quantity of gold and silver is in every country limited by the use which there is for those metals; that their use consists in circulating commodities as coin, and in affording a species of houshold furniture as plate; that the quantity of coin in every country is regulated by the value of the commodities which are to be cir-

---

[18] [Eds. 1–3 read "was it not."]

culated by it: increase that value, and immediately a part of it will be sent abroad to purchase, wherever it is to be had, the additional quantity of coin requisite for circulating them: that the quantity of plate is regulated by the number and wealth of those private families who chuse to indulge themselves in that sort of magnificence: increase the number and wealth of such families, and a part of this increased wealth will most probably be employed in purchasing, wherever it is to be found, an additional quantity of plate: that to attempt to increase the wealth of any country, either by introducing or by detaining in it an unnecessary quantity of gold and silver, is as absurd as it would be to attempt to increase the good cheer of private families, by obliging them to keep an unnecessary number of kitchen utensils. As the expence of purchasing those unnecessary utensils would diminish instead of increasing either the quantity or goodness of the family provisions; so the expence of purchasing an unnecessary quantity of gold and silver must, in every country, as necessarily diminish the wealth which feeds, clothes, and lodges, which maintains and employs the people. Gold and silver, whether in the shape of coin or plate, are utensils, it must be remembered, as much as the furniture of the kitchen. Increase the use for them, increase the consumable commodities which are to be circulated, managed, and prepared by means of them, and you will infallibly increase the quantity; but if you attempt, by extraordinary means, to increase the quantity, you will as infallibly diminish the use and even the quantity too, which in those metals can never be greater than what the use requires. Were they ever to be accumulated beyond this quantity, their transportation is so easy, and the loss which attends their lying idle and unemployed so great, that no law could prevent their being immediately sent out of the country.

Accumulation of gold and silver is not necessary for carrying on distant wars,

It is not always necessary to accumulate gold and silver, in order to enable a country to carry on foreign wars, and to maintain fleets and armies in distant countries. Fleets and armies are maintained, not with gold and silver, but with consumable goods. The nation which, from the annual produce of its domestic industry, from the annual revenue arising out of its lands, labour, and consumable stock, has wherewithal to purchase those consumable goods in distant countries, can maintain foreign wars there.

which may be paid for by exporting: (1) gold and silver, (2) manufactures, or (3) rude produce.

A nation may purchase the pay and provisions of an army in a distant country three different ways; by sending abroad either, first, some part of its accumulated gold and silver; or secondly, some part of the annual produce of its manufactures; or last of all, some part of its annual rude produce.

The gold and silver which can properly be considered as accumulated or stored up in any country, may be distinguished into three parts; first, the circulating motley; secondly, the plate of private families; and last of all, the money which may have been collected by many years parsimony, and laid up in the treasury of the prince.

The gold and silver consists of money in circulation, plate, and money in the treasury.

It can seldom happen that much can be spared from the circulating money of the country; because in that there can seldom be much redundancy. The value of goods annually bought and sold in any country requires a certain quantity of money to circulate and distribute them to their proper consumers, and can give employment to no more. The channel of circulation necessarily draws to itself a sum sufficient to fill it, and never admits any more. Something, however, is generally withdrawn from this channel in the case of foreign war. By the great number of people who are maintained abroad, fewer are maintained at home. Fewer goods are circulated there, and less money becomes necessary to circulate them. An extraordinary quantity of paper money, of some sort or other too, such as exchequer notes, navy bills, and bank bills in England, is generally issued upon such occasions, and by supplying the place of circulating gold and silver, gives an opportunity of sending a greater quantity of it abroad.

Little can be spared from the money in circulation;

All this, however, could afford but a poor resource for maintaining a foreign war, of great expence and several years duration.

The melting down the plate of private families, has upon every occasion been found a still more insignificant one. The French, in the beginning of the last war, did not derive so much advantage from this expedient as to compensate the loss of the fashion.

plate has never yielded much;

The accumulated treasures of the prince have, in former times, afforded a much greater and more lasting resource. In the present times, if you except the king of Prussia, to accumulate treasure seems to be no part of the policy of European princes.

accumulation in the treasury has been abandoned.

The funds which maintained the foreign wars of the present century, the most expensive perhaps which history records, seem to have had little dependency upon the exportation either of the circulating money, or of the plate of private families, or of the treasure of the prince. The last French war cost Great Britain upwards of ninety millions, including not only the seventy-five millions of new debt that was contracted,[19] but the additional two shillings in the pound land tax, and what was annually borrowed of the sinking fund. More than two-thirds of this expence were[20] laid out in distant countries; in Germany, Portugal, America, in the ports of the Mediterranean, in the East and West Indies. The kings of England had no accumulated treasure. We never heard of any extraordinary quantity of plate being melted down. The circulating gold and silver of the country had not been supposed to exceed eighteen millions. Since the late recoinage of the gold, however, it is believed to have been a good deal under-rated. Let us suppose, therefore, according to the most exaggerated computation

The foreign wars of the century have evidently not been paid from the money in circulation

---

[19] [*Present State of the Nation* (see p. 557 and note 23), p. 28.]

[20] [Eds. 1–3 read "was."]

which I remember to have either seen or heard of,[21] that, gold and silver together, it amounted to thirty millions.[22] Had the war been carried on, by means of our money, the whole of it must, even according to this computation, have been sent out and returned again at least twice, in a period of between six and seven years. Should this be supposed, it would afford the most decisive argument to demonstrate how unnecessary it is for government to watch over the preservation of money, since upon this supposition the whole money of the country must have gone from it and returned to it again, two different times in so short a period, without any body's knowing any thing of the matter. The channel of circulation, however, never appeared more empty than usual during any part of this period. Few people wanted money who had wherewithal to pay for it. The profits of foreign trade, indeed, were greater than usual during the whole war; but especially towards the end of it. This occasioned, what it always occasions, a general over-trading in all the ports of Great Britain; and this again occasioned the usual complaint of the scarcity of money, which always follows over-trading. Many people wanted it, who had neither wherewithal to buy it, nor credit to borrow it; and because the debtors found it difficult to borrow, the creditors found it difficult to get payment. Gold and silver, however, were generally to be had for their value, by those who had that value to give for them.

The enormous expence of the late war, therefore, must have been chiefly defrayed, not by the exportation of gold and silver,

but by commodities.

but by that of British commodities of some kind or other. When the government, or those who acted under them, contracted with a merchant for a remittance to some foreign country, he would naturally endeavour to pay his foreign correspondent, upon whom he had granted a bill, by sending abroad rather commodities than gold and silver. If the commodities of Great Britain were not in demand in that country, he would endeav-

[21] [Ed. 1 reads "according to the exaggerated computation of Mr. Horsely."]

[22] [*Lectures*, p. 199.]

our to send them to some other country, in which he could purchase a bill upon that country. The transportation of commodities, when properly suited to the market, is always attended with a considerable profit; whereas that of gold and silver is scarce ever attended with any. When those metals are sent abroad in order to purchase foreign commodities, the merchant's profit arises, not from the purchase, but from the sale of the returns. But when they are sent abroad merely to pay a debt, he gets no returns, and consequently no profit. He naturally, therefore, exerts his invention to find out a way of paying his foreign debts, rather by the exportation of commodities than by that of gold and silver. The great quantity of British goods exported during the course of the late war, without bringing back any returns, is accordingly remarked by the author of *The Present State of the Nation.*[23]

Besides the three sorts of gold and silver above mentioned, there is in all great commercial countries a good deal of bullion alternately imported and exported for the purposes of foreign trade. This bullion, as it circulates among different commercial countries in the same manner as the national coin circulates in every particular country, may be considered as the money of the great mercantile republic. The national coin receives its movement and direction from the commodities circulated within the precincts of each particular country: the money of the mercantile republic, from those circulated between different countries. Both are employed in facilitating exchanges, the one between different individuals of the same, the other between those of different nations. Part of this money of the great mercantile republic may have been, and probably was, employed in carrying on the late war. In time of a general war, it is natural to suppose that a movement and direction should be impressed upon it, different from what it usually follows in profound peace; that it should

Part of the bullion which circulates from country to country may have been employed, but it must have been purchased with commodities.

[23] [*The Present State of the Nation, particularly with respect to its Trade, Finances, etc., etc., addressed to the King and both Houses of Parliament,* 1768 (written under the direction of George Grenville by William Knox), pp. 7, 8.]

circulate more about the seat of the war, and be more employed in purchasing there, and in the neighbouring countries, the pay and provisions of the different armies. But whatever part of this money of the mercantile republic, Great Britain may have annually employed in this manner, it must have been annually purchased, either with British commodities, or with something else that had been purchased with them; which still brings us back to commodities, to the annual produce of the land and labour of the country, as the ultimate resources which enabled us to carry on the war. It is natural indeed to suppose, that so great an annual expence must have been defrayed from a great annual produce. The expence of 1761, for example, amounted to more than nineteen millions. No accumulation could have supported so great an annual profusion. There is no annual produce even of gold and silver which could have supported it. The whole gold and silver annually imported into both Spain and Portugal, according to the best accounts, does not commonly much exceed six millions sterling,[24] which, in some years, would scarce have paid four months expence of the late war.

The commodities most proper for being transported to distant countries, in order to purchase there, either the pay and provisions of an army, or some part of the money of the mercantile republic to be employed in purchasing them, seem to be the finer and more improved manufactures; such as contain a great value in a small bulk, and can, therefore, be exported to a great distance at little expence. A country whose industry produces a great annual surplus of such manufactures, which are usually exported to foreign countries, may carry on for many years a very expensive foreign war, without either exporting any considerable quantity of gold and silver, or even having any such quantity to export. A considerable part of the annual surplus of its manufactures must, indeed, in this case be exported, without bringing back any returns to the country, though it does to

The finer manufactures are the most convenient commodities for the purpose.

[24] [Above, pp. 282, 284.]

the merchant; the government purchasing of the merchant his bills upon foreign countries, in order to purchase there the pay and provisions of an army. Some part of this surplus, however, may still continue to bring back a return.[25] The manufacturers, during the war, will have a double demand upon them, and be called upon, first, to work up goods to be sent abroad, for paying the bills drawn upon foreign countries for the pay and provisions of the army; and, secondly, to work up such as are necessary for purchasing the common returns that had usually been consumed in the country. In the midst of the most destructive foreign war, therefore, the greater part of manufactures may frequently flourish greatly; and, on the contrary, they may decline on the return of the peace. They may flourish amidst the ruin of their country, and begin to decay upon the return of its prosperity. The different state of many different branches of the British manufactures during the late war, and for some time after the peace, may serve as an illustration of what has been just now said.

No foreign war of great expence or duration could conveniently be carried on by the exportation of the rude produce of

Rude produce is inconvenient.

the soil. The expence of sending such a quantity of it to a foreign country as might purchase the pay and provisions of an army, would be too great. Few countries too produce much more rude produce than what is sufficient for the subsistence of their own inhabitants. To send abroad any great quantity of it, therefore, would be to send abroad a part of the necessary subsistence of the people. It is otherwise with the exportation of manufactures. The maintenance of the people employed in them is kept at home, and only the surplus part of their work is exported. Mr. Hume frequently takes notice of the inability of the ancient kings of England to carry on, without interruption, any foreign war of long duration.[26] The English, in those days,

---

[25] [In place of these two sentences ed. 1 reads "A considerable part of the annual surplus of its manufactures must indeed in this case be exported without bringing back any returns. Some part of it, however, may still continue to bring back a return."]

[26] [*History*, chaps. xix. and xx., vol. iii., pp. 103, 104, 165 in ed. of 1773.]

had nothing wherewithal to purchase the pay and provisions of their armies in foreign countries, but either the rude produce of the soil, of which no considerable part could be spared from the home consumption, or a few manufactures of the coarsest kind, of which, as well as of the rude produce, the transportation was too expensive. This inability did not arise from the want of money, but of the finer and more improved manufactures. Buying and selling was transacted by means of money in England then, as well as now. The quantity of circulating money must have borne the same proportion to the number and value of purchases and sales usually transacted at that time, which it does to those transacted at present; or rather it must have borne a greater proportion, because there was then no paper, which now occupies a great part of the employment of gold and silver. Among nations to whom commerce and manufactures are little known, the sovereign, upon extraordinary occasions, can seldom draw any considerable aid from his subjects, for reasons which shall be explained hereafter.[27] It is in such countries, therefore, that he generally endeavours to accumulate a treasure, as the only resource against such emergencies. Independent of this necessity, he is in such a situation naturally disposed to the parsimony requisite for accumulation. In that simple state, the expence even of a sovereign is not directed by the vanity which delights in the gaudy finery of a court, but is employed in bounty to his tenants, and hospitality to his retainers. But bounty and hospitality very seldom lead to extravagance; though vanity almost always does.[28] Every Tartar chief, accordingly, has a treasure. The treasures of Mazepa, chief of the Cossacks in the Ukraine, the famous ally of Charles the XIIth, are said to have been very great. The French kings of the Merovingian race had all treasures. When they divided their kingdom among their different children, they divided their treasure too. The Saxon princes, and the first kings after the conquest, seem likewise to have accumulated treasures. The first exploit of every new reign was commonly to

[27] [Below, pp. 1158–1159.]

[28] [This sentence and the nine words before it are repeated below, p. 1155.]

seize the treasure of the preceding king, as the most essential measure for securing the succession. The sovereigns of improved and commercial countries are not under the same necessity of accumulating treasures, because they can generally draw from their subjects extraordinary aids upon extraordinary occasions. They are likewise less disposed to do so. They naturally, perhaps necessarily, follow the mode of the times, and their expence comes to be regulated by the same extravagant vanity which directs that of all the other great proprietors in their dominions. The insignificant pageantry of their court becomes every day more brilliant, and the expence of it not only prevents accumulation, but frequently encroaches upon the funds destined for more necessary expences. What Dercyllidas said of the court of Persia, may be applied to that of several European princes, that he saw there much splendor but little strength, and many servants but few soldiers.[29]

The importation of gold and silver is not the principal, much less the sole benefit which a nation derives from its foreign trade. Between whatever places foreign trade is carried on, they all of them derive two distinct benefits from it. It carries out that surplus part of the produce of their land and labour for which there is no demand among them, and brings back in return for it something else for which there is a demand. It gives a value to their superfluities, by exchanging them for something else, which may satisfy a part of their wants, and increase their enjoyments. By means of it, the narrowness of the home market does not hinder the division of labour in any particular branch of art or manufacture from being carried to the highest perfection. By opening a more extensive market for whatever part of the produce of their labour may exceed the home consumption, it encourages them to improve its productive powers, and to

The principal benefit of foreign trade is not the importation of gold and silver, but the carrying out of surplus produce for which there is no demand and bringing back something for which there is.

[29] ["Dercyllidas" appears to be a mistake for Antiochus. See Xenophon, *Hellenica*, vii., i., ¶ 38.]

augment its annual produce to the utmost, and thereby to increase[30] the real revenue and wealth of the society. These great and important services foreign trade is continually occupied in performing, to all the different countries between which it is carried on. They all derive great benefit from it, though that in which the merchant resides generally derives the greatest, as he is generally more employed in supplying the wants, and carrying out the superfluities of his own, than of any other particular country. To import the gold and silver which may be wanted, into the countries which have no mines, is, no doubt, a part of the business of foreign commerce. It is, however, a most insignificant part of it. A country which carried on foreign trade merely upon this account, could scarce have occasion to freight a ship in a century.

It is not by the importation of gold and silver, that the discovery of America has enriched Europe. By the abundance of the American mines, those metals have become cheaper. A service of plate can now be purchased for about a third part of the corn, or a third part of the labour, which it would have cost in the fifteenth century. With the same annual expence of labour and commodities, Europe can annually purchase about three times the quantity of plate which it could have purchased at that time. But when a commodity comes to be sold for a third part of what had been its usual price, not only those who purchased it before can purchase three times their former quantity, but it is brought down to the level of a much greater number of purchasers, perhaps to more than ten, perhaps to more than twenty times the former number. So that there may be in Europe at present not only more than three times, but more than twenty or thirty times the quantity of plate which would have been in it, even in its present state of improvement, had the discovery of the American mines never been made. So far Europe has, no doubt, gained a real conveniency, though surely a very trifling one. The cheapness of gold and silver renders those metals

The discovery of America has benefited Europe not by the cheapening of gold and silver,

---

[30] [Ed. 1 reads "thereby increase."]

rather less fit for the purposes of money than they were before. In order to make the same purchases, we must load ourselves with a greater quantity of them, and carry about a shilling in our pocket where a groat would have done before. It is difficult to say which is most trifling, this inconveniency, or the opposite conveniency. Neither the one nor the other could have made any very essential change in the state of Europe. The discovery of America, however, certainly made a most essential one. By opening a new and inexhaustible market to all the commodities of Europe, it gave occasion to new divisions of labour and improvements of art, which, in the narrow circle of the ancient commerce, could never have taken place for want of a market to take off the greater part of their produce. The productive powers of labour were improved, and its produce increased in all the different countries of Europe, and together with it the real revenue and wealth of the inhabitants. The commodities of Europe were almost all new to America, and many of those of America were new to Europe. A new set of exchanges, therefore, began to take place which had never been thought of before, and which should naturally have proved as advantageous to the new, as it certainly did to the old continent. The savage injustice of the Europeans rendered an event, which ought to have been beneficial to all, ruinous and destructive to several of those unfortunate countries.

but by opening up of a new market which improved the productive powers of labour.

The discovery of a passage to the East Indies, by the Cape of Good Hope, which happened much about the same time, opened, perhaps, a still more extensive range to foreign commerce than even that of America, notwithstanding the greater distance. There were but two nations in America, in any respect superior to savages, and these were destroyed almost as soon as discovered. The rest were mere savages. But the empires of China, Indostan, Japan, as well as several others in the East Indies, without having richer mines of gold or silver, were in every

The discovery of the sea passage to the East Indies would have been still more advantageous if the trade to the East Indies had been free.

other respect much richer, better cultivated, and more advanced in all arts and manufactures than either Mexico or Peru, even though we should credit, what plainly deserves no credit, the exaggerated accounts of the Spanish writers, concerning the ancient state of those empires. But rich and civilized nations can always exchange to a much greater value with one another, than with savages and barbarians. Europe, however, has hitherto derived much less advantage from its commerce with the East Indies, than from that with America. The Portuguese monopolized the East India trade to themselves for about a century, and it was only indirectly and through them, that the other nations of Europe could either send out or receive any goods from that country. When the Dutch, in the beginning of the last century, began to encroach upon them, they vested their whole East India commerce in an exclusive company. The English, French, Swedes, and Danes, have all followed their example, so that no great nation in Europe has ever yet had the benefit of a free commerce to the East Indies. No other reason need be assigned why it has never been so advantageous as the trade to America, which, between

The exportation of silver to the East Indies is not harmful.

almost every nation of Europe and its own colonies, is free to all its subjects. The exclusive privileges of those East India companies, their great riches, the great favour and protection which these have procured them from their respective governments, have excited much envy against them. This envy has frequently represented their trade as altogether pernicious, on account of the great quantities of silver, which it every year exports from the countries from which it is carried on. The parties concerned have replied, that their trade, by this continual exportation of silver, might, indeed, tend to impoverish Europe in general, but not the particular country from which it was carried on; because, by the exportation of a part of the returns to other European countries, it annually brought home a much greater quantity of that metal than it carried out. Both the objection and the reply are founded in the popular notion which I have been just now examining. It is, therefore, unnecessary to say any thing further about either. By the annual exportation of silver to the East Indies, plate is probably somewhat dearer in Europe than it otherwise might have been; and coined silver probably purchases a larger quantity both of labour and commodities. The former of these two effects is a very small loss, the latter a very small advantage; both too insignificant to deserve any part of the public attention. The trade to the East Indies, by opening a market to the commodities of Europe, or, what comes nearly to the same thing, to the gold and silver which is purchased with those commodities, must necessarily tend to increase the annual production of European commodities, and consequently the real wealth and revenue of Europe. That it has hitherto increased them so little, is probably owing to the restraints which it every-where labours under.

I thought it necessary, though at the hazard of being tedious, to examine at full length this popular notion that wealth consists in money, or in gold and silver. Money in common language, as I have already observed, frequently signifies wealth; and this ambiguity of expression has rendered this popular notion so familiar to us, that even they, who are convinced of its absurdity, are very apt to forget their own principles, and in the course of their reasonings to take it for granted as a certain and undeniable truth. Some of the best English writers upon commerce set out with observing, that the wealth of a country consists, not in its gold and silver only, but in its lands, houses, and consumable goods of all different kinds. In the course of their reasonings, however, the lands, houses, and consumable goods seem to slip out of their memory, and the strain of their argument frequently supposes that all wealth consists in gold and silver, and that to multiply those metals is the great object of national industry and commerce.

Writers who begin by including lands, houses and consumable goods in wealth often forget them later.

The two principles being established, however, that wealth consisted in gold and silver, and that those metals could be brought into a country which had no mines only by the balance of trade, or by exporting to a greater value than it imported; it neces-

Wealth being supposed to consist in gold and silver,

political economy
endeavoured to
diminish imports
and encourage
exports,

by restraints upon
importation

sarily became the great object of political œconomy to diminish as much as possible the importation of foreign goods for home consumption, and to increase as much as possible the exportation of the produce of domestic industry. Its two great engines for enriching the country, therefore, were restraints upon importation, and encouragements to exportation.

The restraints upon importation were of two kinds.

First, Restraints upon the importation of such foreign goods for home consumption as could be produced at home, from whatever country they were imported.

Secondly, Restraints upon the importation of goods of almost all kinds from those particular countries with which the balance of trade was supposed to be disadvantageous.

Those different restraints consisted sometimes in high duties, and sometimes in absolute prohibitions.

and encourage-
ments to
exportation,

Exportation was encouraged sometimes by drawbacks, sometimes by bounties, sometimes by advantageous treaties of commerce with foreign states, and sometimes by the establishment of colonies in distant countries.

Drawbacks were given upon two different occasions. When the home-manufactures were subject to any duty or excise, either the whole or a part of it was frequently drawn back upon their exportation; and when foreign goods liable to a duty were imported in order to be exported again, either the whole or a part of this duty was sometimes given back upon such exportation.

Bounties were given for the encouragement either of some beginning manufactures, or of such sorts of industry of other kinds as were supposed to deserve particular favour.

By advantageous treaties of commerce, particular privileges were procured in some foreign state for the goods and merchants of the country, beyond what were granted to those of other countries.

By the establishment of colonies in distant countries, not

only particular privileges, but a monopoly was frequently procured for the goods and merchants of the country which established them.

The two sorts of restraints upon importation abovementioned, together with these four encouragements to exportation, constitute the six principal means by which the commercial system proposes to increase the quantity of gold and silver in any country by turning the balance of trade in its favour. I shall consider each of them in a particular chapter, and without taking much further notice of their supposed tendency to bring money into the country, I shall examine chiefly what are likely to be the effects of each of them upon the annual produce of its industry. According as they tend either to increase or diminish the value of this annual produce, they must evidently tend either to increase or diminish the real wealth and revenue of the country.

which restraints and encouragements will be considered in the next six chapters.

CHAPTER II

OF RESTRAINTS UPON THE IMPORTATION
FROM FOREIGN COUNTRIES OF SUCH GOODS
AS CAN BE PRODUCED AT HOME

BY RESTRAINING, either by high duties, or by absolute prohibitions, the importation of such goods from foreign countries as

High duties and prohibitions giving a monopoly to a particular home industry are very common.

can be produced at home, the monopoly of the home market is more or less secured to the domestic industry employed in producing them. Thus the prohibition of importing either live cattle[1] or salt provisions from foreign countries secures to the graziers of Great Britain the monopoly of the home market for

butcher's meat. The high duties upon the importation of corn,[2] which in times of moderate plenty amount to a prohibition, give a like advantage to the growers of that commodity. The prohibition of the importation of foreign woollens is equally favourable to the woollen manufacturers.[3] The silk manufacture, though altogether employed upon foreign materials, has lately obtained the same advantage.[4] The linen manufacture has not yet obtained it, but is making great strides towards it.[5] Many other sorts of manufacturers[6] have, in the same manner, obtained in Great

[1] [See above, p. 532.]

[2] [See below, pp. 676, 677.]

[3] [11 and 12 ed. iii., c. 3; 4 ed. iv., c. 7.]

[4] [6 Geo. III., c. 28.]

[5] [By the additional duties, 7 Geo. III., c. 28.]

[6] [Misprinted "manufactures" in ed. 5.]

Britain, either altogether, or very nearly a monopoly against their countrymen. The variety of goods of which the importation into Great Britain is prohibited, either absolutely, or under certain circumstances, greatly exceeds what can easily be suspected by those who are not well acquainted with the laws of the customs.[7]

That this monopoly of the home-market frequently gives great encouragement to that particular species of industry

They encourage the particular industry, but neither increase general industry nor give it the best direction.

which enjoys it, and frequently turns towards that employment a greater share of both the labour and stock of the society than would otherwise have gone to it, cannot be doubted. But whether it tends either to increase the general industry of the society, or to give it the most advantageous direction, is not, perhaps, altogether so evident.[8]

The general industry of the society never can exceed what the capital of the society can employ. As the number of workmen that can be kept in employment by any particular person

The number of persons employed cannot exceed a certain proportion to the capital of the society.

must bear a certain proportion to his capital, so the number of those that can be continually employed by all the members of a great society, must bear a certain proportion to the whole capital of that society, and never can exceed that proportion. No regulation of commerce can increase the quantity of industry in any society beyond what its capital can maintain. It can only divert a part of it into a direction into which it might not otherwise have gone; and it is by no means certain that this artificial direction is likely to be more advantageous to the society than that into which it would have gone of its own accord.

Every individual is continually exerting himself to find out the most advantageous employment for whatever capital he

and every man's interest leads him to seek that em-

can command. It is his own advantage, indeed, and not that of the society, which he has in view. But the study of his own advan-

---

[7] [This sentence appears first in Additions and Corrections and ed. 3.]

[8] [Ed. 1 reads "certain."]

ployment of capital which is most advantageous to the society.

tage naturally, or rather necessarily leads him to prefer that employment which is most advantageous to the society.

First, every individual endeavours to employ his capital as near home as he can, and consequently as much as he can in the support of domestic industry; provided always that he can thereby obtain the ordinary, or not a great deal less than the ordinary profits of stock.

Thus, upon equal or nearly equal profits, every wholesale merchant naturally prefers the home-trade to the foreign trade

(1) He tries to employ it as near home as possible.

of consumption, and the foreign trade of consumption to the carrying trade. In the home-trade his capital is never so long out of his sight as it frequently is in the foreign

trade of consumption. He can know better the character and situation of the persons whom he trusts, and if he should happen to be deceived, he knows better the laws of the country from which he must seek redress. In the carrying trade, the capital of the merchant is, as it were, divided between two foreign countries, and no part of it is ever necessarily brought home, or placed under his own immediate view and command. The capital which an Amsterdam merchant employs in carrying corn from Konnigsberg to Lisbon, and fruit and wine from Lisbon to Konnigsberg, must generally be the one-half of it at Konnigsberg and the other half at Lisbon. No part of it need ever come to Amsterdam. The natural residence of such a merchant should either be at Konnigsberg or Lisbon, and it can only be some very particular circumstances which can make him prefer the residence of Amsterdam. The uneasiness, however, which he feels at being separated so far from his capital, generally determines him to bring part both of the Konnigsberg goods which he destines for the market of Lisbon, and of the Lisbon goods which he destines for that of Konnigsberg, to Amsterdam: and though this necessarily subjects him to a double charge of loading and unloading, as well as to the payment of some duties and customs, yet for the sake of having some part of his capital always under his own view and command, he willingly submits to this extraordinary charge; and it is in this manner that every country which has any considerable share of the carrying trade, becomes always the emporium, or general market, for the goods of all the different countries whose trade it carries on. The merchant, in order to save a second loading and unloading, endeavours always to sell in the home-market as much of the goods of all those different countries as he can, and thus, so far as he can, to convert his carrying trade into a foreign trade of consumption. A merchant, in the same manner, who is engaged in the foreign trade of consumption, when he collects goods for foreign markets, will always be glad, upon equal or nearly equal profits, to sell as great a part of them at home as he can. He saves himself the risk and trouble of exportation, when, so far as he can, he thus converts his foreign trade of consumption into a home-trade. Home is in this manner the center, if I may say so, round which the capitals of the inhabitants of every country are continually circulating, and towards which they are always tending, though by particular causes they may sometimes be driven off and repelled from it towards more distant employments. But a capital employed in the home-trade, it has already been shown,[9] necessarily puts into motion a greater quantity of domestic industry, and gives revenue and employment to a greater number of the inhabitants of the country, than an equal capital employed in the foreign trade of consumption: and one employed in the foreign trade of consumption has the same advantage over an equal capital employed in the carrying trade. Upon equal, or only nearly equal profits, therefore, every individual naturally inclines to employ his capital in the manner in which it is likely to afford the greatest support to domestic industry, and to give revenue and employment to the greatest number of[10] people of his own country.

(2) He endeavours to produce the greatest possible value.

Secondly, every individual who employs his capital in the support of domestic indus-

---

[9] [Above, pp. 469–474.]

[10] [Ed. 1 reads "the" here.]

try, necessarily endeavours so to direct that industry, that its produce may be of the greatest possible value.

The produce of industry is what it adds to the subject or materials upon which it is employed. In proportion as the value of this produce is great or small, so will likewise be the profits of the employer. But it is only for the sake of profit that any man employs a capital in the support of industry; and he will always, therefore, endeavour to employ it in the support of that industry of which the produce is likely to be of the greatest value, or to exchange for the greatest quantity either of money or of other goods.

But the annual revenue of every society is always precisely equal to the exchangeable value of the whole annual produce of its industry, or rather is precisely the same thing with that exchangeable value. As every individual, therefore, endeavours as much as he can both to employ his capital in the support of domestic industry, and so to direct that industry that its produce may be of the greatest value; every individual necessarily labours to render the annual revenue of the society as great as he can. He generally, indeed, neither intends to promote the public interest, nor knows how much he is promoting it. By preferring the support of domestic to that of foreign industry, he intends only his own security; and by directing that industry in such a manner as its produce may be of the greatest value, he intends only his own gain, and he is in this, as in many other cases, led by an invisible hand to promote an end which was no part of his intention. Nor is it always the worse for the society that it was no part of it. By pursuing his own interest he frequently promotes that of the society more effectually than when he really intends to promote it. I have never known much good done by those who affected to trade for the public good. It is an affectation, indeed, not very common among merchants, and very few words need be employed in dissuading them from it.

What is the species of domestic industry which his capital can employ, and of which the produce is likely to be of the greatest value, every individual, it is evident, can, in his local situation, judge much better than any statesman or lawgiver

He can judge of this much better than the statesman.

can do for him. The statesman, who should attempt to direct private people in what manner they ought to employ their capitals, would not only load himself with a most unnecessary attention, but assume an authority which could safely be trusted, not only to no single person, but to no council or senate whatever, and which would nowhere be so dangerous as in the hands of a man who had folly and presumption enough to fancy himself fit to exercise it.

To give the monopoly of the home-market to the produce of domestic industry, in any particular art or manufacture, is in

High duties and prohibitions direct people to employ capital in producing at home what they could buy cheaper from abroad.

some measure to direct private people in what manner they ought to employ their capitals, and must, in almost all cases, be either a useless or a hurtful regulation. If the produce of domestic can be brought there as cheap as that of foreign industry, the regulation is evidently useless. If it cannot, it must generally be hurtful. It is the maxim of every prudent master of a family, never to attempt to make at home what it will cost him more to make than to buy. The taylor does not attempt to make his own shoes, but buys them of the shoemaker. The shoemaker does not attempt to make his own clothes, but employs a taylor. The farmer attempts to make neither the one nor the other, but employs those different artificers. All of them find it for their interest to employ their whole industry in a way in which they have some advantage over their neighbours, and to purchase with a part of its produce, or what is the same thing, with the price of a part of it, whatever else they have occasion for.

What is prudence in the conduct of every private family, can scarce be folly in that of a great kingdom. If a foreign

It is as foolish for a nation as for an individual to make what can be bought cheaper.

country can supply us with a commodity cheaper than we ourselves can make it, better buy it of them with some part of the produce of our own industry, employed in a way in which we have some advantage. The general industry of the country, being always in proportion to the capital which employs it, will not thereby be diminished, no more than that of the above-mentioned artificers; but only left to find out the way in which it can be employed with the greatest advantage. It is certainly not employed to the greatest advantage, when it is thus directed towards an object which it can buy cheaper than it can make. The value of its annual produce is certainly more or less diminished, when it is thus turned away from producing commodities evidently of more value than the commodity which it is directed to produce. According to the supposition, that commodity could be purchased from foreign countries cheaper than it can be made at home. It could, therefore, have been purchased with a part only of the commodities, or, what is the same thing, with a part only of the price of the commodities, which the industry employed by an equal capital would have produced at home, had it been left to follow its natural course. The industry of the country, therefore, is thus turned away from a more, to a less advantageous employment, and the exchangeable value of its annual produce, instead of being increased, according to the intention of the lawgiver, must necessarily be diminished by every such regulation.

By means of such regulations, indeed, a particular manufacture may sometimes be acquired sooner than it could have

Sometimes by such regulations a manufacture may be established earlier than it would otherwise have been but this would make capital accumulate slower,

been otherwise, and after a certain time may be made at home as cheap or cheaper than in the foreign country. But though the industry of the society may be thus carried with advantage into a particular channel sooner than it could have been otherwise, it will by no means follow that the sum total, either of its industry, or of its revenue, can ever be augmented by any such regulation. The industry of the society can augment only in proportion as its capital augments, and its capital can augment only in proportion to what can be gradually saved out of its revenue. But the immediate effect of every such regulation is to diminish its revenue, and what diminishes its revenue is certainly not very likely to augment its capital faster than it would have augmented of its own accord, had both capital and industry been left to find out their natural employments.

Though for want of such regulations the society should never acquire the proposed manufacture, it would not, upon that account, necessarily be the poorer in any

and the country might always be just as rich if it never acquired the manufacture.

one period of its duration. In every period of its duration its whole capital and industry might still have been employed, though upon different objects, in the manner that was most advantageous at the time. In every period its revenue might have been the greatest which its capital could afford, and both capital and revenue might have been augmented[11] with the greatest possible rapidity.

The natural advantages which one country has over another in producing particular commodities are sometimes so great,

No one proposes that a country should strive against great natural advantages, but it is also absurd to strive against smaller advantages whether natural or acquired.

that it is acknowledged by all the world to be in vain to struggle with them. By means of glasses, hotbeds, and hotwalls, very good grapes can be raised in Scotland, and very good wine too can be made of them at about thirty times the expence for which at least equally good can be brought from foreign countries. Would it be a reasonable law to prohibit the importation of all foreign wines, merely to encourage the making of claret and burgundy in Scotland? But if there

would be a manifest absurdity in turning towards any employment, thirty times more of the capital and industry of the country, than would be necessary to purchase from foreign countries an equal quantity of the commodities wanted, there must be an absurdity, though not altogether so glaring, yet exactly of the same kind, in turning towards any such employment a thirtieth, or even a three hundredth part more of either. Whether the advantages which one country has over another, be natural or acquired, is in this respect of no consequence. As long as the one country has those advantages, and the other

---

[11] [Ed. 1 reads "augmenting," which seems more correct.]

wants them, it will always be more advantageous for the latter, rather to buy of the former than to make. It is an acquired advantage only, which one artificer has over his neighbour, who exercises another trade; and yet they both find it more advantageous to buy of one another, than to make what does not belong to their particular trades.

Merchants and manufacturers are the people who derive the greatest advantage from this monopoly of the home-market.

Merchants and manufacturers get the most benefit from high duties and prohibitions.

The prohibition of the importation of foreign cattle, and of salt provisions, together with the high duties upon foreign corn, which in times of moderate plenty amount to a prohibition,[12] are not near so advantageous to the graziers and farmers of Great Britain, as other regulations of the same kind are to its merchants and manufacturers. Manufactures, those of the finer kind especially, are more easily transported from one country to another than corn or cattle. It is in the fetching and carrying manufactures, accordingly, that foreign trade is chiefly employed. In manufactures, a very small advantage will enable foreigners to undersell our own workmen, even in the home market. It will require a very great one to enable them to do so in the rude produce of the soil. If the free importation of foreign manufactures were[13] permitted, several of the home manufactures would probably suffer, and some of them, perhaps, go to ruin altogether, and a considerable part of the stock and industry at present employed in them, would be forced to find out some other employment. But the freest importation of the rude produce of the soil could have no such effect upon the agriculture of the country.

If the importation of foreign cattle, for example, were made ever so free, so few could be imported, that the grazing trade of Great Britain could be little affected by it. Live cattle are, perhaps, the only commodity of which the transportation is more expensive by sea than by land. By land they carry themselves

---

[12] [Above, p. 532, and below, pp. 676–677.]

[13] [Eds. 1–3 read "was" here and seven lines lower down.]

*The free importa-
tion of foreign cat-
tle would make no
great difference to
British graziers.*

to market. By sea, not only the cattle, but their food and their water too, must be carried at no small expence and inconveniency. The short sea between Ireland and Great Britain, indeed, renders the importation of Irish cattle more easy. But though the free importation of them, which was lately permitted only for a limited time, were rendered perpetual, it could have no considerable effect upon the interest of the graziers of Great Britain. Those parts of Great Britain which border upon the Irish sea are all grazing countries. Irish cattle could never be imported for their use, but must be drove through those very extensive countries, at no small expence and inconveniency, before they could arrive at their proper market. Fat cattle could not be drove so far. Lean cattle, therefore, only could be imported, and such importation could interfere, not with the interest of the feeding or fattening countries, to which, by reducing the price of lean cattle, it would rather be advantageous, but with that of the breeding countries only. The small number of Irish cattle imported since their importation was permitted, together with the good price at which lean cattle still continue to sell, seem to demonstrate that even the breeding countries of Great Britain are never likely to be much affected by the free importation of Irish cattle. The common people of Ireland, indeed, are said to have sometimes opposed with violence the exportation of their cattle. But if the exporters had found any great advantage in continuing the trade, they could easily, when the law was on their side, have conquered this mobbish opposition.

Feeding and fattening countries, besides, must always be highly improved, whereas breeding countries are generally uncultivated. The high price of lean cattle, by

*It might even ben-
efit the cultivated
plains at the
expense of the
rugged mountain-
ous districts.*

augmenting the value of uncultivated land, is like a bounty against improvement. To any country which was highly improved throughout, it would be more advantageous to import its lean cattle than to breed them. The province of Holland, accordingly, is said to follow this maxim at present. The mountains of Scotland,

Wales and Northumberland, indeed, are countries not capable of much improvement, and seem destined by nature to be the breeding countries of Great Britain. The freest importation of foreign cattle could have no other effect than to hinder those breeding countries from taking advantage of the increasing population and improvement of the rest of the kingdom, from raising their price to an exorbitant height, and from laying a real tax upon all the more improved and cultivated parts of the country.

The freest importation of salt provisions, in the same manner, could have as little effect upon the interest of the graziers

The free importa-
tion of salt provi-
sions also would
make little
difference to the
graziers,

of Great Britain as that of live cattle. Salt provisions are not only a very bulky commodity, but when compared with fresh meat, they are a commodity both of worse quality, and as they cost more labour and expence, of higher price. They could never, therefore, come into competition with the fresh meat,

though they might with the salt provisions of the country. They might be used for victualling ships for distant voyages, and such like uses, but could never make any considerable part of the food of the people. The small quantity of salt provisions imported from Ireland since their importation was rendered free, is an experimental proof that our graziers have nothing to apprehend from it. It does not appear that the price of butcher's-meat has ever been sensibly affected by it.

Even the free importation of foreign corn could very little affect the interest of the farmers of Great Britain. Corn is a much

and even the free
importation of
corn would not
much affect the
farmers.

more bulky commodity than butcher's-meat. A pound of wheat at a penny is as dear as a pound of butcher's-meat at four-pence. The small quantity of foreign corn imported even in times of the greatest scarcity, may satisfy our farmers that they can have nothing to

fear from the freest importation. The average quantity imported one year with another, amounts only, according to the very well informed author of the tracts upon the corn trade, to twenty-three thousand seven hundred and twenty-eight quarters of all sorts of grain, and does not exceed the five hundredth and seventy-one part of the annual consumption.[14] But as the bounty upon corn occasions a greater exportation in years of plenty, so it must of consequence occasion a greater importation in years of scarcity, than in the actual state of tillage[15] would otherwise take place. By means of it, the plenty of one year does not compensate the scarcity of another, and as the average quantity exported is necessarily augmented by it, so must likewise, in the actual state of tillage, the average quantity imported. If there were[16] no bounty, as less corn would be exported, so it is probable that, one year with another, less would be imported than at present. The corn merchants, the fetchers and carriers of corn between Great Britain and foreign countries, would have much less employment, and might suffer considerably; but the country gentlemen and farmers could suffer very little. It is in the corn merchants accordingly, rather than in the country gentlemen and farmers, that I have observed the greatest anxiety for the renewal and continuation of the bounty.

Country gentlemen and farmers are, to their great honour, of all people, the least subject to the wretched spirit of monopoly. The undertaker of a great manufactory is

Country gentlemen and farmers are less subject to the spirit of monopoly than merchants and manufacturers.

sometimes alarmed if another work of the same kind is established within twenty miles of him. The Dutch undertaker of the woollen manufacture at Abbeville[17] stipulated, that no work of the same kind should be established within thirty leagues of that city. Farmers and country gentlemen, on the contrary, are generally disposed rather to promote than to obstruct

---

[14] [Charles Smith, *Three Tracts on the Corn-Trade and Corn-Laws*, pp. 144–145. The same figure is quoted below, p. 675.]

[15] [Ed. 1 does not contain the words "in the actual state of tillage."]

[16] [Eds. 1–3 read "was."]

[17] [Joseph Van Robais in 1669.—John Smith, *Memoirs of Wool*, vol. ii., pp. 426, 427, but neither John Smith nor Charles King, *British Merchant*, 1721, vol. ii., pp. 93, 94, gives the particular stipulation mentioned.]

the cultivation and improvement of their neighbours farms and estates. They have no secrets, such as those of the greater part of manufacturers, but are generally rather fond of communicating to their neighbours, and of extending as far as possible any new practice which they have found to be advantageous. *Pius Questus*, says old Cato, *stabilissimusque, minimeque invidiosus; minimeque male cogitantes sunt, qui in eo studio occupati sunt*.[18] Country gentlemen and farmers, dispersed in different parts of the country, cannot so easily combine as merchants and manufacturers, who being collected into towns, and accustomed to that exclusive corporation spirit which prevails in them, naturally endeavour to obtain against all their countrymen, the same exclusive privilege which they generally possess against the inhabitants of their respective towns. They accordingly seem to have been the original inventors of those restraints upon the importation of foreign goods, which secure to them the monopoly of the home-market. It was probably in imitation of them, and to put themselves upon a level with those who, they found, were disposed to oppress them, that the country gentlemen and farmers of Great Britain so far forgot the generosity which is natural to their station, as to demand the exclusive privilege of supplying their countrymen with corn and butcher's-meat. They did not perhaps take time to consider, how much less their interest could be affected by the freedom of trade, than that of the people whose example they followed. To prohibit by a perpetual law the importation of foreign corn and cattle, is in reality to enact, that the population and industry of the country shall at no time exceed what the rude produce of its own soil can maintain.

There seem, however, to be two cases in which it will generally be advantageous to lay some burden upon foreign, for the encouragement of domestic industry. The first is, when some particular sort of industry is necessary for the defence of the country. The defence of Great Britain, for example, depends very much

The prohibition of foreign corn and cattle restrains the population.

[18] [Cato, *De re rustica, ad init.*, but "*Questus*" should of course be "*quæstus*."]

There are two cases which are exceptional,

(1) when a particular industry is necessary for the defence of the country, like shipping, which is properly encouraged by the act of navigation,

upon the number of its sailors and shipping. The act of navigation,[19] therefore, very properly endeavours to give the sailors and shipping of Great Britain the monopoly of the trade of their own country, in some cases, by absolute prohibitions, and in others by heavy burdens upon the shipping of foreign countries. The following are the principal dispositions of this act.

First, all ships, of which the owners, masters, and three-fourths of the mariners are not British subjects, are prohibited, upon pain of forfeiting ship and cargo, from trading to the British settlements and plantations, or from being employed in the coasting trade of Great Britain.[20]

Secondly, a great variety of the most bulky articles of importation can be brought into Great Britain only, either in such ships as are above described, or in ships of the country where those goods are produced, and of which the owners, masters, and three-fourths of the mariners, are of that particular country; and when imported even in ships of this latter kind, they are subject to double aliens duty. If imported in ships of any other country, the penalty is forfeiture of ship and goods.[21] When this act was made, the Dutch were, what they still are, the great carriers of Europe, and by this regulation they were entirely excluded from being the carriers to Great Britain, or from importing to us the goods of any other European country.

Thirdly, a great variety of the most bulky articles of importation are prohibited from being imported, even in British ships, from any country but that in which they are produced;

[19] [12 Car. II., c. 18, "An act for the encouraging and increasing of shipping and navigation."]

[20] [§§ 1 and 6.]

[21] [§§ 8 and 9 Eds. 1 and 2 read "ship and cargo." The alteration was probably made in order to avoid wearisome repetition of the same phrase in the three paragraphs.]

under pain of forfeiting ship and cargo.[22] This regulation too was probably intended against the Dutch. Holland was then, as now, the great emporium for all European goods, and by this regulation, British ships were hindered from loading in Holland the goods of any other European country.

Fourthly, salt fish of all kinds, whale-fins, whale-bone, oil, and blubber, not caught by and cured on board British vessels, when imported into Great Britain, are subjected to double aliens duty.[23] The Dutch, as they are still the principal, were then the only fishers in Europe that attempted to supply foreign nations with fish. By this regulation, a very heavy burden was laid upon their supplying Great Britain.

When the act of navigation was made, though England and Holland were not actually at war, the most violent animosity subsisted between the two nations. It had begun during the government of the long parliament, which first framed this act,[24] and it broke out soon after in the Dutch wars during that of the Protector and of Charles the Second. It is not impossible, therefore, that some of the regulations of this famous act may have proceeded from national animosity. They are as wise, however, as if they had all been dictated by the most deliberate wisdom. National animosity at that particular time aimed at the very same object which the most deliberate wisdom would have recommended, the diminution of the naval power of Holland, the only naval power which could endanger the security of England.

a wise act, though dictated by animosity,

The act of navigation is not favourable to foreign commerce, or to the growth of that opulence which can arise from it. The interest of a nation in its commercial relations to foreign

---

[22] [§ 4, which, however, applies to all such goods of foreign growth and manufacture as were forbidden to be imported except in English ships, not only to bulky goods. The words "great variety of the most bulky articles of importation" occur at the beginning of the previous paragraph, and are perhaps copied here by mistake.]

[23] [§ 5.]

[24] [In 1651, by "An act for the increase of shipping and encouragement of the navigation of this nation," p. 1,449 in the collection of Commonwealth Acts.]

and unfavourable to foreign commerce; nations is, like that of a merchant with regard to the different people with whom he deals, to buy as cheap and to sell as dear as possible. But it will be most likely to buy cheap, when by the most perfect freedom of trade it encourages all nations to bring to it the goods which it has occasion to purchase; and, for the same reason, it will be most likely to sell dear, when its markets are thus filled with the greatest number of buyers. The act of navigation, it is true, lays no burden upon foreign ships that come to export the produce of British industry. Even the ancient aliens duty, which used to be paid upon all goods exported as well as imported, has, by several subsequent acts, been taken off from the greater part of the articles of exportation.[25] But if foreigners, either by prohibitions or high duties, are hindered from coming to sell, they cannot always afford to come to buy; because coming without a cargo, they must lose the freight from their own country to Great Britain. By diminishing the number of sellers, therefore, we necessarily diminish that of buyers, and are thus likely not only to buy foreign goods dearer, but to sell our own cheaper, than if there was a more perfect freedom of trade. As defence, however, is of much more importance than opulence, the act of navigation is, perhaps, the wisest of all the commercial regulations of England.

The second case, in which it will generally be advantageous to lay some burden upon foreign for the encouragement of domestic industry, is, when some tax is imposed at home upon the produce of the latter. *and (2) when there is a tax on the produce of the like home manufacture.* In this case, it seems reasonable that an equal tax should be imposed upon the like produce of the former. This would not give the monopoly of the home market to domestic industry, nor turn towards a particular employment a greater share of the stock and labour of the country, than what would naturally go to it. It would only hinder any part of what

---

[25] [By 25 Car. II., c. 6, § 1, except on coal. The plural "acts" may refer to renewing acts. Anderson, *Commerce*, A.D. 1672.]

would naturally go to it from being turned away by the tax, into a less natural direction, and would leave the competition between foreign and domestic industry, after the tax, as nearly as possible upon the same footing as before it. In Great Britain, when any such tax is laid upon the produce of domestic industry, it is usual at the same time, in order to stop the clamorous complaints of our merchants and manufacturers, that they will be undersold at home, to lay a much heavier duty upon the importation of all foreign goods of the same kind.

This second limitation of the freedom of trade according to some people should, upon some occasions, be extended much

Some people say that this principle justifies a general imposition of duties on imports to counter-balance taxes levied at home on necessaries,

farther than to the precise foreign commodities which could come into competition with those which had been taxed at home. When the necessaries of life have been taxed in any country, it becomes proper, they pretend, to tax not only the like necessaries of life imported from other countries, but all sorts of foreign goods which can come into competition with any thing that is the produce of domestic industry. Subsistence, they say, becomes necessarily dearer in consequence of such taxes; and the price of labour must always rise with the price of the labourers subsistence. Every commodity, therefore, which is the produce of domestic industry, though not immediately taxed itself, becomes dearer in consequence of such taxes, because the labour which produces it becomes so. Such taxes, therefore, are really equivalent, they say, to a tax upon every particular commodity produced at home. In order to put domestic upon the same footing with foreign industry, therefore, it becomes necessary, they think, to lay some duty upon every foreign commodity, equal to this enhancement of the price of the home commodities with which it can come into competition.

but there is a difference,

Whether taxes upon the necessaries of life, such as those in Great Britain upon[26] soap, salt, leather, candles, &c. necessarily

[26] [Ed. 1 contains the words "malt, beer" here.]

raise the price of labour, and consequently that of all other commodities, I shall consider hereafter,[27] when I come to treat of taxes. Supposing, however, in the mean time, that they have this effect, and they have it undoubtedly, this general enhancement of the price of all commodities, in consequence of that of labour, is a case which differs in the two following respects from that of a particular commodity, of which the price was enhanced by a particular tax immediately imposed upon it.

First, it might always be known with great exactness how far the price of such a commodity could be enhanced by such a *since (a) the effect of taxes on necessaries cannot be exactly known,* tax: but how far the general enhancement of the price of labour might affect that of every different commodity about which labour was employed, could never be known with any tolerable exactness. It would be impossible, therefore, to proportion with any tolerable exactness the tax upon every foreign, to this enhancement of the price of every home commodity.

Secondly, taxes upon the necessaries of life have nearly the same effect upon the circumstances of the people as a poor soil *and (b) taxes on necessaries are like poor soil or bad climate: they cannot justify an attempt to give capital an unnatural direction.* and a bad climate. Provisions are thereby rendered dearer in the same manner as if it required extraordinary labour and expence to raise them. As in the natural scarcity arising from soil and climate, it would be absurd to direct the people in what manner they ought to employ their capitals and industry, so is it[28] likewise in the artificial scarcity arising from such taxes. To be left to accommodate, as well as they could, their industry to their situation, and to find out those employments in which, notwithstanding their unfavourable circumstances, they might have some advantage either in the home or in the foreign market, is what in both cases would evidently be most for their advantage. To lay a new tax upon them, because they are already overburdened

[27] [Below, pp. 1102–1109.]

[28] [Ed. 1 reads "it is."]

with taxes, and because they already pay too dear for the necessaries of life, to make them likewise pay too dear for the greater part of other commodities, is certainly a most absurd way of making amends.

Such taxes, when they have grown up to a certain height, are a curse equal to the barrenness of the earth and the inclemency of the heavens; and yet it is in the richest and most industrious countries that they have been most generally imposed. No other countries could support so great a disorder. As the strongest bodies only can live and enjoy health, under an unwholesome regimen; so the nations only, that in every sort of industry have the greatest natural and acquired advantages, can subsist and prosper under such taxes. Holland is the country in Europe in which they abound most, and which from peculiar circumstances continues to prosper, not by means of them, as has been most absurdly supposed; but in spite of them.

Taxes on necessaries are commonest in the richest countries because no others could support them.

As there are two cases in which it will generally be advantageous to lay some burden upon foreign, for the encouragement of domestic industry; so there are two others in which it may sometimes be a matter of deliberation; in the one, how far it is proper to continue the free importation of certain foreign goods; and in the other, how far, or in what manner, it may be proper to restore that free importation after it has been for some time interrupted.

There are two other possible exceptions to the general principle:

The case in which it may sometimes be a matter of deliberation how far it is proper to continue the free importation of certain foreign goods, is, when some foreign nation restrains by high duties or prohibitions the importation of some of our manufactures into their country. Revenge in this case naturally dictates retaliation, and that we should impose the like duties and prohibitions upon the importation of some or all of their manufactures into ours. Nations accordingly seldom fail to retaliate in this manner. The French have been particularly forward to favour their own

(1) Retaliation

manufactures by restraining the importation of such foreign goods as could come into competition with them. In this consisted a great part of the policy of Mr. Colbert, who, notwithstanding his great abilities, seems in this case to have been imposed upon by the sophistry of merchants and manufacturers, who are always demanding a monopoly against their countrymen. It is at present the opinion of the most intelligent men in France that his operations of this kind have not been beneficial to his country. That minister, by the tariff of 1667, imposed very high duties upon a great number of foreign manufactures. Upon his refusing to moderate them in favour of the Dutch, they in 1671 prohibited the importation of the wines, brandies and manufactures of France. The war of 1672 seems to have been in part occasioned by this commercial dispute. The peace of Nimeguen put an end to it in 1678, by moderating some of those duties in favour of the Dutch, who in consequence took off their prohibition. It was about the same time that the French and English began mutually to oppress each other's industry, by the like duties and prohibitions, of which the French, however, seem to have set the first example. The spirit of hostility which has subsisted between the two nations ever since, has hitherto hindered them from being moderated on either side. In 1697 the English prohibited the importation of bonelace, the manufacture of Flanders. The government of that country, at that time under the dominion of Spain, prohibited in return the importation of English woollens. In 1700, the prohibition of importing bonelace into England, was taken off upon condition that the importation of English woollens into Flanders should be put on the same footing as before.[29]

There may be good policy in retaliations of this kind, when there is a probability that they will procure the repeal of the high duties or prohibitions complained of. The recovery of a great foreign market will generally more than compensate the transitory inconveniency of paying dearer during a short time

[29] [The importation of bone lace was prohibited by 13 and 14 Car. II., c. 13, and 9, and 10 W. III., c. 9, was passed to make the prohibition more effectual. By 11 and 12 W. III., c. 11, it was provided that the prohibition should cease three months after English woollen manufactures were readmitted to Flanders.]

may be good policy where it is likely to secure the abolition of foreign restraints.

for some sorts of goods. To judge whether such retaliations are likely to produce such an effect, does not, perhaps, belong so much to the science of a legislator, whose deliberations ought to be governed by general principles which are always the same, as to the skill of that insidious and crafty animal, vulgarly called a statesman or politician, whose councils are directed by the momentary fluctuations of affairs. When there is no probability that any such repeal can be procured, it seems a bad method of compensating the injury done to certain classes of our people, to do another injury ourselves, not only to those classes, but to[30] almost all the other classes of them. When our neighbours prohibit some manufacture of ours, we generally prohibit, not only the same, for that alone would seldom affect them considerably, but some other manufacture of theirs. This may no doubt give encouragement to some particular class of workmen among ourselves, and by excluding some of their rivals, may enable them to raise their price in the home-market. Those workmen, however, who suffered by our neighbours' prohibition will not be benefited by ours. On the contrary, they and almost all the other classes of our citizens will thereby be obliged to pay dearer than before for certain goods. Every such law, therefore, imposes a real tax upon the whole country, not in favour of that particular class of workmen who were injured by our neighbours' prohibition, but of some other class.

The case in which it may sometimes be a matter of deliberation, how far, or in what manner, it is proper to restore the free

(2) It may be desirable to introduce freedom of trade by slow gradations.

importation of foreign goods, after it has been for some time interrupted, is, when particular manufactures, by means of high duties or prohibitions upon all foreign goods which can come into competition with them, have been so far extended as to employ a great multitude of hands. Humanity may in this case require that the freedom of trade should be restored only by slow gra-

---

[30] [Ed. 1 reads "injury ourselves, both to those classes and to."]

dations, and with a good deal of reserve and circumspection. Were those high duties and prohibitions taken away all at once,

But the disorder occasioned by its sudden introduction would be less than is supposed since

cheaper foreign goods of the same kind might be poured so fast into the home market, as to deprive all at once many thousands of our people of their ordinary employment and means of subsistence. The disorder which this would occasion might no doubt be very considerable. It would in all probability, however, be much less than is commonly imagined, for the two following reasons:

First, all those manufactures, of which any part is commonly exported to other European countries without a bounty,

(a) no manufacture which is now exported would be affected;

could be very little affected by the freest importation of foreign goods. Such manufactures must be sold as cheap abroad as any other foreign goods of the same quality and kind, and consequently must be sold cheaper at home. They would still, therefore, keep possession of the home market, and though a capricious man of fashion might sometimes prefer foreign wares, merely because they were foreign, to cheaper and better goods of the same kind that were made at home, this folly could, from the nature of things, extend to so few, that it could make no sensible impression upon the general employment of the people. But a great part of all the different branches of our woollen manufacture, of our tanned leather, and of our hard-ware, are annually exported to other European countries without any bounty, and these are the manufactures which employ the greatest number of hands. The silk, perhaps, is the manufacture which would suffer the most by this freedom of trade, and after it the linen, though the latter much less than the former.

(b) the people thrown out of one employment would easily find another,

Secondly, though a great number of people should, by thus restoring the freedom of trade, be thrown all at once out of their ordinary employment and common method of subsistence, it would by no means follow that they would thereby be deprived either of employment or subsistence. By the reduction of the army and navy at the end of the late war, more than a hundred thousand soldiers and seamen, a number equal to what is employed in the greatest manufactures, were all at once thrown out of their ordinary employment; but, though they no doubt suffered some inconveniency, they were not thereby deprived of all employment and subsistence. The greater part of the seamen, it is probable, gradually betook themselves to the merchant-service as they could find occasion, and in the mean time both they and the soldiers were absorbed in the great mass of the people, and employed in a great variety of occupations. Not only no great convulsion, but no sensible disorder arose from so great a change in the situation of more than a hundred thousand men, all accustomed to the use of arms, and many of them to rapine and plunder. The number of vagrants was scarce any-where sensibly increased by it, even the wages of labour were not reduced by it in any occupation, so far as I have been able to learn, except in that of seamen in the merchant-service. But if we compare together the habits of a soldier and of any sort of manufacturer, we shall find that those of the latter do not tend so much to disqualify him from being employed in a new trade, as those of the former from being employed in any. The manufacturer has always been accustomed to look for his subsistence from his labour only: the soldier to expect it from his pay. Application and industry have been familiar to the one; idleness and dissipation to the other. But it is surely much easier to change the direction of industry from one sort of labour to another, than to turn idleness and dissipation to any. To the greater part of manufactures besides, it has already been observed,[31] there are other collateral manufactures of so similar a nature, that a workman can easily transfer his industry from one of them to another. The greater part of such workmen too are occasionally employed in country labour. The stock which employed them in a particular manufacture before, will still remain in the country to employ an equal number of people in some other way. The capital of the country remaining the

[31] [Above, p. 185.]

same, the demand for labour will likewise be the same, or very nearly the same, though it may be exerted in different places and for different occupations. Soldiers and seamen, indeed, when discharged from the king's service, are at liberty to exercise any trade, within any town or place of Great Britain or Ireland.[32] Let the same natural liberty of exercising what species of industry they please, be restored to all his majesty's subjects, in the same manner as to soldiers and seamen; that is, break down the exclusive privileges of corporations, and repeal the statute of apprenticeship, both which are real encroachments upon natural liberty, and add to these the repeal of the law of settlements, so that a poor workman, when thrown out of employment either in one trade or in one place, may seek for it in another trade or in another place, without the fear either of a prosecution or of a removal, and neither the public nor the individuals will suffer much more from the occasional disbanding some particular classes of manufacturers, than from that of soldiers. Our manufacturers have no doubt great merit with their country, but they cannot have more than those who defend it with their blood, nor deserve to be treated with more delicacy.

especially if the privileges of corporations and the law of settlement were abolished.

To expect, indeed, that the freedom of trade should ever be entirely restored in Great Britain, is as absurd as to expect that an Oceana or Utopia[33] should ever be established in it. Not only the prejudices of the public, but what is much more unconquerable, the private interests of many individuals, irresistibly oppose it. Were the officers of the army to oppose with the same zeal and unanimity any reduction in the number of forces, with which master manufacturers set themselves against every law that is likely to increase the number of their rivals in the home market; were the former to animate their sol-

Private interests are too strong to allow of the restoration of freedom of trade in Great Britain.

---

[32] [12 Car. II., c. 16; 12 Ann., st. 1, § 13; 3 Geo. III., c. 8, gave this liberty after particular wars.]

[33] [Ed. 1 reads "Utopea."]

diers, in the same manner as the latter enflame their workmen, to attack with violence and outrage the proposers of any such regulation; to attempt to reduce the army would be as dangerous as it has now become to attempt to diminish in any respect the monopoly which our manufacturers have obtained against us. This monopoly has so much increased the number of some particular tribes of them, that, like an overgrown standing army, they have become formidable to the government, and upon many occasions intimidate the legislature. The member of parliament who supports every proposal for strengthening this monopoly, is sure to acquire not only the reputation of understanding trade, but great popularity and influence with an order of men whose numbers and wealth render them of great importance. If he opposes them, on the contrary, and still more if he has authority enough to be able to thwart them, neither the most acknowledged probity, nor the highest rank, nor the greatest public services, can protect him from the most infamous abuse and detraction, from personal insults, nor sometimes from real danger, arising from the insolent outrage of furious and disappointed monopolists.

The undertaker of a great manufacture, who, by the home markets being suddenly laid open to the competition of foreigners, should be obliged to abandon his trade, would no doubt suffer very considerably. That part of his capital which had usually been employed in purchasing materials and in paying his workmen, might, without much difficulty, perhaps, find another employment. But that part of it which was fixed in workhouses, and in the instruments of trade, could scarce be disposed of without considerable loss. The equitable regard, therefore, to his interest requires that changes of this kind should never be introduced suddenly, but slowly, gradually, and after a very long warning. The legislature, were it possible that its deliberations could be always directed, not by the clamorous importunity of partial interests, but by an extensive view of the general good, ought upon this very account, perhaps, to

The fact that equitable regard is due to the manufacturer who has fixed capital in his business is an argument against the establishment of new monopolies.

be particularly careful neither to establish any new monopolies of this kind, nor to extend further those which are already established. Every such regulation introduces some degree of real disorder into the constitution of the state, which it will be difficult afterwards to cure without occasioning another disorder.

How far it may be proper to impose taxes upon the importation of foreign goods, in order, not to prevent their importation, but to raise a revenue for government, I shall consider hereafter when I come to treat of taxes.[34] Taxes imposed with a view to prevent, or even to diminish importation, are evidently as destructive of the revenue of the customs as of the freedom of trade.

Customs duties imposed for revenue remain to be considered hereafter.

---

[34] [Below, pp. 1135–1141.]

CHAPTER III

OF THE EXTRAORDINARY RESTRAINTS UPON THE IMPORTATION OF GOODS OF ALMOST ALL KINDS, FROM THOSE COUNTRIES WITH WHICH THE BALANCE IS SUPPOSED TO BE DISADVANTAGEOUS

PART I

OF THE UNREASONABLENESS OF THOSE RESTRAINTS EVEN UPON THE PRINCIPLES OF THE COMMERCIAL SYSTEM[1]

TO LAY extraordinary restraints upon the importation of goods of almost all kinds, from those particular countries with which

British restraints on imports from France are an example.

the balance of trade is supposed to be disadvantageous, is the second expedient by which the commercial system proposes to increase the quantity of gold and silver. Thus in Great Britain, Silesia lawns may be imported for home consumption, upon paying certain duties. But French cambrics and lawns are prohibited to be imported except into the port of London, there to be warehoused for exportation.[2] Higher duties are imposed upon the wines of France than upon those of Portugal, or indeed of any other country. By what is called the impost 1692[3] a duty of five-and-twenty per cent., of the rate or value, was laid upon all French goods;

---

[1] [Ed. 1 contains no part headings and does not divide the chapter into parts.]

[2] [18 Geo. II., c. 36; 7 Geo. III., c. 43.]

[3] [4 W. and M., c. 5, § 2.]

while the goods of other nations were, the greater part of them, subjected to much lighter duties, seldom exceeding five per cent. The wine, brandy, salt and vinegar of France were indeed excepted; these commodities being subjected to other heavy duties, either by other laws, or by particular clauses of the same law. In 1696, a second duty of twenty-five per cent., the first not having been thought a sufficient discouragement, was imposed upon all French goods, except brandy; together with a new duty of five-and-twenty pounds upon the ton of French wine, and another of fifteen pounds upon the ton of French vinegar.[4] French goods have never been omitted in any of those general subsidies, or duties of five per cent., which have been imposed upon all, or the greater part of the goods enumerated in the book of rates. If we count the one third and two third subsidies as making a complete subsidy between them, there have been five of these general subsidies;[5] so that before the commencement of the present war seventy-five per cent. may be considered as the lowest duty, to which the greater part of the goods of the growth, produce, or manufacture of France were liable. But upon the greater part of goods, those duties are equivalent to a prohibition. The French in their turn have, I believe, treated our goods and manufactures just as hardly; though I am not so well acquainted with the particular hardships which they have imposed upon them.

Such restraints are unreasonable on the principles of the mercantile system, since Those mutual restraints have put an end to almost all fair commerce between the two nations, and smugglers are now the principal importers, either of British goods into France, or of French goods into Great Britain. The principles which I have been examining in the foregoing chapter took their origin from private interest and the spirit of monopoly; those which I am going to examine in this, from national prejudice and animos-

---

[4] [7 and 8 W. III., c. 20; but wine and vinegar were excepted from the general increase of 25 per cent. as well as brandy, upon which the additional duty was £30 per ton of single proof and £60 per ton of double proof.]

[5] [See below, pp. 1115, 1116.]

ity.[6] They are, accordingly, as might well be expected, still more unreasonable. They are so, even upon the principles of the commercial system.

First, though it were certain that in the case of a free trade between France and England, for example, the balance would be in favour of France, it would by no means follow that such a trade would be disadvantageous to England, or that the general balance of its whole trade would thereby be turned more against it. If the wines of France are better and cheaper than those of Portugal, or its linens than those of Germany, it would be more advantageous for Great Britain to purchase both the wine and the foreign linen which it had occasion for of France, than of Portugal and Germany. Though the value of the annual importations from France would thereby be greatly augmented, the value of the whole annual importations would be diminished, in proportion as the French goods of the same quality were cheaper than those of the other two countries. This would be the case, even upon the supposition that the whole French goods imported were to be consumed in Great Britain.

(1) if free trade with France did lead to an unfavourable balance with France, it might yet not do so with the world in general,

But, secondly, a great part of them might be re-exported to other countries, where, being sold with profit, they might bring back a return equal in value, perhaps, to the prime cost of the whole French goods imported. What has frequently been said of the East India trade[7] might possibly be true of the

(2) a part of French imports might be re-exported and bring back gold and silver,

---

[6] [Nearly all the matter from the beginning of the chapter to this point appears first in Additions and Corrections and ed. 3. Eds. 1 and 2 contain only the first sentence of the chapter and then proceed, "Thus in Great Britain higher duties are laid upon the wines of France than upon those of Portugal. German linen may be imported upon paying certain duties; but French linen is altogether prohibited. The principles which I have been examining took their origin from private interest and the spirit of monopoly; those which I am going to examine from national prejudice and animosity."]

[7] [See Anderson, *Commerce*, A.D. 1601, and see above, p. 542.]

French; that though the greater part of East India goods were bought with gold and silver, the re-exportation of a part of them to other countries, brought back more gold and silver to that which carried on the trade than the prime cost of the whole amounted to. One of the most important branches of the Dutch trade, at present, consists in the carriage of French goods to other European countries. Some part[8] even of the French wine drank in Great Britain is clandestinely imported from Holland and Zealand. If there was either a free trade between France and England, or if French goods could be imported upon paying only the same duties as those of other European nations, to be drawn back upon exportation, England might have some share of a trade which is found so advantageous to Holland.

Thirdly, and lastly, there is no certain criterion by which we can determine on which side what is called the balance be-

and (3) the balance cannot be certainly known:

tween any two countries lies, or which of them exports to the greatest value. National prejudice and animosity, prompted always by the private interest of particular traders, are the principles which generally direct our judgment upon all questions concerning it. There are two criterions, however, which have frequently been appealed to upon such occasions,

custom-house books are useless,

and the course of exchange is little better.

the custom-house books and the course of exchange. The custom-house books, I think, it is now generally acknowledged, are a very uncertain criterion, on account of the inaccuracy of the valuation at which the greater part of goods are rated in them. The course of exchange[9] is, perhaps, almost equally so.

When the exchange between two places, such as London and Paris, is at par, it is said to be a sign that the debts due from London to Paris are compensated by those due from Paris to London. On the contrary, when a premium is paid at London for a bill upon Paris, it is said to be a sign that the debts due

---

[8] [Ed. 1 reads "a great part."]

[9] [Ed. 1 reads "The course of exchange, at least as it has hitherto been estimated, is, perhaps, almost equally so."]

from London to Paris are not compensated by those due from Paris to London, but that a balance in money must be sent out from the latter place; for the risk, trouble, and expence of exporting which, the premium is both demanded and given. But the ordinary state of debt and credit between those two cities must necessarily be regulated, it is said, by the ordinary course of their dealings with one another. When neither of them imports from the other to a greater amount than it exports to that other, the debts and credits of each may compensate one another. But when one of them imports from the other to a greater value than it exports to that other,[10] the former necessarily becomes indebted to the latter in a greater sum than the latter becomes indebted to it: the debts and credits of each do not compensate one another, and money must be sent out from that place of which the debts over-balance the credits. The ordinary[11] course of exchange, therefore, being an indication of the ordinary state of debt and credit between two places, must likewise be an indication of the ordinary course of their exports and imports, as these necessarily regulate that state.

But though the ordinary course of exchange should be allowed to be a sufficient indication of the ordinary state of debt

A favourable exchange with a particular country does not prove a favourable balance with that country.

and credit between any two places, it would not from thence follow, that the balance of trade was in favour of that place which had the ordinary state of debt and credit in its favour. The ordinary state of debt and credit between any two places is not always entirely regulated by the ordinary course of their dealings with one another; but is often influenced by that of the dealings of either with many other places. If it is usual, for example, for the merchants of England to pay for the goods which they buy of Hamburgh, Dantzic, Riga, &c. by bills upon Holland, the ordinary state of debt and credit between England and Holland will not be regulated entirely by the ordinary course of the dealings of those two coun-

---

[10] [Here and three lines above eds. 1 and 2 read "it" instead of "that other."]

[11] [Ed. 1 reads "common."]

tries with one another, but will be influenced by that of the dealings of England with those other places. England may be obliged to send out every year money to Holland, though its annual exports to that country may exceed very much the annual value of its imports from thence; and though what is called the balance of trade may be very much in favour of England.[12]

In the way, besides, in which the par of exchange has hitherto been computed, the ordinary course of exchange can afford no sufficient indication that the ordinary state of debt and credit is in favour of that country which seems to have, or which is supposed to have, the ordinary course of exchange in its favour: or, in other words, the real exchange may be, and, in fact, often is so very different from the computed one, that from the course of the latter, no certain conclusion can, upon many occasions, be drawn concerning that of the former.[13]

Besides, the ordinary computation of exchange is often misleading, since

When for a sum of money paid in England, containing, according to the standard of the English mint, a certain number of ounces of pure silver, you receive a bill for a sum of money to be paid in France, containing, according to the standard of the French mint, an equal number of ounces of pure silver, exchange is said to be at par between England and France. When you pay more, you are supposed to give a premium, and exchange is said to be against England, and in favour of France. When you pay less, you are supposed to get a premium, and exchange is said to be against France, and in favour of England.

But, first, we cannot always judge of the value of the current money of different countries by the standard[14] of their respec-

---

[12] [This paragraph is absent in ed. 1, but the substance of it occurs in a paragraph lower down, omitted in ed. 2 and later eds. See below, pp. 614–615, note 28.]

[13] [In place of this paragraph ed. 1 reads, "But though this doctrine, of which some part is, perhaps, not a little doubtful, were supposed ever so certain, the manner in which the par of exchange has hitherto been computed renders uncertain every conclusion that has ever yet been drawn from it."]

[14] [Ed. 1 reads "standards" here and ten lines lower.]

(1) money is often below its nominal standard, tive mints. In some it is more, in others it is less worn, clipt, and otherwise degenerated from that standard. But the value of the current coin of every country, compared with that of any other country, is in proportion not to the quantity of pure silver which it ought to contain, but to that which it actually does contain. Before the reformation of the silver coin in king William's time, exchange between England and Holland, computed, in the usual manner, according to the standard of their respective mints, was five and twenty per cent. against England. But the value of the current coin of England, as we learn from Mr. Lowndes, was at that time rather more than five and twenty per cent. below its standard value.[15] The real exchange, therefore, may even at that time have been in favour of England, notwithstanding the computed exchange was so much against it; a smaller number of ounces of pure silver, actually paid in England, may have purchased a bill for a greater number of ounces of pure silver to be paid in Holland, and the man who was supposed to give, may in reality have got the premium. The French coin was, before the late reformation of the English gold coin, much less worn than the English, and was, perhaps, two or three per cent. nearer its standard. If the computed exchange with France, therefore, was not more than two or three per cent. against England, the real exchange might have been in its favour. Since the reformation of the gold coin, the exchange has been constantly in favour of England, and against France.

Secondly, in some countries, the expence of coinage is defrayed by the government; in others, it is defrayed by the private people who carry their bullion to the mint, and the government even derives some revenue from the coinage. In England, it is defrayed by the government, and if you carry a pound weight of standard silver to the mint, you get back sixty-two shillings, containing a pound weight of the like stan-

(2) coin is sometimes raised by seignorage above the value of the bullion contained in it,

[15] [See above, p. 264.]

dard silver. In France, a duty of eight per cent. is deducted for the coinage, which not only defrays the expence of it, but affords a small revenue to the government.[16] In England, as the coinage costs nothing, the current coin can never be much more valuable than the quantity of bullion which it actually contains. In France, the workmanship, as you pay for it, adds to the value, in the same manner as to that of wrought plate. A sum of French money, therefore, containing a certain weight of pure silver, is more valuable than a sum of English money containing an equal weight of pure silver, and must require more bullion, or other commodities, to purchase it. Though the current coin of the two countries, therefore, were equally near the standards of their respective mints, a sum of English money could not well purchase a sum of French money, containing an equal number of ounces of pure silver, nor consequently a bill upon France for such a sum. If for such a bill no more additional money was paid than what was sufficient to compensate the expence of the French coinage, the real exchange might be at par between the two countries, their debts and credits might mutually compensate one another, while the computed exchange was considerably in favour of France. If less than this was paid, the real exchange might be in favour of England, while the computed was in favour of France.

Thirdly, and lastly, in some places, as at Amsterdam, Hamburgh, Venice, &c. foreign bills of exchange are paid in

and (3) bank money bears an agio.

what they call bank money; while in others, as at London, Lisbon, Antwerp, Leghorn, &c. they are paid in the common currency of the country. What is called bank money is always of more value than the same nominal sum of common currency. A thousand guilders in the bank of Amsterdam, for example, are of more value than a thousand guilders of Amsterdam currency. The difference between them is called the agio of the bank,[17] which, at Amsterdam, is generally about

---

[16] [This erroneous statement has already been made, p. 64; see below, pp. 697–698, for details.]

[17] [Already mentioned above, p. 419.]

five per cent. Supposing the current money of two[18] countries equally near to the standard of their respective mints, and that the one pays foreign bills in this common currency, while the other pays them in bank money, it is evident that the computed exchange may be in favour of that which pays in bank money, though the real exchange should be in favour of that which pays in current money; for the same reason that the computed exchange may be in favour of that which pays in better money, or in money nearer to its own standard, though the real exchange should be in favour of that which pays in worse. The computed exchange, before the late reformation of the gold coin, was generally against London with Amsterdam, Hamburgh, Venice, and, I believe, with all other places which pay in what is called bank money. It will by no means follow, however, that the real exchange was against it. Since the reformation of the gold coin, it has been in favour of London even with those places. The computed exchange has generally been in favour of London with Lisbon, Antwerp, Leghorn, and, if you except France, I believe, with most other parts of Europe that pay in common currency; and it is not improbable that the real exchange was so too.

DIGRESSION CONCERNING BANKS OF DEPOSIT, PARTICULARLY CONCERNING THAT OF AMSTERDAM[19]

The currency of a great state, such as France or England, generally consists almost entirely of its own coin. Should this cur-

Small states must admit foreign coin, which is of uncertain value.

rency, therefore, be at any time worn, clipt, or otherwise degraded below its standard value, the state by a reformation of its coin can effectually re-establish its currency. But the currency of a small state, such as Genoa or Hamburgh, can seldom consist altogether in its own coin, but must be made up, in a great measure, of the coins of all the neighbouring states with which its inhabitants have a continual

---

[18] [Ed. 2 and later eds. read erroneously "of the two."]

[19] [See the preface to the 4th ed., above.]

intercourse. Such a state, therefore, by reforming its coin, will not always be able to reform its currency. If foreign bills of exchange are paid in this currency, the uncertain value of any sum, of what is in its own nature so uncertain, must render the exchange always very much against such a state, its currency being, in all foreign states, necessarily valued even below what it is worth.

In order to remedy the inconvenience to which this disadvantageous exchange must have subjected their merchants,

Banks are then established to pay in standard money regardless of the condition of the coin, and this money bears an agio.

such small states, when they began to attend to the interest of trade, have frequently enacted, that foreign bills of exchange of a certain value should be paid, not in common currency, but by an order upon, or by a transfer in the books of a certain bank, established upon the credit, and under the protection of the state; this bank being always obliged to pay, in good and true money, exactly according to the standard of the state. The banks of Venice, Genoa, Amsterdam, Hamburgh, and Nuremberg, seem to have been all originally established with this view, though some of them may have afterwards been made subservient to other purposes. The money of such banks being better than the common currency of the country, necessarily bore an agio, which was greater or smaller, according as the currency was supposed to be more or less degraded below the standard of the state. The agio of the bank of Hamburgh, for example, which is said to be commonly about fourteen per cent. is the supposed difference between the good standard money of the state, and the clipt, worn, and diminished currency poured into it from all the neighbouring states.

Before 1609 the great quantity of clipt and worn foreign

Before 1609 the common currency of Amsterdam was 9 per cent. below the standard.

coin, which the extensive trade of Amsterdam brought from all parts of Europe, reduced the value of its currency about nine per cent. below that of good money fresh from the mint. Such money no sooner appeared than it was melted down or carried away, as it always is in such circumstances. The merchants, with plenty of currency, could not always find a sufficient quantity of good money to pay their bills of exchange; and the value of those bills, in spite of several regulations which were made to prevent it, became in a great measure uncertain.

In order to remedy these inconveniencies, a bank was established in 1609 under the guarantee of the city. This bank received both foreign coin, and the light and worn coin of the country at its real intrinsic value in the good standard money of the country, deducting only so much as was necessary for defraying the expence of coinage, and the other necessary expence of management. For the value which remained, after this small deduction was made, it gave a credit in its books. This credit was called bank money, which, as it represented money exactly according to the standard of the mint, was always of the same real value, and intrinsically worth more than current money. It was at the same time enacted, that all bills drawn upon or negotiated at Amsterdam of the value of six hundred guilders and upwards should be paid in bank money, which at once took away all uncertainty in the value of those bills. Every merchant, in consequence of this regulation, was obliged to keep an account with the bank in order to pay his foreign bills of exchange, which necessarily occasioned a certain demand for bank money.

The bank was then established to receive and pay coin at its intrinsic value in good standard money.

Bank money, over and above both its intrinsic superiority to currency, and the additional value which this demand necessarily gives it, has likewise some other advantages. It is secure from fire, robbery, and other accidents; the city of Amsterdam is bound for it; it can be paid away by a simple transfer, without the trouble of counting, or the risk of transporting it from one place to another. In consequence of those different advantages, it seems from the beginning to have borne an agio, and it is generally believed that all the money

Money in the bank was not only up to the standard, but also secure and easily transferred, so that it bore an agio.

originally deposited in the bank was allowed to remain there, nobody caring to demand payment of a debt which he could sell for a premium in the market. By demanding payment of the bank, the owner of a bank credit would lose this premium. As a shilling fresh from the mint will buy no more goods in the market than one of our common worn shillings, so the good and true money which might be brought from the coffers of the bank into those of a private person, being mixed and confounded with the common currency of the country, would be of no more value than that currency, from which it could no longer be readily distinguished. While it remained in the coffers of the bank, its superiority was known and ascertained. When it had come into those of a private person, its superiority could not well be ascertained without more trouble than perhaps the difference was worth. By being brought from the coffers of the bank, besides, it lost all the other advantages of bank money; its security, its easy and safe transferability, its use in paying foreign bills of exchange. Over and above all this, it could not be brought from those coffers, as it will appear by and by, without previously paying for the keeping.

Those deposits of coin, or those deposits which[20] the bank was bound to restore in coin, constituted the original capital of the bank, or the whole value of what was represented by what is called bank money. At present they are supposed to constitute but a very small part of it. In order to facilitate the trade in bullion, the bank has been for these many years in the practice of giving credit in its books upon deposits of gold and silver bullion. This credit is generally about five per cent. below price of such bullion. The bank grants at the same time what is called a recipice or receipt, intitling the person who makes the deposit, or the bearer, to take out the bullion again at any time within six months, upon retransferring to the bank a quantity of bank money equal to that for which credit had been given in its books when the deposit was

The bank receives bullion as well as coin, giving in exchange a credit in bank money to 95 per cent. of the value.

---

[20] [Ed. 1 reads "Those deposits of coin, or which."]

made, and upon paying one-fourth per cent.
for the keeping, if the deposit was in silver;
and one-half per cent. if it was in gold; but at
the same time declaring, that in default of
such payment, and upon the expiration of
this term, the deposit should belong to the
bank at the price at which it had been received, or for which credit had been given in
the transfer books. What is thus paid for the
keeping of the deposit may be considered as
a sort of warehouse rent; and why this ware-
house rent should be so much dearer for gold than for silver,
several different reasons have been assigned. The fineness of
gold, it has been said, is more difficult to be ascertained than
that of silver. Frauds are more easily practised, and occasion a
greater loss in the more precious metal. Silver, besides, being
the standard metal, the state, it has been said, wishes to encourage more the making of deposits of silver than those of
gold.[21]

*It also gives a re-
ceipt which enti-
tles the bearer to
recover the bullion
on repaying the
sum advanced
and paying ¼ per
cent. for silver and
½ per cent. for
gold.*

Deposits of bullion are most commonly made when the
price is somewhat lower than ordinary; and they are taken
out again when it happens to rise. In Holland
the market price of bullion is generally
above the mint price, for the same reason
that it was so in England before the late
reformation of the gold coin. The difference
is said to be commonly from about six to
sixteen stivers upon the mark, or eight
ounces of silver of eleven parts fine, and one
part alloy. The bank price, or the credit which the bank gives
for deposits of such silver (when made in foreign coin, of
which the fineness is well known and ascertained, such as
Mexico dollars), is twenty-two guilders the mark; the mint
price is about twenty-three guilders, and the market price is
from twenty-three guilders six, to twenty-three guilders sixteen stivers, or from two to three per cent. above the mint

*The receipts are
generally worth
something,
and are renewed
at the end of
each six
months.*

---

[21] [Eds. 1–3 have the more correct but awkward reading "than of those of gold."]

price.[22] The proportions between the bank price, the mint price, and the market price of gold bullion, are nearly the same. A person can generally sell his receipt for the difference between the mint price of bullion and the market price. A receipt for bullion is almost always worth something, and it very seldom happens, therefore, that any body suffers his receipt to expire, or allows his bullion to fall to the bank at the price at which it had been received, either by not taking it out before the end of the six months, or by neglecting to pay the one-fourth or one-half per cent. in order to obtain a new receipt for another six months. This, however, though it happens seldom, is said to happen sometimes, and more frequently with regard to gold, than with regard to silver, on account of the higher warehouse-rent which is paid for the keeping of the more precious metal.

The depositor usually parts with his receipt. The person who by making a deposit of bullion obtains both a bank credit and a receipt, pays his bills of exchange as they become due with his bank credit; and either

---

[22] The following are the prices at which the bank of Amsterdam at present (September 1775) receives bullion and coin of different kinds:

SILVER.

	Guilders.	
Mexico dollars		
French crowns	B—22 per mark.	
English silver coin		
Mexico dollars new coin 21		10
Ducatoons 3		
Rix dollars 2		8

Bar silver containing $\frac{11}{12}$ fine silver 21 per mark, and in this proportion down to ¼ fine, on which 5 guilders are given.
Fine bars, 23 per mark.

GOLD.

Portugal coin	B—310 per mark.	
Guineas		
Louis d'ors new		
Ditto old 300		
New ducats . . . . 4 19 8 per ducat.		

Bar or ingot gold is received in proportion to its fineness compared with the above foreign gold coin. Upon fine bars the bank gives 340 per mark. In general, however, something more is given upon coin of a known fineness, than upon gold and silver bars, of which the fineness cannot be ascertained but by a process of melting and assaying.

sells or keeps his receipt according as he judges that the price of bullion is likely to rise or to fall. The receipt and the bank credit seldom keep long together, and there is no occasion that they should. The person who has a receipt, and who wants to take out bullion, finds always plenty of bank credits, or bank money to buy at the ordinary price; and the person who has bank money, and wants to take out bullion, finds receipts always in equal abundance.

The owners of bank credits, and the holders of receipts, constitute two different sorts of creditors against the bank. The

The bank money and the receipt together equal in value the bullion deposited.

holder of a receipt cannot draw out the bullion for which it is granted, without reassigning to the bank a sum of bank money equal to the price at which the bullion had been received. If he has no bank money of his own, he must purchase it of those who have it. The owner of bank money cannot draw out bullion without producing to the bank receipts for the quantity which he wants. If he has none of his own, he must buy them of those who have them. The holder of a receipt, when he purchases bank money, purchases the power of taking out a quantity of bullion, of which the mint price is five per cent. above the bank price. The agio of five per cent. therefore, which he commonly pays for it, is paid, not for an imaginary, but for a real value. The owner of bank money, when he purchases a receipt, purchases the power of taking out a quantity of bullion of which the market price is commonly from two to three per cent. above the mint price. The price which he pays for it, therefore, is paid likewise for a real value. The price of the receipt, and the price of the bank money, compound or make up between them the full value or price of the bullion.

Receipts for current coin are also given, but these are often of no value and are allowed to expire.

Upon deposits of the coin current in the country, the bank grants receipts likewise as well as bank credits; but those receipts are frequently of no value, and will bring no price in the market. Upon ducatoons, for example, which in the currency pass for three guilders three stivers each, the bank gives a credit of three guilders only, or five per cent. below their current value. It grants a receipt likewise intitling the bearer to take out the number of ducatoons deposited at any time within six months, upon paying one-fourth per cent. for the keeping. This receipt will frequently bring no price in the market. Three guilders bank money generally sell in the market for three guilders three stivers, the full value of the ducatoons, if they were taken out of the bank; and before they can be taken out, one-fourth per cent. must be paid for the keeping, which would be mere loss to the holder of the receipt. If the agio of the bank, however, should at any time fall to three per cent. such receipts might bring some price in the market, and might sell for one and three-fourths per cent. But the agio of the bank being now generally about five per cent. such receipts are frequently allowed to expire, or, as they express it, to fall to the bank. The receipts which are given for deposits of gold ducats fall to it yet more frequently, because a higher warehouse-rent, or one-half per cent. must be paid for the keeping of them before they can be taken out again. The five per cent. which the bank gains, when deposits either of coin or bullion are allowed to fall to it, may be considered as the warehouse-rent for the perpetual keeping of such deposits.

The sum of bank money for which the receipts are expired must be very considerable. It must comprehend the whole original capital of the bank, which, it is generally supposed, has been allowed to remain there from the time it was first deposited, nobody caring either to renew his receipt or to take out his deposit, as, for the reasons already assigned, neither the one nor the other could be done without loss. But whatever may be the amount of this sum, the proportion which it bears to the whole mass of bank money is supposed to be very small. The bank of Amsterdam has for these many years past been the great warehouse of Europe for bullion, for which the receipts are very seldom allowed to expire, or, as they express it, to fall to the bank. The far greater part of the bank money, or of the credits upon the books of the bank, is

So there is a considerable sum of bank money for which the receipts have expired, but it is not a large proportion of the whole.

supposed to have been created, for these many years past, by such deposits which the dealers in bullion are continually both making and withdrawing.

No demand can be made upon the bank but by means of a recipice or receipt. The smaller mass of bank money, for which

This cannot be drawn out of the bank.

the receipts are expired, is mixed and confounded with the much greater mass for which they are still in force; so that, though there may be a considerable sum of bank money, for which there are no receipts, there is no specific sum or portion of it, which may not at any time be demanded by one. The bank cannot be debtor to two persons for the same thing; and the owner of bank money who has no receipt, cannot demand payment of the bank till he buys one. In ordinary and quiet times, he can find no difficulty in getting one to buy at the market price, which generally corresponds with the price at which he can sell the coin or bullion it intitles him to take out of the bank.

It might be otherwise during a public calamity; an invasion,

So that if all the holders of bank money desired to exchange it for coin and bullion receipts might command an exorbitant price,

for example, such as that of the French in 1672. The owners of bank money being then all eager to draw it out of the bank, in order to have it in their own keeping, the demand for receipts might raise their price to an exorbitant height. The holders of them might form extravagant expectations, and, instead of two or three per cent. demand half the bank money for which credit had been given upon the deposits that the receipts had respectively been granted for. The enemy, informed of the constitution of the bank, might even buy them up, in order to prevent the carrying

but it is supposed in an emergency the bank would pay out money or bullion without receipts being offered.

away of the treasure. In such emergencies, the bank, it is supposed, would break through its ordinary rule of making payment only to the holders of receipts. The holders of receipts, who had no bank money, must have received within two or three per cent. of the value of the deposit for which their respective receipts had been granted. The bank, therefore, it is said, would in this case make no scruple of paying, either with money or bullion, the full value of what the owners of bank money who could get no receipts were credited for in its books; paying at the same time two or three per cent. to such holders of receipts as had no bank money, that being the whole value which in this state of things could justly be supposed due to them.

Even in ordinary and quiet times it is the interest of the holders of receipts to depress the agio, in order either to buy bank money (and consequently the bullion, which their receipts would then enable them to take out of the bank) so much cheaper, or to sell their receipts to those who have bank money, and who want to take out bullion, so much dearer; the price of a receipt being

Of late years the bank has always sold bank money at 5 per cent. agio and bought at 4 per cent.

generally equal to the difference between the market price of bank money, and that of the coin or bullion for which the receipt had been granted. It is the interest of the owners of bank money, on the contrary, to raise the agio, in order either to sell their bank money so much dearer, or to buy a receipt so much cheaper. To prevent the stock-jobbing tricks which those opposite interests might sometimes occasion, the bank has of late years come to the resolution to sell at all times bank money for currency, at five per cent. agio, and to buy it in again at four per cent. agio. In consequence of this resolution, the agio can never either rise above five, or sink below four per cent. and the proportion between the market price of bank and that of current money, is kept at all times very near to the proportion between their intrinsic values. Before this resolution was taken, the market price of bank money used sometimes to rise so high as nine per cent. agio, and sometimes to sink so low as par, according as opposite interests happened to influence the market.

The bank of Amsterdam professes to lend out no part of

It professes to lend out no part of the deposits.

what is deposited with it, but, for every guilder for which it gives credit in its books, to keep in its repositories the value of a guilder either in money or bullion. That it keeps in its repositories all the money or bullion for which there are receipts in force, for which it is at all times liable to be called upon, and which, in reality, is continually going from it and returning to it again, cannot well be doubted. But whether it does so likewise with regard to that part of its capital, for which the receipts are long ago expired, for which in ordinary and quiet times it cannot be called upon, and which in reality is very likely to remain with it for ever, or as long as the States of the United Provinces subsist, may perhaps appear more uncertain. At Amsterdam, however, no point of faith is better established than that for every guilder, circulated as bank money, there is a correspondent guilder in gold or silver to be found in the treasure of the bank. The city is guarantee that it should be so. The bank is under the direction of the four reigning burgomasters, who are changed every year. Each new set of burgomasters visits the treasure, compares it with the books, receives it upon oath, and delivers it over, with the same awful solemnity, to the set which succeeds;[23] and in that sober and religious country oaths are not yet disregarded. A rotation of this kind seems alone a sufficient security against any practices which cannot be avowed. Amidst all the revolutions which faction has ever occasioned in the government of Amsterdam, the prevailing party has at no time accused their predecessors of infidelity in the administration of the bank. No accusation could have affected more deeply the reputation and fortune of the disgraced party, and if such an accusation could have been supported, we may be assured that it would have been brought. In 1672, when the French king was at Utrecht, the bank of Amsterdam paid so readily as left no doubt of the fidelity with which it had observed its engagements. Some of the pieces which were then brought from its repositories appeared to have been scorched with the fire which happened in the town-house soon after the bank was established.[24] Those pieces, therefore, must have lain there from that time.

[23] [Ed. 1 reads "it" here.]

[24] [*Lectures*, pp. 193, 194. The story is doubtless in Voltaire, *Siècle de Louis XIV.*, chap. x., and is quoted thence by Anderson, *Commerce*, A.D. 1672.]

What may be the amount of the treasure in the bank, is a question which has long employed the speculations of the curi-

The amount of treasure in the bank is a subject of conjecture.

ous. Nothing but conjecture can be offered concerning it. It is generally reckoned that there are about two thousand people who keep accounts with the bank, and allowing them to have, one with another, the value of fifteen hundred pounds sterling lying upon their respective accounts (a very large allowance), the whole quantity of bank money, and consequently of treasure in the bank, will amount to about three millions sterling, or, at eleven guilders the pound sterling, thirty-three millions of guilders;[25] a great sum, and sufficient to carry on a very extensive circulation; but vastly below the extravagant ideas which some people have formed of this treasure.

The city of Amsterdam derives a considerable revenue from the bank. Besides what may be called the warehouse-rent

The city derives a considerable revenue from the various profits of the bank.

above mentioned, each person, upon first opening an account with the bank, pays a fee of ten guilders; and for every new account three guilders three stivers; for every transfer two stivers; and if the transfer is for less than three hundred guilders, six stivers, in order to discourage the multiplicity of small transactions. The person who neglects to balance his account twice in the year forfeits twenty-five guilders. The person who orders a transfer for more than is upon his account, is obliged to pay three per cent. for the sum overdrawn, and his order is set aside into the bargain. The bank is supposed too to make a considerable profit by the sale of the foreign coin or bullion which sometimes falls to it by the expiring of receipts, and which is always kept till it can be sold with advantage. It makes a profit likewise by selling bank money at five per cent. agio, and buying it in at four. These different emoluments amount to a good deal more than what is

---

[25] [N. Magens, *Universal Merchant*, ed. Horsley, pp. 32, 33, who also protests against the common exaggeration, gives 3,000 as a maximum estimate for the number of accounts, and 60,000,000 guilders as the utmost amount of the treasure.]

necessary for paying the salaries of officers, and defraying the
expence of management. What is paid for the keeping of bullion upon receipts, is alone supposed to amount to a neat annual revenue of between one hundred and fifty thousand and
two hundred thousand guilders. Public utility, however, and not
revenue, was the original object of this institution. Its object
was to relieve the merchants from the inconvenience of a disadvantageous exchange. The revenue which has arisen from it
was unforeseen, and may be considered as accidental. But it is
now time to return from this long digression, into which I have
been insensibly led in endeavouring to explain the reasons why
the exchange between the countries which pay in what is called
bank money, and those which pay in common currency, should
generally appear to be in favour of the former, and against the
latter. The former pay in a species of money of which the intrinsic value is always the same, and exactly agreeable to the
standard of their respective mints; the latter in a species of
money of which the intrinsic value is continually varying, and
is almost always more or less below that standard.[26]

PART II

OF THE UNREASONABLENESS OF THOSE EXTRAORDINARY
RESTRAINTS UPON OTHER PRINCIPLES[27]

In the foregoing Part of this Chapter I have endeavoured to
shew,[28] even upon the principles of the commercial system,

---

[26] [Ed. 1 runs on here as follows, "But though the computed exchange must generally be in favour of the former, the real exchange may frequently be in favour of
the latter."]

[27] [In place of this part heading (see above, p. 594, note 1) ed. 1 reads, in square-
bracketed italics, "End of the Digression concerning Banks of Deposit."]

[28] [In place of this first line ed. 1 reads, "Though the computed exchange between
any two places were in every respect the same with the real, it would not always
follow that what is called the balance of trade was in favour of that place which
had the ordinary course of exchange in its favour. The ordinary course of exchange might, indeed, in this case, be a tolerable indication of the ordinary state of

how unnecessary it is to lay extraordinary restraints upon the

The whole doctrine of the balance of trade is absurd.

importation of goods from those countries with which the balance of trade is supposed to be disadvantageous.

Nothing, however, can be more absurd than this whole doctrine of the balance of trade, upon which, not only these restraints, but almost all the other regulations of commerce are founded. When two places trade with one another, this doctrine supposes that, if the balance be even, neither of them either loses or gains; but if it leans in any degree to one side, that one of them loses, and the other gains in proportion to its declension from the exact equilibrium. Both suppositions are false. A trade which is forced by means of bounties and monopolies, may be, and commonly is disadvantageous to the country in whose favour it is meant to be established, as I shall endeavour to shew hereafter.[29] But that trade which, without force or constraint, is naturally and regularly carried on between any two places, is always advantageous, though not always equally so, to both.

By advantage or gain, I understand, not the increase of the quantity of gold and silver, but that of the exchangeable value of the annual produce of the land and labour of the country, or the increase of the annual revenue of its inhabitants.

If the balance be even, and if the trade between the two

debt and credit between them, and show which of the two countries usually had occasion to send out money to the other. But the ordinary state of debt and credit between any two places is not always entirely regulated by the ordinary course of their dealings with one another, but is influenced by that of the dealings of both with many other countries. If it was usual, for example, for the merchants of England to pay the goods which they buy from Hamburgh, Dantzick, Riga, &c., by bills upon Holland, the ordinary state of debt and credit between England and Holland would not be entirely regulated by the ordinary course of the dealings of those two countries with one another, but would be influenced by that of England with those other places. England might, in this case, be annually obliged to send out money to Holland, though its annual exports to that country exceeded the annual value of its imports from it, and though what is called the balance of trade was very much in favour of England."

"Hitherto I have been endeavouring to shew." See above, p. 599, note 12.]

[29] [Below, pp. 636–638.]

Where there is an even balance and the exchange consists wholly of native commodities two countries trading will gain nearly equally.

places consist altogether in the exchange of their native commodities, they will, upon most occasions, not only both gain, but they will gain equally, or very near equally: each will in this case afford a market for a part of the surplus produce of the other: each will replace a capital which had been employed in raising and preparing for the market[30] this part of the surplus produce of the other, and which had been distributed among, and given revenue and maintenance to a certain number of its inhabitants. Some part of the inhabitants of each, therefore, will indirectly derive their revenue and maintenance from the other. As the commodities exchanged too are supposed to be of equal value, so the two capitals employed in the trade will, upon most occasions, be equal, or very nearly equal; and both being employed in raising the native commodities of the two countries, the revenue and maintenance which their distribution will afford to the inhabitants of each will be equal, or very nearly equal. This revenue and maintenance, thus mutually afforded, will be greater or smaller in proportion to the extent of their dealings. If these should annually amount to an hundred thousand pounds, for example, or to a million on each side, each of them would afford an annual revenue in the one case of an hundred thousand pounds, in the other, of a million, to the inhabitants of the other.

If their trade should be of such a nature that one of them exported to the other nothing but native commodities, while the

If one exported nothing but native commodities, and the other nothing but foreign, both would gain, but the first would gain most.

returns of that other consisted altogether in foreign goods; the balance, in this case, would still be supposed even, commodities being paid for with commodities. They would, in this case too, both gain, but they would not gain equally; and the inhabitants of the country which exported nothing but native commodities would derive the greatest revenue from the trade. If England, for

---

[30] [Ed. 1 does not contain "and preparing for the market."]

example, should import from France nothing but the native commodities of that country, and, not having such commodities of its own as were in demand there, should annually repay them by sending thither a large quantity of foreign goods, tobacco, we shall suppose, and East India goods; this trade, though it would give some revenue to the inhabitants of both countries, would give more to those of France than to those of England. The whole French capital annually employed in it would annually be distributed among the people of France. But that part of the English capital only which was employed in producing the English commodities with which those foreign goods were purchased, would be annually distributed among the people of England. The greater part of it would replace the capitals which had been employed in Virginia, Indostan, and China, and which had given revenue and maintenance to the inhabitants of those distant countries. If the capitals were equal, or nearly equal, therefore, this employment of the French capital would augment much more the revenue of the people of France, than that of the English capital would the revenue of the people of England. France would in this case carry on a direct foreign trade of consumption with England; whereas England would carry on a round-about trade of the same kind with France. The different effects of a capital employed in the direct, and of one employed in the round-about foreign trade of consumption, have already been fully explained.[31]

There is not, probably, between any two countries, a trade which consists altogether in the exchange either of native commodities on both sides, or of native commodities on one side and of foreign goods on the other. Almost all countries exchange with one another partly native and partly foreign goods. That country, however, in whose cargoes there is the greatest proportion of native, and the least of foreign goods, will always be the principal gainer.

Mixed cases conform to the principle.

If it was not with tobacco and East India goods, but with

[31] [Above, pp. 470–471.]

It would be no worse for England to pay in gold and silver than in tobacco.

gold and silver, that England paid for the commodities annually imported from France, the balance, in this case, would be supposed uneven, commodities not being paid for with commodities, but with gold and silver. The trade, however, would, in this case, as in the foregoing, give some revenue to the inhabitants of both countries, but more to those of France than to those of England. It would give some revenue to those of England. The capital which had been employed in producing the English goods that purchased this gold and silver, the capital which had been distributed among, and given revenue to, certain inhabitants of England, would thereby be replaced, and enabled to continue that employment. The whole capital of England would no more be diminished by this exportation of gold and silver, than by the exportation of an equal value of any other goods. On the contrary, it would, in most cases, be augmented. No goods are sent abroad but those for which the demand is supposed to be greater abroad than at home, and of which the returns consequently, it is expected, will be of more value at home than the commodities exported. If the tobacco which, in England, is worth only a hundred thousand pounds, when sent to France will purchase wine which is, in England, worth a hundred and ten thousand pounds, the exchange will augment the capital of England by ten thousand pounds. If a hundred thousand pounds of English gold, in the same manner, purchase French wine, which, in England, is worth a hundred and ten thousand, this exchange will equally augment the capital of England by ten thousand pounds. As a merchant who has a hundred and ten thousand pounds worth of wine in his cellar, is a richer man than he who has only a hundred thousand pounds worth of tobacco in his warehouse, so is he likewise a richer man than he who has only a hundred thousand pounds worth of gold in his coffers. He can put into motion a greater quantity of industry, and give revenue, maintenance, and employment, to a greater number of people than either of the other two. But the capital of the country is equal to the capitals of all its different inhabitants, and the quantity of industry which can be annually maintained in it, is equal to what all those different capitals can maintain. Both the capital of the country, therefore, and the quantity of industry which can be annually maintained in it, must generally be augmented by this exchange. It would, indeed, be more advantageous for England that it could purchase the wines of France with its own hard-ware and broad-cloth, than with either the tobacco of Virginia, or the gold and silver of Brazil and Peru. A direct foreign trade of consumption is always more advantageous than a round-about one. But a round-about foreign trade of consumption, which is carried on with gold and silver, does not seem to be less advantageous than any other equally round-about one. Neither is a country which has no mines, more likely to be exhausted of gold and silver by this annual exportation of those metals, than one which does not grow tobacco by the like annual exportation of that plant. As a country which has wherewithal to buy tobacco will never be long in want of it, so neither will one be long in want of gold and silver which has wherewithal to purchase those metals.

It is a losing trade, it is said, which a workman carries on with the ale-house; and the trade which a manufacturing nation

The arguments against the French wine trade are fallacious.

would naturally carry on with a wine country, may be considered as a trade of the same nature. I answer, that the trade with the ale-house is not necessarily a losing trade. In its own nature it is just as advantageous as any other, though, perhaps, somewhat more liable to be abused. The employment of a brewer, and even that of a retailer of fermented liquors, are as necessary divisions of labour as any other. It will generally be more advantageous for a workman to buy of the brewer the quantity he has occasion for, than to brew[32] it himself, and if he is a poor workman, it will generally be more advantageous for him to buy it, by little and little, of the retailer, than a large quantity of the brewer. He may no doubt buy too much of either, as he may of any other dealers in his neighbourhood, of the butcher, if he is a glutton, or of the draper, if he affects to be a beau among his companions. It is

[32] [Eds. 1 and 2 read "make."]

advantageous to the great body of workmen, notwithstanding, that all these trades should be free, though this freedom may be abused in all of them, and is more likely to be so, perhaps, in some than in others. Though individuals, besides, may sometimes ruin their fortunes by an excessive consumption of fermented liquors, there seems to be no risk that a nation should do so. Though in every country there are many people who spend upon such liquors more than they can afford, there are always many more who spend less. It deserves to be remarked too, that, if we consult experience, the cheapness of wine seems to be a cause, not of drunkenness, but of sobriety. The inhabitants of the wine countries are in general the soberest people in Europe; witness the Spaniards, the Italians, and the inhabitants of the southern provinces of France. People are seldom guilty of excess in what is their daily fare. Nobody affects the character of liberality and good fellowship, by being profuse of a liquor which is as cheap as small beer. On the contrary, in the countries which, either from[33] excessive heat or cold, produce no grapes, and where wine consequently is dear and a rarity, drunkenness is a common vice, as among the northern nations, and all those who live between the tropics, the negroes, for example, on the coast of Guinea. When a French regiment comes from some of the northern provinces of France, where wine is somewhat dear, to be quartered in the southern, where it is very cheap, the soldiers, I have frequently heard it observed, are at first debauched by the cheapness and novelty of good wine; but after a few months residence, the greater part of them become as sober as the rest of the inhabitants. Were the duties upon foreign wines, and the excises upon malt, beer, and ale, to be taken away all at once, it might, in the same manner, occasion in Great Britain a pretty general and temporary drunkenness among the middling and inferior ranks of people, which would probably be soon followed by a permanent and almost universal sobriety. At present drunkenness is by no means the vice of people of fashion, or of those who can easily afford the most expensive liquors. A gentleman drunk

---

[33] [Ed. 1 reads "from either."]

with ale, has scarce ever been seen among us.[34] The restraints upon the wine trade in Great Britain, besides, do not so much seem calculated to hinder the people from going, if I may say so, to the ale-house, as from going where they can buy the best and cheapest liquor. They favour the wine trade of Portugal, and discourage that of France. The Portuguese, it is said, indeed, are better customers for our manufacturers than the French, and should therefore be encouraged in preference to them. As they give us their custom, it is pretended, we should give them ours. The sneaking arts of underling tradesmen are thus erected into political maxims for the conduct of a great empire; for it is the most underling tradesmen only who make it a rule to employ chiefly their own customers. A great trader purchases his goods always where they are cheapest and best, without regard to any little interest of this kind.

The sneaking arts of underling tradesmen have been erected into political maxims and commerce has become a source of discord instead of unity.

By such maxims as these, however, nations have been taught that their interest consisted in beggaring all their neighbours. Each nation has been made to look with an invidious eye upon the prosperity of all the nations with which it trades, and to consider their gain as its own loss. Commerce, which ought naturally to be, among nations, as among individuals, a bond of union and friendship, has become the most fertile source of discord and animosity. The capricious ambition of kings and ministers has not, during the present and the preceding century, been more fatal to the repose of Europe, than the impertinent jealousy of merchants and manufacturers. The violence and injustice of the rulers of mankind is an ancient evil, for which, I am afraid, the nature of human affairs can scarce admit of a remedy. But the mean rapacity, the monopolizing spirit of merchants and manufacturers, who neither are, nor ought to be, the rulers of mankind, though it cannot perhaps be corrected, may very easily be prevented from disturbing the tranquillity of any body but themselves.

[34] [*Lectures*, p. 179.]

That it was the spirit of monopoly which originally both invented and propagated this doctrine, cannot be doubted; and they who first taught it were by no means such fools as they who believed it. In every country it always is and must be the interest of the great body of the people to buy whatever they want of those who sell it cheapest. The proposition is so very manifest, that it seems ridiculous to take any pains to prove it; nor could it ever have been called in question, had not the interested sophistry of merchants and manufacturers confounded the common sense of mankind. Their interest is, in this respect, directly opposite to that of the great body of the people. As it is the interest of the freemen of a corporation to hinder the rest of the inhabitants from employing any workmen but themselves, so it is the interest of the merchants and manufacturers of every country to secure to themselves the monopoly of the home market. Hence in Great Britain, and in most other European countries, the extraordinary duties upon almost all goods imported by alien merchants. Hence the high duties and prohibitions upon all those foreign manufactures which can come into competition with our own. Hence too the extraordinary restraints upon the importation of almost all sorts of goods from those countries with which the balance of trade is supposed to be disadvantageous; that is, from those against whom national animosity happens to be most violently inflamed.

The sophistry of merchants inspired by the spirit of monopoly has confounded the common-sense of mankind.

The wealth of a neighbouring nation, however, though dangerous in war and politics, is certainly advantageous in trade. In a state of hostility it may enable our enemies to maintain fleets and armies superior to our own; but in a state of peace and commerce it must likewise enable them to exchange with us to a greater value, and to afford a better market, either for the immediate produce of our own industry, or for whatever is purchased with that produce. As a rich man is likely to be a better customer to the industrious people in his neighbourhood, than a

Wealthy neighbours are an advantage to a nation as well as an individual.

poor, so is likewise a rich nation. A rich man, indeed, who is himself a manufacturer, is a very dangerous neighbour to all those who deal in the same way. All the rest of the neighbourhood, however, by far the greatest number, profit by the good market which his expence affords them. They even profit by his underselling the poorer workmen who deal in the same way with him. The manufacturers of a rich nation, in the same manner, may no doubt be very dangerous rivals to those of their neighbours. This very competition, however, is advantageous to the great body of the people, who profit greatly besides by the good market which the great expence of such a nation affords them in every other way. Private people who want to make a fortune, never think of retiring to the remote and poor provinces of the country, but resort either to the capital, or to some of the great commercial towns. They know, that, where little wealth circulates, there is little to be got, but that where a great deal is in motion, some share of it may fall to them. The same maxims which would in this manner direct the common sense of one, or ten, or twenty individuals, should regulate the judgment of one, or ten, or twenty millions, and should make a whole nation regard the riches of its neighbours, as a probable cause and occasion for itself to acquire riches. A nation that would enrich itself by foreign trade, is certainly most likely to do so when its neighbours are all rich, industrious, and commercial nations. A great nation surrounded on all sides by wandering savages and poor barbarians might, no doubt, acquire riches by the cultivation of its own lands, and by its own interior commerce, but not by foreign trade. It seems to have been in this manner that the ancient Egyptians and the modern Chinese acquired their great wealth. The ancient Egyptians, it is said, neglected foreign commerce,[35] and the modern Chinese, it is known, hold it in the utmost contempt,[36] and scarce deign to afford it the decent protection of the laws. The modern maxims of foreign commerce, by aiming at the impoverishment of all our neighbours, so far as they are capable of

[35] [Above, pp. 467–468.]

[36] [Below, pp. 864–865.]

producing their intended effect, tend to render that very commerce insignificant and contemptible. It is in
consequence of these maxims that the commerce between France and England has in
both countries been subjected to so many
discouragements and restraints. If those two
countries, however, were to consider their
real interest, without either mercantile jeal-

*The French trade,
if not restrained,
would be much
more advanta-
geous to Great
Britain than the
American.*

ousy or national animosity, the commerce of France might be
more advantageous to Great Britain than that of any other
country, and for the same reason that of Great Britain to
France. France is the nearest neighbour to Great Britain. In the
trade between the southern coast of England and the northern
and north-western coasts of France, the returns might be expected, in the same manner as in the inland trade, four, five, or
six times in the year. The capital, therefore, employed in this
trade, could in each of the two countries keep in motion four,
five, or six times the quantity of industry, and afford employment and subsistence to four, five, or six times the number of
people, which an equal capital could do in the greater part
of the other branches of foreign trade. Between the parts of
France and Great Britain most remote from one another, the returns might be expected, at least, once in the year, and even this
trade would so far be at least equally advantageous as the
greater part of the other branches of our foreign European
trade. It would be, at least, three times more advantageous,
than the boasted trade with our North American colonies, in
which the returns were seldom made in less than three years,
frequently not in less than four or five years. France, besides, is
supposed to contain twenty-four millions of inhabitants.[37] Our
North American colonies were never supposed to contain more
than three millions:[38] And France is a much richer country than
North America; though, on account of the more unequal distribution of riches, there is much more poverty and beggary in
the one country, than in the other. France therefore could af-

---

[37] [See below, p. 1149.]

[38] [See below, pp. 1194–1195.]

ford a market at least eight times more extensive, and, on account of the superior frequency of the returns, four-and-twenty times more advantageous, than that which our North American colonies ever afforded. The trade of Great Britain would be just as advantageous to France, and, in proportion to the wealth, population and proximity of the respective countries, would have the same superiority over that which France carries on with her own colonies. Such is the very great difference between that trade which the wisdom of both nations has thought proper to discourage, and that which it has favoured the most.

But the very same circumstances which would have rendered an open and free commerce between the two countries

But the traders of France and England are jealous of each other.

so advantageous to both, have occasioned the principal obstructions to that commerce. Being neighbours, they are necessarily enemies, and the wealth and power of each becomes, upon that account, more formidable to the other; and what would increase the advantage of national friendship, serves only to inflame the violence of national animosity. They are both rich and industrious nations; and the merchants and manufacturers of each, dread the competition of the skill and activity of those of the other. Mercantile jealousy is excited, and both inflames, and is itself inflamed, by the violence of national animosity: And the traders of both countries have announced, with all the passionate confidence of interested falsehood, the certain ruin of each, in consequence of that unfavourable balance of trade, which, they pretend, would be the infallible effect of an unrestrained commerce with the other.[39]

There is no commercial country in Europe of which the approaching ruin has not frequently been foretold by the pretended doctors of this system, from an unfavourable balance of trade. After all the anxiety, however, which they have excited about this, after all the vain attempts of almost all trading nations to turn that balance in their own favour and against their

[39] [This and the preceding paragraph appear first in Additions and Corrections and ed. 3.]

No country has ever been impoverished by an unfavourable balance, and those which have the freest trade have been the most enriched by foreign trade. neighbours, it does not appear that any one nation in Europe has been in any respect impoverished by this cause. Every town and country, on the contrary, in proportion as they have opened their ports to all nations, instead of being ruined by this free trade, as the principles of the commercial system would lead us to expect, have been enriched by it. Though there are in Europe, indeed, a few towns which in some respects deserve the name of free ports, there is no country which does so. Holland, perhaps, approaches the nearest to this character of any, though still very remote from it; and Holland, it is acknowledged, not only derives its whole wealth, but a great part of its necessary subsistence, from foreign trade.

There is another balance, indeed, which has already been explained,[40] very different from the balance of trade, and *Prosperity and decay depend on the balance of produce and consumption,* which, according as it happens to be either favourable or unfavourable, necessarily occasions the prosperity or decay of every nation. This is the balance of the annual produce and consumption. If the exchangeable value of the annual produce, it has already been observed, exceeds that of the annual consumption, the capital of the society must annually increase in proportion to this excess. The society in this case lives within its revenue, and what is annually saved out of its revenue, is naturally added to its capital, and employed so as to increase still further the annual produce. If the exchangeable value of the annual produce, on the contrary, falls short of the annual consumption, the capital of the society must annually decay in proportion to this deficiency. The expence of the society in this case exceeds its revenue, and necessarily encroaches upon its capital. Its capital, therefore, must necessarily decay, and, together with it, the exchangeable value of the annual produce of its industry.

This balance of produce and consumption is entirely differ-

[40] [Above, pp. 431–432; *Lectures*, p. 207.]

which is quite different from the balance of trade, ent from, what is called, the balance of trade. It might take place in a nation which had no foreign trade, but which was entirely separated from all the world. It may take place in the whole globe of the earth, of which the wealth, population, and improvement may be either gradually increasing or gradually decaying.

The balance of produce and consumption may be constantly in favour of a nation, though what is called the balance *and may be constantly in favour of a nation when the balance of trade is against it.* of trade be generally against it. A nation may import to a greater value than it exports for half a century, perhaps, together; the gold and silver which comes into it during all this time may be all immediately sent out of it; its circulating coin may gradually decay, different sorts of paper money being substituted in its place, and even the debts too which it contracts in the principal nations with whom it deals, may be gradually increasing; and yet its real wealth, the exchangeable value of the annual produce of its lands and labour, may, during the same period, have been increasing in a much greater proportion. The state of our North American colonies, and of the trade which they carried on with Great Britain, before the commencement of the present disturbances,[41] may serve as a proof that this is by no means an impossible supposition.

---

[41] This paragraph was written in the year 1775. [But not exactly as it stands, since ed. 1 reads "the late disturbances" instead of "the present disturbances." We can only conjecture that Smith thought that the disturbances were past either when he was writing or when he returned the proof to the printers, or that they would be past by the time his book was published. The alteration of "late" to "present" was made in ed. 2, and the footnote added in ed. 3. All eds. read "present disturbances" on pp. 727, 742, 781 and "late disturbances" on p. 733. The two expressions could scarcely have been used at the same time, so we must suppose that "late" was corrected into "present" on pp. 727, 742, 781, or that "present" was corrected into "late" on p. 733, but we cannot tell for certain which of the two things happened.]

CHAPTER IV

OF DRAWBACKS

MERCHANTS AND manufacturers are not contented with the monopoly of the home market, but desire likewise the most extensive foreign sale for their goods. Their country has no jurisdiction in foreign nations, and therefore can seldom procure them any monopoly there. They are generally obliged, therefore, to content themselves with petitioning for certain encouragements to exportation.

Merchants demand encouragements to exportation.

Of these encouragements what are called Drawbacks seem to be the most reasonable. To allow the merchant to draw back upon exportation, either the whole or a part of whatever excise or inland duty is imposed upon domestic industry, can never occasion the exportation of a greater quantity of goods than what would have been exported had no duty been imposed. Such encouragements do not tend to turn towards any particular employment a greater share of the capital of the country, than what would go to that employment[1] of its own accord, but only to hinder the duty from driving away any part of that share to other employments. They tend not to overturn that balance which naturally establishes itself among all the various employments of the society; but to hinder it from being overturned by the duty. They tend not to destroy, but to preserve, what it is in most cases advantageous to preserve, the natural division and distribution of labour in the society.

Drawbacks of duty paid on domestic produce are reasonable, as they preserve the natural distribution of labour.

[1] [Eds. 1 and 2 read "go to it."]

The same thing may be said of the drawbacks upon the re-exportation of foreign goods imported; which in Great Britain

So are also drawbacks of duty paid on goods imported.

generally amount to by much the largest part of the duty upon importation.[2] By the second of the rules, annexed to the act of parliament,[3] which imposed, what is now called, the old subsidy, every merchant, whether English or alien, was allowed to draw back half that duty upon exportation; the English merchant, provided the exportation

Under the old subsidy a drawback of one-half is allowed.

took place within twelve months; the alien, provided it took place within nine months. Wines, currants, and wrought silks were the only goods which did not fall within this rule, having other and more advantageous allowances. The duties imposed by this act of parliament were, at that time, the only duties upon the importation of foreign goods. The term within which this, and all other drawbacks, could be claimed, was afterwards (by 7 Geo. I. chap. 21. sect. 10.) extended to three years.[4]

The duties which have been imposed since the old subsidy, are, the greater part of them, wholly drawn back upon exporta-

Of more recent duties the whole is generally allowed,

tion. This general rule, however, is liable to a great number of exceptions, and the doctrine of drawbacks has become a much less simple matter, than it was at their first institution. Upon the exportation of some foreign goods, of which it was expected that the importation would greatly exceed what

and in some cases the whole even of the old subsidy is allowed.

was necessary for the home consumption, the whole duties are drawn back, without retaining even half the old subsidy. Before the revolt of our North American colonies, we had the monopoly of the tobacco of Maryland and Virginia. We imported about ninety-six thou-

---

[2] [The next three pages are not in eds. 1 and 2; see below, p. 633, note 23.]

[3] [12 Car. II., c. 4.]

[4] [Henry Saxby, *The British Customs, Containing an Historical and Practical Account of each branch of that part of the Revenue*, 1757, pp. 10, 308.]

sand hogsheads, and the home consumption was not supposed to exceed fourteen thousand.[5] To facilitate the great exportation which was necessary, in order to rid us of the rest, the whole duties were drawn back, provided the exportation took place within three years.[6]

We still have, though not altogether, yet very nearly, the monopoly of the sugars of our West Indian islands. If sugars are exported within a year, therefore, all the duties upon importation are drawn back[7] and if exported within three years, all the duties, except half the old subsidy, which still continues to be retained upon the exportation of the greater part of goods. Though the importation of sugar exceeds, a good deal, what is necessary for the home consumption, the excess is inconsiderable, in comparison of what it used to be in tobacco.

Some goods, the particular objects of the jealousy of our own manufacturers, are prohibited to be imported for home

In the case of some prohibited goods there is no drawback.

consumption. They may, however, upon paying certain duties, be imported and warehoused for exportation. But upon such exportation, no part of these duties are drawn back. Our manufacturers are unwilling, it seems, that even this restricted importation should be encouraged, and are afraid lest some part of these goods should be stolen out of the warehouse, and thus come into competition with their own. It is under these regulations only that we can import wrought silks,[8] French cambrics and lawns,[9] callicoes painted, printed, stained, or dyed, &c.

We are unwilling even to be the carriers of French goods, and choose rather to forego a profit to ourselves, than to suffer those, whom we consider as our enemies, to make any profit by our means. Not only half the old subsidy, but the second

---

[5] [These figures are also quoted above, p. 475, and below, p. 765.]

[6] [Saxby, *British Customs*, p. 12.]

[7] [*Ibid.*, p. 11.]

[8] [6 Geo. III., c. 28; 11 Geo. III., c. 49.]

[9] [Above, p. 594.]

French imports generally are allowed a smaller drawback on re-exportation.

twenty-five per cent. is retained upon the exportation of all French goods.[10]

By the fourth of the rules annexed to the old subsidy, the drawback allowed upon the exportation of all wines amounted to a great deal more than half the duties which were, at that time, paid upon their importation; and it seems, at that time, to have been the object of the legislature to give some-

Wines have been peculiarly favoured,

what more than ordinary encouragement to the carrying trade in wine. Several of the other duties too, which were imposed, either at the same time, or subsequent to the old

subsidy; what is called the additional duty, the new subsidy, the one-third and two-thirds subsidies, the impost 1692, the coinage on wine, were allowed to be wholly drawn back upon exportation.[11] All those duties, however, except the additional duty and impost 1692,[12] being paid down in ready money, upon importation, the interest of so large a sum occasioned an expence, which made it unreasonable to expect any profitable carrying trade in this article. Only a part, therefore, of the duty called the impost on wine,[13] and no part of the twenty-five pounds the tun upon French wines,[14] or of the duties imposed in 1745,[15] in 1763,[16] and in 1778,[17] were allowed to be drawn back

---

[10] [7 and 8 W. III., c. 20; 1 Geo. I., c. 12, § 3; Saxby, *British Customs*, p. 45; above, pp. 594, 595. The first 25 per cent. was imposed in 1692, the second in 1696.]

[11] [Saxby, *British Customs*, pp. 13, 22, 39, 46. "The additional duty" was imposed in 1703. For the "impost 1692" and the subsidies see above, pp. 594, 595, and below, pp. 1114, 1115. "The coinage on wine" was the duty levied under 18 Car. II., c. 5, for defraying the expenses of the mint.]

[12] [Saxby, *British Customs*, pp. 13, 38.]

[13] [1 Jac. II., c. 3, and continuing Acts: £8 a tun on French and £12 on other wine.]

[14] [7 and 8 W. III., c. 20, § 3; I Geo. I., st. 2, c. 12, § 3.]

[15] [18 Geo. II., c. 9; Saxby, *British Customs*, p. 64: £8 a tun on French and £4 on other wine.]

[16] [? 1762. 3 Geo. III., c. 12: £8 a tun on French and £4 on other wine.]

[17] [18 Geo. III., c. 27: £8 8s. on French and £4 4s. on other wine.]

upon exportation. The two imposts of five per cent., imposed in 1779 and 1781, upon all the former duties of customs,[18] being allowed to be wholly drawn back upon the exportation of all other goods, were likewise allowed to be drawn back upon that of wine. The last duty that has been particularly imposed upon wine, that of 1780,[19] is allowed to be wholly drawn back, an indulgence, which, when so many heavy duties are retained, most probably could never occasion the exportation of a single tun of wine. These rules take place with regard to all places of lawful exportation, except the British colonies in America.

The 15th Charles II. chap. 7. called an act for the encouragement of trade,[20] had given Great Britain the monopoly of supplying the colonies with all the commodities of the growth or manufacture of Europe; and consequently with wines. In a country of so extensive a coast as our North American and West Indian colonies, where our authority was always so very slender, and where the inhabitants were allowed to carry out, in their own ships, their non-enumerated commodities, at first, to all parts of Europe, and afterwards, to all parts of Europe South of Cape Finisterre,[21] it is not very probable that this monopoly could ever be much respected; and they probably, at all times, found means of bringing back some cargo from the countries to which they were allowed to carry out one. They seem, however, to have found some difficulty in importing European wines from the places of their growth, and they could not well import them from Great Britain, where they were loaded with many heavy duties, of which a considerable part was not drawn back upon expor-

especially when exported to the American colonies,

---

[18] [*I.e.*, 5 per cent., not on the value of the goods, but on the amount of the previously existing duties; 19 Geo. III., c. 25, and 22 Geo. III., c. 66.]

[19] [20 Geo. III., c. 30: £8 a tun on French and £4 on other wine.]

[20] [The colonial part of the Act is said in its particular preamble (§ 5) to be for the purpose of "maintaining a greater correspondence and kindness between" the colonies and mother country, and for keeping the colonies "in a firmer dependence."]

[21] [All this is dealt with in greater detail below, pp. 731–735.]

tation. Madeira wine, not being a European commodity,[22] could be imported directly into America and the West Indies, countries which, in all their non-enumerated commodities, enjoyed a free trade to the island of Madeira. These circumstances had probably introduced that general taste for Madeira wine, which our officers found established in all our colonies at the commencement of the war which began in 1755, and which they brought back with them to the mother-country, where that wine had not been much in fashion before. Upon the conclusion of that war, in 1763 (by the 4th Geo. III. Chap. 15. Sect. 12.), all the duties, except 3*l*. 10*s*. were allowed to be drawn back, upon the exportation to the colonies of all wines, except French wines, to the commerce and consumption of which national prejudice would allow no sort of encouragement. The period between the granting of this indulgence and the revolt of our North American colonies was probably too short to admit of any considerable change in the customs of those countries.

The same act, which, in the drawback upon all wines, except French wines, thus favoured the colonies so much more than other countries; in those, upon the greater part of other

though the export of other foreign commodities to those colonies was discouraged.

commodities, favoured them much less. Upon the exportation of the greater part of commodities to other countries, half the old subsidy was drawn back. But this law enacted, that no part of that duty should be drawn back upon the exportation to the colonies of any commodities, of the growth or manufacture either of Europe or the East Indies, except wines, white callicoes and muslins.[23]

[22] [The framers of the Act were not so sure about Madeira being non-European. They excepted wine of the Madeiras and Azores by special provision, § 7 of 15 Car. II., c. 7, § 13.]

[23] [From the words "duty upon importation" at the end of the first sentence of the third paragraph of the chapter to this point is new matter, which appears first in Additions and Corrections and ed. 3. Eds. 1 and 2 read in place of it simply, "Half the duties imposed by what is called the old subsidy, are drawn back universally, except upon goods exported to the British plantations; and frequently the whole, almost always a part of those imposed by later subsidies and imports." The provision of 4 Geo. III., c. 15, taking away drawbacks, is quoted below, p. 740.]

Drawbacks were, perhaps, originally granted for the encouragement of the carrying trade, which, as the freight of the ships is frequently paid by foreigners in money, was supposed to be peculiarly fitted for bringing gold and silver into the country. But though the carrying trade certainly deserves no peculiar encouragement, though the motive of the institution was, perhaps, abundantly foolish, the institution itself seems reasonable enough. Such drawbacks cannot force into this trade a greater share of the capital of the country than what would have gone to it of its own accord, had there been no duties upon importation. They only prevent its being excluded altogether by those duties. The carrying trade, though it deserves no preference, ought not to be precluded, but to be left free like all other trades. It is a necessary resource for those capitals which cannot find employment either in the agriculture or in the manufactures of the country, either in its home trade or in its foreign trade of consumption.

Drawbacks were originally granted to encourage the carrying trade, which was absurd, but they are reasonable enough.

The revenue of the customs, instead of suffering, profits from such drawbacks, by that part of the duty which is retained. If the whole duties had been retained, the foreign goods upon which they are paid, could seldom have been exported, nor consequently imported, for want of a market. The duties, therefore, of which a part is retained, would never have been paid.

The revenue gains by their existence when they do not amount to the whole of the duty paid.

These reasons seem sufficiently to justify drawbacks, and would justify them, though the whole duties, whether upon the produce of domestic industry, or upon foreign goods, were always drawn back upon exportation. The revenue of excise would in this case, indeed, suffer a little, and that of the customs a good deal more; but the natural balance of industry, the natural division and distribution of labour, which is always more or less disturbed by such duties, would be more nearly re-established by such a regulation.

They would be justified even if they always did amount to the whole duty paid

These reasons, however, will justify drawbacks only upon exporting goods to those countries which are altogether foreign and independent, not to those in which our merchants and manufacturers enjoy a monopoly. A drawback, for example, upon the exportation of European goods to our American colonies, will not always occasion a greater exportation than what would have taken place without it. By means of the monopoly which our merchants and manufacturers enjoy there, the same quantity might frequently, perhaps, be sent thither, though the whole duties were retained. The drawback, therefore, may frequently be pure loss to the revenue of excise and customs, without altering the state of the trade, or rendering it in any respect more extensive. How far such drawbacks can be justified, as a proper encouragement to the industry of our colonies, or how far it is advantageous to the mother-country, that they should be exempted from taxes which are paid by all the rest of their fellow-subjects, will appear hereafter[24] when I come to treat of colonies.

but only to independent countries, not to those in respect of which there is a monopoly of trade.

Drawbacks, however, it must always be understood, are useful only in those cases in which the goods for the exportation of which they are given, are really exported to some foreign country and not clandestinely re-imported into our own. That some drawbacks, particularly those upon tobacco, have frequently been abused in this manner, and have given occasion to many frauds equally hurtful both to the revenue and to the fair trader, is well known.

They give rise to frauds.

[24] [Below, pp. 738–742.]

CHAPTER V

OF BOUNTIES

BOUNTIES UPON exportation are, in Great Britain, frequently petitioned for, and sometimes granted to the produce of particular branches of domestic industry.

Foreigners cannot be forced to buy our goods, so it is proposed to pay them to do so.

By means of them our merchants and manufacturers, it is pretended, will be enabled to sell their goods as cheap or cheaper than their rivals in the foreign market. A greater quantity, it is said, will thus be exported, and the balance of trade consequently turned more in favour of our own country. We cannot give our workmen a monopoly in the foreign, as we have done in the home market. We cannot force foreigners to buy their goods, as we have done our own countrymen. The next best expedient, it has been thought, therefore, is to pay them for buying. It is in this manner that the mercantile system proposes to enrich the whole country, and to put money into all our pockets by means of the balance of trade.

Bounties, it is allowed, ought to be given to those branches of trade only which cannot be carried on without them. But

Bounties are not demanded for any but losing trades,

every branch of trade in which the merchant can sell his goods for a price which replaces to him, with the ordinary profits of stock, the whole capital employed in preparing and sending them to market, can be carried on without a bounty. Every such branch is evidently upon a level with all the other branches of trade which are carried on without bounties, and cannot therefore require one more than they. Those trades only require bounties in which the merchant is obliged to sell his goods for a price which does not replace to him his capital, to-

gether with the ordinary profit; or in which he is obliged to sell
them for less than it really costs him to send them to market.
The bounty is given in order to make up this loss, and to encourage him to continue, or perhaps to begin, a trade of which
the expence is supposed to be greater than the returns, of
which every operation eats up a part of the capital employed in
it, and which is of such a nature, that, if all other trades resembled it, there would soon be no capital left in the country.

The trades, it is to be observed, which are carried on by
means of bounties, are the only ones which can be carried on

*and their effect is
to force trade into
disadvantageous
channels.*

between two nations for any considerable
time together, in such a manner as that one
of them shall always and regularly lose, or
sell its goods for less than it really costs to
send them to market. But if the bounty did
not repay to the merchant what he would otherwise lose upon
the price of his goods, his own interest would soon oblige him
to employ his stock in another way, or to find out a trade in
which the price of the goods would replace to him, with the ordinary profit, the capital employed in sending them to market.
The effect of bounties, like that of all the other expedients of
the mercantile system, can only be to force the trade of a country into a channel much less advantageous than that in which it
would naturally run of its own accord.

The ingenious and well-informed author of the tracts upon
the corn-trade[1] has shown very clearly, that since the bounty

*Charles Smith for-
gets the cost of
raising the corn
upon which the
bounty is paid.*

upon the exportation of corn was first established, the price of the corn exported, valued
moderately enough, has exceeded that of the
corn imported, valued very high, by a much
greater sum than the amount of the whole
bounties which have been paid during that
period. This, he imagines, upon the true principles of the mercantile system, is a clear proof that this forced corn trade is
beneficial to the nation; the value of the exportation exceeding

---

[1] [Charles Smith (already described as "very well-informed" above, p. 578), *Three
Tracts on the Corn Trade and Corn Laws*, 2nd ed., 1766, pp. 132–138.]

that of the importation by a much greater sum than the whole
extraordinary expence which the public has been at in order to
get it exported. He does not consider that this extraordinary expence, or the bounty, is the smallest part of the expence which
the exportation of corn really costs the society. The capital
which the farmer employed in raising it, must likewise be
taken into the account. Unless the price of the corn when sold
in the foreign markets replaces, not only the bounty, but this
capital, together with the ordinary profits of stock, the society
is a loser by the difference, or the national stock is so much diminished. But the very reason for which it has been thought
necessary to grant a bounty, is the supposed insufficiency of
the price to do this.

The average price of corn, it has been said, has fallen considerably since the establishment of the bounty. That the aver-

*The fall in the
price of corn since
the establishment
of the bounty is
due to other
causes.*

age price of corn began to fall somewhat
towards the end of the last century, and has
continued to do so during the course of the
sixty-four first years of the present, I have already endeavoured to show. But this event,
supposing it to be as real as I believe it to be,
must have happened in spite of the bounty, and cannot possibly
have happened in consequence of it. It has happened in France,
as well as in England, though in France there was, not only no
bounty, but, till 1764, the exportation of corn was subjected to
a general prohibition.[2] This gradual fall in the average price of
grain, it is probable, therefore, is ultimately owing neither to
the one regulation nor to the other, but to that gradual and insensible rise in the real value of silver, which, in the first book
of this discourse, I have endeavoured to show has taken place
in the general market of Europe, during the course of the present century.[3] It seems to be altogether impossible that the
bounty could ever contribute to lower the price of grain.[4]

---

[2] [Above, pp. 266–270.]

[3] [Above, pp. 268–286, and cp. pp. 548–549.]

[4] [These three sentences beginning with "It has happened in France," appear first
in Additions and Corrections and ed. 3.]

In years of plenty, it has already been observed,[5] the bounty, by occasioning an extraordinary exportation, necessarily keeps

The bounty keeps up the price both in years of plenty and of scarcity.

up the price of corn in the home market above what it would naturally fall to. To do so was the avowed purpose of the institution. In years of scarcity, though the bounty is frequently suspended, yet the great exportation which it occasions in years of plenty, must frequently hinder more or less the plenty of one year from relieving the scarcity of another. Both in years of plenty, and in years of scarcity, therefore, the bounty necessarily tends to raise the money price of corn somewhat higher than it otherwise would be in the home market.

That, in the actual state of tillage, the bounty must necessarily have this tendency, will not, I apprehend, be disputed by

It has been supposed to encourage cultivation and so to lower price.

any reasonable person. But it has been thought by many people that it tends to encourage tillage, and that in two different ways; first, by opening a more extensive foreign market to the corn of the farmer, it tends, they imagine, to increase the demand for, and consequently the production of that commodity; and secondly, by securing to him a better price than he could otherwise expect in the actual state of tillage, it tends, they suppose, to encourage tillage. This double encouragement must, they imagine, in a long period of years, occasion such an increase in the production of corn, as may lower its price in the home market, much more than the bounty can raise it, in the actual state which tillage may, at the end of that period, happen to be in.[6]

I answer, that whatever extension of the foreign market can

[5] [Above, pp. 268–269.]

[6] [Eds. 1 and 2 read (beginning at the third line of the paragraph) "But it has been thought by many people, that by securing to the farmer a better price than he could otherwise expect in the actual state of tillage, it tends to encourage tillage; and that the consequent increase of corn may, in a long period of years, lower its price more than the bounty can raise it in the actual state which tillage may at the end of that period happen to be in." The alteration is given in Additions and Corrections. The next two paragraphs appear first in Additions and Corrections and ed. 3.]

The addition to the price of corn at home caused by the bounty is a heavy tax on the people, which re-strains population and industry and in the long run tends to diminish the consumption of corn.

be occasioned by the bounty, must, in every particular year, be altogether at the expence of the home market; as every bushel of corn which is exported by means of the bounty, and which would not have been exported without the bounty, would have remained in the home market to increase the consumption, and to lower the price of that commodity. The corn bounty, it is to be observed, as well as every other bounty upon exportation, imposes two different taxes upon the people; first, the tax which they are obliged to contribute, in order to pay the bounty; and secondly, the tax which arises from the advanced price of the commodity in the home market, and which, as the whole body of the people are pur-chasers of corn, must, in this particular commodity, be paid by the whole body of the people. In this particular commodity, therefore, this second tax is by much the heaviest of the two. Let us suppose that, taking one year with another, the bounty of five shillings upon the exportation of the quarter of wheat, raises the price of that commodity in the home market only six-pence the bushel, or four shillings the quarter, higher than it otherways would have been in the actual state of the crop. Even upon this very moderate supposition,[7] the great body of the people, over and above contributing the tax which pays the bounty of five shillings upon every quarter of wheat exported, must pay another of four shillings upon every quarter which they themselves consume. But, according to the very well in-formed author of the tracts upon the corn-trade, the average proportion of the corn exported to that consumed at home, is not more than that of one to thirty-one.[8] For every five shillings, therefore, which they contribute to the payment of the first tax, they must contribute six pounds four shillings to the payment

---

[7] [It is really anything but a moderate supposition. It is not at all likely that the in-crease of demand caused by the offer of a bounty on exportation would raise the price of a commodity to the extent of four-fifths of the bounty.]

[8] [C. Smith, *Three Tracts on the Corn Trade*, 2nd ed., p. 144.]

of the second. So very heavy a tax upon the first necessary of life, must either reduce the subsistence of the labouring poor, or it must occasion some augmentation in their pecuniary wages, proportionable to that in the pecuniary price of their subsistence. So far as it operates in the one way, it must reduce the ability of the labouring poor to educate and bring up their children, and must, so far, tend to restrain the population of the country. So far as it operates in the other, it must reduce the ability of the employers of the poor, to employ so great a number as they otherwise might do, and must, so far, tend to restrain the industry of the country. The extraordinary exportation of corn, therefore, occasioned by the bounty, not only, in every particular year, diminishes the home, just as much as it extends the foreign market and consumption, but, by restraining the population and industry of the country, its final tendency is to stunt and restrain the gradual extension of the home market; and thereby, in the long run, rather to diminish, than to augment, the whole market and consumption of corn.

The enhancement of price would encourage production if it was an enhancement of real price, but it is not;

This enhancement of the money price of corn, however, it has been thought, by rendering that commodity more profitable to the farmer, must necessarily encourage its production.[9]

I answer, that this might be the case if the effect of the bounty was to raise the real price of corn, or to enable the farmer, with an equal quantity of it, to maintain a greater number of labourers in the same manner, whether liberal, moderate, or scanty, that other labourers are commonly maintained in his neighbourhood. But neither the bounty, it is evident, nor any other human institution, can have any such effect. It is not the real, but the nominal price of corn, which can in any considerable degree be affected by the bounty.[10] And though the tax which that institution imposes upon the whole body of the people,

[9] [This and the preceding paragraph are not in eds. 1 and 2. See above, p. 639, note 6.]

[10] [See above, pp. 43–54. It does not occur to Smith that the additional corn might require greater labour to produce it than an equal quantity of the old.]

may be very burdensome to those who pay it, it is of very little advantage to those who receive it.[11]

The real effect of the bounty is not so much to raise the real value of corn, as to degrade the real value of silver; or to *it is only a degradation of the value of silver,* make an equal quantity of it exchange for a smaller quantity, not only of corn, but of all other home-made commodities: for the money price of corn regulates that of all other home-made[12] commodities.

It regulates the money price of labour, which must always *for corn regulates the money price of labour,* be such as to enable the labourer to purchase a quantity of corn sufficient to maintain him and his family either in the liberal, moderate, or scanty manner in which the advancing, stationary or declining circumstances of the society oblige his employers to maintain him.

It regulates the money price of all the other parts of the rude produce of land, which, in every period of improvement, must *of all rude produce,* bear a certain proportion to that of corn, though this proportion is different in different periods. It regulates, for example, the money price of grass and hay, of butcher's meat, of horses, and the maintenance of horses, of land carriage consequently, or of the greater part of the inland commerce of the country.

By regulating the money price of all the other parts of the *and of almost all manufactures.* rude produce of land, it regulates that of the materials of almost[13] all manufactures. By regulating the money price of labour, it regulates that of manufacturing art and industry. And by regulating both, it regulates that of the complete manufacture. The money price of labour, and of every thing that is the produce either of

---

[11] [In place of this and the preceding sentence eds. 1 and 2 read only "It is not the real but the nominal price of corn only which can be at all affected by the bounty." The alteration is given in Additions and Corrections.]

[12] ["Home-made" here and in the line above is not in eds. 1 and 2.]

[13] ["Almost" is not in eds. 1 and 2.]

land or labour, must necessarily either rise or fall in proportion to the money price of corn.

Though in consequence of the bounty, therefore, the farmer should be enabled to sell his corn for four shillings the bushel

So farmers and landlords are not benefited by the increased price due to the bounty.

instead of three and sixpence, and to pay his landlord a money rent proportionable to this rise in the money price of his produce; yet if, in consequence of this rise in the price of corn, four shillings will purchase no more home-made[14] goods of any other kind than

three and sixpence would have done before, neither the circumstances of the farmer, nor those of the landlord, will be much[15] mended by this change. The farmer will not be able to cultivate much better: the landlord will not be able to live much[16] better. In the purchase of foreign commodities this enhancement in the price of corn may give them some little advantage. In that of home-made commodities it can give them none at all. And almost the whole expence of the farmer, and the far greater part even of that of the landlord, is in home-made commodities.[17]

That degradation in the value of silver which is the effect of the fertility of the mines, and which operates equally, or very

A worldwide degradation of the value of silver is of little consequence,

near equally, through the greater part of the commercial world, is a matter of very little consequence to any particular country. The consequent rise of all money prices, though it does not make those who receive them really richer, does not make them really

poorer. A service of plate becomes really cheaper, and every thing else remains precisely of the same real value as before.

But that degradation in the value of silver which, being the

---

[14] [Eds. 1 and 2 do not contain "home-made."]

[15] [Eds. 1 and 2 read "in the smallest degree."]

[16] [Neither "much" is in eds. 1 and 2.]

[17] [This and the two preceding sentences from "in the purchase" appear first in Additions and Corrections (which reads "of even" instead of "even of") and ed. 3.]

but degradation confined to one country discourages the industry of that country.

effect either of the peculiar situation, or of the political institutions of a particular country, takes place only in that country, is a matter of very great consequence, which, far from tending to make any body really richer, tends to make every body really poorer. The rise in the money price of all commodities, which is in this case peculiar to that country, tends to discourage more or less every sort of industry which is carried on within it, and to enable foreign nations, by furnishing almost all sorts of goods for a smaller quantity of silver than its own workmen can afford to do, to undersell them, not only in the foreign, but even in the home market.

It is the peculiar situation of Spain and Portugal as proprietors of the mines, to be the distributors of gold and silver to all

In Spain and Portugal gold and silver are naturally cheaper than in the rest of Europe,

the other countries of Europe. Those metals ought naturally, therefore, to be somewhat cheaper in Spain and Portugal than in any other part of Europe. The difference, however, should be no more than the amount of the freight and insurance; and, on account of the great value and small bulk of those metals, their freight is no great matter, and their insurance is the same as that of any other goods of equal value. Spain and Portugal, therefore, could suffer very little from their peculiar situation, if they did not aggravate its disadvantages by their political institutions.

Spain by taxing, and Portugal by prohibiting the exporta-

but by the hindrances to exportation they are made still cheaper,

tion of gold and silver, load that exportation with the expence of smuggling, and raise the value of those metals in other countries so much more above what it is in their own, by the whole amount of this expence.[18] When you dam up a stream of water, as soon as the

[18] [Spain's prohibition of exportation of gold and silver had only been abolished at a recent period. The tax was 3 per cent. till 1768, then 4 per cent. See Raynal, *Histoire philosophique*, Amsterdam ed. 1773, tom. iii., pp. 290, 291. As to the export of gold from Portugal, see below, p. 691, note 3.]

dam is full, as much water must run over the dam-head as if
there was no dam at all. The prohibition of exportation cannot
detain a greater quantity of gold and silver in Spain and
Portugal than what they can afford to employ, than what the annual produce of their land and labour will allow them to employ, in coin, plate, gilding, and other ornaments of gold and
silver. When they have got this quantity the dam is full, and the
whole stream which flows in afterwards must run over. The annual exportation of gold and silver from Spain and Portugal
accordingly is, by all accounts, notwithstanding these restraints, very near equal to the whole annual importation. As
the water, however, must always be deeper behind the dam-
head than before it, so the quantity of gold and silver which
these restraints detain in Spain and Portugal must, in proportion to the annual produce of their land and labour, be greater
than what is to be found in other countries. The higher and
stronger the dam-head, the greater must be the difference in
the depth of water behind and before it. The higher the tax, the
higher the penalties with which the prohibition is guarded, the
more vigilant and severe the police which looks after the execution of the law, the greater must be the difference in the proportion of gold and silver to the annual produce of the land and
labour of Spain and Portugal, and to that of other countries. It
is said accordingly to be very considerable, and that you frequently find there a profusion of plate in houses, where there is
nothing else which would, in other countries, be thought suitable or correspondent to this sort of magnificence. The cheapness of gold and silver, or what is the same thing, the dearness

*and agriculture
and manufactures
are thereby
discouraged.*

of all commodities, which is the necessary
effect of this redundancy of the precious
metals, discourages both the agriculture and
manufactures of Spain and Portugal, and enables foreign nations to supply them with
many sorts of rude, and with almost all sorts of manufactured
produce, for a smaller quantity of gold and silver than what
they themselves can either raise or make them for at home. The
tax and prohibition operate in two different ways. They not
only lower very much the value of the precious metals in Spain

and Portugal, but by detaining there a certain quantity of those
metals which would otherwise flow over other countries, they
keep up their value in those other countries somewhat above
what it otherwise would be, and thereby give those countries a
double advantage in their commerce with Spain and Portugal.
Open the flood-gates, and there will presently be less water
above, and more below, the dam-head, and it will soon come to
a level in both places. Remove the tax and the prohibition, and
as the quantity of gold and silver will diminish considerably in
Spain and Portugal, so it will increase somewhat in other countries, and the value of those metals, their proportion to the annual produce of land and labour, will soon come to a level, or
very near to a level, in all. The loss which Spain and Portugal
could sustain by this exportation of their gold and silver would
be altogether nominal and imaginary. The nominal value of
their goods, and of the annual produce of their land and labour,
would fall, and would be expressed or represented by a smaller
quantity of silver than before: but their real value would be the
same as before, and would be sufficient to maintain, command,
and employ, the same quantity of labour. As the nominal value
of their goods would fall, the real value of what remained of
their gold and silver would rise, and a smaller quantity of those
metals would answer all the same purposes of commerce and
circulation which had employed a greater quantity before. The
gold and silver which would go abroad would not go abroad
for nothing, but would bring back an equal value of goods of
some kind or another. Those goods too would not be all matters of mere luxury and expence, to be consumed by idle people who produce nothing in return for their consumption. As
the real wealth and revenue of idle people would not be augmented by this extraordinary exportation of gold and silver, so
neither would their consumption be much augmented by it.
Those goods would, probably, the greater part of them, and
certainly some part of them, consist in materials, tools, and
provisions, for the employment and maintenance of industrious people, who would reproduce, with a profit, the full value
of their consumption. A part of the dead stock of the society
would thus be turned into active stock, and would put into mo-

tion a greater quantity of industry than had been employed before. The annual produce of their land and labour would immediately be augmented a little, and in a few years would, probably, be augmented a great deal; their industry being thus relieved from one of the most oppressive burdens which it at present labours under.

The bounty upon the exportation of corn necessarily operates exactly in the same way as this absurd policy of Spain and

The corn bounty acts in the same way;

Portugal. Whatever be the actual state of tillage, it renders our corn somewhat dearer in the home market than it otherwise would be in that state, and somewhat cheaper in the foreign; and as the average money price of corn regulates more or less that of all other commodities, it lowers the value of silver considerably in the one, and tends to raise it a little in the other. It enables foreigners, the Dutch in particular, not only to eat our corn cheaper than they otherwise could do, but sometimes to eat it cheaper than even our own people can do upon the same occasions; as we are assured by an excellent authority, that of Sir Matthew Decker.[19] It hinders our own workmen from furnishing their goods for so small a quantity of silver as they otherwise might do; and enables the Dutch to furnish their's for a smaller. It tends to render our manufactures somewhat dearer in every market, and their's somewhat cheaper than they otherwise would be, and consequently to give their industry a double advantage over our own.

The bounty, as it raises in the home market, not so much the

it discourages manufactures without much benefiting farmers and country gentlemen.

real, as the nominal price[20] of our corn, as it augments, not the quantity of labour which a certain quantity of corn can maintain and employ, but only the quantity of silver which it will exchange for, it discourages our manufactures, without rendering any consider-

[19] [*Essay on the Causes of the Decline of the Foreign Trade, consequently of the Value of the Lands of Britain, and on the means to restore both*, 2nd ed., 1750, pp. 55, 171.]

[20] [Eds. 1 and 2 read "not the real but only the nominal price."]

able service[21] either to our farmers or country gentlemen. It puts, indeed, a little more money into the pockets of both, and it will perhaps be somewhat difficult to persuade the greater part of them that this is not rendering them a very considerable service.[22] But if this money sinks in its value, in the quantity of labour, provisions, and home-made[23] commodities of all different kinds which it is capable of purchasing, as much as it rises in its quantity, the service will be little more than nominal[24] and imaginary.

There is, perhaps, but one set of men in the whole commonwealth to whom the bounty either was or could be essentially

It is essentially serviceable only to the corn merchants.

serviceable.[25] These were the corn merchants, the exporters and importers of corn. In years of plenty the bounty necessarily occasioned a greater exportation than would otherwise have taken place; and by hindering the plenty of one year from relieving the scarcity of another, it occasioned in years of scarcity a greater importation than would otherwise have been necessary. It increased the business of the corn merchant in both; and in years of scarcity, it not only enabled him to import a greater quantity, but to sell it for a better price, and consequently with a greater profit than he could otherwise have made, if the plenty of one year had not been more or less hindered from relieving the scarcity of another. It is in this set of men, accordingly, that I have observed the greatest zeal for the continuance or renewal of the bounty.

Our country gentlemen, when they imposed the high duties upon the importation of foreign corn, which in times of moderate plenty amount to a prohibition, and when they established the bounty, seem to have imitated the conduct of our manufacturers. By the one institution, they secured to them-

---

[21] [Eds. 1 and 2 read "the smallest real service."]

[22] [Eds. 1 and 2 read "a very real service."]

[23] ["Home-made" is not in eds. 1 and 2.]

[24] [Eds. 1 and 2 read "will be merely nominal."]

[25] [Eds. 1 and 2 read "could be really serviceable."]

selves the monopoly of the home market, and by the other they

The country gen-
tlemen established
the duties on the
importation of
corn, and the
bounty, in imita-
tion of the manu-
facturers,

endeavoured to prevent that market from ever being overstocked with their commodity. By both they endeavoured to raise its real value, in the same manner as our manufacturers had, by the like institutions, raised the real value of many different sorts of manufactured goods. They did not perhaps attend to the great and essential difference which nature has established between corn and almost every other sort of goods. When, either by the monopoly of the home market, or by a bounty upon exportation, you en-

without attending
to the essential
difference between
corn and other
goods.

able our woollen or linen manufacturers to sell their goods for somewhat a better price than they otherwise could get for them, you raise, not only the nominal, but the real price of those goods. You render them equivalent to a greater quantity of labour and subsis-

tence, you increase not only the nominal, but the real profit, the real wealth and revenue of those manufacturers, and you enable them either to live better themselves, or to employ a greater quantity of labour in those particular manufactures. You really encourage those manufactures, and direct towards them a greater quantity of the industry of the country, than what would probably go to them of its own accord. But when by the like institutions you raise the nominal or money-price of corn, you do not raise its real value. You do not increase the real wealth, the real revenue either of our farmers or country gentlemen. You do not encourage the growth of corn, because you do not enable them to maintain and employ more labourers in raising it. The nature of things has stamped upon corn a real value which cannot be altered by merely altering its money price.[26] No bounty upon exportation, no monopoly of the home market, can raise that value.[27] The freest competition

[26] [Eds. 1 and 2 read "a real value which no human institution can alter." Cp. p. 641.]

[27] [Ed. 1 reads "raise it."]

cannot lower it. Through the world in general that value is equal to the quantity of labour which it can maintain, and in every particular place it is equal to the quantity of labour which it can maintain in the way, whether liberal, moderate, or scanty, in which labour is commonly maintained in that place. Woollen or linen cloth are not the regulating commodities by which the real value of all other commodities must be finally measured and determined; corn is. The real value of every other commodity is finally measured and determined by the proportion which its average money price bears to the average money price of corn. The real value of corn does not vary with those variations in its average money price, which sometimes occur from one century to another. It is the real value of silver which varies with them.

Bounties upon the exportation of any home-made commodity are liable, first, to that general objection which may be

All the expedients of the mercantile system force industry into less advantageous channels: bounties on exports force it into actually disadvantageous channels: the bounty on corn does not encourage its production.

made to all the different expedients of the mercantile system; the objection of forcing some part of the industry of the country into a channel less advantageous than that in which it would run of its own accord: and, secondly, to the particular objection of forcing it, not only into a channel that is less advantageous, but into one that is actually disadvantageous; the trade which cannot be carried on but by means of a bounty being necessarily a losing trade. The bounty upon the exportation of corn is liable to this further objection, that it can in no respect promote the raising of that particular commodity of which it was meant to encourage the production. When our country gentlemen, therefore, demanded the establishment of the bounty, though they acted in imitation of our merchants and manufacturers, they did not act with that complete comprehension of their own interest which commonly directs the conduct of those two other orders of people. They loaded the public revenue with a very considerable expence; they imposed a very heavy tax upon the whole body of the people; but they did not, in any sensible degree, increase[28] the real value of their own commodity; and by lowering somewhat the real value of silver, they discouraged, in some degree, the general industry of the country, and, instead of advancing, retarded more or less the improvement of their own lands, which necessarily depends upon the general industry of the country.

To encourage the production of any commodity, a bounty upon production, one should imagine, would have a more direct operation, than one upon exportation. It would, besides, impose only one tax upon the people, that which they must contribute in order to pay the bounty. Instead of raising, it would tend to lower the price of the commodity in the home market; and thereby, instead of imposing a second tax upon the people, it might, at least in part, repay them for what they had contributed to the first.

A bounty on production would be more effectual than one on exportation and would lower the price of the commodity,

Bounties upon production, however, have been very rarely granted.[29] The prejudices established by the commercial system have taught us to believe, that national wealth arises more immediately from exportation than from production. It has been more favoured accordingly, as the more immediate means of bringing money into the country. Bounties upon production, it has been said too, have been found by experience more liable to frauds than those upon exportation. How far this is true, I know not. That bounties upon exportation have been abused to many fraudulent purposes, is very well known. But it is not the interest of merchants and manufacturers, the great inventors of all these expedients, that the home market should be overstocked with their goods, an

but such bounties have been rare,

owing to the interest of merchants and manufacturers.

---

[28] [Eds. 1 and 2 read "They loaded the public revenue with a very considerable expence, but they did not in any respect increase." The alteration is given in Additions and Corrections.]

[29] [In place of this and the two preceding sentences (beginning "It would besides") eds. 1 and 2 read only "It has, however, been more rarely granted." The alteration is given in Additions and Corrections.]

event which a bounty upon production might sometimes occasion. A bounty upon exportation, by enabling them to send abroad the surplus part, and to keep up the price of what remains in the home market, effectually prevents this. Of all the expedients of the mercantile system, accordingly, it is the one of which they are the fondest. I have known the different undertakers of some particular works agree privately among themselves to give a bounty out of their own pockets upon the exportation of a certain proportion of the goods which they dealt in. This expedient succeeded so well, that it more than doubled the price of their goods in the home market, notwithstanding a very considerable increase in the produce. The operation of the bounty upon corn must have been wonderfully different, if it has lowered the money price of that commodity.

Something like a bounty upon production, however, has been granted upon some particular occasions. The tonnage bounties given[30] to the white-herring and whale-fisheries may, perhaps, be considered as somewhat of this nature.[31] They tend directly, it may be supposed,[32] to render the goods cheaper in the home market than they otherwise would be.[33] In other respects their effects, it must be acknowledged,[34] are the same as those of bounties upon exportation. By means of them a part of the capital of the country is employed in bringing goods to market, of which the price does not repay the cost, together with the ordinary profits of stock.

The herring and whale fishery bounties are in part given on production.

. But though the tonnage[35] bounties to those fisheries do not contribute to the opulence of the nation, it may perhaps be

[30] [Eds. 1 and 2 read "The encouragements given."]

[31] [The whale fishery bounty under 11 Geo. III., c. 38, was 40s. per ton for the first five years, 30s. for the second five years, and 20s. for the third.]

[32] ["It may be supposed" is not in eds. 1 and 2.]

[33] [Eds. 1 and 2 read "would be in the actual state of production."]

[34] ["It must be acknowledged" is not in eds. 1 and 2.]

[35] ["Tonnage" is not in eds. 1 and 2.]

They are supposed to augment the number of sailors and ships.

thought that they contribute to its defence,[36] by augmenting the number of its sailors and shipping. This, it may be alleged, may sometimes be done[37] by means of such bounties at a much smaller expence, than by keeping up a great standing navy, if I may use such an expression,[38] in the same way as a standing army.[39]

In granting the herring bounties Parliament has been imposed on, since (1) the herring buss bounty is too large,

Notwithstanding these favourable allegations, however, the following considerations dispose me to believe, that in granting at least one of these bounties, the legislature has been very grossly imposed upon.

First, the herring buss bounty seems too large.

From the commencement of the winter fishing 1771 to the end of the winter fishing 1781, the tonnage bounty upon the herring buss fishery has been at thirty shillings the ton. During these eleven years the whole number of barrels caught by the herring buss fishery of Scotland amounted to 378,347. The herrings caught and cured at sea, are called sea sticks.[40] In order to render them what are called merchantable herrings, it is necessary to repack them with an additional quantity of salt; and in this case, it is reckoned, that three barrels of sea sticks,

---

[36] [Eds. 1 and 2 read "they may perhaps be defended as conducing to its defence."]

[37] [Eds. 1 and 2 read "This may frequently be done."]

[38] [Eds. 1 and 2 read "in time of peace" here.]

[39] [The next four pages, through p. 658, are not in eds. 1 and 2, which read in place of them: "Some other bounties may be vindicated perhaps upon the same principle. It is of importance that the kingdom should depend as little as possible upon its neighbours for the manufactures necessary for its defence; and if these cannot otherwise be maintained at home, it is reasonable that all other branches of industry should be taxed in order to support them. The bounties upon the importation of naval stores from America, upon British made sail-cloth, and upon British made gunpowder, may perhaps all three be vindicated upon this principle. The first is a bounty upon the production of America, for the use of Great Britain. The two others are bounties upon exportation." The new paragraphs, with the two preceding paragraphs as amended, are given in Additions and Corrections.]

[40] [In Additions and Corrections the term is "seasteeks," as in the Appendix.]

are usually repacked into two barrels of merchantable herrings. The number of barrels of merchantable herrings, therefore, caught during these eleven years, will amount only, according to this account, to 252,231⅓. During these eleven years the tonnage bounties paid amounted to 155,463*l*. 11*s*. or to 8*s*. 2¼*d*. upon every barrel of sea sticks, and to 12*s*. 3¾*d*. upon every barrel of merchantable herrings.

The salt with which these herrings are cured, is sometimes Scotch, and sometimes foreign salt; both which are delivered free of all excise duty to the fish-curers. The excise duty upon Scotch salt is at present 1*s*. 6*d*. that upon foreign salt 10*s*. the bushel. A barrel of herrings is supposed to require about one bushel and one-fourth of a bushel foreign salt. Two bushels are the supposed average of Scotch salt. If the herrings are entered for exportation, no part of this duty is paid up; if entered for home consumption, whether the herrings were cured with foreign or with Scotch salt, only one shilling the barrel is paid up. It was the old Scotch duty upon a bushel of salt, the quantity which, at a low estimation, had been supposed necessary for curing a barrel of herrings. In Scotland, foreign salt is very little used for any other purpose but the curing of fish. But from the 5th April 1771, to the 5th April 1782, the quantity of foreign salt imported amounted to 936,974 bushels, at eighty-four pounds the bushel: the quantity of Scotch salt delivered from the works to the fish-curers, to no more than 168,226, at fifty-six pounds the bushel only. It would appear, therefore, that it is principally foreign salt that is used in the fisheries. Upon every barrel of herrings exported there is, besides, a bounty of 2*s*. 8*d*. and more than two-thirds of the buss caught herrings are exported. Put all these things together, and you will find that, during these eleven years, every barrel of buss caught herrings, cured with Scotch salt when exported, has cost government 17*s*. 11¾*d*.; and when entered for home consumption 14*s*. 3¾*d*.; and that every barrel cured with foreign salt, when exported, has cost government 1*l*. 7*s*. 5¾*d*.; and when entered for home consumption 1*l*. 3*s*. 9¾*d*. The price of a barrel of good merchantable herrings runs from seventeen and eighteen to four and five-and-twenty shillings; about a guinea at an average.[41]

Secondly, the bounty to the white herring fishery is a tonnage bounty; and is proportioned to the burden of the ship, not to her diligence or success in the fishery; and it has, I am afraid, been too common for vessels to fit out for the sole purpose of catching, not the fish, but the bounty. In the year

(2) the bounty is not proportioned to the fish caught,

1759, when the bounty was at fifty shillings the ton, the whole buss fishery of Scotland brought in only four barrels of sea sticks. In that year each barrel of sea sticks cost government in bounties alone 113*l*. 15*s*.; each barrel of merchantable herrings 159*l*. 7*s*. 6*d*.

Thirdly, the mode of fishing for which this tonnage bounty in the white herring fishery has been given (by busses or decked vessels from twenty to eighty tons burthen), seems not so well adapted to the situation of Scotland as to that of Holland; from the practice of which country it appears to have been borrowed. Holland lies at a great distance from the seas to which herrings are known principally to resort; and

(3) the bounty is given to busses, whereas the fishery ought to be carried on by boats,

can, therefore, carry on that fishery only in decked vessels, which can carry water and provisions sufficient for a voyage to a distant sea. But the Hebrides or western islands, the islands of Shetland, and the northern and western coasts of Scotland, the countries in whose neighbourhood the herring fishery is principally carried on, are everywhere intersected by arms of the sea, which run up a considerable way into the land, and which, in the language of the country, are called sea-lochs. It is to these sea-lochs that the herrings principally resort during the seasons in which they visit those seas; for the visits of this, and, I am assured, of many other sorts of fish, are not quite regular and constant. A boat fishery, therefore, seems to be the mode of fishing best adapted to the peculiar situation of

---

[41] See the accounts at the end of the volume. [In Additions and Corrections they are printed in the text.]

Scotland: the fishers carrying the herrings on shore, as fast as they are taken, to be either cured or consumed fresh. But the great encouragement which a bounty of thirty shillings the ton gives to the buss fishery, is necessarily a discouragement to the boat fishery; which, having no such bounty, cannot bring its cured fish to market upon the same terms as the buss fishery. The boat fishery, accordingly, which, before the establishment of the buss bounty, was very considerable, and is said to have employed a number of seamen, not inferior to what the buss fishery employs at present, is now gone almost entirely to decay. Of the former extent, however, of this now ruined and abandoned fishery, I must acknowledge, that I cannot pretend to speak with much precision. As no bounty was paid upon the outfit of the boat-fishery, no account was taken of it by the officers of the customs or salt duties.

Fourthly, in many parts of Scotland, during certain seasons of the year, herrings make no inconsiderable part of the food of the common people. A bounty, which tended to lower their price in the home market, might contribute a good deal to the relief of a great number of our fellow-subjects, whose circumstances are by no means affluent. But the herring buss bounty contributes to no such good purpose. It has ruined the boat fishery, which is, by far, the best adapted for the supply of the home market, and the additional bounty of 2s. 8d. the barrel upon exportation, carries the greater part, more than two thirds, of the produce of the buss fishery abroad. Between thirty and forty years ago, before the establishment of the buss bounty, sixteen shillings the barrel, I have been assured, was the common price of white herrings. Between ten and fifteen years ago, before the boat fishery was entirely ruined, the price is said to have run from seventeen to twenty shillings the barrel. For these last five years, it has, at an average, been at twenty-five shillings the barrel. This high price, however, may have been owing to the real scarcity of the herrings upon the coast of Scotland. I must observe too, that the cask or barrel, which is usually sold with the herrings, and of which the price is included in all the

(4) the bounty has raised, or at any rate not lowered, the price of herrings.

foregoing prices, has, since the commencement of the American war, risen to about double its former price, or from about three shillings to about six shillings. I must likewise observe, that the accounts I have received of the prices of former times, have been by no means quite uniform and consistent; and an old man of great accuracy and experience has assured me, that more than fifty years ago, a guinea was the usual price of a barrel of good merchantable herrings; and this, I imagine, may still be looked upon as the average price. All accounts, however, I think, agree, that the price has not been lowered in the home market, in consequence of the buss bounty.

When the undertakers of fisheries, after such liberal bounties have been bestowed upon them, continue to sell their commodity at the same, or even at a higher price than they were accustomed to do before, it might be expected that their profits should be very great; and it is not improbable that those of some individuals may have been so. In general, however, I have every reason to believe, they have been quite otherwise. The usual effect of such bounties is to encourage rash undertakers to adventure in a business which they do not understand, and what they lose by their own negligence and ignorance, more than compensates all that they can gain by the utmost liberality of government. In 1750, by the same act which first gave the bounty of thirty shillings the ton for the encouragement of the white herring fishery (the 23 Geo. II. chap. 24.), a joint stock company was erected, with a capital of five hundred thousand pounds, to which the subscribers (over and above all other encouragements, the tonnage bounty just now mentioned, the exportation bounty of two shillings and eight pence the barrel, the delivery of both British and foreign salt duty free) were, during the space of fourteen years, for every hundred pounds which they subscribed and paid into the stock of the society, entitled to three pounds a year, to be paid by the receiver-general of the customs in equal half-yearly payments. Besides this great company, the residence of whose governor and directors was to be in London, it was declared lawful to erect different fishing-chambers in all the different out-ports of

Profits in the business have not been high.

the kingdom, provided a sum not less than ten thousand pounds was subscribed into the capital of each, to be managed at its own risk, and for its own profit and loss. The same annuity, and the same encouragements of all kinds, were given to the trade of those inferior chambers, as to that of the great company. The subscription of the great company was soon filled up, and several different fishing-chambers were erected in the different out-ports of the kingdom. In spite of all these encouragements, almost all those different companies, both great and small, lost either the whole, or the greater part of their capitals; scarce a vestige now remains of any of them, and the white herring fishery is now entirely, or almost entirely, carried on by private adventurers.

If any particular manufacture was necessary, indeed, for the defence of the society, it might not always be prudent to depend upon our neighbours for the supply; and if such manufacture could not otherwise be supported at home, it might not be unreasonable that all the other branches of industry should be taxed in order to support it. The bounties upon the exportation of British-made sailcloth, and British-made gunpowder, may, perhaps, both be vindicated upon this principle.

Bounties for manufactures necessary for the defence of the country are not unreasonable.

But though it can very seldom be reasonable to tax the industry of the great body of the people, in order to support that of some particular class of manufacturers; yet in the wantonness of great prosperity, when the public enjoys a greater revenue than it knows well what to do with, to give such bounties to favourite manufacturers, may, perhaps, be as natural, as to incur any other idle expence. In public, as well as in private expences, great wealth may, perhaps, frequently be admitted as an apology for great folly. But there must surely be something more than ordinary absurdity, in continuing such profusion in times of general difficulty and distress.[42]

It is less absurd to give bounties in times of prosperity than in times of distress.

[42] [The ten paragraphs ending here are not in eds. 1 and 2. See above, p. 653, note 39.]

What is called a bounty is sometimes no more than a drawback, and consequently is not liable to the same objections as

Some allowances called bounties are, properly speaking, drawbacks.

what is properly a bounty. The bounty, for example, upon refined sugar exported, may be considered as a drawback of the duties upon the brown and muscovado sugars from which it is made. The bounty upon wrought silk exported, a drawback of the duties upon raw and thrown silk imported. The bounty upon gunpowder exported, a drawback of the duties upon brimstone and saltpetre imported. In the language of the customs those allowances only are called drawbacks, which are given upon goods exported in the same form in which they are imported. When that form has been so altered by manufacture of any kind, as to come under a new denomination, they are called bounties.[43]

Premiums given by the public to artists and manufacturers who excel in their particular occupations, are not liable to the

Prizes to successful artists and manufacturers do not divert industry to less advantageous channels, but encourage perfection.

same objections as bounties. By encouraging extra-ordinary dexterity and ingenuity, they serve to keep up the emulation of the workmen actually employed in those respective occupations, and are not considerable enough to turn towards any one of them a greater share of the capital of the country than what would go to it of its own accord. Their tendency is not to overturn the natural balance of employments, but to render the work which is done in each as perfect and complete as possible. The expence of premiums, besides, is very trifling; that of bounties very great. The bounty upon corn alone has sometimes cost the public in one year more than three hundred thousand pounds.[44]

Bounties are sometimes called premiums, as drawbacks are sometimes called bounties. But we must in all cases attend to the nature of the thing, without paying any regard to the word.

---

[43] [Eds. 1 and 2 read "When that form has been altered by manufacture of any kind, they are called bounties."]

[44] [Above, p. 272.]

DIGRESSION CONCERNING THE CORN TRADE AND CORN LAWS[45]

I cannot conclude this chapter concerning bounties, without observing that the praises which have been bestowed upon the

The corn bounty and corn laws are undeserving of praise.

law which establishes the bounty upon the exportation of corn, and upon that system of regulations which is connected with it, are altogether unmerited. A particular examination of the nature of the corn trade, and of the principal British laws which relate to it, will sufficiently demonstrate the truth of this assertion. The great importance of this subject must justify the length of the digression.

The trade of the corn merchant is composed of four different branches, which, though they may sometimes be all carried

There are four branches of the corn trade:

on by the same person, are in their own nature four separate and distinct trades. These are, first, the trade of the inland dealer; secondly, that of the merchant importer for home consumption; thirdly, that of the merchant exporter of home produce for foreign consumption; and, fourthly, that of the merchant carrier, or of the importer of corn in order to export it again.

1. The interest of the inland dealer, and that of the great body of the people, how opposite soever they may at first sight

I. The Inland Dealer, whose interest is the same as that of the people, viz., that the consumption should be proportioned to the supply available.

appear, are, even in years of the greatest scarcity, exactly the same. It is his interest to raise the price of his corn as high as the real scarcity of the season requires, and it can never be his interest to raise it higher. By raising the price he discourages the consumption, and puts every body more or less, but particularly the inferior ranks of people, upon thrift and good management. If, by raising it too high, he discourages the consumption so much

---

[45] [This heading is not in ed. 1.]

that the supply of the season is likely to go beyond the consumption of the season, and to last for some time after the next crop begins to come in, he runs the hazard, not only of losing a considerable part of his corn by natural causes, but of being obliged to sell what remains of it for much less than what he might have had for it several months before. If by not raising the price high enough he discourages the consumption so little, that the supply of the season is likely to fall short of the consumption of the season, he not only loses a part of the profit which he might otherwise have made, but he exposes the people to suffer before the end of the season, instead of the hardships of a dearth, the dreadful horrors of a famine. It is the interest of the people that their daily, weekly, and monthly consumption, should be proportioned as exactly as possible to the supply of the season. The interest of the inland corn dealer is the same. By supplying them, as nearly as he can judge, in this proportion, he is likely to sell all his corn for the highest price, and with the greatest profit; and his knowledge of the state of the crop, and of his daily, weekly, and monthly sales, enable[46] him to judge, with more or less accuracy, how far they really are supplied in this manner. Without intending the interest of the people, he is necessarily led, by a regard to his own interest, to treat them, even in years of scarcity, pretty much in the same manner as the prudent master of a vessel is sometimes obliged to treat his crew. When he foresees that provisions are likely to run short, he puts them upon short allowance. Though from excess of caution he should sometimes do this without any real necessity, yet all the inconveniencies which his crew can thereby suffer, are inconsiderable, in comparison of the danger, misery, and ruin, to which they might sometimes be exposed by a less provident conduct. Though from excess of avarice, in the same manner, the inland corn merchant should sometimes raise the price of his corn somewhat higher than the scarcity of the season requires, yet all the inconveniencies which the people can suffer from this conduct, which effectually secures

[46] [Not a misprint for "enables." There are two knowledges, one of the state of the crop and the other of the daily sales.]

them from a famine in the end of the season, are inconsiderable, in comparison of what they might have been exposed to by a more liberal way of dealing in the beginning of it. The corn merchant himself is likely to suffer the most by this excess of avarice; not only from the indignation which it generally excites against him, but, though he should escape the effects of this indignation, from the quantity of corn which it necessarily leaves upon his hands in the end of the season, and which, if the next season happens to prove favourable, he must always sell for a much lower price than he might otherwise have had.

Were it possible, indeed, for one great company of merchants to possess themselves of the whole crop of an extensive

The interest of a monopoly might perhaps be to destroy a portion of the crop, but corn cannot be monopolised where the trade is free.

country, it might, perhaps, be their interest to deal with it as the Dutch are said to do with the spiceries of the Moluccas, to destroy or throw away a considerable part of it, in order to keep up the price of the rest.[47] But it is scarce possible, even by the violence of law, to establish such an extensive monopoly with regard to corn; and, wherever the law leaves the trade free, it is of all commodities the least liable to be engrossed or monopolized by the force of a few large capitals, which buy up the greater part of it. Not only its value far exceeds what the capitals of a few private men are capable of purchasing, but supposing they were capable of purchasing it, the manner in which it is produced renders this purchase altogether impracticable. As in every civilized country it is the commodity of which the annual consumption is the greatest, so a greater quantity of industry is annually employed in producing corn than in producing any other commodity. When it first comes from the ground too, it is necessarily divided among a greater number of owners than any other commodity; and these owners can never be collected into one place like a number of independent manufacturers, but are necessarily scattered through all the different corners of the country. These first owners either immediately supply the consumers in their

[47] [Above, p. 217; below, p. 807.]

own neighbourhood, or they supply other inland dealers who supply those consumers. The inland dealers in corn, therefore, including both the farmer and the baker, are necessarily more numerous than the dealers in any other commodity, and their dispersed situation renders it altogether impossible for them to enter into any general combination. If in a year of scarcity therefore, any of them should find that he had a good deal more corn upon hand than, at the current price, he could hope to dispose of before the end of the season, he would never think of keeping up this price to his own loss, and to the sole benefit of his rivals and competitors, but would immediately lower it, in order to get rid of his corn before the new crop began to come in. The same motives, the same interests, which would thus regulate the conduct of any one dealer, would regulate that of every other, and oblige them all in general to sell their corn at a price which, according to the best of their judgment, was most suitable to the scarcity or plenty of the season.

Whoever examines, with attention, the history of the dearths and famines which have afflicted any part of Europe, during either the course of the present or that of the two preceding centuries, of several of which we have pretty exact accounts, will find, I believe, that a dearth never has arisen from any combination among the inland dealers in corn, nor from any other cause but a real scarcity, occasioned sometimes, perhaps, and in some particular places, by the waste of war, but in by far the greatest number of cases, by the fault of the seasons; and that a famine has never arisen from any other cause but the violence of government attempting, by improper means, to remedy the inconveniencies of a dearth.

Dearths are never occasioned by combination, but always by scarcity, and famines are always caused by the supposed remedies for dearths applied by government.

In an extensive corn country, between all the different parts of which there is a free commerce and communication, the scarcity occasioned by the most unfavourable seasons can never be so great as to produce a famine; and the scantiest crop, if managed with frugality and

Scarcities are never great enough to cause famine.

œconomy, will maintain, through the year, the same number of people that are commonly fed in a more affluent manner by one of moderate plenty. The seasons most unfavourable to the crop are those of excessive drought or excessive rain. But, as corn grows equally upon high and low lands, upon grounds that are disposed to be too wet, and upon those that are disposed to be too dry, either the drought or the rain which is hurtful to one part of the country is favourable to another; and though both in the wet and in the dry season the crop is a good deal less than in one more properly tempered, yet in both what is lost in one part of the country is in some measure compensated by what is gained in the other. In rice countries, where the crop not only requires a very moist soil, but where in a certain period of its growing it must be laid under water, the effects of a drought are much more dismal. Even in such countries, however, the drought is, perhaps, scarce ever so universal, as necessarily to occasion a famine, if the government would allow a free trade. The drought in Bengal, a few years ago, might probably have occasioned a very great dearth. Some improper regulations, some injudicious restraints imposed by the servants of the East India Company upon the rice trade, contributed, perhaps, to turn that dearth into a famine.

When the government, in order to remedy the inconveniencies of dearth, orders all the dealers to sell their corn at what it

Governments cause famines by ordering corn to be sold at a reasonable price:

supposes a reasonable price, it either hinders them from bringing it to market, which may sometimes produce a famine even in the beginning of the season; or if they bring it thither, it enables the people, and thereby encourages them to consume it so fast, as must necessarily produce a famine before the end of the season. The unlimited, unrestrained freedom of the corn trade, as it is the only effectual preventative of the miseries of a famine, so it is the best palliative of the inconveniencies of a dearth; for the inconveniencies of a real scarcity cannot be remedied; they can only be palliated. No trade deserves more the full protection of the law, and no trade requires it so much; because no trade is so much exposed to popular odium.

In years of scarcity, the inferior ranks of people impute their distress to the avarice of the corn merchant, who becomes the

The corn merchant is odious to the populace,

object of their hatred and indignation. Instead of making profit upon such occasions, therefore, he is often in danger of being utterly ruined, and of having his magazines plundered and destroyed by their violence. It is in years of scarcity, however, when prices are high, that the corn merchant expects to make his principal profit. He is generally in contract with some farmers to furnish him for a certain number of years with a certain quantity of corn at a certain price. This contract price is settled according to what is supposed to be the moderate and reasonable, that is, the ordinary or average price, which, before the late years of scarcity, was commonly about eight-and-twenty shillings for the quarter of wheat, and for that of other grain in proportion. In years of scarcity, therefore, the corn merchant buys a great part of his corn for the ordinary price, and sells it for a much higher. That this extraordinary profit, however, is no more than sufficient to put his trade upon a fair level with other trades, and to compensate the many losses which he sustains upon other occasions, both from the perishable nature of the commodity itself, and from the frequent and unforeseen fluctuations of its price, seems evident enough, from this single circumstance, that great fortunes are

and this deters respectable people from entering the trade.

as seldom made in this as in any other trade. The popular odium, however, which attends it in years of scarcity, the only years in which it can be very profitable, renders people of character and fortune averse to enter into it. It is abandoned to an inferior set of dealers; and millers, bakers, mealmen, and meal factors, together with a number of wretched hucksters, are almost the only middle people that, in the home market, come between the grower and the consumer.

This popular odium was encouraged by legislation.

The ancient policy of Europe, instead of discountenancing this popular odium against a trade so beneficial to the public, seems, on the contrary, to have authorised and encouraged it.

By the 5th and 6th of Edward VI. cap. 14. it was enacted, That whoever should buy any corn of grain[48] with intent to sell it again, should be reputed an unlawful engrosser, and should, for the first fault suffer two months imprisonment, and forfeit the value of the corn; for the second, suffer six months imprisonment, and forfeit double the value; and for the third, be set in the pillory, suffer imprisonment during the king's pleasure, and forfeit all his goods and chattels. The ancient policy of most other parts of Europe was no better than that of England.

Our ancestors seem to have imagined that the people would buy their corn cheaper of the farmer than of the corn merchant,

Many restraints were imposed on traders.

who, they were afraid, would require, over and above the price which he paid to the farmer, an exorbitant profit to himself. They endeavoured, therefore, to annihilate his trade altogether. They even endeavoured to hinder as much as possible any middle man of any kind from coming in between the grower and the consumer; and this was the meaning of the many restraints which they imposed upon the trade of those whom they called kidders or carriers of corn, a trade which nobody was allowed to exercise without a licence ascertaining his qualifications as a man of probity and fair dealing.[49] The authority of three justices of the peace was, by the statute of Edward VI. necessary, in order to grant this licence. But even this restraint was afterwards thought insufficient, and by a statute of Elizabeth,[50] the privilege of granting it was confined to the quarter-sessions.

[48] ["Any corn growing in the fields, or any other corn or grain, butter, cheese, fish or other dead victuals whatsoever." But grain was exempted when below certain prices, *e.g.*, wheat, 6s. 8d. the quarter.]

[49] [This and the preceding sentence are misleading. The effect of the provisions quoted in the preceding paragraph would have been to "annihilate altogether" the trade of the corn merchant if they had been left unqualified. To avoid this consequence 5 and 6 Ed. VI., c. 14, § 7, provides that badgers, laders, kidders or carriers may be licensed to buy corn with the intent to sell it again in certain circumstances. So that the licensing of kidders was a considerable alleviation, not, as the text suggests, an aggravation.]

[50] [5 Eliz., c. 12, § 4.]

The ancient policy of Europe endeavoured in this manner to regulate agriculture, the great trade of the country, by maxims quite different from those which it established with regard to manufactures, the great trade of the towns. By leaving the farmer no other customers but either the consumers or their immediate factors,[51] the kidders and carriers of corn, it endeavoured to force him to exercise the trade, not only of a farmer, but of a corn merchant or corn retailer. On the contrary, it in many cases prohibited the manufacturer from exercising the trade of a shopkeeper, or from selling his own goods by retail. It meant by the one law to promote the general interest of the country, or to render corn cheap, without, perhaps, its being well understood how this was to be done. By the other it meant to promote that of a particular order of men, the shopkeepers, who would be so much undersold by the manufacturer, it was supposed, that their trade would be ruined if he was allowed to retail at all.

Endeavours were made to force the farmers to be retailers, though manufacturers were forbidden to be so.

The manufacturer, however, though he had been allowed to keep a shop, and to sell his own goods by retail, could not have undersold the common shopkeeper. Whatever part of his capital he might have placed in his shop, he must have withdrawn it from his manufacture. In order to carry on his business on a level with that of other people, as he must have had the profit of a manufacturer on the one part, so he must have had that of a shopkeeper upon the other. Let us suppose, for example, that in the particular town where he lived, ten per cent. was the ordinary profit both of manufacturing and shopkeeping stock; he must in this case have charged upon every piece of his own goods which he sold in his shop, a profit of twenty per cent. When he carried them from his workhouse to his shop, he must have valued them at the price for which he could have sold them to a dealer or shopkeeper, who would have bought them by wholesale. If he valued them lower, he lost a part of the

[51] [Ed. 1 reads "the consumer or his immediate factors." It should be noticed that under 5 and 6 Edward VI., c. 14, § 7, the kidder might sell in "open fair or market" as well as to consumers privately.]

profit of his manufacturing capital. When again he sold them from his shop, unless he got the same price at which a shop-keeper would have sold them, he lost a part of the profit of his shopkeeping capital. Though he might appear, therefore, to make a double profit upon the same piece of goods, yet as these goods made successively a part of two distinct capitals, he made but a single profit upon the whole capital employed about them; and if he made less than this profit, he was a loser, or did not employ his whole capital with the same advantage as the greater part of his neighbours.

What the manufacturer was prohibited to do, the farmer was in some measure enjoined to do; to divide his capital be-tween two different employments; to keep one part of it in his granaries and stack yard, for supplying the occasional de-mands of the market; and to employ the other in the cultivation of his land. But as he could not afford to employ the latter for less than the ordinary profits of farming stock, so he could as little afford to employ the former for less than the ordinary profits of mercantile stock. Whether the stock which really car-ried on the business of the corn merchant belonged to the per-son who was called a farmer, or to the person who was called a corn merchant, an equal profit was in both cases requisite, in order to indemnify its owner for employing it in this manner; in order to put his business upon a level with other trades, and in order to hinder him from having an interest to change it as soon as possible for some other. The farmer, therefore, who was thus forced to exercise the trade of a corn merchant, could not afford to sell his corn cheaper than any other corn mer-chant would have been obliged to do in the case of a free com-petition.

The dealer who can employ his whole stock in one single branch of business has an advantage of the same kind with the workman who can employ his whole labour in one single operation. As the latter acquires a dexterity which enables him, with the same two hands, to perform a much greater quan-tity of work; so the former acquires so easy and ready a method of transacting his business, of buying and

The dealer confined to one branch of business can sell cheaper.

disposing of his goods, that with the same capital he can transact a much greater quantity of business. As the one can commonly afford his work a good deal cheaper, so the other can commonly afford his goods somewhat cheaper than if his stock and attention were both employed about a greater variety of objects. The greater part of manufacturers could not afford to retail their own goods so cheap as a vigilant and active shopkeeper, whose sole business it was to buy them by wholesale, and to retail them again. The greater part of farmers could still less afford to retail their own corn, to supply the inhabitants of a town, at perhaps four or five miles distance from the greater part of them, so cheap as a vigilant and active corn merchant, whose sole business it was to purchase corn by wholesale, to collect it into a great magazine, and to retail it again.

The law which prohibited the manufacturer from exercising the trade of a shopkeeper, endeavoured to force this division in

Laws preventing the manufacturer from being a shopkeeper and compelling the farmer to be a corn merchant were both impolitic and unjust, but the latter was the most pernicious,

the employment of stock to go on faster than it might otherwise have done. The law which obliged the farmer to exercise the trade of a corn merchant, endeavoured to hinder it from going on so fast. Both laws were evident violations of natural liberty, and therefore unjust; and they were both too as impolitic as they were unjust. It is the interest of every society, that things of this kind should never either be forced or obstructed. The man who employs either his labour or his stock in a greater variety of ways than his situation renders necessary, can never hurt his neighbour by underselling him. He may hurt himself, and he generally does so. Jack of all trades will never be rich, says the proverb. But the law ought always to trust people with the care of their own interest, as in their local situations they must generally be able to judge better of it than the legislator can do. The law, however, which obliged the farmer to exercise the trade of a corn merchant, was by far the most pernicious of the two.

It obstructed not only that division in the employment of stock which is so advantageous to every society, but it ob-

by obstructing the improvement of land.

structed likewise the improvement and culti-vation of the land. By obliging the farmer to carry on two trades instead of one, it forced him to divide his capital into two parts, of which one only could be employed in cultivation. But if he had been at liberty to sell his whole crop to a corn merchant as fast as he could thresh it out, his whole capital might have returned immediately to the land, and have been employed in buying more cattle, and hiring more servants, in order to improve and cultivate it better. But by being obliged to sell his corn by re-tail, he was obliged to keep a great part of his capital in his granaries and stack yard through the year, and could not, there-fore, cultivate so well as with the same capital he might other-wise have done. This law, therefore, necessarily obstructed the improvement of the land, and, instead of tending to render corn cheaper, must have tended to render it scarcer, and therefore dearer, than it would otherwise have been.

Corn merchants support the farmers just as wholesale dealers support the manufacturers.

After the business of the farmer, that of the corn merchant is in reality the trade which, if properly protected and encouraged, would contribute the most to the raising of corn. It would support the trade of the farmer, in the same manner as the trade of the wholesale dealer supports that of the manufacturer.

The wholesale dealer, by affording a ready market to the manufacturer, by taking his goods off his hands as fast as he

Wholesale dealers allow manufactur-ers to devote their whole capital to manufacturing.

can make them, and by sometimes even ad-vancing their price to him before he has made them, enables him to keep his whole capital, and sometimes even more than his whole capital, constantly employed in manu-facturing, and consequently to manufacture a much greater quantity of goods than if he was obliged to dis-pose of them himself to the immediate consumers, or even to the retailers. As the capital of the wholesale merchant too is generally sufficient to replace that of many manufacturers, this intercourse between him and them interests the owner of a large capital to support the owners of a great number of small ones, and to assist them in those losses and misfortunes which might otherwise prove ruinous to them.

An intercourse of the same kind universally established between the farmers and the corn merchants, would be attended

So corn merchants should allow farmers to devote their whole capital to cultivation.

with effects equally beneficial to the farmers. They would be enabled to keep their whole capitals, and even more than their whole capitals, constantly employed in cultivation. In case of any of those accidents, to which no trade is more liable than theirs, they would find in their ordinary customer, the wealthy corn merchant, a person who had both an interest to support them, and the ability to do it, and they would not, as at present, be entirely dependent upon the forbearance of their landlord, or the mercy of his steward. Were it possible, as perhaps it is not, to establish this intercourse universally, and all at once, were it possible to turn all at once the whole farming stock of the kingdom to its proper business, the cultivation of land, withdrawing it from every other employment into which any part of it may be at present diverted, and were it possible, in order to support and assist upon occasion the operations of this great stock, to provide all at once another stock almost equally great, it is not perhaps very easy to imagine how great, how extensive, and how sudden would be the improvement which this change of circumstances would alone produce upon the whole face of the country.

The statute of Edward VI., therefore, by prohibiting as

Accordingly the statute of Edward VI. endeavoured to annihilate a trade which is the best palliative and preventative of a dearth.

much as possible any middle man from coming in between the grower and the consumer, endeavoured to annihilate a trade, of which the free exercise is not only the best palliative of the inconveniencies of a dearth, but the best preventative of that calamity: after the trade of the farmer, no trade contributing so much to the growing of corn as that of the corn merchant.

The rigour of this law was afterwards softened by several

Its provisions were moderated by later statutes down to 14 Car. II., c. 7,

subsequent statutes, which successively permitted the engrossing of corn when the price of wheat should not exceed twenty, twenty-four, thirty-two, and forty shillings the quarter.[52] At last, by the 15th of Charles II. c. 7. the engrossing or buying of corn in order to sell it again, as long as the price of wheat did not exceed forty-eight shillings the quarter, and that of other grain in proportion, was declared lawful to all persons not being forestallers, that is, not selling again in the same market within three months.[53] All the freedom which the trade of the inland corn dealer has ever yet enjoyed, was bestowed upon it by this statute. The statute of the twelfth of the present king, which repeals almost all the other ancient laws against engrossers and forestallers, does not repeal the restrictions of this particular statute, which therefore still continue in force.[54]

which is absurd, as it supposes,

This statute, however, authorises in some measure two very absurd popular prejudices.

(1) that engrossing is likely to be hurtful after a certain price has been reached,

First, it supposes that when the price of wheat has risen so high as forty-eight shillings the quarter, and that of other grain in proportion, corn is likely to be so engrossed as to hurt the people. But from what has been already said, it seems evident enough that corn can at no price be so engrossed by the inland dealers as to hurt the people: and forty-

[52] [Diligent search has hitherto failed to discover these statutes.]

[53] [§ 4 incorrectly quoted. The words are "not forestalling nor selling the same in the same market within three months." Under 5 and 6 Ed. VI., c. 14, a person buying and selling again "in any fair or market holden or kept in the same place or in any other fair or market within four miles" was a regrator, while a forestaller was one who bought or contracted to buy things on their way to market, or made any motion for enhancing the price of such things or preventing them going to market.]

[54] [12 Geo. III., c. 71, repeals 5 and 6 Ed. VI., c. 14, but does not mention 15 Car. II., c. 7, which is purely permissive. If 15 Car. II., c. 7, remained of any force in this respect it must have been merely in consequence of the common law being unfavourable to forestalling.]

eight shillings the quarter besides, though it may be considered as a very high price, yet in years of scarcity it is a price which frequently takes place immediately after harvest, when scarce any part of the new crop can be sold off, and when it is impossible even for ignorance to suppose that any part of it can be so engrossed as to hurt the people.

Secondly, it supposes that there is a certain price at which corn is likely to be forestalled, that is, bought up in order to be

(2) that fore-stalling is likely to be hurtful after a certain price has been reached.

sold again soon after in the same market, so as to hurt the people. But if a merchant ever buys up corn, either going to a particular market or in a particular market, in order to sell it again soon after in the same market, it must be because he judges that the market cannot be so liberally supplied through the whole season as upon that particular occasion, and that the price, therefore, must soon rise. If he judges wrong in this, and if the price does not rise, he not only loses the whole profit of the stock which he employs in this manner, but a part of the stock itself, by the expence and loss which necessarily attend[55] the storing and keeping of corn. He hurts himself, therefore, much more essentially than he can hurt even the particular people whom he may hinder from supplying themselves upon that particular market day, because they may afterwards supply themselves just as cheap upon any other market day. If he judges right, instead of hurting the great body of the people, he renders them a most important service. By making them feel the inconveniencies of a dearth somewhat earlier than they otherwise might do, he prevents their feeling them afterwards so severely as they certainly would do, if the cheapness of price encouraged them to consume faster than suited the real scarcity of the season. When the scarcity is real, the best thing that can be done for the people is to divide the inconveniencies of it as equally as possible through all the different months, and weeks, and days of the year. The interest of the corn merchant makes him study to do this as exactly as he can: and as no other person can have ei-

---

[55] [Eds. 1 and 2 read "attends."]

ther the same interest, or the same knowledge, or the same abilities to do it so exactly as he, this most important operation of commerce ought to be trusted entirely to him: or, in other words, the corn trade, so far at least as concerns the supply of the home market, ought to be left perfectly free.

The popular fear of engrossing and forestalling may be compared to the popular terrors and suspicions of witchcraft.

The fear of engrossing and forestalling is as groundless as that of witchcraft.

The unfortunate wretches accused of this latter crime were not more innocent of the misfortunes imputed to them, than those who have been accused of the former. The law which put an end to all prosecutions against witchcraft, which put it out of any man's power to gratify his own malice by accusing his neighbour of that imaginary crime, seems effectually to have put an end to those fears and suspicions, by taking away the great cause which encouraged and supported them. The law which should restore entire freedom to the inland trade of corn, would probably prove as effectual to put an end to the popular fears of engrossing and forestalling.

The 15th of Charles II. c. 7. however, with all its imperfections, has perhaps contributed more both to the plentiful supply of the home market, and to the increase of tillage, than any other law in the statute book. It is from this law that the inland corn trade has derived all the liberty and protection which it has ever yet enjoyed; and both the supply of the home market, and the interest of tillage, are much more effectually promoted by the inland, than either by the importation or exportation trade.

Still, the 15 Car. II., c. 7, is the best of the corn laws, as it gives the inland corn trade all the freedom it possesses.

The proportion of the average quantity of all sorts of grain imported into Great Britain to that of all sorts of grain consumed, it has been computed by the author of the tracts upon the corn trade, does not exceed that of one to five hundred and seventy. For supplying the home market, therefore, the importance of the inland trade must

The inland trade is much more important than the foreign.

be to that of the importation trade as five hundred and seventy to one.[56]

The average quantity of all sorts of grain exported from Great Britain does not, according to the same author, exceed the one-and-thirtieth part of the annual produce.[57] For the encouragement of tillage, therefore, by providing a market for the home produce, the importance of the inland trade must be to that of the exportation trade as thirty to one.

I have no great faith in political arithmetic, and I mean not to warrant the exactness of either of these computations. I mention them only in order to show of how much less consequence, in the opinion of the most judicious and experienced persons, the foreign trade of corn is than the home trade. The great cheapness of corn in the years immediately preceding the establishment of the bounty, may perhaps, with reason, be ascribed in some measure to the operation of this statute of Charles II., which had been enacted about five-and-twenty years before, and which had therefore full time to produce its effect.

A very few words will sufficiently explain all that I have to say concerning the other three branches of the corn trade.

II. The trade of the merchant importer of foreign corn for home consumption, evidently contributes to the immediate *II. The Importer, whose trade benefits the people and does not really hurt the farmers and country gentlemen.* supply of the home market, and must so far be immediately beneficial to the great body of the people. It tends, indeed, to lower somewhat the average money price of corn, but not to diminish its real value, or the quantity of labour which it is capable of maintaining. If importation was at all times free, our farmers and country gentlemen would, probably, one year with another, get less money for their corn than they do at present, when importation is at most times in effect prohibited; but the money which they got would be of more value, would

---

[56] [Charles Smith, *Three Tracts on the Corn Trade and Corn Laws*, 2nd ed., 1766, p. 145. The figures have been already quoted above, p. 579.]

[57] ["The export is bare one thirty-second part of the consumption, one thirty-third part of the growth exclusive of seed, one thirty-sixth part of the growth including the seed."—*Ibid.*, p. 144; quoted above, p. 640.]

buy more goods of all other kinds, and would employ more labour. Their real wealth, their real revenue, therefore, would be the same as at present, though it might be expressed by a smaller quantity of silver; and they would neither be disabled nor discouraged from cultivating corn as much as they do at present. On the contrary, as the rise in the real value of silver, in consequence of lowering the money price of corn, lowers somewhat the money price of all other commodities, it gives the industry of the country, where it takes place, some advantage in all foreign markets, and thereby tends to encourage and increase that industry. But the extent of the home market for corn must be in proportion to the general industry of the country where it grows, or to the number of those who produce something else, and therefore have something else, or what comes to the same thing, the price of something else, to give in exchange for corn. But in every country the home market, as it is the nearest and most convenient, so is it likewise the greatest and most important market for corn. That rise in the real value of silver, therefore, which is the effect of lowering the average money price of corn, tends to enlarge the greatest and most important market for corn, and thereby to encourage, instead of discouraging, its growth.

By the 22d of Charles II. c. 13. the importation of wheat, whenever the price in the home market did not exceed fifty-three shillings and four pence the quarter, was subjected to a duty of sixteen shillings the quarter; and to a duty of eight shillings whenever the price did not exceed four pounds.[58] The former of these two prices has,

The Act of 22 Car. II., c. 13, imposed very high duties on importation

---

[58] [This was not the first law of its kind. 3 Ed. IV., c. 2, was enacted because "the labourers and occupiers of husbandry within this realm of England be daily grievously endamaged by bringing of corn out of other lands and parts into this realm of England when corn of the growing of this realm is at a low price," and forbids importation of wheat when not over 6s. 8d., rye when not over 4s. and barley when not over 3s. the quarter. This Act was repealed by 21 Jac. I., c. 28, and 15 Car. II., c. 7, imposed a duty of 5s. 4d. on imported wheat, 4s. on rye, 2s. 8d. on barley, 2s. on buckwheat, 1s. 4d. on oats and 4s. on pease and beans, when the prices at the port of importation did not exceed for wheat, 48s.; barley and buckwheat, 28s.; oats, 13s. 4d.; rye, pease and beans, 32s. per quarter.]

for more than a century past, taken place only in times of very great scarcity; and the latter has, so far as I know, not taken place at all. Yet, till wheat had risen above this latter price, it was by this statute subjected to a very high duty; and, till it had risen above the former, to a duty which amounted to a prohibition. The importation of other sorts of grain was restrained at rates, and by duties, in proportion to the value of the grain, almost equally[59] high.[60] Subsequent laws still further increased those duties.

[59] [Ed. 1 reads "restrained by duties proportionably."]

[60] Before the 13th of the present king, the following were the duties payable upon the importation of the different sorts of grain:

Grain.	Duties.		Duties.	Duties.
Beans to 28s. per qr.	19s. 10d. after till 40s.		16s. 8d.	then 12d.
Barley to 28s.	19s. 10d.	32s.	16s.	12d.
Malt is prohibited by the annual Malt-tax Bill.				
Oats to 16s.	5s. 10d. after			9½d.
Pease to 40s.	16s. 0d. after			9¾d.
Rye to 36s.	19s. 10d. till	40s.	16s. 8d.	then 12d.
Wheat to 44s.	21s. 9d. till	53s. 4d.	17s.	then 8s.
till 4l. and after that about 1s. 4d.				
Buck wheat to 32s. per qr. to pay 16s.				

These different duties were imposed, partly by the 22d of Charles II. in place of the Old Subsidy, partly by the New Subsidy, by the One-third and Two-thirds Subsidy, and by the Subsidy 1747. [The table of duties in this note is an exact copy of that in Charles Smith, *Three Tracts on the Court Trade*, 2nd ed. 1766. p. 83. That author professes to have taken the figures from "Mr. Saxby, in his Book of Rates" (*i.e.*, Henry Saxby, *The British Customs, containing an Historical and Practical Account of each branch of that Revenue*, 1757, pp. 111–114), but besides rounding off Saxby's fractions of a penny in an inaccurate and inconsistent manner, he has miscopied the second duty on barley, the first on pease and the third on wheat. The "Old Subsidy" consisted of the 5 per cent. or 1s. poundage imposed by 12 Car. II., c. 4, on the values attributed to the various goods by the "Book of Rates" annexed to the Act. According to this, imported beans, barley and malt were to be rated at 26s. 8d. the quarter when the actual price at the place of importation did not exceed 28s. When the actual price was higher than that they were to be rated at 5s. the quarter. Oats and pease were to be rated at 4s. the quarter. Rye when not over 36s. was to be rated at 26s. 8d., and when over that price at 5s. Wheat when not over 44s. was to be rated at 40s., and when over that price at 6s. 8d.

So under the Old Subsidy:—

Beans, barley and malt at prices up to 28s. were to pay 1s. 4d., and when above that price 3d.

but its operation was generally suspended in years of scarcity. The distress which, in years of scarcity, the strict execution of those laws might have brought[61] upon the people, would probably have been very great. But, upon such occasions, its execution was generally suspended by temporary statutes,[62] which permitted, for a limited time, the importation of foreign corn. The necessity of these temporary statutes sufficiently demonstrates the impropriety of this general one.

> Oats and pease to pay 2.4d.
> Rye up to 36s. to pay 1s. 4d., and when above, 3d.
> Wheat up to 44s. to pay 2s., and when above, 4d.
> The Act 22 Car. II., c. 13, took off these duties and substituted the following scheme:—
> Beans to 40s. to pay 16s., and above that price, 3d.
> Barley and malt to 32s. to pay 16s., and above, 3d.
> Oats 16s. to pay 5s. 4d., and above, 2.4d.
> Pease and rye the same as beans.
> Wheat to 53s. 4d. to pay 16s., then to 80s. to pay 8s., and above that price, 4d.
> Buckwheat to 32s. to pay 16s.
> But 9 and 10 Will. III., c. 23, imposed a "New Subsidy" exactly equal to the Old, so that duties equal to those of 12 Car. II., c. 4, were superimposed on those of 22 Car. II., c. 13. By 2 and 3 Ann., c. 9, an additional third, and by 3 and 4 Ann., c. 5, an additional two-thirds of the Old Subsidy were imposed, and by 21 Geo. II., c. 2, another amount equal to the Old Subsidy ("the impost 1747") was further imposed. So between 1747 and 1773 the duties were those of 22 Car. II., c. 13, *plus* three times those of 12 Car. II., c. 4. This gives the following scheme:—
> Beans to 28s. pay 20s. and after till 40s. pay 16s. 9d. then 1s.
> Barley to 28s. pays 20s. and after till 32s. pays 16s. 9d. then 1s.
> Oats to 16s. pay 5s. 11.2d. and then pay 9.6d.
> Pease to 40s. pay 16s. 7.2d. and then pay 9.6d.
> Rye to 36s. pays 20s. and after till 40s. pays 16s. 9d. then 1s.
> Wheat to 44s. pays 22s. and after till 53s. 4d. pays 17s. then 9s. till 80s., and after that 1s. 4d.
> Saxby's figures are slightly less, as they take into account a 5 per cent. discount obtainable on all the subsidies except one. The note appears first in ed. 2.]

[61] [Eds. 1 and 2 do not contain "subsequent laws still further increased those duties," and read "the distress which in years of scarcity the strict execution this statute might have brought."]

[62] [These do not seem to have been numerous. There were cases in 1757 and 1766. See the table in Charles Smith, *Three Tracts upon the Corn Trade and Corn Laws*, 2nd ed., pp. 44, 45.]

These restraints upon importation, though prior to the establishment of the bounty, were dictated by the same spirit, by

Restraint was necessary on account of the bounty.

the same principles, which afterwards enacted that regulation. How hurtful soever in themselves, these or some other restraints upon importation became necessary in consequence of that regulation. If, when wheat was either below forty-eight shillings the quarter, or not much above it, foreign corn could have been imported either duty free, or upon paying only a small duty, it might have been exported again, with the benefit of the bounty, to the great loss of the public revenue, and to the entire perversion of the institution, of which the object was to extend the market for the home growth, not that for the growth of foreign countries.

III. The trade of the merchant exporter of corn for foreign consumption, certainly does not contribute directly to the plen-

III. The Exporter, whose trade indirectly contributes to the plentiful supply of the home market.

tiful supply of the home market. It does so, however, indirectly. From whatever source this supply may be usually drawn, whether from home growth or from foreign importation, unless more corn is either usually grown, or usually imported into the country, than what is usually consumed in it, the supply of the home market can never be very plentiful. But unless the surplus can, in all ordinary cases, be exported, the growers will be careful never to grow more, and the importers never to import more, than what the bare consumption of the home market requires. That market will very seldom be overstocked; but it will generally be understocked, the people, whose business it is to supply it, being generally afraid lest their goods should be left upon their hands. The prohibition of exportation limits the improvement and cultivation of the country to what the supply of its own inhabitants requires. The freedom of exportation enables it to extend cultivation[63] for the supply of foreign nations.

By the 12th of Charles II. c. 4. the exportation of corn was

---

[63] [Eds. 1 and 2 read "extend its cultivation."]

Liberty of exportation was made complete in 1700, permitted whenever the price of wheat did not exceed forty shillings the quarter, and that of other grain in proportion.[64] By the 15th of the same prince,[65] this liberty was extended till the price of wheat exceeded forty-eight shillings the quarter; and by the 22d,[66] to all higher prices. A poundage, indeed, was to be paid to the king upon such exportation. But all grain was rated so low in the book of rates, that this poundage amounted only upon wheat to a shilling, upon oats to four pence, and upon all other grain to six pence the quarter.[67] By the 1st of William and Mary,[68] the act which established the bounty, this small duty was virtually taken off whenever the price of wheat did not exceed forty-eight shillings the quarter; and by the 11th and 12th of William III. c. 20. it was expressly taken off at all higher prices.

though the interest of the exporter sometimes differs from that of the people of his country. The trade of the merchant exporter was, in this manner, not only encouraged by a bounty, but rendered much more free than that of the inland dealer. By the last of these statutes, corn could be engrossed at any price for exportation; but it could not be engrossed for inland sale, except when the price did not exceed forty-eight shillings the quarter.[69] The in-

---

[64] [Earlier statutes are 15 Hen. VI., c. 2; 20 Hen. VI., c. 6; 23 Hen. VI., c. 6; 1 and 2 P. and M., c. 5; 5 Eliz., c. 5, § 26; 13 Eliz., c. 13; and 1 Jac., c. 25, §§ 26, 27. The preamble of the first of these says "by the law it was ordained that no man might carry nor bring corn out of the realm of England without the King's licence, for cause whereof farmers and other men which use manurement of their land may not sell their corn but of a bare price to the great damage of all the realm." Exportation was therefore legalised without licence when grain was above certain prices.]

[65] [C. 7.]

[66] [C. 13.]

[67] [The "Book of Rates" (see above, p. 677, note 60) rated wheat for export at 20s., oats at 6s. 8d., and other grain at 10s. the quarter, and the duty was a shilling in the pound on these values.]

[68] [1 W. and M., c. 12. The bounty was to be given "without taking or requiring anything for custom."]

[69] [Because as to inland sale 15 Car. II., c. 7 (above, pp. 672–673), remained in force.]

terest of the inland dealer, however, it has already been shown, can never be opposite to that of the great body of the people. That of the merchant exporter may, and in fact sometimes is. If, while his own country labours under a dearth, a neighbouring country should be afflicted with a famine, it might be his interest to carry corn to the latter country in such quantities as might very much aggravate the calamities of the dearth. The plentiful supply of the home market was not the direct object of those statutes; but, under the pretence of encouraging agriculture, to raise the money price of corn as high as possible, and thereby to occasion, as much as possible, a constant dearth in the home market. By the discouragement of importation, the supply of that market, even in times of great scarcity, was confined to the home growth; and by the encouragement of exportation, when the price was so high as forty-eight shillings the quarter, that market was not, even in times of considerable scarcity, allowed to enjoy the whole of that growth. The temporary laws, prohibiting for a limited time the exportation of corn, and taking off for a limited time the duties upon its importation, expedients to which Great Britain has been obliged so frequently to have recourse,[70] sufficiently demonstrate the impropriety of her general system. Had that system been good, she would not so frequently have been reduced to the necessity of departing from it.

Were all nations to follow the liberal system of free exportation and free importation, the different states into which a great continent was divided would so far resemble the different provinces of a great empire. As among the different provinces of a great empire the freedom of the inland trade appears, both from reason and experience, not only the best palliative of a dearth, but the most effectual preventative of a famine; so would the freedom of the exportation and importation trade be among the different states into which a

The bad policy of some great countries may sometimes render it necessary for small countries to restrain exportation.

---

[70] [The Acts prohibiting exportation were much more numerous than the others. See above, p. 678, note 62, and the table in Charles Smith there referred to.]

great continent was divided. The larger the continent, the easier the communication through all the different parts of it, both by land and by water, the less would any one particular part of it ever be exposed to either of these calamities, the scarcity of any one country being more likely to be relieved by the plenty of some other. But very few countries have entirely adopted this liberal system. The freedom of the corn trade is almost every where more or less restrained, and, in many countries, is confined by such absurd regulations, as frequently aggravate the unavoidable misfortune of a dearth, into the dreadful calamity of a famine. The demand of such countries for corn may frequently become so great and so urgent, that a small state in their neighbourhood, which happened at the same time to be labouring under some degree of dearth, could not venture to supply them without exposing itself to the like dreadful calamity. The very bad policy of one country may thus render it in some measure dangerous and imprudent to establish what would otherwise be the best policy in another. The unlimited freedom of exportation, however, would be much less dangerous in great states, in which the growth being much greater, the supply could seldom be much affected by any quantity of corn that was likely to be exported. In a Swiss canton, or in some of the little states of Italy, it may, perhaps, sometimes be necessary to restrain the exportation of corn. In such great countries as France or England it scarce ever can. To hinder, besides, the farmer from sending his goods at all times to the best market, is evidently to sacrifice the ordinary laws of justice to an idea of public utility, to a sort of reasons of state; an act of legislative authority which ought to be exercised only, which can be pardoned only in cases of the most urgent necessity. The price at which the exportation of corn is prohibited, if it is ever to be prohibited, ought always to be a very high price.

The laws concerning corn may every where be compared to the laws concerning religion. The people feel themselves so much interested in what relates either to their subsistence in this life, or to their happiness in a life to come, that government must yield to their prejudices, and, in order

The corn laws are like the laws on religion.

to preserve the public tranquillity, establish that system which they approve of. It is upon this account, perhaps, that we so seldom find a reasonable system established with regard to either of those two capital objects.

IV. The trade of the merchant carrier, or of the importer of foreign corn in order to export it again, contributes to the plentiful supply of the home market. It is not indeed the direct purpose of his trade to sell his corn there. But he will generally be willing to do so, and even for a good deal less money than he might expect in a foreign market; because he saves in this manner the expence of loading and unloading, of freight and insurance. The inhabitants of the country which, by means of the carrying trade, becomes the magazine and storehouse for the supply of other countries, can very seldom be in want themselves. Though the carrying trade might thus contribute to reduce the average money price of corn in the home market, it would not thereby lower its real value. It would only raise somewhat the real value of silver.

IV. The Merchant Carrier, whose trade contributes to the plentiful supply of the home market.

The carrying trade was in effect prohibited in Great Britain, upon all ordinary occasions, by the high duties upon the importation of foreign corn, of the greater part of which there was no drawback;[71] and upon extraordinary occasions, when a scarcity made it necessary to suspend those duties by temporary statutes, exportation was always prohibited. By this system of laws, therefore, the carrying trade was in effect prohibited upon all occasions.

British law in effect prohibited the carrying trade in corn.

That system of laws, therefore, which is connected with the establishment of the bounty, seems to deserve no part of the praise which has been bestowed upon it. The improvement and prosperity of Great Britain, which has been so often ascribed to those laws, may very easily be accounted for

The prosperity of Great Britain is not due to the corn bounty, but to the security of enjoying the fruits of labour.

---

[71] [Ed. 1 does not contain "of the greater part of which there was no drawback."]

by other causes. That security which the laws in Great Britain give to every man that he shall enjoy the fruits of his own labour, is alone sufficient to make any country flourish, notwithstanding these and twenty other absurd regulations of commerce; and this security was perfected by the revolution, much about the same time that the bounty was established. The natural effort of every individual to better his own condition, when suffered to exert itself with freedom and security, is so powerful a principle, that it is alone, and without any assistance, not only capable of carrying on the society to wealth and prosperity, but of surmounting a hundred impertinent obstructions with which the folly of human laws too often incumbers its operations; though the effect of these obstructions is always more or less either to encroach upon its freedom, or to diminish its security. In Great Britain industry is perfectly secure; and though it is far from being perfectly free, it is as free or freer than in any other part of Europe.

Though the period of the greatest prosperity and improvement of Great Britain, has been posterior to that system of laws which is connected with the bounty, we must not upon that account impute it to those laws. It has been posterior likewise to the national debt. But the national debt has most assuredly not been the cause of it.

That the greatest prosperity has been subsequent proves nothing.

Though the system of laws which is connected with the bounty, has exactly the same tendency with the police of Spain and Portugal; to lower somewhat the value of the precious metals in the country where it takes place;[72] yet Great Britain is certainly one of the richest countries in Europe, while Spain and Portugal are perhaps among the most beggarly. This difference of situation, however, may easily be accounted for from two different causes. First, the tax in Spain, the prohibition in Portugal of exporting gold and silver,[73] and the vigilant police

Spain and Portugal are poorer than Great Britain because their bad policy is more effectual,

---

[72] [According to the argument above, p. 647.]

[73] [See above, pp. 644–645.]

which watches over the execution of those laws, must, in two very poor countries, which between them import annually upwards of six millions sterling,[74] operate, not only more directly,

and not counteracted by general liberty and security.

but much more forcibly in reducing the value of those metals there, than the corn laws can do in Great Britain. And, secondly, this bad policy is not in those countries counterbalanced by the general liberty and security of the people. Industry is there neither free nor secure, and the civil and ecclesiastical governments of both Spain and Portugal, are such as would alone be sufficient to perpetuate their present state of poverty, even though their regulations of commerce were as wise as the greater part of them are absurd and foolish.

The 13th of the present king, c. 43. seems to have estab-

The 13 Geo. III., c. 43,

lished a new system with regard to the corn laws, in many respects better than the ancient one, but in one or two respects[75] perhaps not quite so good.

By this statute the high duties upon importation for home consumption are taken off so soon as the price of middling

opens the home market at lower prices,

wheat rises to forty-eight shillings the quarter; that of middling rye, pease or beans, to thirty-two shillings; that of barley to twenty-four shillings; and that of oats to sixteen

shillings; and instead[76] of them a small duty is imposed of only six-pence upon the quarter of wheat, and upon that of other grain in proportion. With regard to all these different sorts of grain, but particularly with regard to wheat, the home market is thus opened to foreign supplies at prices considerably lower than before.[77]

---

[74] [Above, pp. 281–285.]

[75] [Ed. 1 reads "in one respect."]

[76] [Ed. 1 reads only "By this statute the high duties upon importation for home consumption are taken off as soon as the price of wheat is so high as forty-eight shillings the quarter, and instead."]

[77] [In place of this sentence ed. 1 reads "The home market is in this manner not so totally excluded from foreign supplies as it was before."]

By the same statute the old bounty of five shillings upon the exportation of wheat ceases so soon as the price rises to forty-four shillings the quarter, instead of forty-eight, the price at which it ceased before; that of two shillings and six-pence upon the exportation of barley ceases so soon as the price rises to twenty-two shillings, instead of twenty-four, the price at which it ceased before; that of two shillings and six-pence upon the exportation of oatmeal ceases so soon as the price rises to fourteen shillings, instead of fifteen, the price at which it ceased before. The bounty upon rye is reduced from three shillings and six-pence to three shillings, and it ceases so soon as the price rises to twenty-eight shillings, instead of thirty-two, the price at which it ceased before.[78] If bounties are as improper as I have endeavoured to prove them to be, the sooner they cease, and the lower they are, so much the better.

stops the bounty earlier,

The same statute permits, at the lowest prices, the importation of corn, in order to be exported again, duty free, provided it is in the meantime lodged in a warehouse under the joint locks of the king and the importer.[79] This liberty, indeed, extends to no more than twenty-five of the different ports of Great Britain. They are, however, the principal ones, and there may not, perhaps, be warehouses proper for this purpose in the greater part of the others.[80]

and admits corn for re-export duty free;

So far this law seems evidently an improvement upon the ancient system.

But by the same law a bounty of two

which are improvements,

[78] [Ed. 1 reads (from the beginning of the paragraph) "By the same statute the old bounty of five shillings upon the quarter of wheat ceases when the price rises so high as forty-four shillings, and upon that of other grain in proportion. The bounties too upon the coarser sorts of grain are reduced somewhat lower than they were before, even at the prices at which they take place."]

[79] [Ed. 1 reads "The same statute permits at all prices the importation of corn in order to be exported again, duty free; provided it is in the meantime lodged in the king's warehouse."]

[80] [Ed. 1 contains an additional sentence, "Some provision is thus made for the establishment of the carrying trade."]

but it gives a bounty on the export of oats, shillings the quarter is given for the exportation of oats whenever the price does not exceed fourteen shillings. No bounty had ever been given before for the exportation of this grain, no more than for that of peas or beans.[81]

By the same law too, the exportation of wheat is prohibited so soon as the price rises to forty-four shillings the quarter; *and prohibits exportation of grain at prices much too low.* that of rye so soon as it rises to twenty-eight shillings; that of barley so soon as it rises to twenty-two shillings; and that of oats so soon as they rise to fourteen shillings. Those several prices seem all of them a good deal too low, and there seems to be an impropriety, besides, in prohibiting exportation altogether at those precise prices at which that bounty, which was given in order to force it, is withdrawn.[82] The bounty ought certainly either to have been withdrawn at a much lower price, or exportation ought to have been allowed at a much higher.

So far, therefore, this law seems to be inferior to the ancient system. With all its imperfections, however, we may perhaps *It is as good a law as can be expected at present.* say of it what was said of the laws of Solon, that, though not the best in itself, it is the best which the interests, prejudices, and temper of the times would admit of. It may perhaps in due time prepare the way for a better.[83]

---

[81] [This paragraph is not in ed. 1.]

[82] [Ed. 1 reads (from the beginning of the paragraph) "But by the same law exportation is prohibited as soon as the price of wheat rises to forty-four shillings the quarter, and that of other grain in proportion. The price seems to be a good deal too low, and there seems to be an impropriety besides in stopping exportation altogether at the very same price at which that bounty which was given in order to force it is withdrawn."]

[83] [These two sentences are not in ed. 1.]

CHAPTER VI

OF TREATIES OF COMMERCE

WHEN A nation binds itself by treaty either to permit the entry of certain goods from one foreign country which it prohibits from all others, or to exempt the goods of one country from duties to which it subjects those of all others, the country, or at least the merchants and manufacturers of the country, whose commerce is so favoured, must necessarily derive great advantage from the treaty. Those merchants and manufacturers enjoy a sort of monopoly in the country which is so indulgent to them. That country becomes a market both more extensive and more advantageous for their goods: more extensive, because the goods of other nations being either excluded or subjected to heavier duties, it takes off a great quantity of theirs: more advantageous, because the merchants of the favoured country, enjoying a sort of monopoly there, will often sell their goods for a better price than if exposed to the free competition of all other nations.

Treaties of commerce are advantageous to the favoured,

Such treaties, however, though they may be advantageous to the merchants and manufacturers of the favoured, are necessarily disadvantageous to those of the favouring country. A monopoly is thus granted against them to a foreign nation; and they must frequently buy the foreign goods they have occasion for, dearer than if the free competition of other nations was admitted. That part of its own produce with which such a nation purchases foreign goods, must consequently be sold cheaper, because when two things are exchanged for one another, the cheapness of the one is a necessary consequence, or

but disadvantageous to the favouring country.

rather is the same thing with the dearness of the other. The exchangeable value of its annual produce, therefore, is likely to be diminished by every such treaty. This diminution, however, can scarce amount to any positive loss, but only to a lessening of the gain which it might otherwise make. Though it sells its goods cheaper than it otherwise might do, it will not probably sell them for less than they cost; nor, as in the case of bounties, for a price which will not replace the capital employed in bringing them to market, together with the ordinary profits of stock. The trade could not go on long if it did. Even the favouring country, therefore, may still gain by the trade, though less than if there was a free competition.

Some treaties of commerce, however, have been supposed advantageous upon principles very different from these; and a commercial country has sometimes granted *Treaties have been concluded with the object of obtaining a favourable balance of trade,* a monopoly of this kind against itself to certain goods of a foreign nation, because it expected that in the whole commerce between them, it would annually sell more than it would buy, and that a balance in gold and silver would be annually returned to it. It is upon this principle that the treaty of commerce between England and Portugal, concluded in 1703, by Mr. Methuen, *e.g., the Methuen treaty,* has been so much commended.[1] The following is a literal translation[2] of that treaty, which consists of three articles only.

ART. I

His sacred royal majesty of Portugal promises, both in his own name, and that of his successors, to admit, for ever hereafter, into Portugal, the woollen cloths, and the rest of the woollen

---

[1] [*E.g.*, in the *British Merchant*, 1721, Dedication to vol. iii.]

[2] [With three small exceptions, "British" for "Britons" and "law" for "laws" in art. 1, and "for" instead of "from" before "the like quantity or measure of French wine," the translation is identical with that given in *A Collection of all the Treaties of Peace, Alliance and Commerce between Great Britain and other Powers from the Revolution in 1688 to the Present Time*, 1772, vol. i., pp. 61, 62.]

manufactures of the British, as was accustomed, till they were prohibited by the law; nevertheless upon this condition:

ART. II

That is to say, that her sacred royal majesty of Great Britain shall, in her own name and that of her successors, be obliged, for ever hereafter, to admit the wines of the growth of Portugal into Britain: so that at no time, whether there shall be peace or war between the kingdoms of Britain and France, any thing more shall be demanded for these wines by the name of custom or duty, or by whatsoever other title, directly or indirectly, whether they shall be imported into Great Britain in pipes or hogsheads, or other casks, than what shall be demanded for the like quantity or measure of French wine, deducting or abating a third part of the custom or duty. But if at any time this deduction or abatement of customs, which is to be made as aforesaid, shall in any manner be attempted and prejudiced, it shall be just and lawful for his scared royal majesty of Portugal, again to prohibit the woollen cloths, and the rest of the British woollen manufactures.

ART. III

The most excellent lords the plenipotentiaries promise and take upon themselves that their above-named masters shall ratify this treaty; and within the space of two months the ratifications shall be exchanged.

By this treaty the crown of Portugal becomes bound to admit the English woollens upon the same footing as before the prohibition; that is, not to raise the duties *which is evidently advantageous to Portugal and disadvantageous to Great Britain.* which had been paid before that time. But it does not become bound to admit them upon any better terms than those of any other nation, of France or Holland for example. The crown of Great Britain, on the contrary, becomes bound to admit the wines of Portugal, upon paying only two-thirds of the duty, which is paid for those of France, the wines most likely to come into competition with them. So far this treaty, therefore, is evidently advantageous to Portugal, and disadvantageous to Great Britain.

It has been celebrated, however, as a masterpiece of the commercial policy of England. Portugal receives annually *Portugal sends much gold to England;* from the Brazils a greater quantity of gold than can be employed in its domestic commerce, whether in the shape of coin or of plate. The surplus is too valuable to be allowed to lie idle and locked up in coffers, and as it can find no advantageous market at home, it must, notwithstanding any prohibition, be sent abroad, and exchanged for something for which there is a more advantageous market at home. A large share of it comes annually to England, in return either for English goods, or for those of other European nations that receive their returns through England. Mr. Baretti was informed that the weekly packet-boat from Lisbon brings, one week with another, more than fifty thousand pounds in gold to England.[3] The sum had probably been exaggerated. It would amount to more than two millions six hundred thousand pounds a year, which is more than the Brazils are supposed to afford.[4]

Our merchants were some years ago out of humour with the crown of Portugal. Some privileges which had been granted *at one time nearly the whole of this gold was said to be on account of other European nations,* them, not by treaty, but by the free grace of that crown, at the solicitation, indeed, it is probable, and in return for much greater favours, defence and protection, from the crown of Great Britain, had been either infringed or revoked. The people, therefore, usually most interested in celebrating the

---

[3] [Joseph Baretti, *Journey from London to Genoa, through England, Portugal, Spain and France*, 3rd ed., 1770, vol. i., pp. 95, 96, but the amount stated is not so large as in the text above: it is "often" from "thirty to fifty and even sixty thousand pounds," and not "one week with another" but "almost every week." The gold all came in the packet boat because it, as a war vessel, was exempt from search.— Raynal, *Histoire philosophique*, Amsterdam ed., 1773, tom. iii., pp. 413, 414.]

[4] [Above, p. 284.]

Portugal trade, were then rather disposed to represent it as less advantageous than it had commonly been imagined. The far greater part, almost the whole, they pretended, of this annual importation of gold, was not on account of Great Britain, but of other European nations; the fruits and wines of Portugal annually imported into Great Britain nearly compensating the value of the British goods sent thither.

Let us suppose, however, that the whole was on account of Great Britain, and that it amounted to a still greater sum than

but even if it were not so, the trade would not be more valuable than another of equal magnitude.

Mr. Baretti seems to imagine: this trade would not, upon that account, be more advantageous than any other in which, for the same value sent out, we received an equal value of consumable goods in return.

It is but a very small part of this importation which, it can be supposed, is employed as an annual addition either to the plate or to the coin of the

Most of the gold must be sent abroad again and exchanged for goods, and it would be better to buy the goods direct with home produce instead of buying gold in Portugal.

kingdom. The rest must all be sent abroad and exchanged for consumable goods of some kind or other. But if those consumable goods were purchased directly with the produce of English industry, it would be more for the advantage of England, than first to purchase with that produce the gold of Portugal, and afterwards to purchase with that gold those consumable goods. A direct foreign trade of consumption is always more advantageous than a round-about one;[5] and

to bring the same value of foreign goods to the home market, requires a much smaller capital in the one way[6] than in the other. If a smaller share of its industry, therefore, had been employed in producing goods fit for the Portugal market, and a greater in producing those fit for the other markets, where those consumable goods for which there is a demand in Great Britain are to be had, it would have been more for the advan-

[5] [Above, pp. 470, 471.]

[6] [Ed. 1 does not contain "way."]

tage of England. To procure both the gold, which it wants for its own use, and the consumable goods, would, in this way, employ a much smaller capital than at present. There would be a spare capital, therefore, to be employed for other purposes, in exciting an additional quantity of industry, and in raising a greater annual produce.

Though Britain were entirely excluded from the Portugal trade, it could find very little difficulty in procuring all the annual supplies of gold which it wants, either for the purposes of plate, or of coin, or of foreign trade. Gold, like every other commodity, is always somewhere or another to be got for its value by those who have that value to give for it. The annual surplus of gold in Portugal, besides, would still be sent abroad, and though not carried away by Great Britain, would be carried away by some other nation, which would be glad to sell it again for its price, in the same manner as Great Britain does at present. In buying gold of Portugal, indeed, we buy it at the first hand; whereas in buying it of any other nation, except Spain, we should buy it at the second, and might pay somewhat dearer. This difference, however, would surely be too insignificant to deserve the public attention.

Britain would find little difficulty in procuring gold even if excluded from trade with Portugal.

Almost all our gold, it is said, comes from Portugal. With other nations the balance of trade is either against us, or not much in our favour. But we should remember, that the more gold we import from one country, the less we must necessarily import from all others. The effectual demand for gold, like that for every other commodity, is in every country limited to a certain quantity. If nine-tenths of this quantity are imported from one country, there remains a tenth only to be imported from all others. The more gold besides that is annually imported from some particular countries, over and above what is requisite for plate and for coin, the more must necessarily be exported to some others; and the more that most insignificant object of modern policy, the bal-

It is said that all our gold comes from Portugal, but if it did not come from Portugal it would come from other countries.

ance of trade, appears to be in our favour with some particular countries, the more it must necessarily appear to be against us with many others.

It was upon this silly notion, however, that England could not subsist without the Portugal trade, that, towards the end of the late war,[7] France and Spain, without pretending either offence or provocation, required the king of Portugal to exclude all British ships from his ports, and for the security of this exclusion, to receive into them French or Spanish garrisons. Had the king of Portugal submitted to those ignominious terms which his brother-in-law the king of Spain proposed to him, Britain would have been freed from a much greater inconveniency than the loss of the Portugal trade, the burden of supporting a very weak ally, so unprovided of every thing for his own defence, that the whole power of England, had it been directed to that single purpose, could scarce perhaps have defended him for another campaign. The loss of the Portugal trade would, no doubt, have occasioned a considerable embarrassment to the merchants at that time engaged in it, who might not, perhaps, have found out, for a year or two, any other equally advantageous method of employing their capitals; and in this would probably have consisted all the inconveniency which England could have suffered from this notable piece of commercial policy.

If the attempt of France and Spain to exclude British ships from Portuguese ports had been successful, it would have been an advantage to England.

The great annual importation of gold and silver is neither for the purpose of plate nor of coin, but of foreign trade. A roundabout foreign trade of consumption can be carried on more advantageously by means of these metals than of almost any other goods. As they are the universal instruments of commerce, they are more readily received in return for all commodities than any other goods; and on account of their small bulk and great value, it costs less to transport them backward and forward from one place to another than almost

The great importation of gold and silver is for foreign trade.

any other sort of merchandize, and they lose less of their value by being so transported. Of all the commodities, therefore, which are bought in one foreign country, for no other purpose but to be sold or exchanged again for some other goods in another, there are none so convenient as gold and silver. In facilitating all the different round-about foreign trades of consumption which are carried on in Great Britain, consists the principal advantage of the Portugal trade; and though it is not a capital advantage, it is, no doubt, a considerable one.

That any annual addition which, it can reasonably be supposed, is made either to the plate or to the coin of the kingdom, could require but a very small annual importation of gold and silver, seems evident enough; and though we had no direct trade with Portugal, this small quantity could always, somewhere or another, be very easily got.

Very little is required for plate and coin.

Though the goldsmiths' trade be very considerable in Great Britain, the far greater part of the new plate which they annually sell, is made from other old plate melted down; so that the addition annually made to the whole plate of the kingdom cannot be very great, and could require but a very small annual importation.

New gold plate is mostly made from old.

It is the same case with the coin. Nobody imagines, I believe, that even the greater part of the annual coinage, amounting, for ten years together, before the late reformation of the gold coin,[8] to upwards of eight hundred thousand pounds a year in gold,[9] was an annual addition to the money before current in the kingdom. In a country where the expence of the coinage is defrayed by the government, the value of the coin, even when it contains its full standard weight of gold and silver, can never be much greater than that of an equal quantity of those metals uncoined; because it requires only the trouble of going to the mint, and the delay

New coin is mostly made from old, as there is a profit on melting good coin.

[8] [See above, pp. 59–60.]

[9] [Above, p. 385, note 12.]

perhaps of a few weeks, to procure for any quantity of un-coined gold and silver an equal quantity of those metals in coin. But, in every country, the greater part of the current coin is almost always more or less worn, or otherwise degenerated from its standard. In Great Britain it was, before the late refor-mation, a good deal so, the gold being more than two per cent. and the silver more than eight per cent. below its standard weight. But if forty-four guineas and a half, containing their full standard weight, a pound weight of gold, could purchase very little more than a pound weight of uncoined gold, forty-four guineas and a half wanting a part of their weight could not purchase a pound weight, and something was to be added in order to make up the deficiency. The current price of gold bul-lion at market, therefore, instead of being the same with the mint price, or 46*l.* 14*s.* 6*d.* was then about 47*l.* 14*s.* and some-times about forty-eight pounds. When the greater part of the coin, however, was in this degenerate condition, forty-four guineas and a half, fresh from the mint, would purchase no more goods in the market than any other ordinary guineas, be-cause when they came into the coffers of the merchant, being confounded with other money, they could not afterwards be distinguished without more trouble than the difference was worth. Like other guineas they were worth no more than 46*l.* 14*s.* 6*d.* If thrown into the melting pot, however, they pro-duced, without any sensible loss, a pound weight of standard gold, which could be sold at any time for between 47*l.* 14*s.* and 48*l.* either in gold or silver, as fit for all the purposes of coin as that which had been melted down. There was an evident profit, therefore, in melting down new coined money, and it was done so instantaneously, that no precaution of government could prevent it. The operations of the mint were, upon this account, somewhat like the web of Penelope; the work that was done in the day was undone in the night. The mint was employed, not so much in making daily additions to the coin, as in replacing the very best part of it which was daily melted down.

Were the private people, who carry their gold and silver to the mint, to pay themselves for the coinage, it would add to the value of those metals in the same manner as the fashion does to

A seignorage raises the value of coin above that of bullion of equal weight, that of plate. Coined gold and silver would be more valuable than uncoined. The seignorage, if it was not exorbitant, would add to the bullion the whole value of the duty; because, the government having every where the exclusive privilege of coining, no coin can come to market cheaper than they think proper to afford it. If the duty was exorbitant indeed, that is, if it was very much above the real value of the labour and expence requisite for coinage, false coiners, both at home and abroad, might be encouraged, by the great difference between the value of bullion and that of coin, to pour in so great a quantity of counterfeit money as might reduce the value of the government money. In France, however, though the seignorage is eight per cent. no sensible inconveniency of this kind is found to arise from it. The dangers to which a false coiner is every where exposed, if he lives in the country of which he counterfeits the coin, and to which his agents or correspondents are exposed if he lives in a foreign country, are by far too great to be incurred for the sake of a profit of six or seven per cent.

The seignorage in France raises the value of the coin higher than in proportion to the quantity of pure gold which it contains. Thus by the edict of January 1726, *as in France.* the[10] mint price of fine gold of twenty-four carats was fixed at seven hundred and forty livres nine sous and one denier one-eleventh, the mark of eight Paris ounces. The gold coin of France, making an allowance for the remedy

[10] See *Dictionaire des Monnoies*, tom ii. article Seigneurage, p. 489. par M. Abot de Bazinghen, Conseiller-Commissaire en la Cour des Monnoies à Paris. [Ed. 1 reads erroneously "tom. i." The book is *Traité des Monnoies et de la jurisdiction de la Cour des Monnoies en forme de dictionnaire*, par M. Abot de Bazinghen, Conseiller-Commissaire en la Cour des Monnoies de Paris, 1764, and the page is not 489, but 589. Garnier, in his edition of *The Wealth of Nations*, vol. v., p. 234, says the book "n'est guère qu'une compilation faite sans soin et sans discernement," and explains that the mint price mentioned above remained in force a very short time. It having failed to bring bullion to the mint, much higher prices were successively offered, and when *The Wealth of Nations* was published the seignorage only amounted to about 3 per cent. On the silver coin it was then about 2 per cent., in place of the 6 per cent. stated by Bazinghen, p. 590.]

of the mint, contains twenty-one carats and three-fourths of fine gold, and two carats one-fourth of alloy. The mark of standard gold, therefore, is worth no more than about six hundred and seventy-one livres ten deniers. But in France this mark of standard gold is coined into thirty Louis-d'ors of twenty-four livres each, or into seven hundred and twenty livres. The coinage, therefore, increases the value of a mark of standard gold bullion, by the difference between six hundred and seventy-one livres ten deniers, and seven hundred and twenty livres; or by forty-eight livres nineteen sous and two deniers.

A seignorage will, in many cases, take away altogether, and will, in all cases, diminish the profit of melting down the new

It diminishes or destroys the profit obtained by melting coin.

coin. This profit always arises from the difference between the quantity of bullion which the common currency ought to contain, and that which it actually does contain. If this difference is less than the seignorage, there will be loss instead of profit. If it is equal to the seignorage, there will neither be profit nor loss. If it is greater than the seignorage, there will indeed be some profit, but less than if there was no seignorage. If, before the late reformation of the gold coin, for example, there had been a seignorage of five per cent. upon the coinage, there would have been a loss of three per cent. upon the melting down of the gold coin. If the seignorage had been two per cent. there would have been neither profit nor loss. If the seignorage had been one per cent. there would have been a profit, but of one per cent. only instead of two per cent. Wherever money is received by tale, therefore, and not by weight, a seignorage is the most effectual preventative of the melting down of the coin, and, for the same reason, of its exportation. It is the best and heaviest pieces that are commonly either melted down or exported; because it is upon such that the largest profits are made.

The law for the encouragement of the coinage, by rendering it duty-free, was first enacted, during the reign of Charles II.[11]

---

[11] ["An act for encouraging of coinage," 18 Car. II., c. 5. The preamble says, "Whereas it is obvious that the plenty of current coins of gold and silver of this kingdom is of great advantage to trade and commerce; for the increase whereof,

The abolition of seignorage in England was probably due to the bank of England,

for a limited time; and afterwards continued, by different prolongations, till 1769, when it was rendered perpetual.[12] The bank of England, in order to replenish their coffers with money, are frequently obliged to carry bullion to the mint; and it was more for their interest, they probably imagined, that the coinage should be at the expence of the government, than at their own. It was, probably, out of complaisance to this great company that the government agreed to render this law perpetual. Should the custom of weighing gold, however, come to be disused, as it is very likely to be on account of its inconveniency; should the gold coin of England come to be received by tale, as it was before the late recoinage, this great company may, perhaps, find that they have upon this, as upon some other occasions, mistaken their own interest not a little.

Before the late recoinage, when the gold currency of England was two per cent. below its standard weight, as there

but the bank would have lost nothing by a seignorage whether it equalled the depreciation,

was no seignorage, it was two per cent. below the value of that quantity of standard gold bullion which it ought to have contained. When this great company, therefore, bought gold bullion in order to have it coined, they were obliged to pay for it two per cent. more than it was worth after the

coinage. But if there had been a seignorage of two per cent. upon the coinage, the common gold currency, though two per cent. below its standard weight, would notwithstanding have been equal in value to the quantity of standard gold which it ought to have contained; the value of the fashion compensating in this case the diminution of the weight. They would indeed have had the seignorage to pay, which being two per cent. their loss upon the whole transaction would have been

your Majesty in our princely wisdom and care hath been graciously pleased to bear out of your revenue half the charge of the coinage of silver money."]

[12] [Originally enacted for five years, it was renewed by 25 Car. II., c. 8, for seven years, revived for seven years by 1 Jac. II., c. 7, and continued by various Acts till made perpetual by 9 Geo. III., c. 25.]

two per cent. exactly the same, but no greater than it actually was.

If the seignorage had been five per cent. and the gold currency only two per cent. below its standard weight, the bank
exceeded it, would in this case have gained three per cent. upon the price of the bullion; but as they would have had a seignorage of five per cent. to pay upon the coinage, their loss upon the whole transaction would, in the same manner, have been exactly two per cent.

If the seignorage had been only one per cent. and the gold currency two per cent. below its standard weight, the bank
or fell short of it. would in this case have lost only one per cent. upon the price of the bullion; but as they would likewise have had a seignorage of one per cent. to pay, their loss upon the whole transaction would have been exactly two per cent. in the same manner as in all other cases.

If there was a reasonable seignorage, while at the same time the coin contained its full standard weight, as it has done very
Nor would it lose if there were no depreciation. nearly since the late re-coinage, whatever the bank might lose by the seignorage, they would gain upon the price of the bullion; and whatever they might gain upon the price of the bullion, they would lose by the seignorage. They would neither lose nor gain, therefore, upon the whole transaction, and they would in this, as in all the foregoing cases, be exactly in the same situation as if there was no seignorage.

When the tax upon a commodity is so moderate as not to encourage smuggling, the merchant who deals in it, though he
A seignorage is paid by no one, advances, does not properly pay the tax, as he gets it back in the price of the commodity. The tax is finally paid by the last purchaser or consumer. But money is a commodity with regard to which every man is a merchant. Nobody buys it but in order to sell it again; and with regard to it there is in ordinary cases no last purchaser or consumer. When the tax upon coinage, therefore, is so moderate as not to encourage false coining, though every body advances the tax, nobody finally pays it; because every body gets it back in the advanced value of the coin.

A moderate seignorage, therefore, would not in any case augment the expence of the bank, or of any other private per-

and could not have augmented the expense of the bank.

sons who carry their bullion to the mint in order to be coined, and the want of a moderate seignorage does not in any case diminish it. Whether there is or is not a seignorage, if the currency contains its full standard weight, the coinage costs nothing to any body, and if it is short of that weight, the coinage must always cost the difference between the quantity of bullion which ought to be contained in it, and that which actually is contained in it.

The government, therefore, when it defrays the expence of

The government loses and nobody gains by the absence of seignorage.

coinage, not only incurs some small expence, but loses some small revenue which it might get by a proper duty; and neither the bank nor any other private persons are in the smallest degree benefited by this useless piece of public generosity.

The directors of the bank, however, would probably be unwilling to agree to the imposition of a seignorage upon the au-

Supposing the coin should again become depreciated, a seignorage would preserve the bank from considerable loss.

thority of a speculation which promises them no gain, but only pretends to insure them from any loss. In the present state of the gold coin, and as long as it continues to be received by weight, they certainly would gain nothing by such a change. But if the custom of weighing the gold coin should ever go into disuse,

as it is very likely to do, and if the gold coin should ever fall into the same state of degradation in which it was before the late recoinage, the gain, or more properly the savings of the bank, in consequence of the imposition of a seignorage, would probably be very considerable. The bank of England is the only company which sends any considerable quantity of bullion to the mint, and the burden of the annual coinage falls entirely, or almost entirely, upon it. If this annual coinage had nothing to do but to repair the unavoidable losses and necessary wear and tear[13] of the

---

[13] [Ed. 1 reads "tear and wear."]

coin, it could seldom exceed fifty thousand or at most a hundred thousand pounds. But when the coin is degraded below its standard weight, the annual coinage must, besides this, fill up the large vacuities which exportation and the melting pot are continually making in the current coin. It was upon this account that during the ten or twelve years immediately preceding the late reformation of the gold coin, the annual coinage amounted at an average to more than eight hundred and fifty thousand pounds.[14] But if there had been a seignorage of four or five per cent. upon the gold coin, it would probably, even in the state in which things then were, have put an effectual stop to the business both of exportation and of the melting pot. The bank, instead of losing every year about two and a half per cent. upon the bullion which was to be coined into more than eight hundred and fifty thousand pounds, or incurring an annual loss of more than twenty-one thousand two hundred and fifty pounds, would not probably have incurred the tenth part of that loss.

The revenue allotted by parliament for defraying the expence of the coinage is but fourteen thousand pounds a year,[15]

The saving to the government may be regarded as too trifling, but that of the bank is worth considerable.

and the real expence which it costs the government, or the fees of the officers of the mint, do not upon ordinary occasions, I am assured, exceed the half of that sum. The saving of so very small a sum, or even the gaining of another which could not well be much larger, are objects too inconsiderable, it may be thought, to deserve the serious attention of government. But the saving of eighteen or twenty thousand pounds a year in case of an event which is not improbable, which has frequently happened before, and which is very likely to happen again, is surely an object which well deserves the serious attention even of so great a company as the bank of England.

Some of the foregoing reasonings and observations might perhaps have been more properly placed in those chapters of the first book which treat of the origin and use of money, and of

---

[14] [Above, p. 695.]

[15] [Under 19 Geo. II., c. 14, § 2, a maximum of £15,000 is prescribed.]

the difference between the real and the nominal price of commodities. But as the law for the encouragement of coinage derives its origin from those vulgar prejudices which have been introduced by the mercantile system; I judged it more proper to reserve them for this chapter. Nothing could be more agreeable to the spirit of that system than a sort of bounty upon the production of money, the very thing which, it supposes, constitutes the wealth of every nation. It is one of its many admirable expedients for enriching the country.

CHAPTER VII

OF COLONIES

PART FIRST

OF THE MOTIVES FOR ESTABLISHING NEW COLONIES

THE INTEREST which occasioned the first settlement of the different European colonies in America and the West Indies, was not altogether so plain and distinct as that which directed the establishment of those of ancient Greece and Rome.

All the different states of ancient Greece possessed, each of them, but a very small territory, and when the people in any one of them multiplied beyond what that territory could easily maintain, a part of them were sent in quest of a new habitation in some remote and distant part of the world; the warlike neighbours who surrounded them on all sides, rendering it difficult for any of them to enlarge very much its territory at home. The colonies of the Dorians resorted chiefly to Italy and Sicily, which, in the times preceding the foundation of Rome, were inhabited by barbarous and uncivilized nations: those of the Ionians and Eolians, the two other great tribes of the Greeks, to Asia Minor and the islands of the Egean Sea, of which the inhabitants seem at that time to have been pretty much in the same state as those of Sicily and Italy. The mother city, though she considered the colony as a child, at all times entitled to great favour and assistance, and owing in return much grati-

Greek colonies were sent out when the population grew too great at home.

The mother city claimed no authority. tude and respect, yet considered it as an emancipated child, over whom she pretended to claim no direct authority or jurisdiction. The colony settled its own form of government, enacted its own laws, elected its own magistrates, and made peace or war with its neighbours as an independent state, which had no occasion to wait for the approbation or consent of the mother city. Nothing can be more plain and distinct than the interest which directed every such establishment.

Rome, like most of the other ancient republics, was originally founded upon an Agrarian law, which divided the public territory in a certain proportion among the different citizens who composed the state. The course of human affairs, by marriage, by succession, and by alienation, necessarily deranged this original division, and frequently threw the lands, which had been allotted for the maintenance of many different families into the possession of a single person. To remedy this disorder, for such it was supposed to be, a law was made, restricting the quantity of land which any citizen could possess to five hundred jugera, about three hundred and fifty English acres. This law, however, though we read of its having been executed upon one or two occasions, was either neglected or evaded, and the inequality of fortunes went on continually increasing. The greater part of the citizens had no land, and without it the manners and customs of those times rendered it difficult for a freeman to maintain his independency. In the present times, though a poor man has no land of his own, if he has a little stock, he may either farm the lands of another, or he may carry on some little retail trade; and if he has no stock, he may find employment either as a country labourer, or as an artificer. But, among the ancient Romans, the lands of the rich were all cultivated by slaves, who wrought under an overseer, who was likewise a slave; so that a poor freeman had little chance of being employed either as a farmer or as a labourer. All trades and manufactures too, even the retail trade, were carried on by the slaves of the rich for the ben-

Roman colonies were sent out to satisfy the demand for lands and to establish garrisons in conquered territories;

efit of their masters, whose wealth, authority, and protection made it difficult for a poor freeman to maintain the competition against them. The citizens, therefore, who had no land, had scarce any other means of subsistence but the bounties of the candidates at the annual elections. The tribunes, when they had a mind to animate the people against the rich and the great, put them in mind of the ancient division of lands, and represented that law which restricted this sort of private property as the fundamental law of the republic. The people became clamorous to get land, and the rich and the great, we may believe, were perfectly determined not to give them any part of theirs. To satisfy them in some measure, therefore, they frequently proposed to send out a new colony. But conquering Rome was, even upon such occasions, under no necessity of turning out her citizens to seek their fortune, if one may say so, through the wide world, without knowing where they were to settle. She assigned them lands generally in the conquered provinces of Italy, where, being within the dominions of the republic, they could never form any independent state; but were at best but a sort of corporation, which, though it had the power of enacting bye-laws for its own government, was at all times subject to the correction, jurisdiction, and legislative authority of the mother city. The sending out a colony of this kind, not only gave some satisfaction to the people, but often established a sort of garrison too in a newly conquered province, of which the obedience might otherwise have been doubtful. A Roman colony, therefore, whether we consider the nature of the establishment itself, or the motives for making it, was altogether different from a Greek one. The words accordingly, which in the original languages denote those different establishments, have very different meanings. The Latin word (*Colonia*) signifies simply a plantation. The Greek word (απoιηια), on the contrary, signifies a separation of dwelling, a departure from home, a going out of the house. But, though the Roman colonies were in many respects different from the Greek ones, the interest which prompted to establish them was equally plain and distinct. Both institutions

they were entirely subject to the mother city.

derived their origin either from irresistible necessity, or from clear and evident utility.

The establishment of the European colonies in America and the West Indies arose from no necessity: and though the utility

The utility of the American colonies is not so evident.

which has resulted from them has been very great, it is not altogether so clear and evident. It was not understood at their first establishment, and was not the motive either of that establishment or of the discoveries which gave occasion to it; and the nature, extent, and limits of that utility are not, perhaps, well understood at this day.

The Venetians, during the fourteenth and fifteenth centuries, carried on a very advantageous commerce in spiceries, and

The Venetians had a profitable trade in East India goods,

other East India goods, which they distributed among the other nations of Europe. They purchased them chiefly[1] in Egypt, at that time under the dominion of the Mammeluks, the enemies of the Turks, of whom the Venetians

were the enemies; and this union of interest, assisted by the money of Venice, formed such a connection as gave the Venetians almost a monopoly of the trade.

The great profits of the Venetians tempted the avidity of the Portuguese. They had been endeavouring, during the course of

which was envied by the Portuguese and led them to discover the Cape of Good Hope passage,

the fifteenth century, to find out by sea a way to the countries from which the Moors brought them ivory and gold dust across the Desart. They discovered the Madeiras, the Canaries, the Azores, the Cape de Verd islands, the coast of Guinea, that of Loango, Congo, Angola, and Benguela,[2] and finally,

the Cape of Good Hope. They had long wished to share in the profitable traffic of the Venetians, and this last discovery opened to them a probable prospect of doing so. In 1497, Vasco de Gama sailed from the port of Lisbon with a fleet of four ships, and, after a navigation of eleven months, arrived

---

[1] ["Chiefly" is not in ed. 1.]

[2] [Ed. 1 reads "that of Congo, Angola and Loango."]

upon the coast of Indostan, and thus completed a course of discoveries which had been pursued with great steadiness, and with very little interruption, for near a century together.

Some years before this, while the expectations of Europe were in suspense about the projects of the Portuguese, of which the success appeared yet to be doubtful, a Genoese pilot formed the yet more daring project of sailing to the East Indies by the West. The situation of those countries was at that time very imperfectly known in Europe. The few European travellers who had been there had magnified the distance; perhaps through simplicity and ignorance, what was really very great, appearing almost infinite to those who could not measure it; or, perhaps, in order to increase somewhat more the marvellous of their own adventures in visiting regions so immensely remote from Europe. The longer the way was by the East, Columbus very justly concluded, the shorter it would be by the West. He proposed, therefore, to take that way, as both the shortest and the surest, and he had the good fortune to convince Isabella of Castile of the probability of his project. He sailed from the port of Palos in August 1492, near five years before the expedition of Vasco de Gama set out from Portugal, and, after a voyage of between two and three months, discovered first some of the small Bahama or Lucayan islands, and afterwards the great island of St. Domingo.

while Columbus endeavoured to reach the East Indies by sailing westwards.

But the countries which Columbus discovered, either in this or in any of his subsequent voyages, had no resemblance to those which he had gone in quest of. Instead of the wealth, cultivation and populousness of China and Indostan, he found, in St. Domingo, and in all the other parts of the new world which he ever visited, nothing but a country quite covered with wood, uncultivated, and inhabited only by some tribes of naked and miserable savages. He was not very willing, however, to believe that they were not the same with some of the countries described by Marco Polo, the first European who had visited, or at least had left behind him

Columbus mistook the countries he found for the Indies.

any description of China or the East Indies; and a very slight resemblance, such as that which he found between the name of Cibao, a mountain in St. Domingo, and that of Cipango, mentioned by Marco Polo, was frequently sufficient to make him return to this favourite prepossession, though contrary to the clearest evidence.[3] In his letters to Ferdinand and Isabella he called the countries which he had discovered, the Indies. He entertained no doubt but that they were the extremity of those which had been described by Marco Polo, and that they were not very distant from the Ganges, or from the countries which had been conquered by Alexander. Even when at last convinced that they were different, he still flattered himself that those rich countries were at no great distance, and in a subsequent voyage, accordingly, went in quest of them along the coast of Terra Firma, and towards the isthmus of Darien.

In consequence of this mistake of Columbus, the name of the Indies has stuck to those unfortunate countries ever since; *Hence the names East and West Indies.* and when it was at last clearly discovered that the new were altogether different from the old Indies, the former were called the West, in contradistinction to the latter, which were called the East Indies.

It was of importance to Columbus, however, that the countries which he had discovered, whatever they were, should be *The countries discovered were not rich* represented to the court of Spain as of very great consequence; and, in what constitutes the real riches of every country, the animal and vegetable productions of the soil, there was at that time nothing which could well justify such a representation of them.

The Cori, something between a rat and a rabbit, and supposed by Mr. Buffon[4] to be the same with the Aperea of Brazil, *in animals* was the largest viviparous quadruped in St. Domingo. This species seems never to have

[3] [P. F. X. de Charlevoix, *Histoire de l'Isle Espagnole ou de S. Domingue*, 1730, tom. i., p. 99.]

[4] [*Histoire Naturelle*, tom. xv. (1750), pp. 160, 162.]

been very numerous, and the dogs and cats of the Spaniards are said to have long ago almost entirely extirpated it, as well as some other tribes of a still smaller size.⁵ These, however, together with a pretty large lizard, called the Ivana or Iguana,⁶ constituted the principal part of the animal food which the land afforded.

The vegetable food of the inhabitants, though from their want of industry not very abundant, was not altogether so *or vegetables,* scanty. It consisted in Indian corn, yams, potatoes, bananes, &c. plants which were then altogether unknown in Europe, and which have never since been very much esteemed in it, or supposed to yield a sustenance equal to what is drawn from the common sorts of grain and pulse, which have been cultivated in this part of the world time out of mind.

The cotton plant indeed afforded the material of a very important manufacture, and was at that time to Europeans undoubtedly the most valuable of all the *cotton being not then considered of great consequence.* vegetable productions of those islands. But though in the end of the fifteenth century the muslins and other cotton goods of the East Indies were much esteemed in every part of Europe, the cotton manufacture itself was not cultivated in any part of it. Even this production, therefore, could not at that time appear in the eyes of Europeans to be of very great consequence.

Finding nothing either in the animals or vegetables of the newly discovered countries, which could justify a very advantageous representation of them, Columbus *So Columbus relied on the minerals.* turned his view towards their minerals; and in the richness of the productions of this third kingdom, he flattered himself, he had found a full compensation for the insignificancy of those of the other two. The little bits of gold with which the inhabitants ornamented their dress, and which, he was informed, they fre-

⁵ [Charlevoix, *Histoire de l'Isle Espagnole*, tom. i., pp. 35, 36.]

⁶ [*Ibid.*, p. 27.]

quently found in the rivulets and torrents that fell from the mountains, were sufficient to satisfy him that those mountains abounded with the richest gold mines. St. Domingo, therefore, was represented as a country abounding with gold, and upon that account (according to the prejudices not only of the present times, but of those times), an inexhaustible source of real wealth to the crown and kingdom of Spain. When Columbus, upon his return from his first voyage, was introduced with a sort of triumphal honours to the sovereigns of Castile and Arragon, the principal productions of the countries which he had discovered were carried in solemn procession before him. The only valuable part of them consisted in some little fillets, bracelets, and other ornaments of gold, and in some bales of cotton. The rest were mere objects of vulgar wonder and curiosity; some reeds of an extraordinary size, some birds of a very beautiful plumage, and some stuffed skins of the huge alligator and manati; all of which were preceded by six or seven of the wretched natives, whose singular colour and appearance added greatly to the novelty of the shew.

In consequence of the representations of Columbus, the council of Castile determined to take possession of countries of which the inhabitants were plainly incapable of defending themselves. The pious purpose of converting them to Christianity sanctified the injustice of the project. But the hope of finding treasures of gold there, was the sole motive which prompted to undertake it; and to give this motive the greater weight, it was proposed by Columbus that the half of all the gold and silver that should be found there should belong to the crown. This proposal was approved of by the council.

The Council of Castile was attracted by the gold, Columbus proposing that the government should have half the gold and silver discovered.

As long as the whole or the far greater part of the gold, which the first adventurers imported into Europe, was got by so very easy a method as the plundering of the defenceless natives, it was not perhaps very difficult to pay even this heavy tax. But when the natives were once fairly stript of all

This was an impossible tax and was soon reduced.

that they had, which, in St. Domingo, and in all the other countries discovered by Columbus, was done completely in six or eight years, and when in order to find more it had become necessary to dig for it in the mines, there was no longer any possibility of paying this tax. The rigorous exaction of it, accordingly, first occasioned, it is said, the total abandoning of the mines of St. Domingo, which have never been wrought since. It was soon reduced therefore to a third; then to a fifth; afterwards to a tenth; and at last to a twentieth part of the gross produce of the gold mines.[7] The tax upon silver continued for a long time to be a fifth of the gross produce. It was reduced to a tenth only in the course of the present century.[8] But the first adventurers do not appear to have been much interested about silver. Nothing less precious than gold seemed worthy of their attention.

All the other enterprises of the Spaniards in the new world, subsequent to those of Columbus, seem to have been prompted

The subsequent Spanish enterprises were all prompted by the same motive.

by the same motive. It was the sacred thirst of gold that carried Oieda, Nicuessa, and Vasco Nugnes de Balboa, to the isthmus of Darien, that carried Cortez to Mexico, and Almagro and Pizzarro to Chile and Peru. When those adventurers arrived upon any unknown coast, their first enquiry was always if there was any gold to be found there; and according to the information which they received concerning this particular, they determined either to quit the country or to settle in it.

Of all those expensive and uncertain projects, however, which bring bankruptcy upon the greater part of the people

A prudent lawgiver would not wish to encourage gold and silver mining,

who engage in them, there is none perhaps more perfectly ruinous than the search after new silver and gold mines. It is perhaps the most disadvantageous lottery in the world, or the one in which the gain of those who

---

[7] [Above, p. 233.]

[8] [Ed. 1 (in place of these two sentences) reads, "The tax upon silver, indeed, still continues to be a fifth of the gross produce." Cp. above, p. 231.]

draw the prizes bears the least proportion to the loss of those who draw the blanks: for though the prizes are few and the blanks many, the common price of a ticket is the whole fortune of a very rich man. Projects of mining, instead of replacing the capital employed in them, together with the ordinary profits of stock, commonly absorb both capital and profit. They are the projects, therefore, to which of all others a prudent law-giver, who desired to increase the capital of his nation, would least chuse to give any extraordinary encouragement, or to turn towards them a greater share of that capital than what would go to them of its own accord. Such in reality is the absurd confidence which almost all men have in their own good fortune, that wherever there is the least probability of success, too great a share of it is apt to go to them of its own accord.

But though the judgment of sober reason and experience concerning such projects has always been extremely un-favourable, that of human avidity has commonly been quite otherwise. The same passion which has suggested to so many people the absurd idea of the philosopher's stone, has suggested to others the equally absurd one of immense rich mines of gold and silver. They did not consider that the value of those metals has, in all ages and nations, arisen chiefly from their scarcity, and that their scarcity has arisen from the very small quantities of them which nature has any where deposited in one place, from the hard and intractable substances with which she has almost every where surrounded those small quantities, and consequently from the labour and expence which are every where necessary in order to penetrate to and get at them. They flattered themselves that veins of those metals might in many places be found as large and as abundant as those which are commonly found of lead, or copper, or tin, or iron. The dream of Sir Walter Raleigh concerning the golden city and country of Eldorado,[9] may satisfy us, that even wise men are not always exempt from such strange delu-

but people have always believed in an Eldorado.

[9] ["That mighty, rich and beautiful empire of Guiana, and . . . that great and golden city which the Spaniards call El Dorado."—Raleigh's *Works*, ed. Thomas Birch, 1751, vol. ii., p. 141.]

sions. More than a hundred years after the death of that great man, the Jesuit Gumila was still convinced of the reality of that wonderful country, and expressed with great warmth, and I dare to say, with great sincerity, how happy he should be to carry the light of the gospel to a people who could so well reward the pious labours of their missionary.[10]

In the countries first discovered by the Spaniards, no gold or silver mines are at present known which are supposed to be worth the working. The quantities of those *In this case expectations were to some extent realised, so far as the Spaniards were concerned,* metals which the first adventurers are said to have found there, had probably been very much magnified, as well as the fertility of the mines which were wrought immediately after the first discovery. What those adventurers were reported to have found, however, was sufficient to inflame the avidity of all their countrymen. Every Spaniard who sailed to America expected to find an Eldorado. Fortune too did upon this what she has done upon very few other occasions. She realized in some measure the extravagant hopes of her votaries, and in the discovery and conquest of Mexico and Peru (of which the one happened about thirty, the other about forty years after the first expedition of Columbus), she presented them with something not very unlike that profusion of the precious metals which they sought for.

A project of commerce to the East Indies, therefore, gave

[10] [P. Jos. Gumilla, *Histoire naturelle civile et géographique de l'Orénoque, etc.*, traduite par M. Eidous, 1758, tom. ii., pp. 46, 117, 131, 132, 137, 138, but the sentiment is apparently attributed to the author who is described on the title page as "de la compagnie de Jésus, supérieur des missions de l'Orénoque," on the strength of a mistranslation of the French or possibly the original Spanish. If "Dieu permit" were mistranslated "God permit," the following passage from pp. 137, 138 would bear out the text: "On cherchait une vallée ou un territoire dont les rochers et les pierres étaient d'or, et les Indiens pour flatter la cupidité des Espagnols, et les éloigner en même temps de chez eux, leur peignaient avec les couleurs les plus vives l'or dont ce pays abondait pour se débarrasser plutôt de ces hôtes incommodes, et Dieu permit que les Espagnols ajoutassent foi à ces rapports, pour qu'ils découvrissent un plus grand nombre de provinces, et que la lumière de l'Evangile pût s'y répandre avec plus de facilité."]

occasion to the first discovery of the West. A project of conquest gave occasion to all the establishments of the Spaniards in those newly discovered countries. The motive which excited them to this conquest was a project of gold and silver mines; and a course of accidents, which no human wisdom could foresee, rendered this project much more successful than the undertakers had any reasonable grounds for expecting.

The first adventures of all the other nations of Europe, who attempted to make settlements in America, were animated by the like chimerical views; but they were not equally successful. It was more than a hundred years after the first settlement of the Brazils, before any silver, gold, or diamond

but the other nations were not so successful.

mines were discovered there. In the English, French, Dutch, and Danish colonies, none have ever yet been discovered; at least none that are at present supposed to be worth the working. The first English settlers in North America, however, offered a fifth of all the gold and silver which should be found there to the king, as a motive for granting them their patents. In the patents to Sir Walter Raleigh, to the London and Plymouth companies, to the council of Plymouth, &c. this fifth was accordingly reserved to the crown. To the expectation of finding gold and silver mines, those first settlers too joined that of discovering a north-west passage to the East Indies. They have hitherto been disappointed in both.

PART SECOND

CAUSES OF THE PROSPERITY OF NEW COLONIES

The colony of a civilized nation which takes possession either of a waste country, or of one so thinly inhabited, that the natives easily give place to the new settlers, advances more rapidly to wealth and greatness than any other human society.

The colonists carry out with them a knowledge of agriculture and of other useful arts, superior to what can grow up of its own accord in the course of many centuries among savage

Colonists take out knowledge and regular government, and barbarous nations. They carry out with them too the habit of subordination, some notion of the regular government which takes place in their own country, of the system of laws which supports[11] it, and of a regular administration of justice; and they naturally establish something of the same kind in the new settlement. But among savage and barbarous nations, the natural progress of law and government is still slower than the natural progress of arts, after law and government have been so far established,

land is plentiful and cheap, as is necessary for their protection. Every colonist gets more land than he can possibly cultivate. He has no rent, and scarce any taxes to pay. No landlord shares with him in its produce, and the share of the sovereign is commonly but a trifle. He has every motive to render as great as possible a produce, which is thus to be almost entirely his own. But his land is commonly so extensive, that with all his own industry, and with all the industry of other people whom he can get to employ, he can seldom make it produce the tenth part of what it is capable of producing. He is eager, therefore, to collect labourers from all quar-

wages are high, ters, and to reward them with the most liberal wages. But those liberal wages, joined to the plenty and cheapness of land, soon make those labourers leave him, in order to become landlords themselves, and to reward, with equal liberality, other labourers, who soon leave them for the same reason that they left their first master. The liberal reward of labour encourages marriage. The chil-

and children are taken care of and are profitable. dren, during the tender years of infancy, are well fed and properly taken care of, and when they are grown up, the value of their labour greatly overpays their maintenance. When arrived at maturity, the high price of labour, and the low price of land, enable them to establish themselves in the same manner as their fathers did before them.

In other countries, rent and profit eat up wages, and the two

[11] [Eds. 1–4 reads "support."]

Population and improvement, which mean wealth and greatness, are encouraged. superior orders of people oppress the inferior one. But in new colonies, the interest of the two superior orders obliges them to treat the inferior one with more generosity and humanity; at least, where that inferior one is not in a state of slavery. Waste lands of the greatest natural fertility, are to be had for a trifle. The increase of revenue which the proprietor, who is always the undertaker, expects from their improvement constitutes his profit; which in these circumstances is commonly very great. But this great profit cannot be made without employing the labour of other people in clearing and cultivating the land; and the disproportion between the great extent of the land and the small number of the people, which commonly takes place in new colonies, makes it difficult for him to get this labour. He does not, therefore, dispute about wages, but is willing to employ labour at any price. The high wages of labour encourage population. The cheapness and plenty of good land encourage improvement, and enable the proprietor to pay those high wages. In those wages consists almost the whole price of the land; and though they are high, considered as the wages of labour, they are low, considered as the price of what is so very valuable. What encourages the progress of population and improvement, encourages that of real wealth and greatness.

The progress of many of the ancient Greek colonies towards wealth and greatness, seems accordingly to have been

The progress of the Greek colonies was very rapid. very rapid. In the course of a century or two, several of them appear to have rivalled, and even to have surpassed their mother cities. Syracuse and Agrigentum in Sicily, Tarentum and Locri in Italy, Ephesus and Miletus in Lesser Asia, appear by all accounts to have been at least equal to any of the cities of ancient Greece. Though posterior in their establishment, yet all the arts of refinement, philosophy, poetry, and eloquence, seem to have been cultivated as early, and to have been improved as highly in them, as in any part of the mother country. The schools of the two oldest Greek philosophers, those of Thales and Pythagoras, were established, it is remarkable, not in ancient Greece, but the one in an Asiatic, the other in an Italian colony.[12] All those colonies had established themselves in countries inhabited by savage and barbarous nations, who easily gave place to the new settlers. They had plenty of good land, and as they were altogether independent of the mother city, they were at liberty to manage their own affairs in the way that they judged was most suitable to their own interest.

The history of the Roman colonies is by no means so brilliant. Some of them, indeed, such as Florence, have in the

That of the Roman colonies much less so.

course of many ages, and after the fall of the mother city, grown up to be considerable states. But the progress of no one of them seems ever to have been very rapid. They were all established in conquered provinces, which in most cases had been fully inhabited before. The quantity of land assigned to each colonist was seldom very considerable, and as the colony was not independent, they were not always at liberty to manage their own affairs in the way that they judged was most suitable to their own interest.

In the plenty of good land, the European colonies established in America and the West Indies resemble, and even

The American colonies have had plenty of land and not very much interference from their mother countries.

greatly surpass, those of ancient Greece. In their dependency upon the mother state, they resemble those of ancient Rome; but their great distance from Europe has in all of them alleviated more or less the effects of this dependency. Their situation has placed them less in the view and less in the power of their mother country. In pursuing their interest their own way, their conduct has, upon many occasions, been overlooked, either because not known or not understood in Europe; and upon some occasions it has been fairly suffered and submitted to, because their distance rendered it difficult to restrain it. Even the violent and arbitrary government of Spain has, upon many

---

[12] [Miletus and Crotona.]

occasions, been obliged to recall or soften the orders which had been given for the government of her[13] colonies, for fear of a general insurrection. The progress of all the European colonies in wealth, population, and improvement, has accordingly been very great.

The crown of Spain, by its share of the gold and silver, derived some revenue from its colonies, from the moment of their first establishment. It was a revenue

The progress of the Spanish colonies, Mexico and Peru, has been very considerable.

too, of a nature to excite in human avidity the most extravagant expectations of still greater riches. The Spanish colonies, therefore, from the moment of their first establishment, attracted very much the attention of their mother country; while those of the other European nations were for a long time in a great measure neglected. The former did not, perhaps, thrive the better in consequence of this attention; nor the latter the worse in consequence of this neglect. In proportion to the extent of the country which they in some measure possess, the Spanish colonies are considered as less populous and thriving than those of almost any other European nation. The progress even of the Spanish colonies, however, in population and improvement, has certainly been very rapid and very great. The city of Lima, founded since the conquest, is represented by Ulloa, as containing fifty thousand inhabitants near thirty years ago.[14] Quito, which had been but a miserable hamlet of Indians, is represented by the same author as in his time equally populous.[15] Gemelli Carreri, a pretended traveller, it is said, indeed, but who seems every where to have writen upon extreme good information, represents the city of Mexico as containing a hundred thousand inhabitants;[16] a number which, in spite of all the exaggerations of the Spanish writers, is, probably, more than

[13] [Ed. 1 reads "its."]

[14] [See above, p. 277.]

[15] [Juan and Ulloa, *Voyage historique*, tom. 1., p. 229.]

[16] [In Awnsham and John Churchill's *Collection of Voyages and Travels*, 1704, vol. iv., p. 508.]

five times greater than what it contained in the time of Montezuma. These numbers exceed greatly those of Boston, New York, and Philadelphia, the three greatest cities of the English colonies. Before the conquest of the Spaniards there were no cattle fit for draught either in Mexico or Peru. The lama was their only beast of burden, and its strength seems to have been a good deal inferior to that of a common ass. The plough was unknown among them. They were ignorant of the use of iron. They had no coined money, nor any established instrument of commerce of any kind. Their commerce was carried on by barter. A sort of wooden spade was their principal instrument of agriculture. Sharp stones served them for knives and hatchets to cut with; fish bones and the hard sinews of certain animals served them for needles to sew with; and these seem to have been their principal instruments of trade.[17] In this state of things, it seems impossible, that either of those empires could have been so much improved or so well cultivated as at present, when they are plentifully furnished with all sorts of European cattle, and when the use of iron, of the plough, and of many of the arts of Europe, has been introduced among them. But the populousness of every country must be in proportion to the degree of its improvement and cultivation. In spite of the cruel destruction of the natives which followed the conquest, these two great empires are, probably, more populous now than they ever were before: and the people are surely very different; for we must acknowledge, I apprehend, the Spanish creoles are in many respects superior to the ancient Indians.

After the settlements of the Spaniards, that of the Portugueze in Brazil is the oldest of any European nation in

The Portuguese colony of Brazil is very populous.

America. But as for a long time after the first discovery, neither gold nor silver mines were found in it, and as it afforded, upon that account, little or no revenue to the crown, it was for a long time in a great measure neglected; and during this state of neglect, it grew up to be a great and powerful

[17] [Cp. above, p. 276.]

colony. While Portugal was under the dominion of Spain, Brazil was attacked by the Dutch, who got possession of seven of the fourteen provinces into which it is divided. They expected soon to conquer the other seven, when Portugal recovered its independency by the elevation of the family of Braganza to the throne. The Dutch then, as enemies to the Spaniards, became friends to the Portugueze, who were likewise the enemies of the Spaniards. They agreed, therefore, to leave that part of Brazil, which they had not conquered, to the king of Portugal, who agreed to leave that part which they had conquered to them, as a matter not worth disputing about with such good allies. But the Dutch Government soon began to oppress the Portugueze colonists, who, instead of amusing themselves with complaints, took arms against their new masters, and by their own valour and resolution, with the connivance, indeed, but without any avowed assistance from the mother country, drove them out of Brazil. The Dutch, therefore, finding it impossible to keep any part of the country to themselves, were contented that it should be entirely restored to the crown of Portugal.[18] In this colony there are said to be more than six hundred thousand people,[19] either Portugueze or descended from Portugueze, creoles, mulattoes, and a mixed race between Portugueze and Brazilians. No one colony in America is supposed to contain so great a number of people of European extraction.

Towards the end of the fifteenth, and during the greater part of the sixteenth century, Spain and Portugal were the two great naval powers upon the ocean: for though the commerce of Venice extended to every part of Europe, its fleets had scarce ever sailed beyond the Mediterranean. The Spaniards, in virtue of the first discovery, claimed all America as their own; and though they could not hinder so great a naval power as that of Portugal from settling in Brazil, such was, at that time, the terror of their name,

When Spain declined, various countries obtained a footing in America.

[18] [Raynal, *Histoire Philosophique*, Amsterdam ed., 1773, tom. iii., pp. 347–352.]

[19] [*Ibid.*, tom. iii., p. 424.]

that the greater part of the other nations of Europe were afraid to establish themselves in any other part of that great continent. The French, who attempted to settle in Florida, were all murdered by the Spaniards.[20] But the declension of the naval power of this latter nation, in consequence of the defeat or miscarriage of, what they called, their Invincible Armada, which happened towards the end of the sixteenth century, put it out of their power to obstruct any longer the settlements of the other European nations. In the course of the seventeenth century, therefore, the English, French, Dutch, Danes, and Swedes, all the great nations who had any ports upon the ocean, attempted to make some settlements in the new world.

The Swedes established themselves in New Jersey; and the number of Swedish families still to be found there, sufficiently

The Swedish colony of New Jersey was prospering when swallowed up by New York.

demonstrates, that this colony was very likely to prosper, had it been protected by the mother country. But being neglected by Sweden it was soon swallowed up by the Dutch colony of New York, which again, in 1674,[21] fell under the dominion of the English.

The small islands of St. Thomas and Santa Cruz are the only countries in the new world that have ever been possessed

The Danish colonies of St. Thomas and Santa Cruz have been very prosperous since the exclusive company was dissolved.

by the Danes. These little settlements too were under the government of an exclusive company, which had the sole right, both of purchasing the surplus produce of the colonists, and of supplying them with such goods of other countries as they wanted, and which, therefore, both in its purchases and sales, had not only the power of oppressing

them, but the greatest temptation to do so. The government of an exclusive company of merchants is, perhaps, the worst of all governments for any country whatever. It was not, however, able to stop altogether the progress of these colonies, though it

[20] [*Ibid.*, tom. vi., p. 8.]

[21] [A mistake for 1664.]

rendered it more slow and languid. The late king of Denmark dissolved this company, and since that time the prosperity of these colonies has been very great.

The Dutch settlements in the West, as well as those in the East Indies, were originally put under the government of an exclusive company. The progress of some of them, therefore,

The Dutch colony of Surinam is prosperous though still under an exclusive company.

though it has been considerable, in comparison with that of almost any country that has been long peopled and established, has been languid and slow in comparison with that of the greater part of new colonies. The colony of Surinam, though very considerable, is still inferior to the greater part of the sugar colonies of the other European nations. The colony of Nova Belgia, now divided into the two provinces of New York and New Jersey, would probably have soon become considerable too, even though it had remained under the government of the Dutch. The plenty and cheapness of good land are such powerful causes of prosperity, that the very worst government is scarce capable of checking altogether the efficacy of their operation. The great distance too from the mother country would enable the colonists to evade more or less, by smuggling, the monopoly which the company enjoyed against them. At present the company allows all Dutch ships to trade to Surinam upon paying two and a half per cent. upon the value of their cargo for a licence; and only reserves to itself exclusively the direct trade from Africa to America, which consists almost entirely in the slave trade. This relaxation in the exclusive privileges of the company, is probably the principal cause of that degree of prosperity which that colony at present enjoys. Curaçoa and Eustatia, the two principal islands belonging to the Dutch, are free ports open to the ships of all nations; and this freedom, in the midst of better colonies whose ports are open to those of one nation only, has been the great cause of the prosperity of those two barren islands.

The French colony of Canada was, during the greater part of the last century, and some part of the present, under the government of an exclusive company. Under so unfavourable an

The French colony of Canada has shown rapid progress since the dissolution of the exclusive company.

administration its progress was necessarily very slow in comparison with that of other new colonies; but it became much more rapid when this company was dissolved after the fall of what is called the Mississippi scheme. When the English got possession of this country, they found in it near double the number of inhabitants which father Charlevoix had assigned to it between twenty and thirty years before.[22] That jesuit had travelled over the whole country, and had no inclination to represent it as less considerable than it really was.

The French colony of St. Domingo was established by pirates and free-booters, who, for a long time, neither required the

St. Domingo, in spite of various obstacles, and the other French sugar colonies, are very thriving.

protection, nor acknowledged the authority of France; and when that[23] race of banditti became so far citizens as to acknowledge this authority, it was for a long time necessary to exercise it with very great gentleness. During this period the population and improvement of this colony increased very fast. Even the oppression of the exclusive company, to which it was for some time subjected, with all the other colonies of France, though it no doubt retarded, had not been able to stop its progress altogether. The course of its prosperity returned as soon as it was relieved from that oppression. It is now the most important of the sugar colonies of the West Indies, and its produce is said to be greater than that of all the English sugar colonies put together.

But the progress of the English colonies has been the most rapid.

The other sugar colonies of France are in general all very thriving.

But there are no colonies of which the progress has been more rapid than that of the English in North America.

[22] [P. F. X. de Charlevoix, *Histoire et description générale de la Nouvelle-France, avec le journal historique d'un voyage dans l'Amérique Septentrionnale*, 1744, tom. ii., p. 390, speaks of a population of 20,000 to 25,000 in 1713. Raynal says in 1753 and 1758 the population, excluding troops and Indians, was 91,000.— *Histoire philosophique*, Amsterdam ed., 1773, tom. vi., p. 137.]

[23] [Ed. 1 reads "the."]

Plenty of good land, and liberty to manage their own affairs their own way, seem to be the two great causes of the prosperity of all new colonies.

In the plenty of good land the English colonies of North America, though, no doubt, very abundantly provided, are, however, inferior to those of the Spaniards and Portugueze, and not superior to some of those possessed by the French before the late war. But the political institutions of the English colonies have been more favourable to the improvement and cultivation of this land, than those of any of the other three nations.

They have not so much good land as the Spanish and Portuguese, but their institutions are more favourable to its improvement.

First, the engrossing of uncultivated land, though it has by no means been prevented altogether, has been more restrained in the English colonies than in any other. The colony law which imposes upon every proprietor the obligation of improving and cultivating, within a limited time, a certain proportion of his lands, and which, in case of failure, declares those neglected lands grantable to any other person; though it has not, perhaps, been very strictly executed, has, however, had some effect.

(1) The engrossing of uncultivated land has been more restrained.

Secondly, in Pennsylvania there is no right of primogeniture, and lands, like moveables, are divided equally among all the children of the family. In three of the provinces of New England the oldest has only a double share, as in the Mosaical law. Though in those provinces, therefore, too great a quantity of land should sometimes be engrossed by a particular individual, it is likely, in the course of a generation or two, to be sufficiently divided again. In the other English colonies, indeed, the right of primogeniture takes place, as in the law of England. But in all the English colonies the tenure of the[24] lands, which are all held by free socage, facilitates alienation, and the grantee of

(2) Primogeniture and entails are less prevalent and alienation more frequent.

---

[24] [Eds. 1 and 2 read "their."]

any extensive tract of land, generally finds it for his interest to alienate, as fast as he can, the greater part of it, reserving only a small quit-rent. In the Spanish and Portugueze colonies, what is called the right of Majorazzo[25] takes place in the succession of all those great estates to which any title of honour is annexed. Such estates go all to one person, and are in effect entailed and unalienable. The French colonies, indeed, are subject to the custom of Paris, which, in the inheritance of land, is much more favourable to the younger children than the law of England. But, in the French colonies, if any part of an estate, held by the noble tenure of chivalry and homage, is alienated, it is, for a limited time, subject to the right of redemption, either by the heir of the superior or by the heir of the family; and all the largest estates of the country are held by such noble tenures, which necessarily embarrass alienation. But, in a new colony, a great uncultivated estate is likely to be much more speedily divided by alienation than by succession. The plenty and cheapness of good land, it has already been observed,[26] are the principal causes of the rapid prosperity of new colonies. The engrossing of land, in effect, destroys this plenty and cheapness.[27] The engrossing of uncultivated land, besides, is the greatest obstruction to its improvement. But the labour[28] that is employed in the improvement and cultivation of land affords the greatest and most valuable produce to the society. The produce of labour, in this case,[29] pays not only its own wages, and the profit of the stock which employs it, but the rent of the land too upon which it is employed. The labour of the English colonists, therefore, being more employed in the improvement and cultivation of land, is likely to afford a greater

[25] [Jus Majoratus. Ed. 1 reads "mayorazzo" in the text and "mayoratus" in the note.]

[26] [Above, pp. 716, 717, and cp. p. 129.]

[27] [This and the preceding sentence, beginning "The plenty," are not in ed. 1.]

[28] [Ed. 1 reads "The engrossing, however, of uncultivated land, it has already been observed, is the greatest obstruction to its improvement and cultivation, and the labour."]

[29] [Ed. 1 reads "Its produce in this case."]

and more valuable produce, than that of any of the other three nations, which, by the engrossing of land, is more or less diverted towards other employments.

Thirdly, the labour of the English colonists is not only likely to afford a greater and more valuable produce, but, in conse-

(3) Taxes are more moderate.

quence of the moderation of their taxes, a greater proportion of this produce belongs to themselves, which they may store up and employ in putting into motion a still greater quantity of labour. The English colonists have never yet contributed any thing towards the defence of the mother country, or towards the support of its civil government. They themselves, on the contrary, have hitherto been defended almost entirely at the expence of the mother country. But the expence of fleets and armies is out of all proportion greater than the necessary expence of civil government. The expence of their own civil government has always been very moderate. It has generally been confined to what was necessary for paying competent salaries to the governor, to the judges, and to some other offices of police, and for maintaining a few of the most useful public works. The expence of the civil establishment of Massachusett's Bay, before the commencement of the present[30] disturbances, used to be but about 18,000*l.* a year. That of New Hampshire and Rhode Island 3,500*l.* each. That of Connecticut 4,000*l.* That of New York and Pennsylvania 4,500*l.* each. That of New Jersey 1,200*l.* That of Virginia and South Carolina 8,000*l.* each. The civil establishments of Nova Scotia and Georgia are partly supported by an annual grant of parliament. But Nova Scotia pays, besides, about 7,000*l.* a year towards the public expence of the colony; and Georgia about 2,200*l.* a year. All the different civil establishments in North America, in short, exclusive of those of Maryland and North Carolina, of which no exact account has been got, did not, before the commencement of the present disturbances, cost the inhabitants above 64,700*l.* a year,[31] an

---

[30] [All eds. read "present" here and on p. 742 and 781, but "late" on p. 733. See above, p. 627, note 41, and below, p. 1195.]

[31] [The figures are evidently from the "very exact account" quoted below, p. 1195.]

ever-memorable example at how small an expence three millions of people may not only be governed, but well governed. The most important part of the expence of government, indeed, that of defence and protection, has constantly fallen upon the mother country. The ceremonial too of the civil government in the colonies, upon the reception of a new governor, upon the opening of a new assembly, &c. though sufficiently decent, is not accompanied with any expensive pomp or parade. Their ecclesiastical government is conducted upon a plan equally frugal. Tithes are unknown among them; and their clergy, who are far from being numerous, are maintained either by moderate stipends, or by the voluntary contributions of the people. The power of Spain and Portugal, on the contrary, derives some support from the taxes levied upon their colonies. France, indeed, has never drawn any considerable revenue from its colonies, the taxes which it levies upon them being generally spent among them. But the colony government of all these three nations is conducted upon a much more expensive plan, and is accompanied with a much more expensive ceremonial. The sums spent upon the reception of a new viceroy of Peru, for example, have frequently been enormous.[32] Such ceremonials are not only real taxes paid by the rich colonists upon those particular occasions, but they serve to introduce among them the habit of vanity and expence upon all other occasions. They are not only very grievous occasional taxes, but they contribute to establish perpetual taxes of the same kind still more grievous; the ruinous taxes of private luxury and extravagance. In the colonies of all those three nations too, the ecclesiastical government is extremely oppressive. Tithes take place in all of them, and are levied with the utmost rigour in those of Spain and Portugal. All of them besides are oppressed with a numerous race of mendicant friars, whose beggary being not only licensed, but consecrated by religion, is a most grievous tax upon the poor people, who are most carefully taught that it is a duty to give, and a very great sin to refuse them their charity.

[32] [Juan and Ulloa, *Voyage historique*, tom. i., pp. 437–441, give a lurid account of the magnificence of the ceremonial.]

Over and above all this, the clergy are, in all of them, the greatest engrossers of land.

Fourthly, in the disposal of their surplus produce, or of what is over and above their own consumption, the

(4) The trade monopoly of the mother country has been less oppressive,

English colonies have been more favoured, and have been allowed a more extensive market, than those of any other European nation. Every European nation has endeavoured more or less to monopolize to itself the commerce of its colonies, and, upon that account, has prohibited the ships of foreign nations from trading to them, and has prohibited them from importing European goods from any foreign nation. But the manner in which this monopoly has been exercised in different nations has been very different.

Some nations have given up the whole commerce of their colonies to an exclusive company, of whom

since there has been no exclusive company with its interest to buy the produce of the colonies as cheap as possible,

the colonies were obliged to buy all such European goods as they wanted, and to whom they were obliged to sell the whole of their own surplus produce. It was the interest of the company, therefore, not only to sell the former as dear, and to buy the latter as cheap as possible, but to buy no more of the latter, even at this low price, than what they could dispose of for a very high price in Europe. It was their interest, not only to degrade in all cases the value of the surplus produce of the colony, but in many cases to discourage and keep down the natural increase of its quantity. Of all the expedients that can well be contrived to stunt the natural growth of a new colony, that of an exclusive company is undoubtedly the most effectual. This, however, has been the policy of Holland, though their company, in the course of the present century, has given up in many respects the exertion of their exclusive privilege. This too was the policy of Denmark till the reign of the late king. It has occasionally been the policy of France, and of late, since 1755, after it had been abandoned by all other nations, on account of its absurdity, it has become the policy of Portugal with regard at least to two of the principal provinces of Brazil, Fernambuco and Marannon.[33]

Other nations, without establishing an exclusive company, have confined the whole commerce of their colonies to a par-

nor any restriction of commerce to a particular port and to particular licensed ships,

ticular port of the mother country, from whence no ship was allowed to sail, but either in a fleet and at a particular season, or, if single, in consequence of a particular licence, which in most cases was very well paid for. This policy opened, indeed, the trade of the colonies to all the natives of the mother country, provided they traded from the proper port, at the proper season, and in the proper vessels. But as all the different merchants, who joined their stocks in order to fit out those licensed vessels, would find it for their interest to act in concert, the trade which was carried on in this manner would necessarily be conducted very nearly upon the same principles as that of an exclusive company. The profit of those merchants would be almost equally exorbitant and oppressive. The colonies would be ill supplied, and would be obliged both to buy very dear, and to sell very cheap. This, however, till within these few years, had[34] always been the policy of Spain, and the price of all European goods, accordingly, is said to have been[35] enormous in the Spanish West Indies. At Quito, we are told by Ulloa, a pound of iron sold for about four and six-pence, and a pound of steel for about six and nine-pence sterling.[36] But it is chiefly in order to purchase European goods, that the colonies part with their own produce. The more, therefore, they pay for the one, the less they really get for the other, and the dearness of the one is the same thing with the cheapness of the other. The policy of Portugal is in this respect the same as the ancient

---

[33] [Maranon in 1755 and Fernambuco four years later.—Raynal, *Histoire philosophique*, Amsterdam ed., 1773, tom. iii., p. 402.]

[34] [Ed. 1 reads "This, however, has."]

[35] [Ed. 1 reads "said to be."]

[36] [Iron sometimes at 100 écus the quintal and steel at 150.—Juan and Ulloa, *Voyage historique*, tom. i., p. 252.]

policy of Spain,[37] with regard to all its colonies, except Fernambuco and Marannon, and with regard to these it has lately adopted a still worse.

Other nations leave the trade of their colonies free to all their subjects, who may carry it on from all the different ports of the mother country, and who have occasion for no other licence than the common dispatches of the customhouse. In this case the number and dispersed situation of the different traders renders it impossible for them to enter into any general combination,

but freedom for every subject to trade with every port in the mother country,

and their competition is sufficient to hinder them from making very exorbitant profits. Under so liberal a policy the colonies are enabled both to sell their own produce and to buy the goods of Europe at a reasonable price. But since the dissolution of the Plymouth company, when our colonies were but in their infancy, this has always been the policy of England. It has generally too been that of France, and has been uniformly so since the dissolution of what, in England, is commonly called their Mississippi company. The profits of the trade, therefore, which France and England carry on with their colonies, though no doubt somewhat higher than if the competition was free to all other nations, are, however, by no means exorbitant; and the price of European goods accordingly is not extravagantly high in the greater part of the colonies of either of those nations.

In the exportation of their own surplus produce too, it is only with regard to certain commodities that the colonies of Great Britain are confined to the market of the mother country. These commodities having been enumerated in the act of navigation and in some other subsequent acts, have upon that account been called *enumerated commodities*.[38] The rest are called *non-enumerated*; and may be exported, directly

and freedom to export everything but the enumerated commodities to other places besides the mother country.

---

[37] [Ed. 1 reads "the same as that of Spain."]

[38] [The commodities originally enumerated in 12 Car. II., c. 18, § 28, were sugar, tobacco-cotton-wool, indigo, ginger, fustic and other dyeing woods.]

to other countries, provided it is in British or Plantation ships, of which the owners and three-fourths of the mariners are British subjects.

Some most important productions are not enumerated, Among the non-enumerated commodities are some of the most important productions of America and the West Indies; grain of all sorts, lumber, salt provisions, fish, sugar, and rum.

Grain is naturally the first and principal object of the culture of all new colonies. By allowing them a very extensive market *as grain,* for it, the law encourages them to extend this culture much beyond the consumption of a thinly inhabited country, and thus to provide beforehand an ample subsistence for a continually increasing population.

In a country quite covered with wood, where timber conse- *timber,* quently is of little or no value, the expence of clearing the ground is the principal obstacle to improvement. By allowing the colonies a very extensive market for their lumber, the law endeavours to facilitate improvement by raising the price of a commodity which would otherwise be of little value, and thereby enabling them to make some profit of what would otherwise be mere expence.

In a country neither half-peopled nor half cultivated, cattle naturally multiply beyond the consumption of the inhabitants, *cattle,* and are often upon that account of little or no value. But it is necessary, it has already been shewn,[39] that the price of cattle should bear a certain proportion to that of corn before the greater part of the lands of any country can be improved. By allowing to American cattle, in all shapes, dead and alive, a very extensive market, the law endeavours to raise the value of a commodity of which the high price is so very essential to improvement. The good effects of this liberty, however, must be somewhat diminished by the 4th of George III. c. 15. which puts hides and skins among the enumerated commodities, and thereby tends to reduce the value of American cattle.

[39] [Above, pp. 203–204, 298–301.]

To increase the shipping and naval power of Great Britain, by the extension of the fisheries of our colonies, is an object

fish, which the legislature seems to have had almost constantly in view. Those fisheries, upon this account, have had all the encouragement which freedom can give them, and they have flourished accordingly. The New England fishery in particular was, before the late[40] disturbances, one of the most important, perhaps, in the world. The whale-fishery which, notwithstanding an extravagant bounty, is in Great Britain carried on to so little purpose, that in the opinion of many people (which I do not, however, pretend to warrant) the whole produce does not much exceed the value of the bounties which are annually paid for it, is in New England carried on without any bounty to a very great extent. Fish is one of the principal articles with which the North Americans trade to Spain, Portugal, and the Mediterranean.

Sugar was originally an enumerated commodity which could be exported only to Great Britain. But in 1731, upon a

sugar, representation of the sugar-planters, its exportation was permitted to all parts of the world.[41] The restrictions,[42] however, with which this liberty was granted, joined to the high price of sugar in Great Britain, have rendered it, in a great measure, ineffectual. Great Britain and her colonies still continue to be almost the sole market for all the sugar produced in the British plantations. Their consumption increases so fast, that, though in consequence of the increasing improvement of Jamaica, as well as of the Ceded Islands,[43] the importation of sugar has increased very greatly

---

[40] [See above, p. 727, note 30.]

[41] [There seems to be some mistake here. The true date is apparently 1739, under the Act 12 Geo. II., c. 30.]

[42] [Ships not going to places south of Cape Finisterre were compelled to call at some port in Great Britain.]

[43] [Garnier, in his note to this passage, tom. iii., p. 323, points out that the islands ceded by the peace of Paris in 1763 were only Grenada and the Grenadines, but that the term here includes the other islands won during the war, St. Vincent, Dominica and Tobago, which are mentioned below, p. 1202.]

within these twenty years, the exportation to foreign countries is said to be not much greater than before.

Rum is a very important article in the trade which the Americans carry on to the coast of Africa, from which they bring back negroe slaves in return.

and rum.

If the whole surplus produce of America in grain of all sorts, in salt provisions, and in fish, had been put into the enumeration, and thereby forced into the market of Great Britain, it would have interfered too much with the produce of the industry of our own people. It was probably not so much from any regard to the interest of America, as from a jealousy of this interference, that those important commodities have not only been kept out of the enumeration, but that the importation into Great Britain of all grain, except rice, and of salt provisions, has, in the ordinary state of the law, been prohibited.

Grain, meat and fish would have competed too strongly with British produce if forced into the British market.

The non-enumerated commodities could originally be exported to all parts of the world. Lumber and rice, having been once put into the enumeration, when they were afterwards taken out of it, were confined, as to the European market, to the countries that lie south of Cape Finisterre.[44] By the 6th of George III. c. 52. all non-enumerated commodities were subjected to the like restriction. The parts of Europe which lie south of Cape Finisterre, are not manufacturing countries, and we were less jealous of the colony ships carrying home from them any manufactures which could interfere with our own.

Originally non-enumerated commodities could be exported to any part of the world. Recently they have been confined to countries south of Cape Finisterre.

The enumerated commodities are of two sorts: first, such as are either the peculiar produce of America, or as cannot be produced, or at least are not produced, in the mother country. Of this kind are, molasses, coffee, cacao-nuts, tobacco, pimento,

---

[44] [Rice was put in by 3 and 4 Ann. c. 5, and taken out by 3 Geo. II., c. 28; timber was taken out by 5 Geo. III., c. 45.]

The enumerated commodities are (1) commodities not produced at all in the mother country, and (2) commodities of which only a small part of the supply is produced in the mother country.

ginger, whale-fins, raw silk, cotton-wool, beaver, and other peltry of America, indigo, fustic, and other dying woods: secondly, such as are not the peculiar produce of America, but which are and may be produced in the mother country, though not in such quantities as to supply the greater part of her demand, which is principally supplied from foreign countries. Of this kind are all naval stores, masts, yards, and bowsprits, tar, pitch, and turpentine, pig and bar iron, copper ore, hides and skins, pot and pearl ashes. The largest importation of commodities of the first kind could not discourage the growth or interfere with the sale of any part of the produce of the mother country. By confining them to the home market, our merchants, it was expected, would not only be enabled to buy them cheaper in the Plantations, and consequently to sell them with a better profit at home, but to establish between the Plantations and foreign countries an advantageous carrying trade, of which Great Britain was necessarily to be the center or emporium, as the European country into which those commodities were first to be imported. The importation of commodities of the second kind might be so managed too, it was supposed, as to interfere, not with the sale of those of the same kind which were produced at home, but with that of those which were imported from foreign countries; because, by means of proper duties, they might be rendered always somewhat dearer than the former, and yet a good deal cheaper than the latter. By confining such commodities to the home market, therefore, it was proposed to discourage the produce, not of Great Britain, but of some foreign countries with which the balance of trade was believed to be unfavourable to Great Britain.

On the importation of naval stores to Great Britain a bounty was given.

The prohibition of exporting from the colonies, to any other country but Great Britain, masts, yards, and bowsprits, tar, pitch, and turpentine, naturally tended to lower the price of timber in the colonies, and consequently to increase the expence of clearing their lands, the principal obstacle to their improvement. But about the beginning of the present century, in 1703, the pitch and tar company of Sweden endeavoured to raise the price of their commodities to Great Britain, by prohibiting their exportation, except in their own ships, at their own price, and in such quantities as they thought proper.[45] In order to counteract this notable piece of mercantile policy, and to render herself as much as possible independent, not only of Sweden, but of all the other northern powers, Great Britain gave a bounty upon the importation of naval stores from America[46] and the effect of this bounty was to raise the price of timber in America, much more than the confinement to the home market could lower it; and as both regulations were enacted at the same time, their joint effect was rather to encourage than to discourage the clearing of land in America.

Though pig and bar iron too have been put among the enumerated commodities, yet as, when imported from America,

American pig iron is exempt from duty.

they are exempted from considerable duties to which they are subject when imported from any other country,[47] the one part of the regulation contributes more to encourage the erection of furnaces in America, than the other to discourage it. There is no manufacture which occasions so great a consumption of wood as a furnace, or which can contribute so much to the clearing of a country over-grown with it.

The tendency of some of these regulations to raise the value

These regulations have raised the value of timber and thus helped to clear the country.

of timber in America, and thereby to faciliate the clearing of the land, was neither, perhaps, intended nor understood by the legislature. Though their beneficial effects, however, have been in this respect accidental, they have not upon that account been less real.

The most perfect freedom of trade is permitted between

---

[45] [Anderson, *Commerce*, A.D. 1703.]

[46] [Details are given below, pp. 818–819, in a chapter not contained in eds. 1 and 2.]

[47] [23 Geo. II., c. 29.]

Freedom of trade prevails between the British American colonies and the British West Indies. the British colonies of America and the West Indies, both in the enumerated and in the non-enumerated commodities. Those colonies are now become so populous and thriving, that each of them finds in some of the others a great and extensive market for every part of its produce. All of them taken together, they make a great internal market for the produce of one another.

The liberality of England, however, towards the trade of her colonies has been confined chiefly to what concerns the market *British liberality does not extend to refined manufactures.* for their produce, either in its rude state, or in what may be called the very first stage of manufacture. The more advanced or more refined manufactures even of the colony produce, the merchants and manufacturers of Great Britain chuse to reserve to themselves, and have prevailed upon the legislature to prevent their establishment in the colonies, sometimes by high duties, and sometimes by absolute prohibitions.

While, for example, Muskovado sugars from the British plantations, pay upon importation only 6s. 4d. the hundred *Manufactured sugar is subject to heavy duty.* weight; white sugars pay 1l. 1s. 1d.; and refined, either double or single, in loaves 4l. 2s. 5d.$\frac{9}{20}$. When those high duties were imposed, Great Britain was the sole, and she still continues to be the principal market to which the sugars of the British colonies could be exported. They amounted, therefore, to a prohibition, at first of claying or refining sugar for any foreign market, and at present of claying or refining it for the market, which takes off, perhaps, more than nine-tenths of the whole produce. The manufacture of claying or refining sugar accordingly, though it has flourished in all the sugar colonies of France, has been little cultivated in any of those of England, except for the market of the colonies themselves. While Grenada was in the hands of the French, there was a refinery of sugar, by claying at least, upon almost every plantation. Since it fell into those of the English, almost all works of this kind have been given up, and there are at present, October 1773, I am assured, not above two or three remaining in the island. At present, however, by an indulgence of the customhouse, clayed or refined sugar, if reduced from loaves into powder, is commonly imported as Muskovado.

While Great Britain encourages in America the manufactures of pig and bar iron, by exempting them from duties to

Steel furnaces and slit-mills may not be erected in the colonies.

which the like commodities are subject when imported from any other country, she imposes an absolute prohibition upon the erection of steel furnaces and slit-mills in any of her American plantations.[48] She will not suffer her colonists to work in those more refined manufactures even for their own consumption; but insists upon their purchasing of her merchants and manufacturers all goods of this kind which they have occasion for.

She prohibits the exportation from one province to another by water, and even the carriage by land upon horseback or in a

Hats, wools and woollen goods produced in America may not be carried in bulk from province to province.

cart, of hats, of wools and woollen goods,[49] of the produce of America; a regulation which effectually prevents the establishment of any manufacture of such commodities for distant sale, and confines the industry of her colonists in this way to such coarse and household manufactures, as a private family commonly makes for its own use, or for that of some of its neighbours in the same province.

To prohibit a great people, however, from making all that they can of every part of their own produce,

Such prohibitions, though a violation of sacred rights, have not as yet been very hurtful.

or from employing their stock and industry in the way that they judge most advantageous to themselves, is a manifest violation of the most sacred rights of mankind. Unjust, however, as such prohibitions may

---

[48] [23 Geo. II., c. 29. Anderson, *Commerce*, A.D. 1750.]

[49] [Hats under 5 Geo. II., c. 22; wools under 10 and 12 W. III., c. 10. See Anderson, *Commerce*, A.D. 1732 and 1699.]

be, they have not hitherto been very hurtful to the colonies. Land is still so cheap, and, consequently, labour so dear among them, that they can import from the mother country, almost all the more refined or more advanced manufactures cheaper than they could make them for themselves. Though they had not, therefore, been prohibited from establishing such manufactures, yet in their present state of improvement, a regard to their own interest would, probably, have prevented them from doing so. In their present state of improvement, those prohibitions, perhaps, without cramping their industry, or restraining it from any employment to which it would have gone of its own accord, are only impertinent badges of slavery imposed upon them, without any sufficient reason, by the groundless jealousy of the merchants and manufacturers of the mother country. In a more advanced state they might be really oppressive and insupportable.

Great Britain too, as she confines to her own market some of the most important productions of the colonies, so in compensation she gives to some of them an advantage in that market; sometimes by imposing higher duties upon the like productions when imported from other countries, and sometimes by giving bounties upon their importation from the colonies. In the first way she gives an advantage in the home-market to the sugar, tobacco, and iron of her own colonies, and in the second to their raw silk, to their hemp and flax, to their indigo, to their naval-stores, and to their building-timber.[50] This second way of encouraging the colony produce by bounties upon importation, is, so far as I have been able to learn, peculiar to Great Britain. The first is not. Portugal does not content herself with imposing higher duties upon the importation of tobacco from any other country, but prohibits it under the severest penalties.

The importation into Great Britain of various colonial productions is encouraged either by abatement of duties or by bounties.

With regard to the importation of goods from Europe,

---

[50] [Details are given below, pp. 818–821, in a chapter which was not in eds. 1 and 2.]

In regard to imports from Europe the British colonies have had more liberal treatment than those of other countries,

England has likewise dealt more liberally with her colonies than any other nation.

Great Britain allows a part, almost always the half, generally a larger portion, and sometimes the whole of the duty which is paid upon the importation of foreign goods, to be drawn back upon their exportation to any foreign country.[51] No independent foreign country, it was easy to foresee, would receive them if they came to it loaded with the heavy duties to which almost all foreign goods are subjected on their importation into Great Britain. Unless, therefore, some part of those duties was drawn back upon exportation, there was an end of the carrying trade; a trade so much favoured by the mercantile system.

Our colonies, however, are by no means independent foreign countries; and Great Britain having assumed to herself the

drawbacks being allowed,

exclusive right of supplying them with all goods from Europe, might have forced them (in the same manner as other countries have done their colonies) to receive such goods, loaded with all the same duties which they paid in the mother country. But, on the contrary, till 1763, the same drawbacks were paid upon the exportation of the greater part of foreign goods to our colonies as to any independent foreign country. In 1763, indeed, by the 4th of Geo. III. c. 15. this indulgence was a good deal abated, and it was enacted, "That no part of the duty called the old subsidy should be drawn back for any goods of the growth, production, or manufacture of Europe or the East Indies, which should be exported from this kingdom to any British colony or plantation in America; wines, white callicoes and muslins excepted."[52] Before this law, many different sorts of foreign goods might have been bought cheaper in the plantations than in the mother country; and some may still.

Of the greater part of the regulations concerning the colony

---

[51] [Above, pp. 628–635.]

[52] [The quotation is not quite *verbatim*. The provision is referred to above, p. 633, where, however, see note 23.]

owing to the advice of interested merchants. trade, the merchants who carry it on, it must be observed, have been the principal advisers. We must not wonder, therefore, if, in the greater part of them, their interest has been more considered than either that of the colonies or that of the mother country. In their exclusive privilege of supplying the colonies with all the goods which they wanted from Europe, and of purchasing all such parts of their surplus produce as could not interfere with any of the trades which they themselves carried on at home, the interest of the colonies was sacrificed to the interest of those merchants. In allowing the same drawbacks upon the re-exportation of the greater part of European and East India goods to the colonies, as upon their re-exportation to any independent country, the interest of the mother country was sacrificed to it, even according to the mercantile ideas of that interest. It was for the interest of the merchants to pay as little as possible for the foreign goods which they sent to the colonies, and consequently, to get back as much as possible of the duties which they advanced upon their importation into Great Britain. They might thereby be enabled to sell in the colonies, either the same quantity of goods with a greater profit, or a greater quantity with the same profit, and, consequently, to gain something either in the one way or the other. It was, likewise, for the interest of the colonies to get all such goods as cheap and in as great abundance as possible. But this might not always be for the interest of the mother country. She might frequently suffer both in her revenue, by giving back a great part of the duties which had been paid upon the importation of such goods; and in her manufactures, by being undersold in the colony market, in consequence of the easy terms upon which foreign manufactures could be carried thither by means of those drawbacks. The progress of the linen manufacture of Great Britain, it is commonly said, has been a good deal retarded by the drawbacks upon the re-exportation of German linen to the American colonies.

But though the policy of Great Britain with regard to the trade of her colonies has been dictated by the same mercantile spirit as that of other nations, it has, however, upon the whole, been less illiberal and oppressive than that of any of them.

In every thing, except their foreign trade, the liberty of the English colonists to manage their own affairs their own way is

Except in regard to foreign trade the English colonies have complete liberty.

complete. It is in every respect equal to that of their fellow-citizens at home, and is secured in the same manner, by an assembly of the representatives of the people, who claim the sole right of imposing taxes for the support of the colony government. The authority of this assembly over-awes the executive power, and neither the meanest nor the most obnoxious colonist, as long as he obeys the law, has any thing to fear from the resentment, either of the governor, or of any other civil or military officer in the province. The colony assemblies, though like the house of commons in England, they are not always a very equal representation of the people, yet they approach more nearly to that character; and[53] as the executive power either has not the means to corrupt them, or, on account of the support which it receives from the mother country, is not under the necessity of doing so, they are perhaps in general more influenced by the inclinations of their constituents. The councils, which, in the colony legislatures, correspond to the house of lords in Great Britain, are not composed of an hereditary nobility. In some of the colonies, as in three of the governments of New England, those councils are not appointed by the king, but chosen by the representatives of the people. In none of the English colonies is there any hereditary nobility. In all of them, indeed, as in all other free countries, the descendant of an old colony family is more respected than an upstart of equal merit and fortune: but he is only more respected, and he has no privileges by which he can be troublesome to his neighbours. Before the commencement of the present disturbances, the colony assemblies had not only the legislative, but a part of the executive power. In Connecticut and Rhode Island, they

---

[53] [Ed. 1 does not contain the words "they approach more nearly to that character; and."]

elected the governor.[54] In the other colonies they appointed
the revenue officers who collected the taxes imposed by those
respective assemblies, to whom those officers were immediately responsible. There is more equality, therefore,
among the English colonists than among the inhabitants of
the mother country. Their manners are more republican, and
their governments, those of three of the provinces of
New England in particular, have hitherto been more republican
too.

The absolute governments of Spain, Portugal, and France,
on the contrary, take place in their colonies; and the discre-

The absolute gov-
ernments of Spain,
of Portugal, and in
a less degree of
France, are even
more violent in the
colonies than at
home.

tionary powers which such governments
commonly delegate to all their inferior officers are, on account of the great distance,
naturally exercised there with more than ordinary violence. Under all absolute governments there is more liberty in the capital
than in any other part of the country. The
sovereign himself can never have either in-
terest or inclination to pervert the order of justice, or to oppress the great body of the people. In the capital his presence
over-awes more or less all his inferior officers, who in the remoter provinces, from whence the complaints of the people are
less likely to reach him, can exercise their tyranny with much
more safety. But the European colonies in America are more
remote than the most distant provinces of the greatest empires
which had ever been known before. The government of the
English colonies is perhaps the only one which, since the
world began, could give perfect security to the inhabitants of
so very distant a province. The administration of the French
colonies, however, has always been conducted with more
gentleness and moderation than that of the Spanish and
Portuguese. This superiority of conduct is suitable both to the
character of the French nation, and to what forms the character

[54] [The Board of Trade and Plantations, in a report to the House of Commons in
1732, insisted on this democratic character of the government of some of the
colonies, and mentioned the election of governor by Connecticut and Rhode
Island: the report is quoted in Anderson, *Commerce*, A.D. 1732.]

of every nation, the nature of their government, which, though arbitrary and violent in comparison with that of Great Britain, is legal and free in comparison with those of Spain and Portugal.

It is in the progress of the North American colonies, however, that the superiority of the English policy chiefly appears.

The sugar colonies of France are more prosperous than the English because they are not discouraged from refining, and slaves are better managed,

The progress of the sugar colonies of France has been at least equal, perhaps superior, to that of the greater part of those of England; and yet the sugar colonies of England enjoy a free government nearly of the same kind with that which takes place in her colonies of North America. But the sugar colonies of France are not discouraged, like those of England, from refining their own sugar; and, what is of still greater importance, the genius of their government naturally introduces a better management of their negro slaves.

In all European colonies the culture of the sugar-cane is carried on by negro slaves. The constitution of those who have been born in the temperate climate of Europe could not, it is supposed, support the labour of digging the ground under the burning sun of the West Indies; and the culture of the sugar-cane, as it is managed at present, is all hand labour, though, in the opinion of many, the drill plough might be introduced into it with great advantage. But, as the profit and success of the cultivation which is carried on by means of cattle, depend very much upon the good management of those cattle; so the profit and success of that which is carried on by slaves, must depend equally upon the good management of those slaves; and in the good management of their slaves the French planters, I think it is generally allowed, are superior to the English. The law, so far as it gives some weak protection to the slave against the violence of his master, is likely to be better executed in a colony where the government is in a great measure arbitrary, than in one where it is altogether free. In every country where the unfortunate law of slavery is

absolute government being more favourable to the slaves than republican, established, the magistrate, when he protects the slave, inter-meddles in some measure in the management of the private property of the master; and, in a free country, where the master is perhaps either a member of the colony assembly, or an elector of such a member, he dare not do this but with the greatest caution and circumspection. The respect which he is obliged to pay to the master, renders it more difficult for him to protect the slave. But in a country where the government is in a great measure arbitrary, where it is usual for the magistrate to intermeddle even in the management of the private property of individuals, and to send them, perhaps, a lettre de cachet if they do not manage it according to his liking, it is much easier for him to give some protection to the slave; and common humanity naturally disposes him to do so. The protection of the magistrate renders the slave less contemptible in the eyes of his master, who is thereby induced to consider him with more regard, and to treat him with more gentleness. Gentle usage renders the slave not only more faithful, but more intelligent, and therefore, upon a double account, more useful. He approaches more to the condition of a free servant, and may possess some degree of integrity and attachment to his master's interest, virtues which frequently belong to free servants, but which never can belong to a slave, who is treated as slaves commonly are in countries where the master is perfectly free and secure.

That the condition of a slave is better under an arbitrary than under a free government, is, I believe, supported by the history of all ages and nations. In the Roman history, the first time we read of the magistrate interposing to protect the slave from the violence of his master, is under the emperors. When Vedius Pollio, in the presence of Augustus, ordered one of his slaves, who had committed a slight fault, to be cut into pieces and thrown into his fish pond in order to feed his fishes, the emperor commanded him, with indignation, to emancipate immediately, not only that slave, but all the others that belonged to him.[55] Under the

as may be seen in Roman history.

---

[55] [The story is told in the same way in *Lectures*, p. 97, but Seneca, *De ira*, lib. iii.,

republic no magistrate could have had authority enough to protect the slave, much less to punish the master.

The stock, it is to be observed, which has improved the sugar colonies of France, particularly the great colony of St.

The superiority of the French sugar colonies is the more remarkable inasmuch as they have accumulated their own stock.

Domingo, has been raised almost entirely from the gradual improvement and cultivation of those colonies. It has been almost altogether the produce of the soil and of the industry[56] of the colonists, or, what comes to the same thing, the price of that produce gradually accumulated by good management, and employed in raising a still greater produce. But the stock which has improved and cultivated the sugar colonies of England has, a great part of it, been sent out from England, and has by no means been altogether the produce of the soil and industry of the colonists.[57] The prosperity of the English sugar colonies has been, in a great measure, owing to the great riches of England, of which a part has overflowed, if one may say so, upon those colonies. But the prosperity of the sugar colonies of France has been entirely owing to the good conduct of the colonists, which must therefore have had some superiority over that of the English; and this superiority has been remarked in nothing so much as in the good management of their slaves.

Such have been the general outlines of the policy of the different European nations with regard to their colonies.

The policy of Europe, therefore, has very little to boast of, either in the original establishment, or, so far as concerns their

cap. 40, and Dio Cassius, *Hist.*, lib. liv., cap. 23, say, not that Augustus ordered all the slaves to be emancipated, but that he ordered all the goblets on the table to be broken. Seneca says the offending slave was emancipated. Dio does not mention emancipation.]

[56] [Ed. 1 reads "and industry."]

[57] [The West India merchants and planters asserted, in 1775, that there was capital worth £60,000,000 in the sugar colonies and that half of this belonged to residents in Great Britain.—See the Continuation of Anderson's *Commerce*, A.D. 1775.]

The policy of Europe has done nothing for the prosperity of the colonies.

internal government,[58] in the subsequent prosperity of the colonies of America.

Folly and injustice seem to have been the principles which presided over and directed the first project of establishing those colonies; the folly of hunting after gold and silver mines, and the injustice of coveting the possession of a country whose harmless natives, far from having ever injured the people of Europe, had received the first adventurers with every mark of kindness and hospitality.

Folly and injustice directed the first project.

The adventurers, indeed, who formed some of the latter establishments, joined, to the chimerical project of finding gold and silver mines, other motives more reasonable and more laudable; but even these motives do very little honour to the policy of Europe.

The more respectable adventurers of later times were sent out by the disorder and injustice of European governments.

The English puritans, restrained[59] at home, fled for freedom to America, and established there the four governments of New England. The English catholics, treated with much greater injustice,[60] established that of Maryland; the Quakers, that of Pennsylvania. The Portugueze Jews, persecuted by the inquisition, stript of their fortunes, and banished to Brazil, introduced, by their example, some sort of order and industry among the transported felons and strumpets, by whom that colony was originally peopled, and taught them the culture of the sugar-cane.[61] Upon all these different occasions it was, not the wisdom and policy, but the disorder and injustice of the European governments, which peopled and cultivated America.

---

[58] [Eds. 1 and 2 do not contain the words "so far as concerns their internal government."]

[59] [Ed. 1 reads "persecuted."]

[60] [Ed. 1 reads "with equal injustice."]

[61] [Raynal, *Histoire philosophique*, Amsterdam ed., 1773, tom. iii., pp. 323, 324, 326, 327. Justamond's English trans., vol. ii., p. 442.]

In effectuating some of the most important of these establishments, the different governments of Europe had as little merit as in projecting them. The conquest of Mexico was the project, not of the council of Spain, but of a governor of Cuba;[62] and it was effectuated by the spirit of the bold adventurer[63] to whom it was entrusted, in spite of every thing which that governor, who soon repented of having trusted such a person, could do to thwart it. The conquerors of Chili and Peru, and of almost all the other Spanish settlements upon the continent of America, carried out with them no other public encouragement, but a general permission to make settlements and conquests in the name of the king of Spain. Those adventures were all at the private risk and expence of the adventurers. The government of Spain contributed scarce any thing to any of them. That of England contributed as little towards effectuating the establishment of some of its most important colonies in North America.

To the actual establishment of the colonies the governments of Europe contributed little,

When those establishments were effectuated, and had become so considerable as to attract the attention of the mother country, the first regulations which she made with regard to them had always in view to secure to herself the monopoly of their commerce; to confine their market, and to enlarge her own at their expence, and, consequently, rather to damp and discourage, than to quicken and forward the course of their prosperity. In the different ways in which this monopoly has been exercised, consists one of the most essential differences in the policy of the different European nations with regard to their colonies. The best of them all, that of England, is only somewhat less illiberal and oppressive than that of any of the rest.

and discouraged rather than encouraged them after they were established.

In what way, therefore, has the policy of Europe contributed either to the first establishment, or to the present grandeur of

[62] [Velasquez.]

[63] [Cortez.]

Europe has done nothing except provide the men who founded the colonies.

the colonies of America? In one way, and in one way only, it has contributed a good deal. *Magna virûm Mater!*[64] It bred and formed the men who were capable of achieving such great actions, and of laying the foundation of so great an empire; and there is no other quarter of the world of which the policy is capable of forming, or has ever actually and in fact formed such men. The colonies owe to the policy of Europe the education and great views of their active and enterprising founders; and some of the greatest and most important of them, so far as concerns their internal government,[65] owe to it scarce any thing else.

PART THIRD

OF THE ADVANTAGES WHICH EUROPE HAS DERIVED FROM THE DISCOVERY OF AMERICA, AND FROM THAT OF A PASSAGE TO THE EAST INDIES BY THE CAPE OF GOOD HOPE

Such are the advantages which the colonies of America have derived from the policy of Europe.

The advantages derived by Europe from America are (1) the advantages of Europe in general, and (2) the advantages of the particular countries which have colonies.

What are those which Europe has derived from the discovery and colonization of America?

Those advantages may be divided, first, into the general advantages which Europe, considered as one great country, has derived from those great events; and, secondly, into the particular advantages which each colonizing country has derived from the colonies which particularly belong to it, in conse-

[64] ["Salve magna parens frugum, Saturnia tellus, Magna virum."—Virgil, *Georg*, ii., 173–174.]

[65] [Eds. 1 and 2 do not contain the words "so far as concerns their internal government." Cp. above, p. 747, note 58.]

quence of the authority or dominion which it exercises over them.

The general advantages which Europe, considered as one great country, has derived from the discovery and colonization of America, consist, first, in the increase of its enjoyments; and secondly, in the augmentation of its industry.

(1) The general advantages to Europe are,

The surplus produce of America, imported into Europe, furnishes the inhabitants of this great continent with a variety of commodities which they could not otherwise have possessed, some for conveniency and use, some for pleasure, and some for ornament, and thereby contributes to increase their enjoyments.

(a) an increase of enjoyments,

The discovery and colonization of America, it will readily be allowed, have contributed to augment the industry, first, of all the countries which trade to it directly; such as Spain, Portugal, France, and England; and, secondly, of all those which, without trading to it directly, send, through the medium of other countries, goods to it of their own produce; such as Austrian Flanders, and some provinces of Germany, which, through the medium of the countries before mentioned, send to it a considerable quantity of linen and other goods. All such countries have evidently gained a more extensive market for their surplus produce, and must consequently have been encouraged to increase its quantity.

(b) an augmentation of industry not only in the countries which trade with America directly, but also in other countries which do not send their produce to America,

But, that those great events should likewise have contributed to encourage the industry of countries, such as Hungary and Poland, which may never, perhaps, have sent a single commodity of their own produce to America, is not, perhaps, altogether so evident. That those events have done so, however, cannot be doubted. Some part of the produce of America is consumed in Hungary and Poland, and there is some demand there for the sugar, chocolate, and tobacco, of that new quarter of the world. But those commodities must be purchased with something which is either the produce of the industry of Hungary and Poland, or with something which had been purchased with some part of that produce. Those commodities of America are new values, new equivalents, introduced into Hungary and Poland to be exchanged there for the surplus produce of those countries. By being carried thither they create a new and more extensive market for that surplus produce. They raise its value, and thereby contribute to encourage its increase. Though no part of it may ever be carried to America, it may be carried to other countries which purchase it with a part of their share of the surplus produce of America; and it may find a market by means of the circulation of that trade which was originally put into motion by the surplus produce of America.

Those great events may even have contributed to increase the enjoyments, and to augment the industry of countries

or even receive any produce from America.

which, not only never sent any commodities to America, but never received any from it. Even such countries may have received a greater abundance of other commodities from countries of which the surplus produce had been augmented by means of the American trade. This greater abundance, as it must necessarily have increased their enjoyments, so it must likewise have augmented their industry. A greater number of new equivalents of some kind or other must have been presented to them to be exchanged for the surplus produce of that industry. A more extensive market must have been created for that surplus produce, so as to raise its value, and thereby encourage its increase. The mass of commodities annually thrown into the great circle of European commerce, and by its various revolutions annually distributed among all the different nations comprehended within it, must have been augmented by the whole surplus produce of America. A greater share of this greater mass, therefore, is likely to have fallen to each of those nations, to have increased their enjoyments, and augmented their industry.

The exclusive trade of the mother countries tends to diminish, or, at least, to keep down below what they would otherwise rise to, both the enjoyments and industry of all those nations in

The exclusive trade of the mother countries reduces the enjoyments and industry of all Europe and America, especially the latter.

general, and of the American colonies in particular. It is a dead weight upon the action of one of the great springs which puts into motion a great part of the business of mankind. By rendering the colony produce dearer in all other countries, it lessens its consumption, and thereby cramps the industry of the colonies, and both the enjoyments and the industry of all other countries, which both enjoy less when they pay more for what they enjoy, and produce less when they get less for what they produce. By rendering the produce of all other countries dearer in the colonies, it cramps, in the same manner, the industry of all other countries, and both the enjoyments and the industry of the colonies. It is a clog which, for the supposed benefit of some particular countries, embarrasses the pleasures, and encumbers the industry of all other countries; but of the colonies more than of any other. It not[66] only excludes, as much as possible, all other countries from one particular market; but it confines, as much as possible, the colonies to one particular market: and the difference is very great between being excluded from one particular market, when all others are open, and being confined to one particular market, when all others are shut up. The surplus produce of the colonies, however, is the original source of all that increase of enjoyments and industry which Europe derives from the discovery and colonization of America; and the exclusive trade of the mother countries tends to render this source much less abundant than it otherwise would be.

The particular advantages which each colonizing country derives from the colonies which particularly belong to it, are of two different kinds; first, those common advantages which every empire derives from the provinces subject to its dominion; and, secondly, those peculiar advantages which are supposed to result from provinces of so very peculiar a nature as the European colonies of America.

[66] ["Not" appears first in ed. 3 and seems to have been inserted in error. The other countries are only excluded from a particular market, but the colonies are confined to one.]

(2) The particular advantages of the colonising countries are (a) the common advantages derived from provinces, (b) the peculiar advantages derived from provinces in America:

The common advantages which every empire derives from the provinces subject to its dominion, consist, first, in the military force which they furnish for its defence; and, secondly, in the revenue which they furnish for the support of its civil government. The Roman colonies furnished occasionally both the one and the other. The Greek colonies, sometimes, furnished a military force; but seldom any revenue.[67] They seldom acknowledged themselves subject to the dominion of the mother city. They were generally her allies in war, but very seldom her subjects in peace.

(a) the common advantages are contributions of military forces and revenue,

The European colonies of America have never yet furnished any military force for the defence of the mother country. Their military force has never yet been sufficient for their own defence; and in the different wars in which the mother countries have been engaged, the defence of their colonies has generally occasioned a very considerable distraction of the military force of those countries. In this respect,

but none of the colonies have ever furnished military force,

therefore, all the European colonies have, without exception, been a cause rather of weakness than of strength to their respective mother countries.

and the colonies of Spain and Portugal alone have contributed revenue;

The colonies of Spain and Portugal only have contributed any revenue towards the defence of the mother country, or the support of her civil government.[68] The taxes which have been levied upon those of other European nations, upon those of England in particular, have seldom been equal to the expence laid out upon them in time of peace, and never sufficient to defray that which they

---

[67] [There is an example of revenue being furnished in Xenophon, *Anab.*, V., v., 7, 10.]

[68] [Above, p. 728.]

occasioned in time of war. Such colonies, therefore, have been a source of expence and not of revenue to their respective mother countries.

The advantages of such colonies to their respective mother countries, consist altogether in those peculiar advantages

(b) the exclusive trade is the sole peculiar advantage.

which are supposed to result from provinces of so very peculiar a nature as the European colonies of America; and the exclusive trade, it is acknowledged, is the sole source of all those peculiar advantages.

In consequence of this exclusive trade, all that part of the surplus produce of the English colonies, for example, which

The exclusive trade of each country is a disadvantage to the other countries,

consists in what are called enumerated commodities,[69] can be sent to no other country but England. Other countries must afterwards buy it of her. It must be cheaper therefore in England than it can be in any other country, and must contribute more to increase the enjoyments of England than those of any other country. It must likewise contribute more to encourage her industry. For all those parts of her own surplus produce which England exchanges for those enumerated commodities, she must get a better price than any other countries can get for the like parts of theirs, when they exchange them for the same commodities. The manufactures of England, for example, will purchase a greater quantity of the sugar and tobacco of her own colonies, than the like manufactures of other countries can purchase of that sugar and tobacco. So far, therefore, as the manufactures of England and those of other countries are both to be exchanged for the sugar and tobacco of the English colonies, this superiority of price gives an encouragement to the former, beyond what the latter can in these circumstances enjoy. The exclusive trade of the colonies, therefore, as it diminishes, or, at least, keeps down below what they would otherwise rise to, both the enjoyments and the industry of the countries which do

[69] [Above, pp. 731, 732.]

not possess it; so it gives an evident advantage to the countries which do possess it over those other countries.

This advantage, however, will, perhaps, be found to be rather what may be called a relative than an absolute advantage; and to give a superiority to the country *rather than an advantage to that country,* which enjoys it, rather by depressing the industry and produce of other countries, than by raising those of that particular country above what they would naturally rise to in the case of a free trade.

The tobacco of Maryland and Virginia, for example, by means of the monopoly which England enjoys of it, certainly comes cheaper to England than it can do to *e.g., England gets tobacco cheaper than France, but not cheaper than it would if there were no exclusive trade.* France, to whom England commonly sells a considerable part of it. But had France, and all other European countries been, at all times, allowed a free trade to Maryland and Virginia, the tobacco of those colonies might, by this time, have come cheaper than it actually does, not only to all those other countries, but likewise to England. The produce of tobacco, in consequence of a market so much more extensive than any which it has hitherto enjoyed, might, and probably would, by this time, have been so much increased as to reduce the profits of a tobacco plantation to their natural level with those of a corn plantation, which, it is supposed, they are still somewhat above.[70] The price of tobacco might, and probably would, by this time, have fallen somewhat lower than it is at present. An equal quantity of the commodities either of England, or of those other countries, might have purchased in Maryland and Virginia a greater quantity of tobacco than it can do at present, and, consequently, have been sold there for so much a better price. So far as that weed, therefore, can, by its cheapness and abundance, increase the enjoyments or augment the industry either of England or of any other country, it would, probably, in the case of a free trade, have produced both these effects in

[70] [Above, p. 215.]

somewhat a greater degree than it can do at present. England, indeed, would not in this case have had any advantage over other countries. She might have bought the tobacco of her colonies somewhat cheaper, and, consequently, have sold some of her own commodities somewhat dearer than she actually does. But she could neither have bought the one cheaper nor sold the other dearer than any other country might have done. She might, perhaps, have gained an absolute, but she would certainly have lost a relative advantage.

In order, however, to obtain this relative advantage in the colony trade, in order to execute the invidious and malignant

To subject other countries to this disadvantage England has made two sacrifices.

project of excluding as much as possible other nations from any share in it, England, there are very probable reasons for believing, has not only sacrificed a part of the absolute advantage which she, as well as every other nation, might have derived from that trade, but has subjected herself both to an absolute and to a relative disadvantage in almost every other branch of trade.

When, by the act of navigation,[71] England assumed to herself the monopoly of the colony trade, the foreign capitals

The withdrawal of foreign capital from the colony trade raised profits in it and drew capital from other British trades and thereby raised profits in them,

which had before been employed in it were necessarily withdrawn from it. The English capital, which had before carried on but a part of it, was now to carry on the whole. The capital which had before supplied the colonies with but a part of the goods which they wanted from Europe, was now all that was employed to supply them with the whole. But it could not supply them with the

whole, and the goods with which it did supply them were necessarily sold very dear. The capital which had before bought but a part of the surplus produce of the colonies, was now all that was employed to buy the whole. But it could not buy the whole at any thing near the old price, and, therefore, whatever it did buy it necessarily bought very cheap. But in an employ-

[71] [Above, pp. 581–583.]

ment of capital in which the merchant sold very dear and bought very cheap, the profit must have been very great, and much above the ordinary level of profit in other branches of trade. This superiority of profit in the colony trade could not fail to draw from other branches of trade a part of the capital which had before been employed in them. But this revulsion of capital, as it must have gradually increased the competition of capitals in the colony trade, so it must have gradually diminished that competition in all those other branches of trade; as it must have gradually lowered the profits of the one, so it must have gradually raised those of the other, till the profits of all came to a new level, different from and somewhat higher than that at which they had been before.

This double effect, of drawing capital from all other trades, and of raising the rate of profit somewhat higher than it other-

and continues to do so.

wise would have been in all trades, was not only produced by this monopoly upon its first establishment, but has continued to be produced by it ever since.

First, this monopoly has been continually drawing capital from all other trades to be employed in that of the colonies.

Though the wealth of Great Britain has increased very

The colony trade has increased faster than the whole British capital,

much since the establishment of the act of navigation, it certainly has not increased in the same proportion as that of the colonies. But the foreign trade of every country natu-rally increases in proportion to its wealth, its surplus produce in proportion to its whole produce; and Great Britain having engrossed

to herself almost the whole of what may be called the foreign trade of the colonies, and her capital not having increased in the same proportion as the extent of that trade, she could not carry it on without continually withdrawing from other branches of trade some part of the capital which had before been employed in them, as well as withholding from them a great deal more which would otherwise have gone to them. Since the establishment of the act of navigation, accordingly, the colony trade has been continually increasing, while many other branches of foreign trade, particularly of that to other parts of Europe, have been continually decaying. Our manufactures for foreign sale, instead of being suited, as before the act of navigation, to the neighbouring market of Europe, or to the more distant one of the countries which lie round the Mediterranean sea, have, the greater part of them, been accommodated to the still more distant one of the colonies, to the market in which they have the monopoly, rather than to that in which they have many competitors. The causes of decay in other branches of foreign trade, which, by Sir Matthew Decker,[72] and other writers, have been sought for in the excess and improper mode of taxation, in the high price of labour, in the increase of luxury, &c. may all be found in the overgrowth of the colony trade. The mercantile capital of Great Britain, though very great, yet not being infinite; and though greatly increased since the act of navigation, yet not being increased in the same proportion as the colony trade, that trade could not possibly be carried on without withdrawing some part of that capital from other branches of trade, nor consequently without some decay of those other branches.

England, it must be observed, was a great trading country, her mercantile capital was very great and likely to become still

and the colonial monopoly has merely changed the direction of British trade.

greater and greater every day, not only before the act of navigation had established the monopoly of the colony trade, but before that trade was very considerable. In the Dutch war, during the government of Cromwel, her navy was superior to that of Holland; and in that which broke out in the beginning of the reign of Charles II. it was at least equal, perhaps superior, to the united navies of France and Holland. Its superiority, perhaps, would scarce appear greater in the present times; at least if the Dutch navy was to bear the same proportion to the Dutch commerce now which it did then. But this great naval power could not, in either of those wars, be owing to the act of navi-

---

[72] [*Essay on the Causes of the Decline of the Foreign Trade, consequently of the Value of the Lands of Britain and on the means to restore both*, 2nd ed., 1750, pp. 28–36, *et passim*.]

gation. During the first of them the plan of that act had been but just formed; and though before the breaking out of the second it had been fully enacted by legal authority; yet no part of it could have had time to produce any considerable effect, and least of all that part which established the exclusive trade to the colonies. Both the colonies and their trade were inconsiderable then in comparison of what they are now. The island of Jamaica was an unwholesome desert, little inhabited, and less cultivated. New York and New Jersey were in the possession of the Dutch: the half of St. Christopher's in that of the French. The island of Antigua, the two Carolinas, Pensylvania, Georgia, and Nova Scotia, were not planted. Virginia, Maryland, and New England were planted; and though they were very thriving colonies, yet there was not, perhaps, at that time, either in Europe or America, a single person who foresaw or even suspected the rapid progress which they have since made in wealth, population and improvement. The island of Barbadoes, in short, was the only British colony of any consequence of which the condition at that time bore any resemblance to what it is at present. The trade of the colonies, of which England, even for some time after the act of navigation, enjoyed but a part (for the act of navigation was not very strictly executed till several years after it was enacted), could not at that time be the cause of the great trade of England, nor of the great naval power which was supported by that trade. The trade which at that time supported that great naval power was the trade of Europe, and of the countries which lie round the Mediterranean sea. But the share which Great Britain at present enjoys of that trade could not support any such great naval power. Had the growing trade of the colonies been left free to all nations, whatever share of it might have fallen to Great Britain, and a very considerable share would probably have fallen to her, must have been all an addition to this great trade of which she was before in possession. In consequence of the monopoly, the increase of the colony trade has not so much occasioned an addition to the trade which Great Britain had before, as a total change in its direction.

Secondly, this monopoly has necessarily contributed to

*The monopoly has keep up the rate of profit in all the different
kept the rate of
profit in British
trade higher than
it naturally would
have been,* keep up the rate of profit in all the different branches of British trade higher than it naturally would have been, had all nations been allowed a free trade to the British colonies.

The monopoly of the colony trade, as it necessarily drew towards that trade a greater proportion of the capital of Great Britain than what would have gone to it of its own accord; so by the expulsion of all foreign capitals it necessarily reduced the whole quantity of capital employed in that trade below what it naturally would have been in the case of a free trade. But, by lessening the competition of capitals in that branch of trade, it necessarily raised the rate of profit[73] in that branch. By lessening too the competition of British capitals in all other branches of trade, it necessarily raised the rate of British profit in all those other branches. Whatever may have been, at any particular period, since the establishment of the act of navigation, the state or extent of the mercantile capital of Great Britain, the monopoly of the colony trade must, during the continuance of that state, have raised the ordinary rate of British profit higher than it otherwise would have been both in that and in all the other branches of British trade. If, since the establishment of the act of navigation, the ordinary rate of British profit has fallen considerably, as it certainly has, it must have fallen still lower, had not the monopoly established by that act contributed to keep it up.

*and this puts the
country at a
disadvantage in
the trades of
which she has no
monopoly,* But whatever raises in any country the ordinary rate of profit higher than it otherwise would be, necessarily subjects that country both to an absolute and to a relative disadvantage in every branch of trade of which she has not the monopoly.

*making her buy
less and sell less,* It subjects her to an absolute disadvantage: because in such branches of trade her merchants cannot get this greater profit, without selling dearer than they otherwise

---

[73] [Ed. 1 reads "rate of the profit."]

would do both the goods of foreign countries which they import into their own, and the goods of their own country which they export to foreign countries. Their own country must both buy dearer and sell dearer; must both buy less and sell less; must both enjoy less and produce less, than she otherwise would do.

It subjects her to a relative disadvantage; because in such branches of trade it sets other countries which are not subject

and enabling other countries to undersell her in foreign markets.

to the same absolute disadvantage, either more above her or less below her than they otherwise would be. It enables them both to enjoy more and to produce more in proportion to what she enjoys and produces. It renders their superiority greater or their inferiority less than it otherwise would be. By raising the price of her produce above what it otherwise would be, it enables the merchants of other countries to undersell her in foreign markets, and thereby to justle her out of almost all those branches of trade, of which she has not the monopoly.

Our merchants frequently complain of the high wages of British labour as the cause of their manufactures being under-

High profits raise the price of manufactures more than high wages.

sold in foreign markets; but they are silent about the high profits of stock. They complain of the extravagant gain of other people; but they say nothing of their own. The high profits of British stock, however, may contribute towards raising the price of British manufactures in many cases as much, and in some perhaps more, than the high wages of British labour.[74]

So British capital has been taken from European and Mediterranean trade,

It is in this manner that the capital of Great Britain, one may justly say, has partly been drawn and partly been driven from the greater part of the different branches of trade of which she has not the monopoly; from the trade of Europe in par-

---

[74] [This passage is much the same as that which appears above, p. 137; but this is the original, as the other was not in ed. 1.]

ticular, and from that of the countries which lie round the Mediterranean sea.

It has partly been drawn from those branches of trade; by the attraction of superior profit in the colony trade in conse-

partly attracted by high profit in the colony trade,

quence of the continual increase of that trade, and of the continual insufficiency of the capital which had carried it on one year to carry it on the next.

It has partly been driven from them; by the advantage which

partly driven out by foreign competition.

the high rate of profit, established in Great Britain, gives to other countries, in all the different branches of trade of which Great Britain has not the monopoly.

As the monopoly of the colony trade has drawn from those other branches a part of the British capital which would other-

While raising British profit, the monopoly has lowered foreign profits.

wise have been employed in them, so it has forced into them many foreign capitals which would never have gone to them, had they not been expelled from the colony trade. In those other branches of trade it has diminished the competition of British capi-

tals, and thereby raised the rate of British profit higher than it otherwise would have been. On the contrary, it has increased the competition of foreign capitals, and thereby sunk the rate of foreign profit lower than it otherwise would have been. Both in the one way and in the other it must evidently have subjected Great Britain to a relative disadvantage in all those other branches of trade.

The colony trade, however, it may perhaps be said, is more advantageous to Great Britain than any other; and the monop-

The colony trade is supposed to be more advanta- geous than others,

oly, by forcing into that trade a greater pro- portion of the capital of Great Britain than what would otherwise have gone to it, has turned that capital into an employment more advantageous to the country than any other

which it could have found.

The most advantageous employment of any capital to the country to which it belongs, is that which maintains there the

but trade with a neighbouring country is more advantageous than with a distant one, and a direct trade is more advantageous than a round-about,

greatest quantity of productive labour, and increases the most the annual produce of the land and labour of that country. But the quantity of productive labour which any capital employed in the foreign trade of consumption can maintain, is exactly in proportion, it has been shewn in the second book,[75] to the frequency of its returns. A capital of a thousand pounds, for example, employed in a foreign trade of consumption, of which the returns are made regularly once in the year, can keep in constant employment, in the country to which it belongs, a quantity of productive labour equal to what a thousand pounds can maintain there for a year. If the returns are made twice or thrice in the year, it can keep in constant employment a quantity of productive labour equal to what two or three thousand pounds can maintain there for a year. A foreign trade of consumption carried on with a neighbouring,[76] is, upon this account, in general, more advantageous than one carried on with a distant country; and for the same reason a direct foreign trade of consumption, as it has likewise been shewn in the second book,[77] is in general more advantageous than a round-about one.

But the monopoly of the colony trade, so far as it has operated upon the employment of the capital of Great Britain, has

while the monopoly has forced capital into (1) a distant and (2) a round-about trade.

in all cases forced some part of it from a foreign trade of consumption carried on with a neighbouring,[78] to one carried on with a more distant country, and in many cases from a direct foreign trade of consumption to a round-about one.

First, the monopoly of the colony trade has in all cases forced some part of the capital of Great Britain from a foreign

[75] [Above, p. 469.]

[76] [Ed. 1 reads "with a neighbouring country."]

[77] [Above, pp. 470, 471.]

[78] [Ed. 1 reads "with a neighbouring country."]

(1) The trade with America and the West Indies is distant and the returns peculiarly infrequent.

trade of consumption carried on with a neighbouring to one carried on with a more distant country.

It has, in all cases, forced some part of that capital from the trade with Europe, and with the countries which lie round the Mediterranean sea, to that with the more distant regions of America and the West Indies, from which the returns are necessarily less frequent, not only on account of the greater distance, but on account of the peculiar circumstances of those countries. New colonies, it has already been observed, are always understocked. Their capital is always much less than what they could employ with great profit and advantage in the improvement and cultivation of their land. They have a constant demand, therefore, for more capital than they have of their own; and, in order to supply the deficiency of their own, they endeavour to borrow as much as they can of the mother country, to whom they are, therefore, always in debt. The most common way in which the colonists contract this debt, is not by borrowing upon bond of the rich people of the mother country, though they sometimes do this too, but by running as much in arrear to their correspondents, who supply them with goods from Europe, as those correspondents will allow them. Their annual returns frequently do not amount to more than a third, and sometimes not to so great a proportion of what they owe. The whole capital, therefore, which their correspondents advance to them is seldom returned to Britain in less than three, and sometimes not in less than four or five years. But a British capital of a thousand pounds, for example, which is returned to Great Britain only once in five years, can keep in constant employment only one-fifth part of the British industry which it could maintain if the whole was returned once in the year; and, instead of the quantity of industry which a thousand pounds could maintain for a year, can keep in constant employment the quantity only which two hundred pounds can maintain for a year. The planter, no doubt, by the high price which he pays for the goods from Europe, by the interest upon the bills which he grants at distant dates, and by the commission upon the renewal of those which he grants at near dates, makes up, and probably more than makes up, all the loss which his correspondent can sustain by this delay. But, though he may make up the loss of his correspondent, he cannot make up that of Great Britain. In a trade of which the returns are very distant, the profit of the merchant may be as great or greater than in one in which they are very frequent and near; but the advantage of the country in which he resides, the quantity of productive labour constantly maintained there, the annual produce of the land and labour must always be much less. That the returns of the trade to America, and still more those of that to the West Indies, are, in general, not only more distant, but more irregular, and more uncertain too, than those of the trade to any part of Europe, or even of the countries which lie round the Mediterranean sea, will readily be allowed, I imagine, by every body who has any experience of those different branches of trade.

(2) It is also largely a round-about trade. Secondly, the monopoly of the colony trade has, in many cases, forced some part of the capital of Great Britain from a direct foreign trade of consumption, into a round-about one.

Among the enumerated commodities which can be sent to no other market but Great Britain, there are several of which the quantity exceeds very much the consumption of Great Britain, and of which a part, therefore, must be exported to other countries. But this cannot be done without forcing some part of the capital of Great Britain into a round-about foreign trade of consumption. Maryland and Virginia, for example, send annually to Great Britain upwards of ninety-six thousand hogsheads of tobacco, and the consumption of Great Britain is said not to exceed fourteen thousand.[79] Upwards of eighty-two thousand hogsheads, therefore, must be exported to other countries, to France, to Holland, and to the countries which lie round the Baltic and Mediterranean seas. But, that part of the capital of Great Britain which brings those eighty-two thousand hogsheads to Great Britain, which re-exports them from

[79] [These figures are given above, pp. 475, 629–630.]

thence to those other countries, and which brings back from those other countries to Great Britain either goods or money in return, is employed in a round-about foreign trade of consumption; and is necessarily forced into this employment in order to dispose of this great surplus. If we would compute in how many years the whole of this capital is likely to come back to Great Britain, we must add to the distance of the American returns that of the returns from those other countries. If, in the direct foreign trade of consumption which we carry on with America, the whole capital employed frequently does not come back in less than three or four years; the whole capital employed in this round-about one is not likely to come back in less than four or five. If the one can keep in constant employment but a third or a fourth part of the domestic industry which could be maintained by a capital returned once in the year, the other can keep in constant employment but a fourth or a fifth part of that industry. At some of the outports a credit is commonly given to those foreign correspondents to whom they export their tobacco. At the port of London, indeed, it is commonly sold for ready money. The rule is, *Weigh and pay*. At the port of London, therefore, the final returns of the whole round-about trade are more distant than the returns from America by the time only which the goods may lie unsold in the warehouse; where, however, they may sometimes lie long enough.[80] But, had not the colonies been confined to the market of Great Britain for the sale of their tobacco, very little more of it would probably have come to us than what was necessary for the home consumption. The goods which Great Britain purchases at present for her own consumption with the great surplus of tobacco which she exports to other countries, she would, in this case, probably have purchased with the immediate produce of her own industry, or with some part of her own manufactures. That produce, those manufactures, instead of being almost entirely suited to one great market, as at present, would probably have been fitted to a great number of smaller

[80] [These four sentences beginning with "At some of the outports" are not in ed. 1.]

markets. Instead of one great round-about foreign trade of consumption, Great Britain would probably have carried on a great number of small direct foreign trades of the same kind. On account of the frequency of the returns, a part, and probably but a small part; perhaps not above a third or a fourth, of the capital which at present carries on this great round-about trade, might have been sufficient to carry on all those small direct ones, might have kept in constant employment an equal quantity of British industry, and have equally supported the annual produce of the land and labour of Great Britain. All the purposes of this trade being, in this manner, answered by a much smaller capital, there would have been a large spare capital to apply to other purposes; to improve the lands, to increase the manufactures, and to extend the commerce of Great Britain; to come into competition at least with the other British capitals employed in all those different ways, to reduce the rate of profit in them all, and thereby to give to Great Britain, in all of them, a superiority over other countries still greater than what she at present enjoys.[81]

The monopoly of the colony trade too has forced some part of the capital of Great Britain from all foreign trade of consumption to a carrying trade; and, consequently, from supporting more or less the industry of Great Britain, to be employed altogether in supporting partly that of the colonies, and partly that of some other countries.

The monopoly has also forced part of the capital of Great Britain into a carrying trade,

The goods, for example, which are annually purchased with the great surplus of eighty-two thousand hogsheads of tobacco annually re-exported from Great Britain, are not all consumed in Great Britain. Part of them, linen from Germany and Holland, for example, is returned to the colonies for their particular consumption. But, that part of the capital of Great Britain which buys the tobacco with which this linen is afterwards bought, is necessarily withdrawn from supporting the industry of Great Britain, to be employed altogether in sup-

---

[81] [Ed. 1 reads "possesses."]

porting, partly that of the colonies, and partly that of the particular countries who pay for this tobacco with the produce of their own industry.

The monopoly of the colony trade besides, by forcing towards it a much greater proportion of the capital of Great

and makes her whole industry and commerce less secure owing to its being driven into one channel.

Britain than what would naturally have gone to it, seems to have broken altogether that natural balance which would otherwise have taken place among all the different branches of British industry. The industry of Great Britain, instead of being accommodated to a great number of small markets, has been principally suited to one great market. Her commerce, instead of running in a great number of small channels, has been taught to run principally in one great channel. But the whole system of her industry and commerce has thereby been rendered less secure; the whole state of her body politic less healthful, than it otherwise would have been. In her present condition, Great Britain resembles one of those unwholesome bodies in which some of the vital parts are overgrown, and which, upon that account, are liable to many dangerous disorders scarce incident to those in which all the parts are more properly proportioned. A small stop in that great blood-vessel, which has been artificially swelled beyond its natural dimensions, and through which an unnatural proportion of the industry and commerce of the country has been forced to circulate, is very likely to bring on the most dangerous disorders upon the whole body politic. The expectation of a rupture with the colonies, accordingly, has struck the people of Great Britain with more terror than they ever felt for a Spanish armada, or a French invasion. It was this terror, whether well or ill grounded, which rendered the repeal of the stamp act,[82] among the merchants at least, a popular measure. In the total exclusion from the colony market, was it to last only for a few years, the greater part of our merchants used to fancy that they foresaw an entire stop to their trade; the greater part of our master

---

[82] [Ed. 1 places "a popular measure" here.]

manufacturers, the entire ruin of their business; and the greater part of our workmen, an end of their employment. A rupture with any of our neighbours upon the continent, though likely too to occasion some stop or interruption in the employments of some of all these different orders of people, is foreseen, however, without any such general emotion. The blood, of which the circulation is stopt in some of the smaller vessels, easily disgorges itself into the greater, without occasioning any dangerous disorder; but, when it is stopt in any of the greater vessels, convulsions, apoplexy, or death, are the immediate and unavoidable consequences. If but one of those overgrown manufactures, which by means either of bounties or of the monopoly of the home and colony markets, have been artificially raised up to an unnatural height, finds some small stop or interruption in its employment, it frequently occasions a mutiny and disorder alarming to government, and embarrassing even to the deliberations of the legislature. How great, therefore, would be the disorder and confusion, it was thought, which must necessarily be occasioned by a sudden and entire stop in the employment of so great a proportion of our principal manufacturers?

Some moderate and gradual relaxation of the laws which give to Great Britain the exclusive trade to the colonies, till it is

The gradual relaxation of the monopoly is desirable.

rendered in a great measure free, seems to be the only expedient which can, in all future times,[83] deliver her from this danger, which can enable her or even force her to withdraw some part of her capital from this overgrown employment, and to turn it, though with less profit, towards other employments; and which, by gradually diminishing one branch of her industry and gradually increasing all the rest, can by degrees restore all the different branches of it to that natural, healthful, and proper proportion which perfect liberty necessarily establishes, and which perfect liberty can alone preserve. To open the colony trade all at once to all nations, might not only occasion some transitory inconveniency, but a

---

[83] [Ed. 1 does not contain "in all future times."]

great permanent loss to the greater part of those whose industry or capital is at present engaged in it. The sudden loss of the employment even of the ships which import the eighty-two thousand hogsheads of tobacco, which are over and above the consumption of Great Britain, might alone be felt very sensibly. Such are the unfortunate effects of all the regulations of the mercantile system! They not only introduce very dangerous disorders into the state of the body politic, but disorders which it is often difficult to remedy, without occasioning, for a time at least, still greater disorders. In what manner, therefore, the colony trade ought gradually to be opened; what are the restraints which ought first, and what are those which ought last to be taken away; or in what manner the natural system of perfect liberty and justice ought gradually to be restored, we must leave to the wisdom of future statesmen and legislators to determine.

Five different events, unforeseen and unthought of, have very fortunately concurred to hinder Great Britain from feeling, so sensibly as it was generally expected *The present exclu-* she would, the total exclusion which has now *sion from the trade* taken place for more than a year (from the *with the twelve* first of December, 1774)[84] from a very im-*provinces would* portant branch of the colony trade, that of *have been more* the twelve associated provinces of North *severely felt but* America. First, those colonies, in preparing *for five transitory* themselves for their non-importation agree-*circumstances.* ment, drained Great Britain completely of all the commodities which were fit for their market: secondly, the extraordinary demand of the Spanish Flota[85] has, this year,

---

[84] [The date at which the non-importation agreement began to operate.]

[85] ["For the greater security of the valuable cargoes sent to America, as well as for the more easy prevention of fraud, the commerce of Spain with its colonies is carried on by fleets which sail under strong convoys. These fleets, consisting of two squadrons, one distinguished by the name of the 'Galeons,' the other by that of the 'Flota,' are equipped annually. Formerly they took their departure from Seville; but as the port of Cadiz has been found more commodious, they have sailed from it since the year 1720."—W. Robertson, *History of America*, bk. viii.; in *Works*, 1825, vol. vii., p. 372.]

drained Germany and the North of many commodities, linen in particular, which used to come into competition, even in the British market, with the manufactures of Great Britain: thirdly, the peace between Russia and Turkey,[86] has occasioned an extraordinary demand from the Turkey market, which, during the distress of the country, and while a Russian fleet was cruizing in the Archipelago, had been very poorly supplied: fourthly, the demand of the North of Europe for the manufactures of Great Britain, has been increasing from year to year for some time past: and, fifthly, the late partition[87] and consequential pacification of Poland, by opening the market of that great country, have this year added an extraordinary demand from thence to the increasing demand of the North. These events are all, except the fourth, in their nature transitory and accidental, and the exclusion from so important a branch of the colony trade, if unfortunately it should continue much longer, may still occasion some degree of distress. This distress, however, as it will come on gradually, will be felt much less severely than if it had come on all at once; and, in the mean time, the industry and capital of the country may find a new employment and direction, so as to prevent this distress[88] from ever rising to any considerable height.

The monopoly of the colony trade, therefore, so far as it has turned towards that trade a greater proportion of the capital of

The monopoly is bad, Great Britain than what would otherwise have gone to it, has in all cases turned it, from a foreign trade of consumption with a neighbouring, into one with a more distant country; in many cases, from a direct foreign trade of consumption, into a round-about one; and in some cases, from all foreign trade of consumption, into a carrying trade. It has in all cases, therefore, turned it, from a direction in which it would have maintained a greater quantity of productive labour, into one, in which it can maintain a much smaller quantity. By suiting, be-

[86] [By the treaty of Kainardji, 1774.]

[87] [In 1773.]

[88] [Ed. 1 reads "prevent it."]

sides, to one particular market only, so great a part of the industry and commerce of Great Britain, it has rendered the whole state of that industry and commerce more precarious and less secure, than if their produce had been accommodated to a greater variety of markets.

We must carefully distinguish between the effects of the colony trade and those of the monopoly of that trade. The for-

but the trade itself is good.

mer are always and necessarily beneficial; the latter always and necessarily hurtful. But the former are so beneficial, that the colony trade, though subject to a monopoly, and notwithstanding the hurtful effects of that monopoly, is still upon the whole beneficial, and greatly beneficial; though a good deal less so than it otherwise would be.

The effect of the colony trade in its natural and free state, is to open a great, though distant market for such parts of the pro-

The trade in its natural state increases the productive labour of Great Britain.

duce of British industry as may exceed the demand of the markets nearer home, of those of Europe, and of the countries which lie round the Mediterranean sea. In its natural and free state, the colony trade, without drawing from those markets any part of the produce which had ever been sent to them, encourages Great Britain to increase the surplus continually, by continually presenting new equivalents to be exchanged for it. In its natural and free state, the colony trade tends to increase the quantity of productive labour in Great Britain, but without altering in any respect the direction of that which had been employed there before. In the natural and free state of the colony trade, the competition of all other nations would hinder the rate of profit from rising above the common level either in the new market, or in the new employment. The new market, without drawing any thing from the old one, would create, if one may say so, a new produce for its own supply; and that new produce would constitute a new capital for carrying on the new employment, which in the same manner would draw nothing from the old one.

The monopoly of the colony trade, on the contrary, by excluding the competition of other nations, and thereby raising the rate of profit both in the new market and in the new em-

The monopoly diminishes it.

ployment, draws produce from the old market and capital from the old employment. To augment our share of the colony trade beyond what it otherwise would be, is the avowed purpose of the monopoly. If our share of that trade were to be no greater with, than it would have been without the monopoly, there could have been no reason for establishing the monopoly. But whatever forces into a branch of trade of which the returns are slower and more distant than those of the greater part of other trades, a greater proportion of the capital of any country, than what of its own accord would go to that branch, necessarily renders the whole quantity of productive labour annually maintained there, the whole annual produce of the land and labour of that country, less than they otherwise would be. It keeps down the revenue of the inhabitants of that country, below what it would naturally rise to, and thereby diminishes their power of accumulation. It not only hinders, at all times, their capital from maintaining so great a quantity of productive labour as it would otherwise maintain, but it hinders it from increasing so fast as it would otherwise increase, and consequently from maintaining a still greater quantity of productive labour.

The natural good effects of the colony trade, however, more than counterbalance to Great Britain the bad effects of the mo-

The natural good effects of the trade more than counterbalance the bad effects of the monopoly.

nopoly, so that, monopoly and all together, that trade, even as it is carried on at present, is not only advantageous, but greatly advantageous. The new market and the new employment[89] which are opened by the colony trade, are of much greater extent than that portion of the old market and of the old employment which is lost by the monopoly. The new produce and the new capital which has been created, if one may say so, by the colony trade, maintain in Great Britain a greater quantity of

[89] [Eds. 1 and 2 read "and employment."]

productive labour, than what can have been thrown out of employment by the revulsion of capital from other trades of which the returns are more frequent. If the colony trade, however, even as it is carried on at present, is advantageous to Great Britain, it is not by means of the monopoly, but in spite of the monopoly.

It is rather for the manufactured than for the rude produce of Europe, that the colony trade opens a new market.

The colonies offer a market for the manufactured rather than the rude produce of Europe,

Agriculture is the proper business of all new colonies; a business which the cheapness of land renders more advantageous than any other. They abound, therefore, in the rude produce of land, and instead of importing it from other countries, they have generally a large surplus to export. In new colonies, agriculture either draws hands from all other employments, or keeps them from going to any other employment. There are few hands to spare for the necessary, and none for the ornamental manufactures. The greater part of the manufactures of both kinds, they find it cheaper to purchase of other countries than to make for themselves. It is chiefly by encouraging the manufactures of Europe, that the colony trade indirectly encourages its agriculture. The manufacturers of Europe, to whom that trade gives employment, constitute a new market for the produce of the land; and the most advantageous of all markets; the home market for the corn and cattle, for the bread and butcher's-meat of Europe; is thus greatly extended by means of the trade to America.

But that the monopoly of the trade of populous and thriving colonies is not alone sufficient to establish, or even to maintain

but the monopoly has not maintained the manufactures of Spain and Portugal,

manufactures in any country, the examples of Spain and Portugal sufficiently demonstrate. Spain and Portugal were manufacturing countries before they had any considerable colonies. Since they had the richest and most fertile in the world, they have both ceased to be so.

In Spain and Portugal, the bad effects of the monopoly, ag-

where the bad effects of the monopoly have nearly over-balanced the good effects of the trade.

gravated by other causes, have, perhaps, nearly over-balanced[90] the natural good effects of the colony trade. These causes seem to be, other monopolies of different kinds; the degradation of the value of gold and silver below what it is in most other countries; the exclusion from foreign markets by improper taxes upon exportation, and the narrowing of the home market, by still more improper taxes upon the transportation of goods from one part of the country to another; but above all, that irregular and partial administration of justice, which often protects the rich and powerful debtor from the pursuit of his injured creditor, and which makes the industrious part of the nation afraid to prepare goods for the consumption of those haughty and great men, to whom they dare not refuse to sell upon credit, and from whom they are altogether uncertain of repayment.

In England, on the contrary, the natural good effects of the colony trade, assisted by other causes, have in a great measure conquered the bad effects of the monopoly.

In England the good effects of the trade have greatly counteracted the bad effects of the monopoly.

These causes seem to be, the general liberty of trade, which, notwithstanding some restraints, is at least equal, perhaps superior, to what it is in any other country; the liberty of exporting, duty free, almost all sorts of goods which are the produce of domestic industry, to almost any foreign country; and what, perhaps, is of still greater importance, the unbounded liberty of transporting them from any one part of our own country to any other, without being obliged to give any account to any public office, without being liable to question or examination of any kind; but above all, that equal and impartial administration of justice which renders the rights of the meanest British subject respectable to the greatest, and which, by securing to every man the fruits of his own industry, gives the greatest and most effectual encouragement to every sort of industry.

---

[90] [Ed. 1 reads "have entirely conquered."]

If the manufactures of Great Britain, however, have been advanced, as they certainly have, by the colony trade, it has not been by means of the monopoly of that trade, but in spite of the monopoly. The effect of the monopoly has been, not to augment the quantity, but to alter the quality and shape of a part of the manufactures of Great Britain, and to accommodate to a market, from which the returns are slow and distant, what would otherwise have been accommodated to one from which the returns are frequent and near. Its effect has consequently been to turn a part of the capital of Great Britain from an employment in which it would have maintained a greater quantity of manufacturing industry, to one in which it maintains a much smaller, and thereby to diminish, instead of increasing, the whole quantity of manufacturing industry maintained in Great Britain.

The trade has benefited British manufactures in spite of the monopoly, not in consequence of it.

The monopoly of the colony trade, therefore, like all the other mean and malignant expedients of the mercantile system, depresses the industry of all other countries, but chiefly that of the colonies, without in the least increasing, but on the contrary diminishing, that of the country in whose favour it is established.

The monopoly hinders the capital of that country, whatever may at any particular time be the extent of that capital, from maintaining so great a quantity of productive labour as it would otherwise maintain, and from affording so great a revenue to the industrious inhabitants as it would otherwise afford. But as capital can be increased only by savings from revenue, the monopoly, by hindering it from affording so great a revenue as it would otherwise afford, necessarily hinders it from increasing so fast as it would otherwise increase, and consequently from maintaining a still greater quantity of productive labour, and affording a still greater revenue to the industrious inhabitants of that country. One great original source of revenue, therefore, the wages of labour, the monopoly must necessarily have ren-

The monopoly reduces wages in the mother country,

dered at all times less abundant than it otherwise would have been.

By raising the rate of mercantile profit, the monopoly discourages the improvement of land. The profit of improvement

raises profits, and thereby tends to lower rents and the price of land.

depends upon the difference between what the land actually produces, and what, by the application of a certain capital, it can be made to produce. If this difference affords a greater profit than what can be drawn from an equal capital in any mercantile employment, the improvement of land will draw capital from all mercantile employments. If the profit is less, mercantile employments will draw capital from the improvement of land. Whatever therefore raises the rate of mercantile profit, either lessens the superiority or increases the inferiority of the profit of improvement; and in the one case hinders capital from going to improvement, and in the other draws capital from it. But by discouraging improvement, the monopoly necessarily retards the natural increase of another great original source of revenue, the rent of land. By raising the rate of profit too, the monopoly necessarily keeps up the market rate of interest higher than it otherwise would be. But the price of land in proportion to the rent which it affords, the number of years purchase which is commonly paid for it, necessarily falls as the rate of interest rises, and rises as the rate of interest falls. The monopoly, therefore, hurts the interest of the landlord two different ways, by retarding the natural increase, first, of his rent, and secondly, of the price which he would get for his land in proportion to the rent which it affords.

The monopoly, indeed, raises the rate of mercantile profit, and thereby augments somewhat the gain of our mer-

It reduces the absolute amount of profit,

chants. But as it obstructs the natural increase of capital, it tends rather to diminish than to increase the sum total of the revenue which the inhabitants of the country derive from the profits of stock; a small profit upon a great capital generally affording a greater revenue than a great profit upon a small one. The monopoly raises the rate of profit, but it hinders the sum of profit from rising so high as it otherwise would do.

All the original sources of revenue, the wages of labour, the

thus rendering all the original sources of revenue less abundant.

rent of land, and the profits of stock, the monopoly renders much less abundant than they otherwise would be. To promote the little interest of one little order of men in one country, it hurts the interest of all other orders of men in that country, and of all men in all other countries.

It is solely by raising the ordinary rate of profit that the monopoly either has proved or could prove advantageous to any

More fatal still, it destroys parsimony.

one particular order of men. But besides all the bad effects to the country in general, which have already been mentioned as necessarily resulting from a high rate of profit; there is one more fatal, perhaps, than all these put together, but which, if we may judge from experience, is inseparably connected with it. The high rate of profit seems every where to destroy that parsimony which in other circumstances is natural to the character of the merchant. When profits are high, that sober virtue seems to be superfluous, and expensive luxury to suit better the affluence of his situation. But the owners of the great mercantile capitals are necessarily the leaders and conductors of the whole industry of every nation, and their example has a much greater influence upon the manners of the whole industrious part of it than that of any other order of men. If his employer is attentive and parsimonious, the workman is very likely to be so too; but if the master is dissolute and disorderly, the servant who shapes his work according to the pattern which his master prescribes to him, will shape his life too according to the example which he sets him. Accumulation is thus prevented in the hands of all those who are naturally the most disposed to accumulate; and the funds destined for the maintenance of productive labour receive no augmentation from the revenue of those who ought naturally to augment them the most. The capital of the country, instead of increasing, gradually dwindles away, and the quantity of productive labour maintained in it grows every day less and less. Have the exorbitant profits of the merchants of Cadiz and Lisbon augmented the capital of Spain and Portugal? Have they alleviated the poverty, have they promoted the industry of those two beggarly countries? Such has been the tone of mercantile expence in those two trading cities, that those exorbitant profits, far from augmenting the general capital of the country, seem scarce to have been sufficient to keep up the capitals upon which they were made. Foreign capitals are every day intruding themselves, if I may say so, more and more into the trade of Cadiz and Lisbon. It is to expel those foreign capitals from a trade which their own[91] grows every day more and more insufficient for carrying on, that the Spaniards and Portuguese endeavour every day to straiten more and more the galling bands of their absurd monopoly. Compare the mercantile manners of Cadiz and Lisbon with those of Amsterdam, and you will be sensible how differently the conduct and character of merchants are affected by the high and by the low profits of stock. The merchants of London, indeed, have not yet generally become such magnificent lords as those of Cadiz and Lisbon; but neither are they in general such attentive and parsimonious burghers as those of Amsterdam. They are supposed, however, many of them, to be a good deal richer than the greater part of the former, and not quite so rich as many of the latter. But the rate of their profit is commonly much lower than that of the former, and a good deal higher than that of the latter. Light come light go, says the proverb; and the ordinary tone of expence seems every where to be regulated, not so much according to the real ability of spending as to the supposed facility of getting money to spend.

It is thus that the single advantage which the monopoly procures to a single order of men, is in many different ways hurtful to the general interest of the country.

To found a great empire for the sole purpose of raising up a people of customers, may at first sight appear a project fit only for a nation of shopkeepers. It is, however, a project altogether

---

[91] [Ed. 1 reads "own capital."]

The policy of the monopoly is a policy of shopkeepers.

unfit for a nation of shopkeepers; but extremely fit for a nation whose government is influenced by shopkeepers. Such statesmen, and such statesmen only,[92] are capable of fancying that they will find some advantage in employing the blood and treasure of their fellow-citizens, to found and maintain[93] such an empire. Say to a shopkeeper, Buy me a good estate, and I shall always buy my clothes at your shop, even though I should pay somewhat dearer than what I can have them for at other shops; and you will not find him very forward to embrace your proposal. But should any other person buy you such an estate, the shopkeeper would be much obliged to your benefactor if he would enjoin you to buy all your clothes at his shop. England purchased for some of her subjects, who found themselves uneasy at home, a great estate in a distant country. The price, indeed, was very small, and instead of thirty years purchase, the ordinary price of land in the present times, it amounted to little more than the expence of the different equipments which made the first discovery, reconnoitred the coast, and took a fictitious possession of the country. The land was good and of great extent, and the cultivators having plenty of good ground to work upon, and being for some time at liberty to sell their produce where they pleased, became in the course of little more than thirty or forty years (between 1620 and 1660) so numerous and thriving a people, that the shopkeepers and other traders of England wished to secure to themselves the monopoly of their custom. Without pretending, therefore, that they had paid any part, either of the original purchase-money, or of the subsequent expence of improvement, they petitioned the parliament that the cultivators of America might for the future be confined to their shop; first, for buying all the goods which they wanted from Europe; and, secondly, for selling all such parts of their own produce as those traders might find it convenient to buy. For they did not

[92] [Ed. 1 reads "extremely fit for a nation that is governed by shopkeepers. Such sovereigns and such sovereigns only."]

[93] [Ed. 1 reads "their subjects, to found and to maintain."]

find it convenient to buy every part of it. Some parts of it imported into England might have interfered with some of the trades which they themselves carried on at home. Those particular parts of it, therefore, they were willing that the colonists should sell where they could; the farther off the better; and upon that account proposed that their market should be confined to the countries south of Cape Finisterre. A clause in the famous act of navigation established this truly shopkeeper proposal into a law.

The maintenance of this monopoly has hitherto been the principal, or more properly perhaps the sole end and purpose of the dominion which Great Britain assumes over her colonies. In the exclusive trade, it is supposed, consists the great advantage of provinces, which have never yet afforded either revenue or military force for the support of the civil government, or the defence of the mother country. The monopoly is the principal badge of their dependency, and it is the sole fruit which has hitherto been gathered from that dependency. Whatever expence Great Britain has hitherto laid out in maintaining this dependency, has really been laid out in order to support this monopoly. The expence of the ordinary peace establishment of the colonies amounted, before the commencement of the present disturbances, to the pay of twenty regiments of foot; to the expence of the artillery, stores, and extraordinary provisions with which it was[94] necessary to supply them; and to the expence of a very considerable naval force which was constantly kept up, in order to guard, from the smuggling vessels of other nations, the immense coast of North America, and that of our West Indian islands. The whole expence of this peace establishment was a charge upon the revenue of Great Britain, and was, at the same time, the smallest part of what the dominion of the colonies has cost the mother country. If we would know the amount of the whole, we must add to the annual expence of this peace estab-

The expenditure of Great Britain on the colonies has all been laid out to support the monopoly, and is enormous.

---

[94] [Ed. 1 reads "is" here and in the next line.]

lishment the interest of the sums which, in consequence of her considering her colonies as provinces subject to her dominion, Great Britain has upon different occasions laid out upon their defence. We must add to it, in particular, the whole expence of the late war, and a great part of that of the war which preceded it.[95] The late war was altogether a colony quarrel, and the whole expence of it, in whatever part of the world it may have been laid out, whether in Germany or the East Indies, ought justly to be stated to the account of the colonies. It amounted to more than ninety millions sterling, including not only the new debt which was contracted, but the two shillings in the pound additional land tax, and the sums which were every year borrowed from the sinking fund. The Spanish war which began in 1739, was principally a colony quarrel. Its principal object was to prevent the search of the colony ships which carried on a contraband trade with the Spanish main. This whole expence is, in reality, a bounty which has been given in order to support a monopoly. The pretended purpose of it was to encourage the manufactures, and to increase the commerce of Great Britain. But its real effect has been to raise the rate of mercantile profit, and to enable our merchants to turn into a branch of trade, of which the returns are more slow and distant than those of the greater part of other trades, a greater proportion of their capital than they otherwise would have done; two events which if a bounty could have prevented, it might perhaps have been very well worth while to give such a bounty.

Under the present system of management, therefore, Great Britain derives nothing but loss from the dominion which she assumes over her colonies.

To propose that Great Britain should voluntarily give up all authority over her colonies, and leave them to elect their own

A voluntary separation would be very advantageous.

magistrates, to enact their own laws, and to make peace and war as they might think proper, would be to propose such a measure as never was, and never will be adopted, by any nation in the world. No nation ever vol-

---

[95] [Ed. 1 reads "and a great part of that which preceded it."]

untarily gave up the dominion of any province, how troublesome soever it might be to govern it, and how small soever the revenue which it afforded might be in proportion to the expence which it occasioned. Such sacrifices, though they might frequently be agreeable to the interest, are always mortifying to the pride of every nation, and what is perhaps of still greater consequence, they are always contrary to the private interest of the governing part of it, who would thereby be deprived of the disposal of many places of trust and profit, of many opportunities of acquiring wealth and distinction, which the possession of the most turbulent, and, to the great body of the people, the most unprofitable province seldom fails to afford. The most visionary enthusiast would scarce be capable of proposing such a measure, with any serious hopes at least of its ever being adopted. If it was adopted, however, Great Britain would not only be immediately freed from the whole annual expence of the peace establishment of the colonies, but might settle with them such a treaty of commerce as would effectually secure to her a free trade, more advantageous to the great body of the people, though less so to the merchants, than the monopoly which she at present enjoys. By thus parting good friends, the natural affection of the colonies to the mother country, which, perhaps, our late dissensions have well nigh extinguished, would quickly revive. It might dispose them not only to respect, for whole centuries together, that treaty of commerce which they had concluded with us at parting, but to favour us in war as well as in trade, and, instead of turbulent and factious subjects, to become our most faithful, affectionate, and generous allies; and the same sort of parental affection on the one side, and filial respect on the other, might revive between Great Britain and her colonies, which used to subsist between those of ancient Greece and the mother city from which they descended.

In order to render any province advantageous to the empire to which it belongs, it ought to afford, in time of peace, a revenue to the public sufficient not only for defraying the whole expence of its own peace establishment, but for contributing its proportion to the support of the general government of the

The colonies do not furnish nearly sufficient revenue to make them advantageous.

empire. Every province necessarily contributes, more or less, to increase the expence of that general government. If any particular province, therefore, does not contribute its share towards defraying this expence, an unequal burden must be thrown upon some other part of the empire. The extraordinary revenue too which every province affords to the public in time of war, ought, from parity of reason, to bear the same proportion to the extraordinary revenue of the whole empire which its ordinary revenue does in time of peace. That neither the ordinary nor extraordinary revenue which Great Britain derives from her colonies, bears this proportion to the whole revenue of the British empire, will readily be allowed. The monopoly, it has been supposed, indeed, by increasing the private revenue of the people of Great Britain, and thereby enabling them to pay greater taxes, compensates the deficiency of the public revenue of the colonies. But this monopoly, I have endeavoured to show, though a very grievous tax upon the colonies, and though it may increase the revenue of a particular order of men in Great Britain, diminishes instead of increasing that of the great body of the people; and consequently diminishes instead of increasing the ability of the great body of the people to pay taxes. The men too whose revenue the monopoly increases, constitute a particular order, which it is both absolutely impossible to tax beyond the proportion of other orders, and extremely impolitic even to attempt to tax beyond that proportion, as I shall endeavour to shew in the following book.[96] No particular resource, therefore, can be drawn from this particular order.

The colonies may be taxed either by their own assemblies, or by the parliament of Great Britain.

That the colony assemblies can ever be so managed as to levy upon their constituents a public revenue sufficient, not only to maintain at all times their own civil and military establishment, but to pay their proper proportion of the expence of

---

[96] [Below, p. 1074.]

The colonial assemblies will never vote enough, the general government of the British empire, seems not very probable. It was a long time before even the parliament of England, though placed immediately under the eye of the sovereign, could be brought under such a system of management, or could be rendered sufficiently liberal in their grants for supporting the civil and military establishments even of their own country. It was only by distributing among the particular members of parliament, a great part either of the offices, or of the disposal of the offices arising from this civil and military establishment, that such a system of management could be established even with regard to the parliament of England. But the distance of the colony assemblies from the eye of the sovereign, their number, their dispersed situation, and their various constitutions, would render it very difficult to manage them in the same manner, even though the sovereign had the same means of doing it; and those means are wanting. It would be absolutely impossible to distribute among all the leading members of all the colony assemblies such a share, either of the offices or of the disposal of the offices arising from the general government of the British empire, as to dispose them to give up their popularity at home, and to tax their constituents for the support of that general government, of which almost the whole emoluments were to be divided among people who were strangers to them. The unavoidable ignorance of administration, besides, concerning the relative importance of the different members of those different assemblies, the offences which must frequently be given, the blunders which must constantly be committed in attempting to manage them in this manner, seems[97] to render such a system of management altogether impracticable with regard to them.

The colony assemblies, besides, cannot be supposed the proper judges of what is necessary for the defence and support of the whole empire. The care of that defence and support is not entrusted to them. It is not their business, and they have no regular means of information concerning it. The assembly of a

[97] [Ed. 1 reads "seem."]

and have no knowledge of what is required. province, like the vestry of a parish, may judge very properly concerning the affairs of its own particular district; but can have no proper means of judging concerning those of the whole empire. It cannot even judge properly concerning the proportion which its own province bears to the whole empire; or concerning the relative degree of its wealth and importance, compared with the other provinces; because those other provinces are not under the inspection and superintendency of the assembly of a particular province. What is necessary for the defence and support of the whole empire, and in what proportion each part ought to contribute, can be judged of only by that assembly which inspects and superintends the affairs of the whole empire.

It has been proposed, accordingly, that the colonies should be taxed by requisition, the parliament of Great Britain determining the sum which each colony ought to pay, and the provincial assembly assessing and levying it in the way that suited best the circumstances of the province. What concerned the whole empire would in this way be determined by the assembly which inspects and superintends the affairs of the whole empire; and the provincial affairs of each colony might still be regulated by its own assembly. Though the colonies should in this case have no representatives in the British parliament, yet, if we may judge by experience, there is no probability that the parliamentary requisition would be unreasonable. The parliament of England has not upon any occasion shown the smallest disposition to overburden those parts of the empire which are not represented in parliament. The islands of Guernsey and Jersey, without any means of resisting the authority of parliament, are more lightly taxed than any part of Great Britain. Parliament in attempting to exercise its supposed right, whether well or ill grounded, of taxing the colonies, has never hitherto demanded of them any thing which even approached to a just proportion to what was paid by their fellow-subjects at home. If the contribution of the colonies, besides, was to rise or fall in propor-

It has been proposed that parliament should tax the colonies by requisition,

tion to the rise or fall of the land tax, parliament could not tax them without taxing at the same time its own constituents, and the colonies might in this case be considered as virtually represented in parliament.

Examples are not wanting of empires in which all the different provinces are not taxed, if I may be allowed the expression, in one mass; but in which the sovereign *as the King of France taxes some of his provinces,* regulates the sum which each province ought to pay, and in some provinces assesses and levies it as he thinks proper; while in others, he leaves it to be assessed and levied as the respective states of each province shall determine. In some provinces of France, the king not only imposes what taxes he thinks proper, but assesses and levies them in the way he thinks proper. From others he demands a certain sum, but leaves it to the states of each province to assess and levy that sum as they think proper. According to the scheme of taxing by requisition, the parliament of Great Britain would stand nearly in the same situation towards the colony assemblies, as the king of France does towards the states of those provinces which still enjoy the privilege of having states of their own, the provinces of France which are supposed to be the best governed.

But though, according to this scheme, the colonies could have no just reason to fear that their share of the public burdens *but parliament has not sufficient authority,* should ever exceed the proper proportion to that of their fellow-citizens at home; Great Britain might have just reason to fear that it never would amount to that proper proportion. The parliament of Great Britain has not for some time past had the same established authority in the colonies, which the French king has in those provinces of France which still enjoy the privilege of having states of their own. The colony assemblies, if they were not very favourably disposed (and unless more skilfully managed than they ever have been hitherto, they are not very likely to be so), might still find many pretences for evading or rejecting the most reasonable requisitions of parliament. A French war breaks out, we shall suppose; ten millions must immediately be raised, in order to defend the seat of the empire. This sum must be borrowed upon the credit of some parliamentary fund mortgaged for paying the interest. Part of this fund parliament proposes to raise by a tax to be levied in Great Britain, and part of it by a requisition to all the different colony assemblies of America and the West Indies. Would people readily advance their money upon the credit of a fund, which partly depended upon the good humour of all those assemblies, far distant from the seat of the war, and sometimes, perhaps, thinking themselves not much concerned in the event of it? Upon such a fund no more money would probably be advanced than what the tax to be levied in Great Britain might be supposed to answer for. The whole burden of the debt contracted on account of the war would in this manner fall, as it always has done hitherto, upon Great Britain; upon a part of the empire, and not upon the whole empire. Great Britain is, perhaps, since the world began, the only state which, as it has extended its empire, has only increased its expence without once augmenting its resources. Other states have generally disburdened themselves upon their subject and subordinate provinces of the most considerable part of the expence of defending the empire. Great Britain has hitherto suffered her subject and subordinate provinces to disburden themselves upon her of almost this whole expence. In order to put Great Britain upon a footing of equality with her own colonies, which the law has hitherto supposed to be subject and subordinate, it seems necessary, upon the scheme of taxing them by parliamentary requisition, that parliament should have some means of rendering its requisitions immediately effectual, in case the colony assemblies should attempt to evade or reject them; and what those means are, it is not very easy to conceive, and it has not yet been explained.

Should the parliament of Great Britain, at the same time, be ever fully established in the right of taxing the colonies, even *and resistance breaks out.* independent of the consent of their own assemblies, the importance of those assemblies would from that moment be at an end, and with it, that of all the leading men of British America. Men desire to have some share in the management of public affairs chiefly on account of the importance which it gives them. Upon the power which the greater part of the leading men, the natural aristocracy of every country, have of preserving or defending their respective importance, depends the stability and duration of every system of free government. In the attacks which those leading men are continually making upon the importance of one another, and in the defence of their own, consists the whole play of domestic faction and ambition. The leading men of America, like those of all other countries, desire to preserve their own importance. They feel, or imagine, that if their assemblies, which they are fond of calling parliaments, and of considering as equal in authority to the parliament of Great Britain, should be so far degraded as to become the humble ministers and executive officers of that parliament, the greater part of their own importance would be at an end. They have rejected, therefore, the proposal of being taxed by parliamentary requisition, and like other ambitious and high-spirited men, have rather chosen to draw the sword in defence of their own importance.

Towards the declension of the Roman republic, the allies of Rome, who had borne the principal burden of defending the state and extending the empire, demanded to *Representation in* be admitted to all the privileges of Roman *parliament in pro-* citizens. Upon being refused, the social war *portion to taxation* broke out. During the course of that war *should be offered.* Rome granted those privileges to the greater part of them, one by one, and in proportion as they detached themselves from the general confederacy. The parliament of Great Britain insists upon taxing the colonies; and they refuse to be taxed by a parliament in which they are not represented. If to each colony, which should detach itself from the general confederacy, Great Britain should allow such a number of representatives as suited the proportion of what it contributed to the public revenue of the empire, in consequence of its being subjected to the same taxes, and in compensation admitted to the same freedom of trade with its fellow-subjects at home; the number of its representatives to be augmented as the proportion of its contribution might afterwards augment; a new method of acquiring importance, a new and more dazzling object of ambition would be presented to the leading men of each colony. Instead of piddling for the little prizes which are to be found in what may be called the paltry raffle of colony faction; they might then hope, from the presumption which men naturally have in their own ability and good fortune, to draw some of the great prizes which sometimes come from the wheel of

Otherwise it seems hopeless to expect submission, the great state lottery of British politics. Unless this or some other method is fallen upon, and there seems to be none more obvious than this, of preserving the importance

and of gratifying the ambition of the leading men of America, it is not very probable that they will ever voluntarily submit to us; and we ought to consider that the blood which must be shed in forcing them to do so, is, every drop of it, the blood either of those who are, or of those whom we wish to have for our fellow-citizens. They are very weak who flatter themselves that, in the state to which things have come, our colonies will be easily conquered by force alone. The persons who now govern the resolutions of what they call their continental congress, feel in themselves at this moment a degree of importance which, perhaps the greatest subjects in Europe scarce feel. From shopkeepers, tradesmen, and attornies, they are become statesmen and legislators, and are employed in contriving a new form of government for an extensive empire, which, they flatter themselves, will become, and which, indeed, seems very likely to become, one of the greatest and most formidable that ever was in the world. Five hundred different people, perhaps, who in different ways act immediately under the continental congress; and five hundred thousand, perhaps, who act under those five hundred, all feel in the same manner a proportionable rise in their own importance. Almost every individual of the governing party in America, fills, at present in his own fancy, a station superior, not only to what he had ever filled before, but to what he had ever expected to fill; and unless some new object of ambition is presented either to him or to his leaders, if he has the ordinary spirit of a man, he will die in defence of that station.

It is a remark of the president Henaut, that we now read with pleasure the account of many little transactions of the

and resistance will be as obstinate as that of Paris.

Ligue, which when they happened were not perhaps considered as very important pieces of news. But every man then, says he, fancied himself of some importance; and the innumerable memoirs which have come down to us from those times were, the greater part of them, written by people who took pleasure in recording and magnifying events in which, they flattered themselves, they had been considerable actors.[98] How obstinately the city of Paris upon that occasion defended itself, what a dreadful famine it supported rather than submit to the best and afterwards[99] the most beloved of all the French kings, is well known. The greater part of the citizens, or those who governed the greater part of them, fought in defence of their own importance, which they foresaw was to be at an end whenever the ancient government should be re-established. Our colonies, unless they can be induced to consent to a union, are very likely to defend themselves against the best of all mother countries, as obstinately as the city of Paris did against one of the best of kings.

The idea of representation was unknown in ancient times. When the people of one state were admitted to the right of citizenship in another, they had no other means of exercising that right but by coming in a body to vote and deliberate with the people of that other state. The admission of the greater part of the inhabitants of Italy to the privileges of Roman citizens, completely ruined the Roman republic. It was no longer possi-

[98] ["Aucun des règnes précédents n'a fourni plus de volumes, plus d'anecdotes, plus d'estampes, plus de pièces fugitives, etc. Il y a dans tout cela bien des choses inutiles; mais comme Henri III. vivait au milieu de son peuple, aucun détail des actions de sa vie n'a échappé à la curiosité; et comme Paris était le théâtre des principaux événements de la ligue, les bourgeois qui y avaient la plus grande part, conservaient soigneusement les moindres faits qui se passaient sous leurs yeux; tout ce qu'ils voyaient leur paraissait grand, parce qu'ils y participaient, et nous sommes curieux, sur parole, de faits dont la plupart ne faisaient peut-être pas alors une grande nouvelle dans le monde,"—C. J. F. Hénault, *Nouvel Abrégé chronologique de l'histoire de France*, nouv. éd., 1768, p. 473, A.D. 1589.]

[99] [Eds. 4 and 5 erroneously insert "to" here.]

The discovery of representation makes the case different from that of Rome and Italy.

ble to distinguish between who was and who was not a Roman citizen. No tribe could know its own members. A rabble of any kind could be introduced into the assemblies of the people, could drive out the real citizens, and decide upon the affairs of the republic as if they themselves had been such. But though America were[100] to send fifty new representatives to parliament, the door-keeper of the house of commons could not find any great difficulty in distinguishing between who was and who was not a member. Though the Roman constitution, therefore, was necessarily ruined by the union of Rome with the allied states of Italy, there is not the least probability that the British constitution would be hurt by the union of Great Britain with her colonies. That constitution, on the contrary, would be completed by it, and seems to be imperfect without it. The assembly which deliberates and decides concerning the affairs of every part of the empire, in order to be properly informed, ought certainly to have representatives from every part of it. That this union, however, could be easily effectuated, or that difficulties and great difficulties might not occur in the execution, I do not pretend: I have yet heard of none, however, which appear insurmountable. The principal perhaps arise, not from the nature of things, but from the prejudices and opinions of the people both on this and on the other side of the Atlantic.

We, on this side the water, are afraid lest the multitude of American representatives should overturn the balance of the constitution, and increase too much either the influence of the crown on the one hand, or the force of the democracy on the other.

The American representatives could be managed.

But if the number of American representatives were[101] to be in proportion to the produce of American taxation, the number of people to be managed would increase exactly in proportion to the means of managing them; and the means of managing, to the number of people to be managed.

[100] [Eds. 1–3 read "was."]

[101] [Eds. 1–3 read "was."]

The monarchical and democratical parts of the constitution would, after the union, stand exactly in the same degree of relative force with regard to one another as they had done before.

The people on the other side of the water are afraid lest their distance from the seat of government might expose them to many oppressions. But their representatives in parliament, of which the number ought from the first to be considerable, would easily be able to protect them from all oppression. The distance could not much weaken the dependency of the representatives upon the constituent, and the former would still feel that he owed his seat in parliament, and all the consequence which he derived from it, to the good-will of the latter. It would be the interest of the former, therefore, to cultivate that good-will by complaining, with all the authority of a member of the legislature, of every outrage which any civil or military officer might be guilty of in those remote parts of the empire. The distance of America from the seat of government, besides, the natives[102] of that country might flatter themselves, with some appearance of reason too, would not be of very long continuance. Such has hitherto been the rapid progress of that country in wealth, population and improvement, that in the course of little more than a century, perhaps, the produce of American might exceed that of British taxation. The seat of the empire would then naturally remove itself to that part of the empire which contributed most to the general defence and support of the whole.

The Americans would not be oppressed.

The discovery of America, and that of a passage to the East Indies by the Cape of Good Hope, are the two greatest and most important events recorded in the history of mankind.[103] Their consequences have already been very great: but, in the

---

[102] [Ed. 1 reads "nations."]

[103] [Raynal begins his *Histoire Philosophique* with the words "Il n'y a point eu d'événement aussi intéressant pour l'espèce humaine en général et pour les peuples de l'Europe en particulier, que la découverte du nouveau monde et le passage aux Indes par le Cap de Bonne-Espérance. Alors a commencé une révolution dans le commerce, dans la puissance des nations, dans les mœurs, l'industrie et le gouvernement de tous les peuples."]

The discovery of America and the Cape passage are the greatest events in history: the misfortunes of the natives of the East and West Indies may be temporary, so the results may be beneficial to all.

short period of between two and three centuries which has elapsed since these discoveries were made, it is impossible that the whole extent of their consequences can have been seen. What benefits, or what misfortunes to mankind may hereafter result from those great events, no human wisdom can foresee. By uniting, in some measure, the most distant parts of the world, by enabling them to relieve one another's wants, to increase one another's enjoyments, and to encourage one another's industry, their general tendency would seem to be beneficial. To the natives, however, both of the East and West Indies, all the commercial benefits which can have resulted from those events have been sunk and lost in the dreadful misfortunes which they have occasioned. These misfortunes, however, seem to have arisen rather from accident than from any thing in the nature of those events themselves. At the particular time when these discoveries were made, the superiority of force happened to be so great on the side of the Europeans, that they were enabled to commit with impunity every sort of injustice in those remote countries. Hereafter, perhaps, the natives of those countries may grow stronger, or those of Europe may grow weaker, and the inhabitants of all the different quarters of the world may arrive at that equality of courage and force which, by inspiring mutual fear, can alone overawe the injustice of independent nations into some sort of respect for the rights of one another. But nothing seems more likely to establish this equality of force than that mutual communication of knowledge and of all sorts of improvements which an extensive commerce from all countries to all countries naturally, or rather necessarily, carries along with it.

In the mean time one of the principal effects of those discoveries has been to raise the mercantile system to a degree of splendour and glory which it could never otherwise have attained to. It is the object of that system to enrich a great nation rather by trade and manufactures than by the improvement and

Meantime the discovery has exalted the mercantile system. cultivation of land, rather by the industry of the towns than by that of the country. But, in consequence of those discoveries, the commercial towns of Europe, instead of being the manufacturers and carriers for but a very small part of the world (that part of Europe which is washed by the Atlantic ocean, and the countries which lie round the Baltic and Mediterranean seas), have now become the manufacturers for the numerous and thriving cultivators of America, and the carriers, and in some respects the manufacturers too, for almost all the different nations of Asia, Africa, and America. Two new worlds have been opened to their industry, each of them much greater and more extensive than the old one, and the market of one of them growing still greater and greater every day.

The countries which possess the colonies of America, and which trade directly to the East Indies, enjoy, indeed, the whole *The countries which possess America and trade to the East Indies appear to get all the advantage, but this is not the case.* shew and splendour of this great commerce. Other countries, however, notwithstanding all the invidious restraints by which it is meant to exclude them, frequently enjoy a greater share of the real benefit of it. The colonies of Spain and Portugal, for example, give more real encouragement to the industry of other countries than to that of Spain and Portugal. In the single article of linen alone the consumption of those colonies amounts, it is said, but I do not pretend to warrant the quantity, to more than three millions sterling a year. But this great consumption is almost entirely supplied by France, Flanders, Holland, and Germany. Spain and Portugal furnish but a small part of it. The capital which supplies the colonies with this great quantity of linen is annually distributed among, and furnishes a revenue to the inhabitants of those other countries. The profits of it only are spent in Spain and Portugal, where they help to support the sumptuous profusion of the merchants of Cadiz and Lisbon.

Even the regulations by which each nation endeavours to secure to itself the exclusive trade of its own colonies, are fre-

The monopoly reg-
ulations some-
times harm the
country which
establishes them
more than others.

quently more hurtful to the countries in favour of which they are established than to those against which they are established. The unjust oppression of the industry of other countries falls back, if I may say so, upon the heads of the oppressors, and crushes their industry more than it does that of those other countries. By those regulations, for example, the merchant of Hamburgh must send the linen which he destines for the American market to London, and he must bring back from thence the tobacco which he destines for the German market; because he can neither send the one directly to America, nor bring back the other directly from thence. By this restraint he is probably obliged to sell the one somewhat cheaper, and to buy the other somewhat dearer than he otherwise might have done; and his profits are probably somewhat abridged by means of it. In this trade, however, between Hamburgh and London, he certainly receives the returns of his capital much more quickly than he could possibly have done in the direct trade to America, even though we should suppose, what is by no means the case, that the payments of America were as punctual as those of London. In the trade, therefore, to which those regulations confine the merchant of Hamburgh, his capital can keep in constant employment a much greater quantity of German industry than it possibly could have done in the trade from which he is excluded. Though the one employment, therefore, may to him perhaps be less profitable than the other, it cannot be less advantageous to his country. It is quite otherwise with the employment into which the monopoly naturally attracts, if I may say so, the capital of the London merchant. That employment may, perhaps, be more profitable to him than the greater part of other employments, but, on account of the slowness of the returns, it cannot be more advantageous to his country.

After all the unjust attempts, therefore, of every country in Europe to engross to itself the whole advantage of the trade of its own colonies, no country has yet been able to engross to itself any thing but the expence of supporting in time of peace

The mother countries have engrossed only the expense and inconveniencies of possessing colonies.

and of defending in time of war the oppressive authority which it assumes over them. The inconveniencies resulting from the possession of its colonies, every country has engrossed to itself completely. The advantages resulting from their trade it has been obliged to share with many other countries.

At first sight, no doubt, the monopoly of the great commerce of America, naturally seems to be an acquisition of the highest value. To the undiscerning eye of giddy ambition, it naturally presents itself amidst the confused scramble of politics and war, as a very dazzling object to fight for. The dazzling splendour of the object, however, the immense greatness of the commerce, is the very quality which renders the monopoly of it hurtful, or which makes one employment, in its own nature necessarily less advantageous to the country than the greater part of other employments, absorb a much greater proportion of the capital of the country than what would otherwise have gone to it.

The monopoly of American trade is a dazzling object.

The mercantile stock of every country, it has been shewn in the second book,[104] naturally seeks, if one may say so, the employment most advantageous to that country. If it is employed in the carrying trade, the country to which it belongs becomes the emporium of the goods of all the countries whose trade that stock carries on. But the owner of that stock necessarily wishes to dispose of as great a part of those goods as he can at home. He thereby saves himself the trouble, risk, and expence of exportation, and he will upon that account be glad to sell them at home, not only for a much smaller price, but with somewhat a smaller profit than he might expect to make by sending them abroad. He naturally, therefore, endeavours as much as he can to turn his carrying trade into a foreign trade of consumption. If his stock again is employed in a foreign trade

The stock of a country naturally seeks the employment most advantageous to the country,

[104] [Above, pp. 458–477.]

of consumption, he will, for the same reason, be glad to dispose of at home as great a part as he can of
preferring the
near to the
more distant
employments,
the home goods, which he collects in order
to export to some foreign market, and he
will thus endeavour, as much as he can, to
turn his foreign trade of consumption into a
home trade. The mercantile stock of every country naturally
courts in this manner the near, and shuns the distant employment; naturally courts the employment in which the returns are
frequent, and shuns that in which they are distant and slow;
naturally courts the employment in which it can maintain the
greatest quantity of productive labour in the country to which
it belongs, or in which its owner resides, and shuns that in
which it can maintain there the smallest quantity. It naturally
courts the employment which in ordinary cases is most advantageous, and shuns that which in ordinary cases is least advantageous to that country.

But if in any of those distant employments, which in ordinary cases are less advantageous to the country, the profit
should happen to rise somewhat higher than
unless profits are
higher in the more
distant, which
indicates that
the more distant
employment is
necessary.
what is sufficient to balance the natural preference which is given to nearer employments, this superiority of profit will draw
stock from those nearer employments, till
the profits of all return to their proper level.
This superiority of profit, however, is a proof
that, in the actual circumstances of the society, those distant employments are somewhat understocked in
proportion to other employments, and that the stock of the society is not distributed in the properest manner among all the
different employments carried on in it. It is a proof that something is either bought cheaper or sold dearer than it ought to
be, and that some particular class of citizens is more or less oppressed either by paying more or by getting less than what is
suitable to that equality, which ought to take place, and which
naturally does take place among all the different classes of
them. Though the same capital never will maintain the same
quantity of productive labour in a distant as in a near employ-

ment, yet a distant employment may be as necessary for the welfare of the society as a near one; the goods which the distant employment deals in being necessary, perhaps, for carrying on many of the nearer employments. But if the profits of those who deal in such goods are above their proper level, those goods will be sold dearer than they ought to be, or somewhat above their natural price, and all those engaged in the nearer employments will be more or less oppressed by this high price. Their interest, therefore, in this case requires that some stock should be withdrawn from those nearer employments, and turned towards that distant one,[105] in order to reduce its profits to their proper level, and the price of the goods which it deals in to their natural price. In this extraordinary case, the public interest requires that some stock should be withdrawn from those employments which in ordinary cases are more advantageous, and turned towards one which in ordinary cases is less advantageous to the public: and in this extraordinary case, the natural interests and inclinations of men coincide as exactly with the public interest as in all other ordinary cases, and lead them to withdraw stock from the near, and to turn it towards the distant employment.

It is thus that the private interests and passions of individuals naturally dispose them to turn their stock towards the employments which in ordinary cases are most advantageous to the society. But if from this natural preference they should turn too much of it towards those employments, the fall of profit in them and the rise of it in all others immediately dispose them to alter this faulty distribution. Without any intervention of law, therefore, the private interests and passions of men naturally lead them to divide and distribute the stock of every society, among all the different employments carried on in it, as nearly as possible in the proportion which is most agreeable to the interest of the whole society.

If too much goes to any employment, profit falls in that employment and the proper distribution is soon restored.

[105] [Ed. 1 reads "distant employment."]

All the different regulations of the mercantile system, necessarily derange more or less this natural and most advantageous distribution of stock. But those which concern the trade to America and the East Indies derange it perhaps more than any other; because the trade to those two great continents absorbs a greater quantity of stock than any two other branches of trade. The regulations, however, by which this derangement is effected in those two different branches of trade are not altogether the same. Monopoly is the great engine of both; but it is a different sort of monopoly. Monopoly of one kind or another, indeed, seems to be the sole engine of the mercantile system.

The mercantile system disturbs this distribution, especially in regard to American and Indian trade.

In the trade to America every nation endeavours to engross as much as possible the whole market of its own colonies, by fairly excluding all other nations from any direct trade to them. During the greater part of the sixteenth century, the Portugueze endeavoured to manage the trade to the East Indies in the same manner, by claiming the sole right of sailing in the Indian seas, on account of the merit of having first found out the road to them. The Dutch still continue to exclude all other European nations from any direct trade to their spice islands. Monopolies of this kind are evidently established against all other European nations, who are thereby not only excluded from a trade to which it might be convenient for them to turn some part of their stock, but are obliged to buy the goods which that trade deals in somewhat dearer, than if they could import them themselves directly from the countries which produce them.

The Portuguese attempted at first to exclude all other nations from trading in the Indian Seas, and the Dutch still exclude all other nations from trade with the Spice Islands.

But since the fall of the power of Portugal, no European nation has claimed the exclusive right of sailing in the Indian seas, of which the principal ports are now open to the ships of all European nations. Except in Portugal,[106] however, and

---

[106] [See below, pp. 803–804.]

Now the principal ports are open, but each country has established an exclusive company.

within these few years in France,[107] the trade to the East Indies has in every European country been subjected to an exclusive company. Monopolies of this kind are properly established against the very nation which erects them. The greater part of that nation are thereby not only excluded from a trade to which it might be convenient for them to turn some part of their stock, but are obliged to buy the goods which that trade deals in, somewhat dearer than if it was open and free to all their countrymen. Since the establishment of the English East India company, for example, the other inhabitants of England, over and above being excluded from the trade, must have paid in the price of the East India goods which they have consumed, not only for all the extraordinary profits which the company may have made upon those goods in consequence of their monopoly, but for all the extraordinary waste which the fraud and abuse, inseparable from the management of the affairs of so great a company, must necessarily have occasioned. The absurdity of this second kind of monopoly, therefore, is much more manifest than that of the first.

Both these kinds of monopolies derange more or less the natural distribution of the stock of the society: but they do not always derange it in the same way.

Monopolies of the American kind always attract, but monopolies of exclusive companies sometimes attract, sometimes repel stock.

Monopolies of the first kind always attract to the particular trade in which they are established, a greater proportion of the stock of the society than what would go to that trade of its own accord.

Monopolies of the second kind may sometimes attract stock towards the particular trade in which they are established, and sometimes repel it from that trade according to different circumstances. In poor countries they naturally attract towards that trade more stock than would otherwise go to

---

[107] [The monopoly of the French East India Company was abolished in 1769.— See the Continuation of Anderson's *Commerce*, 1801, vol. iv., p. 128.]

it. In rich countries they naturally repel from it a good deal of stock which would otherwise go to it.

Such poor countries as Sweden and Denmark, for example, would probably have never sent a single ship to the East Indies,

In poor countries they attract, had not the trade been subjected to an exclusive company. The establishment of such a company necessarily encourages adventurers. Their monopoly secures them against all competitors in the home market, and they have the same chance for foreign markets with the traders of other nations. Their monopoly shows them the certainty of a great profit upon a considerable quantity of goods, and the chance of a considerable profit upon a great quantity. Without such extraordinary encouragement, the poor traders of such poor countries would probably never have thought of hazarding their small capitals in so very distant and uncertain an adventure as the trade to the East Indies must naturally have appeared to them.

Such a rich country as Holland, on the contrary, would probably, in the case of a free trade, send many more ships to

in rich they repel. the East Indies than it actually does. The limited stock of the Dutch East India company[108] probably repels from that trade many great mercantile capitals which would otherwise go to it. The mercantile capital of Holland is so great that it is, as it were, continually overflowing, sometimes into the public funds of foreign countries, sometimes into loans to private traders and adventurers of foreign countries, sometimes into the most roundabout foreign trades of consumption, and sometimes into the carrying trade. All near employments being completely filled up, all the capital which can be placed in them with any tolerable profit being already placed in them, the capital of Holland necessarily flows towards the most distant employments. The trade to the East Indies, if it were[109] altogether free, would probably absorb the greater part of this redundant capital. The East Indies offer

---

[108] [Raynal, *Histoire philosophique*, ed. Amsterdam, 1773, tom. i., p. 203, gives the original capital as 6,459,840 florins.]

[109] [Eds. 1–3 read "if it was."]

a market both for the manufactures of Europe and for the gold and silver as well as for several other productions of America, greater and more extensive than both Europe and America put together.

Every derangement of the natural distribution of stock is necessarily hurtful to the society in which it takes place; whether it be by repelling from a particular trade the stock which would otherwise go to it, or by attracting towards a particular trade that which would not otherwise come to it. If, without any exclusive company, the trade of Holland to the East Indies would be greater than it actually is, that country must suffer a considerable loss by part of its capital being excluded from the employment most convenient for that part. And in the same manner, if, without an exclusive company, the trade of Sweden and Denmark to the East Indies would be less than it actually is, or, what perhaps is more probable, would not exist at all, those two countries must likewise suffer a considerable loss by part of their capital being drawn into an employment which must be more or less unsuitable to their present circumstances. Better for them, perhaps, in their present circumstances, to buy East India goods of other nations, even though they should pay somewhat dearer, than to turn so great a part of their small capital to so very distant a trade, in which the returns are so very slow, in which that capital can maintain so small a quantity of productive labour at home, where productive labour is so much wanted, where so little is done, and where so much is to do.

Both effects are hurtful.

Though without an exclusive company, therefore, a particular country should not be able to carry on any direct trade to the East Indies, it will not from thence follow that such a company ought to be established there, but only that such a country ought not in these circumstances to trade directly to the East Indies. That such companies are not in general necessary for carrying on the East India trade, is sufficiently demonstrated by the experience of the Portugueze, who en-

A country which cannot trade to the East Indies without an exclusive company should not trade there.

joyed almost the whole of it for more than a century together without any exclusive company.

No private merchant, it has been said, could well have capital sufficient to maintain factors and agents in the different ports of the East Indies, in order to provide goods for the ships which he might occasionally send thither; and yet, unless he was able to do this, the difficulty of finding a cargo might frequently make his ships lose the season for returning, and the expence of so long a delay would not only eat up the whole profit of the adventure, but frequently occasion a very considerable loss. This argument, however, if it proved any thing at all, would prove that no one great branch of trade could be carried on without an exclusive company, which is contrary to the experience of all nations. There is no great branch of trade in which the capital of any one private merchant is sufficient, for carrying on all the subordinate branches which must be carried on, in order to carry on the principal one.[110] But when a nation is ripe for any great branch of trade, some merchants naturally turn their capitals towards the principal, and some towards the subordinate branches of it; and though all the different branches of it are in this manner carried on, yet it very seldom happens that they are all carried on by the capital of one private merchant. If a nation, therefore, is ripe for the East India trade, a certain portion of its capital will naturally divide itself among all the different branches of that trade. Some of its merchants will find it for their interest to reside in the East Indies, and to employ their capitals there in providing goods for the ships which are to be sent out by other merchants who reside in Europe. The settlements which different European nations have obtained in the East Indies, if they were taken from the exclusive companies to which they at present belong, and put under the immediate protection of the sovereign, would render this residence both safe and easy, at least to the merchants of the particular nations to whom those settlements belong. If at any particular

The idea that the large capital of a company is necessary is fallacious.

[110] [Ed. 1 reads "the principal branch."]

time that part of the capital of any country which of its own accord tended and inclined, if I may say so, towards the East
India trade, was not sufficient for carrying on all those different branches of it, it would be a proof that, at that particular
time, that country was not ripe for that trade, and that it would
do better to buy for some time, even at a higher price, from
other European nations, the East India goods it had occasion
for, than to import them itself directly from the East Indies.
What it might lose by the high price of those goods could
seldom be equal to the loss which it would sustain by the distraction of a large portion of its capital from other employments more necessary, or more useful, or more suitable to its
circumstances and situation, than a direct trade to the East
Indies.

Though the Europeans possess many considerable settlements both upon the coast of Africa and in the East Indies, they

*There are not
numerous and
thriving colonies
in Africa and
the East Indies,
as in America.*

have not yet established in either of those
countries such numerous and thriving
colonies as those in the islands and continent
of America. Africa, however, as well as several of the countries comprehended under
the general name of the East Indies, are inhabited by barbarous nations. But those nations were by no means so weak and defenceless as the
miserable and helpless Americans; and in proportion to the
natural fertility of the countries which they inhabited, they
were besides much more populous. The most barbarous nations either of Africa or of the East Indies were shepherds;
even the Hottentots were so.[111] But the natives of every part of
America, except Mexico and Peru, were only hunters; and the
difference is very great between the number of shepherds and
that of hunters whom the same extent of equally fertile territory can maintain. In Africa and the East Indies, therefore, it
was more difficult to displace the natives, and to extend the
European plantations over the greater part of the lands of the
original inhabitants. The genius of exclusive companies, be-

---

[111] [Raynal, *Histoire philosophique*, 1773, tom. i., p. 178.]

sides, is unfavourable, it has already been observed,[112] to the growth of new colonies, and has probably been the principal cause of the little progress which they have made in the East Indies. The Portugueze carried on the trade both to Africa and the East Indies without any exclusive companies, and their settlements at Congo, Angola, and Benguela on the coast of Africa, and at Goa in the East Indies, though much depressed by superstition and every sort of bad government, yet bear some faint resemblance to the colonies of America, and are partly inhabited by Portugueze who have been established there for several generations. The Dutch settlements at the Cape of Good Hope and at Batavia, are at present the most considerable colonies which the Europeans have established either in Africa or in the East Indies, and both these[113] settlements are peculiarly fortunate in their situation. The Cape of Good Hope was inhabited by a race of people almost as barbarous and quite as incapable of defending themselves as the natives of America. It is besides the half-way house, if one may say so, between Europe and the East Indies, at which almost every European ship makes some stay both in going and returning. The supplying of those ships with every sort of fresh provisions, with fruit and sometimes with wine, affords alone a very extensive market for the surplus produce of the colonists. What the Cape of Good Hope is between Europe and every part of the East Indies, Batavia is between the principal countries of the East Indies. It lies upon the most frequented road from Indostan to China and Japan, and is nearly about mid-way upon that road. Almost all the ships too that sail between Europe and China touch at Batavia; and it is, over and above all this, the center and principal mart of what is called the country trade of the East Indies; not only of that part of it which is carried on by Europeans, but of that which is carried on by the native Indians; and vessels navigated by the inhabitants of China and Japan, of Tonquin, Malacca, Cochin-China, and the island of Celebes, are frequently to be seen in its port.

[112] [Above, pp. 729–730.]

[113] [Ed. 1 reads "those."]

Such advantageous situations have enabled those two colonies to surmount all the obstacles which the oppressive genius of an exclusive company may have occasionally opposed to their growth. They have enabled Batavia to surmount the additional disadvantage of perhaps the most unwholesome climate in the world.

The English and Dutch companies, though they have established no considerable colonies, except the two above mentioned, have both made considerable conquests in the East Indies. But in the manner in which they both govern their new subjects, the natural genius of an exclusive company has shown itself most distinctly. In the spice islands the Dutch are said to[114] burn all the spiceries which a fertile season produces beyond what they expect to dispose of in Europe with such a profit as they think sufficient. In the islands where they have no settlements, they give a premium to those who collect the young blossoms and green leaves of the clove and nutmeg trees which naturally grow there, but which this savage[115] policy has now, it is said, almost completely extirpated. Even in the islands where they have settlements they have very much reduced, it is said, the number of those trees. If the produce even of their own islands was much greater than what suited their market, the natives, they suspect, might find means to convey some part of it to other nations; and the best way, they imagine, to secure their own monopoly, is to take care that no more shall grow than what they themselves carry to market. By different arts of oppression they have reduced the population of several of the Moluccas nearly to the number which is sufficient to supply with fresh provisions and other necessaries of life their own insignificant garrisons, and such of their ships as occasionally come there for a cargo of spices. Under the government even

The Dutch exclusive company destroys spices and nutmeg trees,

and has reduced the population of the Moluccas.

---

[114] [Ed. 1 does not contain "are said to." The statement has already been twice made, pp. 217, 662.]

[115] [Ed. 1 reads "barbarous."]

The English company has the same tendency.

of the Portuguese, however, those islands are said to have been tolerably well inhabited. The English company have not yet had time to establish in Bengal so perfectly destructive a system. The plan of their government, however, has had exactly the same tendency. It has not been uncommon, I am well assured, for the chief, that is, the first clerk of a factory, to order a peasant to plough up a rich field of poppies, and sow it with rice or some other grain. The pretence was, to prevent a scarcity of provisions; but the real reason, to give the chief an opportunity of selling at a better price a large quantity of opium, which he happened then to have upon hand. Upon other occasions the order has been reversed; and a rich field of rice or other grain has been ploughed up, in order to make room for a plantation of poppies; when the chief foresaw that extraordinary profit was likely to be made by opium. The servants of the company have upon several occasions attempted to establish in their own favour the monopoly of some of the most important branches, not only of the foreign, but of the inland trade of the country. Had they been allowed to go on, it is impossible that they should not at some time or another have attempted to restrain the production of the particular articles of which they had thus usurped the monopoly, not only to the quantity which they themselves could purchase, but to that which they could expect to sell with such a profit as they might think sufficient. In the course of a century or two, the policy of the English company would in this manner have probably proved as completely destructive as that of the Dutch.

Nothing, however, can be more directly contrary to the real interest of those companies, considered as the sovereigns of

This destructive system is contrary to their interest as sovereigns,

the countries which they have conquered, than this destructive plan. In almost all countries the revenue of the sovereign is drawn from that of the people. The greater the revenue of the people, therefore, the greater the annual produce of their land and labour, the more they can afford to the sovereign. It is his interest, therefore, to increase as much as possible that annual produce. But if this is the interest of every sovereign, it is peculiarly so of one whose revenue, like that of the sovereign of Bengal, arises chiefly from a land-rent. That rent must necessarily be in proportion to the quantity and value of the produce, and both the one and the other must depend upon the extent of the market. The quantity will always be suited with more or less exactness to the consumption of those who can afford to pay for it, and the price which they will pay will always be in proportion to the eagerness of their competition. It is the interest of such a sovereign, therefore, to open the most extensive market for the produce of his country, to allow the most perfect freedom of commerce, in order to increase as much as possible the number and the competition of buyers; and upon this account to abolish, not only all monopolies, but all restraints upon the transportation of the home produce from one part of the country to another, upon its exportation to foreign countries, or upon the importation of goods of any kind for which it can be exchanged. He is in this manner most likely to increase both the quantity and value of that produce, and consequently of his own share of it, or of his own revenue.

But a company of merchants are, it seems, incapable of considering themselves as sovereigns, even after they have become such. Trade, or buying in order to sell again, they still consider as their[116] principal business, and by a strange absurdity, regard the character of the sovereign as but an appendix to that of the merchant, as something which ought to be made subservient to it, or by means of which they may be enabled to buy cheaper in India, and thereby to sell with a better profit in Europe. They endeavour for this purpose to keep out as much as possible all competitors from the market of the countries which are subject to their government, and consequently to reduce, at least, some part of the surplus produce of those countries to what is barely sufficient for supplying their own demand, or to what they can expect to sell in Europe with such

but they prefer the transitory profits of the monopolist merchant to the permanent revenue of the sovereign.

116 [Ed. 1 reads "the."]

a profit as they may think reasonable. Their mercantile habits draw them in this manner, almost necessarily, though perhaps insensibly, to prefer upon all ordinary occasions the little and transitory profit of the monopolist to the great and permanent revenue of the sovereign, and would gradually lead them to treat the countries subject to their government nearly as the Dutch treat the Moluccas. It is the interest of the East India company considered as sovereigns, that the European goods which are carried to their Indian dominions, should be sold there as cheap as possible; and that the Indian goods which are brought from thence should bring there as good a price, or should be sold there as dear as possible. But the reverse of this is their interest as merchants. As sovereigns, their interest is exactly the same with that of the country which they govern. As merchants, their interest is directly opposite to that interest.[117]

But if the genius of such a government, even as to what concerns its direction in Europe, is in this manner essentially and

The administra-
tion in India
thinks only of
buying cheap
and selling dear,

perhaps incurably faulty, that of its administration in India is still more so. That administration is necessarily composed of a council of merchants, a profession no doubt extremely respectable, but which in no country in the world carries along with it that sort of authority which naturally over-awes the people, and without force commands their willing obedience. Such a council can command obedience only by the military force with which they are accompanied, and their government is therefore necessarily military and despotical. Their proper business, however, is that of merchants. It is to sell, upon their masters' account, the European goods consigned to them, and to buy in return Indian goods for the European market. It is to sell the one as dear and to buy the other as cheap as possible, and consequently to exclude as much as possible all rivals from the particular market where they keep their shop. The genius of the administration, therefore, so far as concerns the trade of the company, is the

---

[117] [Ed. 1 does not contain these four sentences beginning "It is the interest."]

same as that of the direction. It tends to make government subservient to the interest of monopoly, and consequently to stunt the natural growth of some parts at least of the surplus produce of the country to what is barely sufficient for answering the demand of the company.

All the members of the administration, besides, trade more or less upon their own account, and it is in vain to prohibit them from doing so. Nothing can be more *its members trade* completely foolish than to expect that the *on their own ac-* clerks of a great counting-house at ten thou-*count and cannot* sand miles distance, and consequently al-*be prevented from* most quite out of sight, should, upon a *doing so,* simple order from their masters, give up at once doing any sort of business upon their own account, abandon for ever all hopes of making a fortune, of which they have the means in their hands, and content themselves with the moderate salaries which those masters allow them, and which, moderate as they are, can seldom be augmented, being commonly as large as the real profits of the company trade can afford. In such circumstances, to prohibit the servants of the company from trading upon their own account, can have scarce any other effect than to enable the superior servants, under pretence of executing their masters order, to oppress such of the inferior ones as have had the misfortune to fall under their displeasure. The servants naturally endeavour to establish the same monopoly in favour of their own private trade as of the public trade of the company. If they are suffered to act as they could wish, they will establish this monopoly openly and directly, by fairly prohibiting all other people from trading in the articles in which they chuse to deal; and this, perhaps, is the best and least oppressive way of establishing it. But if by an order from Europe they are prohibited from doing this, they will, notwithstanding, endeavour to establish a monopoly of the same kind, secretly and indirectly, in a way that is much more destructive to the country. They will employ the whole authority of government, and pervert the administration of justice, in order to harass and ruin those who interfere with them in any branch of commerce which, by means

and this private trade is more extensive and harmful than the public trade of the company.

of agents, either concealed, or at least not publicly avowed, they may chuse to carry on. But the private trade of the servants will naturally extend to a much greater variety of articles than the public trade of the company. The public trade of the company extends no further than the trade with Europe, and comprehends a part only of the foreign trade of the country. But the private trade of the servants may extend to all the different branches both of its inland and foreign trade. The monopoly of the company can tend only to stunt the natural growth of that part of the surplus produce which, in the case of a free trade, would be exported to Europe. That of the servants tends to stunt the natural growth of every part of the produce in which they chuse to deal, of what is destined for home consumption, as well as of what is destined for exportation; and consequently to degrade the cultivation of the whole country, and to reduce the number of its inhabitants. It tends to reduce the quantity of every sort of produce, even that of the necessaries of life, whenever the servants of the company chuse to deal in them, to what those servants can both afford to buy and expect to sell with such a profit as pleases them.[118]

The interest of the servants is not, like the real interest of the company, the same as that of the country.

From the nature of their situation too the servants must be more disposed to support with rigorous severity their own interest against that of the country which they govern, than their masters can be to support theirs. The country belongs to their masters, who cannot avoid having some regard for the interest of what belongs to them. But it does

---

[118] [Smith had in his library (see Bonar's *Catalogue*, p. 15) William Bolts, *Considerations on India Affairs, Particularly respecting the present state of Bengal and its Dependencies*, ed. 1772. Pt. i., ch. xiv., of this is "On the general modern trade of the English in Bengal; on the oppressions and monopolies which have been the causes of the decline of trade, the decrease of the revenues, and the present ruinous condition of affairs in Bengal." At p. 215 we find "the servants of the Company . . . directly or indirectly monopolise whatever branches they please of the internal trade of those countries."]

not belong to the servants. The real interest of their masters, if they were capable of understanding it, is the same with that of the country,[119] and it is from ignorance chiefly,[120] and the meanness of mercantile prejudice, that they ever oppress it. But the real interest of the servants is by no means the same with that of the country, and the most perfect information would not necessarily put an end to their oppressions. The regulations accordingly which have been sent out from Europe, though they have been frequently weak, have upon most occasions been well-meaning.[121] More intelligence and perhaps less good-meaning has sometimes appeared in those established by the servants in India. It is a very singular government in which every member of the administration wishes to get out of the

---

[119] The interest of every proprietor of India Stock, however, is by no means the same with that of the country in the government of which his vote gives him some influence. See Book V. Chap. i. Part 3d. [This note appears first in ed. 3; ed. 2 has the following note: "This would be exactly true if those masters never had any other interest but that which belongs to them as Proprietors of India stock. But they frequently have another of much greater importance. Frequently a man of great, sometimes even a man of moderate fortune, is willing to give thirteen or fourteen hundred pounds (the present price of a thousand pounds share in India stock) merely for the influence which he expects to acquire by a vote in the Court of Proprietors. It gives him a share, though not in the plunder, yet in the appointment of the plunderers of India; the Directors, though they make those appointments, being necessarily more or less under the influence of the Court of Proprietors, which not only elects them, but sometimes over-rules their appointments. A man of great or even a man of moderate fortune, provided he can enjoy this influence for a few years, and thereby get a certain number of his friends appointed to employments in India, frequently cares little about the dividend which he can expect from so small a capital, or even about the improvement or loss of the capital itself upon which his vote is founded. About the prosperity or ruin of the great empire, in the government of which that vote gives him a share, he seldom cares at all. No other sovereigns ever were, or from the nature of things ever could be, so perfectly indifferent about the happiness or misery of their subjects, the improvement or waste of their dominions, the glory or disgrace of their administration, as, from irresistible moral causes, the greater part of the Proprietors of such a mercantile Company are, and necessarily must be." This matter with some slight alterations reappears in the portion of bk. v., chap. i., part iii., art. 1st, which was added in ed. 3 below, pp. 954–955.]

[120] [Ed. 1 reads "ignorance only."]

[121] [Ed. 1 reads "have commonly been well meaning."]

country, and consequently to have done with the government, as soon as he can, and to whose interest, the day after he has left it and carried his whole fortune with him, it is perfectly indifferent though[122] the whole country was swallowed up by an earthquake.

I mean not, however, by any thing which I have here said, to throw any odious imputation upon the general character of the servants of the East India company, and much less upon that of any particular persons. It is the system of government, the situation in which they are[123] placed, that I mean to censure; not the character of those who have acted in it. They acted as their situation naturally directed, and they who have clamoured the loudest against them would, probably, not have acted better themselves. In war and negociation, the councils of Madras and Calcutta have upon several occasions conducted themselves with a resolution and decisive wisdom which would have done honour to the senate of Rome in the best days of that republic. The members of those councils, however, had been bred to professions very different from war and politics. But their situation alone, without education, experience, or even example, seems to have formed in them all at once the great qualities which it required, and to have inspired them both with abilities and virtues which they themselves could not well know that they possessed. If upon some occasions, therefore, it has animated them to actions of magnanimity which could not well have been expected from them, we should not wonder if upon others it has prompted them to exploits of somewhat a different nature.

The evils come from the system, not from the character of the men who administer it.

Such exclusive companies, therefore, are nuisances in every respect; always more or less inconvenient to the countries in which they are established, and destructive to those which have the misfortune to fall under their government.

[122] [Ed. 1 reads "if."]

[123] [Eds. 1 and 2 read "were."]

CHAPTER VIII

CONCLUSION OF THE MERCANTILE SYSTEM[1]

THOUGH THE encouragement of exportation, and the discouragement of importation, are the two great engines by which the mercantile system proposes to enrich every country, yet with regard to some particular commodities, it seems to follow an opposite plan: to discourage exportation and to encourage importation. Its ultimate object, however, it pretends, is always the same, to enrich the country by an advantageous balance of trade. It discourages the exportation of the materials of manufacture, and of the instruments of trade, in order to give our own workmen an advantage, and to enable them to undersell those of other nations in all foreign markets: and by restraining, in this manner, the exportation of a few commodities, of no great price, it proposes to occasion a much greater and more valuable exportation of others. It encourages the importation of the materials of manufacture, in order that our own people may be enabled to work them up more cheaply, and thereby prevent a greater and more valuable importation of the manufactured commodities. I do not observe, at least in our Statute Book, any encouragement given to the importation of the instruments of trade. When manufactures have advanced to a certain pitch of greatness, the fabrication of the instruments of trade becomes itself the object of a great number of very im-

The mercantile system discourages the exportation of materials of manufacture and instruments of trade.

It encourages the importation of materials though not of instruments of trade.

---

[1] [This chapter appears first in Additions and Corrections and ed. 3.]

portant manufactures. To give any particular encouragement to the importation of such instruments, would interfere too much with the interest of those manufactures. Such importation, therefore, instead of being encouraged, has frequently been prohibited. Thus the importation of wool cards, except from Ireland, or when brought in as wreck or prize goods, was prohibited by the 3d of Edward IV.;[2] which prohibition was renewed by the 39th of Elizabeth,[3] and has been continued and rendered perpetual by subsequent laws.[4]

The importation of the materials of manufacture has sometimes been encouraged by an exemption from the duties to which other goods are subject, and sometimes by bounties.

The importation of sheep's wool from several different countries,[5] of cotton wool from all countries,[6] of undressed flax,[7] of the greater part of dying drugs,[8] of the greater part of undressed hides from Ireland or the British colonies,[9] of seal skins from the British Greenland fishery,[10] of pig and bar iron from the British colonies,[11] as well as of several other materials of manufacture, has been encouraged by an exemption from all duties, if properly entered at the customhouse. The private interest of our merchants and manufactures may, perhaps, have extorted from the legislature these exemp-

Various materials are exempt from customs duties.

[2] [C. 4.]

[3] [C. 14.]

[4] [3 Car. I., c. 4; 13 and 14 Car. II., c. 19.]

[5] [From Ireland, 12 Geo. II., c. 21; 26 Geo. II., c. 8. Spanish wool for clothing and Spanish felt wool.—Saxby, *British Customs*, p. 263.]

[6] [6 Geo. III., c. 52, § 20.]

[7] [4 Geo. II., c. 27.]

[8] [8 Geo. I., c. 15, § 10; see below, pp. 834–835.]

[9] [9 Geo. III., c. 39, § 1, continued by 14 Geo. III., c. 86, § 11, and 21 Geo. III., c. 29, § 3.]

[10] [15 Geo. III., c. 31, § 10.]

[11] [Above, p. 736.]

tions, as well as the greater part of our other commercial regulations. They are, however, perfectly just and reasonable, and if, consistently with the necessities of the state, they could be extended to all the other materials of manufacture, the public would certainly be a gainer.

The avidity of our great manufacturers, however, has in some cases extended these exemptions a good deal beyond *Yarn, though a* what can justly be considered as the rude ma-*manufactured* terials of their work. By the 24 Geo. II. chap. *article, is free* 46. a small duty of only one penny the pound *from duty,* was imposed upon the importation of foreign brown linen yarn, instead of much higher duties to which it had been subjected before, viz. of sixpence the pound upon sail yarn, of one shilling the pound upon all French and Dutch yarn, and of two pounds thirteen shillings and fourpence upon the hundred weight of all spruce or Muscovia yarn.[12] But our manufacturers were not long satisfied with this reduction. By the 29th of the same king, chap. 15. the same law which gave a bounty upon the exportation of British and Irish linen of which the price did not exceed eighteen pence the yard, even this small duty upon the importation of brown linen yarn was taken away. In the different operations, however, which are necessary for the preparation of linen yarn, a good deal more industry is employed, than in the subsequent operation of preparing linen cloth from linen yarn. To say nothing of the industry of the flax-growers and flax-dressers, three or four spin-*because the spin-* ners, at least, are necessary, in order to keep *ners are poor, un-* one weaver in constant employment; and *protected people,* more than four-fifths of the whole quantity of *and the master* labour, necessary for the preparation of linen *weavers are rich* cloth, is employed in that of linen yarn; but *and powerful.* our spinners are poor people, women commonly, scattered about in all different parts of the country, without support or protection. It is not by the sale of their work, but by that of the complete work of the weavers,

[12] [Smith has here inadvertently given the rates at which the articles were valued in the "Book of Rates," 12 Car. II., c. 4, instead of the duties, which would be 20 per cent. on the rates. See below, pp. 1114–1117.]

that our great master manufacturers make their profits. As it is their interest to sell the complete manufacture as dear, so it is to buy the materials as cheap as possible. By extorting from the legislature bounties upon the exportation of their own linen, high duties upon the importation of all foreign linen, and a total prohibition of the home consumption of some sorts of French linen,[13] they endeavour to sell their own goods as dear as possible. By encouraging the importation of foreign linen yarn, and thereby bringing it into competition with that which is made by our own people, they endeavour to buy the work of the poor spinners as cheap as possible. They are as intent to keep down the wages of their own weavers, as the earnings of the poor spinners, and it is by no means for the benefit of the workman, that they endeavour either to raise the price of the complete work, or to lower that of the rude materials. It is the industry which is carried on for the benefit of the rich and the powerful, that is principally encouraged by our mercantile system. That which is carried on for the benefit of the poor and the indigent, is too often, either neglected, or oppressed.

Both the bounty upon the exportation of linen, and the exemption from duty upon the importation of foreign yarn, which were granted only for fifteen years, but continued by two different prolongations,[14] expire with the end of the session of parliament which shall immediately follow the 24th of June 1786.

This exemption and also the bounty on the exportation of linen are given by a temporary law.

The encouragement given to the importation of the materials of manufacture by bounties, has been principally confined to such as were imported from our American plantations.

The first bounties of this kind were those granted, about the beginning of the present century, upon the importation of naval stores from America.[15] Under this denomination were comprehended timber fit for masts, yards, and bowsprits; hemp; tar,

[13] [Above, p. 594.]

[14] [10 Geo. III., c. 38, and 19 Geo. III., c. 27.]

[15] [3 and 4 Ann., c. 10.—Anderson, *Commerce*, A.D. 1703.]

Bounties on imported materials have been chiefly given to American produce, such as naval stores,

pitch, and turpentine. The bounty, however, of one pound the ton upon masting-timber, and that of six pounds the ton upon hemp, were extended to such as should be imported into England from Scotland.[16] Both these bounties continued without any variation, at the same rate, till they were severally allowed to expire; that upon hemp on the 1st of January 1741, and that upon masting timber at the end of the session of parliament immediately following the 24th June 1781.

The bounties upon the importation of tar, pitch, and turpentine underwent, during their continuance, several alterations. Originally that upon tar was four pounds the ton; that upon pitch the same; and that upon turpentine, three pounds the ton. The bounty of four pounds the ton upon tar was afterwards confined to such as had been prepared in a particular manner; that upon other good, clean, and merchantable tar was reduced to two pounds four shillings the ton. The bounty upon pitch was likewise reduced to one pound; and that upon turpentine to one pound ten shillings the ton.[17]

The second bounty upon the importation of any of the materials of manufacture, according to the order of time, was that

colonial indigo,

granted by the 21 Geo. II. chap. 30. upon the importation of indigo from the British plantations. When the plantation indigo was worth three-fourths of the price of the best French indigo, it was by this act entitled to a bounty of sixpence the pound. This bounty, which, like most others, was granted only for a limited time, was continued by several prolongations, but was reduced to four pence the pound.[18] It was allowed to expire with the end of the session of parliament which followed the 25th March 1781.

---

[16] [Masting-timber (and also tar, pitch and rosin), under 12 Ann, st. 1, c. 9, and masting-timber only under 2 Geo. II., c. 35, § 12. The encouragement of the growth of hemp in Scotland is mentioned in the preamble of 8 Geo. I., c. 12, and is presumably to be read into the enacting portion.]

[17] [8 Geo. I., c. 12; 2 Geo. II., c. 35, §§ 3, 11.]

[18] [3 Geo. III., c. 25.]

The third bounty of this kind was that granted (much about the time that we were beginning sometimes to court and some-

colonial hemp or undressed flax, times to quarrel with our American colonies) by the 4 Geo. III. chap. 26. upon the importation of hemp, or undressed flax, from the British plantations. This bounty was granted for twenty-one years, from the 24th June 1764, to the 24th June 1785. For the first seven years it was to be at the rate of eight pounds the ton, for the second at six pounds, and for the third at four pounds. It was not extended to Scotland, of which the climate (although hemp is sometimes raised there, in small quantities and of an inferior quality) is not very fit for that produce. Such a bounty upon the importation of Scotch flax into England would have been too great a discouragement to the native produce of the southern part of the united kingdom.

The fourth bounty of this kind, was that granted by the 5 Geo. III. chap. 45. upon the importation of wood from

American wood, America. It was granted for nine years, from the 1st January 1766, to the 1st January 1775. During the first three years, it was to be for every hundred and twenty good deals, at the rate of one pound; and for every load containing fifty cubic feet of other squared timber at the rate of twelve shillings. For the second three years, it was for deals to be at the rate of fifteen shillings, and for other squared timber, at the rate of eight shillings; and for the third three years, it was for deals, to be at the rate of ten shillings, and for other squared timber, at the rate of five shillings.

The fifth bounty of this kind, was that granted by the 9 Geo. III. chap. 38. upon the importation of raw silk from the British

colonial raw silk, plantations. It was granted for twenty-one years, from the 1st January 1770, to the 1st January 1791. For the first seven years it was to be at the rate of twenty-five pounds for every hundred pounds value; for the second, at twenty pounds; and for the third at fifteen pounds. The management of the silk-worm, and the preparation of silk, requires so much hand labour; and labour is so very dear in America, that even this great bounty, I have been informed, was not likely to produce any considerable effect.

The sixth bounty of this kind, was that granted by 11 Geo. III. chap. 50. for the importation of pipe, hogshead, and barrel *colonial barrel staves,* staves and heading from the British plantations. It was granted for nine years, from 1st January 1772, to the 1st January 1781. For the first three years, it was for a certain quantity of each, to be at the rate of six pounds; for the second three years, at four pounds; and for the third three years, at two pounds.

The seventh and last bounty of this kind, was that[19] granted by the 19 Geo. III. chap. 37. upon the importation of hemp *Irish hemp.* from Ireland. It was granted in the same manner as that for the importation of hemp and undressed flax from America,[20] for twenty-one years, from the 24th June 1779, to the 24th June 1800. This term is divided, likewise, into three periods of seven years each; and in each of those periods, the rate of the Irish bounty is the same with that of the American. It does not, however, like the American bounty, extend to the importation of undressed flax. It would have been too great a discouragement to the cultivation of that plant in Great Britain. When this last bounty was granted, the British and Irish legislatures were not in much better humour with one another, than the British and American had been before. But this boon to Ireland, it is to be hoped, has been granted under more fortunate auspices, than all those to America.

These commodities were subject to duties when coming from foreign countries. It was alleged that the interest of the colonies and of the mother country was the same. The same commodities upon which we thus gave bounties, when imported from America, were subjected to considerable duties when imported from any other country. The interest of our American colonies was regarded as the same with that of the mother country. Their wealth was considered as our wealth. Whatever money was sent out to them, it was said, came all back to us by the balance of trade, and we could never become

---

[19] [Additions and Corrections omits "that."]

[20] [The third bounty.]

a farthing the poorer, by any expence which we could lay out upon them. They were our own in every respect, and it was an expence laid out upon the improvement of our own property, and for the profitable employment of our own people. It is unnecessary, I apprehend, at present to say any thing further, in order to expose the folly of a system, which fatal experience has now sufficiently exposed. Had our American colonies really been a part of Great Britain, those bounties might have been considered as bounties upon production, and would still have been liable to all the objections to which such bounties are liable, but to no other.

The exportation of the materials of manufacture is sometimes discouraged by absolute prohibitions, and sometimes by high duties.

The exportation of wool and live sheep is forbidden under heavy penalties,

Our woollen manufacturers have been more successful than any other class of workmen, in persuading the legislature that the prosperity of the nation depended upon the success and extension of their particular business. They have not only obtained a monopoly against the consumers by an absolute prohibition of importing woollen cloths from any foreign country; but they have likewise obtained another monopoly against the sheep farmers and growers of wool, by a similar prohibition of the exportation of live sheep and wool. The severity of many of the laws which have been enacted for the security of the revenue is very justly complained of, as imposing heavy penalties upon actions which, antecedent to the statutes that declared them to be crimes, had always been understood to be innocent. But the cruellest of our revenue laws, I will venture to affirm, are mild and gentle, in comparison of some of those which the clamour of our merchants and manufacturers has extorted from the legislature, for the support of their own absurd and oppressive monopolies. Like the laws of Draco, these laws may be said to be all written in blood.

By the 8th of Elizabeth, chap. 3. the exporter of sheep, lambs or rams, was for the first offence to forfeit all his goods for ever, to suffer a year's imprisonment, and then to have his

at one time mutilation and death,

left hand cut off in a market town upon a market day, to be there nailed up; and for the second offence to be adjudged a felon, and to suffer death accordingly. To prevent the breed of our sheep from being propagated in foreign countries, seems to have been the object of this law. By the 13th and 14th of Charles II. chap. 18. the exportation of wool was made felony, and the exporter subjected to the same penalties and forfeitures as a felon.

For the honour of the national humanity, it is to be hoped that neither of these statutes were ever executed. The first of them, however, so far as I know, has never been directly repealed, and Serjeant Hawkins seems to consider it as still in force.[21] It may however, perhaps, be considered as virtually repealed by the 12th of Charles II. chap. 32. sect. 3. which, without expressly taking away the penalties imposed by former statutes,[22] imposes a new penalty, viz. That of twenty shillings for every sheep exported, or attempted to be exported, together with the forfeiture of the sheep and of the owner's share of the ship. The second of them was expressly repealed by the 7th and 8th of William III. chap. 28. sect. 4. By which it is declared that, "Whereas the statute of the 13th and 14th of King Charles II. made against the exportation of wool, among other things in the said act mentioned, doth enact the same to be deemed felony; by the severity of which penalty the prosecution of offenders hath not been so effectually put in execution: Be it, therefore, enacted by the authority foresaid, that so much of the said act, which relates to the making the said offence felony, be repealed and made void."

but now twenty shillings for every sheep with forfeiture of the sheep and the owner's share in the ship,

The penalties, however, which are either imposed by this milder statute, or which, though imposed by former statutes, are not repealed by this one, are still sufficiently severe.

[21] [William Hawkins, *Treatise of the Pleas of the Crown*, 4th ed., 1762, bk. i., chap. 52.]

[22] [So far from doing so, it expressly provides that any greater penalties already prescribed shall remain in force.]

and three shillings for every pound of wool, with other pains and penalties.

Besides the forfeiture of the goods, the exporter incurs the penalty of three shillings for every pound weight of wool either exported or attempted to be exported, that is about four or five times the value. Any merchant or other person convicted of this offence is disabled from requiring any debt or account belonging to him from any factor or other person.[23] Let his fortune be what it will, whether he is, or is not able to pay those heavy penalties, the law means to ruin him completely. But as the morals of the great body of the people are not yet so corrupt as those of the contrivers of this statute, I have not heard that any advantage has ever been taken of this clause. If the person convicted of this offence is not able to pay the penalties within three months after judgment, he is to be transported for seven years, and if he returns before the expiration of that term, he is liable to the pains of felony, without benefit of clergy.[24] The owner of the ship knowing this offence forfeits all his interest in the ship and furniture. The master and mariners knowing this offence forfeit all their goods and chattels, and suffer three months imprisonment. By a subsequent statute the master suffers six months imprisonment.[25]

In order to prevent exportation, the whole inland commerce of wool is laid under very burdensome and oppressive restrictions. It cannot be packed in any box, barrel, cask, case, chest, or any other package, but only in packs of leather or packcloth, on which must be marked on the outside the words *wool* or *yarn*, in large letters not less than three inches long, on pain of forfeiting the same and the package, and three shillings for every pound weight, to be paid by the owner

To prevent clandestine exportation the inland commerce of wool is much hampered by restrictions,

[23] [12 Car. II., c. 32.]

[24] [4 Geo. I., c. 11, § 6.]

[25] [Presumably the reference is to 10 and 11 W. III., c. 10, § 18, but this applies to the commander of a king's ship conniving at the offence, not to the master of the offending vessel.]

or packer.[26] It cannot be loaden on any horse or cart, or carried by land within five miles of the coast, but between sun-rising and sun-setting, on pain of forfeiting the same, the horses and carriages.[27] The hundred next adjoining to the sea coast, out of or through which the wool is carried or exported, forfeits twenty pounds, if the wool is under the value of ten pounds; and if of greater value, then treble that value, together with treble costs, to be sued for within the year. The execution to be against any two of the inhabitants, whom the sessions must reimburse, by an assessment on the other inhabitants, as in the cases of robbery. And if any person compounds with the hundred for less than this penalty, he is to be imprisoned for five years; and any other person may prosecute. These regulations take place through the whole kingdom.[28]

But in the particular counties of Kent and Sussex the restrictions are still more troublesome. Every owner of wool *especially in Kent and Sussex,* within ten miles of the sea-coast must give an account in writing, three days after shearing, to the next officer of the customs, of the number of his fleeces, and of the places where they are lodged. And before he removes any part of them he must give the like notice of the number and weight of the fleeces, and of the name and abode of the person to whom they are sold, and of the place to which it is intended they should be carried. No person within fifteen miles of the sea, in the said counties, can buy any wool, before he enters into bond to the king, that no part of the wool which he shall so buy shall be sold by him to any other person within fifteen miles of the sea. If any wool is found carrying towards the sea-side in the said counties, unless it has been entered and security given as aforesaid, it is forfeited, and

---

[26] [12 Geo. II., c. 21, § 10.]

[27] [13 and 14 Car. II., c. 18, § 9, forbade removal of wool in any part of the country between 8 P.M. and 4 A.M. from March to September, and 5 P.M. and 7 A.M. from October to February. 7 and 8 W. III., c. 28, § 8, taking no notice of this, enacted the pro ision quoted in the text. The provision of 13 and 14 Car. II., c. 18, was repealed by 20 Geo. III., c. 55, which takes no notice of 7 and 8 W. III., c. 28.]

[28] [All these provisions are from 7 and 8 W. III., c. 28.]

the offender also forfeits three shillings for every pound weight. If any person lays any wool, not entered as aforesaid, within fifteen miles of the sea, it must be seized and forfeited; and if, after such seizure, any person shall claim the same, he must give security to the Exchequer, that if he is cast upon trial he shall pay treble costs, besides all other penalties.[29]

When such restrictions are imposed upon the inland trade, the coasting trade, we may believe, cannot be left very free.

and so also is the coasting trade. Every owner of wool who carrieth or causeth to be carried any wool to any port or place on the sea-coast, in order to be from thence transported by sea to any other place or port on the coast, must first cause an entry thereof to be made at the port from whence it is intended to be conveyed, containing the weight, marks, and number of the packages before he brings the same within five miles of that port; on pain of forfeiting the same, and also the horses, carts, and other carriages; and also of suffering and forfeiting, as by the other laws in force against the exportation of wool. This law, however, (1 Will. III. chap. 32.) is so very indulgent as to declare, that "this shall not hinder any person from carrying his wool home from the place of shearing, though it be within five miles of the sea, provided that in ten days after shearing, and before he remove the wool, he do under his hand certify to the next officer of the customs, the true number of fleeces, and where it is housed; and do not remove the same, without certifying to such officer, under his hand, his intention so to do, three days before."[30] Bond must be given that the wool to be carried coastways is to be landed at the particular port for which it is entered outwards; and if any part of it is landed without the presence of an officer, not only the forfeiture of the wool is incurred as in other goods, but the usual additional penalty of three shillings for every pound weight is likewise incurred.

Our woollen manufacturers, in order to justify their demand of such extraordinary restrictions and regulations, confidently

---

[29] [9 and 10 W. III., c. 40.]

[30] [The quotation is not *verbatim.*]

The manufacturers alleged that English wool was superior to all others, which is entirely false.

asserted, that English wool was of a peculiar quality, superior to that of any other country; that the wool of other countries could not, without some mixture of it, be wrought up into any tolerable manufacture; that fine cloth could not be made without it; that England, therefore, if the exportation of it could be totally prevented, could monopolize to herself almost the whole woollen trade of the world; and thus, having no rivals, could sell at what price she pleased, and in a short time acquire the most incredible degree of wealth by the most advantageous balance of trade. This doctrine, like most other doctrines which are confidently asserted by any considerable number of people, was, and still continues to be, most implicitly believed by a much greater number; by almost all those who are either unacquainted with the woollen trade, or who have not made particular enquiries. It is, however, so perfectly false, that English wool is in any respect necessary for the making of fine cloth, that it is altogether unfit for it. Fine cloth is made altogether of Spanish wool. English wool cannot be even so mixed with Spanish wool as to enter into the composition without spoiling and degrading, in some degree, the fabric of the cloth.[31]

It has been shown in the foregoing part of this work,[32] that the effect of these regulations has been to depress the price of

These regulations have depressed the price of wool, as was desired,

English wool, not only below what it naturally would be in the present times, but very much below what it actually was in the time of Edward III. The price of Scots wool, when in consequence of the union it became subject to the same regulations, is said to have fallen about one half. It is observed by the very accurate and intelligent author of the Memoirs of Wool, the Reverend Mr. John Smith, that the price of the best English wool in England is generally below

---

[31] ["It is well known that the real very superfine cloth everywhere must be entirely of Spanish wool." Anderson, *Commerce*, A.D. 1669.]

[32] [Above, pp. 312, 313.]

what wool of a very inferior quality commonly sells for in the
market of Amsterdam.[33] To depress the price of this commodity
below what may be called its natural and proper price, was the
avowed purpose of those regulations; and there seems to be no
doubt of their having produced the effect that was expected
from them.

This reduction of price, it may perhaps be thought, by discouraging the growing of wool, must have reduced very much

but this has not much reduced the quantity of wool grown, the annual produce of that commodity,
though not below what it formerly was,
yet below what, in the present state of things,
it probably would have been, had it, in
consequence of an open and free market,
been allowed to rise to the natural and proper price. I am,
however, disposed to believe, that the quantity of the annual
produce cannot have been much, though it may perhaps have
been a little, affected by these regulations. The growing of
wool is not the chief purpose for which the sheep farmer
employs his industry and stock. He expects his profit, not
so much from the price of the fleece, as from that of the carcase; and the average or ordinary price of the latter, must even,
in many cases, make up to him whatever deficiency there may
be in the average or ordinary price of the former. It has been
observed in the foregoing part of this work, that "Whatever
regulations tend to sink the price, either of wool or of
raw hides, below what it naturally would be, must, in an improved and cultivated country, have some tendency to raise the
price of butchers meat. The price both of the great and small
cattle which are fed on improved and cultivated land, must
be sufficient to pay the rent which the landlord, and the profit
which the farmer has reason to expect from improved and
cultivated land. If it is not, they will soon cease to feed them.
Whatever part of this price, therefore, is not paid by the
wool and the hide, must be paid by the carcase. The less there
is paid for the one, the more must be paid for the other. In

[33] [*Chronicon Rusticum-Commerciale; or Memoirs of Wool*, etc., 1767, vol. ii., p.
418, note.]

what manner this price is to be divided upon the different parts of the beast, is indifferent to the landlords and farmers, provided it is all paid to them. In an improved and cultivated country, therefore, their interest as landlords and farmers cannot be much affected by such regulations, though their interest as consumers may, by the rise in the price of provisions."[34] According to this reasoning, therefore, this degradation in the price of wool is not likely, in an improved and cultivated country, to occasion any diminution in the annual produce of that commodity; except so far as, by raising the price of mutton, it may somewhat diminish the demand for, and consequently the production of, that particular species of butchers meat. Its effect, however, even in this way, it is probable, is not very considerable.

But though its effect upon the quantity of the annual produce may not have been very considerable,
nor its quality, its effect upon the quality, it may perhaps be thought, must necessarily have been very great. The degradation in the quality of English wool, if not below what it was in former times, yet below what it naturally would have been in the present state of improvement and cultivation, must have been, it may perhaps be supposed, very nearly in proportion to the degradation of price. As the quality depends upon the breed, upon the pasture, and upon the management and cleanliness of the sheep, during the whole progress of the growth of the fleece, the attention to these circumstances, it may naturally enough be imagined, can never be greater than in proportion to the recompence which the price of the fleece is likely to make for the labour and expence which that attention requires. It happens, however, that the goodness of the fleece depends, in a great measure, upon the health, growth, and bulk of the animal; the same attention which is necessary for the improvement of the carcase, is, in some respects, sufficient for that of the fleece. Notwithstanding the degradation of price, English wool is said to have been improved considerably

[34] [Above, p. 316.]

during the course even of the present century. The improvement might perhaps have been greater if the price had been better; but the lowness of price, though it may have obstructed, yet certainly it has not altogether prevented that improvement.

The violence of these regulations, therefore, seems to have affected neither the quantity nor the quality of the annual produce of wool so much as it might have been expected to do (though I think it probable that it may have affected the latter a good deal more than the former); and the interest of the growers of wool, though it must have been hurt in some degree, seems, upon the whole, to have been much less hurt than could well have been imagined.

so that the growers of wool have been less hurt than might have been expected.

These considerations, however, will not justify the absolute prohibition of the exportation of wool.[35] But they will fully justify the imposition of a considerable tax upon that exportation.

Though prohibition of exportation cannot be justified, a duty on the exportation of wool might furnish revenue with little inconvenience.

To hurt in any degree the interest of any one order of citizens, for no other purpose but to promote that of some other, is evidently contrary to that justice and equality of treatment which the sovereign owes to all the different orders of his subjects. But the prohibition certainly hurts, in some degree, the interest of the growers of wool, for no other purpose but to promote that of the manufacturers.

Every different order of citizens is bound to contribute to the support of the sovereign or commonwealth. A tax of five, or even of ten shillings upon the exportation of every tod of wool, would produce a very considerable revenue to the sovereign. It would hurt the interest of the growers somewhat less than the prohibition, because it would not probably lower the price of wool quite so much. It would afford a sufficient advantage to the manufacturer, because, though he

---

[35] [Additions and Corrections reads "the wool."]

might not buy his wool altogether so cheap as under the prohibition, he would still buy it, at least, five or ten shillings
cheaper than any foreign manufacturer could buy it, besides
saving the freight and insurance, which the other would
be obliged to pay. It is scarce possible to devise a tax which
could produce any considerable revenue to the sovereign,
and at the same time occasion so little inconveniency to any
body.

The prohibition, notwithstanding all the penalties which
guard it, does not prevent the exportation of wool. It is exported, it is well known, in great quantities. The great difference between the price in the home and that in the foreign
market, presents such a temptation to smuggling, that all the
rigour of the law cannot prevent it. This illegal exportation is
advantageous to nobody but the smuggler. A legal exportation
subject to a tax, by affording a revenue to the sovereign, and
thereby saving the imposition of some other, perhaps, more
burdensome and inconvenient taxes, might prove advantageous to all the different subjects of the state.

The exportation of fuller's earth, or fuller's clay, supposed
to be necessary for preparing and cleansing
The exportation of the woollen manufactures, has been sub-
fuller's earth has jected to nearly the same penalties as the ex-
been subjected to portation of wool.[36] Even tobacco-pipe clay,
the same penalties though acknowledged to be different from
as the exportation fuller's clay, yet, on account of their resem-
of wool. blance, and because fuller's clay might
sometimes be exported as tobacco-pipe clay, has been laid
under the same prohibitions and penalties.[37]

The exportation By the 13th and 14th of Charles II. chap.
of raw hides is 7. the exportation, not only of raw hides, but
forbidden, of tanned leather, except in the shape
of boots, shoes, or slippers, was prohib-

---

[36] [12 Car. II., c. 32; 13 and 14 Car. II., c. 18.]

[37] [13 and 14 Car. II., c. 18, § 8. The preamble to the clause alleges that "great
quantities of fuller's earth or fulling clay are daily carried and exported under the
colour of tobacco-pipe clay."]

ited;[38] and the law gave a monopoly to our boot-makers and shoe-makers, not only against our graziers, but against our tanners. By subsequent statutes, our tanners have got themselves exempted from this monopoly, upon paying a small tax of only one shilling on the hundred weight of tanned leather, weighing one hundred and twelve pounds.[39] They have obtained likewise the drawback of two-thirds of the excise duties imposed upon their commodity, even when exported without further manufacture. All manufactures of leather may be exported duty free; and the exporter is besides entitled to the drawback of the whole duties of excise.[40] Our graziers still continue subject to the old monopoly. Graziers separated from one another, and dispersed through all the different corners of the country, cannot, without great difficulty, combine together for the purpose either of imposing monopolies upon their fellow-citizens, or of exempting themselves from such as may have been imposed upon them by other people.[41] Manufacturers of all kinds, collected together in numerous bodies in all great cities, easily can. Even the horns of cattle are prohibited to be exported;[42] and the two insignificant trades of the horner and combmaker enjoy, in this respect, a monopoly against the graziers.

horns,

Restraints, either by prohibitions or by taxes, upon the exportation of goods which are partially, but not completely

---

[38] [The preamble says that "nowithstanding the many good laws before this time made and still in force, prohibiting the exportation of leather . . . by the cunning and subtlety of some persons and the neglect of others to take care there of; there are such quantities of leather daily exported to foreign parts that the price of leather is grown to those excessive rates that many artificers working leather cannot furnish themselves with sufficient stock thereof for the carrying on of their trades, and the poor sort of people are not able to buy those things made of leather which of necessity they must make use of."]

[39] [20 Car. II., c. 5; 9 Ann., c. 6, § 4.]

[40] [9 Ann., c. 11, § 39, explained by 10 Ann., c. 26, § 6, and 12 Ann., st. 2, c. 9, § 64.]

[41] [Above, p. 174.]

[42] [Except under certain conditions by 4 Ed. IV., c. 8; wholly by 7 Jac. I., c. 14, § 4.]

woollen yarn and worsted, white cloths, watch cases, etc., also manufactured, are not peculiar to the manufacture of leather. As long as any thing remains to be done, in order to fit any commodity for immediate use and consumption, our manufacturers think that they themselves ought to have the doing of it. Woollen yarn and worsted are prohibited to be exported under the same penalties as wool.[43] Even white cloths are subject to a duty upon exportation,[44] and our dyers have so far obtained a monopoly against our clothiers. Our clothiers would probably have been able to defend themselves against it, but it happens that the greater part of our principal clothiers are themselves likewise dyers. Watch-cases, clock-cases, and dial-plates for clocks and watches, have been prohibited to be exported.[45] Our clock-makers and watch-makers are, it seems, unwilling that the price of this sort of workmanship should be raised upon them by the competition of foreigners.

By some old statutes of Edward III., Henry VIII., and Edward VI.,[46] the exportation of all metals was prohibited. *some metals.* Lead and tin were alone excepted; probably on account of the great abundance of those metals; in the exportation of which, a considerable part of the trade of the kingdom in those days consisted. For the encouragement of the mining trade, the 5th of William and Mary, chap. 17. exempted from this prohibition, iron, copper, and mundic metal made from British ore. The exportation of all sorts of copper bars, foreign as well as British, was afterwards permitted by the 9th and 10th of William III. chap. 26.[47] The

[43] [Under 13 and 14 Car. II., c. 18, and 7 and 8 W. III., c. 28; above, pp. 822, 823.]

[44] [See below, next page.]

[45] [9 and 10 W. III., c. 28, professedly to prevent frauds.]

[46] [The preamble to the Act next quoted in the text mentions 28 Ed. III., c. 5 (iron); 33 Hen. VIII., c. 7 (brass, copper, etc.), and 2 and 3 Ed. VI., c. 37 (bell-metal, etc.).]

[47] [This Act is not printed in the ordinary collections, but the provision referred to is in Pickering's index, *s.v.* Copper, and the clause is recited in a renewing Act, 12 Ann., st. 1, c. 18.]

exportation of unmanufactured brass, of what is called gun-metal, bell-metal, and shroff-metal, still continues to be prohibited. Brass manufactures of all sorts may be exported duty free.[48]

On various other materials of manufacture considerable export duties are imposed.

The exportation of the materials of manufacture, where it is not altogether prohibited, is in many cases subjected to considerable duties.

By the 8th George I. chap. 15., the exportation of all goods, the produce or manufacture of Great Britain, upon which any duties had been imposed by former statutes, was rendered duty free. The following goods, however, were excepted: Alum, lead, lead ore, tin, tanned leather, copperas, coals, wool cards, white woollen cloths, lapis calaminaris, skins of all sorts, glue, coney hair or wool, hare's wool, hair of all sorts, horses, and litharge of lead. If you except horses, all these are either materials of manufacture, or incomplete manufactures (which may be considered as materials for still further manufacture), or instruments of trade. This statute leaves them subject to all the old duties which had ever been imposed upon them, the old subsidy and one per cent. outwards.[49]

By the same statute a great number of foreign drugs for dyers' use, are exempted from all duties upon importation. Each of them, however, is afterwards subjected to a certain duty, not indeed a very heavy one, upon exportation.[50] Our dyers, it seems, while they thought it for their interest to encourage the importation of those drugs, by an exemption from all duties, thought it likewise for their interest to throw some small discouragement upon their exportation. The avidity however, which suggested this notable piece of mercantile ingenuity, most probably disappointed itself of its object. It nec-

[48] [Under the general Act, 8 Geo. I., c. 15, mentioned immediately below.]

[49] [12 Car. II., c. 4, § 2, and 14 Car. II., c. 11, § 35. The 1 per cent was due on goods exported to ports in the Mediterranean beyond Malaga, unless the ship had sixteen guns and other warlike equipment. See Saxby, British Customs, pp. 48, 51.]

[50] [Sixpence in the pound on the values at which they are rated in the Act.]

essarily taught the importers to be more careful than they might otherwise have been, that their importation should not exceed what was necessary for the supply of the home market. The home market was at all times likely to be more scantily supplied; the commodities were at all times likely to be somewhat dearer there than they would have been, had the exportation been rendered as free as the importation.

By the above-mentioned statute, gum senega, or gum arabic, being among the enumerated dying drugs, might be

Gum senega has a peculiar history and is subject to a large export duty,

imported duty free. They were subjected, indeed, to a small poundage duty, amounting only to three pence in the hundred weight upon their reexportation. France enjoyed, at that time, an exclusive trade to the country most productive of those drugs, that which lies in the neighbourhood of the Senegal; and the British market could not be easily supplied by the immediate importation of them from the place of growth. By the 25th Geo. II.[51] therefore, gum senega was allowed to be imported (contrary to the general dispositions of the act of navigation), from any part of Europe. As the law, however, did not mean to encourage this species of trade, so contrary to the general principles of the mercantile policy of England, it imposed a duty of ten shillings the hundred weight upon such importation; and no part of this duty was to be afterwards drawn back upon its exportation. The successful war which began in 1755 gave Great Britain the same exclusive trade to those countries which France had enjoyed before.[52] Our manufacturers, as soon as the peace was made, endeavoured to avail themselves of this advantage, and to establish a monopoly in their own favour, both against the growers, and against the importers of this commodity. By the 5th Geo. III. therefore, chap. 37. the exportation of gum senega from his majesty's dominions in Africa was confined to Great Britain, and was subjected to all the same restrictions, regulations, forfeitures and penalties, as that of the enumerated commodities of the British

[51] [C. 32.]

[52] [Anderson, *Commerce*, A.D. 1758.]

colonies in America and the West Indies. Its importation, indeed, was subjected to a small duty of six-pence the hundred weight, but its re-exportation was subjected to the enormous duty of one pound ten shillings the hundred weight. It was the intention of our manufacturers that the whole produce of those countries should be imported into Great Britain, and in order that they themselves might be enabled to buy it at their own price, that no part of it should be exported again, but at such an expence as would sufficiently discourage that exportation. Their avidity, however, upon this, as well as upon many other occasions, disappointed itself of its object. This enormous duty presented such a temptation to smuggling, that great quantities of this commodity were clandestinely exported, probably to all the manufacturing countries of Europe, but particularly to Holland, not only from Great Britain but from Africa. Upon this account,[53] by the 14 Geo. III. chap. 10. this duty upon exportation was reduced to five shillings the hundred weight.

In the book of rates, according to which the old subsidy was levied, beaver skins were estimated at six shillings and

beaver skins exported are charged seven pence,

eight-pence a-piece, and the different subsidies and imposts, which before the year 1722 had been laid upon their importation, amounted to one-fifth part of the rate, or to sixteen-pence upon each skin;[54] all of which, except half the old subsidy, amounting only to two-pence, was drawn back upon exportation.[55] This duty upon the importation of so important a material of manufacture had been thought too high, and, in the year 1722, the rate was reduced to two shillings and six-pence, which reduced the duty upon importation to six-pence, and of this only one half was to be drawn back upon exportation.[56] The same successful war

[53] [As is stated in the preamble.]

[54] [The facts are given in the preamble to 8 Geo. I., c. 15, § 13. The old subsidy, the new, the one-third and the two-third subsidies account for 1s., and the additional impost for 4d.]

[55] [See above, p. 629.]

[56] [8 Geo. I., c. 15. The year should be 1721.]

put the country most productive of beaver under the dominion of Great Britain, and beaver skins being among the enumerated commodities, their exportation from America was consequently confined to the market of Great Britain. Our manufacturers[57] soon bethought themselves of the advantage which they might make of this circumstance, and in the year 1764,[58] the duty upon the importation of beaver-skin was reduced to one penny, but the duty upon exportation was raised to seven-pence each skin, without any drawback of the duty upon importation. By the same law, a duty of eighteen pence the pound was imposed upon the exportation of beaver-wool or wombs, without making any alteration in the duty upon the importation of that commodity, which when imported by British and in British shipping, amounted at that time to between four-pence and five-pence the piece.

Coals may be considered both as a material of manufacture and as an instrument of trade. Heavy duties, accordingly, have
and coals five shillings a ton. been imposed upon their exportation, amounting at present (1783) to more than five shillings the ton, or to more than fifteen shillings the chaldron, Newcastle measure; which is in most cases more than the original value of the commodity at the coal pit, or even at the shipping port for exportation.

The exportation, however, of the instruments of trade, properly so called, is commonly restrained, not by high duties, but
The exportation of the instruments of trade is commonly prohibited. by absolute prohibitions. Thus by the 7th and 8th of William III. chap. 20. sect. 8. the exportation of frames or engines for knitting gloves or stockings is prohibited under the penalty, not only of the forfeiture of such frames or engines, so exported, or attempted to be exported, but of forty pounds, one half to the king, the other to the person who shall inform or sue for the same. In the same manner by the 14th Geo. III. chap. 71. the exportation to foreign parts, of any utensils made use of in the cotton, linen, woollen and silk

[57] [*I.e.* the hatters.]

[58] [4 Geo. III., c. 9.]

manufactures, is prohibited under the penalty, not only of the forfeiture of such utensils, but of two hundred pounds, to be paid by the person who shall offend in this manner, and likewise of two hundred pounds to be paid by the master of the ship who shall knowingly suffer such utensils to be loaded on board his ship. When such heavy penalties were imposed upon the exportation of the dead instruments of trade, it could not well be expected that the living instrument, the artificer, should be allowed to go free.

Similarly it is a grave offence to entice an artificer abroad,

Accordingly, by the 5 Geo. I. chap. 27. the person who shall be convicted of enticing any artificer of, or in any of the manufactures of Great Britain, to go into any foreign parts, in order to practise or teach his trade, is liable for the first offence to be fined in any sum not exceeding one hundred pounds, and to three months imprisonment, and until the fine shall be paid; and for the second offence, to be fined in any sum at the discretion of the court, and to imprisonment for twelve months, and until the fine shall be paid. By the 23 Geo. II. chap. 13. this penalty is increased for the first offence to five hundred pounds for every artificer so enticed, and to twelve months imprisonment, and until the fine shall be paid; and for the second offence, to one thousand pounds, and to two years imprisonment, and until the fine shall be paid.

By the former of those two statutes, upon proof that any person has been enticing any artificer, or that any artificer has promised or contracted to go into foreign parts for the purposes aforesaid, such artificer may be obliged to give security at the discretion of the court, that he shall not go beyond the seas, and may be committed to prison until he give such security.

If any artificer has gone beyond the seas, and is exercising or teaching his trade in any foreign country, upon warning being given to him by any of his majesty's ministers or consuls abroad, or by one of his majesty's secretaries of state for the time being, if he does not, within six months after such warning, return into this realm, and from thenceforth abide and inhabit continu-

and the artificer who exercises or teaches his trade abroad may be ordered to return.

ally within the same, he is from thenceforth declared incapable of taking any legacy devised to him within this kingdom, or of being executor or administrator to any person, or of taking any lands within this kingdom by descent, devise, or purchase. He likewise forfeits to the king, all his lands, goods and chattels, is declared an alien in every respect, and is put out of the king's protection.[59]

It is unnecessary, I imagine, to observe, how contrary such regulations are to the boasted liberty of the subject, of which we affect to be so very jealous; but which, in this case, is so plainly sacrificed to the futile interests of our merchants and manufacturers.

The laudable motive of all these regulations, is to extend our own manufactures, not by their own improvement, but by the depression of those of all our neighbours, and by putting an end, as much as possible, to the troublesome competition of such odious and disagreeable rivals. Our master manufacturers think it reasonable, that they themselves should have the monopoly of the ingenuity of all their countrymen. Though by restraining, in some trades, the number of apprentices which can be employed at one time, and by imposing the necessity of a long apprenticeship in all trades, they endeavour, all of them, to confine the knowledge of their respective employments to as small a number as possible; they are unwilling, however, that any part of this small number should go abroad to instruct foreigners.

The object is to depress the manufactures of our neighbours.

Consumption is the sole end and purpose of all production; and the interest of the producer ought to be attended to, only so far as it may be necessary for promoting that of the consumer. The maxim is so perfectly self-evident, that it would be absurd to attempt to prove it. But in the mercantile system, the interest of the consumer is almost constantly sacrificed to that of the producer; and it seems to consider production, and not

The mercantile system absurdly considers production and not consumption to be the end of industry and commerce.

[59] [Under the same statute, 5 Geo. I., c. 27.]

consumption, as the ultimate end and object of all industry and commerce.

In the restraints upon the importation of all foreign com-

Restraints on importation of competing commodities sacrifice the interest of the consumer to the producer,

modities which can come into competition with those of our own growth, or manufacture, the interest of the home-consumer is evidently sacrificed to that of the producer. It is altogether for the benefit of the latter, that the former is obliged to pay that enhancement of price which this monopoly almost always occasions.

It is altogether for the benefit of the producer that bounties are granted upon the exportation of some of his productions.

and so do bounties on exportation and the provisions of the Methuen treaty,

The home-consumer is obliged to pay, first, the tax which is necessary for paying the bounty, and secondly, the still greater tax which necessarily arises from the enhancement of the price of the commodity in the home market.

By the famous treaty of commerce with Portugal,[60] the consumer is prevented by high duties from purchasing of a neighbouring country, a commodity which our own climate does not produce, but is obliged to purchase it of a distant country, though it is acknowledged, that the commodity of the distant country is of a worse quality than that of the near one. The home-consumer is obliged to submit to this inconveniency, in order that the producer may import into the distant country some of his productions upon more advantageous terms than he would otherwise have been allowed to do. The consumer, too, is obliged to pay, whatever enhancement in the price of those very productions, this forced exportation may occasion in the home market.

But in the system of laws which has been established for the management of our American and West Indian colonies, the interest of the home-consumer has been sacrificed to that of the producer with a more extravagant profusion than in all our other

[60] [Above, p. 689.]

but the most extravagant case of all is that of the management of the American and West Indian colonies.

commercial regulations. A great empire has been established for the sole purpose of raising up a nation of customers who should be obliged to buy from the shops of our different producers, all the goods with which these could supply them. For the sake of that little enhancement of price which this monopoly might afford our producers, the home-consumers have been burdened with the whole expence of maintaining and defending that empire. For this purpose, and for this purpose only, in the two last wars, more than two hundred millions have been spent, and a new debt of more than a hundred and seventy millions has been contracted over and above all that had been expended for the same purpose in former wars. The interest of this debt alone is not only greater than the whole extraordinary profit, which, it ever could be pretended, was made by the monopoly of the colony trade, but than the whole value of that trade, or than the whole value of the goods, which at an average have been annually exported to the colonies.

It cannot be very difficult to determine who have been the contrivers of this whole mercantile system; not the consumers,

The contrivers of the whole mercantile system are the producers and especially the merchants and manufacturers.

we may believe, whose interest has been entirely neglected; but the producers, whose interest has been so carefully attended to; and among this latter class our merchants and manufacturers have been by far the principal architects. In the mercantile regulations, which have been taken notice of in this chapter, the interest of our manufacturers has been most peculiarly attended to; and the interest, not so much of the consumers, as that of some other sets of producers, has been sacrificed to it.[61]

---

[61] [This chapter appears first in Additions and Corrections and ed. 3, and is doubtless largely due to Smith's appointment in 1778 to the Commissionership of Customs (Rae, *Life of Adam Smith*, p. 320). He had in his library W. Sims and R. Frewin, *The Rates of Merchandise*, 1782 (see Bonar, *Catalogue*, p. 27), and probably had access to earlier works such as Saxby's *British Customs*, 1757, which give the duties, etc., at earlier periods as well as references to the Acts of Parliament regulating them.]

CHAPTER IX

OF THE AGRICULTURAL SYSTEMS, OR OF THOSE SYSTEMS OF POLITICAL ŒCONOMY, WHICH REPRESENT THE PRODUCE OF LAND AS EITHER THE SOLE OR THE PRINCIPAL SOURCE OF THE REVENUE AND WEALTH OF EVERY COUNTRY

THE AGRICULTURAL systems of political œconomy will not require so long an explanation as that which I have thought it necessary to bestow upon the mercantile or commercial system.

The agricultural systems will require less lengthy explanation than the mercantile system.

That system which represents the produce of land as the sole source of the revenue and wealth of every country has, so far as I know, never been adopted by any nation, and it at present exists only in the speculations of a few men of great learning and ingenuity in France.[1] It would not, surely, be worth while to examine at great length the errors of a system which never has done, and probably never will do any harm in any part of the world. I shall endeavour to explain, however, as distinctly as I can, the great outlines of this very ingenious system.

Colbert adopted the mercantile system and favoured town industry,

Mr. Colbert, the famous minister of Lewis XIV. was a man of probity, of great industry and knowledge of detail; of great experience and acuteness in the examination of public accounts, and of abilities, in short, every way fitted for introducing method and

[1] [The Économistes or Physiocrats. Quesnay, Mirabeau and Mercier de la Rivière are mentioned below, pp. 856, 863.]

good order into the collection and expenditure of the public revenue. That minister had unfortunately embraced all the prejudices of the mercantile system, in its nature and essence a system of restraint and regulation, and such as could scarce fail[2] to be agreeable to a laborious and plodding man of business, who had been accustomed to regulate the different departments of public offices, and to establish the necessary checks and controls for confining each to its proper sphere. The industry and commerce of a great country he endeavoured to regulate upon the same model as the departments of a public office; and instead of allowing every man to pursue his own interest his own way, upon the liberal plan of equality, liberty and justice, he bestowed upon certain branches of industry extraordinary privileges, while he laid others under as extraordinary restraints. He was not only disposed, like other European ministers, to encourage more the industry of the towns than that of the country; but, in order to support the industry of the towns, he was willing even to depress and keep down that of the country. In order to render provisions cheap to the inhabitants of the towns, and thereby to encourage manufactures and foreign commerce, he prohibited altogether the exportation of corn, and thus excluded the inhabitants of the country from every foreign market for by far the most important part of the produce of their industry. This prohibition, joined to the restraints imposed by the ancient provincial laws of France upon the transportation of corn from one province to another, and to the arbitrary and degrading taxes which are levied upon the cultivators in almost all the provinces, discouraged and kept down the agriculture of that country very much below the state to which it would naturally have risen in so very fertile a soil and so very happy a climate. This state of discouragement and depression was felt more or less in every different part of the country, and many different inquiries were set on foot concerning the causes of it. One of those causes appeared to be the preference given, by the insti-

[2] [Ed. 1 places a full stop at "mercantile system" and continues "That system, in its nature and essence a system of restraint and regulation, could scarce fail."]

tutions of Mr. Colbert, to the industry of the towns above that of the country.

If the rod be bent too much one way, says the proverb, in order to make it straight you must bend it as much the other.

with the result that the French philosophers who support the agricultural system undervalue town industry.

The French philosophers, who have proposed the system which represents agriculture as the sole source of the revenue and wealth of every country, seem to have adopted this proverbial maxim; and as in the plan of Mr. Colbert the industry of the towns was certainly over-valued in comparison with that of the country; so in their system it seems to be as certainly under-valued.

The different orders of people who have ever been supposed to contribute in any respect towards the annual produce of the land and labour of the country, they divide into three classes. The first is the class of the proprietors of land. The second is the class of the cultivators, of farmers and country labourers, whom they honour with the peculiar appellation of the productive class. The third is the class of artificers, manufacturers and merchants, whom they endeavour to degrade by the humiliating appellation[3] of the barren or unproductive class.

There are three classes in their system: (1) proprietors, (2) cultivators, and (3) artificers, manufacturers and merchants.

Proprietors contribute to production by expenses on improvement of land,

The class of proprietors contributes to the annual produce by the expence which they may occasionally lay out upon the improvement of the land, upon the buildings, drains, enclosures and other ameliorations, which they may either make or maintain upon it,

---

[3] [But, see below, p. 850, where the usefulness of the class is said to be admitted. In his exposition of physiocratic doctrine, Smith does not appear to follow any particular book closely. His library contained Du Pont's *Physiocratie, ou constitution naturelle du gouvernement le plus avantageux au genre humain*, 1768 (see Bonar, *Catalogue*, p. 92), and he refers lower down to La Rivière, *L'ordre naturel et essentiel des sociétés politiques*, 1767, but he probably relied largely on his recollection of conversations in Paris; see Rae, *Life of Adam Smith*, pp. 215–222.]

and by means of which the cultivators are enabled, with the same capital, to raise a greater produce, and consequently to pay a greater rent. This advanced rent may be considered as the interest or profit due to the proprietor upon the expence or capital which he thus employs in the improvement of his land. Such expences are in this system called ground expences (depenses foncieres).

The cultivators or farmers contribute to the annual produce by what are in this system called the original and annual expences (depenses primitives et depenses annuelles) which they lay out upon the cultivation of the land. The original expences consist in the instruments of husbandry, in the stock of cattle, in the seed, and in the maintenance of the farmer's family, servants and cattle, during at least a great part of the first year of his occupancy, or till he can receive some return from the land. The annual expences consist in the seed, in the wear and tear[4] of the instruments of husbandry, and in the annual maintenance of the farmer's servants and cattle, and of his family too, so far as any part of them can be considered as servants employed in cultivation. That part of the produce of the land which remains to him after paying the rent, ought to be sufficient, first, to replace to him within a reasonable time, at least during the term of his occupancy, the whole of his original expences, together with the ordinary profits of stock; and, secondly, to replace to him annually the whole of his annual expences, together likewise with the ordinary profits of stock. Those two sorts of expences are two capitals which the farmer employs in cultivation; and unless they are regularly restored to him, together with a reasonable profit, he cannot carry on his employment upon a level with other employments but, from a regard to his own interest, must desert it as soon as possible, and seek some other.[5] That part of the produce of the land which is thus necessary for enabling the farmer to continue his business, ought to be consid-

cultivators, by original and annual expenses of cultivation.

---

[4] [Ed. 1 reads "tear and wear."]

[5] [Ed. 1 reads "some other employment."]

ered as a fund sacred to cultivation, which if the landlord violates, he necessarily reduces[6] the produce of his own land, and in a few years not only disables the farmer from paying this racked rent, but from paying the reasonable rent which he might otherwise have got for his land. The rent which properly belongs to the landlord, is no more than the neat produce which remains after paying in the completest manner all the necessary expences which must be previously laid out in order to raise the gross, or the whole produce. It is because the labour of the cultivators, over and above paying completely all those necessary expences, affords a neat produce of this kind, that this class of people are in this system peculiarly distinguished by the honourable appellation of the productive class. Their original and annual expences are for the same reason called, in this system, productive expences, because, over and above replacing their own value, they occasion the annual reproduction of this neat produce.

The ground expences, as they are called, or what the landlord lays out upon the improvement of his land, are in this system too honoured with the appellation of productive expences. Till the whole of those expences, together with the ordinary profits of stock, have been completely repaid to him by the advanced rent which he gets from his land, that advanced rent ought to be regarded as sacred and inviolable, both by the church and by the king; ought to be subject neither to tithe nor to taxation. If it is otherwise, by discouraging the improvement of land, the church discourages the future increase of her own tithes, and the king the future increase of his own taxes. As in a well-ordered state of things, therefore, those ground expences, over and above reproducing in the completest manner their own value, occasion likewise after a certain time a reproduction of a neat produce, they are in this system considered as productive expences.

These expenses should be free from all taxation.

The ground expences of the landlord, however, together with the original and the annual expences of the farmer, are the

[6] [Ed. 1 reads "degrades."]

All other expenses and orders of people are unproductive, only three sorts of expences which in this system are considered as productive. All other expences and all other orders of people, even those who in the common apprehensions of men are regarded as the most productive, are in this account of things represented as altogether barren and unproductive.

Artificers and manufacturers, in particular, whose industry, in the common apprehensions of men, increases so much the value of the rude produce of land, are in this system represented as a class of people altogether barren and unproductive. Their labour, it is said, replaces only the stock which employs them, together with its ordinary profits. That stock consists in the materials, tools, and wages, advanced to them by their employer; and is the fund destined for their employment and maintenance. Its profits are the fund destined for the maintenance of their employer. Their employer, as he advances to them the stock of materials, tools and wages necessary for their employment, so he advances to himself what is necessary for his own maintenance, and this maintenance he generally proportions to the profit which he expects to make by the price of their work. Unless its price repays to him the maintenance which he advances to himself, as well as the materials, tools and wages which he advances to his workmen, it evidently does not repay to him[7] the whole expence which he lays out upon it. The profits of manufacturing stock, therefore, are not, like the rent of land, a neat produce which remains after completely repaying the whole expence which must be laid out in order to obtain them. The stock of the farmer yields him a profit as well as that of the master manufacturer; and it yields a rent likewise to another person, which that of the master manufacturer does not. The expence, therefore, laid out in employing and maintaining artificers and manufacturers, does no more than continue, if one may say so, the existence of its own value, and does not produce any new value. It is

artificers and manufacturers in particular, and the expense of employing them:

[7] [Ed. 1 reads "repay him."]

therefore altogether a barren and unproductive expence. The expence, on the contrary, laid out in employing farmers and country labourers, over and above continuing the existence of its own value, produces a new value, the rent of the landlord. It is therefore a productive expence.

Mercantile stock is equally barren and unproductive with manufacturing stock. It only continues the existence of its own value, without producing any new value. Its profits are only the repayment of the maintenance which its employer advances to himself during the time that he employs it, or till he receives the returns of it. They are only the repayment of a part of the expence which must be laid out in employing it.

mercantile stock also.

The labour of artificers and manufacturers never adds any thing to the value of the whole annual amount of the rude produce of the land. It adds indeed greatly to the value of some particular parts of it. But the consumption which in the mean time it occasions of other parts, is precisely equal to the value which it adds to those parts; so that the value of the whole amount is not, at any one moment of time, in the least augmented by it. The person who works the lace of a pair of fine ruffles, for example, will sometimes raise the value of perhaps a pennyworth of flax to thirty pounds sterling. But though at first sight he appears thereby to multiply the value of a part of the rude produce about seven thousand two hundred times, he in reality adds nothing to the value of the whole annual amount of the rude produce. The working of that lace costs him perhaps two years labour. The thirty pounds which he gets for it when it is finished, is no more than the repayment of the subsistence which he advances to himself during the two years that he is employed about it. The value which, by every day's, month's, or year's labour, he adds to the flax, does no more than replace the value of his own consumption during that day, month, or year. At no moment of time, therefore, does he add any thing to the value of the whole annual amount of the rude produce of the land: the portion of that produce which he is continually

The labour of artificers and manufacturers adds nothing to the value of the annual produce.

consuming, being always equal to the value which he is continually producing. The extreme poverty of the greater part of the persons employed in this expensive, though trifling manufacture, may satisfy us that the price of their work does not in ordinary cases exceed the value of their subsistence. It is otherwise with the work of farmers and country labourers. The rent of the landlord is a value, which, in ordinary cases, is continually producing, over and above replacing, in the most complete manner, the whole consumption, the whole expence laid out upon the employment and maintenance both of the workmen and of their employer.

Artificers, manufacturers and merchants, can augment the revenue and wealth of their society, by parsimony only; or, as it is expressed in this system, by privation, that is, by depriving themselves of a part of the funds destined for their own subsistence. They annually reproduce nothing but those funds. Unless, therefore, they annually save some part of them, unless they annually deprive themselves of the enjoyment of some part of them, the revenue and wealth of their society can never be in the smallest degree augmented by means of their industry. Farmers and country labourers, on the contrary, may enjoy completely the whole funds destined for their own subsistence, and yet augment at the same time the revenue and wealth of their society. Over and above what is destined[8] for their own subsistence, their industry annually affords a neat produce, of which the augmentation necessarily augments the revenue and wealth of their society. Nations, therefore, which, like France or England, consist in a great measure of proprietors and cultivators, can be enriched by industry and enjoyment. Nations, on the contrary, which, like Holland and Hamburgh, are composed chiefly of merchants, artificers and manufacturers, can grow rich only through parsimony and privation. As the interest of nations so differently circumstanced, is very different, so is likewise the common character of the people. In those of the

Artificers, manufacturers and merchants can augment revenue only by privation.

---

[8] [Ed. 1 reads "above the funds destined."]

former kind, liberality, frankness, and good fellowship, naturally make a part of that common character. In the latter, narrowness, meanness, and a selfish disposition, averse to all social pleasure and enjoyment.

The unproductive class, that of merchants, artificers and manufacturers, is maintained and employed altogether at the

The unproductive class is maintained at the expense of the other two,

expence of the two other classes, of that of proprietors, and of that of cultivators. They furnish it both with the materials of its work and with the fund of its subsistence, with the corn and cattle which it consumes while it is employed about that work. The proprietors and cultivators finally pay both the wages of all the workmen of the unproductive class, and the profits of all their employers. Those workmen and their employers are properly the servants of the proprietors and cultivators. They are only servants who work without doors, as menial servants work within. Both the one and the other, however, are equally maintained at the expence of the same masters. The labour of both is equally unproductive. It adds nothing to the value of the sum total of the rude produce of the land. Instead of increasing the value of that sum total, it is a charge and expence which must be paid out of it.

The unproductive class, however, is not only useful, but greatly useful to the other two classes. By means of the indus-

but is useful to them,

try of merchants, artificers and manufacturers, the proprietors and cultivators can purchase both the foreign goods and the manufactured produce of their own country which they have occasion for, with the produce of a much smaller quantity of their own labour, than what they would be obliged to employ, if they were to attempt, in an awkward and unskilful manner, either to import the one, or to make the other for their own use. By means of the unproductive class, the cultivators are delivered from many cares which would otherwise distract their attention from the cultivation of land. The superiority of produce, which, in consequence of this undivided attention, they are enabled to raise, is fully sufficient to pay the whole expence which the maintenance and employment of the unproductive class costs either the proprietors, or themselves. The industry of merchants, artificers and manufacturers, though in its own nature altogether unproductive, yet contributes in this manner indirectly to increase the produce of the land. It increases the productive powers of productive labour, by leaving it at liberty to confine itself to its proper employment, the cultivation of land; and the plough goes frequently the easier and the better by means of the labour of the man whose business is most remote from the plough.

It can never be the interest of the proprietors and cultivators to restrain or to discourage in any respect the industry of merchants, artificers and manufacturers. The *and it is not their interest to discourage its industry;* greater the liberty which this unproductive class enjoys, the greater will be the competition in all the different trades which compose it, and the cheaper will the other two classes be supplied, both with foreign goods and with the manufactured produce of their own country.

It can never be the interest of the unproductive class to oppress the other two classes. It is the surplus produce of the *nor is it ever the interest of the unproductive class to oppress the others.* land, or what remains after deducting the maintenance, first, of the cultivators, and afterwards, of the proprietors, that maintains and employs the unproductive class. The greater this surplus, the greater must likewise be the maintenance and employment of that class.[9] The establishment of perfect justice, of perfect liberty, and of perfect equality, is the very simple secret which most effectually secures the highest degree of prosperity to all the three classes.

Mercantile states similarly are maintained at the expense of landed states, The merchants, artificers and manufacturers of those mercantile states which, like Holland and Hamburgh, consist chiefly of this unproductive class, are in the same manner maintained and employed altogether at the expence of the proprietors and cultiva-

---

[9] [Ed. 1 reads "the greater must likewise be its maintenance and employment."]

tors of land. The only difference is, that those proprietors and cultivators are, the greater part of them, placed at a most inconvenient distance from the merchants, artificers and manufacturers whom they supply with the materials of their work and the fund of their subsistence, are the inhabitants of other countries, and the subjects of other governments.

Such mercantile states, however, are not only useful, but greatly useful to the inhabitants of those other countries.

but are greatly useful to them, They fill up, in some measure, a very important void, and supply the place of the merchants, artificers and manufacturers, whom the inhabitants of those countries ought to find at home, but whom, from some defect in their policy, they do not find at home.

It can never be the interest of those landed nations, if I may call them so, to discourage or distress the industry of such mercantile states, by imposing high duties upon their trade, or upon the commodities which they furnish. Such duties, by rendering those commodities dearer, could serve only to sink the real value of the surplus produce of their own land, with which, or, what comes to the same thing, with the price of which, those commodities are purchased. Such duties could serve only to discourage the increase of that surplus produce, and consequently the improvement and cultivation of their own land. The most effectual expedient, on the contrary, for raising the value of that surplus produce, for encouraging its increase, and consequently the improvement and cultivation of their own land, would be to allow the most perfect freedom to the trade of all such mercantile nations.

and it is not the interest of landed nations to discourage their industry by high duties.

This perfect freedom of trade would even be the most effectual expedient for supplying them, in due time, with all the artificers, manufacturers and merchants, whom they wanted at home, and for filling up in the properest and most advantageous manner that very important void which they felt there.

Freedom of trade would in due time supply artificers etc., at home,

The continual increase of the surplus produce of their land, would, in due time, create a greater capital than what could be

in consequence of the increase of their capital, which would first employ manufacturers,

employed with the ordinary rate of profit in the improvement and cultivation of land; and the surplus part of it would naturally turn itself to the employment of artificers and manufacturers at home. But those artificers and manufacturers, finding at home both the materials of their work and the fund of their subsistence, might immediately, even with much less art and skill, be able to work as cheap as the like artificers and manufacturers of such mercantile states, who had both to bring from a great[10] distance. Even though, from want of art and skill, they might not for some time be able to work as cheap, yet, finding a market at home, they might be able to sell their work there as cheap as that of the artificers and manufacturers of such mercantile states, which could not be brought to that market but from so great a distance; and as their art and skill improved, they would soon be able to sell it cheaper. The artificers and manufacturers of such mercantile states, therefore, would immediately be rivalled in the market of those landed nations, and soon after undersold and justled out of it altogether. The cheapness of the manufactures of those landed nations, in consequence of the gradual improvements of art and skill, would, in due time, extend their sale beyond the home market, and carry them to many foreign markets, from which they would in the same manner gradually justle out many of the manufactures of such mercantile nations.

This continual increase both of the rude and manufactured produce of those landed nations would in due time create a

and afterwards overflow into foreign trade.

greater capital than could, with the ordinary rate of profit, be employed either in agriculture or in manufactures. The surplus of this capital would naturally turn itself to foreign trade, and be employed in exporting, to foreign countries, such parts of the rude and manufactured produce of its own country,

[10] [Misprinted "greater" in ed. 5.]

as exceeded the demand of the home market. In the exportation of the produce of their own country, the merchants of a landed nation would have an advantage of the same kind over those of mercantile nations, which its artificers and manufacturers had over the artificers and manufacturers of such nations; the advantage of finding at home that cargo, and those stores and provisions, which the others were obliged to seek for at a distance. With inferior art and skill in navigation, therefore, they would be able to sell that cargo as cheap in foreign markets as the merchants of such mercantile nations; and with equal art and skill they would be able to sell it cheaper. They would soon, therefore, rival those mercantile nations in this branch of foreign trade,[11] and in due time would justle them out of it altogether.

According to this liberal and generous system, therefore, the most advantageous method in which a landed nation can

Freedom of trade therefore is best for introducing manufactures and foreign trade.

raise up artificers, manufacturers and merchants of its own, is to grant the most perfect freedom of trade to the artificers, manufacturers and merchants of all other nations. It thereby raises the value of the surplus produce of its own land, of which the continual increase gradually establishes a fund, which in due time necessarily raises up all the artificers, manufacturers and merchants whom it has occasion for.

When a landed nation, on the contrary, oppresses either by high duties or by prohibitions the trade of foreign nations, it

High duties and prohibitions sink the value of agricultural produce, raise mercantile and manufacturing profit,

necessarily hurts its own interest in two different ways. First, by raising the price of all foreign goods and of all sorts of manufactures, it necessarily sinks the real value of the surplus produce of its own land, with which, or, what comes to the same thing, with the price of which, it purchases those foreign goods and manufactures. Secondly, by giving a sort of monopoly of the home market to its own

11 [Ed. 1 reads "of their foreign trade."]

merchants, artificers and manufacturers, it raises the rate of
mercantile and manufacturing profit in proportion to that of
agricultural profit, and consequently either draws from agriculture a part of the capital which had before been employed in
it, or hinders from going to it a part of what would otherwise
have gone to it. This policy, therefore, discourages agriculture
in two different ways; first, by sinking the real value of its produce, and thereby lowering the rate of its profit; and, secondly,
by raising the rate of profit in all other employments. Agriculture is rendered less advantageous, and trade and manufactures more advantageous than they otherwise would be; and
every man is tempted by his own interest to turn, as much as he
can, both his capital and his industry from the former to the latter employments.

Though, by this oppressive policy, a landed nation should
be able to raise up artificers, manufacturers and merchants of

*and could only
raise up
manufacturers
and merchants
prematurely.*

its own, somewhat sooner than it could do by
the freedom of trade; a matter, however,
which is not a little doubtful; yet it would
raise them up, if one may say so, prematurely, and before it was perfectly ripe for
them. By raising up too hastily one species

of industry, it would depress another more valuable species of
industry. By raising up too hastily a species of industry which
only replaces the stock which employs it, together with the ordinary profit, it would depress a species of industry which, over
and above replacing that stock with its profit, affords likewise
a neat produce, a free rent to the landlord. It would depress productive labour, by encouraging too hastily that labour which is
altogether barren and unproductive.

In what manner, according to this system, the sum total of
the annual produce of the land is distributed among the three

*The distribution of
the produce of
land is repre-
sented in the
Economical Table.*

classes above mentioned, and in what manner the labour of the unproductive class does
no more than replace the value of its own
consumption, without increasing in any respect the value of that sum total, is represented by Mr. Quesnai, the very ingenious

and profound author of this system, in some arithmetical formularies. The first of these formularies, which by way of
eminence he peculiarly distinguishes by the name of the
Œconomical Table,[12] represents the manner in which he supposes this distribution takes place, in a state of the most perfect
liberty, and therefore of the highest prosperity; in a state where
the annual produce is such as to afford the greatest possible
neat produce, and where each class enjoys its proper share of
the whole annual produce. Some subsequent formularies represent the manner, in which, he supposes, this distribution is
made in different states of restraint and regulation; in which,
either the class of proprietors, or the barren and unproductive
class, is more favoured than the class of cultivators, and in
which, either the one or the other encroaches more or less upon
the share which ought properly to belong to this productive
class. Every such encroachment, every violation of that natural
distribution, which the most perfect liberty would establish,
must, according to this system, necessarily degrade more or
less, from one year to another, the value and sum total of the
annual produce, and must necessarily occasion a gradual declension in the real wealth and revenue of the society; a declension of which the progress must be quicker or slower,
according to the degree of this encroachment, according as
that natural distribution, which the most perfect liberty would
establish, is more or less violated. Those subsequent formularies represent the different degrees of declension, which, according to this system, correspond to the different degrees in
which this natural distribution of things is violated.

Some speculative physicians seem to have imagined that
the health of the human body could be preserved only by a cer-

*Nations can
prosper in spite
of hurtful
regulations.*

tain precise regimen of diet and exercise, of
which every, the smallest, violation necessarily occasioned some degree of disease or
disorder proportioned to the degree of the
violation. Experience, however, would seem

[12] [See François Quesnay, *Tableau Œconomique*, 1758, reproduced in facsimile
for the British Economic Association, 1894.]

to show, that the human body frequently preserves, to all appearance at least,[13] the most perfect state of health under a vast variety of different regimens; even under some which are generally believed to be very far from being perfectly wholesome. But the healthful state of the human body, it would seem, contains in itself some unknown principle of preservation, capable either of preventing or of correcting, in many respects, the bad effects even of a very faulty regimen. Mr. Quesnai, who was himself a physician, and a very speculative physician, seems to have entertained a notion of the same kind concerning the political body, and to have imagined that it would thrive and prosper only under a certain precise regimen, the exact regimen of perfect liberty and perfect justice. He seems not to have considered that in the political body, the natural effort which every man is continually making to better his own condition, is a principle of preservation capable of preventing and correcting, in many respects, the bad effects of a political œconomy, in some degree both partial and oppressive. Such a political œconomy, though it no doubt retards more or less, is not always capable of stopping altogether the natural progress of a nation towards wealth and prosperity, and still less of making it go backwards. If a nation could not prosper without the enjoyment of perfect liberty and perfect justice, there is not in the world a nation which could ever have prospered. In the political body, however, the wisdom of nature has fortunately made ample provision for remedying many of the bad effects of the folly and injustice of man; in the same manner as it has done in the natural body, for remedying those of his sloth and intemperance.

The system is wrong in representing artificers, etc., as unproductive, since,   The capital error of this system, however, seems to lie in its representing the class of artificers, manufacturers and merchants, as altogether barren and unproductive. The following observations may serve to show the impropriety of this representation.

First, this class, it is acknowledged, reproduces annually the

---

[13] [Ed. 1 reads "at least to all appearance."]

value of its own annual consumption, and continues, at least,

(1) they reproduce at least their annual consumption and continue the capital which employs them,

the existence of the stock or capital which maintains and employs it. But upon this account alone the denomination of barren or unproductive should seem to be very improperly applied to it. We should not call a marriage barren or unproductive, though it produced only a son and a daughter, to replace the father and mother, and though it did not increase the number of the human species, but only continued it as it was before. Farmers and country labourers, indeed, over and above the stock which maintains and employs them, reproduce annually a neat produce, a free rent to the landlord. As a marriage which affords three children is certainly more productive than one which affords only two; so the labour of farmers and country labourers is certainly more productive than that of merchants, artificers and manufacturers. The superior produce of the one class, however, does not render the other barren or unproductive.

Secondly, it seems, upon this account, altogether improper to consider artificers, manufacturers and merchants, in the

(2) they are not like menial servants,

same light as menial servants. The labour of menial servants does not continue the existence of the fund which maintains and employs them. Their maintenance and employment is altogether at the expence of their masters, and the work which they perform is not of a nature to repay that expence. That work consists in services which perish generally in the very instant of their performance, and does not fix or realize itself in any vendible commodity which can replace the value of their wages and maintenance. The labour, on the contrary, of artificers, manufacturers and merchants, naturally does fix and realize itself in some such vendible commodity. It is upon this account that, in the chapter in which I treat of productive and unproductive labour,[14] I have classed artificers, manufacturers and merchants, among the productive

---

[14] [Book II., Chap. III., pp. 422–446.]

labourers, and menial servants among the barren or unproductive.

Thirdly, it seems, upon every supposition, improper to say, that the labour of artificers, manufacturers and merchants,

(3) their labour increases the real revenue of the society,

does not increase the real revenue of the society. Though we should suppose, for example, as it seems to be supposed in this system, that the value of the daily, monthly, and yearly consumption of this class was exactly equal to that of its daily, monthly, and yearly production; yet it would not from thence follow that its labour added nothing to the real revenue, to the real value of the annual produce of the land and labour of the society. An artificer, for example, who, in the first six months after harvest, executes ten pounds worth of work, though he should in the same time consume ten pounds worth of corn and other necessaries, yet really adds the value of ten pounds to the annual produce of the land and labour of the society. While he has been consuming a half yearly revenue of ten pounds worth of corn and other necessaries, he has produced an equal value of work capable of purchasing, either to himself or to some other person, an equal half yearly revenue. The value, therefore, of what has been consumed and produced during these six months is equal, not to ten, but to twenty pounds. It is possible, indeed, that no more than ten pounds worth of this value, may ever have existed at any one moment of time. But if the ten pounds worth of corn and other necessaries, which were consumed by the artificer, had been consumed by a soldier or by a menial servant, the value of that part of the annual produce which existed at the end of the six months, would have been ten pounds less than it actually is in consequence of the labour of the artificer. Though the value of what the artificer produces, therefore, should not at any one moment of time be supposed greater than the value he consumes, yet at every moment of time the actually existing value of goods in the market is, in consequence of what he produces, greater than it otherwise would be.

When the patrons of this system assert, that the consumption of artificers, manufacturers and merchants, is equal to the value of what they produce, they probably mean no more than that their revenue, or the fund destined for their consumption, is equal to it. But if they had expressed themselves more accurately, and only asserted, that the revenue of this class was equal to the value of what they produced, it might readily have occurred to the reader, that what would naturally be saved out of this revenue, must necessarily increase more or less the real wealth of the society. In order, therefore, to make out something like an argument, it was necessary that they should express themselves as they have done; and this argument, even supposing things actually were as it seems to presume them to be, turns out to be a very inconclusive one.

Fourthly, farmers and country labourers can no more augment, without parsimony, the real revenue, the annual produce of the land and labour of their society, than artificers, manufacturers and merchants. The annual produce of the land and labour of any society can be augmented only in two ways; either, first, by some improvement in the productive powers of the useful labour actually maintained within it; or, secondly, by some increase in the quantity of that labour.

(4) for augmenting annual produce parsimony is just as much required from farmers as from them,

The improvement in the productive powers of useful labour depends, first, upon the improvement in the ability of the workman; and, secondly, upon that of the machinery with which he works. But the labour of artificers and manufacturers, as it is capable of being more subdivided, and the labour of each workman reduced to a greater simplicity of operation, than that of farmers and country labourers, so it is likewise capable of both these sorts of improvement in a much higher degree.[15] In this respect, therefore, the class of cultivators can have no sort of advantage over that of artificers and manufacturers.

The increase in the quantity of useful labour actually employed within any society, must depend altogether upon the increase of the capital which employs it; and the increase of that capital again must be exactly equal to the amount of the sav-

---

[15] [See Book I. Chap. I. pp. 11–12.]

ings from the revenue, either of the particular persons who manage and direct the employment of that capital, or of some other persons who lend it to them. If merchants, artificers and manufacturers are, as this system seems to suppose, naturally more inclined to parsimony and saving than proprietors and cultivators, they are, so far, more likely to augment the quantity of useful labour employed within their society, and consequently to increase its real revenue, the annual produce of its land and labour.

Fifthly and lastly, though the revenue of the inhabitants of every country was supposed to consist altogether, as this sys-

and (5) trade and manufactures can procure that subsistence which the system regards as the only revenue.

tem seems to suppose, in the quantity of subsistence which their industry could procure to them; yet even upon this supposition, the revenue of a trading and manufacturing country must, other things being equal, always be much greater than that of one without trade or manufactures. By means of trade and manufactures, a greater quantity of subsistence can be annually imported into a particular country than what its own lands, in the actual state of their cultivation, could afford. The inhabitants of a town, though they frequently possess no lands of their own, yet draw to themselves by their industry such a quantity of the rude produce of the lands of other people as supplies them, not only with the materials of their work, but with the fund of their subsistence. What a town always is with regard to the country in its neighbourhood, one independent state or country may frequently be with regard to other independent states or countries. It is thus that Holland draws a great part of its subsistence from other countries; live cattle from Holstein and Jutland, and corn from almost all the different countries of Europe. A small quantity of manufactured produce purchases a great quantity of rude produce. A trading and manufacturing country, therefore, naturally purchases with a small part of its manufactured produce a great part of the rude produce of other countries; while, on the contrary, a country without trade and manufactures is generally obliged to purchase, at the expence of a great part of its rude produce, a very small part of the manufactured produce of other countries. The one exports what can subsist and accommodate but a very few, and imports the subsistence and accommodation of a great number. The other exports the accommodation and subsistence of a great number, and imports that of a very few only. The inhabitants of the one must always enjoy a much greater quantity of subsistence than what their own lands, in the actual state of their cultivation, could afford. The inhabitants of the other must always enjoy a much smaller quantity.

This system, however, with all its imperfections, is, perhaps, the nearest approximation to the truth that has yet been published upon the subject of political *In spite of its* œconomy, and is upon that account well *errors the system* *has been valuable.* worth the consideration of every man who wishes to examine with attention the principles of that very important science. Though in representing the labour which is employed upon land as the only productive labour, the notions which it inculcates are perhaps too narrow and confined; yet in representing the wealth of nations as consisting, not in the unconsumable riches of money, but in the consumable goods annually reproduced by the labour of the society; and in representing perfect liberty as the only effectual expedient for rendering this annual reproduction the greatest possible, its doctrine seems to be in every respect as just as it is generous and liberal. Its followers are very numerous; and as men are fond of paradoxes, and of appearing to understand what surpasses the comprehension of ordinary people, the paradox which it maintains, concerning the unproductive nature of manufacturing labour, has not perhaps contributed a little to increase the number of its admirers. They have for some years past made a pretty considerable sect, distinguished in the French republic of letters by the name of, The Œconomists. Their works have certainly been of some service to their country; not only by bringing into general discussion, many subjects which had never been well examined before, but by influencing in some measure the public administration in favour of agriculture. It has been in consequence of their representations, accordingly, that the agriculture of France has been delivered from several of the oppressions which it before laboured under. The term during which such a lease can be granted, as will be valid against every future purchaser or proprietor of the land, has been prolonged from nine to twenty-seven years.[16] The ancient provincial restraints upon the transportation of corn from one province of the kingdom to another, have been entirely taken away, and the liberty of exporting it to all foreign countries, has been established as the common law of the kingdom in all ordinary cases.[17] This sect, in their works, which are very numerous, and which treat not only of what is properly called Political Œconomy, or of the nature and causes of the wealth of nations, but of every other branch of the system of civil government, all follow implicitly, and without any sensible variation, the doctrine of Mr. Quesnai. There is upon this account little variety in the greater part of their works. The most distinct and best connected account of this doctrine is to be found in a little book written by Mr. Mercier de la Riviere, sometime Intendant of Martinico, intitled, The natural and essential Order of Political Societies.[18] The admiration of this whole sect for their master, who was himself a man of the greatest modesty and simplicity, is not inferior to that of any of the ancient philosophers for the founders of their respective systems. "There have been, since the world began," says a very diligent and respectable author, the Marquis de Mirabeau, "three great inventions which have principally given stability to political societies, independent of many other inventions which have enriched and adorned them. The first, is the invention of writing, which alone gives human nature the power of transmitting, without alteration, its laws, its contracts, its annals, and its discoveries. The second, is the

---

[16] [Above, p. 499.]

[17] [Above, pp. 269, 638.]

[18] [*L'ordre naturel et essentiel des sociétés politiques*, 1767, a quarto of 511 pages, seems, as G. Schelle (*Du Pont de Nemours et l'école physiocratique*, 1888, p. 46, note) remarks, not entitled to be called a "little book," but Smith may have been thinking of the edition in two vols., 12mo, 1767, nominally printed "à Londres chez Jean Nourse, libraire."]

invention of money, which binds together all the relations between civilized societies. The third, is the Œconomical Table,
the result of the other two, which completes them both by per-
fecting their object; the great discovery of our age, but of
which our posterity will reap the benefit."[19]

As the political œconomy of the nations of modern Europe,
has been more favourable to manufactures and foreign trade,

Some nations have favoured agriculture. the industry of the towns, than to agriculture, the industry of the country; so that of
other nations has followed a different plan,
and has been more favourable to agriculture
than to manufactures and foreign trade.

The policy of China favours agriculture more than all other
employments.[20] In China, the condition of a labourer is said

China, for example, to be as much superior to that of an artificer;
as in most parts of Europe, that of an ar-
tificer is to that of a labourer. In China, the
great ambition of every man is to get possession of some little bit of land, either in property or in
lease; and leases are there said to be granted upon very moderate terms, and to be sufficiently secured to the lessees.
The Chinese have little respect for foreign trade. Your beggarly commerce! was the language in which the Mandarins
of Pekin used to talk to Mr. de Lange,[21] the Russian envoy,

[19] ["Trois grandes inventions principales ont fondé stablement les sociétés,
indépendamment de tant d'autres qui les ont ensuite dotées et décorées. Ces trois
sont, 1° L'invention de l'écriture, qui seule donne à l'humanité le pouvoir
de transmettre, sans altération, ses lois, ses pactes, ses annales et ses découvertes.
2° Celle de la monnaie, qui lie tous les rapports entre les sociétés policées.
La troisième enfin, qui est due à notre âge, et dont nos neveux profiteront, est
un dérivé des deux autres, et les complette également en perfectionnant leur
objet: c'est la découverte du Tableau économique, qui devenant désormais le
truchement universel, embrasse, et accorde toutes les portions ou quotités
correlatives, qui doivent entrer dans tous les calculs généraux de l'ordre
économique."—*Philosophie Rurale ou économie générale et politique de l'agriculture, pour servir de suite à l'Ami des Hommes,* Amsterdam, 1766, tom. i., pp.
52, 53.]

[20] [Du Halde, *Description Géographique, etc., de la Chine,* tom. ii., p. 64.]

[21] [Ed. 1 reads "Mr. Langlet."]

concerning it.[22] Except with Japan, the Chinese carry on, themselves, and in their own bottoms, little or no foreign trade; and it is only into one or two ports of their kingdom that they even admit the ships of foreign nations. Foreign trade, therefore, is, in China, every way confined within a much narrower circle than that to which it would naturally extend itself, if more freedom was allowed to it, either in their own ships, or in those of foreign nations.

Manufactures, as in a small bulk they frequently contain a great value, and can upon that account be transported at less

China is itself of very great extent, but more foreign trade would be advantageous to it.

expence from one country to another than most parts[23] of rude produce, are, in almost all countries, the principal support of foreign trade. In countries, besides, less extensive and less favourably circumstanced for interior commerce than China, they generally require the support of foreign trade. Without an extensive foreign market, they could not well flourish, either in countries so moderately extensive as to afford but a narrow home market; or in countries where the communication between one province and another was so difficult, as to render it impossible for the goods of any particular place to enjoy the whole of that home market which the country could afford. The perfection of manufacturing industry, it must be remembered, depends altogether upon the division of labour; and the degree to which the division of labour can be introduced into any manufacture, is necessarily regulated, it has already been shown,[24] by the extent of the market. But the great extent of the empire of China, the vast multitude of its inhabitants, the variety of climate, and consequently of productions in its different provinces, and the easy

[22] See the Journal of Mr. De Lange in Bell's Travels, vol. ii. p. 258, 276 and 293. [*Travels from St. Petersburg in Russia to Diverse Ports of Asia*, by John Bell of Antermony, Glasgow, 1763. The mandarins requested the Russians to cease "from importuning the council about their beggarly commerce," p. 293. Smith was a subscriber to this book. The note is not in ed. 1.]

[23] [Ed. 1 reads "sorts."]

[24] [Above, pp. 27–32.]

communication by means of water carriage between the greater part of them, render the home market of that country of so great extent, as to be alone sufficient to support very great manufactures, and to admit of very considerable subdivisions of labour. The home market of China is, perhaps, in extent, not much inferior to the market of all the different countries of Europe put together.[25] A more extensive foreign trade, however, which to this great home market added the foreign market of all the rest of the world; especially if any considerable part of this trade was carried on in Chinese ships; could scarce fail to increase very much the manufactures of China, and to improve very much the productive powers of its manufacturing industry. By a more extensive navigation, the Chinese would naturally learn the art of using and constructing themselves all the different machines made use of in other countries, as well as the other[26] improvements of art and industry which are practised in all the different parts of the world. Upon their present plan they have little opportunity of improving themselves by the example of any other nation; except that of the Japanese.

Egypt and the Gentoo government of Indostan favoured agriculture.

The policy of ancient Egypt too, and that of the Gentoo government of Indostan, seem to have favoured agriculture more than all other employments.

The people were divided into castes in these countries.

Both in ancient Egypt and[27] Indostan, the whole body of the people was divided into different casts or tribes, each of which was confined, from father to son, to a particular employment or class of employments. The son of a priest was necessarily a priest; the son of a soldier, a soldier; the son of a labourer, a labourer; the son of a weaver, a weaver; the son of a taylor, a taylor; &c. In both countries, the cast of the priests held the highest rank, and that

[25] [Quesnay went further than this: "L'historien dit que le commerce qui se fit dans l'intérieur de la Chine est si grand que celui de l'Europe ne peut pas lui être comparé."—*Oeuvres*, ed. Oncken, 1888, p. 603.]

[26] [Ed. 1 reads "as well as all the other."]

[27] [Ed. 1 reads "and in."]

of the soldiers the next; and in both countries, the cast of the farmers and labourers was superior to the casts of merchants and manufacturers.

The government of both countries was particularly attentive to the interest of agriculture. The works constructed by the ancient sovereigns of Egypt for the proper distribution of the waters of the Nile were famous in antiquity; and the ruined remains of some of them are still the admiration of travellers. Those of the same kind which were constructed by the ancient sovereigns of Indostan, for the proper distribution of the waters of the Ganges as well as of many other rivers, though they have been less celebrated, seem to have been equally great. Both countries, accordingly, though subject occasionally to dearths, have been famous for their great fertility. Though both were extremely populous, yet, in years of moderate plenty, they were both able to export great quantities of grain to their neighbours.

Irrigation was attended to there.

The ancient Egyptians had a superstitious aversion to the sea; and as the Gentoo religion does not permit its followers to light a fire, nor consequently to dress any victuals upon the water, it in effect prohibits them from all distant sea voyages. Both the Egyptians and Indians must have depended almost altogether upon the navigation of other nations for the exportation of their surplus produce; and this dependency, as it must have confined the market, so it must have discouraged the increase of this surplus produce. It must have discouraged too the increase of the manufactured produce more than that of the rude produce. Manufactures require a much more extensive market than the most important parts of the rude produce of the land. A single shoemaker will make more than three hundred pairs of shoes in the year; and his own family will not perhaps wear out six pairs. Unless therefore he has the custom of at least fifty such families as his own, he cannot dispose of the whole produce of his own labour. The most numerous class of artificers will seldom, in a large country, make more than one in fifty or one in a hundred.

Egypt and India were dependent on other nations for foreign trade.

of the whole number of families contained in it. But in such large countries as France and England, the number of people employed in agriculture has by some authors been computed at a half, by others at a third, and by no author that I know of, at less than a fifth of the whole inhabitants of the country. But as the produce of the agriculture of both France and England is, the far greater part of it, consumed at home, each person employed in it must, according to these computations, require little more than the custom of one, two, or, at most, of [28] four such families as his own, in order to dispose of the whole produce of his own labour. Agriculture, therefore, can support itself under the discouragement of a confined market, much better than manufactures. In both ancient Egypt and Indostan, indeed, the confinement of the foreign market was in some measure compensated by the conveniency of many inland navigations, which opened, in the most advantageous manner, the whole extent of the home market to every part of the produce of every different district of those countries. The great extent of Indostan too rendered the home market of that country very great, and sufficient to support a great variety of manufactures. But the small extent of ancient Egypt, which was never equal to England, must at all times have rendered the home market of that country too narrow for supporting any great variety of manufactures. Bengal, accordingly, the province of Indostan which commonly exports the greatest quantity of rice, has always been more remarkable for the exportation of a great variety of manufactures, than for that of its grain. Ancient Egypt, on the contrary, though it exported some manufactures, fine linen in particular, as well as some other goods, was always most distinguished for its great exportation of grain. It was long the granary of the Roman empire.

The land tax gave eastern sovereigns a particular interest in agriculture. The sovereigns of China, of ancient Egypt, and of the different kingdoms into which Indostan has at different times been divided, have always derived the whole, or by far the most considerable part, of their

---

[28] [Ed. 1 does not contain "of."]

revenue from some sort of land-tax or land-rent. This land-tax or land-rent, like the tithe in Europe, consisted in a certain proportion, a fifth, it is said, of the produce of the land, which was either delivered in kind, or paid in money, according to a certain valuation, and which therefore varied from year to year according to all the variations of the produce. It was natural therefore, that the sovereigns of those countries should be particularly attentive to the interests of agriculture, upon the prosperity or declension of which immediately depended the yearly increase or diminution of their own revenue.[29]

The policy of the ancient republics of Greece, and that of Rome, though it honoured agriculture more than manufactures

Ancient Greece and Rome discouraged manufactures and foreign trade, and carried on manufactures only by slave labour, which is expensive.

or foreign trade, yet seems rather to have discouraged the latter employments, than to have given any direct or intentional encouragement to the former. In several of the ancient states of Greece, foreign trade was prohibited altogether; and in several others the employments of artificers and manufacturers were considered as hurtful to the strength and agility of the human body, as rendering it incapable of those habits which their military and gymnastic exercises endeavoured to form in it, and as thereby disqualifying it more or less for[30] undergoing the fatigues and encountering the dangers of war. Such occupations were considered as fit only for slaves, and the free citizens of the state were prohibited from exercising them.[31] Even in those states where no such prohibition took place, as in Rome and Athens, the great body of the people were in effect excluded from all the trades which are now commonly exercised by the lower sort of the inhabitants of towns. Such trades were, at Athens and Rome, all occupied by the slaves of the rich, who exercised them for the benefit of their masters,

[29] [Below, p. 1059.]

[30] [Ed. 1 reads "from."]

[31] [Montesquieu, *Esprit des lois*, liv. iv., chap. 8.]

whose wealth, power, and protection, made it almost impossible for a poor freeman to find a market for his work, when it came into competition with that of the slaves of the rich. Slaves, however, are very seldom inventive; and all the most important improvements, either in machinery, or in the[32] arrangement and distribution of work, which facilitate and abridge labour, have been the discoveries of freemen. Should a slave propose any improvement of this kind, his master would be very apt to consider the proposal as the suggestion of laziness, and of a desire to save his own labour at the master's expence. The poor slave, instead of reward, would probably meet with much abuse, perhaps with some punishment. In the manufactures carried on by slaves, therefore, more labour must generally have been employed to execute the same quantity of work, than in those carried on by freemen. The work of the former must, upon that account, generally have been dearer than that of the latter. The Hungarian mines, it is remarked by Mr. Montesquieu, though not richer,[33] have always been wrought with less expence, and therefore with more profit, than the Turkish mines in their neighbourhood. The Turkish mines are wrought by slaves; and the arms of those slaves are the only machines which the Turks have ever thought of employing. The Hungarian mines are wrought by freemen, who employ a great deal of machinery, by which they facilitate and abridge their own labour.[34] From the very little that is known about the price of manufactures in the times of the Greeks and Romans, it would appear that those of the finer sort were excessively dear. Silk sold for its weight in gold. It was not, indeed, in those times a European manufacture; and as it was all brought from the East Indies, the distance of the carriage may in some measure account for the greatness of the price. The price, however, which a lady, it is said, would sometimes pay for a piece of very fine linen, seems to have been equally extravagant; and as linen was always either a European, or, at farthest, an

[32] [Ed. 1 reads "that."]

[33] [Ed. 1 reads "more rich."]

[34] [*Lectures*, p. 231; Montesquieu, *Esprit des lois*, liv. xv., chap. 8.]

Egyptian manufacture, this high price can be accounted for only by the great expence of the labour which must have been employed about it, and the expence of this labour again could arise from nothing but the awkwardness of the machinery which it made use of. The price of fine woollens too, though not quite so extravagant, seems however to have been much above that of the present times. Some cloths, we are told by Pliny, dyed in a particular manner, cost a hundred denarii, or three pounds six shillings and eight pence the pound weight.[35] Others dyed in another manner cost a thousand denarii the pound weight, or thirty-three pounds six shillings and eight pence. The Roman pound, it must be remembered, contained only twelve of our avoirdupois ounces. This high price, indeed, seems to have been principally owing to the dye. But had not the cloths themselves been much dearer than any which are made in the present times, so very expensive a dye would not probably have been bestowed upon them. The disproportion would have been too great between the value of the accessory and that of the principal. The price mentioned by the same[36] author of some Triclinaria, a sort of woollen pillows or cushions made use of to lean upon as they reclined upon their couches at table, passes all credibility; some of them being said to have cost more than thirty thousand, others more than three hundred thousand pounds. This high price too is not said to have arisen from the dye. In the dress of the people of fashion of both sexes, there seems to have been much less variety, it is observed by Dr. Arbuthnot, in ancient than in modern times;[37] and the very little variety which we find in that of the ancient statues confirms his observation. He infers from this, that their dress must upon the whole have been cheaper than ours: but the conclusion does not seem to follow. When the expence of fashionable dress is very great, the variety must be very small. But when, by the improve-

---

[35] Plin. [*H.N.*] l. ix. c. 39.

[36] Plin. [*H.N.*] l. viii. c. 48. [Neither this nor the preceding note is in ed. 1.]

[37] [John Arbuthnot, *Tables of Ancient Coins, Weights and Measures*, 2nd ed., 1754, pp. 142–145.]

ments in the productive powers of manufacturing art and industry, the expence of any one dress comes to be very moderate, the variety will naturally be very great. The rich not being able to distinguish themselves by the expence of any one dress, will naturally endeavour to do so by the multitude and variety of their dresses.

The greatest and most important branch of the commerce of every nation, it has already been observed,[38] is that which is

Everything which raises the price of manufactures discourages agriculture,

carried on between the inhabitants of the town and those of the country. The inhabitants of the town draw from the country the rude produce which constitutes both the materials of their work and the fund of their subsistence; and they pay for this rude produce by sending back to the country a certain portion of it manufactured and prepared for immediate use. The trade which is carried on between those two different sets of people, consists ultimately in a certain quantity of rude produce exchanged for a certain quantity of manufactured produce. The dearer the latter, therefore, the cheaper the former; and whatever tends in any country to raise the price of manufactured produce, tends to lower that of the rude produce of the land, and thereby to discourage agriculture. The smaller the quantity of manufactured produce which any given quantity of rude produce, or, which comes to the same thing, which the price of any given quantity of rude produce is capable of purchasing, the smaller the exchangeable value[39] of that given quantity of rude produce; the smaller the encouragement which either the landlord has to increase its quantity by improving, or the farmer by cultivating the land. Whatever, besides, tends to diminish in any country the number of artificers and manufacturers, tends to diminish the home market, the most important of all markets for the rude produce of the land, and thereby still further to discourage agriculture.

Those systems, therefore, which preferring agriculture to

---

[38] [Above, p. 481.]

[39] [Ed. 1 reads "real value."]

and this is done by systems which restrain manufactures and foreign trade.

all other employments, in order to promote it, impose restraints upon manufactures and foreign trade, act contrary to the very end which they propose, and indirectly discourage that very species of industry which they mean to promote. They are so far, perhaps, more inconsistent than even the mercantile system. That system, by encouraging manufactures and foreign trade more than agriculture, turns a certain portion of the capital of the society from supporting a more advantageous, to support a less advantageous species of industry. But still it really and in the end encourages that species of industry which it means to promote. Those agricultural systems, on the contrary, really and in the end discourage their own favourite species of industry.

So all systems of encouragements and restraints retard the progress of society.

It is thus that every system which endeavours, either, by extraordinary encouragements, to draw towards a particular species of industry a greater share of the capital of the society than what would naturally go to it; or, by extraordinary restraints, to force from a particular species of industry some share of the capital which would otherwise be employed in it; is in reality subversive of the great purpose which it means to promote. It retards, instead of accelerating, the progress of the society towards real wealth and greatness; and diminishes, instead of increasing, the real value of the annual produce of its land and labour.

The system of natural liberty leaves the sovereign only three duties: (1) the defence of the country; (2) the administration of justice, and (3) the maintenance of certain public works.

All systems either of preference or of restraint, therefore, being thus completely taken away, the obvious and simple system of natural liberty establishes itself of its own accord. Every man, as long as he does not violate the laws of justice, is left perfectly free to pursue his own interest his own way, and to bring both his industry and capital into competition with those of any other man, or order of men. The sovereign is completely discharged from a duty, in the attempting to perform which he must always be exposed to innumerable delusions, and for the proper performance of which no human wisdom or knowledge could ever be sufficient; the duty of superintending the industry of private people, and of directing it towards the employments most suitable to the interest of the society. According to the system of natural liberty, the sovereign has only three duties to attend to; three duties of great importance, indeed, but plain and intelligible to common understandings: first, the duty of protecting the society from the violence and invasion of other independent societies; secondly, the duty of protecting, as far as possible, every member of the society from the injustice or oppression of every other member of it, or the duty of establishing an exact administration of justice; and, thirdly, the duty of erecting and maintaining certain public works and certain public institutions, which it can never be for the interest of any individual, or small number of individuals, to erect and maintain; because the profit could never repay the expence to any individual or small number of individuals, though it may frequently do much more than repay it to a great society.

The proper performance of those several duties of the sovereign necessarily supposes a certain expence; and this expence again necessarily requires a certain revenue to support it. In the following book, therefore, I shall endeavour to explain; first, what are the necessary expences of the sovereign or commonwealth; and which of those expences ought to be defrayed by the general contribution of the whole society; and which of them, by that of some particular part only, or of some particular members of the society: secondly, what are the different methods in which the whole society may be made to contribute towards defraying the expences incumbent on the whole society, and what are the principal advantages and inconveniences of each of those methods: and, thirdly, what are the reasons and causes which have induced almost all modern governments to mortgage

The next book will treat of the necessary expenses of the sovereign, the methods of contribution towards the expenses of the whole society, and the causes and effects of public debts.

some part of this revenue, or to contract debts, and what have been the effects of those debts upon the real wealth, the annual produce of the land and labour of the society. The following book, therefore, will naturally be divided into three chapters.

BOOK V

OF THE REVENUE OF THE SOVEREIGN OR COMMONWEALTH

CHAPTER I

OF THE EXPENCES OF THE SOVEREIGN OR COMMONWEALTH

PART I

OF THE EXPENCE OF DEFENCE

THE FIRST duty of the sovereign, that of protecting the society from the violence and invasion of other independent societies, can be performed only by means of a military force. But the expence both of preparing this military force in time of peace, and of employing it in time of war, is very different in the different states of society, in the different periods of improvement.

The expense of a military force is different at different periods.

Among nations of hunters, the lowest and rudest state of society, such as we find it among the native tribes of North America, every man is a warrior as well as a hunter. When he goes to war, either to defend his society, or to revenge the injuries which have been done to it by other societies, he maintains himself by his own labour, in the same manner as when he lives at home. His society, for in this state of things there is properly neither sovereign nor commonwealth, is at no sort of expence, either to prepare him for the field, or to maintain him while he is in it.[1]

Among hunters it costs nothing.

---

[1] [*Lectures*, p. 14.]

Among nations of shepherds, a more advanced state of society, such as we find it among the Tartars and Arabs, every

When shepherds go to war the whole nation moves with its property

man is, in the same manner, a warrior. Such nations have commonly no fixed habitation, but live, either in tents, or in a sort of covered waggons which are easily transported from place to place. The whole tribe or nation changes its situation according to the different seasons of the year, as well as according to other accidents. When its herds and flocks have consumed the forage of one part of the country, it removes to another, and from that to a third. In the dry season, it comes down to the banks of the rivers; in the wet season it retires to the upper country. When such a nation goes to war, the warriors will not trust their herds and flocks to the feeble defence of their old men, their women and children, and their old men, their women and children, will not be left behind without defence and without subsistence. The whole nation, besides, being accustomed to a wandering life, even in time of peace, easily takes the field in time of war. Whether it marches as an army, or moves about as a company of herdsmen, the way of life is nearly the same, though the object proposed by it be[2] very different. They all go to war together, therefore, and every one does as well as he can. Among the Tartars, even the women have been frequently known to engage in battle. If they conquer, whatever belongs to the hostile tribe is the recompence of the victory. But if they are vanquished, all is lost, and not only their herds and flocks, but their women and children, become the booty of the conqueror. Even the greater part of those who survive the action are obliged to submit to him for the sake of immediate subsistence. The rest are commonly dissipated and dispersed in the desart.

The ordinary life, the ordinary exercises of a Tartar or Arab, prepare him sufficiently for war. Running, wrestling, cudgel-

and the sovereign is at no expense.

playing, throwing the javelin, drawing the bow, &c. are the common pastimes of those who live in the open air, and are all of them

---

[2] [Ed. 1 reads "is."]

the images of war. When a Tartar or Arab actually goes to war, he is maintained, by his own herds and flocks which he carries with him, in the same manner as in peace. His chief or sovereign, for those nations have all chiefs or sovereigns, is at no sort of expence in preparing him for the field; and when he is in it, the chance of plunder is the only pay which he either expects or requires.

An army of hunters can seldom exceed two or three hundred men. The precarious subsistence which the chace affords could seldom allow a greater number to keep together for any

Shepherds are far more formidable than hunters.

considerable time. An army of shepherds, on the contrary, may sometimes amount to two or three hundred thousand. As long as nothing stops their progress, as long as they can go on from one district, of which they have consumed the forage, to another which is yet entire; there seems to be scarce any limit to the number who can march on together. A nation of hunters can never be formidable to the civilized nations in their neighbourhood. A nation of shepherds may. Nothing can be more contemptible than an Indian war in North America. Nothing, on the contrary, can be more dreadful than a Tartar invasion has frequently been in Asia. The judgment of Thucydides,[3] that both Europe and Asia could not resist the Scythians united, has been verified by the experience of all ages. The inhabitants of the extensive, but defenceless plains of Scythia or Tartary, have been frequently united under the dominion of the chief of some conquering horde or clan; and the havoc and devastation of Asia have always signalized their union. The inhabitants of the inhospitable desarts of Arabia, the other great nation of shepherds, have never been united but once; under Mahomet and his immediate successors.[4] Their union, which was more the effect of religious enthusiasm than of conquest, was signalized in the same manner. If the hunting

---

[3] [What Thucydides says (ii., 97) is that no European or Asiatic nation could resist the Scythians if they were united. Ed. 1 reads here and on p. 883 "Thucidides."]

[4] [*Lectures*, pp. 20, 21.]

nations of America should ever become shepherds, their neighbourhood would be much more dangerous to the European colonies than it is at present.

In a yet more advanced state of society, among those nations of husbandmen who have little foreign commerce, and no other manufactures but those coarse and houshold ones which almost every private family prepares for its own use; every man, in the same manner, either is a warrior, or easily becomes such. They who live by agriculture generally pass the whole day in the open air, exposed to all the inclemencies of the seasons. The hardiness of their ordinary life prepares them for the fatigues of war, to some of which their necessary occupations bear a great[5] analogy. The necessary occupation of a ditcher prepares him to work in the trenches, and to fortify a camp as well as to enclose a field. The ordinary pastimes of such husbandmen are the same as those of shepherds, and are in the same manner the images of war. But as husbandmen have less leisure than shepherds, they are not so frequently employed in those pastimes. They are soldiers, but soldiers not quite so much masters of their exercise. Such as they are, however, it seldom costs the sovereign or commonwealth any expence to prepare them for the field.

Husbandmen with little commerce and only household manufactures are easily converted into soldiers, and it seldom costs the sovereign anything to prepare them for the field,

Agriculture, even in its rudest and lowest state, supposes a settlement; some sort of fixed habitation which cannot be abandoned without great loss. When a nation of mere husbandmen, therefore, goes to war, the whole people cannot take the field together. The old men, the women and children, at least, must remain at home to take care of the habitation. All the men of the military age, however, may take the field, and, in small nations of this kind, have frequently done so. In every nation the men of the military age are supposed to amount to about a fourth or a

or to maintain them when they have taken the field.

---

[5] [Ed. 1 reads "a good deal of."]

fifth[6] part of the whole body of the people. If the campaign too should begin after seedtime, and end before harvest, both the husbandman and his principal labourers can be spared from the farm without much loss. He trusts that the work which must be done in the mean time can be well enough executed by the old men, the women and the children. He is not unwilling, therefore, to serve without pay during a short[7] campaign, and it frequently costs the sovereign or commonwealth as little to maintain him in the field as to prepare him for it. The citizens of all the different states of ancient Greece seem to have served in this manner till after the second Persian war; and the people of Peloponesus till after the Peloponesian war. The Peloponesians, Thucydides observes, generally left the field in the summer, and returned home to reap the harvest.[8] The Roman people under their kings, and during the first ages of the republic, served in the same manner.[9] It was not till the siege of Veii, that they, who staid at home, began to contribute something towards maintaining those who went to war.[10] In the European monarchies, which were founded upon the ruins of the Roman empire, both before and for some time after the establishment of what is properly called the feudal law, the great lords, with all their immediate dependents, used to serve the crown at their own expence. In the field, in the same manner as at home, they maintained themselves by their own revenue, and not by any stipend or pay which they received from the king upon that particular occasion.

Later it becomes necessary to pay those who take the field,

In a more advanced state of society, two different causes contribute to render it altogether impossible that they, who take the field, should maintain themselves

---

[6] [Ed. 1 reads "or fifth."]

[7] [Ed. 1 reads "so short a."]

[8] [VII., 27.]

[9] [Livy, v., 2.]

[10] [Livy, iv., *59 ad fin.*]

at their own expence. Those two causes are, the progress of manufactures, and the improvement in the art of war.

Though a husbandman should be employed in an expedition, provided it begins after seed-time and ends before harvest, the interruption of his business will not always occasion any considerable diminution of his revenue. Without the intervention of his labour, nature does herself the greater part of the work which remains to be done. But the moment that an artificer, a smith, a carpenter, or a weaver, for example, quits his workhouse, the sole source of his revenue is completely dried up. Nature does nothing for him, he does all for himself. When he takes the field, therefore, in defence of the public, as he has no revenue to maintain himself, he must necessarily be maintained by the public. But in a country of which a greater part of the inhabitants are artificers and manufacturers, a great part of the people who go to war must be drawn from those classes, and must therefore be maintained by the public as long as they are employed in its service.

since artificers and manufacturers must be maintained by the public when away from their work,

When the art of war too has gradually grown up to be a very intricate and complicated science, when the event of war ceases to be determined, as in the first ages of society, by a single irregular skirmish or battle, but when the contest is generally spun out through several different campaigns, each of which lasts during the greater part of the year; it becomes universally necessary that the public should maintain those who serve the public in war, at least while they are employed in that service. Whatever in time of peace might be the ordinary occupation of those who go to war, so very tedious and expensive a service would otherwise be by far too heavy a burden upon them. After the second Persian war, accordingly, the armies of Athens seem to have been generally composed of mercenary troops; consisting, indeed, partly of citizens, but partly too of foreigners; and all of them equally hired and paid at the expence of the state. From the time of the

and the greater length of campaigns make service without pay too heavy a burden even for husbandmen.

siege of Veii, the armies of Rome received pay for their service during the time which they remained in the field.[11] Under the feudal governments the military service both of the great lords and of their immediate dependents was, after a certain period, universally exchanged for a payment in money, which was employed to maintain those who served in their stead.

The number of those who can go to war, in proportion to the whole number of the people, is necessarily much smaller in a civilized, than in a rude state of society. In a civilized society,

The possible proportion of soldiers to the rest of the population is much smaller in civilised times.

as the soldiers are maintained altogether by the labour of those who are not soldiers, the number of the former can never[12] exceed what the latter can maintain, over and above maintaining, in a manner suitable to their respective stations, both themselves and the other officers of government, and law, whom they are obliged to maintain. In the little agrarian states of ancient Greece, a fourth or a fifth part of the whole body of the people considered themselves as soldiers, and would sometimes, it is said, take the field. Among the civilized nations of modern Europe, it is commonly computed, that not more than one hundredth part of the inhabitants of any country can be employed as soldiers, without ruin to the country which pays the expence of their service.[13]

The expence of preparing the army for the field seems not to have become considerable in any nation, till long after that of maintaining it in the field had devolved entirely upon the

The expense of preparing for the field was long inconsiderable.

sovereign or commonwealth. In all the different republics of ancient Greece, to learn his military exercises, was a necessary part of education imposed by the state upon every free citizen. In every city there seems

to have been a public field, in which, under the protection of

---

[11] [Above, p. 883.]

[12] [Ed. 1 reads "never can."]

[13] [Ed. 1 reads "at whose expence they are employed." Repeated all but *verbatim* below, p. 979.]

the public magistrate, the young people were taught their different exercises by different masters. In this very simple institution, consisted the whole expence which any Grecian state seems ever to have been at, in preparing its citizens for war. In ancient Rome the exercises of the Campus Martius answered the same purpose with those of the Gymnasium in ancient Greece. Under the feudal governments, the many public ordinances that the citizens of every district should practise archery as well as several other military exercises, were intended for promoting the same purpose, but do not seem to have promoted it so well. Either from want of interest in the officers entrusted with the execution of those ordinances, or from some other cause, they appear to have been universally neglected; and in the progress of all those governments, military exercises seem to have gone gradually into disuse among the great body of the people.

In the republics of ancient Greece and Rome, during the whole period of their existence, and under the feudal governments for a considerable time after their first establishment, the trade of a soldier was not a separate, distinct trade, which constituted the sole or principal occupation of a particular class of citizens. Every subject of the state, whatever might be the ordinary trade or occupation by which he gained his livelihood, considered himself, upon all ordinary occasions, as fit likewise to exercise the trade of a soldier, and upon many extraordinary occasions as bound to exercise it.

Soldiers were not a distinct class in Greece and Rome, nor at first in feudal times.

The art of war, however, as it is certainly the noblest of all arts, so in the progress of improvement it necessarily becomes one of the most complicated among them. The state of the mechanical, as well as of some other arts, with which it is necessarily connected, determines the degree of perfection to which it is capable of being carried at any particular time. But in order to carry it to this degree of perfection, it is necessary that it should become the sole or principal occupation of a particu-

But as war becomes more complicated, division of labour becomes necessary to carry the art to perfection.

lar class of citizens, and the division of labour is as necessary for the improvement of this, as of every other art. Into other arts the division of labour is naturally introduced by the prudence of individuals, who find that they promote their private interest better by confining themselves to a particular trade, than by exercising a great number. But it is the wisdom of the state only which can render the trade of a soldier a particular trade separate and distinct from all others. A private citizen who, in time of profound peace, and without any particular encouragement from the public, should spend the greater part of his time in military exercises, might, no doubt, both improve himself very much in them, and amuse himself very well; but he certainly would not promote his own interest. It is the wisdom of the state only which can render it for his interest to give up the greater part of his time to this peculiar occupation: and states have not always had this wisdom, even when their circumstances had become such, that the preservation of their existence required that they should have it.

A shepherd has a great deal of leisure; a husbandman, in the rude state of husbandry, has some; an artificer or manufacturer

As society advances the people become unwarlike. has none at all. The first may, without any loss, employ a great deal of his time in martial exercises; the second may employ some part of it; but the last cannot employ a single hour in them without some loss, and his attention to his own interest naturally leads him to neglect them altogether. Those improvements in husbandry too, which the progress of arts and manufactures necessarily introduces, leave the husbandman as little leisure as the artificer. Military exercises come to be as much neglected by the inhabitants of the country as by those of the town, and the great body of the people becomes altogether unwarlike. That wealth, at the same time, which always follows the improvements of agriculture and manufactures, and which in reality is no more than the accumulated produce of those improvements, provokes the invasion of all their neighbours. An industrious, and upon that account a wealthy nation, is of all nations the most likely to be attacked; and unless the state takes some new measures for the public defence, the natural habits of the people render them altogether incapable of defending themselves.

In these circumstances, there seem to be but two methods, by which the state can make any tolerable provision for the public defence.

It may either, first, by means of a very rigorous police, and

There are only two methods of providing for defence, (1) to enforce military exercises and service,

in spite of the whole bent of the interest, genius and inclinations of the people, enforce the practice of military exercises, and oblige either all the citizens of the military age, or a certain number of them, to join in some measure the trade of a soldier to whatever other trade or profession they may happen to carry on.

Or secondly, by maintaining and employing a certain number of citizens in the constant practice of military exercises, it

or (2) to make the trade of the soldier a separate one:

may render the trade of a soldier a particular trade, separate and distinct from all others.

If the state has recourse to the first of those two expedients, its military force is said to consist in a militia; if to the second, it

in other words the establishment of a militia or a standing army.

is said to consist in a standing army. The practice of military exercises is the sole or principal occupation of the soldiers of a standing army, and the maintenance or pay

which the state affords them is the principal and ordinary fund of their subsistence. The practice of military exercises is only the occasional occupation of the soldiers of a militia, and they derive the principal and ordinary fund of their subsistence from some other occupation. In a militia, the character of the labourer, artificer, or tradesman, predominates over that of the soldier: in a standing army, that of the soldier predominates over every other character; and in this distinction seems to consist the essential difference between those two different species of military force.

Militias have been of several different kinds. In some countries the citizens destined for defending the state, seem to have been exercised only, without being, if I may say so, regi-

Militias were anciently only exercised and not regimented. mented; that is, without being divided into separate and distinct bodies of troops, each of which performed its exercises under its own proper and permanent officers. In the republics of ancient Greece and Rome, each citizen, as long as he remained at home, seems to have practised his exercises either separately and independently, or with such of his equals as he liked best; and not to have been attached to any particular body of troops till he was actually called upon to take the field. In other countries, the militia has not only been exercised, but regimented. In England, in Switzerland, and, I believe, in every other country of modern Europe, where any imperfect military force of this kind has been established, every militia-man is, even in time of peace, attached to a particular body of troops, which performs its exercises under its own proper and permanent officers.

Before the invention of fire-arms, that army was superior in which the soldiers had, each individually, the greatest skill and dexterity in the use of their arms. Strength and agility of body *Fire-arms brought about the change by making dexterity less important,* were of the highest consequence, and commonly determined the fate of battles. But this skill and dexterity in the use of their arms, could be acquired only, in the same manner as fencing is[14] at present, by practising, not in great bodies, but each man separately, in a particular school, under a particular master, or with his own particular equals and companions. Since the invention of fire-arms, strength and agility of body, or even extraordinary dexterity and skill in the use of arms, though they are far from being of no consequence, are, however, of less consequence. The nature of the weapon, though it by no means puts the awkward upon a level with the skilful, puts him more nearly so than he ever was before. All the dexterity and skill, it is supposed, which are necessary for using it, can be well enough acquired by practising in great bodies.

Regula ity, order, and prompt obedience to command, are

---

[14] [Ed. 1 reads "is acquired."]

qualities which, in modern armies, are of more importance towards determining the fate of battles, than the dexterity and

and discipline much more so.

skill of the soldiers in the use of their arms. But the noise of fire-arms, the smoke, and the invisible death to which every man feels himself every moment exposed, as soon as he comes within cannonshot, and frequently a long time before the battle can be well said to be engaged, must render it very difficult to maintain any considerable degree of this regularity, order, and prompt obedience, even in the beginning of a modern battle. In an ancient battle there was no noise but what arose from the human voice; there was no smoke, there was no invisible cause of wounds or death. Every man, till some mortal weapon actually did approach him, saw clearly that no such weapon was near him. In these circumstances, and among troops who had some confidence in their own skill and dexterity in the use of their arms, it must have been a good deal less difficult to preserve some degree of regularity and order, not only in the beginning, but through the whole progress of an ancient battle, and till one of the two armies was fairly defeated. But the habits of regularity, order, and prompt obedience to command, can be acquired only by troops which are exercised in great bodies.

A militia, however, in whatever manner it may be either disciplined or exercised, must always be much

A militia is always inferior to a standing army, being less expert,

inferior to a well-disciplined and well-exercised standing army.

The soldiers, who are exercised only once a week, or once a month, can never be so expert in the use of their arms, as those who are exercised every day, or every other day; and though this circumstance may not be of so much consequence in modern, as it was in ancient times, yet the acknowledged superiority of the Prussian troops, owing, it is said, very much to their superior expertness in their exercise, may satisfy us that it is, even at this day, of very considerable consequence.

The soldiers, who are bound to obey their officer only once a week or once a month, and who are at all other times at lib-

and less well disciplined. erty to manage their own affairs their own way, without being in any respect accountable to him, can never be under the same awe in his presence, can never have the same disposition to ready obedience, with those whose whole life and conduct are every day directed by him, and who every day even rise and go to bed, or at least retire to their quarters, according to his orders. In what is called discipline, or in the habit of ready obedience, a militia must always be still more inferior to a standing army, than it may sometimes be in what is called the manual exercise, or in the management and use of its arms. But in modern war the habit of ready and instant obedience is of much greater consequence than a considerable superiority in the management of arms.

Those militias which, like the Tartar or Arab militia, go to war under the same chieftains whom they are accustomed to obey in peace, are by far the best. In respect *The best militias are those which go to war under the chieftains who rule in time of peace.* for their officers, in the habit of ready obedience, they approach nearest to standing armies. The highland militia, when it served under its own chieftains, had some advantage of the same kind. As the highlanders, however, were not wandering, but stationary shepherds, as they had all a fixed habitation, and were not, in peaceable times, accustomed to follow their chieftain from place to place; so in time of war they were less willing to follow him to any considerable distance, or to continue for any long time in the field. When they had acquired any booty they were eager to return home, and his authority was seldom sufficient to detain them. In point of obedience they were always much inferior to what is reported of the Tartars and Arabs. As the highlanders too, from their stationary life, spend less of their time in the open air, they were always less accustomed to military exercises, and were less expert in the use of their arms than the Tartars and Arabs are said to be.

A militia of any kind, it must be observed, however, which has served for several successive campaigns in the field, becomes in every respect a standing army. The soldiers are every

A militia kept long enough in the field becomes a standing army.

day exercised in the use of their arms, and, being constantly under the command of their officers, are habituated to the same prompt obedience which takes place in standing armies. What they were before they took the field, is of little importance. They necessarily become in every respect a standing army, after they have passed a few campaigns in it. Should the war in America drag out through another campaign,[15] the American militia may become in every respect a match for that standing army, of which the valour appeared, in the last war,[16] at least not inferior to that of the hardiest veterans of France and Spain.

This distinction being well understood, the history of all ages, it will be found, bears testimony to the irresistible superiority which a well-regulated standing army has over a militia.

History shows the superiority of the standing army.

That of Macedon defeated the Greek militias.

One of the first standing armies of which we have any distinct account, in any well authenticated history, is that of Philip of Macedon. His frequent wars with the Thracians, Illyrians, Thessalians, and some of the Greek cities in the neighbourhood of Macedon, gradually formed his troops, which in the beginning were probably militia, to the exact discipline of a standing army. When he was at peace, which he was very seldom, and never for any long time together, he was careful not to disband that army. It vanquished and subdued, after a long and violent struggle, indeed, the gallant and well exercised militias of the principal republics of ancient Greece; and afterwards, with very little struggle, the effeminate and ill-exercised militia of the great Persian empire. The fall of the Greek republics and of the Persian empire, was the effect of the irresistible superiority which a standing army has over every sort of militia. It is the first great revolu-

---

[15] [As ed. 1 was published at the beginning of March, 1776, this must have been written less than a year after the outbreak of the war, which lasted eight years.]

[16] [The Seven Years' War, 1756–1763. Ed. 1 reads "of which in the last war the valour appeared."]

tion in the affairs of mankind, of which history has preserved any distinct or circumstantial account.

The fall of Carthage, and the consequent elevation of Rome, is the second. All the varieties of the fortune of those two famous republics may very well be accounted for from the same cause.

In the wars of Carthage and Rome standing armies defeated militias.

From the end of the first to the beginning of the second Carthaginian war, the armies of Carthage were continually in the field, and employed under three great generals, who succeeded one another in the command; Amilcar, his son-in-law Asdrubal, and his son Annibal; first in chastising their own rebellious slaves, afterwards in subdu-

The Carthaginian standing army defeated the Roman militia in Italy

ing the revolted nations of Africa, and, lastly, in conquering the great kingdom of Spain. The army which Annibal led from Spain into Italy must necessarily, in those different wars, have been gradually formed to the exact discipline of a standing army. The Romans, in the mean time, though they had not been altogether at peace, yet they had not, during this period, been engaged in any war of very great consequence; and their military discipline, it is generally said, was a good deal relaxed. The Roman armies which Annibal encountered at Trebia, Thrasymenus and Cannæ, were militia opposed to a standing army. This circumstance, it is probable, contributed more than any other to determine the fate of those battles.

The standing army which Annibal left behind him in Spain, had the like superiority over the militia which the Romans sent to oppose it, and in a few years, under the command of his brother, the younger Asdrubal, expelled them almost entirely from that country.

Annibal was ill supplied from home. The Roman militia, being continually in the field, became in the progress of the war a well disciplined and well exercised standing army; and the superiority of Annibal grew every day less and less. Asdrubal judged it necessary to lead the whole, or almost the whole of the standing army which he commanded in Spain, to the assistance of his brother

and Spain.

When the Roman militias became a standing army they defeated the Carthaginian standing army in Italy

in Italy. In this[17] march he is said to have been misled by his guides; and in a country which he did not know, was surprised and attacked by another standing army, in every respect equal or superior to his own, and was entirely defeated.

When Asdrubal had left Spain, the great Scipio found nothing to oppose him but a militia inferior to his own. He conquered and subdued that militia, and, in the course of the war, his own militia necessarily became a well-disciplined and well-exercised standing army. That standing army was afterwards carried to Africa, where it found nothing but a militia to oppose it. In order to defend Carthage it became necessary to recall the standing army of Annibal.

and the Carthaginian militia in Spain, and both standing army and militia in Africa.

The disheartened and frequently defeated African militia joined it, and, at the battle of Zama, composed the greater part of the troops of Annibal. The event of that day determined the fate of the two rival republics.

From the end of the second Carthaginian war till the fall of the Roman republic, the armies of Rome were in every respect standing armies. The standing army of Macedon made some resistance to their arms. In the height of their grandeur, it cost them two great wars, and three great battles, to subdue that little kingdom; of which the conquest would probably have been still more difficult, had it not been for the cowardice of its last king. The militias of all the civilized nations of the ancient world, of Greece, of Syria, and of Egypt, made but a feeble resistance to the standing armies of Rome. The militias of some barbarous nations defended themselves much better. The Scythian or Tartar militia, which Mithridates drew from the countries north of the Euxine and Caspian seas, were the most formida-

Thenceforward the Roman republic had standing armies, which found little resistance except from the standing army of Macedon.

---

[17] ["This" is probably a misprint for "his," the reading of eds. 1–3.]

ble enemies whom[18] the Romans had to encounter after the second Carthaginian war. The Parthian and German militias too were always respectable, and, upon several occasions, gained very considerable advantages over the Roman armies. In general, however, and when the Roman armies were well commanded, they appear to have been very much superior; and if the Romans did not pursue the final conquest either of Parthia or Germany, it was probably because they judged, that it was not worth while to add those two barbarous countries to an empire which was already too large. The ancient Parthians appear to have been a nation of Scythian or Tartar extraction, and to have always retained a good deal of the manners of their ancestors. The ancient Germans were, like the Scythians or Tartars, a nation of wandering shepherds, who went to war under the same chiefs whom they were accustomed to follow in peace. Their militia was exactly of the same kind with that of the Scythians or Tartars, from whom too they were probably descended.

Many different causes contributed to relax the discipline of the Roman armies. Its extreme severity was, perhaps, one of those causes. In the days of their grandeur, when no enemy appeared capable of opposing them, their heavy armour was laid aside as unnecessarily burdensome, their laborious exercises were neglected as unnecessarily toilsome. Under the Roman emperors besides, the standing armies of Rome, those particularly which guarded the German and Pannonian frontiers, became dangerous to their masters, against whom they used frequently to set up their own generals. In order to render them less formidable, according to some authors, Dioclesian, according to others, Constantine, first withdrew them from the frontier, where they had always before been encamped in great bodies, generally of two or three legions each, and dispersed them in small bodies through the different provincial towns, from whence they were scarce ever removed, but when it became necessary to repel an invasion.

Under the emperors these armies degenerated into militias.

---

[18] [Ed. 1 reads "which."]

Small bodies of soldiers quartered in trading and manufacturing towns, and seldom removed from those quarters, became themselves tradesmen, artificers, and manufacturers. The civil came to predominate over the military character; and the standing armies of Rome gradually degenerated into a corrupt, neglected, and undisciplined militia, incapable of resisting the attack of the German and Scythian militias, which soon afterwards invaded the western empire. It was only by hiring the militia of some of those nations to oppose to that of others, that the emperors were for some time able to defend themselves. The fall of the western empire is the third great revolution in the affairs of mankind, of which ancient history has preserved any distinct or circumstantial account. It was brought about by the irresistible superiority which the militia of a barbarous, has over that of a civilized nation; which the militia of a nation of shepherds, has over that of a nation of husbandmen, artificers, and manufacturers. The victories which have been gained by militias have generally been, not over standing armies, but over other militias in exercise and discipline inferior to themselves. Such were the victories which the Greek militia gained over that of the Persian empire; and such too were those which in later times the Swiss militia gained over that of the Austrians and Burgundians.

The military force of the German and Scythian nations who established themselves upon the ruins of the western empire,

Militias were gradually superseded by standing armies in Western Europe.

continued for some time to be of the same kind in their new settlements, as it had been in their original country. It was a militia of shepherds and husbandmen, which, in time of war, took the field under the command of the same chieftains whom it was accustomed to obey in peace. It was, therefore, tolerably well exercised, and tolerably well disciplined. As arts and industry advanced, however, the authority of the chieftains gradually decayed, and the great body of the people had less time to spare for military exercises. Both the discipline and the exercise of the feudal militia, therefore, went gradually to ruin, and standing armies were gradually introduced to supply the place of it. When the expedient of a standing army, besides, had once been adopted by one civilized nation, it became necessary that all its neighbours should follow the example. They soon found that their safety depended upon their doing so, and that their own militia was altogether incapable of resisting the attack of such an army.

The soldiers of a standing army, though they may never have seen an enemy, yet have frequently appeared to possess all the courage of veteran troops, and the very moment that they took the field to have been fit to face the hardiest and most experienced veterans. In 1756, when the Russian army marched into Poland, the valour of the Russian soldiers did not appear inferior to that of the Prussians, at that time supposed to be the hardiest and most experienced veterans in Europe. The Russian empire, however, had enjoyed a profound peace for near twenty years before, and could at that time have very few soldiers who had ever seen an enemy. When the Spanish war broke out in 1739, England had enjoyed a profound peace for about eight and twenty years. The valour of her soldiers, however, far from being corrupted by that long peace, was never more distinguished than in the attempt upon Carthagena, the first unfortunate exploit of that unfortunate war. In a long peace the generals, perhaps, may sometimes forget their skill; but, where a well-regulated standing army has been kept up, the soldiers seem never to forget their valour.

A standing army does not lose its valour in time of peace,

When a civilized nation depends for its defence upon a militia, it is at all times exposed to be conquered by any barbarous nation which happens to be in its neighbourhood. The frequent conquests of all the civilized countries in Asia by the Tartars, sufficiently demonstrates[19] the natural superiority, which the militia of a barbarous, has over that of a civilized nation. A well-regulated standing army is superior to every militia. Such an army, as it can best be maintained by an opulent and civilized nation, so it can alone defend such a na-

and is the only safeguard of a civilised nation,

---

[19] [Almost certainly a misprint for "demonstrate," the reading of ed. 1.]

tion against the invasion of a poor and barbarous neighbour. It is only by means of a standing army, therefore, that the civilization of any country can be perpetuated, or even preserved for any considerable time.

As it is only by means of a well-regulated standing army that a civilized country can be defended; so it is only by means

also the only means of civilising a barbarous one.

of it, that a barbarous country can be suddenly and tolerably civilized. A standing army establishes, with an irresistible force, the law of the sovereign through the remotest provinces of the empire, and maintains some degree of regular government in countries which could not otherwise admit of any. Whoever examines, with attention, the improvements which Peter the Great introduced into the Russian empire, will find that they almost all resolve themselves into the establishment of a well-regulated standing army. It is the instrument which executes and maintains all his other regulations. That degree of order and internal peace, which that empire has ever since enjoyed, is altogether owing to the influence of that army.

Men of republican principles have been jealous of a standing army as dangerous to liberty. It certainly is so, wherever

It is not unfavourable to liberty.

the interest of the general and that of the principal officers are not necessarily connected with the support of the constitution of the state. The standing army of Cæsar destroyed the Roman republic. The standing army of Cromwel turned the long parliament out of doors.[20] But where the sovereign is himself the general, and the principal nobility and gentry of the country the chief officers of the army; where the military force is placed under the command of those who have the greatest interest in the support of the civil authority, because they have themselves the greatest share of that authority, a standing army can never be dangerous to liberty. On the contrary, it may in some cases be favourable to

---

[20] [*Lectures*, p. 29. "Cromwel," which is Hume's spelling, appears first in ed. 4 here, but above, p. 758, it is so spelt in all editions.]

liberty.[21] The security which it gives to the sovereign renders unnecessary that troublesome jealousy, which, in some modern republics, seems to watch over the minutest actions, and to be at all times ready to disturb the peace of every citizen. Where the security of the magistrate, though supported by the principal people of the country, is endangered by every popular discontent; where a small tumult is capable of bringing about in a few hours a great revolution, the whole authority of government must be employed to suppress and punish every murmur and complaint against it. To a sovereign, on the contrary, who feels himself supported, not only by the natural aristocracy of the country, but by a well-regulated standing army, the rudest, the most groundless, and the most licentious remonstrances can give little disturbance. He can safely pardon or neglect them, and his consciousness of his own superiority naturally disposes him to do so. That degree of liberty which approaches to licentiousness can be tolerated only in countries where the sovereign is secured by a well-regulated standing army. It is in such countries only, that the public safety does not require, that the sovereign should be trusted with any discretionary power, for suppressing even the impertinent wantonness of this licentious liberty.

The first duty of the sovereign, therefore, that of defending the society from the violence and injustice of other independ-

Defence thus grows more expensive.

ent societies, grows gradually more and more expensive, as the society advances in civilization. The military force of the society, which originally cost the sovereign no expence either in time of peace or in time of war, must, in the progress of improvement, first be maintained by him in time of war, and afterwards even in time of peace.

The great change introduced into the art of war by the invention of fire-arms, has enhanced still further both the expence of

Fire-arms enhance the expense,

exercising and disciplining any particular number of soldiers in time of peace, and that of employing them in time of war. Both their arms and their ammunition are become more expensive. A

---

[21] [*Lectures*, p. 263.]

musquet is a more expensive machine than a javelin or a bow and arrows; a cannon or a mortar than a balista or a catapulta. The powder, which is spent in a modern review, is lost irrecoverably, and occasions a very considerable expence. The javelins and arrows which were thrown or shot in an ancient one, could easily be picked up again, and were besides of very little value. The cannon and the mortar are, not only much dearer, but much heavier machines than the balista or catapulta, and require a greater expence, not only to prepare them for the field, but to carry them to it. As the superiority of the modern artillery too, over that of the ancients is very great; it has become much more difficult, and consequently much more expensive, to fortify a town so as to resist even for a few weeks the attack of that superior artillery. In modern times many different causes contribute to render the defence of the society more expensive. The unavoidable effects of the natural progress of improvement have, in this respect, been a good deal enhanced by a great revolution in the art of war, to which a mere accident, the invention of gunpowder, seems to have given occasion.

In modern war the great expence of fire-arms gives an evident advantage to the nation which can best afford that expence; and consequently, to an opulent and civilized over a poor and barbarous nation. In ancient times the opulent and civilized found it difficult to defend themselves against the poor and barbarous nations. In modern times the poor and barbarous find it difficult to defend themselves against the opulent and civilized. The invention of fire-arms, an invention which at first sight appears to be so pernicious, is certainly favourable both to the permanency and to the extension of civilization.[22]

and so give an advantage to rich nations, which is favourable to civilisation.

---

[22] [Hume, *History*, ed. of 1773, vol. ii., p. 432, says the "furious engine," artillery, "though it seemed contrived for the destruction of mankind and the overthrow of empires, has in the issue rendered battles less bloody, and has given greater stability to civil societies," but his reasons are somewhat different from those in the text above. This part of the chapter is evidently adapted from Part iv. "Of Arms" in the *Lectures*, pp. 260–264, and the dissertation on the rise, progress and fall of militarism in Part i., pp. 26–34.]

PART II

OF THE EXPENCE OF JUSTICE

The second duty of the sovereign, that of protecting, as far as possible, every member of the society from the injustice or oppression of every other member of it, or the duty of establishing an exact administration of justice requires two very different degrees of expence in the different periods of society.

The expense of justice is different at different periods.

Among nations of hunters, as there is scarce any property, or at least none that exceeds the value of two or three days labour; so there is seldom any established magistrate or any regular administration of justice. Men who have no property can injure one another only in their persons or reputations. But when one man kills, wounds, beats, or defames another, though he to whom the injury is done suffers, he who does it receives no benefit. It is otherwise with the injuries to property. The benefit of the person who does the injury is often equal to the loss of him who suffers it. Envy, malice, or resentment, are the only passions which can prompt one man to injure another in his person or reputation. But the greater part of men are not very frequently under the influence of those passions; and the very worst men are so only occasionally. As their gratification too, how agreeable soever it may be to certain characters, is not attended with any real or permanent advantage, it is in the greater part of men commonly restrained by prudential considerations. Men may live together in society with some tolerable degree of security, though there is no civil magistrate to protect them from the injustice of those passions. But avarice and ambition in the rich, in the poor the hatred of labour and the love of present ease and enjoyment, are the passions which prompt to invade property, passions much more steady in their operation, and much more universal in their influence. Wherever

Civil government was first rendered necessary by the introduction of property.

there is great property, there is great inequality. For one very rich man, there must be at least five hundred poor, and the affluence of the few supposes the indigence of the many. The affluence of the rich excites the indignation of the poor, who are often both driven by want, and prompted by envy, to invade his possessions. It is only under the shelter of the civil magistrate that the owner of that valuable property, which is acquired by the labour of many years, or perhaps of many successive generations, can sleep a single night in security. He is at all times surrounded by unknown enemies, whom, though he never provoked, he can never appease, and from whose injustice he can be protected only by the powerful arm of the civil magistrate continually held up to chastise it. The acquisition of valuable and[23] extensive property, therefore, necessarily requires the establishment of civil government. Where there is no property, or at least none that exceeds the value of two or three days labour, civil government is not so necessary.

Civil government supposes a certain subordination. But as

Property strengthens the causes of subordination.

the necessity of civil government gradually grows up with the acquisition of valuable property, so the principal causes which naturally introduce subordination gradually grow up with the growth of that valuable property.

The causes or circumstances which naturally introduce sub-

There are four causes of subordination,

ordination, or which naturally, and antecedent to any civil institution, give some men some superiority over the greater part of their brethren, seem to be four in number.

The first of those causes or circumstances is the superiority of personal qualifications, of strength, beauty, and agility of

(1) superiority of personal qualifications,

body; of wisdom, and virtue, of prudence, justice, fortitude, and moderation of mind. The qualifications of the body, unless supported by those of the mind, can give little authority in any period of society. He is a very strong man, who, by mere strength of body, can force two weak ones to

[23] [Ed. 1 reads "or."]

obey him. The qualifications of the mind can alone give very great authority. They are, however, invisible qualities; always disputable, and generally disputed. No society, whether barbarous or civilized, has ever found it convenient to settle the rules of precedency of rank and subordination, according to those invisible qualities; but according to something that is more plain and palpable.

The second of those causes or circumstances is the superiority of age. An old man, provided his age is not so far advanced as to give suspicion of dotage, is every where more respected than a young man of equal rank, fortune, and abilities. Among nations of hunters, such as the native tribes of North America, age is the sole foundation of rank and precedency. Among them, father is the appellation of a superior; brother, of an equal; and son, of an inferior. In the most opulent and civilized nations, age regulates rank among those who are in every other respect equal, and among whom, therefore, there is nothing else to regulate it. Among brothers and among sisters, the eldest always take place; and in the succession of the paternal estate every thing which cannot be divided, but must go entire to one person, such as a title of honour, is in most cases given to the eldest. Age is a plain and palpable quality which admits of no dispute.

(2) superiority of age,

The third of those causes or circumstances is the superiority of fortune. The authority of riches, however, though great in every age of society, is perhaps greatest in the rudest age of society which admits of any considerable inequality of fortune. A Tartar chief, the increase of whose herds and flocks is sufficient to maintain a thousand men, cannot well employ that increase in any other way than in maintaining a thousand men. The rude state of his society does not afford him any manufactured produce, any trinkets or baubles of any kind, for which he can exchange that part of his rude produce which is over and above his own consumption. The thousand men whom he thus maintains, depending entirely upon him for their subsistence, must both obey his orders in war, and submit to his jurisdiction

(3) superiority of fortune,

in peace. He is necessarily both their general and their judge, and his chieftainship is the necessary effect of the superiority of his fortune. In an opulent and civilized society a man may possess a much greater fortune, and yet not be able to command a dozen of people. Though the produce of his estate may be sufficient to maintain, and may perhaps actually maintain, more than a thousand people, yet as those people pay for every thing which they get from him, as he gives scarce any thing to any body but in exchange for an equivalent, there is scarce any body who considers himself as entirely dependent upon him, and his authority extends only over a few menial servants. The authority of fortune, however, is very great even in an opulent and civilized society. That it is much greater than that, either of age, or of personal qualities, has been the constant complaint of every period of society which admitted of any considerable inequality of fortune. The first period of society, that of hunters, admits of no such inequality. Universal poverty establishes there[24] universal equality, and the superiority, either of age, or of personal qualities, are the feeble, but the sole foundations of authority and subordination. There is therefore little or no authority or subordination in this period of society. The second period of society, that of shepherds, admits of very great inequalities of fortune, and there is no period in which the superiority of fortune gives so great authority to those who possess it. There is no period accordingly in which authority and subordination are more perfectly established. The authority of an Arabian scherif is very great; that of a Tartar khan altogether despotical.

The fourth of those causes or circumstances is the superiority of birth. Superiority of birth supposes an ancient superiority of fortune in the family of the person who claims it. All families are equally ancient; and the ancestors of the prince, though they may be better known, cannot well be more numerous than those of the beggar. Antiquity of family means every where the antiquity either of wealth, or of that greatness which is com-

and (4) superiority of birth.

---

[24] [Misprinted "their" in eds. 4 and 5.]

monly either founded upon wealth, or accompanied with it. Upstart greatness is every where less respected than ancient greatness.[25] The hatred of usurpers, the love of the family of an ancient monarch, are, in a great measure, founded upon the contempt which men naturally have for the former, and upon their veneration for the latter. As a military officer submits without reluctance to the authority of a superior by whom he has always been commanded, but cannot bear that his inferior should be set over his head; so men easily submit to a family to whom they and their ancestors have always submitted; but are fired with indignation when another family, in whom they had never acknowledged any such superiority, assumes a dominion over them.

The distinction of birth, being subsequent to the inequality of fortune, can have no place in nations of hunters, among whom all men, being equal in fortune, must likewise be very nearly equal in birth. The son of a wise and brave man may, indeed, even among them, be somewhat more respected than a man of equal merit who has the misfortune to be the son of a fool or a coward. The difference, however, will not be very great; and there never was, I believe, a great family in the world whose illustration was entirely derived from the inheritance of wisdom and virtue.

The distinction of birth is not present among hunters,

The distinction of birth not only may, but always does take place among nations of shepherds. Such nations are always strangers to every sort of luxury, and great wealth can scarce ever be dissipated among them by improvident profusion. There are no nations accordingly who abound more in families revered and honoured on account of their descent from a long race of great and illustrious ancestors; because there are no nations among whom wealth is likely to continue longer in the same families.

but always among shepherds.

Birth and fortune are evidently the two circumstances which principally set one man above another. They are the two great sources of personal distinction, and are therefore the

[25] [*Lectures*, p. 10.]

Distinctions of birth and fortune are both most powerful among shepherds.

principal causes which naturally establish authority and subordination among men. Among nations of shepherds both those causes operate with their full force. The great shepherd or herdsman, respected on account of his great wealth, and of the great number of those who depend upon him for subsistence, and revered on account of the nobleness of his birth, and of the immemorial antiquity of his illustrious family, has a natural authority over all the inferior shepherds or herdsmen of his horde or clan. He can command the united force of a greater number of people than any of them. His military power is greater than that of any of them. In time of war they are all of them naturally disposed to muster themselves under his banner, rather than under that of any other person, and his birth and fortune thus naturally procure to him some sort of executive power. By commanding too the united force of a greater number of people than any of them, he is best able to compel any one of them who may have injured another to compensate the wrong. He is the person, therefore, to whom all those who are too weak to defend themselves naturally look up for protection. It is to him that they naturally complain of the injuries which they imagine have been done to them, and his interposition in such cases is more easily submitted to, even by the person complained of, than that of any other person would be. His birth and fortune thus naturally procure him some sort of judicial authority.

It is in the age of shepherds, in the second period of society, that the inequality of fortune first begins to take place, and in-

Among shepherds inequality of fortune arises and introduces civil government,

troduces among men a degree of authority and subordination which could not possibly exist before. It thereby introduces some degree of that civil government which is indispensably necessary for its own preservation: and it seems to do this naturally, and even independent of the consideration of that necessity. The consideration of that necessity comes no doubt afterwards to contribute very much to maintain and secure that authority and subordination. The rich, in particular, are necessarily interested to support that order of things, which can alone secure them in the possession of their own advantages. Men of inferior wealth combine to defend those of superior wealth in the possession of their property, in order that men of superior wealth may combine to defend them in the possession of theirs. All the inferior shepherds and herdsmen feel that the security of their own herds and flocks depends upon the security of those of the great shepherd or herdsman; that the maintenance of their lesser authority depends upon that of his greater authority, and that upon their subordination to him depends his power of keeping their inferiors in subordination to them. They constitute a sort of little nobility, who feel themselves interested to defend the property and to support the authority of their own little sovereign, in order that he may be able to defend their property and to support their authority. Civil government, so far as it is instituted for the security of property, is in reality instituted for the defence of the rich against the poor, or of those who have some property against those who have none at all.[26]

The judicial authority of such a sovereign, however, far from being a cause of expence, was for a long time a source of

but the judicial authority was long a source of revenue rather than expense,

revenue to him. The persons who applied to him for justice were always willing to pay for it, and a present never failed to accompany a petition. After the authority of the sovereign too was thoroughly established, the person found guilty, over and above the satisfaction which he was obliged to make to the party, was likewise forced to pay an amercement to the sovereign. He had given trouble, he had disturbed, he had broke the peace of his lord the king, and for those offences an amercement was thought due. In the Tartar governments of Asia, in the governments of Europe which were founded by the German and Scythian nations who overturned the Roman empire, the ad-

---

[26] [*Lectures*, p. 15: "Till there be property there can be no government, the very end of which is to secure wealth and to defend the rich from the poor." Cp. Locke, *Civil Government*, § 94, "government has no other end but the preservation of property."]

ministration of justice was a considerable source of revenue, both to the sovereign, and to all the lesser chiefs or lords who exercised under him any particular jurisdiction, either over some particular tribe or clan, or over some particular territory or district. Originally both the sovereign and the inferior chiefs used to exercise this jurisdiction in their own persons. Afterwards they universally found it convenient to delegate it to some substitute, bailiff, or judge. This substitute, however, was still obliged to account to his principal or constituent for the profits of the jurisdiction. Whoever reads the[27] instructions which were given to the judges of the circuit in the time of Henry II. will see clearly that those judges were a sort of itinerant factors, sent round the country for the purpose of levying certain branches of the king's revenue. In those days the administration of justice, not only afforded a certain revenue to the sovereign, but to procure this revenue seems to have been one of the principal advantages which he proposed to obtain by the administration of justice.

This scheme of making the administration of justice subservient to the purposes of revenue, could scarce fail to be

which produced great abuses,

productive of several very gross abuses. The person, who applied for justice with a large present in his hand, was likely to get something more than justice; while he, who applied for it with a small one, was likely to get something less. Justice too might frequently be delayed, in order that this present might be repeated. The amercement, besides, of the person complained of, might frequently suggest a very strong reason for finding him in the wrong, even when he had not really been so. That such abuses were far from being uncommon, the ancient history of every country in Europe bears witness.

When the sovereign or chief exercised his judicial authority in his own person, how much soever he might abuse it, it must have been scarce possible to get any redress; because

---

[27] [They are to be found in Tyrrell's History of England. *General History of England, both Ecclesiastical and Civil*, by James Tyrrell, vol. ii., 1700, pp. 576–579. The king is Richard I., not Henry II.]

whether the sovereign exercised the judicial authority in person or by deputy.

there could seldom be any body powerful enough to call him to account. When he exercised it by a bailiff, indeed, redress might sometimes be had. If it was for his own benefit only, that the bailiff had been guilty of any act of injustice, the sovereign himself might not always be unwilling to punish him, or to oblige him to repair the wrong. But if it was for the benefit of his sovereign, if it was in order to make court to the person who appointed him and who might prefer him, that he had committed any act of oppression, redress would upon most occasions be as impossible as if the sovereign had committed it himself. In all barbarous governments, accordingly, in all those ancient governments of Europe in particular, which were founded upon the ruins of the Roman empire, the administration of justice appears for a long time to have been extremely corrupt; far from being quite equal and impartial even under the best monarchs, and altogether profligate under the worst.

Among nations of shepherds, where the sovereign or chief is only the greatest shepherd or herdsman of the horde or

These abuses could not be remedied so long as the sovereign depended only on land revenue and court fees,

clan, he is maintained in the same manner as any of his vassals or subjects, by the increase of his own herds or flocks. Among those nations of husbandmen who are but just come out of the shepherd state, and who are not much advanced beyond that state; such as the Greek tribes appear to have been about the time of the Trojan war, and our German and Scythian ancestors when they first settled upon the ruins of the western empire; the sovereign or chief is, in the same manner, only the greatest landlord of the country, and is maintained, in the same manner as any other landlord, by a revenue derived from his own private estate, or from what, in modern Europe, was called the demesne of the crown. His subjects, upon ordinary occasions, contribute nothing to his support, except when, in order to protect them from the oppression of some of their fellow-subjects, they stand in need of his authority.[28] The presents which they make him upon such occasions, constitute the whole ordinary revenue, the whole of the emoluments which, except perhaps upon some very extraordinary emergencies, he derives from his dominion over them. When Agamemnon, in Homer, offers to Achilles for his friendship the sovereignty of seven Greek cities, the sole advantage which he mentions as likely to be derived from it, was, that the people would honour him with presents.[29] As long as such presents, as long as the emoluments of justice, or what may be called the fees of court, constituted in this manner the whole ordinary revenue which the sovereign derived from his sovereignty, it could not well be expected, it could not even decently be proposed, that he should give them up altogether. It might, and it frequently was proposed, that he should regulate and ascertain them. But after they had been so regulated and ascertained, how to hinder a person who was all-powerful from extending them beyond those regulations, was still very difficult, not to say impossible. During the continuance of this state of things, therefore, the corruption of justice, naturally resulting from the arbitrary and uncertain nature of those presents, scarce admitted of any effectual remedy.

But when from different causes, chiefly from the continually increasing expence of defending the nation against the invasion of other nations, the private estate of the sovereign had become altogether insufficient for defraying the expence of the sovereignty; and when it had become necessary that the people should, for their own security, contribute towards this expence by taxes of different kinds, it seems to have been very commonly stipulated, that no present for the administration of justice should, under any pretence, be accepted either by the sovereign, or by his bailiffs and substitutes, the judges. Those

but when taxes became necessary, the people stipulated that no presents should be taken by judges.

---

[28] [Ed. 1 reads "except when they stand in need of the interposition of his authority in order to protect them from the oppression of some of their fellow subjects."]

[29] [*Iliad*, ix., 149–156, but the presents are not the "sole advantage" mentioned.]

presents, it seems to have been supposed, could more easily be abolished altogether, than effectually regulated and ascertained. Fixed salaries were appointed to the judges, which were supposed to compensate to them the loss of whatever might have been their share of the ancient emoluments of justice; as the taxes more than compensated to the sovereign the loss of his. Justice was then said to be administered gratis.

Justice, however, never was in reality administered gratis in any country. Lawyers and attornies, at least, must always be *Justice is never administered gratis.* paid by the parties; and, if they were not, they would perform their duty still worse than they actually perform it. The fees annually paid to lawyers and attornies amount, in every court, to a much greater sum than the salaries of the judges. The circumstance of those salaries being paid by the crown, can no-where much diminish the necessary expence of a law-suit. But it was not so much to diminish the expence, as to prevent the corruption of justice, that the judges were prohibited from receiving any present or fee from the parties.

The office of judge is in itself so very honourable, that men are willing to accept of it, though accompanied with very *The salaries of judges are a small part of the expense of civilised government,* small emoluments. The inferior office of justice of peace, though attended with a good deal of trouble, and in most cases with no emoluments at all, is an object of ambition to the greater part of our country gentlemen. The salaries of all the different judges, high and low, together with the whole expence of the administration and execution of justice, even where it is not managed with very good œconomy, makes, in any civilized country, but a very inconsiderable part of the whole expence of government.

The whole expence of justice too might easily be defrayed by the fees of court; and, without exposing the administration of justice to any real hazard of corruption, the public revenue might thus be entirely discharged from a certain, though, perhaps, but a small incumbrance. It is difficult to regulate the fees of court effectually, where a person so powerful as the sovereign is to share in them, and to derive any considerable part

and might be defrayed by fees of court. of his revenue from them. It is very easy, where the judge is the principal person who can reap any benefit from them. The law can very easily oblige the judge to respect the regulation, though it might not always be able to make the sovereign respect it. Where the fees of court are precisely regulated and ascertained, where they are paid all at once, at a certain period of every process, into the hands of a cashier or receiver, to be by him distributed in certain known proportions among the different judges after the process is decided, and not till it is decided, there seems to be no more danger of corruption than where such fees are prohibited altogether. Those fees, without occasioning any considerable increase in the expence of a law-suit, might be rendered fully sufficient for defraying the whole expence of justice. By not being paid to the judges till the process was determined, they might be some incitement to the diligence of the court in examining and deciding it. In courts which consisted of a considerable number of judges, by proportioning the share of each judge to the number of hours and days which he had employed in examining the process, either in the court or in a committee by order of the court, those fees might give some encouragement to the diligence of each particular judge. Public services are never better performed than when their reward comes only in consequence of their being performed, and is proportioned to the diligence employed in performing them. In the different parliaments of France, the fees of court (called Epicès[30] and vacations) constitute the far greater part of the emoluments of the judges. After all deductions are made, the neat salary paid by the crown to a counsellor or judge in the parliament of Toulouse, in rank and dignity the second parliament of the Kingdom, amounts only to a hundred and fifty livres, about six pounds eleven shillings sterling a year. About seven years ago[31] that sum was in the

---

[30] [The extraordinary accent here and eight lines lower down appears first in ed. 2.]

[31] [Smith was in Toulouse from February or March, 1764, to August, 1765.—Rae, *Life of Adam Smith*, pp. 174, 175, 188.]

same place the ordinary yearly wages of a common footman. The distribution of those Epicès too is according to the diligence of the judges. A diligent judge gains a comfortable, though moderate, revenue by his office: An idle one gets little more than his salary. Those parliaments are perhaps, in many respects, not very convenient courts of justice; but they have never been accused; they seem never even to have been suspected of corruption.

The fees of court seem originally to have been the principal support of the different courts of justice in England. Each

The English courts were originally maintained by fees, and this led to their encroachments.

court endeavoured to draw to itself as much business as it could, and was, upon that account, willing to take cognizance of many suits which were not originally intended to fall under its jurisdiction. The court of king's bench, instituted for the trial of criminal causes only, took cognizance of civil suits; the plaintiff pretending that the defendant, in not doing him justice, had been guilty of some trespass or misdemeanor. The court of exchequer, instituted for the levying of the king's revenue, and for enforcing the payment of such debts only as were due to the king, took cognizance of all other contract debts; the plaintiff alleging that he could not pay the king, because the defendant would not pay him. In consequence of such fictions it came, in many cases, to depend altogether upon the parties before what court they would chuse to have their cause tried; and each court endeavoured, by superior dispatch and impartiality, to draw to itself as many causes as it could. The present admirable constitution of the courts of justice in England was, perhaps, originally in a great measure, formed by this emulation, which anciently took place between their respective judges; each judge endeavouring to give, in his own court, the speediest and most effectual remedy, which the law would admit, for every sort of injustice. Originally the courts of law gave damages only for breach of contract. The court of chancery, as a court of conscience, first took upon it to enforce the specific performance of agreements. When the breach of contract consisted in the non-payment of money, the damage sustained could be compensated in no other way than by ordering payment, which was equivalent to a specific performance of the agreement. In such cases, therefore, the remedy of the courts of law was sufficient. It was not so in others. When the tenant sued his lord for having unjustly outed him of his lease, the damages which he recovered were by no means equivalent to the possession of the land. Such causes, therefore, for some time, went all to the court of chancery, to the no small loss of the courts of law. It was to draw back such causes to themselves that the courts of law are said to have invented the artificial and fictitious writ of ejectment, the most effectual remedy for an unjust outer or dispossession of land.[32]

A stamp-duty upon the law proceedings of each particular court, to be levied by that court, and applied towards the maintenance of the judges and other officers belonging to it, might, in the same manner, afford a revenue sufficient for defraying the expence of the administration of justice, without bringing any burden upon the general revenue of the society. The judges indeed might, in this case, be under the temptation of multiplying unnecessarily the proceedings upon every cause, in order to increase, as much as possible, the produce of such a stamp-duty. It has been the custom in modern Europe to regulate, upon most occasions, the payment of the attorneys and clerks of court, according to the number of pages which they had occasion to write; the court, however, requiring that each page should contain so many lines, and each line so many words. In order to increase their payment, the attorneys and clerks have contrived to multiply words beyond all necessity, to the corruption of the law language of, I believe, every court of justice in Europe. A like temptation might perhaps occasion a like corruption in the form of law proceedings.

Courts might be maintained by a stamp duty on proceedings before them, but this would tempt them to multiply such proceedings.

But whether the administration of justice be so contrived as to defray its own expence, or whether the judges be maintained by fixed salaries paid to them from some other fund, it does not seem necessary that the person or persons entrusted with the executive power should be charged with the management of that fund, or with the payment of those salaries. That fund might arise

Another way of securing independence would be to endow the courts with a revenue from property.

from the rent of landed estates, the management of each estate being entrusted to the particular court which was to be maintained by it. That fund might arise even from the interest of a sum of money, the lending out of which might, in the same manner, be entrusted to the court which was to be maintained by it. A part, though indeed but a small part, of the salary of the judges of the court of session in Scotland, arises from the interest of a sum of money. The necessary instability of such a fund seems, however, to render it an improper one for the maintenance of an institution which ought to last for ever.

The separation of the judicial from the executive power seems originally to have arisen from the increasing business of

The separation of the judicial from the executive power is due to the increase of executive business.

the society, in consequence of its increasing improvement. The administration of justice became so laborious and so complicated a duty as to require the undivided attention of the persons to whom it was entrusted. The person entrusted with the executive power, not having leisure to attend to the decision

of private causes himself, a deputy was appointed to decide them in his stead. In the progress of the Roman greatness, the consul was too much occupied with the political affairs of the state, to attend to the administration of justice. A prætor, therefore, was appointed to administer it in his stead. In the progress of the European monarchies which were founded upon the ruins of the Roman empire, the sovereigns and the great lords came universally to consider the administration of justice as an office, both too laborious and too ignoble for them to execute in their own persons. They universally, therefore, discharged themselves of it by appointing a deputy, bailiff, or judge.

When the judicial is united to the executive power, it is scarce possible that justice should not frequently be sacrificed

The judicial should be not only separate but independent of the executive power.

to, what is vulgarly called, politics. The persons entrusted with the great interests of the state may, even without any corrupt views, sometimes imagine it necessary to sacrifice to those interests the rights of a private man. But upon the impartial administration of justice depends the liberty of every individual, the sense which he has of his own security. In order to make every individual feel himself perfectly secure in the possession of every right which belongs to him, it is not only necessary that the judicial should be separated from the executive power, but that it should be rendered as much as possible independent of that power. The judge should not be liable to be removed from his office according to the caprice of that power. The regular payment of his salary should not depend upon the good-will, or even upon the good economy of that power.

PART III

OF THE EXPENCE OF PUBLIC WORKS AND PUBLIC INSTITUTIONS

The third and last duty of the sovereign or commonwealth is that of erecting and maintaining those public institutions and

The third duty of the sovereign is the erection and maintenance of those public works and institutions which are useful but not capable of bringing in a profit to individuals.

those public works, which, though they may be in the highest degree advantageous to a great society, are, however, of such a nature, that the profit could never repay the expence to any individual or small number of individuals, and which it therefore cannot be expected that any individual or small number of individuals should erect or maintain. The performance of this duty requires too very different degrees of expence in the different periods of society.

After the public institutions and public works necessary for the defence of the society, and for the administration of justice,

These are chiefly institutions for facilitating commerce and promoting instruction.

both of which have already been mentioned, the other works and institutions of this kind are chiefly those for facilitating the commerce of the society, and those for promoting the instruction of the people. The institutions for instruction are of two kinds; those for the education of the youth, and those for the instruction of people of all ages. The consideration of the manner in which the expence of those different sorts of public works and institutions may be most properly defrayed, will divide this third part of the present chapter into three different articles.

ARTICLE I

Of the public Works and Institutions for facilitating the Commerce of the Society

And, first, of those which are necessary for facilitating Commerce in general[33]

That the erection and maintenance of the public works which facilitate the commerce of any country, such as good roads,

The expense of such institutions increases.

bridges, navigable canals, harbours, &c. must require very different degrees of expence in the different periods of society, is evident without any proof. The expence of making and maintaining the public roads of any country must evidently increase with the annual produce of the land and labour of that country, or with the quantity and weight of the goods which it becomes necessary to fetch and carry upon those roads. The strength of a bridge must be suited to the number and weight of the carriages, which are likely to pass over it. The depth and the supply of water for a navigable canal

---

[33] [These two lines are not in eds. 1 and 2. See below, p. 928, note 45.]

must be proportioned to the number and tunnage of the lighters, which are likely to carry goods upon it; the extent of a harbour to the number of the shipping which are likely to take shelter in it.

It does not seem necessary that the expence of those public works should be defrayed from that public revenue, as it is

The expense need not be defrayed from the general public revenue,

commonly called, of which the collection and application are[34] in most countries assigned to the executive power. The greater part of such public works may easily be so managed, as to afford a particular revenue

sufficient for defraying their own expence, without bringing any burden upon the general revenue of the society.

A highway, a bridge, a navigable canal, for example, may in most cases be both made and maintained by a small toll upon

but may be raised by tolls and other particular charges.

the carriages which make use of them: a harbour, by a moderate port-duty upon the tunnage of the shipping which load or unload in it. The coinage, another institution for facilitating commerce, in many countries, not

only defrays its own expence, but affords a small revenue or seignorage to the sovereign. The post-office, another institution for the same purpose, over and above defraying its own expence, affords in almost all countries a very considerable revenue to the sovereign.

When the carriages which pass over a highway or a bridge, and the lighters which sail upon a navigable canal, pay toll in

Tolls according to weight of carriages and capacity of boats are very equitable.

proportion to their weight or their tunnage, they pay for the maintenance of those public works exactly in proportion to the wear and tear[35] which they occasion of them. It seems scarce possible to invent a more equitable way of maintaining such works. This tax or

toll too, though it is advanced by the carrier, is finally paid by the consumer, to whom it must always be charged in the price

[34] [Eds. 1–4 read "is"; cp. below, p. 962, note 110.]

[35] [Ed. 1 reads "tear and wear."]

of the goods. As the expence of carriage, however, is very much reduced by means of such public works, the goods, notwithstanding the toll, come cheaper to the consumer than they could otherwise have done; their price not being so much raised by the toll, as it is lowered by the cheapness of the carriage. The person who finally pays this tax, therefore, gains by the application, more than he loses by the payment of it. His payment is exactly in proportion to his gain. It is in reality no more than a part of that gain which he is obliged to give up in order to get the rest. It seems impossible to imagine a more equitable method of raising a tax.

When the toll upon carriages of luxury, upon coaches, postchaises, &c. is made somewhat higher in proportion to their weight, than upon carriages of necessary use, such as carts, waggons, &c. the indolence and vanity of the rich is made to contribute in a very easy manner to the relief of the poor, by rendering cheaper the transportation of heavy goods to all the different parts of the country.

If the tolls are higher on carriages of luxury, the rich contribute in an easy manner to the relief of the poor.

When high roads, bridges, canals, &c. are in this manner made and supported by the commerce which is carried on by means of them, they can be made only where that commerce requires them, and consequently where it is proper to make them. Their expence too, their grandeur and magnificence, must be suited to what that commerce can afford to pay. They must be made consequently as it is proper to make them. A magnificent high road cannot be made through a desart country where there is little or no commerce, or merely because it happens to lead to the country villa of the intendant of the province, or to that of some great lord to whom the intendant finds it convenient to make his court. A great bridge cannot be thrown over a river at a place where nobody passes, or merely to embellish the view from the windows of a neighbouring palace: things which sometimes happen, in countries where works of this kind are carried on by any other

Roads and canals, etc., thus paid for cannot be made except where they are wanted.

revenue than that which they themselves are capable of affording.

In several different parts of Europe the toll or lock-duty upon a canal is the property of private persons, whose private interest

Canals are better in the hands of private persons than of commissioners.

obliges them to keep up the canal. If it is not kept in tolerable order, the navigation necessarily ceases altogether, and along with it the whole profit which they can make by the tolls. If those tolls were put under the management of commissioners, who had themselves no interest in them, they might be less attentive to the maintenance of the works which produced them. The canal of Languedoc cost the king of France and the province upwards of thirteen millions of livres, which (at twenty-eight livres the mark of silver, the value of French money in the end of the last century) amounted to upwards of nine hundred thousand pounds sterling. When that great work was finished, the most likely method, it was found, of keeping it in constant repair was to make a present of the tolls to Riquet the engineer, who planned and conducted the work. Those tolls constitute at present a very large estate to the different branches of the family of that gentleman, who have, therefore, a great interest to keep the work in constant repair. But had those tolls been put under the management of commissioners, who had no such interest, they might perhaps have been dissipated in ornamental and unnecessary expences, while the most essential parts of the work were allowed to go to ruin.

The tolls for the maintenance of a high road, cannot with any

But tolls on a high road cannot safely be made private property and must be committed to trustees.

safety be made the property of private persons. A high road, though entirely neglected, does not become altogether impassable, though a canal does. The proprietors of the tolls upon a high road, therefore, might neglect altogether the repair of the road, and yet continue to levy very nearly the same tolls. It is proper, therefore, that the tolls for the maintenance of such work should be put under the management of commissioners or trustees.

In Great Britain, the abuses which the trustees have committed in the management of those tolls, have in many cases been

The prevalence of complaints against British turnpike tolls is not remarkable.

very justly complained of. At many turnpikes, it has been said, the money levied is more than double of what is necessary for executing, in the completest manner, the work which is often executed in a very slovenly manner, and sometimes not executed at all. The system of repairing the high roads by tolls of this kind, it must be observed, is not of very long standing. We should not wonder, therefore, if it has not yet been brought to that degree of perfection of which it seems capable.[36] If mean and improper persons are frequently appointed trustees; and if proper courts of inspection and account have not yet been established for controlling their conduct, and for reducing the tolls to what is barely sufficient for executing the work to be done by them; the recency of the institution both accounts and apologizes for those defects, of which, by the wisdom of parliament, the greater part may in due time be gradually remedied.

The money levied at the different turnpikes in Great Britain is supposed to exceed so much what is necessary for repairing the roads, that the savings, which, with proper œconomy, might be made from it, have been considered, even by some

It has been proposed that the government should manage the turnpikes and make a revenue from them.

ministers, as a very great resource which might at some time or another be applied to the exigencies of the state. Government, it has been said, by taking the management of the turnpikes into its own hands, and by employing the soldiers, who would work for a very small addition to their pay, could keep the roads in good order at a much less expence than it can be done by trustees, who have no other workmen to employ, but such as derive their whole subsistence from their wages. A great revenue, half a million, perhaps,[37] it has

---

[36] [Ed. 1 reads "seems to be capable."]

[37] Since publishing the two first editions of this book, I have got good reasons to believe that all the turnpike tolls levied in Great Britain do not produce a neat revenue that amounts to half a million; a sum which, under the management of Government, would not be sufficient to keep in repair five of the principal roads in the kingdom. [This and the next note appear first in ed. 3.]

been pretended, might in this manner be gained without laying any new burden upon the people; and the turnpike roads might be made to contribute to the general expence of the state, in the same manner as the post-office does at present.

That a considerable revenue might be gained in this man-

This plan is open to the following objections,

ner, I have no doubt, though probably not near so much, as the projectors of this plan have supposed. The plan itself, however, seems liable to several very important objections.

First, if the tolls which are levied at the turnpikes should

(1) the tolls would be raised and become a great encumbrance to commerce,

ever be considered as one of the resources for supplying the exigencies of the state, they would certainly be augmented as those exigencies were supposed to require. According to the policy of Great Britain, therefore, they would probably be augmented very fast. The

facility with which a great revenue could be drawn from them, would probably encourage administration to recur very frequently to this resource. Though it may, perhaps, be more than doubtful, whether half a million could by any œconomy be saved out of the present tolls, it can scarce be doubted but that a million might be saved out of them, if they were doubled; and perhaps two millions, if they were tripled.[38] This great revenue too might be levied without the appointment of a single new officer to collect and receive it. But the turnpike tolls being continually augmented in this manner, instead of facilitating the inland commerce of the country, as at present, would soon become a very great incumbrance upon it. The expence of transporting all heavy goods from one part of the country to another would soon be so much increased, the market for all such goods, consequently, would soon be so much narrowed, that their production would be in a great measure discouraged, and the most important branches of the domestic industry of the country annihilated altogether.

[38] I have now good reasons to believe that all these conjectural sums are by much too large.

Secondly, a tax upon carriages in proportion to their weight, though a very equal tax when applied to the sole purpose of re-

(2) a tax on carriages in proportion to weight falls principally on the poor,

pairing the roads, is a very unequal one, when applied to any other purpose, or to supply the common exigencies of the state. When it is applied to the sole purpose above mentioned, each carriage is supposed to pay exactly for the wear and tear[39] which that carriage occasions of the roads. But when it

is applied to any other purpose each carriage is supposed to pay for more than that wear and tear, and contributes to the supply of some other exigency of the state. But as the turnpike toll raises the price of goods in proportion to their weight, and not to their value, it is chiefly paid by the consumers of coarse and bulky, not by those of precious and light commodities. Whatever exigency of the state therefore this tax might be intended to supply, that exigency would be chiefly supplied at the expence of the poor, not of the rich; at the expence of those who are least able to supply it, not of those who are most able.

Thirdly, if government should at any time neglect the reparation of the high roads, it would be still more difficult, than it

and (3) the roads would be neglected.

is at present, to compel the proper application of any part of the turnpike tolls. A large revenue might thus be levied upon the people, without any part of it being applied to

the only purpose to which a revenue levied in this manner ought ever to be applied. If the meanness and poverty of the trustees of turnpike roads render it sometimes difficult at present to oblige them to repair their wrong; their wealth and greatness would render it ten times more so in the case which is here supposed.

In France, the funds destined for the reparation of the high roads are under the immediate direction of the executive power. Those funds consist, partly in a certain number of days labour[40] which the country people are in most parts of Europe

[39] [Ed. 1 reads here and three lines lower down "tear and wear."]

[40] [Ed. 1 reads "partly in the six days' labour."]

High roads are under the executive in France,

obliged to give to the reparation of the high-ways; and partly in such a portion of the general revenue of the state as the king chuses to spare from his other expences.

By the ancient law of France, as well as by that of most other parts of Europe, the labour of the country people[41] was under

and great post roads are generally good, but all the rest entirely neglected.

the direction of a local or provincial magistracy, which had no immediate dependency upon the king's council. But by the present practice both the labour of the country people, and whatever other fund the king may chuse to assign for the reparation of the high

roads in any particular province or generality, are entirely under the management of the intendant; an officer who is appointed and removed by the king's council, who receives his orders from it, and is in constant correspondence with it. In the progress of despotism the authority of the executive power gradually absorbs that of every other power in the state, and assumes to itself the management of every branch of revenue which is destined for any public purpose. In France, however, the great post-roads, the roads which make the communication between the principal towns of the kingdom, are in general kept in good order; and in some provinces are even a good deal superior to the greater part of the turnpike roads of England. But what we call the cross-roads, that is, the far greater part of the roads in the country, are entirely neglected, and are in many places absolutely impassable for any heavy carriage. In some places it is even dangerous to travel on horseback, and mules are the only conveyance which can safely be trusted. The proud minister of an ostentatious court may frequently take pleasure in executing a work of splendour and magnificence, such as a great highway, which is frequently seen by the principal nobility, whose applauses not only flatter his vanity, but even contribute to support his interest at court. But to execute a great number of little works, in which nothing that can be done can

---

[41] [Here and in the next sentence for "the labour of the country people," ed. 1 reads "the six days' labour."]

make any great appearance, or excite the smallest degree of admiration in any traveller, and which, in short, have nothing to recommend them but their extreme utility, is a business which appears in every respect too mean and paultry to merit the attention of so great a magistrate. Under such an administration, therefore, such works are almost always entirely neglected.

In China, and in several other governments of Asia, the executive power charges itself both with the reparation of the high roads, and with the maintenance of the navigable canals. In the instructions which are given to the governor of each province, those objects, it is said, are constantly recommended to him, and the judgment which the court forms of his conduct is very much regulated by the attention which he appears to have paid to this part of his instructions. This branch of public police accordingly is said to be very much attended to in all those countries, but particularly in China, where the high roads, and still more the navigable canals, it is pretended, exceed very much every thing of the same kind which is known in Europe. The accounts of those works, however, which have been transmitted to Europe, have generally been drawn up by weak and wondering travellers; frequently by stupid and lying missionaries. If they had been examined by more intelligent eyes, and if the accounts of them had been reported by more faithful witnesses, they would not, perhaps, appear to be so wonderful. The account which Bernier gives of some works of this kind in Indostan, falls very much short of what had been reported of them by other travellers, more disposed to the marvellous than he was.[42] It may too, perhaps, be in those countries, as it is in France,

The executive in China and other parts of Asia maintains both high roads and canals, it is said, in good condition, but this would not be the case in Europe.

---

[42] [*Voyages de François Bernier*, Amsterdam, 1710, can scarcely be said to discredit the ordinary eulogy of Indian roads and canals by an account of any particular works, but it does so by not mentioning them in places where it would be natural to do so if they had existed or been remarkable. See tom. ii., p. 249, "les grandes rivières qui en ces quartiers n'ont ordinairement point de ponts."]

where the great roads, the great communications which are likely to be the subjects of conversation at the court and in the capital, are attended to, and all the rest neglected. In China, besides, in Indostan, and in several other governments of Asia, the revenue of the sovereign arises almost altogether from a land-tax or land-rent, which rises or falls with the rise and[43] fall of the annual produce of the land. The great interest of the sovereign, therefore, his revenue, is in such countries necessarily and immediately connected with the cultivation of the land, with the greatness of its produce, and with the value of its produce. But in order to render that produce both as great and as valuable as possible, it is necessary to procure to it as extensive a market as possible, and consequently to establish the freest, the easiest, and the least expensive communication between all the different parts of the country; which can be done only by means of the best roads and the best navigable canals. But the revenue of the sovereign does not, in any part of Europe, arise chiefly from a land-tax or land-rent. In all the great kingdoms of Europe, perhaps, the greater part of it may ultimately depend upon the produce of the land: But that dependency is neither so immediate, nor so evident. In Europe, therefore, the sovereign does not feel himself so directly called upon to promote the increase, both in quantity and value, of the produce of the land, or, by maintaining good roads and canals, to provide the most extensive market for that produce. Though it should be true, therefore, what I apprehend is not a little doubtful, that in some parts of Asia this department of the public police is very properly managed by the executive power, there is not the least probability that, during the present state of things, it could be tolerably managed by that power in any part of Europe.

Public works of a local nature should be maintained by local revenue.

Even those public works which are of such a nature that they cannot afford any revenue for maintaining themselves, but of which the conveniency is nearly confined to

---

[43] [Ed. 1 reads "or."]

some particular place or district, are always better maintained by a local or provincial revenue, under the management of a local and provincial administration, than by the general revenue of the state, of which the executive power must always have the management. Were the streets of London to be lighted and paved at the expence of the treasury, is there any probability that they would be so well lighted and paved as they are at present, or even at so small an expence? The expence, besides, instead of being raised by a local tax upon the inhabitants of each particular street, parish, or district in London, would, in this case, be defrayed out of the general revenue of the state, and would consequently be raised by a tax upon all the inhabitants of the kingdom, of whom the greater part derive no sort of benefit from the lighting and paving of the streets of London.

The abuses which sometimes creep into the local and provincial administration of a local and provincial revenue, *The abuses of local administration are small compared with those of the administration of the general revenue.* how enormous soever they may appear, are in reality, however, almost always very trifling, in comparison of those which commonly take place in the administration and expenditure of the revenue of a great empire. They are, besides, much more easily corrected. Under the local or provincial administration of the justices of the peace in Great Britain, the six days labour which the country people are obliged to give to the reparation of the highways, is not always perhaps very judiciously applied, but it is scarce ever exacted with any circumstance of cruelty or oppression. In France, under the administration of the intendants, the application is not always more judicious, and the exaction is frequently the most cruel and oppressive. Such Corvées, as they are called, make one of the principal instruments of tyranny by which those officers chastise any parish or communeauté which has had the misfortune to fall under their displeasure.[44]

---

[44] [Ed. 1 reads "tyranny by which the intendant chastises any parish or communauté which has had the misfortune to fall under his displeasure."]

*Of the Public Works and Institutions which are necessary for
facilitating particular Branches of Commerce*[45]

The object of the public works and institutions above mentioned is to facilitate commerce in general. But in order to facilitate some particular branches of it, particular institutions are necessary, which again require a particular and extraordinary expence.

Some particular institutions are required to facilitate particular branches of commerce, as trade with barbarous nations requires forts, and trade with other nations requires ambassadors.

Some particular branches of commerce, which are carried on with barbarous and uncivilized nations, require extraordinary protection. An ordinary store or counting-house could give little security to the goods of the merchants who trade to the western coast of Africa. To defend them from the barbarous natives, it is necessary that the place where they are deposited, should be, in some measure, fortified. The disorders in the government of Indostan have been supposed to render a like precaution necessary even among that mild and gentle people; and it was under pretence of securing their persons and property from violence, that both the English and French East India Companies were allowed to erect the first forts which they possessed in that country. Among other nations, whose vigorous government will suffer no strangers to possess any fortified place within their territory, it may be necessary to maintain some ambassador, minister, or consul, who may both decide, according to their own customs, the differences arising among his own countrymen; and, in their disputes with the natives, may, by means of his public character, interfere with more authority, and afford them a more powerful protection, than they could expect from any private man. The interests of commerce have frequently made it necessary to maintain ministers in foreign countries, where the purposes,

[45] [This section (ending on p. 962) appears first in Additions and Corrections and ed. 3.]

either of war or alliance, would not have required any. The commerce of the Turkey Company first occasioned the establishment of an ordinary ambassador at Constantinople.[46] The first English embassies to Russia arose altogether from commercial interests.[47] The constant interference which those interests necessarily occasioned between the subjects of the different states of Europe, has probably introduced the custom of keeping, in all neighbouring countries, ambassadors or ministers constantly resident even in the time of peace. This custom, unknown to ancient times, seems not to be older than the end of the fifteenth or beginning of the sixteenth century; that is, than the time when commerce first began to extend itself to the greater part of the nations of Europe, and when they first began to attend to its interests.

It seems not unreasonable, that the extraordinary expence, which the protection of any particular branch of commerce may occasion, should be defrayed by a moderate tax upon that particular branch; by a moderate fine, for example, to be paid by the traders when they first enter into it, or, what is more equal, by a particular duty of so much per cent. upon the goods which they either import into, or export out of, the particular countries with which it is carried on.

Branches of commerce which require extraordinary expense for their protection may reasonably bear a particular tax.

The protection of trade in general, from pirates and freebooters, is said to have given occasion to the first institution of the duties of customs. But, if it was thought reasonable to lay a general tax upon trade, in order to defray the expence of protecting trade in general, it should seem equally reasonable to lay a particular tax upon a particular branch of trade, in order to defray the extraordinary expence of protecting that branch.

The protection of trade in general has always been considered as essential to the defence of the commonwealth, and, upon that account, a necessary part of the duty of the executive

---

[46] [Anderson, *Commerce*, A.D. 1606.]

[47] [*Ibid.*, A.D. 1620, and cp. A.D. 1623.]

The proceeds of such taxes should be at the disposal of the executive, but have often been given to companies of merchants,

power. The collection and application of the general duties of customs, therefore, have always been left to that power. But the protection of any particular branch of trade is a part of the general protection of trade; a part, therefore, of the duty of that power; and if nations always acted consistently, the particular duties levied for the purposes of such particular protection, should always have been left equally to its disposal. But in this respect, as well as in many others, nations have not always acted consistently; and in the greater part of the commercial states of Europe, particular companies of merchants have had the address to persuade the legislature to entrust to them the performance of this part of the duty of the sovereign, together with all the powers which are necessarily connected with it.

These companies, though they may, perhaps, have been useful for the first introduction of some branches of commerce, by

which have always proved in the long run burdensome or useless.

making, at their own expence, an experiment which the state might not think it prudent to make, have in the long-run proved, universally, either burdensome or useless, and have either mismanaged or confined the trade.

When those companies do not trade upon a joint stock, but are obliged to admit any person, properly qualified, upon pay-

They are either regulated or joint stock companies.

ing a certain fine, and agreeing to submit to the regulations of the company, each member trading upon his own stock, and at his own risk, they are called regulated companies. When they trade upon a joint stock, each member sharing in the common profit or loss in proportion to his share in this stock, they are called joint stock companies.[48] Such companies, whether regulated or joint stock, sometimes have, and sometimes have not, exclusive priviliges.

---

[48] [Sir Josiah Child; *New Discourse of Trade*, etc., chap. iii., divides companies into those in joint stock and those "who trade not by a joint stock, but only are under a government and regulation."]

Regulated companies resemble, in every respect, the corporations of trades, so common in the cities and towns of all

Regulated compa-
nies are like cor-
porations of trades
and act like them.

the different countries of Europe; and are a sort of enlarged monopolies of the same kind. As no inhabitant of a town can exercise an incorporated trade, without first obtaining his freedom in the corporation, so in most cases no subject of the state can lawfully carry on any branch of foreign trade, for which a regulated company is established, without first becoming a member of that company. The monopoly is more or less strict according as the terms of admission are more or less difficult; and according as the directors of the company have more or less authority, or have it more or less in their power to manage in such a manner as to confine the greater part of the trade to themselves and their particular friends. In the most ancient regulated companies the privileges of apprenticeship were the same as in other corporations; and entitled the person who had served his time to a member of the company, to become himself a member, either without paying any fine, or upon paying a much smaller one than what was exacted of other people. The usual corporation spirit, wherever the law does not restrain it, prevails in all regulated companies. When they have been allowed to act according to their natural genius, they have always, in order to confine the competition to as small a number of persons as possible, endeavoured to subject the trade to many burdensome regulations. When the law has restrained them from doing this, they have become altogether useless and insignificant.

The regulated companies for foreign commerce, which at

There are five ex-
isting regulated
companies,

present subsist in Great Britain, are, the ancient merchant adventurers company,[49] now commonly called the Hamburgh Company, the Russia[50] Company, the Eastland Company, the Turkey Company, and the African Company.

---

[49] [The company or society of the Merchant Adventurers of England.]

[50] [Additions and Corrections reads "Russian," probably a misprint, though "Russian," which is incorrect, appears on the next page.]

The terms of admission into the Hamburgh Company, are now said to be quite easy; and the directors either have it not in their power to subject the trade to any burdensome restraint[51] or regulations, or, at least, have not of late exercised that power. It has not always been so. About the middle of the last century, the fine for admission was fifty, and at one time one hundred pounds,[52] and the conduct of the company was said to be extremely oppressive. In 1643, in 1645, and in 1661, the clothiers and free traders of the West of England complained of them to parliament, as of monopolists who confined the trade and oppressed the manufactures of the country.[53] Though those complaints produced no act of parliament, they had probably intimidated the company so far, as to oblige them to reform their conduct. Since that time, at least, there have[54] been no complaints against them. By the 10th and 11th of William III. c. 6.[55] the fine for admission into the Russian Company was reduced to five pounds; and by the 25th of Charles II. c. 7. that for admission into the Eastland Company, to forty shillings, while, at the same time, Sweden, Denmark and Norway, all the countries on the north side of the Baltic, were exempted from their exclusive charter.[56] The conduct of those companies had probably given occasion to those two acts of parliament. Before that time, Sir Josiah Child had represented both these and the Hamburgh Company as extremely oppressive, and imputed to their bad management the low state of the trade,

of which the Hamburg, Russian and Eastland Companies are merely useless.

---

[51] [Eds. 1–3 read "restraints."]

[52] [Anderson, *Commerce*, A.D. 1643: the fine was doubled in that year, being raised to £100 for Londoners and £50 for others.]

[53] [Anderson, *Commerce*, A.D. 1661, under which the other two years are also mentioned.]

[54] [Additions and Corrections and eds. 3 and 4 read "has." Smith very probably wrote "there has been no complaint."]

[55] [The preamble recites the history of the company.]

[56] [Anderson, *Commerce*, A.D. 1672.]

which we at that time carried on to the countries comprehended within their respective charters.[57] But though such companies may not, in the present times, be very oppressive, they are certainly altogether useless. To be merely useless, indeed, is perhaps the highest eulogy which can ever justly be bestowed upon a regulated company; and all the three companies above mentioned seem, in their present state, to deserve this eulogy.

The fine for admission into the Turkey Company, was formerly twenty-five pounds for all persons under twenty-six

The Turkey Company is an oppressive monopoly.

years of age, and fifty pounds for all persons above that age. Nobody but mere merchants could be admitted; a restriction which excluded all shop-keepers and retailers.[58] By a bye-law, no British manufactures could be exported to Turkey but in the general ships of the company; and as those ships sailed always from the port of London, this restriction confined the trade to that expensive[59] port, and the traders, to those who lived in London and in its neighbourhood. By another bye-law, no person living within twenty miles of London, and not free of the city, could be admitted a member; another restriction, which, joined to the foregoing, necessarily excluded all but the freemen of London.[60] As the time for the loading and sailing of those general ships depended altogether upon the directors, they could easily fill them with their own goods and those of their particular friends, to the exclusion of others, who, they might pretend, had made their proposals too late. In this state of things, therefore, this company was in every respect a strict and oppressive monopoly. Those abuses gave occasion to the act of the 26th of George II. c. 18. reducing the fine for admission to twenty

[57] [*New Discourse of Trade*, chap. iii., quoted by Anderson, *Commerce*, A.D. 1672. This part of the book was not published till long after 1672, but seems to have been written before the closing of the Exchequer in that year.]

[58] [Anderson, *Commerce*, A.D. 1605, 1643, 1753.]

[59] [Additions and Corrections reads "extensive."]

[60] [See the preamble to 26 Geo. II., c. 18.—Anderson, *Commerce*, A.D. 1753.]

pounds for all persons, without any distinction of ages, or any restriction, either to mere merchants, or to the freemen of London; and granting to all such persons the liberty of exporting, from all the ports of Great Britain to any port in Turkey, all British goods of which the exportation was not prohibited; and of importing from thence all Turkish goods, of which the importation was not prohibited, upon paying both the general duties of customs, and the particular duties assessed for defraying the necessary expences of the company; and submitting, at the same time, to the lawful authority of the British ambassador and consuls resident in Turkey, and to the bye-laws of the company duly enacted. To prevent any oppression by those bye-laws, it was by the same act ordained, that if any seven members of the company conceived themselves aggrieved by any bye-law which should be enacted after the passing of this act, they might appeal to the Board of Trade and Plantations (to the authority of which, a committee of the privy council has now succeeded), provided such appeal was brought within twelve months after the bye-law was enacted; and that if any seven members conceived themselves aggrieved by any bye-law which had been enacted before the passing of this act, they might bring a like appeal, provided it was within twelve months after the day on which this act was to take place. The experience of one year, however, may not always be sufficient to discover to all the members of a great company the pernicious tendency of a particular bye-law; and if several of them should afterwards discover it, neither the Board of Trade, nor the committee of council, can afford them any redress. The object, besides, of the greater part of the bye-laws of all regulated companies, as well as of all other corporations, is not so much to oppress those who are already members, as to discourage others from becoming so; which may be done, not only by a high fine, but by many other contrivances. The constant view of such companies is always to raise the rate of their own profit as high as they can; to keep the market, both for the goods which they export, and for those which they import, as much understocked as they can: which can be done only by restraining the competition, or by discouraging new adventurers from entering into the trade. A fine even of twenty pounds, besides, though it may not, perhaps, be sufficient to discourage any man from entering into the Turkey trade, with an intention to continue in it, may be enough to discourage a speculative merchant from hazarding a single adventure in it. In all trades, the regular established traders, even though not incorporated, naturally combine to raise profits, which are no-way so likely to be kept, at all times, down to their proper level, as by the occasional competition of speculative adventurers. The Turkey trade, though in some measure laid open by this act of parliament, is still considered by many people as very far from being altogether free. The Turkey Company contribute to maintain an ambassador and two or three consuls, who, like other public ministers, ought to be maintained altogether by the state, and the trade laid open to all his majesty's subjects. The different taxes levied by the company, for this and other corporation purposes, might afford a revenue much more than sufficient to enable the state to maintain such ministers.

Regulated companies, it was observed by Sir Josiah Child, though they had frequently supported public ministers, had never maintained any forts or garrisons in the countries to which they traded; whereas joint stock companies frequently had.[61] And in reality the former seem to be much more unfit for this sort of service than the latter. First, the directors of a regulated company have no particular interest in the prosperity of the general trade of the company, for the sake of which such forts and garrisons are maintained. The decay of that general trade may even frequently contribute to the advantage of their own private trade; as by diminishing the number of their competitors, it may enable them both to buy cheaper, and to sell dearer. The directors of a joint stock company, on the contrary, having only their share in the profits which are made upon the common stock committed to their management, have no private trade of their

Regulated companies are more unfit to maintain forts than joint stock companies,

---

[61] [*New Discourse of Trade*, chap. iii.]

own, of which the interest can be separated from that of the general trade of the company. Their private interest is connected with the prosperity of the general trade of the company; and with the maintenance of the forts and garrisons which are necessary for its defence. They are more likely, therefore, to have that continual and careful attention which that maintenance necessarily requires. Secondly, The directors of a joint stock company have always the management of a large capital, the joint stock of the company, a part of which they may frequently employ, with propriety, in building, repairing, and maintaining such necessary forts and garrisons. But the directors of a regulated company, having the management of no common capital, have no other fund to employ in this way, but the casual revenue arising from the admission fines, and from the corporation duties, imposed upon the trade of the company. Though they had the same interest, therefore, to attend to the maintenance of such forts and garrisons, they can seldom have the same ability to render that attention effectual. The maintenance of a public minister requiring scarce any attention, and but a moderate and limited expence, is a business much more suitable both to the temper and abilities of a regulated company.

Long after the time of Sir Josiah Child, however, in 1750, a regulated company was established, the present company of

but the African company was charged with this duty.

merchants trading to Africa, which was expressly charged at first with the maintenance of all the British forts and garrisons that lie between Cape Blanc and the Cape of Good Hope, and afterwards with that of those only which lie between Cape Rouge and the Cape of Good Hope. The act which establishes this company (the 23d of George II. c. 31.) seems to have had two distinct objects in view; first, to restrain effectually the oppressive and monopolizing spirit which is natural to the directors of a regulated company; and secondly, to force them, as much as possible, to give an attention, which is not natural to them, towards the maintenance of forts and garrisons.[62]

[62] [Below, pp. 942–943.]

For the first of these purposes, the fine for admission is limited to forty shillings. The company is prohibited from trading in their corporate capacity, or upon a joint stock; from borrowing money upon common seal, or from laying any restraints
upon the trade which may be carried on freely from all places, and by all persons being British subjects, and paying the fine. The government is in a committee of nine persons who meet at London, but who are chosen annually by the freemen of the company at London, Bristol and Liverpool; three from each place. No committee-man can be continued in office for more than three years together. Any committee-man might be removed by the Board of Trade and Plantations; now by a committee of council, after being heard in his own defence. The committee are forbid to export negroes from Africa, or to import any African goods into Great Britain. But as they are charged with the maintenance of forts and garrisons, they may, for that purpose, export from Great Britain to Africa, goods and stores of different kinds. Out of the monies which they shall receive from the company, they are allowed a sum not exceeding eight hundred pounds for the salaries of their clerks and agents at London, Bristol and Liverpool, the house-rent of their office at London, and all other[63] expences of management, commission and agency in England. What remains of this sum, after defraying these different expences, they may divide among themselves, as compensation for their trouble, in what manner they think proper. By this constitution, it might have been expected, that the spirit of monopoly would have been effectually restrained, and the first of these purposes sufficiently answered. It would seem, however, that it had not. Though by the 4th of George III. c. 20. the fort of Senegal, with all its dependencies, had been vested in the company of merchants trading to Africa, yet in the year following (by the 5th of George III. c. 44.), not only Senegal and its dependencies, but the whole coast from the port of Sallee,

The statute establishing the company endeavoured ineffectually to restrain the spirit of monopoly,

---

[63] [*Additions and Corrections* reads "all the other."]

in south Barbary, to Cape Rouge, was exempted from the jurisdiction of that company, was vested in the crown, and the trade to it declared free to all his majesty's subjects. The company had been suspected of restraining the trade, and of establishing some sort of improper monopoly. It is not, however, very easy to conceive how, under the regulations of the 23d George II. they could do so. In the printed debates of the House of Commons, not always the most authentic records of truth, I observe, however, that they have been accused of this. The members of the committee of nine being all merchants, and the governors and factors in their different forts and settlements being all dependent upon them, it is not unlikely that the latter might have given peculiar attention to the consignments and commissions of the former, which would establish a real monopoly.

For the second of these purposes, the maintenance of the forts and garrisons, an annual sum has been allotted to them

and Parliament allots £13,000 a year to the company for forts, which sum they misapply.

by parliament, generally about 13,000*l.* For the proper application of this sum, the committee is obliged to account annually to the Cursitor Baron of Exchequer; which account is afterwards to be laid before parliament. But parliament, which gives so little attention to the application of millions, is not likely to give much to that of 13,000*l.* a-year; and the Cursitor Baron of Exchequer, from his profession and education, is not likely to be profoundly skilled in the proper expence of forts and garrisons. The captains of his majesty's navy, indeed, or any other commissioned officers, appointed by the Board of Admiralty, may enquire into the condition of the forts and garrisons, and report their observations to that board. But that board seems to have no direct jurisdiction over the committee, nor any authority to correct those whose conduct it may thus enquire into; and the captains of his majesty's navy, besides, are not supposed to be always deeply learned in the science of fortification. Removal from an office, which can be enjoyed only for the term of three years, and of which the lawful emoluments, even during that term, are so very small,

seems to be the utmost punishment to which any committee-
man is liable, for any fault, except direct malversation, or embezzlement, either of the public money, or of that of the
company; and the fear of that punishment can never be a motive of sufficient weight to force a continual and careful attention to a business, to which he has no other interest to attend.
The committee are accused of having sent out bricks and
stones from England for the reparation of Cape Coast Castle
on the coast of Guinea, a business for which parliament had
several times granted an extraordinary sum of money. These
bricks and stones too, which had thus been sent upon so long a
voyage, were said to have been of so bad a quality, that it was
necessary to rebuild from the foundation the walls which had
been repaired with them. The forts and garrisons which lie
north of Cape Rouge, are not only maintained at the expence
of the state, but are under the immediate government of the executive power; and why those which lie south of that Cape,
and which too are, in part at least, maintained at the expence
of the state, should be under a different government, it seems
not very easy even to imagine a good reason. The protection of
the Mediterranean trade was the original purpose or pretence
of the garrisons of Gibraltar and Minorca, and the maintenance and government of those garrisons has always been,
very properly, committed, not to the Turkey Company, but to
the executive power. In the extent of its dominion consists, in a
great measure, the pride and dignity of that power; and it is not
very likely to fail in attention to what is necessary for the defence of that dominion. The garrisons at Gibraltar and
Minorca, accordingly, have never been neglected; though
Minorca has been twice taken, and is now probably lost for
ever, that disaster was never even imputed to any neglect in
the executive power. I would not, however, be understood to
insinuate, that either of those expensive garrisons was ever,
even in the smallest degree, necessary for the purpose for
which they were originally dismembered from the Spanish
monarchy. That dismemberment, perhaps, never served any
real purpose than to alienate from England her natural ally
the King of Spain, and to unite the two principal branches

of the house of Bourbon in a much stricter and more permanent alliance than the ties of blood could ever have united them.

Joint stock companies, established either by royal charter or by act of parliament, differ in several respects, not only from regulated companies, but from private co-partneries.

Joint stock companies differ from private partnerships:

First, In a private copartnery, no partner, without the consent of the company, can transfer his share to another person, or introduce a new member into the company. Each member, however, may, upon proper warning, withdraw from the copartnery, and demand payment from them of his share of the common stock. In a joint stock company, on the contrary, no member can demand payment of his share from the company; but each member can, without their consent, transfer his share to another person, and thereby introduce a new member. The value of a share in a joint stock is always the price which it will bring in the market; and this may be either greater or less, in any proportion, than the sum which its owner stands credited for in the stock of the company.

(1) withdrawals are by sale of shares;

Secondly, In a private copartnery, each partner is bound for the debts contracted by the company to the whole extent of his fortune. In a joint stock company, on the contrary, each partner is bound only to the extent of his share.[64]

(2) liability is limited to the share held.

The trade of a joint stock company is always managed by a court of directors. This court, indeed, is frequently subject, in many respects, to the control of a general court of proprietors. But the greater part of those proprietors seldom pretend to understand any thing of the business of the company; and when the spirit of faction happens not to prevail among them, give themselves

Such companies are managed by directors, who are negligent and profuse.

[64] [A joint-stock company here is an incorporated or chartered company. The common application of the term to other companies is later.]

no trouble about it, but receive contentedly such half yearly or yearly dividend, as the directors think proper to make to them. This total exemption from trouble and from risk, beyond a limited sum, encourages many people to become adventurers in joint stock companies, who would, upon no account, hazard their fortunes in any private copartnery. Such companies, therefore, commonly draw to themselves much greater stocks than any private copartnery can boast of. The trading stock of the south Sea Company, at one time, amounted to upwards of thirty-three millions eight hundred thousand pounds.[65] The dividend capital of the Bank of England amounts, at present, to ten millions seven hundred and eighty thousand pounds.[66] The directors of such companies, however, being the managers rather of other people's money than of their own, it cannot well be expected, that they should watch over it with the same anxious vigilance with which the partners in a private copartnery frequently watch over their own. Like the stewards of a rich man, they are apt to consider attention to small matters as not for their master's honour, and very easily give themselves a dispensation from having it. Negligence and profusion, therefore, must always prevail, more or less, in the management of the affairs of such a company. It is upon this account that joint stock companies for foreign trade have seldom been able to maintain the competition against private adventurers. They have, accordingly, very seldom succeeded without an exclusive privilege; and frequently have not succeeded with one. Without an exclusive privilege they have commonly mismanaged the trade. With an exclusive privilege they have both mismanaged and confined it.

The Royal African Company, the predecessors of the present African Company, had an exclusive privilege by charter; but as that charter had not been confirmed by act of parliament, the trade, in consequence of the declaration of rights, was, soon after

[65] [Anderson, *Commerce*, A.D. 1723.]

[66] [It stood at this amount from 1746 to the end of 1781, but was then increased by a call of 8 per cent.—Anderson, *Commerce*, A.D. 1746, and (Continuation) A.D. 1781.]

Some have and some have not exclusive privileges. the revolution, laid open to all his majesty's subjects.[67] The Hudson's Bay Company are, as to their legal rights, in the same situation as the Royal African Company.[68] Their exclusive charter has not been confirmed by act of parliament. The South Sea Company, as long as they continued to be a trading company, had an exclusive privilege confirmed by act of parliament; as have likewise the present United Company of Merchants trading to the East Indies.

The Royal African Company soon found that they could not maintain the competition against private adventurers, whom, notwithstanding the declaration of rights, they contin-*The Royal African Company, having lost exclusive privileges, failed.* ued for some time to call interlopers, and to persecute as such. In 1698, however, the private adventurers were subjected to a duty of ten per cent. upon almost all the different branches of their trade, to be employed by the company in the maintenance of their forts and garrisons. But, notwithstanding this heavy tax, the company were still unable to maintain the competition.[69] Their stock and credit gradually declined. In 1712, their debts had become so great, that a particular act of parliament was thought necessary, both for their security and for that of their creditors. It was enacted, that the resolution of two-thirds of these creditors in number and value, should bind the rest, both with regard to the time which should be allowed to the company for the payment of their debts; and with regard to any other agreement which it might be thought proper to make with them concerning those debts.[70] In 1730, their affairs were in so great disorder, that they were altogether incapable of maintaining their forts and garrisons, the sole purpose and pretext of their institution. From that year, till their final dissolution, the parliament judged it necessary to allow the annual sum of ten thousand

[67] [Anderson, *Commerce*, A.D. 1672 and A.D. 1698.]

[68] [*Ibid.*, A.D. 1670.]

[69] [*Ibid.*, A.D. 1698.]

[70] [10 Ann., c. 27. Anderson, *Commerce*, A.D. 1712.]

pounds for that purpose.[71] In 1732, after having been for many years losers by the trade of carrying negroes to the West Indies, they at last resolved to give it up altogether; to sell to the private traders to America the negroes which they purchased upon the coast; and to employ their servants in a trade to the inland parts of Africa for gold dust, elephants teeth, dying drugs, &c. But their success in this more confined trade was not greater than in their former extensive one.[72] Their affairs continued to go gradually to decline, till at last, being in every respect a bankrupt company, they were dissolved by act of parliament, and their forts and garrisons vested in the present regulated company of merchants trading to Africa.[73] Before the erection of the Royal African Company, there had been three other joint stock companies successively established, one after another, for the African trade.[74] They were all equally unsuccessful. They all, however, had exclusive charters, which, though not confirmed by act of parliament, were in those days supposed to convey a real exclusive privilege.

The Hudson's Bay Company, before their misfortunes in the late war, had been much more fortunate than the Royal African Company. Their necessary expence is much smaller. The whole number of people whom they maintain in their different settlements and habitations, which they have honoured with the name of forts, is said not to exceed a hundred and twenty persons.[75] This number, however, is sufficient to prepare beforehand the cargo of furs and other goods necessary for loading their ships,

The Hudson's Bay Company have been moderately successful, having in fact an exclusive trade and a very small number of proprietors.

---

[71] [*Ibid.*, A.D. 1730. The annual grant continued till 1746.]

[72] [Anderson, *Commerce*, A.D. 1733.]

[73] [23 Geo. II., c. 31; 25 Geo. II., c. 40; Anderson, *Commerce*, A.D. 1750, 1752; above, p. 936.]

[74] [Anderson, *Commerce*, A.D. 1618, 1631 and 1662.]

[75] [*Ibid.*, A.D. 1743, quoting Captain Christopher Middleton.]

which, on account of the ice, can seldom remain above six or eight weeks in those seas. This advantage of having a cargo ready prepared, could not for several years be acquired by private adventurers, and without it there seems to be no possibility of trading to Hudson's Bay. The moderate capital of the company, which, it is said, does not exceed one hundred and ten thousand pounds,[76] may besides be sufficient to enable them to engross the whole, or almost the whole, trade and surplus produce of the miserable, though extensive country, comprehended within their charter. No private adventurers, accordingly, have ever attempted to trade to that country in competition with them. This company, therefore, have always enjoyed an exclusive trade in fact, though they may have no right to it in law. Over and above all this, the moderate capital of this company is said to be divided among a very small number of proprietors.[77] But a joint stock company, consisting of a small number of proprietors, with a moderate capital, approaches very nearly to the nature of a private copartnery, and may be capable of nearly the same degree of vigilance and attention. It is not to be wondered at, therefore, if in consequence of these different advantages, the Hudson's Bay Company had, before the late war, been able to carry on their trade with a considerable degree of success. It does not seem probable, however, that their profits ever approached to what the late Mr. Dobbs imagined them.[78] A much more sober and judicious writer, Mr. Anderson, author of *The Historical and Chronological Deduction of Commerce*, very justly observes, that upon examining the accounts which Mr. Dobbs himself has given for several years together, of their exports and imports, and upon making proper allowances for their extraordi-

[76] [Anderson, *Commerce*, A.D. 1670.]

[77] ["Eight or nine private merchants do engross nine-tenth parts of the company's stock." Anderson, *Commerce*, A.D. 1743, quoting from *An Account of the Countries Adjoining to Hudson's Bay ... with an Abstract of Captain Middleton's Journal and Observations upon his Behaviour*, by Arthur Dobbs, Esq., 1744, p. 58.]

[78] [In his *Account*, pp. 3 and 58, he talks of 2,000 per cent., but this, of course, only refers to the difference between buying and selling prices.]

nary risk and expence, it does not appear that their profits deserve to be envied, or that they can much, if at all, exceed the ordinary profits of trade.[79]

The South Sea Company never had any forts or garrisons to maintain, and therefore were entirely exempted from one great

The South Sea Company failed to make any profit by their annual ship to the Spanish West Indies,

expence, to which other joint stock companies for foreign trade are subject. But they had an immense capital dividend among an immense number of proprietors. It was naturally to be expected, therefore, that folly, negligence, and profusion should prevail in the whole management of their affairs. The knavery and extravagance of their stock-jobbing projects are sufficiently known, and the explication of them would be foreign to the present subject. Their mercantile projects were not much better conducted. The first trade which they engaged in was that of supplying the Spanish West Indies with negroes, of which (in consequence of what was called the Assiento contract granted them by the treaty of Utrecht) they had the exclusive privilege. But as it was not expected that much profit could be made by this trade, both the Portugueze and French companies, who had enjoyed it upon the same terms before them, having been ruined by it, they were allowed, as compensation, to send annually a ship of a certain burden to trade directly to the Spanish West Indies.[80] Of the ten voyages which this annual ship was allowed to make, they are said to have gained considerably by one, that of the Royal Caroline in 1731, and to have been losers, more or less, by almost all the rest. Their ill success was imputed, by their factors and agents, to the extortion and oppression of the Spanish government; but was, perhaps, principally owing to the profusion and depredations of those very factors and agents; some of whom are said to have acquired great fortunes even in one year. In 1734, the company petitioned the king, that they might be allowed to dis-

---

[79] [*Commerce*, A.D. 1743, but the examination is not nearly so comprehensive, nor the expression of opinion so ample as is suggested by the text.]

[80] [Anderson, *Commerce*, A.D. 1713.]

pose of the trade and tunnage of their annual ship, on account of the little profit which they made by it, and to accept of such equivalent as they could obtain from the king of Spain.[81]

In 1724, this company had undertaken the whale-fishery. Of this, indeed, they had no monopoly; but as long as they carried

lost £237,000 in their whale fishery,

it on, no other British subjects appear to have engaged in it. Of the eight voyages which their ships made to Greenland, they were gainers by one, and losers by all the rest. After their eighth and last voyage, when they had sold their ships, stores, and utensils, they found that their whole loss, upon this branch, capital and interest included, amounted to upwards of two hundred and thirty-seven thousand pounds.[82]

In 1722, this company petitioned the parliament to be allowed to divide their immense capital of more than thirty-three million eight hundred thousand pounds, the whole of which

and finally ceased to be a trading company.

had been lent to government, into two equal parts: The one half, or upwards of sixteen millions nine hundred thousand pounds, to be put upon the same footing with other government annuities, and not to be subject to the debts contracted, or losses incurred, by the directors of the company, in the prosecution of their mercantile projects; the other half to remain, as before, a trading stock, and to be subject to those debts and losses. The petition was too reasonable not to be granted.[83] In 1733, they again petitioned the parliament, that three-fourths of their trading stock might be turned into annuity stock, and only one-fourth remain as trading stock, or exposed to the hazards arising from the bad management of their directors.[84] Both their annuity and trading stocks had, by this time, been reduced more than two millions each, by several different payments from government; so that this

---

[81] [*Ibid.*, A.D. 1731, 1732 and 1734.]

[82] [*Ibid.*, A.D. 1724 and 1732. But there was no successful voyage; the company were "considerable losers in every one" of the eight years.]

[83] [By 9 Geo. I., c. 6. Anderson, *Commerce*, A.D. 1723.]

[84] [This was done by 6 Geo. II., c. 28. *Ibid.*, A.D. 1733.]

fourth amounted only to 3,662,784*l.* 8*s.* 6*d.*[85] In 1748, all the demands of the company upon the king of Spain, in consequence of the Assiento contract, were, by the treaty of Aix-la-Chapelle, given up for what was supposed an equivalent. An end was put to their trade with the Spanish West Indies, the remainder of their trading stock was turned into an annuity stock, and the company ceased in every respect to be a trading company.[86]

It ought to be observed, that in the trade which the South Sea Company carried on by means of their annual ship, the *They had competitors in the trade of the annual ship.* only trade by which it ever was expected that they could make any considerable profit, they were not without competitors, either in the foreign or in the home market. At Carthagena, Porto Bello, and La Vera Cruz, they had to encounter the competition of the Spanish merchants, who brought from Cadiz, to those markets, European goods, of the same kind with the outward cargo of their ship; and in England they had to encounter that of the English merchants, who imported from Cadiz goods of the Spanish West Indies, of the same kind with the inward cargo. The goods both of the Spanish and English merchants, indeed, were, perhaps, subject to higher duties. But the loss occasioned by the negligence, profusion, and malversation of the servants of the company, had probably been a tax much heavier than all those duties. That a joint stock company should be able to carry on successfully any branch of foreign trade, when private adventurers can come into any sort of open and fair competition with them, seems contrary to all experience.

The old English East India Company was established in *The old East India Company, unable to support competition,* 1600, by a charter from Queen Elizabeth. In the first twelve voyages which they fitted out for India, they appear to have traded as a regulated company, with separate stocks, though only in the general ships of the com-

---

[85] [*Ibid.*, A.D. 1732 and A.D. 1733.]

[86] [*Ibid.*, A.D. 1748 and A.D. 1750.]

pany. In 1612, they united into a joint stock.[87] Their charter was exclusive, and though not confirmed by act of parliament, was in those days supposed to convey a real exclusive privilege. For many years, therefore, they were not much disturbed by interlopers. Their capital which never exceeded seven hundred and forty-four thousand pounds,[88] and of which fifty pounds was a share,[89] was not so exorbitant, nor their dealings so extensive, as to afford either a pretext for gross negligence and profusion, or a cover to gross malversation. Notwithstanding some extraordinary losses, occasioned partly by the malice of the Dutch East India Company, and partly by other accidents, they carried on for many years a successful trade. But in process of time, when the principles of liberty were better understood, it became every day more and more doubtful how far a royal charter, not confirmed by act of parliament, could convey an exclusive privilege. Upon this question the decisions of the courts of justice were not uniform, but varied with the authority of government and the humours of the times. Interlopers multiplied upon them; and towards the end of the reign of Charles II. through the whole of that of James II. and during a part of that of William III. reduced them to great distress.[90] In 1698, a proposal was made to parliament of advancing two millions to government at eight per cent. provided the subscribers were erected into a new East India Company with exclusive privileges. The old East India Company offered seven hundred thousand pounds, nearly the amount of their capital, at four per cent. upon the same conditions. But such was at that time the state of public credit, that it was more convenient for government to borrow two millions at eight per cent. than seven hundred thousand pounds at four.

The proposal of the new subscribers was accepted, and a

[87] ["Until this time the English East India trade was carried on by several separate stocks, making particular running voyages; but in this year they united all into one general joint-capital stock." Anderson, *Commerce*, A.D. 1612.]

[88] [*Ibid.*, A.D. 1693.]

[89] [*Ibid.*, A.D. 1676.]

[90] [*Ibid.*, A.D. 1681 and A.D. 1685.]

was superseded by the present company, new East India Company established in consequence. The old East India Company, however, had a right to continue their trade till 1701. They had, at the same time, in the name of their treasurer, subscribed, very artfully, three hundred and fifteen thousand pounds into the stock of the new. By a negligence in the expression of the act of parliament, which vested the East India trade in the subscribers to this loan of two millions, it did not appear evident that they were all obliged to unite into a joint stock.[91] A few private traders, whose subscriptions amounted only to seven thousand two hundred pounds, insisted upon the privilege of trading separately upon their own stocks and at their own risk.[92] The old East India Company had a right to a separate trade upon their old stock till 1701; and they had likewise, both before and after that period, a right, like that of other private traders, to a separate trade upon the three hundred and fifteen thousand pounds, which they had subscribed into the stock of the new company. The competition of the two companies with the private traders, and with one another, is said to have well nigh ruined both. Upon a subsequent occasion, in 1730, when a proposal was made to parliament for putting the trade under the management of a regulated company, and thereby laying it in some measure open, the East India Company, in opposition to this proposal, represented in very strong terms, what had been, at this time, the miserable effects, as they thought them, of this competition. In India, they said, it raised the price of goods so high, that they were not worth the buying; and in England, by overstocking the market, it sunk their price so low, that no profit could be made by them.[93] That by a more plentiful supply, to the great advantage and conveniency of the public, it must have reduced, very much, the price of India goods in the English market, cannot well be doubted; but that it should have raised very much their price in the India market, seems not very probable, as all the

[91] [The whole of this history is in Anderson, *Commerce*, A.D. 1698.]

[92] [Anderson, *Commerce*, A.D. 1701.]

[93] [*Ibid.*, A.D. 1730.]

extraordinary demand which that competition could occasion, must have been but as a drop of water in the immense ocean of Indian commerce. The increase of demand, besides, though in the beginning it may sometimes raise the price of goods, never fails to lower it in the long run. It encourages production, and thereby increases the competition of the producers, who, in order to undersell one another, have recourse to new divisions of labour and new improvements of art, which might never otherwise have been thought of. The miserable effects of which the company complained, were the cheapness of consumption and the encouragement given to production, precisely the two effects which it is the great business of political economy to promote. The competition, however, of which they gave this doleful account, had not been allowed to be of long continuance. In 1702, the two companies, were, in some measure, united by an indenture tripartite, to which the queen was the third party;[94] and in 1708, they were, by act of parliament, perfectly consolidated into one company by their present name of the United Company of Merchants trading to the East Indies. Into this act it was thought worth while to insert a clause, allowing the separate traders to continue their trade till Michaelmas 1711, but at the same time empowering the directors, upon three years notice, to redeem their little capital of seven thousand two hundred pounds, and thereby to convert the whole stock of the company into a joint stock. By the same act, the capital of the company, in consequence of a new loan to government, was augmented from two millions to three millions two hundred thousand pounds.[95] In 1743, the company advanced another million to government. But this million being raised, not by a call upon the proprietors, but by selling annuities and contracting bond-debts, it did not augment the stock upon which the proprietors could claim a dividend. It augmented, however, their trading stock, it being equally liable

---

[94] ["This coalition was made on the 22nd of July, 1702, by an indenture tripartite between the Queen and the said two companies."—Anderson, *Commerce*, A.D. 1702.]

[95] [6 Ann., c. 17. Anderson, *Commerce*, A.D. 1708.]

with the other three millions two hundred thousand pounds to the losses sustained, and debts contracted, by the company in

which with exclusive privileges has traded successfully,

but has conquered large territories,

prosecution of their mercantile projects. From 1708, or at least from 1711, this company, being delivered from all competitors, and fully established in the monopoly of the English commerce to the East Indies, carried on a successful trade, and from their profits made annually a moderate dividend to their proprietors. During the French war which began in 1741, the ambition of Mr. Dupleix, the French governor of Pondicherry, involved them in the wars of the Carnatic, and in the politics of the Indian princes. After many signal successes, and equally signal losses, they at last lost Madras, at that time their principal settlement in India. It was restored to them by the treaty of Aix-la-Chapelle; and about this time the spirit of war and conquest seems to have taken possession of their servants in India, and never since to have left them. During the French war which began in 1755, their arms partook of the general good fortune of those of Great Britain. They defended Madras, took Pondicherry, recovered Calcutta, and acquired the revenues of a rich and extensive territory, amounting, it was then said, to upwards of three millions a-year. They remained for several years in quiet possession of this revenue: But in 1767, administration laid claim to their territorial acquisitions, and the revenue arising from them, as of right belonging to the crown; and the company, in compensation for this claim, agreed to pay to government four hundred thousand pounds a-year. They had before this gradually augmented their dividend from about six to ten per cent.; that is, upon their capital of three millions two hundred thousand pounds, they had increased it by a hundred and twenty-eight thousand pounds, or had raised it from one hundred and ninety-two thousand, to three hundred and twenty thousand pounds a-year. They were attempting about this time to raise it still further, to twelve and a half per cent. which would have made their annual payments to their proprietors equal to what they had agreed to pay annually to government, or to four hundred thousand pounds a-year. But during the two years in which their agreement with government was to take place, they were restrained from any further increase of dividend by two successive acts of parliament,[96] of which the object was to enable them to make a speedier progress in the payment of their debts, which were at this time estimated at upwards of six or seven millions sterling. In 1769, they renewed their agreement with government for five years more, and stipulated, that during the course of that period they should be allowed gradually to increase their dividend to twelve and a half per cent.; never increasing it, however, more than one per cent. in one year. This increase of dividend, therefore, when it had risen to its utmost height, could augment their annual payments, to their proprietors and government together, but by six hundred and eight thousand pounds, beyond what they had been before their late territorial acquisitions. What the gross revenue of those territorial acquisitions was supposed to amount to, has already been mentioned; and by an account brought by the Cruttenden East Indiaman in 1768, the nett revenue, clear of all deductions and military charges, was stated at two million forty-eight thousand seven hundred and forty-seven pounds. They were said at the same time to possess another revenue, arising partly from lands, but chiefly from the customs established at their different settlements, amounting to four hundred and thirty-nine thousand pounds. The profits of their trade too, according to the evidence of their chairman before the House of Commons, amounted at this time to at least four hundred thousand pounds a-year; according to that of their accomptant, to at least five hundred thousand; accord-

and mismanaged them, ing to the lowest account, at least equal to the highest dividend that was to be paid to their proprietors. So great a revenue might certainly have afforded an augmentation of six hundred and eight thousand pounds in their annual payments; and at the same time have a large sinking fund sufficient for the speedy reduction of their debts. In 1773, however, their debts, instead

[96] [7 Geo. III., c. 49, and 8 Geo. III., c. 11.]

of being reduced, were augmented by an arrear to the treasury in the payment of the four hundred thousand pounds, by another to the custom-house for duties unpaid, by a large debt to the bank for money borrowed, and by a fourth for bills drawn upon them from India, and wantonly accepted, to the amount of upwards of twelve hundred thousand pounds. The distress which these accumulated claims brought upon them, obliged them not only to reduce all at once their dividend to six per cent. but to throw themselves upon the mercy of government, and to supplicate, first, a release from the further payment of the stipulated four hundred thousand pounds a-year; and, secondly, a loan of fourteen hundred thousand, to save them from immediate bankruptcy. The great increase of their fortune had,

so that Parliament has been obliged to make alterations, it seems, only served to furnish their servants with a pretext for greater profusion, and a cover for greater malversation, than in proportion even to that increase of fortune. The conduct of their servants in India, and the general state of their affairs both in India and in Europe, became the subject of a parliamentary inquiry;[97] in consequence of which several very important alterations were made in the constitution of their government, both at home and abroad. In India their principal settlements of Madras, Bombay, and Calcutta, which had before been altogether independent of one another, were subjected to a governor-general, assisted by a council of four assessors, parliament assuming to itself the first nomination of this governor and council who were to reside at Calcutta; that city having now become, what Madras was before, the most important of the English settlements in India. The court of the mayor of Calcutta, originally instituted for the trial of mercantile causes, which arose in the city and neighbourhood, had gradually extended its jurisdiction with the extension of the empire. It was now reduced and confined to the original purpose of its institution. Instead of it a new supreme court of judicature was established, consisting of a chie. justice and three judges to be appointed by the

[97] [In 1772–3. Additions and Corrections and ed. 3 read "subjects."]

crown. In Europe, the qualification necessary to entitle a proprietor to vote at their general courts was raised, from five hundred pounds, the original price of a share in the stock of the company, to a thousand pounds. In order to vote upon this qualification too, it was declared necessary that he should have possessed it, if acquired by his own purchase, and not by inheritance, for at least one year, instead of six months, the term requisite before. The court of twenty-four directors had before been chosen annually; but it was now enacted that each director should, for the future, be chosen for four years; six of them, however, to go out of office by rotation every year, and not to be capable of being re-chosen at the election of the six new directors for the ensuing year.[98] In consequence of these alterations, the courts, both of the proprietors and directors, it was expected, would be likely to act with more dignity and steadiness than they had usually done before. But it seems impossible, by any alterations, to render those courts, in any respect, fit to govern, or even to share in the government of a great empire; because the greater part of their members must always have too little interest in the prosperity of that empire, to give any serious attention to what may promote it. Frequently a man of great, sometimes even a man of small fortune, is willing to purchase a thousand pounds share in India stock, merely for the influence which he expects to acquire by a vote in the court of proprietors. It gives him a share, though not in the plunder, yet in the appointment of the plunderers of India; the court of directors, though they make that appointment, being necessarily more or less under the influence of the proprietors, who not only elect those directors, but sometimes overrule the appointments of their servants in India. Provided he can enjoy this influence for a few years, and thereby provide for a certain number of his friends, he frequently cares little about the dividend; or even about the value of the stock upon which his vote is founded. About the prosperity of the great empire, in the government of which that vote gives him a share, he seldom cares at all. No other sovereigns ever were, or, from the nature

[98] [13 Geo. III., c. 63.]

of things, ever could be, so perfectly indifferent about the happiness or misery of their subjects, the improvement or waste of their dominions, the glory or disgrace of their administration; as, from irresistible moral causes, the greater part of the proprietors of such a mercantile company are, and necessarily must be. This indifference too was more likely to be increased than diminished by some of the new regulations which were made in consequence of the parliamentary inquiry. By a resolution of the House of Commons, for example, it was declared, that when the fourteen hundred thousand pounds lent to the company by government should be paid, and their bond-debts be reduced to fifteen hundred thousand pounds, they might then, and not till then, divide eight per cent. upon their capital; and that whatever remained of their revenues and neat profits at home, should be divided into four parts; three of them to be paid into the exchequer for the use of the public, and the fourth to be reserved as a fund, either for the further reduction of their bond-debts, or for the discharge of other contingent exigencies, which the company might labour under.[99]

But if the company were bad stewards, and bad sovereigns,

which are not likely to be of service. when the whole of their nett[100] revenue and profits belonged to themselves, and were at their own disposal, they were surely not likely to be better, when three-fourths of them were to belong to other people, and the other fourth, though to be laid out for the benefit of the company, yet to be so, under the inspection, and with the approbation, of other people.

It might be more agreeable to the company that their own servants and dependants should have either the pleasure of

They tend to encourage waste, wasting, or the profit of embezzling whatever surplus might remain, after paying the proposed dividend of eight per cent., than that it should come into the hands of a set of people with whom

---

[99] [*House of Commons Journals*, April 27, 1773.]

[100] [The spelling in other parts of the work is "neat." The Additions and Corrections read "nett" both here and seven lines above. The discrepancy was obviously noticed in one case and not in the other.]

those resolutions could scarce fail to set them, in some measure, at variance. The interest of those servants and dependants might so far predominate in the court of proprietors, as sometimes to dispose it to support the authors of depredations which had been committed in direct violation of its own authority. With the majority of proprietors, the support even of the authority of their own court might sometimes be a matter of less consequence, than the support of those who had set that authority at defiance.

The regulations of 1773, accordingly, did not put an end to the disorders of the company's government in India.

and the company is now in greater distress than ever.

Notwithstanding that, during a momentary fit of good conduct, they had at one time collected, into the treasury of Calcutta, more than three millions sterling; notwithstanding that they had afterwards extended, either their dominion, or their depredations over a vast accession of some of the richest and most fertile countries in India; all was wasted and destroyed. They found themselves altogether unprepared to stop or resist the incursion of Hyder Ali; and, in consequence of those disorders, the company is now (1784) in greater distress than ever; and, in order to prevent immediate bankruptcy, is once more reduced to supplicate the assistance of government. Different plans have been proposed by the different parties in parliament, for the better management of its affairs. And all those plans seem to agree in supposing, what was indeed always abundantly evident, that it is altogether unfit to govern its territorial possessions. Even the company itself seems to be convinced of its own incapacity so far, and seems, upon that account, willing to give them up to government.

With the right of possessing forts and garrisons in distant and barbarous countries, is necessarily connected the right of

Companies misuse the right of making peace and war.

making peace and war in those countries. The joint stock companies which have had the one right, have constantly exercised the other, and have frequently had it expressly conferred upon them. How unjustly, how capriciously, how cruelly they have commonly exercised it, is too well known from recent experience.

When a company of merchants undertake, at their own risk and expence, to establish a new trade with some remote and barbarous nation, it may not be unreasonable to incorporate them into a joint stock company, and to grant them, in case of their success, a monopoly of the trade for a certain number of years. It is the easiest and most natural way in which the state can recompense them for hazarding a dangerous and expensive experiment, of which the public is afterwards to reap the benefit. A temporary monopoly of this kind may be vindicated upon the same principles upon which a like monopoly of a new machine is granted to its inventor, and that of a new book to its author. But upon the expiration of the term, the monopoly ought certainly to determine; the forts and garrisons, if it was found necessary to establish any, to be taken into the hands of government, their value to be paid to the company, and the trade to be laid open to all the subjects of the state. By a perpetual monopoly, all the other subjects of the state are taxed very absurdly in two different ways; first, by the high price of goods, which, in the case of a free trade, they could buy much cheaper; and, secondly, by their total exclusion from a branch of business, which it might be both convenient and profitable for many of them to carry on. It is for the most worthless of all purposes too that they are taxed in this manner. It is merely to enable the company to support the negligence, profusion, and malversation of their own servants, whose disorderly conduct seldom allows the dividend of the company to exceed the ordinary rate of profit in trades which are altogether free, and very frequently makes it fall even a good deal short of that rate. Without a monopoly, however, a joint stock company, it would appear from experience, cannot long carry on any branch of foreign trade. To buy in one market, in order to sell, with profit, in another, when there are many competitors in both; to watch over, not only the occasional variations in the demand, but the

The grant of a temporary monopoly to a joint stock company may sometimes be reasonable, but a perpetual monopoly creates an absurd tax.

much greater and more frequent variations in the competition, or in the supply which that demand is likely to get from other people, and to suit with dexterity and judgment both the quantity and quality of each assortment of goods to all these circumstances, is a species of warfare of which the operations are continually changing, and which can scarce ever be conducted successfully, without such an unremitting exertion of vigilance and attention, as cannot long be expected from the directors of a joint stock company. The East India Company, upon the redemption of their funds, and the expiration of their exclusive privilege, have a right, by act of parliament, to continue a corporation with a joint stock, and to trade in their corporate capacity to the East Indies in common with the rest of their fellow-subjects. But in this situation the superior vigilance and attention of private adventurers would, in all probability, soon make them weary of the trade.

An eminent French author, of great knowledge in matters of political œconomy, the Abbé Morellet, gives a list of fifty-five joint stock companies for foreign trade, which have been established in different parts of Europe since the year 1600, and which, according to him, have all failed from mismanagement, notwithstanding they had exclusive privileges.[101] He has been misinformed with regard to the history of two or three of them, which were not joint stock companies and have not failed. But, in compensation, there have been several joint stock companies which have failed, and which he has omitted.

A list of fifty-five companies with exclusive privileges for foreign trade which have failed has been collected by Abbé Morellet.

Only four trades can be well carried on by a company with no exclusive privilege, namely,

The only trades which it seems possible for a joint stock company to carry on successfully, without an exclusive privilege, are those, of which all the operations are capable of being reduced to what is called a routine, or to such a uniformity of method as

[101] [*Examen de la réponse de M. N** [Necker] au Mémoire de M. l'Abbé Morellet, sur la Compagnie des Indes: par l'auteur du Mémoire*, 1769, pp. 35–38.]

admits of little or no variation. Of this kind is, first, the banking trade; secondly, the trade of insurance from fire, and from sea risk and capture in time of war; thirdly, the trade of making and maintaining a navigable cut or canal; and, fourthly, the similar trade of bringing water for the supply of a great city.

Though the principles of the banking trade may appear somewhat abstruse, the practice is capable of being reduced to strict rules. To depart upon any occasion from those rules, in *banking,* consequence of some flattering speculation of extraordinary gain, is almost always extremely dangerous, and frequently fatal to the banking company which attempts it. But the constitution of joint stock companies renders them in general more tenacious of established rules than any private copartnery. Such companies, therefore, seem extremely well fitted for this trade. The principal banking companies in Europe, accordingly, are joint stock companies, many of which manage their trade very successfully without any exclusive privilege. The Bank of England has no other exclusive privilege, except that no other banking company in England shall consist of more than six persons.[102] The two banks of Edinburgh are joint stock companies without any exclusive privilege.

The value of the risk, either from fire, or from loss by sea, or *insurance,* by capture, though it cannot, perhaps, be calculated very exactly, admits, however, of such a gross estimation as renders it, in some degree, reducible to strict rule and method. The trade of insurance, therefore, may be carried on successfully by a joint stock company, without any exclusive privilege. Neither the London Assurance, nor the Royal Exchange Assurance companies, have any such privilege.[103]

When a navigable cut or canal has been once made, the management of it becomes quite simple and easy, and[104] is reducible to strict rule and method. Even the making of it is so,

[102] [6 Ann., c. 22.]

[103] [At least as against private persons, Anderson, *Commerce*, A.D. 1720.]

[104] [Eds. 4 and 5 insert "it" here, by a misprint.]

canal and aque-duct management and construction.
as it may be contracted for with undertakers at so much a mile, and so much a lock. The same thing may be said of a canal, an aqueduct, or a great pipe for bringing water to supply a great city. Such undertakings, therefore, may be, and accordingly frequently are, very successfully managed by joint stock companies without any exclusive privilege.

To establish a joint stock company, however, for any undertaking, merely because such a company might be capable of managing it successfully; or to exempt a particular set of dealers from some of the general laws which take place with regard to all their neighbours, merely because they might be capable of thriving if they had such an exemption, would certainly not be reasonable. To render such an establishment perfectly reasonable, with the circumstance of being reducible to strict rule and method, two other circumstances ought to concur. First, it ought to appear with the clearest evidence, that the undertaking is of greater and more general utility than the greater part of common trades; and secondly, that it requires a greater capital than can easily be collected into a private copartnery. If a moderate capital were[105] sufficient, the great utility of the undertaking would not be a sufficient reason for establishing a joint stock company; because, in this case, the demand for what it was to produce, would readily and easily be supplied by private adventurers. In the four trades above mentioned, both those circumstances concur.

A joint stock company ought not to be established except for some purpose of remarkable utility, requiring a larger capital than can be provided by a private partnership.

The great and general utility of the banking trade when prudently managed, has been fully explained in the second book of this inquiry.[106] But a public bank which is to support public credit, and upon particular emergencies to advance to government the whole produce of a tax, to the amount, per-

These conditions are fulfilled by banking,

---

[105] [Additions and Corrections and ed. 3 read "was."]

[106] [Above, pp. 372–382.]

haps, of several millions, a year or two before it comes in, requires a greater capital than can easily be collected into any
private copartnery.

The trade of insurance gives great security to the fortunes
of private people, and by dividing among a great many that

insurance, loss which would ruin an individual, makes
it fall light and easy upon the whole society.
In order to give this security, however, it is
necessary that the insurers should have a very large capital.
Before the establishment of the two joint stock companies for
insurance in London, a list, it is said, was laid before the
attorney-general, of one hundred and fifty private insurers who
had failed in the course of a few years.

That navigable cuts and canals, and the works which are
sometimes necessary for supplying a great city with water, are

canals and water works, of great and general utility; while at the
same time they frequently require a greater
expence than suits the fortunes of private
people, is sufficiently obvious.

Except the four trades above mentioned, I have not been
able to recollect any other in which all the three circumstances,

but not by anything else. requisite for rendering reasonable the establishment of a joint stock company, concur.
The English copper company of London, the
lead smelting company, the glass grinding company, have not
even the pretext of any great or singular utility in the object
which they pursue; nor does the pursuit of that object seem to
require any expence unsuitable to the fortunes of many private
men. Whether the trade which those companies carry on, is reducible to such strict rule and method as to render it fit for the
management of a joint stock company, or whether they have
any reason to boast of their extraordinary profits, I do not pretend to know. The mine-adventurers company has been long
ago bankrupt.[107] A share in the stock of the British Linen
Company of Edinburgh sells, at present, very much below par,
though less so than it did some years ago. The joint stock com-

---

[107] [Anderson, *Commerce*, A.D. 1690, 1704, 1710, 1711.]

panies, which are established for the public-spirited purpose of promoting some particular manufacture, over and above managing their own affairs ill, to the diminution of the general stock of the society, can in other respects scarce ever fail to do more harm than good. Notwithstanding the most upright intentions, the unavoidable partiality of their directors to particular branches of the manufacture, of which the undertakers mislead and impose upon them, is a real discouragement to the rest, and necessarily breaks, more or less, that natural proportion which would otherwise establish itself between judicious industry and profit, and which, to the general industry of the country, is of all encouragements the greatest and the most effectual.[108]

ARTICLE II

Of the Expence of the Institutions for the Education of Youth[109]

Institutions for education may also be made to furnish their own expense, The institutions for the education of the youth may, in the same manner, furnish a revenue sufficient for defraying their own expence. The fee or honorary which the scholar pays to the master naturally constitutes a revenue of this kind.

Even where the reward of the master does not arise altogether from this natural revenue, it still is not necessary that it should be derived from that general revenue of the society, of which the collection and application are,[110] in most countries, assigned to the executive power. Through the greater part of Europe, accordingly, the endowment of schools and colleges makes either no charge upon that general revenue, or but a very small one. It every where arises chiefly from some local or provincial revenue, from the rent of some landed estate, or from the interest

or may be endowed.

---

[108] [This section, beginning on p. 928, appears first in *Additions and Corrections* and ed. 3.]

[109] [Ed. 1 reads "the youth" as in the first line of the text.]

[110] [Eds. 1–4 read "is."]

of some sum of money allotted and put under the management of trustees for this particular purpose, sometimes by the sovereign himself, and sometimes by some private donor.

Have those public endowments contributed in general to promote the end of their institution? Have they contributed to

Have endowments really promoted useful education? encourage the diligence, and to improve the abilities of the teachers? Have they directed the course of education towards objects more useful, both to the individual and to the public, than those to which it would naturally have gone of its own accord? It should not seem very difficult to give at least a probable answer to each of those questions.

In every profession, the exertion of the greater part of those who exercise it, is always in proportion to the necessity they

Exertion is always in proportion to its necessity. are under of making that exertion. This necessity is greatest with those to whom the emoluments of their profession are the only source from which they expect their fortune, or even their ordinary revenue and subsistence. In order to acquire this fortune, or even to get this subsistence, they must, in the course of a year,[111] execute a certain quantity of work of a known value; and, where the competition is free, the rivalship of competitors, who are all endeavouring to justle one another out of employment, obliges every man to endeavour to execute his work with a certain degree of exactness. The greatness of the objects which are to be acquired by success in some particular professions may, no doubt, sometimes animate the exertion of a few men of extraordinary spirit and ambition. Great objects, however, are evidently not necessary in order to occasion the greatest exertions. Rivalship and emulation render excellency, even in mean professions, an object of ambition, and frequently occasion the very greatest exertions. Great objects, on the contrary, alone and unsupported by the necessity of application, have seldom been sufficient to occasion any considerable exertion. In England, success in the profession of the law leads to some very great objects of ambition; and yet how

---

[111] [Ed. 1 reads "the year."]

few men, born to easy fortunes, have ever in this country been eminent in that profession?

The endowments of schools and colleges have necessarily diminished more or less the necessity of application in the

Endowments diminish the necessity of application,

teachers. Their subsistence, so far as it arises from their salaries, is evidently derived from a fund altogether independent of their success and reputation in their particular professions.

In some universities the salary makes but a part, and frequently but a small part of the emoluments of the teacher, of

which is not entirely removed where the teacher receives part of his emoluments from fees, but is entirely absent when his whole revenue arises from endowments.

which the greater part arises from the honoraries or fees of his pupils. The necessity of application, though always more or less diminished, is not in this case entirely taken away.[112] Reputation in his profession is still of some importance to him, and he still has some dependency upon the affection, gratitude, and favourable report of those who have attended upon his instructions; and these favourable sentiments he is likely to gain in no way so well as by deserving them, that is, by the abilities and diligence with which he discharges every part of his duty.

In other universities the teacher is prohibited from receiving any honorary or fee from his pupils, and his salary constitutes the whole of the revenue which he derives from his office. His interest is, in this case, set as directly in opposition to his duty as it is possible to set it. It is the interest of every man to live as much at his ease as he can; and if his emoluments are to be precisely the same, whether he does, or does not perform some very laborious duty, it is certainly his interest, at least as interest is vulgarly understood, either to neglect it altogether, or, if he is subject to some authority which will not suffer him to do this, to perform it in as careless and slovenly a manner as

---

[112] [Rae, *Life of Adam Smith*, p. 48, thinks Smith's salary at Glasgow may have been about £70 with a house, and his fees near £100.]

that authority will permit. If he is naturally active and a lover of labour, it is his interest to employ that activity in any way, from which he can derive some advantage, rather than in the performance of his duty, from which he can derive none.

If the authority to which he is subject resides in the body corporate, the college, or university, of which he himself is a

Members of a college or university are indulgent to their fellow members.

member, and in which the greater part of the other members are, like himself, persons who either are, or ought to be teachers; they are likely to make a common cause, to be all very indulgent to one another, and every man to consent that his neighbour may neg-

lect his duty, provided he himself is allowed to neglect his own. In the university of Oxford, the greater part of the public professors have, for these many years, given up altogether even the pretence of teaching.

If the authority to which he is subject resides, not so much in the body corporate of which he is a member, as in some

External control is ignorant and capricious.

other extraneous persons, in the bishop of the diocese for example; in the governor of the province; or, perhaps, in some minister of state; it is not indeed in this case very

likely that he will be suffered to neglect his duty altogether. All that such superiors, however, can force him to do, is to attend upon his pupils a certain number of hours, that is, to give a certain number of lectures in the week or in the year. What those lectures shall be, must still depend upon the diligence of the teacher; and that diligence is likely to be proportioned to the motives which he has for exerting it. An extraneous jurisdiction of this kind, besides, is liable to be exercised both ignorantly and capriciously. In its nature it is arbitrary and discretionary, and the persons who exercise it, neither attending upon the lectures of the teacher themselves, nor perhaps understanding the sciences which it is his business to teach, are seldom capable of exercising it with judgment. From the insolence of office too they are frequently indifferent how they exercise it, and are very apt to censure or deprive him of his office wantonly, and without any just cause. The person subject to such jurisdiction is necessarily degraded by it, and, instead of being one of the most respectable, is rendered one of the meanest and most contemptible persons in the society. It is by powerful protection only that he can effectually guard himself against the bad usage to which he is at all times exposed; and this protection he is most likely to gain, not by ability or diligence in his profession, but by obsequiousness to the will of his superiors, and by being ready, at all times, to sacrifice to that will the rights, the interest, and the honour of the body corporate of which he is a member. Whoever has attended for any considerable time to the administration of a French university, must have had occasion to remark the effects which naturally result from an arbitrary and extraneous jurisdiction of this kind.

Whatever forces a certain number of students to any college or university, independent of the merit or reputation of the teachers, tends more or less to diminish the necessity of that merit or reputation.

To compel young men to attend a unversity has a bad effect on the teachers.

The privileges of graduates in arts, in law, physic[113] and divinity, when they can be obtained only by residing a certain number of years in certain universities, necessarily force a certain number of students to such universities, independent of the merit or reputation of the teachers. The privileges of graduates are a sort of statutes of apprenticeship, which have contributed to the improvement of education, just as the[114] other statutes of apprenticeship have to that of arts and manufactures.

The privileges of graduates are thus like apprenticeship.

The charitable foundations of scholarships, exhibitions, bursaries, &c. necessarily attach a certain number of students to certain colleges, independent altogether of the merit of those particular colleges. Were the students upon such charitable foundations left free to chuse what college they liked best, such liberty might perhaps

Scholarships,

---

[113] [Eds. 1 and 2 read "in physic."]

[114] [Ed. 1 does not contain "the."]

contribute to excite some emulation among *regulations against migration,* different colleges. A regulation, on the contrary, which prohibited even the independent members of every particular college from leaving it, and going to any other, without leave first asked and obtained of that which they meant to abandon, would tend very much to extinguish that emulation.

If in each college the tutor or teacher, who was to instruct each student in all arts and sciences, should not be voluntarily chosen by the student, but appointed by the *and assignment of students to particular tutors are equally pernicious.* head of the college; and if, in case of neglect, inability, or bad usage, the student should not be allowed to change him for another, without leave first asked and obtained; such a regulation would not only tend very much to extinguish all emulation among the different tutors of the same college, but to diminish very much in all of them the necessity of diligence and of attention to their respective pupils. Such teachers, though very well paid by their students, might be as much disposed to neglect them, as those who are not paid by them at all, or who have no other recompence but their salary.

If the teacher happens to be a man of sense, it must be an unpleasant thing to him to be conscious, while he is lecturing *Where such regulations prevail a teacher may avoid or suppress all visible signs of disapprobation on the part of his pupils.* his students, that he is either speaking or reading nonsense, or what is very little better than nonsense. It must too be unpleasant to him to observe that the greater part of his students desert his lectures; or perhaps attend upon them with plain enough marks of neglect, contempt, and derision. If he is obliged, therefore, to give a certain number of lectures, these motives alone, without any other interest, might dispose him to take some pains to give tolerably good ones. Several different expedients, however, may be fallen upon, which will effectually blunt the edge of all those incitements to diligence. The teacher, instead of explaining to his pupils himself the science in which he proposes to instruct them, may read some book upon it; and if this book is written in a foreign and dead language, by interpreting it to them into their own; or, what would give him still less trouble, by making them interpret it to him, and by now and then making an occasional remark upon it, he may flatter himself that he is giving a lecture. The slightest degree of knowledge and application will enable him to do this, without exposing himself to contempt or derision, or saying any thing that is really foolish, absurd, or ridiculous. The discipline of the college, at the same time, may enable him to force all his pupils to the most regular attendance upon this sham-lecture, and to maintain the most decent and respectful behaviour during the whole time of the performance.

The discipline of colleges and universities is in general contrived, not for the benefit of the students, but for the interest, or *University and college discipline is contrived for the ease of the teachers, and quite unnecessary if the teachers are tolerably diligent.* more properly speaking, for the ease of the masters. Its object is, in all cases, to maintain the authority of the master, and whether he neglects or performs his duty, to oblige the students in all cases to behave to him as if he performed it with the greatest diligence and ability. It seems to presume perfect wisdom and virtue in the one order, and the greatest weakness and folly in the other. Where the masters, however, really perform their duty, there are no examples, I believe, that the greater part of the students ever neglect theirs. No discipline is ever requisite to force attendance upon lectures which are really worth the attending, as is well known wherever any such lectures are given. Force and restraint may, no doubt, be in some degree requisite in order to oblige children, or very young boys, to attend to those parts of education which it is thought necessary for them to acquire during that early period of life; but after twelve or thirteen years of age, provided the master does his duty, force or restraint can scarce ever be necessary to carry on any part of education. Such is the generosity of the greater part of young men, that, so far from being disposed to neglect or despise the instructions of their master, provided he shows some serious intention of being of use to them, they are generally inclined to pardon a great deal of incorrectness in the performance of his duty, and sometimes even to conceal from the public a good deal of gross negligence.

Those parts of education, it is to be observed, for the teaching of which there are no public institutions, are generally the

The parts of education that are not conducted by public institutions are better taught.

best taught. When a young man goes to a fencing or a dancing school, he does not indeed always learn to fence or to dance very well; but he seldom fails of learning to fence or to dance. The good effects of the riding school are not commonly so evident. The expence of a riding school is so great, that in most places it is a public institution. The three most essential parts of literary education, to read, write, and account, it still continues to be more common to acquire in private than in public schools; and it very seldom happens that any body fails of acquiring them to the degree in which it is necessary to acquire them.

In England the public schools are much less corrupted than the universities. In the schools the youth are taught, or at least

English public schools, where the teachers depend more upon fees, are less corrupt than the universities.

may be taught, Greek and Latin; that is, every thing which the masters pretend to teach, or which, it is expected, they should teach. In the universities the youth neither are taught, nor always can find any proper means of being taught, the sciences, which it is the business of those incorporated bodies to teach. The reward of the schoolmaster in most cases depends principally, in some cases almost entirely, upon the fees or honoraries of his scholars. Schools have no exclusive privileges. In order to obtain the honours of graduation, it is not necessary that a person should bring a certificate of his having studied a certain number of years at a public school. If upon examination he appears to understand what is taught there, no questions are asked about the place where he learnt it.

The parts of education which are commonly taught in universities, it may, perhaps, be said are not very well taught. But

What the universities teach badly would not be commonly taught at all but for them.

had it not been for those institutions they would not have been commonly taught at all, and both the individual and the public would have suffered a good deal from the want of those important parts of education.

The present universities of Europe were originally, the greater part of them, ecclesiastical corporations;

They were originally instituted for the education of churchmen in theology;

instituted for the education of churchmen. They were founded by the authority of the pope, and were so entirely under his immediate protection, that their members, whether masters or students, had all of them what was then called the benefit of clergy, that is, were exempted from the civil jurisdiction of the countries in which their respective universities were situated, and were amenable only to the ecclesiastical tribunals. What was taught in the greater part of those universities was suitable to the end of their institution, either theology, or something that was merely preparatory to theology.

When christianity was first established by law, a corrupted Latin had become the common language of all the western

for this Latin was necessary,

parts of Europe. The service of the church accordingly, and the translation of the Bible which was read in churches, were both in that corrupted Latin; that is, in the common language of the country. After the irruption of the barbarous nations who overturned the Roman empire, Latin gradually ceased to be the language of any part of Europe. But the reverence of the people naturally preserves the established forms and ceremonies of religion, long after the circumstances which first introduced and rendered them reasonable are no more. Though Latin, therefore, was no longer understood any where by the great body of the people, the whole service of the church still continued to be performed in that language. Two different languages were thus established in Europe, in the same manner as in ancient Egypt; a language of the priests, and a language of the people; a sacred and a profane; a learned and an unlearned language. But it was necessary that the priests should understand something of that sacred and learned language in which they were to officiate; and the study of the Latin language therefore made, from the beginning, an essential part of university education.

It was not so with that either of the Greek, or of the Hebrew language. The infallible decrees of the church had pronounced

but not Greek or Hebrew, which were introduced by the Reformation.

the Latin translation of the Bible, commonly called the Latin Vulgate, to have been equally dictated by divine inspiration, and therefore of equal authority with the Greek and Hebrew originals. The knowledge of those two languages, therefore, not being indispensably requisite to a churchman, the study of them did not for a long time make a necessary part of the common course of university education. There are some Spanish universities, I am assured, in which the study of the Greek language has never yet made any part of that course. The first reformers found the Greek text of the new testament, and even the Hebrew text of the old, more favourable to their opinions, than the vulgate translation, which, as might naturally be supposed, had been gradually accommodated to support the doctrines of the catholic church. They set themselves, therefore, to expose the many errors of that translation, which the Roman catholic clergy were thus put under the necessity of defending or explaining. But this could not well be done without some knowledge of the original languages, of which the study was therefore gradually introduced into the greater part of universities; both of those which embraced, and of those which rejected, the doctrines of the reformation. The Greek language was connected with every part of that classical learning, which, though at first principally cultivated by catholics and Italians, happened to come into fashion much about the same time that the doctrines of the reformation were set on foot. In the greater part of universities, therefore, that language was taught previous to the study of philosophy, and as soon as the student had made some progress in the Latin. The Hebrew language having no connection with classical learning, and, except the holy scriptures, being the language of not a single book in any esteem, the study of it did not commonly commence till after that of philosophy, and when the student had entered upon the study of theology.

Originally the first rudiments both of the Greek and Latin languages were taught in universities, and in some universities they still continue to be so.[115] In others it is expected that the student should have previously acquired at least the rudiments of one or both of those languages, of which the study continues to make every where a very considerable part of university education.

Greek and Latin continue to be a considerable part of university education.

The ancient Greek philosophy was divided into three great branches; physics, or natural philosophy; ethics, or moral philosophy; and logic. This general division seems perfectly agreeable to the nature of things.

There are three branches of Greek philosophy,

The great phenomena of nature, the revolutions of the heavenly bodies, eclipses, comets; thunder, lightning, and other extraordinary meteors; the generation, the life, growth, and dissolution of plants and animals; are objects which, as they necessarily excite the wonder, so they naturally[116] call forth the curiosity, of mankind to enquire into their causes. Superstition first attempted to satisfy this curiosity, by referring all those wonderful appearances to the immediate agency of the gods. Philosophy afterwards endeavoured to account for them, from more familiar causes, or from such as mankind were better acquainted with, than the agency of the gods. As those great phenomena are the first objects of human curiosity, so the science which pretends to explain them must naturally have been the first branch of philosophy that was cultivated. The first philosophers, accordingly, of whom history has preserved any account, appear to have been natural philosophers.

(1) physics or natural philosophy,

In every age and country of the world men must have at-

---

[115] [Ed. 1 reads "and they still continue to be so in some universities."]

[116] ["Necessarily" and "naturally" are transposed in ed. 1.]

(2) ethics or moral philosophy, tended to the characters, designs, and actions of one another, and many reputable rules and maxims for the conduct of human life, must have been laid down and approved of by common consent. As soon as writing came into fashion, wise men, or those who fancied themselves such, would naturally endeavour to increase the number of those established and respected maxims, and to express their own sense of what was either proper or improper conduct, sometimes in the more artificial form of apologues, like what are called the fables of Æsop; and sometimes in the more simple one of apophthegms, or wise sayings, like the Proverbs of Solomon, the verses of Theognis and Phocyllides, and some part of the works of Hesiod. They might continue in this manner for a long time merely to multiply the number of those maxims of prudence and morality, without even attempting to arrange them in any very distinct or methodical order, much less to connect them together by one or more general principles, from which they were all deducible, like effects from their natural causes. The beauty of a systematical arrangement of different observations connected by a few common principles, was first seen in the rude essays of those ancient times towards a system of natural philosophy. Something of the same kind was afterwards attempted in morals. The maxims of common life were arranged in some methodical order, and connected together by a few common principles, in the same manner as they had attempted to arrange and connect the phenomena of nature. The science which pretends to investigate and explain those connecting principles, is what is properly called moral philosophy.

Different authors gave different systems both of natural and moral philosophy. But the arguments by which they supported *and (3) logic.* those different systems, far from being always demonstrations, were frequently at best but very slender probabilities, and sometimes mere sophisms, which had no other foundation but the inaccuracy and ambiguity of common language. Speculative systems have in all ages of the world been adopted for reasons too frivolous to have determined the judgment of any man of common sense, in a mat-

ter of the smallest pecuniary interest. Gross sophistry has
scarce ever had any influence upon the opinions of mankind,
except in matters of philosophy and speculation; and in these it
has frequently had the greatest. The patrons of each system of
natural and moral philosophy naturally endeavoured to expose
the weakness of the arguments adduced to support the systems
which were opposite to their own. In examining those arguments, they were necessarily led to consider the difference between a probable and a demonstrative argument, between a
fallacious and a conclusive one; and Logic, or the science of
the general principles of good and bad reasoning, necessarily
arose out of the observations which a scrutiny of this kind gave
occasion to. Though in its origin, posterior both to physics and
to ethics, it was commonly taught, not indeed in all, but in the
greater part of the ancient schools of philosophy, previously to
either of those sciences. The student, it seems to have been
thought, ought to understand well the difference between good
and bad reasoning, before he was led to reason upon subjects of
so great importance.

This ancient division of philosophy into three parts was in
the greater part of the universities of Europe,
changed for another into five.

*Philosophy was
afterwards divided
into five branches,
Metaphysics or
pneumatics were
added to physics,*

In the ancient philosophy, whatever was
taught concerning the nature either of the
human mind or of the Deity, made a part of
the system of physics. Those beings, in
whatever their essence might be supposed to
consist, were parts of the great system of the universe, and
parts too productive of the most important effects. Whatever
human reason could either conclude, or conjecture, concerning them, made, as it were, two chapters, though no doubt two
very important ones, of the science which pretended to give an
account of the origin and revolutions of the great system of the
universe. But in the universities of Europe, where philosophy
was taught only as subservient to theology, it was natural to
dwell longer upon these[117] two chapters than upon any other of

[117] [Ed. 1 reads "those."]

the science. They were[118] gradually more and more extended, and were divided into many inferior chapters, till at last the doctrine of spirits, of which so little can be known, came to take up as much room in the system of philosophy as the doctrine of bodies, of which so much can be known. The doctrines concerning those two subjects were considered as making two distinct sciences. What are called Metaphysics or Pneumatics were set in opposition to Physics, and were cultivated[119] not only as the more sublime, but, for the purposes of a particular profession, as the more useful science of the two. The proper subject of experiment and observation, a subject in which a careful attention is capable of making so many useful discoveries, was almost entirely neglected. The subject in which, after a few very simple and almost obvious truths, the most careful attention can discover nothing but obscurity and uncertainty, and can consequently produce nothing but subtleties and sophisms, was greatly cultivated.

When those two sciences had thus been set in opposition to one another, the comparison between them naturally gave birth to a third, to what was called Ontology, or the science which *and gave rise to Ontology.* treated of the qualities and attributes which were common to both the subjects of the other two sciences. But if subtleties and sophisms composed the greater part of the Metaphysics or Pneumatics of the schools, they composed the whole of this cobweb science of Ontology, which was likewise sometimes called Metaphysics.

Wherein consisted the happiness and perfection of a man, considered not only as an individual, but as the member of a *Moral philosophy degenerated into casuistry and an ascetic morality,* family, of a state, and of the great society of mankind, was the object which the ancient moral philosophy proposed to investigate. In that philosophy the duties of human life were treated of as subservient to the happi-

[118] [Ed. 1 reads "Those two chapters were."]

[119] [Ed. 1 reads, "What was called Metaphysics or Pneumatics was set in opposition to Physics, and was cultivated."]

ness and perfection of human life. But when moral, as well as natural philosophy, came to be taught only as subservient to theology, the duties of human life were treated of as chiefly subservient to the happiness of a life to come. In the ancient philosophy the perfection of virtue was represented as necessarily productive, to the person who possessed it, of the most perfect happiness in this life. In the modern philosophy it was frequently represented as generally, or rather as almost always inconsistent with any degree of happiness in this life; and heaven was to be earned only by penance and mortification, by the austerities and abasement of a monk; not by the liberal, generous, and spirited conduct of a man. Casuistry and an ascetic morality made up, in most cases, the greater part of the moral philosophy of the schools. By far the most important of all the different branches of philosophy, became in this manner by far the most corrupted.

Such, therefore, was the common course of philosophical education in the greater part of the universities in[120] Europe. Logic was taught first: Ontology came in the second place: Pneumatology, comprehending the doctrine concerning the nature of the human soul and of the Deity, in the third: In the fourth followed a debased system of moral philosophy, which was considered as immediately connected with the doctrines of Pneumatology, with the immortality of the human soul, and with the rewards and punishments which, from the justice of the Deity, were to be expected in a life to come: A short and superficial system of Physics usually concluded the course.

the order being (1) logic, (2) ontology, (3) pneumatology, (4) a debased moral philosophy, (5) physics.

The alterations which the universities of Europe thus introduced into the ancient course of philosophy, were all meant for the education of ecclesiastics, and to render it a more proper introduction to the study of theology. But the additional quantity of subtlety and sophistry;

University education was thus made less likely to produce men of the world.

---

[120] [Ed. 1 reads "of."]

the casuistry and the ascetic morality which those alterations introduced into it, certainly did not render it more proper for the education of gentlemen or men of the world, or more likely either to improve the understanding, or to mend the heart.

This course of philosophy is what still continues to be taught in the greater part of the universities of Europe; with

This course is still taught in most universities with more or less diligence.

more or less diligence, according as the constitution of each particular university happens to render diligence more or less necessary to the teachers. In some of the richest and best endowed universities, the tutors content themselves with teaching a few unconnected shreds and parcels of this corrupted course; and even these they commonly teach very negligently and superficially.

The improvements which, in modern times, have been made in several different branches of philosophy, have not, the

Few improvements in philosophy have been made by universities, and fewest by the richest universities.

greater part of them, been made in universities; though some no doubt have. The greater part of universities have not even been very forward to adopt those improvements, after they were made; and several of those learned societies have chosen to remain, for a long time, the sanctuaries in which exploded systems and obsolete prejudices found shelter and protection, after they had been hunted out of every other corner of the world. In general, the richest and best endowed universities have been the slowest in adopting those improvements, and the most averse to permit any considerable change in the established plan of education. Those improvements were more easily introduced into some of the poorer universities, in which the teachers, depending upon their reputation for the greater part of their subsistence, were obliged to pay more attention to the current opinions of the world.[121]

But though the public schools and universities of Europe were originally intended only for the education of a particular

[121] [Above, p. 964.]

In spite of all this the universities drew to themselves the education of gentlemen and men of fortune,

profession, that of churchmen; and though they were not always very diligent in instructing their pupils even in the sciences which were supposed necessary for that profession, yet they gradually drew to themselves the education of almost all other people, particularly of almost all gentlemen and men of fortune. No better method, it seems, could be fallen upon of spending, with any advantage, the long interval between infancy and that period of life at which men begin to apply in good earnest to the real business of the world, the business which is to employ them during the remainder of their days. The greater part of what is taught in schools and universities, however, does not seem to be the most proper preparation for that business.

In England, it becomes every day more and more the custom to send young people to travel in foreign countries immediately upon their leaving school, and without sending them to

but in England it is becoming more usual to send young men to travel abroad, a plan so absurd that nothing but the discredit of the universities could have brought it into repute.

any university. Our young people, it is said, generally return home much improved by their travels. A young man who goes abroad at seventeen or eighteen, and returns home at one and twenty, returns three or four years older than he was when he went abroad; and at that age it is very difficult not to improve a good deal in three or four years. In the course of his travels, he generally acquires some knowledge of one or two foreign languages; a knowledge, however, which is seldom sufficient to enable him either to speak or write them with propriety. In other respects, he commonly returns home more conceited, more unprincipled, more dissipated, and more incapable of any serious application either to study or to business, than he could well have become in so short a time, had he lived at home. By travelling so very young, by spending in the most frivolous dissipation the most precious years of his life, at a distance from the inspection and control of his parents and relations, every useful habit, which the earlier parts of his education might have had some tendency to form in him, instead of being rivetted and confirmed, is almost necessarily either weakened or effaced. Nothing but the discredit into which the universities are allowing themselves to fall, could ever have brought into repute so very absurd a practice as that of travelling at this early period of life. By sending his son abroad, a father delivers himself, at least for some time, from so disagreeable an object as that of a son unemployed, neglected, and going to ruin before his eyes.

Such have been the effects of some of the modern institutions for education.

Different plans and different institutions for education seem to have taken place in other ages and nations.

In the republics of ancient Greece, every free citizen was instructed, under the direction of the public magistrate, in gymnastic exercises and in music. By gymnastic exercises it was intended to harden his body, to sharpen his courage, and to prepare him for the fatigues and dangers of war; and as the Greek militia was, by all accounts, one of the best that ever was in the world, this part of their public education must have answered completely the purpose for which it was intended. By the other part, music, it was proposed, at least by the philosophers and historians who have given us an account of those institutions, to humanize the mind, to soften the temper, and to dispose it for performing all the social and moral duties both of public and private life.

In Greece the state directed education in gymnastics and music.

The Romans had the Campus Martius, resembling the gymnasium, but no music. They were none the worse for its absence.

In ancient Rome the exercises of the Campus Martius answered the same purpose as those of the Gymnazium in ancient Greece,[122] and they seem to have answered it equally well. But among the Romans there was nothing which corresponded to the musical education of the Greeks. The morals of the Romans, however, both in private and

---

[122] [Repeated all but *verbatim* from above, p. 886.]

public life, seem to have been, not only equal, but, upon the whole, a good deal superior to those of the Greeks. That they were superior in private life, we have the express testimony of Polybius[123] and of Dionysius of Halicarnassus,[124] two authors well acquainted with both nations; and the whole tenor of the Greek and Roman history bears witness to the superiority of the public morals of the Romans. The good temper and moderation of contending factions seems to be the most essential circumstance in the public morals of a free people. But the factions of the Greeks were almost always violent and sanguinary; whereas, till the time of the Gracchi, no blood had ever been shed in any Roman faction; and from the time of the Gracchi the Roman republic may be considered as in reality dissolved. Notwithstanding, therefore, the very respectable authority of Plato,[125] Aristotle,[126] and Polybius,[127] and notwithstanding the very ingenious reasons by which Mr. Montesquieu endeavours to support that authority,[128] it seems probable that the musical education of the Greeks had no great effect in mending their morals, since, without any such education, those of the Romans were upon the whole superior. The respect of those ancient sages for the institutions of their ancestors, had probably disposed them to find much political wisdom in what was, perhaps, merely an ancient custom, continued, without interruption, from the earliest period of those societies, to the times in which they had arrived at a considerable degree of refinement. Music and dancing are the great amusements of almost all barbarous nations, and the great accomplishments which are supposed to fit any man for entertaining his society. It is so at this day among the negroes on the

---

[123] [*Hist.*, vi., 56; xviii., 34.]

[124] [*Ant. Rom.*, ii., xxiv. to xxvii., esp. xxvi.]

[125] [*Repub.*, iii., 400–401.]

[126] [*Politics*, 1340 *a*.]

[127] [*Hist.*, iv., 20.]

[128] [*Esprit des lois*, liv. iv., chap. viii., where Plato, Aristotle and Polybius are quoted.]

coast of Africa. It was so among the ancient Celtes, among the ancient Scandinavians, and, as we may learn from Homer, among the ancient Greeks in the times preceding the Trojan war.[129] When the Greek tribes had formed themselves into little republics, it was natural that the study of those accomplishments should, for a long time, make a part of the public and common education of the people.

The masters who instructed the young people either in music or in military exercises, do not seem to have been

The teachers of military exercises and music were not paid or appointed by the state.

paid, or even appointed by the state, either in Rome or even in Athens, the Greek republic of whose laws and customs we are the best informed. The state required that every free citizen should fit himself for defending it in war, and should, upon that account, learn his military exercises. But it left him to learn them of such masters as he could find, and it seems to have advanced nothing for this purpose, but a public field or place of exercise, in which he should practise and perform them.

In the early ages both of the Greek and Roman republics, the other parts of education seem to have consisted in learning to

Reading, writing and arithmetic were taught privately.

read, write, and account according to the arithmetic of the times. These accomplishments the richer citizens seem frequently to have acquired at home, by the assistance of some domestic pedagogue, who was generally, either a slave, or a freedman; and the poorer citizens, in the schools of such masters as made a trade of teaching for hire. Such parts of education, however, were abandoned altogether to the care of the parents or guardians of each individual. It does not appear that the state ever assumed any inspection or direction of them. By a law of Solon, indeed, the children were acquitted from maintaining those parents in their old age,[130] who

---

[129] [*Iliad*, xiii., 137; xviii., 494, 594; *Odyssey*, i., 152; viii., 265; xviii., 304; xxiii., 134.]

[130] [Ed. 1 places "those parents" here.]

had neglected to instruct them in some profitable trade or business.[131]

In the progress of refinement, when philosophy and rhetoric came into fashion, the better sort of people used to send
their children to the schools of philosophers and rhetoricians, in order to be instructed in these fashionable sciences. But those schools were not supported by the public. They were for a long time barely tolerated by it. The demand for philosophy and rhetoric was for a long time so small, that the first professed teachers of either could not find constant employment in any one city, but were obliged to travel about from place to place. In this manner lived Zeno of Elea, Protagoras, Gorgias, Hippias, and many others. As the demand increased, the schools both of philosophy and rhetoric became stationary; first in Athens, and afterwards in several other cities. The state, however, seems never to have encouraged them further than by assigning to some of them a particular place to teach in, which was sometimes done too by private donors. The state seems to have assigned the Academy to Plato, the Lyceum to Aristotle, and the Portico to Zeno of Citta, the founder of the Stoics. But Epicurus bequeathed his gardens to his own school. Till about the time of Marcus Antoninus, however, no teacher appears to have had any salary from the public, or to have had any other emoluments, but what arose from the honoraries or fees of his scholars. The bounty which that philosophical emperor, as we learn from Lucian, bestowed upon one of[132] the teachers of philosophy, probably lasted no longer than his own life. There was nothing equivalent to the privileges of graduation, and to have attended any of those schools was not necessary, in order to be permitted to practise any particular trade or profession. If the opinion of their own utility could not draw scholars to them,

Philosophical education was independent of the state.

---

[131] [Plutarch, *Life of Solon*, quoted by Montesquieu, *Esprit des Lois*, liv., xxvi., ch. v.]

[132] [The words "one of" do not occur in eds. 1 and 2. They are perhaps a misprint for "some of" or a misreading suggested by a failure to understand that "his own life" is that of Marcus Antoninus. See Lucian, *Eunuchus*, iii.]

the law neither forced any body to go to them, nor rewarded any body for having gone to them. The teachers had no jurisdiction over their pupils, nor any other authority besides that natural authority, which superior virtue and abilities never fail to procure from young people towards those who are entrusted with any part of their education.

At Rome, the study of the civil law made a part of the education, not of the greater part of the citizens, but of some particular families. The young people, however, who wished to acquire knowledge in the law, had no public school to go to, and had no other method of studying it, than by frequenting the company of such of their relations and friends, as were supposed to understand it. It is perhaps worth while to remark, that though the laws of the twelve tables were, many of them, copied from those of some ancient Greek republics, yet law never seems to have grown up to be a science in any republic of ancient Greece. In Rome it became a science very early, and gave a considerable degree of illustration to those citizens who had the reputation of understanding it. In the republics of ancient Greece, particularly in Athens, the ordinary courts of justice consisted of numerous, and therefore disorderly, bodies of people, who frequently decided almost at random, or as clamour, faction and party spirit happened to determine. The ignominy of an unjust decision, when it was to be divided among five hundred, a thousand, or fifteen hundred people (for some of their courts were so very numerous), could not fall very heavy upon any individual. At Rome, on the contrary, the principal courts of justice consisted either of a single judge, or of a small number of judges, whose characters, especially as they deliberated always in public, could not fail to be very much affected by any rash or unjust decision. In doubtful cases, such courts, from their anxiety to avoid blame, would naturally endeavour to shelter themselves under the example, or precedent, of the judges who had sat before them, either in the same, or in some other court. This attention to practice and precedent, necessarily formed the Roman law

No public institutions for teaching law existed at Rome, where law was first developed into an orderly system.

into that regular and orderly system in which it has been delivered down to us; and the like attention has had the like effects upon the laws of every other country where such attention has taken place. The superiority of character in the Romans over that of the Greeks, so much remarked by Polybius and Dionysius of Halicarnassus,[133] was probably more owing to the better constitution of their courts of justice, than to any of the circumstances to which those authors ascribe it. The Romans are said to have been particularly distinguished for their superior respect to an oath. But the people who were accustomed to make oath only before some diligent and well-informed court of justice, would naturally be much more attentive to what they swore, than they who were accustomed to do the same thing before mobbish and disorderly assemblies.

The abilities, both civil and military, of the Greeks and Romans, will readily be allowed to have been, at least, equal to those of any modern nation. Our prejudice is perhaps rather to overrate them. But except in what related to military exercises, the state seems to have been at no pains to form those great abilities: for I cannot be induced to believe, that the musical education of the Greeks could be of much consequence in forming them. Masters, however, had been found, it seems, for instructing the better sort of people among those nations in every art and science in which the circumstances of their society rendered it necessary or convenient for them to be instructed. The demand for such instruction produced, what it always produces, the talent for giving it; and the emulation which an unrestrained competition never fails to excite, appears to have brought that talent to a very high degree of perfection. In the attention which the ancient philosophers excited, in the empire which they acquired over the opinions and principles of their auditors, in the faculty which they possessed of giving a certain tone and character to the conduct and conversation of those auditors; they appear to have been much

The ancient system was more successful than the modern, which corrupts public teaching and stifles private.

[133] [Above, pp. 979–980.]

superior to any modern teachers. In modern times, the diligence of public teachers is more or less corrupted by the circumstances, which render them more or less independent of their success and reputation in their particular professions. Their salaries too put the private teacher, who would pretend to come into competition with them, in the same state with a merchant who attempts to trade without a bounty, in competition with those who trade with a considerable one. If he sells his goods at nearly the same price, he cannot have the same profit, and poverty and beggary at least, if not bankruptcy and ruin will infallibly be his lot. If he attempts to sell them much dearer, he is likely to have so few customers that his circumstances will not be much mended. The privileges of graduation, besides, are in many countries necessary, or at least extremely convenient to most men of learned professions; that is, to the far greater part of those who have occasion for a learned education. But those privileges can be obtained only by attending the lectures of the public teachers. The most careful attendance upon the ablest instructions of any private teacher, cannot always give any title to demand them. It is from these different causes that the private teacher of any of the sciences which are commonly taught in universities, is in modern times generally considered as in the very lowest order of men of letters. A man of real abilities can scarce find out a more humiliating or a more unprofitable employment to turn them to. The endowments of schools and colleges have, in this manner, not only corrupted the diligence of public teachers, but have rendered it almost impossible to have any good private ones.

Were there no public institutions for education, no system, no science would be taught for which there was not some demand; or which the circumstances of the times did not render it either necessary, or convenient, or at least fashionable, to learn. A private teacher could never find his account in teaching, either an exploded and antiquated system of a science acknowledged to be useful, or a science universally believed to be a mere useless and pedantic heap of sophistry and

If there were no public institutions for education nothing except what was useful would be taught.

nonsense. Such systems, such sciences, can subsist no where, but in those incorporated societies for education whose prosperity and revenue are in a great measure independent of their reputation, and altogether independent of their industry. Were there no public institutions for education, a gentleman, after going through, with application and abilities, the most complete course of education which the circumstances of the times were supposed to afford, could not come into the world completely ignorant of every thing which is the common subject of conversation among gentlemen and men of the world.

There are no public institutions for the education of women, and there is accordingly nothing useless, absurd, or fantastical in the common course of their education.

Women's education is excellent in consequence of the absence of public institutions.

They are taught what their parents or guardians judge it necessary or useful for them to learn; and they are taught nothing else. Every part of their education tends evidently to some useful purpose; either to improve the natural attractions of their person, or to form their mind to reserve, to modesty, to chastity, and to œconomy; to render them both likely to become the mistresses of a family, and to behave properly when they have become such. In every part of her life a woman feels some conveniency or advantage from every part of her education. It seldom happens that a man, in any part of his life, derives any conveniency or advantage from some of the most laborious and troublesome parts of his education.

Ought the public, therefore, to give no attention, it may be asked, to the education of the people? Or if it ought to give any,

Ought the state to give no attention to education?

what are the different parts of education which it ought to attend to in the different orders of the people? and in what manner ought it to attend to them?

In some cases the state of the society necessarily places the greater part of individuals in such situations

In some cases it ought, in others it need not.

as naturally form in them, without any attention of government, almost all the abilities and virtues which that state requires, or perhaps can admit of. In other cases the state of the society does not place the greater part of individuals in such situations, and some attention of government is necessary in order to prevent the almost entire corruption and degeneracy of the great body of the people.

In the progress of the division of labour, the employment of the far greater part of those who live by labour, that is, of the great body of the people, comes to be

Division of labour destroys intellectual, social and martial virtues unless government takes pains to prevent it,

confined to a few very simple operations, frequently to one or two. But the understandings of the greater part of men are necessarily formed by their ordinary employments. The man whose whole life is spent in performing a few simple operations, of which the effects too are, perhaps, always the same, or very nearly the same, has no occasion to exert his understanding, or to exercise his invention in finding out expedients for removing difficulties which never occur. He naturally loses, therefore, the habit of such exertion, and generally becomes as stupid and ignorant as it is possible for a human creature to become. The torpor of his mind renders him, not only incapable of relishing or bearing a part in any rational conversation, but of conceiving any generous, noble, or tender sentiment, and consequently of forming any just judgment concerning many even of the ordinary duties of private life. Of the great and extensive interests of his country he is altogether incapable of judging; and unless very particular pains have been taken to render him otherwise, he is equally incapable of defending his country in war. The uniformity of his stationary life naturally corrupts the courage of his mind, and makes him regard with abhorrence the irregular, uncertain, and adventurous life of a soldier. It corrupts even the activity of his body, and renders him incapable of exerting his strength with vigour and perseverance, in any other employment than that to which he has been bred. His dexterity at his own particular trade seems, in this manner, to be acquired at the expence of his intellectual, social, and martial virtues. But in every improved and civilized society this is the state into which the labouring poor, that is, the great body of the people, must necessarily fall, unless government takes some pains to prevent it.

It is otherwise in the barbarous societies, as they are commonly called, of hunters, of shepherds, and even of husbandmen in that rude state of husbandry which precedes the improvement of manufactures, and the extension of foreign commerce. In such societies the varied occupations of every man oblige every man to exert his capacity; and to invent expedients for removing difficulties which are continually occurring. Invention is kept alive, and the mind is not[134] suffered to fall into that drowsy stupidity, which, in a civilized society, seems to benumb the understanding of almost all the inferior ranks of people. In those barbarous societies, as they are called, every man, it has already been observed, is a warrior. Every man too is in some measure a statesman, and can form a tolerable judgment concerning the interest of the society, and the conduct of those who govern it. How far their chiefs are good judges in peace, or good leaders in war, is obvious to the observation of almost every single man among them. In such a society indeed, no man can well acquire that improved and refined understanding, which a few men sometimes possess in a more civilized state. Though in a rude society there is a good deal of variety in the occupations of every individual, there is not a great deal in those of the whole society. Every man does, or is capable of doing, almost every thing which any other man does; or is capable of doing. Every man has a considerable degree of knowledge, ingenuity, and invention; but scarce any man has a great degree. The degree, however, which is commonly possessed, is generally sufficient for conducting the whole simple business of the society. In a civilized state, on the contrary, though there is little variety in the occupations of the greater part of individuals, there is an almost infinite variety in those of the whole society. These varied occupations present an almost infinite variety of objects to the contemplation of those few, who,

whereas in barbarous societies those virtues are kept alive by constant necessity.

[134] [Ed. 1 reads "the minds of men are not."]

being attached to no particular occupation themselves, have leisure and inclination to examine the occupations of other people. The contemplation of so great a variety of objects necessarily exercises their minds in endless comparisons and combinations, and renders their understandings, in an extraordinary degree, both acute and comprehensive. Unless those few, however, happen to be placed in some very particular situations, their great abilities, though honourable to themselves, may contribute very little to the good government or happiness of their society. Notwithstanding the great abilities of those few, all the nobler parts of the human character may be, in a great measure, obliterated and extinguished in the great body of the people.

The education of the common people requires, perhaps, in a civilized and commercial society, the attention of the public more than that of people of some rank and fortune. People of some rank and fortune are generally eighteen or nineteen years of age before they enter upon that particular business, profession, or trade, by which they propose to distinguish themselves in the world. They have before that full time to acquire, or at least to fit themselves for afterwards acquiring, every accomplishment which can recommend them to the public esteem, or render them worthy of it. Their parents or guardians are generally sufficiently anxious that they should be so accomplished, and are, in most cases, willing enough to lay out the expence which is necessary for that purpose. If they are not always properly educated, it is seldom from the want of expence laid out upon their education; but from the improper application of that expence. It is seldom from the want of masters; but from the negligence and incapacity of the masters who are to be had, and from the difficulty, or rather from the impossibility which there is, in the present state of things, of finding any better. The employments too in which people of some rank or fortune spend the greater part of their lives, are not, like those of

The education of the common people requires attention from the state more than that of people of rank and fortune, whose parents can look after their interests, and who spend their lives in varied occupations chiefly intellectual,

the common people, simple and uniform. They are almost all of them extremely complicated, and such as exercise the head more than the hands. The understandings of those who are engaged in such employments can seldom grow torpid for[135] want of exercise. The employments of people of some rank and fortune, besides, are seldom such as harass them from morning to night. They generally have a good deal of leisure, during which they may perfect themselves in every branch either of useful or ornamental knowledge of which they may have laid the foundation, or for which they may have acquired some taste in the earlier part of life.

It is otherwise with the common people. They have little time to spare for education. Their parents can scarce afford to maintain them even in infancy. As soon as they are able to work, they must apply to some trade by which they can earn their subsistence. That trade too is generally so simple and uniform as to give little exercise to the understanding; while, at the same time, their labour is both so constant and so severe, that it leaves them little leisure and less inclination to apply to, or even to think of any thing else.

unlike the children of the poor.

But though the common people cannot, in any civilized society, be so well instructed as people of some rank and fortune, the most essential parts of education, however, to read, write, and account, can be acquired at so early a period of life, that the greater part even of those who are to be bred to the lowest occupations, have time to acquire them before they can be employed in those occupations. For a very small expence the public can facilitate, can encourage, and can even impose upon almost the whole body of the people, the necessity of acquiring those most essential parts of education.

The state can encourage or insist on the general acquirement of reading, writing, and arithmetic,

The public can facilitate this acquisition by establishing in every parish or district a little school, where children may be taught

by establishing parish schools,

---

[135] [Ed. 1 reads "from."]

for a reward so moderate, that even a common labourer may afford it; the master being partly, but not wholly paid by the public; because, if he was wholly, or even principally paid by it, he would soon learn to neglect his business. In Scotland the establishment of such parish schools has taught almost the whole common people to read, and a very great proportion of them to write and account. In England the establishment of charity schools has had an effect of the same kind, though not so universally, because the establishment is not so universal. If in those little schools the books, by which the children are taught to read, were a little more instructive than they commonly are; and if, instead of a[136] little smattering of Latin, which the children of the common people are sometimes taught there, and which can scarce ever be of any use to them; they were instructed in the elementary parts of geometry and mechanics, the literary education of this rank of people would perhaps be as complete as it can be.[137] There is scarce a common trade which does not afford some opportunities of applying to it the principles of geometry and mechanics, and which would not therefore gradually exercise and improve the common people in those principles, the necessary introduction to the most sublime as well as to the most useful sciences.

The public can encourage the acquisition of those most essential parts of education by giving small premiums, and little badges of distinction, to the children of the common people who excel in them.

giving prizes,

The public can impose upon almost the whole body of the people the necessity of acquiring those most essential parts of education, by obliging every man to undergo an examination or probation in them before he can obtain the freedom in any corporation, or be allowed to set up any trade either in a village or town corporate.

and requiring men to pass an examination before setting up in trade.

It was in this manner, by facilitating the acquisition of their military and gymnastic exercises, by encouraging it, and even

---

[136] [Ed. 1 reads "the."]

[137] [Ed. 1 reads "as it is capable of being."]

In this way the Greeks and Romans maintained a martial spirit.

by imposing upon the whole body of the people the necessity of learning those exercises, that the Greek and Roman republics maintained the martial spirit of their respective citizens. They facilitated the acquisition of those exercises by appointing a certain place for learning and practising them, and by granting to certain masters the privilege of teaching in that place. Those masters do not appear to have had either salaries or exclusive privileges of any kind. Their reward consisted altogether in what they got from their scholars; and a citizen who had learnt his exercises in the public Gymnasia, had no sort of legal advantage over one who had learnt them privately, provided the latter had learnt them equally well. Those republics encouraged the acquisition of those exercises, by bestowing little premiums and badges of distinction upon those who excelled in them. To have gained a prize in the Olympic, Isthmian or Nemæan games gave illustration, not only to the person who gained it, but to his whole family and kindred. The obligation which every citizen was under to serve a certain number of years, if called upon, in the armies of the republic, sufficiently imposed the necessity of learning those exercises without which he could not be fit for that service.

That in the progress of improvement the practice of military exercises, unless government takes proper pains to support it,

Martial spirit in the people would diminish both the necessary size and the danger of a standing army.

goes gradually to decay, and, together with it, the martial spirit of the great body of the people, the example of modern Europe sufficiently demonstrates. But the security of every society must always depend, more or less, upon the martial spirit of the great body of the people. In the present times, indeed, that martial spirit alone, and unsupported by a well-disciplined standing army, would not, perhaps, be sufficient for the defence and security of any society. But where every citizen had the spirit of a soldier, a smaller standing army would surely be requisite. That spirit, besides, would necessarily diminish very much the dangers to liberty, whether real or imaginary, which are commonly apprehended from a standing army. As it would very much facilitate the operations of that army against a foreign invader, so it would obstruct them as much if unfortunately they should ever be directed against the constitution of the state.

The ancient institutions of Greece and Rome seem to have been much more effectual, for maintaining the martial spirit of the great body of the people, than the estab-

The Greek and Roman institutions were more effectual than modern militias, which only include a small portion of the people.

lishment of what are called the militias of modern times. They were much more simple. When they were once established, they executed themselves, and it required little or no attention from government to maintain them in the most perfect vigour. Whereas to maintain, even in tolerable execution, the complex regulations of any modern militia, requires the continual and painful attention of government, without which they are constantly falling into total neglect and disuse. The influence, besides, of the ancient institutions was much more universal. By means of them the whole body of the people was completely instructed in the use of arms. Whereas

It is the duty of government to prevent the growth of cowardice,

it is but a very small part of them who can ever be so instructed by the regulations of any modern militia; except, perhaps, that of Switzerland. But a coward, a man incapable either of defending or of revenging himself,

evidently wants one of the most essential parts of the character of a man. He is as much mutilated and deformed in his mind as another is in his body, who is either deprived of some of its most essential members, or has lost the use of them.[138] He is evidently the more wretched and miserable of the two; because happiness and misery, which reside altogether in the mind, must necessarily depend more upon the healthful or unhealthful, the mutilated or entire state of the mind, than upon that of the body. Even though the martial spirit of the people were of no use towards the defence of the society, yet to prevent that

[138] [Ed. 1 reads "the use of those members."]

sort of mental mutilation, deformity, and wretchedness, which cowardice necessarily involves in it, from spreading themselves through the great body of the people, would still deserve the most serious attention of government; in the same manner as it would deserve its most serious attention to prevent a leprosy or any other loathsome and offensive disease, though neither mortal nor dangerous, from spreading itself among them; though, perhaps, no other public good might result from such attention besides the prevention of so great a public evil.

The same thing may be said of the gross ignorance and stupidity which, in a civilized society, seem so frequently to benumb the understandings of all the inferior ranks of people. A
gross ignorance and stupidity. man without the proper use of the intellectual faculties of a man, is, if possible, more contemptible than even a coward, and seems to be mutilated and deformed in a still more essential part of the character of human nature. Though the state was to derive no advantage from the instruction of the inferior ranks of people, it would still deserve its attention that they should not be altogether uninstructed. The state, however, derives no inconsiderable advantage from their instruction. The more they are instructed, the less liable they are to the delusions of enthusiasm and superstition, which, among ignorant nations, frequently occasion the most dreadful disorders. An instructed and intelligent people besides, are always more decent and orderly than an ignorant and stupid one. They feel themselves, each individually more respectable, and more likely to obtain the respect of their lawful superiors, and they are therefore more disposed to respect those superiors. They are more disposed to examine, and more capable of seeing through, the interested complaints of faction and sedition, and they are, upon that account, less apt to be misled into any wanton or unnecessary opposition to the measures of government. In free countries, where the safety of government depends very much upon the favourable judgment which the people may form of its conduct, it must surely be of the highest importance that they should not be disposed to judge rashly or capriciously concerning it.

ARTICLE III

*Of the Expence of the Institutions for the Instruction
of People of all Ages*

The institutions for the instruction of people of all ages are
chiefly those for religious instruction. This is a species of instruction of which the object is not so much
to render the people good citizens in this
world, as to prepare them for another and a
better world in a life to come. The teachers
of the doctrine which contains this instruction, in the same manner as other teachers,
may either depend altogether for their subsistence upon the voluntary contributions of
their hearers; or they may derive it from
some other fund to which the law of their country may entitle
them; such as a landed estate, a tythe or land tax, an established salary or stipend. Their exertion, their zeal and industry,
are likely to be much greater in the former situation than in the
latter. In this respect the teachers of new religions have always
had a considerable advantage in attacking those ancient and
established systems of which the clergy, reposing themselves
upon their benefices, had neglected to keep up the fervour of
faith and devotion in the great body of the people; and having
given themselves up to indolence, were become altogether incapable of making any vigorous exertion in defence even of
their own establishment. The clergy of an established and well-
endowed religion frequently become men of learning and elegance, who possess all the virtues of gentlemen, or which can
recommend them to the esteem of gentlemen; but they are apt
gradually to lose the qualities, both good and bad, which gave
them authority and influence with the inferior ranks of people,
and which had perhaps been the original causes of the success
and establishment of their religion. Such a clergy, when attacked by a set of popular and bold, though stupid and ignorant

*These institutions
are chiefly for reli-
gious instruction.
Religious like
other teachers are
more vigorous if
unestablished and
unendowed.*

enthusiasts, feel themselves as perfectly defenceless as the indolent, effeminate, and full-fed nations of the southern parts of Asia, when they were invaded by the active, hardy, and hungry Tartars of the North. Such a clergy, upon such an emergency, have commonly no other resource than to call upon the civil magistrate to persecute, destroy, or drive out their adversaries, as disturbers of the public peace. It was thus that the Roman catholic clergy called upon the civil magistrate to persecute the protestants; and the church of England, to persecute the dissenters; and that in general every religious sect, when it has once enjoyed for a century or two the security of a legal establishment, has found itself incapable of making any vigorous defence against any new sect which chose to attack its doctrine or discipline. Upon such occasions the advantage in point of learning and good writing may sometimes be on the side of the established church. But the arts of popularity, all the arts of gaining proselytes, are constantly on the side of its adversaries. In England those arts have been long neglected by the well-endowed clergy of the established church, and are at present chiefly cultivated by the dissenters and by the methodists. The independent provisions, however, which in many places have been made for dissenting teachers, by means of voluntary subscriptions, of trust rights, and other evasions of the law, seem very much to have abated the zeal and activity of those teachers. They have many of them become very learned, ingenious, and respectable men; but they have in general ceased to be very popular preachers. The methodists, without half the learning of the dissenters, are much more in vogue.

The inferior clergy of the Church of Rome are more stimulated by self-interest than those of any established Protestant Church.

In the church of Rome, the industry and zeal of the inferior clergy are[139] kept more alive by the powerful motive of self-interest, than perhaps in any established protestant church. The parochial clergy derive, many of them, a very considerable part of their subsistence from the voluntary oblations of the people; a source of revenue which confes-

---

[139] [Eds. 1–3 read "is."]

sion gives them many opportunities of improving. The mendicant orders derive their whole subsistence from such oblations. It is with them, as with the hussars and light infantry of some armies; no plunder, no pay. The parochial clergy are like those teachers whose reward depends partly upon their salary, and partly upon the fee or honoraries which they get from their pupils; and these must always depend more or less upon their industry and reputation. The mendicant orders are like those teachers whose subsistence depends altogether upon their industry. They are obliged, therefore, to use every art which can animate the devotion of the common people. The establishment of the two great mendicant orders of St. Dominic and St. Francis, it is observed by Machiavel,[140] revived, in the thirteenth and fourteenth centuries, the languishing faith and devotion of the catholic church. In Roman catholic countries the spirit of devotion is supported altogether by the monks and by the poorer parochial clergy. The great dignitaries of the church, with all the accomplishments of gentlemen and men of the world, and sometimes with those of men of learning, are careful enough to maintain the necessary discipline over their inferiors, but seldom give themselves any trouble about the instruction of the people. "Most of the arts and professions in a state," says by far the most illustrious philosopher and historian of the present age, "are of such a nature, that, while they promote the interests of the society, they are also useful or agreeable to some individuals; and in that case, the constant rule of the magistrate, except, perhaps, on the first introduction of any art, is, to leave the profession to itself, and trust its encouragement to the individuals who reap the benefit of it. The artizans, finding their profits to rise by the favour of their customers, increase, as much as possible, their skill and industry; and as matters are not disturbed by any injudicious tampering, the commodity is always sure to be at all times nearly proportioned to the demand.

Hume says the state may leave the promotion of some arts to individuals who benefit by them,

---

[140] [In "Discourses on the First Decade of Titus Livius," book iii., chap. i.]

"But there are also some callings, which, though useful and even necessary in a state, bring no advantage or pleasure to any individual, and the supreme power is obliged to alter its conduct with regard to the retainers of those professions. It must give them public encouragement in order to their subsistence; and it must provide against that negligence to which they will naturally be subject, either by annexing particular honours to the profession, by establishing a long subordination of ranks and a strict dependance, or by some other expedient. The persons employed in the finances, fleets,[141] and magistracy, are instances of this order of men.

others must be promoted by the state;

"It may naturally be thought, at first sight, that the ecclesiastics belong to the first class, and that their encouragement, as well as that of lawyers and physicians, may safely be entrusted to the liberality of individuals, who are attached to their doctrines, and who find benefit or consolation from their spiritual ministry and assistance. Their industry and vigilance will, no doubt, be whetted by such an additional motive; and their skill in the profession, as well as their address in governing the minds of the people, must receive daily increase, from their increasing practice, study, and attention.

it might be thought that the teaching of religion belonged to the first class,

"But if we consider the matter more closely, we shall find, that this interested diligence of the clergy is what every wise legislator will study to prevent; because, in every religion except the true, it is highly pernicious, and it has even a natural tendency to pervert the true, by infusing into it a strong mixture of superstition, folly, and delusion. Each ghostly practitioner, in order to render himself more precious and sacred in the eyes of his retainers, will inspire them with the most violent abhorrence of all other sects, and continually endeavour, by some novelty, to excite the languid devotion of his audience. No regard will be

but it does not, because the interested zeal of the clergy should be discouraged.

---

[141] [The original reads "finances, armies, fleets."]

paid to truth, morals, or decency in the doctrines inculcated. Every tenet will be adopted that best suits the disorderly affections of the human frame. Customers will be drawn to each conventicle by new industry and address in practising on the passions and credulity of the populace. And in the end, the civil magistrate will find, that he has dearly paid for his pretended frugality, in saving a fixed establishment for the priests; and that in reality the most decent and advantageous composition, which he can make with the spiritual guides, is to bribe their indolence, by assigning stated salaries to their profession, and rendering it superfluous for them to be farther active, than merely to prevent their flock from straying in quest of new pastures. And in this manner ecclesiastical establishments, though commonly they arose at first from religious views, prove in the end advantageous to the political interests of society."[142]

But whatever may have been the good or bad effects of the independent provision of the clergy; it has, perhaps, been very seldom bestowed upon them from any view to those effects. Times of violent religious controversy have generally been times of equally violent political faction. Upon such occasions, each political party has either found it, or imagined it, for its interest, to league itself with some one or other of the contending religious sects. But this could be done only by adopting, or at last by favouring, the tenets of that particular sect. The sect which had the good fortune to be leagued with the conquering party, necessarily shared in the victory of its ally, by whose favour and protection it was soon enabled in some degree to silence and subdue all its adversaries. Those adversaries had generally leagued themselves with the enemies of the conquering party, and were therefore the enemies of that party. The clergy of this particular sect having thus become complete masters of the field, and their influence and authority with the great body of the people being in

Establishments and public endowments have not been due to reasoning like this, but to the needs of political faction.

[142] [Hume, *History*, chap. xxix., vol. iv., pp. 30, 31, in ed. of 1773, which differs verbally both from earlier and from later editions.]

its highest vigour, they were powerful enough to over-awe the chiefs and leaders of their own party, and to oblige the civil magistrate to respect their opinions and inclinations. Their first demand was generally, that he should silence and subdue all their adversaries; and their second, that he should bestow an independent provision on themselves. As they had generally contributed a good deal to the victory, it seemed not unreasonable that they should have some share in the spoil. They were weary, besides, of humouring the people, and of depending upon their caprice for a subsistence. In making this demand therefore they consulted their own ease and comfort, without troubling themselves about the effect which it might have in future times upon the influence and authority of their order. The civil magistrate, who could comply with this demand only by giving them something which he would have chosen much rather to take, or to keep to himself, was seldom very forward to grant it. Necessity, however, always forced him to submit at last, though frequently not till after many delays, evasions, and affected excuses.

But if politics had never called in the aid of religion, had the conquering party never adopted the tenets of one sect more than those of another, when it had gained the victory, it would probably have dealt equally and impartially with all the different sects, and have allowed every man to chuse his own priest and his own religion as he thought proper. There would in this case, no doubt, have been a great multitude of religious sects. Almost every different congregation might probably have made a little sect by itself, or have entertained some peculiar tenets of its own. Each teacher would no doubt have felt himself under the necessity of making the utmost exertion, and of using every art both to preserve and to increase the number of his disciples. But as every other teacher would have felt himself under the same necessity, the success of no one teacher, or sect of teachers, could have been very great. The interested and active zeal of religious teachers can be dangerous and troublesome only

If politics had never called in the aid of religion, sects would have been so numerous that they would have learnt to tolerate each other,

where there is, either but one sect tolerated in the society, or where the whole of a large society is divided into two or three great sects; the teachers of each[143] acting by concert, and under a regular discipline and subordination. But that zeal must be altogether innocent where the society is divided into two or three hundred, or perhaps into as many thousand small sects, of which no one could be considerable enough to disturb the public tranquillity. The teachers of each sect, seeing themselves surrounded on all sides with more adversaries than friends, would be obliged to learn that candour and moderation which is so seldom to be found among the teachers of those great sects, whose tenets, being supported by the civil magistrate, are held in veneration by almost all the inhabitants of extensive kingdoms and empires, and who therefore see nothing round them but followers, disciples, and humble admirers. The teachers of each little sect, finding themselves almost alone, would be obliged to respect those of almost every other sect, and the concessions which they would mutually find it both convenient and agreeable to make to one another, might in time probably reduce the doctrine of the greater part of them to that pure and rational religion, free from every mixture of absurdity, imposture, or fanaticism, such as wise men have in all ages of the world wished to see established; but such as positive law has perhaps never yet established, and probably never will establish in any country: because, with regard to religion, positive law always has been, and probably always will be, more or less influenced by popular superstition and enthusiasm. This plan of ecclesiastical government, or more properly of no ecclesiastical government, was what the sect called Independents, a sect no doubt of very wild enthusiasts, proposed to establish in England towards the end of the civil war. If it had been established, though of a very unphilosophical origin, it would probably by this time have been productive of the most philosophical good temper and moderation with regard to every sort of religious principle. It has been established in Pennsylvania, where, though the Quakers happen to be the

---

[143] [Ed. 1 reads "of each sect."]

and if they did not, their zeal could do no harm. most numerous,[144] the law in reality favours no one sect more than another, and it is there said to have been productive of this philosophical good temper and moderation.

But though this equality of treatment should not be productive of this good temper and moderation in all, or even in the greater part of the religious sects of a particular country; yet provided those sects were sufficiently numerous, and each of them consequently too small to disturb the public tranquillity, the excessive zeal of each[145] for its particular tenets could not well be productive of any very hurtful effects, but, on the contrary, of several good ones: and if the government was perfectly decided both to let them all alone, and to oblige them all to let alone one another, there is little danger that they would not of their own accord subdivide themselves fast enough, so as soon to become sufficiently numerous.

In every civilized society, in every society where the distinction of ranks has once been completely established, there *Of the two systems of morality, the strict or austere and the liberal or loose, the first is favoured by the common people, the second by the people of fashion.* have been always two different schemes or systems of morality current at the same time; of which the one may be called the strict or austere; the other the liberal, or, if you will, the loose system. The former is generally admired and revered by the common people: the latter is commonly more esteemed and adopted by what are called people of fashion. The degree of disapprobation with which we ought to mark the vices of levity, the vices which are apt to arise from great prosperity, and from the excess of gaiety and good humour, seems to constitute the principal distinction between those two opposite schemes or systems. In the liberal or loose system, luxury, wanton and even disorderly mirth, the pursuit of pleasure to some degree of intemperance, the breach of chastity, at least in one of the two sexes, &c. provided they are not accompanied with gross

---

[144] [Ed. 1 reads "the most numerous sect."]

[145] [Ed. 1 reads "of each sect."]

indecency, and do not lead to falshood or injustice, are generally treated with a good deal of indulgence, and are easily either excused or pardoned altogether. In the austere system, on the contrary, those excesses are regarded with the utmost abhorrence and destestation. The vices of levity are always ruinous to the common people, and a single week's thoughtlessness and dissipation is often sufficient to undo a poor workman for ever, and to drive him through despair upon committing the most enormous crimes. The wiser and better sort of the common people, therefore, have always the utmost abhorrence and detestation of such excesses, which their experience tells them are so immediately fatal to people of their condition. The disorder and extravagance of several years, on the contrary, will not always ruin a man of fashion, and people of that rank are very apt to consider the power of indulging in some degree of excess as one of the advantages of their fortune, and the liberty of doing so without censure or reproach, as one of the privileges which belong to their station. In people of their own station, therefore, they regard such excesses with but a small degree of disapprobation, and censure them either very slightly or not at all.

Almost all religious sects have begun among the common people, from whom they have generally drawn their earliest, as

Religious sects usually begin with the austere system,

well as their most numerous proselytes. The austere system of morality has, accordingly, been adopted by those sects almost constantly, or with very few exceptions; for there have been some. It was the system by which they could best recommend themselves to that order of people to whom they first proposed their plan of reformation upon what had been before established. Many of them, perhaps the greater part of them, have even endeavoured to gain credit by refining upon this austere system, and by carrying it to some degree of folly and extravagance; and this excessive rigour has frequently recommended them more than any thing else to the respect and veneration of the common people.

A man of rank and fortune is by his station the distinguished member of a great society, who attend to every part of

and in small religious sects morals are regular and orderly and even disagreeably rigorous and unsocial.

his conduct, and who thereby oblige him to attend to every part of it himself. His authority and consideration depend very much upon the respect which this society bears to him. He dare not do any thing which would disgrace or discredit him in it, and he is obliged to a very strict observation of that species of morals, whether liberal or austere, which the general consent of this society prescribes to persons of his rank and fortune. A man of low condition, on the contrary, is far from being a distinguished member of any great society. While he remains in a country village his conduct may be attended to, and he may be obliged to attend to it himself. In this situation, and in this situation only, he may have what is called a character to lose. But as soon as he comes into a great city, he is sunk in obscurity and darkness. His conduct is observed and attended to by nobody, and he is therefore very likely to neglect it himself, and to abandon himself to every sort of low profligacy and vice. He never emerges so effectually from this obscurity, his conduct never excites so much the attention of any respectable society, as by his becoming the member of a small religious sect. He from that moment acquires a degree of consideration which he never had before. All his brother sectaries are, for the credit of the sect, interested to observe his conduct, and if he gives occasion to any scandal, if he deviates very much from those austere morals which they almost always require of one another, to punish him by what is always a very severe punishment, even where no civil effects attend it, expulsion or excommunication from the sect. In little religious sects, accordingly, the morals of the common people have been almost always remarkably regular and orderly; generally much more so than in the established church. The morals of those little sects, indeed, have frequently been rather disagreeably rigorous and unsocial.

There are two possible remedies,

There are two very easy and effectual remedies, however, by whose joint operation the state might, without violence, correct whatever was unsocial or disagreeably rigorous in the morals of all the little sects into which the country was divided.

The first of those remedies is the study of science and philosophy, which the state might render almost universal among all people of middling or more than middling rank and fortune;

(1) the requirement of a knowledge of science and philosophy from candidates for professions and offices;

not by giving salaries to teachers in order to make them negligent and idle, but by instituting some sort of probation, even in the higher and more difficult sciences, to be undergone by every person before he was permitted to exercise any liberal profession, or before he could be received as a candidate for any honourable office of trust or profit. If the state imposed upon this order of men the necessity of learning, it would have no occasion to give itself any trouble about providing them with proper teachers. They would soon find better teachers for themselves than any whom the state could provide for them. Science is the great antidote to the poison of enthusiasm and superstition; and where all the superior ranks of people were secured from it, the inferior ranks could not be much exposed to it.

The second of those remedies is the frequency and gaiety of public diversions. The state, by encouraging, that is by giving

and (2) the encouragement of public diversions.

entire liberty to all those who for their own interest would attempt, without scandal or indecency, to amuse and divert the people by painting, poetry, music, dancing; by all sorts of dramatic representations and exhibitions, would easily dissipate, in the greater part of them, that melancholy and gloomy humour which is almost always the nurse of popular superstition and enthusiasm. Public diversions have always been the objects of dread and hatred, to all the fanatical promoters of those popular frenzies. The gaiety and good humour which those diversions inspire were altogether inconsistent with that temper of mind, which was fittest for their purpose, or which they could best work upon. Dramatic representations besides, frequently exposing their artifices to public ridicule, and sometimes even to public execration, were upon that account, more than all other diversions, the objects of their peculiar abhorrence.

In a country where the law favoured the teachers of no one religion more than those of another, it would not be necessary

Where no religion was favoured the sovereign would not require to influence the teachers of religion,

that any of them should have any particular or immediate dependency upon the sovereign or executive power; or that he should have any thing to do, either in appointing, or in dismissing them from their offices. In such a situation he would have no occasion to give himself any concern about them, further than to keep the peace among them, in the same manner as among the rest of his subjects; that is, to hinder them from persecuting, abusing, or oppressing one another. But it is quite otherwise in countries where there is an established or governing religion. The sovereign can in this case never be secure, unless he has the means of influencing in a considerable degree the greater part of the teachers of that religion.

The clergy of every established church constitute a great incorporation. They can act in concert, and pursue their interest

as he must where there is an established church,

upon one plan and with one spirit, as much as if they were under the direction of one man; and they are frequently too under such direction. Their interest as an incorporated body is never the same with that of the sovereign, and is sometimes directly opposite to it. Their great interest is to maintain their authority with the people; and this authority depends upon the supposed certainty and importance of the whole doctrine which they inculcate, and upon the supposed necessity of adopting every part of it with the most implicit faith, in order to avoid eternal misery. Should the sovereign have the imprudence to appear either to deride or doubt himself of the most trifling part of their doctrine, or from humanity attempt to protect those who did either the one or the other, the punctilious honour of a clergy who have no sort of dependency upon him, is immediately provoked to proscribe him as a profane person, and to employ all the terrors of religion in order to oblige the people to transfer their allegiance to some more orthodox and obedient prince. Should he oppose any of their pretensions or usurpations, the danger is equally great. The princes who have dared in this manner to rebel against the church, over and above this crime of rebellion, have generally been charged too with the additional crime of heresy, notwithstanding their solemn protestations of their faith and humble submission to every tenet which she thought proper to prescribe to them. But the authority of religion is superior to every other authority. The fears which it suggests conquer all other fears. When the authorised teachers of religion propagate through the great body of the people doctrines subversive of the authority of the sovereign, it is by violence only, or by the force of a standing army, that he can maintain his authority. Even a standing army cannot in this case give him any lasting security; because if the soldiers are not foreigners, which can seldom be the case, but drawn from the great body of the people, which must almost always be the case, they are likely to be soon corrupted by those very doctrines. The revolutions which the turbulence of the Greek clergy was continually occasioning at Constantinople, as long as the eastern empire subsisted; the convulsions which, during the course of several centuries, the turbulence of the Roman clergy was continually occasioning in every part of Europe, sufficiently demonstrate how precarious and insecure must always be the situation of the sovereign who has no proper means of influencing the clergy of the established and governing religion of his country.

Articles of faith, as well as all other spiritual matters, it is evident enough, are not within the proper department of a temporal sovereign, who, though he may be very well qualified for protecting, is seldom supposed to be so for instructing the people. With regard to such matters, therefore, his authority can seldom be sufficient to counterbalance the united authority of the clergy of the established church. The public tranquillity, however, and his own security, may frequently depend upon the doctrines which they may think proper to propagate concerning such matters. As he can seldom directly oppose their decision, therefore, with proper

since he cannot directly oppose the doctrines of the clergy.

weight and authority, it is necessary that he should be able to influence it; and he can influence it only by the fears and expectations which he may excite in the greater part of the individuals of the order. Those fears and expectations may consist in the fear of deprivation or other punishment, and in the expectation of further preferment.

In all Christian churches the benefices of the clergy are a sort of freeholds which they enjoy, not during pleasure, but during life, or good behaviour. If they held them by a more precarious tenure, and were liable to be turned out upon every slight disobligation either of the sovereign or of his ministers, it would perhaps be impossible for them to maintain their authority with the people, who would then consider them as mercenary dependents upon the court, in the sincerity of whose instructions they could no longer have any confidence. But should the sovereign attempt irregularly, and by violence, to deprive any number of clergymen of their freeholds, on account, perhaps, of their having propagated, with more than ordinary zeal, some factious or seditious doctrine, he would only render, by such persecution, both them and their doctrine ten times more popular, and therefore ten times more troublesome and dangerous than they had been before. Fear is in almost all cases a wretched instrument of government, and ought in particular never to be employed against any order of men who have the smallest pretensions to independency. To attempt to terrify them, serves only to irritate their bad humour, and to confirm them in an opposition which more gentle usage perhaps might easily induce them, either to soften, or to lay aside altogether. The violence which the French government usually employed in order to oblige all their parliaments, or sovereign courts of justice, to enregister any unpopular edict, very seldom succeeded. The means commonly employed, however, the imprisonment of all the refractory members, one would think were forcible enough. The princes of the house of Stewart sometimes employed the like means in order to influence some of the mem-

The clergy hold their benefices for life, and violence used against them would be ineffectual; so management must be resorted to.

bers of the parliament of England; and they generally found them equally intractable. The parliament of England is now managed in another manner; and a very small experiment, which the duke of Choiseul made about twelve years ago upon the parliament of Paris, demonstrated sufficiently that all the parliaments of France might have been managed still more easily in the same manner. That experiment was not pursued. For though management and persuasion are always the easiest and the safest instruments of government, as force and violence are the worst and the most dangerous, yet such, it seems, is the natural insolence of man, that he almost always disdains to use the good instrument, except when he cannot or dare not use the bad one. The French government could and durst use force, and therefore disdained to use management and persuasion. But there is no order of men, it appears, I believe, from the experience of all ages, upon whom it is so dangerous, or rather so perfectly ruinous, to employ force and violence, as upon the respected clergy of any established church. The rights, the privileges, the personal liberty of every individual ecclesiastic, who is upon good terms with his own order, are, even in the most despotic governments, more respected than those of any other person of nearly equal rank and fortune. It is so in every gradation of despotism, from that of the gentle and mild government of Paris, to that of the violent and furious government of Constantinople. But though this order of men can scarce ever be forced, they may be managed as easily as any other; and the security of the sovereign, as well as the public tranquillity, seems to depend very much upon the means which he has of managing them; and those means seem to consist altogether in the preferment which he has to bestow upon them.

Bishops were originally elected by the clergy and people, afterwards by the clergy alone,

In the ancient constitution of the Christian church,[146] the bishop of each diocese was elected by the joint votes of the clergy and of the people of the episcopal city. The people did not long retain their

---

[146] [Ed. 1 reads "Roman catholic church."]

right of election; and while they did retain it, they almost always acted under the influence of the clergy, who in such spiritual matters appeared to be their natural guides. The clergy, however, soon grew weary of the trouble of managing them, and found it easier to elect their own bishops themselves. The abbot, in the same manner, was elected by the monks of the monastery, at least in the greater part of abbacies. All the inferior ecclesiastical benefices comprehended within the diocese were collated by the bishop, who bestowed them upon such ecclesiastics as he thought proper. All church preferments were in this manner in the disposal of the church. The sovereign, though he might have some indirect influence in those elections, and though it was sometimes usual to ask both his consent to elect, and his approbation of the election, yet had no direct or sufficient means of managing the clergy. The ambition of every clergyman naturally led him to pay court, not so much to his sovereign, as to his own order, from which only he could expect preferment.

Through the greater part of Europe the Pope gradually drew to himself first the collation of almost all bishoprics and abbacies, or of what were called Consistorial benefices, and afterwards, by various machinations and pretences, of the greater part of inferior benefices comprehended within each diocese; little more being left to the bishop than what was barely necessary to give him a decent authority with his own clergy. By this arrangement the condition of the sovereign was still worse than it had been before. The clergy of all the different countries of Europe were thus formed into a sort of spiritual army, dispersed in different quarters, indeed, but of which all the movements and operations could now be directed by one head, and conducted upon one uniform plan. The clergy of each particular country might be considered as a particular detachment of that army, of which the operations could easily be supported and seconded by all the other detachments quartered in the different countries round about. Each detachment was not only independent of the sovereign of the country in which it was quartered, and by which it was maintained, but depen-

still later to a large extent by the Pope.

dent upon a foreign sovereign, who could at any time turn its arms against the sovereign of that particular country, and support them by the arms of all the other detachments.

Those arms were the most formidable that can well be imagined. In the ancient state of Europe, before the establishment of arts and manufactures, the wealth of the clergy gave them the same sort of influence over the common people, which that of the great barons gave them over their respective vassals, tenants, and retainers. In the great landed estates, which the mistaken piety both of princes and private persons had bestowed upon the church, jurisdictions were established of the same kind with those of the great barons; and for the same reason. In those great landed estates, the clergy, or their bailiffs, could easily keep the peace without the support or assistance either of the king or of any other person; and neither the king nor any other person could keep the peace there without the support and assistance of the clergy. The jurisdictions of the clergy, therefore, in their particular baronies or manors, were equally independent, and equally exclusive of the authority of the king's courts, as those of the great temporal lords. The tenants of the clergy were, like those of the great barons, almost all tenants at will, entirely dependent upon their immediate lords, and therefore liable to be called out at pleasure, in order to fight in any quarrel in which the clergy might think proper to engage them. Over and above the rents of those estates, the clergy possessed, in the tythes, a very large portion of the rents of all the other estates in every kingdom of Europe. The revenues arising from both those species of rents were, the greater part of them, paid in kind, in corn, wine, cattle, poultry, &c. The quantity exceeded greatly what the clergy could themselves consume; and there were neither arts nor manufactures for the produce of which they could exchange the surplus. The clergy could derive advantage from this immense surplus in no other way than by employing it, as the great barons employed the like surplus of their revenues, in the most profuse hospitality, and in the most extensive charity. Both the hospitality and

This, joined with the great wealth of the clergy, rendered them exceedingly formidable.

the charity of the ancient clergy, accordingly, are said to have been very great. They not only maintained almost the whole poor of every kingdom, but many knights and gentlemen had frequently no other means of subsistence than by travelling about from monastery to monastery, under pretence of devotion, but in reality to enjoy the hospitality of the clergy. The retainers of some particular prelates were often as numerous as those of the greatest lay-lords; and the retainers of all the clergy taken together were, perhaps, more numerous than those of all the lay-lords. There was always much more union among the clergy than among the lay-lords. The former were under a regular discipline and subordination to the papal authority. The latter were under no regular discipline or subordination, but almost always equally jealous of one another, and of the king. Though the tenants and retainers of the clergy, therefore, had both together been less numerous than those of the great lay-lords, and their tenants were probably much less numerous, yet their union would have rendered them more formidable. The hospitality and charity of the clergy too, not only gave them the command of a great temporal force, but increased very much the weight of their spiritual weapons. Those virtues procured them the highest respect and veneration among all the inferior ranks of people, of whom many were constantly, and almost all occasionally, fed by them. Every thing belonging or related to so popular an order, its possessions, its privileges, its doctrines, necessarily appeared sacred in the eyes of the common people, and every violation of them, whether real or pretended, the highest act of sacrilegious wickedness and profaneness. In this state of things, if the sovereign frequently found it difficult to resist the confederacy of a few of the great nobility, we cannot wonder that he should find it still more so to resist the united force of the clergy of his own dominions, supported by that of the clergy of all the neighbouring dominions. In such circumstances the wonder is, not that he was sometimes obliged to yield, but that he ever was able to resist.

The privileges of the clergy in those ancient times (which to us who live in the present times appear the most absurd), their

Benefit of clergy and other privileges were the natural result. total exemption from the secular jurisdiction, for example, or what in England was called the benefit of clergy; were the natural or rather the necessary consequences of this state of things. How dangerous must it have been for the sovereign to attempt to punish a clergyman for any crime whatever, if his own order were disposed to protect him, and to represent either the proof as insufficient for convicting so holy a man, or the punishment as too severe to be inflicted upon one whose person had been rendered sacred by religion? The sovereign could, in such circumstances, do no better than leave him to be tried by the ecclesiastical courts, who, for the honour of their own order, were interested to restrain, as much as possible, every member of it from committing enormous crimes, or even from giving occasion to such gross scandal as might disgust the minds of the people.

In the state in which things were through the greater part of Europe during the tenth, eleventh, twelfth, and thirteenth cen-

The Church of Rome in the Middle Ages was the most formidable combination against liberty, reason and happiness. turies, and for some time both before and after that period, the constitution of the church of Rome may be considered as the most formidable combination that ever was formed against the authority and security of civil government, as well as against the liberty, reason, and happiness of mankind, which can flourish only where civil government is able to protect them. In that constitution the grossest delusions of superstition were supported in such a manner by the private interests of so great a number of people as put them out of all danger from any assault of human reason: because though human reason might perhaps have been able to unveil, even to the eyes of the common people, some of the delusions of superstition; it could never have dissolved the ties of private interest. Had this constitution been attacked by no other enemies but the feeble efforts of human reason, it must have endured for ever. But that immense and well-built fabric, which all the wisdom and virtue of man could never have shaken, much less have overturned, was by the natural course of things, first weakened, and[147] afterwards in part destroyed, and is now likely, in the course of a few centuries more, perhaps, to crumble into ruins altogether.

The gradual improvements of arts, manufactures, and commerce, the same causes which destroyed the power of the great barons, destroyed in the same manner, through the greater part of Europe, the whole temporal power of the clergy. In the produce of arts, manufactures, and commerce, the clergy, like the great barons, found something for which they could exchange their rude produce, and thereby discovered the means of spending their whole revenues upon their own persons, without giving any considerable share of them to other people. Their charity became gradually less extensive, their hospitality less liberal or less profuse. Their retainers became consequently less numerous, and by degrees dwindled away altogether. The clergy too, like the great barons, wished to get a better rent from their landed estates, in order to spend it, in the same manner, upon the gratification of their own private vanity and folly. But this increase of rent could be got only by granting leases to their tenants, who thereby became in a great measure independent of them. The ties of interest, which bound the inferior ranks of people to the clergy, were in this manner gradually broken and dissolved. They were even broken and dissolved sooner than those which bound the same ranks of people to the great barons: because the benefices of the church being, the greater part of them, much smaller than the estates of the great barons, the possessor of each benefice was much sooner able to spend the whole of its revenue upon his own person. During the greater part of the fourteenth and fifteenth centuries the power of the great barons was, through the greater part of Europe, in full vigour. But the temporal power of the clergy, the absolute command which they had once had over the great body of the people, was very much decayed. The power of the church was by that time very nearly re-

Its power was destroyed by the improvement of arts, manufactures and commerce.

[147] [Ed. 1 does not contain "and."]

duced through the greater part of Europe to what arose from her spiritual authority; and even that spiritual authority was much weakened when it ceased to be supported by the charity and hospitality of the clergy. The inferior ranks of people no longer looked upon that order, as they had done before, as the comforters of their distress, and the relievers of their indigence. On the contrary, they were provoked and disgusted by the vanity, luxury, and expence of the richer clergy, who appeared to spend upon their own pleasures what had always before been regarded as the patrimony of the poor.

In this situation of things, the sovereigns in the different states of Europe endeavoured to recover the influence which they had once had in the disposal of the great benefices of the church, by procuring to the deans and chapters of each diocese the restoration of their ancient right of electing the bishop, and to the monks of each abbacy that of electing the abbot. The re-establishing of this ancient order was the object of several statutes enacted in England during the course of the fourteenth century, particularly of what is called the statute of provisors;[148] and of the Pragmatic sanction established in France in the fifteenth century. In order to render the election valid, it was necessary that the sovereign should both consent to it before-hand, and afterwards approve of the person elected; and though the election was still supposed to be free, he had, however, all the indirect means which his situation necessarily afforded him, of influencing the clergy in his own dominions. Other regulations of a similar tendency were established in other parts of Europe. But the power of the pope in the collation of the great benefices of the church seems, before the reformation, to have been nowhere so effectually and so universally restrained as in France and England. The Concordat afterwards, in the sixteenth century, gave to the kings of France the absolute right of presenting to all the great,

The sovereigns endeavoured to deprive the Pope of the disposal of the great benefices, and succeeded, especially in France and England.

---

[148] [These nine words are not in ed. 1.]

or what are called the consistorial[149] benefices of the Gallican church.[150]

Since the establishment of the Pragmatic sanction and of the Concordat, the clergy of France have in general shown less re-

Ever since the French clergy have been less devoted to the Pope.

spect to the decrees of the papal court than the clergy of any other catholic country. In all the disputes which their sovereign has had with the pope, they have almost constantly taken party with the former. This independency of the clergy of France upon the court of Rome, seems to be principally founded upon the Pragmatic sanction and the Concordat. In the earlier periods of the monarchy, the clergy of France appear to have been as much devoted to the pope as those of any other country. When Robert, the second prince of the Capetian race, was most unjustly excommunicated by the court of Rome, his own servants, it is said, threw the victuals which came from his table to the dogs, and refused to taste any thing themselves which had been polluted by the contact of a person in his situation.[151] They were taught to do so, it may very safely be presumed, by the clergy of his own dominions.

The claim of collating to the great benefices of the church, a claim in defence of which the court of Rome had frequently shaken, and sometimes overturned the thrones of some of the

So even before the Reformation the clergy had less power and inclination to disturb the state.

greatest sovereigns in Christendom, was in this manner either restrained or modified, or given up altogether, in many different parts of Europe, even before the time of the reformation. As the clergy had now less influence over the people, so the state had more influence over the clergy. The clergy therefore had both less power and less inclination to disturb the state.

[149] [Ed. 1 reads "great and consistorial."]

[150] [Daniel, *Histoire de France*, 1755, tom. vii., pp 158, 159; tom. ix., p. 40.]

[151] ["Il ne lui resta que deux domestiques pour le servir et lui préparer à manger, encore faisaient-ils passer par le feu les plats où il mangeait, et les vases où il buvait pour les purifier, comme ayant été fouillés par un homme retranché de la communion des fidèles."—Ibid., tom. iii., pp. 305, 306. Hénault's account is similar, *Nouvel Abrégé chronologique*, 1768, tom. i., p. 114, A.D. 996.]

The authority of the church of Rome was in this state of declension, when the disputes which gave birth to the reformation, began in Germany, and soon spread themselves through every part of Europe. The new doctrines were every where received with a high degree of popular favour. They were propagated with all that enthusiastic zeal which commonly animates the spirit of party, when it attacks established authority. The teachers of those doctrines, though perhaps in other respects not more learned than many of the divines who defended the established church, seem in general to have been better acquainted with ecclesiastical history, and with the origin and progress of that system of opinions upon which the authority of the church was established, and they had thereby some advantage in almost every dispute. The austerity of their manners gave them authority with the common people, who contrasted the strict regularity of their conduct with the disorderly lives of the greater part of their own clergy. They possessed too in a much higher degree than their adversaries, all the arts of popularity and of gaining proselytes, arts which the lofty and dignified sons of the church had long neglected, as being to them in a great measure useless. The reason of the new doctrines recommended them to some, their novelty to many; the hatred and contempt of the established clergy to a still greater number; but the zealous, passionate, and fanatical, though frequently coarse and rustic, eloquence with which they were almost every where inculcated, recommended them to by far the greatest number.

The Reformation doctrines were recommended to the common people by the zeal of their teachers

The success of the new doctrines was almost every where so great, that the princes who at that time happened to be on bad terms with the court of Rome, were by means of them easily enabled, in their own dominions, to overturn the church, which, having lost the respect and veneration of the inferior ranks of people, could make scarce any resistance. The court of Rome had disobliged some of the smaller princes in the northern parts of

and enabled sovereigns on bad terms with Rome to overturn the Church with ease,

Germany, whom it had probably considered as too insignificant to be worth the managing. They universally, therefore, established the reformation in their own dominions. The tyranny of Christiern II. and of Troll, archbishop of Upsal, enabled Gustavus Vasa to expel them both from Sweden. The pope favoured the tyrant and the archbishop, and Gustavus Vasa found no difficulty in establishing the reformation in Sweden: Christiern II. was afterwards deposed from the throne of Denmark, where his conduct had rendered him as odious as in Sweden. The pope, however, was still disposed to favour him, and Frederic of Holstein, who had mounted the throne in his stead, revenged himself by following the example of Gustavus Vasa. The magistrates of Berne and Zurich, who had no particular quarrel with the pope, established with great ease the reformation in their respective cantons, where just before some of the clergy had, by an imposture somewhat grosser than ordinary, rendered the whole order both odious and contemptible.

In this critical situation of its affairs, the papal court was at sufficient pains to cultivate the friendship of the powerful sovereigns of France and Spain, of whom the latter was at that time emperor of Germany. With their assistance it was enabled, though not without great difficulty and much bloodshed, either to suppress altogether, or to obstruct very much the progress of the reformation in their dominions. It was well enough inclined too to be complaisant to the king of England. But from the circumstances of the times, it could not be so without giving offence to a still greater sovereign, Charles V. king of Spain and emperor of Germany. Henry VIII. accordingly, though he did not embrace himself the greater part of the doctrines of the reformation, was yet enabled, by their general prevalence,[152] to suppress all the monasteries, and to abolish the authority of the church of Rome in his dominions. That he should go so far, though he went no further, gave some satisfaction to the patrons of the reformation,

while in countries the sovereigns of which were friendly to Rome the Reformation was suppressed or obstructed.

---

[152] [Ed. 1 reads "by the general prevalence of those doctrines."]

who having got possession of the government in the reign of his son and successor, completed without any difficulty the work which Henry VIII. had begun.

In some countries, as in Scotland, where the government

In some countries the Reformation overturned both church and state.

was weak, unpopular, and not very firmly established, the reformation was strong enough to overturn, not only the church, but the state likewise for attempting to support the church.

Among the followers of the reformation, dispersed in all the different countries of Europe, there was no general tribunal,

The followers of the Reformation had no common authority like the court of Rome, and divided into Lutherans and Calvinists.

which, like that of the court of Rome, or an ecumenical council, could settle all disputes among them, and with irresistible authority prescribe to all of them the precise limits of orthodoxy. When the followers of the reformation in one country, therefore, happened to differ from their brethren in another, as they had no common judge to appeal to, the

dispute could never be decided; and many such disputes arose among them. Those concerning the government of the church, and the right of conferring ecclesiastical benefices, were perhaps the most interesting to the peace and welfare of civil society. They gave birth accordingly to the two principal parties or sects among the followers of the reformation, the Lutheran and Calvinistic sects, the only sects among them, of which the doctrine and discipline have ever yet been established by law in any part of Europe.

The followers of Luther, together with what is called the church of England, preserved more or less of the epis-

The Lutherans and the Church of England preferred episcopacy, and gave the disposal of benefices to the sovereign and other lay patrons.

copal government, established subordination among the clergy, gave the sovereign the disposal of all the bishoprics, and other consistorial benefices within his dominions, and thereby rendered him the real head of the church; and without depriving the bishop of the right of collating to the smaller benefices within his diocese, they, even to those benefices, not only admitted, but favoured the right of presentation both in the sovereign and in all other lay patrons. This system of church government was from the beginning favourable to peace and good order, and to submission to the civil sovereign. It has never, accordingly, been the occasion of any tumult or civil commotion in any country in which it has once been established. The church of England in particular has always valued herself, with great reason, upon the unexceptionable loyalty of her principles. Under such a government the clergy naturally endeavour to recommend themselves to the sovereign, to the court, and to the nobility and gentry of the country, by whose influence they chiefly expect to obtain preferment. They pay court to those patrons, sometimes, no doubt, by the vilest flattery and assentation, but frequently too by cultivating all those arts which best deserve, and which are therefore most likely to gain them the esteem of people of rank and fortune; by their knowledge in all the different branches of useful and ornamental learning, by the decent liberality of their manners, by the social good humour of their conversation, and by their avowed contempt of those absurd and hypocritical austerities which fanatics inculcate and pretend to practise, in order to draw upon themselves the veneration, and upon the greater part of men of rank and fortune, who avow that they do not practise them, the abhorrence of the common people. Such a clergy, however, while they pay their court in this manner to the higher ranks of life, are very apt to neglect altogether the means of maintaining their influence and authority with the lower. They are listened to, esteemed and respected by their superiors; but before their inferiors they are frequently incapable of defending, effectually and to the conviction of such hearers, their own sober and moderate doctrines against the most ignorant enthusiast who chuses to attack them.

The followers of Zuinglius, or more properly those of Calvin, on the contrary, bestowed upon the people of each parish, whenever the church became vacant, the right of electing their own pastor; and established at the same time the most perfect equality among the clergy. The former part of this institution, as long as it remained in vigour, seems to have been

Zwinglians and Calvinists gave the right of election to the people, and established equality among the clergy.

productive of nothing but disorder and confusion, and to have tended equally to corrupt the morals both of the clergy and of the people. The latter part seems never to have had any effects but what were perfectly agreeable.

As long as the people of each parish preserved the right of electing their own pastors, they acted almost always under the influence of the clergy, and generally of the most factious and fanatical of the order. The

Election by the people gave rise to great disorders,

clergy, in order to preserve their influence in those popular elections, became, or affected to become, many of them, fanatics themselves, encouraged fanaticism among the people, and gave the preference almost always to the most fanatical candidate. So small a matter as the appointment of a parish priest occasioned almost always a violent contest, not only in one parish, but in all the neighbouring parishes, who seldom failed to take part[153] in the quarrel. When the parish happened to be situated in a great city, it divided all the inhabitants into two parties; and when that city happened either to

and after trial was abolished in Scotland, though the concurrence of the people is still required.

constitute itself a little republic, or to be the head and capital of a little republic, as is the case with many of the considerable cities in Switzerland and Holland, every paltry dispute of this kind, over and above exasperating the animosity of all their other factions, threatened to leave behind it both a new schism in the church, and a new faction in the state. In those small republics, therefore, the magistrate very soon found it necessary, for the sake of preserving the public peace, to assume to himself the right of presenting to all vacant benefices. In Scotland, the most extensive country in which this presbyterian form of church government has ever been established, the rights of patronage were in effect abolished by the act which established presbytery in the beginning of the reign of William

[153] [Eds. 1 and 2 read "take party."]

III.[154] That act at least put it in the power of certain classes of people in each parish, to purchase, for a very small price, the right of electing their own pastor. The constitution which this act established was allowed to subsist for about two and twenty years, but was abolished by the 10th of queen Anne, ch. 12. on account of the confusions and disorders which this more popular mode of election had almost every where occasioned.[155] In so extensive a country as Scotland, however, a tumult in a remote parish was not so likely to give disturbance to government, as in a smaller state. The 10th of queen Anne restored the rights of patronage. But though in Scotland the law gives the benefice without any exception to the person presented by the patron; yet the church requires sometimes (for she has not in this respect been very uniform in her decisions) a certain concurrence of the people, before she will confer upon the presentee what is called the cure of souls, or the ecclesiastical jurisdiction in the parish. She sometimes at least, from an affected concern for the peace of the parish, delays the settlement till this concurrence can be procured. The private tampering of some of the neighbouring clergy, sometimes to procure, but more frequently to prevent this concurrence, and the popular arts which they cultivate in order to enable them upon such occasions to tamper more effectually, are perhaps the causes which principally keep up whatever remains of the old fanatical spirit, either in the clergy or in the people of Scotland.

The equality which the presbyterian form of church government establishes among the clergy, consists, first, in the equality of authority or ecclesiastical jurisdiction; and, secondly, in the equality of benefice. In all presbyterian churches the equality of authority is perfect: that of benefice is not so. The difference, however,

The equality of the Presbyterian clergy makes them independent and respectable.

---

[154] [The "Act concerning Patronages," 53rd of the second session of the first parliament of William and Mary, is doubtless meant, but this is a separate Act from the "Act ratifying the Confession of Faith and settling Presbyterian Church Government," *Acts of the Parliaments of Scotland*, 1822, vol. ix., pp. 133, 196.]

[155] [The preamble of the Act mentions "the great hardship upon the patrons" as well as the "great heats and divisions."]

between one benefice and another, is seldom so considerable as commonly to tempt the possessor even of the small one[156] to pay court to his patron, by the vile arts of flattery and assentation, in order to get a better. In all the presbyterian churches, where the rights of patronage are thoroughly established, it is by nobler and better arts that the established clergy in general endeavour to gain the favour of their superiors; by their learning, by the irreproachable regularity of their life, and by the faithful and diligent discharge of their duty. Their patrons even frequently complain of the independency of their spirit, which they are apt to construe into ingratitude for past favours, but which at worst, perhaps, is seldom any more than that indifference which naturally arises from the consciousness that no further favours of the kind are ever to be expected. There is scarce perhaps to be found any where in Europe a more learned, decent, independent, and respectable set of men, than the greater part of the presbyterian clergy of Holland, Geneva, Switzerland, and Scotland.

Where the church benefices are all nearly equal, none of them can be very great, and this mediocrity of benefice, though

The mediocrity of their benefices gives them influence with the common people.

it may no doubt be carried too far, has, however, some very agreeable effects. Nothing but the most exemplary morals can give dignity to a man of small fortune. The vices of levity and vanity necessarily render him ridiculous, and are, besides, almost as ruinous to him as they are to the common people. In his own conduct, therefore, he is obliged to follow that system of morals which the common people respect the most. He gains their esteem and affection by that plan of life which his own interest and situation would lead him to follow. The common people look upon him with that kindness with which we naturally regard one who approaches somewhat to our own condition, but who, we think, ought to be in a higher. Their kindness naturally provokes his kindness. He becomes careful to instruct them, and attentive to assist and relieve them. He does not even despise the preju-

---

[156] [Ed. 1 reads "small benefice."]

dices of people who are disposed to be so favourable to him, and never treats them with those contemptuous and arrogant airs which we so often meet with in the proud dignitaries of opulent and well-endowed churches. The presbyterian clergy, accordingly, have more influence over the minds of the common people than perhaps the clergy of any other established church. It is accordingly in presbyterian countries only that we ever find the common people converted, without persecution, completely, and almost to a man, to the established church.

In countries where church benefices are the greater part of them very moderate, a chair in a university is generally a better establishment than a church benefice. The universities have, in this case, the picking and chusing of their members from all the *It also enables the universities to draw on them for professors, who are thus the most eminent men of letters.* churchmen of the country, who, in every country, constitute by far the most numerous class of men of letters. Where church benefices, on the contrary, are many of them very considerable, the church naturally draws from the universities the greater part of their eminent men of letters; who generally find some patron who does himself honour by procuring them church preferment. In the former situation we are likely to find the universities filled with the most eminent men of letters that are to be found in the country. In the latter we are likely to find few eminent men among them, and those few among the youngest members of the society, who are likely too to be drained away from it, before they can have acquired experience and knowledge enough to be of much use to it. It is observed by Mr. de Voltaire, that father Porrée, a jesuit of no great eminence in the republic of letters, was the only professor they had ever had in France whose works were worth the reading.[157] In a country which has produced so many eminent men of letters, it must appear somewhat singular, that scarce one of them should

[157] [Voltaire's expression is not quite so strong as it is represented. He says in the catalogue of writers in the *Siècle de Louis XIV.*, "Porée (Charles) né en Normandie en 1675, Jésuite, du petit nombre des professeurs qui ont eu de la célébrité chez les gens du monde. Eloquent dans le goût de Sénèque poëte et très bel esprit. Son plus grand mérite fut de faire aimer les lettres et la vertu à ses disciples. Mort en 1741."]

have been a professor in a university. The famous Gassendi was, in the beginning of his life, a professor in the university of Aix. Upon the first dawning of his genius, it was represented to him, that by going into the church he could easily find a much more quiet and comfortable subsistence, as well as a better situation for pursuing his studies; and he immediately followed the advice. The observation of Mr. de Voltaire may be applied, I believe, not only to France, but to all other Roman catholic countries. We very rarely find, in any of them, an eminent man of letters who is a professor in a university, except, perhaps, in the professions of law and physic; professions from which the church is not so likely to draw them. After the church of Rome, that of England is by far the richest and best endowed church in Christendom. In England, accordingly, the church is continually draining the universities of all their best and ablest members; and an old college tutor who is known and distinguished in Europe as an eminent man of letters, is as rarely to be found there as in any Roman catholic country. In Geneva, on the contrary, in the protestant cantons of Switzerland, in the protestant countries of Germany, in Holland, in Scotland, in Sweden, and Denmark, the most eminent men of letters whom those countries have produced, have, not all indeed, but the far greater part of them, been professors in universities. In those countries the universities are continually draining the church of all its most eminent men of letters.

It may, perhaps, be worth while to remark, that, if we except the poets, a few orators, and a few historians, the far greater

Eminent men of letters in Greece and Rome were mostly teachers.

part of the other eminent men of letters, both of Greece and Rome, appear to have been either public or private teachers; generally either of philosophy or of rhetoric. This remark will be found to hold true from the days of Lysias and Isocrates, of Plato and Aristotle, down to those of Plutarch and Epictetus, of Suetonius and Quintilian.[158]

---

[158] [*Quaere* as to Suetonius. Ed. 1 continues here "Several of those whom we do not know with certainty to have been public teachers appear to have been private tutors. Polybius, we know, was private tutor to Scipio Æmilianus; Dionysius of Halicarnassus, there are some probable reasons for believing, was so to the children of Marcus and Quintus Cicero."]

To impose upon any man the necessity of teaching, year after year, any particular branch of science, seems, in reality, to be the most effectual method of rendering him completely master of it himself. By being obliged to go every year over the same ground, if he is good for any thing, he necessarily becomes, in a few years, well acquainted with every part of it: and if upon any particular point he should form too hasty an opinion one year, when he comes in the course of his lectures to re-consider the same subject the year thereafter, he is very likely to correct it.[159] As to be a teacher of science is certainly the natural employment of a mere man of letters; so is it likewise, perhaps, the education which is most likely to render him a man of solid learning and knowledge. The mediocrity of church benefices naturally tends to draw the greater part of men of letters, in the country where it takes place, to the employment in which they can be the most useful to the public, and, at the same time, to give them the best education, perhaps, they are capable of receiving. It tends to render their learning both as solid as possible, and as useful as possible.

The revenue of every established church, such parts of it excepted as may arise from particular lands or manors, is a

The revenue of the church except that part which arises from endowments is a branch of that of the state.

branch, it ought to be observed, of the general revenue of the state, which is thus diverted to a purpose very different from the defence of the state. The tythe, for example, is a real land-tax, which puts it out of the power of the proprietors of land to contribute so largely towards the defence of the state as they otherwise might be able to do. The rent of land, however, is, according to some, the sole fund, and according to others, the principal fund, from which, in all great monarchies, the exigencies of the state must be ultimately supplied. The more of this fund that is given to the church, the less, it is evident, can be spared to the state. It may be laid down as a certain maxim, that, all other things being supposed equal, the richer the church, the poorer must necessarily be, either the sovereign

---

[159] [The *Lectures* leave little doubt that this is a fragment of autobiography.]

on the one hand, or the people on the other; and, in all cases, the less able must the state be to defend itself. In several

In some cantons of Switzerland the old revenue of the church now maintains both church and state.

protestant countries, particularly in all the protestant cantons of Switzerland, the revenue which anciently belonged to the Roman catholic church, the tythes and church lands, has been found a fund sufficient, not only to afford competent salaries to the established clergy, but to defray, with little or no addition, all the other expences of the state. The magistrates of the powerful canton of Berne, in particular, have accumulated out of the savings from this fund a very large sum, supposed to amount to several millions, part of which is deposited in a public treasure, and part is placed at interest in what are called the public funds of the different indebted nations of Europe; chiefly in those of France and Great Britain. What may be the amount of the whole expence which the

The whole revenue of the Church of Scotland is a trifling amount, but that church produces all possible good effects.

church, either of Berne, or of any other protestant canton, costs the state, I do not pretend to know. By a very exact account it appears, that, in 1755, the whole revenue of the clergy of the church of Scotland, including their glebe or church lands, and the rent of their manses or dwelling-houses, estimated according to a reasonable valuation, amounted only to 68,514*l*. 1*s*. 5*d*.½. This very moderate revenue affords a decent subsistence to nine hundred and forty-four ministers. The whole expence of the church, including what is occasionally laid out for the building and reparation of churches, and of the manses of ministers, cannot well be supposed to exceed eighty or eighty-five thousand pounds a-year. The most opulent church in Christendom does not maintain better the uniformity of faith, the fervour of devotion, the spirit of order, regularity, and austere morals in the great body of the people, than this very poorly endowed church of Scotland. All the good effects, both civil and religious, which an established church can be supposed to produce, are produced by it as completely as by any other. The greater part of the protestant churches of Switzerland, which in general are not better endowed than the church of Scotland, produce those effects in a still higher degree. In the greater part of the protestant cantons, there is not a single person to be found who does not profess himself to be of the established church. If he professes himself to be of any other, indeed, the law obliges him to leave the canton. But

This is also true in a still higher degree of the Swiss Protestant churches.

so severe, or rather indeed so oppressive a law, could never have been executed in such free countries, had not the diligence of the clergy before-hand converted to the established church the whole body of the people, with the exception of, perhaps, a few individuals only. In some parts of Switzerland, accordingly, where, from the accidental union of a protestant and Roman catholic country, the conversion has not been so complete, both religions are not only tolerated but established by law.

The proper performance of every service seems to require that its pay or recompence should be, as exactly as possible, proportioned to the nature of the service. If any service is very much under-paid, it is very apt to suffer by the meanness and incapacity of the greater part of those who are employed in it. If it is very much over-paid, it

Large revenue is unsuitable to the office of clergymen.

is apt to suffer, perhaps, still more by their negligence and idleness. A man of a large revenue, whatever may be his profession, thinks he ought to live like other men of large revenues; and to spend a great part of his time in festivity, in vanity, and in dissipation. But in a clergyman this train of life not only consumes the time which ought to be employed in the duties of his function, but in the eyes of the common people destroys almost entirely that sanctity of character which can alone enable him to perform those duties with proper weight and authority.

PART IV

OF THE EXPENCE OF SUPPORTING THE DIGNITY
OF THE SOVEREIGN

Over and above the expence[160] necessary for enabling the sovereign to perform his several duties, a certain expence is requisite for the support of his dignity. This expence varies both with the different periods of improvement, and with the different forms of government.

The expense of supporting the dignity of the sovereign increases as the expenditure of the people increases,

In an opulent and improved society, where all the different orders of people are growing every day more expensive in their houses, in their furniture, in their tables, in their dress, and in their equipage; it cannot well be expected that the sovereign should alone hold out against the fashion. He naturally, therefore, or rather necessarily becomes more expensive in all those different articles too. His dignity even seems to require that he should become so.

As in point of dignity, a monarch is more raised above his subjects than the chief magistrate of any republic is ever supposed to be above his fellow-citizens; so a greater expence is necessary for supporting that higher dignity. We naturally expect more splendor in the court of a king, than in the mansion-house of a doge or burgomaster.

and is greater in a monarchy than in a republic.

CONCLUSION

The expence of defending the society, and that of supporting the dignity of the chief magistrate, are both laid out for the general benefit of the whole society. It is reasonable, therefore,

[160] [Ed. 5 reads "expences," but this seems to be a misprint or misreading suggested by the fact that several expenses have been mentioned.]

The expense of defence and of maintaining the dignity of the sovereign should be paid by general contribution.

that they should be defrayed by the general contribution of the whole society, all the different members contributing, as nearly as possible, in proportion to their respective abilities.

The expence of the administration of justice too, may, no doubt, be considered as laid out for the benefit of the whole society. There is no impropriety, therefore, in its being defrayed by the general contribution of the whole society. The persons, how-

But the expense of justice may be defrayed by fees of court,

ever, who give occasion to this expence are those who, by their injustice in one way or another, make it necessary to seek redress or protection from the courts of justice. The persons again most immediately benefited

by this expence, are those whom the courts of justice either restore to their rights, or maintain in their rights. The expence of the administration of justice, therefore, may very properly be defrayed by the particular contribution of one or other, or both of those two different sets of persons, according as different occasions may require, that is, by the fees of court. It cannot be necessary to have recourse to the general contribution of the whole society, except for the conviction of those criminals who have not themselves any estate or fund sufficient for paying those fees.

Those local or provincial expences of which the benefit is local or provincial (what is laid out, for example, upon the po-

and expenses of local benefit ought to be defrayed by local revenue.

lice of a particular town or district) ought to be defrayed by a local or provincial revenue, and ought to be no burden upon the general revenue of the society. It is unjust that the whole society should contribute towards an

expence of which the benefit is confined to a part of the society.

The expence of maintaining good roads and communications is, no doubt, beneficial to the whole society, and may, therefore, without any injustice, be defrayed by the general contribution of the whole society. This expence, however, is

The expense of roads may not unjustly be defrayed by general contribution, but better by tolls.

most immediately and directly beneficial to those who travel or carry goods from one place to another, and to those who consume such goods. The turnpike tolls in England, and the duties called peages in other countries, lay it altogether upon those two different sets of people, and thereby discharge the general revenue of the society from a very considerable burden.

The expence of the institutions for education and religious instruction, is likewise, no doubt, beneficial to the whole society,

The expense of education and religious instruction may also be defrayed by general contribution, but better by fees and voluntary contribution.

and may, therefore, without injustice, be defrayed by the general contribution of the whole society. This expence, however, might perhaps with equal propriety, and even with some advantage, be defrayed altogether by those who receive the immediate benefit of such education and instruction, or by the voluntary contribution of those who think they have occasion for either the one or the other.

When the institutions or public works which are beneficial to the whole society, either cannot be maintained altogether, or

Any deficiencies in the revenue of institutions beneficial to the whole society must be made up by general contribution.

are not maintained altogether by the contribution of such particular members of the society as are most immediately benefited by them, the deficiency must in most cases be made up by the general contribution of the whole society. The general revenue of the society, over and above defraying the expence of defending the society, and of supporting the dignity of the chief magistrate, must make up for the deficiency of many particular branches of revenue. The sources of this general or public revenue, I shall endeavour to explain in the following chapter.

CHAPTER II

OF THE SOURCES OF THE GENERAL OR PUBLIC REVENUE OF THE SOCIETY

THE REVENUE which must defray, not only the expence of defending the society and of supporting the dignity of the chief magistrate, but all the other necessary expences of government, for which the constitution of the state has not provided any particular revenue, may be drawn, either, first, from some fund which peculiarly belongs to the sovereign or commonwealth, and which is independent of the revenue of the people; or, secondly, from the revenue of the people.

All revenue comes from one or two sources: (1) property belonging to the sovereign; (2) the revenue of the people.

PART I

OF THE FUNDS OR SOURCES OF REVENUE WHICH MAY PECULIARLY BELONG TO THE SOVEREIGN OR COMMONWEALTH

The property may be in stock or land.

The funds or sources of revenue which may peculiarly belong to the sovereign or commonwealth must consist, either in stock, or in land.

Revenue from stock may be profit or interest.

The sovereign, like any other owner of stock, may derive a revenue from it, either by employing it himself, or by lending it. His revenue is in the one case profit, in the other interest.

Tartar and Arabian chiefs make profit from herds and flocks, Hamburg from a wine cellar and apothecary's shop, and many states from banks

The revenue of a Tartar or Arabian chief consists in profit. It arises principally from the milk and increase of his own herds and flocks, of which he himself superintends the management, and is the principal shepherd or herdsman of his own horde or tribe. It is, however, in this earliest and rudest state of civil government only that profit has ever made the principal part of the public revenue of a monarchical state.

Small republics have sometimes derived a considerable revenue from the profit of mercantile projects. The republic of Hamburgh is said to do so from the profits of a public wine cellar and apothecary's shop.[1] The state cannot be very great of which the sovereign has leisure to carry on the trade of a wine merchant or apothecary. The profit of a public bank has been a source of revenue to more considerable states. It has been so not only to Hamburgh, but to Venice and Amsterdam. A revenue of this kind has even by some people been thought not below the attention of so great an empire as that of Great Britain. Reckoning the ordinary dividend of the bank of England at five and a half per cent. and its capital at ten millions seven hundred and eighty thousand pounds, the neat annual profit, after paying the expence of management, must amount, it is said, to five hundred and ninety-two thousand nine hundred pounds. Government, it is pretended, could bor-

[1] See *Memoires concernant les Droits & Impositions en Europe*: tome i. page 73. This work was compiled by the order of the court for the use of a commission employed for some years past in considering the proper means for reforming the finances of France. The account of the French taxes, which takes up three volumes in quarto, may be regarded as perfectly authentic. That of those of other European nations was compiled from such informations as the French ministers at the different courts could procure. It is much shorter, and probably not quite so exact as that of the French taxes. [The book is by Moreau de Beaumont, Paris, 1768–9, 4 vols. 4to. The correct title of vol. i. is *Mémoires concernant les Impositions et Droits en Europe*; vols. ii.–iv. are *Mémoires concernant les Impositions et Droits*, 2de. Ptie., *Impositions et Droits en France*. Smith obtained his copy through Turgot, and attached great value to it, believing it to be very rare. See Bonar, *Catalogue*, p. 10.]

row this capital at three per cent. interest, and by taking the management of the bank into its own hands, might make a clear profit of two hundred and sixty-nine thousand five hundred pounds a year. The orderly, vigilant, and parsimonious administration of such aristocracies as those of Venice and Amsterdam, is extremely proper, it appears from experience, for the management of a mercantile project of this kind. But whether such a government as that of England; which, whatever may be its virtues, has never been famous for good œconomy; which, in time of peace, has generally conducted itself with the slothful and negligent profusion that is perhaps natural to monarchies; and in time of war has constantly acted with all the thoughtless extravagance that democracies are apt to fall into; could be safely trusted with the management of such a project, must at least be a good deal more doubtful.

The post office is properly a mercantile project. The government advances the expence of establishing the different of-

and post offices.   fices, and of buying or hiring the necessary horses or carriages, and is repaid with a large profit by the duties upon what is carried. It is perhaps the only mercantile project which has been successfully managed by, I believe, every sort of government. The capital to be advanced is not very considerable. There is no mystery in the business. The returns are not only certain, but immediate.

Princes, however, have frequently engaged in many other mercantile projects, and have been willing, like private per-

But generally princes are unsuccessful as traders.   sons, to mend their fortunes by becoming adventurers in the common branches of trade. They have scarce ever succeeded. The profusion with which the affairs of princes are always managed, renders it almost impossible that they should. The agents of a prince regard the wealth of their master as inexhaustible; are careless at which price they buy; are careless at what price they sell; are careless at what expence they transport his goods from one place to another. Those agents frequently live with the profusion of princes, and sometimes too, in spite of that profusion, and by a proper method of making up their accounts, acquire the fortunes of princes. It was

thus, as we are told by Machiavel, that the agents of Lorenzo of Medicis, not a prince of mean abilities, carried on his trade. The republic of Florence was several times obliged to pay the debt into which their extravagance had involved him. He found it convenient, accordingly, to give up the business of merchant, the business to which his family had originally owed their fortune, and in the latter part of his life to employ both what remained of that fortune, and the revenue of the state of which he had the disposal, in projects and expences more suitable to his station.[2]

No two characters seem more inconsistent than those of trader and sovereign. If the trading spirit of the English East India company renders them very bad sovereigns; the spirit of sovereignty seems to have rendered them equally bad traders. While they were traders only, they managed their trade successfully, and were able to pay from their profits a moderate dividend to the proprietors of their stock. Since they became sovereigns, with a revenue which, it is said, was originally more than three millions sterling, they have been obliged to beg the extraordinary assistance of government in order to avoid immediate bankruptcy.[3] In their former situation, their servants in India considered themselves as the clerks of merchants: in their present situation, those servants consider themselves as the ministers of sovereigns.

The two characters are inconsistent.

A state may sometimes derive some part of its public revenue from the interest of money, as well as from the profits of stock. If it has amassed a treasure, it may lend a part of that treasure, either to foreign states, or to its own subjects.

Treasure may be lent to subjects or foreign states:

The canton of Berne derives a considerable revenue by lending a part of its treasure to foreign states; that is, by placing it in the public funds of the different indebted nations of

---

[2] [*Hist. of Florence*, bk. viii., *ad fin.*]

[3] [Details are given above, pp. 952–953, but that is in a passage which appears first in ed. 3.]

Berne lends to foreign states, Europe, chiefly in those of France and England.[4] The security of this revenue must depend, first, upon the security of the funds in which it is placed, or upon the good faith of the government which has the management of them; and, secondly, upon the certainty or probability of the continuance of peace with the debtor nation. In the case of a war, the very first act of hostility, on the part of the debtor nation, might be the forfeiture of the funds of its creditor. This policy of lending money to foreign states is, so far as I know, peculiar to the canton of Berne.

The city of Hamburgh[5] has established a sort of public pawn-shop, which lends money to the subjects of the state upon pledges at six per cent. interest. This pawn-shop or *Hamburg has a pawn-shop.* Lombard, as it is called, affords a revenue, it is pretended, to the state of a hundred and fifty thousand crowns, which, at four-and-sixpence the crown, amounts to 33,750*l.* sterling.

The government of Pennsylvania, without amassing any treasure, invented a method of lending, not money indeed, but what is equivalent to money, to its subjects. By advancing to *Pennsylvania lent paper money on land security.* private people, at interest, and upon land security to double the value, paper bills of credit to be redeemed fifteen years after their date, and in the mean time made transferrable from hand to hand like bank notes, and declared by act of assembly to be a legal tender in all payments from one inhabitant of the province to another, it raised a moderate revenue, which went a considerable way towards defraying an annual expence of about 4,500*l.* the whole ordinary expence of that frugal and orderly government. The success of an expedient of this kind must have depended upon three different circumstances; first, upon the demand for some other instrument of commerce, besides gold and silver money; or upon the demand for such a quantity of consumable stock, as could not be had without sending abroad the greater part of their gold and

---

[4] [Above, p. 1027.]

[5] [See *Memoires concernant les Droits & Impositions en Europe*; tome i. p. 73.]

silver money, in order to purchase it; secondly, upon the good credit of the government which made use of this expedient; and, thirdly, upon the moderation with which it was used, the whole value of the paper bills of credit never exceeding that of the gold and silver money which would have been necessary for carrying on their circulation, had there been no paper bills of credit. The same expedient was upon different occasions adopted by several other American colonies: but, from want of this moderation, it produced, in the greater part of them, much more disorder than conveniency.

The unstable and perishable nature of stock and credit, however, render them unfit to be trusted to, as the principal

No great revenue can be derived from such a source.

funds of that sure, steady and permanent revenue, which can alone give security and dignity to government. The government of no great nation, that was advanced beyond the shepherd state, seems ever to have derived the greater part of its public revenue from such sources.

Land is a fund of a more stable and permanent nature; and the rent of public lands, accordingly, has been the principal

Revenue from land is much more important,

source of the public revenue of many a great nation that was much advanced beyond the shepherd state. From the produce or rent of the public lands, the ancient republics of Greece and Italy derived, for a long time, the greater part of that revenue which defrayed the necessary expences of the commonwealth. The rent of the crown lands constituted for a long time the greater part of the revenue of the ancient sovereigns of Europe.

War and the preparation for war, are the two circumstances which in modern times occasion the greater part of the neces-

especially when war cost little, as in ancient Greece and Italy,

sary expence of all great states. But in the ancient republics of Greece and Italy every citizen was a soldier, who both served and prepared himself for service at his own expence. Neither of those two circumstances, therefore, could occasion any very considerable expence to the state. The rent of a very moderate landed estate might be fully sufficient for defraying all the other necessary expences of government.

In the ancient monarchies of Europe, the manners and customs of the times sufficiently prepared the great body of the

and in feudal times, when all expenses were small.

people for war; and when they took the field, they were, by the condition of their feudal tenures, to be maintained, either at their own expence, or at that of their immediate lords, without bringing any new charge upon the sovereign. The other expences of government were, the greater part of them, very moderate. The administration of justice, it has been shown, instead of being a cause of expence, was a source of revenue. The labour of the country people, for three days before and for three days after harvest, was thought a fund sufficient for making and maintaining all the bridges, highways, and other public works which the commerce of the country was supposed to require. In those days the principal expence of the sovereign seems to have consisted in the maintenance of his own family and houshold. The officers of his houshold, accordingly were then the great officers of state. The lord treasurer received his rents. The lord steward and lord chamberlain looked after the expence of his family. The care of his stables was committed to the lord constable and the lord marshal. His houses were all built in the form of castles, and seem to have been the principal fortresses which he possessed. The keepers of those houses or castles might be considered as a sort of military governors. They seem to have been the only military officers whom it was necessary to maintain in time of peace. In these circumstances the rent of a great landed estate might, upon ordinary occasions, very well defray all the necessary expences of government.

The present rent of all the land in the country would not suffice for the ordinary expenditure

In the present state of the greater part of the civilized monarchies of Europe, the rent of all the lands in the country, managed as they probably would be if they all belonged to one proprietor, would scarce perhaps amount to the ordinary revenue which they levy upon the people even in peaceable times. The ordinary revenue of Great Britain, for example, including not only what is necessary for defraying the current expence of the year, but for paying the interest of the public debts, and for sinking a part of the capital of those debts, amounts to upwards of ten millions a year. But the land tax, at four shillings in the pound, falls short of two millions a year. This land tax, as it is called, however, is supposed to be one-fifth, not only of the rent of all the land, but of that of all the houses, and of the interest of all the capital stock of Great Britain, that part of it only excepted which is either lent to the public, or employed as farming stock in the cultivation of land. A very considerable part of the produce of this tax arises from the rent of houses, and the interest of capital stock. The land-tax of the city of London, for example, at four shillings in the pound, amounts to 123,399*l*. 6*s*. 7*d*. That of the city of Westminster, to 63,092*l*. 1*s*. 5*d*. That of the palaces of Whitehall and St. James's, to 30,754*l*. 6*s*. 3*d*.[6] A certain proportion of the land-tax is in the same manner assessed upon all the other cities and towns corporate in the kingdom, and arises almost altogether, either from the rent of houses, or from what is supposed to be the interest of trading and capital stock. According to the estimation, therefore, by which Great Britain is rated to the land-tax, the whole mass of revenue arising from the rent of all the lands, from that of all the houses, and from the interest of all the capital stock, that part of it only excepted which is either lent to the public, or employed in the cultivation of land, does not exceed ten millions sterling a year, the ordinary revenue which government levies upon the people even in peaceable times. The estimation by which Great Britain is rated to the land-tax is, no doubt, taking the whole kingdom at an average, very much below the real value; though in several particular counties and districts it is said to be nearly equal to that value. The rent of the lands alone, exclusive of that of houses, and of the interest of stock, has by many people been estimated at twenty millions, an estimation made in a great measure at random, and which, I apprehend, is as likely to be

[6] [The figures are those of the Land Tax Acts.]

but if the whole of the land of the country were under the extravagant management of state, the rent would be much reduced,

above as below the truth.[7] But if the lands of Great Britain, in the present state of their cultivation, do not afford a rent of more than twenty millions a year, they could not well afford the half, most probably not the fourth part of that rent, if they all belonged to a single proprietor, and were put under the negligent, expensive, and oppressive management of his factors and agents. The crown lands of Great Britain do not at present afford the fourth part of the rent, which could probably be drawn from them if they were the property of private persons. If the crown lands were more extensive, it is probable they would be still worse managed.

The revenue which the great body of the people derives from land is in proportion, not to the rent, but to the produce of

and the revenue of the people would be reduced by a still greater amount.

the land. The whole annual produce of the land of every country, if we except what is reserved for seed, is either annually consumed by the great body of the people, or exchanged for something else that is consumed by them. Whatever keeps down the produce of the land below what it would otherwise rise to, keeps down the revenue of the great body of the people, still more than it does that of the proprietors of land. The rent of land, that portion of the produce which belongs to the proprietors, is scarce anywhere in Great Britain supposed to be more than a third part of the whole produce. If the land, which in one state of cultivation affords a rent of ten millions sterling a year, would in another afford a rent of twenty millions; the rent being, in both cases, supposed a third part of the produce; the revenue of the proprietors would be less than it otherwise might be by ten millions a year only; but the revenue of the great body of the people would be less than it otherwise might be by thirty millions a year, deducting only what would be necessary for seed. The population of the country would be less by

[7] [See on these estimates Sir Robert Giffen, *Growth of Capital*, 1889, pp. 89, 90.]

the number of people which thirty millions a year, deducting always the seed, could maintain, according to the particular mode of living and expence which might take place in the different ranks of men among whom the remainder was distributed.

Though there is not at present, in Europe, any civilized state of any kind which derives the greater part of its public revenue from the rent of lands which are the property of the state; yet, in all the great monarchies of Europe, there are still many large tracts of land which belong to the crown. They are generally forest; and sometimes forest where, after travelling several miles, you will scarce find a single tree; a mere waste and loss of country in respect both of produce and population. In every great monarchy of Europe the sale of the crown lands would produce a very large sum of money, which, if applied to the payment of the public debts, would deliver from mortgage a much greater revenue than any which those lands have ever afforded to the crown. In countries where lands, improved and cultivated very highly, and yielding at the time of sale as great a rent as can easily be got from them, commonly sell at thirty years purchase; the unimproved, uncultivated, and low-rented crown lands might well be expected to sell at forty, fifty, or sixty years purchase. The crown might immediately enjoy the revenue which this great price would redeem from mortgage. In the course of a few years it would probably enjoy another revenue. When the crown lands had become private property, they would, in the course of a few years, become well-improved and well-cultivated. The increase of their produce would increase the population of the country, by augmenting the revenue and consumption of the people. But the revenue which the crown derives from the duties of customs and excise, would necessarily increase with the revenue and consumption of the people.

The sale of crown lands would benefit both sovereign and people.

The revenue which, in any civilized monarchy, the crown derives from the crown lands, though it appears to cost nothing to individuals, in reality costs more to the soci-

The revenue from crown lands costs the people more than any other.

ety than perhaps any other equal revenue which the crown enjoys. It would, in all cases, be for the interest of the society to
replace this revenue to the crown by some other equal revenue,
and to divide the lands among the people, which could not well
be done better, perhaps, than by exposing them to public sale.

Lands, for the purposes of pleasure and magnificence,

Public parks, etc.,
are the only lands
which should
belong to the
sovereign.

parks, gardens, public walks, &c. possessions which are every where considered as
causes of expence, not as sources of revenue, seem to be the only lands which, in a
great and civilized monarchy, ought to belong to the crown.

Public stock and public lands, therefore, the two sources of
revenue which may peculiarly belong to the sovereign or com-

The greater part
of the sovereign's
expense must be
defrayed by taxes.

monwealth, being both improper and insufficient funds for defraying the necessary
expence of any great and civilized state; it
remains that this expence must, the greater
part of it, be defrayed by taxes of one kind or
another; the people contributing a part of their own private revenue in order to make up a public revenue to the sovereign or
commonwealth.

PART II

Of Taxes

The private revenue of individuals, it has been shewn in the
first book of this Inquiry, arises ultimately from three different

Taxes may be
intended to fall
on rent, profit, or
wages, or upon all
three sorts of
revenue.

sources; Rent, Profit, and Wages. Every tax
must finally be paid from some one or other
of those three different sorts of revenue, or
from all of them indifferently. I shall endeavour to give the best account I can, first, of
those taxes which, it is intended, should fall
upon rent; secondly, of those which, it is in-
tended, should fall upon profit; thirdly, of those which, it is in-

tended, should fall upon wages; and, fourthly, of those which, it is intended, should fall indifferently upon all those three different sources of private revenue. The particular consideration of each of these four different sorts of taxes will divide the second part of the present chapter into four articles, three of which will require several other subdivisions. Many of those taxes, it will appear from the following review, are not finally paid from the fund, or source of revenue, upon which it was intended they should fall.

There are four maxims with regard to taxes in general,

Before I enter upon the examination of particular taxes, it is necessary to premise the four following maxims with regard to taxes in general.

(1) equality,

I. The subjects of every state ought to contribute towards the support of the government, as nearly as possible, in proportion to their respective abilities; that is, in proportion to the revenue which they respectively enjoy under the protection of the state. The expence of government to the individuals of a great nation, is like the expence of management to the joint tenants of a great estate, who are all obliged to contribute in proportion to their respective interests in the estate. In the observation or neglect of this maxim consists, what is called the equality or inequality of taxation. Every tax, it must be observed once for all, which falls finally upon one only of the three sorts of revenue above mentioned, is necessarily unequal, in so far as it does not affect the other two. In the following examination of different taxes I shall seldom take much further notice of this sort of inequality, but shall, in most cases, confine my observations to that inequality which is occasioned by a particular tax falling unequally even upon that particular sort of private revenue which is affected by it.

II. The tax which each individual is bound to pay ought to be certain, and not arbitrary. The time of payment, the manner *(2) certainty,* of payment, the quantity to be paid, ought all to be clear and plain to the contributor, and to every other person. Where it is otherwise, every person subject to the tax is put more or less in the power of the tax-gatherer, who can either aggravate the tax upon any obnoxious contributor, or extort, by the terror of such aggravation, some present or perquisite to himself. The uncertainty of taxation encourages the insolence and favours the corruption of an order of men who are naturally unpopular, even where they are neither insolent nor corrupt. The certainty of what each individual ought to pay is, in taxation, a matter of so great importance, that a very considerable degree of inequality, it appears, I believe, from the experience of all nations, is not near so great an evil as a very small degree of uncertainty.

III. Every tax ought to be levied at the time, or in the manner, in which it is most likely to be convenient for the contrib-

(3) convenience of payment, utor to pay it. A tax upon the rent of land or of houses, payable at the same term at which such rents are usually paid, is levied at the time when it is most likely to be convenient for the contributor to pay; or, when he is most likely to have wherewithal to pay. Taxes upon such consumable goods as are articles of luxury, are all finally paid by the consumer, and generally in a manner that is very convenient for him. He pays them by little and little, as he has occasion to buy the goods. As he is at liberty too, either to buy, or not to buy, as he pleases, it must be his own fault if he ever suffers any considerable inconveniency from such taxes.

IV. Every tax ought to be so contrived as both to take out and to keep out of the pockets of the people as little as possi-

and (4) economy in collection, ble, over and above what it brings into the public treasury of the state. A tax may either take out or keep out of the pockets of the people a great deal more than it brings into the public treasury, in the four following ways. First, the levying of it may require a great number of officers, whose salaries may eat up the greater part of the produce of the tax, and whose perquisites may impose another additional tax upon the people. Secondly, it may obstruct the industry of the people, and discourage them from applying to certain branches of business which might give maintenance and employment to great multitudes. While it obliges the people to pay, it may thus diminish, or perhaps destroy, some of the funds which might enable them more easily to do so. Thirdly, by the forfeitures and other penalties which those unfortunate individuals incur who attempt unsuccessfully to evade the tax, it may frequently ruin them, and thereby put an end to the benefit which the community might have received from the employment of their capitals. An injudicious tax offers a great temptation to smuggling. But the penalties of smuggling must rise in proportion to the temptation. The law, contrary to all the ordinary principles of justice, first creates the temptation, and then punishes those who yield to it; and it commonly enhances the punishment too in proportion to the very circumstance which ought certainly to alleviate it, the temptation to commit the crime.[8] Fourthly, by subjecting the people to the frequent visits and the odious examination of the tax-gatherers, it may expose them to much unnecessary trouble, vexation, and oppression; and though vexation is not, strictly speaking, expence, it is certainly equivalent to the expence at which every man would be willing to redeem himself from it. It is in some one or other of these four different ways that taxes are frequently so much more burdensome to the people than they are beneficial to the sovereign.

The evident justice and utility of the foregoing maxims have recommended them more or less to the attention of all nations. All nations have endeavoured, to the best of their judgment, to render their taxes as equal as they could contrive; as

---

[8] See *Sketches of the History of Man* [1774, by Henry Home, Lord Kames, vol. i.] page 474 & seq. [This author at the place quoted gives six "general rules" as to taxation:—

1. "That wherever there is an opportunity of smuggling taxes ought to be moderate."

2. "That taxes expensive in the levying ought to be avoided."

3. "To avoid arbitrary taxes."

4. "To remedy" inequality of riches "as much as possible, by relieving the poor and burdening the rich."

5. "That every tax which tends to impoverish the nation ought to be rejected with indignation."

6. "To avoid taxes that require the oath of party."]

which have recommended themselves to all nations. certain, as convenient to the contributor, both in the time and in the mode of payment, and in proportion to the revenue which they brought to the prince, as little burdensome to the people.[9] The following short review of some of the principal taxes which have taken place in different ages and countries will show, that the endeavours of all nations have not in this respect been equally successful.

ARTICLE I

Taxes upon Rent. Taxes upon the Rent of Land

A tax upon the rent of land may either be imposed according to *A tax on the rent of land may be on a constant or variable valuation.* a certain canon, every district being valued at a certain rent, which valuation is not afterwards to be altered; or it may be imposed in such a manner as to vary with every variation in the real rent of the land, and to rise or fall with the improvement or declension of its cultivation.

A land-tax which, like that of Great Britain, is assessed upon each district according to[10] a certain invariable canon, *If on a constant valuation it becomes unequal, like the British land tax.* though it should be equal at the time of its first establishment, necessarily becomes unequal in process of time, according to the unequal degrees of improvement or neglect in the cultivation of the different parts of the country. In England, the valuation according to which the different counties and parishes were assessed to the land-tax by the 4th of William and Mary was very unequal even at its first establishment. This tax, therefore, so far offends against the first of the four maxims above-mentioned. It is perfectly agreeable to the other three. It is perfectly certain.

[9] [In ed. 1 "as they could contrive" comes here instead of five lines earlier.]

[10] [Ed. 1 reads "is imposed according to." For the origin of the stereotyped assessment of the land tax, see Cannan, *Hist. of Local Rates in England*, 1896, pp. 114–119.]

The time of payment for the tax, being the same as that for the rent, is as convenient as it can be to the contributor. Though the landlord is in all cases the real contributor, the tax is commonly advanced by the tenant, to whom the landlord is obliged to allow it in the payment of the rent. This tax is levied by a much smaller number of officers than any other which affords nearly the same revenue. As the tax upon each district does not rise with the rise of the rent, the sovereign does not share in the profits of the landlord's improvements. Those improvements sometimes contribute,[11] indeed, to the discharge of the other landlords of the district. But the aggravation of the tax, which this may sometimes occasion upon a particular estate, is always so very small, that it never can discourage those improvements,[12] nor keep down the produce of the land below what it would otherwise rise to. As it has no tendency to diminish the quantity, it can have none to raise the price of that produce. It does not obstruct the industry of the people. It subjects the landlord to no other inconveniency besides the unavoidable one of paying the tax.

The advantage, however, which the landlord has derived *Circumstances have made the constant valuation favourable to the British landlords, the country having prospered and rents risen,* from the invariable constancy of the valuation by which all the lands of Great Britain are rated to the land-tax, has been principally owing to some circumstances altogether extraneous to the nature of the tax.

It has been owing in part to the great prosperity of almost every part of the country, the rents of almost all the estates of Great Britain having, since the time when this valuation was first established, been continually rising, and scarce any of them having fallen. The landlords, therefore, have almost all gained the difference between the tax which they would have paid, according to the present rent of their estates, and that

---

[11] [Ed. 2 reads "They contribute."]

[12] [Ed. 1, beginning after "the same revenue," six lines higher up, reads "As the tax does not rise with the rise of the rent, the sovereign does not share in the profits of the landlord's improvements. The tax therefore does not discourage those improvements."]

which they actually pay according to the ancient valuation. Had the state of the country been different, had rents been gradually falling in consequence of the declension of cultivation, the landlords would almost all have lost this difference. In the state of things which has happened to take place since the revolution, the constancy of the valuation has been advantageous to the landlord and hurtful to the sovereign. In a different state of things it might have been advantageous to the sovereign and hurtful to the landlord.

As the tax is made payable in money, so the valuation of the land is expressed in money. Since the establishment of this val-

and the value of money and silver remained uniform.

uation the value of silver has been pretty uniform, and there has been no alteration in the standard of the coin either as to weight or fineness. Had silver risen considerably in its value, as it seems to have done in the course of the two centuries which preceded the discovery of the mines of America, the constancy of the valuation might have proved very oppressive to the landlord. Had silver fallen considerably in its value, as it certainly did for about a century at least after the discovery of those mines, the same constancy of valuation would have reduced very much this branch of the revenue of the sovereign. Had any considerable alteration been made in the standard of the money, either by sinking the same quantity of silver to a lower denomination, or by raising it to a higher; had an ounce of silver, for example, instead of being coined into five shillings and twopence, been coined, either into pieces which bore so low a denomination as two shillings and seven-pence, or into pieces which bore so high a one as ten shillings and four-pence, it would in the one case have hurt the revenue of the proprietor, in the other that of the sovereign.

The constancy of valuation might have been very inconvenient to one or other of the parties.

In circumstances, therefore, somewhat different from those which have actually taken place, this constancy of valuation might have been a very great inconveniency, either to the contributors, or to the common-wealth. In the course of ages such circumstances, however, must, at some time or other, happen. But though empires, like all the other works of men, have all hitherto proved mortal, yet every empire aims at immortality. Every constitution, therefore, which it is meant should be as permanent as the empire itself, ought to be convenient, not in certain circumstnaces only, but in all circumstances; or ought to be suited, not to those circumstances which are transitory, occasional, or accidental, but to those which are necessary and therefore always the same.

A tax upon the rent of land which varies with every variation of the rent, or which rises and falls according to the improvement or neglect of cultivation, is recommended by that sect of men of letters in France, who call themselves the œconomists, as the most equitable of all taxes. All taxes, they pretend, fall ultimately upon the rent of land, and ought therefore to be imposed equally upon the fund which must finally pay them. That all taxes ought to fall as equally as possible upon the fund which must finally pay them, is certainly true. But without entering into the disagreeable discussion of the metaphysical arguments by which they support their very ingenious theory, it will sufficiently appear, from the following review, what are the taxes which fall finally upon the rent of the land, and what are those which fall finally upon some other fund.

The French economists recommend a tax varying with the rent.

In the Venetian territory all the arable lands which are given in lease to farmers are taxed at a tenth of the rent.[13] The leases are recorded in a public register which is kept by the officers of revenue in each province or district. When the proprietor cultivates his own lands, they are valued according to an equitable estimation, and he is allowed a deduction of one-fifth of the tax, so that for such lands he pays only eight instead of ten per cent. of the supposed rent.

In the Venetian territory rented lands are taxed 10 per cent. and lands cultivated by the proprietor 8 per cent.

A land-tax of this kind is certainly more equal than the land-tax of England. It might not, perhaps, be altogether so

---

[13] *Memoires concernant les Droits* [tom. i.] p. 240, 241.

Such a land tax is
more equal but is
not so certain,
and is more
troublesome and
expensive than
the British.

certain, and the assessment of the tax might
frequently occasion a good deal more trouble to the landlord. It might too be a good
deal more expensive in the levying.

Such a system of administration, however, might perhaps be contrived as would,
in a great measure, both prevent this uncertainty and moderate this expence.

The uncertainty
and expense could
be diminished.

The landlord and tenant, for example,
might jointly be obliged to record their lease
in a public register. Proper penalties might

Leases should be
registered,

be enacted against concealing or misrepre-
senting any of the conditions; and if part of
those penalties were to be paid to either of
the two parties who informed against and convicted the other
of such concealment or misrepresentation, it would effectually
deter them from combining together in order to defraud the
public revenue. All the conditions of the lease might be sufficiently known from such a record.

Some landlords, instead of raising the rent, take a fine for
the renewal of the lease. This practice is in most cases the ex-

fines taxed higher
than rent,

pedient of a spendthrift, who for a sum of
ready money sells a future revenue of much
greater value. It is in most cases, therefore,
hurtful to the landlord. It is frequently hurtful to the tenant, and
it is always hurtful to the community. It frequently takes from
the tenant so great a part of his capital, and thereby diminishes
so much his ability to cultivate the land, that he finds it more
difficult to pay a small rent than it would otherwise have been
to pay a great one. Whatever diminishes his ability to cultivate,
necessarily keeps down, below what it would otherwise have
been, the most important part of the revenue of the community.
By rendering the tax upon such fines a good deal heavier than
upon the ordinary rent, this hurtful practice might be discouraged, to the no small advantage of all the different parties concerned, of the landlord, of the tenant, of the sovereign, and of
the whole community.

Some leases prescribe to the tenant a certain mode of culti-

conditions of culti-
vation should be
discouraged by
high valuation,

vation, and a certain succession of crops
during the whole continuance of the lease.
This condition, which is generally the effect
of the landlord's conceit of his own superior
knowledge (a conceit in most cases very ill
founded), ought always to be considered as an additional rent;
as a rent in service instead of a rent in money. In order to discourage the practice, which is generally a foolish one, this
species of rent might be valued rather high, and consequently
taxed somewhat higher than common money rents.

Some landlords, instead of a rent in money, require a rent in
kind, in corn, cattle, poultry, wine, oil, &c. others again require

rents payable in
kind should be
valued high,

a rent in service. Such rents are always more
hurtful to the tenant than beneficial to the
landlord. They either take more or keep
more out of the pocket of the former, than
they put into that of the latter. In every country where they take
place, the tenants are poor and beggarly, pretty much according to the degree in which they take place. By valuing, in the
same manner, such rents rather high, and consequently taxing
them somewhat higher than common money rents, a practice
which is hurtful to the whole community might perhaps be sufficiently discouraged.

When the landlord chose to occupy himself a part of his
own lands, the rent might be valued according to an equitable

and an abatement
given to landlords
cultivating a
certain extent of
their land.

arbitration of the farmers and landlords in
the neighbourhood, and a moderate abatement of the tax might be granted to him, in
the same manner as in the Venetian territory;
provided the rent of the lands which he occupied did not exceed a certain sum. It is of importance that the landlord should be encouraged to cultivate a
part of his own land. His capital is generally greater than that
of the tenant, and with less skill he can frequently raise a
greater produce. The landlord can afford to try experiments,
and is generally disposed to do so. His unsuccessful experiments occasion only a moderate loss to himself. His successful
ones contribute to the improvement and better cultivation of

the whole country. It might be of importance, however, that the abatement of the tax should encourage him to cultivate to a certain extent only. If the landlords should, the greater part of them, be tempted to farm the whole of their own lands, the country (instead of sober and industrious tenants, who are bound by their own interest to cultivate as well as their capital and skill will allow them) would be filled with idle and profligate bailiffs, whose abusive management would soon degrade the cultivation, and reduce the annual produce of the land, to the diminution, not only of the revenue of their masters, but of the most important part of that of the whole society.

Such a system of administration might, perhaps, free a tax of this kind from any degree of uncertainty which could occasion either oppression or inconveniency to *Such a system* the contributor; and might at the same time *would free the tax* serve to introduce into the common manage- *from inconvenient* ment of land such a plan or policy, as might *uncertainty and* contribute a good deal to the general im- *encourage* provement and good cultivation of the coun- *improvement.* try.

The expence of levying a land-tax, which varied with every variation of the rent, would no doubt be somewhat greater than *The extra expense* that of levying one which was always rated *of levying the* according to a fixed valuation. Some addi- *tax would be* tional expence would necessarily be in- *inconsiderable.* curred both by the different register offices which it would be proper to establish in the different districts of the country, and by the different valuations which might occasionally be made of the lands which the proprietor chose to occupy himself. The expence of all this, however, might be very moderate, and much below what is incurred in the levying of many other taxes, which afford a very inconsiderable revenue in comparison of what might easily be drawn from a tax of this kind.

The discouragement which a variable land-tax of this kind might give to the improvement of land, seems to be the most important objection which can be made to it. The landlord would certainly be less disposed to improve, when the

The value of improvements should be for a fixed term exempt from taxation, sovereign, who contributed nothing to the expence, was to share in the profit of the improvement. Even this objection might perhaps be obviated by allowing the landlord, before he began his improvement, to ascertain, in conjunction with the officers of revenue, the actual value of his lands, according to the equitable arbitration of a certain number of landlords and farmers in the neighbourhood, equally chosen by both parties; and by rating him according to this valuation for such a number of years, as might be fully sufficient for his complete indemnification. To draw the attention of the sovereign towards the improvement of the land, from a regard to the increase of his own revenue, is one of the principal advantages proposed by this species of land-tax. The term, therefore, allowed for the indemnification of the landlord, ought not to be a great deal longer than what was necessary for that purpose; lest the remoteness of the interest should discourage too much this attention. It had better, however, be somewhat too long than in any respect too short. No incitement to the attention of the sovereign can ever counterbalance the smallest discouragement to that of the landlord. The attention of the sovereign can be at best but a very general and vague consideration of what is likely to contribute to the better cultivation of the greater part of his dominions. The attention of the landlord is a particular and minute consideration of what is likely to be the most advantageous application of every inch of ground upon his estate. The principal attention of the sovereign ought to be to encourage, by every means in his power, the attention both of the landlord and of the farmer; by allowing both to pursue their own interest in their own way, and according to their own judgment; by giving to both the most perfect security that they shall enjoy the full recompence of their own industry; and by procuring to both the most extensive market for every part of their produce, in consequence of establishing the easiest and safest communications both by land and by water, through every part of his own dominions, as well as the most unbounded freedom of exportation to the dominions of all other princes.

If by such a system of administration a tax of this kind could be so managed as to give, not only no discouragement,

and the tax would then be as little inconvenient as is possible.

but, on the contrary, some encouragement to the improvement of land, it does not appear likely to occasion any other inconveniency to the landlord, except always the unavoidable one of being obliged to pay the tax.

In all the variations of the state of the society, in the improvement and in the declension of agriculture; in all the vari-

It would adjust itself to all changes.

ations in the value of silver, and in all those in the standard of the coin, a tax of this kind would, of its own accord and without any attention of government, readily suit itself to the actual situation of things, and would be equally just and equitable in all those different changes. It would, therefore, be much more proper to be established as a perpetual and unalterable regulation, or as what is called a fundamental law of the commonwealth, than any tax which was always to be levied according to a certain valuation.

Some states, instead of the simple and obvious expedient of a register of leases, have had recourse to the laborious and ex-

Some states make a survey and valuation for the land tax,

pensive one of an actual survey and valuation of all the lands in the country. They have suspected, probably, that the lessor and lessee, in order to defraud the public revenue, might combine to conceal the real terms of the lease. Dooms-day-book seems to have been the result of a very accurate survey of this kind.

In the ancient dominions of the king of Prussia, the land-tax is assessed according to an actual survey and valuation, which

for example, Prussia,

is reviewed and altered from time to time.[14] According to that valuation, the lay proprietors pay from twenty to twenty-five per cent. of their revenue. Ecclesiastics from forty to forty-five per cent.

The survey and valuation of Silesia was made by order of

---

[14] *Memoires concernant les Droits, &c.* tome i. p. 114, 115, 116, &c.

Silesia, the present king; it is said with great accuracy. According to that valuation, the lands belonging to the bishop of Breslaw are taxed at twenty-five per cent. of their rent. The other revenues of the ecclesiastics of both religions, at fifty per cent. The commanderies of the Teutonic order, and of that of Malta, at forty per cent. Lands held by a noble tenure, at thirty-eight and one-third per cent. Lands held by a base tenure, at thirty-five and one-third per cent.[15]

The survey and valuation of Bohemia is said to have been the work of more than a hundred years. It was not perfected *and Bohemia.* till after the peace of 1748, by the orders of the present empress queen.[16] The survey of the dutchy of Milan, which was begun in the time of Charles VI., was not perfected till after 1760. It is esteemed one of the most accurate that has ever been made. The survey of Savoy and Piedmont was executed under the orders of the late king of Sardinia.[17]

In the dominions of the king of Prussia the revenue of the church is taxed much higher than that of lay proprietors.[18] The *Under the Prussian land tax the church lands are taxed higher than the rest; in some states they are taxed lower than the rest.* revenue of the church is, the greater part of it, a burden upon the rent of land. It seldom happens that any part of it is applied towards the improvement of land; or is so employed as to contribute in any respect towards increasing the revenue of the great body of the people. His Prussian majesty had probably, upon that account, thought it reasonable, that it should contribute a good deal more towards relieving the exigencies of the state. In some countries the lands of the church are exempted from all taxes. In others they are taxed more lightly than other lands. In the dutchy of

[15] [*Ibid.,* pp. 117–119.]

[16] *Memoires concernant les Droits, &c.* tome i. p. 83, 84 [and 79.]

[17] Ibid. p. 280, &c. also p. 287, &c. to 316.

[18] [See above note 17; previous page.]

Milan, the lands which the church possessed before 1575, are rated to the tax at a third only of their value.[19]

In Silesia, lands held by a noble tenure are taxed three per cent. higher than those held by a base tenure. The honours and privileges of different kinds annexed to the former, his Prussian majesty had probably imagined, would sufficiently compensate to the proprietor a small aggravation of the tax; while at the same time the humiliating inferiority of the latter would be in some measure alleviated by being taxed somewhat more lightly. In other countries, the system of taxation, instead of alleviating, aggravates this inequality. In the dominions of the king of Sardinia, and in those provinces of France which are subject to what is called the real or predial taille, the tax falls altogether upon the lands held by a base tenure. Those held by a noble one are exempted.

Differences are often made between land held by noble and base tenures.

A land-tax assessed according to a general survey and valuation, how equal soever it may be at first, must in the course of a very moderate period of time, become unequal. To prevent its becoming so would require the continual and painful attention of government to all the variations in the state and produce of every different farm in the country. The governments of Prussia, of Bohemia, of Sardinia, and of the dutchy of Milan, actually exert an attention of this kind; an attention so unsuitable to the nature of government, that it is not likely to be of long continuance, and which, if it is continued, will probably in the long-run occasion much more trouble and vexation than it can possibly bring relief to the contributors.

A land tax assessed according to a general survey and valuation soon becomes unequal,

In 1666, the generality of Montauban was assessed to the Real or predial taille[20] according, it is said, to a very exact survey and valuation.[21] By 1727, this assessment had become al-

---

[19] [*Mémoires*, tom. i., p. 282.]

[20] [Misprinted "tallie" here and seven lines lower down in eds. 2–5.]

[21] *Memoires concernant les Droits &c.* tome ii. p. 139, &c. [pp. 145–147.]

as in Montauban. together unequal. In order to remedy this inconveniency, government has found no better expedient than to impose upon the whole generality an additional tax of a hundred and twenty thousand livres. This additional tax is rated upon all the different districts subject to the taille according to the old assessment. But it is levied only upon those which in the actual state of things are by that assessment under-taxed, and it is applied to the relief of those which by the same assessment are over-taxed. Two districts, for example, one of which ought in the actual state of things to be taxed at nine hundred, the other at eleven hundred livres, are by the old assessment both taxed at a thousand livres. Both these districts are by the additional tax rated at eleven hundred livres each. But this additional tax is levied only upon the district under-charged, and it is applied altogether to the relief of that over-charged, which consequently pays only nine hundred livres. The government neither gains nor loses by the additional tax, which is applied altogether to remedy the inequalities arising from the old assessment. The application is pretty much regulated according to the discretion of the intendant of the generality, and must, therefore, be in a great measure arbitrary.

Taxes which are proportioned, not to the Rent,
but to the Produce of Land

Taxes upon the produce of land are in reality taxes upon the rent; and though they may be originally advanced by the farmer, are finally paid by the landlord. *Taxes on the produce are finally paid by the landlord,* When a certain portion of the produce is to be paid away for a tax, the farmer computes, as well as he can, what the value of this portion is, one year with another, likely to amount to, and he makes a proportionable abatement in the rent which he agrees to pay to the landlord. There is no farmer who does not compute beforehand what the church tythe, which is a land-tax of this kind, is, one year with another, likely to amount to.

The tythe, and every other land-tax of this kind, under the appearance of perfect equality, are very unequal taxes; a cer-

and are very unequal taxes,

tain portion of the produce being, in differ-ent situations, equivalent to a very different portion of the rent. In some very rich lands the produce is so great, that the one half of it is fully sufficient to replace to the farmer his capital employed in cultivation, to-gether with the ordinary profits of farming stock in the neigh-bourhood. The other half, or, what comes to the same thing, the value of the other half, he could afford to pay as rent to the landlord, if there was no tythe. But if a tenth of the produce is taken from him in the way of tythe, he must require an abate-ment of the fifth part of his rent, otherwise he cannot get back his capital with the ordinary profit. In this case the rent of the landlord, instead of amounting to a half, or five-tenths of the whole produce, will amount only to four-tenths of it. In poorer lands, on the contrary, the produce is sometimes so small, and the expence of cultivation so great, that it requires four-fifths of the whole produce to replace to the farmer his capital with the ordinary profit. In this case, though there was no tythe, the rent of the landlord could amount to no more than one-fifth or two-tenths of the whole produce. But if the farmer pays one-tenth of the produce in the way of tythe, he must require an equal abatement of the rent of the landlord, which will thus be reduced to one-tenth only of the whole produce. Upon the rent of rich lands, the tythe may sometimes be a tax of no more than one-fifth part, or four shillings in the pound; whereas upon that of poorer lands, it may sometimes be a tax of one-half, or of ten shillings in the pound.

The tythe, as it is frequently a very unequal tax upon the rent, so it is always a great discouragement both to the im-

which discourage both improvement and good cultivation.

provements of the landlord and to the culti-vation of the farmer. The one cannot venture to make the most important, which are gen-erally the most expensive improvements; nor the other to raise the most valuable, which are generally too the most expensive crops; when the church, which lays out no part of the expence, is to share so very largely in the profit. The cultivation of madder was for a long time confined by the tythe to the United Provinces, which, being presbyterian countries, and upon that account exempted from this destructive tax, enjoyed a sort of monopoly of that useful dying drug against the rest of Europe. The late attempts to introduce the culture of this plant into England, have been made only in consequence of the statute which enacted that five shillings an acre should be received in lieu of all manner of tythe upon madder.[22]

As through the greater part of Europe, the church, so in many different countries of Asia, the state, is principally sup-

They form the principal revenue of the state in many Asiatic countries,

ported by a land-tax, proportioned, not to the rent, but to the produce of the land. In China, the principal revenue of the sovereign consists in a tenth part of the produce of all the lands of the empire. This tenth part, how-

ever, is estimated so very moderately, that, in many provinces, it is said not to exceed a thirtieth part of the ordinary produce. The land-tax or land-rent which used to be paid to the Mahometan government of Bengal, before that country fell into the hands of the English East India company, is said to have amounted to about a fifth part of the produce. The land-tax of ancient Egypt is said likewise to have amounted to a fifth part.[23]

In Asia, this sort of land-tax is said to interest the sovereign in the improvement and cultivation of land.[24] The sovereigns of

and are said to interest the sovereign in the improvement and cultivation of land there.

China, those of Bengal while under the Mahometan government, and those of ancient Egypt, are said accordingly to have been extremely attentive to the making and maintaining of good roads and navigable canals, in order to increase, as much as pos-

sible, both the quantity and value of every part of the produce of the land, by procuring to every part of it

---

[22] [31 Geo. II., c. 12, continued by 5 Geo. III., c. 18.]

[23] [Genesis xlvii. 26.]

[24] [Above, pp. 868–869.]

the most extensive market which their own dominions could afford. The tythe of the church is divided into such small portions, that no one of its proprietors can have any interest of this kind. The parson of a parish could never find his account in making a road or canal to a distant part of the country, in order to extend the market for the produce of his own particular parish. Such taxes, when destined for the maintenance of the state, have some advantages which may serve in some measure to balance their inconveniency. When destined for the maintenance of the church, they are attended with nothing but inconveniency.

They may be in kind or in money.

Taxes upon the produce of land may be levied, either in kind; or, according to a certain valuation, in money.

Collection in kind is quite unsuitable for public revenue.

The parson of a parish, or a gentleman of small fortune who lives upon his estate, may sometimes, perhaps, find some advantage in receiving, the one his tythe, and the other his rent, in kind. The quantity to be collected, and the district within which it is to be collected, are so small, that they both can oversee, with their own eyes, the collection and disposal of every part of what is due to them. A gentleman of great fortune, who lived in the capital, would be in danger of suffering much by the neglect, and more by the fraud of his factors and agents, if the rents of an estate in a distant province were to be paid to him in this manner. The loss of the sovereign, from the abuse and depredation of his tax-gatherers, would necessarily be much greater. The servants of the most careless private person are, perhaps, more under the eye of their master than those of the most careful prince; and a public revenue, which was paid in kind, would suffer so much from the mismanagement of the collectors, that a very small part of what was levied upon the people would ever arrive at the treasury of the prince. Some part of the public revenue of China, however, is said to be paid in this manner. The Mandarins and other tax-gatherers will, no doubt, find their advantage in continuing the practice of a payment which is so much more liable to abuse than any payment in money.

A tax upon the produce of land which is levied in money, may be levied either according to a valuation which varies with all the variations of the market price; or according to a fixed valuation, a bushel of wheat, for example, being always valued at one and the same money price, whatever may be the state of the market. The produce of a tax levied in the former way, will vary only according to the variations in the real produce of the land according to the improvement or neglect of cultivation. The produce of a tax levied in the latter way will vary, not only according to the variations in the produce of the land, but according to both those in the value of the precious metals, and those in the quantity of those metals which is at different times contained in coin of the same denomination. The produce of the former will always bear the same proportion to the value of the real produce of the land. The produce of the latter may, at different times, bear very different proportions to that value.

A money tax on produce may be always the same or may vary with the market price of produce.

When, instead either of a certain portion of the produce of land, or of the price of a certain portion, a certain sum of money is to be paid in full compensation for all tax or tythe; the tax becomes, in this case, exactly of the same nature with the land-tax of England. It neither rises nor falls with the rent of the land. It neither encourages nor discourages improvement. The tythe in the greater part of those parishes which pay what is called a modus in lieu of all other tythe, is a tax of this kind. During the Mahometan government of Bengal, instead of the payment in kind of the fifth[25] part of the produce, a modus, and, it is said, a very moderate one, was established in the greater part of the districts or zemindaries of the country. Some of the servants of the East India company, under pretence of restoring the public revenue to its proper value, have, in some provinces, exchanged this modus for a

When a certain sum of money is to be paid in compensation for the tax it becomes exactly like the English land tax.

[25] [Eds. 1–4 read "a fifth."]

payment in kind. Under their management this change is likely both to discourage cultivation, and to give new opportunities for abuse in the collection of the public revenue, which has fallen very much below what it was said to have been, when it first fell under the management of the company. The servants of the company may, perhaps, have profited by this change, but at the expence, it is probable, both of their masters and of the country.

Taxes upon the Rent of Houses

The rent of a house may be distinguished into two parts, of

House rent consists of two parts,

which the one may very properly be called the Building rent; the other is commonly called the Ground rent.

building rent,

The building rent is the interest or profit of the capital expended in building the house. In order to put the trade of a builder upon a level with other trades, it is necessary that this rent should be sufficient, first, to pay him the same interest which he would have got for his capital if he had lent it upon good security; and, secondly, to keep the house in constant repair, or, what comes to the same thing, to replace, within a certain term of years, the capital which had been employed in building it. The building rent, or the ordinary profit of building, is, therefore, every where regulated by the ordinary interest of money. Where the market rate of interest is four per cent. the rent of a house which, over and above paying the ground rent, affords six, or six and a half per cent. upon the whole expence of building, may perhaps afford a sufficient profit to the builder. Where the market rate of interest is five per cent., it may perhaps require seven or seven and a half per cent. If, in proportion to the interest of money, the trade of the builder affords at any time a much greater profit than this, it will soon draw so much capital from other trades as will reduce the profit to its proper level. If it affords at any time much less than this, other trades will soon draw so much capital from it as will again raise that profit.

Whatever part of the whole rent of a house is over and

and ground rent. above what is sufficient for affording this reasonable profit, naturally goes to the ground-rent; and where the owner of the ground and the owner of the building are two different persons, is, in most cases, completely paid to the former. This surplus rent is the price which the inhabitant of the house pays for some real or supposed advantage of the situation. In country houses, at a distance from any great town, where there is plenty of ground to chuse upon, the ground rent is scarce any thing, or no more than what the ground which the house stands upon would pay if employed in agriculture. In country villas in the neighbourhood of some great town, it is sometimes a good deal higher; and the peculiar conveniency or beauty of situation is there frequently very well paid for. Ground rents are generally highest in the capital, and in those particular parts of it where there happens to be the greatest demand for houses, whatever be the reason of that demand, whether for trade and business, for pleasure and society, or for mere vanity and fashion.

A tax upon house-rent, payable by the tenant and proportioned to the whole rent of each house, could not, for any considerable time at least, affect the building rent. If the builder did not get his reasonable profit, he would be obliged to quit the trade; which, by raising the demand for building, would in a short time bring back his profit to its proper level with that of other trades. Neither would such a tax fall altogether upon the ground-rent; but it would divide itself in such a manner as to fall, partly upon the inhabitant of the house, and partly upon the owner of the ground.

A tax on house rent paid by the tenant falls partly on the inhabitant and partly on the owner of the ground,

Let us suppose, for example, that a particular person judges that he can afford for house-rent an expence of sixty pounds a year; and let us suppose too that a tax of four shillings in the pound, or of one-fifth, payable by the inhabitant, is laid upon house-rent. A house of sixty pounds rent will in this case cost him seventy-two pounds a year, which is twelve pounds

as may be shown by an example.

more than he thinks he can afford. He will, therefore, content himself with a worse house, or a house of fifty pounds rent, which, with the additional ten pounds that he must pay for the tax, will make up the sum of sixty pounds a year, the expence which he judges he can afford; and in order to pay the tax he will give up a part of the additional conveniency which he might have had from a house of ten pounds a year more rent. He will give up, I say, a part of this additional conveniency; for he will seldom be obliged to give up the whole, but will, in consequence of the tax, get a better house for fifty pounds a year, than he could have got if there had been no tax. For as a tax of this kind, by taking away this particular competitor, must diminish the competition for houses of sixty pounds rent, so it must likewise diminish it for those of fifty pounds rent, and in the same manner for those of all other rents, except the lowest rent, for which it would for some time increase the competition. But the rents of every class of houses for which the competition was diminished, would necessarily be more or less reduced. As no part of this reduction, however, could, for any considerable time at least, affect the building rent; the whole of it must in the long-run necessarily fall upon the ground-rent. The final payment of this tax, therefore, would fall, partly upon the inhabitant of the house, who, in order to pay his share, would be obliged to give up a part of his conveniency; and partly upon the owner of the ground, who, in order to pay his share, would be obliged to give up a part of his revenue. In what proportion this final payment would be divided between them, it is not perhaps very easy to ascertain. The division would probably be very different in different circumstances, and a tax of this kind might, according to those different circumstances, affect very unequally both the inhabitant of the house and the owner of the ground.

The inequality with which a tax of this kind might fall upon the owners of different ground-rents, would arise altogether from the accidental inequality of this division. But the inequality with which it might fall upon the inhabitants of different houses would arise, not only from this, but from

On the inhabitants it would be an unequal tax, falling heaviest on the rich.

another cause. The proportion of the expence of house-rent to the whole expence of living, is different in the different degrees of fortune. It is perhaps highest in the highest degree, and it diminishes gradually through the inferior degrees, so as in general to be lowest in the lowest degree. The necessaries of life occasion the great expence of the poor. They find it difficult to get food, and the greater part of their little revenue is spent in getting it. The luxuries and vanities of life occasion the principal expence of the rich; and a magnificent house embellishes and sets off to the best advantage all the other luxuries and vanities which they possess. A tax upon house-rents, therefore, would in general fall heaviest upon the rich; and in this sort of inequality there would not, perhaps, be any thing very unreasonable. It is not very unreasonable that the rich should contribute to the public expence, not only in proportion to their revenue, but something more than in that proportion.

The rent of houses, though it in some respects resembles the rent of land, is in one respect essentially different from it.

It would be like a tax on any other consumable commodity, it would be very much in proportion to men's whole expense, and it would produce considerable revenue.

The rent of land is paid for the use of a productive subject. The land which pays it produces it. The rent of houses is paid for the use of an unproductive subject. Neither the house nor the ground which it stands upon produce any thing. The person who pays the rent, therefore, must draw it from some other source of revenue, distinct from and independent of this subject.[26] A tax upon the rent of houses, so far as it falls upon the inhabitants, must be drawn from the same source as the rent itself, and must be paid from their revenue, whether derived from the wages of labour, the profits of stock, or the rent of land. So far as it falls upon the inhabitants, it is one of those taxes which fall, not upon one only, but indiffer-

---

[26] [Above, pp. 356–357.]

ently upon all the three different sources of revenue; and is in every respect of the same nature as a tax upon any other sort of consumable commodities. In general there is not, perhaps, any one article of expence or consumption by which the liberality or narrowness of a man's whole expence can be better judged of, than by his house-rent. A proportional tax upon this particular article of expence might, perhaps, produce a more considerable revenue than any which has hitherto been drawn from it in any part of Europe. If the tax indeed was very high, the greater part of people would endeavour to evade it, as much as they could, by contenting themselves with smaller houses, and by turning the greater part of their expence into some other channel.

The rent of houses might easily be ascertained with sufficient accuracy, by a policy of the same kind with that

The rent could be easily ascertained. Empty houses should be exempt, and houses occupied by their proprietor should be assessed at their letting value.

which would be necessary for ascertaining the ordinary rent of land. Houses not inhabited ought to pay no tax. A tax upon them would fall altogether upon the proprietor, who would thus be taxed for a subject which afforded him neither conveniency nor revenue. Houses inhabited by the proprietor ought to be rated, not according to the expence which they might have cost in building, but according to the rent which an equitable arbitration might judge them likely to bring, if leased to a tenant. If rated according to the expence which they may have cost in building, a tax of three or four shillings in the pound, joined with other taxes, would ruin almost all the rich and great families of this, and, I believe, of every other civilized country. Whoever will examine, with attention, the different town and country houses of some of the richest and greatest families in this country, will find that, at the rate of only six and a half, or seven per cent. upon the original expence of building, their house-rent is nearly equal to the whole neat rent of their estates. It is the accumulated expence of several successive generations, laid out upon objects of great beauty and magnificence, indeed; but, in proportion to what they cost, of very small exchangeable value.[27]

Ground-rents are a still more proper subject of taxation than the rent of houses. A tax upon ground-rents would not raise the rents of houses. It would fall altogether upon *Ground rent is a still more proper subject of taxation than building rent,* the owner of the ground-rent, who acts always as a monopolist, and exacts the greatest rent which can be got for the use of his ground. More or less can be got for it according as the competitors happen to be richer or poorer, or can afford to gratify their fancy for a particular spot of ground at a greater or smaller expence. In every country the greatest number of rich competitors is in the capital, and it is there accordingly that the highest ground-rents are always to be found. As the wealth of those competitors would in no respect be increased by a tax upon ground-rents, they would not probably be disposed to pay more for the use of the ground. Whether the tax was to be advanced by the inhabitant, or by the owner of the ground, would be of little importance. The more the inhabitant was obliged to pay for the tax, the less he would incline to pay for the ground; so that the final payment of the tax would fall altogether upon the owner of the ground-rent. The ground-rents of uninhabited houses ought to pay no tax.

Both ground-rents and the ordinary rent of land are a species of revenue which the owner, in many cases, enjoys *as no discouragement is given to industry by the taxation of the rent of land.* without any care or attention of his own. Though a part of this revenue should be taken from him in order to defray the expences of the state, no discouragement will thereby be given to any sort of industry. The annual produce of the land and labour of the

[27] Since the first publication of this book, a tax nearly upon the above-mentioned principles has been imposed. [This note appears first in ed. 3. The tax was first imposed by 18 Geo. III., c. 26, and was at the rate of 6d. in the pound on houses of £5 and under £50 annual value, and 1s. in the pound on houses of higher value, but by 19 Geo. III., c. 59, the rates were altered to 6d. in the pound on houses of £5 and under £20 annual value, 9d. on those of £20 and under £40, and 1s. on those of £40 and upwards.]

society, the real wealth and revenue of the great body of the people, might be the same after such a tax as before. Ground-rents, and the ordinary rent of land, are, therefore, perhaps, the species of revenue which can best bear to have a peculiar tax imposed upon them.

Ground-rents seem, in this respect, a more proper subject of peculiar taxation than even the ordinary rent of land. The ordi-

Ground rents are even a more proper subject of taxation than ordinary land rents.

nary rent of land is, in many cases, owing partly at least to the attention and good management of the landlord. A very heavy tax might discourage too much this attention and good management. Ground-rents, so far as they exceed the ordinary rent of land, are altogether owing to the good government of the sovereign, which, by protecting the industry either of the whole people, or of the inhabitants of some particular place, enables them to pay so much more than its real value for the ground which they build their houses upon; or to make to its owner so much more than compensation for the loss which he might sustain by this use of it. Nothing can be more reasonable than that a fund which owes its existence to the good government of the state, should be taxed peculiarly, or should contribute something more than the greater part of other funds, towards the support of that government.

Though, in many different countries of Europe, taxes have been imposed upon the rent of houses, I do not know of any in

Ground rents are nowhere separately taxed, but might be.

which ground-rents have been considered as a separate subject of taxation. The contrivers of taxes have, probably, found some difficulty in ascertaining what part of the rent ought to be considered as ground-rent, and what part ought to be considered as building-rent. It should not, however, seem very difficult to distinguish those two parts of the rent from one another.

In Great Britain the rent of houses is supposed to be taxed in the same proportion as the rent of land, by what is called the annual land-tax. The valuation, according to which each different parish and district is assessed to this tax, is always the

House rent is legally liable to the British land tax.

same. It was originally extremely unequal, and it still continues to be so. Through the greater part of the kingdom this tax falls still more lightly upon the rent of houses than upon that of land. In some few districts only, which were originally rated high, and in which the rents of houses have fallen considerably, the land-tax of three or four shillings in the pound, is said to amount to an equal proportion of the real rent of houses.[28] Untenanted houses, though by law subject to the tax, are, in most districts, exempted from it by the favour of the assessors; and this exemption sometimes occasions some little variation in the rate of particular houses, though that of the district is always the same. Improvements of rent, by new buildings, repairs, &c.; go to the discharge of the district, which occasions still further variations in the rate of particular houses.[29]

In the province of Holland[30] every house is taxed at two and a half per cent. of its value, without any regard either to the

In Holland there is a tax on the capital value of houses.

rent which it actually pays, or to the circumstance of its being tenanted or untenanted. There seems to be a hardship in obliging the proprietor to pay a tax for an untenanted house, from which he can derive no revenue, especially so very heavy a tax. In Holland, where the market rate of interest does not exceed three per cent. two and a half per cent. upon the whole value of the house, must, in most cases, amount to more than a third of the building-rent, perhaps of the whole rent. The valuation, indeed, according to which the houses are rated, though very unequal, is said to be always below the real value. When a house is rebuilt, improved or enlarged, there is a new valuation, and the tax is rated accordingly.

The contrivers of the several taxes which in England have, at different times, been imposed upon houses, seem to have

[28] [Ed. 1 reads "the houses."]

[29] [Ed. 1 does not contain this sentence.]

[30] *Memoires concernant les Droits, &c.* [tom. i.], p. 223.

House taxes in England have not been proportioned to the rent, imagined that there was some great difficulty in ascertaining, with tolerable exactness, what was the real rent of every house. They have regulated their taxes, therefore, according to some more obvious circumstance, such as they had probably imagined would, in most cases, bear some proportion to the rent.

The first tax of this kind was hearth-money; or a tax of two shillings upon every hearth. In order to ascertain how many *but first to the number of hearths,* hearths were in the house, it was necessary that the tax-gatherer should enter every room in it. This odious visit rendered the tax odious. Soon after the revolution, therefore, it was abolished, as a badge of slavery.

The next tax of this kind was, a tax of two shillings upon every dwelling house inhabited. A house with ten windows to *and later to the number of windows.* pay four shillings more. A house with twenty windows and upwards to pay eight shillings. This tax was afterwards so far altered, that houses with twenty windows, and with less than thirty, were ordered to pay ten shillings, and those with thirty windows and upwards to pay twenty shillings. The number of windows can, in most cases, be counted from the outside, and, in all cases, without entering every room in the house. The visit of the tax-gatherer, therefore, was less offensive in this tax than in the hearth-money.

This tax was afterwards repealed, and in the room of it was established the window-tax, which has undergone too several *The present window tax augments gradually from 2d. per window to 2s.* alterations and augmentations. The window-tax, as it stands at present (January, 1775), over and above the duty of three shillings upon every house in England, and of one shilling upon every house in Scotland, lays a duty upon every window, which, in England, augments gradually from two-pence, the lowest rate, upon houses with not more than seven windows; to two shillings, the highest rate, upon houses with twenty-five windows and upwards.

The principal objection to all such taxes is their inequality,

Window taxes are objectionable, chiefly on the ground of inequality.

an inequality of the worst kind, as they must frequently fall much heavier upon the poor than upon the rich. A house of ten pounds rent in a country town may sometimes have more windows than a house of five hundred pounds rent in London; and though the inhabitant of the former is likely to be a much poorer man than that of the latter, yet so far as his contribution is regulated by the window-tax, he must contribute more to the support of the state. Such taxes are, therefore, directly contrary to the first of the four maxims above mentioned. They do not seem to offend much against any of the other three.

The natural tendency of the window-tax, and of all other taxes upon houses, is to lower rents. The more a man pays for

Taxes on houses lower rents.

the tax, the less, it is evident, he can afford to pay for the rent. Since the imposition of the window-tax, however, the rents of houses have upon the whole risen, more or less, in almost every town and village of Great Britain, with which I am acquainted. Such has been almost every where the increase of the demand for houses, that it has raised the rents more than the window-tax could sink them; one of the many proofs of the great prosperity of the country, and of the increasing revenue of its inhabitants. Had it not been for the tax, rents would probably have risen still higher.

ARTICLE II

Taxes upon Profit, or upon the Revenue arising from Stock

The revenue or profit arising from stock naturally divides itself into two parts; that which pays the interest, and which belongs

Profit is divided into interest and surplus over interest.

to the owner of the stock; and that surplus part which is over and above what is necessary for paying the interest.

This latter part of profit is evidently a subject not taxable directly. It is the compensation, and in most cases it is no more than a very moderate

The surplus is not taxable. compensation, for the risk and trouble of employing the stock. The employer must have this compensation, otherwise he cannot, consistently with his own interest, continue the employment. If he was taxed directly, therefore, in proportion to the whole profit, he would be obliged either to raise the rate of his profit, or to charge the tax upon the interest of money; that is, to pay less interest. If he raised the rate of his profit in proportion to the tax, the whole tax, though it might be advanced by him, would be finally paid by one or other of two different sets of people, according to the different ways in which he might employ the stock of which he had the management. If he employed it as a farming stock in the cultivation of land, he could raise the rate of his profit only by retaining a greater portion, or, what comes to the same thing, the price of a greater portion of the produce of the land; and as this could be done only by a reduction of rent, the final payment of the tax would fall upon the landlord. If he employed it as a mercantile or manufacturing stock, he could raise the rate of his profit only by raising the price of his goods; in which case the final payment of the tax would fall altogether upon the consumers of those goods. If he did not raise the rate of his profit, he would be obliged to charge the whole tax upon that part of it which was allotted for the interest of money. He could afford less interest for whatever stock he borrowed, and the whole weight of the tax would in this case fall ultimately upon the interest of money. So far as he could not relieve himself from the tax in the one way, he would be obliged to relieve himself in the other.

The interest of money seems at first sight a subject equally capable of being taxed directly as the rent of land. Like the rent

Interest at first sight seems as fit to be taxed as rent, of land, it is a neat produce which remains after completely compensating the whole risk and trouble of employing the stock. As a tax upon the rent of land cannot raise rents; because the neat produce which remains after replacing the stock of the farmer, together with his reasonable profit, cannot be greater after the tax than before it: so, for the same reason, a tax upon the interest of money could not raise the rate of interest; the quantity of stock or money in the country, like the quantity of land, being supposed to remain the same after the tax as before it. The ordinary rate of profit, it has been shewn in the first book,[31] is every where regulated by the quantity of stock to be employed in proportion to the quantity of the employment, or of the business which must be done by it. But the quantity of the employment, or of the business to be done by stock, could neither be increased nor diminished by any tax upon the interest of money. If the quantity of the stock to be employed therefore, was neither increased nor diminished by it, the ordinary rate of profit would necessarily remain the same. But the portion of this profit necessary for compensating the risk and trouble of the employer, would likewise remain the same; that risk and trouble being in no respect altered. The residue, therefore, that portion which belongs to the owner of the stock, and which pays the interest of money, would necessarily remain the same too. At first sight, therefore, the interest of money seems to be a subject as fit to be taxed directly as the rent of land.

There are, however, two different circumstances which render the interest of money a much less proper subject of direct taxation than the rent of land.

but it is not, since,

First, the quantity and value of the land which any man possesses can never be a secret, and can always be ascertained with great exactness. But the whole amount of the capital stock which he possesses is almost always a secret, and can scarce ever be ascertained with tolerable exactness. It is liable, besides, to almost continual variations. A year seldom passes away, frequently not a month, sometimes scarce a single day, in which it does not rise or fall more or less. An inquisition into every man's private circumstances, and an inquisition which, in order to accommodate the tax to them, watched over all the fluctuations of his

(1) the amount received by an individual cannot be readily and exactly ascertained,

[31] [Chap. ix.]

fortune, would be a source of such continual and endless vexation as no people could support.

Secondly, land is a subject which cannot be removed, whereas stock easily may. The proprietor of land is necessarily

and (2) stock may be removed from the country imposing the tax.

a citizen of the particular country in which his estate lies. The proprietor of stock is properly a citizen of the world, and is not necessarily attached to any particular country. He would be apt to abandon the country in which he was exposed to a vexatious inquisition, in order to be assessed to a burdensome tax, and would remove his stock to some other country where he could either carry on his business, or enjoy his fortune more at his ease. By removing his stock he would put an end to all the industry which it had maintained in the country which he left. Stock cultivates land; stock employs labour. A tax which tended to drive away stock from any particular country, would so far tend to dry up every source of revenue, both to the sovereign and to the society. Not only the profits of stock, but the rent of land and the wages of labour, would necessarily be more or less diminished by its removal.

The nations, accordingly, who have attempted to tax the revenue arising from stock, instead of any severe inquisition of

Where such a tax exists it is levied on a loose and very low valuation,

this kind, have been obliged to content themselves with some very loose, and, therefore, more or less arbitrary estimation. The extreme inequality and uncertainty of a tax assessed in this manner, can be compensated only by its extreme moderation, in consequence of which every man finds himself rated so very much below his real revenue, that he gives himself little disturbance though his neighbour should be rated somewhat lower.

By what is called the land-tax in England, it was intended that stock should be taxed in the same proportion as land.

as under the English land tax.

When the tax upon land was at four shillings in the pound, or at one-fifth of the supposed rent, it was intended that stock should be taxed at one-fifth of the supposed interest. When the present annual land-tax was first imposed, the legal rate of interest was six per cent. Every hundred pounds stock, accordingly, was supposed to be taxed at twenty-four shillings, the fifth part of six pounds. Since the legal rate of interest has been reduced to five per cent.[32] every hundred pounds stock is supposed to be taxed at twenty shillings only. The sum to be raised, by what is called the land-tax, was divided between the country and the principal towns. The greater part of it was laid upon the country; and of what was laid upon the towns, the greater part was assessed upon the houses. What remained to be assessed upon the stock or trade of the towns (for the stock upon the land was not meant to be taxed) was very much below the real value of that stock or trade. Whatever inequalities, therefore, there might be in the original assessment, gave little disturbance. Every parish and district still continues to be rated for its land, its houses, and its stock, according to the original assessment; and the almost universal prosperity of the country, which in most places has raised very much the value of all these, has rendered those inequalities of still less importance now. The rate too upon each district continuing always the same, the uncertainty of this tax, so far as it might be assessed upon the stock of any individual, has been very much diminished, as well as rendered of much less consequence. If the greater part of the lands of England are not rated to the land-tax at half their actual value, the greater part of the stock of England is, perhaps, scarce rated at the fiftieth part of its actual value. In some towns the whole land-tax is assessed upon houses; as in Westminster, where stock and trade are free. It is otherwise in London.

Inquisition is avoided. In all countries a severe inquisition into the circumstances of private persons has been carefully avoided.

At Hamburgh[33] every inhabitant is obliged to pay to the state, one-fourth per cent. of all that he possesses; and as the wealth of the people of Hamburgh consists principally in

---

[32] [Above, p. 124.]

[33] *Memoires concernant les Droits*, tome i. p. 74.

At Hamburg each inhabitant privately assesses himself on oath.

stock, this tax may be considered as a tax upon stock. Every man assesses himself, and, in the presence of the magistrate, puts annually into the public coffer a certain sum of money, which he declares upon oath to be one-fourth per cent. of all that he possesses, but without declaring what it amounts to, or being liable to any examination upon that subject.[34] This tax is generally supposed to be paid with great fidelity. In a small republic, where the people have entire confidence in their magistrates, are convinced of the necessity of the tax for the support of the state, and believe that it will be faithfully applied to that purpose, such conscientious and voluntary payment may sometimes be expected. It is not peculiar to the people of Hamburgh.

The canton of Underwald[35] in Switzerland is frequently ravaged by storms and inundations, and[36] is thereby exposed to extraordinary expences. Upon such occasions

In some Swiss cantons each man assesses himself publicly,

the people assemble, and every one is said to declare with the greatest frankness what he is worth, in order to be taxed accordingly. At Zurich the law orders, that, in cases of necessity, every one should be taxed in proportion to his revenue; the amount of which, he is obliged to declare upon oath. They have no suspicion, it is said, that any of their fellow-citizens will deceive them. At Basil the principal revenue of the state arises from a small custom upon goods exported. All the citizens make oath that they will pay every three months all the taxes imposed by the law. All merchants and even all inn-

[34] [The *Mémoires* only say "La taille consiste dans le quart pour cent que tout habitant, sans exception, est obligé de payer de tout ce qu'il possède en meubles et immeubles. Il ne se fait aucune répartition de cette taille. Chaque bourgeois se cottise lui-même et porte son imposition à la maison de ville, et on n'exige autre chose de lui, sinon le serment qu'il est obligé de faire que ce qu'il paye forme véritablement ce qu'il doit acquitter." But Lord Kames, *Sketches of the History of Man*, vol. i., p. 476, says, "Every merchant puts privately into the public chest, the sum that, in his own opinion, he ought to contribute."]

[35] [Ed. 1 reads "Underwold."]

[36] [Ed. 5 adds "it" here, doubtless a misprint.]

keepers are trusted with keeping themselves the account of the goods which they sell either within or without the territory. At the end of every three months they send this account to the treasurer, with the amount of the tax computed at the bottom of it. It is not suspected that the revenue suffers by this confidence.[37]

To oblige every citizen to declare publicly upon oath the amount of his fortune, must not, it seems, in those Swiss can-

which would be a hardship at Hamburg.

tons, be reckoned a hardship. At Hamburgh it would be reckoned the greatest. Merchants engaged in the hazardous projects of trade, all tremble at the thoughts of being obliged at all times to expose the real state of their circumstances. The ruin of their credit and the miscarriage of their projects, they foresee, would too often be the consequence. A sober and parsimonious people, who are strangers to all such projects, do not feel that they have occasion for any such concealment.

In Holland, soon after the exaltation of the late prince of Orange to the stadtholdership, a tax of two per cent. or the fifti-

Holland once adopted the Hamburg practice.

eth penny, as it was called, was imposed upon the whole substance of every citizen. Every citizen assessed himself and paid his tax in the same manner as at Hamburgh; and it was in general supposed to have been paid with great fidelity. The people had at that time the greatest affection for their new government, which they had just established by a general insurrection. The tax was to be paid but once; in order to relieve the state in a particular exigency. It was, indeed, too heavy to be permanent. In a country where the market rate of interest seldom exceeds three per cent., a tax of two per cent. amounts to thirteen shillings and four-pence in the pound upon the highest neat revenue which is commonly drawn from stock. It is a tax which very few people could pay without encroaching more or less upon their capitals. In a particular exigency the people may, from great public zeal, make a great effort, and

[37] *Memoires concernant les Droits*, tome i. p. 163, 166, 171. [The statements as to the confidence felt in these self-assessments are not taken from the *Mémoires*.]

give up even a part of their capital, in order to relieve the state. But it is impossible that they should continue to do so for any considerable time; and if they did, the tax would soon ruin them so completely as to render them altogether incapable of supporting the state.

The tax upon stock imposed by the land-tax bill in England, though it is proportioned to the capital, is not intended to di-

On that occasion the tax was meant to be a tax on the capital.

minish or take away any part of that capital. It is meant only to be a tax upon the interest of money proportioned to that upon the rent of land; so that when the latter is at four shillings in the pound, the former may be at four shillings in the pound too. The tax at Hamburgh, and the still more moderate taxes of Underwald and Zurich, are meant, in the same manner, to be taxes, not upon the capital, but upon the interest or neat revenue of stock. That of Holland was meant to be a tax upon the capital.

Taxes upon the Profit of particular Employments

In some countries extraordinary taxes are imposed upon the profits of stock; sometimes when employed in particular

Taxes are sometimes imposed on particular profits,

branches of trade, and sometimes when employed in agriculture.

Of the former kind are in England the tax upon hawkers and pedlars, that upon hack-

such as those on hawkers, pedlars, etc.

ney coaches and chairs, and that which the keepers of ale-houses pay for a licence to retail ale and spirituous liquors. During the late war, another tax of the same kind was proposed upon shops.[38] The war having been undertaken, it was said, in defence of the trade of the country, the merchants, who were to profit by it, ought to contribute towards the support of it.

A tax, however, upon the profits of stock employed in any

[38] [Proposed by Legge in 1759. See Dowell, *History of Taxation and Taxes in England*, 1884, vol. ii., p. 137.]

These fall not on the dealers but on the consumers of the goods, particular branch of trade, can never fall finally upon the dealers (who must in all ordinary cases have their reasonable profit, and, where the competition is free, can seldom have more than that profit), but always upon the consumers, who must be obliged to pay in the price of the goods the tax which the dealer advances; and generally with some overcharge.

A tax of this kind when it is proportioned to the trade of the dealer, is finally paid by the consumer, and occasions no oppression to the dealer. When it is not so proportioned, but is the same upon all dealers, though in this case too it is finally paid by the consumer, yet it favours the great, and occasions some oppression to the small dealer. The tax of five shillings a week upon every hackney coach, and that of ten shillings a year upon every hackney chair, so far as it is advanced by the different keepers of such coaches and chairs, is exactly enough proportioned to the extent of their respective dealings. It neither favours the great, nor oppresses the smaller dealer. The tax of twenty shillings a year for a licence to sell ale; of forty shillings for a licence to sell spirituous liquors; and of forty shillings more for a licence to sell wine, being the same upon all retailers, must necessarily give some advantage to the great, and occasion some oppression to the small dealers. The former must find it more easy to get back the tax in the price of their goods than the latter. The moderation of the tax, however, renders this inequality of less importance, and it may to many people appear not improper to give some discouragement to the multiplication of little ale-houses. The tax upon shops, it was intended, should be the same upon all shops. It could not well have been otherwise. It would have been impossible to proportion with tolerable exactness the tax upon a shop to the extent of the trade carried on in it, without such an inquisition as would have been altogether insupportable in a free country. If the tax had been considerable, it would have oppressed the small, and forced almost the whole retail trade into

but when not proportioned to the trade of the dealer they oppress the small and favour the great dealer.

the hands of the great dealers. The competition of the former being taken away, the latter would have enjoyed a monopoly of the trade; and like all other monopolists would soon have combined to raise their profits much beyond what was necessary for the payment of the tax. The final payment, instead of falling upon the shopkeeper, would have fallen upon the consumer, with a considerable over-charge to the profit of the shopkeeper. For these reasons, the project of a tax upon shops was laid aside, and in the room of it was substituted the subsidy 1759.

The personal taille in France on the profits of agriculture is arbitrary and uncertain.

What in France is called the personal taille is, perhaps, the most important tax upon the profits of stock employed in agriculture that is levied in any part of Europe.

In the disorderly state of Europe during the prevalence of the feudal government, the sovereign was obliged to content himself with taxing those who were too weak to refuse to pay taxes. The great lords, though willing to assist him upon particular emergencies, refused to subject themselves to any constant tax, and he was not strong enough to force them. The occupiers of land all over Europe were, the greater part of them, originally bond-men. Through the greater part of Europe they were gradually emancipated. Some of them acquired the property of landed estates which they held by some base or ignoble tenure, sometimes under the king, and sometimes under some other great lord, like the ancient copyholders of England. Others, without acquiring the property, obtained leases for terms of years, of the lands which they occupied under their lord, and thus became less dependent upon him. The great lords seem to have beheld the degree of prosperity and independency which this inferior order of men had thus come to enjoy, with a[39] malignant and contemptuous indignation, and willingly consented that the sovereign should tax them.[40] In some countries this tax was confined to the lands which were held in property by an ignoble tenure; and, in this

[39] [Ed. 1 does not contain "a."]

[40] [Above, pp. 500–501.]

case, the taille was said to be real. The land-tax established by the late king of Sardinia, and the taille in the provinces of Languedoc, Provence, Dauphiné, and Brittany; in the generality of Montauban, and in the elections of Agen and Condom, as well as in some other districts of France, are taxes upon lands held in property by an ignoble tenure.[41] In other countries the tax was laid upon the supposed profits of all those who held in farm or lease lands belonging to other people, whatever might be the tenure by which the proprietor held them; and in this case the taille was said to be personal. In the greater part of those provinces of France, which are called the Countries of Elections, the taille is of this kind. The real taille, as it is imposed only upon a part of the lands of the country, is necessarily an unequal, but it is not always an arbitrary tax, though it is so upon some occasions. The personal taille, as it is intended to be proportioned to the profits of a certain class of people, which can only be guessed at, is necessarily both arbitrary and unequal.

In France the personal taille at present (1775) annually imposed upon the twenty generalities, called the Countries of Elections, amounts to 40,107,239 livres, 16 sous.[42] The proportion in which this sum is assessed upon those different provinces, varies from year to year, according to the reports which are made to the king's council concerning the goodness or badness of the crops, as well as other circumstances, which may either increase or diminish their respective abilities to pay. Each generality is divided into a certain number of elections, and the proportion in which the sum imposed upon the whole generality is divided among those different elections, varies likewise from year to year, according to the reports made to the council concerning their respective abilities. It seems impossible that the council, with the best inten-

The authority which assesses it is always ignorant of the real abilities of the contributors and often misled by friendship, party animosity and private resentment.

[41] [Above, p. 1056.]

[42] *Memoires concernant les Droits, &c.* tome ii. p. 17.

tions, can ever proportion with tolerable exactness, either of those two assessments to the real abilities of the province or district upon which they are respectively laid. Ignorance and misinformation must always, more or less, mislead the most upright council. The proportion which each parish ought to support of what is assessed upon the whole election, and that which each individual ought to support of what is assessed upon his particular parish, are both in the same manner varied, from year to year, according as circumstances are supposed to require. These circumstances are judged of, in the one case, by the officers of the election; in the other by those of the parish; and both the one and the other are, more or less, under the direction and influence of the intendant. Not only ignorance and misinformation, but friendship, party animosity, and private resentment, are said frequently to mislead such assessors. No man subject to such a tax, it is evident, can ever be certain, before he is assessed, of what he is to pay. He cannot even be certain after he is assessed. If any person has been taxed who ought to have been exempted; or if any person has been taxed beyond his proportion, though both must pay in the mean time, yet if they complain, and make good their complaints, the whole parish is reimposed next year in order to reimburse them. If any of the contributors become bankrupt or insolvent, the collector is obliged to advance his tax, and the whole parish is reimposed next year in order to reimburse the collector. If the collector himself should become bankrupt, the parish which elects him must answer for his conduct to the receiver-general of the election. But, as it might be troublesome for the receiver to prosecute the whole parish, he takes at his choice five or six of the richest contributors, and obliges them to make good what had been lost by the insolvency of the collector. The parish is afterwards reimposed in order to reimburse those five or six. Such reimpositions are always over and above the taille of the particular year in which they are laid on.

When a tax is imposed upon the profits of stock in a particular branch of trade, the traders are all careful to bring no more goods to market than what they can sell at a price sufficient to reimburse them for advancing the tax. Some of them withdraw

Taxes on the profits of agriculture do not, like those on profits of other trades, fall on the consumer, but on the landlord.

a part of their stocks from the trade, and the market is more sparingly supplied than before. The price of the goods rises, and the final payment of the tax falls upon the consumer. But when a tax is imposed upon the profits of stock employed in agriculture, it is not the interest of the farmers to withdraw any part of their stock from that employment. Each farmer occupies a certain quantity of land, for which he pays rent. For the proper cultivation of this land a certain quantity of stock is necessary; and by withdrawing any part of this necessary quantity, the farmer is not likely to be more able to pay either the rent or the tax. In order to pay the tax, it can never be his interest to diminish the quantity of his produce, nor consequently to supply the market more sparingly than before. The tax, therefore, will never enable him to raise the price of his produce, so as to[43] reimburse himself by throwing the final payment upon the consumer. The farmer, however, must have his reasonable profit as well as every other dealer, otherwise he must give up the trade. After the imposition of a tax of this kind, he can get this reasonable profit only by paying less rent to the landlord. The more he is obliged to pay in the way of tax, the less he can afford to pay in the way of rent. A tax of this kind imposed during the currency of a lease may, no doubt, distress or ruin the farmer. Upon the renewal of the lease it must always fall upon the landlord.

In the countries where the personal taille takes place, the farmer is commonly assessed in proportion to the stock which

The discouragement to good cultivation caused by the personal taille injures the public, the farmer and the landlord.

he appears to employ in cultivation. He is, upon this account, frequently afraid to have a good team of horses or oxen, but endeavours to cultivate with the meanest and most wretched instruments of husbandry that he can. Such is his distrust in the justice of his assessors, that he counterfeits poverty, and wishes to appear scarce able to pay any thing

[43] [Ed. 1 reads "nor to."]

for fear of being obliged to pay too much. By this miserable policy he does not, perhaps, always consult his own interest in the most effectual manner; and he probably loses more by the diminution of his produce than he saves by that of his tax. Though, in consequence of this wretched cultivation the market is, no doubt, somewhat worse supplied; yet the small rise of price which this may occasion, as it is not likely even to indemnify the farmer for the diminution of his produce, it is still less likely to enable him to pay more rent to the landlord. The public, the farmer, the landlord, all suffer more or less by this degraded cultivation. That the personal taille tends, in many different ways, to discourage cultivation, and consequently to dry up the principal source of the wealth of every good country, I have already had occasion to observe in the third book of this Inquiry.[44]

What are called poll-taxes in the southern provinces of North America, and in the West Indian[45] islands, annual taxes

Per capita taxes on negro slaves fall on the landlords.

of so much a head upon every negroe, are properly taxes upon the profits of a certain species of stock employed in agriculture. As the planters are, the greater part of them, both farmers and landlords, the final payment of the tax falls upon them in their quality of landlords without any retribution.

Taxes of so much a head upon the bondmen employed in cultivation, seem anciently to have been common all over

Poll taxes have been represented as badges of slavery, but, to the taxpayer every tax is a badge of liberty.

Europe. There subsists at present a tax of this kind in the empire of Russia. It is probably upon this account that poll-taxes of all kinds have often been represented as badges of slavery.[46] Every tax, however, is to the person who pays it a badge, not of slavery, but of liberty. It denotes that he is subject to government, indeed, but that, as he has some property, he cannot

---

[44] [Above, pp. 500–501.]

[45] [Ed. 1 reads "West India."]

[46] [*E.g.*, by Montesquieu, *Esprit des lois*, liv. xiii., chap. xiv.]

himself be the property of a master. A poll-tax upon slaves is altogether different from a poll-tax upon freemen. The latter is paid by the persons upon whom it is imposed; the former by a different set of persons. The latter is either altogether arbitrary or altogether unequal, and in most cases is both the one and the other; the former, though in some respects unequal, different slaves being of different values, is in no respect arbitrary. Every master who knows the number of his own slaves, knows exactly what he has to pay. Those different taxes, however, being called by the same name, have been considered as of the same nature.

The taxes which in Holland are imposed upon men and maid servants, are taxes, not upon stock, but upon expence;

Taxes on menial servants are like taxes on consumable commodities.

and so far resemble the taxes upon consumable commodities. The tax of a guinea a head for every man servant, which has lately been imposed in Great Britain,[47] is of the same kind. It falls heaviest upon the middling rank. A man of two hundred a year may keep a single man servant. A man of ten thousand a year will not keep fifty. It does not affect the poor.[48]

Taxes upon the profits of stock in particular employments can never affect the interest of money. Nobody will lend his

Taxes on particular profits cannot affect interest.

money for less interest to those who exercise the taxed, than to those who exercise the untaxed employments. Taxes upon the revenue arising from stock in all employments, where the government attempts to levy them with any degree of exactness, will, in many cases, fall upon the interest of money. The Vingtieme, or twentieth penny, in France, is a tax of the same kind with what is called the land-tax in England, and is assessed, in the same manner, upon the revenue arising from land, houses, and stock. So far as it affects stock it is assessed, though not with great rigour, yet with much more exactness than that part of the land-tax of England which is

[47] [17 Geo. III., c. 39.]

[48] [This paragraph is not in ed. 1.]

imposed upon the same fund. It, in many cases, falls altogether upon the interest of money. Money is frequently sunk in France upon what are called Contracts for the constitution of a rent; that is, perpetual annuities redeemable at any time by the debtor upon repayment of the sum originally advanced, but of which this redemption is not exigible by the creditor except in particular cases. The Vingtieme seems not to have raised the rate of those annuities, though it is exactly levied upon them all.

APPENDIX TO ARTICLES I AND II

Taxes upon the Capital Value of Land, Houses, and Stock

While property remains in the possession of the same person, whatever permanent taxes may have been imposed upon it,

Taxes on the transmission of property often necessarily take a part of the capital value.

they have never been intended to diminish or take away any part of its capital value, but only some part of the revenue arising from it. But when property changes hands, when it is transmitted either from the dead to the living, or from the living to the living, such taxes have frequently been imposed upon it as necessarily take away some part of its capital value.

The transference of all sorts of property from the dead to the living, and that of immoveable property, of lands and

Transfers from the dead to the living and all transfers of immovable property can be taxed directly; transfers by way of loan of money have been taxed by stamp duties or duties on registration.

houses, from the living to the living, are transactions which are in their nature either public and notorious, or such as cannot be long concealed. Such transactions, therefore, may be taxed directly. The transference of stock or moveable property, from the living to the living, by the lending of money, is frequently a secret transaction, and may always be made so. It cannot easily, therefore, be taxed directly. It has been taxed indirectly in two different ways; first, by requiring that the deed, containing the obligation to repay, should be written upon paper or parchment which had paid a certain stamp-duty, otherwise not to be valid; secondly, by requiring, under the like penalty of invalidity, that it should be recorded either in a public or secret register, and by imposing certain duties upon such registration. Stamp-duties and duties of registration have frequently been imposed likewise upon the deeds transferring property of all kinds from the dead to the living, and upon those transferring immoveable property from the living to the living, transactions which might easily have been taxed directly.

The Vicesima Hereditatum, the twentieth penny of inheritances, imposed by Augustus upon the ancient Romans, was a

Transfers from the dead to the living were taxed by the Vicesima Hereditatum,

tax upon the transference of property from the dead to the living. Dion Cassius,[49] the author who writes concerning it the least indistinctly, says, that it was imposed upon all successions, legacies, and donations, in case of death, except upon those to the nearest relations, and to the poor.

Of the same kind is the Dutch tax upon successions.[50] Collateral successions are taxed, according to the degree of re-

and the Dutch tax on successions.

lation, from five to thirty per cent. upon the whole value of the succession. Testamentary donations, or legacies to collaterals, are subject to the like duties. Those from husband to wife, or from wife to husband, to the fifteenth[51] penny. The Luctuosa Hereditas, the mournful succession of ascendents to descendents, to the twentieth penny only. Direct successions, or those of descendents to ascendents, pay no tax. The death of a father, to such of his children as live in the same house with him, is

---

[49] Lib. 55 [(25) quoted by Burman and Bouchaud]. See also Burman de Vectigalibus Pop. Rom. cap. xi. [in *Utriusque thesauri antiquitatum romanarum graecarumque nova supplementa congesta ab* Joanne Poleno, Venice, 1737, vol. i., p. 1032B] and Bouchaud de l'impôt du vingtieme sur les successions [*et de l'impôt sur les marchandises chez les Romains*; nouv. ed., 1772, pp. 10 *sqq.*]

[50] See *Memoires concernant les Droits, &c.* tome i. p. 225.

[51] [All eds. read "fiftieth," but the *Mémoires* say "quinzième" and the "only" in the next sentence shows that Smith intended to write "fifteenth."]

seldom attended with any increase, and frequently with a considerable diminution of revenue; by the loss of his industry, or his office, or of some life-rent estate, of which he may have been in possession. That tax would be cruel and oppressive which aggravated their loss by taking from them any part of his succession. It may, however, sometimes be otherwise with those children who, in the language of the Roman law, are said to be emancipated; in that of the Scotch law, to be forisfamiliated; that is, who have received their portion, have got families of their own, and are supported by funds separate and independent of those of their father. Whatever part of his succession might come to such children, would be a real addition to their fortune, and might therefore, perhaps, without more inconveniency than what attends all duties of this kind, be liable to some tax.

The casualties of the feudal law were taxes upon the trans-

The feudal law taxed the transference of land,

ference of land, both from the dead to the living, and from the living to the living. In ancient times they constituted in every part of Europe one of the principal branches of the revenue of the crown.

The heir of every immediate vassal of the crown paid a certain duty, generally a year's rent, upon receiving the investiture

by wardships and reliefs,

of the estate. If the heir was a minor, the whole rents of the estate, during the continuance of the minority, devolved to the superior without any other charge, besides the maintenance of the minor, and the payment of the widow's dower, when there happened to be a dowager upon the land. When the minor came to be of age, another tax, called Relief, was still due to the superior, which generally amounted likewise to a year's rent. A long minority, which in the present times so frequently disburdens a great estate of all its incumbrances, and restores the family to their ancient splendour, could in those times have no such effect. The waste, and not the disincumbrance of the estate, was the common effect of a long minority.

By the feudal law the vassal could not alienate without the consent of his superior, who generally extorted a fine or com-

and fines on alienation, which last still form a considerable branch of revenue in many countries.

position for granting it. This fine, which was at first arbitrary, came in many countries to be regulated at a certain portion of the price of the land. In some countries, where the greater part of the other feudal customs have gone into disuse, this tax upon the alienation of land still continues to make a very[52] considerable branch of the revenue of the sovereign. In the canton of Berne it is so high as a sixth part of the price of all noble fiefs; and a tenth part of that of all ignoble ones.[53] In the canton of Lucerne the tax upon the sale of lands is not universal, and takes place only in certain districts. But if any person sells his land, in order to remove out of the territory, he pays ten per cent. upon the whole price of the sale.[54] Taxes of the same kind upon the sale either of all lands, or of lands held by certain tenures, take place in many other countries, and make a more or less considerable branch of the revenue of the sovereign.

Such transactions may be taxed indirectly, by means either of stamp-duties, or of duties upon registration; and those du-

These taxes on the sale of land may be levied by stamps or duties on registration.

ties either may or may not be proportioned to the value of the subject which is transferred.

In Great Britain the duties are not proportioned to the value of the property.

In Great Britain the stamp-duties are higher or lower, not so much according to the value of the property transferred (an eighteen penny or half crown stamp being sufficient upon a bond for the largest sum of money) as according to the nature of the deed. The highest do not exceed six pounds upon every sheet of paper, or skin of parchment; and these high duties fall chiefly upon grants from the crown, and upon certain law proceedings, without any regard to the value of the subject. There are in Great Britain no duties on the registration of deeds or writings, except the fees of the

[52] [Ed. 1 does not contain "very."]

[53] *Memoires concernant les Droits, &c.* tome i. p. 154.

[54] Id. p. 157.

officers who keep the register; and these are seldom more than a reasonable recompence for their labour. The crown derives no revenue from them.

In Holland[55] there are both stamp-duties and duties upon registration; which in some cases are, and in some are not pro-

In Holland some are proportioned and others not.

portioned to the value of the property transferred. All testaments must be written upon stamped paper of which the price is proportioned to the property disposed of, so that there are stamps which cost from three pence, or three stivers a sheet, to three hundred florins, equal to about twenty-seven pounds ten shillings of our money. If the stamp is of an inferior price to what the testator ought to have made use of, his succession is confiscated. This is over and above all their other taxes on succession. Except bills of exchange, and some other mercantile bills, all other deeds, bonds, and contracts, are subject to a stamp-duty. This duty, however, does not rise in proportion to the value of the subject. All sales of land and of houses, and all mortgages upon either, must be registered, and, upon registration, pay a duty to the state of two and a half per cent. upon the amount of the price or of the mortgage.[56] This duty is extended to the sale of all ships and vessels of more than two tons burthen, whether decked or undecked. These, it seems, are considered as a sort of houses upon the water. The sale of moveables, when it is ordered by a court of justice, is subject to the like duty of two and a half per cent.

In France there are both stamp-duties and duties upon registration. The former are considered as a branch of the aides or

In France different sets of officers collect the stamp duties and the registration duties.

excise, and in the provinces where those duties take place, are levied by the excise officers. The latter are considered as a branch of the domain of the crown, and are levied by a different set of officers.

Those modes of taxation, by stamp-duties and by duties upon registration, are of very modern invention.

---

[55] *Memoires concernant les Droits, &c.* tome i. p. 223, 224, 225.

[56] [Ed. 1 reads "or the mortgage."]

Both stamps and registration duties are modern methods of taxation.

In the course of little more than a century, however, stamp-duties have, in Europe, become almost universal, and duties upon registration extremely common. There is no art which one government sooner learns of another, than that of draining money from the pockets of the people.

Taxes upon the transference of property from the dead to the living, fall finally as well as immediately upon the person

Taxes on transfers from the dead to the living fall on the person who acquires the property; taxes on sales of land fall on the seller;

to whom the property is transferred. Taxes upon the sale of land fall altogether upon the seller. The seller is almost always under the necessity of selling, and must, therefore, take such a price as he can get. The buyer is scarce ever under the necessity of buying, and will, therefore, only give[57] such a price as he likes. He considers what the land will cost him in tax and price together. The more

he is obliged to pay in the way of tax, the less he will be disposed to give in the way of price. Such taxes, therefore, fall almost always upon a necessitous person, and

taxes on the sale of new buildings fall on the buyer;

must, therefore, be frequently very cruel and oppressive. Taxes upon the sale of new-built houses, where the building is sold without the ground, fall generally upon the buyer, because the builder

must generally have his profit; otherwise he must give up the trade. If he advances the tax, therefore, the

taxes on the sale of old houses fall on the seller;

buyer must generally repay it to him. Taxes upon the sale of old houses, for the same reason as those upon the sale of land, fall

generally upon the seller; whom in most cases either conveniency or necessity obliges to sell. The number of new-built houses that are annually brought to market, is more or less regulated by the demand. Unless the demand is such as to afford the builder his profit, after paying all expences, he will build no more houses. The number of old houses which happen at

[57] [Ed. 1 reads "give only."]

taxes on the sale of ground rents fall on the seller;

taxes on loans fall on the borrower;

taxes on law proceedings fall on the suitors.

any time to come to market is regulated by accidents of which the greater part have no relation to the demand. Two or three great bankruptcies in a mercantile town, will bring many houses to sale, which must be sold for what can be got for them. Taxes upon the sale of ground rents fall altogether upon the seller; for the same reason as those upon the sale of land. Stamp-duties, and duties upon the registration of bonds and contracts for borrowed money, fall altogether upon the borrower, and, in fact, are always paid by him. Duties of the same kind upon law proceedings fall upon the suitors. They reduce to both the capital value of the subject in dispute. The more it costs to acquire any property, the less must be the neat[58] value of it when acquired.

All taxes on transfers, so far as they diminish the capital value, are unthrifty.

All taxes upon the transference of property of every kind, so far as they diminish the capital value of that property, tend to diminish the funds destined for the maintenance of productive labour. They are all more or less unthrifty taxes that increase the revenue of the sovereign, which seldom maintains any but unproductive labourers; at the expence of the capital of the people, which maintains none but productive.

Even when proportioned to the value of the property they are unequal, because the frequency of transfer varies. They are certain, convenient and inexpensive.

Such taxes, even when they are proportioned to the value of the property transferred, are still unequal; the frequency of transference not being always equal in property of equal value. When they are not proportioned to this value, which is the case with the greater part of the stamp-duties, and duties of registration, they are still more so. They are in no respect arbitrary, but are or may be in all cases perfectly clear and certain. Though they sometimes fall upon the person who is not very able to

---

[58] [Ed. 1 does not contain "neat."]

pay; the time of payment is in most cases sufficiently convenient for him. When the payment becomes due, he must in most cases have the money to pay. They are levied at very little expence, and in general subject the contributors to no other inconveniency besides always the unavoidable one of paying the tax.

In France the stamp-duties are not much complained of. Those of registration, which they call the Contrôle, are. They give occasion, it is pretended, to much extortion in the officers of the farmers-general who collect the tax, which is in a great measure arbitrary and uncertain. In the greater part of the libels[59] which have been written against the present system of finances in France, the abuses of the Contrôle make a principal article. Uncertainty, however, does not seem to be necessarily inherent in the nature of such taxes. If the popular complaints are well founded, the abuse must arise, not so much from the nature of the tax, as from the want of precision and distinctness in the words of the edicts or laws which impose it.

French stamp-duties on transfers are not much complained of, but the registration duties (or Contrôle) are said to be arbitrary and uncertain.

The registration of mortgages, and in general of all rights upon immoveable property, as it gives great security both to creditors and purchasers, is extremely advantageous to the public. That of the greater part of deeds of other kinds is frequently inconvenient and even dangerous to individuals, without any advantage to the public. All registers which, it is acknowledged, ought to be kept secret, ought certainly never to exist. The credit of individuals ought certainly never to depend upon so very slender a security as the probity and religion of the inferior officers of revenue. But where the fees of registration have been made a source of revenue to the sovereign, register offices have com-

Public registration of mortgages and all rights to immovable property is advantageous, but secret registers ought not to exist.

---

[59] [The word is used in its older sense, equivalent to the modern "pamphlets." See Murray, *Oxford English Dictionary, s.v.*]

monly been multiplied without end, both for the deeds which ought to be registered, and for those which ought not. In France there are several different sorts of secret registers. This abuse, though not perhaps a necessary, it must be acknowledged, is a very natural effect of such taxes.

Such stamp-duties as those in England upon cards and dice, upon news-papers and periodical pamphlets, &c. are properly

Many stamp-duties are duties on consumption.

taxes upon consumption; the final payment falls upon the persons who use or consume such commodities. Such stamp-duties as those upon licences to retail ale, wine, and spirituous liquors, though intended, perhaps, to fall upon the profits of the retailers, are likewise finally paid by the consumers of those liquors. Such taxes, though called by the same name, and levied by the same officers and in the same manner with the stamp-duties above mentioned upon the transference of property, are however of a quite different nature, and fall upon quite different funds.

ARTICLE III

Taxes upon the Wages of Labour

The wages of the inferior classes of workmen, I have endeavoured to show in the first book, are every where necessarily

A tax on wages must raise wages by rather more than the amount of the tax.

regulated by two different circumstances; the demand for labour, and the ordinary or average price of provisions. The demand for labour, according as it happens to be either increasing, stationary, or declining; or to require an increasing, stationary, or declining population, regulates the subsistence of the labourer, and determines in what degree it shall be, either liberal, moderate, or scanty. The ordinary or average price of provisions determines the quantity of money which must be paid to the workman in order to enable him, one year with another, to purchase this liberal, moderate, or scanty subsistence. While the demand for labour and the price of provisions, therefore, remain the same, a direct tax upon the wages of labour can have no other effect than to raise them somewhat higher than the tax. Let us suppose, for example, that in a particular place the demand for labour and the price of provisions were such, as to render ten shillings a week the ordinary wages of labour; and that a tax of one-fifth, or four shillings in the pound, was imposed upon wages. If the demand for labour and the price of provisions remained the same, it would still be necessary that the labourer should in that place earn such a subsistence as could be bought only for ten shillings a week, or that after paying the tax he should have ten shillings a week free wages. But in order to leave him such free wages after paying such a tax, the price of labour must in that place soon rise, not to twelve shillings a week only, but to twelve and sixpence; that is, in order to enable him to pay a tax of one-fifth, his wages must necessarily soon rise, not one-fifth part only, but one-fourth. Whatever was the proportion of the tax, the wages of labour must in all cases rise, not only in that proportion, but in a higher proportion. If the tax, for example, was one-tenth, the wages of labour must necessarily soon rise, not one-tenth part only, but one-eighth.

A direct tax upon the wages of labour, therefore, though the labourer might perhaps pay it out of his hand, could not properly be said to be even advanced by him; at least if the demand for labour and the average price of provisions remained the same after the tax as before it. In all such cases, not only the tax, but something more than the tax, would in reality be advanced by the person who immediately employed him. The final payment would in different cases fall upon different persons. The rise which such a tax might occasion in the wages of manufacturing labour would be advanced by the master manufacturer, who would both be entitled and obliged to charge it, with a profit, upon the price of his goods. The final payment of this rise of wages, therefore, together with the additional profit of the master manufacturer, would fall upon the consumer. The rise

The rise in the wages of manufacturing labour would be advanced by the employers and paid by the consumers, and the rise in agricultural wages advanced by the farmers and paid by the landlords.

which such a tax might occasion in the wages of country labour would be advanced by the farmer, who, in order to maintain the same number of labourers as before, would be obliged to employ a greater capital. In order to get back this greater capital, together with the ordinary profits of stock, it would be necessary that he should retain a larger portion, or what comes to the same thing, the price of a larger portion, of the produce of the land, and consequently that he should pay less rent to the landlord. The final payment of this rise of wages, therefore, would in this case fall upon the landlord, together with the additional profit of the farmer who had advanced it. In all cases a direct tax upon the wages of labour must, in the long-run, occasion both a greater reduction in the rent of land, and a greater rise in the price of manufactured goods, than would have followed from the proper assessment of a sum equal to the produce of the tax, partly upon the rent of land, and partly upon consumable commodities.

If direct taxes upon the wages of labour have not always occasioned a proportionable rise in those wages, it is because

The effect of the tax in raising wages is generally disguised by the fall in the demand for labour which it occasions.

they have generally occasioned a considerable fall in the demand for labour. The declension of industry, the decrease of employment for the poor, the diminution of the annual produce of the land and labour of the country, have generally been the effects of such taxes. In consequence of them, however, the price of labour must always be higher than it otherwise would have been in the actual state of the demand: and this enhancement of price, together with the

A tax on agricultural wages raises prices no more than one on farmers' profits.

profit of those who advance it, must always be finally paid by the landlords and consumers.

A tax upon the wages of country labour does not raise the price of the rude produce of land in proportion to the tax;[60] for the

---

[60] [Ed. 1 does not contain "in proportion to the tax."]

same reason that a tax upon the farmer's profit does not raise that price in that proportion.[61]

Absurd and destructive as such taxes are, however, they take place in many countries. In France that part of the taille

Many countries have such taxes, e.g., France and Bohemia.

which is charged upon the industry of workmen and day-labourers in country villages, is properly a tax of this kind. Their wages are computed according to the common rate of the district in which they reside, and that they may be as little liable as possible to any overcharge, their yearly gains are estimated at no more than two hundred working days in the year.[62] The tax of each individual is varied from year to year according to different circumstances, of which the collector or the commissary, whom the intendant appoints to assist him, are the judges. In Bohemia, in consequence of the alteration in the system of finances which was begun in 1748, a very heavy tax is imposed upon the industry of artificers. They are divided into four classes. The highest class pay a hundred florins a year; which, at two-and-twenty-pence halfpenny a florin, amounts to 9l. 7s. 6d. The second class are taxed at seventy; the third at fifty; and the fourth, comprehending artificers in villages, and the lowest class of those in towns, at twenty-five florins.[63]

The recompence of ingenious artists and of men of liberal professions, I have endeavoured to show in

A tax on the recompense of the liberal professions, etc., would also raise that recompense, but a tax on government offices would not raise salaries.

the first book,[64] necessarily keeps a certain proportion to the emoluments of inferior trades. A tax upon this recompence, therefore, could have no other effect than to raise it somewhat higher than in proportion to the tax. If it did not rise in this manner, the ingenious arts and the liberal professions, being no longer upon a level with other

[61] [Ed. 1 does not contain "in that proportion."]

[62] *Memoires concernant les Droits, &c.* tom. ii. p. 108.

[63] Ibid. tom. iii. [really i.] p. 87.

[64] [Above, pp. 139–153.]

trades, would be so much deserted that they would soon return to that level.

The emoluments of officers are not, like those of trades and professions, regulated by the free competition of the market, and do not, therefore, always bear a just proportion to what the nature of the employment requires. They are, perhaps, in most countries, higher than it requires; the persons who have the administration of government being generally disposed to reward both themselves and their immediate dependents rather more than enough. The emoluments of officers, therefore, can in most cases very well bear to be taxed. The persons, besides, who enjoy public offices, especially the more lucrative, are in all countries the objects of general envy; and a tax upon their emoluments, even though it should be somewhat higher than upon any other sort of revenue, is always a very popular tax. In England, for example, when by the land-tax every other sort of revenue was supposed to be[65] assessed at four shillings in the pound, it was very popular to lay a real tax of five shillings and sixpence in the pound upon the salaries of offices which exceeded a hundred pounds a year; the pensions of the younger branches of the royal family, the pay of the officers of the army and navy, and a few others less obnoxious to envy excepted.[66] There are in England no other direct taxes upon the wages of labour.

[65] ["Was supposed to be" is equivalent to "was nominally but not really."]

[66] [Eds. 1 and 2 read "a real tax of five shillings in the pound upon the salaries of offices which exceeded a hundred pounds a year; those of the judges and a few others less obnoxious to envy excepted." Under 31 Geo. II., c. 22, a tax of 1s. in the pound was imposed on all offices worth more than £100 a year, naval and military offices excepted. The judges were not excepted, but their salaries were raised soon afterwards. See Dowell, *History of Taxation and Taxes*, vol. ii., pp. 135–136. The 6d. seems a mistake; the 5s. is arrived at by adding the 4s. land tax (which was "real" in the case of offices) and the 1s.]

Article IV

*Taxes which, it is intended, should fall indifferently
upon every different Species of Revenue*

The taxes which, it is intended, should fall indifferently upon every different species of revenue, are capitation taxes, and

These are capitation taxes and taxes on consumable commodities.

taxes upon consumable commodities. These must be paid indifferently from whatever revenue the contributors may possess; from the rent of their land, from the profits of their stock, or from the wages of their labour.

Capitation Taxes

Capitation taxes, if it is attempted to proportion them to the

Capitation taxes ostensibly proportioned to revenue are altogether arbitrary.

fortune or revenue of each contributor, become altogether arbitrary. The state of a man's fortune varies from day to day, and without an inquisition more intolerable than any tax, and renewed at least once every year, can only be guessed at. His assessment,

therefore, must in most cases depend upon the good or bad humour of his assessors, and must, therefore, be altogether arbitrary and uncertain.

If proportioned to rank they are unequal.

Capitation taxes, if they are proportioned not to the supposed fortune, but to the rank of each contributor, become altogether unequal; the degree of fortune being frequently

unequal in the same degree of rank.

In the first case they are always grievous and in the second they are intolerable unless they are light.

Such taxes, therefore, if it is attempted to render them equal, become altogether arbitrary and uncertain; and if it is attempted to render them certain and not arbitrary, become altogether unequal. Let the tax be light or heavy, uncertainty is always a great grievance. In a light tax a considerable degree of inequality may be supported; in a heavy one it is altogether intolerable.

In the different poll-taxes which took place in England during the reign of William III.[67] the contributors were, the greater

In the poll taxes of William III. assessment was chiefly according to rank.

part of them, assessed according to the degree of their rank; as dukes, marquisses, earls, viscounts, barons, esquires, gentlemen, the eldest and youngest sons of peers, &c. All shopkeepers and tradesmen, worth more than three hundred pounds, that is, the better sort of them, were subject to the same assessment; how great soever might be the different in their fortunes.[68] Their rank was more considered than their fortune. Several of those who in the first poll-tax were rated according to their supposed fortune, were afterwards rated according to their rank. Serjeants, attornies, and proctors at law, who in the first poll-tax were assessed at three shillings in the pound of their supposed income, were afterwards assessed as gentlemen.[69] In the assessment of a tax which was not very heavy, a considerable degree of inequality had been found less insupportable than any degree of uncertainty.

In the capitation which has been levied in France without any interruption since the beginning of the present century, the highest orders of people are rated according to their rank, by an invariable tariff; the lower orders of people, according to what is supposed to be their fortune, by an assessment which

---

[67] [The first of these is under 1 W. and M., sess. 1, c. 13.]

[68] [1 W. and M., sess. 2, c. 7, § 2.]

[69] [Under 1 W. and M., c. 13, § 4, serjeants, attorneys and proctors, as well as certain other classes, were to pay 3s. in the pound on their receipts. Under 1 W. and M., sess. 2, c. 7, § 2, attorneys and proctors and others were to pay 20s. in addition to the sums already charged. Under 2 W. and M., sess. 1, c. 2, § 5, serjeants-at-law were to pay £15, apparently in addition to the 3s. in the pound. Under 3 W. and M., c. 6, the poundage charge does not appear at all. The alterations were doubtless made in order to secure certainty, but purely in the interest of the government, which desired to be certain of getting a fixed amount. Under the Land Tax Act of 8 and 9 W. III., c. 6, § 5, serjeants, attorneys, proctors, etc., are again charged to an income tax.]

In France the assessment is by rank in the higher and by supposed fortune in the lower orders of people.

varies from year to year. The officers of the king's court, the judges and other officers in the superior courts of justice, the officers of the troops, &c. are assessed in the first manner. The inferior ranks of people in the provinces are assessed in the second. In France the great easily submit to a considerable degree of inequality in a tax which, so far as it affects them, is not a very heavy one; but could not brook the arbitrary assessment of an intendant. The inferior ranks of people must, in that country, suffer patiently the usage which their superiors think proper to give them.

In England the different poll-taxes never produced the sum which had been expected from them, or which, it was supposed, they might have produced, had they been exactly levied. In France the capitation always produces the sum expected from it. The mild government of England, when it assessed the different ranks of people to the poll-tax, contented itself with what that assessment happened to produce; and required no compensation for the loss which the state might sustain either by those who could not pay, or by those who would not pay (for there were many such), and who, by the indulgent execution of the law, were not forced to pay. The more severe government of France assesses upon each generality a certain sum, which the intendant must find as he can. If any province complains of being assessed too high, it may, in the assessment of next year, obtain an abatement proportioned to the overcharge of the year before. But it must pay in the mean time. The intendant, in order to be sure of finding the sum assessed upon his generality, was impowered to assess it in a larger sum, that the failure or inability of some of the contributors might be compensated by the over-charge of the rest; and till 1765, the fixation of this surplus assessment was left altogether to his discretion. In that year indeed the council assumed this power to itself. In the capitation of the provinces, it is observed by the perfectly well-informed author of the Memoirs upon the impositions in

The French tax is more rigorously exacted than the English taxes were.

France, the proportion[70] which falls upon the nobility, and upon those whose privileges exempt them from the taille, is the least considerable. The largest falls upon those subject to the taille, who are assessed to the capitation at so much a pound of what they pay to that other tax.[71]

Capitation taxes, so far as they are levied upon the lower ranks of people, are direct taxes upon the wages of labour, and are attended with all the inconveniences of such taxes.

Capitation taxes on the lower orders of people are like taxes on wages.

Capitation taxes are levied at little expence; and, where they are rigorously exacted, afford a very sure revenue to the state. It is upon this account that in countries where the ease, comfort, and security of the inferior ranks of people are little attended to, capitation taxes are very common. It is in general, however, but a small part of the public revenue, which, in a great empire, has ever been drawn from such taxes; and the greatest sum which they have ever afforded, might always have been found in some other way much more convenient to the people.

They are inexpensive and afford a sure revenue.

Taxes upon consumable Commodities

The impossibility of taxing the people, in proportion to their revenue, by any capitation, seems to have given occasion to the invention of taxes upon consumable commodities. The state not knowing how to tax, directly and proportionably, the revenue of its subjects, endeavours to tax it indirectly by taxing their expence, which, it is supposed, will in most cases be nearly in proportion to their revenue. Their expence is taxed by taxing the consumable commodities upon which it is laid out.

Consumable commodities are either necessaries or luxuries.

By necessaries I understand, not only the commodities which are indispensably necessary for the support of life, but

[70] [Ed. 1 reads "portion."]

[71] [*Mémoires*, tom. ii., p. 421.]

The impossibility of taxation according to revenue has given rise to taxation according to expenditure on consumable commodities, either necessaries or luxuries, necessaries including all that creditable people of the lowest order cannot decently go without.

whatever the custom of the country renders it indecent for creditable people, even of the lowest order, to be without. A linen shirt, for example, is, strictly speaking, not a necessary of life. The Greeks and Romans lived, I suppose, very comfortably, though they had no linen.[72] But in the present times, through the greater part of Europe, a creditable day-labourer would be ashamed to appear in public without a linen shirt, the want of which would be supposed to denote that disgraceful degree of poverty, which, it is presumed, no body can well fall into without extreme bad conduct. Custom, in the same manner, has rendered leather shoes a necessary of life in England. The poorest creditable person of either sex would be ashamed to appear in public without them. In Scotland, custom has rendered them a necessary of life to the lowest order of men; but not to the same order of women, who may, without any discredit, walk about bare-footed. In France, they are necessaries neither to men nor to women; the lowest rank of both sexes appearing there publicly, without any discredit, sometimes in wooden shoes, and sometimes bare-footed. Under necessaries therefore, I comprehend, not only those things which nature, but those things which the established rules of decency have rendered necessary to the lowest rank of people. All other things I call luxuries; without meaning by this appellation, to throw the smallest degree of reproach upon the temperate use of them. Beer and ale, for example, in Great Britain, and wine, even in the wine countries, I call luxuries.[73] A man of any rank may, without any reproach, abstain totally from tasting such liquors. Nature does

[72] [Dr. John Arbuthnot, in his *Tables of Ancient Coins, Weights and Measures*, 2nd ed., 1754, p. 142, says that linen was not used among the Romans, at least by men, till about the time of Alexander Severus.]

[73] [In *Lectures*, p. 179, and above in ed. 1., p. 432 note, beer seems to be regarded as a necessary of life rather than a luxury.]

not render them necessary for the support of life; and custom nowhere renders it indecent to live without them.

As the wages of labour are every where regulated, partly by the demand for it, and partly by the average price of the neces-

What raises the price of subsistence must raise wages.

sary articles of subsistence; whatever raises this average price must necessarily raise those wages, so that the labourer may still be able to purchase that quantity of those neces-sary articles which the state of the demand for labour, whether increasing, stationary, or declining, re-quires that he should have.[74] A tax upon those articles neces-sarily raises their price somewhat higher than the amount of the tax, because the dealer who advances the tax, must gener-ally get it back with a profit. Such a tax must, therefore, occa-sion a rise in the wages of labour proportionable to this rise of price.

It is thus that a tax upon the necessaries of life, operates ex-actly in the same manner as a direct tax upon the wages of

So that a tax on necessaries, like a tax on wages, raises wages.

labour. The labourer, though he may pay it out of his hand, cannot, for any considerable time at least, be properly said even to ad-vance it. It must always in the long-run be advanced to him by his immediate employer in the advanced rate of his wages. His employer, if he is a man-ufacturer, will charge upon the price of his goods this rise of wages, together with a profit; so that the final payment of the tax, together with this over-charge, will fall upon the con-sumer. If his employer is a farmer, the final payment, together with a like over-charge, will fall upon the rent of the landlord.

It is otherwise with taxes upon which I call luxuries; even upon those of the poor. The rise in the price of the taxed com-

Taxes on luxuries even if consumed by the poor have no such effect,

modities, will not necessarily occasion any rise in the wages of labour. A tax upon to-bacco, for example, though a luxury of the poor as well as of the rich, will not raise wages. Though it is taxed in England at three times, and in France at fifteen times its original price, those high duties seem to have no effect upon the wages of labour. The same thing may be said of the taxes upon tea and sugar; which in England and Holland have become luxuries of the lowest ranks of people; and of those upon chocolate, which in Spain is said to have become so. The different taxes which in Great Britain have in the course of the present century been imposed upon spirituous liquors, are not supposed to have had any effect upon the wages of labour. The rise in the price of porter, occasioned by an additional tax of three shillings upon the barrel of strong beer,[75] has not raised the wages of common labour in London. These were about eighteen pence and twenty-pence a day before the tax, and they are not more now.

The high price of such commodities does not necessarily diminish the ability of the inferior ranks of people to bring up

as they act like sumptuary laws, and so do not diminish the ability of the poor to bring up useful families,

families. Upon the sober and industrious poor, taxes upon such commodities act as sumptuary laws, and dispose them either to moderate, or to refrain altogether from the use of superfluities which they can no longer easily afford. Their ability to bring up families, in consequence of this forced frugality, instead of being diminished, is frequently, perhaps, increased by the tax. It is the sober and industrious poor who generally bring up the most numerous families, and who principally supply the demand for useful labour. All the poor indeed are not sober and industrious, and the dissolute and disorderly might continue to indulge themselves in the use of such commodities after this rise of price in the same manner as before; without regarding the distress which this indulgence might bring upon their families. Such disorderly persons, however, seldom rear up numerous families; their children generally perishing from neglect, mismanagement, and the scantiness or unwholesomeness of their food. If by the strength of their constitution they survive the hardships to which the bad conduct of their parents exposes them; yet the example of

[75] [1 Geo. III., c. 7.]

that bad conduct commonly corrupts their morals; so that, instead of being useful to society by their industry, they become public nuisances by their vices and disorders. Though the advanced price of the luxuries of the poor, therefore, might increase somewhat the distress of such disorderly families, and thereby diminish somewhat their ability to bring up children; it would not probably diminish much the useful population of the country.

Any rise in the average price of necessaries, unless it is compensated by a proportionable rise in the wages of labour,

whereas a rise in the price of necessaries diminishes the ability of the poor to bring up useful families and supply the demand for labour.

must necessarily diminish more or less the ability of the poor to bring up numerous families, and consequently to supply the demand for useful labour; whatever may be the state of that demand, whether increasing, stationary, or declining; or such as requires an increasing, stationary, or declining population.

Taxes on necessaries are contrary to the interest of the middle and superior ranks of people.

Taxes upon luxuries have no tendency to raise the price of any other commodities except that of the commodities taxed. Taxes upon necessaries, by raising the wages of labour, necessarily tend to raise the price of all manufactures, and consequently to diminish the extent of their sale and consumption. Taxes upon luxuries are finally paid by the consumers of the commodities taxed, without any retribution. They fall indifferently upon every species of revenue, the wages of labour, the profits of stock, and the rent of land. Taxes upon necessaries, so far as they affect the labouring poor, are finally paid, partly by landlords in the diminished rent of their lands, and partly by rich consumers, whether landlords or others, in the advanced price of manufactured goods; and always with a considerable over-charge. The advanced price of such manufactures as are real necessaries of life, and are destined for the consumption of the poor, of coarse woollens, for example, must be compensated to the poor by a farther advancement of their wages. The middling and superior ranks of people, if they understood their own interest, ought always to oppose all taxes upon the necessaries of life, as well as all direct taxes upon the wages of labour. The final payment of both the one and the other falls altogether upon themselves, and always with a considerable over-charge. They fall heaviest upon the landlords, who always pay in a double capacity; in that of landlords, by the reduction of their rent; and in that of rich consumers, by the increase of their expence. The observation of Sir Matthew Decker, that certain taxes are, in the price of certain goods, sometimes repeated and accumulated four or five times, is perfectly just with regard to taxes upon the necessaries of life. In the price of leather, for example, you must pay, not only for the tax upon the leather of your own shoes, but for a part of that upon those of the shoe-maker and the tanner. You must pay too for the tax upon the salt, upon the soap, and upon the candles which those workmen consume while employed in your service, and for the tax upon the leather, which the salt-maker, the soap-maker, and the candle-maker consume while employed in their service.[76]

The chief British taxes on necessaries are those on salt, leather, soap and candles,

In Great Britain, the principal taxes upon the necessaries of life are those upon the four commodities just now mentioned, salt, leather, soap, and candles.

Salt is a very ancient and a very universal subject of taxation. It was taxed among the Romans, and it is so at present in, I believe, every part of Europe. The quantity annually consumed by any individual is so small, and may be purchased so gradually, that nobody, it seems to have been thought, could feel very sensibly even a pretty heavy tax upon it. It is in England taxed at three shillings and four-pence a bushel; about three times the original price of the commodity. In some other countries the tax is still higher. Leather is a real necessary of life. The use of linen renders soap such. In countries where the winter nights are long, candles are a necessary instrument of trade.

[76] [Leather is Decker's example, *Essay on the Decline of the Foreign Trade*, 2nd ed., 1750, pp. 29, 30. See also p. 10.]

Leather and soap are in Great Britain taxed at three half-pence a pound; candles at a penny;[77] taxes which, upon the original price of leather, may amount to about eight or ten per cent.; upon that of soap to about twenty or five and twenty per cent.; and upon that of candles to about fourteen or fifteen per cent.; taxes which, though lighter than that upon salt, are still very heavy. As all those four commodities are real necessaries of life, such heavy taxes upon them must increase somewhat the expence of the sober and industrious poor, and must consequently raise more or less the wages of their labour.

In a country where the winters are so cold as in Great Britain, fuel is, during that season, in the strictest sense of
and also seaborne coal. the word, a necessary of life, not only for the purpose of dressing victuals, but for the comfortable subsistence of many different sorts of workmen who work within doors; and coals are the cheapest of all fuel. The price of fuel has so important an influence upon that of labour, that all over Great Britain manufactures have confined themselves principally to the coal countries; other parts of the country, on account of the high price of this necessary article, not being able to work so cheap. In some manufactures, besides, coal is a necessary instrument of trade; as in those of glass, iron, and all other metals. If a bounty could in any case be reasonable, it might perhaps be so upon the transportation of coals from those parts of the country in which they abound, to those in which they are wanted. But the legislature, instead of a bounty, has imposed a tax of three shillings and threepence a ton upon coal carried coastways;[78] which upon most sorts of coal is more than sixty per cent. of the original price at the coal-pit. Coals carried either by land or by inland navigation pay no duty. Where they are naturally cheap, they are consumed duty free: where they are naturally dear, they are loaded with a heavy duty.

Such taxes, though they raise the price of subsistence, and

[77] [See Dowell, _History of Taxation and Taxes_, 1884, vol. iv., pp. 318, 322, 330.]

[78] [Saxby, _British Customs_, p. 307. 8 Ann., c. 4; 9 Ann., c. 6.]

Such taxes at any rate bring in revenue, which is more than can be said of the regulations of the corn trade, etc., which produce equally bad effects.

consequently the wages of labour, yet they afford a considerable revenue to government, which it might not be easy to find in any other way. There may, therefore, be good reasons for continuing them. The bounty upon the exportation of corn, so far as it tends in the actual state of tillage to raise the price of that necessary article, produces all the like bad effects; and instead of affording any revenue, frequently occasions a very great expence to government. The high duties upon the importation of foreign corn, which in years of moderate plenty amount to a prohibition; and the absolute prohibition of the importation either of live cattle or of salt provisions, which takes place in the ordinary state of the law, and which, on account of the scarcity, is at present suspended for a limited time with regard to Ireland and the British plantations,[79] have all the bad effects of taxes upon the necessaries of life, and produce no revenue to government. Nothing seems necessary for the repeal of such regulations, but to convince the public of the futility of that system in consequence of which they have been established.

Taxes upon the necessaries of life are much higher in many other countries than in Great Britain. Duties upon flour

Much higher taxes on necessaries prevail in many other countries. There are taxes on bread,

and meal when ground at the mill, and upon bread when baked at the oven, take place in many countries. In Holland the money price of the bread consumed in towns is supposed to be doubled by means of such taxes. In lieu of a part of them, the people who live in the country pay every year so much a head, according to the sort of bread they are supposed to consume. Those who consume wheaten bread, pay three guilders fifteen stivers; about six shillings and ninepence halfpenny. These, and some other taxes of the same kind, by raising the price of labour, are said to have ruined the greater part of the manufactures of

[79] [Above, vol. i., p. 392.]

Holland.[80] Similar taxes, though not quite so heavy, take place in the Milanese, in the states of Genoa, in the dutchy of Modena, in the dutchies of Parma, Placentia, and Guastalla, and in the ecclesiastical state. A French[81] author of some note has proposed to reform the finances of his country, by substituting in the room of the greater part of other taxes, this most ruinous of all taxes. There is nothing so absurd, says Cicero, which has not sometimes been asserted by some philosophers.[82]

Taxes upon butchers meat are still more common than those upon bread. It may indeed be doubted whether butchers meat

and meat.

is any where a necessary of life. Grain and other vegetables, with the help of milk, cheese, and butter, or oil, where butter is not to be had, it is known from experience, can, without any butchers meat, afford the most plentiful, the most wholesome, the most nourishing, and the most invigorating diet. Decency no where requires that any man should eat butchers meat, as it in most places requires that he should wear a linen shirt or a pair of leather shoes.

Consumable commodities, whether necessaries or luxuries,

A tax on a consumable commodity may be levied either periodically from the consumer or once for all from the dealer when the consumer acquires it.

may be taxed in two different ways. The consumer may either pay an annual sum on account of his using or consuming goods of a certain kind; or the goods may be taxed while they remain in the hands of the dealer, and before they are delivered to the consumer. The consumable goods which last a considerable time before they are consumed altogether, are most properly taxed in the

---

[80] *Memoires concernant les Droits, &c.* p. 210, 211 [and 233. See below, p. 1150.]

[81] *Le Reformateur.* [Amsterdam, 1756. Garnier in his note on this passage, *Recherches,* etc., tom. iv., p. 387, attributes this work to Clicquot de Blervache, French Inspector-general of Manufactures and Commerce, 1766–90, but later authorities doubt or deny Clicquot's authorship. See Jules de Vroil, *Étude sur Clicquot-Blervache,* 1870, pp. xxxi–xxxiii.]

[82] [*De Divinatione,* ii., 58, "Sed nescio quomodo nihil tam absurde dici potest quod non dicatur ab aliquo philosophorum."]

one way. Those of which the consumption is either immediate or more speedy, in the other. The coach-tax and plate-tax are examples of the former method of imposing: the greater part of the other duties of excise and customs, of the latter.

A coach may, with good management, last ten or twelve years. It might be taxed, once for all, before it comes out of the hands of the coach-maker. But it is certainly more convenient for the buyer to pay four pounds a year for the privilege of keeping a coach, than to pay all at once forty or forty-eight pounds additional price to the coach-maker; or a sum equivalent to what the tax is likely to cost him during the time he uses the same coach. A service of plate, in the same manner, may last more than a century. It is certainly easier for the consumer to pay five shillings a year for every hundred ounces of plate, near one per cent. of the value, than to redeem this long annuity at five and twenty or thirty years purchase, which would enhance the price at least five and twenty or thirty per cent. The different taxes which affect houses are certainly more conveniently paid by moderate annual payments, than by a heavy tax of equal value upon the first building or sale of the house.

The first method is best when the commodity is durable.

It was the well-known proposal of Sir Matthew Decker, that all commodities, even those of which the consumption is either immediate or very speedy, should be taxed in this manner; the dealer advancing nothing, but the consumer paying a certain annual sum for the licence to consume certain goods.[83] The object of his scheme was to promote all the different branches of foreign trade, particularly the carrying trade, by taking away all duties upon importation and exportation, and thereby enabling the merchant to employ his whole capital and credit in the purchase of

Sir M. Decker proposed to adapt it also to other commodities by issuing annual licences to consume them, but this would be liable to greater objections than the second and usual method.

[83] [*Essay on the Causes of the Decline of the Foreign Trade*, 2nd ed., 1750, pp. 78–163.]

goods and the freight of ships, no part of either being diverted towards the advancing of taxes. The project, however, of taxing, in this manner, goods of immediate or speedy consumption, seems liable to the four following very important objections. First, the tax would be more unequal, or not so well proportioned to the expence and consumption of the different contributors, as in the way in which it is commonly imposed. The taxes upon ale, wine, and spirituous liquors, which are advanced by the dealers, are finally paid by the different consumers exactly in proportion to their respective consumption. But if the tax were[84] to be paid by purchasing a licence to drink those liquors, the sober would, in proportion to his consumption, be taxed much more heavily than the drunken consumer. A family which exercised great hospitality would be taxed much more lightly than one who[85] entertained fewer guests. Secondly, this mode of taxation, by paying for an annual, half-yearly, or quarterly licence to consume certain goods, would diminish very much one of the principal conveniences of taxes upon goods of speedy consumption; the piece-meal payment. In the price of three-pence halfpenny, which is at present paid for a pot of porter, the different taxes upon malt, hops, and beer, together with the extraordinary profit which the brewer charges for having advanced them, may perhaps amount to about three halfpence. If a workman can conveniently spare those three halfpence, he buys a pot of porter. If he cannot, he contents himself with a pint, and, as a penny saved is a penny got, he thus gains a farthing by his temperance. He pays the tax piecemeal, as he can afford to pay it, and when he can afford to pay it; and every act of payment is perfectly voluntary, and what he can avoid if he chuses to do so. Thirdly, such taxes would operate less as sumptuary laws. When the licence was once purchased, whether the purchaser drunk much or drunk little, his tax would be the same. Fourthly, if a workman were[86] to pay all at once, by yearly, half-yearly or quarterly payments, a tax equal to what he

---

[84] [Eds. 1–3 read "was."]

[85] [Eds. 1 and 2 read "which."]

[86] [Eds. 1–3 read "was."]

at present pays, with little or no inconveniency, upon all the different pots and pints of porter which he drinks in any such period of time, the sum might frequently distress him very much. This mode of taxation, therefore, it seems evident, could never, without the most grievous oppression, produce a revenue nearly equal to what is derived from the present mode without any oppression. In several countries, however, commodities of an immediate or very speedy consumption are taxed in this manner. In Holland, people pay so much a head for a licence to drink tea. I have already mentioned a tax upon bread, which, so far as it is consumed in farm-houses and country villages, is there levied in the same manner.

The duties of excise are imposed chiefly upon goods of home produce destined for home consumption. They are imposed only upon a few sorts of goods of the most general use. There can never be any doubt either concerning the goods which are subject to those duties, or concerning the particular duty which each species of goods is subject to. They fall almost altogether upon what I call luxuries, excepting always the four duties above mentioned, upon salt, soap, leather, candles, and, perhaps, that upon green glass.

Excepting the four mentioned above, British excise duties fall chiefly on luxuries.

The duties of customs are much more ancient than those of excise. They seem to have been called customs, as denoting customary payments which had been in use from time immemorial. They appear to have been originally considered as taxes upon the profits of merchants. During the barbarous times of feudal anarchy, merchants, like all the other inhabitants of burghs, were considered as little better than emancipated bondmen, whose persons were despised, and whose gains were envied. The great nobility, who had consented that the king should tallage the profits of their own tenants, were not unwilling that he should tallage likewise those of an order of men whom it was much less their interest to protect. In those ignorant times, it was not understood, that the profits of merchants are a subject not taxable directly; or that

Customs were originally regarded as taxes on merchants' profits, the final payment of all such taxes must fall, with a considerable over-charge, upon the consumers.

The gains of alien merchants were looked upon more unfavourably than those of English merchants. It was natural, therefore, that those of the former should be taxed more heavily than those of the latter.[87] This distinction between the duties upon aliens and those upon English merchants, which was begun from ignorance, has been continued from the spirit of monopoly, or in order to give our own merchants an advantage both in the home and in the foreign market.

those of aliens being taxed more heavily.

With this distinction, the ancient duties of customs were imposed equally upon all sorts of goods, necessaries as well as luxuries, goods exported as well as goods imported. Why should the dealers in one sort of goods, it seems to have been thought, be more favoured than those in another? or why should the merchant exporter be more favoured than the merchant importer?

So originally customs were imposed equally on all sorts of goods, and on exports as well as imports.

The ancient customs were divided into three branches. The first, and perhaps the most ancient of all those duties, was that upon wool and leather. It seems to have been chiefly or altogether an exportation duty. When the woollen manufacture came to be established in England, lest the king should lose any part of his customs upon wool by the exportation of woollen cloths, a like duty was imposed upon them. The other two branches were, first, a duty upon wine, which, being imposed at so much a ton, was called a tonnage; and, secondly, a duty upon all other goods, which, being imposed at so much a pound of their supposed value, was called a poundage. In the forty-seventh year of Edward III. a duty of six-pence in the pound was imposed upon all goods exported and imported, except

The first was that on wool and leather, and the second tonnage (on wine) and poundage (on all other goods). Subsidies were additions to poundage.

[87] [Above, pp. 583–584, 622.]

wools, wool-fells, leather, and wines, which were subject to particular duties. In the fourteenth of Richard II. this duty was raised to one shilling in the pound; but three years afterwards, it was again reduced to six-pence. It was raised to eight-pence in the second year of Henry IV.; and in the fourth year of the same prince, to one shilling. From this time to the ninth year of William III. this duty continued at one shilling in the pound. The duties of tonnage and poundage were generally granted to the king by one and the same act of parliament, and were called the Subsidy of Tonnage and Poundage. The subsidy of poundage having continued for so long a time at one shilling in the pound, or at five per cent.; a subsidy came, in the language of the customs, to denote a general duty of this kind of five per cent. This subsidy, which is now called the Old Subsidy, still continues to be levied according to the book of rates established in the twelfth of Charles II. The method of ascertaining, by a book of rates, the value of goods subject to this duty, is said to be older than the time of James I.[88] The new subsidy imposed by the ninth and tenth of William III.,[89] was an additional five per cent. upon the greater part of goods. The one-third and the two-third subsidy[90] made up between them another five per cent. of which they were proportionable parts. The subsidy of 1747[91] made a fourth five per cent. upon the greater part of goods; and that of 1759,[92] a fifth upon some particular sorts of goods. Besides those five subsidies, a great variety of other duties have occasionally been imposed upon particular sorts of goods, in order sometimes to relieve the exigencies of the state, and sometimes to regulate

[88] [Gilbert, *Treatise on the Court of Exchequer*, 1758, p. 224, mentions a Book of Rates printed in 1586. Dowell, *History of Taxation and Taxes*, 1884, vol. i., pp. 146, 165, places the beginning of the system soon after 1558.]

[89] [C. 23.]

[90] [2 and 3 Ann. c. 9; 3 and 4 Ann., c. 5.]

[91] [21 Geo. II., c. 2.]

[92] [32 Geo. II., c. 10, on tobacco, linen, sugar and other grocery, except currants, East India goods (except coffee and raw silk), brandy and other spirits (except colonial rum), and paper.]

the trade of the country, according to the principles of the mercantile system.

That system has come gradually more and more into fashion. The old subsidy was imposed indifferently upon expor-

The prevalence of the principles of the mercantile system has led to the removal of nearly all the export duties, tation as well as importation. The four subsequent subsidies, as well as the other duties which have since been occasionally imposed upon particular sorts of goods, have, with a few exceptions, been laid altogether upon importation. The greater part of the ancient duties which had been imposed upon the exportation of the goods of home produce and manufacture, have either been lightened or taken away altogether. In most cases they have been taken away. Bounties have even been given upon the exportation of some of them. Drawbacks too, sometimes of the whole, and, in most cases, of a part of the duties which are paid upon the importation of foreign goods, have been granted upon their exportation. Only half the duties imposed by the old subsidy upon importation are drawn back upon exportation: but the whole of those imposed by the latter[93] subsidies and other imposts are, upon the greater part of goods, drawn back in the same manner.[94] This growing favour of exportation, and discouragement of importation, have suffered only a few exceptions, which chiefly concern the materials of some manufactures. These, our merchants and manufacturers are willing should come as cheap as possible to themselves, and as dear as possible to their rivals and competitors in other countries. Foreign materials are, upon this account, sometimes allowed to be imported duty free; Spanish wool, for example, flax, and raw linen yarn. The exportation of the materials of home produce, and of those which are the particular[95] produce of our colonies, has sometimes been prohibited, and sometimes subjected to higher duties. The

[93] [Ed. 1 reads, more intelligibly, "later." Another example of this unfortunate change occurs below, p. 1186.]

[94] [Above, p. 629, written after the present passage.]

[95] [Eds. 1–3 read "peculiar," and "particular" is perhaps a misprint.]

exportation of English wool has been prohibited.[96] That of beaver skins, of beaver wool, and of gum senega,[97] has been subjected to higher duties; Great Britain, by the conquest of Canada and Senegal, having got almost the monopoly of those commodities.

That the mercantile system has not been very favourable to the revenue of the great body of the people, to the annual produce of the land and labour of the country, I have endeavoured to shew in the fourth book of this Inquiry. It seems not to have been more favourable to the revenue of the sovereign; so far at least as that revenue depends upon the duties of customs.

and has been unfavourable to the revenue of the state,

In consequence of that system, the importation of several sorts of goods has been prohibited altogether. This prohibition has in some cases entirely prevented, and in others has very much diminished the importation of those commodities, by reducing the importers to the necessity of smuggling. It has entirely prevented the importation of foreign woollens; and it has very much diminished that of foreign silks and velvets. In both cases it has entirely annihilated the revenue of customs which might have been levied upon such importation.

annihilating parts of it by prohibitions of importation,

The high duties which have been imposed upon the importation of many different sorts of foreign goods, in order to discourage their consumption in Great Britain, have in many cases served only to encourage smuggling; and in all cases have reduced the revenue of the customs below what more moderate duties would have afforded. The saying of Dr. Swift, that in the arithmetic of the customs two and two, instead of making four, make sometimes only one,[98] holds perfectly true

and reducing other parts by high duties.

---

[96] [Above, pp. 822–827.]

[97] [Above, pp. 835–836.]

[98] [Swift attributes the saying to an unnamed commissioner of customs. "I will tell you a secret, which I learned many years ago from the commissioners of the cus-

with regard to such heavy duties, which never could have been imposed, had not the mercantile system taught us, in many cases, to employ taxation as an instrument, not of revenue, but of monopoly.

The bounties which are sometimes given upon the exportation of home produce and manufactures, and the drawbacks

Bounties and drawbacks (great part of which is obtained by fraud) and expenses of management make a large deduction from the customs revenue.

which are paid upon the re-exportation of the greater part of foreign goods, have given occasion to many frauds, and to a species of smuggling more destructive of the public revenue than any other. In order to obtain the bounty or drawback, the goods, it is well known, are sometimes shipped and sent to sea; but soon afterwards clandestinely re-landed in some other part of the country. The defalcation of the revenue of customs occasioned by bounties and drawbacks, of which a great part are obtained fraudulently, is very great. The gross produce of the customs in the year which ended on the 5th of January 1755, amounted to 5,068,000*l*. The bounties which were paid out of this revenue, though in that year there was no bounty upon corn, amounted to 167,800*l*. The drawbacks which were paid upon debentures and certificates, to 2,156,800*l*. Bounties and drawbacks together, amounted to 2,324,600*l*. In consequence of these deductions the revenue of the customs amounted only to 2,743,400*l*.: from which, deducting 287,900*l*. for the expence of management in salaries and other incidents, the neat revenue of the customs for that year comes out to be 2,455,500*l*.

toms in London: they said when any commodity appeared to be taxed above a moderate rate, the consequence was to lessen that branch of the revenue by one-half; and one of these gentlemen pleasantly told me that the mistake of parliaments on such occasions was owing to an error of computing two and two make four; whereas in the business of laying impositions, two and two never made more than one; which happens by lessening the import, and the strong temptation of running such goods as paid high duties, at least in this kingdom."—"Answer to a Paper Called a Memorial of the Poor Inhabitants, Tradesmen and Labourers of the Kingdom of Ireland" (in *Works*, ed. Scott, 2nd ed., 1883, vol. vii., pp. 165–166. The saying is quoted from Swift by Hume in his *Essay on the Balance of Trade*, and by Lord Kames in his *Sketches of the History of Man*, 1774, vol. i., p. 474).]

The expence of management amounts in this manner to between five and six per cent. upon the gross revenue of the customs, and to something more than ten per cent. upon what remains of that revenue, after deducting what is paid away in bounties and drawbacks.

Heavy duties being imposed upon almost all goods imported, our merchant importers smuggle as much, and make entry of as little as they can. Our merchant exporters, on the contrary, make entry of more than they export; sometimes out of vanity, and to pass for great dealers in goods which pay no duty; and sometimes to gain a bounty or a drawback. Our exports, in consequence of these different frauds, appear upon the customhouse books greatly to overbalance our imports; to the unspeakable comfort of those politicians who measure the national prosperity by what they call the balance of trade.

In the customs returns the imports are minimised and the exports exaggerated.

All goods imported, unless particularly exempted, and such exemptions are not very numerous, are liable to some duties of customs. If any goods are imported not mentioned in the book of rates, they are taxed at 4s. 9%/20d. for every twenty shillings value,[99] according to the oath of the importer, that is, nearly at five subsidies, or five poundage duties. The book of rates is extremely comprehensive, and enumerates a great variety of articles, many of them little used, and therefore not well known. It is upon this account frequently uncertain under what article a particular sort of goods ought to be classed, and consequently what duty they ought to pay. Mistakes with regard to this sometimes ruin the customhouse officer, and frequently occasion much trouble, expence, and vexation to the importer. In point of perspicuity, precision, and distinctness, therefore, the duties of customs are much inferior to those of excise.

The customs are very numerous and much less perspicuous and distinct than the excise duties.

In order that the greater part of the members of any society

---

[99] [Saxby, *British Customs*, p. 266.]

They might with great advantage be confined to a few articles.

should contribute to the public revenue in proportion to their respective expence, it does not seem necessary that every single article of that expence should be taxed. The revenue, which is levied by the duties of excise, is supposed to fall as equally upon the contributors as that which is levied by the duties of customs; and the duties of excise are imposed upon a few articles only of the most general use and consumption. It has been the opinion of many people, that, by proper management, the duties of customs might likewise, without any loss to the public revenue, and with great advantage to foreign trade, be confined to a few articles only.

The foreign articles, of the most general use and consumption in Great Britain, seem at present to consist chiefly in for-

Foreign wines and brandies and East and West Indian products at present yield most of the customs revenue.

eign wines and brandies; in some of the productions of America and the West Indies, sugar, rum, tobacco, cocoanuts, &c. and in some of those of the East Indies, tea, coffee, china-ware, spiceries of all kinds, several sorts of piece-goods, &c. These different articles afford, perhaps, at present, the greater part of the revenue which is drawn from the duties of customs. The taxes which at present subsist upon foreign manufactures, if you except those upon the few contained in the foregoing enumeration, have the greater part of them been imposed for the purpose, not of revenue, but of monopoly, or to give our own merchants an advantage in the home market. By removing all prohibitions, and by subjecting all foreign manufactures to such moderate taxes, as it was found from experience afforded upon each article the greatest revenue to the public, our own workmen might still have a considerable advantage in the home market, and many articles, some of

The yield of high duties is often lessened by smuggling or diminished consumption.

which at present afford no revenue to government, and others a very inconsiderable one, might afford a very great one.

High taxes, sometimes by diminishing the consumption of the taxed commodities, and sometimes by encouraging smuggling, frequently afford a smaller revenue to government than what might be drawn from more moderate taxes.

When the diminution of revenue is the effect of the diminution of consumption, there can be but one remedy, and that is the lowering of the tax.

In the first case the only remedy is to lower the duty.

When the diminution of the revenue is the effect of the encouragement given to smuggling, it may perhaps be remedied in two ways; either by diminishing the temptation to smuggle, or by increasing the difficulty of smuggling. The temptation to smuggle can be diminished only by the lowering of the tax; and the difficulty of smuggling can be increased only by establishing that system of administration which is most proper for preventing it.

For smuggling the remedy is to lower the tax or increase the difficulty of smuggling.

The excise laws, it appears, I believe, from experience, obstruct and embarrass the operations of the smuggler much more effectually than those of the customs. By introducing into the customs a system of administration as similar to that of the excise as the nature of the different duties will admit, the difficulty of smuggling might be very much increased. This alteration, it has been supposed by many people, might very easily be brought about.

Excise laws are more embarrassing to the smuggler than the customs.

The importer of commodities liable to any duties of customs, it has been said, might at his option be allowed either to carry them to his own private warehouse, or to lodge them in a warehouse provided either at his own expence or at that of the public, but under the key of the customhouse officer, and never to be opened but in his presence. If the merchant carried them to his own private warehouse, the duties to be immediately paid, and never afterwards to be drawn back; and that warehouse to be at all times subject to the visit and examination of the customhouse officer, in order to ascertain how far the quantity contained in it corresponded with that for which the

If customs were confined to a few articles, a system of excise supervision of stores could be instituted.

duty had been paid. If he carried them to the public warehouse, no duty to be paid till they were taken out for home consumption. If taken out for exportation, to be duty-free; proper security being always given that they should be so exported. The dealers in those particular commodities, either by wholesale or retail, to be at all times subject to the visit and examination of the customhouse officer; and to be obliged to justify by proper certificates the payment of the duty upon the whole quantity contained in their shops or warehouses. What are called the excise-duties upon rum imported are at present levied in this manner, and the same system of administration might perhaps be extended to all duties upon goods imported; provided always that those duties were, like the duties of excise, confined to a few sorts of goods of the most general use and consumption. If they were extended to almost all sorts of goods, as at present, public warehouses of sufficient extent could not easily be provided, and goods of very delicate nature, or of which the preservation required much care and attention, could not safely be trusted by the merchant in any warehouse but his own.

If by such a system of administration smuggling, to any considerable extent, could be prevented even under pretty high du-

Great simplification without loss of revenue would then be secured, ties; and if every duty was occasionally either heightened or lowered according as it was most likely, either the one way or the other, to afford the greatest revenue to the state; taxation being always employed as an instrument of revenue and never of monopoly; it seems not improbable that a revenue, at least equal to the present neat revenue of the customs, might be drawn from duties upon the importation of only a few sorts of goods of the most general use and consumption; and that the duties of customs might thus be brought to the same degree of simplicity, certainty, and precision, as those of excise. What the revenue at present loses, by drawbacks upon the re-exportation of foreign goods which are afterwards relanded and consumed at home, would under this system be saved altogether. If to this saving, which would alone be very considerable, were[100]

---

[100] [Eds. 1–3 read "was."]

added the abolition of all bounties upon the exportation of home-produce; in all cases in which those bounties were not in reality drawbacks of some duties of excise which had before been advanced; it cannot well be doubted but that the neat revenue of customs might, after an alteration of this kind, be fully equal to what it had ever been before.

If by such a change of system the public revenue suffered no loss, the trade and manufactures of the country would certainly gain a very considerable advantage.

while the trade and manufactures of the country would gain greatly.

The trade in the commodities not taxed, by far the greatest number, would be perfectly free, and might be carried on to and from all parts of the world with every possible advantage. Among those commodities would be comprehended all the necessaries of life, and all the materials of manufacture. So far as the free importation of the necessaries of life reduced their average money price in the home market, it would reduce the money price of labour, but without reducing in any respect its real recompence. The value of money is in proportion to the quantity of the necessaries of life which it will purchase. That of the necessaries of life is altogether independent of the quantity of money which can be had for them. The reduction in the money price of labour would necessarily be attended with a proportionable one in that of all home-manufactures, which would thereby gain some advantage in all foreign markets. The price of some manufactures would be reduced in a still greater proportion by the free importation of the raw materials. If raw silk could be imported from China and Indostan duty-free, the silk manufacturers in England could greatly undersell those of both France and Italy. There would be no occasion to prohibit the importation of foreign silks and velvets. The cheapness of their goods would secure to our own workmen, not only the possession of the home, but a very great command of the foreign market. Even the trade in the commodities taxed would be carried on with much more advantage than at present. If those commodities were delivered out of the public warehouse for foreign exportation, being in this case exempted from all taxes, the trade in them would be perfectly free. The carrying trade in all sorts of goods would under this system enjoy every possible advantage. If those commodities were delivered out for home-consumption, the importer not being obliged to advance the tax till he had an opportunity of selling his goods, either to some dealer, or to some consumer, he could always afford to sell them cheaper than if he had been obliged to advance it at the moment of importation. Under the same taxes, the foreign trade of consumption even in the taxed commodities, might in this manner be carried on with much more advantage than it can at present.

It was the object of the famous excise scheme of Sir Robert Walpole to establish, with regard to wine and tobacco, a

Sir Robert Walpole's excise scheme was something of this kind so far as wine and tobacco are concerned.

system not very unlike that which is here proposed. But though the bill which was then brought into parliament, comprehended those two commodities only; it was generally supposed to be meant as an introduction to a more extensive scheme of the same kind. Faction, combined with the interest of smuggling merchants, raised so violent, though so unjust, a clamour against that bill, that the minister thought proper to drop it; and from a dread of exciting a clamour of the same kind, none of his successors have dared to resume the project.

The duties on foreign luxuries fall chiefly on the middle and upper ranks.

The duties upon foreign luxuries imported for home-consumption, though they sometimes fall upon the poor, fall principally upon people of middling or more than middling fortune. Such are, for example, the duties upon foreign wines, upon coffee, chocolate, tea, sugar, &c.

Those on the luxuries of home produce fall on people of all ranks.

The duties upon the cheaper luxuries of home-produce destined for home-consumption, fall pretty equally upon people of all ranks in proportion to their respective expence. The poor pay the duties upon malt, hops, beer, and ale, upon their own consumption: The rich, upon both[101] their own consumption and that of their servants.

The whole consumption of the inferior ranks of people, or of those below the middling rank, it must be observed, is in every country much greater, not only in quantity, but in value,

Taxes on the consumption of the inferior ranks are much more productive than those on the consumption of the rich.

than that of the middling and of those above the middling rank. The whole expence of the inferior is much greater than that of the superior ranks. In the first place, almost the whole capital of every country is annually distributed among the inferior ranks of people, as the wages of productive labour. Secondly, a great part of the revenue arising from both[102] the rent of land and[103] the profits of stock, is annually distributed among the same rank, in the wages and maintenance of menial servants, and other unproductive labourers. Thirdly, some part of the profits of stock belongs to the same rank, as a revenue arising from the employment of their small capitals. The amount of the profits annually made by small shopkeepers, tradesmen, and retailers of all kinds, is every where very considerable, and makes a very considerable portion of the annual produce. Fourthly, and lastly, some part even of the rent of land belongs to the same rank; a considerable part to those who are somewhat below the middling rank, and a small part even to the lowest rank; common labourers sometimes possessing in property an acre or two of land. Though the expence of those inferior ranks of people, therefore, taking them individually, is very small, yet the whole mass of it, taking them collectively, amounts always to by much the largest portion of the whole expence of the society; what remains, of the annual produce of the land and labour of the country for the consumption of the superior ranks, being always much less, not only in quantity but in value. The taxes upon expence, therefore, which fall chiefly upon that of the su-

[101] [Ed. 1 reads "both upon."]

[102] [Ed. 1 reads "both from."]

[103] [Ed. 1 reads "and from."]

perior ranks of people, upon the smaller portion of the annual
produce, are likely to be much less productive than either those
which fall indifferently upon the expence of all ranks, or even
those which fall chiefly upon that of the inferior ranks; than either those which fall indifferently upon the whole annual produce, or those which fall chiefly upon the larger portion of it.
The excise upon the materials and manufacture of home-made
fermented and spirituous liquors is accordingly, of all the different taxes upon expence, by far the most productive; and this
branch of the excise falls very much, perhaps principally, upon
the expence of the common people. In the year which ended on
the 5th of July 1775, the gross produce of this branch of the excise amounted to 3,341,837*l*. 9*s*. 9*d*.[104]

It must always be remembered, however, that it is the luxu-
rious and not the necessary expence of the inferior ranks of

*But such taxes
must never be on
the necessary
consumption of
the inferior ranks.*

people that ought ever to be taxed. The final
payment of any tax upon their necessary expence would fall altogether upon the superior ranks of people; upon the smaller
portion of the annual produce, and not upon
the greater. Such a tax must in all cases ei-
ther raise the wages of labour, or lessen the demand for it. It
could not raise the wages of labour, without throwing the final
payment of the tax upon the superior ranks of people. It could
not lessen the demand for labour, without lessening the annual
produce of the land and labour of the country, the fund from
which all taxes must be finally paid. Whatever might be the
state to which a tax of this kind reduced the demand for labour,
it must always raise wages higher than they otherwise would
be in that state; and the final payment of this enhancement of
wages must in all cases fall upon the superior ranks of people.

Fermented liquors brewed, and spirituous liquors distilled,
not for sale, but for private use, are not in Great Britain liable
to any duties of excise. This exemption, of which the object is
to save private families from[105] the odious visit and examina-

---

[104] [Ed. 1 reads "£3,314,223 18s. 10¾d."]

[105] [Ed. 1 reads "is not to expose private families to."]

Liquors brewed or distilled for private use are exempt from excise, though a composition must be paid for malting.

tion of the tax-gatherer, occasions the burden of those duties to fall frequently much lighter upon the rich than upon the poor. It is not, indeed, very common to distil for private use, though it is done sometimes. But in the country, many middling and almost all rich and great families brew their own beer. Their strong beer, therefore, costs them eight shillings a barrel less than it costs the common brewer, who must have his profit upon the tax, as well as upon all the other expence which he advances. Such families, therefore, must drink their beer at least nine or ten shillings a barrel cheaper than any liquor of the same quality can be drunk by the common people, to whom it is every where more convenient to buy their beer, by little and little, from the brewery or the alehouse. Malt, in the same manner, that is made for the use of a private family, is not liable to the visit or examination of the tax-gatherer; but in this case the family must compound at seven shillings and sixpence a head for the tax. Seven shillings and sixpence are equal to the excise upon ten bushels of malt; a quantity fully equal to what all the different members of any sober family, men, women, and children, are at an average likely to consume. But in rich and great families, where country hospitality is much practised, the malt liquors consumed by the members of the family make but a small part of the consumption of the house. Either on account of this composition, however, or for other reasons, it is not near so common to malt as to brew for private use. It is difficult to imagine any equitable reason why those who either brew or distil for private use, should not be subject to a composition of the same kind.

It is said that a tax on malt smaller than the present taxes on malt, beer and ale taken together would bring in more revenue,

A greater revenue than what is at present drawn from all the heavy taxes upon malt, beer, and ale, might be raised, it has frequently been said, by a much lighter tax upon malt; the opportunities of defrauding the revenue being much greater in a brewery than in a malt-house; and those who brew for private use being exempted from all duties or composition for duties, which is not the case with those who malt for private use.

In the porter brewery of London, a quarter of malt is commonly brewed into more than two barrels and a half, sometimes into three barrels of porter. The different taxes upon malt amount to six shillings a quarter; those upon strong beer and ale to eight shillings a barrel. In the porter brewery, therefore, the different taxes upon malt, beer, and ale, amount to between twenty-six and thirty shillings upon the produce of a quarter of malt. In the country brewery for common country sale, a quarter of malt is seldom brewed into less than two barrels of strong and one barrel of small beer; frequently into two barrels and a half of strong beer. The different taxes upon small beer amount to one shilling and four-pence a barrel. In the country brewery, therefore, the different taxes upon malt, beer, and ale, seldom amount to less than twenty-three shillings and four-pence, frequently to twenty-six shillings upon the produce of a quarter of malt. Taking the whole kingdom at an average, therefore, the whole amount of the duties upon malt, beer, and ale, cannot be estimated at less than twenty-four or twenty-five shillings upon the produce of a quarter of malt. But by taking off all the different duties upon beer and ale, and by tripling the malt-tax, or by raising it from six to eighteen shillings upon the quarter of malt, a greater revenue, it is said, might be raised by this single tax than what is at present drawn from all those heavier taxes.

and figures are quoted to prove it.

Under the old malt tax, indeed, is comprehended a tax of four shillings upon the hogshead of cyder, and another of ten shillings upon the barrel of mum. In 1774, the tax upon cyder produced only 3083*l*. 6*s*. 8*d*. It probably fell somewhat short of its usual amount; all the different taxes upon cyder having, that year, produced less than ordinary. The tax upon mum, though much heavier, is still less productive, on account of the smaller consumption of that liquor. But to balance whatever may be the ordinary amount of those two taxes; there is comprehended under what is

Taxes on cyder and mum included in the old malt tax are counterbalanced by the "country excise" duty on cyder, verjuice, vinegar and mead.

called The country excise, first, the old excise of six shillings and eight-pence upon the hogshead of cyder; secondly, a like tax of six shillings and eight-pence upon the hogshead of verjuice; thirdly, another of eight shillings and nine-pence upon the hogshead of vinegar; and, lastly, a fourth tax of eleven-pence upon the gallon of mead or metheglin: the produce of those different taxes will probably much more than counterbalance that of the duties imposed, by what is called The annual malt tax upon cyder and mum.

	l.	*s.*	*d.*
In 1772 the old malt-tax produced	722,023	11	11
The additional	356,776	7	9¾
In 1773, the old tax produced	561,627	3	7½
The additional	278,650	15	3¾
In 1774, the old tax produced	624,614	17	5¾
The additional	310,745	2	8½
In 1775, the old tax produced	657,357	—	8¼
The additional	323,785	12	6¼
4)3,835,580 12		–¾	
Average of these four years	958,895	3	–3/16
In 1772, the country excise produced	1,243,128	5	3
The London brewery	408,260	7	2¾
In 1773, the country excise	1,245,808	3	3
The London brewery	405,406	17	10½
In 1774, the country excise	1,246,373	14	5½
The London brewery	320,601	18	–¼
In 1775, the country excise	1,214,583	7	1
The London brewery	463,670	7	–¼
	4)6,547,832	19	2¼
Average of these four years	1,636,958	4	9½
To which adding the average malt tax, or	958,895	3	–3/16
The whole amount of these different taxes comes out to be	2,595,853	7	9 11/16
But by tripling the malt tax, or by raising it from six to eighteen shillings upon the quarter of malt, that single tax would produce	2,876,685	9	–9/16
A sum which exceeds the foregoing by	280,832	1	2 14/16

Malt is consumed not only in the brewery of beer and ale, but in the manufacture of low wines and spirits. If the malt tax were[106]

[106] [Eds. 1–3 read "was."]

If the malt tax were raised, it would be proper to reduce the excises on wines and spirits containing malt, to be raised to eighteen shillings upon the quarter, it might be necessary to make some abatement in the different excises which are imposed upon those particular sorts of low wines and spirits of which malt makes any part of the materials. In what are called Malt spirits, it makes commonly but a third part of the materials; the other two-thirds being either raw barley, or one-third barley and one-third wheat. In the distillery of malt spirits, both the opportunity and the temptation to smuggle, are much greater than either in a brewery or in a malt-house; the opportunity, on account of the smaller bulk and greater value of the commodity; and the temptation, on account of the superior height of the duties, which amount to $3s.$ $10\frac{2}{3}d.$[107] upon the gallon of spirits. By increasing the duties upon malt, and reducing those upon the distillery, both the opportunities and the temptation to smuggle would be diminished, which might occasion a still further augmentation of revenue.

It has for some time past been the policy of Great Britain to discourage the consumption of spirituous liquors, on account *but not so as to reduce the price of spirits.* of their supposed tendency to ruin the health and to corrupt the morals of the common people. According to this policy, the abatement of the taxes upon the distillery ought not to be so great as to reduce, in any respect, the price of those liquors. Spirituous liquors might remain as dear as ever; while at the same time the wholesome and invigorating liquors of beer and ale might be considerably reduced in their price. The people might thus be in part relieved from one of the burdens of which they at present complain the most; while at the same time the revenue might be considerably augmented.

The objections of Dr. Davenant to this alteration in the pres-

[107] Though the duties directly imposed upon proof spirits amount only to 2s. 6d. per gallon, these added to the duties upon the low wines, from which they are distilled, amount to 3s. 10⅔d. Both low wines and proof spirits are, to prevent frauds, now rated according to what they gauge in the wash. [This note appears first in ed. 3; ed. 1 reads "2s. 6d." in the text instead of "3s. 10⅔d."]

Dr. Davenant objects that the maltster's profits would be unfairly taxed, and the rent and profit of barley land reduced, but the change would make malt liquors cheaper, and so be likely to increase the consumption,

ent system of excise duties, seem to be without foundation. Those objections are, that the tax, instead of dividing itself as at present pretty equally upon the profit of the maltster, upon that of the brewer, and upon that of the retailer, would, so far as it affected profit, fall altogether upon that of the maltster; that the maltster could not so easily get back the amount of the tax in the advanced price of his malt, as the brewer and retailer in the advanced price of their liquor; and that so heavy a tax upon malt might reduce the rent and profit of barley land.[108]

No tax can ever reduce, for any considerable time, the rate of profit in any particular trade, which must always keep its level with other trades in the neighbourhood. The present duties upon malt, beer, and ale, do not affect the profits of the dealers in those commodities, who all get back the tax with an additional profit, in the enhanced price of their goods. A tax indeed may render the goods upon which it is imposed so dear as to diminish the consumption of them. But the consumption of malt is in malt liquors; and a tax of eighteen shillings upon the quarter of malt could not well render those liquors dearer than the different taxes, amounting to twenty-four or twenty-five

---

[108] [*Political and Commercial Works*, ed. Sir Charles Whitworth, 1771, vol. i., pp. 222, 223. But Davenant does not confine the effect of the existing tax to the maltster, the brewer and the retailer. The tax, he says, "which seems to be upon malt, does not lie all upon that commodity, as is vulgarly thought. For a great many different persons contribute to the payment of this duty, before it comes into the Exchequer. First, the landlord, because of the excise, is forced to let his barley land at a lower rate; and, upon the same score, the tenant must sell his barley at a less price; then the maltster bears his share, for because of the duty, he must abate something in the price of his malt, or keep it; in a proportion it likewise affects the hop merchant, the cooper, the collier, and all trades that have relation to the commodity. The retailers and brewers bear likewise a great share, whose gains of necessity will be less, because of that imposition; and, lastly, it comes heaviest of all upon the consumers." If the duty were put upon the maltster, it would be "difficult for him to raise the price of a dear commodity a full ½d at once: so that he must bear the greatest part of the burden himself, or throw it upon the farmer, by giving less for barley, which brings the tax directly upon the land of England."]

shillings, do at present. Those liquors, on the contrary, would probably become cheaper, and the consumption of them would be more likely to increase than to diminish.

It is not very easy to understand why it should be more difficult for the maltster to get back eighteen shillings in the advanced price of his malt, than it is at present for the brewer to get back twenty-four or twenty-five, sometimes thirty shillings, in that of his liquor. The maltster, indeed, instead of a tax of six shillings, would be obliged to advance one of eighteen shillings upon every quarter of malt. But the brewer is at present obliged to advance a tax of twenty-four or twenty-five, sometimes thirty shillings upon every quarter of malt which he brews. It could not be more inconvenient for the maltster to advance a lighter tax, than it is at present for the brewer to advance a heavier one. The maltster doth not always keep in his granaries a stock of malt which it will require a longer time to dispose of, than the stock of beer and ale which the brewer frequently keeps in his cellars. The former, therefore, may frequently get the returns of his money as soon as the latter. But whatever inconveniency might arise to the maltster from being obliged to advance a heavier tax, it[109] could easily be remedied by granting him a few months longer credit than is at present commonly given to the brewer.

and the maltster could recover eighteen shillings as easily as the brewer at present recovers twenty-four or thirty and might be given longer credit.

Nothing could reduce the rent and profit of barley land which did not reduce the demand for barley. But a change of system, which reduced the duties upon a quarter of malt brewed into beer and ale from twenty-four and twenty-five shillings to eighteen shillings, would be more likely to increase than diminish that demand. The rent and profit of barley land, besides, must always be nearly equal to those of other equally fertile and equally

The consumption of barley not being reduced, the rent and profit of barley land could not be reduced, as there is no monopoly.

[109] [Ed. 1 does not contain "it."]

well cultivated land. If they were less, some part of the barley land would soon be turned to some other purpose; and if they were greater, more land would soon be turned to the raising of barley. When the ordinary price of any particular produce of land is at what may be called a monopoly price, a tax upon it necessarily reduces the rent and profit of the land which grows it. A tax upon the produce of those precious vineyards, of which the wine falls so much short of the effectual demand, that its price is always above the natural proportion to that of the produce of other equally fertile and equally well cultivated land, would necessarily reduce the rent and profit of those vineyards. The price of the wines being already the highest that could be got for the quantity commonly sent to market, it could not be raised higher without diminishing that quantity; and the quantity could not be diminished without still greater loss, because the lands could not be turned to any other equally valuable produce. The whole weight of the tax, therefore, would fall upon the rent and profit; properly upon the rent of the vineyard. When it has been proposed to lay any new tax upon sugar, our sugar planters have frequently complained that the whole weight of such taxes fell, not upon the consumer, but upon the producer; they never having been able to raise the price of their sugar after the tax, higher than it was before. The price had, it seems, before the tax been a monopoly price; and the argument adduced to shew that sugar was an improper subject of taxation, demonstrated, perhaps, that it was a proper one; the gains of monopolists, whenever they can be come at, being certainly of all subjects the most proper. But the ordinary price of barley has never been a monopoly price; and the rent and profit of barley land have never been above their natural proportion to those of other equally fertile and equally well cultivated land. The different taxes which have been imposed upon malt, beer, and ale, have never lowered the price of barley; have never reduced the rent and profit of barley land. The price of malt to the brewer has constantly risen in proportion to the taxes imposed upon it; and those taxes, together with the different duties upon beer and ale, have constantly either raised the price, or what comes to the same thing, reduced the quality of those commodities to the consumer. The final payment of those taxes has fallen constantly upon the consumer, and not upon the producer.

The only people likely to suffer by the change of system here proposed, are those who brew for their own private use.

The only sufferers would be those who brew for prvate use.

But the exemption, which this superior rank of people at present enjoy, from very heavy taxes which are paid by the poor labourer and artificer, is surely most unjust and unequal, and ought to be taken away, even though this change was never to take place. It has probably been the interest of this superior order of people, however, which has hitherto prevented a change of system that could not well fail both to increase the revenue and to relieve the people.

Besides such duties as those of customs and excise abovementioned, there are several others which affect the price of goods more unequally and more indirectly.

Tolls on goods carried from place to place affect prices unequally.

Of this kind are the duties which in French are called Péages, which in old Saxon times were called Duties of Passage, and which seem to have been originally established for the same purpose as our turnpike tolls, or the tolls upon our canals and navigable rivers, for the maintenance of the road or of the navigation. Those duties, when applied to such purposes, are most properly imposed according to the bulk or weight of the goods. As they were originally local and provincial duties, applicable to local and provincial purposes, the administration of them was in most cases entrusted to the particular town, parish, or lordship, in which they were levied; such communities being in some way or other supposed to be accountable for the application. The sovereign, who is altogether unaccountable, has in many countries assumed to himself the administration of those duties; and though he has in most cases enhanced very much the duty, he has in many entirely neglected the application. If the turnpike tolls of Great Britain should ever become one of the resources of government, we may learn, by the example of many other nations, what would probably be the consequence. Such tolls are no doubt finally paid by the consumer; but the consumer is not taxed in proportion to his expence when he pays, not according to the value, but according to the bulk or weight of what he consumes. When such duties are imposed, not according to the bulk or weight, but according to the supposed value of the goods, they become properly a sort of inland customs or excises, which obstruct very much the most important of all branches of commerce, the interior commerce of the country.

In some small states duties similar to those passage duties are imposed upon goods carried across the territory, either by

Some countries levy transit duties on foreign goods.

land or by water, from one foreign country to another. These are in some countries called transit-duties. Some of the little Italian states, which are situated upon the Po, and the rivers which run into it, derive some revenue from duties of this kind, which are paid altogether by foreigners, and which, perhaps, are[110] the only duties that one state can impose upon the subjects of another, without obstructing in any respect the industry or commerce of its own. The most important transit-duty in the world is that levied by the king of Denmark upon all merchant ships which pass through the Sound.

Such taxes upon luxuries as the greater part of the duties of customs and excise, though they all[111] fall indifferently upon

Taxes on luxuries do not reach absentees, but the fact that they are paid voluntarily recommends them.

every different species of revenue, and are paid finally, or without any retribution, by whoever consumes the commodities upon which they are imposed, yet they do not always fall equally or proportionably upon the revenue of every individual. As every man's humour regulates the degree of his consumption, every man contributes rather according to his humour than in proportion to his revenue; the profuse contribute more, the parsimonious less, than their proper proportion. During the minority of a man of great fortune, he contributes commonly very little, by his consumption, towards the support

---

[110] [Ed. 1 reads "are perhaps."]

[111] [Ed. 1 does not contain "all."]

of that state from whose protection he derives a great revenue. Those who live in another country contribute nothing, by their consumption, towards the support of the government of that country, in which is situated the source of their revenue. If in this latter country there should be no land-tax, nor any considerable duty upon the transference either of moveable or of immoveable property, as in the case in Ireland, such absentees may derive a great revenue from the protection of a government to the support of which they do not contribute a single shilling. This inequality is likely to be greatest in a country of which the government is in some respects subordinate and dependent upon that of some other. The people who possess the most extensive property in the dependent, will in this case generally chuse to live in the governing country. Ireland is precisely in this situation, and we cannot therefore wonder that the proposal of a tax upon absentees should be so very popular in that country. It might, perhaps, be a little difficult to ascertain either what sort, or what degree of absence would[112] subject a man to be taxed as an absentee, or at what precise time the tax should either begin or end. If you except, however, this very peculiar situation, any inequality in the contribution of individuals, which can arise from such taxes, is much more than compensated by the very circumstance which occasions that inequality; the circumstance that every man's contribution is altogether voluntary; it being altogether in his power either to consume or not to consume the commodity taxed. Where such taxes, therefore, are properly assessed and upon proper commodities, they are paid with less grumbling than any other. When they are advanced by the merchant or manufacturer, the consumer, who finally pays them, soon comes to confound them with the price of the commodities, and almost forgets that he pays any tax.

Such taxes are or may be perfectly certain, or may be assessed so as to leave no doubt concerning either what ought to be paid, or when it ought to be paid; concerning either the quantity or

They are also certain

---

[112] [Ed. 1 reads "should."]

the time of payment. Whatever uncertainty there may sometimes be, either in the duties of customs in Great Britain, or in
other duties of the same kind in other countries, it cannot arise
from the nature of those duties, but from the inaccurate or unskilful manner in which the law that imposes them is expressed.

Taxes upon luxuries generally are, and always may be, paid
piece-meal, or in proportion as the contributors have occasion

and payable at convenient times,

to purchase the goods upon which they are
imposed. In the time and mode of payment
they are, or may be, of all taxes the most
convenient. Upon the whole, such taxes, therefore, are, perhaps, as agreeable to the three first of the four general maxims
concerning taxation, as any other. They offend in every respect
against the fourth.

but take much more from the people than they yield to the state, since

Such taxes, in proportion to what they
bring into the public treasury of the state, always take out or keep out of the pockets of
the people more than almost any other taxes.
They seem to do this in all the four different
ways in which it is possible to do it.

First, the levying of such taxes, even when imposed in the
most judicious manner, requires a great number of custom-

(1) the salaries and perquisites of customs and excise officers take a large proportion of what is collected;

house and excise officers, whose salaries
and perquisites are a real tax upon the people, which brings nothing into the treasury
of the state. This expence, however, it must
be acknowledged, is more moderate in Great
Britain than in most other countries. In the
year which ended on the fifth of July 1775,
the gross produce of the different duties, under the management of the commissioners of excise in England, amounted to
5,507,308*l.* 18*s.* 8¼*d.*[113] which was levied at an expence of little
more than five and a half per cent. From this gross produce,
however, there must be deducted what was paid away in bounties and drawbacks upon the exportation of exciseable goods,

---

[113] [Ed. 1 reads "£5,479695 7s. 10d."]

which will reduce the neat produce below five millions.[114] The levying of the salt duty, an excise duty, but under a different management, is much more expensive. The neat revenue of the customs does not amount to two millions and a half, which is levied at an expence of more than ten per cent. in the salaries of officers, and other incidents. But the perquisites of custom-house officers are every where much greater than their salaries; at some ports more than double or triple those salaries. If the salaries of officers, and other incidents, therefore, amount to more than ten per cent. upon the neat revenue of the customs; the whole expence of levying that revenue may amount, in salaries and perquisites together, to more than twenty or thirty per cent. The officers of excise receive few or no perquisites: and the administration of that branch of the revenue being of more recent establishment, is in general less corrupted than that of the customs, into which length of time has introduced and authorised many abuses. By charging upon malt the whole revenue which is at present levied by the different duties upon malt and malt liquors, a saving, it is supposed, of more than fifty thousand pounds might be made in the annual expence of the excise. By confining the duties of customs to a few sorts of goods, and by levying those duties according to the excise laws, a much greater saving might probably be made in the annual expence of the customs.

Secondly, such taxes necessarily occasion some obstruction or discouragement to certain branches of industry. As they al-

(2) particular branches of industry are discouraged;

ways raise the price of the commodity taxed, they so far discourage its consumption, and consequently its production. If it is a commodity of home growth or manufacture, less labour comes to be employed in raising and producing it. If it is a foreign commodity of which the tax increases in this manner the price, the commodities of the same kind which are made at home may thereby, indeed, gain some advantage in the home market, and a greater quantity of domes-

---

[114] The neat produce of that year, after deducting all expences and allowances, amounted to 4,975,652*l.* 19*s.* 6*d.* [This note appears first in ed. 2.]

tic industry may thereby be turned toward preparing them. But though this rise of price in a foreign commodity may encourage domestic industry in one particular branch, it necessarily discourages that industry in almost every other. The dearer the Birmingham manufacturer buys his foreign wine, the cheaper he necessarily sells that part of his hardware with which, or, what comes to the same thing, with the price of which he buys it. That part of his hardware, therefore, becomes of less value to him, and he has less encouragement to work at it. The dearer the consumers in one country pay for the surplus produce of another, the cheaper they necessarily sell that part of their own surplus produce with which, or, what comes to the same thing, with the price of which they buy it. That part of their own surplus produce becomes of less value to them, and they have less encouragement to increase its quantity. All taxes upon consumable commodities, therefore, tend to reduce the quantity of productive labour below what it otherwise would be, either in preparing the commodities taxed, if they are home commodities; or in preparing those with which they are purchased, if they are foreign commodities. Such taxes too always alter, more or less, the natural direction of national industry, and turn it into a channel always different from, and generally less advantageous than that in which it would have run of its own accord.

Thirdly, the hope of evading such taxes by smuggling gives frequent occasion to forfeitures and other penalties, which en-

(3) smuggling is encouraged;

tirely ruin the smuggler; a person who, though no doubt highly blameable for violating the laws of his country, is frequently incapable of violating those of natural justice, and would have been, in every respect, an excellent citizen, had not the laws of his country made that a crime which nature never meant to be so. In those corrupted governments where there is at least a general suspicion of much unnecessary expence, and great misapplication of the public revenue, the laws which guard it are little respected. Not many people are scrupulous about smuggling, when, without perjury, they can find any easy and safe opportunity of doing so. To pretend to have any scruple about buying smuggled goods, though a manifest encouragement to the violation of the revenue laws, and to the perjury which almost always attends it, would in most countries be regarded as one of those pedantic pieces of hypocrisy which, instead of gaining credit with any body, serve only to expose the person who affects to practise them, to the suspicion of being a greater knave than most of his neighbours. By this indulgence of the public, the smuggler is often encouraged to continue a trade which he is thus taught to consider as in some measure innocent; and when the severity of the revenue laws is ready to fall upon him, he is frequently disposed to defend with violence, what he has been accustomed to regard as his just property. From being at first, perhaps, rather imprudent than criminal, he at last too often becomes one of the hardiest and most determined violators of the laws of society. By the ruin of the smuggler, his capital, which had before been employed in maintaining productive labour, is absorbed either in the revenue of the state or in that of the revenue-officer, and is employed in maintaining unproductive, to the diminution of the general capital of the society, and of the useful industry which it might otherwise have maintained.

Fourthly, such taxes, by subjecting at least the dealers in the taxed commodities to the frequent visits and odious exam-

and (4) vexation equivalent to expense is caused by the tax-gatherers' examinations and visits.

ination of the tax-gatherers, expose them sometimes, no doubt, to some degree of oppression, and always to much trouble and vexation; and though vexation, as has already been said,[115] is not strictly speaking expence, it is certainly equivalent to the expence at which every man would be willing to redeem himself from it. The laws of excise, though more effectual for the purpose for which they were instituted, are, in this respect, more vexatious than those of the customs. When a merchant has imported goods subject to certain duties of customs, when he has paid those duties, and lodged the goods in his warehouse, he is not in most cases liable to any further trouble or vexation from the customhouse officer. It is other-

[115] [Above, p. 1045.]

wise with goods subject to duties of excise. The dealers have no respite from the continual visits and examination of the excise officers. The duties of excise are, upon this account, more unpopular than those of the customs; and so are the officers who levy them. Those officers, it is pretended, though in general, perhaps, they do their duty fully as well as those of the customs; yet, as that duty obliges them to be frequently very troublesome to some of their neighbours, commonly contract a certain hardness of character which the others frequently have not. This observation, however, may very probably be the mere suggestion of fraudulent dealers, whose smuggling is either prevented or detected by their diligence.

The inconveniencies, however, which are, perhaps, in some degree inseparable from taxes upon consumable commodities,

Great Britain suffers less than other countries from these inconveniencies.

fall as light upon the people of Great Britain as upon those of any other country of which the government is nearly as expensive. Our state is not perfect, and might be mended; but it is as good or better than that of most of our neighbours.

In consequence of the notion that duties upon consumable goods were taxes upon the profits of merchants, those duties

Duties on commodities are sometimes repeated on each sale, as by the Spanish Alcavala,

have, in some countries, been repeated upon every successive sale of the goods. If the profits of the merchant importer or merchant manufacturer were taxed, equality seemed to require that those of all the middle buyers, who intervened between either of them and the consumer, should likewise be taxed. The

famous Alcavala of Spain seems to have been established upon this principle. It was at first a tax of ten per cent., afterwards of fourteen per cent., and is at present of only six per cent. upon the sale of every sort of property, whether moveable or immoveable; and it is repeated every time the property is sold.[116]

---

[116] *Memoires concernant les Droits, &c.* tom. i. p. 455. ["La première branche, connue sous la dénomination de Alcavala y Cientos, consiste dans un droit qui se perçoit sur toutes les choses mobiliaires et immobiliaires qui sont vendues, échangées et négociées: ce droit qui dans le principe avoit été fixé à quatorze pour

The levying of this tax requires a multitude of revenue-officers sufficient to guard the transportation of goods, not only from one province to another, but from one shop to another. It subjects, not only the dealers in some sorts of goods, but those in all sorts, every farmer, every manufacturer, every merchant and shopkeeper, to the continual visits and examination of the tax-gatherers. Through the greater part of a country in which a tax of this kind is established, nothing can be produced for distant sale. The produce of every part of the country must be proportioned to the consumption of the neighbourhood. It is to the Alcavala, accordingly, that Ustaritz imputes the ruin of the manufactures of Spain.[117] He might have imputed to it likewise the declension of agriculture, it being imposed not only upon manufactures, but upon the rude produce of the land.

In the kingdom of Naples there is a similar tax of three per cent. upon the value of all contracts, and consequently upon

and the 3 per cent. tax at Naples. that of all contracts of sale. It is both lighter than the Spanish tax, and the greater part of towns and parishes are allowed to pay a composition in lieu of it. They levy this composition in what manner they please, generally in a way that gives no interruption to the interior commerce of the place. The Neapolitan tax, therefore, is not near so ruinous as the Spanish one.

The uniform system of taxation, which, with a few exceptions of no great consequence, takes place in all the different parts of the united kingdom of Great Britain, leaves the interior commerce of the country, the inland and coasting trade, almost entirely free. The inland trade is almost perfectly free, and the

cent a été depuis réduit à six pour cent." The rest of the information is probably from Uztariz, *Theory and Practice of Commerce and Maritime Affairs*, trans. by John Kippax, 1751, chap. 96, *ad init.*, vol. ii., p. 236. "It is so very oppressive as to lay 10 per cent. for the primitive Alcavala, and the four 1 per cents. annexed to it, a duty not only chargeable on the first sale, but on every future sale of goods, I am jealous, it is one of the principal engines, that contributed to the ruin of most of our manufactures and trade. For though these duties are not charged to the full in some places, a heavy tax is paid."]

[117] [See the preceding note. Uztariz' opinion is quoted by Lord Kames, *Sketches of the History of Man*, 1774, vol. i., p. 516.]

Great advantage is obtained by the uniformity of taxation in Great Britain.

greater part of goods may be carried from one end of the kingdom to the other, without requiring any permit or let-pass, without being subject to question, visit, or examination from the revenue officers. There are a few exceptions, but they are such as can give no interruption to any important branch of the inland commerce of the country. Goods carried coastwise, indeed, require certificates or coast cockets. If you except coals, however, the rest are almost all duty-free. This freedom of interior commerce, the effect of the uniformity of the system of taxation, is perhaps one of the principal causes of the prosperity of Great Britain; every great country being necessarily the best and most extensive market for the greater part of the productions of its own industry. If the same freedom, in consequence of the same uniformity, could be extended to Ireland and the plantations, both the grandeur of the state and the prosperity of every part of the empire, would probably be still greater than at present.

In France, the different revenue laws which take place in the different provinces, require a multitude of revenue-officers to

In France the diversity of taxes in different provinces occasions many hindrances to internal trade,

surround, not only the frontiers of the kingdom, but those of almost each particular province, in order either to prevent the importation of certain goods, or to subject it to the payment of certain duties, to the no small interruption of the interior commerce of the country. Some provinces are allowed to compound for the gabelle or salt-tax. Others are exempted from it altogether. Some provinces are exempted from the exclusive sale of tobacco, which the farmers-general enjoy through the greater part of the kingdom. The aids, which correspond to the excise in England, are very different in different provinces. Some provinces are exempted from them, and pay a composition or equivalent. In those in which they take place and are in farm, there are many local duties which do not extend beyond a particular town or district. The Traites, which correspond to our customs, divide the kingdom into three great parts; first, the provinces subject to the tarif of 1664, which are called the provinces of the five great farms, and under which are comprehended Picardy, Normandy, and the greater part of the interior provinces of the kingdom; secondly, the provinces subject to the tarif of 1667, which are called the provinces reckoned foreign, and under which are comprehended the greater part of the frontier provinces; and, thirdly, those provinces which are said to be treated as foreign, or which, because they are allowed a free commerce with foreign countries, are in their commerce with the other provinces of France subjected to the same duties as other foreign countries. These are Alsace, the three bishopricks of Metz, Toul, and Verdun, and the three cities of Dunkirk, Bayonne, and Marseilles. Both in the provinces of the five great farms (called so on account of an ancient division of the duties of customs into five great branches, each of which was originally the subject of a particular farm, though they are now all united into one), and in those which are said to be reckoned foreign, there are many local duties which do not extend beyond a particular town or district. There are some such even in the provinces which are said to be treated as foreign, particularly in the city of Marseilles. It is unnecessary to observe how much, both the restraints upon the interior commerce of the country, and the number of the revenue officers must be multiplied, in order to guard the frontiers of those different provinces and districts, which are subject to such different systems of taxation.

Over and above the general restraints arising from this complicated system of revenue laws, the commerce of wine, after

and the commerce in wine is subject to particular restraints.

corn perhaps the most important production of France, is in the greater part of the provinces subject to particular restraints, arising from the favour which has been shewn to the vineyards of particular provinces and districts, above those of others. The provinces most famous for their wines, it will be found, I believe, are those in which the trade in that article is subject to the fewest restraints of this kind. The extensive market which such provinces enjoy, encourages good management both in the cultivation of their vineyards, and in the subsequent preparation of their wines.

Such various and complicated revenue laws are not peculiar to France. The little dutchy of Milan is divided into six

Milan and Parma are still more absurdly managed.

provinces, in each of which there is a different system of taxation with regard to several different sorts of consumable goods. The still smaller territories of the duke of Parma are divided into three or four, each of which has, in the same manner, a system of its own. Under such absurd management, nothing, but the great fertility of the soil and happiness of the climate, could preserve such countries from soon relapsing into the lowest state of poverty and barbarism.

Taxes upon consumable commodities may either be levied by an administration of which the officers are appointed by

The collection of taxes by government officers is much superior to letting the taxes to farm.

government and are immediately accountable to government, of which the revenue must in this case vary from year to year, according to the occasional variations in the produce of the tax; or they may be let in farm for a rent certain, the farmer being allowed to appoint his own officers, who, though obliged to levy the tax in the manner directed by the law, are under his immediate inspection, and are immediately accountable to him. The best and most frugal way of levying a tax can never be by farm. Over and above what is necessary for paying the stipulated rent, the salaries of the officers, and the whole expense of administration, the farmer must always draw from the produce of the tax a certain profit proportioned at least to the advance which he makes, to the risk which he runs, to the trouble which he is at, and to the knowledge and skill which it requires to manage so very complicated a concern. Government, by establishing an administration under their own immediate inspection, of the same kind with that which the farmer establishes, might at least save this profit, which is almost always exorbitant. To farm any considerable branch of the public revenue, requires either a great capital or a great credit; circumstances which would alone restrain the competition for such an undertaking to a very small number of people. Of the few who have this capital or credit, a still smaller number have the necessary knowledge or experience; another circumstance which restrains the competition still further. The very few, who are in condition to become competitors, find it more for their interest to combine together; to become co-partners instead of competitors, and when the farm is set up to auction, to offer no rent, but what is much below the real value. In countries where the public revenues are in farm, the farmers are generally the most opulent people. Their wealth would alone excite the public indignation, and the vanity which almost always accompanies such upstart fortunes, the foolish ostentation with which they commonly display that wealth, excites that indignation still more.

The farmers of the public revenue never find the laws too severe, which punish any attempt to evade the payment of

Farmers of taxes require sanguinary revenue laws.

a tax. They have no bowels for the contributors, who are not their subjects, and whose universal bankruptcy, if it should happen the day after their farm is expired, would not much affect their interest. In the greatest exigencies of the state, when the anxiety of the sovereign for the exact payment of his revenue is necessarily the greatest, they seldom fail to complain that without laws more rigorous than those which actually take place, it will be impossible for them to pay even the usual rent. In those moments of public distress their demands cannot be disputed. The revenue laws, therefore, become gradually more and more severe. The most sanguinary are always to be found in countries where the greater part of the public revenue is in farm. The mildest, in countries where it is levied under the immediate inspection of the sovereign. Even a bad sovereign feels more compassion for his people than can ever be expected from the farmers of his revenue. He knows that the permanent grandeur of his family depends upon the prosperity of his people and he will never knowingly ruin that prosperity for the sake of any momentary interest of his own. It is otherwise with the farmers of his revenue, whose grandeur may frequently be the effect of the ruin, and not of the prosperity of his people.

A tax is sometimes, not only farmed for a certain rent,[118] but the farmer has, besides, the monopoly of the commodity taxed.

Taxation by monopolies let to farm is even worse. In France, the duties[119] upon tobacco and salt are levied in this manner. In such cases the farmer, instead of one, levies two exorbitant profits upon the people; the profit of the farmer, and the still more exorbitant one of the monopolist. Tobacco being a luxury, every man is allowed to buy or not to buy as he chuses. But salt being a necessary, every man is obliged to buy of the farmer a certain quantity of it; because, if he did not buy this quantity of the farmer, he would, it is presumed, buy it of some smuggler. The taxes upon both commodities are exorbitant. The temptation to smuggle consequently is to many people irresistible, while at the same time the rigour of the law, and the vigilance of the farmer's officers, render the yielding to that temptation almost certainly ruinous. The smuggling of salt and tobacco sends every year several hundred people to the gallies, besides a very considerable number whom it sends to the gibbet. Those taxes levied in this manner yield a very considerable revenue to government. In 1767, the farm of tobacco was let for twenty-two millions five hundred and forty-one thousand two hundred and seventy-eight livres a year. That of salt, for thirty-six millions four hundred and ninety-two thousand four hundred and four livres. The farm in both cases was to commence in 1768, and to last for six years. Those who consider the blood of the people as nothing in comparison with the revenue of the prince, may perhaps approve of this method of levying taxes. Similar taxes and monopolies of salt and tobacco have been established in many other countries; particularly in the Austrian and Prussian dominions, and in the greater part of the states of Italy.

In France, the greater part of the actual revenue of the crown is derived from eight different sources; the taille, the

[118] [Ed. 1 reads "rent certain."]

[119] [Ed. 1 reads "the taxes."]

In France the three branches of revenue which are levied by government officers are much more economical.
capitation, the two vingtiemes, the gabelles, the aides, the traites, the domaine, and the farm of tobacco. The five last are, in the greater part of the provinces, under farm. The three first are every where levied by an administration under the immediate inspection and direction of government, and it is universally acknowledged that, in proportion to what they take out of the pockets of the people, they bring more into the treasury of the prince than the other five, of which the administration is much more wasteful and expensive.

The finances of France seem, in their present state, to admit of three very obvious reformations. First, by abolishing the
The taille and capitations should be abolished, the vingtièmes increased, the taxes on commodities made uniform, and farming abolished.
taille and the capitation, and by encreasing the number of vingtiemes, so as to produce an additional revenue equal to the amount of those other taxes, the revenue of the crown might be preserved; the expence of collection might be much diminished; the vexation of the inferior ranks of people, which the taille and capitation occasion, might be entirely prevented; and the superior ranks might not be more burdened than the greater part of them are at present. The vingtieme, I have already observed,[120] is a tax very nearly of the same kind with what is called the land-tax of England. The burden of the taille, it is acknowledged, falls finally upon the proprietors of land; and as the greater part of the capitation is assessed upon those who are subject to the taille at so much a pound of that other tax, the final payment of the greater part of it must likewise fall upon the same order of people. Though the number of the vingtiemes, therefore, was increased so as to produce an additional revenue equal to the amount of both those taxes, the superior ranks of people might not be more burdened than they are at present. Many individuals no doubt would, on account of the great inequalities with

[120] [Above, p. 1085.]

which the taille is commonly assessed upon the estates and tenants of different individuals. The interest and opposition of such favoured subjects are the obstacles most likely to prevent this or any other reformation of the same kind. Secondly, by rendering the gabelle, the aides, the traites,[121] the taxes upon tobacco, all the different customs and excises, uniform in all the different parts of the kingdom, those taxes might be levied at much less expence, and the interior commerce of the kingdom might be rendered as free as that of England. Thirdly, and lastly, by subjecting all those taxes to an administration under the immediate inspection and direction of government, the exorbitant profits of the farmers general might be added to the revenue of the state. The opposition arising from the private interest of individuals, is likely to be as effectual for preventing the two last as the first mentioned scheme of reformation.

The French system of taxation seems, in every respect, inferior to the British. In Great Britain ten millions sterling are annually levied upon less than eight millions of people, without its being possible to say that any particular order is oppressed. From the collections of the Abbé Expilly,[122] and the observations of the author of the Essay upon the legislation and commerce of corn,[123] it appears probable, that France, including the provinces of Lorraine and Bar, contains about twenty-three or twenty-four millions of people;

The French system is in every respect inferior to the British.

---

[121] [Ed. 1 does not contain "the traites."]

[122] [These estimates seem to have been quoted in England at the time, since the Continuation of Anderson's *Commerce*, under the year 1773, mentions "the calculations of the Abbé D'Expilly published about this time in Paris," which gave 8,661,381 births and 6,664,161 deaths as the number taking place in the nine years, 1754 to 1763, in France, inclusive of Lorraine and Bar. In his *Dictionnaire géographique, historique et politique des Gaules et de la France*, tom. v. (1768), *s.v.* Population, Expilly estimated the population at 22,014,357. See Levasseur, *La Population française*, tom. i., 1889, pp. 215 and 216 note.]

[123] [*Sur la législation et le commerce des grains* (by Necker), 1775, ch. viii., estimates the population at 24,181,333 by the method of multiplying the deaths by 31.]

three times the number perhaps contained in Great Britain. The soil and climate of France are better than those of Great Britain. The country has been much longer in a state of improvement and cultivation, and is, upon that account, better stocked with all those things which it requires a long time to raise up and accumulate, such as great towns, and convenient and well-built houses, both in town and country. With these advantages, it might be expected that in France a revenue of thirty millions might be levied for the support of the state, with as little inconveniency as a revenue of ten millions is in Great Britain. In 1765 and 1766, the whole revenue paid into the treasury of France, according to the best, though, I acknowledge, very imperfect, accounts which I could get of it, usually run between 308 and 325 millions of livres; that is, it did not amount to fifteen millions sterling; not the half of what might have been expected, had the people contributed in the same proportion to their numbers as the people of Great Britain. The people of France, however, it is generally acknowledged, are much more oppressed by taxes than the people of Great Britain. France, however, is certainly the great empire in Europe which, after that of Great Britain, enjoys the mildest and most indulgent government.

In Holland the heavy taxes upon the necessaries of life have ruined, it is said, their principal manufactures,[124] and

In Holland heavy taxes on necessaries have ruined manufactures. are likely to discourage gradually even their fisheries and their trade in shipbuilding. The taxes upon the necessaries of life are inconsiderable in Great Britain, and no manufacture has hitherto been ruined by them. The British taxes which bear hardest on manufactures are some duties upon the importation of raw materials, particularly upon that of raw silk. The revenue of the states general and of the different cities, however, is said to amount to more than five millions two hundred and fifty thousand pounds sterling; and as the inhabitants of the

[124] [Above, pp. 1109–1110.]

United Provinces cannot well be supposed to amount to more than a third part of those of Great Britain, they must, in proportion to their number, be much more heavily taxed.

After all the proper subjects of taxation have been exhausted, if the exigencies of the state still continue to require new taxes, they must be imposed upon improper ones.[125] The taxes upon the necessaries of life, therefore, may be no impeachment of the wisdom of that republic, which, in order to acquire and to maintain its independency, has, in spite of its great frugality, been involved in such expensive wars as have obliged it to contract great debts. The singular countries of Holland and Zealand, besides, require a considerable expence even to preserve their existence, or to prevent their being swallowed up by the sea, which must have contributed to increase considerably the load of taxes in those two provinces. The republican form of government seems to be the principal support of the present grandeur of Holland. The owners of great capitals, the great mercantile families, have generally either some direct share, or some indirect influence, in the administration of that government. For the sake of the respect and authority which they derive from this situation, they are willing to live in a country where their capital, if they employ it themselves, will bring them less profit, and if they lend it to another, less interest; and where the very moderate revenue which they can draw from it will purchase less of the necessaries and conveniencies of life than in any other part of Europe. The residence of such wealthy people necessarily keeps alive, in spite of all disadvantages, a certain degree of industry in the country. Any public calamity which should destroy the republican form of government, which should throw the whole administration into the hands of nobles and of soldiers, which should annihilate altogether the importance of those wealthy merchants would soon

But perhaps Holland has done the best possible.

---

[125] [Below, p. 1183.]

render it disagreeable to them to live in a country where they were no longer likely to be much respected. They would remove both their residence and their capital to some other country, and the industry and commerce of Holland would soon follow the capitals which supported them.

CHAPTER III

OF PUBLIC DEBTS

IN THAT rude state of society which precedes the extension of commerce and the improvement of manufactures, when those

When expensive luxuries are unknown, persons with large revenue are likely to hoard savings.

expensive luxuries which commerce and manufactures can alone introduce, are altogether unknown, the person who possesses a large revenue, I have endeavoured to show in the third book of this Inquiry,[1] can spend or enjoy that revenue in no other way than by maintaining nearly as many people as it can maintain. A large revenue may at all times be said to consist in the command of a large quantity of the necessaries of life. In that rude state of things it is commonly paid in a large quantity of those necessaries, in the materials of plain food and coarse clothing, in corn and cattle, in wool and raw hides. When neither commerce nor manufactures furnish any thing for which the owner can exchange the greater part of those materials which are over and above his own consumption, he can do nothing with the surplus but feed and clothe nearly as many people as it will feed and clothe. A hospitality in which there is no luxury, and a liberality in which there is no ostentation, occasion, in this situation of things, the principal expences of the rich and the great. But these, I have likewise endeavoured to show in the same book,[2] are expences by which people are not very apt to ruin themselves. There is not, perhaps, any selfish pleasure so frivolous, of which the pursuit has not sometimes

[1] [Above, pp. 521–522.]

[2] [Above, p. 529.]

ruined even sensible men. A passion for cock-fighting has ruined many. But the instances, I believe, are not very numerous of people who have been ruined by a hospitality or liberality of this kind; though the hospitality of luxury and the liberality of ostentation have ruined many. Among our feudal ancestors, the long time during which estates used to continue in the same family, sufficiently demonstrates the general disposition of people to live within their income. Though the rustic hospitality, constantly exercised by the great land-holders, may not, to us in the present times, seem consistent with that order, which we are apt to consider as inseparably connected with good œconomy, yet we must certainly allow them to have been at least so far frugal as not commonly to have spent their whole income. A part of their wool and raw hides they had generally an opportunity of selling for money. Some part of this money, perhaps, they spent in purchasing the few objects of vanity and luxury, with which the circumstances of the times could furnish them; but some part of it they seem commonly to have hoarded. They could not well indeed do anything else but hoard whatever money they saved. To trade was disgraceful to a gentleman, and to lend money at interest, which at that time was considered as usury and prohibited by law, would have been still more so. In those times of violence and disorder, besides, it was convenient to have a hoard of money at hand, that in case they should be driven from their own home, they might have something of known value to carry with them to some place of safety. The same violence, which made it convenient to hoard, made it equally convenient to conceal the hoard. The frequency of treasure-trove, or of treasure found of which no owner was known, sufficiently demonstrates the frequency in those times both of hoarding and of concealing the hoard. Treasure-trove was then considered as an important branch of the revenue of the sovereign.[3] All the treasure-trove of the kingdom would scarce perhaps in the present times make an important branch of the revenue of a private gentleman of a good estate.

[3] [Cp. pp. 361–362.]

The same disposition to save and to hoard prevailed in the sovereign, as well as in the subjects. Among nations to whom

So the ancient sovereigns of Europe amassed treasures.

commerce and manufactures are little known, the sovereign, it has already been observed in the fourth book,[4] is in a situation which naturally disposes him to the parsimony requisite for accumulation. In that situation the expence even of a sovereign cannot be directed by that vanity which delights in the gaudy finery of a court. The ignorance of the times affords but few of the trinkets in which that finery consists. Standing armies are not then necessary, so that the expence even of a sovereign, like that of any other great lord, can be employed in scarce any thing but bounty to his tenants, and hospitality to his retainers. But bounty and hospitality very seldom lead to extravagance; though vanity almost always does.[5] All the ancient sovereigns of Europe accordingly, it has already been observed, had treasures. Every Tartar chief in the present times is said to have one.

In a commercial country abounding with every sort of expensive luxury, the sovereign, in the same manner as almost all

When luxuries are introduced, the sovereign's expenditure equals his revenue in time of peace,

the great proprietors in his dominions, naturally spends a great part of his revenue in purchasing those luxuries. His own and the neighbouring countries supply him abundantly with all the costly trinkets which compose the splendid, but insignificant pageantry of a court. For the sake of an inferior pageantry of the same kind, his nobles dismiss their retainers, make their tenants independent, and become gradually themselves as insignificant as the greater part of the wealthy burghers in his dominions. The same frivolous passions, which influence their conduct, influence his. How can it be supposed that he should be the only rich man in his dominions who is insensible to pleasures of this kind? If he does not, what he is very likely to do, spend upon those pleasures so great a part of

[4] [Above, p. 560.]

[5] [Repeated *verbatim* from p. 560.]

his revenue as to debilitate very much the defensive power of the state, it cannot well be expected that he should not spend upon them all that part of it which is over and above what is necessary for supporting that defensive power. His ordinary expence becomes equal to his ordinary revenue, and it is well if it does not frequently exceed it. The amassing of treasure can no longer be expected, and when extraordinary exigencies require extraordinary expences, he must necessarily call upon his subjects for an extraordinary aid. The present and the late king of Prussia are the only great princes of Europe, who, since the death of Henry IV. of France in 1610, are supposed to have amassed any considerable treasure.[6] The parsimony which leads to accumulation has become almost as rare in republican as in monarchical governments. The Italian republics, the United Provinces of the Netherlands, are all in debt. The canton of Berne is the single republic in Europe which has amassed any considerable treasure.[7] The other Swiss republics have not. The taste for some sort of pageantry, for splendid buildings, at least, and other public ornaments, frequently prevails as much in the apparently sober senate-house of a little republic, as in the dissipated court of the greatest king.

The want of parsimony in time of peace, imposes the necessity of contracting debt in time of war. When war comes, there

and in time of war he contracts debts. is no money in the treasury but what is necessary for carrying on the ordinary expence of the peace establishment. In war an establishment of three or four times that expence becomes necessary for the defence of the state, and consequently a revenue three or four times greater than the peace revenue. Supposing that the sovereign should have, what he scarce ever has, the immediate means of augmenting his revenue in proportion to the augmentation of his expence, yet still the produce of the taxes, from which this increase of revenue must be drawn, will not begin to come into the treasury till perhaps ten or twelve months after they are imposed. But the moment in which war

[6] [Above, p. 555.]

[7] [Above, pp. 1035–1036.]

begins, or rather the moment in which it appears likely to begin, the army must be augmented, the fleet must be fitted out, the garrisoned towns must be put into a posture of defence; that army, that fleet, those garrisoned towns must be furnished with arms, ammunition, and provisions. An immediate and great expence must be incurred in that moment of immediate danger, which will not wait for the gradual and slow returns of the new taxes. In this exigency government can have no other resource but in borrowing.

The same commercial state of society which, by the operation of moral causes, brings government in this manner into

The same causes which make borrowing necessary make it possible.

the necessity of borrowing, produces in the subjects both an ability and an inclination to lend. If it commonly brings along with it the necessity of borrowing, it likewise brings along[8] with it the facility of doing so.

A country abounding with merchants and manufacturers, necessarily abounds with a set of people through whose hands

Merchants and manufacturers are able to lend,

not only their own capitals, but the capitals of all those who either lend them money, or trust them with goods, pass as frequently, or more frequently, than the revenue of a private man, who, without trade or business, lives upon his income, passes through his hands. The revenue of such a man can regularly pass through his hands only once in a year. But the whole amount of the capital and credit of a merchant, who deals in a trade of which the returns are very quick, may sometimes pass through his hands two, three, or four times in a year. A country abounding with merchants and manufacturers, therefore, necessarily abounds with a set of people who have it at all times in their power to advance, if they chuse to do so, a very large sum of money to government. Hence the ability in the subjects of a commercial state to lend.

Commerce and manufactures can seldom flourish long in

and also willing.

any state which does not enjoy a regular administration of justice, in which the people

[8] [Ed. 5 omits "along," doubtless by a misprint.]

do not feel themselves secure in the possession of their property, in which the faith of contracts is not supported by law, and in which the authority of the state is not supposed to be regularly employed in enforcing the payment of debts from all those who are able to pay. Commerce and manufactures, in short, can seldom flourish in any state in which there is not a certain degree of confidence in the justice of government. The same confidence which disposes great merchants and manufacturers, upon ordinary occasions, to trust their property to the protection of a particular government; disposes them, upon extraordinary occasions, to trust that government with the use of their property. By lending money to government, they do not even for a moment diminish their ability to carry on their trade and manufactures. On the contrary, they commonly augment it. The necessities of the state render government upon most occasions willing to borrow upon terms extremely advantageous to the lender. The security which it grants to the original creditor, is made transferable to any other creditor, and, from the universal confidence in the justice of the state, generally sells in the market for more than was originally paid for it. The merchant or monied man makes money by lending money to government, and instead of diminishing, increases his trading capital. He generally considers it as a favour, therefore, when the administration admits him to a share in the first subscription for a new loan. Hence the inclination or willingness in the subjects of a commercial state to lend.

The government of such a state is very apt to repose itself

A government dispenses itself from saving if it knows it can borrow,

upon this ability and willingness of its subjects to lend it their money on extraordinary occasions. It foresees the facility of borrowing, and therefore dispenses itself from the duty of saving.

In a rude state of society there are no great mercantile or

whereas if there is no possibility of borrowing, it feels it must save.

manufacturing capitals. The individuals, who hoard whatever money they can save, and who conceal their hoard, do so from a distrust of the justice of government, from a fear that if it was known that they had a hoard, and where that hoard was to be found, they would quickly be plundered. In such a state of things few people would be able, and no body would be willing, to lend their money to government on extraordinary exigencies. The sovereign feels that he must provide for such exigencies by saving, because he foresees the absolute impossibility of borrowing. This foresight increases still further his natural disposition to save.

The progress of the enormous debts which at present oppress, and will in the long-run probably ruin, all the great nations of Europe, has been pretty uniform.

Nations have begun to borrow without special security and have afterwards mortgaged particular funds.

Nations, like private men, have generally begun to borrow upon what may be called personal credit, without assigning or mortgaging any particular fund for the payment of the debt; and when this resource has failed them, they have gone on to borrow upon assignments or mortgages of particular funds.

What is called the unfunded debt of Great Britain, is contracted in the former of those two ways. It consists partly in a debt which bears, or is supposed to bear, no interest, and which resembles the debts that a private man contracts upon account; and partly in a debt which bears interest, and which resembles what a private man contracts upon his bill or promissory note. The debts which are due either for extraordinary services, or for services either not provided for, or not paid at the time when they are performed; part of the extraordinaries of the army, navy, and ordnance, the arrears of subsidies to foreign princes, those of seamen's wages, &c. usually constitute a debt of the first kind. Navy and Exchequer bills, which are issued sometimes in payment of a part of such debts and sometimes for other purposes, constitute a debt of the second kind; Exchequer bills bearing interest from the day on which they are issued, and navy bills six months after they are issued. The bank of England, either by voluntarily discounting those bills at their current value, or by

The unfunded debt of Great Britain is contracted in the first way.

agreeing with government for certain considerations to circulate Exchequer bills, that is, to receive them at par, paying the interest which happens to be due upon them, keeps up their value and facilitates their circulation, and thereby frequently enables government to contract a very large debt of this kind. In France, where there is no bank, the state bills (billets d'état[9]) have sometimes sold at sixty and seventy per cent. discount. During the great re-coinage in King William's time, when the bank of England thought proper to put a stop to its usual transactions, Exchequer bills and tallies are said to have sold from twenty-five to sixty per cent. discount;[10] owing partly, no doubt, to the supposed instability of the new government established by the Revolution, but partly too to the want of the support of the bank of England.

When this resource is exhausted, and it becomes necessary, in order to raise money, to assign or mortgage some particular branch of the public revenue for the payment of the debt, government has upon different occasions done this in two different ways. Sometimes it has made this assignment or mortgage for a short period of time only, a year, or a few years, for example; and sometimes for perpetuity. In the one case, the fund was supposed sufficient to pay, within the limited time, both principal and interest of the money borrowed. In the other, it was supposed sufficient to pay the interest only, or a perpetual annuity equivalent to the interest, government being at liberty to redeem at any time this annuity, upon paying back the principal sum borrowed. When money was raised in

Mortgages of particular branches of revenue are either for a term of years, when money is said to be raised by anticipation, or in perpetuity, when it is said to be raised by funding.

---

[9] See *Examen des Reflexions politiques sur les Finances.* [P. J. Duverney, *Examen du livre intitulé Réflexions politiques sur les finances et le commerce* (by Du Tot), tom. i., p. 225.]

[10] [James Postlethwayt, *History of the Public Revenue*, 1759, pp. 14, 15, mentions discounts of 25 and 55 per cent. The discount varied with the priority of the tallies and did not measure the national credit in general, but the probability of particular taxes bringing in enough to pay the amounts charged upon them. See also above, p. 406.]

the one way, it was said to be raised by anticipation; when in the other, by perpetual funding, or, more shortly, by funding.

In Great Britain the annual land and malt taxes are regularly anticipated every year, by virtue of a borrowing clause con-

The annual land and malt taxes are always anticipated.

stantly inserted into the acts which impose them. The bank of England generally advances at an interest, which since the Revolution has varied from eight to three per cent. the sums for which those taxes are granted, and receives payment as their produce gradually comes in. If there is a deficiency, which there always is, it is provided for in the supplies of the ensuing year. The only considerable branch of the public revenue which yet remains unmortgaged is thus regularly spent before it comes in. Like an improvident[11] spendthrift, whose pressing occasions will not allow him to wait for the regular payment of his revenue, the state is in the constant practice of borrowing of its own factors and agents, and of paying interest for the use of its own money.

In the reign of king William, and during a great part of that of queen Anne, before we had become so familiar as we are

Under William III. and Anne antici- pations gave rise to deficiencies,

now with the practice of perpetual funding, the greater part of the new taxes were imposed but for a short period of time (for four, five, six, or seven years only), and a great part of the grants of every year consisted in loans upon anticipations of the produce of those taxes. The produce being frequently insufficient for paying within the limited term the principal and interest of the money borrowed, deficiencies arose, to make good which it became necessary to prolong the term.

In 1697, by the 8th of William III. c. 20. the deficiencies of several taxes were charged upon what was then called the first

and the term of the mortgage taxes was prolonged in 1697,

general mortgage or fund, consisting of a prolongation to the first of August, 1706, of several different taxes, which would have expired within a shorter term, and of which

---

[11] [Ed. 1 reads "unprovident," as do all editions, see also below, p. 1164.]

the produce was accumulated into one general fund. The deficiencies charged upon this prolonged term amounted to 5,160,459*l.* 14*s.* 9¼*d.*[12]

In 1701, those duties, with some others, were still further prolonged for the like purposes till the first of August, 1710,

in 1701, and were called the second general mortgage or fund.[13] The deficiencies charged upon it amounted to 2,055,999*l.* 7*s.* 11½*d.*

In 1707, those duties were still further prolonged, as a fund for new loans, to the first of August, 1712, and were called the

in 1707, third general mortgage or fund. The sum borrowed upon it was 983,254*l.* 11*s.* 9¼*d.*

In 1708, those duties were all (except the old subsidy of tonnage and poundage, of which one moiety only was made a

in 1708, part of this fund, and a duty upon the importation of Scotch linen, which had been taken off by the articles of union) still further continued, as a fund for new loans, to the first of August, 1714, and were called the fourth general mortgage or fund.[14] The sum borrowed upon it was 925,176*l.* 9*s.* 2¼*d.*[15]

In 1709, those duties were all (except the old subsidy of tonnage and poundage, which was now left out of this fund alto-

in 1709, together) still further continued for the same purpose to the first of August, 1716 and were called the fifth general mortgage or fund.[16] The sum borrowed upon it was 922,029*l.* 6*s.* 0*d.*

In 1710, those duties were again prolonged to the first of August, 1720, and were called the sixth gen-

and in 1710. eral mortgage or fund.[17] The sum borrowed upon it was 1,296,552*l.* 9*s.* 11¾*d.*

---

[12] [Postlethwayt, *op. cit.*, p. 38. Ed. 5 misprints "9½*d.*"]

[13] [Postlethwayt, *op. cit.*, p. 40.]

[14] [*Ibid.*, p. 59.]

[15] [*Ibid.*, pp. 63, 64.]

[16] [*Ibid.*, p. 68.]

[17] [*Ibid.*, p. 71.]

In 1711, the same duties (which at this time were thus subject to four different anticipations), together

*In 1711 the taxes
were continued for
ever and made
into a fund for
paying the interest
on £9,177,968.*

with several others, were continued for ever,
and made a fund for paying the interest of
the capital of the South Sea company, which
had that year advanced to government, for
paying debts and making good deficiencies,
the sum of 9,177,967*l.* 15*s.* 4*d.*;[18] the greatest loan which at that time had ever been made.

Before this period, the principal, so far as I have been able
to observe, the only taxes which in order to pay the interest of

*The only earlier
taxes imposed in
perpetuity to pay
interest on debt
were those for
paying interest on
the advances of
the Bank and East
India Company.*

a debt had been imposed for perpetuity, were
those for paying the interest of the money
which had been advanced to government by
the Bank and East India Company, and of
what it was expected would be advanced, but
which was never advanced, by a projected
land bank. The bank fund at this time
amounted to 3,375,027*l.* 17*s.* 10½*d.* for

which was paid an annuity or interest of
206,501*l.*13*s.*5*d.*[19] The East India fund amounted to
3,200,000*l.* for which was paid an annuity or interest of
160,000*l.*;[20] the bank fund being at six per cent.,[21] the East
India fund at five per cent. interest.

In 1715, by the first of George I. c. 12. the different taxes
which had been mortgaged for paying the bank annuity, to-

*In 1715 several
taxes were accu-
mulated into the
Aggregate Fund,*

gether with several others which by this act
were likewise rendered perpetual, were accumulated into one common fund called The
Aggregate Fund, which was charged, not
only with the payments[22] of the bank annuity,

---

[18] [*Ibid.*, p. 311.]

[19] [*Ibid.*, pp. 301–303, and see above, p. 407.]

[20] [*Ibid.*, pp. 319, 320.]

[21] [The odd £4,000 of the £206.501 13s. 5d. was for expenses of management. See above, p. 406.]

[22] [Ed. I reads "payment," perhaps correctly.]

but with several other annuities and burdens of different kinds. This fund was afterwards augmented by the third of George I. c. 8. and by the fifth of George I. c. 3. and the different duties which were then added to it were likewise rendered perpetual.[23]

In 1717, by the third of George I. c. 7.[24] several other taxes

and in 1717 several others into the General Fund.

were rendered perpetual, and accumulated into another common fund, called The General Fund, for the payment of certain annuities, amounting in the whole to 724,849*l.* 6*s.* 10½*d.*

In consequence of those different acts, the greater part of

Thus most of the anticipated taxes were made into a fund for paying interest only.

the taxes which before had been anticipated only for a short term of years, were rendered perpetual as a fund for paying, not the capital, but the interest only, of the money which had been borrowed upon them by different successive anticipations.

Had money never been raised but by anticipation, the course of a few years would have liberated the public revenue,

When once become familiar, perpetual funding is preferred to anticipation.

without any other attention of government besides that of not overloading the fund by charging it with more debt than it could pay within the limited term, and of not anticipating a second time before the expiration of the first anticipation. But the greater part of European governments have been incapable of those attentions. They have frequently overloaded the fund even upon the first anticipation; and when this happened not to be the case, they have generally taken care to overload it, by anticipating a second and a third time before the expiration of the first anticipation. The fund becoming in this manner altogether insufficient for paying both principal and interest of the money borrowed upon it, it became necessary to charge it with the interest only, or a perpetual annuity equal to the interest, and such improvident anticipations necessarily gave birth to the

[23] [Postlethwayt, *History of the Public Revenue*, p. 305.]

[24] [This Act belongs to 1716, not 1717.]

more ruinous practice of perpetual funding. But though this practice necessarily puts off the liberation of the public revenue from a fixed period to one so indefinite that it is not very likely ever to arrive; yet as a greater sum can in all cases be raised by this new practice than by the old one of anticipations, the former, when men have once become familiar with it, has in the great exigencies of the state been universally preferred to the latter. To relieve the present exigency is always the object which principally interests those immediately concerned in the administration of public affairs. The future liberation of the public revenue, they leave to the care of posterity.

During the reign of queen Anne, the market rate of interest had fallen from six to five per cent., and in the twelfth year of her reign five per cent. was declared to be the highest rate which could lawfully be taken for money borrowed upon private security.[25] Soon after the greater part of the temporary taxes of Great Britain had been rendered perpetual, and distributed into the Aggregate, South Sea, and General Funds, the creditors of the public, like those of private persons, were induced to accept of five per cent. for the interest of their money,[26] which occasioned a saving of one per cent. upon the capital of the greater part of the debts which had been thus funded for perpetuity, or of one-sixth of the greater part of the annuities which were paid out of the three great funds above mentioned. This saving left a considerable surplus in the produce of the different taxes which had been accumulated into those funds, over and above what was necessary for paying the annuities which were now charged upon them, and laid the foundation of what has since been called the Sinking Fund. In 1717, it amounted to 323,434l. 7s. 7½d.[27] In 1727, the interest of the greater part of the public debts was still further reduced to four per

A fall in the market rate of interest led to a saving, which gave rise to the Sinking Fund.

---

[25] [Above, p. 124.]

[26] [In 1717, under the provisions of 3 Geo. I., c. 7. Postlethwayt, *History of the Public Revenue*, pp. 120, 145.]

[27] [Anderson, *Commerce*, A.D. 1717.]

cent.;[28] and in 1753[29] and 1757, to three and a half and three per cent.; which reductions still further augmented the sinking fund.

A sinking fund, though instituted for the payment of old, facilitates very much the contracting of new debts. It is a sub-

A sinking fund facilitates the contraction of new debt.

sidiary fund always at hand to be mortgaged in aid of any other doubtful fund, upon which money is proposed to be raised in any exigency of the state. Whether the sinking fund of Great Britain has been more frequently applied to the one or to the other of those two purposes, will sufficiently appear by and by.

Besides those two methods of borrowing, by anticipations

Money is also borrowed by terminable and life annuities.

and by perpetual funding, there are two other methods, which hold a sort of middle place between them. These are, that of borrowing upon annuities for terms of years, and that of borrowing upon annuities for lives.

During the reigns of king William and queen Anne, large sums were frequently borrowed upon annuities for terms of

Under William III. and Anne large sums were borrowed on annuities for terms of years.

years, which were sometimes longer and sometimes shorter. In 1693, an act was passed for borrowing one million upon an annuity of fourteen per cent.,[30] or of 140,000*l*. a year, for sixteen years. In 1691, an act was passed for borrowing a million upon annuities for lives, upon terms which in the present times would appear very advantageous. But the subscription was not filled up. In the following year[31] the deficiency was made good by borrowing upon annuities for lives at fourteen per cent., or at little more than seven years purchase. In 1695, the persons who had purchased those annuities were

[28] [*Ibid.*, A.D. 1727.]

[29] [This should be 1750. Anderson, *Commerce*, A.D. 1749.]

[30] [5 and 6 W. and M., c. 7.]

[31] [4 W. and M., c. 3.]

allowed to exchange them for others of ninety-six years, upon paying into the Exchequer sixty-three pounds in the hundred; that is, the difference between fourteen per cent. for life, and fourteen per cent. for ninety-six years, was sold for sixty-three pounds, or for four and a half years purchase. Such was the supposed instability of government, that even these terms procured few purchasers. In the reign of queen Anne, money was upon different occasions borrowed both upon annuities for lives, and upon annuities for terms of thirty-two, of eighty-nine, of ninety-eight, and of ninety-nine years. In 1719, the proprietors of the annuities for thirty-two years were induced to accept in lieu of them South Sea stock to the amount of eleven and a half years purchase of the annuities, together with an additional quantity of stock equal to the arrears which happened then to be due upon them.[32] In 1720, the greater part of the other annuities for terms of years both long and short were subscribed into the same fund. The long annuities at that time amounted to 666,821*l*. 8*s*. 3½*d*. a year.[33] On the 5th of January, 1775, the remainder of them, or what was not subscribed at that time, amounted only to 136,453*l*. 12*s*. 8*d*.

During the two wars which begun in 1739 and in 1755, little money was borrowed either upon annuities for terms of years, or upon those for lives. An annuity for ninety-eight or ninety-nine years, however, is worth nearly as much money as a perpetuity, and should, therefore, one might think, be a fund for borrowing nearly as much. But those who, in order to make family settlements, and to provide for remote futurity, buy into the public stocks, would not care to purchase into one of which the value was continually diminishing; and such people make a very considerable proportion both of the proprietors and purchasers of stock. An annuity for a long term of years, therefore, though its intrinsic value may be very nearly the same with that of a per-

But little money was so borrowed in the wars of the middle of the eighteenth century, most people preferring a perpetual annuity,

[32] [Anderson, *Commerce*, A.D. 1719.]

[33] [*Ibid.*, A.D. 1720.]

petual annuity, will not find nearly the same number of purchasers. The subscribers to a new loan, who mean generally to sell their subscription as soon as possible, prefer greatly a perpetual annuity redeemable by parliament, to an irredeemable annuity for a long term of years of only equal amount. The value of the former may be supposed always the same, or very nearly the same; and it makes, therefore, a more convenient transferable stock than the latter.

During the two last mentioned wars, annuities, either for terms of years or for lives, were seldom granted but as premiums to the subscribers to a new loan, over and above the redeemable annuity or interest upon the credit of which the loan was supposed to be made. They were granted, not as the proper fund upon which the money was borrowed; but as an additional encouragement to the lender.

and annuities for terms and for lives were only given as premiums.

Annuities for lives have occasionally been granted in two different ways; either upon separate lives, or upon lots of lives, which in French are called Tontines, from the name of their inventor. When annuities are granted upon separate lives, the death of every individual annuitant disburthens the public revenue so far as it was affected by his annuity. When annuities are granted upon tontines, the liberation of the public revenue does not commence till the death of all the annuitants comprehended in one lot, which may sometimes consist of twenty or thirty persons, of whom the survivors succeed to the annuities of all those who die before them; the last survivor succeeding to the annuities of the whole lot. Upon the same revenue more money can always be raised by tontines than by annuities for separate lives. An annuity, with a right of survivorship, is really worth more than an equal annuity for a separate life, and from the confidence which every man naturally has in his own good fortune, the principle upon which is founded the success of all lotteries, such an annuity generally sells for something more than it is worth. In countries where it is usual for government to raise money by granting annuities,

Tontines are preferred to annuities on separate lives, though they do not liberate the public revenue so quickly.

tontines are upon this account generally preferred to annuities for separate lives. The expedient which will raise most money, is almost always preferred to that which is likely to bring about in the speediest manner the liberation of the public revenue.

In France, a much greater proportion of the public debts consists in annuities for lives than in England. According to a

In France a much greater proportion of the whole debt is in life annuities than in England;

memoir presented by the parliament of Bourdeaux to the king in 1764, the whole public debt of France is estimated at twenty-four hundred millions of livres; of which the capital for which annuities for lives had been granted, is supposed to amount to three hundred millions, the eighth part of the whole public debt. The annuities themselves are computed to amount to thirty millions a year, the fourth part of one hundred and twenty millions, the supposed interest of that whole debt. These estimations, I know very well, are not exact, but having been presented by so very respectable a body as approximations to the truth, they may, I apprehend, be considered as such. It is not the different degrees of anxiety in the two governments of France and England for the liberation of the public revenue, which occasions this difference in their respective modes of borrowing. It arises altogether from the different views and interests of the lenders.

In England, the seat of government being in the greatest mercantile city in the world, the merchants are generally the

the difference is due to the fact that in England the lenders are merchants,

people who advance money to government. By advancing it they do not mean to diminish, but, on the contrary, to increase their mercantile capitals; and unless they expected to sell with some profit their share in the subscription for a new loan, they never would subscribe. But if by advancing their money they were to purchase, instead of perpetual annuities, annuities for lives only, whether their own or those of other people, they would not always be so likely to sell them with a profit. Annuities upon their own lives they would always sell with loss; because no man will give for an annuity upon the life of another, whose age and state of health are nearly the same with his own, the same price which he would give for one upon his own. An annuity upon the life of a third person, indeed, is, no doubt, of equal value to the buyer and the seller; but its real value begins to diminish from the moment it is granted, and continues to do so more and more as long as it subsists. It can never, therefore, make so convenient a transferable stock as a perpetual annuity, of which the real value may be supposed always the same, or very nearly the same.

In France the seat of government not being in a great mercantile city, merchants do not make so great a proportion of the people who advance money to government. *whereas in France they are persons engaged in the farming and collection of the taxes, who are chiefly bachelors.* The people concerned in the finances, the farmers general, the receivers of the taxes which are not in farm, the court bankers, &c. make the greater part of those who advance their money in all public exigencies. Such people are commonly men of mean birth, but of great wealth, and frequently of great pride. They are too proud to marry their equals, and women of quality disdain to marry them. They frequently resolve, therefore, to live bachelors, and having neither any families of their own, nor much regard for those of their relations, whom they are not always very fond of acknowledging, they desire only to live in splendour during their own time, and are not unwilling that their fortune should end with themselves. The number of rich people, besides, who are either averse to marry, or whose condition of life renders it either improper or inconvenient for them to do so, is much greater in France than in England. To such people, who have little or no care for posterity, nothing can be more convenient than to exchange their capital for a revenue, which is to last just as long,[34] and no longer than they wish it to do.

The ordinary expence of the greater part of modern governments in time of peace being equal or nearly equal to their ordinary revenue, when war comes, they are both unwilling and unable to increase their revenue in proportion to the increase of

[34] [Ed. 1 reads "just as long as."]

The system of perpetual funding prevents the people from feeling distinctly the burden of war.

their expence. They are unwilling, for fear of offending the people, who by so great and so sudden an increase of taxes, would soon be disgusted with the war; and they are unable, from not well knowing what taxes would be sufficient to produce the revenue wanted. The facility of borrowing delivers them from the embarrassment which this fear and inability would otherwise occasion. By means of borrowing they are enabled, with a very moderate increase of taxes, to raise, from year to year, money sufficient for carrying on the war, and by the practice of perpetual funding they are enabled, with the smallest possible increase of taxes, to raise annually the largest possible sum of money. In great empires the people who live in the capital, and in the provinces remote from the scene of action, feel, many of them, scarce any inconveniency from the war; but enjoy, at their ease, the amusement of reading in the newspapers the exploits of their own fleets and armies. To them this amusement compensates the small difference between the taxes which they pay on account of the war, and those which they had been accustomed to pay in time of peace. They are commonly dissatisfied with the return of peace, which puts an end to their amusement, and to a thousand visionary hopes of conquest and national glory, from a longer continuance of the war.

The return of peace, indeed, seldom relieves them from the greater part of the taxes imposed during the war.

These are mortgaged for the interest of the debt contracted in order to carry it on. If, over and above paying the interest of this debt, and defraying the ordinary expence of government,

Their burdens are not reduced on the conclusion of peace.

the old revenue, together with the new taxes, produce some surplus revenue, it may perhaps be converted into a sinking fund for paying off the debt. But, in the first place, this sinking fund, even supposing it should be applied to no other purpose, is generally altogether inadequate for paying, in the course of any period during which it can reasonably be expected that peace should continue, the whole debt contracted during the war; and, in the second place, this fund is almost always applied to other purposes.

The new taxes were imposed for the sole purpose of paying the interest of the money borrowed upon them. If they produce

Any new taxes imposed are rarely sufficient to do more than pay the new interest. Sinking funds arise generally from reductions of interest,

more, it is generally something which was neither intended nor expected, and is therefore seldom very considerable. Sinking funds have generally arisen, not so much from any surplus of the taxes which was over and above what was necessary for paying the interest or annuity originally charged upon them, as from a subsequent reduction of that interest. That of Holland in 1655, and that of the ecclesiastical state in 1685, were both formed in this manner.[35] Hence the usual insufficiency of such funds.

During the most profound peace, various events occur which require an extraordinary expence, and government finds

and are constantly misapplied.

it always more convenient to defray this expence by misapplying the sinking fund than by imposing a new tax. Every new tax is immediately felt more or less by the people. It occasions always some murmur, and meets with some opposition. The more taxes may have been multiplied, the higher they may have been raised upon every different subject of taxation; the more loudly the people complain of every new tax, the more difficult it becomes too either to find out new subjects of taxation, or to raise much higher the taxes already imposed upon the old. A momentary suspension of the payment of debt is not immediately felt by the people, and occasions neither murmur nor complaint. To borrow of the sinking fund is always an obvious and easy expedient for getting out of the present difficulty. The more the public debts may have been accumulated, the more necessary it may have become to study to reduce them, the more dangerous, the more ruinous it may be to misapply any part of the sinking fund; the less likely is the public debt to be

---

[35] [Anderson, *Commerce*, mentions these reductions under their dates, and recalls them in reference to the British reduction in 1717.]

reduced to any considerable degree, the more likely, the more certainly is the sinking fund to be misapplied towards defraying all the extraordinary expences which occur in time of peace. When a nation is already overburdened with taxes, nothing but the necessities of a new war, nothing but either the animosity of national vengeance, or the anxiety for national security, can induce the people to submit, with tolerable patience, to a new tax. Hence the usual misapplication of the sinking fund.

In Great Britain, from the time that we had first recourse to the ruinous expedient of perpetual funding, the reduction of the public debt in time of peace, has never borne any proportion to its accumulation in time of war. It was in the war which began in 1688, and was concluded by the treaty of Ryswick in 1697, that the foundation of the present enormous debt of Great Britain was first laid.

The British debt had its origin in the war of 1688–97,

On the 31st of December 1697, the public debts of Great Britain, funded and unfunded, amounted to 21,515,742*l.* 13*s.* 8½*d.* A great part of those debts had been contracted upon short anticipations, and some part upon annuities for lives; so that before the 31st of December 1701, in less than four years, there had partly been paid off, and partly reverted to the public, the sum of 5,121,041*l.* 12*s.* 0¾*d.*; a greater reduction of the public debt than has ever since been brought about in so short a period of time. The remaining debt, therefore, amounted only to 16,394,701*l.* 1*s.* 7¼*d.*

which left a debt of twenty-one and a half millions. This was reduced by five millions in 1697–1701. From 1702 to 1722 the increase was thirty-nine millions, and from 1722 to 1739 the reduction was only eight and one-third millions.

In the war which began in 1702, and which was concluded by the treaty of Utrecht, the public debts were still more accumulated. On the 31st of December 1714, they amounted to 53,681,076*l.* 5*s.* 6½*d.* The subscription into the South Sea fund of the short and long[36] annuities increased the capital of the public debts, so that on the 31st of December

---

[36] [Ed. 1 reads "long and short."]

1722, it amounted to 55,282,978*l*. 1*s*. 3⅚*d*. The reduction of the debt began in 1723, and went on so slowly that, on the 31st of December 1739, during seventeen years of profound peace, the whole sum paid off was no more than 8,328,354*l*. 17*s*. 11½²*d*. the capital of the public debt at that time amounting to 46,954,623*l*. 3*s*. 4½²*d*.

The Spanish war, which began in 1739, and the French war which soon followed it, occasioned a further increase of the debt, which, on the 31st of December 1748, after the

From 1739 to 1748 the increase was thirty-one and one-third millions.

war had been concluded by the treaty of Aix la Chapelle, amounted to 78,293,313*l*. 1*s*. 10¾*d*. The most profound peace of seventeen years continuance had taken no more than 8,328,354*l*. 17*s*. 11½²*d*. from it. A war of less than nine years continuance added 31,338,689*l*. 18*s*. 6⅛*d*. to it.[37]

During the administration of Mr. Pelham, the interest of the public debt was reduced, or at least measures were taken for reducing it, from four to three per cent.;[38] the sinking fund was

During the peace of 1748–55 the reduction was six millions, and the seven years' war added more than seventy-five.

increased, and some part of the public debt was paid off. In 1755, before the breaking out of the late war, the funded debt of Great Britain amounted to 72,289,673*l*.[39] On the 5th of January 1763, at the conclusion of the peace, the funded debt amounted to 122,603,336*l*. 8*s*. 2¼*d*.[40] The unfunded debt

has been stated at 13,927,589*l*. 2*s*. 2*d*. But the expence occasioned by the war did not end with the conclusion of the peace;[41] so that though, on the 5th of January 1764, the funded debt was increased (partly by a new loan, and partly by funding

[37] See James Postlethwayt's history of the public revenue. [Pp. 42, 143–145, 147, 224, 300. The reference covers the three paragraphs in the text above.]

[38] [Above, pp. 1165–1166.]

[39] [*Present State of the Nation* (above, p. 557), p. 28.]

[40] [Anderson, *Commerce*, postscript *ad init.*]

[41] ["But the expenses of the war did not cease with its operations."— *Considerations* (see a few lines below), p. 4.]

a part of the unfunded debt)[42] to 129,586,789*l*. 10*s*. 1¾*d*.[43] there still remained (according to the very well informed author of the Considerations on the trade and finances of Great Britain)[44] an unfunded debt which was brought to account in that and the following year, of 9,975,017*l*. 12*s*. 2¹⁵⁄₄₄*d*. In 1764, therefore, the public debt of Great Britain, funded and unfunded together, amounted, according to this author, to 139,561,807*l*. 2*s*. 4*d*.[45] The annuities for lives too, which had been granted as premiums to the subscribers to the new loans in 1757, estimated at fourteen years purchase, were valued at 472,500*l*.; and the annuities for long terms of years, granted as premiums likewise, in 1761 and 1762, estimated at 27½ years purchase, were valued at 6,826,875*l*.[46] During a peace of about seven years continuance, the prudent and truly patriot administration of Mr. Pelham, was not able to pay off an old debt of six millions. During a war of nearly the same continuance, a new debt of more than seventy-five millions was contracted.

On the 5th of January 1775, the funded debt of Great Britain amounted to 124,996,086*l*. 1*s*. 6¼*d*. The unfunded, exclusive of a large civil list debt, to 4,150,236*l*. 3*s*. 11⅞*d*. Both together, to 129,146,322*l*. 5*s*. 6*d*. According to this account the whole debt paid off during eleven years profound peace amounted only to 10,415,474*l*. 16*s*. 9⅞*d*. Even this small reduction of debt, however, has not been all made from the savings out of the ordinary revenue of the state. Several extraneous sums, altogether independent of that ordinary revenue,

---

[42] [*Ibid.*, p. 5.]

[43] [The account is given in the Continuation of Anderson's *Commerce*, A.D. 1764, vol. iv., p. 58, in ed. of 1801. The "¾d." should be "¼d."]

[44] [*Considerations on the Trade and Finances of this Kingdom and on the measures of administration with respect to those great national objects since the conclusion of the peace*, by Thomas Whately, 1766 (often ascribed to George Grenville), p. 22.]

[45] [This is the amount obtained by adding the two items mentioned, and is the reading of ed. 1. Eds. 2–5 all read "£139,516,807 2s. 4d.," which is doubtless a misprint. The total is not given in *Considerations*.]

[46] [*Considerations*, p. 4.]

have contributed towards it. Amongst[47] these we may reckon an additional shilling in the pound land tax for three years; the two millions received from the East India company, as indemnification for their territorial acquisitions; and the one hundred and ten thousand pounds received from the bank for the renewal of their charter. To these must be added several other sums which, as they arose out of the late war, ought perhaps to be considered as deductions from the expences of it. The principal are,

In the eleven years of peace before January 1775 the reduction was only ten and a half millions, and most of this was due to reductions of interest.

	l.	s.	d.
The produce of French prizes	690,449	18	9
Composition for French prisoners	670,000	0	0
What has been received from the sale of the ceded islands[48]	95,500	0	0
Total,	1,455,949	18	9

If we add to this sum the balance of the earl of Chatham's and Mr. Calcraft's accounts, and other army savings of the same kind, together with what has been received from the bank, the East India company, and the additional shilling in the pound land tax; the whole must be a good deal more than five millions. The debt, therefore, which since the peace has been paid out of the savings from the ordinary revenue of the state, has not, one year with another, amounted to half a million a year. The sinking fund has, no doubt, been considerably augmented since the peace, by the debt which has been paid off, by the reduction of the redeemable four per cents. to three per cents., and by the annuities for lives which have fallen in, and, if peace were[49] to continue, a million, perhaps, might now be annually spared out of it towards the discharge of the debt. Another million, accordingly, was paid in the course of last year; but, at the same time, a large civil list debt was left unpaid, and we are

[47] [Ed. 1 reads "Among."]

[48] [Above, p. 733, note 43.]

[49] [Eds. 1–3 read "was."]

now involved in a new war which, in its progress, may prove as expensive as any of our former wars.[50] The new debt which will probably be contracted before the end of the next campaign, may perhaps be nearly equal to all the old debt which has been paid off from the savings out of the ordinary revenue of the state. It would be altogether chimerical, therefore, to expect that the public debt should ever be completely discharged by any savings which are likely to be made from that ordinary revenue as it stands at present.

The public funds of the different indebted nations of Europe, particularly those of England, have by one author been represented as the accumulation of a great capital superadded

The opinion that the national debt is an additional capital is altogether erroneous.

to the other capital of the country, by means of which its trade is extended, its manufactures multiplied, and its lands cultivated and improved much beyond what they could have been by means of that other capital only.[51] He does not consider that the capital which the first creditors of the public advanced to government, was, from the moment in which they advanced it, a certain portion of the annual produce turned away from serving in the function of a capital, to serve in that of a revenue; from maintaining productive labourers to maintain unproductive ones, and to be spent and wasted, generally in the course of the year, without even the hope of any future reproduction. In return for the capital which they advanced they obtained, indeed, an annuity in the public funds in most cases of more than equal value. This annuity, no doubt, replaced to them their capital,

[50] It has proved more expensive than any of our former wars; and has involved us in an additional debt of more than one hundred millions. During a profound peace of eleven years, little more than ten millions of debt was paid; during a war of seven years, more than one hundred millions was contracted. [This note appears first in ed. 3.]

[51] [Garnier's note, *Recherches etc.*, tom. iv., p. 501, is "Pinto: *Traité de la Circulation et du Crédit*," a work published in 1771 ("Amsterdam"), "par l'auteur de l'essai sur le luxe," of which see esp. pp. 44, 45, 209–211. But an English essay of 1731 to the same effect is quoted by Melon, *Essai Politique sur le Commerce*, chap. xxiii., ed. of 1761, p. 296, and Melon seems to be referred to below, p. 1180. Cp. *Lectures*, p. 210.]

and enabled them to carry on their trade and business to the same or perhaps to a greater extent than before; that is, they were enabled either to borrow of other people a new capital upon the credit of this annuity, or by selling it to get from other people a new capital of their own, equal or superior to that which they had advanced to government. This new capital, however, which they in this manner either bought or borrowed of other people, must have existed in the country before, and must have been employed as all capitals are, in maintaining productive labour. When it came into the hands of those who had advanced their money to government, though it was in some respects a new capital to them, it was not so to the country; but was only a capital withdrawn from certain employments in order to be turned towards others. Though it replaced to them what they had advanced to government, it did not replace it to the country. Had they not advanced this capital to government, there would have been in the country two capitals, two portions of the annual produce, instead of one, employed in maintaining productive labour.

When for defraying the expence of government a revenue is raised within the year from the produce of free or unmortgaged taxes, a certain portion of the revenue of private people is only turned away from maintaining one species

When necessary expenditure is met by taxes, it only diverts unproductive labour from one unproductive employment to another.

of unproductive labour, towards maintaining another. Some part of what they pay in those taxes might no doubt have been accumulated into capital, and consequently employed in maintaining productive labour; but the greater part would probably have been spent and consequently employed in maintaining unproductive labour. The public expence, however, when defrayed in this manner, no doubt hinders more or less the further accumulation of new capital; but it does not necessarily occasion the destruction of any actually existing capital.

When the public expence is defrayed by funding, it is defrayed by the annual destruction of some capital which had before existed in the country; by the perversion of some portion of the annual produce which had before been destined for the

When it is met by borrowing, it diverts labour from productive to unproductive employment, and the only advantage is that people can continue to save more during the war,

maintenance of productive labour, towards that of unproductive labour. As in this case, however, the taxes are lighter than they would have been, had a revenue sufficient for defraying the same expence been raised within the year; the private revenue of individuals is necessarily less burdened, and consequently their ability to save and accumulate some part of that revenue into capital is a good deal less impaired. If the method of funding destroy[52] more old capital, it at the same time hinders less the accumulation or acquisition of new capital, than that of defraying the public expence by a revenue raised within the year. Under the system of funding, the frugality and industry of private people can more easily repair the breaches which the waste and extravagance of government may occasionally make in the general capital of the society.

It is only during the continuance of war, however, that the system of funding has this advantage over the other system. Were the expence of war to be defrayed always by a revenue

which advantage disappears immediately peace is concluded. Under the other system, too, wars would be shorter and periods of peace longer.

raised within the year, the taxes from which that extraordinary revenue was drawn would last no longer than the year. The ability of private people to accumulate, though less during the war, would have been greater during the peace than under the system of funding. War would not necessarily have occasioned the destruction of any old capitals, and peace would have occasioned the accumulation of many more new. Wars would in general be more speedily concluded, and less wantonly undertaken. The people feeling, during the continuance of the war, the complete burden of it, would soon grow weary of it, and government, in order to humour them, would not be under the necessity of carrying it on longer than it was necessary to do so. The foresight of the heavy and unavoidable burdens of war would hinder the

[52] [Eds. 1–3 read the indicative, "destroys."]

people from wantonly calling for it when there was no real or solid interest to fight for. The seasons during which the ability of private people to accumulate was somewhat impaired, would occur more rarely, and be of shorter continuance. Those on the contrary, during which that ability was in the highest vigour, would be of much longer duration than they can well be under the system of funding.

When funding, besides, has made a certain progress, the multiplication of taxes which it brings along with it sometimes impairs as much the ability of private people to accumulate

Moreover funding at length burdens the revenue so greatly that the ordinary peace expenditure exceeds that which would under the other system have been sufficient in war.

even in time of peace, as the other system would in time of war. The peace revenue of Great Britain amounts at present to more than ten millions a year. If free and unmortgaged, it might be sufficient, with proper management and without contracting a shilling of new debt, to carry on the most vigorous war. The private revenue of the inhabitants of Great Britain is at present as much encumbered in time of peace, their

ability to accumulate is[53] as much impaired as it would have been in the time of the most expensive war, had the pernicious system of funding never been adopted.

In the payment of the interest of the public debt, it has been said, it is the right hand which pays the left.[54] The money does not go out of the country. It is only a part of the revenue of one set of the inhabitants which is transferred to another; and the nation is not a farthing the poorer. This apology is founded altogether in the sophistry of the mercantile system, and after the long examination which I have already bestowed upon that system, it may perhaps be unnecessary to say any thing further about it. It supposes, besides, that the whole public debt is owing to the inhabitants of the country, which happens not to

[53] [Misprinted "it" in ed. 5.]

[54] ["Les Dettes d'un État sont des dettes de la main droite à la main gauche, dont le corps ne se trouvera point affaibli, s'il à la quantité d'aliments nécessaires, et s'il sait les distribuer." —Melon, *Essai politique sur le Commerce*, chap. xxiii., ed. of 1761, p. 296.]

The fact of part or the whole of the debt being held at home makes no difference.

be true; the Dutch, as well as several other foreign nations, having a very considerable share in our public funds. But though the whole debt were owing to the inhabitants of the country, it would not upon that account be less pernicious.

Land and capital stock are the two original sources of all revenue both private and public. Capital stock pays the wages

Land and capital, the two original sources of all revenue, are managed by landlords and owners of capital.

of productive labour, whether employed in agriculture, manufactures, or commerce. The management of those two original sources of revenue belongs to two different sets of people; the proprietors of land, and the owners or employers of capital stock.

Taxation may diminish or destroy the landlord's ability to improve his land,

The proprietor of land is interested for the sake of his own revenue to keep his estate in as good condition as he can, by building and repairing his tenants' houses, by making and maintaining the necessary drains and enclosures, and all those other expensive improvements which it properly belongs to the landlord to make and maintain. But by different land-taxes the revenue of the landlord may be so much diminished;

and by different duties upon the necessaries and conveniences of life, that diminished revenue may be rendered of so little real value, that he may find himself altogether unable to make or maintain those expensive improvements. When the landlord, however, ceases to do his part, it is altogether impossible that the tenant should continue to do his. As the distress of the landlord increases, the agriculture of the country must necessarily decline.

When, by different taxes upon the necessaries and conveniences of life, the owners and employers of capital stock find,

and induce the owner of the capital to remove it from the country.

that whatever revenue they derive from it, will not, in a particular country, purchase the same quantity of those necessaries and conveniences which an equal revenue would in almost any other, they will be disposed to remove to some other. And when, in order to raise those taxes, all or the greater part of merchants and manufacturers, that is, all or the greater part of the employers of great capitals, come to be continually exposed to the mortifying and vexatious visits of the tax-gatherers, this disposition to remove will soon be changed into an actual removal. The industry of the country will necessarily fall with the removal of the capital which supported it, and the ruin of trade and manufactures will follow the declension of agriculture.

To transfer from the owners of those two great sources of revenue, land and capital stock, from the persons immediately interested in the good condition of every particular portion of

The transference of the sources of revenue from the owners of particular portions of them to the creditors of the public must occasion neglect of land and waste or removal of capital.

land, and in the good management of every particular portion of capital stock, to another set of persons (the creditors of the public, who have no such particular interest), the greater part of the revenue arising from either, must, in the long-run, occasion both the neglect of land, and the waste or removal of capital stock. A creditor of the public has no doubt a general interest in the prosperity of the agriculture, manufactures, and commerce of the country; and consequently in the good condition of its lands, and in the good management of its capital stock. Should there be any general failure or declension in any of these things, the produce of the different taxes might no longer be sufficient to pay him the annuity or interest which is due to him. But a creditor of the public, considered merely as such, has no interest in the good condition of any particular portion of land, or in the good management of any particular portion of capital stock. As a creditor of the public he has no knowledge of any such particular portion. He has no inspection of it. He can have no care about it. Its ruin may in some[55] cases be unknown to him, and cannot directly affect him.

The practice of funding has gradually enfeebled every state

---

[55] [Ed. 1 reads "most."]

which has adopted it. The Italian republics seem to have begun it. Genoa and Venice, the only two remaining which can pretend

The practice of funding has always enfeebled states.

to an independent existence, have both been enfeebled by it. Spain seems to have learned the practice from the Italian republics, and (its taxes being probably less judicious than theirs) it has, in proportion to its natural

strength, been still more enfeebled. The debts of Spain are of very old standing. It was deeply in debt before the end of the sixteenth century, about a hundred years before England owed a shilling. France, notwithstanding all its natural resources, languishes under an oppressive load of the same kind. The republic of the United Provinces is as much enfeebled by its debts as either Genoa or Venice. Is it likely that in Great Britain alone a practice, which has brought either weakness or desolation into every other country, should prove altogether innocent?

The system of taxation established in those different countries, it may be said, is inferior to that of England. I believe it is so. But it ought to be remembered, that when the wis-

The superiority of the British system of taxation will not enable Britain to support an unlimited burden.

est government has exhausted all the proper subjects of taxation, it must, in cases of urgent necessity, have recourse to improper ones.[56] The wise republic of Holland has upon some occasions been obliged to have recourse to taxes as inconvenient as the greater part of those of Spain. Another war

begun before any considerable liberation of the public revenue had been brought about, and growing in its progress as expensive as the last war, may, from irresistible necessity, render the British system of taxation as oppressive as that of Holland, or even as that of Spain. To the honour of our present system of taxation, indeed, it has hitherto given so little embarrassment to industry, that, during the course even of the most expensive wars, the frugality and good conduct of individuals seem[57] to have been able, by saving and accumulation, to repair

[56] [Above, p. 1151.]

[57] [Eds. 1 and 2 read "seems."]

all the breaches which the waste and extravagance of government had made in the general capital of the society. At the conclusion of the late war, the most expensive that Great Britain ever waged, her agriculture was as flourishing, her manufacturers as numerous and as fully employed, and her commerce as extensive, as they had ever been before. The capital, therefore, which supported all those different branches of industry, must have been equal to what it had ever been before. Since the peace, agriculture has been still further improved, the rents of houses have risen in every town and village of the country, a proof of the increasing wealth and revenue of the people; and the annual amount of the greater part of the old taxes, of the principal branches of the excise and customs in particular, has been continually increasing, an equally clear proof of an increasing consumption, and consequently of an increasing produce, which could alone support that consumption. Great Britain seems to support with ease, a burden which, half a century ago, nobody believed her capable of supporting. Let us not, however, upon this account rashly conclude that she is capable of supporting any burden; nor even be too confident that she could support, without great distress, a burden a little greater than what has already been laid upon her.

When national debts have once been accumulated to a certain degree, there is scarce, I believe, a single instance of their having been fairly and completely paid. The *Bankruptcy is always the end of great accumulation of debt.* liberation of the public revenue, if it has ever been brought about at all, has always been brought about by a bankruptcy; sometimes by an avowed one, but always by a real one, though frequently by a pretended payment.[58]

The raising of the denomination of the coin has been the most usual expedient by which a real public bankruptcy has

---

[58] [Raynal says "L'évidence autorise seulement à dire que les gouvernements qui pour le malheur des peuples ont adopté le détestable système des emprunts doivent tôt ou tard l'abjurer: et que l'abus qu'ils en ont fait les forcera vraisemblablement à être infidèles."—*Histoire philosophique*, Amsterdam, 1773, tom. iv., p. 274.]

Raising the coin has been the usual method of disguising bankruptcy though this expedient has much worse consequences than open bankruptcy.

been disguised under the appearance of a pretended payment. If a sixpence, for example, should either by act of parliament or royal proclamation be raised to the denomination of a shilling, and twenty sixpences to that of a pound sterling; the person who under the old denomination had borrowed twenty shillings, or near four ounces of silver, would, under the new, pay with twenty sixpences, or with something less than two ounces. A national debt of about a hundred and twenty-eight millions, nearly the capital of the funded and unfunded debt of Great Britain, might in this manner be paid with about sixty-four millions of our present money. It would indeed be a pretended payment only, and the creditors of the public would really be defrauded of ten shillings in the pound of what was due to them. The calamity too would extend much further than to the creditors of the public, and those of every private person would suffer a proportionable loss; and this without any advantage, but in most cases with a great additional loss, to the creditors of the public. If the creditors of the public indeed were generally much in debt to other people, they might in some measure compensate their loss by paying their creditors in the same coin in which the public had paid them. But in most countries the creditors of the public are, the greater part of them, wealthy people, who stand more in the relation of creditors than in that of debtors towards the rest of their fellow-citizens. A pretended payment of this kind, therefore, instead of alleviating, aggravates in most cases the loss of the creditors of the public; and without any advantage to the public, extends the calamity to a great number of other innocent people. It occasions a general and most pernicious subversion of the fortunes of private people; enriching in most cases the idle and profuse debtor at the expence of the industrious and frugal creditor, and transporting a great part of the national capital from the hands which were likely to increase and improve it, to those which are likely to dissipate and destroy it. When it becomes necessary for a state to declare itself bankrupt, in the same manner as when it becomes necessary for an individual to do so, a fair, open, and avowed bankruptcy is always the measure which is both least dishonourable to the debtor, and least hurtful to the creditor. The honour of a state is surely very poorly provided for, when, in order to cover the disgrace of a real bankruptcy, it has recourse to a juggling trick of this kind, so easily seen through, and at the same time so extremely pernicious.

Almost all states, however, ancient as well as modern, when reduced to this necessity, have, upon some occasions, played this very juggling trick. The Romans, at the end of the

It has been adopted by many states, including ancient Rome,

first Punic war, reduced the As, the coin or denomination by which they computed the value of all their other coins, from containing twelve ounces of copper to contain only two ounces: that is, they raised two ounces of copper to a denomination which had always before expressed the value of twelve ounces. The republic was, in this manner, enabled to pay the great debts which it had contracted with the sixth part of what it really owed. So sudden and so great a bankruptcy, we should in the present times be apt to imagine, must have occasioned a very violent popular clamour. It does not appear to have occasioned any. The law which enacted it was, like all other laws relating to the coin, introduced and carried through the assembly of the people by a tribune, and was probably a very popular law. In Rome, as in all the other ancient republics, the poor people were constantly in debt to the rich and the great, who, in order to secure their votes at the annual elections, used to lend them money at exorbitant interest, which, being never paid, soon accumulated into a sum too great either for the debtor to pay, or for any body else to pay for him. The debtor, for fear of a very severe execution, was obliged, without any further gratuity, to vote for the candidate whom the creditor recommended. In spite of all the laws against bribery and corruption, the bounty of the candidates, together with the occasional distributions of corn, which were ordered by the senate, were the principal funds from which, during the latter[59] times of the Roman re-

[59] [Eds. 1 and 2 read "later"; cp. above, p. 1116.]

public, the poorer citizens derived their subsistence. To deliver themselves from this subjection to their creditors, the poorer citizens were continually calling out either for an entire abolition of debts, or for what they called New Tables; that is, for a law which should entitle them to a complete acquittance, upon paying only a certain proportion of their accumulated debts. The law which reduced the coin of all denominations to a sixth part of its former value, as it enabled them to pay their debts with a sixth part of what they really owed, was equivalent to the most advantageous new tables. In order to satisfy the people, the rich and the great were, upon several different occasions, obliged to consent to laws both for abolishing debts, and for introducing new tables; and they probably were induced to consent to this law, partly for the same reason, and partly that, by liberating the public revenue, they might restore vigour to that government of which they themselves had the principal direction. An operation of this kind would at once reduce a debt of a hundred and twenty-eight millions to twenty-one millions three hundred and thirty-three thousand three hundred and thirty-three pounds six shillings and eight-pence. In the course of the second Punic war the As was still further reduced, first, from two ounces of copper to one ounce; and afterwards from one ounce to half an ounce; that is, to the fourth part of its original value.[60] By combining the three Roman operations into one, a debt of a hundred and twenty-eight millions of our present money, might in this manner be reduced all at once to a debt of five millions three hundred and thirty-three thousand three hundred and thirty-three pounds six shillings and eight-pence. Even the enormous debt of Great Britain might in this manner soon be paid.

By means of such expedients the coin of, I believe, all nations has been gradually reduced more and more below its original value, and the same nominal sum has been gradu-

---

[60] [This chapter of Roman history is based on a few sentences in Pliny, *H.N.*, lib. xxxiii., cap. iii. Modern criticism has discovered the facts to be not nearly so simple as they are represented in the text.]

and has led to the universal reduction of the value of the coin.

ally brought to contain a smaller and a smaller quantity of silver.

Nations have sometimes, for the same purpose, adulterated the standard of their coin; that is, have mixed a greater quantity of alloy in it. If in the pound weight of our silver coin, for example, instead of eighteen penny-weight, according to the present standard, there was mixed eight ounces of alloy; a pound sterling, or twenty shillings of such coin, would be worth little more than six shillings and eight-pence of our present money. The quantity of silver contained in six shillings and eight-pence of our present money, would thus be raised very nearly to the denomination of a pound sterling. The adulteration of the standard has exactly the same effect with what the French call an augmentation, or a direct raising of the denomination of the coin.

Another expedient is to adulterate the coin,

An augmentation, or a direct raising of the denomination of the coin, always is, and from its nature must be, an open and avowed operation. By means of it pieces of a smaller weight and bulk are called by the same name which had before been given to pieces of a greater weight and bulk. The adulteration of the standard, on the contrary, has generally been a concealed operation. By means of it pieces were issued from the mint of the same denominations, and, as nearly as could be contrived, of the same weight, bulk, and appearance, with pieces which had been current before of much greater value. When king John of France,[61] in order to pay his debts, adulterated his coin, all the officers of his mint were sworn to secrecy. Both operations are unjust. But a simple augmentation is an injus-

but this is a treacherous fraud which occasions such indignation that it usually fails.

---

[61] See du Cange Glossary, voce Moneta; the Benedictine edition. [This gives a table of the alterations made in the coin and refers to Le Blanc, *Traité historique des Monnoyes de France*, 1792, in which the fact that the officers were adjured by their oaths to keep the matter secret is mentioned on p. 218, but the adjuration is also quoted in the more accessible Melon, *Essai politique sur le Commerce*, chap. xiii., ed. of 1761, p. 177.]

tice of open violence; whereas an adulteration is an injustice of treacherous fraud. This latter operation, therefore, as soon as it has been discovered, and it could never be concealed very long, has always excited much greater indignation than the former. The coin after any considerable augmentation has very seldom been brought back to its former weight; but after the greatest adulterations it has almost always been brought back to its former fineness. It has scarce ever happened that the fury and indignation of the people could otherwise be appeased.

In the end of the reign of Henry VIII. and in the beginning of that of Edward VI. the English coin was not only raised in its denomination, but adulterated in its standard. The like frauds were practised in Scotland during the minority of James VI. They have occasionally been practised in most other countries.

It has been tried in England, Scotland and most other countries.

That the public revenue of Great Britain can ever[62] be completely liberated, or even that any considerable progress can ever be made towards that liberation, while the surplus of that revenue, or what is over and above defraying the annual expence of the peace establishment, is so very small, it seems altogether in vain to expect. That liberation, it is evident, can never be brought about without either some very considerable augmentation of the public revenue, or some equally considerable reduction of the public expence.

For the paying off or reduction of the British debt a very considerable increase of revenue or diminution of expense is necessary.

A more equal land tax, a more equal tax upon the rent of houses, and such alterations in the present system of customs and excise as those which have been mentioned in the foregoing chapter, might, perhaps, without increasing the burden of the greater part of the people, but only distributing the weight of it more equally upon the whole, produce a considerable augmentation of revenue. The most sanguine projector, however,

Alterations in taxation might increase the revenue considerably but not sufficiently.

---

[62] [Misprinted "never" in eds. 2–5.]

could scarce flatter himself that any augmentation of this kind would be such as could give any reasonable hopes, either of liberating the public revenue altogether, or even of making such progress towards that liberation in time of peace, as either to prevent or to compensate the further accumulation of the public debt in the next war.

By extending the British system of taxation to all the different provinces of the empire inhabited by people of either[63] British or European extraction, a much greater augmentation of revenue might be expected. This, however, could scarce, perhaps, be done, consistently with the principles of the British constitution, without admitting into the British parliament, or if you will into the states-general of the British empire, a fair and equal representation of all those different provinces, that of each province bearing the same proportion to the produce of its taxes, as the representation of Great Britain might bear to the produce of the taxes levied upon Great Britain. The private interest of many powerful individuals, the confirmed prejudices of great bodies of people seem, indeed, at present, to oppose to so great a change such obstacles as it may be very difficult, perhaps altogether impossible, to surmount. Without, however, pretending to determine whether such a union be practicable or impracticable, it may not, perhaps, be improper, in a speculative work of this kind, to consider how far the British system of taxation might be applicable to all the different provinces of the empire; what revenue might be expected from it if so applied, and in what manner a general union of this kind might be likely to affect the happiness and prosperity of the different provinces comprehended within it. Such a speculation can at worst be regarded but as a new Utopia, less amusing certainly, but not more useless and chimerical than the old one.

An extension of taxation to Ireland and the colonies would afford a larger increase.

The land-tax, the stamp-duties, and the different duties of customs and excise, constitute the four principal branches of the British taxes.

---

[63] [Ed. 1 reads "neither of."]

Ireland is certainly as able, and our American and West Indian plantations more able to pay a land-tax than Great Britain. Where the landlord is subject neither to tithe nor poors rate, he must certainly be more able to pay such a tax, than where he is subject to both those other burdens. The tithe,

The land-tax could well be extended to Ireland, America and the West Indies.

where there is no modus, and where it is levied in kind, diminishes more what would otherwise be the rent of the landlord, than a land-tax which really amounted to five shillings in the pound. Such a tithe will be found in most cases to amount to more than a fourth part of the real rent of the land, or of what remains after replacing completely the capital of the farmer, together with his reasonable profit. If all moduses and all impropriations were taken away, the complete church tithe of Great Britain and Ireland could not well be estimated at less than six or seven millions. If there was no tithe either in Great Britain or Ireland, the landlords could afford to pay six or seven millions additional land-tax, without being more burdened than a very great part of them are at present. America pays no tithe, and could therefore very well afford to pay a land-tax. The lands in America and the West Indies, indeed, are in general not tenanted nor[64] leased out to farmers. They could not therefore be assessed according to any rent-roll. But neither were the lands of Great Britain, in the 4th of William and Mary, assessed according to any rent-roll, but according to a very loose and inaccurate estimation. The lands in America might be assessed either in the same manner, or according to an equitable valuation in consequence of an accurate survey, like that which was lately made in the Milanese, and in the dominions of Austria, Prussia, and Sardinia.[65]

Stamp-duties, it is evident, might be levied without any

Stamp duties could easily be extended.

variation in all countries where the forms of law process, and the deeds by which property both real and personal is transferred, are the same or nearly the same.

[64] [Ed. 1 reads "or."]

[65] [Above, pp. 1046, 1055–1056.]

The extension of the custom-house laws of Great Britain to Ireland and the plantations, provided it was accompanied, as in justice it ought to be, with an extension of the freedom of trade, would be in the highest degree advantageous to both. All the invidious restraints which at present oppress the trade of Ireland, the distinction between the enumerated and non-enumerated commodities of America, would be entirely at an end.[66] The countries north of Cape Finisterre would be as open to every part of the produce of America, as those south of that Cape are to some parts of that produce at present. The trade between all the different parts of the British empire would, in consequence of this uniformity in the custom-house laws, be as free as the coasting trade of Great Britain is at present. The British empire would thus afford within itself an immense internal market for every part of the produce of all its different provinces. So great an extension of market would soon compensate both to Ireland and the plantations, all that they could suffer from the increase of the duties of customs.

The extension of the customs would be of great advantage to all, as it would be accompanied by an extension of free trade.

The excise is the only part of the British system of taxation, which would require to be varied in any respect according as it was applied to the different provinces of the empire. It might be applied to Ireland without any variation; the produce and consumption of that kingdom being exactly of the same nature with those of Great Britain. In its application to America and the West Indies, of which the produce and consumption are so very different from those of Great Britain, some modification might be necessary, in the same manner as in its application to the cyder and beer counties of England.

Excise duties would require some variation,

A fermented liquor, for example, which is called beer, but which, as it is made of melasses, bears very little resemblance to our beer, makes a considerable part of the common drink of

[66] [Above, pp. 731–732.]

the people in America. This liquor, as it can be kept only for a few days, cannot, like our beer, be prepared and stored up for sale in great breweries; but every private family must brew it for their own use, in the same manner as they cook their victuals. But to subject every private family to the odious

as for example in the case of American beer.

visits and examination of the tax-gatherers, in the same manner as we subject the keepers of alehouses and the brewers for public sale, would be altogether inconsistent with liberty. If for the sake of equality it was thought necessary to lay a tax upon this liquor, it might be taxed by taxing the material of which it is made, either at the place of manufacture, or, if the circumstances of the trade rendered such an excise improper, by laying a duty upon its importation into the colony in which it was to be consumed. Besides the duty of one penny a gallon imposed by the British parliament upon the importation of melasses into America; there is a provincial tax of this kind upon their importation into Massachusetts Bay, in ships belonging to any other colony, of eight-pence the hogshead; and another upon their importation, from the northern colonies, into South Carolina, of five-pence the gallon. Or if neither of these methods was found convenient, each family might compound for its consumption of this liquor, either according to the number of persons of which it consisted, in the same manner as private families compound for the malt-tax in England; or according to the different ages and sexes of those persons, in the same manner as several different taxes are levied in Holland; or nearly as Sir Matthew Decker proposes that all taxes upon consumable commodities should be levied in England.[67] This mode of taxation, it has already been observed, when applied to objects of a speedy consumption, is not a very convenient one. It might be adopted, however, in cases where no better could be done.

Sugar, rum, and tobacco, are commodities which are no where necessaries of life, which are become objects of almost universal consumption, and which are therefore extremely

[67] [Above, p. 1111.]

proper subjects of taxation. If a union with the colonies were[68] to take place, those commodities might be taxed either before

Sugar, rum and tobacco could be made subject to excise.

they go out of the hands of the manufacturer or grower; or if this mode of taxation did not suit the circumstances of those persons, they might be deposited in public warehouses both at the place of manufacture, and at all the different ports of the empire to which they might afterwards be transported, to remain there, under the joint custody of the owner and the revenue officer, till such time as they should be delivered out either to the consumer, to the merchant retailer for home-consumption, or to the merchant exporter, the tax not to be advanced till such delivery. When delivered out for exportation, to go duty free; upon proper security being given that they should really be exported out of the empire. These are perhaps the principal commodities with regard to which a union with the colonies might require some considerable change in the present system of British taxation.

What might be the amount of the revenue which this system of taxation extended to all the different provinces of the empire

The increase of revenue thus obtained, if proportionate to the increased population taxed, would yield six millions and a quarter to be applied in reduction of debt, and this sum would of course be a growing one.

might produce, it must, no doubt, be altogether impossible to ascertain with tolerable exactness. By means of this system there is annually levied in Great Britain, upon less than eight millions of people, more than ten millions of revenue. Ireland contains more than two millions of people, and according to the accounts laid before the congress,[69] the twelve associated provinces of America contain more than three. Those accounts, however, may have been exaggerated, in order, perhaps, either to encourage their own people, or to intimidate those of this country, and we shall suppose therefore that our North American

---

[68] [Eds. 1–3 read "was."]

[69] [Given in the Continuation of Anderson's *Commerce*, A.D. 1774, vol. iv., p. 178, in ed. of 1801.]

and West Indian colonies taken together contain no more than three millions; or that the whole British empire, in Europe and America, contains no more than thirteen millions of inhabitants. If upon less than eight millions of inhabitants this system of taxation raises a revenue of more than ten millions sterling; it ought upon thirteen millions of inhabitants to raise a revenue of more than sixteen millions two hundred and fifty thousand pounds sterling. From this revenue, supposing that this system could produce it, must be deducted, the revenue usually raised in Ireland and the plantations for defraying the expence of their respective civil governments. The expence of the civil and military establishment of Ireland, together with the interest of the public debt, amounts, at a medium of the two years which ended March 1775, to something less than seven hundred and fifty thousand pounds a year. By a very exact account[70] of the revenue of the principal colonies of America and the West Indies, it amounted, before the commencement of the present[71] disturbances, to a hundred and forty-one thousand eight hundred pounds. In this account, however, the revenue of Maryland, of North Carolina, and of all our late acquisitions both upon the continent and in the islands, is omitted, which may perhaps make a difference of thirty or forty thousand pounds. For the sake of even numbers therefore, let us suppose that the revenue necessary for supporting the civil government of Ireland and the plantations, may amount to a million. There would remain consequently a revenue of fifteen millions two hundred and fifty thousand pounds, to be applied towards defraying the general expence of the empire, and towards paying the public debt. But if from the present revenue of Great Britain a million could in peaceable times be spared towards the payment of that debt, six millions two hundred and fifty thousand pounds could very well be spared from this improved revenue. This great sinking fund too might be augmented every year by the interest of the debt which had been discharged the year before, and might in this manner increase so

[70] [Above, p. 727.]

[71] [Ed. 1 reads "late"; cp. above, p. 627.]

very rapidly, as to be sufficient in a few years to discharge the whole debt, and thus to restore completely the at present debilitated and languishing vigour of the empire. In the mean time the people might be relieved from some of the most burdensome taxes; from those which are imposed either upon the necessaries of life, or upon the materials of manufacture. The labouring poor would thus be enabled to live better, to work cheaper, and to send their goods cheaper to market. The cheapness of their goods would increase the demand for them, and consequently for the labour of those who produced them. This increase in the demand for labour, would both increase the numbers and improve the circumstances of the labouring poor. Their consumption would increase, and together with it the revenue arising from all those articles of their consumption upon which the taxes might be allowed to remain.

The revenue arising from this system of taxation, however, might not immediately increase in proportion to the number of people who were subjected to it. Great indulgence would for some time be due to those provinces of the empire which were thus subjected to burthens to which they had not before been accustomed, and even when the same taxes came to be levied every where as exactly as possible, they would not every where produce a revenue proportioned to the numbers of the people. In a poor country the consumption of the principal commodities subject to the duties of customs and excise is very small; and in a thinly inhabited country the opportunities of smuggling are very great. The consumption of malt liquors among the inferior ranks of people in Scotland is very small, and the excise upon malt, beer, and ale, produces less there than in England in proportion to the numbers of the people and the rate of the duties, which upon malt is different on account of a supposed difference of quality. In these particular branches of the excise, there is not, I apprehend, much more smuggling in the one country than in the other. The duties upon the distillery, and the greater part of the duties of customs, in proportion to

Some necessary deductions from this estimate would be counterbalanced by additions resulting from a few simple alterations.

the numbers of people in the respective countries, produce less in Scotland than in England, not only on account of the smaller consumption of the taxed commodities, but of the much greater facility of smuggling. In Ireland, the inferior ranks of people are still poorer than in Scotland, and many parts of the country are almost as thinly inhabited. In Ireland, therefore, the consumption of the taxed commodities might, in proportion to the number of the people, be still less than in Scotland, and the facility of smuggling nearly the same. In America and the West Indies the white people even of the lowest rank are in much better circumstances than those of the same rank in England, and their consumption of all the luxuries in which they usually indulge themselves is probably much greater. The blacks, indeed, who make the greater part of the inhabitants both of the southern colonies upon the continent and of the West India[72] islands, as they are in a state of slavery, are, no doubt, in a worse condition than the poorest people either in Scotland or Ireland. We must not, however, upon the account, imagine that they are worse fed, or that their consumption of articles which might be subjected to moderate duties, is less than that even of the lower ranks of people in England. In order that they may work well, it is the interest of their master that they should be fed well and kept in good heart, in the same manner as it is his interest that his working cattle should be so. The blacks accordingly have almost every where their allowance of rum and of melasses or spruce beer, in the same manner as the white servants; and this allowance would not probably be withdrawn, though those articles should be subjected to moderate duties. The consumption of the taxed commodities, therefore, in proportion to the number of inhabitants, would probably be as great in America and the West Indies as in any part of the British empire. The opportunities of smuggling indeed, would be much greater; America, in proportion to the extent of the country, being much more thinly inhabited than either Scotland or Ireland. If the revenue, however, which is at present raised by the different du-

[72] [Eds. 1 and 2 read "West Indian."]

ties upon malt and malt liquors, were[73] to be levied by a single duty upon malt, the opportunity of smuggling in the most important branch of the excise would be almost entirely taken away: And if the duties of customs, instead of being imposed upon almost all the different articles of importation, were confined to a few of the most general use and consumption, and if the levying of those duties were subjected to the excise laws, the opportunity of smuggling, though not so entirely taken away, would be very much diminished. In consequence of those two, apparently, very simple and easy alterations, the duties of customs and excise might probably produce a revenue as great in proportion to the consumption of the most thinly inhabited province, as they do at present in proportion to that of the most populous.

The Americans, it has been said, indeed, have no gold or silver money; the interior commerce of the country being carried on by a paper currency, and the gold and silver which occasionally come among them being all sent to Great Britain in return for the commodities which they receive from us. But without gold and silver, it is added, there is no possibility of paying taxes. We already get all the gold and silver which they have. How is it possible to draw from them what they have not?

The Americans have little gold and silver,

The present scarcity of gold and silver money in America is not the effect of the poverty of that country, or of the inability of the people there to purchase those metals. In a country where the wages of labour are so much higher, and the price of provisions so much lower than in England, the greater part of the people must surely have wherewithal to purchase a greater quantity, if it were[74] either necessary or convenient for them to do so. The scarcity of those metals therefore, must be the effect of choice, and not of necessity.

but this is the effect of choice, not necessity.

It is for transacting either domestic or foreign business, that gold and silver money is either necessary or convenient.

---

[73] [Eds. 1–3 read "was" here and five lines below.]

[74] [Eds. 1–3 read "was."]

The domestic business of every country, it has been shewn in the second book of this Inquiry,[75] may, at least in peaceable times, be transacted by means of a paper currency, with nearly the same degree of conveniency as by gold and silver money. It

Paper is more convenient to the Americans for home trade,

is convenient for the Americans, who could always employ with profit in the improvement of their lands a greater stock than they can easily get, to save as much as possible the expence of so costly an instrument of

commerce as gold and silver, and rather to employ that part of their surplus produce which would be necessary for purchasing those metals, in purchasing the instruments of trade, the materials of clothing, several parts of household furniture, and the iron-work necessary for building and extending their settlements and plantations; in purchasing, not dead stock, but active and productive stock. The colony governments find it for their interest to supply the[76] people with such a quantity of paper-money as is fully sufficient and generally more than sufficient for transacting their domestic business. Some of those governments, that of Pennsylvania particularly, derive a revenue from lending this paper-money to their subjects at an interest of so much per cent. Others, like that of Massachusett's Bay, advance upon extraordinary emergencies a paper-money of this kind for defraying the public expence, and afterwards, when it suits the conveniency of the colony, redeem it at the depreciated value to which it gradually falls. In 1747[77] that colony paid, in this manner, the greater part of its public debts, with the tenth part of the money for which its bills had been granted. It suits the conveniency of the planters to save the expence of employing gold and silver money in their domestic transaction; and it suits the conveniency of the colony governments to supply them with a medium, which, though attended with some very considerable disadvantages, enables them to

[75] [Above, pp. 372–378.]

[76] [Ed. 1 omits "the."]

[77] See Hutchinson's *Hist. of Massachusett's Bay, Vol. II.*, page 436 & seq. [*History of the Colony of Massachusetts Bay*, 2nd ed., 1765–8.]

save that expence. The redundancy of paper-money necessarily banishes gold and silver from the domestic transactions of the colonies, for the same reason that it has banished those metals from the greater part of the domestic transactions in[78] Scotland; and in both countries it is not the poverty, but the enterprizing and projecting spirit of the people, their desire of employing all the stock which they can get as active and productive stock, which has occasioned this redundancy of paper-money.

while for their external trade they use as much gold and silver as is necessary.

In the exterior commerce which the different colonies carry on with Great Britain, gold and silver are more or less employed, exactly in proportion as they are more or less necessary. Where those metals are not necessary, they seldom appear. Where they are necessary, they are generally found.

In the commerce between Great Britain and the tobacco colonies, the British goods are generally advanced to the

In the trade between Great Britain and Virginia and Maryland tobacco is a more convenient currency than gold and silver.

colonists at a pretty long credit, and are afterwards paid for in tobacco, rated at a certain price. It is more convenient for the colonists to pay in tobacco than in gold and silver. It would be more convenient for any merchant to pay for the goods which his correspondents had sold to him in some other sort of goods which he might happen to deal in, than in money. Such a merchant would have no occasion to keep any part of his stock by him unemployed, and in ready money, for answering occasional demands. He could have, at all times, a larger quantity of goods in his shop or warehouse, and he could deal to a greater extent. But it seldom happens to be convenient for all the correspondents of a merchant to receive payment for the goods which they sell to him, in goods of some other kind which he happens to deal in. The British merchants who trade to Virginia and Maryland happen to be a particular set of correspondents, to whom it is more convenient to receive payment for the goods which they sell to those colonies in tobacco than in gold and silver. They expect to make a profit by the sale of the tobacco. They could make none by that of the gold and silver. Gold and silver, therefore, very seldom appear in the commerce between Great Britain and the tobacco colonies. Maryland and Virginia have as little occasion for those metals in their foreign as in their domestic commerce. They are said, accordingly, to have less gold and silver money than any other colonies in America. They are reckoned, however, as thriving, and consequently as rich, as any of their neighbours.

In the northern colonies, Pennsylvania, New York, New Jersey, the four governments of New England, &c. the value of their own produce which they export to Great Britain is not

The northern colonies generally find the gold and silver necessary to pay the balance on their trade with Great Britain.

equal to that of the manufactures which they import for their own use, and for that of some of the other colonies to which they are the carriers. A balance, therefore, must be paid to the mother country in gold and silver, and this balance they generally find.

In the sugar colonies the value of the produce annually exported to Great Britain is much greater than that of all the goods imported from thence. If the sugar and rum annually sent to the mother country were

The sugar colonies generally find the gold and silver necessary to pay the balance to Great Britain which arises from the sugar planters being absentees.

paid for in those colonies, Great Britain would be obliged to send out every year a very large balance in money, and the trade to the West Indies would, by a certain species of politicians, be considered as extremely disadvantageous. But it so happens, that many of the principal proprietors of the sugar plantations reside in Great Britain. Their rents are remitted to them in sugar and rum, the produce of their estates. The sugar

and rum which the West India merchants purchase in those colonies upon their own account, are not equal in value to the goods which they annually sell there. A balance therefore must necessarily[79] be paid to them in gold and silver, and this balance too is generally found.

The difficulty and irregularity of payment from the different colonies to Great Britain, have not been at all in proportion to the greatness or smallness of the balances which were respectively due from them. Payments have in general been more regular from the northern than from the tobacco colonies, though the former have generally paid a pretty large balance in money, while the latter have either paid[80] no balance, or a much smaller one. The difficulty of getting payment from our different sugar colonies has been greater or less in proportion, not so much to the extent of the balances respectively due from them, as to the quantity of uncultivated land which they contained; that is, to the greater or smaller temptation which the planters have been under of over-trading, or of undertaking the settlement and plantation of greater quantities of waste land than suited the extent of their capitals. The returns from the great island of Jamaica, where there is still much uncultivated land, have, upon this account, been in general more irregular and uncertain, than those from the smaller islands of Barbadoes, Antigua, and St. Christophers, which have for these many years been completely cultivated, and have, upon that account, afforded less field for the speculations of the planter. The new acquisitions of Grenada, Tobago, St. Vincents, and Dominica,[81] have opened a new field for speculations of this kind; and the returns from those islands have of late been as irregular and uncertain as those from the great island of Jamaica.

Any difficulties have not been proportionate to the size of the balance due,

It is not, therefore, the poverty of the colonies which occasions, in the greater part of them, the present scarcity of gold and silver money. Their great demand for active and productive stock makes it convenient for them to have as little dead stock as possible; and disposes them upon that account to content them-

---

[79] [Ed. 1 reads "must generally."]

[80] [Ed. 1 reads "paid either."]

[81] [Above, p. 733, note 43.]

and have arisen from unnecessary and excessive enterprise. selves with a cheaper, though less commodious instrument of commerce than gold and silver. They are thereby enabled to convert the value of that gold and silver into the instruments of trade, into the materials of clothing, into household furniture, and into the iron work necessary for building and extending their settlements and plantations. In those branches of business which cannot be transacted without gold and silver money, it appears, that they can always find the necessary quantity of those metals; and if they frequently do not find it, their failure is generally the effect, not of their necessary poverty, but of their unnecessary and excessive enterprize. It is not because they are poor that their payments are irregular and uncertain; but because they are too eager to become excessively rich. Though all that part of the produce of the colony taxes, which was over and above what was necessary for defraying the expence of their own civil and military establishments, were to be remitted to Great Britain in gold and silver, the colonies have abundantly wherewithal to purchase the requisite quantity of those metals. They would in this case be obliged, indeed, to exchange a part of their surplus produce, with which they now purchase active and productive stock, for dead stock. In transacting their domestic business they would be obliged to employ a costly instead of a cheap instrument of commerce; and the expence of purchasing this costly instrument might damp somewhat the vivacity and ardour of their excessive enterprize in the improvement of land. It might not, however, be necessary to remit any part of the American revenue in gold and silver. It might be remitted in bills drawn upon and accepted by particular merchants or companies in Great Britain, to whom a part of the surplus produce of America had been consigned, who would pay into the treasury the American revenue in money, after having themselves received the value of it in goods; and the whole business might frequently be transacted without exporting a single ounce of gold or silver[82] from America.

---

[82] [Ed. 1 reads "gold and silver."]

It is not contrary to justice that both Ireland and America should contribute towards the discharge of the public debt of Great Britain. That debt has been contracted

It is justice that Ireland and America should contribute to the discharge of the British debt.

in support of the government established by the Revolution, a government to which the protestants of Ireland owe, not only the whole authority which they at present enjoy in their own country, but every security which they possess for their liberty, their property, and their religion; a government to which several of the colonies of America owe their present charters, and consequently their present constitution, and to which all the colonies of America owe the liberty, security, and property which they have ever since enjoyed. That public debt has been contracted in the defence, not of Great Britain alone, but of all the different provinces of the empire; the immense debt contracted in the late war in particular, and a great part of that contracted in the war before, were both properly contracted in defence of America.

By a union with Great Britain, Ireland would gain, besides the freedom of trade, other advantages much more important,

Union would deliver Ireland from an oppressive aristocracy founded on religious and political prejudices.

and which would much more than compensate any increase of taxes that might accompany that union. By the union with England, the middling and inferior ranks of people in Scotland gained a complete deliverance from the power of an aristocracy which had always before oppressed them. By an union with Great Britain, the greater part of the people of all ranks in Ireland would gain an equally complete deliverance from a much more oppressive aristocracy; an aristocracy not founded, like that of Scotland, in the natural and respectable distinctions of birth and fortune; but in the most odious of all distinctions, those of religious and political prejudices; distinctions which, more than any other, animate both the insolence of the oppressors and the hatred and indignation of the oppressed, and which commonly render the inhabitants of the same country more hostile to one another than those of different countries ever are. Without a union with Great Britain, the inhabitants of Ireland are not likely for many ages to consider themselves as one people.

No oppressive aristocracy has ever prevailed in the colonies. Even they, however, would, in point of happiness and tranquillity, gain considerably by a union with Great Britain. It would, at least, deliver them from those rancorous and virulent factions which are inseparable from small democracies, and which have so frequently divided the affections of their people, and disturbed the tranquillity of their governments, in their form so nearly democratical. In the case of a total separation from Great Britain, which, unless prevented by a union of this kind, seems very likely to take place, those factions would be ten times more virulent than ever. Before the commencement of the present disturbances, the coercive power of the mother-country had always been able to restrain those factions from breaking out into any thing worse than gross brutality and insult. If that coercive power were[83] entirely taken away, they would probably soon break out into open violence and bloodshed. In all great countries which are united under one uniform government, the spirit of party commonly prevails less in the remote provinces than in the centre of the empire. The distance of those provinces from the capital, from the principal seat of the great scramble of faction and ambition, makes them enter less into the views of any of the contending parties, and renders them more indifferent and impartial spectators of the conduct of all. The spirit of party prevails less in Scotland than in England. In the case of a union it would probably prevail less in Ireland than in Scotland, and the colonies would probably soon enjoy a degree of concord and unanimity at present unknown in any part of the British empire. Both Ireland and the colonies, indeed, would be subjected to heavier taxes than any which they at present pay. In consequence, how-

The colonies would be delivered from rancorous factions which are likely to lead to bloodshed in case of separation from Great Britain.

[83] [Eds. 1–3 read "was."]

ever, of a diligent and faithful application of the public revenue towards the discharge of the national debt, the greater part of those taxes might not be of long continuance, and the public revenue of Great Britain might soon be reduced to what was necessary for maintaining a moderate peace establishment.

The territorial acquisitions of the East India company, the undoubted right of the crown, that is, of the state and people of

East India with lighter taxes and less corrupt administration might yield an even larger addition of revenue.

Great Britain, might be rendered another source of revenue more abundant, perhaps, than all those already mentioned. Those countries are represented as more fertile, more extensive; and, in proportion to their extent, much richer and more populous than Great Britain. In order to draw a great revenue from them, it would not probably be necessary, to introduce any new system of taxation into countries which are already sufficiently and more than sufficiently taxed. It might, perhaps, be more proper to lighten, than to aggravate, the burden of those unfortunate countries, and to endeavour to draw a revenue from them, not by imposing new taxes, but by preventing the embezzlement and misapplication of the greater part of those which they already pay.

If it should be found impracticable for Great Britain to draw any considerable augmentation of revenue from any of the re-

If no such augmentation of revenue can be obtained Great Britain should reduce her expenses by ridding herself of the cost of the colonies in peace and war.

sources above mentioned; the only resource which can remain to her is a diminution of her expence. In the mode of collecting, and in that of expending the public revenue; though in both there may be still room for improvement; Great Britain seems to be at least as œconomical as any of her neighbours. The military establishment which she maintains for her own defence in time of peace, is more moderate than that of any European state which can pretend to rival her either in wealth or in power. None of those articles, therefore, seem to admit of any considerable reduction of expence. The expence of the peace establishment of the colonies was, before the commencement of the present disturbances, very considerable, and is an expence which may, and if no revenue can be drawn from them, ought certainly to be saved altogether. This constant expence in time of peace, though very great, is insignificant in comparison with what the defence of the colonies has cost us in time of war. The last war, which was undertaken altogether on account of the colonies, cost Great Britain, it has already been observed, upwards of ninety millions.[84] The Spanish war of 1739 was principally undertaken on their account; in which, and in the French war that was the consequence of it, Great Britain spent upwards of forty millions, a great part of which ought justly to be charged to the colonies. In those two wars the colonies cost Great Britain much more than double the sum which the national debt amounted to before the commencement of the first of them. Had it not been for those wars that debt might, and probably would by this time, have been completely paid; and had it not been for the colonies, the former of those wars might not, and the latter certainly would not have been undertaken. It was because the colonies were supposed to be provinces of the British empire, that this expence was laid out upon them. But countries which contribute neither revenue nor military force towards the support of the empire, cannot be considered as provinces. They may perhaps be considered as appendages, as a sort of splendid and showy equipage of the empire. But if the empire can no longer support the expence of keeping up this equipage, it ought certainly to lay it down; and if it cannot raise its revenue in proportion to its expence, it ought, at least, to accommodate its expence to its revenue. If the colonies, notwithstanding their refusal to submit to British taxes, are still to be considered as provinces of the British empire, their defence in some future war may cost Great Britain as great an expence as it ever has done in any former war. The rulers of Great Britain have, for more than a century past, amused the people with the imagination that they possessed a great empire on the west side of the Atlantic. This empire, however, has hitherto existed in imagination only. It has hith-

---

[84] [Above, p. 555.]

erto been, not an empire, but the project of an empire; not a gold mine, but the project of a gold mine; a project which has cost, which continues to cost, and which, if pursued in the same way as it has been hitherto, is likely to cost, immense expence, without being likely to bring any profit; for the effects of the monopoly of the colony trade, it has been shewn,[85] are, to the great body of the people, mere loss instead of profit. It is surely now time that our rulers should either realize this golden dream, in which they have been indulging themselves, perhaps, as well as the people; or, that they should awake from it themselves, and endeavour to awaken the people. If the project cannot be completed, it ought to be given up. If any of the provinces of the British empire cannot be made to contribute towards the support of the whole empire, it is surely time that Great Britain should free herself from the expence of defending those provinces in time of war, and of supporting any part of their civil or military establishments in time of peace, and endeavour to accommodate her future views and designs to the real mediocrity of her circumstances.

[85] [Above, pp. 749–814.]

APPENDIX[1]

THE TWO following Accounts are subjoined in order to illustrate and confirm what is said in the Fifth Chapter of the Fourth Book,[2] concerning the Tonnage bounty to the White Herring Fishery. The Reader, I believe, may depend upon the accuracy of both Accounts.

An Account of Busses fitted out in Scotland for Eleven Years, with the Number of Empty Barrels carried out, and the Number of Barrels of Herrings caught; also the Bounty at a Medium on each Barrel of Seasteeks, and on each Barrel when fully packed.

Years	Number of Busses.	Empty Barrels carried out.	Barrels of Herrings caught.	Bounty paid on the Busses.		
				£.	s.	d.
1771	29	5948	2832	2085	0	0
1772	168	41316	22237	11055	7	6
1773	190	42333	42055	12510	8	6
1774	248	59303	56365	16952	2	6
1775	275	69144	52879	19315	15	0
1776	294	76329	51863	21290	7	6
1777	240	62679	43313	17592	2	6
1778	220	56390	40958	16316	2	6
1779	206	55194	29367	15287	0	0
1780	181	48315	19885	13445	12	6
1781	135	33992	16593	9613	12	6
Total,	2186	550943	378347	155463	11	0

[1] [See above, p. 655.]

[2] [In Additions and Corrections this matter is printed in the text, and consequently the reading here is "confirm what is said above."]

Seasteeks	378347	Bounty at a medium for each barrel of seasteeks, ... £. 0 8 2¼ But a barrel of seasteeks being only reckoned two-thirds of a barrel fully packed, one-third is deducted,
⅓ deducted	126115⅔	which brings the bounty to. . . . . . £. 0 12 3¾
Barrels full packed,	252231⅓	

And if the herrings are exported, there is besides a premium of	0	2	8
So that the bounty paid by Government in money for each barrel, is	£. 0	14	11¾
But if to this, the duty of the salt usually taken credit for as expended in curing each barrel, which at a medium is of foreign, one bushel and one-fourth of a bushel, at 10 *s.* a bushel, be added, viz.	0	12	6
The bounty on each barrel would amount to	£. 1	7	5¾
If the herrings are cured with British salt, it will stand thus, viz. Bounty as before	£. 0	14	11¾
—but if to this bounty the duty of two bushels of Scots salt at 1 *s.* 6 *d.* per bushel, supposed to be the quantity at a medium used in curing each barrel is added, to wit,	0	3	0
The bounty on each barrel will amount to	£. 0	17	11¾
And,			
When buss herrings are entered for home consumption in Scotland, and pay the shilling a barrel of duty, the bounty stands thus, to wit as before	£. 0	12	3¾
From which the 1 *s.* a barrel is to be deducted	0	1	0
	0	11	3¾
But to that there is to be added again, the duty of the foreign salt used in curing a barrel of herrings, viz.	0	12	6
So that the premium allowed for each barrel of herrings entered for home consumption is	£. 1	3	9¾
If the herrings are cured with British salt, it will stand as follows, viz.			
Bounty on each barrel brought in by the busses as above	£. 0	12	3¾
From which deduct the 1 *s.* a barrel paid at the time they are entered for home consumption	0	1	0
	£. 0	11	3¾
But if to the bounty the duty on two bushels of Scots salt at 1 *s.* 6 *d.* per bushel, supposed to be the quantity at a medium used in curing each barrel, is added, to wit,	0	3	0
The premium for each barrel entered for home consumption will be	£. 0	14	3¾

Though the loss of duties upon herrings exported cannot, perhaps, properly be considered as bounty; that upon herrings entered for home consumption certainly may.

An Account of the Quantity of Foreign Salt imported into Scotland, and of Scots Salt delivered Duty free from the Works there for the Fishery, from the 5th of April 1777 to the 5th of April 1782, with a Medium of both for one Year.

PERIOD.	Foreign Salt imported.	Scots Salt delivered from the Works.
	Bushels.	Bushels.
From the 5th of April 1771 to the 5th of April 1782.	936974	168226
Medium for one Year	85179⅗₁	15293⅗₁

It is to be observed that the Bushel of Foreign Salt weighs 84 lb. that of British Salt 56 1b. only.

AFTERWORD

EDWIN CANNAN

THE TEXT of the present edition is copied from that of the fifth, the last published before Adam Smith's death. The fifth edition has been carefully collated with the first, and wherever the two were found to disagree the history of the alteration has been traced through the intermediate editions. With some half-dozen utterly insignificant exceptions such as a change of "these" to "those," "towards" to "toward," and several haphazard substitutions of "conveniences" for "conveniencies," the results of this collation are all recorded in the footnotes, unless the difference between the editions is quite obviously and undoubtedly the consequence of mere misprints, such as "is" for "it," "that" for "than," "becase" for "because." Even undoubted misprints are recorded if, as often happens, they make a plausible misreading which has been copied in modern texts, or if they present any other features of interest.

As it does not seem desirable to dress up an eighteenth century classic entirely in twentieth century costume, I have retained the spelling of the fifth edition and steadily refused to attempt to make it consistent with itself. The danger which would be incurred by doing so may be shown by the example of "Cromwel." Few modern readers would hesitate to condemn this as a misprint, but it is, as a matter of fact, the spelling affected by Hume in his *History*, and was doubtless adopted from him by Adam Smith, though in the second of the two places where the name is mentioned inadvertence or the obstinacy of the printers allowed the usual "Cromwell" to appear till the fourth edition was reached. I have been equally rigid in following the original in the matter of the use of capitals and italics, except that in deference to modern fashion I have allowed the initial words of paragraphs to appear in small letters instead of capitals, the chapter headings to be printed in capitals instead of italics, and the abbreviation "Chap." to be replaced with "Chapter" in full. I have also allowed each chapter to begin on a fresh page, as the old practices of beginning a new chapter below the end of the preceding one is inconvenient to a student who desires to use the book for reference.

The original index,* with some slight unavoidable changes of typography, is reprinted as it appeared in the third, fourth and fifth editions. I have added to it a large number of new articles and references. I have endeavoured by these additions to make it absolutely complete in regard to names of places and persons, except that it seemed useless to include the names of kings and others when used merely to indicate dates, and altogether vain to hope to deal comprehensively with "Asia," "England," "Great Britain" and "Europe." I have inserted a few catchwords which may aid in the recovery of particularly striking passages, such as "Invisible hand," "Pots and pans," "Retaliation," "Shopkeepers, nation of." I have not thought it desirable to add to the more general of the headings in the original index, such as "Commerce" and "Labour," since these might easily be enlarged till they included nearly everything in the book. Authorities expressly referred to either in the text or the Author's notes are included, but as it would have been inconvenient and confusing to add references to the Editor's notes, I have appended a second index in which all the authorities referred to in the text, in the Author's notes, and in the Editor's notes are collected together. This will, I hope, be found useful by students of the history of economics.

The Author's references to his footnotes are placed exactly where he placed them, though their situation is often somewhat curiously selected, and the footnotes themselves are printed exactly as in the fifth edition. Critics will probably

---

* [EDITOR'S NOTE: The original index has been removed because of its length, and replaced with one more general and concise.]

complain of the trivial character of many of the notes which record the result of the collation of the editions, but I would point out that if I had not recorded all the differences, readers would have had to rely entirely on my expression of opinion that the unrecorded differences were of no interest. The evidence having been once collected at the expense of very considerable labour, it was surely better to put it on record, especially as these trivial notes, though numerous, if collected together would not occupy more than three or four pages of the present work. Moreover, as is shown in the Editor's Introduction, the most trivial of the differences often throw interesting light upon Smith's way of regarding and treating his work.

The other notes consist chiefly of references to sources of Adam Smith's information. Where he quotes his authority by name, no difficulty ordinarily arises. Elsewhere there is often little doubt about the matter. The search for authorities has been greatly facilitated by the publication of Dr. Bonar's *Catalogue of the Library of Adam Smith* in 1894, and of Adam Smith's *Lectures* in 1896. The *Catalogue* tells us what books Smith had in his possession at his death, fourteen years after the *Wealth of Nations* was published, while the *Lectures* often enable us to say that a particular piece of information must have been taken from a book published before 1763. As it is known that Smith used the Advocates' Library, the Catalogue of that library, of which Part II was printed in 1776, has also been of some use. Of course a careful comparison of words and phrases often makes it certain that a particular statement must have come from a particular source. Nevertheless many of the references given must be regarded as indicating merely a possible source of information or inspiration. I have refrained from quoting or referring to parallel passages in other authors when it is impossible or improbable that Smith ever saw them. That many more references might be given by an editor gifted with omniscience I know better than any one. To discover a reference has often taken hours of labour: to fail to discover one has often taken days.

When Adam Smith misquotes or clearly misinterprets his

authority, I note the fact, but I do not ordinarily profess to decide whether his authority is right or wrong. It is neither possible nor desirable to rewrite the history of nearly all economic institutions and a great many other institutions in the form of footnotes to the *Wealth of Nations*.

Nor have I thought well to criticise Adam Smith's theories in the light of modern discussions. I would beseech any one who thinks that this ought to have been done to consider seriously what it would mean. Let him review the numerous portly volumes which modern inquiry has produced upon every one of the immense number of subjects treated by Adam Smith, and ask himself whether he really thinks the order of subjects in the *Wealth of Nations* a convenient one to adopt in an economic encyclopædia. The book is surely a classic of great historical interest which should not be overlaid by the opinions and criticisms of any subsequent moment—still less of any particular editor.

Much of the heavier work involved in preparing the present edition, especially the collation of the original editions, has been done by my friend Mrs. Norman Moor, without whose untiring assistance the book could not have been produced.

Numerous friends have given me the benefit of their knowledge of particular points, and my hearty thanks are due to them.

London School of Economics, 1904

INDEX

ASK YOUR BOOKSELLER FOR THESE
BANTAM CLASSICS

BEOWULF AND OTHER ENGLISH POEMS, 0-553-21347-4

THE BHAGAVAD-GITA: KRISHNA'S COUNSEL IN TIME OF WAR,
0-553-21365-2

THE DECLARATION OF INDEPENDENCE and
THE CONSTITUTION OF THE UNITED STATES, 0-553-21482-9

THE FEDERALIST PAPERS, 0-553-21340-7

GREEK DRAMA, 0-553-21221-4

JO'S BOYS, Louisa May Alcott, 0-553-21449-7

LITTLE WOMEN, Louisa May Alcott, 0-553-21275-3

WINESBURG, OHIO, Sherwood Anderson, 0-553-21439-X

THE COMPLETE PLAYS, Aristophanes, 0-553-21343-1

EMMA, Jane Austen, 0-553-21273-7

MANSFIELD PARK, Jane Austen, 0-553-21276-1

NORTHANGER ABBEY, Jane Austen, 0-553-21197-8

PERSUASION, Jane Austen, 0-553-21137-4

PRIDE AND PREJUDICE, Jane Austen, 0-553-21310-5

SENSE AND SENSIBILITY, Jane Austen, 0-553-21334-2

PETER PAN, J. M. Barrie, 0-553-21178-1

BRADBURY CLASSIC STORIES, Ray Bradbury, 0-553-28637-4

THE MARTIAN CHRONICLES, Ray Bradbury, 0-553-27822-3

JANE EYRE, Charlotte Brontë, 0-553-21140-4

VILLETTE, Charlotte Brontë, 0-553-21243-5

WUTHERING HEIGHTS, Emily Brontë, 0-553-21258-3

THE SECRET GARDEN, Frances Hodgson Burnett, 0-553-21201-X

ALICE'S ADVENTURES IN WONDERLAND &
THROUGH THE LOOKING-GLASS, Lewis Carroll, 0-553-21345-8

MY ÁNTONIA, Willa Cather, 0-553-21418-7

O PIONEERS!, Willa Cather, 0-553-21358-X

THE CANTERBURY TALES, Geoffrey Chaucer, 0-553-21082-3

STORIES, Anton Chekhov, 0-553-38100-8

THE AWAKENING, Kate Chopin, 0-553-21330-X

THE WOMAN IN WHITE, Wilkie Collins, 0-553-21263-X

HEART OF DARKNESS and THE SECRET SHARER, Joseph Conrad,
0-553-21214-1

LORD JIM, Joseph Conrad, 0-553-21361-X

THE DEERSLAYER, James Fenimore Cooper, 0-553-21085-8

THE LAST OF THE MOHICANS, James Fenimore Cooper,
0-553-21329-6

MAGGIE: A GIRL OF THE STREETS AND OTHER SHORT FICTION, Stephen Crane, 0-553-21355-5

THE RED BADGE OF COURAGE, Stephen Crane, 0-553-21011-4

THE INFERNO, Dante, 0-553-21339-3

PARADISO, Dante, 0-553-21204-4

PURGATORIO, Dante, 0-553-21344-X

THE ORIGIN OF SPECIES, Charles Darwin, 0-553-21463-2

MOLL FLANDERS, Daniel Defoe, 0-553-21328-8

ROBINSON CRUSOE, Daniel Defoe, 0-553-21373-3

BLEAK HOUSE, Charles Dickens, 0-553-21223-0

A CHRISTMAS CAROL, Charles Dickens, 0-553-21244-3

DAVID COPPERFIELD, Charles Dickens, 0-553-21189-7

GREAT EXPECTATIONS, Charles Dickens, 0-553-21342-3

HARD TIMES, Charles Dickens, 0-553-21016-5

OLIVER TWIST, Charles Dickens, 0-553-21102-1

THE PICKWICK PAPERS, Charles Dickens, 0-553-21123-4

A TALE OF TWO CITIES, Charles Dickens, 0-553-21176-5

THREE SOLDIERS, John Dos Passos, 0-553-21456-X

THE BROTHERS KARAMAZOV, Fyodor Dostoevsky, 0-553-21216-8

CRIME AND PUNISHMENT, Fyodor Dostoevsky, 0-553-21175-7

THE ETERNAL HUSBAND AND OTHER STORIES, Fyodor Dostoevsky, 0-553-21444-6

THE IDIOT, Fyodor Dostoevsky, 0-553-21352-0

NOTES FROM UNDERGROUND, Fyodor Dostoevsky, 0-553-21144-7

SHERLOCK HOLMES VOL I, Sir Arthur Conan Doyle, 0-553-21241-9

SHERLOCK HOLMES VOL II, Sir Arthur Conan Doyle, 0-553-21242-7

SISTER CARRIE, Theodore Dreiser, 0-553-21374-1

THE SOULS OF BLACK FOLK, W. E. B. Du Bois, 0-553-21336-9

THE COUNT OF MONTE CRISTO, Alexandre Dumas, 0-553-21350-4

THE THREE MUSKETEERS, Alexandre Dumas, 0-553-21337-7

MIDDLEMARCH, George Eliot, 0-553-21180-3

SILAS MARNER, George Eliot, 0-553-21229-X

SELECTED ESSAYS, LECTURES, AND POEMS, Ralph Waldo Emerson, 0-553-21388-1

TEN PLAYS BY EURIPIDES, Euripides, 0-553-21363-6

APRIL MORNING, Howard Fast, 0-553-27322-1

MADAME BOVARY, Gustave Flaubert, 0-553-21341-5

HOWARDS END, E. M. Forster, 0-553-21208-7

A ROOM WITH A VIEW, E. M. Forster, 0-553-21323-7

THE DIARY OF A YOUNG GIRL, Anne Frank, 0-553-57712-3

ANNE FRANK'S TALES FROM THE SECRET ANNEX, Anne Frank, 0-553-58638-6

THE ADVENTURES OF HUCKLEBERRY FINN, Mark Twain, 0-553-21079-3
THE ADVENTURES OF TOM SAWYER, Mark Twain, 0-553-21128-5
THE COMPLETE SHORT STORIES OF MARK TWAIN, Mark Twain,
    0-553-21195-1
A CONNECTICUT YANKEE IN KING ARTHUR'S COURT, Mark Twain,
    0-553-21143-9
LIFE ON THE MISSISSIPPI, Mark Twain, 0-553-21349-0
THE PRINCE AND THE PAUPER, Mark Twain, 0-553-21256-7
PUDD'NHEAD WILSON, Mark Twain, 0-553-21158-7
20,000 LEAGUES UNDER THE SEA, Jules Verne, 0-553-21252-4
AROUND THE WORLD IN EIGHTY DAYS, Jules Verne, 0-553-21356-3
FROM THE EARTH TO THE MOON, Jules Verne, 0-553-21420-9
THE AENEID OF VIRGIL, Virgil, 0-553-21041-6
CANDIDE, Voltaire, 0-553-21166-8
THE INVISIBLE MAN, H. G. Wells, 0-553-21353-9
THE ISLAND OF DR. MOREAU, H. G. Wells, 0-553-21432-2
THE TIME MACHINE, H. G. Wells, 0-553-21351-2
THE WAR OF THE WORLDS, H. G. Wells, 0-553-21338-5
THE AGE OF INNOCENCE, Edith Wharton, 0-553-21450-0
THE CUSTOM OF THE COUNTRY, Edith Wharton, 0-553-21393-8
ETHAN FROME AND OTHER SHORT FICTION, Edith Wharton, 0-553-21255-9
THE HOUSE OF MIRTH, Edith Wharton, 0-553-21320-2
SUMMER, Edith Wharton, 0-553-21422-5
LEAVES OF GRASS, Walt Whitman, 0-553-21116-1
THE ACCIDENT, Elie Wiesel, 0-553-58170-8
DAWN, Elie Wiesel, 0-553-22536-7
NIGHT, Elie Wiesel, 0-553-27253-5
THE PICTURE OF DORIAN GRAY AND OTHER WRITINGS, Oscar Wilde,
    0-553-21254-0
THE SWISS FAMILY ROBINSON, Johann David Wyss, 0-553-21403-9
EARLY AFRICAN-AMERICAN CLASSICS, 0-553-21379-2
FIFTY GREAT SHORT STORIES, 0-553-27745-6
FIFTY GREAT AMERICAN SHORT STORIES, 0-553-27294-2
SHORT SHORTS, 0-553-27440-6
GREAT AMERICAN SHORT STORIES, 0-440-33060-2
SHORT STORY MASTERPIECES, 0-440-37864-8
THE VOICE THAT IS GREAT WITHIN US, 0-553-26263-7
THE BLACK POETS, 0-553-27563-1
THREE CENTURIES OF AMERICAN POETRY, (Trade) 0-553-37518-0,
    (Hardcover) 0-553-10250-8